Philosophy of Education

Advisory Board

Philosophy of Education
An Encyclopedia

Editor
J.J. Chambliss

GARLAND PUBLISHING, INC.
New York & London
1996

Library of Congress Cataloging-in-Publication Data

Philosophy of education :   an encyclopedia / editor, J.J. Chambliss.
               p.   cm. — (Garland reference library of the humanities ;
       vol. 1671)
           Includes bibliographical references and index.
           ISBN 0-8153-1177-X
           1. Education—Philosophy—Encyclopedias.   I. Chambliss, J. J. (Joseph
       James), 1929–   . II. Series.
       LB17. P485   1996
       370'.1—dc20   96-18393
                                                                      CIP

Cover by Lawrence Wolfson Design, New York. Photograph credit: Jeffry Myers/
FPG International Corp. Reprinted by permission. Photograph research: Diane
Cook.

Printed on acid-free, 250-year-life paper
Manufactured in the United States of America

Contents

Introduction

Philosophy of Education: An Encyclopedia is a reference work addressed to general readers, university students, and scholars. To our knowledge, no other encyclopedia exists that is devoted entirely to the philosophy of education.

The encyclopedia contains 228 signed articles written by 184 authors; it is designed to show the diversity of topics that contribute to the study of the philosophy of education. The core of the encyclopedia is its coverage of philosophical points of view that have had the greatest influence on educational thinking, from ancient Greece to the present. This core consists of philosophers such as Plato, Abelard, Descartes, Locke, and Dewey, along with topics from the field of philosophy, such as epistemology, metaphysics, rationalism, and realism. Yet the scope of the encyclopedia is much broader than its core, because many ideas and thinkers influencing education come from outside the field of philosophy. Articles are thus included from such fields as politics, religion, poetry, rhetoric, and the social sciences. The range of sources that contribute to the philosophy of education can be seen in the variety of academic departments in which our contributors work (see Contributors). While the largest number are in departments, colleges, and schools of education and departments of philosophy, also represented are departments of anthropology, the classics, English, history, psychology, religion, and sociology. There are also contributors from the Institute for Critical Thinking, the Institute of Jesuit Sources, and the University of Judaism. There are entries on antiquity, such as those on Homer, Sappho, and *Arete*, alongside others on more recent subjects, including Colonialism and Post-Colonialism, Feminism, and Modernism and PostModernism. Most of the authors are teachers and scholars in the United States and Canada; others are from Australia, Britain, Israel, and the Czech Republic.

While the emphasis of most articles is on the theory rather than the practice of education, many articles show the significance of theory for practice. The inclusion of ideas and thinkers beginning with the ancient, medieval, and Renaissance periods has been deliberate, with the intention of showing something of the history of the philosophy of education. In addition, two articles treat this history in an explicit way. One, Philosophy of Education, History of, begins with the idea that philosophy and educational theory had a common origin in the Greek Sophists and Plato's response to them. It sketches out various relationships between philosophy and educational thinking, down to the origins of the philosophy of education as a distinct discipline in the nineteenth century. The other article, Philosophy of Education, Professional Organizations in, treats the professional development of the philosophy of education as a result of the evolution of moral and social philosophy into the social sciences, and the social discourse over the part that education should play in the industrialized world of the twentieth century. This development has taken place mainly in the United States, Britain, and Australasia.

With the exception of one article that is eighty-five hundred words in length, the articles vary from six hundred to five thousand words, with only fourteen articles of more than three thousand words. Each article has a bibliography and a list of "see also" references. A comprehensive name and subject index provides easy access to information on topics that do not have individual entries.

We are sure that our readers will understand that this encyclopedia, like all reference works, cannot be complete, for the philosophy of education is not a completed but an ongoing activity. Also, this encyclopedia is an invitation to pursue further the enterprise in which its authors are engaged.

J.J. Chambliss

Acknowledgments

The editor wishes to acknowledge the contributors and advisory board, the first for taking their writing seriously and contributing first-rate articles, the second for helping the editor to settle upon a workable list of entries. Members of the advisory board also suggested prospective contributors, as did many authors as well as other scholars who did not write for us but took the time to help. Such enthusiasm and encouragement have been most gratifying, and if the editor could do so without appearing to be presumptuous, he would dedicate the encyclopedia to all who have helped.

The Department of Educational Theory, Policy, and Administration of the Rutgers Graduate School of Education has supported the project from the beginning. Thanks especially go to James M. Giarelli, department chairperson during the early phases of the project, and James R. Bliss, chairperson during the later phases.

Christopher Collins was most helpful in getting the project under way, and his enthusiasm for it almost exceeded my own. Marie Ellen Larcada and Marianne Lown, editors at Garland Publishing who shepherded the work along, and Eunice Petrini, who worked as editor during the final phases of the project, have also been helpful and resourceful. We thank them and the production staff at Garland Publishing.

The one individual who deserves the most thanks and highest praise is Sandra Chubrick. She has done superb work in many ways, most of all in organizing and maintaining a filing system for the project and in preparing the manuscript for submission to Garland. Without her contribution, the project would still have many miles to go.

J.J. Chambliss

Contributors

Entries written by contributor are denoted by *italic* and follow affiliation.

Donald C. Abel Department of Philosophy, St. Norbert College. *Human Nature*

H.A. Alexander University of Judaism, Los Angeles. *Judaism*

Donald G. Arnstine Division of Education, University of California, Davis. *Aesthetics*

Robert L. Arrington Department of Philosophy, Georgia State University, Atlanta. *Realism*

Thomas Auxter Department of Philosophy, University of Florida. *Kant*

Maryann Ayim Faculty of Education, University of Western Ontario. *Gender and Sexism*

Sharon Bailin Faculty of Education, Simon Fraser University. *Critical Thinking*

Bruce F. Baker School of Education, University of Missouri, Kansas City. *Makarenko*

Bertram Bandman Department of Philosophy, Long Island University. *Rights*

Ermanno Bencivenga Department of Philosophy, University of California, Irvine. *Montaigne*

John Hardin Best Department of Educational Policy Studies, Pennsylvania State University. *Franklin*

David Blacker College of Education, Illinois State University. *Technology*

William D. Blattner Philosophy Department, Georgetown University. *Heidegger*

Lawrence A. Blum University of Massachusetts, Boston. *Community*

David Blumenfeld Department of Philosophy, Georgia State University. *Rationalism*

Deanne Bogdan Department of History and Philosophy of Education, Ontario Institute for Studies in Education. *Literacy*

Raymond D. Boisvert Department of Philosophy, Siena College. *Metaphysics*

Florence Boos Department of English, University of Iowa. *Davies; Macaulay*

William Boos Department of Philosophy, William Paterson College. *Cynics; Cyrenaics*

C.A. Bowers School of Education, Portland State University. *Conservatism*

Eric Bredo Department of Educational Studies, University of Virginia. *Positivism; Sociology*

John Channing Briggs Department of English, University of California, Riverside. *Bacon*

Angela Brown Department of History, Stanford University. *King*

Diana Brydon Department of English, University of Guelph. *Colonialism and Post-colonialism*

Nicholas Burbules College of Education, University of Illinois. *Social and Political Philosophy*

Joan N. Burstyn School of Education, Syracuse University. *Higher Education*

Charles E. Butterworth Department of Government and Politics, University of Maryland at College Park. *Alfarabi; Averroes; Avicenna*

Eamonn Callan Faculty of Education, University of Alberta. *Academic Freedom*

Dagmar Capkova Pedagogicky ustav J. A. Komenskeho, Prague. *Comenius*

Clayborne Carson Department of History, Stanford University. *King*

Joseph S. Catalano New York City. *Sartre*

John C. Cavadini Department of Theology, Notre Dame University. *Augustine*

Robert Cavalier Center for the Advancement of Applied Ethics, Carnegie Mellon University. *Computers*

J.J. Chambliss Graduate School of Education, Rutgers University. *Aristotle; Condillac; Condorcet; Helvetius; Herbart; John of Salisbury; Peter Lombard; Philosophy of Education, History of; Progress, Idea of, and Progressive Education; Romanticism*

Richard P. Chaney Department of Anthropology, University of Oregon. *Anthropology*

Shih-chuan Chen Graduate School of Philosophy, Tunghai University, Taichung, Taiwan. *Confucianism*

Hsueh-Li Cheng Department of Philosophy and Religion, University of Hawaii at Hilo. *Buddhism*

Clinton Collins Department of Educational Policy Studies, University of Kentucky. *Existentialism*

John F. Covaleskie Northern Michigan University. *Discipline*

Randall R. Curren Department of Philosophy and Margaret Warner Graduate School of Edu-

cation, Rochester University. Arete; Paideia; *Practical Wisdom*

Frederick C. Dahlstrand Department of Social Sciences, Ohio State University, Mansfield. *Alcott*

James DeFronzo Department of Sociology, University of Connecticut. *Revolution*

Joseph L. DeVitis School of Education and Human Development, Binghamton University. *Freud*

Ana-Marie Diaz-Stevens Union Theological Seminary. *Hostos y Bonilla*

Allan F. DiBiase College of Staten Island. *Emerson*

Ann Diller Department of Education, University of New Hampshire. *Mysticism*

Donald Dippo Faculty of Education, York University. *Possibility*

Gerard Elfstrom Department of Philosophy, Auburn University. *Toleration*

Richard Leo Enos Department of English, Texas Christian University. *Rhetoric*

Claudia Eppert Ontario Institute for Studies in Education. *Literacy*

Stephen M. Fallon Program of Liberal Studies, University of Notre Dame. *Milton*

Peter Figueroa School of Education, University of Southampton. *Pluralism; Race and Racism*

Esther Fine Faculty of Education, York University. *Possibility*

William A. Frank Department of Philosophy, University of Dallas. *Anselm of Canterbury; Bonaventure; Duns Scotus*

Susan Douglas Franzosa Department of Education, University of New Hampshire. *Civic Education; Peabody*

James W. Fraser Center for Innovation in Urban Education, Northeastern University. *Democracy*

Michael Gane Department of Social Sciences, Loughborough University. *Durkheim*

James W. Garrison Division of Curriculum and Instruction, Virginia Polytechnic Institute. *Abelard; Luther; Science, Philosophy of; Social Sciences, Philosophy of*

James M. Giarelli Graduate School of Education, Rutgers University. *Ethics and Morality; Reconstructionism*

Leon Golden Department of Classics, Florida State University. *Comedy; Tragedy*

Louis Goldman Department of Curriculum and Instruction, Wichita State University. *Homer*

Michael F. Goodman Department of Philosophy, Humboldt State University. *Person, Concept of*

Roger S. Gottlieb Department of Humanities, Worcester Polytechnic Institute. *Marx*

Ignacio L. Götz New College, Hofstra University. *Alienation; Hypatia*

James Gouinlock Department of Philosophy, Emory University. *Hook; Mill*

D. Bob Gowin Professor Emeritus, Cornell University. *Whitehead*

Thomas F. Green Pompey, New York. *Common Sense; Norm*

Maxine Greene Teachers College, Columbia University. *Philosophy and Literature*

Michael H. Grimmitt School of Education, University of Birmingham. *Religious Education*

Gerald L. Gutek School of Education, Loyola University, Chicago. *Froebel; Pestalozzi*

David Hawkins Boulder, Colorado. *Intelligence*

Graham Haydon History and Philosophy, Institute of Education, University of London. *Aims of Education*

Felicity Haynes Graduate School of Education, University of Western Australia. *Epistemology; Meaning*

Arthur L. Herman Department of Philosophy, University of Wisconsin, Stevens Point. *Hinduism*

Robert D. Heslep College of Education, University of Georgia. *Analytic Philosophy*

Richard W. Hibler State University of New York, College at Potsdam. *Epicureanism*

Larry A. Hickman Center for Dewey Studies, Southern Illinois University, Carbondale. *Dewey*

Kathleen Marie Higgins Department of Philosophy, University of Texas at Austin. *Nietzsche*

Barbara Houston Department of Education, University of New Hampshire. *Feminism*

Kenneth E. Howe School of Education, University of Colorado. *Equality*

Thomas C. Hunt Division of Curriculum and Instruction, Virginia Polytechnic Institute. *Abelard; Luther*

Georg G. Iggers Department of History, State University of New York, Buffalo. *Historicism*

Erwin V. Johanningmeier School of Education, University of South Florida. *Rosenkranz; School*

Joseph Kahne College of Education, University of Illinois, Chicago. *Justice*

James S. Kaminsky Educational Foundations, Leadership, and Technology, Auburn University. *Philosophy of Education, Professional Organizations in*

George B. Kerferd Emeritus Professor of Greek, University of Manchester. *Sophists*

Bruce A. Kimball School of Education, University of Rochester. *Liberal Education*

Russell Kirkland Department of Religion, University of Georgia. *Taoism*

Wendy Kohli Department of Curriculum and Instruction, Louisiana State University. *Critical Theory*

Christine M. Korsgaard Department of Philosophy, Harvard University. *Conscience; Formalism*

R. Scott Kretchmar College of Health and Human Development, Pennsylvania State University. *Physical Education*

Walter P. Krolikowski Loyola University of Chicago. *Thomas Aquinas; William of Ockham*

Susan Laird Educational Leadership and Policy Studies, University of Oklahoma. *Beecher; Domestic Education; Girls and Women, Education of*

Oliver Leaman Education and Community Studies, Liverpool John Morris University. *Islam*

Deborah M. Licht Department of Psychology, Harvard University. *Hall*

Christopher J. Lucas College of Education, University of Arkansas. *Humanism;* Studia Humanitatis

David Lyons School of Law, Boston University. *Civil Disobedience; Utilitarianism*

Joseph M. McCarthy Department of Education and Human Services, Suffolk University. *Philo of Alexandria; Quintilian*

James E. McClellan, Jr. College of Arts and Humanities, Corpus Christi State University. *Dialectic; Scientism*

Terrance McConnell Department of Philosophy, University of North Carolina, Greensboro. *Intuitionism*

Michael McDuffie Department of Religion and Philosophy, Muskingum College. *Phenomenology*

Lynne McFall Department of Philosophy, Syracuse University. *Happiness*

Tibor R. Machan Department of Philosophy, Auburn University. *Capitalism*

Peter McLaren Graduate School of Education, University of California, Los Angeles. *Indoctrination*

C.J.B. Macmillan Center for Policy Studies in Education, Florida State University. *Teaching and Learning*

Karen E. Maloney Harvard Educational Review. *Gilman*

Frank Margonis Department of Educational Studies, University of Utah. *Nationalism*

Gordon D. Marino Department of Philosophy, St. Olaf College. *Kierkegaard; Love*

Jane Roland Martin Professor of Philosophy Emerita, University of Massachusetts, Boston. *Home and Family; Montessori*

Michael Martin Department of Philosophy, Boston University. *Atheism*

P. Rudy Mattai Educational Foundations, State University of New York, College at Buffalo. *Elitism*

Michael R. Matthews School of Education Studies, University of New South Wales. *Darwin*

Barry Mehler Department of Humanities, Ferris State College. *Heredity and Hereditarianism*

Parviz Morewedge Institute of Global Cultural Studies, Binghamton University. *Neoplatonism*

Christopher W. Morris Department of Philosophy, Bowling Green State University. *Right, Theories of the*

Paul K. Moser Philosophy Department, Loyola University, Chicago. *Truth*

Paul Nash Formerly President, Civic Education Foundation. *Arnold; Freedom and Determinism*

Thomas Whitson Nelson Department of Educational Administration and Foundations, Illinois State University. *Philosophy of Education, Literature in*

Jan Nespor Division of Curriculum and Instruction, Virginia Polytechnic Institute. *Social Sciences, Philosophy of*

Joseph W. Newman Department of Educational Leadership and Foundations, University of South Alabama. *Mann*

Carol J. Nicholson Department of Philosophy, Rider College. *Modernism and Postmodernism*

Frederick W. Norris Department of Religion and Philosophy, Emmanuel School of Religion. *Jesus of Nazareth*

Michael A. Oliker Independent Scholar. *Censorship; Educational Policy and Administration*

Richard Olmsted Department of Philosophy, Rhode Island College. *Harris*

Donald Oppewal Education Department, Calvin College. *Calvinism*

David B. Owen College of Education, Iowa State University. *Rousseau*

John W. Padberg Institute of Jesuit Sources. *Ignatius of Loyola*

Graham Parkes Department of Philosophy, University of Hawaii, Manoa. *Nihilism*

Andres I. Perez y Mena New York City. *Marti-Perez; Multiculturalism*

Stephen Perkins Kent, England. *Marxism*

Henry J. Perkinson Department of Cultural Foundations, New York University. *Evolution*

F. Michael Perko Loyola University, Chicago. *Scholasticism*

Richard H. Popkin Professor Emeritus, Washington University. *Skepticism*

Jerome A. Popp Southern Illinois University, Edwardsville. *Learning, Theories of*

Madhu Suri Prakash Administration, Policy, Foundations, and Comparative/International Education, Pennsylvania State University. *Gandhi*

Samuel D. Proctor Martin Luther King, Jr. Emeritus Professor, Rutgers University. *Washington*

Marc Pruyn Graduate School of Education, University of California, Los Angeles. *Indoctrination*

Rupert J. Read Faculty of Humanities and Social Science, Manchester Metropolitan University. *Wittgenstein*

Nicholas Rescher Department of Philosophy, University of Pittsburgh. *Idealism*

John Martin Rich Department of Curriculum and Instruction, University of Texas, Austin. *Emotivism*

Emily Robertson School of Education, Syracuse University. *Relativism*

Michael J. Rockler National Lewis University. *Russell*

Sandra Rosenthal Department of Philosophy, Loyola University, New Orleans. *Pragmatism*

Edward G. Rozycki Center for Education, Widener University. *Behaviorism*

Erika Rummel Department of History, Wilfrid Laurier University. *Erasmus*

Virginia Sapiro Department of Political Science, University of Wisconsin, Madison. *Wollstonecraft*

Jean Schmittau School of Education and Human Development, Binghamton University. *Cognitive Development*

Peter A. Schouls Philosophy Department, Massey University. *Descartes; Locke*

Samuel Scolnicov Department of Philosophy, Hebrew University of Jerusalem. *Plato*

John R. Scudder, Jr. Department of Philosophy, Lynchburg College. *Buber*

Robert Sessions Kirkwood Community College, Iowa. *Work*

Robert R. Sherman College of Education, University of Florida. *Stoicism*

Mwalimu J. Shujaa School of Education, State University of New York, Buffalo. *DuBois*

Betty A. Sichel College of Education, University of Houston. *Socrates*

Harvey Siegel Department of Philosophy, University of Miami. *Reason and Rationality*

Audrey Smedley Department of Sociology and Anthropology, Virginia Commonwealth University. *Slavery*

Philip L. Smith College of Education, Ohio State University. *Empiricism*

K. Alan Snyder Indiana Wesleyan University. *Webster*

D.R. Steg Department of Psychology, Sociology, and Anthropology, Drexel University. *Cybernetics; Moral Development; Values and Evaluation*

Eva M. Stehle Department of Classics, University of Maryland. *Sappho*

Kenneth A. Strike Department of Education, Cornell University. *Liberalism*

John R. Suler Department of Psychology, Rider College. *Psychoanalysis*

Daniel Tanner Graduate School of Education, Rutgers University. *Curriculum and Instruction*

Kenneth Teitelbaum School of Education and Human Development, Binghamton University. *Socialism*

Mariam G. Thalos Department of Philosophy, State University of New York, Buffalo. *Naturalism*

Lucy F. Townsend Department of Leadership and Educational Policy Studies, Northern Illinois University. *Willard*

Barry Troyna Department of Education, University of Warwick. *Minorities*

Jonathan H. Turner Department of Sociology, University of California, Riverside. *Spencer*

Wayne Urban College of Education, Georgia State University. *Public Education*

Donald Phillip Verene Department of Philosophy, Emory University. *Hegel; Vico*

Paul C. Violas College of Education, University of Illinois. *Cicero; Isocrates*

Walter H. Wagner Department of Religion, Muhlenberg College. *Clement of Alexandria*

Jennings L. Wagoner, Jr. Curry School of Education, University of Virginia. *Jefferson*

Russell Wahl Department of English and Philosophy, Idaho State University. *Arnauld*

Andrea Walton Teachers College, Columbia University. *Addams*

Richard Warner Chicago-Kent College of Law, Illinois Institute of Technology. *Pleasure*

Rodman B. Webb College of Education, University of Florida. *Experience*

Mark Weinstein Institute for Critical Thinking, Montclair State College. *Logic*

Danny G. Wells Doraville, Georgia. *Calvin*

Bruce W. Wilshire Department of Philosophy, Rutgers University. *James*

Tom H. Winnifrith University of Warwick. *Leisure*

Arthur G. Wirth Professor Emeritus, Department of Education, Washington University. *Vocational Education*

Robert Wokler Department of Government, University of Manchester. *Diderot*

Victor L. Worsfold School of Arts and Humanities, University of Texas, Dallas. *Children's Rights; Individualism*

Philosophy of Education

Abelard, Peter (1079–1142)

Peter Abelard cleared the path for the coming of the Scholastic era of Christian rationalism. Abelard also did more than any other scholar to prepare the ground for the founding of the great universities of Europe.

Personalities as well as principles transform ages, just as teachers' personalities as much as their precepts influence students. Abelard educated his age in both ways. He took teaching, learning, and scholarship beyond the passive transmission of unquestioned church dogma by developing a dialectical method of inquiry that did not proceed according to authority. Abelard eagerly questioned everything; for him, nothing was beyond the domain of rational inquiry. He was a staunch defender of the right to consult reason and to be persuaded by its dictates alone. He emphasized the method of systematic doubt:

> In truth, constant or frequent questioning is the first key to wisdom; and it is, indeed, to the acquiring of this questioning with absorbing eagerness that the famous philosopher, Aristotle . . . urges the studious. . . . For through doubting we come to inquiry, and through inquiry we perceive truth. *(Sic et Non)*

By his rational method he sought to place belief on a firmer foundation than that of faith alone.

Abelard's major works include (i) his *Theologia Christiana,* in which he argued that faith and revelation are the beginning of belief but that they can not be inconsistent with reason, because our finite reason was made in God's image, even if it shines by a lesser light. Abelard placed the assent of faith on an intel-lectual rather than a voluntarist foundation; (ii) his *Scito Teipsum,* in which he argued that sin lies in our intentions alone and that deeds add nothing to the morality of what was purposed; and (iii) *Sic et Non,* written as a text for students, in which Abelard asked difficult theological questions, cited "authorities" on both sides, and then left it to the students to resolve the dialectical problem. Examples of questions in *Sic et Non* include "Should human faith be based on reason, or no?" and "Is God the author of evil, or no?"

Abelard was a compelling personality. Many that knew him commented on his attractive appearance, self-confidence, eloquence, and enthusiasm. He was a quick-witted master of subtle logic and was known as "a master of universal knowledge." In debate he was intrepid, aggressive, and unrelenting. His effect was devastating to opponents and attractive to his young admirers, who flocked to him by the thousands.

By 1108 Abelard was ensconced at Paris at a site that lay within the confines of the future University of Paris. Unlike the ecclesiastical schools, which prepared monks and priests for church service, Abelard's "school" was open to all. When interrupted by the scandal of his liaison with Heloise, his Parisian school numbered nearly five thousand students. When in 1120 he started another school in Champagne, its numbers reached three thousand students. Wherever he taught he established a community of scholars that lived and learned together. Originally the term *university* referred not to the disciplines taught but to the university of persons, teachers, and students that establish a community of study.

Abelard's rebellious attitudes did not endear him to church authorities. He was arraigned and condemned of heresy before two councils—at Soissons in 1121 A.D. and in 1140 A.D. at Sens, under the assault of Bernard of Clairvaux (1091–1153).

James W. Garrison
Thomas C. Hunt

See also SCHOLASTICISM

Bibliography

Abelard. *Ethics*. Translated by D.E. Luscombe. Oxford: Oxford University Press, 1971.

———. *Sic et Non*. Translated by D.E. Luscombe. Oxford: Oxford University Press, 1971.

Compayre, Gabriel. *Abelard and the Origin and Early History of Universities*. New York: Greenwood Press, 1963. Originally published by Charles Scribner's Sons, 1893.

Luscombe, D.E. *The School of Peter Abelard*. Cambridge: Cambridge University Press, 1969.

McCallum, J.R. *Abelard's Christian Theology*. Oxford: Oxford University Press, 1935.

Sikes, J.G. *Peter Abailard*. New York: Russell and Russell, 1965.

Academic Freedom

The right to academic freedom is commonly ascribed to teachers and researchers in the educational institutions of liberal democratic societies. Academic freedom is also claimed, though less often and more controversially, by students in the same institutions. Although the precise content of the right has long been disputed, there is wide agreement on the central idea of a right to noninterference in the responsible pursuit of academic ends.

The right to academic freedom is in some ways similar to other rights closely connected to liberal democracy—in particular, rights to freedom of conscience and speech. Like those other socially protected liberties, academic freedom marks out an area of conduct where the right-holder is free to act according to convictions that others may regard as false or otherwise objectionable. Even if those who disagree with the right-holder are correct to do so, it is assumed that this fact cannot by itself justify any infringement on the right. Reasons of special weight are needed to warrant infringements on academic freedom, just as reasons of special urgency are needed to justify restricting free speech; such reasons are not supplied merely by the fact that the right-holder is mistaken, or thought to be mistaken. Broadly similar moral arguments are used to justify these rights, such as the useful role of unconventional views in helping to test and refine accepted theories.

Yet important differences and tensions exist between academic freedom and the common liberties of citizens. First, the academic freedom of teachers and researchers belongs only to those whose demonstrated competence supposedly entitles them to specialized roles in educational institutions; the liberties they enjoy as occupants of these roles are not a universal prerogative of citizenship, like freedom of conscience. Second, the social consequences of respect for academic freedom may restrict the liberties of ordinary citizens in significant ways. If respect for the academic freedom of science teachers requires that we permit them to dismiss religious views as scientifically irrelevant, this will be perceived by some as a violation of the freedom of conscience of students and parents who believe it is sinful to divorce science from religion. Whether this is an unjustified restriction on students' and parents' liberty is controversial. What cannot be denied is that significant restriction of the liberty of others is inevitable so long as we insist on the teacher's academic freedom in such cases. There is also potential for moral conflict between academic freedom and the free speech of participants within educational institutions. The risks of conflict are more substantial for teachers than for students, and so it is best to discuss the two separately.

The role of teacher characteristically involves a large asymmetry of power with students. One implication of this is that the boundaries of the academic freedom we assign to teachers must be limited by the need to protect students against the abuse of power. If the boundaries are marked too narrowly, teachers lack the freedom to teach in imaginative and intellectually provocative ways. If the boundaries are too wide, students are left vulnerable to irresponsible individuals who might practice indoctrination or otherwise abuse their powers. There is room here for reasonable disagreement about where distinctions should be made. But teachers in the classroom cannot defensibly claim a freedom of expression of the same scope they might enjoy as ordinary citizens. The scope of an ordinary citizen's freedom of speech is determined in part by the assumption that others are free not to listen if they so choose, and are under no special social pressure to accept what is said to them. Neither of these assumptions is true of students in their dealings with teachers, and so the case is far weaker for granting teachers in the classroom freedom of speech of the scope that ordinary citizens enjoy.

Furthermore, some views that would be protected by the right to free speech when voiced by an ordinary citizen cannot be protected by the academic freedom of teachers, when such views indicate gross intellectual incompetence. Individuals are entitled to the academic freedom that befits the role of teacher only so long as they show the requisite competence. When their speech in the classroom shows that they lack such competence, they forfeit any legitimate claim to the protections of academic freedom.

Students are not under the same social pressure to accept the views of fellow students as they are to accept the views of their teachers. Thus the case for granting them a larger scope for free speech in educational institutions looks strong. Similarly, they do not forfeit the right to whatever academic freedom befits the role of student when their speech in the classroom indicates gross intellectual incompetence. However, the expression of convictions, such as racist or sexist prejudices, that are in fundamental conflict with the purposes of the institution creates a strong argument for restriction in some circumstances. That argument is often used in defense of speech codes for students in schools and universities. But restrictions on student speech must be tempered by recognition of the educational benefits of bringing morally noxious views into the open so that teachers and other students can subject them to the public criticism they deserve.

The various controversies that revolve around the issue of academic freedom are inseparable from arguments about the proper purposes of educational institutions. In diverse and complex societies, unanimity on educational values is unattainable, but a partial consensus is entailed by a shared commitment to the basic principles of liberal democracy. The survival of liberty and democracy as social ideals is often said to depend on a vigorous intellectual culture in which dissent is welcome and opposing views can clash and compete for adherents in a free marketplace of ideas. A culture of that sort is stifled when those who participate in educational institutions are compelled to adhere to established orthodoxies. That is why academic freedom is an alien principle to authoritarian societies. The intellectual culture that academic freedom encourages is a threat to regimes that repudiate liberal democratic values.

The defense of academic freedom as a bulwark of liberal democracy is widely though not universally shared in contemporary educational debate. But the defense can be developed in two contrasting directions, each with divergent implications for the detailed interpretation of academic freedom. On the one hand, it may be argued that if educational institutions are to nurture genuinely free and informed thought, those working within them must be insulated from pressures exerted by outside agencies. This argument supports a strong emphasis on the professional autonomy of teachers and professors. Insofar as students or other interested parties are regarded as incapable of reasonable academic judgment, demands for their participation in educational decision-making will be condemned as a pernicious encroachment on the academic freedom of the professional elite. Alternatively, the intellectual culture of liberal democracy may be understood in a more egalitarian spirit. This second interpretation rejects the elitist premises of the first and suggests that schools that welcome a high level of community and student participation in decision-making will embody the kind of academic freedom worth having.

The two interpretations of academic freedom are not mutually exclusive alternatives, because a variety of intermediate views are possible. It may be argued that some decisions within schools are heavily dependent on special expertise. That being so, those particular decisions are properly matters for the academic freedom of certified professionals; other decisions can and should be determined by a more inclusive process of deliberation. This view is subject to many variations, as the line between the professional autonomy of the expert and the democratic participation of parents, students, and others can be drawn in numerous ways. The chief difficulty in developing any version of the intermediate view is drawing that line in a clear and defensible way. For example, academic expertise is highly relevant to the selection of texts for a curriculum, and therefore it is argued that text selection must be left to educational professionals if their academic freedom is to be respected. Nevertheless, moral considerations are also relevant to text selection, and, as teachers can claim no special expertise in morality, it is also plausibly claimed that teachers cannot arrogate exclusive authority over the choice of texts. The resolution of such disputes will depend on how moral and other considerations are balanced in our vision of the purposes of schools, and on who is thought to be in the best position to advance those purposes.

Eamonn Callan

See also CENSORSHIP; CHILDREN'S RIGHTS; DEMOCRACY; INDOCTRINATION; LIBERAL EDUCATION; RIGHTS; TOLERATION

Bibliography
Gewirth, Alan. "Human Rights and Academic Freedom." In *Morality, Responsibility, and the University*, edited by Steven M. Cahn. Philadelphia: Temple University Press, 1990.
Gutmann, Amy. *Democratic Education.* Princeton: Princeton University Press, 1988.
Strike, Kenneth. *Liberty and Learning.* Oxford: Martin Robertson, 1982.

Addams, Jane (1860–1935)

Leader in the social settlement movement, social worker, progressive reformer, suffragist, pacifist, and educational thinker. Born and raised in Cedarville, Illinois, Addams received her bachelor's degree from Rockford College in 1882. Seven years later, she established a social settlement (area where reformers lived as neighbors to the working poor, sharing their lives and helping to work out their problems), Hull-House, in Chicago's Nineteenth Ward. It was not the nation's first settlement, but Hull-House soon emerged as the vanguard of what became a national movement. Equally important, Addams herself attained international prominence as an educator and was admired by many people as a cultural heroine.

Addams's ideas on education, social reform, culture, and democracy were deeply intertwined. They generally reflected the faith many thinkers of the Progressive Era expressed in democracy, the capacity of all individuals to grow and contribute to society, and the inevitability of social progress. In Addams's view, a social settlement, both in its living arrangements

and programs, embodied an educational philosophy designed to meet the social needs created by urban, industrial life. Hull-House defined education broadly, hoping to extend education to all social groups and to all levels and types of students, and rejected religious dogma and old absolutes about learning and culture. The settlement was a fundamentally new social institution that was, Addams asserted, "attempting to learn from life itself" (*Second Twenty Years at Hull-House:* 408).

Addams conceived of education as an integral part of any reform effort to lessen the social pressures brought by industrialization and immigration and to alleviate the squalor and exploitation faced by immigrants in the nation's cities. It was also a first step in building a new social morality and in integrating immigrant cultures into American society. By promoting various types of education, settlement workers could meet the pressing needs of their immigrant neighbors and also help build a sense of community.

To Addams, the idea of a social settlement went beyond the notion of physical proximity to embrace the interconnectedness of daily human relations. The ultimate goal of the social settlement, she believed, was to help people live together in a way that built upon their diversity and gave concrete meaning to the ideals of democratic theory. Education was a vehicle for cultivating the civic spirit needed to spark public debate; thus it was vital to the settlements' mission of promoting the social reforms needed to achieve a more harmonious, equitable, and just American society.

It would be myopic to view Addams's philosophy of education apart from the circumstances of her own life. She derived many of her early educational ideas and her goals for settlement work from her personal experiences as an educated, middle-class, Christian woman who came of age in the 1880s. Addams's father was a successful mill owner, a well-respected citizen, and a state senator whose example of public leadership she deeply admired and hoped to emulate. Like many of the first generation of female college graduates, however, she struggled to reconcile her education and religiously inspired desire to help others with the domestic expectations most people held for young women. These constraints, which Addams later referred to as the "family claim," and her father's untimely death in 1881 left the idealistic Addams searching restlessly for a suitable vocation. She enrolled at the Women's Medical College of Philadelphia, but soon withdrew because of a recurring ailment. She eventually concluded that her frail health was connected to her unfulfilled need for a career that would be socially useful and personally satisfying. She devoted the next eight years to self-cultivation. She read the social ideas of Ruskin, Morris, and Tolstoy, studied the arts and languages, and traveled abroad.

During a trip to Europe in 1887, Addams and her college friend Ellen Gates Starr visited London's Toynbee Hall, a settlement run by Oxford University students and overseen by Canon Samuel A. Barnett. Toynbee Hall residents translated their Christian values into their communal living and daily work among London's poor. Addams and Starr returned to Chicago inspired by this model and firmly convinced that they too would dedicate themselves to social service. Together they rented an old mansion on Chicago's Halsted Street and founded Hull-House. Forgoing marriage, Addams devoted herself to organizing and promoting settlement work. In the process, she figured prominently in the creation of a new profession for women and oversaw one of the nation's most important efforts to bring the religious value of universality into secular life and to put democratic theory and progressive educational ideas into practice.

Recognized as the spokeswoman for the settlement movement, Addams wrote numerous articles and lectured throughout the country to educate others about the aims and purposes of the social settlements. In her early address "The Subjective Necessity for the Social Settlements" (1892), she elaborated upon the three broad ideas that animated the growing settlement movement: (1) an effort to infuse democracy into social relationships and community affairs; (2) a desire to ensure social unity and a higher civic life by bringing the benefits of tradition and culture to the masses (reflecting the temper of her times, Addams naively referred to these achievements as the "race life," but she increasingly emphasized the richness and coherence immigrants brought to American culture); and (3) a widespread, renewed commitment to the values of Christian humanitarianism.

Addams believed that a social settlement like Hull-House could provide a bridge or a meeting point between the "objective" needs of the urban poor and the "subjective" needs of many well-educated, religious-minded individuals who, like herself, were searching for a worthy social cause to embrace. Settlement work brought immediate help and training to struggling poor and immigrant families. It also gave the settlement residents ample opportunity to test the validity of their social ideas and to apply their education to the practical experiences and problems of everyday life. The meeting of these two distinct social groups and the fulfillment of their respective needs was education in action and a way to overcome the physical and cultural segregation that characterized nineteenth-century American cities.

Addams's philosophy of education, which she tried to translate into residential life and activities at Hull-House, was both pluralistic and pragmatic. It was rooted in a notion of social interdependence, an empathy with the common person, and an appreciation of what men and women of different classes, cultures, and generations might learn from each other. Drawing a contrast between settlement work and then-existing philanthropic and charity efforts, which tended to pass moral judgment on the poor, Addams viewed Hull-House as an experiment in social education. She and other Hull-House residents accepted the needs and conditions of the neighborhood as the starting point for their work and hoped to build a partnership with those they helped. Addams believed that the value of educational methods lay in the adequacy of their results. Settlement programs and approaches to problems therefore needed to be evaluated continually and, if necessary, changed accordingly.

From its founding, Hull-House thus both reflected and tested Addams's educational theories and ideas about the intimate ties between education and democracy. In her view, democracy is not just a political form of government; it is a form of social relations having education as its foundation. Achieving and sustaining democracy amid rapid urbanization and industrialization meant fostering a civic consciousness among all people. Addams and other settlement workers hoped to restore communication between different parts of society and thereby mend the broken social ties between people, to foster a sense of mutual need and benefit, and to overcome the social distinctions between the rich and poor, or the native-born and the foreign-born. The settlement movement encouraged the more privileged members of society to respect and reach out to the immigrants and the uneducated in an effort to ensure them access to cultural resources, but also to appreciate the unique culture of each group. In all, the settlement activity hoped to counter what many social critics saw as the dehumanizing isolation of urban life and the industrial age. In contrast to those who feared rising immigration or who asserted the superiority of Anglo-Saxon American culture, Addams affirmed what she often described as the "solidarity of the human race." As she explained in her introduction to *Democracy and Social Ethics* (1902), democracy must be a "rule of living as well as a test of faith."

Addams shared with many pragmatic thinkers and progressive educators, perhaps most notably her friend, the University of Chicago philosopher John Dewey (1859–1952), a belief that education is a broad, lifelong process. It encompasses more than instruction or the period of youth and formal schooling. The settlements were, in Addams's words, a "protest" against a narrow or "restricted" view of education (Addams in Lagemann, 55). She voiced concern about school's narrow, limiting vocational curriculum and its isolation from other parts of the community. She urged educators to draw upon the child's own experiences and to affirm the child's social value. She was similarly critical of the orientation of American universities and the academic knowledge and elite culture they valued to the exclusion of other forms.

Addams's autobiography, *Twenty Years at Hull-House* (1910), offers a rich account of the wide-ranging settlement projects. As Ellen Condliffe Lagemann has discussed most fully, the educational programs Hull-House sponsored, at times in collaboration with Chicago's University Extension, reflected Addams's developing ideas about education, culture, and the possibilities for "socialized democracy." Addams emphasized a blending of intellectual and emotional life and believed in the uplifting creativity and moral inspiration that could be drawn from art and aesthetic experience. She was initially inspired to share a refined "college type" of culture with her immigrant neighbors. Soon she realized that culture should not separate or categorize people, and she therefore began to sponsor educational activities such as current-event discussions, cultural pageants, and immigrant theater productions, which were better suited to the residents of urban Chicago.

Central to all Hull-House educational activities, both in content and method, was the theme of connectedness. Reflecting the pervasive influence of the educational ideas of Friedrich Froebel (1782–1852), the Hull-House kindergarten, like many progressive educational ventures, emphasized the importance of creative play and exposed the children to music and art. Moreover, Addams urged public schools to rethink their curriculum and to offer a broad type of education that would prepare an immigrant child for work without alienating the child from family and cultural traditions. Addams, in fact, believed that children could help their parents make the often difficult transition to American life. The innovative Labor Museum at Hull-House, which displayed the history of spinning and weaving, was designed to convey the dignity of manual labor and traditional handicrafts and to capture the meaningful contributions of workers to history. Addams regarded the museum as exemplifying Dewey's concept of education as "a continuing reconstruction of experience" (*Twenty Years:* 172). Having once embraced a refined notion of culture, Addams increasingly appreciated that culture was continually remaking itself and that it could be found in daily, ordinary life. Moreover, she came to respect immigrant cultures on their own terms. She argued that the immigrant populations "through their very diversity have in their power to unify American experience" (Addams in Lagemann: 210).

Addams's conceptualization of social life, like her view of education, was organic. It affirmed the links between individuals, and between individuals and the greater society. Thus, from her perspective, the needs or problems of any social group were the concern of all citizens. "But on what basis beyond good will could people act wisely to improve social conditions?" she and her contemporaries asked. Addams and the Hull-House residents believed that reform activity should be guided by practical, applied knowledge and that a settlement should be a center for social research. The *Hull-House Maps and Papers* (1895) was a pioneering effort to survey a city ward and to collect data that could inform policy decisions and legislation.

Related to Addams's holistic educational views and her support for research was her feminist belief that women have a unique perspective to bring to social reform. Addams argued that the humane qualities and moral insights culturally associated with women needed to be incorporated into social reform and legislation. She underscored the link between what were often seen as women's concerns, such as child welfare, and the well-being of the entire society. Hull-House and the other settlements attracted many college-educated women who also believed that women had a special role to play in "municipal housekeeping." Several Hull-House residents, among them Florence Kelley, Julia Lathrop, Alice Hamilton, and Edith and Grace Abbott, gained national prominence for their efforts concerning tenement living conditions, sanitation, public schools, playgrounds, labor unions, child-labor legislation, day nurseries, and other reforms. Addams herself tried, with varying success and public receptivity, to extend her feminine vision to politics, race relations, and international affairs.

In all, Addams remains a social thinker whose attempts to apply progressive educational ideas and whose views on democracy and cultural diversity are still relevant to the problems of urban life and education. Like Dewey, Addams believed that the action needed for meaningful and permanent social change could come only through the enlightened participation of the masses, the public. Settlements, in fulfilling their educational role in an industrial society, helped to provide a basis for democracy. They offered the means of self-development and liberty necessary for individuals to take part in public debate. Education thus was the basis for any collective movement toward new social values and a better society. As Addams wrote in her chapter on "Educational Methods" in *Democracy and Social Ethics*, "We have learned to say that the good must be extended to all of society before it can be held secure by any one person or any one class; but we have not yet learned to add to that statement, that unless all men and all classes contribute to a good, we cannot even be sure that it is worth having" (p. 220).

Andrea Walton

See also DEMOCRACY; DEWEY; FEMINISM; PLURALISM; PRAGMATISM; SOCIAL SCIENCES, PHILOSOPHY OF; SOCIOLOGY

Bibliography

Addams, Jane. *Democracy and Social Ethics.* New York: Macmillan, 1920.
———. *Second Twenty Years at Hull-House.* New York: Macmillan, 1930.
———. *The Spirit of Youth and City Streets.* New York: Macmillan, 1909.
———. *Twenty Years at Hull-House.* New York: Macmillan, 1910.
Conway, Kathryn Jill. *The First Generation of American Women Graduates.* New York: Garland, 1987.
Davis, F. Allen. *American Heroine.* New York: Oxford Press, 1973.
———. *Spearheads for Reform.* New Brunswick, N.J.: Rutgers University Press, 1984.
Deegan, Mary Jo. *Jane Addams and the Men of the Chicago School, 1892–1918.* New Brunswick, N.J.: Transaction Books, 1988.
Lagemann, Ellen Condliffe, ed. *Jane Addams on Education.* New York: Teachers College University Press, 1985.

A

Aesthetics

Aesthetics has traditionally dealt with taste and the study of beauty in nature and art. Since 1750, when Alexander Baumgarten (1714–1762) coined the term *aesthetics,* it has also dealt with the felt qualities of experience. Because Baumgarten aimed at producing a science of beauty based on sense perception, his attention shifted from the study of things (especially art works) to the study of people's responses to those things. The questions of classical antiquity, "What makes a thing beautiful?" and "What makes it a work of art?" became "What makes a response an aesthetic one?" and "Under what conditions does experience become aesthetic in quality?"

Aesthetic qualities are held to be valuable, and since they are not always easy to achieve, the answers to the latter questions are of interest to educators. Educators are also interested in the classical questions "What makes a thing beautiful, or a work of art?" because curriculum content cannot be developed without answers to them. Different answers to these questions result in different approaches to aesthetic education: the content of the curriculum, ways of cultivating taste, and the conditions that render experience aesthetic in quality.

Aesthetic inquiry can, therefore, guide educational practice. And while aestheticians hold conflicting theories, the results of some investigations have been widely accepted. For example, although the content of courses in the various arts has become standardized over the generations, there are reasons to reexamine and alter that content. That is because the concept of art itself has been conceived more loosely since the publication of Morris Weitz's classic essay "The Role of Theory in Aesthetics" (1956). Weitz argued that "art" is an open concept because it cannot be defined by a set of necessary and sufficient conditions. Examination of diverse works of art reveals a variety of characteristics, none of which are essential to all works of art yet which possess "family resemblances" to one another. Thus what makes something "art" is as flexible as what makes something a game (in games, too, there are "family resemblances" but no single feature that will be found in all things properly called games). The practical guidance afforded by this conceptualization would be an opening up of the content of courses in English, art, music, and so forth. Many teachers, refusing to consider graphic novels, the lyrics of popular music, or even movies as "art," consider them unworthy of serious study. This suggests that school practice lags considerably behind the established work of aestheticians.

Aesthetic education in Western culture can be traced at least as far back as Plato (c. 427–347 B.C.). In his work on the ideal state, the *Republic,* everyone was to be educated until the age of seventeen or eighteen, and that education was dominantly aesthetic in character. Physical education emphasized grace of body, and what are now academic studies—history, social studies, citizenship—are taught by means of poetry, song, dance, myth, and dramatization. Even mathematics are taught by means of play, games, and practical activities. Only later would promising students be selected for further intellectual studies. Plato mistrusted the fancies of artists and poets, but he was prepared to censor their work and utilize it in the education of the young. For him, the arts were inherently educative: "Rhythm and harmony sink deep into the recesses of the soul and take the strongest hold there, bringing . . . grace of body and mind. . . . All that is ugly and disgraceful [the child] will rightly condemn and abhor while he is still too young to understand the reason; and when reason comes, he will greet her as a friend with whom his education has made him long familiar."

In spite of Plato, the aesthetic has been treated in Western culture more as entertainment than as a fundamental dimension of living. Johann C. Friedrich Schiller (1759–1805) argued two centuries ago, in *On the Aesthetic Education of Man,* that the enjoyment of art and the perception of beauty are a necessary stage in the development of rationality and freedom. But European and (especially) American traditions continued to conceive of education in the arts as a diversion for upper-class women and as vocational training for a limited number of men.

In the last third of the twentieth century, aesthetic education has taken two different directions. One approach, based on the concerns of classical antiquity, emphasizes academic understanding and focuses on works of art, particularly exemplary works recognized as "great." The other approach is largely concerned with the quality of students' experience; it focuses on aesthetic responses not only to the arts but also to nonartistic activities and events. In subsequent discussion, the former approach will be referred to as "academic" and the latter as "integrative."

The academic approach to aesthetic education is exemplified in a movement called discipline-based art education (DBAE). Described in detail by Clark, Day, and Greer (1987), DBAE reacted against trends long current in education in the arts: a tendency to conceive art as therapy or an escape from serious concerns; a tendency to treat art as merely decorative; and a tendency to treat art as purely affective, without any cognitive or intellectual dimension. As a corrective, DBAE conceives of four components to aesthetic education: art history, art criticism, aesthetics, and the production of art. Students can thereby acquire a broad historical and cultural context for the arts, and aesthetic principles and critical standards that bring richer meaning to art and a more discriminating appreciation of it.

That approach to aesthetic education brings greater depth and academic rigor to the study of the arts. On the other hand, an academic approach to aesthetic education risks failing to engage students in the immediate pleasures and fulfillments without which the arts become just one more thing to be studied and then tested on. Critics also note that DBAE's emphasis on the fine arts, particularly classics of the Western heritage, may fail to instruct students about the arts to which they are already responding, and it may fail to illuminate the relationships between contemporary art and society. A growing number of aesthetic educators, represented in works like Blandy's and Congdon's *Art in a Democracy* (1987), have emphasized the ways in which social and economic conditions affect the production of art and the ways in which the arts—popular and folk arts as well as fine arts—provide insight into those social and economic conditions.

The concern for people's responses to the arts that characterizes contemporary aesthetics became, in the integrative approach to aesthetic education, a concern for the quality of people's experience. That approach can be found in

Plato, but its first modern spokesman was Sir Herbert Read (1943). He claimed that the psychological disturbances that lead individuals to insanity and societies to war result from an education that overemphasizes cognitive processes at the expense of affective processes and creative activities. Because he believed that "the secret of our collective ills is to be traced to the suppression of spontaneous creative ability," he urged that personal integration and social health be achieved by "a method of education which is formally and fundamentally aesthetic." For Read, the whole of primary education should be based on creative and constructive forms of play: drama, design, dance, music, and crafts. Pupils would begin with no academic subjects as such. But the aforementioned activities, developing poise, zest, and personal integration, would quite naturally develop into literature, math, science, and technology. For Read, aesthetic education should constitute the whole of primary education, aimed not at producing artists or scholars but at developing integrated, healthy personalities.

John Dewey (1859–1952) provided additional direction and depth to an integrative approach to aesthetic education. Casual readers of Dewey's work have tended to confuse his pragmatic philosophy with a purely instrumental approach to the problems and experiences of living. But in his influential *Art as Experience* (1934), he argued for the paramount importance of the aesthetic, or consummatory, dimension of experience. The aesthetic, he claimed, characterizes experience carried to completion, brought to fulfillment. Ordinary, everyday events (and not simply works of art) are capable of rendering experience aesthetic in quality, and they fail to do so only insofar as they become routinized, dull, or arbitrarily directed by others. Thus, for Dewey, the aesthetic became a criterion for judging the worth not simply of individual experience, but of social forms and institutions as well. Authoritarian societies and schools cannot create conditions for the appearance of aesthetic quality in experience; thus they cannot promote democratic citizenship or effective learning, either.

The implications of Dewey's thought for aesthetic education are immense. In a more thoroughgoing way than Read, Dewey implied that all of education (except its specialized, vocational aspects) should strive to be aesthetic. That is, all serious attempts to teach should aim at creating conditions in which the experience of the learner is aesthetic in quality. While students of Dewey's views quite properly focus on his account of problem-solving in education, Dewey also emphasized, in *Democracy and Education* (1916), that the first phase of learning in any subject or area should involve what he called an "appreciative realization." That term is close in meaning to his use of the term "aesthetic," and, like the latter, was meant to apply through the curriculum—not just to courses in the fine arts. Dewey wrote in *Democracy and Education* that "living has its own intrinsic quality and . . . the business of education is with that quality." In other words, it is not instrumental—not just "what works"—but rather the consummatory—what is fulfilling—that needs to be focal in education. The consummatory is the aesthetic, and there may be no more powerful argument than this for the value and the nature of aesthetic education.

Donald G. Arnstine

See also DEWEY; EXPERIENCE; PLATO

Bibliography

Blandy, Doug, and Kristin G. Congdon. *Art in a Democracy*. New York: Teachers College Press, 1987.

Clark, Gilbert A., Michael D. Day, and W. Dwaine Greer. "Discipline-Based Art Education: Becoming Students of Art." *Journal of Aesthetic Education* 21 (1987): 129–93.

Dewey, John. *Art as Experience*. New York: Minton, Balch, 1934.

———. *Democracy and Education*. New York: Macmillan, 1916.

Plato. *The Republic*. Translated by F.M. Cornford. London: Oxford University Press, 1941.

Read, Sir Herbert. *Education through Art*. London: Faber and Faber, 1943. Rev. ed., 1958.

Schiller, Johann C. Friedrich. *On the Aesthetic Education of Man*. Translated by Reginald Snell. New Haven: Yale University Press, 1954.

Weitz, Morris. "The Role of Theory in Aesthetics." *Journal of Aesthetics and Art Criticism* 15 (1956): 27–35.

Aims of Education

The phrase "aims of education," at its most general, is a way of referring to whatever it is that educators try to achieve, or should try to achieve, when they undertake education as a deliberate activity. John Dewey (1859–1952) said that education as such has no aims; it is people involved in education, teachers and others, who have aims. But people have often tried to clarify or defend their own aims by asking what are, or what should be, the aims of education.

Most of the classic philosophical writings about education, from Plato (c. 427–347 B.C.) onwards, contain at least implicit answers to this question—arguably one of the most fundamental questions in the philosophy of education. But writings devoted explicitly to the aims of education are more recent and still not extensive. Examples earlier in the twentieth century include a chapter (first published in 1917) in *The Aims of Education* by A.N. Whitehead (1861–1947) and a chapter in Dewey's *Democracy and Education* (1916). The analytical work of R.S. Peters in the 1960s and 1970s helped to clarify the nature—and complexity—of the questions that can be raised under the heading of "the aims of education."

To ask what the aims of education are—when this is a philosophical question and not an empirical question about what actual teachers and others are aiming at—is to suppose that certain aims are implicit in the concept of education. On this supposition, questions about the aims of education are to be settled by conceptual analysis. For Peters, an educational process must (among other conditions) be aiming at the initiation of persons into worthwhile activities that involve knowledge and understanding. He meant this as a conceptual point: Any process which does not have such an aim could not count as education. Thus Peters and some of his critics were in effect engaging in a debate about the central features, and the boundaries, of the concept of education.

It would be widely agreed now that there was a degree of stipulation in that approach: both stipulation about what is to count as an acceptable use of the word *education* and, often, an insufficiently defended assumption that the central concern of schools, or related social institutions and practices, must be education (in the sense articulated). Most philosophers of education now would probably agree that the important question about the aims of education is a normative one: What should teachers (and others in related positions of influence) be aiming at? Debate around this question is effectively debate about what the aims of schooling ought to be.

Within this broad question, the articulation of a concept of education may well furnish a central part of the answer. There may in fact be quite wide agreement, within the literate cultures in which philosophers of education operate, about the features that distinguish what is called "education" from what would be labeled with terms such as "socialization," "training," and "indoctrination"; those features will be related to such qualities as rationality, critical reflectiveness, breadth of intellectual interest, commitment to truth, and independent-mindedness. Analytical philosophy is of value in delineating such qualities. But the defense of such qualities as specially desirable, and deserving of a central place among the aims pursued by teachers and schools, must be by normative argument, which cannot be conducted by analysis alone.

Contemporary philosophical debate about the aims of education, then, articulates different possible aims and argues their importance, which may be their importance not in an abstract, universal sense, but within a given form of society. In the late twentieth century, the conception of educational aims as associated with the idea of liberal education—the concept that Peters among others articulated—is still prominent; alongside it, the idea of vocational education puts forward another set of aims. The contemporary setting of much education within pluralistic democracies gives many accounts of educational aims a concreteness in their application that purely analytical accounts lack.

Positions taken on the aims of education may be conveniently classified in three major categories, though there are overlaps among them. These categories emphasize aims having to do with the realization of qualities that are seen as intrinsically good; aims having to do with promoting the good of the individual; and aims having to do with the good of society.

The first position would have it that goals such as knowledge and understanding—whether or not they are seen as conceptually linked with education—are themselves intrinsically good and should be pursued just for that reason. There are perhaps two major problems with positions of this sort: (1) that the claim that knowledge and understanding (and perhaps other qualities such as the appreciation of art) are intrinsically good, independently of their instrumental value, seems inevitably an appeal to intuition rather than something for which further argument can be given; and (2) that even if it is accepted that these things are intrinsically good, a further normative argument is needed to establish the extent, if any, to which schools should be devoted to the pursuit of them, rather than to the pursuit of other things that can be clearly defended as improving the quality of life.

The second position allows for diverse accounts of those aspects of the good of individuals that can and should be promoted through education. This position can also refer to the promotion of knowledge and understanding, when they are seen as valuable for the individual in enhancing the quality of life or serving instrumentally in the pursuit of other goals. It can include the acquisition of skills that will help the individual to fill vocational roles. It can, and in many contemporary accounts of liberal education does, include the promotion of the individual's autonomy (as is prominent in the writings of John White in Britain and many contemporary North American writers). It is clear that the justification for any of these aims, or the establishing of priorities among them, requires that an underlying account of the good of the individual be articulated.

The third position stresses that the goal of the education of each person is to promote, not only the good of that person, but also the good of others—others being educated at the same time, adult members of society who are no longer being educated, or even future generations. Within this category is one of the longest-established aims of education: that education include the development of moral qualities and dispositions, so that society as a whole will be made, through education, more peaceful and harmonious than it might otherwise be. Within the same category can be included more specific aims, such as promoting social justice, racial harmony, and equality of opportunity between the sexes.

All such aims will be seen as tending to make the society in question a better society (according to criteria that must be specified within a full justification). Within one influential subcategory, a society is judged better to the extent that its economy is growing; that education should enable one society to compete economically with others is a theme commonly heard in modern political rhetoric, though less often defended explicitly by philosophers.

While the good of society and the good of individuals can be given interpretations that would make the pursuit of both mutually in-compatible, that is by no means necessarily the case. Thus vocational aims may benefit both the individuals who are enabled to get more rewarding jobs and the society that benefits from their skills. The aim of equipping individuals to be active, informed, and reflective citizens may directly help individuals defend their own rights and promote their own interests, and may also help to produce and maintain a flourishing democracy that indirectly will benefit everyone within it.

The conceptions of the good life and of the good society that are now increasingly invoked in accounts of the aims of education are themselves, of course, contestable; thus in this area philosophers of education are increasingly drawing on writings within ethics and political philosophy, including the ongoing debate between individualist and communitarian accounts of the good life.

Graham Haydon

See also ANALYTIC PHILOSOPHY; COMMUNITY; DEWEY; INDIVIDUALISM; LIBERAL EDUCATION; VOCATIONAL EDUCATION; WHITEHEAD

Bibliography
Dewey, John. *Democracy and Education.* New York: Macmillan, 1916.
Peters, R.S., J. Woods, and W.H. Dray. "Aims of Education—A Conceptual Inquiry." In *The Philosophy of Education*, edited by R.S. Peters. Oxford: Oxford University Press, 1973.
White, John. *The Aims of Education Restated.* London: Routledge, 1982.
Whitehead, A.N. *The Aims of Education and Other Essays.* London: Williams and Norgate, 1932.
Wringe, Colin. *Understanding Educational Aims.* London: Unwin Hyman, 1988.

Alcott, Amos Bronson (1799–1888)
American philosopher, educator, and reformer. Along with Ralph Waldo Emerson (1803–1882), Henry David Thoreau (1817–1862), and several other New England literati, he helped form the nucleus of what came to be known as American Transcendentalism.

Having had only a sketchy formal education, Alcott nonetheless set out to reform education in the United States, believing that such change would be the key to the progress of humanity. Guided by the ideas of the English philosopher John Locke (1632–1704), the Swiss educator Johann Pestalozzi (1746–1827), and the English reformer Robert Owen (1771–1858), he used techniques in his early common school classrooms that reflected a mechanistic and strongly environmentalist theory of learning. Assuming the existence of predictable laws of nature that dictate the growth of the human mind, he argued that the mind initially receives ideas through the interaction of the senses with external objects. In the process of thinking, the mind has the ability to select and discriminate among the received simple ideas to produce more complex ones. He believed that the successful educator had to follow the laws of mental growth meticulously, attending carefully to the classroom environment that shapes the process.

For Alcott, the primary purpose of education was the inculcation of moral values. Accordingly, he confronted his students with objects that suggested such values as love, reverence, and gratitude. The objects would, he believed, encourage the development of corresponding values in the child. Similarly, objects of art would promote aesthetic values. A spontaneous, varied, and nonthreatening classroom atmosphere would encourage a love of learning, and the positive moral values and behavior of the instructor and classmates would encourage the same in each student.

During the 1830s, Alcott turned toward Platonic idealism to find greater support for his faith in human improvement through education. While he did not completely forsake Lockean epistemology, his newfound Platonism stressed those innate qualities in the human mind that enable it to intuit eternal truths without the aid of sense perception. Thus endowed, humans could transcend the limitations of the physical world, sharing in a universal divine spirit of which the physical world is a mere reflection.

At his Temple School, founded in Boston in 1834, Alcott publicized what he called "spiritual culture." While much of his curriculum and his teaching practices from earlier schools remained in place, he spent great energy trying to nurture what he believed was the essential, Godlike nature of his young students' souls. As before, he exposed his students to objects, attitudes, writings, and behavior—the Christian Gospels, for example—that he felt were emblematic of "spiritual" values. He hoped that these external impressions would awaken the intuitive spiritual tendencies in the children, perfecting their souls while sharpening their intellects.

Alcott's later educational writings shed the arcane idealism of his Transcendentalist phase. As superintendent of the Concord, Massachusetts, public schools, he celebrated the more practical methods of his early schools and emphasized concern for the desires, needs, and creative abilities of the student. He called for variety in classroom activities, pleasant surroundings, expressive writing and conversation, the abolition of corporal punishment, the avoidance of rote learning, the inductive method, and experiential learning.

Alcott's educational philosophy was largely derivative, although he was not a devotee of any one school of thought, nor could he present a coherent and logically consistent ideology. But he was a gifted practitioner, and his prescription for reform in the schools touched upon many of the diverse elements that would come to be known as progressive education.

Frederick C. Dahlstrand

See also LOCKE; PEABODY; PESTALOZZI; PROGRESS, IDEA OF

Bibliography

Alcott, Amos Bronson. "Elementary Instruction." *American Journal of Education* 3 (1828): 369–74, 440–43.

———. *Essays on Education (1830–1862).* Edited by Walter Harding. Gainesville, Fla.: Scholar's Facsimiles and Reprints, 1960.

———. "Pestalozzi's Principle and Methods of Instruction." *American Journal of Education* 4 (1829): 97–107.

———. "Primary Education: Account of the Method of Instruction in the Primary School No. 1, of Cheshire, Connecticut." *American Journal of Education* 3 (1828): 26–31, 86–94.

Dahlstrand, Frederick C. *Amos Bronson Alcott, an Intellectual Biography.* Rutherford, N.J.: Fairleigh Dickinson University Press, 1982.

McCuskey, Dorothy. *Bronson Alcott, Teacher.* New York: Macmillan, 1940.

Peabody, Elizabeth Palmer, ed. *Record of a School.* Boston: James Munroe and Co., 1835. 3rd ed., Roberts Brothers, 1874.

Alfarabi (870–950)

Generally known as "the second teacher"—that is, second after Aristotle—Abu Nasr Muhammad Ibn Muhammad Ibn Tarkham Ibn Awzalagh al-Farabi is generally heralded as having founded political philosophy within the Islamic cultural tradition. Born in the village of Farab in Turkestan, he resided in Bukhara, Marv, Haran, Baghdad, Constantinople, Aleppo, Cairo, and Damascus, where he died. The son of an army officer in the service of the Samanids, Alfarabi first studied Islamic jurisprudence and music in Bukhara and then moved to Marv, where he began to study logic with a Nestorian Christian monk, Yuhanna Ibn Haylan. While in his early twenties, Alfarabi went to Baghdad, where he continued to study logic and philosophy with Ibn Haylan. At the same time, he improved his grasp of Arabic by studying with the prominent philologist Ibn al-Sarraj, and he is said to have followed the courses of the famous Nestorian Christian translator and student of Aristotle, Matta Ibn Yunus.

Around 905 to 910 Alfarabi left Baghdad for Constantinople, where he remained for about eight years studying Greek sciences and philosophy. On his return to Baghdad he busied himself with teaching and writing, until political upheavals in 942 forced him to seek refuge in Damascus. Two or three years later political turmoil there drove him to Egypt, where he stayed until returning to Damascus in 948 or 949—that is, a little more than a year before his death.

Alfarabi's writings, charming and alluringly deceptive, are couched in remarkably simple language with quite uncomplicated sentences. More often than not, he sets forth something resembling a narrative, a story of sorts about the way things are—the natural as well as the conventional—that is simply unobjectionable. As the narrative unfolds, the reader slowly begins to realize that Alfarabi has accounted for the natural order, political leadership, prophecy, moral virtue, civic order, the order of the sciences, even the philosophical pursuits of Plato or Aristotle—in short, for all the major subjects of interest to humans—in a completely unprecedented and seemingly unproblematic manner. Frequently, the account explains the reasons for which human beings live in civic association, how it can best be ordered to meet the highest human needs, the way in which most actual regimes differ from this best order, and why philosophy and religion deem this order best.

These writings, extraordinary in their breadth as well as their deep learning, extend through all of the sciences and embrace every part of philosophy. Alfarabi's interest in mathematics is evidenced in commentaries on the *Elements* of Euclid and *Almagest* of Ptolemy, as well as several writings on the history and theory of music. Indeed, his *Kitab al-Musiqa al-Kabir* ("Large Book on Music") may well be the most significant work in Arabic on that subject. He also wrote numerous commentaries on Aristotle's logic, was knowledgeable about the Stagirite's physical writings, and is credited with an extensive commentary on the *Nicomachean Ethics* that is no longer extant. In addition to writing accounts of Plato's and Aristotle's philosophy, he also composed a commentary on Plato's *Laws*.

As the first philosopher within the tradition of Islam to explore the challenge to traditional philosophy presented by revealed religion, especially in its claims that the Creator provides for human well-being by means of an inspired prophet/legislator, Alfarabi has come to be known as the founder of Islamic political philosophy. In the *Enumeration of the Sciences* he sets forth two accounts of the old political science. Both presuppose the validity of the traditional separation between the practical and the theoretical sciences, but neither is adequate for the radically new situation created by the appearance of revealed religion. The two accounts explain in detail the actions and ways of life required for sound political rule to flourish, but they are utterly silent about opinions—especially the kind of theoretical opinions now set forth in religion—and thus are unable to point to the kind of rulership needed now that religion holds sway. Nor can either speak about the opinions or actions addressed by the jurisprudence and theology of revealed religion. These tasks require a political science that combines theoretical and practical sciences along with prudence and shows how they are to be ordered in the soul of the ruler.

In his other writings—most notably in his *Book of Religion* but also in the *Political Regime,* the *Aphorisms of the Statesman,* and the *Principles of the Opinions of the Inhabitants of the Virtuous City*—Alfarabi develops this broader political science. It speaks of religious beliefs as opinions and of acts of worship as actions, noting that both are prescribed for a community by a supreme ruler or prophet. The new political science views religion as centered in a political community whose supreme ruler is distinct in no way from the founder of a religion. Indeed, the goals and prescriptions of the supreme ruler are identical to those of the prophet/lawgiver. Everything said or done by this supreme ruler finds constant justification in philosophy, and religion thus appears to depend on philosophy—theoretical as well as practical. Similarly, by presenting the art of jurisprudence as a means to identify particular details the supreme ruler did not regulate before his death, Alfarabi makes it depend upon practical philosophy and thus to be part of this broader political science. At least once, he presents a political science that offers a comprehensive view of the universe and thus indicates what kind of practical acumen permits the one who possesses this understanding, either the supreme ruler or a successor endowed with all of his qualities, to rule wisely. Able to explain the various ranks of all the beings, this political science also stresses the importance of religion for uniting the citizens and for helping them attain the virtues that prolong decent political life. Near the end of the *Philosophy of Plato and Aristotle,* Part One, this understanding of political matters leads Alfarabi to declare in a voice more like Plato's than Aristotle's that "the idea of the philosopher, supreme ruler, prince, legislator, and imam is but a single idea" (para. 58).

Charles E. Butterworth

See also ARISTOTLE; AVERROES; AVICENNA; ISLAM; PLATO

Bibliography

Alfarabi. *Alfarabi's Philosophy of Plato and Aristotle.* Translated by Muhsin Mahdi. Glencoe: Free Press, 1962.
———. "Enumeration of the Sciences." Translated by Fauzi M. Najjar. In *Medieval Political Philosophy: A Sourcebook,* edited by Ralph Lerner and Muhsin Mahdi, 22–30. New York: Free Press of Glencoe, 1963.
Butterworth, Charles E. "The Rhetorician and His Relationship to the Community: Three Accounts of Aristotle's Rhetoric." In *Islamic Theology and Philosophy: Studies in Honor of George F. Hourani,* edited by Michael E. Marmura, 111–36. Albany: SUNY Press, 1984.
Mahdi, Muhsin S. "Alfarabi." In *History of Political Philosophy,* edited by Leo Strauss and Joseph Cropsey, 160–80. Chicago: Rand McNally and Co., 1963.
———. "Al-Farabi." In *Dictionary of Scientific Biography.* Vol. 4, edited by C.C. Gillispie, 523–26. New York: Charles Scribner's, 1971.
———. "Al-Farabi and the Foundation of Islamic Philosophy." In *Islamic Philosophy and Mysticism,* edited by Parviz Morewedge, 3–21. Delmar, N.Y.: Caravan Books, 1981.

Alienation

Latin *alienatio,* from *alienare,* to make something another's, often in a legal sense; used also in medicine, meaning loss of reason, as in shock or madness; hence "alienist," an early term for specialists in mental disorders. Contemporary philosophical meanings are complex and have developed over a long period of time.

The term appears first in Gnostic designations of the divinity and the divine life, implying that it is transcendent or "radically other." Adherents, therefore, must regard this world as alien and seek constantly for the divine, to which they properly belong.

Alienation appears early in Christian scripture and theology, meaning the breaking of the soul's union with God through sin. The context is the Judaic concept that God's relation to his people is that of a father to his family (*Hosea* 11:1–8). Thus, Gentiles converting to Christianity are reminded that they were once alienated from the people of God (*Ephesians* 2:12), and believers are taught that they become alienated from him through sin: "Spiritual death is nothing else than the alienation of the soul from God" (Calvin). Within Christian theology, therefore, alienation is a more or less permanent condition that religion cures by effecting a reconciliation with God.

Alienation appears first in a secular and philosophical garb in social contract theory, where it describes the transfer of one's powers and rights to another to create the sovereign as well as the body politic (Grotius; Rousseau). By the use of the term, which carries a pejorative connotation, the constitution of government is seen as something of a necessary evil, and this may be the reason why it is generally avoided by Hobbes and Locke.

During the Enlightenment, alienation reappears with a touch of Gnostic meaning as the human reaction to a physical world that seems unconcerned and uncaring. "The eternal silence of these infinite spaces frightens me," confesses

Pascal, capturing the feelings of modern humanity cast adrift in an expanding universe.

Alienation begins its modern career in the work of Johann Fichte, for whom it means the mind's objectification and creation of the phenomenal world, which is thus taken to be "other," or "alien." The companion term, "objectification," derives literally from "object" (Latin *ob-jectum,* thrown-in-front).

This new meaning is expanded by G.W.F. Hegel in *The Phenomenology of Mind* (1807). Given Hegel's idealistic monism, to conceive the world as independent is to alienate it—that is, to split it from the integral essence of the subject-object by making it purely and independently an "object." Fundamentally, "the world" is not external or a stranger to Thought. To deem it so is to alienate it from us, and us from it.

Hegel's idea of alienation is developed by his followers in new, original ways. First, the religious consciousness is analyzed and found wanting, for it splits the human consciousness by introducing the separate power of God unto whom all power is alienated. All forms of thinking that project an object as independent from a subject are thought to be alienating, and so all alienation becomes self-alienation (Bauer). The most extreme form of self-alienation or objectification of the self is taken to be the religious concept of God. In it are summed up all human capacities and aspirations, and insofar as it is given independent existence and endowed with absolute power, it represents the supreme alienation of humanity from itself (Feuerbach). It must be remembered that from its inception Christianity had preached the human incapacity to do good without the aid of divine grace, and had condemned as heretical Pelagius's arguments to the contrary. Still, the study, if not the practice, of religion remains useful because it leads back to the human subject. Therefore, the study of theology becomes the study of what humans would like to become and achieve, and theology, thus, resolves itself into anthropology and psychology, in much the same way as theosophy gives way to anthroposophy (Steiner).

Further analyses lead to the generalization that anything that is given independent, objective value marks an alienation of the human essence, not just consciousness. Moreover, the concept of alienation becomes increasingly used to critique social and political realities. Thus the concept is applied to money (Hess; Marx) and the state (Marx), and institutional religion, with its warring denominations, is seen as an artificial factor that alienates humans from each other (Marx) and not just from themselves.

Alienation becomes a crucial term in Karl Marx, especially in the *Paris Manuscripts of 1844.* It is the major theme of all his writings.

Marx uses mostly two terms: *Entfremdung,* simple estrangement or divorce, and *Entausserung,* the externalization and objectification or reification of aspects of the self, but the alienated object is conceived in more dynamic and antagonistic terms, so that, as a result of alienation, "man's own deed becomes an alien power opposed to him, which enslaves him instead of being controlled by him" (*The German Ideology*).

Marx analyzes alienation in four interrelated areas: alienation from the *product* of human activity, which is controlled by others and which makes the human agents dependent on, and even subservient to, it in some sort of idolatry; alienation in the *process* of production, about which much has been written; alienation from *nature,* resulting in the abuse of nature rather than in a symbiotic relationship with it; and alienation from *species-life*—that is, from one's fellow human beings, so that competition overshadows cooperation and the selfish interests of the individual are given value over and even against those of the collectivity and the species. Contemporary writers have extended this critical idea to other areas of socioeconomic relations in which our essential humanness is obliterated, such as consumerism and authority (Fromm), racism (Harrington; Fanon; Manganyi), sexism (de Beauvoir), education (Leight; Freire; Sarup), grades (Götz), art (Marcuse; Sternig), and sexuality (May; Marcuse).

By embedding the concept of alienation in the socioeconomic realm, Marx made it more easily accessible to psychologists and sociologists. Psychologists use the term *alienation* to describe the feeling of not being in control of one's life and fate (Horney; Fromm) and the split between one's real and one's ideal self. Through psychology, the concept of alienation has been popularized, and it has come to mean any kind of lack of fit, any feelings of isolation, and the inability to belong or to find meaning in life.

In sociology, alienation stands for the depersonalization of relationships and the distance between persons (Tonnies). It encompasses also the anomie generated by displacement caused by war (Pire), major social upheavals, the speed of social change (Toffler), and the confinement of institutions, from factories to schools, resulting in indifference, loneliness (Riesman; Slater), disaffection, and ultimately lack of commitment (Keniston). The concept has also been used as a tool to critique the mechanization, standardization, and fragmentation of much of contemporary life.

As with Marxism, alienation has a technical meaning in existentialism, one that generally hearkens back to Hegel's use of it in *The Phenomenology of Mind*. Thus, it sometimes designates inauthenticity—that is, living without regard to "one's ownmost potentiality-for-being" (Heidegger). This happens, for example, when one's involvement in the present blocks or obliterates one's openness to the future and to possibility. On the other hand, for Jean-Paul Sartre (in *Being and Nothingness*), alienation describes the split between the self one knows one is and the impression one strives to present to others; between the self and its masks. It describes, also, the self's experience of being objectified, of being rendered into an object like other objects in the world, by "the Other's Look." This meaning is often explored in Sartre's stories, novels, and plays. In later philosophical work, however, Sartre adopted a meaning of alienation more akin to Marx's.

Curiously, especially given its importance in Marx, alienation has not been an important tool in the American Left's critique of capitalism. Rather, the analysis has turned almost exclusively on class distinctions and on the unequal distribution of the means of production.

It must also be pointed out that there is an abundant literature, spanning more than a hundred years, that purports to explore combinations of the various meanings of alienation in the lives of fictitious characters. The works of Dostoevsky, Tolstoy, Melville, Ibsen, Kafka, Chopin, Lawrence, Gide, Malraux, Sarraute, Camus, Ionesco, Ellison, O'Connor, Welty, Percy, and Walker may be cited as examples.

Undeniably, alienation has a pejorative meaning. But the question may be asked whether or not all forms of alienation are evil and must be overcome. For example, it may be that the self-objectification involved in *self*-consciousness is both constitutive of thought and necessary, and, therefore, at worst neutral (Kaufmann). Alienation may also be the price we pay for clarity of thought, or nothing more than a temporary estrangement as we traverse from paradigm to paradigm (McDermott). Similarly, belief in the radical otherness of God need not entail a diminution of the human, but may be a simple acknowledgment of the difference between the Absolute and the relative. After all, admission of difference does not necessarily entail valuation judgments.

Ignacio L. Götz

See also HEGEL; HEIDEGGER; MARX; PHENOMENOLOGY; SARTRE

Bibliography

American Journal of Psychoanalysis 21, no. 2 (1961). The entire issue is dedicated to alienation.

Bell, Daniel. "The 'Rediscovery' of Alienation." *Journal of Philosophy* 56, no. 24 (1959): 933–52.

Fromm, Erich. *The Sane Society*. New York: Fawcett Publications, 1967.

Horney, Karen. *Neurosis and Human Growth*. New York: Norton, 1950.

Johnson, Frank. *Alienation: Concept, Term, and Meanings*. New York: Seminar Press, 1973.

Leight, Robert L., ed. *Philosophers Speak on Alienation in Education*. Danville, Ill.: Interstate Printers and Publishers, 1974.

Levi, Albert W. "Existentialism and the Alienation of Man." In *Phenomenology and Existentialism,* edited by Edward N. Lee and Maurice Mandelbaum. Baltimore: Johns Hopkins Press, 1967.

Ollman, Bertell. *Alienation*. New York: Cambridge University Press, 1971.

Sarup, Madan. *Marxism and Education*. London: Routledge and Kegan Paul, 1978.

Schacht, Richard. *Alienation*. New York: Doubleday, Anchor, 1971.

Analytic Philosophy

Seeks to clarify meaning, linguistic or conceptual. It appeared and flourished, mainly in English-speaking countries, during the first seven decades of the twentieth century. Around the middle of the century, it began to influence the philosophy of education in at least some of those countries, and during the 1960s and 1970s it was a major force in educational philosophy in many of them.

Philosophers historically have sought to understand linguistic expressions and concepts, but they have not been analytic philosophers as such for that reason alone. Analytic philosophy focuses upon language as its subject matter, or area of inquiry, thereby departing from the many philosophies that have concentrated upon substance (such as Aristotelianism), existence (such as existentialism), perception (such as phenomenology), and action (such as pragmatism). Despite its subject matter, analytic philosophy differs from linguistics, lexicography, philology, and other empirical investigations. The latter examine language so as to establish facts, laws, and theories about it; whereas the former investigates language in order to address philosophical issues. The methods of analytic philosophy are of two major sorts, logical analysis and ordinary language analysis. By the former, one tries to clarify meanings according to the principles and forms of symbolic logic; by the latter, one attempts to explicate meanings according to the uses of terms and the functions of statements in standard discourse.

History of Analytic Philosophy

G.E. Moore (1873–1958) and Bertrand Russell (1872–1970), faculty members at Cambridge University, started the "analytic revolution" in philosophy, during the early years of this century, with their discussions of certain traditional philosophical views. While they concurred that understanding the language in which these views had been expressed was crucial, they disagreed over how to explain the meaning of philosophical language. Moore maintained that the language of philosophers could be understood sufficiently by appeals to ordinary language—that is, by reference to the normal uses and functions of terms and statements. Russell, on the other hand, held that the language of philosophers could be comprehended fully only by examining it according to the principles and forms of symbolic logic. Moore's approach, then, may be seen as the root of ordinary language analysis while Russell's may be seen as the source of logical analysis.

In his *Tractatus Logico-Philosophicus* (1921), Ludwig Wittgenstein (1889–1951), who had been a student of Russell's, presented a theory of propositional meaning that, along with a similar view held by Moritz Schlick (1882–1936) at the University of Vienna, helped shape the philosophical movement known as logical positivism. It notably departed from Moore's and Russell's thinking in that it rejected metaphysical and other traditional philosophical questions as legitimate ones for philosophy. According to Wittgenstein's theory, a proposition is meaningful only if it is empirical—that is, only if it asserts a fact. Metaphysical propositions, Wittgenstein claimed, are not empirical and therefore are nonsense. Logical positivists concluded the same also about moral and aesthetic principles and judgments. According to logical positivism, consequently, philosophy must abandon its traditional efforts to provide understanding of the world and direction to human life; it must content itself with clarifying language with the techniques of symbolic logic. If people want to know about the world, they will do well to consult science; if they want guidance for their lives, they will do well to consult their feelings, customs, and laws, as informed by logic and science.

Logical positivism initially had its strongest following in Germany and Austria, where its early adherents were known as the Vienna Circle. In England the movement had its most famous spokesman in A.J. Ayer (1910–1989), whose *Language, Truth and Logic* (1936) brought the philosophy's tenets to the attention of philosophers and nonphilosophers alike. While Ayer's work was influential in the United States also, it by no means was the only inspiration of logical positivism there. Because of political conditions in Germany and Austria before World War II, some philosophers in those countries, including logical positivists, immigrated to England, and the United States. Karl Popper and Friedrich Waismann, for example, went to England, while Rudolph Carnap, Herbert Feigl, Hans Reichenbach, Carl Hempel, and Gustav Bergmann went to the United States. American philosophers sympathetic to logical positivism were not always faithful devotees. Some, such as W.V.O. Quine, were seriously attracted to pragmatism as well.

Shortly after joining the Cambridge faculty in 1930, Wittgenstein renounced most of the major ideas in his *Tractatus,* thus abandoning logical positivism as it started to gain wide acceptance. One dismissed idea was his contention that all discourse, including everyday speech, could be analyzed by logical analysis. Wittgenstein, then, undertook to develop a new approach to philosophy. Looking this time to Moore rather than Russell, Wittgenstein constructed an orientation to philosophy that emphasized the analysis of the forms of ordinary language. This approach was set forth in his posthumous *Philosophical Investigations* (1953). While Wittgenstein now agreed with Moore that ordinary language analysis was a fruitful philosophical method, he did not agree that such analysis could solve metaphysical and normative problems. For the later Wittgenstein, metaphysical questions—in truth, all traditional philosophical issues—arose from the failure of people to understand their language fully. That is, metaphysical and other traditional philosophical questions were phantasms produced by "linguistic anxiety," which in turn was caused by linguistic ignorance. So, once philosophy finished its task of describing the workings of ordinary language, it should have eliminated any need for "linguistic anxiety" and, consequently, should have rendered itself otiose.

By the time of World War II, logical positivism, having suffered criticism by many philosophers, was losing its appeal in the philosophical community. Accordingly, Wittgenstein's new approach to philosophy soon began to attract interest among British and American philosophers. While contemporaries sympathetic to the later Wittgenstein's views did not always agree what his specific positions were on certain questions, they were not hesitant to do ordinary language analysis. For instance, in his book *The Concept of Mind* (1949), Gilbert Ryle, at Oxford, argued that the traditional separation of mind and body into different substances rested upon confusions in talk about mental matters. J.L. Austin, the leader of the "Oxford movement" in linguistic analysis, devoted extensive and technical attention to grammatical distinctions in the English language, pointing out thereby changes in meaning that accompany even small shifts in grammar. Peter F. Strawson, at Oxford mainly after the breakup of the Oxford movement, contended in *Individuals: An Essay in Descriptive Metaphysics* (1959) that the analysis of ordinary language has metaphysical significance in that it can provide some knowledge of the world. And in *Theory of Knowledge* (1965), Roderick M. Chisholm at Brown University examined the issues, problems, and terms involved in talk about knowledge.

Ordinary language analysts, however, had an impact upon more than metaphysics and epistemology. They also recast moral and political philosophy as the study of moral and political discourse. Thus, in *Ethics and Language* (1944), Charles L. Stevenson sought to clarify the meaning of the stock terms of moral language and to describe the methods by which ethical judgments can be proved or supported. In *The Language of Morals* (1952), Richard M. Hare took ethics to be "the logical study of the language of morals." And in *The Vocabulary of Politics* (1953), T.D. Weldon aimed at articulating the logic of statements typical in discourse about politics.

Philosophers in the ordinary language tradition eventually went beyond describing the normal uses and functions of linguistic expressions. Beginning with Ryle, they increasingly transformed ordinary language analysis into conceptual analysis; that is, they saw the study of the uses and functions of linguistic utterances as a way for clarifying concepts. Instead of conceiving of a concept as a term of some sort, they viewed it as a set of criteria by which matters may be classified together and distinguished from one another. And they held that the criteria constituting a concept were the rules governing the uses and functions of linguistic utterances related to that concept. Thus, there have been analytic philosophers who have sought to explain the concepts of the natural and social sciences by examining the language of those disciplines, while others have sought to explain ethical, political, historical, legal, and aesthetic concepts by studying the respective cognate discourses.

In political philosophy and ethics, some philosophers have pursued conceptual analysis as a tool for determining normative principles. That is, some have examined certain political and moral concepts in order to discover normative principles logically implied by those concepts. For instance, in *The Theory of Justice* (1972), John Rawls argued that the concept of justice logically commits people to a society organized according to certain egalitarian norms. And in *Reason and Morality* (1978), Alan Gewirth contended that the concept of voluntary action logically entails that the features of such action are morally worthy and that each and every moral agent has rights to those features. With its renewed interest in normative questions as well as metaphysical ones, analytic philosophy came full circle in at least one respect: It now was concerned with the sorts of issues that it had discussed during its formative years.

Since the 1970s, analytic philosophy has continued largely as conceptual analysis. What transformation it might undergo next is not evident. Meanwhile, it competes with existentialism, phenomenology, neopragmatism, and several postmodernist views in trying to solve the enduring problems of philosophy.

Impact of Analytic Philosophy upon the Philosophy of Education

Analytic philosophy started, in England, to enter philosophical thinking about education with the publication of Charles D. Hardie's *Truth and Fallacy in Educational Theory* (1942). In that work, Hardie, who had studied with C.D. Broad and I.A. Richards at Cambridge University, attempted to resolve disagreements among major educational theories by several devices of philosophical analysis—mainly elucidation of concepts, articulation of theories, and reconstruction of theories. Partly because of the distractions of World War II, however, the initial impact of Hardie's pioneering work was neither deep nor long lasting. The volume went out of print after a while, and another book-length philosophical analysis of education did not appear in England for fifteen years.

It was during the middle 1950s that analytic philosophy began to make, indelibly, an impression upon the philosophy of education in the United States. Shortly after World War II, the public schools and their ideology of progressive education came under increasing political attack: They were often charged with failing to provide students with substantial academic knowledge and skills. And by the early 1950s, influential proposals were being made to organize the curricula of public schools and colleges of education along the lines of academic disciplines. Accordingly, philosophers of education in the United States started to reconceive the philosophy of education as an academic discipline, which they did formally through the publication of the Philosophy of Education Society's 1953 pamphlet "The Distinctive Nature of the Discipline of the Philosophy of Education." In rethinking their field as an academic discipline, American philosophers of education perforce paid much attention to the dominant philosophical views in philosophy departments, which at the time were, among others, ordinary language analysis.

In 1954, the journal *Harvard Educational Review* devoted an issue to articles discussing the philosophy of education. Most of them, such as those by Harry Broudy and Kingsley Price, allowed that philosophy has an analytic, or critical, function for education as well as a synthetic, or constructive, one, but stressed that the former should not overshadow the latter. In his piece, however, Israel Scheffler, noting that philosophy of education is "rarely, if ever, construed as the rigorous logical analysis of key concepts related to the practice of education," argued that the analytic approach to philosophy of education is quite fruitful.

Five years later, the publication, both in England and the United States, of D.J. O'Connor's *Introduction to the Philosophy of Education* signaled that interest in an analytic approach to the philosophy of education had revived in England, and it also strengthened the interaction between English and American philosophers of education. Even though O'Connor, at the University of Liverpool, emphasized criticism and clarification, he allowed that analytic philosophy had a constructive as well as a critical function. He explained, however, that theory construction in analytic philosophy was different from what it had been in traditional philosophy. It was, like the solution of a jigsaw puzzle, a reshuffling of the items of experience into a pattern. It differed, then, from traditional metaphysics, which often invoked unknown and unknowable entities to account for puzzlements about the everyday world. At the same time, theory construction by analytic philosophy, unlike the work of the scientist, does not give any new knowledge; it provides only an understanding of what we already know.

During the late 1950s, articles favoring an analytic approach to the philosophy of education appeared in various professional publications in the United States, such as the Proceedings of the Philosophy of Education Society; *Educational Theory; Harvard Educational Review; School Review;* and *Teachers College Record.* Most of these pieces were by newer members of the Philosophy of Education Society, such as Reginald Archambault, Joe R. Burnett, Robert H. Ennis, B. Paul Komisar, James E. McClellan, and George L. Newsome, Jr. Also at this time, Israel Scheffler published the first edition of *Philosophy of Education: Modern Readings,* which was the first anthology of readings taking an analytic approach to the philosophy of education. Before 1960 in England, not many articles taking the analytic view appeared, although Richard S. Peters published a collection of his essays in philosophy of education, *Authority, Responsibility, and Education,* in 1959. Not only was Peters another analytic philosopher in England who brought out a volume on education; but he, more than anyone else, also established philosophy of education as an academic discipline in England. In addition to publishing numerous articles and books on the philosophy of education, he organized the philosophy of education graduate program at the University of London's Institute of Education. He helped in the creation of the Philosophy of Education Society of Great Britain, and his discussions of numerous issues were well received in the United States, Canada, Australia, and elsewhere.

It was during the 1960s that the analytic approach to the philosophy of education reached the peak of its influence. Many monographs, anthologies, and textbooks reflecting this viewpoint appeared. Hardie's *Truth and Fallacy in Educational Theory* appeared in an American edition (1962) that contained a special preface by McClellan and Komisar discussing the status of analytic philosophy of education. The journal *Studies in Philosophy and Education,* which published lengthy essays with an analytic orientation, came into being, and the *British Journal of Educational Studies* began to publish analytic pieces on education and eventually became the publisher of the Proceedings of the Philosophy of Education Society of Great Britain. Eminent members of philosophy departments, such as William Frankena, Michael Scriven, Abraham Edel, Anthony Flew, and William Blackstone, published papers on education and addressed conferences on the philosophy of education. John Wilson, an analyst, began publishing and teaching advanced studies in the philosophy of education at Oxford University, while Paul H. Hirst, also an analyst, started to do the same at Cambridge University. In the United States, doctoral programs in the philosophy of education with an analytic streak were offered not only at Harvard University, Teachers College, and the University of Illinois but also were established at Temple University, Cornell University, Syracuse University, the University of Wisconsin, the University of Georgia, the Ohio State University, Florida State University, and elsewhere. In Canada, similar programs were created at the Ontario Institute of Studies in Education and at the University of British Columbia. And in Australia, an analytic approach to the philosophy of education was taken at the University of New South Wales and also at the University of Tasmania.

During the 1960s and 1970s, other analytic philosophers of education—for example, Jane Roland Martin, Charles Brauner, Thomas F. Green, Robert F. Dearden, Brian Crittenden, C.J.B. Macmillan, and Robin Barrow—addressed many topics and issues. The following list is only a sampling: In analyzing the concept of education, these philosophers raised the question of whether or not education is normatively neutral, what sort of knowledge it involves, and whether or not it excludes certain

kinds of pedagogical methods. In examining the concept of knowledge, they distinguished between skill knowledge and propositional knowledge, clarified the concept of understanding, discussed whether or not there are different ways of knowing, and theorized about the structure and organization of the intellectual disciplines. In inquiries into teaching, they were especially concerned with its intentionality, with whether or not it logically implies the occurrence of learning, and how it differs from indoctrination and conditioning. In discussions of moral education, they examined the theories of developmental psychologists and articulated the structure of moral thinking. In investigations of mental concepts, they discussed what critical thinking is and whether or not it is subject-specific. They analyzed such psychological concepts as need, interest, motivation, and want, and they attempted to determine whether or not mental states and acts are necessarily nonphysical and, if so, how such states and acts are to be dealt with in education. And in inquiries into educational research, they examined the logic of theories of such research and proposed reconstructions of them.

Some of the concepts and issues examined by analytic philosophers related directly to educational policies. These philosophers discussed what it means for schools to be neutral and whether or not they should be. They looked at policies of educational equality to see whether they were policies of equal opportunity or policies of equal results. They considered whether certain school policies violate the rights of students. They criticized policies insisting upon the expression of all educational objectives in behavioral terms. And they analyzed the concept of justice and its relevance for policies of affirmative action.

By shortly after the 1970s, the analytic movement in the philosophy of education plainly had lost its position of dominance. The number of books and articles in the analytic tradition sharply declined, whereas the number with phenomenological and postmodernist viewpoints increased. The number of analytic philosophers featured at philosophy of education conferences dropped sharply. And the analytic approach had increasingly become subject to criticism not only by philosophers of education with different orientations but also by educators and some philosophers of education working within the analytic tradition.

But even in reduced circumstances, philosophers of education with an analytic bent continue today in doing notable work on a variety of problems relevant to education. While this contemporary work has extensively employed conceptual analysis, it has attempted also to use such analysis as a means for the construction of theories. Robert H. Ennis, John McPeck, and Stephen Norris have argued theories of critical thinking. C.J.B. Macmillan and James W. Garrison have advanced a comprehensive theory of teaching. Denis C. Phillips has written on the theoretical foundations of science education and of educational research. Eamonn Callan has set forth a reconstructed theory of child-centered education. Kenneth A. Strike, John P. White, and Robert D. Heslep have offered social and political theories.

Appraisal

The analytic approach to philosophy of education has been subject to various criticisms. Some were made before the approach was well established, others when it was flourishing. Some were expressed by educators, others by philosophers of education with different viewpoints, and still others by analytic philosophers of education themselves. Some were uninformed while others were cogent.

A charge made early and persistently was that the analytic philosophy of education provided no vision of life, dealing with education and the rest of life only in a piecemeal fashion—concept by concept, statement by statement, and in haphazard order. This objection was silly if it was doing nothing more than pointing out that analysis necessarily breaks things into their parts. But it was wrongheaded if it meant that analysis is incompatible with obtaining a synoptic view through the synthesizing of parts. Beginning at least with Descartes's writing of his *Regulae*, philosophers have recognized that analysis and synthesis are complementary methods. Moreover, as indicated above, O'Connor had contended that analytic philosophy of education is capable of synthesizing its piecemeal findings into wholes. Still further, later critics of the analytic orientation to philosophy of education complained that it *does* have a vision of life—namely, a rationalistic one. Also, even though analytic philosophy of education during the 1960s and 1970s frequently stressed analysis rather than synthesis, some, such as Peters, used their analytic work as a means for constructing broad theories. Finally, during the 1980s some philosophers of education working

in the analytic tradition largely oriented their analyses toward theory construction, formulating general views of education, teaching, the curriculum, and education in democracy.

Another early charge was that analytic philosophy of education was nondirective; it did not offer prescriptions. An early answer was that the objection erroneously conflated analytic philosophy of education with nothing but analysis. To be sure, so this answer went, analytic philosophy of education does not prescribe when it is clarifying; but analytic philosophers of education, unlike their counterparts in philosophy departments, have to be prescriptive. In truth, the literature contains numerous policy recommendations by analytic philosophers of education. A much later answer to this criticism came when normative conceptual analysis began to operate in the philosophy of education. That form of analysis set itself a twofold task: the clarification of the values, rights, duties, and virtues embedded in certain concepts (such as democracy and voluntary action) and the formulation of recommendations based upon those norms.

A criticism that occurred during the early 1970s came from Jonas F. Soltis, himself an analytic philosopher. He held that some of the analyses done on important educational concepts, such as learning, were uninteresting to education, and that analytic philosophers had yet to show that they could deal effectively with enduring value questions in education. Response to this charge came from Abraham Edel. He agreed with the criticism but then proposed a solution. Far from holding that the analytic approach is in principle a sterile one for the philosophy of education, he argued that analytic philosophers of education must put language in its human relations. In other words, philosophers have to be especially cognizant of the valuational and sociohistorical components of the contexts that give meaning to the language they are analyzing. Indeed, Edel allowed that some analytic philosophers of education had already begun to do this.

During the 1980s, the analytic viewpoint of philosophy of education was the subject of objections from critical theorists and those concerned with feminist issues in the philosophy of education. The thrust of the critical theorist's contention was that analytic philosophy was an instrument whereby societies dominated by modern Anglo-Saxon culture deprived their members with subjugated cultures from attaining legitimacy. Because such philosophy regarded science, purportedly the epistemology of modern Anglo-Saxon culture, and ordinary discourse, supposedly the language of that culture, as the sources of empirical truth and of meaning, it rejected the nonscientific ways of knowing and the nonstandard meanings from dominated cultures and thus rendered those cultures intellectually worthless. The central point of the feminist's argument was that analytic philosophy of education betrays a deep, perhaps ineradicable, masculine bias. Its preoccupation with logical rigor, precision, and objectivity; its emphasis upon theoretical reason in education; its neglect of the practical and the affective in the curriculum; its disregard of nurturing, caring, sensitivity, and the other feminine qualities of human character—these are telltale signs of a masculine orientation.

Because analytic philosophy originated in and has flourished in modern Anglo-Saxon societies, it might have led some, if not many, of its practitioners to confuse the ways of such societies with those of the analytic approach to philosophy. This does not mean, however, that analytic philosophy was necessarily a regulatory tool of modern Anglo-Saxon societies. Analytic philosophy neither rises nor falls upon the position of science in the world. Science happens to be widely accepted as a great source of knowledge about the physical world, but it is not essential to analytic philosophy, which is compatible, at least in its forms other than logical positivism, with other modes of knowing about the physical world. Moreover, while analytic philosophy does often appeal to ordinary usages often shaped by modern Anglo-Saxon culture, it does not have to. Different cultures may employ the same words when expressing different concepts; but even when they do, they respectively tend to have something like ordinary uses of their terms. Because analytic philosophy is concerned theoretically with the normal uses or functions of any linguistic expression in any context, it is not committed logically to favoring linguistic use or function in the contexts of hegemonic cultures over that in the contexts of subjugated cultures.

It is true that logical positivists, looking to mathematics and physical science as models of knowing, made a virtual fetish of logical rigor, precision, and objectivity. But it is also true that ordinary language analysis, especially as practiced by Austin and others in the Oxford movement, deemphasized those qualities. Moreover, while it is true that early analyses of the concept

of education reflected a preference for the abstract and academic, it also is true that later ones shed that preference and included the practical and the affective as aspects of education. Finally, while it is true that many attempts to clarify the concept of moral education failed to allow for the feminine virtues, other attempts, especially some by feminists from the analytic tradition, showed that these virtues are not necessarily excluded by an analytic understanding of moral education.

The last critical point to be mentioned here about analytic philosophy of education is that it never gained a constituency among educators. That it did not attract a following among practitioners was indicated by the fact that professional education societies and governmental education agencies rarely consulted analytic philosophers on policy matters. Also, a reason occasionally put forth as to why this approach did not captivate practitioners is quite plausible. While analytic philosophers frequently provided scattered positions on parts of education, educators uniformly wanted a systematic body of principles about all of education. Moreover, while analytic philosophers often saw the problems of education as problems of language, educators always regarded them as problems of institutions and action.

This charge, however, is open to counterargument. Except for Thomism, which continues to have an influence in Roman Catholic schools, no philosophy of education has had much of a following among educators since World War II. For decades, public school educators have increasingly switched from philosophy to the social sciences in a search for guiding principles. Hence, a failure to have a constituency among practitioners is not a problem specific to analytic philosophy of education. It is, rather, a problem for recent philosophy of education in general. Moreover, it is arguable that the philosophy of education is not bound to have a following among educators. Harvey Siegel, for instance, has maintained that the philosophy of education seeks knowledge for its own sake and thus is not the worse if practitioners do not employ its findings.

While it is questionable that any of the foregoing criticisms of the analytic approach to philosophy of education are substantial, it does seem plain, in view of the literature, that the approach has made several distinct contributions. First, the approach has shown that the clarification of educational discourse must receive special and concerted attention if theorizing is not to be vague and muddled. Second, the approach has yielded a large body of studies of educational language, including theories as well as terms, statements, and concepts. And third, the approach has resulted in the reconstruction of existing theories and the construction of new ones that have benefited from attention to the details of meaning.

Robert D. Heslep

See also CRITICAL THINKING; EMPIRICISM; EPISTEMOLOGY; LOGIC; POSITIVISM; REASON AND RATIONALITY; RUSSELL; TEACHING AND LEARNING; WITTGENSTEIN

Bibliography

Callan, Eamonn. *Autonomy and Schooling.* Montreal: McGill-Queen's University Press, 1988.

International Library of the Philosophy of Education. Twenty-two works with an analytic orientation published by Routledge and Kegan Paul between 1972 and 1986.

Lucas, Christopher J. *What Is Philosophy of Education?* London: Macmillan, 1969.

Macmillan, C.J.B., and James W. Garrison. *A Logical Theory of Teaching: Erotetics and Intentionality.* Boston: Kluwer Academic Publishers, 1988.

Philosophy of Education Society, proceedings of the society's conferences, 1958–present.

Philosophy of Education Society of Great Britain, proceedings of the society's conferences, 1966–present.

Soltis, Jonas F. *An Introduction to the Analysis of Educational Concepts.* Reading, Mass.: Addison-Wesley, 1968. 2nd ed., 1978.

———, ed. *Philosophy and Education: Eightieth Yearbook of the National Society for the Study of Education, Part I.* Chicago: University of Chicago Press, 1981.

Urmson, J.O. *Philosophical Analysis: Its Development between the Two World Wars.* New York: Oxford University Press, 1971.

White, John P. *Education and the Good Life: Autonomy, Altruism, and the National Curriculum.* New York: Teachers College Press, 1991.

Anselm of Canterbury (1033–1109)

A

Benedictine monk and abbot of Bec, archbishop of Canterbury, whose innovative thought helped usher in the scholastic revolution of the twelfth and thirteenth centuries.

Born in Aosta, northern Italy, Anselm joined the Benedictine monastery at Bec in Normandy in 1060. Shortly thereafter, he rose to the office of prior and was subsequently elected abbot in 1078. Consecrated archbishop of Canterbury in 1093, he was the chief antagonist in turbulent relations with two of England's kings, William II and Henry I, both sons of William the Conqueror (c. 1028–1087). Anselm left a body of works that include some sixteen treatises and meditations, nineteen lengthy prayers, and an extensive correspondence. Although the subjects he took up were commonplace for a medieval theologian (for example, the existence of God and his attributes, freedom of choice, the Incarnation, original sin, divine foreknowledge, the Trinity), Anselm dealt with them in a style that was epoch-making. He thought in a way that provoked the German philosopher Karl Jaspers (1883–1969) to remark that "in Anselm philosophy is reborn."

In a fashion that was to characterize most of his subsequent philosophico-theological works, Anselm wrote his first treatise, the *Monologion* (1076), as a response to his monastic brothers who wanted him to put down in a systematic way the ideas they had been discussing over a period of time both formally and informally. The purpose of these conversations and, perforce, of this treatise was to set the monks' minds to rest in their worries over basic beliefs about the divine being and human existence, but to do so with simple arguments that rested on reason alone, forsaking the persuasive powers of embellished rhetoric and appeals to either Scripture or the Church fathers. For the duration of his life, Anselm carried on such dialectical conversations, the residues of which appear in the variety of his works.

From a methodological point of view, the salient characteristics of his thought are the following: First, his interlocutors, confreres, and students, ask the questions. They establish the subject matter. Their concerns are almost always their confusion and doubts regarding the content of their basic Christian beliefs. The teacher's task is to settle the issues by dissipating confusion, thereby returning the students to their doctrinal starting points, but with the difference that the intervening inquiry enables them to rest their beliefs on the light of understanding rather than only to assent to them on the basis of blind faith. Secondly, in his response, Anselm appeals exclusively to the evidence of reason. He tries to show the rational necessity by virtue of which things must be as they have been presented in the essential doctrines of the Christian faith. Finally, insofar as Anselm's inquiries inevitably continue and extend either his ongoing monastic instruction of his confreres or more informal conversations rooted in spiritual friendships, they are ordered toward intensification of the hope and joy that results from meditating upon Christian truths about God and human destiny.

Accordingly, Anselm's thinking inevitably expresses a form of teaching that derives from his vocation as a Christian monk. But it is a teaching that appeals to the hard witness of reason in the expectation that his interlocutors or readers will experience intellectual insight. This reasoned intuition is meant to foster the deeply satisfying activity of meditation or contemplation, which itself, in turn, is ordered toward rousing a more complete love of God. Anselm considers any experience of the love of God in this life, however, as but an analogical anticipation of one's future beatitude in the Heavenly City.

Perhaps no thinker before or since Anselm has had such confidence in the power of reason to demonstrate the conformity of its findings to the doctrines of the Christian faith. Indeed, it was a culture rooted in the conviction that the life of reason is fully compatible with the doctrines of the Christian faith that gave rise to the medieval universities, out of which subsequently developed modern natural science and the modern university. According to Anselm's principles, every aspect of reality, spiritual as well as physical, would be subject to the inquiring light of reason. In fact, for the mature Christian the search for understanding is an obligation. Anselm stands at the pole opposite to those who have come to think of the academy as an institution created by the liberation of reason from revelation, of science from religion, of facts from values.

Anselm's doctrines on freedom and truth bear special mention in a consideration of the philosophy of education. He defines truth as "rightness perceptible to the mind alone" (*On Truth:* c. 11). The idea is that words and propositions, actions, the human will, and things themselves each have their own defining powers or capabilities and they are true to the degree that in their use or existence they conform to the divine measure of their reality. Anselm thinks of all things, save God, as in some way "signs," whose reality consists in pointing beyond themselves toward their own more complete reality. Thus a spoken or written word points to and is verified by an interior, conceptual word, which in turn points to and is verified by the independent or exterior thing. But even the thing is a "sign," in that it points to and is verified by its corresponding idea in the mind of God. The task of learning, therefore, becomes a matter of elevating one's mind toward the experience of the higher measures of reality. Learning is a process of assimilating or "living into" the more ultimate reality of things.

Anselm defines freedom as "the ability to keep uprightness of will for its own sake" (*On Freedom of Choice:* c. 13). Since uprightness of will amounts to justice that is loved simply for its intrinsic attractiveness, persons are free to the degree that they can transcend their selfish interests and bring their actions and affections into conformity with the transcendent measure of things. In so doing, human beings complete themselves as images of God, who is the ultimate autonomous agent. God's freedom manifests itself in his ability to love others in unforced generosity. Human freedom, therefore, imitates divine liberality.

To come to truth and to exercise freedom, therefore, were the great ends of Anselm the teacher. His philosophy and especially his method of inquiry were ordered toward inducing others to these specifically human activities.

William A. Frank

See also FREEDOM AND DETERMINISM; SCHOLASTICISM; TRUTH

Bibliography

Adams, Marilyn McCord. *"Fides Quaerens Intellectum:* St. Anselm's Method in Philosophical Theology." *Faith and Philosophy* 9 (1992): 409–35.

Anselm. *Anselm of Canterbury.* 4 vols. Translated by Jasper Hopkins and Herbert W. Richardson. Toronto: Edwin Mellen, 1974–1976.

———. *Anselm Opera Omnia.* 6 vols. Edited by F.S. Schmitt. Rome/Edinburgh: Thomas Nelson, 1938–1968.

———. *The Prayers and Meditations of Saint Anselm.* Translated by Benedicta Ward.

New York: Penguin, 1973.

Hopkins, Jaspar. *A Companion to the Study of St. Anselm.* Minneapolis: University of Minnesota Press, 1972.

Southern, Richard. *Saint Anselm: A Portrait in a Landscape.* New York: Cambridge University Press, 1990.

Anthropology

Anthropology is concerned with the emergence of humanity and its manner of living. Anthropology as a unifying science has embraced the four fields of physical anthropology (the study of the emergence of self-awareness and the physical evolution of humanity), archaeology (the study of the remains of prehistoric cultures), anthropological linguistics (the comparative, historical study of the five thousand or so mutually unintelligible languages of the world), and cultural anthropology (the study of living cultures as historically created forms of life).

Alfred Kroeber, in 1901 the first American to receive a Ph.D. in anthropology, helped to shape the contemporary idea of the field beyond its earlier antiquarian interests:

> After all, the subject matter of anthropology is limited only by man. It is not restricted by time—it goes back into geology as far as man can be traced. It is not restricted by region but is world-wide in scope. It has specialized on the primitives because no other science would deal seriously with them, but it has never renounced its intent to understand the high civilizations also. Anthropology is interested in what is most exotic in mankind but equally in ourselves, here, now, at home. (Kroeber 1953: xiii)

The following will be concerned with cultural anthropology and its relationship to the philosophy of education.

During this century, the concept of "culture" has become the foundation stone for the human, social, and behavioral sciences. The idea of culture has its historical roots in the German intellectual world of Immanuel Kant, Johann Herder, and Wilhelm von Humboldt during the latter part of the eighteenth century and the early part of the nineteenth century. The emergence of historical consciousness in the twofold sense of our consciousness of making history and our consciousness of belonging to history was already widespread in the Enlightenment philosophy of the eighteenth century. The essential historical and cultural contextualization of all human life and consciousness was proposed by von Humboldt: "Man lives with his objects chiefly—in fact, since his feeling and acting depends on his perceptions, one may say exclusively—as language presents them to him. By the same process whereby he spins language out of his being, he ensnares himself in it; and each language draws a magic circle around the people to which there is no escape save by stepping out of it into another." Essentially, von Humboldt said that the languages of the world do not differ merely in terms of sounds and grammatical structures, but rather create diverse *Weltanschauungen,* or world views, that shape what we call human thinking, consciousness, values, reality, and forms of life. His keystone idea of the enormous plurality of cultural perspectives is behind the dominant intellectual-humanistic concept of the last two centuries: perspectivism. In this century the idea of perspectivism has been interpreted as cultural relativity and is behind the contemporary concern with multiculturalism.

The profound implication of perspectivism for the philosophy of education is that it led to a transformation in how we understand the emergent quality of human life as "self-awareness." Human beings have not merely possessed self-awareness, but rather a specific, culturally transmitted context for self-awareness. Such reflection has made us aware that what historically has been treated as the power of human "judgment" is really a specific cultural "prejudgment."

This emerging idea concerning the dynamics of cultural history led to the development of the German university system known as the Humboldt-University, the basis of modern university education. The task and structure of this new model for university education were principally formulated and put into effect by Wilhelm von Humboldt, who held the post of chief of the departments of religion, public instruction, and health. The fundamental principles of the Humboldt-University were the unity of research and teaching and academic freedom. The model of the Humboldt-University changed the function of teaching in a university. In the medieval and the absolutist university, teaching meant the transmission of a basically static body of knowledge structured by the works of well-known authorities. The new Humboldt-

University model treated scientific knowledge as something in continual process; scientific knowledge is something to pursue unremittingly.

The Humboldt-University took a momentous step in the history of university education, from the idea of a fixed body of knowledge to the idea that the process of research itself is what is to be taught. It is in the teaching of the process of research itself that the "unity of research and teaching" is realized. The idea of process and growth in human history and education also infused the emergence of anthropology.

It is most significant that Kant was the person who introduced anthropology as a branch of education in 1772–1773. It was Kant who helped to take the humanistic enterprise out of a mystic darkness subject to merely theological traditions. Kant maintained that we are able to transcend the existing local contexts of human life through an exploration of the diverse forms of thought and methods found in the history of humanity. Kant's *Anthropology from a Pragmatic Point of View* called for a comparative, empirical study of ethics as contrasted with merely a rational ethics. For the German authors of this period, the term *Kultur* (culture) is employed to mean cultivating or becoming cultured, which was also the older meaning of civilization. The profound implication was that the quality of cultural transmission and education was intimately intertwined with the quality of the cultural life of the human being.

The word *culture* was established in the English-speaking world by E.B. Tylor in his 1871 book *Primitive Culture: Researches into the Development of Mythology, Philosophy, Religion, Language, Art, and Custom*: "Culture or Civilization, taken in its wide ethnographic sense, is that complex whole which includes knowledge, belief, act, morals, law, custom, and any other capabilities and habits acquired by man as a member of society" (p. 1). Influenced by the concept of organic evolution, Tylor and Lewis Henry Morgan thought of all cultures as stages in a single course of development from savagery through barbarism toward scientific civilization.

The seed for the creative transformation of how to represent and interpret the peoples of the world and their forms of life occurred in the work of Franz Boas. Fundamentally, he initiated a redefinition of the articulation of the ideas of "context," "culture," "creativity" and "lived experience." Boas drew attention to the incredible diversity of contexts of human life that have defined what human beings have taken as "reality." In 1911, Boas defined ethnology as "the science dealing with the mental phenomena of the peoples of the world."

The diversity of categories of experiencing became the focus of study. The diversity of "reality" created by the diversity in human signification became central, owing to language being "one of the most important manifestations of mental life." Essentially, Boas was linking the idea of the "language-centric predicament" of humanity proposed a century earlier by von Humboldt to a reconceptualization of what a cultural tradition means for life. The major implication was a transformation of how the diversity of cultural worlds was conceived. Although an image of progressive development from savagery to civilization revealed the potential enlightenment of mankind, it concealed the enormous variability in the extrasomatic cultural shaping of what human beings think about themselves and what they apprehend about their possibilities. Boas's historical relativism was further expanded to the question of the relationship of culture to personality. This was best exemplified in Ruth Benedict's *Patterns of Culture*.

During this century, participant-observation and formal fieldwork became the methods of cultural anthropology. Fieldwork became centered on discerning the world view and form of life generated by the native categories of language use. The idea of doing fieldwork from the "native point of view" is best exemplified in the contemporary "interpretive anthropology" of *Local Knowledge* by Clifford Geertz (1983).

It is the idea of cultural plurality and the methodology of participant observation that have had the biggest impact on the study of cultural transmission in education. The work of people like Margaret Mead, Jules Henry, the Spindlers, and the Whitings was antecedent to the creation of an educational anthropology. The potential of the articulation of education and anthropology is best exemplified in the journal *Anthropology and Education Quarterly*.

The fieldwork of the twentieth century has created an expanding record of humanity. The amassing data has led to the problem of creating a comparative methodology. The forerunner of such a methodology was George Peter Murdock, who created the *Human Relations*

Area Files and the *Atlas of World Cultures.* Within education, the awareness of diversity of cultural transmission among the peoples of the world has led to the comparative methodological concerns exemplified in Dobbert et al. (pp. 275–367) in "Cultural Transmission in Three Societies: Testing a Systems-Based Field Guide."

Contemporary anthropology is concerned with the globalization process that we are living through. The major shift of humanity during the past two centuries (and the next) is the shift from a traditional local context to a postmodern global context for the shaping and evaluation of one's life. Traditionally, the context of the individual-universal was in terms of the local knowledge of a specific cultural context in space-time. The emerging anthropological and educational global context is a transient step into a new world of the totality of world culture-history as the problematic domain of the individual-universal. One's relationship to this new totality of humanity is the potential context for one's enculturation and individuation.

Richard P. Chaney

See also KANT; MULTICULTURALISM; RELATIVISM; SOCIOLOGY

Bibliography

Benedict, Ruth. *Patterns of Culture.* Boston: Houghton Mifflin, 1934.
Clifford, James. *The Predicament of Culture.* Cambridge: Harvard University Press, 1988.
Dobbert, Marion Lundy, et al. "Cultural Transmission in Three Societies: Testing a Systems-Based Field Guide." *Anthropology and Education Quarterly* 15 (1984): 275–367.
Geertz, Clifford. *Local Knowledge.* New York: Basic Books, 1983.
Hannerz, Ulf. *Cultural Complexity.* New York: Columbia University Press, 1992.
Harris, Marvin. *The Rise of Anthropological Theory.* New York: Thomas S. Crowell, 1969.
Honigmann, John. *Handbook of Social and Cultural Anthropology.* Chicago: Rand McNally, 1973.
Kroeber, Alfred L. *Anthropology Today.* Chicago: University of Chicago Press, 1953.
Shweder, Richard A., and Robert A. LeVine, eds. *Culture Theory.* Cambridge: Cambridge University Press, 1984.
Turner, Victor. *On the Edge of the Bush.* Tucson: University of Arizona Press, 1985.
Tylor, E.B. *Primitive Culture.* 5th ed. London: J. Murray, 1929.

Arete

The central concept in ancient Greek ethical and educational thought, translated most often as "virtue," but also as "goodness" or "excellence." In common use, the term *arete* generally denoted the quality or disposition of a thing or person that makes it effective in some role or enables it to do its work well or outstandingly well. In this relative or qualified use of the term, one could speak of the *arete* of many things both animate and inanimate, but always with reference to some role or task. One could speak in this way of military or domestic *arete* or excellence, or again of the *arete* or virtue of a wrestler, archer, or scribe, but not of *arete* per se, or the virtue of a man or person as such.

Used without qualification, or qualified by the adjective *anthropine* (human), *arete* acquires a more contentious aspect, signifying the form of excellence that either does, or arguably should, command the greatest respect or social recognition in a society. The former and more conservative variant of this notion of human virtue, or virtue per se, was closely linked to the notions of fame (*kleos*) and honor (*time*). Understood in this way, *arete* consists in part or even in large measure of good reputation and the honors bestowed in recognition of outward success or outstanding accomplishment. Failure and dishonor entail a corresponding loss of *arete*, experienced as shame (*aidos*). Thus, Homer (c. 800–700 B.C.) could hold that defeat and enslavement entail an immediate loss of half one's goodness.

Even in its progressive variant, the possession and exercise of *arete* was often understood to depend in some measure upon gifts of fortune that many people lacked. Most notably, it was widely supposed that a person could not be good without being born into a good family, and without the advantages of wealth, strength, and social position.

The virtues (*aretai*) most admired in Greek popular morality were those of the warrior hero: strength, courage, cunning, and endurance. Those heroic virtues, and the hero's competitive or agonistic ethic (from *agon*, or "contest"), were captured most influentially by Homer in his poems the *Iliad* and *Odyssey,* and are thus referred to as "Homeric virtues" and "Homeric ethics." The Homeric virtues give the appearance of being eminently valuable to those who possess them, given their utility in securing power, status, and success. Yet their untrammeled exercise invites aggression, conflict, and a substantial disregard for the interests of others, and those disadvantages not only work to the detriment of the lower classes but also preclude any secure enjoyment of success by the most excellent.

An alternative conception of *arete* developed in opposition to this dominant one, taking as its starting point the image of Zeus as a god who cared not only about his own honor and success but also about justice among human beings. Hesiod, a near contemporary of Homer's, defended the place of justice among the virtues, and the idea that Zeus will not permit success through injustice, in his *Works and Days* (c. 700 B.C.). Solon (c. 640–560 B.C.) promoted the virtues of restraint, both through his poems and by establishing the first written law of the Athenian state. His goal was to limit the power of the ruling aristocracy and restrain their abuse of the lower classes. Advocacy of the virtues of moderation and justice prompted a question that did not seem to arise for Homeric virtue—namely, Why would one want to be virtuous, if virtue involves self-restraint or moderation in the pursuit of one's own success? Hesiod and Solon answered this challenge with divine and legal sanctions, respectively, and the moral theorists of the fifth and fourth centuries B.C. developed the defense of these virtues further with arguments for the desirability of virtue even in the absence of external rewards.

Systematic inquiry into the nature of *arete* began in the fifth century B.C. with Protagoras (c. 490–c. 421 B.C.) and Socrates (c. 470–399 B.C.). Protagoras developed a form of relativism according to which justice, piety, courage, and other virtues are whatever they are generally taken to be in one's own city. He took human virtue in general to be a capacity to reason well in practical matters both public and personal, and held that this capacity could be refined and enhanced through teaching. Rejecting the relativism of Protagoras, Socrates held that the virtues have universal natures that can be identified and known through reasoned inquiry. While holding that he did not possess the moral knowledge attainable in that way, he did hold that the virtues are the greatest good one can possess; that they cannot be possessed independently of one another; that virtue is a state of knowing the best way to act and live; and that no one in the possession of such knowledge can willingly do what is wrong.

Plato (c. 427–347 B.C.) developed and modified this Socratic conception of virtue through holding that knowledge of moral particulars rests on knowledge of the transcendent "Form" of goodness itself, and through an account of motivation that identifies appetites and emotions as springs of action that may compete with reasoned thought. He identified virtue as a state of psychic harmony or health in which emotion and appetite are aligned with reason's dictates.

The Socratic tradition culminated in the development by Aristotle (384–322 B.C.) of a highly systematic and subtle account of human excellence. Adopting an account of motivation much like Plato's but rejecting the Platonic account of moral knowledge in favor of one that places fundamental importance in the grasp of particulars, he defined excellence of character as a disposition entailing desires for good ends and the capacities of perception, judgment, and choice necessary for choosing well with respect to those ends.

The Socratic conception of *aretai* as traits required by the best way of life found later expression in the Stoic definition of virtue as "living according to nature."

Randall R. Curren

See also ARISTOTLE; HOMER; PLATO; SOCRATES; SOPHISTS

Bibliography
Adkins, A.W.H. "Homeric Values and Homeric Society." *Journal of Hellenic Studies* 91 (1971): 1–14.
———. *Merit and Responsibility: A Study in Greek Values.* Oxford: Oxford University Press, 1960.
Aristotle. *Eudemian Ethics, Nicomachean Ethics.*
Dover, K.J. *Greek Popular Morality in the Time of Plato and Aristotle.* Berkeley: University of California Press, 1974.
Plato. *Charmides, Euthyphro, Laches, Protagoras, Meno, Republic.*

Aristotle (384–322 B.C.)

Philosopher and scientist; for twenty years, student and member of Plato's Academy; from 348/47, teacher of philosophy, first in Assos, next in Mytilene, and then tutor of Alexander at the court of Macedon. In 335/34, he founded a school of philosophy in Athens, the Lyceum.

Aristotle's early dialogues and a protreptic on the ideal of the philosophic life have survived only in fragmentary form. The main body of writings that has come down to us consists of treatises on a wide range of subjects. It is thought that these were originally presented as lectures; some of them may be notes on lectures taken down by students. Cicero (106–43 B.C.) called them "notebooks."

Aristotle's treatises are investigative reports, describing a method of inquiry and the results reached. They were part of the extensive program of investigation undertaken in the Lyceum, which was a research institution, a library, and a museum as well as a school. In Aristotle's practice of taking into account his predecessors' ideas and opinions as points of departure for his own thinking, we see the origins of the history of philosophy. This interest in mining the work of others in order to find the origins of our own customs and thinking was characteristic of the research activities of the Lyceum. In giving attention to the collecting of materials as empirical findings and illustrations for the developing sciences, the Lyceum was a new kind of institution in ancient Greece, a forerunner of the museums in Hellenistic times at Alexandria, Pergamus, and Rhodes. Aristotle broke new ground by researching various archives for materials in the history of culture and literature. Examples include compiling a *List of Pythian Winners;* researching the records of dramatic performances at Athens; collecting 158 constitutions, of which the *Constitution of Athens* has survived; preparing a literary and philological study called *Homeric Problems;* and putting together a collection of maps and a museum of objects to serve as illustrations for lectures in the natural sciences. The research continued in the work of Aristotle's successor as head of the Lyceum, Theophrastus (c. 370– c. 287 B.C.), who is best known for his study of botany, the *History of Plants.*

The Intellectual Virtues and Scientific Investigation

Aristotle's treatises may be described as the research reports of an investigator at work, developing distinct sciences. Each treatise included (1) a statement of the object of the science under investigation; (2) a consideration of other thinkers' ideas on the subject; (3) an examination of proposed principles, in order to find the one that has the best prospect of explaining the subject matter; (4) a search for the facts in which the proposed principles can be seen; and (5) an explanation of the subject matter by showing how the proposed principles explain the observed facts.

Thus Aristotle's approach to the sciences embodied a general method common to all of them. At the same time, his investigations led him to find differences among them that enabled him to organize the sciences according to three categories. The origin of the three categories of science may be found in Aristotle's analysis of the "intellectual virtues," the states of mind by which the soul arrives at the truth. The intellectual virtues are activities of the rational part of the mind, which is capable of knowing two kinds of subject matter. One activity of mind is concerned with necessary and eternal things, whose principles are invariable; the other is concerned with contingent things, which are neither necessary nor eternal, and whose principles are variable. The knowing of necessary and eternal things manifests itself as *nous* (intuition), *episteme* (scientific knowledge), and *sophia* (wisdom). *Nous* is the state of mind that apprehends the primary principles of knowledge. *Episteme* is the state of mind that demonstrates the truth from primary principles. And *Sophia* is the state of mind able to combine *nous* and *episteme;* it apprehends first principles and argues deductively to conclusions. The knowing of contingent things manifests itself as *techne* (art, or technical skill) and *phronesis* (practical wisdom, or prudence). *Techne* is concerned with bringing things into being, with making, with craftsmanship. *Phronesis* is concerned with doing, with making judgments about what is to be done, and with actions to be taken.

The intellectual virtues concerned with subject matters whose principles are invariable led Aristotle to three theoretical sciences, which aim to know for the sake of knowing—metaphysics, mathematics, and physics. One intellectual virtue concerned with contingent subject matter led to the productive sciences, which aim to know for the sake of making useful or beautiful things—poetics and rhetoric, as examples. The other intellectual virtue concerned with contingent subject matter led to the practical sciences, ethics and politics, which aim to know for the sake of doing, for conduct. To summarize: The theoretical sciences are capable of being understood by principles that are certain and cannot be other than they are; as objects of study their subject matters are necessary and eternal. The productive sciences and the practical sciences are capable of being understood by principles that are less than certain; as objects of study their subject matters are contingent.

Aristotle's idea of distinct sciences—approached by a general method of inquiry, with the nature of each determined by principles found in the midst of the facts of its subject matter—objected to the Idea of the Good as espoused by Plato (c. 427–347 B.C.) in the *Republic* as the highest object in the hierarchy of Being, capable of unifying all knowledge claims. For Aristotle, there is no one science capable of determining one truth to which all other truths are subordinate. Instead, he held, to work on questions about subject matters whose nature is necessary and eternal, one must go to the appropriate theoretical sciences; to work on questions about subject matters whose nature is contingent, one must go to the appropriate productive or practical sciences. Many subject matters exist, and there are a corresponding plurality of principles explaining specific sets of facts. Principles explaining the facts of one subject matter thereby speak for that subject matter; a hierarchy of subject matters, in which the principles of the higher explain the lower, is an unnecessary assumption.

To be true to Aristotle's method of investigation is to follow the lead of each subject matter, and let its facts lead us to its principles. The principles of one make no claims on the facts of another. What get to be called the facts are, empirically, the facts in whose midst the principles of the subject matter under investigation get to be seen. The principles explain more than the facts, yet the facts are required in finding the principles that explain them. Aristotle held that metaphysics is the "most honorable" and the "most divine" science, because it deals with objects that are necessary and eternal, rather than contingent. Yet the principles of metaphysics make no claim on the facts whose principles are sought in the subject matter of ethics.

At the same time, Aristotle's method recognized the usefulness of findings in one science for the pursuit of the ends of another. As an example, in the science of politics questions arise as to the place of mathematics and poetry in the pursuit of the good life in the community.

Here the investigator is not concerned with the study of mathematics and poetry for their own sake, but with determining their place in the science and art of politics. Thus each science may be pursued for its own sake, and the findings of certain sciences also may be found useful in the pursuit of other sciences.

As reasoning has a large place in establishing the criteria for what can be taken to be knowledge, and being the method for gaining knowledge, the nature of logic needs to be addressed. According to Aristotle, logic is not a substantive science, but a study that is essential to undertaking investigations in the theoretical, productive, and practical sciences. Aristotle did not know the term *logic;* his own name for the study of reasoning was *analytics*. This term refers to the analysis of reasoning into the kinds of syllogism; in practice, analytics has also included analyzing syllogisms into propositions and propositions into terms. For Aristotle, logic is not involved in the study of words in the same ways as grammar, philology, and rhetoric are; instead, logic is a study of the thinking in which words are signs. Aristotle's logical treatises may be divided into three main parts: (1) the *Prior Analytics*, which sets out the structure that he thinks is common to all reasoning. This is essentially a formal logic, a study of the varieties of the syllogism, which hold whatever the nature of the subject matter under consideration. (2) the *Posterior Analytics*, which treats the kinds of reasoning that pertain to truth as well as consistency. This logic treats scientific knowledge. Its reasoning is "demonstration" when its primary premises are true; "induction" is the reasoning that comes to know the primary premises of knowledge. (3) the *Topics* and *Sophistic Elenchi*, which consider types of reasoning that are not demonstrations or inductions. For example, dialectical reasoning argues from probable rather than certain premises and is appropriate to studies such as the productive and practical sciences, whose subject matters are contingent rather than necessary.

Education and the Master-Craft

Unlike Plato's *Republic* and *Laws*, Aristotle's treatises do not contain lengthy discussions of education. His most explicit discussion of educational theory and practice, in Books VII and VIII of the *Politics*, ends without being completed; either it is an unfinished work or the remainder has been lost. Yet, like Plato, Aristotle's educational thinking was inseparable from his account of pursuing the highest good for human beings in the life of a community. For both Plato and Aristotle, the subject matter of *politike,* the science of politics, takes into account the conduct of the individual along with the conduct of the group. Thus we may say that ethics is a part of politics; and equally, politics is a part of ethics. That is why Aristotle's *Nicomachean Ethics* and *Politics* constitute a continuous work, each marking a distinct emphasis in the science of politics, which Aristotle called the master-craft. Aristotle put it succinctly: "The end of individuals and the states is the same." Inasmuch as human beings cannot become good apart from the social life that is necessary for shaping the good, an investigation into the nature of society is a necessary companion to an investigation into the nature of ethics. Aristotle, again like his teacher Plato, did not write a separate work on education; conceiving of education as a natural part of civic life, he wrote about education in the context of the master-craft, which addresses the nature of the mind and character of individuals, which is to be shaped to serve and be served by a community of individuals. For Aristotle, "The Good of man must be the end of the science of Politics."

Inasmuch as pursuing the human good as the end of ethics and politics is an activity of education, and this pursuit constitutes the practical sciences that Aristotle called the master-craft, the pursuit of the human good is "practical," "scientific," and the "craft" of making human beings and the community in which they live. Although Aristotle's distinction between the productive and practical sciences is clear, maintaining that distinction is not easy to do when considering Aristotle's educational thinking. While the subject matters of both sciences are contingent, which means that the principles of both are probable, not certain, the probabilities are of two kinds. In the productive sciences, the art of making aims to bring into existence something that stands apart from the making— a poem, a statue, a house. In the practical sciences, the activity of doing is the act itself. Doing cannot bring into existence something apart from itself; it can only "end" in further doing. And education, as one of the activities of doing, does not "produce" anything apart from education, but must be a continuing process that has no ends outside of itself. Yet there appears to be an art to education as well, in the sense that in the activity itself, we attempt to "make"

character and mind. The potentiality that exists in human beings must be actualized; it must be formed, it must take on its shape, in educative activities.

In Aristotle's explicit remarks about the aims of education, it is clear that, like all activities in pursuit of the good life, education is "practical" in that it involves activities of doing. At the same time, the master-craft is a science that aims to know the nature of the best state and the highest virtues of which human beings are capable. Such knowledge enables us to have a sense of what is possible in education. Educational activity is also a "craft" in the sense that determining the means appropriate for pursuing that which is possible is a kind of making as well as a kind of doing. For example, it is commonplace to say that, in doing, we try and "make things happen." The master-craft is an attempt to find the kind of unity of doing and making that works; Aristotle's pursuit of the good is a sophisticated example of "making do."

The *Politics* ends by citing three aims of education: in addition to the possible and the appropriate, there is the "happy mean." The idea of a happy mean is worked out in the *Nicomachean Ethics,* in which Aristotle characterizes human conduct as consisting of two kinds of virtues—moral and intellectual. The intellectual virtues, which we have already discussed in the context of scientific investigations, are produced by teaching. The moral virtues are produced by habit. For example, we are not courageous or temperate by nature; but by nature we have the potentiality to become courageous and temperate. This potentiality can be brought to maturity by the appropriate habits; by taking certain actions we learn to actualize our potential moral virtues. Thus children learn habits of conduct before they know what they are doing or why they are doing it. It is because very young children cannot control their conduct by intellectual principles that Aristotle emphasized habit in training them. The long-term aim is for children first to learn the moral virtues by habit; later, as their intellectual powers mature, they can learn to conduct themselves in terms of what they know through exercising the intellectual virtues. Ultimately, Aristotle's highest aim is "happiness," a way of being in which human beings conduct themselves in *cooperation* with the highest principles of their moral and intellectual nature, not merely in *conformity* with those principles. In so doing, they will be conducting their lives in such a way that their reason determines the disposition of the moral virtues that are natural to them. This is to say that, while the moral virtues are necessary for virtuous action, their uses in specific individual and social actions must be determined by the intellectual virtue called practical wisdom.

A closer examination of Aristotle's definition of the moral virtues and their relationship to the intellectual virtue of practical wisdom enables us to understand that the master-craft is a rational investigation with a practical aim. Aristotle thought that a moral virtue is exercised when one hits the mean between two extremes; as examples, courage is the mean between rashness and cowardice, temperance is the mean between licentiousness and insensibility. It is not easy to hit the mean, Aristotle thought, because "goodness" (hitting the mean) is simple, but "badness" (missing the mean) comes in many guises. The ultimate aim of conducting ourselves in cooperation with the highest principles cannot be learned entirely by habit, because such cooperation involves the use of reason in specific instances of conduct. Thus, in one sense—what is learned by habit—one who hits the means of the moral virtues exhibits goodness. Yet in another sense—what is learned by reason—such goodness lacks a rational quality, and one must go beyond virtue learned by habit and use reason to exercise practical wisdom. Put differently, the ethical-political-educational aim is to combine the moral and intellectual virtues by enabling the principles of reason to cooperate with the mean that is hit upon in actions taken. It is the person of practical wisdom, then, who illustrates cooperation of this kind of actions learned by habit and determined by reason. Again, we see that reason is employed in pursuit of a practical aim. And "cooperating" must be reason *in* action, not apart from action.

Now we can understand more fully how the science of ethics and politics aims not to "know" in a purely theoretical sense what the nature of virtue is, but to determine in a "practical" sense how human beings are to act in cooperation with that virtue that their reason holds to be the highest principle of action. As Aristotle put it, "We are not investigating the nature of virtue for the sake of knowing what it is, but in order that we may become good." Even though our reason may propose what is possible, what is appropriate, and what is the happy mean, only in the actions taken may we find out what our reason means: Our actions simply are the means by which our reason strives to actualize itself.

In summary, we may say that Aristotle's legacy in educational theory is threefold. First is his conception of distinct sciences, having a general method of inquiry in common, with the particular nature of each to be determined by the facts of its subject matter as they are subjected to the appropriate logic of investigation. Second is the research program undertaken in order to collect empirical findings needed to determine whether the nature of the sciences can be demonstrated or illustrated to be what Aristotle hypothesized them as being. The third, and arguably Aristotle's most significant contribution to educational thinking, lies in his insistence on the conjoint activities of ethics and politics, leading to the practical wisdom that teaches us that the end of the science of ethics and politics can be realized only if we learn what is good for us. Thus the end of the master-craft is naturally an educational end. What is more, while we know in a general way what the highest virtue is—what reason requires—we will not actually find out what it is until we learn to live in cooperation with reason's highest principles. In that sense, the highest virtue is never completely known, but may come to us in the pursuit of knowing, a process that has no end but further knowing. The contingent nature of social existence makes it necessary to find out what is good for us in what we do.

Aristotle the scientist had his poetic and speculative yearnings. In Book X of the *Nicomachean Ethics* he claims that the life of the intellect is the best for human beings; by living in accord with the highest principle in us we strive "to achieve immortality." Yet Aristotle's practical wisdom prevailed, reminding him that the good we seek can come to pass only from what we do. And in our striving for the good we must settle for principles that are merely probable.

J.J. Chambliss

See also LOGIC; PLATO; PRACTICAL WISDOM; REALISM; THOMAS AQUINAS

Bibliography
Aristotle. *Complete Works of Aristotle: The Revised Oxford Translation.* Edited by J. Barnes. 2 vols. Princeton: Princeton University Press, 1984.
———. *Nicomachean Ethics.* Translated by

H. Rackham. Loeb Classical Library. Cambridge: Harvard University Press, 1975.

———. *Politics.* Translated by H. Rackham. Loeb Classical Library. Cambridge: Harvard University Press, 1944.

Edel, Abraham. *Aristotle and His Philosophy.* Chapel Hill: University of North Carolina Press, 1982.

Fisch, Max H. "The Poliscraft: A Dialogue." In *Philosophy and the Civilizing Arts: Essays Presented to Herbert W. Schneider,* edited by Craig Walton and John P. Anton. Athens: Ohio University Press, 1975.

Jaeger, Werner. *Aristotle: Fundamentals of the History of His Development.* Translated by Richard Robinson. 2nd ed. New York: Oxford University Press, 1948.

Lynch, John Patrick. *Aristotle's School: A Study of a Greek Educational Institution.* Berkeley: University of California Press, 1972.

Randall, John Herman, Jr. *Aristotle.* New York: Columbia University Press, 1960.

Ross, W.D. *Aristotle: A Complete Exposition of His Works and Thought.* Cleveland: World Publishing, 1959.

Arnauld, Antoine (1612–1694)

French philosopher and theologian, associate of Port-Royal (a community of reclusives, devoted to the writings of St. Augustine, formed in the early seventeenth century) and principal author of the *Port-Royal Logic*. Besides the *Port-Royal Logic,* Arnauld is also known for his objections to Descartes' *Meditations,* his dispute with Malebranche over the nature of ideas, and his correspondence with Leibniz. His association with Jansenism and Port-Royal caused him to be the center of controversy for most of his life. Dismissed from the Sorbonne and forced to flee Paris, he eventually went into exile in Belgium, where he remained until he died.

Arnauld's philosophical position can be seen as a blend of two very different currents: the religious doctrines of Jansenism and the philosophical views of Descartes. His views on education, like those of others associated with Port-Royal, were influenced by the actual practice at the "little schools" of Port-Royal (so-called to distinguish them from the universities). Although not formally a master at the schools, Arnauld was closely associated with them and did some teaching there. The *Port-Royal Logic* and the *Port-Royal Grammar* (co-authored by Arnauld and Claude Lancelot) grew out of courses done at the schools, although they were not published until after the schools had been closed.

The Jansenists held an extremely anti-Pelagian view with respect to the question of divine grace and emphasized the sinfulness of the world. They tended to be very suspicious of anything worldly and as a consequence concerned themselves not just with the academic training of the students, but rather with their entire environment. This suspicion extended to any worldly authority, a position that coincided nicely with the Cartesian distrust of tradition and that led the Port-Royalists to place an emphasis on the individual's ability to come to the truth by reason and reflection.

Arnauld agreed with Descartes that, for matters concerning the world, the human mind is capable of coming to know the world around it, not because the world grafts itself onto a passive mind but because the mind is equipped with concepts which, when used properly, can enable it to understand the world. The proper method involves breaking things down to their simplest components, carefully distinguishing the known from the unknown, and then moving from the known to the less known. The *Port-Royal Logic* embodied this method, being quite free of jargon and the scholastic complexities of earlier works on logic and emphasizing the reader's coming to understand things over the ability to dispute well or speak well. The little schools of Port-Royal were quite innovative for their time in applying this method; in particular, all subjects were initially taught not in Latin, which the students did not know when they arrived, but in French.

Arnauld adopted the Cartesian philosophy of ideas, but he was strongly critical of Malebranche's position that ideas were the objects of our mental perceptions. Arnauld held that an idea was the mental activity of representing rather than a representative entity perceived by the mind. He did not, therefore, see ideas as in any sense a veil between the world and the mind, but rather as the connection between the two. His views on ideas thus differed from those of later empiricists who thought of ideas as the objects of mental perception.

Arnauld saw education as a therapy for the bad thinking and confusion wrought by the sinful outside world's imposing itself haphazardly on the mind; he was thus critical of empiricists for being concerned solely with what is imposed. The emphasis in the *Port-Royal Logic* is on the mind's ability to think critically, clarifying concepts and removing its prejudices. This concern is especially evident in the discussion of fallacies one encounters in ordinary life. The discussion focuses on the prejudices that lead to the fallacies, and on ways of guarding against them. In many respects, the discussion compares quite favorably with modern textbooks on critical thinking.

The influence of the *Port-Royal Logic* was enormous. It was a success not only in France but also in England, and it was in print continuously from its first publication, in 1662, until the end of the nineteenth century. Most logic textbooks from the eighteenth century borrowed heavily from it, and John Locke adopted some of its organization and much of its terminology in his own work.

Russell Wahl

See also DESCARTES; LOCKE; LOGIC

Bibliography

Arnauld, Antoine. *On True and False Ideas.* Translated by E. Kremer. Lewiston, N.Y.: Edwin Mellen, 1990.
————, and Claude Lancelot. *General and Rational Grammar: The Port-Royal Grammar.* Translated by J. Rieux and B. Rollin. The Hague: Mouton, 1975.
————, and Pierre Nicole. *The Art of Thinking (Port-Royal Logic).* Translated by Dickoff and James. Indianapolis: Bobbs-Merrill, 1964.
Barnard, H.C. *The Port-Royalists on Education.* Cambridge: Cambridge University Press, 1918.
Nadler, Steve. *Arnauld and the Cartesian Philosophy of Ideas.* Princeton: Princeton University Press, 1989.

Arnold, Matthew (1822–1888)

English Victorian poet, critic, and inspector of schools, seen by some to be the founder of comparative education, apostle of "culture," and advocate of the reform of middle-class education as the best safeguard of democracy in an era of rapid change.

Matthew Arnold was born on Christmas Eve, 1822. He was the eldest son of Thomas Arnold (1795–1842), the renowned headmaster of Rugby, where Matthew was a student from age fourteen to eighteen before going on to Balliol College, Oxford.

In 1851, in order to raise money for his marriage to Frances Lucy Wightman, he accepted an appointment as one of Her Majesty's inspectors of schools, a position he retained for thirty-five years. His poetry and criticism, for which he is best known, had to be written in his spare time.

Arnold's views on philosophy and education were set out over his lifetime in his best-known work, *Culture and Anarchy* (1869), in his *Essays in Criticism* (First Series 1865; Second Series 1888), in his annual reports on the state of schools in England, and in his excellent reports on education on the Continent, especially France, Germany, Holland, and Switzerland.

He was a major critic of the Victorian age and its problems. In *Culture and Anarchy,* he analyzed the cultural problems of Victorian England with a metaphor that became famous. He saw English society as divided into three classes: the Barbarians (the aristocracy), the Philistines (the middle class), and the Populace (the lower class). He admired a healthy aristocracy because it has "a grand style," by which he meant elevated character and nobility of thinking and acting. England had enjoyed such leadership in the past, but now things were changing. Members of the the aristocracy were becoming Barbarians, who read nothing, lacked culture, and were ceasing to be an elevating influence on the masses. The class on which he pinned his hopes was the middle class, at present Philistines because of their inadequate schooling, but capable of becoming the carriers of culture if properly educated. The Barbarians and Philistines had created a complacent, insular, and ignorant society in Victorian England, in Arnold's view, and it was necessary now to educate the Philistines well because they were becoming the most influential sector of society.

Inasmuch as the aristocracy had ceased, in England, to be an elevating influence, what could now take its place in the task, necessary in a democracy, of introducing the majority of the population to culture, which Arnold defined as "the best that has been said and thought in the world"? His answer was, always, the State, which (with Edmund Burke) he defined as "the nation in its collective and corporate character." There was much resistance to such an idea in laissez-faire Victorian England. But Arnold saw this laissez-faire attitude (dominant in economics and extended by emulation to education) as "anarchy"—an attitude that had brought England to its uncultured condition.

This use of State intervention to bring about social improvement had been achieved by countries on the Continent, argued Arnold, and it could be done in England, too. He had traveled to the Continent several times to examine patterns of schooling for several commissions on education. In a number of eloquent, authoritative, and widely influential reports—for the Newcastle Commission (1858), the Taunton Commission (1865), and the Cross Commission (1885–1886)—Arnold argued that England must follow the Continental example (especially that of France, Germany, and Switzerland) and use the power of the State to organize systematic secondary education for the middle classes and bring democratic unity to all classes through cultural assimilation.

Arnold's influence on shaping the English tradition of education was immense. His views on educational reform were frequently cited in subsequent educational disputes, in minutes of parliamentary committees, and in the reports of royal commissions. Although few of his major recommendations were enacted in his lifetime, many of them were incorporated into the English educational structure after his death. The system of "payment by results," which he consistently condemned, was abandoned in 1890. His recommendation for the appointment of a minister of education, like Alexander von Humboldt (1769–1859) in Prussia or Francois Guizot (1787–1874) in France, both of whom he greatly admired, was eventually followed: In 1899, a board of education, with minister of cabinet rank, was created. His advocacy of municipal control of education, such as he had seen on the Continent, was reflected in the Local Government Act of 1888, which created county councils, and in the Education Act of 1902, which made the county councils the local education authorities. His arguments for the organization of secondary education and the articulation of education at all levels were accepted by the Bryce Commission in 1895 and enacted by the Board of Education Act of 1899 and the Education Act of 1902, which brought both secondary and elementary education under the auspices of the local education authorities.

Arnold's moderation, objectivity, and lack of ethnocentrism did much to bring English education into the mainstream of European thought and practice. His prestige as a poet and critic gave his views on education additional weight and helped to direct the attention of his fellow countrymen to the deficiencies in English education.

Not surprisingly, as a son of Thomas Arnold and a product of a traditional "public school" and Oxford education, he was to a large extent a prisoner of his own Victorian culture. This both rendered his voice more acceptable to fellow prisoners of his era and limited the range of his vision. Although he was aware of the need for drastic reforms in English education, he was too much a product of Protestant, middle-class, Victorian culture and gentlemanly schooling to be able to envision the new world that was coming to birth around him. In his insistent focus on the middle class, he failed to anticipate the growing power, importance, and educational needs of the working class. When he discussed the three parts of education as primary, secondary, and superior, he did not have in mind a progression through those three stages for all children. He saw secondary and university education as suitable for children of a different class than those who attended elementary schools. His was a class system of education, with all its concomitant limitations.

Paul Nash

See also CONSERVATISM; DEMOCRACY; HIGHER EDUCATION; PUBLIC EDUCATION

Bibliography

Arnold, Matthew. *Culture and Anarchy*. Edited by J. Dover Wilson. Cambridge: Cambridge University Press, 1946.
———. *Essays in Criticism*. Boston: Ticknor and Fields, 1865.
———. *A French Eton*. London: Macmillan, 1864.
———. *Schools and Universities on the Continent*. London: Macmillan, 1868.
Connell, W.F. *The Educational Thought and Influence of Matthew Arnold*. London: Routledge and Kegan Paul, 1950.
Nash, Paul. *Culture and the State: Matthew Arnold and Continental Education*. New York: Columbia University Teachers College Press, 1966.
Trilling, Lionel. *Matthew Arnold*. New York: Norton, 1939.

Atheism

A nonbeliever is someone who does not believe in God. This includes *positive atheists*—people who disbelieve in God—and *negative atheists*—people without a belief in God. Although dictionaries typically define "atheism" in the positive sense, the negative meaning is more in keeping with its Greek roots. In Greek *a* means "without" or "not," and *theos* means "god." Furthermore, a number of well-known atheists of the past, for instance Baron d'Holbach, Richard Carlile, Charles Southwell, Charles Bradlaugh, and Anne Besant, have either assumed or have explicitly characterized "atheism" in this negative sense. A broad and narrow sense of both negative and positive atheism can be distinguished. In the broad sense atheism is nonbelief or disbelief in all gods; in the narrow sense it is nonbelief or disbelief in the theistic God.

Negative atheists in the narrow sense defend their position by either refuting the traditional arguments for the existence of God—that is, the cosmological and teleological arguments—or by maintaining that religious language is factually meaningless. Positive atheists in the narrow sense go beyond this to argue that the existence of God is impossible or unlikely. Thus, they attempt to demonstrate that the concept of God is inconsistent or that the existence of seemingly gratuitous evil makes the existence of a good and all-powerful God unlikely. In addition to arguing for the truth of their views, both kinds of atheists defend their position against alleged problems: for example, that they are committed to moral nihilism or to the assumption that life is meaningless.

Nonbelief in the existence of God is a worldwide phenomenon with a long and distinguished history. For example, philosophers of the ancient world such as Epicurus and Lucretius were nonbelievers, and leading thinkers of the Enlightenment such as Baron d'Holbach and Diderot were professed atheists. Even in the Middle Ages there were skeptical and naturalistic currents of thought. Expressions of nonbelief are found, moreover, in the literature of the Western world: in the writings of Mark Twain and Upton Sinclair; Shelley, Byron, and Thomas Hardy; Voltaire and Jean-Paul Sartre; and Turgenev. Today, nonbelievers are found from the Netherlands to New Zealand, from Canada to China, from Spain to South America. According to the *1993 World Almanac*, in 1991 there were about 1.2 billion nonbelievers in the world. This means that about 22 percent of the world's population are nonbelievers.

Atheism should not be confused with other "isms" such as humanism, rationalism, naturalism, skepticism, and agnosticism, or with movements such as Ethical Culture and Free Thought. Although the relation between atheism and these other positions is complicated, atheism is not identical with any of them. For example, there have been atheists who were not humanists and humanists who were not atheists; not all members of the Free Thought or Ethical Culture movements were atheists; rationalists have sometimes been believers, and followers of so-called atheistic religions have not always been naturalists. Furthermore, negative atheism (not having a belief in God) is compatible with agnosticism, while positive atheism (affirming the nonexistence of God) is incompatible with neither affirming nor denying the existence of God.

Some religions, such as Jainism, certain forms of Buddhism, and Auguste Comte's religion of Humanity, do not include a belief in a theistic God. Whether these warrant the title "atheistic" depends on the meaning of atheism. In the case of Jainism, although there is no belief in a creator God, there is belief in numerous gods within the cosmos. Thus, Jainism is an atheistic religion in the narrow but not the broad sense. Comte's religion is atheistic in both senses.

Michael Martin

See also BUDDHISM; DIDEROT; NIHILISM; SKEPTICISM

Bibliography

Edwards, Paul. "Atheism." In *The Encyclopedia of Philosophy*. Vol. 1, edited by Paul Edwards. New York: Macmillan, 1967.

Gaskin, J.C.A., ed. *Varieties of Unbelief*. New York: Macmillan, 1989.

Martin, Michael. *Atheism: A Philosophical Justification*. Philadelphia: Temple University Press, 1990.

Nielsen, Kai. *Philosophy and Atheism*. Buffalo, N.Y.: Prometheus Books, 1985.

Stein, Gordon. "Atheism." In *The Encyclopedia of Unbelief*. Vol. 1, edited by Gordon Stein. Buffalo, N.Y.: Prometheus Books, 1985.

Augustine, Saint (354–430)

Bishop of Hippo in North Africa from 395. His influence on educational theory and practice in the Middle Ages and beyond was decisive and profound, although this is something of a paradox, for Augustine was not strictly speaking an educational theorist, at least not in the style or scope of Quintilian or Martianus Capella. Yet in one form or another throughout his life, first in the classroom and finally in his bishop's seat in church, Augustine spent his whole life teaching ("carried away by a love of tracking down truth") and sharing his conclusions, however tentative ("a slave of those who desire this of me," as he says, "by right of charity" [*On the Trinity*: 1.9]). It is fair to say that Augustine was preoccupied by issues associated with the processes of "tracking down the truth" and communicating the results to others. That preoccupation often surfaces in his work, sometimes tangentially, sometimes more centrally.

We know about Augustine's own education, acquired at great expense and through the determination of his parents, from his autobiography, the *Confessions*. Born to a Christian mother (Monica) and a pagan father (Patricius), Augustine was educated until age fifteen in his hometown of Thagaste in North Africa. He continued his studies at nearby Madaura. After a year-long interruption for lack of funds, he left at age seventeen for higher studies in the provincial capital, Carthage. The aim of Augustine's education was to make him a *rhetor*, an eloquent and persuasive public speaker. The content of this education was undistinguished, limited largely to minute and repeated literary analyses of Virgil, Cicero, and a few other Latin authors. It was heavily oriented toward memorization. Nevertheless, though parochial, such an education had its strengths. Steeped in a reservoir of literary images, Augustine had available to him a whole set of deeply cultivated, standard empathies for the plights of personages both fictive and historical (such as Dido and Lucretia), a huge repertoire of characters and ideals, dilemmas and paradoxes, quips and quotes. Paradoxically, this highly conventional education had been a real training of the imagination, and it permitted Augustine the *rhetor* to understand and appeal to the wellsprings of emotion and motivation in his hearers, their ideals and fears, hopes and aspirations. At the fullest urging of his art, Augustine could move people to tears (*De doctrina*: 4.24.53). Although Augustine spends most of *Confessions* 1 criticizing his education, the *Confessions* themselves, with their moving depictions of loss and return, are impossible to imagine apart from such an education.

At age nineteen Augustine underwent a kind of educational conversion. As part of the

syllabus in the advanced schools of rhetoric, Augustine was introduced to Cicero's dialogue *Hortensius* (now lost), an exhortation to philosophy or the "love of wisdom." Augustine reports that he was immediately converted to philosophy and to the pursuit of wisdom, which he now opposed to the pursuit of mere elegance of rhetorical style. Nevertheless, he soon returned to Thagaste in 375, himself a teacher of rhetoric. In a way, his formal educational practice now lagged behind his actual educational ideals, and this tension was to remain with him for the next eleven years. Augustine continued to teach rhetoric, at Carthage from 376, at Rome in 383, and from 384 at Milan, an imperial residence, where he received a spectacular civic appointment as professor of rhetoric.

All this time, Augustine carried out his pursuit of "wisdom" apart from his career as a teacher. After his reading of the *Hortensius* at age nineteen he became a Manichee, an adherent of the (illegal) Manichaean religion, which promised its followers religious knowledge and understanding apart from faith. Disillusioned, however, when Faustus, a prominent Manichaean teacher, came to Carthage in 383 but could not resolve Augustine's growing doubts, Augustine dismissed him as just another person trained, like himself, in elegance of diction without substance. Augustine began to look for some other venue for the pursuit of wisdom. This he found in Milan, where he was introduced both to Ambrose, the eloquent and learned bishop, and at the same time to certain "Platonist books," most probably the works of Plotinus. Augustine felt that he had found in the Platonist books the wisdom for which he had so long been seeking, and, when Ambrose's sermons showed him how the Scriptures could be interpreted philosophically, he decided finally to abandon the teaching of rhetoric and to devote himself full time to the pursuit of wisdom as a celibate Catholic Christian. He retired at the end of term in August 386 to prepare for baptism.

Together with an intimate circle of friends and family, including his mother, son, brother, and two students, he withdrew to the villa of a friend at Cassiciacum, there to live a common life in pursuit of philosophy. Some of his most important writings concerning education come oddly enough from this short period of his life— Augustine had just quite publicly left education behind as a profession. But the closer one examines the early writings, the more one realizes

Augustine is still teaching—working closely with students and using his favorite school-texts, among them the *Aeneid* and (especially) the *Hortensius*. Augustine had not given up teaching at all; rather his teaching had in a way finally been reconciled to his educational ideals concerning the pursuit of wisdom. Clearly it was his new-found enthusiasm for Neoplatonic philosophy that permitted this reconciliation, for Platonism gave him a way of integrating the study of the liberal arts, including rhetoric, into a unified curriculum specifically oriented toward the pursuit of "wisdom."

This new educational vision finds its most important articulation in the early dialogues *De ordine* (*On Order*) and *Soliloquia* (*Soliloquies*), the *De beata vita* (*On the Happy Life*) and the *Contra Academicos* (*Against the Skeptics*). For Augustine the Platonist enthusiast, attainment of "wisdom" meant attainment of a contemplative vision of the incorporeal beauty of divine essence (Truth itself). This goal ordered the liberal arts into a regimen of intellectual *purification*—disciplines or "exercises" for the mind prompting it to abandon its customary reliance on sense knowledge of temporal things and to rise progressively to a spiritual vision of eternal things. In other words, in this scheme the aim of the liberal arts is to bring the student to the "port of philosophy" (*De beata vita:* 1), to which the other arts and sciences are all a prerequisite or propaedeutic. In *Contra academicos* (2.3.8), Augustine prepares his student Licentius for philosophy by the study of the liberal arts; in *De ordine,* where he styles himself as "teacher" (2.10.28), Augustine tells his students that "order" requires that instruction in the liberal arts precede the embrace of truth (1.8.24). "For it is the duty of good education to arrive at wisdom by means of a definite order" (*Soliloquies:* 1.14). And this order is laid out in Book 2 of the *De ordine:* Grammar (or Literature), Dialectics, Rhetoric, Music (which presupposes Numbers), Geometry, and Astronomy (2.12–15). Training in these disciplines purifies the mind to the point where it can once again see Truth itself, lying within each of us, as if forgotten, in our memories (*Soliloquies:* 2.19.35).

Pursuant to this vision, Augustine soon began work on an "encyclopedia," or complete and ordered curriculum, of the liberal arts, with one treatise planned for each subject. The only surviving treatise from this educational platform is the *De musica,* written between 387 and 391, although Augustine also finished a treatise on Grammar, as he tells us in his *Retractations* (1.5). It was already lost in Augustine's own lifetime, as were the beginnings of other treatises meant to belong to the *Encyclopedia* (including one on philosophy, which Augustine here treats as the last in the series). The object of study is consistent with the ideals presented in the *De ordine:* "to pass from corporeal to incorporeal things"—that is, to philosophy.

The *De magistro* (ca. 389), a dialogue between Augustine and his son Adeodatus, is also consistent with these ideals, but specifies much more fully the view of the process of teaching and of learning which they imply. The dialogue focuses on the role of words in teaching and learning. What Adeodatus discovers under his father's guidance is that neither the words of the teacher nor of anyone else actually teach. Words are "signs" that can impart belief, but they cannot impart knowledge (*scientia*), for knowledge strictly speaking pertains to incorporeal realities, and they cannot be represented but only "seen" or recognized within. Words serve to admonish the hearer to consult the truth within, to remind the reader of what one may have forgotten or lost sight of, but it is the incorporeal truth within that alone can be said to teach: "Those who are called pupils consider within themselves whether what has been explained has been said truly; looking of course to that interior truth, according to the measure of which each is able" (*De magistro:* 14.45). The Truth within, the interior teacher, is Christ, "the unchangeable excellence of God and His everlasting wisdom, which every rational soul does indeed consult" (*De magistro:* 11.38), and one learns only from him. One can note in passing that the depiction of the impotence of words in this text reflects, in part, Augustine's rejection of the theory and profession of rhetoric.

The next few years, 392 to 395, were a watershed in Augustine's life, for the experiments in Christian monasticism which had occupied his attention since his baptism were interrupted by his (virtually forced) ordination to the priesthood during a church service he was attending in Hippo; in 395 he was consecrated as bishop. He began his duties of preaching even before he became a bishop, requesting a short period of time off to study the Scriptures. His work soon immersed him in intractable disputes—between Donatist schismatics and Catholic congregations, and between himself and his own people, upon whom the clergy were attempting to impose certain unpopular reforms. Perhaps the new dilemmas he experienced as a preacher regarding how to motivate people to change and, in particular, how to interpret the text of Scripture such that it might motivate people to change, had an effect on his educational thinking. For we find that by the last decade of the fourth century it has in fact changed, a change most evident in three works from the period between 397 and 400, the *De doctrina christiana* ("On Christian Doctrine," 396), the *Confessions* (397–401), and the little treatise *De catechizandis rudibus* ("On the Cathechesis of the Uninstructed," 399–400).

From the point of view of the history of education, the *De doctrina* is the most important of these and perhaps the most important and influential of all of Augustine's works. The title is somewhat deceiving to English readers, since the word *doctrine* in English has the connotation of a body of fixed teachings, while in Latin it can refer to "teaching" more broadly, including method as well as content, almost approaching the English word *education* and certainly the Greek word *paideia*.

For Augustine the bishop, Christian "teaching" is above all Scriptural, and the *De doctrina* is above all a book about how to interpret Scripture and how to teach what one has learned in interpretation. It is divided into four books, the first three on "discovering" the "things" (*res*) that Scripture teaches, and the fourth (added, together with the last part of the present Book 3, much later, ca. 426) on the means of "presenting" one's discoveries in rhetorically effective preaching. As in the *De magistro*, the discussion is formatted around the distinction between "signs" and "things"; where "signs" are essentially equivalent to words, and "things" what the words refer to. We need to interpret the signs so that we can discover the things to which they refer. Unlike the *De magistro*, however, the *De doctrina* is much more willing to consider "external" realities, such as the life, death, and resurrection of Jesus, as "things" to be learned. Book 1 presents a summary of the "things" Scripture teaches, finally reducing these to one thing, "charity" or love (1.40–41). Correspondingly, the aim of *De doctrina christiana* is less to teach contemplative ascent to incorporeal truth, and more to "discover" charity in the Scriptures and to "teach" that. Our attention is focused not on the Teacher within, but on a text, a set of "signs" like any other book, albeit an inspired one, and this means that we must also focus on the education in "signs"—that is, in words and

their meanings and usage, which is required to understand this text.

Thus, in Book 2 Augustine turns to a treatment of signs. Learning of languages is essential for understanding unknown signs, as is knowledge of natural history (which also helps in the interpretation of figurative signs). For the same reasons, knowledge of arithmetic and music, history, dialectic, rhetoric, geometry, and even astronomy is not only desirable but necessary for the exegete, although astrological and other superstitious sciences are to be avoided (2.16–57). Augustine cautions students that "they should not pursue those studies which are taught outside of the Church of Christ as though they might lead to the happy life" (2.58)—that is, as though the liberal arts, education, or "culture" were ends in themselves. And this in itself is nothing new for the Augustine who fifteen years earlier had learned to integrate the liberal arts into a cohesive curriculum by ordering them toward the philosophical pursuit of wisdom. But what is new in the *De doctrina* is that philosophy itself is no longer the goal of education. Philosophy, like all the other branches of learning, is subordinated to the exegesis of Scripture. Philosophy, like the gold of the Egyptians which was despoiled by the escaping Israelites and turned to God's purposes (2.60–61), is no longer an end in itself, the "portal" to the blessed life of incorporeal vision of God, but is just another tool, even if the most noble one of all, available to the exegete. In other words, philosophy, or the search for incorporeal vision, is no longer the integrating principle of education. In its place is a literary, textual practice, that of exegesis or interpretation. That Augustine's plans for a philosophically construed "encyclopedia" of the liberal arts never materialized is not an accident: It was abandoned because its rationale was abandoned. The *De doctrina* is in a way its replacement, it *is* the new "encyclopedia," offering Augustine's new and final version of the integration of the arts and sciences and thus indeed of cultural endeavor as a totality.

Often this shift is expressed as a subordination of education to "theology," but that is misleading. Augustine has no word for "theology." He does not think of theology as a separate subject, closely allied with philosophy and systematic in character, as it will later be understood. He has in mind not the creation of a new school subject, but a new use for all school studies, a new integration of learning, in which all of education in its broadest sense of cultural endeavor and formation now has a new, exegetical character. Culture becomes as it were itself a literary and textual practice focused on the Bible and oriented toward preaching. For Augustine, this means he has in a way gone back to his roots, to his early and profound formation in rhetoric, replacing a philosophical paradigm for cultural endeavor with a rhetorical and literary paradigm. If anything, it is philosophy that has become a new "subject" among subjects like all the others—the "love of wisdom" and the search for truth are now primarily a literary, exegetical pursuit. This shift is also visible in the *Confessions,* where, despite Augustine's enthusiastic recounting of his conversion to philosophy, the whole autobiography ends with three books of exegesis as the integration and fruition of all of Augustine's education and reading.

The roughly contemporaneous text *De catechizandis rudibus* focuses more narrowly on the method of teaching the Christian faith to those applying for baptism, although its connection with the *De doctrina* is evident in Augustine's remarks that the sum total of the catechism is the love that God has for us, and that the aim of the catechist is to teach in such a way that love is engendered in response (4.8). This little treatise is the closest Augustine will come to a handbook on what we might call practical educational method. Augustine advises that the teacher should work in such a way that he or she enjoys the work, for such a teacher will prove more engaging (2.4). He instructs the catechist to adapt the style of discourse to the character and mood of the audience, to provide different sorts of instruction for those with different starting points, and not to worry too much about the inadequacy of words to express thoughts as we would like. In his comforting advice that our words are more effective than we think (2.3), we realize how far we have come from the *De magistro,* where the power of words to teach or even to reveal the mind of the speaker was emphatically denied (13.42) while "exterior" realities, such as the histories Scripture narrates and the catechist interprets, were not even considered within the realm of knowledge.

Augustine's influence was immediate and widespread. The mandate that the *De doctrina* gave for Christians to study the liberal arts found one of its most responsive readers in Cassiodorus, who organized a monastery dedicated to learning on his estate Vivarium. His *Institutiones* (ca. 550), written for the benefit of his monks, takes the *De doctrina* as a paradigm and, in a way, institutionalizes its educational vision. Cassiodorus's lead was followed by many, including the encylopedist Isidore of Seville (d. 636), whose *Etymologiae* is a compendium of classical and patristic learning, dependent on the *De doctrina* not only at specific points regarding the liberal arts, but also for its dedication to preserving and organizing the best of classical arts and sciences for the Christian scholar. The Venerable Bede (ca. 672–735) carried on the Augustinian synthesis of education and exegesis (Augustine's explicit influence is especially visible in Bede's *De rerum natura*) as the basis for the monastic school at the monasteries of Wearmouth and Jarrow, where Egbert, future Archbishop of York, was educated. Alcuin (ca. 734–804), educated by Egbert at the school of York and steeped in Augustinian educational ideals, brought the influence of Augustine to the Carolingian renaissance as the leading teacher at Charlemagne's palace school and principal enactor of Charlemagne's cultural reforms. His pupil, Rabanus Maurus (c. 776–c. 836), known as the "praeceptor Germaniae" for his educational work in Germany, exhibits a heavy and explicit indebtedness to Augustine in his *On the Education of the Clergy*. It is clear that the educational foundations of the Middle Ages were Augustinian. And when it is remembered that all of the figures just named, with the exception of Isidore, were exegetes, and that in the case of Isidore his work became one of the most important resources for exegetes, one gains further insight into the broader cultural influence of the *De doctrina*. Its vision of the Christian search for wisdom as essentially a search for an understanding of the Bible, and its insistence upon an education sufficient to produce skilled exegetes came to define the cultural preoccupations of the Middle Ages. In the sermons of Bernard of Clairvaux on the Song of Songs, and even in Thomas Aquinas's characterization of *sacra doctrina* as essentially a project of Scriptural interpretation, we can see the persistence of Augustine's vision, and we are reminded of his stature as the true founder of the educational and cultural edifice of the medieval Latin West.

John C. Cavadini

See also RHETORIC; SCHOLASTICISM; THOMAS AQUINAS

Bibliography

Alfaric, P. L'Evolution intellectuelle de S. Augustin. Paris: Nourry, 1918.

Augustine's De doctrina christiana: A Classic of Western Civilization. 2 vols. Edited by Duane Arnold and Pamela Bright (vol. 1), and by Edward English (vol. 2). South Bend, Ind.: University of Notre Dame Press, forthcoming.

Brown, Peter. *Augustine of Hippo.* Berkeley: University of California Press, 1967.

Hadot, Ilsetraut. *Arts liberaux et philosophie dans la pensee antique.* Paris: Etudes Augustiniennes, 1984.

Howe, George. *Educational Theory and Practice in St. Augustine.* New York: Teachers College Press, 1969.

Marrou, H.I. *A History of Education in Antiquity.* Translated by George Lamb. New York: Sheed and Ward, 1956.

———. *St. Augustin et la fin de la culture antique.* Paris: de Boccard, 1938. 4th ed., 1958.

Press, Gerald A. "The Subject and Structure of Augustine's *De Doctrina Christiana.*" *Augustinian Studies* 11 (1980): 99–124.

Averroes (1126–1198)

Thanks to Thomas Aquinas (1225–1274) and Dante (1265–1321), Abu al-Walid Muhammad Ibn Ahmad Ibn Rushd, or Averroes as he is more commonly called in the West, is well known as the foremost commentator on Aristotle. Much as he deserves that appellation, he must also be recognized as an accomplished commentator on Plato, physician, practicing judge, jurist, and spokesman for theoretical problems of his day—the latter addressed in independent treatises and commentaries on Alghazali (1058–1111). We learn of Averroes's life from a few personal references scattered throughout his writings, traditional Arabic biographies, and histories of the Maghreb. In the latter two sources, his intellectual acumen and profound accomplishments in jurisprudence, medicine, poetry, philosophy, natural science, and theology are praised extravagantly. The autobiographical references we do encounter in Averroes's writings serve mainly to explain the imperfect character of the work being offered to the public, but show thereby how busily engaged he was in other activities.

He was born in Cordoba, the son and grandson of noted cadis—his grandfather having served as the chief cadi of Cordova and of Andalusia. During the first two decades of Averroes's life, the ruling Almoravid dynasty was so wracked by internal dissension that it fell to the emergent Almohad forces. The sources describe this as a period of study for Averroes, one in which he devoted himself to jurisprudence, medicine, theology, and the natural sciences. Indeed, his desire for learning is said to have been so intense that he relaxed from his philosophical studies by passing to the reading of poetry or history. Two biographers even go so far as to claim he studied all but two nights of his life, that of his marriage and of his father's death.

Although Averroes is known as much for his practical activity as a cadi and advisor to rulers as for his theoretical accomplishments, we hear nothing of his political activity until he was nearly thirty. Called to Marrakesh in 1153 by Abd al-Mumin, then ruler of the Almohad dynasty, Averroes was named advisor to the grandiose project of building schools and literary institutions throughout the realm. Some sixteen years later, he was appointed cadi of Seville and held that post until called again to Marrakesh in 1182 as personal physician to Abd al-Mumin's successor, Abu Yagub. Abd al-Mumin ruled from 1128 until his death in 1163. His eldest son, Muhammad, had been named his successor, but Muhammad was such a profligate that he was able to rule only forty-five days before being deposed. The brother next in line, Umar, willingly stepped aside and allowed the next brother, Abu Yagub Yusuf, to succeed because he discerned so clearly Abu Yagub's merits.

The treatise *On the Substance of the Celestial Sphere,* dated 1178 in Marrakesh, and references in the *Meteorologica* to earthquakes occurring in Cordoba show that Averroes traveled extensively during those years. Averroes served as personal physician to Abu Yagub only a matter of months before being appointed cadi of Cordoba. Killed two years afterwards in the siege of Santarem, Abu Yagub was succeeded by his son Yagub ibn Yusuf, a ruler praised as a great warrior and builder. Averroes had a very close relationship with him, almost one of intimate friendship, but he was nonetheless punished in 1195, along with other notable scholars, for being overly occupied with philosophy and "the sciences of the ancients." The reason for this unusual action by a supposedly philosophically minded ruler—to punish Averroes for insolence or to calm zealous partisans of religion within the court—is unclear. Averroes's punishment was banishment to Lucena, a small town near Cordoba, but it lasted only two years. Having returned to the court in Marrakesh, Averroes died shortly afterwards.

By the age of thirty, Averroes had already composed some treatises on logic. Then after having been presented to Abu Yagub in 1168 as the one most qualified to undertake the task of commenting on Aristotle's works, he began the work for which he is so noted. From about 1169 to 1182 he composed middle commentaries on all of Aristotle's logical works, including the *Rhetoric* and the *Poetics*, on most of the major works having to do with physical science (the *Physics, On the Heavens, On Generation and Corruption, Meteorologica,* and *On the Soul),* on the *Metaphysics,* and on the *Nicomachean Ethics.* Moreover, he wrote short commentaries on or summaries of some of Aristotle's other works in natural science (the *Parts of Animals, Generation of Animals,* and *Parva Naturalia)* as well as two treatises, *On the Application of the Intellect and Intelligibles* and *On the Substance of the Celestial Sphere.* Averroes also composed a large commentary on Aristotle's *Posterior Analytics.* In addition to these writings related to Aristotle and Aristotelian investigations, Averroes composed treatises on topics of more immediate concern to fellow Muslims: the *Decisive Treatise,* with its introduction (*al-Damimah*) and sequel (*Kashf an Manahij al-Adillah*), or *Uncovering of the Ways to the Signs,* and the famous refutation of Alghazali, the *Tahafut al-Tahafut,* or *Incoherence of the Incoherence.* When banished in 1195, he had also composed large commentaries on Aristotle's *Physics, On the Heavens, On the Soul,* and *Metaphysics;* a middle commentary on Galen's *On Fevers;* a short or middle commentary on Plato's *Republic;* and a small book entitled *On the Happiness of the Soul.*

Averroes differs from Avicenna (980–1037) in his style of writing as well as in his personal habits. He is both more direct in what he has to say and less given to whimsical comparisons between religion and philosophy. Equally concerned as Avicenna about the relationship between revelation and reason or prophecy and prudence, he is less willing to suggest facile similarities that might lead to confusion. Like Alfarabi (870–950), Averroes was persuaded that science and with it philosophy had been completed by Aristotle but still needed to be re-

covered and, above all, protected in each age. These are the goals to which he addressed himself in all of his works. The commentaries on Aristotle and Plato are intended to recover or rediscover the ancient teaching and explain it to those who can profit from it; the public writings—that is, those written to address issues of the day—seek to preserve the possibility of philosophical pursuits in an increasingly hostile religious environment. For Averroes, philosophy is ever the friend of religion; it seeks to discover the same truth as religion and to bring the learned to respect divine revelation.

Charles E. Butterworth

See also ALFARABI; ARISTOTLE; AVICENNA; PLATO

Bibliography

Averroes. al-Alawi, Jamal al-Din. *al-Matn al-Rushdi: Madkhal li-Qira ah Jadidah.* Casablanca: Les Editions Toubkal, 1986.

———. *Averroes' Middle Commentary on Aristotle's Poetics.* Translated by Charles E. Butterworth. Princeton: Princeton University Press, 1986.

———. *Averroes on Plato's "Republic."* Translated by Ralph Lerner. Ithaca, N.Y.: Cornell University Press, 1974.

———. *The Decisive Treatise.* Translated by George F. Hourani. In George F. Hourani, *Averroes on the Harmony of Religion and Philosophy.* London: Luzac, 1976.

Butterworth, Charles E. *Philosophy, Ethics, and Virtuous Rule: A Study of Averroes' Commentary on Plato's "Republic."* Cairo Papers in Social Science, vol. 9, monograph 1. Cairo: AUC Press, 1986.

———. "The Study of Arabic Philosophy Today" and "Appendix (1983–87)." In *Arabic Philosophy and the West: Continuity and Interaction,* edited by Therese-Anne Druart, 81–90 and 131–37. Washington: Center for Contemporary Arab Studies, 1988.

Avicenna (980–1037)

Of the three great political philosophers within the medieval Islamic tradition—Abu Nasr Muhammad Alfarabi (870–950), Abu Ali al-Husayn Ibn Sina, or Avicenna, and Abu al-Walid Muhammad Ibn Ahmad Ibn Rushd, or Averroes—Avicenna is best known to us. Thanks to the efforts of his devoted pupil and long-time companion Abu Ubayd Abd al-Wahid al-Juzjani, we have something resembling an autobiography of Avicenna with a biographical appendix by al-Juzjani. We learn from it that Avicenna was an assiduous and devoted learner from the days of his youth to the time of his death.

Born in Afshanah, Avicenna's family soon moved to nearby Bukhara, where he began his studies. Having proved himself in the study of the Quran and related works of literature by the age of ten, he turned to Indian mathematics and Islamic jurisprudence, then to the study of philosophy. Afterwards, he set about reading Porphyry's *Isagoge,* logic in general, Euclid, Ptolemy's *Almagest,* and eventually undertook the natural sciences and metaphysics. For the latter two pursuits, he claims to have read both the original texts—presumably Aristotle—and the commentaries. Such theoretical inquiries soon gave way to more practical ones as he focused his attention upon medicine. Avicenna found "medicine . . . not one of the difficult sciences," and he "excelled in it in a very short time" (*Life*: 24–26). Having thoroughly mastered the forms of the syllogisms and their various premises by sixteen, he moved on to metaphysics. These studies occupied Avicenna until the age of eighteen, at which time he found an occasion to present himself as a physician to the ailing ruler of Bukhara, Nuh Ibn Mansur, and gained access to that ruler's well-stocked library.

Avicenna composed his numerous works under unusually trying circumstances at an intense, almost frenetic, pace and used his medical knowledge to push his body beyond normal limits. Yet tales of his pursuit of bodily pleasure must be judged in light of his ascetic moral teaching. Such activities in no way kept this gifted scholar from his all-consuming pursuit of learning.

Presumably, Avicenna's first exposure to politics came from his father, a village administrator for Nuh Ibn Mansur, owner of the magnificent library. After his father's death, Avicenna first accepted an administrative post from Mansur, then moved to other locales where he served as a jurist or practiced the art of politics in service to different minor rulers. He occasionally also managed the affairs of the widows of rulers and eventually came to serve as physician to Shams al-Dawlah, the Buyid prince of Hamadhan and Qirmisin. On two separate occasions he was named chief minister or vizier to Shams al-Dawlah. Avicenna also tried his hand,

unsuccessfully, at deceptive politics, when he tried to leave the service of Shams al-Dawlah's son in order to join up with the rising Ala al-Dawlah. Forced into hiding and then imprisoned for four months, Avicenna was finally able to reach Ala al-Dawlah in Isfahan only by slipping away dressed in Sufi garb. He remained in the service of that prince, living as an intimate companion and learned advisor, until dying in Hamadhan.

In the first chapter of the introductory volume to the logical part of his famous *Kitab al-Shifa,* or *Healing,* the logical part being at the same time the beginning part, Avicenna explains the general order of the whole work. After the part on logic is another devoted to natural science. It is followed by a third that sets forth mathematics, and the whole compendium concludes with Avicenna's explanation of the divisions and aspects of the science pertaining to metaphysics. From this account of its scope, one might think that Avicenna's *Shifa* was devoted solely to theoretical philosophy or science, that it had nothing to say about practical philosophy or science. Indeed, it is not until the very end of his discussion of metaphysics that he speaks of the practical sciences or arts of ethics and politics. As he puts it, this "summary of the science of ethics and of politics" is placed there "until I compose a separate, comprehensive book about them" (*Madkhal:* 11:12–13).

Avicenna's fuller teaching reveals, however, that ethical and political science belong after divine science intrinsically and not provisionally. Indeed, they are the human manifestation of divine sciences—its practical proof. They testify to divine providence for humanity and thus to the truth of revelation more clearly than any of the other sciences investigated in the *Shifa.* Yet because the correctness of what they teach can also be verified by Aristotelian or pagan reasoning processes, Avicenna must elucidate the relationship he discerns between pagan philosophy and the revelation accorded the Prophet Muhammad.

Avicenna's description of Plato's *Laws* as a treatise on prophecy provides a clue to how interrelated he deems philosophy and revelation. Indeed, with one exception, he consistently presents the revelation of Islam in terms that admit of rational defense. The exception concerns the question of ultimate happiness. Even there, however, he preserves philosophy's role, never insisting upon the character of that happiness and thus forcing readers to ponder over what they could propose in its stead.

Similarly, the attention he gives to the political aspects of prophecy and divine law leads to reflection upon the most fundamental political questions: the nature of law, the purpose of political community, the need for sound moral life among the citizens, the importance of providing for divorce as well as for marriage, the conditions for just war, the considerations that lie behind penal laws, and the end of human life. Although he does not address the origin of private property any more than he explains how future successors to the prophet-lawgiver might be raised so that they will have the moral habits and character traits suitable to such a position, he does provide the basic principles for readers to pursue those issues on their own. In this respect, Avicenna's political teaching is propaedeutic rather than provisional: It provides an introduction to the fundamentals of political science and alerts readers to the need to think carefully about the strong affinity between the vision of political life set forth by the pagan Greek philosophers and that exceptional individual who surpasses philosophic virtue by acquiring prophetic qualities.

Charles E. Butterworth

See also ARISTOTLE; AVERROES; ISLAM; PLATO

Bibliography

Avicenna. *Healing: Metaphysics X.* Translated by Michael E. Marmura. In *Medieval Political Philosophy: A Sourcebook,* edited by Ralph Lerner and Muhsin Mahdi, 99–111. New York: Free Press of Glencoe, 1963.

———. *Kitab al-Shifa, al-Mantiq, al-Madkhal.* Edited by G. Anawati, M. El-Khodeiri, and F. El-Ahwani. Cairo: al-Matba ah al-Amiriyyah, 1952.

———. *The Life of Ibn Sina.* Edited and translated by William E. Gohlman. Albany, N.Y.: SUNY Press, 1974.

Butterworth, Charles E. "Ethics in Medieval Islamic Philosophy." *Journal of Religious Ethics* 11 (1983): 224–39.

———. "Medieval Islamic Philosophy and the Virtue of Ethics." *Arabica* 34 (1987): 221–50.

Galston, Miriam. "Realism and Idealism in Avicenna's Political Philosophy." *Review of Politics* 41 (1979): 561–77.

Marmura, Michael E. "Avicenna on Primary Concepts in the *Metaphysics* of his *al-Shifa.*" In *Logos Islamikos: Studia Islamica in Honorem Georgii Michaelis Wickens,* edited by Roger M. Savory and Dionisius A. Agius, 219–40. Toronto: Pontifical Institute of Mediaeval Studies, 1984.

B

Bacon, Francis (1561–1626)

Best known as the author of *The Advancement of Learning,* Francis Bacon was a courtier, barrister, member of Parliament, essayist, lord high chancellor under James I, historian, and natural philosopher. It remains an open question whether his greatest achievement, the forceful championing of a conception of scientific inquiry that has come to characterize modern science, is essentially scientific in the conventional modern sense, or a mixture of eloquence, traditional lore, and daring adaptations of Biblical religion for purposes that have not yet been fully appreciated.

Bacon's new learning incorporates yet separates itself from contemplative, deductive, imaginative, and theological habits of mind associated with Plato, Aristotle, the rhetoricians and poets, and medieval scholastics. *The Advancement of Learning* generally follows this outline: Book I is a defense of learning, especially the old learning, while Book II advocates ambitious renovations in almost all fields.

Thomas Sprat's 1667 history of the Royal Society, that fabled seedbed of modern science, invokes Bacon's vision of the new learning in the paradoxical terms of Moses' vision of the promised land. The Baconian Moses is supposed to inspire and sustain a new association of persons dedicated to free, truthful, and useful inquiry into the laws of nature—inquiry that Sprat thought would leave behind the religious and political differences that had wreaked destruction in the recent civil wars. Honest (that is, nonverbal) demonstrations of natural laws and practical (that is, unarguably beneficial) applications of those laws were supposed to introduce a new age of comprehensive yet charitable mastery over nature and politics.

Bacon is extremely careful not to impugn theological learning, which is one of the few types of learning he says is not wanting. But he repeatedly argues that war, faction, and delusion derive from misguided religious enthusiasm. Superstitions are the pseudoreligious delusions of the mob, which—linked with many religious reformers' overzealous iconoclasm—are the chief threats to the enlightened iconoclasm of the new sciences.

Bacon's famous inductive method, though it treats a topic at least as old as the works of Aristotle, is unusual in its requiring a quasi-religious discipline so that true induction distinguishes itself from false worship. Baconian induction first systematically beats nature's fields for game, collecting experimentally forced evidence as well as encyclopedic tabulations, and then rigorously eliminates superficial findings until laws of nature's construction become evident and available for charitable ends. Most important, the new induction is also supposed to do contradictory things: (1) scourge and test the sons of science, purging them of the vanities of appetite and aspiration, and (2) enable them to indulge themselves—without their becoming corrupt—in the pleasures of their unprecedented, scientific mastery over nature and the utilitarian comforts of the new scientific age.

Bacon's famous doctrine of the four idols, which he outlines in the *Novum Organon* (1620), is a detailed indictment of common habits of mind that he argues are intellectual heresies injurious to scientific progress. Here again, Bacon displays his strategy of using religious language and ideas to fend off enemies of the new learning. Opponents are worshipers of false gods, and the new sciences are the means of smashing those idols. The true

Baconian iconoclasm imitates Moses' destruction of the Golden Calf in Exodus 32. (He notes the resemblance in a remark recorded by William Rawley.) In a poem by Abraham Cowley (1618–1667) quoted by Sprat, Bacon is likened to the law-giving, iconoclastic prophet who led the Hebrews into the promised land.

Moses taught an arduous patience and hope in a wilderness that was only occasionally and selectively illuminated by divine revelation. Bacon urges the sons of science across another divide, where they must sacrifice their embrace of appearances and anticipate what their own relentless, inhuman "machine" of scientific induction prevents them from anticipating: an "apocalypse" or revelation of the laws of matter that would make possible the mastery of all the arts of rhetorical, political, and material manipulation.

Mathematics and poetry, which (one would think) might contribute a great deal to this enterprise, pale in Bacon's preoccupation with the deeper project, which is to glimpse the laws of the forms. Thus he sometimes associates mathematics and poetry with a love of the occult and imaginative self-indulgence, even though elsewhere he pays both arts respect. Conversely, what are today considered to be hard-headed experimental breakthroughs in Renaissance science, such as the discovery of the circulation of the blood by William Harvey (1578–1657) and the seminal experiments with the powers of the magnet by William Gilbert (1540–1603), are—by Bacon's standards—narrow researches and tinkerings that fail to conceive of or endure the harsh grandeur of the Mosaic vision.

The only way to overcome idolatry and advance the new sciences decisively is to undergo a self-denying "experience" in a trackless wilderness of scientific inquiry, stripped of presuppositions and desire yet somehow driven by a yearning for world-transforming wisdom. In order to reveal the few deep laws that would enable the sons of science to transform everything into everything else (a goal Bacon strangely gleans from the writings of the Apostle Paul), nature itself must ultimately be purged of those lesser tendencies that Aristotle attributed to natural desires for merely appropriate natural ends. This is the double meaning of Bacon's famous dictum in the *Novum Organon* that inquiry into nature must be a submission to nature's ways: Both man and nature must eventually prostrate themselves to the few laws of the forms, which man can then use to remake the visible world even as nature works toward birth and death.

Those who do not know Moses' paradoxical way to the promised land fall into four idolatries which, according to Bacon, embrace the vanities of appearance and of easy persuasion rather than the purgative, revelatory ordeal of experience. *The Idols of the Tribe* arise from weakness in "human nature itself," especially the propensity to find order in appearances where there is none. The idolatrous understanding gathers evidence to support first impressions, seizes upon positive evidence rather than searching out exceptions, looks in vain for extremely distant "final" causes rather than practical applications; indulges its flattering affections; and relies on the immediate sensations of the senses or the aid of deceptive, simplistic instruments.

The Idols of the Cave are illusions that dominate individual minds, not just because the human understanding is prone to make real what is illusory, but because self-isolated minds develop their own heresies. These are merely idiosyncratic associations and inferences depending upon accident and habit rather than the rigors of self-abashing, probing inquiry.

The Idols of the Market-Place are "the most troublesome" because they come from words, which are powerful indulgers of vanity because they give their users a false sense of control. Since users of words rely upon language to control words, especially in the process of defining terms, they are victims of language's origins in the vulgar whims of the common people. Deception is certain unless the idolatrous linguistic medium of trade (like filthy lucre) can be destroyed by a new wisdom of how the forms of things make the world. Things rather than words must be the focus of the new learning. Hence the motto of the Royal Society: *Nullius in Verba*: "Of nothing in words."

The Idols of the Theater are the collections of ideas and arguments amassed by academies, pseudoscientists, and other schools of thought in ancient as well as modern times. (Here Bacon comes close to removing any basis for his praise of the old learning.) They presume to explain such phenomena as logic, the elements, and animal life; yet they do not deign to engage in experiments to test their ideas. When these idolaters discuss the nature of the heavens, which Bacon says are open to innumerable and vain interpretations, they mix inquiry with rhetoric, and theology with science, thereby creating endless controversies that resemble religious warfare.

Given the nearly overwhelming power of these idolatrous delusions, how can they be overcome? Simple empiricism is not the answer, since the senses' dependence upon appearances makes them unreliable, more so when they depend upon the convenience of instruments that simply magnify or distance the observer. Bacon's call to a higher learning is itself suspect (as he observes) insofar as it uses eloquence to raise hopes, the chief sources of idolatrous misapprehensions. Most important, what is to be done when the "sons" achieve unprecedented power over appearances, having the ability not only to satisfy their unsaintly deviations from charitable perfection, but to give or deny the mass of mankind what its idolatrous heart hardly dares to hope for?

Given the dangers of these possible developments, Bacon selects another extraordinary biblical figure to be a model for scientific conduct: King Solomon. The wise and fabulously wealthy ruler is also a naturalist and the author of the enigmatical *Book of Proverbs* and the *Wisdom of Solomon*. Most important, he can luxuriate in the fruits of his inquiries without being corrupted by them, at least in his prime. The secret of his ability seems to be contained in his forceful, enigmatic aphorisms: moral teachings that are in fact broken bits of wisdom that suggest a deeper encryption of the laws of nature. In both mode and substance, the Solomonic books protectively hide and yet promise a paradigm for changing the world to satisfy human needs with God's blessing—at least as long as Solomon remains God's favorite.

The world itself, Bacon argues, must be read as code, and must be put to the test so that it too gives up vain appearances and yields to utility at the command of Solomonic masters of the new sciences. Hence Bacon's collection of aphoristic bits of learning in the *Sylva Sylvarum* and the treatises on winds, tides, and the nature of matter. Perhaps the most intriguing example of this effort is the *Wisdom of the Ancients,* a wrenching, experimental reading of ancient myth that assumes that the old stories are scatterings and encryptions of natural laws so deep they were unknown even to the ancients who made the myths.

The best evidence for the new sciences, according to Bacon, comes from the antipodes: the extremes of place, time, and circumstance. He uses this principle to venture hypotheses that later science has confirmed: the moon's influence on the tides, and the existence of continental drift. Experiments are useful for a similar reason. They tell us what seemingly ordinary things do under the adversity of extremes. The world of appearances is an untamed Proteus that tells us everything we falsely desire to know but nothing obviously true. To detect and use its deeper laws, Proteus must be captured, tortured, interrogated.

The users of the new sciences must therefore be exceedingly wise so as not to be cruel, especially when their researches begin to control human subjects (as Bacon anxiously and enthusiastically hints they will). Solomon was able to conduct himself wisely as God's chosen king, but in the end the Bible says he became corrupt; will the sons of science need to be so fortunate and yet end up so debauched? What happens to the sciences and their champions when the strenuous and perplexing experience of scientific inquiry routinely yields luxuries (potential idols) that render hardship unnecessary? And what makes wisdom worth knowing if everyone knows it (or thinks everyone can know it) as automatic laws of action that seem to make everything convenient?

For all its charitable dedication and cautious concealment, the new learning's emphasis upon power and secret codes expands the temptation to deceive and coerce, to allow ends to justify means in a new, profoundly Machiavellian rhetoric of power. One gets a glimpse of these trends in the *Essays,* which teach a sort of prudence to the general reader but intimate a "wise" reading of deeper laws of political and ethical manipulation beneath their conventional advice. Most illustratively, *The New Atlantis* shows us the House of Solomon, which seems to rule almost imperceptibly and charitably over its island, amassing a world-transforming arsenal of knowledge capable of creating wonders like the unearthly wind that drives the sailors to utopia's shore. Imitating and improving upon the latter days of Genesis while seeming to leave religion to the founders of Christianity, Bensalem's College of the Six Days' Work is an institution whose extreme benevolence is matched by its power to awe and control.

These tensions severely qualify, or at least greatly complicate, the hope that Bacon's new learning will spread a tradition of free inquiry and open communication that is liberated from illusion and ambition. In the effort to do away with the vanity of the old occult sciences, idolatrous imaginings, and the dominating influence of ancient philosophy, the great practical benefits promised by Bacon's works are mixed up with new forms of coercion and dissimulation that confine and dangerously excite the imagination.

What seems to be gained most of all from Bacon's great project is the nerve to hope for a new degree of security from the ravages of mortality. What tends to be lost is patience with and knowledge of some things that traditionally have helped to proportion and perfect such a hope: the complicated, largely intractable exigencies of political life and the gradual nature of philosophical enlightenment. For all Bacon's interest in vernacular opinions, political and ethical prudence, and divinity, the gist of his arguments unties the connections between common sense and higher truths, melts the distinction between persuasion and coercion, and severely discounts the old idea that nature and supernature (or divinity) might be significantly accessible to unaided reason.

Bacon's works are especially compelling because they incorporate into his practical sciences a remarkably persistent quest for the deeper truths in ancient texts and in nature. His interest in the unobstructed contemplation of those truths, not just their application, keeps open the discussion of what the new sciences really are and what they should be as they are put into practice. The new Baconian sciences are not only technologies; they make elaborate claims about the nature of the world. Thus Bacon continues to present to us something that is now easily obscured: the original, problematic character of the new sciences as charitable, truth-seeking manipulations of nature and of man. If our imagination is open to the premodern as well as the modern qualities of Bacon's writings, they present us with philosophically prodigious innovations that call out for more discussion of their meaning and implications.

John Channing Briggs

See also ARISTOTLE; CALVINISM; CIVIC EDUCATION; COMENIUS; COMMON SENSE; CRITICAL THINKING; DEWEY; DIDEROT; EMPIRICISM; EXPERIENCE; JEFFERSON; LOCKE; PLATO; RHETORIC; SCIENCE, PHILOSOPHY OF; SKEPTICISM; SOPHISTS

Bibliography

Bacon, Francis. *The New Atlantis and the Great Instauration.* Edited by Jerry Weinberger. Arlington Heights, Ill.: Harlan Davidson, 1989.

————. *Works.* Edited and translated by James Spedding. New York: Garrett Press, 1857–1874. Reprint. 1968.

Briggs, John C. *Francis Bacon and the Rhetoric of Nature.* Cambridge: Harvard University Press, 1989.

Jardine, Lisa. *Francis Bacon: Discovery and the Art of Discourse.* Cambridge: Cambridge University Press, 1974.

Kocher, Paul H. *Science and Religion in Elizabethan England.* San Marino, Calif: Huntington Library, 1953.

Quinton, Anthony. *Francis Bacon.* Oxford: Oxford University Press, 1980.

Whitney, Charles. *Francis Bacon and Modernity.* New Haven: Yale University Press, 1986.

Beecher, Catharine Esther (1800–1878)

New England philosopher of religion, education, and gender, who repudiated the Augustinian foundation of Calvinist doctrine to formulate a "common sense" religion and a professional "ministry for women" in teaching, nursing, and homemaking. This sister of Harriet Beecher Stowe (1811–1896) and great aunt of Charlotte Perkins Gilman (1860–1935) founded three academies for women, published more than two dozen books, and wrote many shorter pieces between 1827 and 1874—often recapitulating arguments she had articulated in *A Treatise on Domestic Education for the Use of Young Ladies at Home and at School* (1841) and in *The True Remedy for the Wrongs of Women* (1851).

Embracing love rather than fear as a basis for Christian childrearing, Beecher (1) argued that learned moral conduct rather than conversion was essential to a soul's salvation; (2) reconceptualized teaching within the home and the school as professional mothering; (3) constructed a new subject of school study for girls and women, "Domestic Economy"; and (4) formulated a utopian vision of the Christian home and neighborhood as fundamental to democracy in the United States.

Beecher's critique of the sternly introspective New England religious tradition was integral to her reformulations of education and womanhood. With all seven brothers in the ministry, she questioned women's exclusion from that profession. As the eldest daughter of evangelist Lyman Beecher (1775–1863), she shared the assessment of Horace Mann (1796–1859) of Calvinistic education: "an unspeakable calamity . . . a dreadful thing it was for me!" Aimed at purifying the child's soul of its Original Sin, that education cultivated fear of God and required conversion as a young adult, a spiritual rebirth without which virtue was deemed meaningless and the soul's salvation impossible.

In her unpublished *Elements of Mental and Moral Philosophy* (1831) and in her published *Letters on the Difficulties of Religion* (1836), *Common Sense Applied to Religion* (1857), and *Religious Training of Children in the School, the Family, and the Church* (1864), Beecher developed a critique of Calvinism that was, like the later religious inquiry of William James (1842–1910), simultaneously psychological. Granting epistemological authority to reason and to the evidence of both sensory and revelatory experience, she rejected the doctrine of natural depravity of Jonathan Edwards (1703–1758) as a theological fiction unsupported by either the Word of God or common sense. Defining evil as needless destruction of human happiness or infliction of pain, locating happiness in "mutual relations of minds" rather than individual pleasure, and locating sin only in voluntary action, she argued that everyone is born with perfect mental constitution and must be properly educated—not through fear, but through love, patience, gentleness, sympathy, self-denying labors, and care—to seek perfection through controlled voluntary action, especially self-sacrifice. Toward that end, she articulated developmental phases of children's education and theorized that records of experience are indispensable to successful Christian educational practice in both homes and schools.

Having debunked the Calvinist call to conversion, Beecher regarded the family state as the best earthly illustration of the heavenly kingdom and claimed for women a special calling within it to civilize men. Her revised Christian ethics thus constructed a soul-saving purpose for her concept of the "ministry of women" as school teachers, nurses, and homemakers. Women's ministerial authority to educate men's minds, bodies, and souls must derive from professional education and from learned emulation of Christ's self-sacrifice, which entailed women's submission to patriarchal authority but not their subservience. For it required women's intelligent, indirect exertions of "influence," rather than their votes or other direct exertions of power, as means of teaching others Christian self-denial on behalf of the ignorant and weak.

Paradoxically, however, Beecher also advocated rendering women's ministerial vocation both honorable and remunerative so that not only married women, but single women as well, might own homes of their own, marrying only as a choice, not from economic necessity. Toward this end, she remade motherhood as a profession that exceeded the boundaries of biological motherhood—to include childless and unmarried women as its practitioners and to include orphans, the sick and homeless, the sinful, husbands, brothers, friends, and children in the uncivilized western United States as its beneficiaries. If rhetoric could so effectively glorify men's profession of "killing our fellow creatures," she argued, why not women's profession? In order to achieve lives for intellectual women something like men's lives as professors, she claimed that only women should be appointed to faculties of institutions charged with educating women for their "true" profession.

She believed that, apart from boys and men, all girls and women should be taught "Domestic Economy" in schools and institutions of higher education, a curriculum embodied in textbook form as Beecher, the author of textbooks in various subjects, thought other curricula should be as well. This curricular innovation responded to her perception that women had never been properly educated for mothering and homemaking. Besides instructive reflections on democracy, Christianity, and marriage, domestic economy included both broad theoretical principles and minute technical details concerning the judicious management and care of home and garden, their myriad appointments, and their inhabitants' minds, bodies, dispositions, habits, relationships, and acts of charity. Among those inhabitants she included domestic servants, girls and women whose distinctive education she also formulated, to be taught by their employers.

A forerunner of home economics, domestic economy reflected Beecher's debt to the account by Alexis de Tocqueville (1805–1859) of gender in the United States as differentiating the sexes' labors without renouncing the possibility of their equality. Her utopian vision of neighborhood and home made Christ's self-denying example a paradigm of democratic social relations among independent but congenial families who valued health, happiness, and economy of time, labor, and money. She thought that such social reform must depend on the ministry of women, albeit women of a prosperous class.

Susan Laird

See also CALVINISM; DOMESTIC EDUCATION; GIRLS AND WOMEN, EDUCATION OF; RELIGIOUS EDUCATION

Bibliography

Beecher, Catharine Esther. *The Evils Suffered by American Women and American Children: The Causes and the Remedy.* New York: Harper and Brothers, 1846.

————. *A Treatise on Domestic Economy.* Introduction by Kathryn Kish Sklar. New York: Schocken, 1977.

————. *The True Remedy for the Wrongs of Women.* Boston: Phillips, Sampson, 1851.

Beecher, Catharine Esther, Margaret Fuller, and M. Carey Thomas. *The Educated Woman in America: Selected Writings of Catharine Beecher, Margaret Fuller, and M. Carey Thomas,* edited by Barbara M. Cross. New York: Teachers College Press, 1965.

Biester, Charlotte E. "Prelude—Catharine Beecher." *Journal of Home Economics* 51 (1959): 549–51.

Boydston, Jeanne, Mary Kelly, and Anne Margolis. *The Limits of Sisterhood: The Beecher Sisters on Women's Rights and Woman's Sphere.* Chapel Hill: University of North Carolina Press, 1988.

Harveson, Mae Elizabeth. *Catharine Esther Beecher: Pioneer Educator.* Doctoral dissertation, University of Pennsylvania, 1932.

Sklar, Kathryn Kish. *Catharine Beecher: A Study in American Domesticity.* New York: W.W. Norton and Company, 1973.

Behaviorism

The Behaviorist Enterprise

In education, behaviorism has been both a research program and a philosophy of psychology. As a research program, it undertakes to explain and predict an organism's behavior solely in terms of the effects of its present environment and the conditioning history of that individual organism. Put in simple mathematical form, it asserts that

$$(1)\ B = f(E,H),$$

that is, that behavior, B, is a function of environment, E, and conditioning history, H. In more colloquial terms, what formula (1) says is that specific pairs of values, that of an environmental variable and that of a conditioning history variable, specify a unique value of a behavioral variable. Or, in stronger causal language, a specific environmental state, given a specific conditioning history, is sufficient to cause an organism to act in a unique way. Thus, a different environment may cause an organism to behave differently, or a different conditioning history may cause an organism to behave differently in the same environment. Behaviorism disallows the possibility that the organism could behave consistently differently given the same environment and no new conditioning history. For the behaviorist, organisms do not develop independently of environmental stimuli.

As the functional formula shows, E and H are assumed to be noninteractive, because such interaction would have to be done by some theoretically disallowed internal process. Thus, any formula of the form

$$(2)\ B = f(E,H,\ g[E,H])$$

where f and g are functions, is disallowed. The reason for this dismissal, given for example by B.F. Skinner, is that the behaviorist researcher needs to be able to assume that behavioral types, B, can be simply mapped back to environmental states, E, that presumably affect them, without worrying about physiological processes of the observed organism.

As a doctrine, behaviorism presumes to say what psychology should do. It demands of that discipline that no internal states of organism be treated as indispensable to explaining that organism's behavior. Thus, any formulation that includes internal states, for example, X, for expectations, yielding

$$(3)\ B = f(E,H,X)$$

must be disallowed. For the behaviorist, the organism is "empty."

The theoretical viability of behaviorist theory depends upon the possibility of defining such things as behavioral, environmental, and conditioning history variables, B, E, and H. The definitional requirements for being a variable are that a variable be a partitioned set—that is, that it represent a class of event-types that are mutually exclusive and together exhaustive of all events in its class. This partitionability condition is a requirement of the mathematical foundations of measurement.

A further assumption of behaviorism is that B, E, and H can be adequately and interestingly defined extensionally—that is, without reference to the beliefs of perceptions of the behaving organism. Those would be, after all, represented by additional internal variables. Thus the behaviorist discards the generally practical distinction between "John's left biceps twitched" and "John twitched his left biceps" unless it could be made out in terms of measurable characteristics of the observed event.

Intensional definition—that is, definition that invokes beliefs or perceptions of the subject—is avoided, one might presume, by characterizing type-defining events in terms of the responses of measuring devices. So it is that behavior, or environment, or conditioning history types will be identified by sets of numbers generated on certain devices. (How one would calibrate such a device from within the framework of behaviorist theory is an interesting question.)

Can a Consistent Behaviorist Finish an Experiment?

Suppose the experimenter were going to apply the same theoretical restrictions upon his own behavior—that is, be a "consistent behaviorist"—as upon the experimental subjects. According to behaviorist theory, an organism can be shown to be able to discriminate between two environmental event-types, say, e_1 and e_2, only if it can be conditioned to respond differentially upon their presentation. If the experimenter's apparatus can discriminate n environmental-event types, it would take

$$(4) \quad \frac{n!}{2(n-2)!}$$

experiments to map out the perceptual capabilities of the subject organism. (This is the number of combinations of pairs of contrastive events given n. If the order of presentation were crucial, then the even greater measure of the number of permutations of pairs would be the number of experiments required.)

So for a paltry ten environmental types, it would take forty-five experiments to map out the organism's respondent capabilities, assuming the organism to have only two response types. For m behavior-types, the stimulus-presentation set must be presented $m-1$ times.

It is easy to measure stimulus variation to the hundredth of a unit, and easy to measure,

say, ten simultaneous potential stimulus-properties of an environment—say, intensity of illumination, temperature, density of magnetic flux, speed relative to the Earth's surface, and so on. (No a priori restrictions on possible physical variables is consistent with behaviorist doctrine.) If we suppose that an organism is capable of ten behavioral types, then the "consistent behaviorist," to determine the behavioral variability of the organism, has an enormous number of experiments to perform. There are 100^{10} "environments" to be tested out for each of the ten response types.

It may take at least ten training trials for the organism to "learn" to differentiate its responses in a given environment (a very steep learning curve!). Putting all these considerations together and given that most reported conditioning experiments concluded within months of their initiation, one may assume that there were never any "consistent behaviorists" at work. The experimental results offered in evidence of behaviorist theory must have been carried out with the surreptitious support of other theoretical scaffolding.

Is the Behaviorist's Concept of Behavior Useful to Educators?

Consider the following generally useful and possibly both educationally and legally important distinctions between emitting sound, saying, telling, informing, and surprising. Consider Harry to be the person who is our subject of investigation. From a behaviorist perspective, Harry has behaved, b_1, in a way described (using adapted phonetic notation) as follows:

(a) Harry emitted/²aym+gowin howm¹/.

But other descriptions of b_1 are available. For example:

(b) Harry said, "I'm goin' home."
(c) Harry told John he was going home.
(d) Harry informed John that he, Harry, was going home.
(e) Harry surprised John with the statement that he was going home.

Does this mean that the behaviorist has a chance of reducing descriptions (b), (c), (d), and (e) to (a)? Not at all. We can easily imagine a situation in which all of these descriptions are true of Harry's behavior. But if Harry is a babbling idiot, (a) might be true and none of the rest. If Harry is reading aloud a line from a script, (a) and (b) might be true and none of the rest. If John already knew that Harry was going home, (a), (b), and (c) might be true but none of the rest. If John is never surprised by what Harry does, (a), (b), (c), and (d) might be true, but not (e).

What these alternative descriptions show is the following:

(1) If circumstances determine how behavior is to be described, we must take care to separate such circumstances from environmental conditions that supposedly explain that same behavior, otherwise our variables are not independent; and

(2) Behavior is not, in natural language, a partitioned set of events, therefore it is not a variable in the mathematical sense. Thus, it cannot be measured, nor can it be conditioned—that is, be subject to a procedure that requires it to be assigned a probability distribution. (Such an assignment requires a partition.)

Thus the would-be behaviorist bears the burden of defining a behavior-partition rather than assuming that behavioral categories in our natural language—those categories with which we express our educational, legal, and moral concerns—will do for a start. This burden, however, is not the behaviorist's uniquely, but is borne also by theorists of any persuasion who would attempt to analyze human behavior as a causal consequence. If no behavior-partition can be constructed, no global measurement of behavior can be made, and thus no global correlational analysis of human behavior.

Why Has Behaviorism Survived in Education?

The behaviorist theorist who has had the greatest influence on education is B.F. Skinner. The plausibility of the Skinnerian doctrine in education depends on the viability of the behaviorist program. With the proliferation of devices such as handheld calculators and computers containing internal processing devices, hidden internal processors—anathema to Skinner—have become a commonplace explanatory hypothesis.

Because the "behavior" of such computing devices cannot be explained and predicted solely in terms of environmental variables or their history of influence on the individual "organism,"

and also because the enthusiasm with which the behaviorist program was promoted has not been met with corresponding empirical results, the behaviorist program has been largely abandoned in empirical psychological research—except in cases where severely dysfunctioning individuals are concerned. Indeed, the development of computers provides a major impetus for the ascent of the cognitivist psychological theories that have largely replaced behaviorism in experimental psychology.

As a philosophical theory, behaviorism is passé. However, its influence in education cannot be understood merely in terms of the viability of the scientific or philosophical standing of behaviorism as a general theory of psychology.

Ideologically, behaviorism serves several kinds of interests: first, those of radical educational interventionists who want to discount influences external to the school environment, such as genetics or the influence of parents, in the hope that the school can be a major agent of social reconstruction. Second, behaviorist theory has provided the rationale for a variety of marketable although short-lived teaching devices. Educational budgets have long proven to be easy prey for scientific-sounding entrepreneurs. Third, the idea of control within the school environment feeds the aspirations of educators to professional independence. Gaining control over the in-school behavior of children without having to worry about their out-of-school circumstances is a seductive idea.

Finally, behaviorism, with its experimental superficialities and laboratory seemings, has served the academic aspirations of psychologists of all stripes who find it necessary to insist to this day—as many an introductory text in that discipline will attest—that psychology covers academic territory substantially different from the ancient realm of philosophy from which it has evolved.

Edward G. Rozycki

See also EPISTEMOLOGY; FREEDOM AND DETERMINISM; HUMAN NATURE; INTELLIGENCE; LEARNING, THEORIES OF; TECHNOLOGY

Bibliography

Chomsky, Noam. Book Review of *Verbal Behavior* by B.F. Skinner. *Language* 35 (1959): 26–58.

Hocutt, Max. "Skinner on the Word 'Good': A Naturalistic Semantics for Ethics." *Ethics* 87 (1977): 319–38.

Kaufman, Arnold S. "Behaviorism." In *The Encyclopedia of Philosophy*. Vol. 1, edited by Paul Edwards. 268–73. New York: Collier-MacMillan, 1967.

McKeachie, W.J. "The Decline and Fall of the Laws of Learning." *Educational Researcher* 3 (1974): 7–11.

Mischel, Theodore, ed. *Human Action: Conceptual and Empirical Issues*. New York: Academic Press, 1969.

Rozycki, Edward G. "The Functional Analysis of Behavior." *Educational Theory* 25 (1975): 278–302.

———. "Human Behavior: Measurement and Cause. Can There Be a Science of Education?" Ed.D. dissertation, Temple University, 1974. In *Dissertation Abstracts International*. Vol. 35, no. 3. Ann Arbor, Mich.: Xerox University Microfilms, 1974.

———. "Measurability and Educational Concerns." *Educational Theory* 24 (1974): 52–60.

———. "More on Rewards and Reinforcers." *Ethics* 84 (1974): 354–58.

———. "Rewards, Reinforcers and Voluntary Behavior." *Ethics* 84 (1973): 38–47.

Schick, Karl. "Operants." *Journal of the Experimental Analysis of Behavior* 15 (1971): 413–23.

Skinner, B.F. "The Genetic Nature of the Concepts of Stimulus and Response." *Journal of General Psychology* 12 (1935): 40–65.

———. *Science and Human Behavior*. New York: Free Press, 1953.

Spence, Kenneth W. "The Postulates and Methods of 'Behaviorism.'" In *Readings in the Philosophy of Science*, edited by Herbert Feigl and May Brodbeck. New York: Appleton-Century Crofts, 1953.

Bonaventure (1217–1274)

Franciscan theologian, whose intellectual synthesis was paralleled for its comprehensiveness and influence in the medieval Christian West only by those of Thomas Aquinas (1225–1274) and Duns Scotus (c. 1266–1308). For the artistry of his vision he is exceeded in the Middle Ages only by Dante (1265–1321).

Born John of Fidanza in Tuscany, he was schooled in the arts and theology at Paris. In 1244 he joined the Franciscan Order and was given the name Bonaventure. From 1254 to 1257 he taught as a master at Paris. His scholastic career was abandoned when he was elected minister general of the Franciscans, an office he held until 1273 when he became a cardinal bishop. The large body of his writings fall into three categories: those dating from his academic career (1252–1257), in which he commented and disputed as a schoolman, the spiritual works of the middle period (1257–1267), in which he writes as a moral and spiritual leader of the burgeoning Franciscan Order, and the final, controversial period (1267–1274), during which time he weighed in as a voice against radical Aristotelianism in the cultural debate that shook Christendom at its intellectual foundations.

Bonaventure's professional life was devoted to the intellectual and spiritual formation of others. He had a keen sense of the drama of human development. For him, all education was at root ethical and religious. His philosophy of education is integrated throughout the whole of his work, and especially in his *Commentary on the Sentences* and various disputed questions. Several works, however, bear special mention. In his *Journey of the Mind into God*, Bonaventure synthesizes the whole of human cognitive powers and of the arts and sciences (for example, perception, logic, physics, mathematics, metaphysics, and theology) within the narrative context of a personal, spiritual pilgrimage. The short but dense *Reduction of the Arts to Theology*, ordering the medieval curriculum, demonstrates how the arts, from drama and medicine to agriculture and warfare, the five powers of sense perception, and the various liberal arts and philosophical sciences manifest, each in its own way, the dynamics of Bonaventure's metaphysics. The total effect is to enable one to see the world of learning as a vast book whose literal meaning (that is, what the sciences tell us) is open to a deeper moral and spiritual interpretation, teaching men and women about ultimate realities and their destiny within it.

In *Six Wings of the Seraph*, Bonaventure, speaking to those who are newly placed in charge of the care and formation of the souls of others, clues them in on the diversities of personalities and characters they will find among their wards and warns them of the personal temptations they will likely face in their duties. His overriding concern is to identify for these new "shepherds of souls" the virtues they must acquire if they are to perfect themselves in the office of forming others in the intellectual and moral virtues. Finally, in "Christ, the One Teacher of All," Bonaventure presents Jesus Christ as the exemplary teacher, whose action lies behind all successful learning. In the process, he sketches the main problems and chief virtues of learners.

His richly textured, comprehensive thought contains principles that bear directly on the tasks and purposes of education. At the center of his thought lies the special relationship between the world and its First Principle. As he put it: "The sum total of our metaphysics [is] . . . emanation, exemplarity, and consummation." The idea here is that every entity exists and is to be understood within a three-stage movement: It first proceeds from God as an overflow of the divine plentitude of being and goodness; then it persists as an image of its exemplar, the divine principle. Finally, it is impelled to its source as a consummating end point.

Accordingly, the task of learning is epitomized in what Bonaventure called "reduction," a process of resolving ("leading back into again") each thing to its First Principle. Almost the antithesis of a modern "reductivist" account, in which the meaning of a thing is fractured into its component elements and forces, which are less than the original whole, Bonaventure's "reduction" is a matter of interpreting each entity as an image by seeing it alongside that of which it is an image. Hence, to understand something is to grasp it as more than it is. In other words, as a symbolic reality, each thing has a surplus of meaning that is grasped only when one understands it against its more stable, more real exemplar. "Contuition" is the word he uses for this important "stereoscopic" vision, which is the acme of ordinary human understanding.

Bonaventure was perhaps the last great exponent of the doctrine of illumination. According to this doctrine, the quest for knowledge escapes a final skepticism and achieves certitude only through the influence of the Divine Being exposing its own ideas, its exemplars of worldly reality, to the human intellect. As the argument would have it, the human intellect is by its nature subject to error, and worldly realities are intrinsically changeable. Thus, apart from exposure to what cannot change (namely, divine ideas) by what cannot err (the Divine Mind), human knowledge cannot be certain. Yet certitude is the intellect's natural desideratum. Therefore, Bonaventure insists that human understanding culminates with the "contuition" of the Divine Art; that is to say, knowledge reaches its perfection in this life in the simultaneous grasp of the human idea against the measure of the divine idea.

From a personal or subjective point of view, this act of understanding perfects the knower. By engaging in such inquiry, human beings perform as images of God himself. For Bonaventure, however, knowledge is not an end in itself; rather, it is to be subordinated to the operations of the will and the affections. Ultimately, one seeks to know in order to love more fully. Hence, formation of the will and disciplining of the affections are essential components of education. Supporting this view is Bonaventure's idea that the soul is constituted by three distinct parts: intellect, will, and power. As a result of a good education, the intellect is able to avoid wasting itself in vain curiosity or dissipating its energies in endless questions because it has opened itself up to the higher Truth of the "reduction." Correspondingly, the will escapes the despair of a life drained of meaning by the restless exploits of cupidity because it has learned to turn itself to the ultimate Goodness that is the source of all that is desirable, just as the soul's power eludes the entrapment of a career of manipulation and violence by joining itself to the Creativity of the divine artist.

William A. Frank

See also DUNS SCOTUS; SCHOLASTICISM; THOMAS AQUINAS

Bibliography

Bonaventure. "Christ, the One Teacher of All." In *What Manner of Man?* Translated by Zachary Hayes. Chicago: Franciscan Herald, 1974.

———. *De Reductione Artium and Theologiam.* Translated by Emma Therese Healy. St. Bonaventure, N.Y.: Franciscan Institute, 1955.

———. *Itinerarium Mentis in Deum.* Translated by Philotheus Boehner. St. Bonaventure, N.Y.: Franciscan Institute, 1956.

———. *Opera Omnia.* 10 vols. Quaracchi: College of St. Bonaventure, 1882–1902.

———. *Six Wings of the Seraph.* In *The Works of Bonaventure.* Vol. 3, translated by Jose de Vinck. Paterson, N.J.: St. Anthony Guild, 1966.

Bougerol, J. Guy. *Introduction to "The Works of Bonaventure."* Translated from the French by Jose de Vinck. Paterson, N.J.: St. Anthony Guild, 1961.

Hayes, Zachary. "Toward a Philosophy of Education in the Spirit of St. Bonaventure." In *Proceedings of the Seventh Centenary Celebration of the Death of Saint Bonaventure*. St. Bonaventure, N.Y.: Franciscan Institute, 1975.

Quinn, John Francis. *The Historical Constitution of St. Bonaventure's Philosophy*. Toronto: Pontifical Institute of Medieval Studies, 1973.

Buber, Martin (1878–1965)

Through his seminal work, *Ich und Du* (1923), translated *I and Thou*, this Jewish philosopher fixed the distinction between I and Thou and I and It relationships in the consciousness of philosophers, theologians, psychiatrists, and many others in continental Europe before World War II and in the English-speaking world thereafter. Buber wrote several short pieces on education, the most important of which are contained in *Between Man and Man* (1956), in which he rejects both progressivism and traditionalism on the grounds that they stress objective thought and methodology rather than personal relationships. He advocated dialogical relationships that would include the way of being of particular students, confirm their worth, and realize their potential for being. As insightful as these works are, the implications of Buber's treatments of I-Thou and I-It and of dialogue for education are the richest sources for educational philosophy.

These implications were introduced to English-speaking philosophers of education by Maurice Friedman in 1956 in a way that should have sparked interest in Buber's contributions to the philosophy of education and fostered sound interpretations of his thought. Unfortunately, treatments of Buber's educational philosophy appeared much later and were few in number, especially considering how often educational literature mentioned I-It and I-Thou relationships. Those that did appear often reduced Buber's ontological encounters and phenomenological methodology to fit into the objective thought of contemporary education. They tended to use his thought to resolve problems in education or to support favorite themes, such as humanistic and wholistic education.

John R. Scudder, Jr., for example, attempted to resolve the problem of freedom and author-

ity in education with a Buber model of education. Actually, rather than a Buber model, Scudder developed a dialogical model, aspects of which were generated by an encounter with Buber's thought. Unfortunately, the model itself was based on a misinterpretation of I-Thou as meaning respect for the dignity and worth of the person rather than an ontological encounter between persons. Equally unfortunate has been the tendency to treat Buber's thought in critical response to those who, like Scudder, inadequately interpreted him. Instead, philosophers of education need straightforward interpretations of the implications of Buber's philosophy for education, such as those of Adir Cohen (1983) and Daniel Murphy (1988), whose works unfortunately did not appear until nearly three decades after Friedman's article.

Buber's poetic work *I and Thou* challenged the exclusive domination of I-It objective thinking that has dominated the Western world. For Buber, an I-It relationship is one in which persons detach themselves from other persons, gain knowledge about other persons, and use that knowledge to achieve their own goals. Further, in I-It relationships persons do not relate to each other with their whole being but categorically—that is, say, teaching a retarded student rather than Susie Smith. These relationships are obviously one-sided rather than mutual. Mutuality, for Buber, is central in I-Thou relationships, hence the importance of dialogue. In I-Thou relationships, the partners relate to each other as whole persons. Rather than subsuming the other under a category, the partners deal with each other as they appear to each other. In addition, they accept the legitimacy of the other's being. Rather than objective knowledge about the other, knowledge of each other grows out of mutual relationship. Friedman calls such knowledge ineffable because I-Thou relationships cannot be fully grasped in language. They can be known only through meeting.

Obviously, Buber's I-Thou relationships have much to contribute to an educational system that tends to be objective and instrumental. Those who have attempted to explore education from Buber's perspective in ways that can be meaningfully related to contemporary education have encountered serious obstacles. Haim Gordon, for example, has used Buber's dialogue to foster understanding between Jews and Arabs. Although dialogue did foster understanding, Gordon concluded that it was inadequate for preparing students to bring about the changes required for fostering peace in the I-It world. Scudder and Mickunas also contend that Buber's dialogue inadequately deals with I-It relationships in the world. They believe that, in addition to I-Thou and I-It, an I-It (Thou) relationship is necessary for education to ensure that students are treated with dignity and respect in I-It relationships. Scudder and Mickunas also believe that Buber's dyadic dialogue should be replaced with triadic dialogue, in which student and teacher learn about the world together. Unlike dyadic dialogue, which has no end other than the relationship itself, in triadic dialogue the student learns from and with his teacher how to understand and confront the world. In so doing, the teacher's discipline, understanding, and skill are transferred to the student, thus overcoming Gordon's criticism that Buber's dialogue fails to teach students the disciplines needed to live in the world. Triadic dialogue is similar to that in Paulo Freire's liberation philosophy, where it is articulated as mutual interaction between student and teacher mediated by the world.

The reason that Buber's philosophy has had limited effect on the philosophy of education, in spite of the popularity of I-It and I-Thou terminology, stems from distortion of his philosophy by incorporating it into the objective thought of contemporary education. Buber did not advocate a new methodology called dialogue, but instead called for relational encounters that transformed human beings by calling persons out of I-It relationships. Although it is difficult to incorporate his philosophy into contemporary education, his distinction between I-Thou and I-It relationships reminds educators that relying solely on I-It relationships in education fosters loss of humanity. Buber puts it in this way: "Without *It* man cannot live. But he who lives with *It* alone is not a man."

John R. Scudder, Jr.

See also PHENOMENOLOGY; PROGRESS, IDEA OF, AND PROGRESSIVE EDUCATION

Bibliography

Buber, Martin. *Between Man and Man.* Translated by R.G. Smith. New York: Macmillan, 1965.

———. *I and Thou.* Translated by R.G. Smith. New York: Charles Scribner's Sons. 1937. 2nd ed., 1958. Originally published as *Ich und Du,* 1923.

Cohen, Adir. *The Educational Philosophy of Martin Buber.* Rutherford, N.J.: Fairleigh Dickinson University Press, 1983.

Friedman, Maurice. "Martin Buber's Philosophy of Education." *Educational Theory* 6 (1956): 93–109.

Gordon, Haim. "Buberian Learning Groups: Existentialist Philosophy as an Ariadne Thread for Education for Peace—A Final Report." *Teachers College Record* 85 (1983): 73–87.

———. "Would Martin Buber Endorse the Buber Model?" *Educational Theory* 23 (1973): 240–59.

Kiner, Eduard D. "Some Problems in a Buber Model for Teaching." *Educational Theory* 19 (1969): 369–403.

Murphy, Daniel. *Martin Buber's Philosophy of Education.* Dublin: Irish Academic Press, 1988.

Scudder, John R., Jr. "Freedom with Authority: A Buber Model for Teaching." *Educational Theory* 18 (1968): 133–42.

———, and Algis Mickunas. *Meaning, Dialogue, and Enculturation: Phenomenological Philosophy of Education.* Washington, D.C.: Center for Advanced Research in Phenomenology and University Press of America, 1985.

Buddhism

Buddhism is based on the life and teachings of Gautama Buddha (563–483 B.C.). The Buddha was a prince of the Sakya kingdom in what is today southern Nepal. He lived a luxurious life when he was young, but, tiring of material pleasures, he renounced his palace and started pursuing a religious life at the age of twenty-nine. Thus, the aim of Buddhist education is not to help people obtain worldly well-being, although it does not encourage retreat to a rigorously ascetic lifestyle either.

After leaving his home, Gautama first devoted himself to the study of traditional religious teachings and practiced the most extreme forms of self-denial and self-mortification for six years. But he became disappointed with strict asceticism. He went his own way and established a new religious movement. His first teaching was on the Middle Way. Buddhist education is about the Middle Way, which teaches people to live neither a hedonistic, worldly life nor a pessimistic, ascetic one. The Buddha is reported to have said: "I stand above these two extremes, though my heart is kept in the Middle. Sufferings in me have come to an end; having become free of errors and defilements, I have now attained peace." The Buddha's discipline is a middle way between indulgence and austerity.

Unlike many other religions, Buddhism has not been concerned with the problems of the existence of God or the immortality of the soul. In fact, the Buddha avoided discussing any purely theoretical or metaphysical issues. For him, such study offered few benefits and did not have to do with the fundamentals of religion. One who engages himself in the examination of such a problem would be like a man wounded by a poison arrow. Instead of getting medical help, he wastes his time in investigating the origin, essence, and reality of the arrow, and will die from the poison. The Buddha's teaching is predominantly practical in nature. Its chief purpose is to enlighten people about the problem of suffering, its origin, its cessation, and the way leading to its cessation.

The main curriculum in Buddhist education is instruction in the Four Noble Truths: (1) Life is suffering. (2) Suffering is caused. (3) Suffering can be extinguished by eliminating the causes of suffering. (4) The way leading to the cessation of suffering is the Eightfold Path, which is also known as the Middle Way.

The First Noble Truth lists the facts of familiar sufferings such as birth, old age, illness, death, the presence of what we may hate, separation from what we love, and not obtaining what we desire. The Buddha did not deny that happiness exists and that we value sensual pleasures in life. What he wanted to teach is that the pleasures of one person are often the pains of another. Further, the so-called happiness or pleasure by itself entails unhappiness or displeasure. For example, we experience happy times with parents and friends, but sooner or later our loved ones will die or depart from us. The happier the times we have had with them, the more miserable feelings we will have after their departure. Really, happiness leads to unhappiness. The First Noble Truth teaches that all things are conditioned and transitory. Nothing is absolute and hence all, including happiness and pleasure, is suffering.

Buddhism was in part a reaction against Hinduism, yet Buddhists have inherited many tenets from traditional Hindu teachings and practices. Like Hindu believers, Buddhists hold that the causes of suffering are craving and ignorance. The Second Noble Truth stresses that we are slaves of our blind passions. We appear to be free in making daily decisions, but actually our conscious behavior is controlled by unconscious desire. This is why life is suffering. This instruction embodies the doctrine of karma. Our present existence is the effect of the past, and the future will be the effect of the present existence. A good deed will produce a good effect, and a bad deed will have negative consequences. Life is a process of causes and effects, and human beings are not unchanging and do not have immortal souls. A belief in the existence of a permanent self or soul represents ignorance that creates suffering in life.

For whatever exists there must be a cause. If the cause is taken away, the effect will disappear. The Third Noble Truth teaches that suffering can be extinguished by eliminating its causes: desire and ignorance. When suffering is eradicated, one achieves Nirvana, the main goal of Buddhist discipline.

The Fourth Noble Truth shows the way leading to Nirvana. Its prescription is the doctrine of the Middle Way, which is also called the Noble Eightfold Path because it is built upon eight principles. The first two principles, right view and right resolution, aim to eliminate ignorance so as to produce wisdom. But theory and practice in Buddhism are understood as inseparable: One cannot obtain right knowledge without right behavior and a living experience. For that reason, the principles of right speech, right action, and right livelihood are given to guide the religious life. Finally, ethical conduct results from mental motives and feelings, so the three principles of right effort, right mindfulness, and right concentration are taught.

In Buddhism, being, knowing, doing, and feeling are interdependent. One is what one knows, what one does, as well as what one thinks. Training in wisdom, ethical conduct, and mental discipline should occur simultaneously. To achieve Nirvana, Buddhists should avoid extremes and imbalance, and try to live the Middle Way, or a holistic way of life. Buddhist education is a kind of values education. It does not merely offer wisdom but seeks to help a person become enlightened. For the Buddha, wisdom springs from moral conduct and mental discipline, and vice versa. Buddhism is briefly conveyed as follows:

Avoid evil,
Do good,
Purify one's mind.
This is the teaching of all Buddhas.

Like Western Christianity, Buddhism has been divided into two major schools, Hinayana (small vehicle) and Mahayana (great vehicle). The split occurred between the first century B.C. and the first century A.D. It was the result of clashes of attitude and opinion among Buddhists over the method, content, and purpose of Buddhist education.

Hinayana Buddhism is also known as Theravada (school of the elders) and is the conservative Buddhist school. It has been popular in Burma, Thailand, Cambodia, Laos, and Sri Lanka. Theravada Buddhists regard themselves as guardians of the orthodox teachings and practices of traditional Buddhism. In their education, the emphasis is on self-discipline and individual achievement. Salvation has to be accomplished by each person. No merit can be transferred from one person to another. Even the Buddha cannot offer salvation, but merely shows his followers the right way to salvation. According to Theravada, no other human being can become a Buddha, and only the historical founder of Buddhism achieved Buddhahood. The highest goal of Theravada discipline is to become an *arhat* (revered person), a good disciple of the Buddha who has extinguished the fires of craving by his own efforts.

For Theravada Buddhism, the traditional Sangha (Buddhist organization or monastery) is the main place to seek salvation. The temple is an educational center where monks are teachers and trainers. It is essential for Buddhists to enter a monastery and to receive monastic education for at least a short period during their lifetimes. To be a thoroughly good Buddhist, one must become a monk and study. In the Theravada tradition studying often leads to being ordained a monk, and being ordained is for the sake of study. Theravada Buddhists accept the ancient Pali canon as their chief scripture. The Pali Tripitaka texts, and instruction in the Pali language, are important parts of Theravada education.

The temple or monastery, as a core of Theravada activity, is not only a school but also a dormitory for the brotherhood and a place of meditation. The observation of the *vinaya* (monastic rules of conduct) is central to the Theravada lifestyle. In fact, it is a requirement for attaining *arhat*ship. Strict rules of discipline are prescribed for the members of the order. The ordained monks must take vows of celibacy, chastity, and poverty, and should observe ten basic precepts. Among them are not taking life, not taking what is not given, not engaging in impure practices, not telling lies, not drinking intoxicating liquors, not eating like a glutton, and not dancing or singing.

Mahayana Buddhism is the later, liberal Buddhist school. Although Mahayana monks observe the same basic precepts, they have a different and new interpretation of Buddhism. In their discipline, emphasis is on *prajna* (wisdom) and *karuna* (compassion) rather than *vinaya*. This new Buddhist movement has been popular in China, Korea, Japan, Tibet, Mongolia, and Vietnam. According to Mahayana Buddhism, salvation can be achieved outside the Sangha. An enlightened person is not necessarily one who devotes himself to preserving traditional Buddhism and observing the monastic *vinaya*. For Mahayana Buddhists, blind obedience to tradition is a hindrance to salvation. For that reason, one Mahayana Zen master even claimed, "when you meet the Buddha, kill the Buddha; When you meet the Patriarch, kill the Patriarch."

Mahayana masters would not confine their instruction to the Pali canon, but have many new scriptures written in Sanskrit and other languages. In fact, different Mahayana sects have adopted different scriptures as the chief texts that convey the Buddha's Dharma (truth). There is no unified canon or scriptural source in Mahayana Buddhism. Among Mahayana Buddhists, some have been devoted to extensive scriptural study. Yet Zen masters especially dislike the blind acceptance of the written word. They may dismiss all scriptures and declare that "the entire sutra (scripture) from beginning to end is nothing but deceitful words." The truth is not to be found by a literal recitation and exposition of scripture, nor can it be apprehended by conceptual analysis. The key to *prajna* (wisdom) is one's own mind. Enlightenment is an opening of the mind-flower.

According to Zen, a form of Mahayana that flourished in China, Korea and Japan, the mind is the spring of knowledge. Truth is not a set of propositions to be objectively and intellectually perceived, but rather is something concrete, living, and personal. Genuine education really doesn't offer new information to disciples but reminds them of the wisdom within. To identify the Buddha's teaching with external verbal statements is to make the Dharma abstract and dead. Effective instruction leads to an opening of one's mind. Thus the role of teachers is not to help disciples receive, but to know when the opening will occur and to provide an occasion for it.

Yet for Zen, the human mind is often polluted by external factors in the environment, and hence human beings become corrupted and ignorant. The mind cannot easily be reopened unless extraordinary pedagogic means are used to shock and stimulate a person. Zen masters have sometimes given their disciples a hard time by shouting, beating, kicking, or using other unorthodox methods to enlighten them.

Gautama Buddha was indeed a great and skillful teacher himself, using a variety of means to help others achieve Nirvana. However, according to Mahayana Buddhism, he is not the only person in this world who may become a buddha. In Mahayana, everyone is regarded as having buddha-nature or buddha-mind and can become a buddha. As for the present life, the goal of Mahayana Buddhist education is to become not merely an *arhat* but a bodhisattva (being of wisdom). The bodhisattva is a buddha-to-be who has the virtues of compassion and wisdom. Although he may attain salvation now, he stays in this troubled world to help other sentient beings attain salvation. All good Buddhist teachers should be like bodhisattvas, who dedicate themselves to the salvation and well-being of others.

For many Mahayana Buddhists, salvation does not depend solely upon one's own effort. Good merit can be transferred from one person to others. All things are interdependent and hence are devoid of any self-sufficient nature. No one can exist by himself physically and spiritually. Mahayanists regard the egoistic approach to salvation as unrealistic, impossible, as well as unethical. Therefore, a bodhisattva rather than an *arhat* becomes the ideal one seeks to achieve by religious discipline. In the process of obtaining this goal, one realizes that all beings can benefit each other because they all depend upon each other. Salvation depends on the help of others. A good teacher can assist students on the path to salvation.

Mahayana Pure Land Buddhists even hold that the human mind is so degraded by sin that one cannot do anything good enough to deserve salvation. It is due to the compassion, power, and grace of Amitabha (the Buddha of boundless light) that human beings may hope for salvation. According to Pure Land Buddhism, the Dharma is given not to encourage good and avoid evil, but rather to acknowledge the sinfulness of the human mind. For Pure Land Buddhists, genuine education is not an opening of one's mind-flower, but an expression of gratitude to Amitabha. Thus in Pure Land education, a great teacher is or could become a great savior. Teaching is not merely a redemptive process, but an outcome of presumed redemption through the grace of Amitabha. Instead of struggling painfully for Nirvana, Pure Land students are supposed to live a joyful life of thanksgiving.

Hsueh-li Cheng

See also CONFUCIANISM; HINDUISM; TAOISM

Bibliography

Bloom, Alfred. *Shinran's Gospel of Pure Grace*. Tucson, Ariz.: University of Arizona Press, 1977.

Buasri, Saroj. *A Philosophy of Education for Thailand: The Confluence of Buddhism and Democracy*. Thailand: Ministry of Education, 1970.

Cheng, Hsueh-li. *Empty Logic: Madhyamika Buddhism from Chinese Sources*. New York: Philosophical Library, 1983.

——. *Exploring Zen*. New York: Peter Lang, 1991.

Don Peter, W.L.A. *Buddhist and Benedictine Monastic Education*. Colombo, Sri Lanka: Evangel Press, 1990.

Jayatilleke, K.N. *The Message of the Buddha*. New York: Free Press, 1975.

Mookerji, Radha Kumud. *Ancient Indian Education (Brahmanical and Buddhist)*. Delhi: Motilal Banarsidass, 1960.

Suzuki, Daisetz Teitaro. *The Training of the Zen Buddhist Monk*. Kyoto: Eastern Buddhist Society, 1934.

Welch, Holmes. *The Buddhist Revival in China*. Boston: Harvard University Press, 1968.

Calvin, John (1509–1564)

John Calvin was born in Noyon, Picardy, in northern France. His father was an ecclesiastical and civil notary, and his mother was a woman of exceptional beauty and piety. She died when Calvin was a small child.

As a young boy, Calvin attended a school for boys in Noyon. Following the educational plan his father had established for him, the twelve-year-old Calvin attended the University of Paris and received a master's degree in classical and humanist studies early in 1528. To improve young Calvin's economic potential, his father instructed him to turn from clerical to legal studies later that year. Calvin reluctantly but dutifully complied and entered the study of law at Orleans and Bourges. In 1532 he completed a doctorate in law, despite his deep reservations about law as a profession. Calvin served briefly as an annual deputy of proctor for Picardy, but except for his contributions to the reform of the laws of Geneva in 1543, he was not otherwise engaged in the legal profession.

In 1536 Calvin returned to Paris before moving to Strasbourg, where he planned to resume the life of a scholarly interpreter. On the way to Strasbourg, however, he was forced to detour south to Geneva. While there, Calvin met William Farel (1489–1565), who persuaded him to stay in Geneva and to lead the reform movement with the title of "Professor of Sacred Letters." In a short time, Calvin found himself embroiled in a religious and political controversy, and, in 1537, the council of Geneva ordered Calvin and Farel to depart from the city. Calvin stopped briefly in Zurich, and then went to Basel to pursue his scholarly interests. His scholarly paradise was short-lived, however, and, in 1537, Calvin left Basel to accept a pastoral call in Strasbourg. During his three-year stay in Strasbourg, Calvin accepted a position at an academy as a "Lecturer in Holy Scripture." The curriculum was weighted heavily in humanist and classical studies and was dedicated to training young men for the Gospel ministry. This academy served as a model for the one Calvin would later begin in Geneva. In 1540, the Little Council in Geneva voted to recall Calvin. He reluctantly returned to Geneva in 1541, where the public received him with acclaim.

Calvin converted to Protestantism, a movement begun by Martin Luther (1483–1546) in opposition to the Roman Catholic Church. Calvin began a tradition known as the "Reformed faith," one of several movements originating in the Protestant Reformation. Very little is known about Calvin's conversion other than that it was a sudden and pivotal event in his life. Calvin's writings and those of his friends suggest that his conversion probably occurred between late 1532 and 1534. In 1534 Calvin returned to Noyon, resigned the clerical benefices that his father had secured for him as a child, and severed his relationship with the unreformed church. His participation in the Protestant Reformation subsequently intensified.

Calvin was primarily a theologian, and his theology opposed the official teachings of the Roman Catholic Church. During the sixteenth century, the Roman Church was the predominant force in European education and society. Calvin's theological pursuits, therefore, placed him in the role of reforming not only theological doctrine, but society and politics as well. Since Calvin's reforms had broad ramifications for society, education took on preeminent importance.

Calvin saw his social and political thought,

including that on education, as stemming directly from his theology and as originating in the same source—Holy Scripture. Calvin's theology, along with his social, political, and educational thought, was humanist and evangelical in character. His evangelicalism rested on two basic tenets: justification by faith, and the authority of Holy Scripture as the final rule of faith and practice.

The Protestant Reformation led to the collapse of Roman Catholicism in certain territories and resulted in social, political, and religious upheaval. Since the Roman Church had dominated education, many Reformation leaders sought to fill the vacuum by making education, at least in part, a responsibility of civil government. Calvin believed that God had ordained civil government to promote and defend true religion, to ensure a semblance of law and order, to promote public justice, and to protect private property. Calvin understood civil rulers to be vicegerents of God, therefore guardians of the religious, moral, and intellectual welfare of their citizens. In Geneva, Calvin fostered an educational system that functioned as a cooperative relationship between civil government, the church, and the family. Civil government made education compulsory and provided buildings and resources at public expense. The church greatly influenced the curriculum, and parents supported the schools and their children.

Calvin's educational reforms in Geneva included the establishment of one of the first free and compulsory public educational systems. Later, he began a college of higher education where young men prepared for service in the ministry and civil government.

Under Calvin's guidance, moderate discipline and a challenging curriculum characterized Geneva's school system. There were four school districts; each school consisted of seven grades, starting with beginners in grade seven. Promotions were not necessarily annual, with students progressing to more advanced grades on evidence of academic achievement at any point within the school year.

In grade seven, the students progressed from the French alphabet to fluent French reading. This grade also included an introduction to Latin. Grade six consisted of Latin grammar and simple composition. In grade five, students read Virgil and Cicero, and grade four introduced the students to Greek grammar. Grades one to three contained an abundance of Latin

and Greek literature. The curriculum also required that all students listen to a reading of the Greek New Testament for an hour each Saturday. Classical texts formed the basis for the teaching of Rhetoric and Dialectic. Reviews and disputations were frequent, and pupils regularly participated in debating exercises in groups of ten. School began at six in the summer and seven in the winter, and closed at four in the afternoon. Except Wednesdays and Saturdays, the students were escorted home during a brief recess from nine to eleven. The students enjoyed two hours of supervised recreation on Wednesdays, and Saturday breaks from noon to three. They sang the Psalms daily for two hours, not in Latin, but in French. Abundant catechism exercises evidenced the emphasis on memorization. Calvin believed that education should be administered with gentleness, and should seek to avoid fallacies, vain questions, and excessive curiosity. Education began with the simple and advanced to the more complex.

Calvin's philosophy of education was strongly antiauthoritarian and exhorted teachers not to sit above their students and merely prescribe, but to walk along with them as companions. Calvin insisted that teachers avoid harshness because it intimidates students and prevents them from achieving their educational potential in a liberal arts environment. The goal of a teacher is to encourage, not discourage.

The dominance of the classics in the curriculum demonstrated the Renaissance character of the school. Calvin encouraged students to study a wide range of materials, including those of secular philosophers. This broad curriculum was based on the principle that truth should be appreciated wherever it is found, since God is the sole fountain from which all truth flows.

As a reformer and an educator, Calvin was a prolific and penetrating writer. Calvin's writings include *The Institutes of the Christian Religion,* his multivolume *Commentary* on the Bible, and his numerous tracts and letters. Without question, his most significant work is *The Institutes of the Christian Religion,* first published in 1534. Few Christian works equal Calvin's *Institutes* in comprehensiveness and depth, and it remains a benchmark for subsequent writings of Christian scholars.

Calvin divides the *Institutes* into four parts, in which he treats God as creator, as redeemer, and as inspirer of individuals, and describes the church as the focus of God's redemptive plan for His people and creation. The influences of such thinkers as Saint Augustine (354–430) and Desiderius Erasmus (1467–1536) on Calvin's thinking are evident in the *Institutes*. Virtually all of Calvin's religious thought (or philosophy, for Calvin would have seen little difference between the two) is contained in the *Institutes*. Calvin argued that God has been revealing Himself from the beginning by His creation and by special revelation in the Holy Scriptures.

Central to Calvin's theology are the doctrines of the sovereignty of God and the total depravity of human beings. These doctrines are foundational to Calvin's views on predestination and election, but they have much broader ramifications for Calvin's philosophy. To Calvin, God's sovereignty directly relates to His creative activity. God created everything; therefore, He by right governs all things, including human activities. Calvin's understanding of total depravity stems from the doctrine of "original sin"—that human beings are created in the image of God but that image has been marred by Adam's fall. By total depravity, Calvin does not mean that human beings are as bad as they could be, but that every human faculty, including the intellect, and every aspect of human life has been tainted by Adam's fall. In Calvin's estimation, the scope of redemption is as wide as the fall, and the scope of the fall is as wide as creation. Calvin's choice of the word "institutes," from the Latin *institutios,* in the title of *The Institutes of the Christian Religion* indicates the importance he places on education for human redemption and social reformation, since the word *institutio* may be translated "education" or "instruction."

Danny G. Wells

See also CALVINISM; LUTHER; RELIGIOUS EDUCATION

Bibliography

Breen, Q. "John Calvin and the Rhetorical Tradition." *Church History* 26 (1957): 3–21.

Bouwsma, William J. *John Calvin: A Sixteenth Century Portrait.* New York: Oxford University Press, 1988.

Calvin, John. *Commentaries.* Twenty-two vols. Grand Rapids, Mich.: Baker Book House, 1989. See especially commentaries on Acts 26:25, Psalms 22:31, Isaiah 2:3, Colossians 3:20, and Hebrews 6:9.

———. *The Institutes of the Christian Religion.* 2 vols. Edited by John T. McNeill. Translated by Ford Louis Battles. Philadelphia: Westminster Press, 1960.

———. *Selected Works of John Calvin: Tracts and Letters.* Edited by Henry Beveridge and Jules Bonnet. Grand Rapids, Mich.: Baker Book House, 1983.

Clark, Gordon H. *A Christian Philosophy of Education.* Grand Rapids, Mich.: William B. Eerdmans, 1946.

McNeill, John T. *The History and Character of Calvinism.* New York: Oxford University Press, 1954.

Wolin, Sheldon. "Calvin: The Political Education of Protestantism." In *Politics and Vision: Continuity and Innovation in Western Political Thought.* Boston: Little, Brown, 1960.

Calvinism

Calvinism, since its origins in the thought of John Calvin (1509–1564) of sixteenth-century Geneva, Switzerland, has had its central tenets elaborated upon in several political contexts, especially in France, the Netherlands, England, and America. In each of these countries, as a religio-philosophical movement, it has affected not only specifically ecclesiastical life and practice, but social and political life as well. Although it has assumed different shapes and different roles in each of these countries, in none of them has it operated simply as a set of specifically doctrinal or liturgical beliefs: It has always found cultural expressions and produced implications for economics, politics, and education.

R.H. Tawney's *Religion and the Rise of Capitalism,* Max Weber's *Protestant Ethic and the Spirit of Capitalism,* and Ralph Barton Perry's *Puritanism and Democracy* are just a few of the standard works that have described Calvinism in its social and economic forms. It is not surprising therefore to find that in many countries Calvinism has also found institutional expression in education. Previous reference works have recognized this power of Calvinism, as in the following: "One of the fairest and most permanent influences of Calvinists in Geneva, France, Holland, Scotland, England and America was their contribution to education (Monroe's *Cyclopedia of Education,* vol. 1, 1911)."

The interest of Calvinists in education had been more than simply that of church extension and doctrinal instruction. The reference work cited above contains also the following: "The remarkable development of colleges and free schools among Calvinists was not entirely due to any single theological tenet. . . . Their common program and their social insight demanded education for all as instruments of Providence for church and commonwealth."

The last sentence reflects the conception of the purpose of education, and the whole quotation is a commentary upon what Calvinists have called the "Kingdom of God." Broader than the "Church of Christ" concept, it includes not only the institutionalized church within its scope but all human relations, social, political, economic.

At least three interrelated educational positions are undergirded by Calvinist theology. The first is that the locus of educational authority is neither the church nor the state but resides in the family. This has led to the founding and propagation of schools owned and operated by societies of like-minded parents and citizens. The second is that education can be neither neutral toward all world views nor devoted simply to indoctrination in the creeds of one religion, but rather that a religious world view would be integrated into all curriculum content. This has led to serious attempts to produce textbooks and other teaching materials that incorporate this outlook. Thirdly, the aim of such education is not evangelization for church membership, nor is it value-free information giving. Rather, its aim is to prepare the learner for living a Christian life in society in all areas of life—familial, civic, and economic.

Five theological concepts, most of them peculiar to Calvinism, are the undergirding for the educational positions that set off Calvinist schools from public, parochial, or private schools. While other theist world views have their respective rationales for directing educational policy, these collectively provide the Calvinist rationale.

The Sovereignty of God

The most pervasive, but also the most abstract, is the doctrine of the sovereignty of God. Whatever else this doctrine has meant for soteriology or other ecclesiastical issues, for education it has meant that schools exhibit more than a secular concern. In Calvinism, schools are the instruments of social transformation in all areas of life.

The term *sovereign,* suggesting a sociopolitical authority, indicates that in the Calvinist thought system God is the central figure, calling for loyalty and obedience. The term *kingdom* is used similarly to suggest a whole network of social and political relationships that are under the sovereignty of God.

Sphere Sovereignty

A second doctrine, derived from the first and more directly decisive in shaping educational policy, is sphere sovereignty. According to this view, numerous social spheres or institutions operate within their own areas, with what are called creation ordinances governing each. None is subordinate to any other, or under their control. Academies or schools constitute one of the spheres, having its own sovereignty. This renders both the parochial, church-owned school and the public, state-owned school a violation of sphere sovereignty. This doctrine underlies the Calvinist educational belief that the locus of educational authority is neither the church nor the state, but the parent community. It explains why Calvinist schools are protest institutions in America, rejecting not this or that isolated practice in public schools but their overall increasing tendency to treat education like simply another government agency.

Covenant

Another doctrine especially relevant to parental control of schools is that of covenant. While this term carries much meaning in ecclesiastical settings, the effect of it on the conception of schooling is that God uses the institution of the family to carry forward the Kingdom of God. "Family" in this setting refers not simply to the biological family but to the total spiritual community of adults who provide funds and support for children, theirs and the children of others like-minded.

General and Special Revelation

Another central doctrine is that of commitment to both general and special revelation as sources of truth. This "two book" theory of the sources of knowledge identifies the Bible as one book and the book of nature or creation as the second. The evidences and conclusions of investigations in both are held to be in tension and interpenetration with each other. It holds that there is no basic dichotomy between the sacred and the secular, between Scripture and nature as sources of dependable knowledge. Both emanate from one sovereign God, both are trustworthy sources of truth.

Given this distinction, areas of cooperation and specialization are mapped out between the church and the day school. The church as institution is the expert in interpreting special revelation, and the school provides leadership in interpreting general revelation. The school, through teachers trained in the investigations of history, science, and psychology, among others, aims at cultural involvement and social transformation, not mastery of church doctrine or evangelization. Those functions belong to the church. This division of labor legitimizes a liberal arts curriculum for the school as a means of discovering the creation ordinances, with the aid and direction of the Bible. This educational goal has more to do with community membership than with church membership. In the curriculum, Bible study becomes one among many academic areas for exploration, with biblical insights related to each curriculum area but occupying neither a higher nor lower status than other areas of investigation to discover God's truth.

Cultural Mandate

A final doctrine and, one arising out of the previous four, is that of cultural mandate. Seen as rooted in the Genesis account and command to till the soil, exercise dominion over creation, and to shape society and its institutions, the cultural mandate gives the Calvinist school an aim that distinguishes it from other theistically grounded world views. The aim is to train Christian citizens, workers in the world of business, politics, art, and science. More recent statements put the aim generically thus: To live the Christian life in contemporary society. This goal distinguishes the Calvinist vision from others that express more socially isolationistic goals or more narrowly evangelistic goals, as in some theistic Protestant or Roman Catholic thought about education.

This school task, of helping the young to exercise cultural dominion rather than cultural isolation, has important consequences for the curriculum. The doctrine has caused Calvinists to translate their aim into textbooks and other teaching materials designed specifically for schools founded on these five doctrines of Calvinism.

The implications of Calvinism for educational thought and practice, the connections between the network of peculiarly Calvinist doctrines and educational policy, have not been codified in any single official document, but are compiled from numerous books and treatises, mostly in this century.

Donald Oppewal

See also CALVIN; RELIGIOUS EDUCATION

Bibliography

Bieler, A. *The Social Humanism of John Calvin.* Richmond, Va.: John Knox, 1964.

DeBoer, Peter, and Donald Oppewal. "Calvinist Day Schools: Root and Branches." In *Religious Schooling in America,* edited by James Carper and Thomas Hunt, 58–84. Birmingham, Ala.: Religious Education Press, 1984.

Hill, Walter. "The Influence of Calvinism on Education." MST dissertation, Western Theological Seminary, Pittsburgh,1987.

McCarthy, Rockne, et al. *Society, State, and Schools: A Case for Structural and Confessional Pluralism.* Grand Rapids, Mich.: Wm. B. Eerdmans, 1981.

McNeill, John T. *History and Character of Calvinism.* New York: Oxford University Press, 1954.

Meeter, H. Henry. *American Calvinism: A Survey.* Grand Rapids, Mich.: Baker Book House, 1956.

———. *The Basic Ideas of Calvinism.* 5th ed. Grand Rapids, Mich.: Baker Book House, 1975.

VanTil, Henry. *The Calvinistic Concept of Culture.* Grand Rapids, Mich.: Baker Book House, 1959.

Capitalism

Capitalism is the political economic system in which the institution of the right to private property—that is, to own anything of value (not, of course, other human beings, who are themselves owners)—is fully respected. There is dispute about the label, of course, mostly because its definition is often a precondition of having either a favorable or unfavorable view of the system.

By itself, capitalism is an economic arrangement of an organized human community or policy. Often, however, entire societies are called capitalist, mainly to stress their thriving commerce and industry. More rigorously understood, however, capitalism presupposes a type of legal order governed by the rule of law in which the principle of private property rights plays a central role. Such a system of laws is usually grounded on *classical liberal* ideals in political thinking. These ideals may incorporate positivism, utilitarianism, natural rights theory and individualism, as well as notions about the merits of laissez-faire (no government interference in commerce), the "invisible hand" (as a principle of spontaneous social organization), prudence and industriousness (as significant virtues), the price system as distinct from central planning (for registering supply and demand), and so forth.

Put a bit differently, *capitalism* is the term used to mean that feature of a human community whereby citizens are understood to have the basic right to make their own (more or less wise or prudent) decisions concerning what they will do with their labor and property, whether they will engage in trade with one another involving nearly anything they may value. Thus capitalism includes freedom of trade and contract, the free movement of labor, and protection of property rights against both criminal and official intrusiveness.

The concept of freedom plays a central role in the understanding of capitalism. There are two prominent ways of understanding the nature of freedom as it pertains to human relationships. The one that fits with capitalism is negative freedom—namely, that everyone in society not be ruled by others with respect to the use and disposal of themselves and what belongs to them. Citizens are free, in this sense, when no other adult person has authority over them that they have not granted of their own volition. In short, in capitalism one enjoys negative freedom, which amounts to being free from others' intrusiveness. The other meaning of freedom is that citizens have their goals and purposes supported by others or the government so as to prosper. Under that conception of freedom, one is free to progress, advance, develop, or flourish only when one is enabled to do so by the efforts of capable others.

In international political discussions, the term *capitalist* is used very loosely, so that such diverse types of societies as Italy, New Zealand, the U.S.A., Sweden, and France are all considered capitalist. Clearly, no country today is completely capitalist. None enjoys a condition of economic laissez-faire in which governments stay out of people's commercial transactions except when conflicting claims over various valued items are advanced and the dispute needs to be resolved in line with due process of law. But many Western-type societies protect a good deal of free trade, even if they also regulate most of it as well. (The extent of such regulation in the U.S.A. alone, thus the divergence from pure capitalism, is chronicled in Jonathan R.T. Hughes, *The Governmental Habit*, 2nd ed. [1991].) Still, just as those countries are called "democratic" if there is substantial suffrage—even though many citizens may be prevented from voting—so if there exists substantial free trade and private ownership of the major means of production (labor, capital, intellectual creations, and so forth), the country is usually designated as capitalist.

The most common reason among political theorists and economists for supporting capitalism is the system's support of wealth creation. (See Adam Smith, *The Wealth of Nations* [1976]; Milton Friedman, *Capitalism and Freedom* [1962]; F.A. Hayek, *The Road To Serfdom* [1944].) This is not to say that such theorists do not also credit capitalism with other worthwhile traits, such as encouragement of progress, political liberty, and innovation.

Those who defend the system for its utilitarian virtues—its propensity to encourage the production of wealth—are distinct from others who champion the system—or the broader framework within which it exists—because they consider it morally just. (See, for example, Ayn Rand, *Capitalism: The Unknown Ideal* [1966]; John Hospers, *Libertarianism* [1972]; Robert Nozick, *Anarchy, State, and Utopia* [1974].)

The first group of supporters argue that a free market or capitalist economic system is of great public benefit, even though this depends on private or even social vice, such as greed, ambition, or exploitation. As Bernard Mandeville, the author of *The Fable of the Bees,* put it, this system produces "private vice, public benefit." Many moral theorists see nothing virtuous in efforts to improve one's own life. They believe, however, that enhancing the overall wealth of a human community is a worthwhile goal.

Those who stress the moral or normative merits of capitalism say the system rewards hard work, ingenuity, industry, entrepreneurship, and personal or individual responsibility, and that is all to the good. That alone makes the system morally preferable to the alternatives. Yet, another reason given why capitalism is not only useful but a morally preferable system is that it makes possible the exercise of personal choice, something that would be obliterated in noncapitalist, collectivist systems or economic organizations.

The most influential critic of capitalism is the nineteenth-century German thinker and social activist Karl Marx. He did not oppose capitalism but argued that it occupies only a specific period of humanity's development. Capitalism, as Marx saw it, is the adolescent period of humanity, as it were. Socialism is the young adulthood, while communism is full maturity. Marx believed that supporters are wrong to assume that the system has universal relevance and validity. Instead, Marx held, the system must be accepted as a temporary fact of the life of humanity—two or perhaps four hundred years long.

Capitalism's defenders have argued, in response, that the system—that is, economic liberty—is best suited to human beings because human nature is reasonably stable over time. Human beings, in turn, tend always to be motivated by self-interest. They will always want to be rewarded for their work and will not likely develop into creatures who are loyal primarily to humanity or society.

Others have responded to Marx by claiming that not only is his position untenable but actually morally despicable. The vision of human life Marx champions cuts directly against what is best about human beings—namely, their individuality, uniqueness, and resulting multifaceted creativity, their often single-minded vision. Capitalism accords more with the idea of human excellence exemplified by the great artists, scientists, and industrialists of the world, not the vision exemplified by members of a stagnant commune. Capitalism is feared only by the lethargic or cowardly, who do not prefer the hustle-bustle of nature, including human life.

Capitalism is an economic organization based on some very limited rules or principles. People are at liberty to do everything other than intrude on the sovereignty of other human beings and what they own. As such, it is a system said to be well suited to human nature, whereby one may embark on various tasks and do well or badly at them but avoid intruding on others. This is best done when one's own sphere of authority—one's private property rights—is clearly identifiable.

With the 1989 collapse of the centrally planned economy of the Soviet Union, the debate about the ultimate merits of capitalism heated up once again. It had been somewhat lukewarm earlier because of the dominance and apparent success of the welfare state. But that system be-

gan to falter from the malaise of stagflation—that is, both inflation and recession at the same time. Such Eastern European scholars as Janos Kornai have argued in favor of moving toward a full-fledged free market system (see *The Road to the Free Economy* [1990]), instead of attempting to institute the welfare state, mainly because they believed that the latter is possible, at least for a while, only in robust economies that can support the redistribution of wealth. But Kornai argued that the Eastern European countries—indeed, all those with serious economic deficiencies—require robust economic activity, something the welfare state tends to stifle.

Others have urged that a "third way" be found—for example, communitarianism or market socialism. They argue that capitalism is too harsh a system to be fully adopted in any decent society, echoing what earlier critics said about the system (for example, John Maynard Keynes in his book *The End of Laissez-Faire* [1926]). Indeed one such warning comes from Robert Kuttner, himself the author of a recent book entitled *The End of Laissez-Faire* (1991). In all of these criticisms, despite protestations to the contrary, the conception of capitalism the critics embrace differs only minimally from Karl Marx's. Only what to do about it is different, closer to the pre-Marxist utopian socialist solutions.

Marx had argued, in his *Das Kapital* (1863) and other works, that although unavoidable, capitalism leads to the alienation of the members of its community, not to mention the exploitation of the working class. In the end that will be the immediate cause of its necessary demise—namely, workers' disenchantment. Marx also argued that capitalism, like all societies prior to socialism and communism, is essentially a class system, so that the working and the capitalist classes are locked in an irresolvable conflict that can be overcome only by way of fundamental change—either a peaceful or a violent revolution leading to a socialist system.

The more recent critics wish to forge some kind of hybrid between capitalism and socialism. Yet the welfare state is just that hybrid, and it is suffering from the inconsistencies that such systems wish to live with but that also haunt them. To try to preserve both negative and positive liberty is futile. It means some have a bit of one, others a bit of the other, some of the time, and the disorder tends to slow everything down. By only partially protecting private property, for example, the welfare state or market socialism or communitarianism instills major uncertainties into people's lives, some of whom set property aside only to find it confiscated for some public cause just when they wish to make it useful to them.

Those who champion capitalism have different answers to Marx and his friends, the welfare statists. Mainly they argue that although capitalism permits some harshness of treatment, it need not cultivate it at all. Nor need economic and social classes be rigidly formed—people travel from one economic level to the other more often than the critics imagine. Exploitation is really just a way to meet the needs of differently positioned members of the community: Some need more of certain goods and services at one time than at others. Some have too much and some lack even elementary survival resources, but it is still best to leave things to the marketplace of free trade.

Capitalist theorists also note that most critics of capitalism demean wealth. Indeed, they virtually attack the pursuit of human well-being itself and, especially, luxury, anytime there are needy people left anywhere on earth, as well as, more recently, if any portion of nature is overrun by human beings (as if they were not natural creatures). But, the champions of capitalism argue, this stems from utopian thinking and has the consequences of begrudging anyone a measure of welfare, since some people will always be poor some of the time and nature will continue to be transformed by people.

Yet the capitalist advocate need not be seen as reckless toward the environment. Arguably, the strict and consistent institution of the principle of private property rights—through, for example, privatization and prohibition of dumping waste into other private or public realms—may indeed solve the environmental problems we face better than any solutions central-planning champions of the environment tend to propose. (In this connection, see the works of such free-market environmentalists as John Baden, Richard Stroup, Fred Singer, and Tibor R. Machan.)

Finally, critics of capitalism do not credit owners of wealth with any moral virtues—not even for their industry or prudence (often denying that these are virtues at all). This, its champions maintain, is a grave and indeed tragic mistake. We all depend on the wealth creation of our fellow human beings, even as we try to do this ourselves, and yet the activity is without much appreciation. Business has a very bad press, indeed.

Capitalism has experienced widespread disrespect in part because throughout human history there has been a powerful intellectual tradition of *otherworldliness*. In the Bible, Jesus decries wealth-acquisition when he asks, rhetorically, "For what shall it profit a man, if he shall gain the whole world, and lose his own soul?" This suggests that a profitable life cannot go hand in hand with being a decent person or having moral character. And, again, the Bible states that sooner will a camel go through the eye of the needle than the rich man enter the kingdom of heaven. Socrates, Plato, and even Aristotle (who had his feet planted mostly on the ground), tended to denigrate wealth production, regarding trade and commerce as lowly and base. Throughout much of Western history, taking interest on money has been deemed usurious, hoarding miserly, and profiteering greedy or avaricious. Marx's criticism was different not in the standards he employed to judge the system but by his claim that it is a necessary but soon to be superseded evil, nothing more.

Some supporters of the system argue that this view is untrue to the facts of human nature and has misled us about the moral merits of commerce and business and, thus, of capitalism itself as a vital human institution. Because of its challenge of some central ideas of the past, it is arguable that capitalism is far more radical than even communism. The commune has always been around, in its relatively small versions, and it has much in common with the prominent social organization of primitive times, tribalism (both as idealized and as actually manifest).

Capitalism, on the other hand, rests in large part on the belief that human beings are essentially individuals and a society's laws must value individuals above all else. Contrast this with Marx's conservative view: "The human essence is the true collectivity of man" ("On the Jewish Question"). Most historians of ideas admit that whether the importance of human individuality should have been recognized in earlier times, it certainly was not much needed until the modern age. Even in our time it is more often that groups—ethnic, religious, racial, sexual, national, cultural—are taken to have greater significance than individuals. The latter are constantly asked to make sacrifices for the former. In capitalism, however, the individual, as the sovereign citizen or the consumer, is king. Undoubtedly a capitalist system does not give prime place to economic equality among people, something that group thinking seems to favor, because in groups all are deemed to be entitled to a fair share.

Capitalism's champions take it as more reasonable that people may be different in their abilities, talents, and willingness pertaining to economic achievement. So what is crucial is that they should be *equally unimpeded by the aggressiveness of others*—whether criminals or bureaucrats—in their access to the marketplace or, indeed, to any other place in a human community whenever they gain permission to enter or reach satisfactory terms of agreement. From this it is proposed that they will not only benefit in the long run, collectively, but will have their individuality as human beings, with dignity and choice, more respected than in alternative systems.

Capitalism tends to be favored most by academic economists, even more so than by members of the commercial community (who often do not understand and even wish to subvert the system). They are unique in the academic world and are often met with severe criticism from outside their field. (See, for example, Amitai Etzioni, *The Moral Dimension* [1988], Kenneth Lux, *Adam Smith's Mistake* [1990], and Andrew Bard Schmookler, *The Illusion of Choice* [1993].)

The most prominent academic economists who champion capitalism are known as members of the neoclassical or Chicago school. Another that stands foursquare behind capitalism is the Austrian school. (For a collection of nontechnical essays by such thinkers and others who favor capitalism, see Lawrence S. Stepelevich, ed., *The Capitalist Reader* [1977].) Others include the well-known Public Choice and the Law and Economists theorists. With certain variations in their approach, all these believe that capitalism is well suited to people living in communities, mainly because any other system places obstacles before the natural inclination of human beings to advance their own lot and thus improve the world.

But is that enough? An economic organization of society needs to appeal to what people believe is just and proper; it may not offend moral sensibilities. Unless supporters of capitalism reconcile their vision of economic life with the demands most people make for their society to conform to a sound view of justice, they will not succeed. Despite the demise of centrally planned socialism and the great deal of skepticism about socialism of any kind, capitalism is by no means the hands down winner in the race for the hearts and minds of people in the world regarding the kind of community they ought to support.

Tibor R. Machan

See also CONSERVATISM; INDIVIDUALISM; LIBERALISM; MARX; MARXISM; NATIONALISM; SOCIAL AND POLITICAL PHILOSOPHY

Bibliography

Chamberlain, John. *The Roots of Capitalism.* Princeton, N.J.: Van Nostrand, 1968.

Etzioni, Amitai. *The Moral Dimension.* New York: Free Press, 1988.

Friedman, Milton. *Capitalism and Freedom.* Chicago: University of Chicago Press, 1962.

Hospers, John. *Libertarianism.* Los Angeles: Nash, 1972.

Hughes, Jonathan R.T. *The Governmental Habit.* 2nd ed. Princeton: Princeton University Press, 1991.

Kelso, Louis O., and Mortimer J. Adler. *The Capitalist Manifesto.* New York: Random House, 1958.

Keynes, John Maynard. *The End of Laissez-Faire.* London: L. and Virginia Woolf, 1926.

Kornai, Janos. *The Road to the Free Economy.* New York: W.W. Norton, 1990.

Kristol, Irving. *Two Cheers for Capitalism.* New York: Basic Books, 1978.

Kuttner, Robert. *The End of Laissez-Faire.* New York: Alfred Knopf, 1991.

Lux, Kenneth. *Adam Smith's Mistake.* Boston: Shambhala, 1990.

Machan, Tibor R. *Capitalism and Individualism.* New York: St. Martin's Press, 1990.

Mandeville, Bernard. *The Fable of the Bees,* 5th ed. London: J. Toson, 1728–29.

Marx, Karl. *Das Kapital.* New York: International Publishers, 1967.

Nozick, Robert. *Anarchy, State, and Utopia.* New York: Basic Books, 1974.

Rand, Ayn. *Capitalism: The Unknown Ideal.* New York: New American Library, 1966.

Schmookler, Andrew Bard. *The Illusion of Choice.* Albany, N.Y.: State University of New York Press, 1993.

Smith, Adam. *The Wealth of Nations.* Oxford: Clarendon Press, 1976.

Stepelevich, Lawrence S., ed. *The Capitalist Reader.* New Rochelle, N.Y.: Arlington House, 1977.

C

von Hayek, F.A. *The Road to Serfdom*. Chicago: University of Chicago Press, 1944.
———, ed. *Capitalism and the Historians*. Chicago: University of Chicago Press, 1954.
von Mises, Ludwig. *The Anti-Capitalist Mentality*. Princeton, N.J.: Von Nostrand, 1956.

Censorship

The term has two meanings. At one time, *censorship* could be defined as the function of a public official—a censor—in protecting the public from such offenses as obscenity, blasphemy, or slander against public officials. In contemporary society, the censor has become either a sinister or a ridiculous figure, and *censorship* has become a pejorative term. The contemporary meaning might be "illegitimate forms of control of public communication." In education, accusations of "censorship" often arise in disputes over the content of student publications, academic publishing (including textbooks and scholarly journals), the selection of materials for school libraries, and the coverage of education by the mass media.

The two meanings of *censorship* correspond roughly to the philosophical treatments of the topic by Plato (c. 427–347 B.C.) and John Stuart Mill (1806–1873). Plato—who opposed democracy and favored censorship—wrote about the art of his day as a moralist rather than as an aesthetician. His dialogue *Ion* portrays a confrontation between a popular entertainer and the philosopher Socrates (470–399 B.C.). In Plato's *Apology*, he suggests that the portrayal of Socrates in a popular play by Aristophanes (448–380 B.C.) encouraged the factions who were eventually able to have Socrates tried and executed for blasphemy. For Plato, popular entertainers entice the masses to confuse image and reality. Censorship—Plato argues—enables the public to see the truth and not be misled by fleeting images. Mill inspired a powerful metaphor that continues to appeal to opponents of censorship: the "marketplace of ideas." For Mill, censorship must be opposed because of its consequences. Left to its natural operation, the marketplace of ideas will sort out good and bad ideas. The censor can impose artificial criteria that interfere with the natural sorting process. Recent critics of Mill such as Ronald Dworkin typically share Mill's opposition to censorship but question the notion of the marketplace of ideas as inadequate in an age of emerging international media monopolies. Joel Spring has shown that the censor and the educator have often found themselves allies in opposing the mass media's "marketplace of ideas."

School librarians often find themselves at the center of conflicts among public librarians, educators, and censors. The public librarian regards public demand for books as imposing a professional obligation. The listing of a book as a best seller often obligates the public librarian to add it to the collection and make it available to the patrons. Advocates of censorship may argue that the librarian should also consider whether a given book will harm the public. (Historically, as Bonk and Magrill point out, courts have sided with the censor—although criteria of "harm" have changed.) Educators may also side with censors against librarians who cater to the tastes of the public rather than seeking to improve them. The educator and the librarian may stand together in favoring "literacy" even if "literacy" conflicts with the censor's criterion of "harm" or "obscenity." Until recently, both the librarian and the educator might seek to defeat the censor by retreating to the high ground of "professional standards." But in recent years professional standards have come under attack from racial, ethnic, and sexual minorities who see professional standards as biased against them (see Raywid 1979).

While librarians have the American Library Association and the American Association of School Librarians to speak out against censorship and for the profession, editors and advisors of student publications have no comparable avenue of appeal. In the past, student editors commonly sought freedom from censorship by school administrators, with faculty advisors caught in the middle. A frequent bone of contention in discussions of censorship of the student press was whether the school administrator, faculty advisor, or student editor was the "real" publisher of the student publication. In their attempt to make connections between Mill's philosophy and the problems of the student press, Strike and Soltis simply treat the faculty advisor as having the authority of a publisher rather than considering whether that authority is properly that of a school administrator or the student editor. The claim that the faculty advisor is the publisher has been defended on such grounds as: (1) student publications (SPs) are reflections of school policy; (2) SPs are part of the school's public relations program; (3) SPs reach a "captive audience"; and (4) SPs are a training ground for professional journalism (see Oliker 1972). Nearly thirty years ago, Roger Ebert—now a noted film critic—urged student editors of college newspapers to bypass advisors, administrators, and censors by finding the legal means to establish the student publication as an autonomous corporation. This had been done at several major universities and did free university administrators from any legal obligations. But is that a sufficient response to minority students who see themselves as being denied access to the student media by student editors? Can student editors themselves practice censorship?

While there is little further discussion of these issues with respect to the student press by philosophers of education, their discussions of the academic press are relevant. Of course, academic publishers may not face censorship from school administrators, but the academic press—including publishers of scholarly books, journals, and textbooks—can be accused of censorship itself on the grounds that a publisher has denied a work publication on other than academic grounds. By contrast, there is the argument that academic publishers may be practicing censorship by applying stringent stylistic standards that have the consequence of excluding competent work from publication solely on the basis of style of writing. Both Richard D. Mohr and George L. Newsome discuss cases of academic publishers' abandoning academic standards. Mohr charges that his recent scholarly book on the photography of male homosexual acts was rejected by several publishers who substituted a criterion of obscenity for the favorable opinions of academic reviewers. Newsome takes a similar position on the abandonment of academic standards in the face of demands from minority groups but retreats from a defense of academic standards in cases of obscenity. Ronald Swartz does not make a charge of censorship, but does cast serious doubt on claims by academic publishers that they can avoid charges of bias simply by appealing to academic standards. Swartz maintains that the specialized vocabularies of academic disciplines function as mechanisms for enforcing conformity by scholars who have lost any sense of the utility of one vocabulary as opposed to another. Kenneth Strike attempts to steer a middle course by urging academic publishers to reject Mill's "marketplace of ideas" and consider the ideal of "equal time" in the face of complaints by minority scholars and textbook writers.

The contemporary use of *censorship* as meaning "illegitimate forms of the control of public communication" allows for a discussion of Mary Anne Raywid's 1984 paper on biases of the mass media in their portrayals of education. She argues that: (1) education reporters are commonly the least experienced and most biased with regard to their subject; (2) education reporters see themselves as holding views on education that are shared by the public as a whole; (3) education reporters commonly lack any historical or sociological perspective on education and become preoccupied with details of particular events; and (4) with respect to public education, reporting typically reveals an adversarial stance toward the public sector. If the mass media are systematically biased in education reporting and if these biases are misinforming the public, then can it be said that the mass media are themselves engaged in censorship?

Michael A. Oliker

See also ACADEMIC FREEDOM; AESTHETICS; CIVIC EDUCATION; INDOCTRINATION; MILL; PLATO; SOCRATES

Bibliography

Bonk, Wallace John, and Rose Mary Magrill. "Censorship and Selection." In *Building Library Collections*. 5th ed. Metuchen, N.J.: Scarecrow, 1979.

Dworkin, Ronald. "A New Map of Censorship." *Index on Censorship* 23 (May/June 1994): 9–15.

Ebert, Roger. "Plain Talk on College Newspaper Freedom." In *Freedom and Censorship of the College Press*, edited by Herman A. Estrin and Arthur M. Sanderson. Dubuque, Iowa: Wm. C. Brown, 1966.

Mohr, Richard D. "When University Presses Give in to Bias, Academic Principle Will Be Disregarded." *Chronicle of Higher Education*, July 15, 1992, A44.

Nehamas, Alexander. "Plato and the Mass Media." *Monist* 71 (1988): 214–34.

Newsome, George L. "Bias, Censorship, and Freedom of the Academic Press." *Educational Theory* 29 (1979): 229–36.

Oliker, Michael A. "The College Newspaper: A Descriptive Definition." *College Press Review* 11 (1972): 9–12.

C

Raywid, Mary Anne. "Censorship: New Wrinkles in an Old Problem." *High School Journal* 62 (1979): 332–38.

———. "Education and the Media or Why They Keep Raining on Your Parade." *Contemporary Education* 55 (1984): 206–11.

Spring, Joel. *Images of American Life*. Albany, N.Y.: State University of New York Press, 1992.

Strike, Kenneth. "Liberality and Censorship: A Philosophy of Textbook Controversies." In *Philosophy of Education 1977*. Urbana, Ill.: Philosophy of Education Society, 1977.

———, and Jonas F. Soltis. "Intellectual Freedom." In *The Ethics of Teaching*. New York: Teachers College Press, 1985.

Swartz, Ronald. "The Publication Game and the Education of Future Scholars." In *Scientific Information Transfer: The Editor's Role*, edited by Miriam Balaban. Dordrecht, Holland: D. Reidel, 1978.

Waugh, J.M. Beil. "Art and Morality: The End of an Ancient Rivalry?" *Journal of Aesthetic Education* 20 (1986): 5–17.

Children's Rights

The idea that children themselves, on their own behalves, or that children's advocates, on behalf of the children, may make claims to fair treatment, either morally or, increasingly, legally. The notion of children's rights is a recent one, for, historically, children have not been thought to possess such rights but have been treated paternalistically. Thus, according rights to children, whether morally or legally, marks a change of children's status in society.

Writing in the seventeenth century, Thomas Hobbes (1588–1679) provides an example of the kind of paternalistic thinking typical of much Western thought about children's rights. Hobbes wrote, "Like the imbecile, the crazed and the beasts, over . . . children . . . there is no law" (*Leviathan*: 257). Fathers have absolute power over their children because children, lacking rationality, cannot understand the consequences of their actions and so cannot undertake the obligations of participating in the social contract that binds society together. For Hobbes's contemporary John Locke (1632–1704), although he wanted to constrain parental dominance by attributing natural rights to children, children's welfare was still decided by

their father. Both philosophers, then, view children as dependent upon their fathers; therefore, children are prevented from making claims, either moral or legal, on their own. As a result, society did not deem children individuals, worthy of respect in their own right.

This last view is the view of the nineteenth-century British philosopher John Stuart Mill (1806–1873). Despite his libertarian stance toward individuals, Mill believed that children, unlike adults, should not be permitted the right to interpret their own good because they cannot understand, and thus might not act in accordance with, the public good. To grant children rights would, therefore, be fundamentally against utilitarianism. Children, once again, must be treated paternalistically.

Taken together, these three representative philosophers argued that children have no basis on which to be accorded rights because they lack the rationality necessary to develop a perspective of their own. Recently, however, using the work of John Rawls, an argument for children's rights has emerged. This argument brushes aside arguments for children's rights based on the idea that children, like adults, are beings capable of suffering, or once more like adults, are human beings and so must be ascribed rights. Rather, Rawls argues that children, as they develop the ability to reason for themselves, should participate as fully as they can in the formation and perpetuation of society. For Rawls, what matters in deciding who is to count as a rights-bearing member of a just society is the capacity for accepting and living under the principle of fairness. To the extent that children possess this capacity, which depends crucially on rationality, children should be accorded rights.

Rawls's conception of society is an ideal conception designed to function as a benchmark for determining how near actual societies are to realizing justice. As such, Rawls's argument can be dismissed as merely theoretical and impractical. But, Rawls's argument, albeit theoretical, may also be challenged on the ground that it encourages a confrontational moral relationship between children and adults. For, even when adults act on behalf of children, believing that they will gain the children's consent to those actions at some future date, Rawls's view allows children to claim moral rights of their own on such matters as choosing which school to attend or what kind of vacation to take. And, some confrontations have led to children's claiming legal rights against society and even against their parents. (1967: *in re Gault.* The Supreme Court extended to children Fourteenth Amendment rights of due process in deliquency proceedings. 1989: *T.W. vs. State of Florida.* Florida Supreme Court ruled the state constitutional right to privacy applies to girls, giving them the right to abortions without parental consent.) Such cases have produced a call for a moratorium on granting rights to children because, as Hobbes had said, children lack the responsibility to live with the consequences of possessing them.

Victor L. Worsfold

See also COMMUNITY; INDIVIDUALISM; LIBERALISM; RIGHTS

Bibliography

Etzioni, Amitai. *The Spirit of Community: Rights, Responsibilities and the Communitarian Agenda.* New York: Crown Publishers, 1993.

Hawes, Joseph M. *The Children's Rights Movement: A History of Advocacy and Protection.* Boston: Twayne Publishers, 1991.

Rawls, John. *A Theory of Justice.* Cambridge: Harvard University Press, 1972.

The Rights of Children. Harvard Educational Review Reprint Series no. 9. Cambridge: Harvard University Press, 1974.

Wringe, C.A. *Children's Rights: A Philosophical Study.* London: Routledge and Kegan Paul, 1981.

Cicero, Marcus Tullius (106–43 B.C.)

Roman rhetor, statesman, politician, philosopher, linguist, and educational theorist whose writings have provided significant information on the Greco-Roman world and inspired European educational renovation in varying degrees for nineteen hundred years. He was born in Arpinum, a village approximately sixty miles southeast of Rome. His family was affluent and of the Equestrian Order. The *Equites,* however, were not of the nobility. Thus Cicero was a "new man" in Roman politics. During the last one hundred and fifty years of the Republic only ten *novi* reached councilship, and during his generation Cicero was the only one. *Novi* status seriously affected his reception among the ruling class and his own sense of self.

Cicero's early education most probably was typical of that of an upper-class Roman boy. There were four distinct stages. Most authorities, with good reason, presume that he studied with Greek teachers during the first three stages. During the elementary stage, he learned the Greek language and literacy skills, most likely from Greek tutors. Subsequently, he studied literature with a Greek *grammaticus.* The latter involved a careful reading of mostly Greek texts, especially Homer and the tragic poets. The third stage, which Cicero describes in his *Brutus,* was training in rhetoric. It began about age fifteen, when his family was living at their city home in Rome. His rhetorical training was at a "school" in the home of Lucius Crassus, and again probably from Greek teachers. Cicero, unlike most Roman boys, also received instruction in philosophy at that time. His teachers were the Epicurean Pharedrus and the Stoic Diodotus.

Most notable about the first three stages of this education was the strong Greek influence, both in language and materials. It must be remembered that at this time Rome lacked a Latin literary culture. In her biography entitled *Cicero,* Elizabeth Rawson ably summarized this situation: "Education at Rome was probably more Greek at this time than ever before or after; for when Cicero himself had enriched the Latin language and brought rhetorical training to full maturity there was less need for rhetorical training to use Greek models and, in the generation after his, Virgil and Horace provided the *grammaticus* too with texts that could rank with and even to some extent replace Greek literature" (p. 8).

At age sixteen Cicero received the *toga virilis,* the white toga, which symbolized entry into manhood. That time also marked the beginning of the fourth stage of his education. Roman elder statesmen often became mentors for aspiring young men. The youths would attend their mentor for a year or more. They would follow, listen, and observe as the elders received clients, offered advice, participated in the Senate, or argued cases in the courts. Cicero began his apprenticeship with a renowned jurist, the eighty-year-old Q. Mucius Scaevola, "Augur," and, after Augur's death with Q. Scaevola, "Pontifex." His was a practical apprenticeship in the law and politics. Young Cicero not only learned the law, but was also introduced into the world of Roman politics, acquiring what a later era would call "old school ties."

Unlike most contemporaries, Cicero engaged in these preparatory activities for nearly a decade, interrupted only by a short stint in the army during the Social War. During the eighties B.C., Cicero continued his study of law. Additionally, he found time to attend the philosophic lectures of Philo of Larisa and to study rhetoric with Milon of Rhodes, both of whom were visiting Rome. It was not until 81 or 80 B.C., at about age twenty-five, that he defended his first case in the courts. Within two years he left Rome for an extended visit to Greece and Asia Minor. While there he studied philosophy at the Academy with Antiochus and at Rhodes with the Stoic Posidonius. While at Rhodes, Cicero renewed his study of rhetoric with Milon. This prolonged education provided both depth and breadth to his preparation. Undoubtedly, Cicero was the best educated Roman of his time, and perhaps of any time. His subsequent careers were ample testimony to its effectiveness.

In 76 B.C., Cicero returned to Rome and his career in the courts. He entered politics, winning the Quaestorship at age thirty. From there, the bottom rung of Roman politics, Cicero climbed to the highest offices available during the troubled next thirty years. As the Republic lurched from one crisis to the next, Cicero was in the midst of the fray. His political career saw stunning successes and dismal defeats as he tried to steer a middle course between the "popularis" and the "optimates." As the Republic lurched to its final demise at the hands of Anthony and Octavian, Cicero delivered the fourteen speeches entitled *Philippic* against Anthony. In retaliation, Anthony's henchmen murdered him near one of his country homes. During his entire career, Cicero had strenuously defended the Senate and upheld the status of what he called the "good men." This effort gained him throughout subsequent history the enmity of both those who championed the causes of the "common people" as well as those who favored authoritarian rule. Ultimately, the economic and social ills of the Republic were beyond the ability of Cicero or his contemporaries to solve.

Cicero's major contributions to education were in the areas of philosophy and rhetoric. Interestingly, although he had a lifelong interest in philosophy, his eight major philosophical works were written in a brief period of less than two years during the last three years of his life. Such fecundity was possible, in part, because of Cicero's forty years of philosophical study. He was eclectic in the sources of his readings and

was influenced by a variety of Hellenistic schools and philosophers, including Antiochus of the "New Academy," Pharedrus the Epicurean, Posidonius the Platonist, and the Stoics Diodotus and Chrysippus. It has long been fashionable to belittle his philosophical work as unimportant because it was unoriginal, merely summarizing Greek and Hellenistic philosophic efforts. H.A.K. Hunt's *Humanism of Cicero* and A.E. Douglas's "Cicero the Philosopher," however, lay such criticism to rest.

The focus of Cicero's philosophical writings was on how to lead a "good life." His effort was to provide a guide to moral behavior as a social and political being. He began with epistemology and perception. What can we know of the world? After careful consideration, he rejected the Stoic arguments for "perfect" perception and the idea that perception directly corresponds to material reality. Rather, he held that imperfect human perception could yield a calculation of probability that was a reasonable guide to truth. This conclusion required all conclusions to be held as tentative rather than final. Cicero's very method of inquiry assaults dogmatism, and he continually chides those who uncritically accept authority.

A second problem for his moral philosophy was human nature. Cicero, like most in the ancient world, believed that humanity alone is endowed by nature with reason. He argued that because humans are an intimate part of an essentially benevolent nature, human nature must also be essentially good. A human's true nature is to move toward moral perfection, which, because humans are by nature social beings, requires altruism and implies the brotherhood of all humans. This linking of all individuals to a common humanity led Cicero to assert the necessity of obedience to a higher common law that transcends the laws of individual states. The ideal of universal human brotherhood bound through altruism and higher law, although honored more in the abstract than in the concrete, has been one of Cicero's more significant legacies to Western Europe.

The issue of human responsibility was directly addressed by Cicero. He rejected the common belief that fate or the gods intervene in human affairs. Thus while absolving the fates and gods of responsibility for human actions, he developed a theory of human freedom and responsibility for choices. While imperfect human perception always means provisional knowledge, Cicero argued that humans' movement to their true perfection involves making choices that respect fellow humans. The drive for private gain must not injure other humans if one is to achieve virtue—that is, moral perfection that is the true human nature. Only the making of ethical choices can lead humans to true happiness, which is harmony with the true self. It is practical conduct that leads to virtue.

Hunt summarized Cicero's philosophy: "Cicero had a coherent system and it deserves the name of humanism because it was concerned with man first and foremost. . . . First it inquired into man's nature, the validity of his perceptions, the nature of his highest virtue, the condition of his happiness, the degree of his freedom and his relation to the forces which control the world; it ended by asserting a theory of freedom and a rule of conduct enjoying the highest respect for man and systematically based in the theory of human nature" (188–89).

Closely related to his moral philosophy was Cicero's second contribution to Western education, his rhetorical theory. By Cicero's time, rhetorical training had become the principal vehicle of Roman education. Most of the schools of rhetoric were excessively pedantic, too concerned with rules and techniques of style while slavishly aping previous models of composition with spirit-dulling exercises. Rhetoric had become synonymous with eloquence and principally concerned with persuasion, especially in the courts and the senate. Cicero's major writings on rhetoric began with his *De Inventione,* written in his youth, and continued with his later *De Oratore, Brutus,* and *Orator.* Each represented a concerned condemnation of the schools of rhetoric, the school masters, and their methods of instruction.

Cicero's writings on rhetoric were not without technical content. For example, he outlined the principal subdivisions of rhetoric. Rhetoric begins with an investigation of the subject *(inventio),* proceeds to an arrangement of the material for the argument *(dispositio),* and concludes with the presentation in correct and pleasing style *(elocutio).* Each of these has almost infinite subdivisions. He also noted that there are three major types of style: (a) plain, best for simple exposition of factual data; (b) middle, most appropriate for conciliating; and (c) the grand, used to heighten the emotions of the listener. This categorizing of styles was to deeply influence Augustine's *De Doctrina Christiana,* and thus much of subsequent Christian humanism.

For all the mass of technical content, however, Cicero's overriding concern was the philosophy of rhetoric and the educational theory embedded within it. For Cicero, the most critical issue of his time was how Rome should educate its leaders. Like most of the ancients, he was interested in the education of only that small percentage from the upper class who would exercise political power. It was they who would determine the fate of the society.

Cicero was very clear about the fundamental cause of the Roman educational failure. It stemmed from the divorce of rhetoric from philosophy, which, he claimed, began with Socrates. Isolation from philosophy resulted in exclusive attention on the techniques of rhetoric. Such a narrow focus led to vacuous speech, deceit, a narrowness of outlook, an obsessive concern for show, a concentration on private rather than on public good, and a general decline in public spiritedness among Roman rhetors. Above all, Cicero wished to identify the rhetor with the statesman, and not with the court pleader of special interest. And that could be accomplished only with a new conception of rhetoric and rhetorical education. The orator-statesman must understand his responsibility for the welfare, security, and happiness of the whole society. Cicero put it succinctly: "Upon the prudence and abilities of an accomplished orator, not only his own dignity, but the welfare of vast numbers of individuals, nay of the whole government rests." The orator's education, Cicero charged, was fatally incomplete without a thorough grounding in moral philosophy and ethics. In his first work on rhetoric, Cicero noted, "Wisdom without eloquence is of little use to the community, but eloquence without wisdom mostly does great harm, and never does good." The more mature Cicero stated the case even more sharply as he asserted that if we train men in rhetoric without philosophy "we shall not have made orators of them but shall have put weapons into the hands of madmen."

Cicero noted in *De Oratore* that while many youths were studying rhetoric under the direction of numerous teachers, there were few good orators. The reason was partly that the objective of rhetoric training was exclusively focused on the production of eloquence. For this the "tricks of the oratorical trade," as taught by the school masters, would suffice. But to educate the Ciceronian orator, a longer, more rigorous curriculum was required. Besides moral philosophy, it required the inclusion of all subjects that have any bearing on human life and society. Cicero demanded the systematic inclusion of law, literature, and history in rhetorical education. In defense of history he argued, "Not to know what happened before you were born is to remain forever a child." To the queries, Why study all these subjects? Will they really be utilized by the orator? Cicero answered, "No man ought to be accounted an orator who is not thoroughly accomplished in all those arts that become a gentleman; and if we do not make a show of them upon every turn of discourse, yet it may be plainly and evidently perceived whether we possess them or not." He understood that true education is neither easily nor quickly accomplished. In essence, he recommended an education much like his own, which had occupied over a decade of his adolescence. In the middle of the first century, Cicero gave theoretical expression to what became known in Western education as the "Classical Tradition." It was firmly rooted in "Classical Humanism," insisting upon a breadth of study that encompasses all human knowledge.

Cicero's educational ideas, like his political values, engender little resonance in the twentieth century. Two kinds of arguments have been advanced against them. While both have been effective, neither seems to have much logical force. The first argument claims that with the modern "knowledge explosion," it is impossible for anyone to know all the available facts, and pursuit of a broad education is therefore a fool's errand. This seems to confuse Cicero's demand for knowledge with facts. Cicero never asserted that the student should have command of all the available facts or data; rather, he argued for knowledge of all areas of human inquiry. Ciceronian education would seek to equip the student to understand what is important, to acquire necessary facts, and to make moral decisions. These understandings and abilities hardly seem less important today than in the first century B.C.

The second argument assumes that education for an aristocracy must be different from a democratic education. Cicero, like most of the ancients, was concerned with the education of an elite whose role would be societal leadership. He was most concerned that this leadership be prepared to make ethical decisions based on social justice for the benefit of all society. Surprisingly, many modern educational theorists seem to believe that because the ancients were thus concerned, their educational ideas are inappropriate for a democratic society in which the masses exercise political power. One might wonder why educational theories appropriate for preparing the upper class for effective exercise of political power would be inappropriate for preparing the masses to exercise similar power.

Cicero's influence on Western European education has flowed in three distinct and not always complementary channels. The most well known has been stylistic. Ciceronianism became synonymous for elegant, ornate, long sentences, pedantic diction, and overbearing concern for grammar. In the hands of mediocre schoolmasters, Ciceronianism was, all too often, a crude weapon used to bludgeon students' curiosity and love for learning. These small-minded schoolmasters, no doubt, would have been scandalized by Cicero's comment that all the Romans he knew spoke Latin, but none spoke grammar. A second channel of Ciceronian influence was Cicero's moral philosophy. His moral philosophy inspired many later educators who also believed that education should inspire virtue, patriotism, and the good life. The third, and perhaps most important, stream of Cicero's influence was Ciceronian *humanitatus*. Cicero's discussions on the kind of education that produces an educated gentleman echoes loudly over the centuries in most of the noblest statements of educational ideals. Ciceronian *humanitatus* easily brings to mind the words of Cardinal Newman's Dublin lecture on literature or John Stuart Mill's "Inaugural Address" at St. Andrews.

Paul C. Violas

See also AUGUSTINE; ETHICS AND MORALITY; HUMAN NATURE; HUMANISM; RHETORIC; STOICISM

Bibliography

Bonner, Stanley F. *Education in Ancient Rome.* Berkeley: University of California Press, 1977.

Cicero. *Brutus.* Translated by G.L. Hendrickson. London: Loeb Classic Library, 1939, 1988.

———. *De Inventione.* Translated by H.M. Hubbell. London: Loeb Classic Library, 1949, 1976.

———. *De Officiis.* Translated by Walter Miller. London: Loeb Classic Library, 1913, 1930.

———. *De Oratore.* Vol. 1, translated by E.W. Sutton and H. Rackham. London:

Loeb Classic Library, 1967.

———. *De Oratore*. Vol. 2, translated by H. Rackham. London: Loeb Classic Library, 1942, 1982.

———. *Orator*. Translated by H.M. Hubbell. London: Loeb Classic Library, 1939, 1988.

Clarke, M.L. "Cicero at School." *Greece & Rome* 14–15 (1967–68): 18–22.

———. "Ciceronian Oratory." *Greece & Rome* 40 (January 1945): 72–81.

———. "Non Hominis Nomen, Sed Eloquentiae." In *Cicero*, edited by T.A. Dorey. London: Routledge and Kegan Paul, 1965.

Douglas, A.E. *Cicero*. Oxford: Clarendon Press, 1968.

———. "Cicero the Philosopher." In *Cicero*, edited by T.A. Dorey. London: Routledge and Kegan Paul, 1965.

Grube, G.M.A. "Educational, Rhetorical, and Literary Theory in Cicero." *Phoenix* 16 (1962): 3234–57.

Hunt, H.A.K. *The Humanism of Cicero*. Carlton, Victoria: Melbourne University Press, 1954.

Meador, Prentice A. "Rhetoric and Humanism in Cicero." *Philosophy and Rhetoric* 1 (Winter 1970): 1–12.

Rawson, Elizabeth. *Cicero: A Portrait*. London: Penguin Books, 1975.

Smethurst, S.E. "Cicero and Isocrates." *Transactions and Proceedings of the American Philological Association* 84 (1953): 262–320.

Civic Education

Civic education refers to education that is concerned with the development of citizenship or civic competence. The word "civic" is derived from the Greek *civitas*, meaning "of the city," and denotes life within a sociopolitical community. The content and nature of civic education is thus context specific. Its goals are necessarily understood in relation to expectations for members of particular nations and societies as they transmit the knowledge, dispositions, values, and skills associated with participation in civic, or public, life. While all sociopolitical groups can be said to practice some form of civic preparation as they socialize the next generation, the term *civic education* more often refers to a society's or nation's explicit provisions for inculcating civic virtues through formal schooling. This may be carried out through a curriculum that focuses on instruction in history, government, and public affairs, through organized routines, ceremonies, and rituals, or through participation in group interactions and activities.

Civic education has long been a concern of philosophers of education. Central to its discussion are definitions of the nature of the political state, the citizen, and the relation of individual and society. The ancient Greek philosopher Plato (c. 427–347 B.C.) introduced the topic in the *Republic* in his depiction of a model for preparing the youth of Athens for a virtuous public life. For Plato, the continuity and strength of the political state was dependent on an education that could mold future members to its ideal purposes.

Since the time of Plato, subsequent works have tended to dispute the assumption of the primacy of the political state's rights over the rights of the individual. An education that emphasizes maintaining the stability of the state for the general good against the interests and needs of individuals has been frequently understood to have the potential to become a form of coercive indoctrination. Further, since Plato places his ideal education within an ideal state, his system was designed to produce citizens who would preserve rather that seek to improve or change that state. Modern writers have seen the need to provide models for a civic education that would produce individuals who could participate in social and political progress and reform.

The most influential and striking contrast to Plato's treatment of civic education appeared in *Emile* (1762) by the Enlightenment theorist Jean-Jacques Rousseau. In Rousseau's view, the rights of "natural man" rather than the rights of the state have primacy. The goal of an ideal education, according to Rousseau, should be to counter the influences of what he believed to be a corrupt political order and society. In *Emile* he described how fostering a child's natural development through nondirective methods would produce a virtuous citizen capable of acting for political and social change.

The sharply drawn alternatives presented in the *Republic* and the *Emile* have continued to characterize discussions of the social and political aims of education and are particularly relevant to debates concerning the nature and goals of civic education. Understandings of the requirements for responsible participation in civic life, fundamental to the design of civic education, are necessarily connected to perspectives on state power, individual rights and duties, and the desirability of social and political change. Responsible civic participation within particular sociopolitical contexts may mean no more than conformity to law. In others, it might involve the responsibility to evaluate government policies critically and work toward their improvement and change.

Civic education can be seen as encompassing more than preparation for full legal citizenship. During periods in which a country is at war or involved in ideological conflict with other countries, allegiance to the state and patriotism may be stressed. In nations in which those in power fear that social dissent or political unrest threatens the state, civic education may be used to promote adherence to a traditional culture, a state religion, or nationalism. Within countries characterized by ethnic, cultural, and socioeconomic class differences, civic education might involve attempts to assimilate all students within a dominant culture, or alternatively, to recognize the value of multiculturalism and diversity. Civic education may also emphasize the worth of particular forms of knowledge and technical skills related to meeting those needs. That is, within a nation that has identified specific social or economic needs, the civic curriculum may seek to alter student attitudes toward the family and work or teach the importance of science and technology.

In early arguments for public schooling in the United States, the education of the common people and electorate was seen as integral to the nation's well-being. However, an education that served merely to maintain the state's power or indoctrinate its future citizens was clearly contrary to the principle of government by and for the people. Proponents of public education thus began to define education not only as a means to political continuity but also as a way of cultivating individual improvement to ensure one's rights and liberty.

Following national independence in 1776, the initial focus of concern of political theorists in the United States was training in citizenship. Thomas Jefferson (1743–1826), a disciple of Rousseau's, saw the need for schools that would teach the rights and duties of citizenship as well as basic literacy. Contending that ignorance was incompatible with freedom, Jefferson introduced a proposal for publicly supported state schools in the Virginia legislature in 1779. Like most political theorists of his time, Jefferson

defined citizenship narrowly as applying only to the white male property holders who formed the electorate. In Jefferson's plan, white children of both sexes would receive three years of primary education. This he believed would be sufficient to educate girls to assume their duties in the home and prepare less talented boys of the lower classes for the paid labor force. Boys who had proven themselves as scholars during these three years would be supported by the state in their further education, with the hope that they would distinguish themselves in the professions or as political leaders.

Jefferson's proposals for state-supported education were taken up by the members of the common school movement in the mid nineteenth century. The common schoolers however placed less emphasis on the instruction of the future citizen in individual rights and liberties than had Jefferson. Horace Mann (1796–1859) stressed the need to teach social obligations and responsibilities to all students. Mann saw common schooling as a process that could uplift character, inculcate a work ethic, and lead to the social and economic improvement of the "general public."

While education of an informed electorate was still a goal for the common schoolers, unlike their predecessors they included women and the unpropertied in their vision of the general public that would be served by public schooling. Their rationales for civic education were thus more broadly conceived. A student's civic education was thought to be integrated throughout the curriculum. Students of both sexes and all classes would receive lessons in reading, writing, numeracy, and United States government and history. They would also be presented with stories of exemplary cases of bravery, thrift, honesty, hard work, and self-sacrifice that they could emulate in school and later life. Their teachers would be expected to model these virtues as they instructed their students.

During the 1880s and 1890s, as public schooling was increasingly extended to provide secondary education, the term "civics" began to be used more frequently to describe instruction in United States history, civil government, and the framework of the constitution. The question of what should constitute the study of civics as a distinct school subject took place during an era of unprecedented immigration. While some writers of the period continued to contend that lessons in civics should concentrate on United

States history and government, many others called for an education that would foster "social likemindedness" by teaching the public school's increasingly diverse population of students dominant cultural values, social etiquette, and manners. In contrast, and in the minority, Jane Addams (1860–1935) argued that immigrant children would be more fully integrated within American public life if the value of their cultural traditions were acknowledged and represented in the curriculum.

Within this context, the National Education Association (NEA) formed a series of committees to evaluate the civics curriculum of the public schools. This initiated debates within the NEA as well as among the American History Teachers Association, American Political Science Association, and regional teachers organizations that centered on (1) whether facts or interpretation should be stressed in history and government, (2) whether textbooks and lectures or group projects and field trips should be the medium of instruction, (3) whether it is more valuable to teach the workings of local community government or the laws and constitution of the United States, and (4) whether a separate course in civics was needed in the elementary and secondary schools.

No effective or lasting consensus was reached on the first two of these questions. In regard to the third and fourth, by 1920 most upper elementary levels included civics in the social studies or history curriculum that focused on community life and local government. Secondary students were routinely required to complete a course specifically designed to teach the principles and processes of American government.

Although there is now general agreement that civic responsibilities and values should be taught in public schools, profound differences exist among contemporary writers on what those responsibilities and values are and how they should be taught. A series of reports during the 1970s and 1980s issued by the United States Department of Education, National Assessment of Educational Progress, and professional educational associations indicated that students were not being adequately prepared for life in the twenty-first century. The cumulative impact of these reports, as well as a concern to address the needs of an increasingly diverse population, initiated a new interest in defining the purposes, goals, and content of the civic curriculum.

One group of theorists has tended to concentrate its analyses on the importance of teaching democratic principles. R. Freeman Butts suggests, for example, that a national standard be set for the civics curriculum, in which instruction in core democratic values, obligations, and rights would be required of all students. Only a national standard, Butts contends, would be able to counter the disruptive effects of contemporary tendencies toward cultural and racial separation and enable students "to play their parts as informed, responsible, committed, and effective members of a modern democratic society." Richard Pratte, while also placing major focus on principles of democracy, proposes a more participatory model for both the determination of policies governing civic education and its content. He advocates promoting public discussion and debate on the nature of power, conflict, social change, and the relation between individual and society within both local educational communities and classrooms.

A second group of writers focuses on the methods that should be used to teach civic education. Judith Torney-Purta, basing her conclusions on the findings of the national Assessment of Educational Progress, describes how higher achievement in civic understanding is correlated with classrooms in which open discussion and students' opinions are valued above lectures and memorization. She argues that students who are guided in solving hypothetical problems develop a firmer grasp of political and social principles. In a similar vein, Frederick Newmann advances models for social studies classrooms that include group problem solving, promote thoughtful consideration of issues, require the practice of critical thinking, and teach decision-making.

Departing from these approaches to method, C. Finn critiques reliance on discussion and decision-making as appropriate classroom methods. In his view, they serve to train students to accept cultural relativism and rely on subjective judgment. Finn's solution is closely associated with the work of E.D. Hirsch, Jr., whose *Cultural Literacy* (1987) defines cultural literacy as dependent on knowledge of a prescribed list of persons, events, and terms every American should learn. For Finn, the chief responsibility of civic education is to teach the facts of American history and government.

A final group of theorists is concerned with developing a more culturally sensitive and inclusive civic education. Writers within this group stress the need to represent the accomplishments, contributions, and experience of minorities within the course of study and advocate forms of teaching that are responsive to individual students' needs. George Wood, for example, discusses how the inclusion of stories of the lives of ordinary people, minorities, and women, as well as discussions of their roles in social reform movements, can serve to empower students and promote civic engagement. Jane Martin, responding in part to the proponents of core standards for cultural literacy, offers an alternative that addresses the deterioration of the social conditions in which many students now live. Care, concern, and connection become the governing principles within what Martin calls a "school home" designed to support students as they learn to value both their commonalities and differences and develop toward adulthood.

While debates between educational philosophers about civic education continue, and wide variations in state and local practices exist, Newmann's, James Shaver's, and Torney-Purta's research suggests that there is currently a dominant trend in American civic education within the schools. In the vast majority of classrooms, lectures and reliance on textbooks are the medium of instruction and established cultural norms; patriotism, civic tradition, and the structure of American government are the standard topics of study. Although projects sponsored by professional educational associations have sought to initiate changes, large-scale reform of the contemporary civic education curriculum has yet to occur.

Susan Douglas Franzosa

See also: ADDAMS; JEFFERSON; MANN; PLATO; RIGHTS; ROUSSEAU

Bibliography

Anderson, L., et al. *The Civic Report Card: Trends in Achievement for 1976 to 1988*. Princeton, N.J.: National Assessment of Educational Progress, 1990.

Butts, R. Freeman. *The Revival of Civic Learning: A Rationale for Citizenship Education in American Schools*. Bloomington, Ind.: Phi Delta Kappan Educational Foundation, 1980.

Finn, C. "Among the Educationaloids: The Social Studies Debacle." *American Spectator* 21(5) (1988): 35–36.

Franzosa, Susan Douglas, ed. *Civic Education: Its Limits and Conditions*. Ann Arbor, Mich.: Prakken Publications, 1988.

Hirsch, E.D., Jr. *Cultural Literacy*. New York: Vintage Books, 1987.

Ichilov, O., ed. *Political Socialization, Citizenship Education, and Democracy*. New York: Teachers College Press, 1990.

Martin, Jane R. *The School Home*. Boston: Harvard University Press, 1993.

Newmann, Frederick. "Higher Order Thinking in Teaching Social Studies: A Rationale for the Assessment of Classroom Thoughtfulness." *Journal of Curriculum Studies* 22 (1990): 41–56.

Pratte, Richard. *The Civic Imperative: Examining the Need for Civic Education*. New York: Teacher's College Press, 1988.

Shaver, James, ed. *Handbook of Research on Social Studies Teaching and Learning*. New York: Macmillan, 1991.

Torney-Purta, Judith, and J. Schwille. "Civic Values Learned in School: Policy and Practice in Industrialized Nations." *Comparative Education Review* 30(1) (1986): 30–49.

Wood, George. "Civic Education for Participatory Democracy." In *Civic Education: Its Limits and Conditions*, edited by Susan Douglas Franzosa, 68–98. Ann Arbor, Mich.: Prakken Publications, 1988.

Civil Disobedience

Conduct contrary to established authority, in response to perceived injustice. Examples are found in drama, history, and today's news reports. They range from Antigone's defiance of the king's decree that her slain brother be left unburied to Rosa Parks's noncompliance with racial segregation in Montgomery, Alabama, and the organized bus boycott that followed.

Thoreau initiated theoretical discussion of the subject. Because of Massachusetts' support of the Mexican War, chattel slavery, and wrongs to Native Americans, he refused to pay the poll tax and was jailed. In his subsequent lecture on "Resistance to Civil Government," Thoreau argued that one is not morally required to battle injustice generally, but one must refrain from helping a government commit injustice.

Thoreau's essay made an impact on Mohandas Gandhi, who led mass campaigns against racism in South Africa and against British colonial domination of India. Gandhi developed the notion of *satyagraha*, which stresses a series of disciplined actions. One first tries to win opponents over by persuasion and, if necessary, suffering. If that fails, one seeks change by nonviolent measures that put pressure on those in power.

Gandhi in turn influenced Martin Luther King, Jr., who led the Montgomery bus boycott and later helped organize or supported many other campaigns, including an economic boycott to end racist store policies in Birmingham, which led to his arrest and to his famous "Letter from Birmingham Jail."

Surprisingly, none of these examples fit under theorists' current definitions of civil disobedience. Theorists begin by distinguishing civil disobedience not only from ordinary criminal activity but also from actions aimed at revolutionary change. Civil disobedients are assumed to accept the prevailing system as morally sound and to aim only at reform. They seek to change law or public policy by moral persuasion. To convince others of their sincerity, their limited aims, and their respect for law, they act openly and nonviolently and willingly accept the legal penalties.

Theorists distinguish civil disobedience, so defined, from "conscientious refusal"—such as Thoreau's tax resistance or a conscientious objector's refusal to serve in the military—and from "conscientious evasion"—such as covert assistance to fugitive slaves or the Sanctuary Movement's aid to refugees excluded by restrictive immigration policies. Conscientious refusal aims to avoid complicity with injustice, conscientious evasion seeks to aid its victims, and civil disobedience tries to motivate officials to change the law by means of moral pressure.

According to these definitions, the act for which King was jailed does not count as civil disobedience because it aimed at changing neither law nor public policy but a practice of private store owners. Indeed, disobedience to law was not essential to the action, and his act could only barely be considered unlawful. He led a march to promote a store boycott. Because the march defied a court order, the Supreme Court upheld his conviction, even though the order itself was unlawful: It enforced an unconstitutionally discriminatory denial of a parade permit under an unconstitutionally vague statute.

Theorists might think they have a reason for placing special emphasis on disobedience to law. They might believe there is a general obligation to obey the law but no general obligation to comply with social norms that are not backed by law. Contemporary theories of civil disobedience do seem to take that obligation for granted. It means that substantial justification is required for disobedience to any law, whatever it requires or allows. Disobedience might be justified, but not easily.

But the idea of a general obligation to obey the law is widely discredited by political philosophers. To be sure, there are many good reasons for obeying many laws. But no one has constructed an argument making it reasonable to conclude that those reasons apply to all laws and to all persons under them. It is implausible to suppose, for example, that the intended victims of pervasive, systematic discrimination are under any obligation to obey the specific laws that enforce those wrongs. It might therefore be reasonable to think of civil disobedience broadly as resistance to any form of established authority.

What about the notion that civil disobedients accept the prevailing system as morally sound and aim only at reform? Given the entrenched character of racial discrimination in American society, there is reason to take seriously King's suggestion that genuine reform would amount to a "revolution." If that seems inconclusive, then consider the campaigns against British colonial rule led by Gandhi. They had a revolutionary aim—the same aim that Americans had earlier achieved by violence. If those campaigns—which are commonly called civil disobedience—were revolutionary as well as nonviolent, it is unclear why we should insist that something cannot count as civil disobedience unless it has reformist aims.

Theorists may do so for various reasons. Caught in a pun, they may assume that disobedience cannot be *civil* unless it is nonviolent. They may assume that political violence must be uncontrolled and indiscriminate. Forgetful of the Indian example, they may assume that political violence seeks an overthrow of the prevailing system.

This seems mistaken on more than one count. Consider someone who with measured violence delays a slave catcher in order to help a fugitive achieve freedom, and who thus violates the Fugitive Slave Act. He may think of slavery as an outrageous, morally indefensible practice, but he might not want to overthrow the system. His doubly unlawful assault might not count for theorists as "civil" disobedience, but it is arguably justifiable. And justification is the central issue.

Theorists appear to assume that the category of conduct that they call civil disobedience is capable of effecting change by pure persuasion. But it typically involves an element of coercion. Massive or individually dramatic nonconformist action commands attention. As King observed, it produces a "creative tension" that obliges those in power to decide how much violence they are willing to use, or how much they might use with impunity if they wish to overcome the resistance of committed disobedients. It forces those in power to consider negotiation, compromise, and accommodation. That is sometimes the only way to achieve needed change.

David Lyons

See also GANDHI; KING

Bibliography

Bedau, Hugo Adam, ed. *Civil Disobedience in Focus.* New York: Routledge, 1991.

Harris, Paul, ed. *Civil Disobedience.* Lanham, Md.: University Press of America, 1989.

Clement of Alexandria (c. 160–215)

Titus Flavius Alexandrinus is often regarded as the first Christian theologian and ethicist. His biography by Eusebius of Caesarea (269–340) in *Ecclesiastical History* (6.6–14) is problematic in that it has been embellished by others. Eusebius depicted Clement as the second teacher of the official Christian catechetical school in Alexandria, who instructed Origen (185–c. 254), the controversial theologian whom Eusebius championed.

Eusebius did not indicate where Clement was born or whether he was raised a Christian or converted to Christianity from paganism. It is not clear if he was a member of the clergy or held any official position in a congregation. He reflected only that he traveled extensively and studied with Christian philosophers who came from Italy, Greece, Palestine, and Mesopotamia. Some traditions mention his departure from Egypt during a persecution, his taking refuge with former students in Cappadocia, and his possibly being martyred. It appears that he headed an independent school in Alexandria in which he presented Christianity as the true philosophy. He posited that while the river of truth was broad and that many tributaries from philosophy and world cultures flowed into it, the whole moved toward fulfillment (*syntelia,* or consummation) in knowing God through Jesus. Jesus is God's Word (*Logos*) through whom God made, sustains, guides, and fulfills the cosmos. Clement avoided mentioning eternal punishment, hell, apocalyptic descriptions, a worldwide day of judgment, and a resurrection of physical bodies. He did so by understanding divinity, humanity, and the world through education (*paideia*). His three major works (*Exhortation to the Greeks,* or *Protreptikos, Instructor,* or *Paidagogos,* and *Miscellanies,* or *Stromateis*) plus the tract *Who is the Rich Man Being Saved,* a brief sermon, and notes on a work by a heretical teacher (*Excerpts from Theodotos*) fit into his education, or *paideia,* pattern.

For Clement, education (*paideia* or *paidagogia*) is God's will and program to human salvation. God created nothing that God hates, and, above all, God is human-loving (*philanthropia*). In brief, the *Logos* is in the image and likeness of God, while women and men are in the image of *Logos* and are developing through *paideia* into being in the likeness of *Logos.* Humans are destined to live eternally among the highest rank of angels, ever joyfully learning about and communing with God's love. Adam and Eve were only playful children in Eden, the first classroom. God intended them to develop and move on to higher places. The devil, exploiting their immaturity, misled them into sin (ignorance). Consequently, the primal couple and all their descendants have to go through a rigorous curriculum in this earthly sphere by means of which they are supposed to gain, as much as possible, mastery over their actions, habits, and passions. Students who are relatively successful now are initiated by spiritually enlightened teachers into some of the divine, esoteric higher knowledge (*gnosis*). Those teachers and their advanced students have graduated to a plane of superior self-control and wisdom under the tutelage of *Logos*-inspired teachers. These "true gnostics," as contrasted to heretical, or "false," gnostics, know cosmological secrets and are privy to secret teachings, which *Logos*-Jesus gave to his disciples and which now are to be pulled from Scripture by those who have the eyes and ears to discern them. Because the full course of study is eternal, earthly death is actually a transition to another classroom or campus. Those whose souls are not sufficiently disciplined will not be sent back to earth in a reincarnated form but will have remedial lessons in the next venue. Progress continues until the soul reaches a prepared mansion in the high reaches of the heavens.

Clement only hinted about the heavenly aspects of his teachings because these were part of the esoteric tradition that awaited the initiated. He concentrated on *paideia* in the present. Adapting a melange of middle Platonic and Aristotelian ideas subsumed under biblical auspices (especially Sirach and the Wisdom of Solomon), Clement structured the ethical-pedagogical curriculum in middle Stoic categories. *Logos* was the real Exhorter, Instructor, and Teacher *(Didaskalos)* who spoke through human counterparts. Works by pagan poets, dramatists, and philosophers were criticized on moral grounds but affirmed as vehicles through which truth is conveyed in other cultures. Wherever there is love, goodness, and truth, there the *Logos* had been as the planter and cultivator of God's gifts. While the teacher (both *Logos* and the human counterpart) could speak in tones that ranged from public denunciation and private admonition to ringing praise and gentle comfort, the educational goal always was to aid the person's progress into being the image and likeness of *Logos*. Intellectual attainments were seen as inseparable from a person's growth toward ethical-human excellence. Education, then, is the path to truth, love, and eternal life.

Clement used graphic images (such as the Father's becoming female and *Logos* as the Father's breasts) and gave advice on a myriad of details (such as belching at parties and frequency of bathing). Sometimes he spoke favorably about rival Christian schools that he and others considered heretical, and he praised as well as lampooned pagan philosophers. While these factors could have led to his condemnation, his amiable and deliberately cryptic rhetoric made him too obscure for later authorities to anathematize. Even some modern commentators hold he is more Buddhist than Christian, or on the left wing of orthodoxy teetering over the border into heresy. In the West, he was overshadowed by Augustinian understandings of corrupted human nature. Elements of his views of God and humanity, however, echo in mystics like Meister Eckhart (c. 1260–c. 1327). His works were republished in fifteenth-century Florence, gained some popularity among eighteenth- and nineteenth-century Anglicans, Unitarians, and Methodists, and are receiving attention now. Some contemporary attention is attracted by his rhetoric, while most is connected to Western society's attempts to relate faith to culture and to reaffirm positive dimensions within human nature.

Walter H. Wagner

See also JESUS; *PAIDEIA;* STOICISM

Bibliography
Clement of Alexandria. *Alexandrian Christianity*. Translated by H. Chadwick. Philadelphia: Library of Christian Classics, 1954.
———. *Christ the Educator*. Translated by S. Wood. New York: Fathers of the Church, 1954.
———. "Clement of Alexandria." In *Encyclopedia of Early Christianity*, edited by E. Ferguson, 214–16. New York: Garland, 1990.
Osborn, E. *The Philosophy of Clement of Alexandria*. Cambridge: Cambridge University Press, 1957.
von Campenhausen, H. *Father of the Greek Church*. London: Blackwells, 1962.
Wagner, W.H. *After the Apostles: Christianity in the Second Century*. Minneapolis: Fortress, 1993.

Cognitive Development

The attainment and substantiation of knowledge were concerns of philosophy long before the emergence of psychology as an empirical science. The branch of philosophy known as epistemology was concerned not only with everyday cognition generative of common knowledge, but also with the theoretical cognition represented by both the mathematical knowledge and natural sciences that emerged in the seventeenth century. Descartes (1595–1650) was the first to attempt the substantiation of the entire range of common and theoretical knowledge. Questioning both the reliability of sense perceptions and the truth of the classical philosophy that served as a basis for the natural sciences, Descartes concluded that the only certain knowledge resides in the individual's own subjective state, to which self-consciousness provides immediate access ("I think, therefore I am"). Although Descartes' analysis formed the basis for introspectionist psychology, subjectivist epistemological perspectives in general proved inadequate for an experimental psychology faced with the problem of deducing knowledge about the world of objects from the consciousness of the cognizing subject.

It became increasingly apparent that the cognizing subject is initially confronted with orienting itself within a system of objects and others, and that self-reflection emerges only after the subject has first freed itself from its initial tendency to merge with its surroundings, objectified its own body, and distinguished itself from other subjects as well. Since the cognizing subject and the cognized object exist within a system of relations, differing views concerning the nature of the system were assumed by the various theories of cognition and cognitive development that made their appearance early in the twentieth century.

Behaviorism and Reflexology

Reacting against introspectionism, several variations of physiologically reductionist psychology emerged early in the twentieth century, emphasizing the action of the object on the reactive subject. These included both behaviorism in America and Pavlovian reflexology in the former Soviet Union. Within those systems, complex forms of behavior are considered to progress from simple forms, which result from a response on the part of the subject to a stimulus from the object. Learning is conditioned by positive reinforcement, and sequences of experiences may be programmed in order to direct and facilitate the learning process. Behavioral and reflexological reductionism are epistemologically grounded in the empiricism of John Locke (1632–1704) and reflect a mechanistic world view. Locke identified knowledge with sense perceptions. Phenomena such as optical illusions, or the sensation of pain in an amputated limb, challenge the simplicity of Locke's view. In addition, modern neuropsychological research has identified complex mechanisms involved in the formation of sense perceptions. Also, it is now known that conceptual frameworks can affect what is perceived, so that perception appears to be more of a constructive than a replicative process.

Locke also distinguished between primary and secondary qualities of objects, the former consisting of qualities that inhere in the object, such as color, and the latter designating those that emerge through the action of the object on the subject, such as quantity and form. These latter have been shown to belong to the category of scientific concepts, however, and studies such as David R. Olson's *Cognitive Development: The Child's Acquisition of Diagonality* (1970) document a complex process of conceptual development necessary to attain even the relatively simple understanding of the diagonal of a square. That challenges Locke's notion that such "secondary qualities" can be apprehended at the perceptual or phenomenological level. In addition, acquisition of scientific knowledge is mediated by technological and measurement devices and, as Thomas Kuhn's *Structure of Scientific Revolutions* (1962) reveals, by conceptual and theoretical systems as well. Scientific knowledge is thus unattainable by the empirical abstraction envisioned by Locke, and reductionist psychology is inadequate to account for its development. Finally, quantum physics issues perhaps the ultimate challenge to a theory of knowledge predicated on Lockean empiricism and structural elementalism, in that macroscopic forms perceived as temporally and spatially stable appear to be only temporary instantiations of matter-energy transformations.

More recent investigations into problem-solving behavior through information-processing approaches endeavor to model such behavior on computer operations and employ task analyses that proceed from encoded stimulus dimensions to complex problem-solving processes. These share the same Lockean empiricist-epistemological framework, structural-elementalist philosophical basis, and mechanistic world view as their reductionist predecessors. They have illumined a number of more or less localized cognitive phenomena and revealed important limitations to human memory and information-processing capacity. Their contribution to the understanding of cognitive processes may be expected to increase with the availability of parallel processing, but they continue to reflect the shortcomings of other reductionist-psychological perspectives—that is, the inability to account for the development of the higher psychological functions through what is essentially a bootstrapping approach to human cognition.

Piaget's Theory of Cognitive Development

A radically different theory of cognition was advanced early in the twentieth century by the Swiss psychologist Jean Piaget (1896–1980), who emphasized the active role of the subject in the transformation of the object and posited a biological rather than a mechanistic model of cognition. Piaget wrote voluminously, and his experimental research has contributed greatly to our understanding of the nature of children's interactions with their environment. A biologist whose observations convinced him that organismic development is the result not only of maturation but of adaptation to the environment as well, Piaget extended this biological model to cognitive development. He envisioned cognition progressing through assimilation of or accommodation to the environment, with the subject achieving equilibrium with the environment through the interiorization of actions as stable cognitive operations. Piaget's "genetic epistemology" links cognitive development (the formation of stable and reversible cognitive structures) with progress toward the immutability of object characteristics, and hence, with criteria for the substantiation of knowledge.

In Piaget's theory, the internal formation of cognitive structures progresses through four major stages, beginning in infancy with sensorimotor activity and culminating in adolescence with the formation of formal logical operations. Development is maturational, and learning—which creates a construct rather than a copy of real-world phenomena—is contingent upon the existing level of development. More recent cross-cultural research supports the existence of stagelike periods of cognitive development, although the attainment of the fourth and final stage is problematic in virtually all cultures studied. Further research points to extensions of cognitive ability beyond those characterizing Piagetian stages and suggests inadequacies in the Piagetian tasks themselves. Margaret Donaldson's *Children's Minds* (1978) presents a representational survey of some of this research. A study by R. Gelman (1972), for example, found that children between the ages of three and four years could distinguish between number and perceptual arrangement for a small number of objects. When confronted with the classical Piagetian tasks for conservation of number, however, which require children to notice that the number of objects in a line remains constant whether the objects are arranged close together or far apart, these same children could not discriminate the number of objects from their spatial configuration.

Theories of cognitive development must be critiqued, however, not only with respect to their experimental confirmation, but also in relation to the more generalized philosophical and scientific frameworks within which they are defined. Here Piaget's theory has exhibited internal contradictions, especially with respect to his concept of equilibrium and its relation to general systems theory. Initially defining equilibrium—a concept central to the development of progressively higher cognitive structures—in terms applicable only to closed systems, Piaget was forced to revise his theory, but with somewhat less than satisfactory results. In the attainment of conservation of volume, for example, as a liquid is poured from one container into another that is taller and more narrow, a child's cognitive processes may be described as first successively, then alternately, attending to the stimulus dimensions of container height and width, and finally attaining equilibrium by coordinating both to arrive at the invariance of volume with respect to the shape of the container. Piaget attributes this advancement through a succession of progressively more successful strategies to a lack of satisfaction with prior strategies, thereby introducing an element of subjectivity into what is presumably the interaction of naturalistic systems. Further, the reversibility of cognitive structures that enables the alternate consideration of stimulus dimensions that makes equilibrium possible at the same time places it at variance with its physical analogue, as equilibrium in open systems is generally attained not when the potential for reversibility within the system is maximal, but when the system has reached an irreversible state.

In addition to these problems, the terminus of development envisioned by Piaget has been criticized both for its premature convergence toward formal logic and for being inadequate to represent the full range of thought.

Vygotsky's Theory of Cognitive Development

A third view of cognitive development, proposed by the Russian psychologist Lev Vygotsky (1896–1934), is derived from a theory of activity grounded in the social and historical context of human development. For Vygotsky, the cognizing subject is not only individual but also collective. The forms of knowledge produced by the activity of a cooperating mankind reflect the fully universal categories of thought identified by Aristotle, which transcend the formally general categories produced by the empirical abstraction of phenomenological properties. The former embody scientific as opposed to everyday knowledge, and their appropriation by the individual subject leads the subject's cognitive development. Consequently, Vygotsky's successors argue that the historically objectified forms of knowledge, including semiotic systems such as mathematical notation and language, must become the subject both of epistemological analysis, in order to uncover the laws of their development and formulation, and of psychological analysis in order to reveal the requisite actions through which such knowledge may be appropriated by the individual subject.

Because the genesis of the higher psychological functions follows from the mastery of scientific (but not everyday) concepts, and because scientific concepts are typically introduced in formal educational settings, Vygotsky's theoretical formulations have important pedagogical implications. His successor, V.V. Davydov, in *Types of Generalization in Instruction* (1972/1990), further elucidates the differences between these two types of concepts. Unlike everyday concepts, which can be developed in naturalistic settings and for which Lockean empirical abstraction is sufficient, Davydov asserts that scientific concepts require the development of a theoretical mode of thinking, which is qualitatively discontinuous from the method of empirical abstraction. Schools must deliberately cultivate this mode of thought, which is necessary for cognitive development. Here Vygotsky's theory differs from that of Piaget, which predicates cognitive development on the mastery of everyday concepts, acquired in naturalistic settings, through modes of thinking that do not transcend Lockean empiricism.

Vygotsky is virtually alone among developmental theorists in focusing on higher psychological processes and in deriving from them explanations for the development of lower forms. Indeed, he began his psychological career in 1924 by challenging reflexologists to account for the development of these higher forms and for consciousness itself. Vygotsky, although sharing with Piaget an emphasis on the interiorization of action as cognition, differs from Piaget in viewing cognition as mediated, a view compatible with that of operationalism in physics, which emphasizes the mediatory role of measuring devices in the construction of scientific knowledge. Vygotsky, however, views cognition as mediated by psychological tools, such as semiotic systems which, in contrast to mechanical tools that are directed outward toward mastery of the environment, are instead directed inward toward the subject's mastery of his own behavior in accord with societal norms.

Vygotsky assigns a central role in the development of cognition to language, a psychological tool enabling the interiorization of objective norms of human behavior. When the infant's primitive sounds and grasping gestures are re-warded by adults with the object toward which the child reaches, she responds to the communicative intent attributed to her efforts, developing speech in order to enlist the aid of adults on her behalf. As her ability to communicate progresses, similarly encouraging attributions of conceptual content are made with respect to her verbalizations, though these may reflect only primitive and incomplete levels of conceptualizations despite their correspondence with the forms of adult speech. Through a continuing dialectic between the individual and the social context, both language and concepts move progressively from the interpsychological to the intrapsychological plane. Thus, speech possesses a social function from the beginning, and its progressive interiorization reflects Vygotsky's insistence on the primacy of the social dimension of cognitive development and the derivative nature of individual development. Here again, Vygotsky's theory is in conflict at a deep level with that of Piaget, and their differing interpretations of the phenomenon of egocentric speech highlight the nature of this conflict. Piaget regards this truncated and mainly predicative speech as an undeveloped form reflecting the child's egocentrism prior to the emergence of its communicative function. Vygotsky views speech as social from its incipience, and egocentric speech as an abbreviated form appearing prior to the internalization of speech to the plane of thought. His research found children unable to execute multistep problem-solving tasks successfully when deprived of the opportunity to use egocentric speech, which they employed to direct their own activity.

Vygotsky also identified a zone of proximal development with respect to scientific concepts in particular. Within this zone, which marked the distance between a subject's actual and potential development, the subject could, through dialectical interactions with one more knowledgeable, accomplish intellectual tasks that he would only later be capable of performing independently. The learning taking place within the zone of proximal development again reflects movement from the interpsychological to the intrapsychological plane, and provides additional evidence of the influence of Hegelian dialectics on Vygotsky's theory of cognitive development. From a Vygotskian perspective, testing in educational settings, rather than assessing the subject's mastery of everyday concepts, ought to determine the zone of proximal development for scientific concepts.

Clearly, the field of cognitive development

is in a preparadigmatic state in the Kuhnian sense, and it is arguable whether its competing theories are even mutually translatable, because they reflect differing philosophical perspectives. However, it is interesting that Vygotsky not only put forth a critique of the psychologies of his day that many believe is still apt, but also set out to formulate a metatheoretical basis for psychology. This goal has still not been achieved, and attempts to merge aspects of the various theories of cognitive development more often reflect a superficial eclecticism than a true integration within which each perspective might be reinterpreted while retaining its own contributory validity.

However, activity within the field of cognitive development, both theoretical and experimental, has reflexively impacted the epistemological presumptions of antiquity from whose foundations psychology emerged as a science. Like mathematics, the pure scientific knowledge for which it attempted to account, epistemology has become subject to foundational revision. Mathematics, presumed from antiquity to represent absolute truth about the real world until challenged by the non-Euclidean geometries of the nineteenth century, attempted unsuccessfully to reestablish its foundations on logic and formalism in the twentieth century. The historical account of the two-hundred-year proof of Euler's theorem, presented in Imre Lakatos's *Proofs and Refutations* (1976), reveals the social nature of the construction of mathematical knowledge. Similarly, through its own activity as an emergent science, cognitive development has challenged epistemological assumptions dating back to antiquity. Vygotsky's views, especially, suggest that epistemological norms for the substantiation of knowledge cannot be metaphysically posited, but must be sought where they are established, within the sociohistorical process of cognitive development itself.

Jean Schmittau

See also BEHAVIORISM; DESCARTES; EPISTEMOLOGY; LEARNING, THEORIES OF; LOCKE; MORAL DEVELOPMENT

Bibliography

Davydov, V.V. *Types of Generalization in Instruction: Logical and Psychological Problems in the Structuring of School Curricula*. Reston, Va.: National Council of Mathematics, 1990.

Donaldson, Margaret. *Children's Minds.* New York: Norton, 1978.

Gelman, R. "Logical Capacity of Very Young Children: Number Invariance Rules." *Child Development* 43 (1972): 75–90.

Kuhn, Thomas S. *The Structure of Scientific Revolutions*. Chicago: University of Chicago Press, 1962.

Lakatos, Imre. *Proofs and Refutations*. Cambridge: Cambridge University Press, 1976.

Olson, David R. *Cognitive Development: The Child's Acquisition of Diagonality*. New York: Academic Press, 1970.

Piaget, J. *The Principles of Genetic Epistemology*. New York: Basic Books, 1972.

Vygotsky, Lev. *Thought and Language*. Cambridge: M.I.T. Press, 1986.

C

Colonialism and Post-Colonialism

Colonialism is primarily a political and economic system in which a technologically powerful country conquers and then rules or settles other countries, called colonies, for its own profit. Such a system creates its own forms of knowledge, based on the assumption that the colonizing power must be superior to those colonized. Although there have always been empires based on some form of colonialism throughout human history, the term *colonialism* is most often used today to refer to the age of European expansion that began with Columbus's voyage to America in 1492 and experienced its heyday in the period from 1875 to 1947. Eurocentrism (the prejudiced belief in the superiority of Europe) is the justifying ideology of this form of colonialism, and capitalism is its motive force.

The terms *imperialism* and *colonialism* are often used interchangeably, particularly in referring to the European empires of the nineteenth century that were gradually dismantled after the Second World War. However, unlike colonialism, imperialism need not involve the establishment of actual colonies (subordinate territories governed from the imperial center). Today, the term *imperialism* is often used to refer to a capitalist penetration and dominance of other markets that no longer relies on a formally established colonialism. This new system of imperialism is often termed neocolonialism, recognizing that it has been made possible by the former colonial system it is replacing. Under colonialism, power was maintained through direct control of the government, military, and other institutions of the colony. Under neocolonialism, this control is exerted in less open fashion through international money markets, the World Bank and the International Monetary Fund, and the news media. Media penetration of the margins from the center is often termed cultural imperialism.

Whereas the term *neocolonialism* refers specifically to continuing economic dominance of former colonies after official decolonization, the term *postcolonialism* is both wider and vaguer in its reference. It is more proper to speak of various postcolonialisms. Each academic discipline employs the term differently, and no consensus has yet been reached, even within individual disciplines. Historians see postcolonialism in relation to time, as the period following official decolonization. But others use it for the study of colonialism and its aftermath, stressing the complicity and continuity between the two terms. Some thinkers within anthropology, geography, or literature, may use the term *postcolonialism* in relation to place. For them, it involves study of the entire culture and history of those parts of the world once colonized. Some omit settler-invader colonies from its terms of reference, using the term *postcolonial* interchangeably with the term *Third World*. Some apply the term to people, but disagree about which people: It is sometimes applied to everyone living within formerly colonized territory; it sometimes refers to everyone belonging to formerly colonized races and ethnic groups, even if they live within an imperial center. Or it may be reserved to describe migrant intellectuals from former colonies now living in metropolitan centers. Each of these usages marks out the boundaries of postcolonialism as a field of study.

But even more controversially, postcolonialism may also refer to a particular methodology, committed to decolonizing Western understanding of other cultures and of itself, understandings that were distorted by colonial assumptions of European superiority and by the colonial interventions they justified. In Africa, Chinua Achebe and wa Thiong'o Ngugi have analyzed the tyranny of English as literature and language, while in the Caribbean Frantz Fanon and Edward Kamau Brathwaite have revealed the denigrating images of Africans and of their history and language in French and English culture respectively. Edward Said has initiated such a study on a more ambitious scale in the West by arguing that "Orientalism" was a Western style of knowledge "for dominating, restructuring, and having authority over the Orient" (*Orientalism*: 3). To initiate a decolonizing methodology, some follow Said in focusing on the discursive systems of the colonizer, leading to the subdiscipline of "colonial discourse analysis" (study of the linguistic system structuring writing and speech—what can and cannot be thought, under colonialism). Alternatively, study may focus on the dynamic of relations between colonizer and colonized, stressing psychoanalytic readings of ambivalence, complicity, or mimicry, or more overt acts of resistance or opposition. Finally, such study may choose to downplay the role of the colonizer, to highlight instead the autonomous achievements of the colonized, before, after, and during colonization.

Although postcolonialism as a new cross-disciplinary field of study has been criticized as a potential master narrative for homogenizing world cultures, it can also be used to reaffirm local cultural differences that were denied under colonialism. Many postcolonial studies investigate the different forms of colonialism practiced by the various European colonial powers and acknowledge that, even within a single empire, different kinds of colonies were established. In settler-invader colonies, such as the United States (a colony before independence in 1776), Canada, Australia, Latin America, and New Zealand, genocide was practiced against the indigenous populations, who were displaced and marginalized and their languages and cultural practices forbidden. In Australia and North America, residential schools for Native children were designed to facilitate full assimilation into the dominant imported culture. The plantation economies of the Caribbean and the South Pacific were based on imported slave and indentured labor. An imported European educational system suppressed Creole speech and denied African, Asian, and indigenous cultural achievements. In India, colonialism developed over several centuries, with the colonizer recognizing, ambivalently, the achievements of Oriental scholarship and establishing a dual educational system, one in English and the other in indigenous languages. In Africa, where indigenous cultural achievements went largely unappreciated, foreign rule never fully penetrated the fabric of local life, but took on radically different forms across the continent. West Africa was disrupted by the slave trade; South

Africa, Zimbabwe (formerly Rhodesia), and Kenya, by white settlement. Further differences arose from the priorities of the different colonizing powers.

Yet despite these differences, education remained in each instance an important tool for the manufacturing of consent under colonialism. Therefore, the implications of postcolonialism for the philosophy of education are substantial. The impact should be felt at several levels: in terms of disciplinary methodologies and values, curriculum design, institutional reform, and pedagogical practice.

Many modern disciplines, such as anthropology, art history, and English, attained academic status during the height of colonialism, and all were shaped in their current forms by the ideologies of colonialism. As postcolonial critics study the colonial histories of their disciplines, they are questioning ethnographic practices employing fieldwork and the use of "native informants," as well as assumptions about orality and literacy that have led to damaging cultural generalizations. The role of colonialism in the rise of modernism and its contribution to theories of nationalism and racism are now being examined. Similar work is being undertaken within scientific theory and applied science technology, medicine, and public health policy to understand how colonialist assumptions within these disciplines have affected racial, sexual, national, and international relations within the postcolonial world (see Alvarez, Bishop, and Meade and Walker).

Modern educational institutions as varied as the Boy Scout movement, art galleries, museums, schools, journals like *National Geographic,* and the literary canon, all require rethinking in light of their participation in colonialist assumptions about value. There is tremendous potential within postcolonial studies for developing a revised curriculum, taught through a redesigned pedagogy that rejects authoritarian structures, within a more multiculturally diverse and inclusive educational system, all of which together might make possible a "decolonizing of the mind" (Ngugi).

Diana Brydon

See also ANTHROPOLOGY; CRITICAL THEORY; FEMINISM; GANDHI; LITERACY; MINORITIES; MODERNISM AND POST-MODERNISM; MULTICULTURALISM; NATIONALISM; RACE AND RACISM; SLAVERY

Bibliography

Achebe, Chinua. *Morning Yet on Creation Day: Essays.* Garden City: Anchor Press, 1975.

Alvarez, Claude. *Decolonizing History: Technology and Culture in India, China and the West 1492 to the Present Day.* New York: Apex Press, 1991.

Aschroft, Bill, Gareth Griffiths, and Helen Tiffin. *The Empire Writes Back: Theory and Practice in Post-Colonial Literatures.* London and New York: Routledge, 1989.

Bishop, Alan J. "Western Mathematics: The Secret Weapon of Cultural Imperialism." *Race and Class* 32, no. 2 (October–December 1990): 51–65.

Brathwaite, Edward Kamau. *History of the Voice: The Development of Nation Language in Anglophone Caribbean Poetry.* London: New Beacon, 1984.

Carnoy, M. *Education as Cultural Imperialism.* London: Longman, 1974.

Fanon, Frantz. *Black Skin, White Masks.* Translated by Charles Lam Markmann. New York: Grove, 1967.

Mangan, J.A., ed. *The Imperial Curriculum: Racial Images and Education in the British Colonial Experience.* New York and London: Routledge, 1993.

Meade, Teresa, and Mark Walker, eds. *Science, Medicine and Cultural Imperialism.* New York: St. Martin's Press, 1991.

Nandy, Ashis. *The Intimate Enemy: Loss and Recovery of Self under Colonialism.* New York: Oxford University Press, 1983.

Ngugi, wa Thiong'o. *Decolonising the Mind: The Politics of Language in African Literature.* London: James Currey, 1986.

Said, Edward. *Orientalism.* New York: Vintage, 1979.

Trinh, T. Minh-ha. *Woman, Native, Other: Writing Postcoloniality and Feminism.* Bloomington and Indianapolis: Indiana University Press, 1989.

Viswanathan, Gauri. *Masks of Conquest: Literary Study and British Rule in India.* New York: Columbia University Press, 1989.

Young, Robert. *White Mythologies: Writing History and the West.* London and New York: Routledge, 1990.

Comedy

We know little about the earliest history of comedy because, according to Aristotle, it was not at first considered to be as significant a genre as tragedy. Aristotle, however, was aware that comedy evolved from a primitive form consisting of satiric lampoons to the dramatic representation of "the ridiculous." He recognized Homer's lost epic the *Margites* as having played a critical role, analogous to the relationship of the *Iliad* and the *Odyssey* to tragedy, in this evolution of the genre toward a mature dramatic form.

In the *Poetics* Aristotle does not treat comedy fully, but he does offer a concise and perceptive framework for establishing a theory of conduct. (A document of unknown origin and unusual in content and form, the *Tractatus Coislinianus* purports to offer an Aristotelian theory of comedy, but it clashes in significant detail with statements made about comedy in the *Poetics;* its actual relationship to Aristotelian theory is controversial.) Aristotle informs us that comedy is representation of inferior *(phauloi)* human beings, not inferior in regard to every kind of vice but in regard to the "ridiculous," which is a species of psychological or physical ugliness. For Aristotle, an important characteristic of the "ridiculous," is that, although it involves spiritual or physical deformity, it does not cause pain; he cites the comic masks of Greek actors to illustrate his point.

For other theorists, such as Henri Bergson (1859–1941) and Sigmund Freud (1856–1939) an element of pain is or can be involved in comedy. Bergson argued that the essential purpose of comedy is to punish and alter the mechanical and rigid behavior of individuals whose actions frustrate society. Societal laughter, Bergson argues, is a potent weapon to force such individuals, the world's hypocrites, lechers, misers, and so on, to conform to the needs and standards of society. Freud perceived that comedy can be used to express aggression and degrade another human being. C.L. Barber, followed by Erich Segal, emphasized the escapist aspect of at least some kinds of comedy, and Segal cites the description of comedy by psychiatrist Ernst Kris: a "holiday for the superego." Students of comic theory generally recognize that two fundamental principles lie at the core of our response to comedy: (1) a sense of *superiority* evoked by our exposure to the representation of comic action and character, and (2) a recognition of the incongruity and inappropriateness of that comic action and character.

Comedy reached a high point of development in the Greco-Roman period. Greek "Old Comedy," represented for us today only by the extant work of Aristophanes (middle of the fifth century to early fourth century B.C.), offers an almost unrestrictedly sharp satire of Athenian politics and society. Examples are the savage attack on sophistry in the *Clouds* and the incisive critique of Athens's conduct of the Peloponnesian War in the *Lysistrata*. Comedy of this type required considerable tolerance for free artistic expression, and that tolerance came to an end after Athens was defeated in 404 B.C. Old Comedy was succeeded by "Middle Comedy," which began, and "New Comedy," which completed, the process of turning away from political and social satire to the representation of comic character, action, and manners. The greatest writer of Greek New Comedy was Menander (342/1–293/89 B.C.). We know his work best from the twentieth century discovery of a nearly complete play, the *Dyskolos,* a representation of the archetypal comic misanthrope.

The greatest writers of Roman comedy, Plautus (c. 254–184 B.C.) and Terence (c. 190–159 B.C.) both were significantly influenced by Greek New Comedy but made differing adaptations of this source. Plautus, for the most part, developed a comic style that emphasized farcical action and ridiculous characters, although it is also possible to discern in some of his works a more serious, darker representation of humanity. Terence for the most part avoids extreme farce and concentrates on a more sober comedy of manners.

Roman comedy exercised a strong influence on the development of later, European comedy. Lodovico Ariosto (1474–1533) and Niccolo Machiavelli (1469–1527) created an Italian comic form that was modeled on Roman comedy. Machiavelli used Plautus's *Casina,* recognized as one of that author's dark comedies, as the basis of his *La Clizia.* While still employing many of the external characteristics of Roman comedy, he went well beyond the originals in his exploration of human corruptibility in *La Mandragola.* The themes and characters used by the great Spanish dramatist Lope de Vega (1562–1635) are often similar to those regularly found in Roman comedy. Roman models were used by a number of early French writers, and Moliere (1622–1763), one of the greatest of all comic dramatists, made significant use of Roman comedy by adapting a number of classical plots to his own use. One of his masterpieces,

L'Avare, is based on Plautus's *Aulularia* but creates situations and characters of far greater psychological complexity and emotional depth. From its inception, English comedy reflected its debt to Roman comedy, and that influence can be traced in the work of the greatest English comic dramatists. Both William Shakespeare (1564–1616) (see, for example, *The Comedy of Errors)* and Ben Jonson (c. 1573–1637) (see, for example, *Every Man in His Humour* and *Volpone)* creatively adapted Roman models for their own unique purposes.

Interest in works of art that represent the "ridiculous" in character and action remains strong in more recent times and indicates that comedy, like tragedy, has universal human appeal and relevance. This interest is evident in regard to both its farcical and escapist dimensions, as well as its more serious and darker aspects. Popular culture, through much that appears on film and television, offers, of course, a superabundance of escapist comedy. In the comic dramas, however, of such nineteenth- and twentieth-century artists as Anton Chekhov and George Bernard Shaw, and in a number of important films, such as Woody Allen's *Crimes and Misdemeanors*, we recognize that the role of comedy as an insightful commentary on humanity's foibles and as an instrument of trenchant social criticism is very much alive and well.

Leon Golden

See also TRAGEDY

Bibliography

Barber, C.L. *Shakespeare's Festive Comedy: A Study of Dramatic Form and Its Relation to Social Custom*. Princeton: Princeton University Press, 1959.

Bergson, Henri. "Laughter." In *Comedy*, edited by W. Sypher. Garden City, N.Y.: Doubleday, Anchor Books, 1956.

Duckworth, George. *The Nature of Roman Comedy: A Study in Popular Entertainment*. Princeton: Princeton University Press, 1971.

Feibleman, James. *In Praise of Comedy*. New York: Horizon Press, 1970.

Freud, Sigmund. *Jokes and Their Relations to the Unconscious*. Translated by J. Strachey. New York: W.W. Norton, 1963.

Golden, Leon. *Aristotle on Tragic and Comic Mimesis*. Atlanta: Scholars Press, 1992.

Heilman, Robert. *The Ways of the World: Comedy and Society*. Seattle: University of Washington Press, 1978.

Janko, Richard. *Aristotle on Comedy: Towards a Reconstruction of Poetics II*. Berkeley and Los Angeles: University of California Press, 1984.

Kern, Edith. *The Absolute Comic*. New York: Columbia University Press, 1980.

Konstan, David. *Roman Comedy*. Ithaca, N.Y.: Cornell University Press, 1983.

Levin, Harry. *Playboys and Killjoys: An Essay on the Theory and Practice of Comedy*. New York: Oxford University Press, 1987.

Nelson, T.G.A. *Comedy: An Introduction to Comedy in Literature, Drama, and Cinema*. Oxford and New York: Oxford University Press, 1990.

Segal, Erich. *Roman Laughter: The Comedy of Plautus*. Cambridge: Harvard University Press, 1970.

Torrance, Robert. *The Comic Hero*. Cambridge: Harvard University Press, 1978.

Comenius, John Amos (1592–1670)

Czech educator, philosopher and theologian, and social reformer. His work was a remarkable contribution to the reform of education in seventeenth-century Europe, a great endeavor to change society into a peaceful, harmonious, creative, and cooperating community. Although Comenius's projects to reform education simultaneously with far-reaching social reconstruction were utopian in his time, his concept of a universal culture of all individuals and the whole of society succeeded in indicating a relevant line of European thought.

His respect for education and his yearning to reform education and society grew from his life experience before, during, and after the Thirty Years' War (1618–1648). His various literary inspirations were in Antiquity and Christianity as interpreted in Renaissance, humanist, and Reformation thought.

In his native Moravia, Comenius showed an interest in the problems of teaching, in the improvement of social, religious, and political life, and in encyclopedic activities designed to enrich the national culture. After the successful struggle to create the Czech state of Estates (the model for the Netherlands), Bohemia and Moravia lost political, religious, and cultural freedom. With the Protestant majority, Comenius became an outcast in his homeland, and, in 1628, after the sharpest edict against non-Catholics, he was also forced into exile. He then worked in Poland (1628–1656), in England (1641–1642), and for the reform of Swedish schools (1642–1648), establishing a pansophical school in Sarospatak (1650–1654) and, between 1656 and 1670, in Amsterdam.

In the period between 1620 and 1630, in urgent need to find a way out of so many labyrinths of life, his approach to the problems of the time became more profound. He came close to the Neoplatonism he found in Augustine, in N. Cusanus, Paracelsus, J. Boehme, the Rosicrucians, J.V. Andreae, and others. Simultaneously, Comenius found himself strengthened in the conviction current in the Unitas Fratrum that it is necessary to begin with man himself if we want to deal with inhumanities, with all that goes to ruin life; it is necessary to begin with education—complete, thorough, and effective.

After writing about the importance of the inner transformation of man by self-sacrificing love *(The Labyrinth of the World and the Paradise of the Heart)* and the necessity of getting rid of violence, selfishness, superficiality, and partiality, seeking the road toward highest perfection, which is God *(Centrum securitatis),* and after producing several other works, Comenius began to write his *Didactic* (1627—1630).

In the Neoplatonic conception, Comenius saw man as an integral part of a world that is an organic, harmonic entity, likened to a tree with the roots in God, from whom flow wisdom, goodness, and strength, and in whom man can find perfection, certainty, and order. Facing the problem of evil in the world, Comenius stressed the idea that evil cannot be attributed to God but to men and their failure to grow in the image of God. Unlike the Lutheran conception but close to that of the Czech Reformation, what is called for by Comenius is activity preceded by thorough self-examination. This line of thought reappears in his observations on human history and the role given to man within cosmic development. As an image of the Creator, man has been awarded a chance for creative activity. Comenius emphasized the role of Jesus as a Redeemer who had made it possible for all men and women to redeem man's falling away from his original unity with God. Therefore, to play a part in the redemption is also a religious duty of all men. In his stress on human activity, Comenius came close to Francis Bacon, who inspired him to seek a unified method that could not be offered by encyclopedism. Similarly, he found the reform of Latin learning and teaching a part of the reform of education in general.

In his *Didactic,* written in Czech as a theoretical part of his first project to reform education and society in his homeland, Comenius made the philosophy of man in man's relation to the entire world a basis for proposed educational principles of certain, easy, thorough, concise, and rapid learning and teaching. This philosophy was later called *pansophia* (the word used also by the Rosicrucians). Pansophy became philosophy of the world, philosophy of man and man's education. By pansophy's clear demand that all should be educated in schools in all things essential for human life, in all ways corresponding to man's natural development, and by all means that respect it, Comenius went much further than his contemporaries. These educational principles (later called *omnes omnia omnino*) answered the question of who should be educated, in what subjects, and how. According to those principles, a firm system of the goals, content, and methods of education needed to be developed. Well-organized schools should be everywhere, and education should start right after the birth of the child (while also respecting the child's prenatal period) and continue in elementary school (based on the vernacular), in Latin secondary school, and in the academy. All schools should become "workshops of humanity" *(officinae humanitatis).* The Czech *Didactic* represents the first phase of the Comenian philosophy of education, a philosophy of national education. It was meant to educate all the children of the Czech nation.

The content and methods of education should correspond, too, to the structure of the world as a whole—Nature, man, and God. In getting to know Nature, the human world, and God, it is necessary to develop typically human qualities—reason, speech, and conscious acting—and to develop the intellectual, moral, and religious capacities. The meaning of pansophy, as applied to education, was not only epistemological (the search for the maximum of knowledge), but also moral, social, and religious. Comenius believed in the panharmony of the universe. This led him to seek the harmonious order, where observation is most readily possible—Nature—since parallelism between the strata of the universe can be discovered by syncrisis, a particular way of comparison, revealing the relationships in the world. That is why the educational principles of the *Didactic* are based on the conception that art should imitate Nature; it should go from the simple to the more complex, from that which is near to that which is farther away, to work by degrees and without sharp leaps—all that goes to make up the natural method. If the macrocosm had evolved from the lowest forms in Nature to the higher human level and on to the highest, the spiritual, then Comenius concluded that the same procedure must apply to the microcosm, starting from physical and sensory abilities and going on to higher expressions of the ways in which man is superior to the other creatures—to the training of the mind, of speech, of skills to act, to work.

Neoplatonist ideas led Comenius to stress the idea of the whole, an a priori religious and idealistic concept. However, applying syncrisis to education, he also adopted the a posteriori approach: moving from the senses to reason, from the physical to the spiritual, from the concrete to the abstract, from learning the mother tongue to learning foreign languages, from preschool to school education. Not only in his *Didactic* but also in his theory of preschool education (the first six years of a child's age)—that is, in the Czech School of Infancy (1632; *Informatorium skoly materske*)—Comenius proved to be an empirical psychologist, respecting each child as a personality, as we would put it today, and stressing the significance of childhood. He was aware of individual differences in development, of talents and capabilities, and was ready to deal with children afflicted with various handicaps. He firmly believed that every individual is capable of being educated, even if the results are not always of the same standard because of differences in previous development, home background, and so forth. His belief in innate ideas meant that everybody, as the image of God and as an integral part of the harmonious macrocosm, has a chance to develop into humanity. He saw the importance of activity not only in what it does to develop the body and the senses, but as an essential element in the training of the mind, in ethical and social education. He recommended play as one of the best means to education—collective games.

At a time when children were generally regarded as miniature adults and education was viewed as an artificial process of passing on knowledge mainly by word of mouth, Comenius came forward with the idea that the specific characteristics of childhood from birth to six years should be taken into account. He developed and systematized some ideas of the humanists, the Baconian stress on the unity of things and words. Bacon was searching for a uniform approach to perform research into natural laws, while Comenius sought the key to all-round development of body and mind, theory and practice, individual and society. For school education, he was founder of the class as a unit, with pupils of the same age and with one teacher instructing and paying attention to individual differences and, on the other hand, to the whole of the curriculum, which should include selected results of human culture. Comenius combined the sensualist, empiricist, and rationalist approaches, and stressed activity and utility for life, with careful division of time for effective teaching. His metaphor of school as a clock, or as a well-oiled machine, expressed his belief in order and discipline. At the same time, the harmony between the intentions of the educator and the natural development of the child showed that education should be a vital process in its own right.

Among his manifold activities while in exile, Comenius was constantly improving on his educational conceptions. Between 1630 and 1641, the second phase in his philosophy of education developed. When the hope to return home disappeared, he translated the Czech *Didactic* into international Latin (1638, published in 1657 as *Didactica magna*) to offer this theory of education for the benefit of all nations, to educate all children and youth in all nations.

At the same time, the Latin text was supplemented and somewhat revised. The recommendation concerning the stages of schooling was developed in several chapters into a system of schooling in periods of six years, from birth until twenty-four years of age: preschool education in the family, primary school in the vernacular, secondary Latin school, academy (or university), including traveling. The revision concerned a deeper application of pansophy to the content of education. Comenius stressed the understanding of interrelations between the whole and its particular parts, the understanding of causes and their essential features; everything must be presented in general, not only in particular. Language was considered in its general meaning, as an instrument of acquiring knowledge, wisdom, and education to be passed on to others.

Now Comenius considered the application of pansophy to the content of education and pansophy as a more complex methodology in two ways. The curriculum *(omnia)* was planned as (a) the selection from the knowledge of individual things and phenomena; and (b) the selection from the knowledge of general principles on which the world is built. Suggesting that reality is a highly complex phenomenon, a complex methodology—a combination of analysis, synthesis, induction and deduction, and syncrisis (comparisons)—was elaborated for presenting the curriculum. For all-round education of everybody *(omnino)*, the interrelations between *ratio* (beginning with sensual education), *oratio,* and *operatio* were deeply considered. Human creative activity, work (developing from play), was stressed as the criterion of improvement. Man by his own activity was to lay the foundations for future regeneration of all human beings. Practice was an important criterion of the theory.

Comenius realized task (a) by means of his *Janua linguarum* (1631), a language textbook (later accompanied by a grammar) based on factual knowledge of individual things or phenomena of the natural, human, and divine world, with the criterion of utility and profit to human life. The conception of the textbook corresponded to contemporary requirements to integrate the teaching of things and words, and *Janua linguarum* was enormously successful, then as well as in later centuries. So was the whole system of textbooks for younger pupils *(Vestibulum)* and for advanced pupils *(Atrium)*. Comenius called the whole project for Latin study *Templum latinitatis*. It also included the training of teachers *(Didactica dissertatio,* 1637), school dramas (such as *Diogenes cynicus redivivus)*, and later, *Schola ludus*.

Much more difficult was task (b) as elaborated in *Janua rerum,* a textbook of philosophy presenting a selection of general principles. To remove the fragmentation and scattering of knowledge, and to combat the one-sided specialization of the branches of knowledge ("separate kingdoms") and the lack of integration in the subjects of the school curriculum, Comenius outlined this aspect of pansophy in *Prodromus pansophiae (Pansophiae praeludium,* 1637). Later this aspect was called pansophical metaphysics, which should present all branches of knowledge with a methodological, philosophical basis. He believed that such a general foundation would help prevent the disputes and misunderstandings between scholars working in different fields, and that science would thereby

not avoid problems of human life, both individual and social. Pansophical metaphysics differed from all traditional metaphysical conceptions; in the methodological function, it resembled Bacon's *prima philosophia,* in the stress on the practice in Bacon's metaphysics. However, pansophy did not concern the problems of a better knowledge only, but of the whole man. Every individual should realize that all human activity requires a philosophy of life: the meaning of life, both in general and in particular activities. Unlike Bacon or other contemporary philosophers, Comenius did not believe that liberating human reason would suffice to bring happiness to mankind. Pansophical metaphysics should help integrate general education and specialization. This was an innovation to which the time turned a deaf ear. Disagreement with contemporary scientists and theologians, because of the broad and many-sided function of pansophy, led him to defend his pansophy *(Pansophiae dilucidatio)*. This work delayed the editing of *Didactica magna*.

Nevertheless, Comenius did not give up pansophy but developed it in still a deeper and broader way in the third stage of his philosophy of education. This began during his stay in England (1641–1642), where educational and social reform was discussed during the revolution. In *Via lucia* (1642, edited in 1668), Comenius outlined the reform of education connected with the reform of the whole society. Then, simultaneously with his work for school reform in Sweden (1642–1648), he elaborated his greatest work, in which the third stage was fully contained—*The General Consultation on the Reform of Human Affairs (De rerum humanarum emendatione consultatio catholica,* 1643–1670, edited in 1966), in seven parts *(Panegersia, Panaugia, Pansophia* or *Pantaxia, Pampaedia, Panglottia, Panorthosia, Pannuthesia)*.

Within *Consultatio* the aspects of the philosophy of education, *omnes omnia omnino,* were called *cultura universalis, (Pampaedia),* a process as well as the result of developing full humanity in every individual. In social wholes— family, school, state, church, *(Panorthosia)*—by the reform of all human affairs, but especially the main ones—philosophy, politics, religion; by means of international communication in language understandable to all (world languages or an international language, *Panglottia,* and by means of international bodies for spreading education to help underdeveloped nations (college of light), for political peace (court of justice), for religious peace *(consistorium oecumenicum, Panorthosia),* full humanity is to be pursued. *Omnes* here meant the lifelong education of "every human being born on earth" in the schools of life; reform of human affairs based on avoiding past mistakes in social development.

The whole of human life was divided into eight schools of life: the school of birth (prenatal period), school of early childhood or infancy (first six years of age), school of childhood, school of adolescence, school of youth, school of adult age, school of old age, school of death. All schools are bound by the common principles of knowing the world, as explained in *Pantaxia,* the interrelation between general and particular things and phenomena, of developing all the qualities directed toward full humanity, and relationships between children, adults, and the elderly. In all the schools of life the hierarchy of right values obtains, for this is what raises life above mere consumerism while avoiding one-sided intellectualism with no human warmth. The specific problems of each school of life relate to the context of the whole, to the meaning of life, for common good.

That is why Comenius stressed respect for life and the defense of it and why he wanted man not only to master Nature but also to take care of it and to master himself. He supplemented his concept of interrelations between intellect, speech, and acting by the requirement to educate will, feeling, and conscience. He did not want to investigate the processes of human mind only (like Rene Descartes) but the process of how man becomes positively human. Having characterized man as a being of liberal action, Comenius appreciated freedom as belonging to the essentials of humanity, so that to deny it was to do violence to the very essence of human nature. However, freedom must not become arbitrary: A lack of order leading to anarchy is as harmful as the lack of freedom is, both individually and socially. Education should help human beings correctly use their wills on the basis of understanding causes, similarities, differences, and the manner of existence of things and phenomena. The relation of freedom and order, spontaneity and discipline, was central to Comenian educational philosophy: The greater use made of creative human activity, the more man's desire for knowledge; and if varied and pleasureful employment is afforded, the more effectively can we ensure that people do not feel any contradiction between freedom and disciplined order. The triads to know, to will, and to

be able to act, and universality, essentiality, and spontaneity, became more and more important principles in *Consultatio,* a part of always more deeply elaborated principles of the interrelations between the whole and the parts, the general and the particular, and a more deeply considered concept of human nature.

These principles became evident also in educational works written as a part of *Consultatio* after 1643: in *Methodus linguarum novissima* (1648), discussing the interrelations between philosophy of language and the practice and general methodology of education; in the particular didactics of language *(Schola pansophica),* stating the interrelations between general and specialized education and gathering fresh powers in rest or recreation; in *De culture ingeniorum oratio* (1651), summarizing the results of education in schools as workshops of humanity; in *Orbis pictus,* the most successful, illustrated, textbook by Comenius (1654); in *E. scholasticis labyrinthis exitus in planum* (1657); in *Paradisus juventuti christianae reducendus* (1657); and in many other writings collected by the author in the third and fourth part of *Opera didactica omnia* (1657–1658).

While the interest in the pansophical textbooks by Comenius was great in his century and in later ones, one-sided rationalist thinkers rejected his pansophical philosophy of education, with his conception of education for all, based on a philosophy of life, with the many-sided function of pansophy aiming at an integration of all human activities—theory, practice, and his methodological concept of the whole. The prophets of the ideal of humanity in the late eighteenth and nineteenth centuries (J.G. Herder, K. Ch. Fr. Krause, Fr. Palacky, and others) began to appreciate Comenius as a philosopher. After the discovery of the whole *Consultatio* (1934) and the first publication of the complete text, the educational philosophy of Comenius could be supplemented.

Dagmar Capkova

See also BACON; DESCARTES; HUMAN NATURE

Bibliography

Blekastad, Milada. *Comenius.* Versuch eines Umrisses von Leben, Werk und Schicksal des Jan Amos Komesky. Oslo, Universitetsforlaget-Praha: Academia, 1969.

Capkova, Dagmar. *Myslitelsko-Vychovatelsky Odkaz Jana Amose*

Komenskeho. Philosophical and Educational Heritage of Jan Amos Komensky. Phaha: Academia, 1987.

———, Jaromir Cervenka, Pavel Floss, and Robert Kalivoda. *The Philosophical Significance of the Work of Comenius*, 5-16. Acta Comeniana 8/32. Praha: Academic, 1989.

Comenius, John Amos. *De Rerum Humanarum Emandatione Consultatio Catholica*. 2 folio vol. Praha: Academia, 1966.

———. *The Great Didactic*. Translated and edited by M.W. Keating. London: Adam and Charles Black, 1896.

———. *Obecna Porado o Naprave Veci Lidskych*. De Rerum Humanarum Emendatione Consultatio Catholica. 3 vols. Praha: Nakladatelstivi Svoboda, 1992.

———. *Opera Omnia*. Dilo J.A. Komenskeho. Vols. 1, 2, 3, 4, 9, 11, 12, 13, 14, 15, 17, 18, 23. Praha: Academia, 1969– .

———. *Pampaedia. Allerziehung*. In deutscher Übersetzung herausgegeben von Klaus Schaller. Sankt Augustin: Academia Verlag, 1991. Veroffentlichungen der Comeniusforschungstelle im Institut fur Padagogik der Ruhr-Universitat Bochum.

———. *Pampaedia or Universal Education*. Translated by A.M.O. Dobbie. London: Buckland Publications, 1986.

———. *Panaugia or Universal Light*. Translated by A.M.O. Dobbie. Shipston-on-Stour: Peter I. Drinkwater, 1989.

———. *Panegersia or Universal Awakening*. Translated by A.M.O. Dobbie. Shipston-on-Stour: Peter I. Drinkwater, 1990.

———. *Panglottia or Universal Language*. Translated by A.M.O. Dobbie: Shipston-on-Stour: Peter I. Drinkwater, 1990.

———. *Panguthesia or Universal Warning*. Translated by A.M.O. Dobbie. Shipston-on-Stour: Peter I. Drinkwater, 1991.

———. *Panorthosia or Universal Reform*. Chapters 19 and 26. Translated by A.M.O. Dobbie. Sheffield: Academic Press, 1993.

———. *Selections*. Introduction by Jean Piaget. Paris: Unesco, 1957.

Homage to J.A. Comenius. Edited by J. Peskova, J. Cach, and M. Svatos. Praha: Univerzita Karlova, 1991.

Jan Amos Comenius. 1592–1670. Special issue on the occasion of the quatercentenary of J.A. Comenius's birth. Edited by Dagmar Capkova and Willem Frijhoff. *Paedagogica Historica* 28, no. 2 (1992).

Patocka, Jan. *Jan Amos Komensky*. Gesammelte Schriften zur Comenius Forschung. Comenius forschungstelle, Institut fur Padagogik, Ruhr-Universitat. Veroffentlichungen no. 12. Bochum: 1981.

Schaller, Klaus. *Comenius 1992*. Sankt Augustin: Academia Verlag Richarz, 1992. Schriften zur Comeniusforschung, Band 22. Veroffentlichungen der Comeniusforschungstelle im Institut der Padagogik der Ruhr-Universitat Bocum.

———. *Herder und Comenius*. Sankt Augustin: Academia Verlag Richarz, 1988. Veroffentlichungen der Comeniusforschungstelle. Im Institut fur Padagogik, Ruhr-Universitat, Bochum, no. 12.

Common Sense

Something called "common sense" occupies a position of unusual importance in the history of philosophy. Examine the treatment it accords to common sense and you will understand a great deal about any system of philosophical thought. Neither in common parlance, however, nor in the uncommon vocabulary of philosophy does the phrase "common sense" have a single meaning.

(1) By "common sense" might be meant something like the popular opinion of humankind or the shared beliefs of persons in a community at a particular time and place. This kind of common sense will include, no doubt, a blend of superstition, fact, illusion, and folklore. This is common sense of the kind that C.D. Broad (1887–1971) had in mind when urging that when facts or theory contradict common sense, "we can only advise common-sense to 'go out' and hang itself." Common sense, of this sort, includes a great deal that is false.

(2) By common sense might be meant instead a body of common knowledge possessed by human beings simply as a consequence of their living as human beings, such claims as that fire burns, that ice is cold, that food is necessary to survival, or that I have my shoes on (when I do). That there are some things I ought to do or ought to refrain from doing, that it is good to

have friends, that pleasure is better than pain, these are bits of knowledge accessible to everyone. Sometimes they are described as immediate or direct knowledge to convey the idea that they are not the consequence of any sort of inference. These are the sorts of claims that G.E. Moore (1873–1958) had in mind when saying that the common sense view of the world, is "in certain fundamental features *wholly* true," or that Thomas Reid (1710–1796) meant by saying, "It is absurd to conceive that there can be any opposition between reason and common sense."

(3) By "common sense," instead of something ordinary and possessed by everyone, might be meant something fairly rare, a quite specific virtue, described sometimes as "good sense" in contrast to "foolishness" or "ineptness." Says the *Oxford English Dictionary* in an example from 1726, "There is not . . . a more uncommon thing in the world than common sense. By common sense we usually and justly understand the faculty to discern one thing from another, and the ordinary ability to keep ourselves from being imposed upon by gross contradictions, palpable inconsistencies, and unmask'd imposture. By a man of common sense we mean one who knows, as we say, chalk from cheese." To have or to exercise common sense of this sort is to have or exercise excellent judgment in practical affairs.

Philosophers have said harsh things about common sense in the first of these meanings. Yet they also appeal to common sense, cheerfully embracing, from time to time, the prospect that common sense might be on their side, thinking apparently that if it is, that would be a good thing. In this appeal, they turn to the second of these meanings, even going so far as to suggest that common sense offers at once both a test of philosophical truth and a marker as to where philosophy ought properly to begin and where it must eventually return. Perhaps because of this dual service to philosophy, the appeal to common sense is most apt to appear whenever philosophers seem tempted by views that depart, not a little but a lot, from the shared intelligence of mankind—that is, from the plain truth of common sense in the second of our meanings.

The appeal to common sense functions, in short, as a barrier against entrapment by wild speculations. Any epistemology advancing the claim that all knowledge is subjective and socially constructed, for example, cannot be correct if it sheds doubt on my common-sense ability to know whether I am wearing shoes. If anyone sincerely doubts that such knowledge is knowledge or sees nothing peculiar in the claim that it is subjective and socially constructed, then the need is not for philosophical wisdom, but perhaps for some kind of therapy. The appropriate response is simply, "You couldn't really mean it!" Such a call to common sense is a call to keep in touch with the most simple tests of reality.

In the conduct of philosophy, however, the appeal to common sense plays a more expansive role. Common sense is often construed to identify the beginning point, the end point, and thus, perhaps even the subject matter of philosophy. Neither inquiry nor, for that matter, intelligent conduct of any sort can go forward in the absence of common sense, understood as common knowledge of undoubted truths—that is, common sense of the second sort. Even arguments of the most unbridled skeptic, although rebutted by an appeal to common sense, are also advanced and owe their persuasiveness entirely to the fact that they appeal to common sense—that is, to knowledge and to experiences it is presumed we share. Without such common sense, not even skeptical doubts could be seriously entertained.

Nor can moral reflection of a critical sort make any sense at all but to those who already have some developed moral sense—some sense of what is good or bad, right or wrong. We do not gain our introduction to the moral life through philosophy. It is rather through philosophy that we seek to understand that life that we already share with other human beings. Aristotle (384–322 B.C.), who might be described as the first common-sense philosopher, begins every inquiry in ethics or politics, for example, by asking what it is that human beings generally believe about it. What do they think is happiness, for instance, or virtue, or friendship, or pleasure? He holds that one must begin by setting "the observed facts before us, and after first discussing the difficulties, go on to prove, if possible, the truth of all the common opinions . . . , or failing this, of the greater number and the most authoritative; for if we both refute the objections and leave the common opinions undisturbed, we shall have proved the case sufficiently" *(Nicomachean Ethics, 7, 1145b2–7)*. Here philosophy begins with the claims of common sense, advances by the refinement of common sense, and returns to common sense.

This again was also a central aim of Henry Sidgwick (1838–1900) in *The Methods of Ethics*. He sought to reconcile the arguments of reason offered in support of intuitionism, utilitarianism, egoism, and Kantian formalism, discovering how the principles of each are discoverable in a kind of common-sense morality, how each is thus commended by common-sense, can be measured against that morality, and, at the same time can be used in critical review of common-sense morality. In short, he tended to view common-sense morality as offering a rich lode of insight, albeit fraught with ambiguity, vagueness, compromises, and in need of clarification and refinement. Common sense is seen thus as the starting point, the subject matter, and the end point of philosophical ethics.

This philosophical role of common sense, to provide not only a barrier against nonsense but also to mark the boundaries of the subject itself, is evident not only in ethics and other subjects of practical reason, but also in epistemology. Thomas Reid, the most prominent philosopher in the Scottish school of common sense, directed his analysis primarily against the arguments of David Hume (1711–1776) on causation and the foundations of knowledge, setting in opposition to Hume an account of perception and of the intellectual powers of human beings that affirmed the foundations of ordinary knowledge possessed by ordinary persons. His was not only a call to common sense, but also a philosophical approach that begins in an attempt to understand what is already known to common sense. Common sense, thought Reid, has so fundamentally shaped the character of ordinary language that anyone seeking to depart from it very far will have almost to invent a different language. There is much greater chance for error, thought Reid, in the intricate reasoning needed to carry off such a project than there is in a judicious adherence to common sense.

Such a philosophical attitude always produces a distinctive formulation of what might be called "the philosophical project." The significance of philosophical systems lies in their capacity to elucidate, clarify, and set in ordered array the everyday problems implicit, but often concealed, in the everyday experiences of everyday life among ordinary persons. It is, in other words, to explicate the experience of common sense. The consistency or completeness of such systems of thought is another matter. By such a view, philosophy cannot teach anyone anything they do not already know, but it may call to their attention what they had not noticed, remind them of what they had forgotten, and bring to understanding what had been taken for granted. In doing these things, there can be great surprises.

Thomas F. Green

See also ANALYTIC PHILOSOPHY; ARISTOTLE; INTUITIONISM; POSITIVISM; REALISM; REASON AND RATIONALITY; WITTGENSTEIN

Bibliography

Malcolm, Norman. "Defending Common Sense." *Philosophical Review* 58 (1949): 201–20.

———. "Moore and Ordinary Language." In *The Philosophy of G.E. Moore*, edited by P.A. Schilpp, 345–68. Evanston and Chicago: Northwestern University Press, 1942.

Moore, G.E. "A Defense of Common Sense." In *Philosophical Papers*. London: George Allan and Unwin, 1959.

Reid, Thomas. *Essays on the Intellectual Powers of Man*, edited by A.D. Woozley. London: Macmillan, 1941. 1st ed. 1785.

Sidgwick, Henry. *The Methods of Ethics*. 6th ed. London: Macmillan, 1902.

———. *Philosophy, Its Scope and Relations*. London: Macmillan, 1902.

Singer, M.G. "Ethics and Common Sense." *Revue Internationale de Philosophie*, no. 158, pp. 221–58. Presses Universitaires de France.

———. "Sidgwick and Nineteenth-Century British Ethical Thought." In *Essays on Henry Sidgwick*, edited by Bart Schultz. Cambridge: Cambridge University Press, 1992.

White, Alan R. "Common Sense: Moore and Wittgenstein." *Revue Internationale de Philosophie*, no. 158, pp. 350–62. Presses Universitaires de France.

Woozley, A.D. "Ordinary Language and Common Sense." *Mind* 62 (1953): 301–12.

Community

The notion of community can have a purely descriptive sense—referring to virtually any grouping of persons who share some common characteristic or condition ("the law enforcement community," "the community of students at Lincoln University")—or it can have an evaluative one, where to call something a community implies that it realizes some value(s). Community in the latter sense has been a concern of social and political thought since the Greeks (with Aristotle [384–322 B.C.] and G.W.F. Hegel [1770–1831] being especially noteworthy) and was revived in the 1980s in the philosophical tendency known as "communitarianism."

What are the values that community realizes? A "universalist" approach sees certain core values realized by all communities—a sense of belonging, of rootedness, of mutual trust, of connection to others. A "particularist" approach emphasizes that different communities can realize distinct and divergent values. For example, some communities are devoted to a strict division between female and male roles, others to a military form of honor, others to a vision of equality among their members, others to the realization of some good external to that community. The particularist approach may take a step beyond this value-diversity to a form of relativism, claiming that persons inside one community are not in a position to assess the values of other distinct communities.

A related claim, often linked with the particularist approach, is that every community (with its attendant values) deserves the positive *respect* of those outside of it; the aforementioned relativism involves only a refraining from judging communities positively or negatively. Both claims have been associated with multicultural education and are the source of charges of relativism leveled against it. Yet (even apart from the fact that the principle of respect is not itself relative) the notion of respect for a community's values can be interpreted in such a way as to involve no affirming of divergent values at all. For example, teachers can have respect for the differing communities from which their students come, not in the sense that they positively affirm the worth of those communities' values, but in that they respect the students' valuing of and attachments to their own communities and cultures. The principle is thus one of respect for persons in light of their communal attachments, rather than respect for the communities' own values in their own right.

Ultimately, there need be no conflict between the universalistic and the particularistic dimensions of community values. For no matter how divergent the specific values of different communities, it can be argued that all communities embody the core communitarian values of belonging, connection, and rootedness.

A related distinction within communitarian thought is this: Community can be a set of specific values to be aimed at, which values can be of either a particularistic or universalistic character (or both). A contrasting communitarian strand of thought emphasizes, in Philip Selznick's words, "the primacy of the particular"—that is, according some degree of respect to the traditional values of existing communities, and a consequent reluctance to press too relentlessly for change in the direction of principle or value where doing so runs counter to those existing values. The principles or values that raise this problem can be justice-based, such as achieving racial integration through busing, or the teaching of respect for homosexual students in schools; in certain communities, such policies run up against existing values and folkways.

The values that may conflict with existing community-based values may themselves be communitarian ones; racial integration, for example, can be a communitarian value (as well as a justice-based one), serving the goal of creating a sense of belonging and connection between students of different races. Here the "value" strand of communitarianism may be in direct conflict with the "primacy of the particular" strand. Philip Selznick's book, *The Moral Commonwealth: Social Theory and the Promise of Community,* the most sustained and important contemporary articulation of a communitarian social philosophy, strives to balance and reconcile the claims of both strands of communitarianism.

The primacy of the particular has an inherently conservative thrust, which has been insightfully criticized by feminists such as Marilyn Friedman. Friedman points out that many of the communities of place, religion, and cultural tradition valorized by proponents of community relegate women to subordinate and limited roles. Some of the values of community, then (in either particularistic or universalistic modes), may come at the expense of women. At the same time, there is an affinity between communitarianism and some versions of feminism in that both place value on a sense of interpersonal connectedness, and both are critical of social theories and values with strong individualist foundations, such as the social contract, economic rationality, and libertarianism.

Friedman attempts to combine the value of connectedness with her concern for women's equality by emphasizing voluntary associations rather than unchosen ones as sites of community. She thereby points to an important further dimension of differentiation within types of communities. Many proponents of community focus on bases of community that are generally unchosen by members. For many, communities of neighborhood, village, nation, and other place-based entities (in regard to those born into them) epitomize the notion of "community," though family, ethnicity, and religious tradition are other nonchosen forms of community prominent among proponents of traditional community. Yet Friedman is right to emphasize the possibilities for a sense of community in voluntary groups and associations—such as professions, organizations, schools, and intentional communities—and right to think that by and large these are more likely than traditional communities to preserve personal autonomy and to be receptive to the claims of equality in general and gender equality in particular.

A traditionalist rejoinder is that community that is consciously and deliberately sought can never sustain the sense of rootedness and belonging that comes with nonchosen communities, where membership is taken for granted and unquestioned. But, apart from the troubling risk to personal freedom attendant upon making too much of this point, the contrast between the two types of communities may not be so sharp. We may initially enter into marriages, choose professions, and join organizations voluntarily; but after many years, commitments to them come to take on much of the taken-for-granted character that traditional communities embody. Exit from them is no longer so purely voluntary as was entrance. On the other side, persons can to some extent exit from traditional, nonvoluntary communities.

Moreover, even when not so deeply and permanently grounded in a person's sense of identity, the realization of community in many domains and institutions—schools, classrooms, workplaces, offices, cities—is a great advance over its absence. This is partly for instrumental reasons; being a responsible member of a community involves the development of traits, skills, and sensibilities—a sense of loyalty and commitment, of caring and responsibility for others, of mutual trust, of compromise—that contribute to the forming of responsible citizens in the wider polity. But, in addition, these traits of character and their embodiment in communal entities are good in their own right.

Finally, communities differ on the dimension of heterogeneity and homogeneity. Many writers on community—both proponents (Alasdair MacIntyre, for example) and opponents—emphasize commonalities among the members of a community, such as shared beliefs and values; these thinkers give the impression that communities must be strongly homogeneous. But many communities of place and institution in modern societies include persons of differing races, ethnicities, cultures, and religions. If the commonality that communities require is broadened (beyond shared beliefs and values) to include shared experiences, activities, goals, and institutional commitments, differences of ethnicity and the like can be encompassed within community. Members of a school class, or of a workplace, share a range of activities and goals that provide a foundation for some sense of community. From this base a sense of shared commitment, concern for others, loyalty to the group, and responsibility for the success of the enterprise (whether educational or work-related) may be generated and sustained. Cultural differences can be brought into the communal context (a classroom, for example) as a source of enrichment of the shared enterprise and thereby of the community itself. The diversity itself can become a further source of loyalty and attachment to, and pride in, the community. This is a potential source of hope for racially and ethnically integrated schools as sites of community, though this hope has often remained unrealized.

No doubt pluralistic and heterogeneous communities lack some of the forces of cohesion that purely homogenous ones contain. Nevertheless, some differences pose a greater threat to the cohesion of community than do others. For historical and social reasons, race, for example, and some forms of ethnicity and religion, are identities whose presence often occasions fear, hatred, and discomfort, constituting obstacles to the achievement of community. A multiracial school aspiring to create or nurture a sense of community needs to face up explicitly to the forces of racial divisiveness. From a philosophical point of view, tying community to sameness and pure homogeneity rules this aspiration out by definition.

Lawrence A. Blum

See also DEMOCRACY; EQUALITY; MULTICULTURALISM; PUBLIC EDUCATION

Bibliography

Friedman, Marilyn. "Feminism and Modern Friendship: Dislocating the Community." In *What Are Friends For: Feminist Perspectives on Personal Relationships and Moral Theory,* 225–49. Ithaca, N.Y.: Cornell University Press, 1993.

MacIntyre, Alasdair. *After Virtue.* Notre Dame, Ind.: University of Notre Dame Press, 1981, 1984.

Nisbet, Robert A. *The Quest for Community.* London: Oxford University Press, 1953.

Sandel, Michael. *Liberalism and the Limits of Justice.* New York: Cambridge University Press, 1982.

Selznick, Philip. *The Moral Commonwealth: Social Theory and the Promise of Community.* Berkeley: University of California Press, 1982.

Computers

The origins of a mechanical "computer" can be traced to the calculations of the thirteenth-century Spanish cleric Ramon Lull, to the "Plate of Conjunctions" attributed to the fourteenth-century Moslem astronomer al-Kashi (1393–1449), to the mechanical calculators of Blaise Pascal (1623–1662) and Gottfried Leibniz (1646–1716), and to the nineteenth-century "Analytical Engine" of Charles Babbage (1791–1871). But it is only with the advent of the digital computer and the introduction of transistors in the twentieth century that the technological evolution of today's computer comes into being. In fact, during the period of World Wars I and II, a "computer" meant someone who calculated, and the calculations were often of numerical rows determining artillery trajectories. The initial designs of the electrical computers of the 1940s were intended to replace the work of these human computers.

In the 1950s, the newly emerging mainframe computer expanded the military use of the computer into the industrial arena. Computers were then seen as capable of automating payroll departments and managing numerous kinds of data produced by large corporations. By the 1960s, the emergence of minimainframes put computers into the hands of academic institutions, and the beginnings of work in "educational" computing could be seen. By the 1970s, the Plato Project at the University of Illinois, the development of BASIC at Dartmouth, and the DoD-sponsored research network called ARPAnet were in place.

Some early models of educational computing envisioned the development of "computer-assisted instruction (CAI)" programs on time-sharing computers used by students sitting in front of terminals. The creation of such programs required teams of developers including content experts, instructional designers, programmers, and project managers.

The use of silicon chips to replace transistors created the conditions for the development of the "microcomputer"; by the early 1980s, "personal" computers arrived on the desktop. The standard CAI model of educational software was now implemented on new machines from Apple and IBM: drill and practice programs using Keller-method branching techniques ("if 9 out of 10 correct, then go to next level"). Soon, simulations and educational games were also appearing on these machines, along with Seymour Papert's LOGO language.

By the mid to late 1980s, more powerful machines and the appearance of graphical user interfaces (GUI) enabled the function of computers to approach that of a tool box and communication device. Today, educators can select from an ever-increasing variety of off-the-shelf CAI programs; discipline-specific tools and applications; programming and authoring languages; general-purpose tools like spreadsheets customized for curricular needs; and presentation software, including multimedia tool kits.

As a result of greater power, diverse applications, and user-friendliness, every academic discipline has undergone its own "computational turn" in both teaching and research. The computer has now become an indispensable tool for both knowledge acquisition and knowledge dissemination.

In the trenches of the teaching process, the computer is used far more for "composing" or preparing classroom materials than for programming CAI lessons. For administrative tasks, it is used in course management and report writing. For professional life, it is used to do research, produce articles, and correspond with colleagues.

In many ways, the computer has itself become transformed into an icon for the Information Age. Its meaning as a machine has receded and it is now emerging as a generalized infor-

C

mation medium in an increasingly "networked" society.

Robert Cavalier

See also TEACHING AND LEARNING; TECHNOLOGY

Bibliography

Bolter, David. *Turing's Man: Western Culture in the Computer Age.* Chapel Hill: University of North Carolina Press, 1984.

Chambers, Jack, and Jerry Sprecher. *Computer-Assisted Instruction: Its Use in the Classroom.* Englewood Cliffs, N.J.: Prentice-Hall, 1983.

Goldstine, Herman. *The Computer from Pascal to von Neumann.* Princeton, N.J.: Princeton University Press, 1972.

Nelson, Ted. *Computer Lib.* Redmond, Wash.: Microsoft Press, 1974, 1987.

Weiser, Mark. "The Computer for the 21st Century." *Scientific American* 265 (1991): 94–104.

Condillac, Etienne Bonnot de (1705–1780)

French *philosophe,* logician, psychologist, grammarian, and tutor, Condillac led a plain life compared with those of other *philosophes.* He was not politically involved, and, although he wore the robes of the Church, he seems not to have been involved with its obligations. Condillac gained his reputation by developing a literary style exhibiting clarity of expression and precision of thinking. As he kept no diary, did not write any memoirs, and seldom corresponded, he is known almost entirely by his published writings.

Condillac's *Essay on the Origin of Human Knowledge* (1756) was a commentary on John Locke's *Essay on Human Understanding.* While Locke had referred to two "fountains" of experience by which we come to know—sensation and reflection—Condillac gave expression to a more sensationalistic epistemology by arguing that sensation alone was the basis of all knowledge and that Locke's "reflection" is not necessary to account for knowledge. In his *Treatise on Sensations* (1754), Condillac asks his readers to imagine a "statue-man," made of marble in human form but without human spirit. The statue-man can experience no sensation from an inner source, but must be enabled to accept only those sensations that have an external source. Endowing the statue-man with the senses of smell, hearing, taste, sight, and touch, Condillac shows how sensations alone can lead to comparison, memory, desire, and to more complex ideas. The point of his demonstration is to "see that sensation encompasses all the powers of the mind."

The kind of natural necessity by which human sensations lead to knowledge is found also in Condillac's writings on the origin and formation of language. There he writes of the earliest language symbols developing through a natural necessity, first through sounds and gestures, and then in more complex forms. He calls this natural process "the language of action," by which gestures, facial expressions, and body movements were the first ways human beings communicated their thoughts. It is not simply the case that actions preceded thinking; more exactly, the actions by which human beings learned to communicate were themselves a kind of thinking.

Condillac's sensationalism, along with his idea of the natural development of language, contributed to his criticism of those system-makers who, he thought, invented false systems based on *a priori* reasoning. From Condillac's perspective, system-makers should proceed as human beings naturally did in developing languages and as children do in learning according to nature: They move from certain knowledge gained through their senses to more and more complex forms of knowledge. We move from what is known toward what is unknown in such a manner that the latter becomes known in relation to the former. His definition of "system" follows from a strong belief that the knowledge gained from the senses can lead to further knowledge, if only we continue to depend on sensory experience and not invent explanations prior to our experience of them: "A system is none other than the arrangement of the different parts of a body of knowledge so that they are mutually related and the last parts are involved in explanations of the first parts."

In 1758, Condillac was chosen to be tutor to the Prince of Parma, and until 1766 the tutor worked with a real-life "statue-boy." What is most memorable about that experience is not whether the prince lived up to expectations, but the way in which Condillac elaborated his thinking on language, logic, and analysis, and made explicit the ways in which this thinking contributed to an educational theory. In working on the twofold aim of elaborating his thinking and tutoring the prince, Condillac wrote works on grammar, writing, reasoning, thinking, ancient history, and modern history; they were subdivisions of his *Cours d' etudes,* published in 1775. While this is a rather imposing course of study, Condillac's way of using it and his discussions of its various parts show us that Condillac did not propose to provide the prince with all the knowledge he would need to become educated. Rather, he attempted to provide the means of acquiring that knowledge when it is needed. Thus Condillac shared with his more-famous contemporary Jean-Jacques Rousseau the idea that an important aim of education is to learn how to make knowledge for oneself, rather than merely to possess what others already know.

In Condillac's little work on logic, published in 1780, he makes clear the sense in which thinking—as an art that we can learn from nature—and conducting ourselves so that we may pursue the truth are different ways of talking about the same kind of activity. The theme emphasized in this work tells us, first, that nature gives us lessons; second, if we learn the lessons nature gives, we can conduct ourselves according to our nature. To learn the lessons of nature is to learn the true lessons of conduct and of education. In his *Logic,* Condillac repeats his criticisms of *a priori* reasoning by saying that he will not begin with "definitions, axioms, or principles; we shall begin by observing the lessons which nature gives us." The method of analysis was learned from nature, and is the method which will be used to explain the origin of ideas and faculties of the mind. Condillac compares the activity of learning to direct our senses truly to the activities of children when they acquire knowledge without the help of adults. The very fact that children do learn how to know is proof, Condillac says, that nature teaches those who are able to pay attention to what nature says. In this natural way of knowing, children "have then an art by which they acquire knowledge. It is true, they follow its rules without knowing it, but they follow them." The relation between nature, sensory experience, and communication of truth had been put this way in the *Essay on the Origin of Human Knowledge*: "Nature itself points out the order we ought to follow in the communication of truth; for if all our ideas come from the senses, it is manifest that the perception of abstract notions must be prepared by sensible ideas."

Condillac sees the analytic method as an art, insofar as it is undertaken without consulting its rules. It is also a logic insofar as it constitutes a way of doing things that can serve as a source of rules whenever we are unable to proceed artfully. Thus the analytical method as art-and-logic is not just a way of knowing, for knowing does not take place apart from doing. It is also a way of doing by which we make the arts and sciences become a part of our conduct. Condillac did not waver from his strong sense that human beings are capable of taking the lessons that nature gives.

J.J. Chambliss

See also CONDORCET; EMPIRICISM; EPISTEMOLOGY; LOCKE; ROUSSEAU

Bibliography
Chambliss, J.J. "Condillac's Natural Logic." Chapter 10 in *Educational Theory as Theory of Conduct.* Albany: State University of New York Press, 1987.
Condillac, Etienne Bonnot de. *Cours d' etudes pour l'instruction du prince de Parme.* Geneva: Du Villead fils and Nouffer, 1770–1780.
———. *An Essay on the Origin of Human Knowledge, Being a Supplement to Mr. Locke's Essay on the Human Understanding.* Translated by Thomas Nugent. London: J. Nourse, 1756.
———. *The Logic of Condillac.* Translated by Joseph Neef. Philadelphia, 1809.
———. *Oeuvres Completes.* Vols. 1–16. Geneva: Slatkine Reprints, 1970.
Kagdis, Nicholas J. *Etienne Bonnot de Condillac's Cours D'Etudes: Analysis and Implications.* Doctoral diss., Rutgers University, 1984.
Knight, Isabel F. *The Geometric Spirit: The Abbe de Condillac and the French Enlightenment.* New Haven: Yale University Press, 1968.
Levy-Bruhl, Lucien. "Condillac." Chapter 10 in *History of Modern Philosophy in France.* Translated by G. Coblence. Chicago: Open-Court Publishing, 1899.
Schaupp, Zora. *The Naturalism of Condillac.* Lincoln: University of Nebraska Press, 1926.

Condorcet, Marie-Jean-Antoine-Nicolas Caritat de (1743–1794)

Mathematician, political theorist, and social reformer, Condorcet was the only prominent *philosophe* to participate actively in the French Revolution. At the age of twenty-one, he published a work on integral calculus; it and other mathematical writings drew the attention of Jean le Rond D'Alembert, one of the foremost mathematicians of the eighteenth century, who had written the *Preliminary Discourse* to Denis Diderot's *Encyclopedia* of 1751. After serving as assistant secretary of the Royal Academy of Sciences, at that time the most influential scientific body of Europe, Condorcet was elected to the position of permanent secretary in 1776. This was a position critical to the mobilization of science for research in military affairs, navigation, animal diseases, reforming weights and measures, and other applications of science to matters furthering the public good.

His position in the Academy of Sciences, and his friendship with prominent scientists and philosophers, moved Condorcet into the midst of a campaign to show that the certainty attained in the language and methods of the physical sciences could be gained in the moral and political sciences as well. Holding that our political and moral actions can be made rational by an analysis of mathematical probability in decision-making, Condorcet argued that "I must not act according to what I myself believe to be reasonable, but according to that which everyone—like me, setting aside his own opinion—must regard as in conformity with reason and truth." Thus it is justifiable for citizens in a republic to be subjected to decisions with which a minority of them disagree, so long as everyone acts as if that decision were a rational one. The aim of Condorcet's analysis was to investigate the nature of the conditions in which people's wants could be expressions of "public reason."

Condorcet's political aim for a reformed French society recognized the existence of two distinct groups of people: (1) the more enlightened few, who would be obligated to make decisions "in conformity with reason and truth"; and (2) the less enlightened many, who would be willing to entrust their right of decision-making to their more enlightened fellow citizens. This political aim acknowledged that individuals in both groups are equal in their rights as human beings and in their obligations as citizens, while holding that they are unequal in abilities and enlightenment. Addressing education in his *Sketch for a Historical Picture of the Progress of the Human Mind*, Condorcet wrote, "A well-directed system of education rectifies natural inequality in ability instead of strengthening it." Condorcet's plans for public education emphasized the necessity of working out social relations among all citizens, so that public reason would serve the common good, rather than the interests of certain classes at the expense of others. Their lack of natural ability means that many are not capable of attaining the scientific knowledge of their more enlightened fellow citizens, Condorcet thought, yet all citizens are capable of developing their critical powers so that they will be reasonably free from prejudice, passion, and superstition. Thus all children must receive a primary education. The curriculum Condorcet advocated put the physical and moral sciences in place of the classical curriculum: The need to move toward a more rational society would be better served by the written words of science than by the spoken words of rhetoric. The invention of printing has made available a rational way in which citizens can make decisions, in contrast to the way in which orators appeal to the passions of the unenlightened. The aim is to "substitute reason for eloquence, books for talkers, and finally bring to the moral sciences the philosophy and the method of the physical sciences."

The teaching of the moral and political sciences is necessary if both the less enlightened and the more enlightened are to have their rights secured and to make their duties as citizens a part of their minds and characters. And Condorcet argued that because women, like men, "are sentient beings, capable of acquiring moral ideas and reasoning concerning these ideas," women should enjoy rights equal to those of men. By "moral sciences," Condorcet meant, first, those involving the analysis of sensations and ideas (such as logic, mathematics, psychology, and epistemology); second, those involving social relations (such as ethics, politics, legislation, and statistics). Condorcet came to call the second kind of studies "social sciences." The idea of a social science could be realized in three kinds of investigation. The first, what Condorcet called "the natural history of man," would be an empirical investigation into the conditions of social life, by which observational and statistical data would contribute to the establishment of a science of human beings in society. The second, moving from social "facts" to social "principles," included the natural rights of humans together with the theory of social organization needed to bring actual conditions of social existence into line with the social principles established. The third was a "social art," working out the forms of conduct by which individual citizens participate in their social life in a rational and scientific manner. Establishing a social science, which must be translated into an art if there is to be an increasingly enlightened and scientific society in which our natural rights are to be respected, is what Condorcet had in mind in his *Sketch,* when he wrote: "Until men progress in the practice as well as in the science of morality, it will be impossible for them to attain any insight into either the nature and development of the moral sentiments, the principles of morality, the natural motives that prompt their actions, or their own true interests either as individuals or as members of society." Condorcet's social science-and-art puts us in mind of a democratic version of Aristotle's argument in the *Nicomachean Ethics,* that it is not sufficient to know what practical wisdom is, but necessary actually to become wise in the practical affairs of everyday life.

Condorcet was elected to the Legislative Assembly in 1791, but his plans for public education, as well as his draft Constitution, went down in defeat to the voices of unenlightened passion, which his education for reason and enlightenment was intended to ameliorate. Condemned by the National Convention, in July of 1793 Condorcet went into hiding in the midst of the Terror; in the eight months left to him, wrote the *Sketch for a Historical Picture of the Progress of the Human Mind.* Condorcet portrayed history as the servant of social science, identifying the progress that has been made in developing that science, pointing out errors made and obstacles placed in the way of its development. Finally, in showing that rational and moral progress is a very part of our past, Condorcet makes a passionate argument on behalf of the future prospects of the social art. Human beings, not gods, have made their past; by learning the social art, they can remake the present for the indefinite improvement of the human condition. What Condorcet had written of the human mind at the time of Descartes might well be said of Condorcet's own mind at the time he was drafting the *Sketch:* "The human mind was not yet free but it knew that it was formed to be so."

J.J. Chambliss

See also CIVIC EDUCATION; CONDILLAC; DIDEROT; HELVETIUS; PROGRESS, IDEA OF, AND PROGRESSIVE EDUCATION

Bibliography
Baker, Keith Michael. *Condorcet: From Natural Philosophy to Social Mathematics.* Chicago: University of Chicago Press, 1975.
Condorcet, Nicolas Caritat. *Condorcet: Selected Writings.* Edited by Keith Baker. Indianapolis, Ind.: Bobbs Merrill, 1976.
———. *Essai sur l'application de l'analyse a la probabilite des decisions rendues a la pluralite des voix.* Paris: De l'imprimerie royale, 1785.
———. *Oeuvres de Condorcet.* 12 vols. Edited by A. Condorcet-O'Connor and F. Arago. Paris: Firmin Dodot freres, 1847–1849.
———. *Sketch for a Historical Picture of the Progress of the Human Mind.* Translated by June Barraclough. New York: Noonday Press, 1955.
Gay, Peter. *The Enlightenment: An Interpretation.* Vol. 2. *The Science of Freedom,* 108–25. New York: Alfred A. Knopf, 1969.
Goodell, Edward. *The Noble Philosopher: Condorcet and the Enlightenment.* Buffalo, N.Y.: Prometheus Books, 1994.
Vial, Francisque. *Condorcet et l'education democratique.* Paris: P. Delaplane, 1903.

C

Confucianism

Confucius was born in 551 B.C. and died in 479 B.C. during the time when the Chou Dynasty was in decline. The authority of the Chou house was disregarded by the feudal lords, and the feudal states were engaged in wars of hegemony against each other. The whole country was in a great turmoil, and the Duke of Chou's concept of the perfect humanity through proprieties and music collapsed. Observing proprieties at proper occasions had been neglected by both the royal courts and the ordinary people. It was recorded by the historian of the Chou that the ceremonial vessels were misplaced and that the music was played at improper occasions during the ceremonies of ancestral worship at the temples of the feudal lords. It was regarded by Confucius that it should be his life's ambition to restore the Duke of Chou's political institutions and to renew his cultural ideals.

When Confucius, however, finally found that the feudal lord of the Lu and his powerful subordinates would not seek advice from him, he left the state for more than thirteen years, visiting many feudal lords in the country, with the hope that he might be employed. Apparently, his itinerary failed and he returned to his native state, Lu, to teach when he was about sixty-eight years of age. Many of his disciples were from poor families; in later years, they became important officials in the courts of the feudal lords.

The materials used in his teachings were the ancient archival documents, the popular odes, and the written decorums, which he had collected. In later years, they became the Classics: the *Book of Change* (the *I*), the *Book of the Ancient Documents* (the *Shu*), the *Book of Odes* (the *Shih*), the *Book of Proprieties* (the *Li*), the *Book of Music* (the *Yueh*), and the *Spring-and-Autumn Annals* (the *Ch'un-Hsiu*). The Classics have survived to the present day, all except for the *Book of Music*, which was lost. Confucianists were required to learn the Classics by heart, and, in later years, they became sourcebooks for providing topics for the civil-service examinations by means of which the royal courts selected their officials, high and low. This civil-service examination system lasted in China until 1906.

Confucianism was merely one of the schools of philosophy before and during the time of Confucius. Others were Taoism and Legalism. Confucianism has always been known as "Ju Chia" in China. During the reign of Wu-ti of the Han Dynasty, about 150 years prior to the Christian era, a royal decree made Confucianism the official philosophy, the highest principles for ruling the country. There were, of course, variations in Confucianism during the more than two thousand years following, but its essential teachings, the perfection of human nature through cultural refinement, remained the same.

Though Confucius did appreciate the ancient traditions, he was not a traditionalist. As he said in the *Analects,* after his long years' investigation of the *Li* (proprieties) of the Three Ancient Dynasties, the Hsia, the Shang, and the Chou, he concluded that no matter what changes of the *Li* were made during the Three Dynasties, the concept of humanity, as the basis of the *Li,* would not change, even in the coming hundred generations. Then what is the concept of humanity he cherished?

Trying to define his concept of humanity, Confucius once said to his disciples, "The humans and the humanity are identical. Humanity is the quality which makes the humans human." At another instance he said, "If a person lacks humanity, I don't know how to address him!"

Though this human quality does not change, even while its expression in the form of habits or customs may be different in different times, it needs education to bring it up to one's consciousness. In other words, as human beings, each of us is endowed with the quality of humanity; through education the quality may be recovered if it is forgotten, or strengthened when it calls for its perfection.

To Confucius, education means learning, while learning means more than mere book-reading, meditation, collecting information, or sharing others' experiences. Confucius once said:

> To love virtue and not learning: a
>   simpleton.
> To love knowing and not learning:
>   shallowness.
> To love honesty and not learning:
>   naivete.
> To love plain speech and not learning: a
>   boor.
> To love physical strength and not learning:
>   a rebel.
> To love determination and not learning:
>   recklessness.
> Without learning the wise become foolish;
>   by learning, the foolish wise.

At another occasion he said, "I have spent a whole day and night without eating and sleeping, in meditation. And I find it is of no use and that it is better to learn." To him, apparently, learning is directly incorporated into one's personality, showing in one's moral character and one's deeds. Though humans are by nature very much alike, it is circumstances that draw them apart. To Confucius there were two types of humans: the perfect gentleman and the small man, the inferior person. This happened not because they were unequal by nature but because some people made the best of themselves, while the others only "eat their fill and fix their minds on nothing."

However, in his teaching Confucius did not leave a foothold for the formation of rigid social classes or castes. He once told one of his disciples, Tze Lu, "With earnest and careful cultivation of oneself, a person would realize his responsibility toward his fellow men." Of course, he disclaimed that he was a sage, the superior type of person, one like the Duke of Chou, but he said:

The perfect gentleman, the superior man, loves quality; the small man, the inferior type of person, loves comfort.

The perfect gentleman awaits the will of Heaven; the small man anxiously awaits a stroke of luck.

The perfect gentleman brings out the best in others; the small man does the opposite.

The perfect gentleman thinks of what is right; the small man thinks of what is profitable.

The perfect gentleman demands much of himself; a small man demands much of others.

All these remarks show the contrast between the perfect gentleman and the small man. Furthermore, Confucius made the following demands on the perfect gentleman:

The perfect gentleman is modest, generous, open-hearted, industrious, and kind.

The perfect gentleman is watchful of these things: his eyes, so that he may observe; his ears, that he may learn; his face, that it may reflect kindness always; his manners, that they might show respect for others; his words, that they may be true; his business dealings, that they may be fair; his doubts, that he may resolve them; his emotions, that he may control them; his money, that he may earn it honestly.

From his teachings, Confucius showed clearly that he was a thoroughgoing humanist whose concern was basically the welfare of human beings. He never thought that to live was to serve the welfare of human beings; he never thought that to live was to take part in a tragedy. Instead, he thought that to live was to fulfill one's responsibility. When one of his disciples once asked him about death, he quipped, "You do not know how to live yet, why should you so bother about death?" On another occasion, the same disciple asked him about ghosts and gods, and Confucius bade him to keep a distance from them. He requested his disciple to pay more attention to the living than to offer sacrifices to the ghosts and gods.

Confucius avoided discussing whether there is survival after death or whether gods exist. He thought that religious worship of whatever form was originally designed by the ancient sages for educational purposes. As long as the religious practice brings about improvement in human character, it matters not whether the ghosts or gods exist.

Confucius believed in three ways by which a person could achieve his immortality: good deeds, moral excellence, and words of wisdom. Though he regretted that he had no chance to demonstrate his good deeds by administering a state or country, as the Duke of Chou did, he often reminded himself that the good qualities of his behavior and speech would equal the fame that might be bestowed upon him after his death as a ruler.

Finally, we should credit Confucius for his concept of the *Great Harmony of the World*, which has exercised a tremendous influence on the Chinese mind, much like that of Plato's *Republic*, or Thomas More's *Utopia* in the West. Herewith, the words of his wisdom, handed down to us almost twenty-five-hundred years after his passing:

When the Great Principle prevails, the world is a Commonwealth in which rulers are selected according to their wisdom and ability. Mutual confidence is promoted and good neighborliness cultivated. Hence, men do not regard as parents only their own parents, nor do they treat as children only their own children. Provision is secured for the aged until death, employment for the able-bodied, and the means of growing up for the young. Helpless widows and widowers, orphans and the lonely, as well as the sick and the disabled, are well cared for. Men have their respective occupations and women their homes. They do not like to see wealth lying idle, yet they do not keep it for their own gratification. They despise indolence, yet they do not use their energies for their own benefit. In this way, selfish schemings are repressed, and robbers, thieves and other lawless men no longer exist, and there is no need for people to shut their outer doors.

Shih-chuan Chen

See also HUMAN NATURE; TAOISM

Bibliography

Chen, Shih-chuan. *The Confucian Analects: A New Translation of the Corrected Text of Lun Yü.* Taipei, Taiwan: Li

C

Ming Cultural Enterprise, 1986.

Legge, James. *Book of Ancient Document (Shang Shu)*. London: Series of the Sacred Book of China, 1907.

———. *Book of Proprieties (Li-Chi)*. London: Series of the Sacred Book of China, 1907.

———. *I Ching, Book of Change*. Secaucus, N.J.: Citadel Press, 1948.

———. *The Spring-and-Autumn Annals*. London: Series of the Sacred Book of China, 1907.

Pound, Ezra. *The Odes of Confucius*. Boston: Harvard University Press, 1948.

Conscience

Conscience is the psychological faculty by which we are aware of and respond to the moral character of our own actions. It is most commonly thought of as the source of pains we suffer as a result of doing what we believe is wrong—the pains of guilt, or "pangs of conscience." It may also be seen, more controversially, as the source of our knowledge of what is right and wrong, or as a motive for moral conduct. Thus a person who is motivated to act on principle is said to act "conscientiously."

These terms come from the Latin *conscientia*, a direct translation of the Greek *syneidesis*. These terms range in meaning from being aware of something (hence our "consciousness") to "knowing something in common with" someone. Knowing something in common with someone can mean sharing his secret, and that puts you in a position to serve as a witness against him. Thus the term came to have a judicial use, to describe one who could bear witness. In certain contexts, *syneidesis* came to mean a state of knowing in common with oneself, and so of bearing witness against oneself.

Although these terms appear in Stoic and Epicurean works, conscience did not receive extensive philosophical treatment until the medieval period, when treatises on conscience became standard. Medieval philosophers distinguished two aspects of conscience, *conscientia* and *synderesis*. Roughly, *synderesis* (a technical term of uncertain origin) refers to the ineradicable and infallible basis of conscience in human nature; *conscientia* refers to the more particular judgments we make about our actions. There are various ways of specifying the two ideas further. In the account by Thomas Aquinas (1225–1274), which became standard, synderesis en-compasses the basic moral principles that are the first premises of practical reasoning. Conscientia is the conclusion, the act of judging that one ought to perform a particular action. Synderesis is infallible, but conscientia can be mistaken, because of mistaken factual premises or faulty reasoning. Medieval philosophers raised a variety of questions about these two aspects of conscience: whether they are inborn powers, learned dispositions, or actions; whether they are intellectual, motivational, or affective; and whether conscience is a manifestation of practical reason or a separate faculty. Above all, medieval thinkers were interested in the question of whether conscience is fallible, and, if it is fallible, to what extent one is responsible for (or sins in) acting in accordance with an erring conscience.

Modern moral philosophers of the seventeenth and eighteenth centuries did little with the concept of conscience except to identify it with whatever they took to be the basic moral faculty, or with that faculty when it operates in judgment upon one's own actions. Thus, for rationalist philosophers, conscience is the voice of reason judging one's motives and actions; for sentimentalists and later utilitarians, conscience consists in the second-order sentiments of approval and disapproval we feel toward our own motives and sentiments. An important exception is the eclectic philosopher Joseph Butler (1692–1752), who brought together insights from sentimentalism and rationalism and emphasized the connection of these philosophical ideas with more popular and religious conceptions of morality. Butler identified conscience with a natural disposition to approve or disapprove of our motives and actions in accordance with reason and to act accordingly. But conscience is not only a part of our nature: It claims a special authority over other principles equally natural to us, an authority it retains even when it lacks the power to execute its commands. To explain the distinction between power and authority, Butler argued, we must understand human nature as a constitution, in the political as well as the biological sense, in which there is a hierarchy of principles, some having the right to control others. Just as we act contrary to our natural constitution when we gratify a strong but destructive passion at the expense of our long-term interests, so we act contrary to our nature when we pursue passion or self-interest in violation of conscience.

The advent of evolutionary thought in the late nineteenth and early twentieth centuries brought with it a new set of questions about conscience. If human beings evolved from the "lower" animals, then those attributes that seem to distinguish human beings from other animals must also have evolved from more primitive characteristics. An account of how conscience, along with other distinctive human attributes, such as reason, language, and aesthetic sensibilities, could have evolved seems to be required. In *The Descent of Man* (1871), Charles Darwin (1809–1882) argued that the development of conscience in social animals was inevitable once they developed the powers of reflection and memory. The altruistic and cooperative instincts that characterize social animals are frequently less strong than appetitive insights such as fear, hunger, or lust; but they make more persistent and enduring claims on the animal's mind. Appetites, by contrast, no longer seem important once they have been satisfied. An animal that gratifies its appetites at the expense of its young or its comrades, once able to reflect back on what it has done, will experience remorse. When reason and language enable the animal to remember these experiences, the social instincts acquire the special authority of conscience: We come to believe that we ought to obey them.

Other thinkers, especially Friedrich Nietzsche (1844–1900) and Sigmund Freud (1856–1939), saw the acquisition of conscience as a more decisive break with our animal past. Both believed that conscience resulted from a process of "internalization." When our natural aggressive instincts are suppressed for the sake of social life, we find an outlet for them by turning them against ourselves, inflicting pain on ourselves in the form of guilt. The resulting psychological formation, the existence in the psyche of a superego or conscience that can punish us for giving way to our natural impulses, makes self-mastery possible. Because it is society and, in particular, our parents that train us to suppress aggression, self-mastery is exercised for the sake of social requirements or obedience to parental command: The conscience is a kind of internally authoritative voice of one's society and parents. These accounts of the origin of conscience are sometimes viewed as attacks on morality. But it is possible to understand them simply as explanations of how human beings acquired the self-mastery, or control of one part of the soul by another, that philosophers from Plato to Kant have identified with our moral nature. Nietzsche and Freud did raise important questions,

however, about the price humanity has paid for our distinctive self-mastery. Both saw internalization as having a natural dynamic that causes guilt to grow, so that the better we become, the more guilt we feel, and the more inclined we become to reject our aggressive and sexual natures altogether, with potentially disastrous results. If they are right, the vindication of our moral nature depends on whether the self-mastery we get from conscience can be detached from social and parental authority, and exercised instead in the name of a set of sane and realistic standards derived from reason.

Christine M. Korsgaard

See also CIVIL DISOBEDIENCE; DARWIN; FREUD; HUMAN NATURE; MORAL DEVELOPMENT; NIETZSCHE; PSYCHOANALYSIS; THOMAS AQUINAS

Bibliography

Butler, Joseph. *Five Sermons Preached at the Rolls Chapel.* Edited by Stephen Darwall. Indianapolis, Ind.: Hackett Publishing Company, 1983.

Darwin, Charles. *The Descent of Man, and Selection in Relation to Sex.* Princeton: Princeton University Press, 1981.

Freud, Sigmund. *Civilization and Its Discontents.* Translated by James Strachey. New York: Norton, 1961.

———. *Totem and Taboo.* Translated by James Strachey. New York: Norton, 1950.

Nietzsche, Friedrich. *On the Genealogy of Morals.* Translated by Walter Kaufmann and R.J. Hollingdale. New York: Random House, 1967.

Potts, Timothy C. *Conscience in Medieval Philosophy.* Commentary with translations from Jerome, Augustine, Peter Lombard, Philip the Chancellor, Bonaventure, and Aquinas. Cambridge: Cambridge University Press, 1980.

Thomas Aquinas. *Commentary on the Sentences* (of Peter Lombard), 2.24.2.3–4; *Disputed Questions on Truth,* 16–17; *Summa Theologica,* I.79.11–II.19.5–8.

Conservatism

The word conservatism is often used by academics and the popular press as a way of referring to people who adhere to traditional beliefs and values. These groups often use it as a pejorative term to designate groups that cannot be categorized as having a liberal ideological orientation.

In the United States, the word *conservatism* has many connotations, depending upon the cultural group using the term or being designated by it. It also has different meanings in different parts of the world. Because of its many connotations, it is important to use the term precisely by identifying the specific ideas, values, and cultural practices it is being identified with. Much confusion in social and educational thinking has resulted from the failure to recognize the complexity of human embeddedness, and thus what aspects of human and cultural experience are being conserved. The following are different ways in which the term may be used.

Cultural Conservatism

As the languages of a cultural group reproduce in thought and behavior the accepted patterns that give order and predictability to everyday life, every cultural group can be considered as an example of cultural conservatism. Even modern cultures with strong antitradition traditions, as well as cultures undergoing a phase of revolutionary change, reproduce and thus conserve the accepted cultural patterns that are not the focus of political and educational reform. One way to understand the depth and complexity of cultural conservatism is to view it as being as encompassing as the traditions of a cultural group; that is, a culture conserves itself through the ideas, values, practices, institutions, technologies, art forms, and so forth, that are handed down from the past to the present.

Temperamental Conservatism

Every person who experiences meaning and has a sense of self-identity rooted in the accepted cultural patterns and beliefs is a temperamental conservative. This more psychological and existential expression of conservatism is often not recognized because of the traditions of Western thought that have emphasized the explicit forms of knowledge and the rational process as the source of individual autonomy, and the belief that people are more fully realized when they constantly experience change. But temperamental conservatism encompasses every aspect of a person's life, including preferences for certain foods, music, topics of conversation, clothes, forms of work, leisure activities, and all the conventions that regulate different forms of communication (paralinguistic cues, proxemics, kinesic patterns, and so forth). Even theorists who explain why people's humanness can be realized only through constant critical reflection and change are temperamental conservatives in the sense of feeling personally more comfortable with the established routines and norms that underlie everyday life.

Economic Conservatism

This form of "conservatism" is often associated with individuals and social groups who advocate free market economic principles, competitive individualism, and other beliefs and practices associated with economic success, privilege, and the view that the fittest should survive. Although the word "conservatism" is widely used to designate groups who want to retain or recover their former economic and political advantages, their beliefs and values have a more direct linkage with Classical Liberalism.

Philosophic Conservatism

Unlike cultural and temperamental conservatism, philosophic conservatism is based on critical reflection about the conditions and prospects of human existence. The tradition of conservatism began with the writings of Edmund Burke (1729–1797). His defense of the American Revolution and carefully argued criticisms of the French Revolution laid out the philosophical conservative's basic way of understanding the possibilities and limitations of the political process, and thus of the educational process. In a public letter to his constituents about the true character of civil freedom, Burke wrote "that the disposition of the people of America is wholly averse to any other than a free government; and this is indication enough to any honest statesman, how he ought to adapt whatever power he finds in his hands to their case. If any ask me what a free government is, I answer that, for any practical purpose, it is what the people think so, and that they, and not I, are the natural, lawful, and competent judges of the matter" (1982: 4). In his most famous book, *Reflections on the Revolution in France* (1962), Burke reaffirmed the philosophical conservative's commitment to social change, with the only qualification being that the change must meet the test of conserving still viable traditions while reforming those traditions that had become outmoded. According to Burke, "A state without the means of change is without the means of its conservation" (1962: 37). His criticism of basing social change on abstract theories, which he saw as contributing to the political extremism and violence that characterized the French Revolution, was based on his belief that "the nature of man is intricate; the objects of society are of the greatest possible complexity; and therefore no simple disposition or direction of power can be suitable either to man's nature or to the quality of his affairs" (1962: 92).

Other philosophical conservatives include Samuel T. Coleridge (1772–1834), who criticized the dehumanizing effects of the Industrial Revolution; Alexander Hamilton (1755–1804), who articulated why the Constitution was needed to protect human freedom; Alexis de Tocqueville (1805–1859), who recognized the Cartesian and secularizing tendencies in early American society; T.S. Eliot (1888–1965), who warned that cultural accomplishments achieved over generations of collective effort were being overturned by the shallow interests of an increasingly rootless form of individualism; Hannah Arendt (1906–1975), who was concerned with the modern forms of totalitarianism and the loss of the private sphere of existence; and Michael Oakeshott, who criticized the growing influence of a technological form of consciousness and the loss of mentor relationships. Today, a wide range of contemporary thinkers, including Robert Heilbroner, Ivan Illich, John Berger, and Alasdair MacIntyre, while not calling themselves philosophical conservatives, analyze social issues by utilizing the insights and form of dialectical thinking that have roots in the thinking of Burke.

The form of dialectical thinking of the philosophic conservative involves tensions, double meanings, and the possibility of reversals where an idea or social institutions, when carried to an extreme, turn into a new form of oppression. It is not the dialectical process of liberal theorists that equates change with social progress. The dialectical quality of philosophical conservative thinking can be seen in how they refuse to base social and educational practices on abstractions—such as the ideal of the autonomous individual or the current myth of progress. Burke's statement about the complexity of human nature and social life is reaffirmed in the philosophical conservative's proclivity to place issues in a cultural context and to explore the tensions and possibilities of reversals. For the philosophical conservative, thinking about the needs of the individual cannot be separated from a consideration of the interdependencies

within a healthy community. The reality constituted at the level of abstract thought has to be weighed against the complexity and proven nature of experience, the promise of change judged in terms of the empowerment of living traditions.

Unlike the various streams of liberal thought, where human nature is represented either as inherently good or shaped by the environment, philosophical conservatives view humans as multidimensional—capable of altruism, fairness, and a sense of responsibility to the larger community. And as the historical record also demonstrates, humans can be selfish, irrational, and even demonic. This mixed view of human nature leads philosophical conservatives to argue for a political and educational system that has checks and balances built in, like a tripartite system of government (including a constitution), an educational system that balances learning from experience with a knowledge of the cultural achievements of the past.

Given the philosophical conservative's proclivity toward understanding political and educational issues in terms of what represents a balance of interests and ways of thinking, their writings are not formulistic in the sense of always upholding a particular set of values or guiding principles. For example, if community traditions become rigid and threaten to repress the rights and critical judgment of the individual, philosophical conservatives will align themselves with the need to maintain intellectual, creative, and personal freedoms. Similarly, if they think society is relying excessively on the authority of rational forms of procedural thinking (a technicist orientation), they will argue for a greater recognition of and appreciation for other forms of knowledge that are more experiential and communal based. What unifies philosophical conservatives is their sensitivity to Burke's dictums that the "nature of man is intricate" and that the processes of a just and well-organized community are "of the greatest possible complexity," which in turn leads them to oppose forms of extremism.

Religious Conservatism

This form of conservatism is complex and varied in its forms of expression—as varied as the forms of sacred authority (doctrines, texts, teachings) that characterize different religious traditions. As the fundamental metanarratives that underlie each religious tradition vary widely, no attempt will be made here to explain either the commonalities or differences. As a distinct form of conservatism, it is widespread, deeply rooted in the life of individuals and communities, and a powerful force in shaping political and educational policies and practices.

Cultural/Bio-Conservatism

This tradition has also been called "eco-conservatism," which is a metaphorical construction that hides that it is really an ecologically centered form of cultural conservatism. With the growing awareness that the stability of the earth's ecosystems are being threatened, a new form of conservatism has emerged that challenges philosophical conservatism as being too anthropocentric. It also challenges the various traditions of liberalism as expressions of the reactionary ideas and values associated with the rise of modern consciousness and the ecologically destructive Industrial Revolution. Early American cultural/bio-conservative thinkers include Henry David Thoreau (1817–1862) and John Muir (1838–1914). More recent cultural/bio-conservative thinkers include Aldo Leopold (1886–1948), Gregory Bateson (1904–1980), Wendell Berry, and Gary Snyder.

The central principle of this form of conservatism is that ideas, values, technologies, and all other cultural practices must meet the test of contributing to the long-term sustainability of the human/biotic community relationship. Alan Durning states the principle in terms of a new Golden Rule: "Each generation should meet its needs without jeopardizing the prospects of future generations to meet their own needs" (1991: 165). Cultural/bio-conservatives also stress that the forms of technology and economic practice should contribute to the development of a person's abilities and a sense of interdependency within the biotic community. Furthermore, technology and economic practices should not destroy the forms of intergenerational knowledge that have enabled the cultural group to meet its material, psychological, and spiritual needs without destroying the environment upon which it depends. This sensitivity to the connections among meeting human needs, preserving traditions that enhance the well-being of the extended human/biotic community, and the need for self-limitation in the context of fragile and limited ecosystems is clearly articulated in the following statement by Wendell Berry: "A healthy culture is a communal order of memory, insight, value, work, conviviality, reverence, aspiration. It reveals the

human necessities and the human limits. It clarifies our inescapable bonds to the earth and to each other. It assures that the necessary restraints are observed, that the work is done, and that it is done well" (1986: 43).

As an ecologically centered form of conservatism, cultural/bio-conservatism leads to a radical reframing of how both liberals and philosophical conservatives have understood the nature of progress, individualism, intelligence, and the rational process as a source of individual empowerment and social advancement. Whereas the philosophical conservative wants to emphasize the tensions (which vary from being complementary to being oppositional) between progress and tradition, individualism and community, and rational thought and the contextual knowledge of experience—and the various traditions of liberalism emphasize specific human attributes and potentialities (freedom, emancipation, rational planning, and so forth)—the cultural/bio-conservative understands human attributes and possibilities in terms of an ecological model. This leads to profoundly different ways of understanding progress, individualism, intelligence, creativity, and forms of knowledge that are to have authority in the life of the culture. In effect, the rejection of the anthropocentric foundations shared by both philosophic conservatives and the various genres of liberalism leads to emphasizing the interactive relationships between living beings and their physical environments.

This leads to thinking of progress in terms of cultural achievements that contribute to the long-term sustainability of both the human culture and natural systems. It also shifts the emphasis from progress in the technological ability to exploit natural resources and control the forces of nature to progress in meeting basic human needs in ways that reduce the adverse impact of humans on the environment. It leads to an emphasis on progress in understanding our moral relationship to the rest of the biotic community, and in how to represent these relationships in languages that provide the conceptual schemata for thought and behavior. Intelligence understood within an ecological framework takes account of the conceptual schemata encoded in the language systems of a culture, as well as how these recursive expressions of intelligence influence the person's ability to recognize and interpret the information exchanges that both sustain the structural coupling of other entities and systems that make up an ecology, and, depending upon the nature of the perturbations, lead to fundamental changes—like the decline of a species or changes in the chemical characteristics of the soil that, in turn, will alter the types of vegetation that will grow. Individualism is similarly reframed, with the emphasis shifting from autonomous individuals who look out upon an external world, think, and make value judgments relative to how they are going to act upon it, to an emphasis on understanding individuals as evolving through relationships, with their ultimate well-being depending upon the nondestructive quality of the relationships.

Forms of Conservatism and the Educational Process

As part of the process of how cultures reproduce themselves, education is an inherently conserving process—even when it is part of a modern form of culture that has a strong antitradition orientation. The goals of education, the form of pedagogy, and the curriculum will vary depending upon the epistemology encoded in the language of the cultural group, the metanarratives that frame how progress and other fundamental relationships are understood, and the more explicit ideology that guides the thought and cultural practices of those groups who are more oriented toward accepting the authority of abstract ideas than the more contextual forms of knowledge that characterize living traditions. Thus there is no one conservative form of education. But there is always a relationship between the deep metanarratives of a cultural group (which can also be understood as a world view or paradigm) and the educational process. Unless these deep cultural ways of knowing and interpreting the world (that is, the root metaphors upon which the metaphorical languages of everyday life are based) are made explicit, the culturally specific orientations in a philosophy of education will remain hidden.

C.A. Bowers

See also CAPITALISM; INDIVIDUALISM; LIBERALISM; NATIONALISM; PROGRESS, IDEA OF, AND PROGRESSIVE EDUCATION; RELIGIOUS EDUCATION; REVOLUTION; SOCIAL AND POLITICAL PHILOSOPHY

Bibliography

Bateson, Gregory. *Steps to an Ecology of Mind.* New York: Ballantine, 1972.
Berry, Wendell. *The Unsettling of America: Culture and Agriculture.* San Francisco: Sierra Club Books, 1986.
Bowers, C.A. *Education, Cultural Myths, and the Ecological Crisis: Toward Deep Changes.* Albany, N.Y.: State University of New York Press, 1993.
———. *Elements of a Post-Liberal Theory of Education.* New York: Teachers College Press, 1987.
Burke, Edmund. *Reflections on the Revolution in France.* Chicago: Gateway Editions, 1962.
———. "The Truth about Civil Liberty." In *The Portable Conservative Reader,* edited by Russell Kirk, 3–7. New York: Penguin Books, 1982.
Durning, Alan. "Asking How Much Is Enough." In *State of the World 1991,* edited by Lester R. Brown, 153–69. New York: Norton, 1991.
Leopold, Aldo. *A Sand County Almanac.* San Francisco/New York: Sierra Club/ Ballantine Book, 1970.
Nisbet, Robert. *Conservatism: Dream and Reality.* Minneapolis: University of Minnesota Press, 1986.
Rossiter, Clinton. *Conservatism in America.* New York: Vintage, 1962.
Shils, Edward. *Tradition.* Chicago: University of Chicago Press, 1981.
Snyder, Gary. *The Practice of the Wild.* San Francisco: North Point, 1991.

Critical Theory

Critical theory is a school of social and political thought that had its origins in Weimar Germany. Also known as the Frankfurt School because of the theoretical and empirical work done at the Institute of Social Research in Frankfurt, Germany, it includes such eminent (and disparate) thinkers as Max Horkheimer, Theodor Adorno, Herbert Marcuse, Erich Fromm, and, later, Jürgen Habermas. Their scholarship brought together philosophy and social theory in the interest of transforming society and ending all forms of domination.

Troubled by the increasing influence of monopoly capitalism on German institutions, the rise of Nazism, and the problematic socialism of the Soviet Union, these theorists began asking fundamental questions about the nature of social change, the role of reason in modern society, and the connections between theory and practice. Although committed to a Marxist critique of capitalism, they drew on non-Marxist thinking, especially that of Max Weber and Sigmund Freud. There was no unanimity among them, but they all shared a commitment to systematic, interdisciplinary, and multifaceted analyses of modernity. At the same time, they developed analyses that resisted closure: They did not want to replicate the kind of German philosophical systems in which they had been steeped as students.

As part of their commitment to openness, critical theorists questioned the intellectual traditions around them, including much of Western philosophy, mainstream social science, and orthodox Marxism. But these were not dogmatic challenges. Even though they criticized traditional philosophy, they remained committed to many of the central concerns of Enlightenment thought, including reason, freedom, and truth. Their project was to transform and rehabilitate these concepts to aid the creation of a more just and democratic society. And although they targeted positivist social science for criticism, they did not eschew empirical work. In fact, they believed that empirical studies must be done, along with cogent theoretical analysis, in order to better explain the social movements of the time. As for their relationship to Marxism, they still embraced Marx's commitment to human liberation through praxis and his understanding of political economy; however, they wanted to extend his analysis beyond the economic to include all spheres of life, including the family, the environment, bureaucratic institutions, and mass culture.

Critical theory was most often expressed as a series of critiques of positivism, Marxism, and other philosophical schools of thought. The members of the Institute of Social Research developed their work in dialogue with these other traditions, employing their own dialectical method as they did.

The Early Frankfurt School: The Work of Horkheimer and Adorno

Max Horkheimer (1895–1971) and Theodor Adorno (1903–1969) are, arguably, the most important early figures associated with critical theory. Although the Frankfurt Institute was established in 1923, it was Horkheimer, in his role as director starting in 1931, who significantly influenced the quality and scope of the institute's work. He attracted an array of intellectuals from many different disciplines who were given relative autonomy to work on their own research. There was no "party line" at the institute. There were, however, some common interests that these thinkers addressed in unique ways, including what they saw as the crisis of capitalism, the collapse of traditional liberalism, and the rising authoritarian threat, particularly Nazism. The study of fascism, with the hope of ending it, preoccupied these men through the thirties. It was the increasing power of the Nazi party that forced the predominantly Jewish institute to move: first to Geneva in 1933, then to New York City in 1934–1935, and to California in 1941. After the war, Horkheimer and Adorno returned to West Germany, reestablishing the institute in 1953, while Marcuse and others stayed on in California.

While in New York, Horkheimer published "Traditional and Critical Theory" in 1937, an essay that established "critical theory" as a unique school of thought. Critical theory, as laid out by Horkheimer in this and other early essays, is a direct attack on positivist social science and on "bourgeois thought" in general. As for traditional social science, Horkheimer criticized its "fetishization of knowledge" and its lack of interest in action. He also undercut the social scientist's belief in prediction by arguing that it is impossible to predict the future of an irrational society. Horkheimer argued for a dialectical social science that was grounded historically and able to accommodate dynamically the "negative" moments latent in contemporary reality.

As for "bourgeois thought" in general, rather than perpetuate the "illusion" of the bourgeois individual as perfectly free and autonomous, Horkheimer promoted critical theory as ideology critique. This form of critique, combining Marx and Freud, was intended to help people understand their "true" interests as opposed to culturally created "false" ones, and to enable them to act on them in reflective, and even revolutionary, ways.

With his colleague Adorno, Horkheimer argued that traditional social theory reinforced the status quo, particularly a consumerist status quo that was complicit in the domination of human society and the natural world. In their influential book *Dialectic of Enlightenment*, written during the war but first published in 1947, they sought to undermine the Enlightenment belief in progress that informed most contemporary thought, even Marxism. In this, as well as in Horkheimer's *Eclipse of Reason*, they continued to believe in the power of reason to enlighten and liberate. However, heavily influenced by the work of Weber and Freud, they came to a pessimistic clarity about the underside of enlightenment. They could see how reason had been "eclipsed" by technical interests, and, when allied with capitalism, became more identified with domination and mastery than with freedom and justice. But their critique did not stop with capitalism. They understood how technological reason, signified by the means-ends relationships that shape much of modern industrial culture, corrupted the utopian socialist goals of the Soviet Union as well.

In addition to their interest in technical rationality and the domination of nature, Horkheimer and Adorno also developed a critique of popular culture. They were concerned with the way film, television, and radio, for example, could affect the consciousness of individuals in advanced capitalist societies. Along with this analysis of mass culture, they developed a sophisticated critical theory of aesthetics that paid attention to the meaning and function of art and how that meaning changes in different historical periods. Adorno, in particular, integrated his compelling philosophical talents with his aesthetic sensibilities to become one of the institute's leading aestheticians.

In addition to his interest in the arts, particularly modern music, Adorno focused on developing an "immanent critique" of philosophy. This involved an examination of the antagonisms and tensions of particular theories in an effort to see the way structures of society are expressed through them. Adorno was among the more pessimistic thinkers of the Frankfurt School, yet held on to some hope that society could change. Anticipating Foucault's poststructuralist analysis of regimes of power, Adorno, in his most developed work, *Negative Dialectics* of 1966, suggested that a negative stance and method can help to disrupt the influence of dominant conceptual systems and avoid totalizing theory. He made problematic any attempt to resolve the inherent tensions present in a dialectical analysis of reason in modern society.

A Generational Bridge: Herbert Marcuse

Herbert Marcuse (1898–1978) is perhaps the member of the Frankfurt School best known in the United States, particularly among students who came of age in the 1960s. With the publication of *One Dimensional Man* in 1964, he gained popularity and strongly influenced the development of New Left theory and political praxis. Elaborating on the theses put forward by Horkheimer and Adorno in *Dialectic of Enlightenment,* Marcuse focused on the pervasiveness of the technical apparatus of production and distribution in advanced industrial society. He warned against a "one-dimensional" society that eliminated all forms of opposition and resistance and showed how the natural and social sciences were complicit in this process.

In order to better explain advanced industrial, consumer societies, Marcuse drew heavily on Freud. He understood the contradictory power of sublimation in modern society, taking the form, for example, of wasteful yet apparently pleasurable consumerism. And he put forward a revised edition of Marx's notion of false consciousness, pointing to the difficulty, in heavily administered societies, of attaining the kind of freedom necessary to make truly rational choices about one's real as opposed to manufactured needs.

This development in Marcuse's thinking led him to underscore the role of language in everyday life and how it is distorted through mass media. His understanding of the explicitly ideological role language can play in any society was echoed in the work of Jürgen Habermas.

Critical Theory and Communicative Competence: Jürgen Habermas

Although Marcuse gained wide popularity during the 1960s and 1970s and rejuvenated politics on the Left, Jurgen Habermas is currently the most widely read of the critical theorists, especially in English-speaking countries. He has become identified as the main voice of a new generation of critical theorists that includes Claus Offe, Albrecht Wellmer, and Karl-Otto Apel.

Since the 1950s, when he was an assistant to Adorno in Frankfurt, Habermas has been gradually reformulating critical theory while remaining anchored to its commitment: helping people gain self-understanding through practically oriented social theory that will lead to their emancipation from domination. His work reflects more of the optimism of Horkheimer and Marcuse than the later pessimism of his mentor Adorno. And unlike Adorno, who abhorred overly systematic analysis and deliberately wrote in fragments, Habermas has become increasingly systematic and analytically precise in his theorizing.

In one of his most important works, *Knowl-*

edge and Human Interests, he carried on the tradition of critical theory by looking at the relationship between science, emancipation, and ideological critique. However, instead of grounding his theory in universal human interests, as had his former Frankfurt colleagues, he developed a theory of knowledge-constitutive interests to better articulate the conditions for the possibility of knowledge. These "interests" are technical, practical, and emancipatory, and are connected to different kinds of human action and to particular means of social organization. Although Habermas agreed with Marcuse that language is vulnerable to ideological distortion, he held out hope for the realization of ideal speech situations, characterized by reciprocity and autonomy of and for the participating speakers. He insisted that, through these self-reflective dialogues, people would come to distinguish "distorted" from "nondistorted" forms of communication, and act accordingly in the interest of emancipation.

Remaining committed to the concept of ideal speech situations, Habermas recognized, however, that there were some problems with his theory of systematically distorted communication. This led to the development of his most recent work in communicative, or discourse, ethics. In this ongoing, complex endeavor, Habermas argues for the necessary linkage between rational consensus through dialogue and democratic participation in society. His discourse ethic functions as "a regulative ideal" to guide the establishment of a just society and to make individual participants accountable to the agreements and commitments they have made in conversation with their peers. He brings together social theory with moral-cognitive developmental theory to better understand communicative competence in the modern world. In his recent two-volume project, *The Theory of Communicative Action,* Habermas offers a systematic analysis of the concept of rationality, constructs a two-tier view of society, and provides a redirection of critical theory that does not lead to the abandonment of Enlightenment hope and values.

Critical Theory and Educational Thought

Since the late 1960s, educational theorists have become increasingly critical of the schooling system. Marxist analyses of social reproduction, such as those offered by Samuel Bowles and Herbert Gintis in *Schooling in Capitalist America,* were helpful in explaining some aspects of inequality in capitalist societies. The

work of the "new sociologists of education" in Britain and the United States opened up new avenues to study the relationships between and among ideology, education, and society. And Paulo Freire, the renowned Brazilian, has had an enormous impact on educational theorists and practitioners with the development of "critical pedagogy."

The Frankfurt School has been another important source of critique for scholars in the field of educational studies. For those disenchanted with the correspondence theory of Bowles and Gintis, Habermas and his colleagues offered a more subtle and comprehensive analysis of the relationship between education and the dominant society. Habermas's theory of knowledge and interests, and his critique of technical rationality, were taken up by Henry Giroux, Thomas Popkewitz, and Maxine Greene, among others, and applied to the educational system in powerful ways. In addition to these theoretical contributions of critical theory to educational critique, Habermas has had some impact on the actual practice of schooling. Robert Young, in *Critical Theory and Classroom Talk,* for example, appropriates Habermas's critical discourse theory to classroom interaction between teachers and students.

This is not to say, however, that Habermas's work is problem-free for us in the philosophy of education or that it should be accepted uncritically. Certain feminist theorists like Seyla Benhabib and Iris Young have pointed out his lack of attention to "difference." In particular, the effects of gender on communicative situations is given little or no consideration by Habermas. Nor does he address the way "reason" is culturally defined. He offers scarce acknowledgment of the effects of institutionalized and internalized oppression, such as racism, classism, and sexism, on how "rationally communicative" a person is at any given historical time or with any particular group.

Yet, it would be shortsighted to discount the whole of Habermas's project because of these limitations. At this time in intellectual history, when battles are being fought between modernists and postmodernists, Habermas's systematic analysis of modernity provides a rich source for understanding the rationalization of the lifeworld in advanced capitalist societies. And his work in communicative ethics remains promising for those committed to furthering democratic participation and rational dialogue in hierarchical, bureaucratic institutions like schools. By transforming the structures and processes of communication within these institutions, those committed to liberatory practice may see the spheres of democracy and justice expand.

Wendy Kohli

See also CAPITALISM; DEMOCRACY; DIALECTIC; FEMINISM; FREUD; MARX; MODERNISM AND POSTMODERNISM; POSITIVISM; REVOLUTION; SOCIAL AND POLITICAL PHILOSOPHY; SOCIAL SCIENCES, PHILOSOPHY OF; SOCIALISM

Bibliography

Adorno, Theodor. *Negative Dialectics*. New York: Seabury Press, 1973.

Benhabib, Seyla. *Situating the Self: Gender, Community and Postmodernism in Contemporary Ethics*. New York: Routledge, 1992.

Bowles, Samuel, and Herbert Gintis. *Schooling in Capitalist America*. New York: Basic Books, 1976.

Gibson, Rex. *Critical Theory and Education*. London: Hodder and Stoughton, 1986.

Habermas, Jürgen. *Knowledge and Human Interests*. Boston: Beacon Press, 1968.

Held, David. *Introduction to Critical Theory: Horkheimer to Habermas*. Berkeley: University of California Press, 1980.

Horkheimer, Max. *Critical Theory: Selected Essays*. New York: Herder and Herder, 1972.

———. *Eclipse of Reason*. New York: Seabury Press, 1974.

———, and Theodor Adorno. *Dialectic of Enlightenment*. New York: Herder and Herder, 1972.

Ingram, David. *Critical Theory and Philosophy*. New York: Paragon House, 1990.

Jay, Martin. *The Dialectical Imagination: A History of the Frankfurt School and the Institute of Social Research, 1923–1950*. Boston: Little, Brown, 1973.

Marcuse, Herbert. *Eros and Civilization: A Philosophical Inquiry into Freud*. Boston: Beacon Press, 1966.

———. *One Dimensional Man: Studies in the Ideology of Advanced Industrial Society*. Boston: Beacon Press, 1964.

Young, Iris. *Justice and the Politics of Difference*. Princeton: Princeton University Press, 1990.

Young, Robert. *Critical Theory and Classroom Talk*. Clevedan, England: Multilingual Matters, 1992.

Critical Thinking

Critical thinking, though variously defined, refers to good thinking and is connected with rationality and the appeal to reason. Many theorists view critical thinking as central to the aims of education, and it has become the focus for an educational reform movement accompanied by curricular and pedagogical innovations and the development of teaching materials and evaluation procedures. Considerable philosophical debate has centered on how critical thinking should be conceptualized, and discussions regarding critical thinking raise and connect with fundamental issues regarding the nature and aims of education and the nature of rationality.

Philosophers of education have traditionally viewed the fostering of good thinking as an aim of education, and the views of John Dewey, John Passmore, and Israel Scheffler are precursors to contemporary work on critical thinking. Contemporary interest in and debate about critical thinking was initiated largely by the work of Robert Ennis, in particular "A Concept of Critical Thinking" (1962), in which he put forward a detailed conception of critical thinking.

Theorists working in the field of informal logic also contributed significantly to the development of critical thinking theory and practice. The approach that they have taken to critical thinking centers on argumentation. A recognition of the limitations of formal deductive logic has prompted them to focus on the interpretation, evaluation, and construction of arguments in natural language.

The issue of how critical thinking should be conceptualized is a primary philosophical issue in this area. Although a variety of definitions and conceptualizations have been proposed, there are some common features that distinguish philosophical conceptions from more psychologically inspired accounts. All the main philosophical conceptions of critical thinking have as a central concept the idea of good reasons; they are, thus, explicitly normative. Psychological views, on the other hand, focus on the processes or mental operations involved in thinking. These views have been criticized by philosophers on a number of grounds. First, it is impossible to determine what mental operations correlate with particular cases of good thinking. Second, any particular operation can be performed critically or uncritically. What determines whether thinking is critical is the quality of the reasoning and not whether particular mental operations have been performed. All the main philosophical accounts of critical thinking depend, thus, on the concept of reason, and focus on the norms and standards of good thinking.

Robert Ennis, for example, highlights the assessment of reasons in his conception of critical thinking. In his 1962 paper, Ennis defines critical thinking as "the correct assessing of statements." He described twelve aspects involved in critical thinking, which he categorized according to three dimensions: the logical (understanding relationships between meanings of words and statements), the criterial (having knowledge of the criteria for judging statements), and the pragmatic (judging sufficiency in light of the purpose of the judgment). Ennis subsequently broadened the scope of critical thinking, and by 1985 he was defining critical thinking as "reasonable reflective thinking that is focused on deciding what to believe or do." The list of abilities he proposes as basic to critical thinking is categorized under the headings elementary clarification, basic support, inference, advanced clarification, and strategies and tactics. They include the following: (1) focusing on a question; (2) analyzing arguments; (3) asking and answering questions of clarification and challenge; (4) judging the credibility of a source; (5) observing and judging observation reports; (6) deducing and judging deductions; (7) inducing and judging inductions; (8) making and judging value judgments; (9) defining terms and judging definitions; (10) identifying assumptions; (11) deciding on an action; and (12) interacting with others. Ennis also views judgment as necessary to critical thinking.

Harvey Siegel also puts reason at the center of his account of critical thinking. For Siegel, the critical thinker is one who is appropriately moved by reasons, and one of the main aspects of critical thinking for Siegel is the reason assessment component. This means that the critical thinker is able to properly assess reasons and their ability to warrant beliefs, claims, and actions. Siegel views critical thinking as the educational correlate to rationality.

The assessment of reasons is also central to the conception of critical thinking put forward by Richard Paul, but for Paul such assessment must go beyond finding weaknesses in views with which one disagrees in order to reinforce one's own views. The latter Paul characterizes as critical thinking in the weak sense. He advocates, instead, critical thinking in the strong sense, which is thinking that probes the egocentric and sociocentric assumptions that underpin beliefs, including one's own, and that examines the world views in which beliefs are embedded. Strong-sense critical thinking involves dealing with issues from multiple perspectives and is, thus, dialectical and dialogical.

Criteria and standards are particularly prominent in the account of critical thinking proposed by Matthew Lipman. Lipman's view differs from the views previously described in that it focuses on judgment rather than on belief and action. He defines critical thinking as thinking that facilitates judgment because it relies on criteria, is self-correcting, and is sensitive to context.

John McPeck defines critical thinking as the appropriate use of reflective skepticism within the problem area under consideration. This definition limits the domain of critical thinking somewhat in that, for McPeck, critical thinking is not coextensive with rationality, but is a subspecies of rational thought that is used only when one encounters problems in the normal course of reasoning. According to McPeck, all rational thinking is not critical thinking.

Another commonality among the main philosophical conceptions of critical thinking is that dispositions are seen as constituting an important dimension of critical thinking. Siegel proposes the notion of the critical spirit to capture this dispositional dimension, which he sees as being of equal importance with the reason assessment component. The critical spirit indicates that a critical thinker values good reasoning and is disposed to assess reasons and to govern beliefs and actions on the basis of such assessment. Ennis includes a list of tendencies or dispositions in his conception of critical thinking. It includes the disposition to seek a clear statement of the statement or question, to seek reasons, to try to be well-informed, to use credible sources and mention them, to take into account the total situation, to try to remain relevant to the main point, to keep in mind the original or basic concern, to look for alternatives, to be open-minded, to take a position when the evidence and reasons are sufficient, to seek as much precision as the subject permits, to deal in an orderly manner with the parts of a complex whole, and to be sensitive to the feelings, level of knowledge, and degree of sophistication of others. And dispositions, values, and traits of character are central to Paul's strong-sense critical thinking. Strong sense critical thinking involves not just a set of intellectual or technical skills but certain central dispositions or habits of mind. These include open-mindedness, sensitivity to the possibility of self-deception, and willingness to empathetically understand points of view with which one disagrees.

Another issue with respect to the conceptualization of critical thinking involves the relationship between critical thinking and creative thinking. Early accounts, (such as that of Ennis, 1962), tended to view them as distinct, but theorists have begun to argue that they are interrelated, and that good thinking has both generative and evaluative dimensions. For example, Lipman maintains that critical thinking has an intuitive, spontaneous dimension and that creative thinking has rational aspects.

The relationship between informal logic and critical thinking is another important issue. Informal logic has been defined by J.A. Blair and R.H. Johnson as the normative study of argument, which involves the development of standards, criteria, and procedures for the interpretation, evaluation, and construction of arguments and argumentation used in natural language. Most theorists see logic and argumentation as important and necessary but not sufficient for critical thinking, the scope of critical thinking extending beyond the analysis of arguments. McPeck, however, argues that argument analysis plays a relatively minor role in critical thinking.

The main area of philosophical contention with respect to critical thinking relates to the issue of whether critical thinking is generalizable—that is, whether there are criteria, principles, or skills of critical thinking that apply across domains or subjects. Ennis, an upholder of generalizability, argues that the proficiencies and dispositions he describes are relevant to a variety of areas. McPeck deploys a number of arguments against the existence of general skills: (1) Because all thinking is thinking about something, the idea of a general skill that is not applied to any particular subject is incoherent; (2) Because knowledge of the particular subject is necessary for critical thinking, a general ability to think critically can not exist; and (3) Different fields rely on different epistemologies, using different kinds of reasons and different types of arguments, so what is involved in critical thinking varies from field to field.

In response to these arguments, Ennis, Siegel, and others have argued the following: (1) The fact that critical thinking must have an object does not imply that there cannot be critical thinking principles that are relevant to more than one area; (2) Supporters of generalizability acknowledge that knowledge is necessary for critical thinking, but the necessity of knowledge does not imply that there are no general skills; (3) The fact that there are some types of reasons and arguments that are specific to particular fields does not preclude the possibility that there are also principles that apply to many fields.

The issue of generalizability has implications for how critical thinking can best be fostered through education. The subject-specificity thesis would seem to point to the conclusion that students would have to learn to think critically through actually engaging in an in-depth and critical manner with the particular subject matter. The existence of general principles might seem to lend support to the use of separate courses or instructional units designed specifically to develop critical thinking (for example, informal logic courses). Nonetheless, it might be that general principles are best learned in particular contexts, a conclusion that might support an infusion approach in which particular subject matter is taught in a manner that highlights the relevant critical principles and encourages the relevant dispositions. A different approach to developing critical thinking takes the form of attempts to engage children in philosophical inquiry. Such inquiry is thought to be useful in the development of an inquiring attitude, the ability to be self-critical, and the ability to reflect on methodology, and thus, ultimately, in the development of judgment. The choice of approach would be dependent on whether there are general principles of critical thinking, the importance of the epistemologies of particular disciplines, the role of background knowledge, and the extent to which principles of critical thinking will transfer between areas and to everyday contexts. These are to some extent empirical as well as conceptual questions.

The issue of how and to what extent critical thinking can be evaluated has also been the subject of philosophical investigation. The most widely used instruments for assessing critical thinking are the Cornell Critical Thinking Tests and the Watson-Glaser Critical Thinking Appraisal, but their multiple-choice format has been criticized for failing to capture the reasoning involved and for missing some important dimensions of critical thinking. New methods for assessment, such as essay tests, multiple-choice tests requiring written justifications, and various types of authentic measures are being developed.

Much current debate about critical thinking centers on issues of justification. Although the ideal of critical thinking is implicit in some prominent philosophical conceptions of education (such as those of Israel Scheffler and R.S. Peters), one of the few theorists to tackle the issue of justification explicitly is Siegel. The justification that Siegel offers rests on the following grounds: (1) The principle of respect for persons entails respect for students' right to question and to seek reasons and justification; (2) Critical thinking is necessary for the development of the independent judgment required for self-sufficiency in adulthood; (3) Critical thinking contributes to the development of skills and dispositions necessary for initiation into the rational traditions; and (4) The ability to think critically is vital for citizens in a democracy.

Much recent discussion about critical thinking has taken the form of challenges to the prevailing conceptions and to their justification. One criticism is that prevailing conceptions are excessively individualistic and that critical thinking is better viewed as a social practice that is constituted through dialogue and community.

Another form of challenge takes the form of charges that critical thinking is biased, in particular with respect to gender and culture. Thus it is claimed that current conceptions conceive of critical thinking in terms that favor traditionally advantaged groups and thus fail to recognize certain important aspects of critical thinking. For example, it is claimed that current conceptions neglect emotion, are overly confrontational, privilege personal autonomy over relationships, downplay concrete experience, and fail to acknowledge subjectivity and situational differences.

Another sort of challenge is to the place claimed for critical thinking as universal and as the primary educational ideal. It has been argued that there are other ideals, for example caring, that are at least equally important, and further, that to propose critical thinking as a universal idea is culturally biased because critical thinking is not central to all cultures. Thus critical thinking is viewed as one ideology among others and its advocacy viewed as a kind of cultural imposition. These types of criticisms raise fundamental philosophical issues regarding the nature and role of rationality. Responses on the part of advocates of critical thinking point to the self-correcting nature of reason, the fallibilist nature of critical thinking (that the standards are themselves subject to improvement), that there may be numerous ways to be rational, that reason is presupposed in any criticisms, even of reason itself, and that any proposed alternatives to critical thinking would themselves have to be assessed on the basis of standards and principles of critical thinking.

Sharon Bailin

See also AIMS OF EDUCATION; DEWEY; LIBERAL EDUCATION; LOGIC; REASON AND RATIONALITY

Bibliography

Bailin, Sharon. "Critical and Creative Thinking." *Informal Logic* 9 (1987): 23–30.

Blair, J.A., and R.H. Johnson. "The Current State of Informal Logic and Critical Thinking." *Informal Logic* 9 (1987): 147–51.

Ennis, Robert. "A Concept of Critical Thinking: A Proposed Basis for Research in the Teaching and Evaluation of Critical Thinking Ability." *Harvard Educational Review* 32 (1962): 81–111.

———. "A Taxonomy of Critical Thinking Dispositions and Abilities." In *Teaching Thinking: Theory and Practice*, edited by J. Baron and R. Sternberg. New York: W.H. Freeman, 1987.

Lipman, Matthew. *Thinking in Education.* Cambridge: Cambridge University Press, 1991.

McPeck, John. *Critical Thinking and Education.* New York: St. Martin's Press, 1981.

Norris, Stephen, and Robert Ennis. *Evaluating Critical Thinking.* Pacific Grove, Calif.: Midwest Publications, 1989.

Paul, Richard. *Critical Thinking: What Every Person Needs to Survive in a Rapidly Changing World.* Rohnert Park, Calif.: Center for Critical Thinking and Moral Critique, 1990.

Scriven, Michael. *Reasoning.* New York: McGraw-Hill, 1976.

Siegel, Harvey. *Educating Reason: Rationality, Critical Thinking, and Education.* New York: Routledge, 1988.

Thayer-Bacon, Barbara. "Caring and Its Relationship to Critical Thinking." *Educational Theory* 43 (1993): 323–40.

Curriculum and Instruction

Curriculum and instruction have come to be regarded in academia as separate realms from research and scholarship. This separation stems from several developments, not the least of which is the burgeoning body of research on instruction and the technology of instruction. The bias toward specialization and division in university scholarship throughout the twentieth century has led to the separation of the study of the act of teaching from that of the curriculum to be taught and from the learning that ensues. This division is explicitly indicated, for example, in the separate research handbooks produced under the auspices of the American Educational Research Association—one on teaching and one on curriculum. That this division is dysfunctional is reflected in the inevitable treatment of curriculum in the *Handbook of Research on Teaching* and in the inevitable inclusion of teaching in the *Handbook of Research on Curriculum*. Yet curriculum continues to be seen by many teachers and school administrators simply as subject matter, or "content," whereas instruction is ascribed to "methods." This dualism between content and method is illustrated in the research literature on reading, for example, in which is found such terminology as "reading of content materials" and "content textbooks"—indicating that reading is also taught as a skill apart from "content" or ideas.

The dualism between curriculum and method was anathema to John Dewey. As early as 1900, Dewey attacked the separation of curriculum from method as a survival of the medieval philosophic dualism that held to the separation of mind from activity, the separation of ends from means, and the separation of knowledge from the processes of inquiry through which knowledge is generated and tested on the anvil of experience. To Dewey, an end or aim implies an orderly activity in which the order consists of the progressive completion of a process. Thus, in shooting at a target, the end in view is hitting the target, not the target per se. In the same vein, in defining his own realm of physics, Einstein pointed out that physics had become so expanded that it seems to be limited only by the limitations of the methods through which physics advances. Hence physics cannot be defined merely as a body of codified knowledge, but must be seen as deriving from the methods of inquiry through which one becomes knowledgeable and through which knowledge of physical science is advanced.

Curriculum, then, is more than an organized body of knowledge or subject matter to be imparted to the learner through methods of instruction. Dewey went so far as to express a preference for the concept of teaching over the concept of instruction, in that the latter term derives from a narrower meaning reflecting traditional education—literally a building into mind from without—whereas the idea of teaching, in the broader sense, is seen as a vitally shared experience in the art of communication that enables the learner to become increasingly knowledgeable. Although acknowledging the contributions of Johann Friedrich Herbart, Dewey criticized Herbartian instructional method for missing the vital consideration that the environment defining the teaching-learning process involves a personal sharing in common experiences. To Dewey, Herbartian instruction takes everything educational into account except its essence.

Mark Van Doren pointed out that it has not been fashionable to ponder over curriculum, and few oddities are more suspect than being rational about the curriculum. At first blush, Van Doren's observation may seem outlandish when one considers that there can be no such institution as a school, college, or university without a curriculum. Yet the school typically regards the process of formal education as defined merely by the subjects or courses to be taken. Teachers and professors may devote considerable attention to devising and revising their courses, but give relatively little attention to the necessary interaction and interdependence of courses that, taken together, constitute a curriculum.

The Question of Questions: "What Knowledge is of Most Worth?"

Considering the long history of philosophy and the significance given to epistemology in philosophic thought, it would seem that the problems and issues of curriculum would be of central concern in philosophy. Indeed, the concept of curriculum is implicit even in the earliest prescriptions, programs, and disputations on schooling and the acculturation of the young in all civilized societies. "As things are," observed Aristotle, "mankind are by no means agreed about the things to be taught. . . . Again about the means there is no agreement." Over the centuries, this dispute has marked differences in philosophic outlook and the sociopolitical priorities affecting the schools and institutions of higher education.

In posing a question as the title of his 1859 essay "What knowledge is of Most Worth?" Herbert Spencer held that this was "the question of questions" in education. "Before there can be a rational *curriculum*," proposed Spencer, "we must settle which things it most concerns us to know."

The German philosopher Hans Vaihinger described how knowledge systems or thought edifices have been devised in academia in order to keep from drowning in an ever-expanding sea of knowledge and information (1935). These knowledge edifices or disciplines were developed to meet the practical need for making the world more comprehensible and to facilitate the production of new knowledge. Vaihinger noted, however, that these thought edifices are fictional constructs, and although they are useful for advancing scholarship, scholars make the error of treating them as though the real world were so organized. As a consequence, these isolated, compartmentalized, and departmentalized disciplinary constructs are treated as self-serving entities or as accomplishments in themselves, thereby undermining the very purpose for which they were conceived—to facilitate communication and action.

In *The Structure of Scientific Revolutions* (1970), Thomas S. Kuhn proposed that the advancement of scientific knowledge has been generated through paradigmatic inquiry or through a disciplinary matrix of values, models, and processes for systematic inquiry. To Kuhn, the social sciences remain in a preparadigmatic stage. Regardless of the issues generated by Kuhn's thesis, the divide between the thought edifices of the discipline-centered university and the concerns of a mission-oriented society remains a continuing and growing problem. At the same time, where the disciplines may serve the function of academic specialization, they do not serve the wider curriculum functions of general education, exploratory education, and enrichment education.

A Distinct Field of Study

Paradoxically, despite its long past the term *curriculum* is a relatively modern one, according to the *Oxford English Dictionary,* dating from the nineteenth century. The term *peda-*

gogy, however, dates back to the early seventeenth century. Thus curriculum can be said to have a long past but a short history.

According to Lawrence A. Cremin, the rapid growth of professional teacher education during the progressive period gave impetus to the creation of a burgeoning literature on curriculum development and the emergence of curriculum as a distinct field of study. In the closing chapter of his two-volume classic *Dynamic Sociology, or Applied Social Science* (1883), Lester F. Ward prophetically called for the systematic development of three universal curriculums: a core of generalized knowledge common to all citizens; guided electives for exploratory studies; and specialized studies for life pursuits. With regard to Ward's first universal curriculum, the lines of philosophic disputation were to be drawn throughout the twentieth century, marking the essentialism of basic education, the perennialism of liberal education, and the experimentalism of general education—not to mention the issues in secondary and higher education connected with electives and specialization.

Dewey's *School and Society* (1900) and *The Child and the Curriculum* (1902), coupled with the laboratory school movement through the early decades of the twentieth century, stimulated interest in the pursuit of professional work on curriculum and instruction. But it was Dewey's *Democracy and Education* (1916) that laid the groundwork for curriculum as a field of specialized study. In it he repeatedly attacked the philosophic dualisms separating content and method, ends and means, the how and the what, and the division separating mind, method, and matter. In this work, Dewey offered a technical definition of education that seemed to fit his conception of curriculum perfectly: namely "that reconstruction or reorganization of experience which adds to the meaning of experience, and which increases ability to direct the course of subsequent experience."

The growing recognition of the need for systematic study of curriculum was evidenced in the publication of *The Curriculum* by Franklin Bobbitt (1918) and *Curriculum Construction* by Wallace W. Charters (1923). However, the monumental effort to develop a sense of consensus for curriculum as a field of professional study was to be found in the two-volume yearbook of the National Society for the Study of Education under the chairmanship of Harold Rugg (1926). During the late 1920s, a group of university professors and field leaders were meeting regularly to explore common concerns on curriculum, eventuating in the establishment of the Society for Curriculum Study in 1932, which later merged with the Department of Supervision and Directors of Instruction of the National Education Association to form the Association of Supervision and Curriculum Development in 1941. The establishment of the Department of Curriculum and Teaching at Teachers College, Columbia, in 1938, under the leadership of Hollis Caswell, was followed by the organization of similar departments in schools of education throughout North America and elsewhere.

Nationalizing Influences

Since the middle of the twentieth century, curriculum has increasingly become an arena for nationalizing influences. The initial premise undergirding the national curriculum projects in the wake of the cold war and space race was "course-content improvement" for the schools. It was assumed that the Achilles' heel of the teacher was the lack of subject matter knowledge. However, it was soon realized that content and method are functionally inseparable from teaching and learning. Epistemologically, the leaders behind these national curriculum projects realized that the very rationale undergirding scholarship is method—and so they began to herald the inquiry-discovery method as integral to their curriculum rationale. This was commonly and erroneously associated in much of the curriculum literature of that era with Dewey's reflective thinking or method of intelligence. But Dewey's methodology was not directed at abstract academic knowledge as opposed to practical, life-related knowledge—an opposition reflected in the national discipline-centered curriculum projects led by university scholars.

Compounding the problem was the distortion of the nature of the learner as a miniature scholar concerned with the pursuit of the abstract body of knowledge that defines an academic discipline, coupled with the curriculum fragmentation and imbalance created by nationalistic priorities favoring the physical sciences and mathematics. Oddly, few philosophers challenged the dualism between specialized abstract knowledge and general practical knowledge, or the priority given to specialized abstract knowledge in the national discipline-centered curriculum projects, an issue so aptly addressed by Alfred North Whitehead in his Lowell Lecture of

1925 entitled "Dangers of Specialization." And few philosophers challenged the narrow nationalizing influences on the curriculum extending from the era of the cold war and space race to the contemporary scene of global economic competition. The dangers of subordinating the individual interest and the wider democratic-social interest to the superior nationalistic interest was central to the writings of Dewey, Boyd H. Bode, Harold Rugg, and Robert Maynard Hutchins—and it remains a vital problem to this day.

The divorce between content and method has been greatly widened in contemporary times through the vastly expanding industry of standardized testing, in which the tests determine the curriculum, and teachers feel impelled to teach the test. Under such conditions, students seek to learn what they will be held responsible for on the test. Subject matter is regarded as an end in itself rather than as raw material for growth in social power and insight because the curriculum is isolated from life experience. Curriculum is seen increasingly as a matter of policy mandated from the White House and the state house, as filtered by the local school board. Instruction is seen as the means of implementing the curriculum—the task of the teacher being "curriculum delivery," to use the current parlance. Not only is this division of labor dysfunctional, it also reduces the teacher to a kind of technician.

The problem of curriculum fragmentation, reflecting the artificially divided knowledge domains in academia, highlights the real, continuing, and inescapable educational problem of the fragmentation of society. Educational institutions are incessantly making segmental curriculum decisions, while neglecting to consider the curriculum as a whole. Yet somehow through the medium of that thing that has come to be called curriculum, the immature learner is expected to grow in knowledge and ability—in the social power and insight required of the good person leading the good life in the good society.

Daniel Tanner

See also DEWEY; HERBART; LEARNING, THEORIES OF; LIBERAL EDUCATION; SPENCER; TEACHING AND LEARNING

Bibliography

Aristotle. *Politics*. In *Aristotle on Education*, edited by J. Burnet. London: Cambridge University Press, 1913.

Bobbitt, Franklin. *The Curriculum*. Boston: Houghton Mifflin, 1918.

Bode, Boyd H. *Modern Educational Theories*. New York: Macmillan, 1927.

Bruner, Jerome S. *Toward a Theory of Instruction*. Cambridge: Harvard University Press, 1966.

Charters, Wallace W. *Curriculum Construction*. New York: Macmillan, 1923.

Cremin, Lawrence A. "Curriculum Making in the United States." *Teachers College Record* 73 (December 1971): 207–12.

Dewey, John. *Democracy and Education*. New York: Macmillan, 1916.

———. *How We Think*. Rev. ed. Lexington, Mass.: D.C. Heath, 1933.

———. *The School and Society/The Child and the Curriculum*. Chicago: University of Chicago Press, 1900, 1915/1902; combined ed., 1990.

Harvard Committee on General Education. *General Education in a Free Society*. Cambridge: Harvard University Press, 1945.

Hutchins, Robert Maynard. "The Great Anti-School Campaign." In *The Great Ideas Today*, edited by Robert M. Hutchins and Mortimer J. Adler. Chicago: Encyclopedia Britannica, 1972.

Jackson, Philip W., ed. *Handbook of Research on Curriculum*. New York: Macmillan, 1992.

Kuhn, Thomas S. *The Structure of Scientific Revolutions*. 2nd ed. Chicago: University of Chicago Press, 1970.

National Society for the Study of Education. *Curriculum Making: Past and Present*. Twenty-sixth Yearbook, Part 2. Bloomington, Ill.: Public School Publishing, 1927.

———. *The Foundations of Curriculum Making*. Twenty-sixth Yearbook, Part 1. Bloomington, Ill.: Public School Publishing, 1927.

Spencer, Herbert. "What Knowledge Is of Most Worth?" In *Education: Intellectual, Moral, and Physical* [1859]. New York: Appleton, 1883.

Tanner, Daniel, and Laurel Tanner. *Curriculum Development: Theory into Practice*. 3rd ed. Englewood Cliffs, N.J.: Prentice-Hall, 1995.

———. *History of the School Curriculum*. New York: Macmillan, 1990.

Tyler, Ralph W. *Basic Principles of Curriculum and Instruction*. Chicago: University of Chicago Press, 1949.

U.S. Department of Education. *America 2000: An Education Strategy*. Washington, D.C.: The Department, 1991.

Vaihinger, Hans. *The Philosophy of "As If."* Translated by C.K. Odgen. London: Routledge and Kegan Paul, 1935.

Van Doren, Mark. *Liberal Education*. Boston: Beacon Press, 1943.

Ward, Lester F. *Dynamic Sociology, or Applied Social Science*, vols. 1 and 2. New York: D. Appleton, 1883.

Whitehead, Alfred North. *The Aims of Education and Other Essays*. New York: Macmillan, 1929.

———. *Science and the Modern World*. The Lowell Lectures. New York: Macmillan, 1925.

Wittrock, Merlin C., ed. *Handbook of Research on Teaching*. 3rd ed. New York: Macmillan, 1986.

Cybernetics

As early as 1896, in his article on "The Reflex Arc Concept in Psychology," John Dewey notes the total inadequacy of a stimulus-response model to explicate human behavior or action. He emphasizes the dichotomous nature of stimulus and response in behaviorism and makes the case that it is totally antithetical to an understanding of human behavior and activity. Dewey can thus be considered a precursor of cybernetics—a proto-cybernetician. While the meaning of stimulus and response is totally different, the language and meaning of control theory and systems are already there. The notion of systems was thus introduced in 1896, and the terms *communication* and *control* in *Democracy and Education* (1916). Norbert Wiener's term *cybernetics* called attention to the study of human control mechanism and the principle of feedback control. Wiener derived cybernetics from *kybernetes*, the Greek word for the art of steering. Upon the advice of his mentor, Bertrand Russell, Norbert Wiener studied with Dewey, and, in his 1948 volume *Cybernetics: Control and Communication in the Animal and the Machine*, he fused and built upon the work of Russell and Dewey to launch the contemporary revolution in the management of information.

Feedback control visualizes an elementary system of control by which the sensing elements of an organism can obtain information and feed it back internally for guidance of its operative motor nerve centers. Such feedback was widely recognized by biologists and physiologists long before the engineer-physicist found common ground with the concept in cybernetics. This principle of steersmanship by feedback has played an important evolutionary role in animal life.

Behavior: Adaptive vs. Adapting

Human beings are built as an error-detecting system. Reflective thinking stems from the conditions of the environment, whether it be thinking in philosophy, the physical sciences, or any other field of inquiry. It begins with the perception of a disturbance, such as a signal from noise, and sensed by an individual. Bateson calls it the difference that makes a difference, and thus defines a "bit" of information (Bateson 1972).

The mechanism involving human activity is one of error-detection and subsequent controlled behavior to correct the detected error. Activities are triggered by a signal of some unsatisfactory situation. The feeling of hot or cold or sensations of hunger and thirst are all detected errors requiring some action to eliminate discomfort. Thus, when we act on a hunch, the error-detecting receptor feeds it into the control system for possible reaction to the detected area that calls for correction.

Negative feedback is illustrated in the following case. When the speed of an engine varies beyond a certain range, the governor operates to maintain the speed within that range. The work done by the feedback mechanism opposes, or counteracts, the direction of the main system. Positive feedback occurs when the feedback mechanism acts so that it amplifies the work of the main system. For instance, automobile power brakes amplify foot pressure (Handy and Kurtz 1964).

Adaptive

Automatic activity of man, animal, or machine is an adaptive control system. It is safe to assume that, as with the laws of physics, the laws governing control systems apply equally to animal, man, or machine. In the language of the system engineer, this is a close-loop control system. The control system pattern consists of an input signal that triggers some action; a feedback signal of the result of the action to be compared with the input signal; a closing of the loop and a summation of the two signals; and effec-

tive action to counteract any resulting signal. An input signal is controlled by variations in the output. It is a reference signal. A persistent residuary signal can be made to affect memory, which results in "learning." In a control system, work is triggered as a result of an actual error input. The error is essential to the activity of any control system. These mechanical patterns apply equally to automatic machinery, animal behavior, and man's everyday automatic activity.

To recapitulate, an adaptive control system is subject to the effect of the environment on its sensing elements and has no freedom to control the effect of the environment on its sensing elements. It can only adapt to the system by using its own energy to satisfy the requirement from the environment conveyed through its sensors.

Adapting

An important deviation from the automatic pattern occurs when the automaticity of a system is eliminated. Nonautomatic activity will not necessarily be subjected to the adaptive nature of the control system and trigger its own sources of energy internally available to cancel the disturbance. With the automaticity eliminated, the response to a disturbance is chosen after the disturbance has been analyzed as to its source, the energy involved in the disturbance, the possible response and resulting consequences, including analysis and assessment of energy sources and energy balances. In other words, understanding and creativity are replacing automatic response. In this case the system exhibits adapting behavior. Generally, in people one can observe a mixture of adaptive and adapting behavior. To date, clear-cut adapting behavior has been observed only in people. In a hierarchical system, such as in human behavior and activity, the signal does not originate from sensory inputs, but from the outputs of higher systems inside the behaving systems.

Human beings have the ability of adapting (creating) an environment by means that extend human reach in a specific fashion, including the use of tools and machines, and psychological, sociopolitical, economic, educational, historical, and other instruments. Specifically, the human mechanism directs the signal-triggered action with a view to the adaptation of the environment to eliminate the differential between the feedback signal resulting from the modified environment and the original input signal. The mechanism involved in the latter system of disturbance is subject to the filter of intelligence, thus creating an art image of the environment to serve as a blueprint, or as a guideline, for the adapting (creative) process. The system involved in specifically human activity is operable only when an action is triggered to adapt the existing, given, objective environment to an art or dream image.

As defined by Dewey, art is to select what is significant and to reject by the very same impulse what is irrelevant, and thereby compressing and intensifying the significant (Dewey 1934). We should add to the statement that both the significant and the irrelevant are dynamic concepts that continuously change position. Because machines have only automatic, adaptive responses, and thus have built-in qualitative aspects, or significant aspects, creativity is impossible.

Education, formal or informal, is the phenomenon that initiates a control activity, triggered by the element of relation, association, or construction that appears, for example, when an artist produces an image unlike the one achieved by a camera. It also appears in all scientific discovery, as a change from the accepted previous concept. In other words, education centers on the art-created image and its involvement in control system activity. Adapting, creative behavior depends on education and not training alone. Training involves learning some specified patterns of behavior, be it prestidigitation or tightrope walking, while education is a new concept formation. The result of education is creativity, while the result of training is performance involving skills.

If the adapting, creative, control process "filters" disturbances, or input signals, in the closed-loop servo-system that controls human action, education is then taking place. The servo-mechanism of the human control system continuously develops and grows as thinking develops and grows. Inquiry and correlation of experience are tools used in this process of education. They are elements that trigger the controls. As for experience itself, we can no more know what a particular experience will do to education than what a pencil will write. Experience, of course, is a prerequisite, just as one needs a pencil or something else with which to write. Any realization of something being wrong or different than expected is a discovery. It contradicts the previously assumed satisfactory order. Anything that has seemed logical up to this point becomes illogical, becomes wrong,

becomes an error, and will make room for the elimination of error—for a new logic—for the *ought* instead of the *is*. This realization that something is wrong or different (which initiates the process) is a prerequisite required for new concept formation. There is a difference between man and animals, or man and the machine that is made to simulate man's behavior. The computer essentially accomplishes its function by operating on multitudes of types of problems with techniques for solving them. Thus, a problem fed into the computer in a sense triggers an answer that was originally built into it. But, to reiterate, human problem-solving is a matter of education and growth. It creates or formulates problems and at times their solutions.

The philosophical and cybernetic model of thinking presented herein contains quality as an essential element and operates pragmatically as a closed self-organizing loop. It accounts in a new way for teleological processes like problem-solving, planning, and mechanistic behavior and allows for an infinite variety of perceptual feedback systems.

An Overview of Some Relevant Aspects of Cybernetics in Learning Theory

Cybernetics, or modern communication theory, points out that there are two kinds of messages that get sent between systems or organisms. One kind of message simply travels from a sender to a receiver in such a way that the effects of the message on the receiver have no effect on the sender. Most mechanical systems work in this way. Turning on a switch affects the device to which it is switched, but the device does not thereby affect the switch, unless the device and the switch are parts of, say, a thermostat. The second kind of message is one in which the reaction of the recipient of the message feeds information back to the sender in such a way as to affect the subsequent behavior of the sender, as in a thermostat.

In human beings, communication is of the second sort. Messages are affected by the responses they elicit and are modified by the feedback of information from the receiver of information. Furthermore, the receiver is not only able to choose from several options the response that is most suitable; the receiver also can and does initiate his own desired action.

One parallel we can draw is in the source of the individual's behavior. In many situations, external conditions impel us to respond in a certain way, and usually we do so, changing our behavior to satisfy those external pressures. Such behavior can be quite mechanical. Training programs often produce behavior of this sort. We may, for example, be trained to drive an automobile with little knowledge or understanding of how it works. As noted above, Steg (1962, 1964a, 1964b, 1973, 1993) distinguishes "adaptive" from "adapting" behavior. Adapting behavior, of necessity, must, in the long run, also be adaptive. Generally, all human behavior can be found on a continuum of adaptive to adapting behavior.

Adaptive activity describes the mechanical or automatic response to external messages. Adapting activity is the effort to redefine the message and to feed back to the sender information or responses that in turn can change the sender's subsequent behavior. It is this second kind of behavior that is at the heart of creativity, exploration, and discovery, and that is the essence of thinking. This second kind of behavior is usually keyed by a sense of discomfort with an existing situation. If all seems well, an automatic response is the easiest response. Automatic behavior can take place within a feedback loop when there are no error messages, doubt, or noise in the system. Turning a doorknob to open a door requires the most exquisite feedback of information but, unless the knob or the door react in unexpected ways, requires no reflective thought. Dewey (1916, 1933) recognized this aspect of the thinking process when he described thinking as that behavior that takes place when in the presence of doubt and dissatisfaction. In the language of cybernetics, we would say that an error message is necessary for thinking, curiosity, and discovery to get started. How then, does the individual proceed from dissatisfaction or curiosity to learning and understanding?

There appear to be two necessary conditions for learning and for understanding. First of all, the learner must be able to determine, to choose the pathways he will follow, the trials he can take, the pace of the learning, the self-organization and self-regulation that can occur. In short, the learner must have some control over the learning situation. Second, the learner must receive continuous dynamic feedback from his every effort to solve the puzzle he faces, the task he wants to understand, the process he is exploring.

Notice that there are some major differences in these conditions from, say, operant conditioning. There does not need to be an extrinsic motivator or reward as long as the learner is free to explore and discover. Safe exploration, discovery, invention, and understanding are reward enough, as long as continuous dynamic feedback helps on his quest. It is a given that learning is virtually a cellular imperative. Organisms will learn unless they are prevented from doing so. Humans will seek to explore, discover, invent, and understand, and will do so when permitted.

Transformation of Control and Some Substantiation in Education Feedback vs. Reinforcement

Behavioral scientists have indicated a rather widespread acceptance of the principle of feedback. However, "feedback" and "knowledge of results" are being used synonymously, mainly by psychologists and educators. Knowledge of results is thought to function as reward as well as information. In *Psychological Abstracts,* feedback is indexed as "See also knowledge of results: Reinforcement." One can thus see why many theoreticians took the term feedback to mean reinforcement. In the analogy, the feedback signal is interpreted as having reinforcing properties. The smaller the magnitude of the error, the greater the reinforcement value of the signal. It is understood that the response that minimizes error is presumably strengthened or learned. It has been observed experimentally that providing knowledge of results rather than reducing or withholding such knowledge does lead to more effective learning. It is also true that immediate knowledge is more effective than delayed knowledge. However, this does not automatically enhance efficiency of performance or learning, nor what is categorically stated as competence or mastery. In other words, dynamic sensory feedback provides an intrinsic means of regulating motion in relation to the environment while knowledge of results, given after a response, is a static aftereffect that may give information about accuracy but does not give dynamic regulation of information. Dynamic feedback indication of "error" or selection of what is "taken from the environment" would thus be expected to be more effective in performance and learning than static knowledge of results. Dynamic feedback is not the same phenomenon as reinforcement, although feedback often does also serve to support the desire to continue an activity. Furthermore, the efficacy of reinforcement assumes an active need or drive state while feedback theory assumes that the organism is built as an active

C

system and thus energizes itself. Hence, body needs are satisfied by behavior that is structured primarily according to perceptual organizational mechanism and require programs that communicate (Bruner 1968, 1970; Steg 1962). Systematic transformation of sensory-feedback patterns is affected by the use of tools, be they symbolic, sociopsychological, economic, or other instruments. Opposed to this, reinforcement theory describes learning as the result of the effects of reinforcement that bear no systematic relation to the different kinds of behavior learned.

Reinforcement theories assume an essentially mechanical connection between the reinforcement and the response. There need be no rational or structural connection between them other than their spatial-temporal relationship. An alternative is the notion that learning and understanding require that meaningful feedback inform the behaving individual. For this to take place, the content of the feedback must be intrinsically related to the behavior and its outcome. Purpose can then be seen as an outgrowth of the activity, not as a predetermined goal to be reached by the learner.

D.R. Steg

See also Cognitive Development; Curriculum and Instruction; Learning, Theories of; Moral Development

Bibliography

Ashby, W.R. *An Introduction to Cybernetics.* London: Methuen, 1964.

Bateson, G. *Mind and Nature: A Necessary Unity.* New York: E.P. Dutton, 1979.

———. *Steps to an Ecology of Mind.* Navato, Calif.: Chandler Publishing Company, 1972.

Beer, S. *Cybernetics and Management.* London and New York, 1959.

Bruner, J.S. *Studies in Cognitive Growth, Infancy.* Werner Lecture Series, vol. 3. Worcester, Mass.: Clark University Press with Barre Publishers, 1968.

———. "Up from Helplessness." In *Readings in Educational Psychology,* edited by J.P. De Cecco. Del Mar, Calif.: CMR Books, 1970.

Dewey, J. *Art as Experience.* New York: Minton Balch, 1934.

———. *Democracy and Education.* New York: Macmillan, 1916.

———. *How We Think.* Rev. ed. Boston: D.C. Heath, 1933.

———. "The Reflex Arc Concept in Psychology." *Psychological Review* 4 (1896): 357–70.

———, and A.F. Bentley. *Knowing and the Known.* Boston: Beacon Press, 1949.

Handy, R., and P. Kurtz. *A Current Appraisal of the Behavioral Sciences.* Great Barrington, Mass.: Behavioral Research Council, 1964.

Keiny, Shoshana. *Promoting Higher Levels of Learning through School-Based-Curriculum-Development.* Philadelphia: American Society for Cybernetics, 1993.

Krippendorff, K. *Cybernetics. International Encyclopedia of Communications,* vol. 1. New York: Oxford University Press, 1989.

Papert, S. *The Children's Machine: Rethinking School in the Age of the Computer.* New York: Basic Books, 1993.

Steg, D.R. *A Philosophical and Cybernetic Model of Thinking.* Doctoral diss., University of Pennsylvania, 1962.

———. "Programmed Teaching and Learning." In *Proceedings of Philosophy of Education Society,* edited by F.T. Villemain, 274–81. Chicago: Southern Illinois University, 1964a.

———. "Some Aspects of Teaching and Learning." In *Proceedings of Philosophy of Education Society,* edited by F.T. Villemain, 132–39. Chicago: Southern Illinois University, 1964b.

———. *Some System Concepts in the Human System and a Review of Some Recent Experiments in Infant Behavior.* Proceedings of the Seventh International Congress of Cybernetics, Namur, Belgium, 1973.

———, and C. Fox. *Early Intervention through SCILS: A Communication Model.* Philadelphia: Drexel University Press, 1991.

———, I. Lazar, and C. Boyce. *Computer Assisted Education: A Communication Approach.* Philadelphia: University of Pennsylvania, 1993.

———, I. Lazar, and C. Boyce. "A Cybernetic Approach to Early Education." *Journal of Educational Computing Research* 10 (1994): 1–27.

Wiener, N. *Ex-prodigy: My Childhood and Youth.* 2nd ed. Cambridge: MIT Press, 1966.

————. *The Human Use of Human Beings: Cybernetics and Society.* Boston: Houghton Mifflin, 1954.

Cynics

The philosophical tradition we call Cynicism (from *kuon,* or dog) survived in the ancient world for most of a millennium after its inception in the fourth century B.C. Its fundamental ideas have influenced or anticipated radical social and political movements ever since.

Antisthenes (c. 445–365 B.C.), the tradition's reputed founder, devoted himself to a life of altruism, meditation, and material simplicity, in conscious emulation of his teacher Socrates. He wrote many works that found copyists for a few centuries but are now lost.

Diogenes (d. 323 B.C.), the first so-called "canine" philosopher *(kunikos),* lived on in legend as the searcher for a wise person *(sophos)* with a lantern in broad daylight. He also preached (and practiced) blunt "free speech" *(parresia;* compare both the Quaker injunction to "speak truth to power" and the Berkeley "free-speech" movement of the 1960s), and called for an ethical "restriking of the coinage" *(paracharattein to nomisma*; compare the classical scholar Friedrich Nietzsche's call for a "revaluation of all values"). Plato—an Athenian aristocrat by birth—is said to have characterized Diogenes as "Socrates gone mad." He himself compared his practice with that of choral trainers who "pitch the note too high so others can get it right."

Onesicratus (with Alexander in India, 327–326 B.C.), one of Diogenes' more gifted students, later became the principal navigator of Alexander's fleet through the Persian gulf, and observed strong parallels between cynical teachings and those of the fakirs and "gymnosophists" he encountered during his commander's forays into India. In one extant fragment, he also described some of the social practices he encountered in terms that strongly anticipated Hythlodaye's descriptions of "utopian" mores in Thomas More's *Utopia.*

Crates (c. 365–285 B.C.), a hunchback and student of Diogenes, renounced a considerable fortune for philosophy, as later (in effect) did Hipparchia (c. 335 B.C.), his wife. The two lived amicably together in straitened circumstances, in what may have been the first recorded egalitarian marriage between philosophers, an egalitarianism they tried to carry through in the education of their children. Their example seems to have provided later generations of Stoic and Cynic philosophers with an allegedly unattainable model of happiness *(eudaimonia),* independence *(autarkeia),* wisdom *(sophia),* and other aspects of the idealized "cynic life" *(kunikos bios).* A collective counterpart of this ideal appears in an extant fragment attributed to Crates, which describes a utopian "city of Pera, in the middle of a wine-colored sea of illusion, . . . where people do not fight each other, or take up arms for petty gain or glory."

The conjunction of a Cynic world view and literary talent led naturally to forms of political homiletic, on the one hand, and politically and ethically tinged satire on the other. Bion (c. 325–255 B.C.), Menippus (fl. c. 250 B.C.), and Cercidas (c. 290–220 B.C.), all cynically educated during the third century B.C., wrote pointed anecdotal "diatribes" *(diatribai)* and developed new forms of political and satirical prose as well as verse. Cercidas also drafted bitter denunciations of political and social inequality and engaged in complicated and dangerous political negotiations on behalf of his native city-state of Megalopolis.

Zeno of Citium (c. 335–263 B.C.), the founder of Stoicism, and later Stoic writers such as Seneca (c. 4–65) and Epictetus (c. 55–135), often professed their admiration for cynic "sages" *(sophoi)* such as Antisthenes and Crates (though not for the more bluntly iconoclastic Diogenes), and drew heavily on Cynic ideals of personal integrity, cosmopolitanism (most Cynics characterized themselves as "*kosmopolitai,*" or "citizens-of-the-world"), and ethical self-determination.

Indeed, a plausible case can be made that ancient Stoic ethicians effectively offered more "respectable" counterparts of "radical" Cynic doctrines (parallels might be found in the contrasts between institutional Christian practices and Jesus' reported injunction to "sell all and give to the poor").

In any case, both Stoics and Cynics subsequently found themselves in opposition to the more egregious excesses of several Roman emperors—Nero and Domitian, among them—during the first and second centuries A.D. Among these oppositional figures were the Roman Demetrius (c. 5–c. 80), the Bithynian Dio Chrysostom (c. 40–115), and the Cypriot/Athenian Demonax (c. 70–c. 170).

Demetrius was an exemplar of dissident

integrity, and Demonax an admirable and much-beloved conciliator after the model of Crates. Dio Chrysostom, however, was probably the most remarkable of the three, if only for the enormous range of his personal experiences. Initially an arrogant young aristocrat, he wandered in exile as a humble philosopher-mendicant for fifteen years before he returned to imperial favor, drafted an earnest analysis of the origins of social injustice, and served as an unimpeachable adviser to Trajan after Domitian's death.

Subsequent figures of interest included the second-century skeptical litterateur Oenomaus (fl. 120–140), and the sometime Christian and cult figure Peregrinus, who announced in advance his own public suicide at the Olympic games of 167.

Common to most strands of the complex tradition of ancient Cynicism was an essentially ethical conception of philosophy-as-spiritual-exercise *(askesis)*—more or less austere or rigoristic as temperament prompted or circumstances required. Aspects of this conception and its practice survive in the practice of many who know nothing of historical Cynicism.

Umberto Eco's "William of Baskerville," for example, was a clear Cynic, as were many of the Franciscan and minorite friars he defended. Henry Thoreau was also a Cynic, along with assorted hippies, and the Diggers and Levellers of seventeenth-century England. Mary Wollstonecraft and Heinrich Heine, finally, were Cynics, along with their fellow political dissidents, freethinkers, and radical democrats of (almost) every sort. Cynicism lives.

William Boos

See also Cyrenaics; Socrates; Stoicism

Bibliography
Dudley, Donald. *A History of Cynicism*. London: Methuen, 1937.
Giannantoni, Gabriele, ed. *Socratis et Socraticorum Reliquiae*. Napoli: Bibliopolis, 1990.
Malherbe, Abraham, ed. *The Cynic Epistles, A Study Edition*. Missoula, Mont.: Scholars, 1977.
Paguet, Leonce. *Les Cyniques grecs: Fragments et temoignages*. Ottawa: les Presses de l'Universite d'Ottawa, 1988.
Zeller, Eduard. *Die Philosophie der Grieche in ihrer geschichtlichen Entwicklung dargestellt*. Leipzig: Reisland, 1888. Funfte Auflage, 1922.

Cyrenaics

The Cyrenaics, a succession of "minor" Socratic philosophers, took their name after the native city Cyrene of Aristippus (c. 435–365 B.C.), a devoted student of Socrates and the school's apparent founder. Aristippus imparted his teachings to his daughter Arete, who developed and transmitted them in turn to her son, also named Aristippus, sometimes Aristippus Metrodidaktos ("mother-taught").

The latter tag obviously served to distinguish the younger Aristippus from his grandfather, but the latter's philosophical opponents and unsympathetic observers may also have used it to mark the (then) anomalous role played by his philosophically educated mother. There is, in any case, a scholarly dispute about the distribution of credit for Cyrenaic doctrines (preserved now in a few score pages of scattered fragments) among the school's three founders.

Later figures associated with the Cyrenaic school or tradition included Annikeris, Hegesias, and Theodorus Atheos ("atheist") (fl. c. 300), the latter a student of the younger Aristippus. Much as aspects of philosophical Cynicism were eventually co-opted by the Stoics, substantial elements of the Cyrenaic viewpoint blended into the positions of the Epicureans, in ways sketched below.

The Cyrenaics were proto-empiricists of a rather strong sort, who believed that all forms of human understanding—of facts, values, and whatever else there may be—arise from immediate sensory experience. They embraced, moreover, what in twentieth-century philosophy would be called phenomenalism, the view that we have access only to the direct presentations of our senses, about which alone, therefore, we have any measure of certainty.

In consequence, for example, some Cyrenaics expressed open skepticism about the (officially sanctioned) gods and other spirits, since we lack direct sensory evidence for such entities' existence.

More significantly, the Cyrenaics also held that goodness and ethical value can be directly correlated with pleasure *(hedone)*, suitably modulated and directed, and that such pleasure is not static or passive, but a form of (physiological) motion or *kinesis*.

Further implications of these views appear in the Cyrenaic texts that have survived. Others emerged in the writings of later empiricists, positivists, and other theorists who might be considered the Cyrenaics' collateral descendents.

The Cyrenaics themselves, for example, skeptically dismissed the scientific investigation of their time in all its (rudimentary) forms. Less radical empiricists later argued that science does indeed repay study, but only to the extent it mediates between the phenomena of immediate sensory experience in coherent and useful ways—a view that is sometimes called "coherentism" or "instrumentalism" in the philosophy of science.

The Cyrenaics also gave strong priority to ethical questions, which they interpreted almost entirely in terms of our natural desires to enlarge and refine the range of pleasurable feelings *(pathe)*. Empiricist defenders of such ethical "hedonism" later argued that we should seek to maximize some sort of "utilitarian" aggregate of such pleasures, and sometimes suggested that we have an immediate, pleasure-giving moral "sense" for what will do this, and therefore for what is right for us to do.

Finally, the original Cyrenaics (like their opponents, the Cynics) considered themselves "citizens-of-the-world" *(kosmopolitai),* and they strongly valued freedom *(eleutheria),* for themselves and for others. This latter valuation, with the Cyrenaics' "hedonism," may have inclined them to develop the (quasi-Socratic) view that what would now be called "positive reinforcement" is essential not only to successful living, but also to persuasive argumentation and good teaching at every level (including "mother-teaching"). However "obvious" this view may be, it is one that more recent empiricists and pragmatists have taken care to affirm.

The elder Aristippus's successors gradually broadened the notion of "pleasure" so extensively that Theodorus (for example) found common cause with his Cynic contemporaries, and the Cyrenaics' views eventually blended into the materialism of the Epicureans, who interpreted sensory phenomena "scientifically"—in atomistic terms—as have most of their empiricist and materialist successors.

The Cyrenaics' phenomenalism and distaste for metaphysical abstraction reemerges from time to time, however, as do variants of their hedonism, which lives on in social and educational psychology, and in the refinements of utilitarian ethics that underlie much of contemporary welfare-economics and social and political theory.

William Boos

See also CYNICS; EPICUREANISM; SOCRATES; STOICISM

Bibliography

Giannantoni, Gabriele. *I Cirenaici.* Firenze: Sansoni, 1958.

———, ed. *Socratis et Socraticorum Reliquiae.* Napoli: Bibliopolis, 1990.

Guthrie, W.K.C. *A History of Greek Philosophy. Volume III: The Fifth Century Enlightenment.* Cambridge: Cambridge University Press, 1969.

Mannebach, Erich. *Aristippi et Cyrenaicorum Fragmenta.* Leiden: Brill, 1961.

Robin, Leon. *La Pensee grecque et les origines de l'esprit scientifique.* Paris: Albin Michel, 1948.

Zeller, Eduard. *Die Philosophie der Griechen in ihrer geschichtlichen Entwicklung dargestellt.* Leipzig: Reisland, 1888. Funfte Auflage, 1922.

C

Darwin, Charles (1809–1882)

Charles Darwin, although not seeking or antici-pating it, had enormous influence on the mod-ern world. Very shortly after the publication of his *Origin of Species* (1859), his architectonic idea of evolution by natural selection, and its associated naturalist or materialist world view, began to permeate, affect, and in many cases transform, the academic disciplines of zoology, botany, physiology, geology, anthropology, psy-chology, philosophy, literature, and theology. The nature of these effects, and the debates they occasioned, can be found in numerous standard works and anthologies on "Darwinian Im-pacts," such as those of Appleman (1970), Kohn (1985), Oldroyd (1980), and Oldroyd and Langham (1983). It is noteworthy that these works of the "Darwin Industry," as it has been called, routinely omit reference to Darwin's impact on educational theory and practice. This is a peculiar lacuna.

Overwhelmingly, in both the popular and scholarly world, the beginning and end of Dar-win's influence on education is the controversy precipitated by the teaching of evolution in schools. The Scopes Trial of 1925 was the har-binger of a political and intellectual debate that has simmered away ever since with periodic eruptions, the most recent being the Arkansas trial of 1981 in which Judge Overton over-turned state statutes that compelled schools to give equal time to Creationist accounts of evo-lution. This "Evolution in Education" or "Cre-ationism versus Science" controversy has been well documented by Godfrey (1983), Ruse (1988), McMullin (1985), and Numbers (1992), among others. The issues canvassed have included the nature of science, the demar-cation between science and pseudoscience, the legitimate role of parents and community in the determination of the curriculum, the relation-ship between education and culture, and the pedagogical worth of bringing controversy into the classroom.

One contentious philosophical issue that divided the professional philosophy-of-science community in the Arkansas trial was whether Creationism in science classes ought to be op-posed because it is not a science (Michael Ruse) or because it is an inadequate science (Larry Laudan, Eran McMullin, and others). Judge Overton endorsed Ruse's view and declared against Creationism on the grounds that it is not a science, and thus should not be given time in a state-funded science classroom.

But something more needs to be said about Darwin and education than just the issues oc-casioned by the Creationist debate. Education does deserve a spot in the standard roll-call of Darwinian influences. This claim can begin to be appreciated when it is recalled how many of Darwin's immediate disciples played influential roles in the theory and practice of education.

Darwin's self-proclaimed "bull-dog," Tho-mas Huxley (1825–1895), wrote numerous tracts on educational issues and was actively engaged in curriculum reform and educational administration from 1854 to his final days. A selection of these writings, along with an illumi-nating introductory essay, are contained in Bibby (1971). Huxley was an early advocate of techni-cal and scientific education in a milieu where proper education was identified with literary and classical studies. Furthermore, he championed the education of all classes in society; education was not just for the elite. A central paper of Huxley's, contained in Cyril Bibby's collection, is "A Liberal Education; and Where to Find It"

(1868), which was his address at the opening of the South London Working Men's College. He was scathing in his condemnation of British education, saying that "the best of our schools and the most complete of our university trainings give but a narrow, one-sided, and essentially illiberal education—while the worst give what is really no education at all."

Huxley's address on "Science and Culture" (1880), also in Bibby, provoked an important debate with Matthew Arnold over the merits of a scientific versus a literary education for the development of a cultured person. Huxley wanted both science and the humanities included in the curriculum, maintaining that the absence of either impoverished education and, ultimately, culture. This debate was in certain ways resurrected almost a century later in C.P. Snow's *Two Cultures*. Huxley defended Darwinism against charges that it dissolved the basis for morality. Such charges maintained that if we are descended from the apes, and seriously a part of the animal kingdom, then our notions of good and bad, right and wrong, can have no intellectual foundation. In defending ethics as a legitimate inquiry, he did not embrace any version of naturalism, the idea that ethics amounts to looking for progressive trends in nature and modeling life on them. He also defended Darwinism against the excesses of the Social Darwinists, who maintained that in nature the weak go to the wall, therefore it is unnatural for the state or charitable institutions to interfere with social processes.

Herbert Spencer (1820–1903), although an unorthodox disciple of Darwin in that he retained significant Lamarckism—the view that environmental changes cause structural changes in living things that are transmitted to offspring—was also influential in educational theory. His *Essays on Education,* containing four essays written prior to Darwin's *Origin,* was published in 1861. To many people, this collection became identified with Darwin's educational theory: For them, Spencer was the educational face of Darwinism. Spencer asked in the opening chapter of his *Essays:* "What knowledge is of most worth?" He was unashamedly utilitarian and scientific in his answer: The most important knowledge bears directly upon self-preservation, the next most important bears upon the acquisition of the necessities of life, then knowledge of the rearing and caring of children, next knowledge of social affairs, and bringing up the rear was

knowledge pertinent to and enabling of cultural pursuits. Spencer opposed the domination of the curriculum by the classics. His individualism and Lamarckism led him to a form of child-centered pedagogy: The individual had to survive in his environment, and so education should promote informed self-determination and decision-making.

As well as being a convert to Darwinism, Spencer was an enthusiast of the positivist Auguste Comte (1798–1857), who maintained, among other things, that educational regimes for individuals should be based upon the broad principles that can be discerned in the intellectual development of the species. Comte, and then Spencer, articulated the idea of ontogeny recapitulating phylogeny in the development of mind. Walter Humes, in a well-documented essay on "Evolution and Educational Theory," has observed that Spencer's *Essays* were translated into fifteen languages within twenty years of their publication, that as early as 1868 Spencer was featured in books on educational theory, and that he was "set reading" in teacher-training institutions.

Francis Galton (1822–1911), Darwin's cousin and a founder of the mental-testing movement, is a clear bridge between Darwin and important aspects of twentieth-century educational theory and practice. Galton coined the distinction between nature and nurture, and came down firmly on the side of nature. He was an avowed hereditarian about mental capacity, a thesis that he thought was vindicated with the publication of his *Hereditary Genius* in 1869. When biologists established that physical characteristics—such as weight, height, and skull size—were statistically normally distributed in populations, Galton's naturalism led him to assert that mental capacity must also be normally distributed. This assumption underlay all developments in intelligence testing from that time to the present.

Walter Humes, in the above-cited article, mentions how Charles Spearman (1863–1945) and Cyril Burt (1883–1971)—founding fathers of British educational psychology—both worked with Galton, who used his influence to have Burt appointed as a psychologist to the London County Council. Humes also traces Galton's influence in the United States through James Cattell (1860–1944)—who described Galton as the "greatest man I have ever known"—Cattell's student, E.L. Thorndike (1874–1949), and Lewis Terman (1877–1956), the mastermind of the Stanford-Binet intelligence test. John Dewey (1859–1952) was an enthusiast for Darwinian ideas and stressed, in contrast to Galton, the interactions of individuals with their environment.

Darwin's immediate disciples certainly cast a long educational shadow. But did Darwin himself explicitly write or agitate on educational matters? The answer is no. The excellent biography of Darwin by Adrian Desmond and James Moore, and the extensive study of Darwinian thought by Ernst Mayr, are both silent on Darwin's educational views or activities.

Michael R. Matthews

See also EVOLUTION; PROGRESS, IDEA OF, AND PROGRESSIVE EDUCATION; SCIENTISM; SPENCER

Bibliography

Appleman, P., ed. *Darwin*. New York: Norton, 1970.

Bibby, C., ed. *T. H. Huxley on Education*. Cambridge: Cambridge University Press, 1971.

Desmond, Adrian, and James Moore. *Darwin*. London: Penguin Books, 1992.

Godfrey, L.R., ed. *Scientists Confront Creationism*. New York: Norton, 1983.

Humes, Walter. "Evolution and Educational Theory." In *The Wider Domain of Evolutionary Thought*, edited by D. Oldroyd and I. Landham, 27–56. Dordrecht: Reidel, 1983.

Kohn, D., ed. *The Darwinian Heritage*. Princeton: Princeton University Press, 1985.

McMullin, E., ed. *Evolution and Creation*. Notre Dame: University of Notre Dame Press, 1985.

Mayr, Ernst. *One Long Argument*. London: Penguin, 1991.

Numbers, R.L. *The Creationists*. New York: Alfred A. Knopf, 1992.

Oldroyd, D.R. *Darwinian Impacts: An Introduction to the Darwinian Revolution*. Sydney: University of New South Wales, 1980.

——, and I. Langham, eds. *The Wider Domain of Evolutionary Thought*. Dordrecht: Reidel, 1983.

Ruse, M., ed. *But Is It Science? The Philosophical Question in the Creation/Evolution Controversy*. Albany, N.Y.: Prometheus Books, 1988.

Snow, C.P. *The Two Cultures and the Scientific Revolution*. New York: Cambridge University Press, 1951.

Spencer, H. *Education: Intellectual, Moral and Physical* [1861]. New York: D. Appleton, 1860.

D

Davies, (Sarah) Emily (1830–1921)

An English pioneer of women's education and author of *The Higher Education of Women* (1866), campaigned successfully for the foundation of Girton College, Cambridge, and served as its first mistress from 1873 to 1875. Davies solicited aid from well-established supporters and showed little interest in issues of educational reform per se, but her firm defense of a common education for both sexes was exemplary in a period when opponents posed every imaginable objection to the university education of women.

Davies was the fourth of five children of John Davies, an Anglican clergyman, and his wife, Mary Hopkinson. The family settled in Gateshead near Newcastle when Emily was ten. Davies's three brothers attended well-known public schools and went up to Cambridge, but Emily, eager to study science and classical languages, was permitted only brief attendance at a local day school and occasional lessons in languages and music.

Emily's elder brother Llewellyn Davies, however, shared many of her interests and convictions. A Broad-Church clergyman and Christian Socialist, he taught in the Working Men's College, and aided in the campaigns to make higher education available for women. Through him, Davies developed connections with progressive circles in London and became one of the "lady visitors" who chaperoned women students at Bedford College. Also valuable were her encounters with Barbara Leigh Smith Bodichon, whom she met during the late 1850s, and with Elizabeth Garrett Anderson and other prominent members of the Langham Place Circle. After three of her siblings died, Emily returned to live with her parents and struggled to maintain her activities from Gateshead, making short visits to London whenever possible. After her father's death in 1861, she moved with her mother to London, and began work from an office in Langham Place.

Emily Davies became an indefatigable member of the women's movement for much of the next half century. She served as editor of the *English Women's Journal*, secretary of a committee to open the University of London matriculation examination to women, and founder and secretary of the London Schoolmistresses' Association from 1866 to 1888. She also campaigned successfully for the inclusion of girls' education in an 1864 government inquiry on education, helped organize the first suffrage petition presented by John Stuart Mill to Parliament in 1866, served on the London School Board from 1870 to 1873, and led a deputation to Parliament to demand votes for women in 1906.

Davies's most important contribution, however, was her role in the foundation and growth of Girton College. In 1863, she persuaded Cambridge University to hold a local examination for girls, and she began to raise money to found a college for women at Benslow House, Hitchin, Hertfordshire, which opened in 1869 with five students and Davies as honorary secretary. These students were permitted to take Cambridge examinations privately, and when the school moved to Cambridge as Girton College in 1873, Davies became its first mistress from 1873 to 1875 and remained its secretary for the next thirty years. All Cambridge University examinations were opened to women in 1884, though graduates of women's colleges did not receive university degrees until 1948. Emily Davies made her last public appearance at age 89 in 1919, when she attended the Girton College Jubilee.

Davies's major contribution to educational theory was *The Higher Education of Women* (1866), a short work in which she canvassed the grim state of contemporary women's education and called for a feminist interpretation of the "doctrine which teaches educators to seek in every human soul for that divine image which it is their work to call out and to develop."

Contemporary middle-class women, Davies observed, were forced to betray their natural aspirations and sense of discipline for a life of "idle" domestic self-effacement. In response to such repression, Davies proposed a system of secondary and university education to prepare women for all the duties of life—civic, domestic, and professional. Thus trained, she argued, women might work "with great advantage to themselves, and at least without injury to any one else" in medicine, pharmacy, law, farming, marketing, and aspects of what one might now call "social work," including visitation and inspection of workhouses, hospitals, and penitentiaries. Daughters would be apprenticed to the family business in the same way as sons, and "ladies" would manage factories.

To rebut claims that married women needed no such education, Davies pointed to the administrative aspects of household management and problems of widowhood, and even made bold to suggest that some married women might continue to practice their professions. Paralleling arguments of Harriet Taylor and J.S. Mill, she also observed that equal access to higher education would permit a more natural range of human preferences to develop: "It seems likely that a more healthy diversified type of character will be obtained by cultivating the common human element, and leaving individual differences free to develop themselves, than by dividing mankind into two great sections and forcing each into a mould." "A man who should carry one of his arms in a sling, in order to secure greater efficiency and importance to the other, would be regarded as a lunatic." "'Women's work,' it is said, 'is helping work.' . . . And is it men's work to hinder?"

The higher education she advocated, finally, should also be of unimpeachable quality, she asserted, for "it matters less what is nominally taught, than that . . . it . . . be taught in the best way." For this reason, she sought with special ardor to open technical and medical schools as well as advanced examinations to women. Mindful of students' need for material support, she also suggested that some endowments for secondary and higher education be made available to both sexes, and that larger day schools provide inexpensive accommodations for female students.

Emily Davies's most enduring contribution to the discussion of women's education may have been the unwavering ardor of her conviction that women and men are essentially alike in their aptitudes for inquiry and achievement of every sort. She acknowledged, of course, with other Victorian feminists, that "until artificial appliances are removed, we cannot know anything certain about the native distinctions." But she remained unshakably committed to the view that "a great part of the difficulties which beset every question concerning women would be at once removed by a frank recognition of the fact, that there is between the sexes a deep and broad basis of likeness." Her analytic prose, discreetly sardonic presentation, and belief in stringent standards for women's education made Emily Davies a pioneering figure in the history of nineteenth- and early twentieth-century feminism and educational reform.

Florence Boos

See also FEMINISM; GIRLS AND WOMEN, EDU-
CATION OF; MILL

Bibliography

Caine, Barbara. *Victorian Feminists*. New
York: Oxford University Press, 1992.

Davies, Emily. *The Application of Funds to
the Education of Girls*. London:
Longman, 1865.

———. *The Higher Education of Women*.
London and New York: Strahan, 1866.

———. *Medicine as a Profession for Women*.
London: Emily Faithfull, 1862.

———. *On Secondary Instruction as Relating
to Girls*. London: William Ridgeway,
1864.

———. *Thoughts on Some Questions Relating to Women*. Cambridge: Bowes and
Bowes, 1910.

———. *Women in the Universities of England and Scotland*. Cambridge:
Macmillan and Bowes, 1896.

Sheets, Robin. "Emily Davies." In *Victorian
Britain: An Encyclopedia*. New York:
Garland, 1988.

Stephen, Barbara. *Emily Davies and Girton
College*. Westport, Conn.: Hyperion
Press, 1975.

Vicinus, Martha. *Independent Women: Work
and Community for Single Women,
1850–1920*. Chicago: University of Chicago Press, 1985.

Democracy

Democracy has been defined many different
ways by different people in different historical
contexts. At the most fundamental level, the
term *democracy* refers to a government based
on the consent of the governed as opposed to
dictatorship or oligarchy, based on birth,
wealth, or simple power. There are, however, a
number of variables that appear along the spectrum of the differing definitions of democracy.
The consent of the governed can be a fairly
passive acceptance of the rule of a leadership
class. On the other hand, it can mean active
involvement in the business of government by
citizens at every level, not merely through voting but through the development of communities of active and equal citizens. In most governments that have called themselves democratic,
the ranks of citizens whose consent was required has also been significantly smaller than
the people as a whole. Women, slaves, and

people without property or birth rights have
more often than not been excluded from the
government of states referred to as democratic.
And the contests over inclusion and over the
rights and responsibilities of citizenship continue to be at the heart of current debates about
democracy.

The link between democracy and education has also been a matter of debate since at
least the time of Aristotle (384–322 B.C.). And
since the time of Aristotle, the definitions of
both democracy and education have been fluid.
Aristotle defended democracy on the grounds
that the many were, on average, likely to be
wiser than the few, and also because a state in
which the majority are excluded would be, of
necessity, full of enemies. Because the Aristotelian state was based on the wisdom and virtue
of the rulers, democracy demanded a widespread education that would ensure both the
wisdom and the virtue of the next generation of
citizens, both those called to specific office and
those doing the calling.

At the same time, however, the great contradiction of Aristotle's definition of democracy
was the limited base of citizenship. Citizens
were free men; women, slaves, and foreigners
were excluded. And the exclusion by sex and by
caste was as central to Aristotle's definition of
democracy as the inclusion of the free citizen.
Both the inclusive and the exclusive elements of
Greek democracy influenced the education
needed for citizenship. The free man needed a
preparation in the exercise of freedom and leadership, while women and slaves needed preparation in the virtues of submission to their respective roles. Thus Aristotle argued that
virtue—and education for the virtuous life—
depends on one's position in the society. Democratic education was a very different thing for
a free citizen and for a dependent noncitizen.

In Western Europe, the century between
the Glorious Revolution in England (1689) and
the revolution in France (1789) produced a generation of philosophers who sought to refine the
definition of democracy in terms of the political arrangements they wanted. In England, John
Locke (1632–1704) defended the overthrow of
Charles II by declaring the legislature the supreme power in a rational state. Locke also saw
that an essential link between democracy and
education was necessary to prepare good citizens, who would create and maintain the democratic ideals of a just, rational, and equitable
society. In France, the intellectual base of the

D

ancien regime was undermined by a generation of philosophers, among them Francois Voltaire (1694–1778), Charles de Montesquieu (1689–1755), and Denis Diderot (1713–1784), who chronicled the irrational nature of aristocracy while laying the base for revolution and for a state governed by the many rather than the few. Thus, well before the time of the American revolution, the philosophical stage had been set for grafting some form of Aristotelian democratic polity onto the emerging nation state in the political and intellectual ferment of early modern Europe.

The leaders of the American revolution were readers and correspondents of their counterparts in England and France. Locke's defense of the revolution that brought William and Mary to the English throne became, a century later, a key defense of the revolution that would end George III's reign in a significant number of his North American colonies.

In what became the United States, both the inclusive and the exclusive definitions of democracy also continued to influence democratic education. Among the nation's founders, Thomas Jefferson (1743–1826) provided perhaps the best definition of democracy, as a form of government in which all authorities derive "their just powers from the consent of the governed." Jefferson was equally clear that the kind of democracy he articulated needed a new kind of education to prepare citizens fit for the new free and democratic nation. Throughout Jefferson's long career, the themes of expanding democracy, and of education as central to democracy, appear again and again. The best way to protect against tyranny, Jefferson insisted, is to "illuminate, as far as practicable, the minds of the people at large," while at the same time, ensuring that "those who form and administer" the laws and the government, "are wise and honest." And, as with Aristotle, the contradictions of exclusion—of women, of slaves, of indigenous peoples—also remained in place in Jefferson's world.

Unlike many of his contemporaries, Jefferson understood the contradiction between his call for liberty and democracy, and the second-class status of women and the slave status of African-Americans. More fundamentally, of course, those who were excluded understood all too well the limits of the democracy espoused by the revolution of 1776. Whether it was Abigail Adams, reminding her husband to "remember the ladies," or Langston Hughes in *Freedom's*

Plow, giving voice to the slaves who also believed Jefferson's words "And silently took for granted; That what he said was meant for them," the struggle to expand democracy paralleled the development of the new government.

In 1779 Jefferson proposed, unsuccessfully, that Virginia revise its educational system to fit the needs of the democracy for which its soldiers were fighting. There were two elements in Jefferson's "Bill for the More General Diffusion of Knowledge," both of which fit his own Aristotelian world view. As a means of safeguarding against a return to tyranny, Jefferson proposed a system of schooling throughout the Commonwealth that would ensure that every free male child would receive at least three years of basic instruction and thus be able to read, write, and participate in the democratic political process. At the same time, Jefferson also proposed a restructuring of the College of William and Mary to ensure that citizens of all ranks would be able to attend, thus perpetuating a leadership class of virtue and wisdom, regardless of the wealth of their families of origin.

For Jefferson, as for Benjamin Franklin (1706–1790), Noah Webster (1758–1843), and others of the revolutionary generation, education for democracy included schooling for all and higher education for the preparation of ever new generations of democratic leaders steeped in classical notions of democracy, wisdom, and virtue. It also included the development of a new republican character with a new language (hence Webster's dictionary, which was designed to define a separate American version of the English language), new literature, and new understandings of culture.

It was left to a generation after Jefferson's to begin to systematize an educational system based on this notion of democracy. Horace Mann (1796–1859) was but the most articulate of a generation of school reformers who called for a system of common schools throughout the North and in the emerging West, founded on the need to prepare democratic citizens. As Mann and his counterparts never tired of noting, a republican form of government without widespread education in republican ideals was a receipt for disaster. And in making these appeals, Mann and others were able to persuade reluctant state legislatures to provide the financial base for a loosely federated system of education to ensure a significant level of literacy and exposure to the rhetoric of democracy for many of the citizens of the North and West by the time of the Civil War. Around the same time, William Holmes McGuffey and his editors were successful in producing textbooks to provide the curriculum for these schools, a curriculum that reflected democratic pieties and republican virtue, while ignoring the divisions of race, class, and gender that so limited democracy in antebellum America.

Learning and literacy were also growing in importance in the slave communities of the South, however. In spite of increasingly harsh legislation prohibiting slaves from learning to read and write that was adopted by Southern legislatures following the uprisings led by Nat Turner (1800–1831) and other literate slaves, groups of slaves found ways to acquire literacy. They were willing to risk their lives for something that to them was an essential element in the political and social liberation they sought.

Perhaps the most dramatic expansion of education, in the name of democracy in the United States, came at the time of emancipation. With the end of the Civil War, the great contradiction between Aristotelian and Jeffersonian democracy began to take a different shape. The two pictures of education—education for full and active citizenship and education for second-class citizenship and obedience—were challenged in fresh ways. For newly freed slaves, going to school, learning to read and write, were essential steps in the process of freedom. Seldom had the language of democracy been so central to the development of literacy and schools. As W.E.B. DuBois (1868–1963) asserted, the system of public education in the South was a creation of newly freed African-Americans seeking to embrace a democratic ideal.

In the first decade after the Civil War, when newly freed slaves were able to control their own schools, and in many cases the legislatures of the states of the old Confederacy, the creation of a democratic system of education that ensured not only literacy and technical mastery, but also full-scale citizenship, was the goal. With the end of Reconstruction after 1876, these themes were masked as reactionary forces gained power, but they would emerge again a century later in the educational agenda of the Civil Rights movement.

At the beginning of the twentieth century, John Dewey (1859–1952) emerged as one of the leaders in linking and also expanding the notions of democracy and democratic education. For Dewey, the commitment of democracy to education was only superficially explained by the belief that popular suffrage required well-educated electors. At a much more fundamental level, Dewey insisted, democracy is more than a form of government; it is a way of building up the common good and the common community. If democracy is more than a system of government, but rather a whole way of understanding and living in the great community, then the implications for education are significant. The progressive education movement, as defined by Dewey, was a means of preparing self-confident, active citizens ready to engage in the continuing process of social evolution and community building. Active learning, self-directed study, participation in school governance—all of these for Dewey were not merely new and more effective means of instruction; they were ways of creating in the school the small-scale model of the larger democratic society, a society not only well governed, but "worthy, lovely, and harmonious." In a sense, Dewey was the first American philosopher of education to take seriously Alexis de Tocqueville's observation in his 1835 *Democracy in America* that the American democracy always threatened to degenerate into an anarchic individualism unless the forces of community were as central to democracy as those of individual liberty.

Though often called the father of progressive education, Dewey actually found himself highly critical of much that used the name. Dewey continually warned of the danger of progressivism declining into mere techniques of instruction and concerns for the successful development of individual children—often the children of those wealthy enough to send their offspring to expensive private schools. He also engaged in political battles with those who, also in the name of progressivism, sought to centralize educational authority in increasingly elite superintendents' offices and school boards. For Dewey, democracy required the full participation of all citizens—children in the life of their classes and teachers and communities in the development of curriculum and school policies and practices.

DuBois spent a long and illustrious career expanding the borders of both democracy and education. Known best for his militant rejection of gradualism and his commitment to immediate and full emancipation of African-Americans, DuBois regularly returned to the issues of democracy and education. Most significantly, DuBois rejected the exclusion that had been

D

part of the definition of democracy from the time of Aristotle. For DuBois, democracy worked for all or it worked for none, embraced all or embraced none. Writing while the Ku Klux Klan was an open and powerful force in national politics and even the best of white progressives, including Dewey, often wrote as if African-Americans were invisible, DuBois gave intellectual voice to the yearnings of the nation's excluded. In that voice the stage was set for both the Civil Rights movement and for many of the struggles that have been waged over education in the twentieth century.

For DuBois, a democratic education contained the double elements of skill-building and the development of character and wisdom. From the days of his famous debates with Booker T. Washington (1856–1915), DuBois rejected manual education for African-Americans as a sure means of continuing second-class citizenship. Writing during the Second World War, DuBois noted that the technical skills, the manual skills, were in higher order than ever before, and yet the world was in chaos. He called for an education that would teach both how and why, both mastery of technique and the character to use techniques for human good. The combination of both was required if democracy were to flourish.

In the United States in the 1950s, 60s, and 70s, the Civil Rights movement became the chief arena in which democracy continued to be defined and the links between democracy and education fought out. From the 1954 United States Supreme Court decision in *Brown vs. Board of Education* of Topeka, Kansas, through the struggles to integrate school systems throughout the country, to the passage of the first Civil Rights act since Reconstruction, and expanding provisions to meet the needs of bilingual and special education students, and the campaigns for equal resources to educate all citizens, the Civil Rights agenda has been at the forefront of school politics in the second half of the twentieth century. Also beginning in the 1960s, but expanding rapidly in the 1980s and 1990s, the struggle around the school curriculum, the struggle for the culture to be taught and passed on in school, has expanded the debates about the nature of a democratic education.

Of course, linking democracy and education has not been confined to the United States. The most widely read exponent of a link between democracy and education in the second half of the twentieth century has been the Bra-

zilian educator Paulo Freire. Beginning with his work in adult literacy in Brazil, Freire developed a conceptualization of education in which the struggle for democracy, for the illiterate student to become a free subject participating in the transformation of society, is the key to both democracy and literacy. Expanding on Dewey's notion of the link between democratic education and community building, Freire has insisted that the process of liberation becomes both the reason for literacy and the means to literacy.

On the brink of the twenty-first century, debates about democracy and education continue. In the arguments about multicultural education, "political correctness," and the kind of history to be taught in schools, the much older arguments about the nature of democracy are reflected yet again. While few today openly argue that democracy should be the preserve of a limited number of male citizens, there are great debates about the kind of democratic culture that should be taught in the schools. On the one hand are those who see democracy and culture as emerging in Western Europe and flourishing in North America and who thus teach a conception of culture that is Eurocentric in its core while adding the stories of other peoples and cultures around the margins. On the other hand are those who argue that the only culture worthy of a democracy is one that fully and equally embraces all of the people, female and male, from all races and classes, and thus teaches a multicultural view of history in which the contributions of the many—as well as the repeated attempts by various elites to control power and culture—make up the heart of the history and the school's curriculum.

Systems of public education in the United States that were originally expanded to include more and more citizens in the democratic ideal have also come increasingly to be the key to entry into the world of work. At the same time, new and greater inequities are appearing in the nation's schools, in the resources available to rich and poor school districts, and in the opportunities and expectations for different students in different areas, and often—through tracking—in a single school. At the same time, the number of private schools, and a variety of schemes for funding private schools with public money, are growing. In the increasing separation between the well-educated "haves" and the undereducated "have nots," the future of an inclusive society remains in question.

Throughout the debates of the last decades, public discussion of the link between education and democracy has also declined. For the first time since Jefferson, educational reformers, from many different perspectives, seem unwilling to cast their appeals in the language of democracy. Part of this is the result of growing cynicism about the term, and part is an increasing link between schools and immediate economic concerns. The result, however, could be an impoverishment of the democratic process unless a new generation recaptures a vision of and a commitment to a society governed by and for all.

James W. Fraser

See also ARISTOTLE; DEWEY; DUBOIS; EQUALITY; JEFFERSON; LOCKE; MANN; MULTICULTURALISM

Bibliography

Anderson, James D. *The Education of Blacks in the South, 1860–1935.* Chapel Hill: University of North Carolina Press, 1988.

Aristotle. *Complete Works of Aristotle: The Revised Oxford Translation.* 2 vols. Edited by J. Barnes. Princeton: Princeton University Press, 1984.

Dewey, John. *Democracy and Education.* New York: Macmillan, 1916.

DuBois, W.E.B. *Against Racism: Unpublished Essays, Papers, Addresses, 1887–1961.* Edited by Herbert Aptheker. Amherst: University of Massachusetts Press, 1985.

Finkelstein, Barbara. "Education and the Retreat from Democracy in the United States, 1979–198?" *Teachers College Record* 86 (1984).

Freire, Paulo. *Pedagogy of the Oppressed.* New York: Seabury Press, 1970.

Giroux, Henry. *Schooling and the Struggle for Public Life.* Minneapolis: University of Minnesota Press, 1988.

Gutmann, Amy. *Democratic Education.* Princeton: Princeton University Press, 1987.

Hughes, Langston. "Freedom's Plow." In *Selected Poems.* New York: Alfred A. Knopf, 1959.

Jefferson, Thomas. *The Papers of Thomas Jefferson.* Edited by Julian P. Boyd. Princeton: Princeton University Press, 1950 ff.

Marable, Manning. *The Crisis of Color and Democracy: Essays on Race, Class and Power.* Monroe, Maine: Common Courage Press, 1992.

Tocqueville, Alexis de. *Democracy in America.* 2 vols., 1835, 1839. Translated by George Lawrence. Garden City, N.Y.: Doubleday, 1969.

D

Descartes, René (1596–1650)

French philosopher, mathematician, and scientist, who lived most of his productive period in the Netherlands and died in Sweden, where he spent his last year at the court of Queen Christina (1626–1689) as her private tutor. He is justly called the father of modern Western philosophy. His philosophy, and that of his closer followers, is often called "Cartesianism."

Descartes wrote no work exclusively on education, and there are no commentaries devoted to him as a thinker who profoundly influenced educational theory and practice. Nevertheless, Descartes changed people's ways of thinking and, with it, the educational practice of much of Europe.

His writings commanded immediate attention. His first publication, the *Discourse on the Method* (1637), established his reputation to the extent that thinkers such as Thomas Hobbes (1588–1679) and Antoine Arnauld (1612–1694) were willing to comment on his second publication, the *Meditations on First Philosophy* (1641), and have their comments, with Descartes's replies, published together with the original work as the *Objections and Replies.* A measure of both Descartes's immediate influence and of the extent of his break with the major traditions of his day is indicated by the fact that, within a decade of the publication of the *Discourse* and *Meditations,* the Protestant magistrates and university officials of both Leiden and Utrecht condemned his philosophy and prohibited its public discussion. That did not prevent him from publishing additional influential works, most notably the *Principles of Philosophy* (1644) and *The Passions of the Soul* (1649). Well before the century was out, the Catholic Church had placed his works on the *Index.*

Censure generally has effects opposite to those intended, and it was not long before the Cartesian position became dominant in much of Europe. The entry on Locke (1632–1704) in this volume indicates the extensive influence Descartes exerted on him, particularly in Locke's influential educational writings. The theological school of John Calvin (1509–1564) in Geneva was dominated by Cartesianism a generation after Calvin's death; through the Calvinistic influence in Protestant countries, a good deal of Cartesian rationalism entered into Europe's consciousness from pulpit through pew. In Italy, in the face of the growing imperiousness of exact scientific thought, Giambattista Vico (1668–1744) published *On the Study Methods of Our Time* (1709), opposing the Cartesianism that by then had become pervasive—a Cartesianism that emphasized formalistic science.

The most radical change Descartes brought about concerned both the status of human beings and the way in which human beings in their new status could achieve truth, goodness, and wisdom. For Plato (c. 427–347 B.C.), truth had been a transcendent form: Truth is not found—let alone made—in the human world, and whatever is true is so in relation to eternal, unchangeable Forms. In the Christian medieval world, one pervasive influence was that of Saint Augustine (354–430). For Augustine, too, truth and goodness come from without, ultimately from a transcendent God in whose light only can we see light. This view became the founding vision of Europe's great medieval universities, often—as at Oxford—expressed in their very mottos: *Dominus illuminatio mea.*

Descartes's radical turnabout is that, from now on, truth is to be established by individual human beings who can achieve goodness unaided by external sources, and for whom wisdom is their own creation. The change required of education was profound. It begins with ascribing autonomy to individuals; this autonomy involves rejection of tradition, a different role for knowledge, and a change in how to view the realm of nature.

Descartes insists on the rejection of tradition from the *Discourse* on: He has no use for conventional "oratory," "poetry," "morals," "theology," and "philosophy." The best he can say for "jurisprudence," "medicine," and "other sciences" is that they "bring honors and riches to those who cultivate them." That statement amounts to a charge of fraudulence, but it also contains a hint of the grounds for Descartes's dismissal of traditional so-called knowledge: It is not *useful to humanity.* During his own education at one of France's outstanding schools, he had been "nourished upon letters" because he had been persuaded that "by their means one could acquire a clear and certain knowledge of all that is useful in life." However, at the end of this training, he realized that "there was no knowledge in the world such as I had previously been led to hope for." The best traditional education available is useless "in life." The one exception is mathematics because it has potential "to further all the arts and lessen man's labors," although during his student days neither he nor his teachers had "yet noticed its real use."

This stress on utility that accompanies the rejection of traditional knowledge sounds a new note that has reverberated through Western culture ever since. It drastically changed the role of knowledge; no longer was it pursued for the sake of contemplating the object of knowledge, but it was sought for the sake of application beneficial to the subject.

Implicit is an equally drastic change in the status accorded to that object of knowledge called "nature" or "the physical world." For centuries, nature had been contemplated as God's creation, greater knowledge of which served as a way to greater knowledge of its Maker. Now, nature's value becomes purely instrumental in an immanent sense: Nature exists to serve humanity, and this stress on utility requires knowledge to make nature serve human temporal needs. As Descartes writes in the last part of the *Discourse,* his eyes were opened "to the possibility of gaining knowledge which would be very useful in life, and of discovering a practical philosophy . . . and thus make ourselves, as it were, the lords and masters of nature . . . and so enjoy without any trouble the fruits of the earth and . . . the maintenance of health."

How to achieve this knowledge which promises mastery? The second part of the *Discourse* states four rules which, if they are scrupulously followed, will firmly place the knower on the path of progress. These four rules are (i) Never jump to conclusions; always avoid prejudice (that is, never accept anything on faith or on the authority of someone else); affirm or deny only that which is so clear and distinct that it is not open to doubt. (ii) Whatever you seek to understand you must divide into its parts until no further division is possible. (iii) Then, beginning with the simplest parts, you can develop knowledge of complex items, as long as each step in this (re)construction is clear and distinct to you so that no obscurity enters along the way. (iv) When the (re)construction is complete, check to make sure that you have left out nothing, and go over it several times so that the whole argument becomes distinct.

These rules, which together constitute Descartes's *method,* are presented as a functional definition of reason. In other words, these rules are reason articulating how it goes—and only can go—about its business in achieving power-giving knowledge. They are absolutely valid and are to be applied to any subject matter whatsoever. Upon his belief that a rational God created a rational universe with rational human beings in it, Descartes bases the position that human reason is infallible, being the right tool with which to gain the useful knowledge sought. Human beings can now use their infallible reason to start them on the road of progress to ever increasing well-being. Their destiny is in their own hands, and the focus of their longing shifts from a paradise lost to a future one to be gained through applied scientific knowledge.

Descartes's position is not that of the skeptic. Although doubt is explicitly mentioned in the first rule, it is only a part of the method. Doubt pushes the thinker to divide the problems that confront the mind into ever simpler parts until no further division is possible. That process is not to lead to skepticism but to certainty, for the parts no longer open to division are simplest parts and, as simplest, are clear and distinct. By "clear" Descartes means that all of it is before the mind, and by "distinct" that nothing but what pertains to having it clear is before the mind. With respect to a simplest part, no mistake is possible, for one either understands it or one does not; and since, if it is before the mind at all, all of it is before the mind, it then cannot but be understood. Such knowledge is incontrovertible, absolutely beyond doubt. Over items so known, the knower has absolute intellectual power.

Descartes expands the role of clarity and distinctness to become the criteria for all knowledge. The fourth rule implies as much in its insistence on review: That nothing relevant may be omitted is the insistence on clarity, that nothing irrelevant may be present is the insistence on distinctness. Thus, Descartes's method is not the method of doubt but of reason, and reason leads to certainty. The certainty attaching to knowledge indicates the power of the knower over the item known. Application of such knowledge in the realm of nature results in mastery over nature and amelioration of humanity's lot. Again, how to attain this power-giving knowledge? That is to say, how do we get to know about, and become proficient in the use of, these rules? How do we educate ourselves, and the next generation, to travel the road leading to mastery? Descartes's answers to these questions are in many ways more implicit than explicit.

Descartes expected the required change in thinking to come about through following the examples given in his own writings. The absence of treatises on education is therefore deliberate. All must think for themselves; none can think for others or have others think for them. No one can be taught how to think through imposition of formal rules: If one did not already think, one would not be able to understand the rules in any case. The uselessness of thinking along formal lines is well illustrated in syllogistic thought, which can never lead to discovery of anything new but only to explication of what is already contained in the premises. And since the syllogistic rules contain no guidance as to how one obtains the premises, they are useless in the pursuit of new knowledge. Since he takes his examples to be instances of reasoning, following Descartes's examples is in fact following the examples of reason itself.

No one can achieve proficiency in thinking except through self-education; we must all teach ourselves to think for ourselves. It is for this reason that Descartes called his first publication a "discourse" rather than a "treatise" on method: He wanted to present readers with a "preface" to their own methodic procedure, of which they would become aware through following examples. The examples in the *Discourse* do not remain abstract; Descartes actually shows these rules at work in three scientific treatises he appended to the *Discourse,* one each on geometry, optics, and meteorology. His claim that these treatises could not have been developed without his method is hardly surprising: Descartes believes them to be parts of the new science. No such science can be developed except through reason, and reason functions as described in the rules of the *Discourse.*

Practice in these treatises will make the practitioner self-conscious of the procedures of reason. And of more than reason itself. For necessary to reason are the tools of imagination, sensation, and memory: imagination in order to advance hypotheses; sensation in order to gain initial information on the world in which we live, and in order to test reason's conclusions through experimentation so that the results obtained are indeed useful knowledge; and memory because without it no knowledge of any complexity can be developed.

For those too young to practice on the advanced material of Descartes's *Discourse* and its *Treatises,* there are the simpler mathematical problems of arithmetic and geometry. For the young, these are the best of all initial training grounds for seeing reason at work. This is because, in these sciences, it is obvious that there can be no knowledge of any complexity without reduction of that complexity to the utterly simple, necessarily clear and distinct foundational items such as "unity" (out of which the entire number series is to be generated) and "point" (out of which is to be developed the concept "line" and so all geometrical relationships). Moreover, in developing the number series and the relationships between numbers, as well as in developing relationships between lines, angles, and figures, it is very clear that no next step can be omitted without loss of understanding. If such an omission occurs, it is generally easy to see what the required missing item is.

There is one exercise in the method to which all thinkers must submit themselves "once in the course of their lives." It is the exercise presented as the *Meditations on First Philosophy.* This exercise in the method is Descartes's metaphysics, the necessary prelude to power-giving scientific knowledge. In it, Descartes asks and answers what he takes to be all basic questions a skeptic might conceivably ask about the possibility of the Cartesian project: Can reason be trusted as the developer of useful knowledge? And can imagination, sensation, and memory in fact function as reason requires them to? As in the *Discourse,* so in the *Meditations:* The readers have to follow Descartes's—which is reason's—path for themselves. As they do so, each of them asks these questions, and each will give reason's affirmative answer. In the process, each becomes aware of autonomy as thinker. For each experiences that truth is ultimately founded on the Archimedean point that is reached in the awareness of the fact that not even God can invalidate the fact that "if I think, then I am."

On this foundational subjective certainty—the *cogito*—all of philosophy rests. Philosophy, in turn, serves as the foundation of pure physics, which is itself the foundation of mechanics, medicine, and morals. Those who are proficient in this "tree of knowledge" possess the wisdom of travelers on the road toward mastery. They are busy undoing what the church taught to be the inescapable outcome of humanity's fall into sin. At the end of the road, there will be no more sweat: Machines will subdue the earth for humanity's enjoyment. There will be no more pain: Medical science will prevent illness and prolong what will have become enjoyable life. Conflicts will cease: The science of morals will enable all to keep their passions firmly under control and to allow expression to only such passions as lead to personal or communal well-being.

In Europe's fertile soil, Descartes sowed the seeds of the Enlightenment's enthusiasm for progress: As long as we are willing to reeducate ourselves, paradise lies within humanity's grasp. Error and sin will be no more, and even the final limitation of "three score years and ten" will have been overcome.

Peter A. Schouls

See also AIMS OF EDUCATION; HUMAN NATURE; LOCKE; PROGRESS, IDEA OF, AND PROGRESSIVE EDUCATION; RATIONALISM; REASON AND RATIONALITY

Bibliography

Blom, John J. *Descartes: His Moral Philosophy and Psychology.* Hassocks, Sussex: Harvester Press, 1978.

Descartes, René. *The Philosophical Writings of Descartes, Volume I and II.* Edited by John Cottingham, Robert Stoothoff, and Dugald Murdoch. Cambridge: Cambridge University Press, 1985.

Schouls, Peter A. *Descartes and the Enlightenment.* Edinburgh, Kingston, and Montreal: Edinburgh University Press and McGill–Queen's University Press, 1989.

Dewey, John (1859–1952)

American philosopher and educator widely regarded as the "father of progressive education" and one of the most influential educational philosophers of the twentieth century. Born and raised in Burlington, Vermont, Dewey attended the University of Vermont. After a brief period as a secondary school teacher, he enrolled in the new graduate school at Johns Hopkins University, where he received his Ph.D. in 1884. During the next decade, Dewey taught at the University of Michigan and, briefly, at the University of Minnesota.

While at Michigan, Dewey's interest in secondary education was stimulated by his membership on a committee that evaluated the state's high schools. But it was not until his move to the University of Chicago in 1894 as head professor of the department of philosophy, which included psychology and pedagogy, that he turned his attention to the philosophy of education in a systematic way. Shortly after his arrival he helped establish a separate department of pedagogy, which he also chaired. Dewey also founded the University Laboratory School, which opened in 1896 with sixteen pupils and two teachers and later became known informally as the "Dewey School."

The Laboratory School was a laboratory in fact as well as in name. Dewey never intended for it to be a model that other schools should follow. It was instead to be a place where experiments in educational thinking could take place. It was, he wrote, a place where "the student of education sees theories and ideas demonstrated, tested, criticized, enforced, and the evolution of the new truths" (MW1: 56). It was to be a place where the education of children could be viewed "in the light of the principles of mental activity and the processes of growth made known by modern psychology" (MW1: 67). Drawing on the results of his experiments, Dewey published several highly influential works on education during his Chicago years. These include "Interest in Relation to Training of the Will" (1896), "My Pedagogic Creed" (1897), *The School and Society* (1900), and *The Child and the Curriculum* (1902).

In these works Dewey attempted both to set out his practical pedagogy and to explain the wider psychological and philosophical insights on which it was based. He discussed matters such as stages of development and learning in children, the relationship of the native interests of the child to the subject matter of the curriculum, and the importance of history and geography as tools for helping pupils recognize and develop their interests.

Dewey's educational theories were colored by his insight, rare among philosophers of his time, that late nineteenth- and early twentieth-century America was rapidly evolving from an agricultural society to one dominated by industrial technology. He argued that the nation's schools must reflect this change. Schools devoted entirely to the transmission of vocational skills or to the development of discipline were no longer adequate to the new milieu. The new schools, he argued, must be places of interaction with the life of the new technological culture. To that end, the actual interests of the child must be nurtured and developed: interests in communication, in finding out about things, in making things, and in artistic expression. There must be a reciprocal relationship between the school and the wider society. What goes on outside the school must be the subject of education, and what goes on inside the school must be applicable within the society beyond its walls.

Dewey also argued that improved educational practice must rest on an improved psychology. Breaking with the mainstream psychology of his time, Dewey rejected the prevailing idea of mind as a "purely individual affair." He viewed mind instead as a function of social life. He also rejected the idea that psychology deals only with knowledge. Taking his cue from philosopher and psychologist William James (1842–1910), whose groundbreaking work, *The Principles of Psychology*, had appeared in 1890, he argued that emotion and action also play an important role in learning. Mind, then, should not be regarded as a fixed thing or entity, but rather as a process by means of which the organism can continue to grow and develop.

Another of Dewey's enduring insights was that pedagogy tends to oscillate between two extreme positions. Educators at one extreme are preoccupied with the subject matter of the curriculum. There is consequently little concern for the development of the child's own experiences. This view holds that education involves the rote memory of facts and formulae and that the goal of education is little more than training for the professional or commercial activities of adult life. "Discipline" is both means and ends of this view of education.

Dewey was highly critical of this view. What such "passive absorption of academic and theoretic material" (LW8: 153) lacks, he argued, is the active experimentation that allows children, working with their teacher, to discover their own individual talents and their own best techniques for learning.

At the other pedagogical extreme is the view that it is the independent self-expression of the child, and not mastery of subject matter, that is the main goal of education. In its extreme form, as Dewey described it, this view holds that "almost any kind of spontaneous activity inevitably secures the desired or desirable training of mental power" (LW8: 153).

In his rejection of that view, Dewey argued

that the teacher must play an active role in the educational process. The task of the teacher is to guide children in their own quests, to direct their energies away from what is debilitating or destructive, to focus their attention on important themes and problems, and to help them develop the tools needed to play a full and productive role in society.

Dewey's own view of the relationship of the child to the curriculum holds that education should emphasize both the child and the curriculum. Wherever one element is emphasized at the expense of the other, he argued, education remains one-sided and out of balance. Neither the child's interests (the psychological side of the education process) nor the teaching of subject matter, which enables the child to understand the present and the prospects of civilization (education's sociological side), should be neglected at the expense of the other. Dewey wrote that these two aspects of education are "organically related and that education cannot be regarded as a compromise between the two, or a superimposition of one upon the other" (EW5: 85).

Following a series of disagreements with University of Chicago's president, William Rainey Harper (1856–1906), concerning the administration of the Laboratory School, Dewey resigned his position in 1904 and accepted a joint appointment on the faculty of philosophy and the faculty of Teachers College at Columbia University in New York City. He continued to develop his educational theory in a series of works that included *Moral Principles in Education* (1909), *How We Think* (1910), *Schools of Tomorrow* (1915), *Democracy and Education* (1916), *Experience and Education* (1938), and dozens of essays and reviews.

Dewey was a strong advocate of professional teachers' unions. He helped organize the Teachers League of New York and encouraged its alignment with the American Federation of Labor. Educational leaders throughout the world sought his advice. He was a frequent speaker at the meetings of educational societies and he traveled widely, visiting schools in the Soviet Union, Turkey, South Africa, Mexico, Japan, and China. He died at his home in New York City on June 1, 1952.

In Dewey's philosophy of education, as well as in his wider philosophy, several important and recurring strands are notable. One of them is his deep intellectual debt to the German philosopher G.W.F. Hegel (1770–1831). Even though he had abandoned most of the tenets of Hegelian idealism by the time of his arrival in Chicago, Dewey's earlier devotion to the works of Hegel had nevertheless left what he later termed a "permanent deposit in his thinking." His reading of Hegel had convinced him that cultures and societies are in continual flux and that progress, when it occurs, is the result of a reconstructive synthesis of trends and ideas that are often fiercely opposed to one another.

As his own thought matured, however, Dewey rejected Hegel's view that progress occurs on a grand scale and as a result of historical forces that are the work of an Absolute or World Spirit. He argued instead that when progress occurs it tends to be piecemeal and that it results from the work of individuals and groups who are engaged in a conscious reconstruction of their situations. Dewey thought that the most basic tool available to a society for such reconstruction is the education of its children.

It is by means of education, he argued, that "the individual gradually comes to share in the intellectual and moral resources which humanity has succeeded in getting together. He becomes an inheritor of the funded capital of civilization" (EW5: 84), and an active participant in the formation of its future. Sound education is thus for Dewey the most effective means of effecting social progress.

Dewey's thought was also strongly influenced by the naturalism of Charles Darwin (1809–1882). It was from Darwin's *Origin of Species,* published in 1859, that Dewey got his concept of the human being as a highly complex natural organism that continually accommodates itself to some environmental conditions and alters others to meet its needs. Dewey conceived of education as virtually synonymous with this evolutionary process.

Education is evolutionary in that it is an ongoing experiment in which the teacher leads students to discover ways in which they can actively adjust to novel circumstances. Consequently, there can be no set rules for education. Dewey did think, however, that there are sound methods for educational experimentation and that those methods themselves evolve as they are applied in an intelligent fashion.

Not everyone interpreted Darwin in the way that Dewey did. Some, including the American industrialist Andrew Carnegie (1835–1919), had interpreted Darwinism as a justification for the predatory treatment of workers. "Social Darwinism," as their view was known, held that the rich are the product of natural selection. Financial success was thus viewed as a mark of individual fitness, and poverty as a sign of individual failure. In one form or another, Social Darwinism has remained a durable residue within American social and political life.

Dewey rejected Social Darwinism as both self-serving and antidemocratic. He wrote that the "rugged individualism" advanced by Social Darwinists was dangerous, especially when applied to education. Instead of an individualism of people looking out only for themselves, a new concept of individualism was needed. This would be an individualism in which social cooperation would liberate children from the constraints that prevented them from developing as individuals. The principal instrument of such liberation would be schools, in which children were guided to develop their own latent talents and capacities and thus to sharpen their own unique instruments of adjustment within the life of the wider society.

Dewey's Darwinian naturalism led him to adopt several views that were highly controversial. The first was that manual training should be an integral part of primary and secondary education. He argued that learning involves coordination of all of the capacities of the living organism, not just the intellect. Children should be taught weaving, carpentry, cooking, and gardening not only as examples of problem-solving, but also because such skills involve the embodiment of knowledge and provide tools for further discovery and learning. If education is adjustment within an environment, as Dewey thought, then it is the whole person that adjusts, and not just the whole function or aspect of the organism we call the "intellect."

It was on precisely these grounds that Dewey rejected the two-track system of education proposed by some educators during the period immediately prior to World War I. Their suggestion was that children should be tested at an early age and then routed on the basis of aptitude into either "vocational" or "academic" schools. Dewey replied that such a system would undermine democracy by sanctioning the separation of "bookish" from "mechanical" education and by creating a social chasm across which communication would be difficult. In his view, the two-track strategy would serve to reinforce the worst practices of the industrial system rather than reform them. "I object," he wrote, "to regarding as voca-tional education any training which does not have as its supreme regard the development of such intelligent initiative, ingenuity, and executive capacity as shall make workers, as far as they may be, the masters of their own industrial fate" (MW8: 412).

Dewey also rejected the notion that intelligence tests should be used as a justification for two-track education, let alone a criterion for its application. Intelligence tests, along with other types of tests, might serve educators as tools for analysis. But they should not be used to compare one child with another any more than should medical tests. "The notion that intelligence is a personal endowment or personal attainment," Dewey wrote, "is the great conceit of the intellectual class, as that of the commercial class is that wealth is something which they personally have wrought and possess" (LW2: 367).

Dewey's target in these remarks was most likely one of his colleagues at Columbia, the educational psychologist E.L. Thorndike (1874–1949). Like Dewey, Thorndike thought that traditional notions of education were inadequate and in need of reform. But unlike Dewey, he argued that children learn in much the same mechanical way that he thought laboratory animals are conditioned to perform rote tasks. He also held the view that intelligence is more or less innate, and that precisely quantifiable tests afford the educator the means of separating more educable pupils from those that are less so.

Dewey also rejected another form of two-track education. During a time when many educators considered women intellectually inferior to men and coeducation was thought to do serious damage to the education of boys and young men by distracting them from their work and by lowering instructional standards, Dewey mounted forceful arguments in defense of both equal education for women and coeducational classrooms.

Underlying Dewey's rejection of any form of two-track educational system was his revolutionary stance with respect to the problem traditionally known to philosophers as the "mind-body problem." His Darwinian naturalism is nowhere more evident than in his view that "body" and "mind" are just ways of describing different functions of a whole organism, and not separate entities between which there exists some unbridgeable gap or mysterious relationship. When human beings examine their experiences, he argued, they find no immediate experience indicating body and mind as separate. When such a distinction is made, it is only the result of an inference that differentiates among features of experience for some specific purpose. An important consequence of Dewey's naturalism was that he rejected arguments for the existence of a transcendent or immortal "soul." This position put him at odds with some of the more conservative religious thinkers of his time.

It was Dewey's view that most of the philosophers who have taken up the "mind-body problem" have tended to get matters backward. Since the time of Plato there has been a tendency to accept the result of inquiry—in this case the differentiation of two functions of the whole organism, mind and body—as what must have existed as separate substances or entities prior to inquiry. Because of the prevalence of this fallacy in the history of philosophy, Dewey termed it "the philosopher's fallacy."

In *Experience and Nature* (1925), Dewey coined the term "body-mind" to help express his own view of the "mind-body problem." "Body-mind" he wrote, "simply designates what actually takes place when a living body is implicated in situations of discourse, communication and participation" (LW1: 217). Mind is thus, for Dewey, a function of highly complex and evolved organisms, and not, as it is for Plato (c. 427–347 B.C.) and Descartes (1596–1650), a substance or entity somehow separate from or locked up inside the body. Dewey sometimes used the verb "to mind" in place of the noun "mind" to refer to the mental functions of the organism.

Dewey's philosophy of education also represents a continuation and development of themes first advanced in the work of the American pragmatists Charles Sanders Peirce (1839–1914) and William James (1842–1910). One of the central themes of pragmatism was the view that inquiry should be undertaken in a controlled and experimental manner. Peirce had argued that all other methods of settling belief, such as just holding fast to old ideas, reliance on authority, or the acceptance of whatever seems amenable to reason, are inferior to thought that is experimental and thus self-corrective.

Because of his high regard for the experimental method, some of Dewey's critics accused him of espousing "scientism," or the view that the methods of physical science should serve as standards for all other types of thinking. But Dewey replied that this was a mistaken reading of his work as well as that of the other pragma-

tists. For Dewey, inquiry within the arts, history, and law, to take just three examples, is also experimental and by no means inferior to scientific inquiry. Inquiry in each of these fields contributes to and is in turn nourished by an over-arching "general method of intelligence." It is by means of their participation in this general method of intelligence that the various disciplines and subject matters are able to communicate with one another. Dewey thought that logic is best characterized as the study of this general method of intelligence.

Together with the other pragmatists, Dewey argued that all inquiry is initiated by doubt. Doubt is best described as an uneasy state of the organism in which equilibrium is lost and irritation is felt. The pragmatists thus rejected the claims of Descartes, that it is possible to doubt everything except one's own existence and that it is possible to doubt just by deciding to do so.

Dewey presented his version of the pragmatic theory of inquiry to teachers in his widely read book *How We Think* (1910). In this work he advanced a five-step analysis of effective learning. In the first phase, there is an organic, emotional response to a situation that is unsettled or perhaps even threatening. What would be a normal course of action is inhibited by one circumstance or another. But since something is at stake, the organism leaps to various suggestions for alleviating the irritation and regaining equilibrium.

Second, there is an intellectual response to the confused situation. There is an attempt to gather the strands of emotional response and immediate suggestions into a precise formulation of the problem at hand. Certain facts and the principles of their interpretation are selected as appropriate to the case under review, and others are rejected as irrelevant. In most cases there are no rules for the selection of facts and principles. Children may be taught to judge the relevance or irrelevance of data and their interpretation, however, even in the absence of rules. This is accomplished by teaching them good habits of inquiry. Dewey lists alertness, flexibility, and curiosity as tools that are essential to this phase of inquiry.

Third, after the problem has been clarified, some hypothesis or guiding idea must be produced which, if true, would lead to the resolution of the problem. This hypothesis is much more definite than a simple suggestion. It must be formulated with care and based on the analysis undertaken in the previous phase of inquiry. Unlike a mere suggestion, it must be testable. Dewey thought it of the utmost importance that children be taught the distinction between a suggestion based on an emotional response and a carefully formulated hypothesis. The former is haphazard and unregulated. The latter is a tool whose use requires control and skill.

In the fourth stage of inquiry, the hypothesis must be subjected to reasoning, or "thought experiments." It must be elaborated, its possible consequences worked out, and its value relative to competing hypotheses calculated. Inferences must be drawn and connections made. Dewey thought that quantitative analysis often plays an important role in this stage of inquiry. This is because quantification often permits generalization to and from other, better-known cases. But it is also important, he noted, that quantitative measurement be understood as a tool that leads to further results. If quantification becomes an end in itself, as is often the case in teaching to a test, for example, then full reach of inquiry is prematurely terminated and education suffers.

Once the hypothesis is tested by thought-experiments or reasoning in the fourth stage of inquiry, then the fifth and final stage of inquiry is devoted to tests that involve overt action. As Dewey put it, "Conditions are deliberately arranged in accord with the requirements of an idea or hypothesis to see whether the results theoretically indicated by the idea actually occur" (LW8: 205). If results turn out as predicted, new habits of action are produced and the irritation of doubt ceases. But even if the experiments fail, the exercise may still prove instructive.

Dewey thought that some form of this five-step experimental method of inquiry is apparent wherever true thinking and learning occur. Because it is the only self-corrective method of inquiry so far devised, it forms the basis for sound educational theory and practice and it serves as a primary tool for the development of democratic institutions.

Dewey exhibited a lifelong concern with the problems and prospects of democracy as a form of social organization. He was aware that democracy is sometimes fragile and that it has many detractors. Nevertheless, he tirelessly advanced democracy as a means to more effective and harmonious social arrangements and as a goal to be worked for.

There is perhaps no one book in which Dewey's philosophy of education is presented more clearly, and its connections to his wider philosophy and his concept of democracy made with more precision, than *Democracy and Education* (1916). A decade and a half after its publication, in a brief autobiographical essay, Dewey declared that it was the one book in which his philosophy was "most fully expounded." He added that it is in the philosophy of education that "other problems, cosmological, moral, logical, come to a head" (LW5: 156).

Dewey contended that all social life rests on communication, and that all communication is a form of education. But informal communication, and therefore informal education, tends to be haphazard. In order to control more effectively those environmental conditions that are not what we wish them to be, especially the ever-changing technological environment, education itself must be carefully thought out and systematically undertaken. This means that it is no longer sufficient to teach children "Great Books," or the accumulated knowledge of a society. They must also be taught to develop new tools for discovery and learning that will enable them to work together with other members of their society toward the goals of ascertaining and realizing the common good.

Dewey's naturalism is evident in his characterization of education. Human life, like all other forms of life, is concerned with growth. Education is just the most efficient means of effecting growth. Its goal is the enrichment of the capacity for continuing renewal. Dewey explicitly rejected the view that education is just preparation for some future occupation. He likewise denied that its proper concern is the absorption of accumulated knowledge or the unfolding of capacities that already lie dormant in the child.

For Dewey, education is both a tool and an outcome of democratic practice. Education equips individuals for full participation in social life, and in its finest form it is the result of free and open social interaction. It is by means of education that individuals come to have a stake in society, and it is by means of the strengthened democratic institutions that result from education that the tools and techniques of education are improved. In education, just as in other forms of democratic practice, means and ends are continually adjusted to one another and are made to stand in a relation of cooperation with one another. Where means dominate ends, life becomes menial. Where ends dominate means, rigid ideologies and dogmas stifle creative thinking and learning.

D

Dewey's remarks in *Democracy and Education* also represent a further development of his concept of the place of values in education. He held that education requires no specific subject matter within the curriculum designated as "values," since the entire educational process is permeated with values. One of the principal aims of education is the development of critical tools that can be used to advance the growth and refinement of the student's appreciation of values.

It is the business of education, Dewey thought, to teach the child to appraise what is just "valued" with a view to determining what may prove to be "valuable." These terms, he suggested, are analogous to "eaten" and "edible." Just as it is the case that some things that have been eaten do not prove to be edible, some things that are valued do not prove to be valuable. What is merely "valued" remains private and personal. It is subject to the vagaries of subjectivistic or egoistic interpretation. As such it tends to cut short interchange between individuals. On the other hand, what is "valuable" is what has been experimentally tested and proven to be of value. Since the very notion of experimental proof depends on communication within a democratic community of inquiry, what proves to be "valuable" will have been worked over, debated, refined, and reconstructed in a public forum.

It was Dewey's contention that one of the most important issues in education is the relation of knowledge to conduct. Knowledge that does not affect conduct is of little or no value. Education is thus a training of character and a training for citizenship. Character, for Dewey, is built up as the individual comes to understand and appreciate the consequences of conduct and the relationships that such conduct involves. The school, as a miniature community, serves as a laboratory in which relations and connections can be explored. Good citizenship is one of the expressions of character. Because of his belief that education develops the capacities of the student to share effectively in social life, Dewey argued that all meaningful education is moral education.

By the 1920s, a generation of Dewey's students had become teachers and administrators in primary and secondary schools throughout the United States. In their zeal to reform the traditional "fundamentals and discipline" approach to education, however, an approach that Dewey had sharply criticized, some went to the opposite extreme. In their eagerness to construct a new "child-centered curriculum," focus was sometimes lost and the academic side of education dangerously diminished. "Progressive education," a term that had once described Dewey's own moderate and inclusive pedagogical views, came to be used to describe an education of "self-expression," an extreme view that Dewey had sharply criticized. During the 1920s, Dewey was put in the position of criticizing some of his own former students for what he regarded as their pedagogical excesses.

This situation grew even worse as the economic and social upheavals brought about by the Great Depression of the 1930s precipitated major debates concerning the role and function of education in society. Polarization between educational theorists on the competing extremes became acute. On one extreme there was a call for a return to the fundamentals of the "Three Rs," religious training in the public schools, the curtailment of academic freedom, and the dismissal of educators with "radical" views. On the other extreme, some educators argued that the traditional division of the curriculum into subjects was antiquated and counterproductive, that the child should have complete freedom to decide what to study, and that students should have extensive liberty of behavior so as to prevent "personality maladjustment."

As he had done since his years at Chicago, Dewey continued to criticize both of these views as one-sided and extreme. He argued that the proponents of the "discipline" or "fundamentals" approach were in danger of substituting indoctrination for education. He added that their program would have the effect of de-democratizing education by splitting off one religious community from another and by graduating students who were ill equipped to assess the wider context of their lives in a technical society and to contribute to its reform. In addition, he thought that the proponents of the "fundamentals" approach had placed themselves in an untenable position. Not only are fundamentals of any subject precisely what is most difficult for the beginning student to grasp; they are also the things that are the most disputed.

Dewey also criticized the other side, or what he termed the "would-be progressive teachers" (LW9: 198). He charged that their pedagogical lassitude treated the raw materials of the child's interests in ways that "fixated" those interests in their primitive state. Such teachers tended to overlook their own responsibility for providing guidance for their pupils.

Their desire to respect the "individuality" of the child, though admirable as an ideal, often had the effect of stunting development. Like the good gardener or the good metal worker, Dewey argued, the good teacher is one who cultivates and develops potentialities. The raw materials of the child's interests require skillful reconstruction and refinement.

The most succinct formulation of Dewey's educational theory is found in "My Pedagogic Creed," published in 1897. In that essay he stated his belief that education is the development of children's capacities in ways that enable them to become active and constructive participants in the life of society. The school is thus a form of community life, and not merely a preparation for something further. The subject matter of the school should involve the gradual differentiation of disciplinary studies out of "the primitive unconscious unity of social life" (EW5: 88). Educational methods should aim at developing the child's capacities and interests. Finally, education is "the fundamental method of social progress and reform." It is therefore the most basic moral duty of a community to provide its educators with the requisite resources with which to perform their tasks. In return, a community should demand that its educational system be a primary agent of social progress.

Larry A. Hickman

See also COMMUNITY; DEMOCRACY; EVOLUTION; INTELLIGENCE; NATURALISM; PRAGMATISM; PROGRESS, IDEA OF, AND PROGRESSIVE EDUCATION

Bibliography
Cremin, Lawrence. *The Transformation of the School.* New York: Alfred A. Knopf, 1961.
Dewey, John. *The Collected Works of John Dewey.* Edited by Jo Ann Boydston. Carbondale and Edwardsville: Southern Illinois University Press, 1969–1991. Standard references are to *The Early Works* (EW), *The Middle Works* (MW), and *The Later Works* (LW). In citations, these designations are followed by volume and page number (for example, LW1: 253).
Dykhuizen, George. *The Life and Mind of John Dewey.* Introduction by Harold Taylor. Edited by Jo Ann Boydston. Carbondale and Edwardsville: Southern Illinois University Press, 1973.
Feiffer, Andrew. *The Chicago Pragmatists and American Progressivism.* Ithaca, N.Y.: Cornell University Press, 1993.
Westbrook, Robert. *John Dewey and American Democracy.* Ithaca, N.Y.: Cornell University Press, 1991.
Zilversmit, Arthur. *Changing Schools: Progressive Education Theory and Practice, 1930–1960.* Chicago: University of Chicago Press, 1993.

D

Dialectic

A protean word designating a number of different philosophical activities, all, however, activities touching upon dialogue, thus "dialect"— that is, language as actually spoken, whatever linguistic group it happens to be a dialect of. Wherever "dialectic" has a central position in a philosophical tradition, there the activity of question-and-answer (as opposed to, say, listening to the voice of God or contemplating essences) is central to the search for truth and justice. Many major schools or traditions of Western philosophy, from pre-Socratic to the latest version of postmodernism, put question-and-answer at the center of philosophical activities and use some derivative from the Greek *dialektiks* as a central concept. The meanings assigned are so varied in different systems of thought, however, that any effort to trace a continuing tradition of "dialectical philosophy" would be forced and unprofitable. But among the many philosophical traditions where something called "dialectic" has an honored place, two touch upon educational theory and practice most directly and profoundly.

Dialectic in Plato's *Republic*

By the time Plato (c. 427–347 B.C.) chose "dialectic" to play the role assigned it in Book 7 of the *Republic,* the word had already been used in various senses by Zeno, the Eleatics, the sophists, and Socrates. It enters the *Republic* when Socrates and Glaucon consider the final stage in the education of the republic's guardian-rulers. Having emerged at the top of a carefully designed and rigidly selective program of physical, moral, and intellectual education, these guardians must continue their study of higher mathematics, astronomy, and harmonics. Before describing the final step in their education, Socrates introduces the well-known myth of the cave, where human beings know only what they can infer from images cast by flickering firelight on the cave wall. From there a select few may be led, by stages, into the light of the sun, where, blinded at first, they look upon shadows of real things till at last they can look upon things as they are. Socrates says: "Isn't this at last the song itself that dialectic performs? It is in the realm of the intelligible, but it is imitated by the power of sight. We said that sight at last tries to look at the animals themselves and at stars themselves and then finally at the sun itself. So, also, when a man tries by discussion—by means of argument without the use of any of the senses—to attain to each thing itself that *is* and doesn't give up before he grasps by intellection itself that which is good itself, he comes to the very end of the intelligible realm" (*Republic: 532a–b*). This "journey" he calls dialectic.

To understand Plato here, look upon dialectic as the "other side" of logic. Logic (inductive) considers how from many particular statements a more general conclusion may be drawn, or (deductive) how from one or more statements some particular conclusion may be derived. The activity he calls dialectic seeks to go behind, beyond particular and general truths, searching for the more basic, universal principles of reality—for example, the principles underlying logic itself. Such universal principles are to be discovered, Plato believed, by the activity of pure intellect. All ignoble passions have been burned away in the souls of Plato's guardian-rulers. Their intellectual power has been sharpened to a razor edge, their courage tested and confirmed in combat; they alone are prepared for the social activity of question-and-answer that delves ever more deeply into the mysteries of existence. They alone, but no one of them alone, may undertake that journey. And most significantly, they alone, as a ruling elite, have the power to apply what emerges from dialectic to fine tune the republic's laws and maintain social stability.

As capstone for an educational program, then, Platonic dialectic not only fulfills human potential for personal development to its highest level but also prepares a leadership class for effective use of political power. In a democracy, every child is educated for membership in society's ruling class. Have we a capstone conception of intellectual activity to fulfill each child's full potential and release the imagination and creativity required for effective citizenship today? One is here reminded of John Dewey's conception of the "complete act of thought."

Thinking begins with an existential problem and stops not with the problem's solution but with reflection on the more general features of the world revealed in the activity itself. In short, what Plato reserves as a capstone for a few individuals at the conclusion of life, Dewey's activity curriculum would make the capstone of each concrete instance of full intellectual activity, from kindergarten through in-service professional training.

Marxist Dialectic

Between Plato and Karl Marx (1818–1883), "dialectic" played a number of different philosophical roles, finally becoming in G.W.F. Hegel's *Logic* (1812) a single, universe-creating process, that by which Absolute Idea becomes manifest as Reason-and-Reality. Dialectic as a structure is visible, for example, in Book 1 of Plato's *Republic;* there an obviously accurate definition of "justice" is proposed and rebutted by an equally obvious counterexample. Logic notes only their contradiction; dialectic seeks a more general vision of justice in which that contradiction may be transcended—that is, resolved without loss of the partial truth in either of the contending claims. With Hegel that structure—contradiction and transcendence—becomes the activity by which the world itself is created and animated.

Like all German intellectuals of his time, Marx was deeply influenced by Hegel. In a famous passage, Marx claims that he found Hegel standing on his head and turned him right side up, meaning that emergence-and-transcendence-of-contradiction is indeed the basic dynamic of the world. It begins, however, not in the realm of Ideas but in the hard reality of material existence. Where Hegel had seen the history of Western civilization as the emergence of the Idea of Freedom, Marx saw it as the unremitting, still far-from-won struggle of the working class to liberate itself from successive forms—slavery, serfdom, wage-labor—of exploitation.

Marxist dialectic today focuses on the fundamental contradiction of capitalism: Capitalist production can provide sufficient material goods to satisfy the basic needs of all human beings; in fact, a huge proportion of production is allocated to waste, war, and preparation for war, at the cost of tragic deprivation for the majority of humanity. This contradiction stands forth in cyclical economic crises; to this point in history such crises have been more or less contained, either by renewed outbreak of warfare or by orgies of consumer spending on some new technological device, but always with ever sterner exploitation of the working class worldwide and by ever increasing, irreversible degradation of the natural environment.

The Marxist dialectic concludes that the basic contradiction in capitalist production cannot be resolved until capitalism itself is transcended and new modes of social production instituted. The challenge to democratic educators is to bring that hypothesis into the critical consciousness of youth now under the sway of capitalist-owned mass media. This challenge evokes critical theory in education.

James E. McClellan, Jr.

See also ALIENATION; CAPITALISM; CRITICAL THEORY; DEWEY; HEGEL; MARX; PLATO; SOCRATES

Bibliography

Engels, Frederick. *The Dialectics of Nature.* New York: International Publishers, 1940.

Irwin, T.H. "Socratic Inquiry and Politics." *Ethics* 96 (1986): 400–415.

Marquit, Erwin. "Contradictions in Dialectics and Formal Logic." In *Dialectical Contradictions: Contemporary Marxist Discussions,* edited by E. Marquit, P. Moran, and W.H. Truitt. Minneapolis, Minn.: Marxist Educational Press, 1982.

Meyer, Michel. "Dialectic and Questioning: Socrates and Plato." *American Philosophical Quarterly* 17 (1980): 281–90.

Plato. *The Republic.* Translated by Allan Bloom. New York: Basic Books, 1968.

Ruben, David-Hillel. "Marxism and Dialectics." In *Issues in Marxist Philosophy, Volume One: Dialectics and Method,* edited by J. Mepham and D-H Hillel. Atlantic Highlands, N.J.: Humanities Press, 1979.

Diderot, Denis (1713–1784)

At the heart of the Enlightenment all his mature life, Diderot achieved greatest distinction among his contemporaries as the principal animator of the French *Encyclopedie,* which celebrated an Age of Reason and Invention, much as the Crystal Palace built in London a century later would pay tribute to an Age of Industry and Commerce. In his capacity as chief editor of that collective enterprise of men of letters, he mainly assembled the ideas of other thinkers for recirculation in a work of reference, guarding against official censors who frequently threatened to bring publication to a halt. He had begun his literary career around 1743 as a translator, and, as late as the 1770s, he still produced some of his most spirited passages anonymously, by way of contributions to the writings of other authors. Perhaps equally because so much of his own best work would only be published posthumously, largely in the form of fictional dialogues, Diderot has for all these reasons come to be seen as the Enlightenment's most eclectic thinker. Unlike his equally celebrated contemporaries—Montesquieu, Voltaire, and Rousseau—he did not espouse one great doctrine or devote all his attention to a comprehensive intellectual crusade.

The tensions manifest within his work correspond to the clash of principles and personalities that he perceived in the world at large. At once a materialist and an atheist, he was determined to describe human behavior empirically, in all its diverse, contrasting, and irregular forms. Such diversity and contrast were features of human nature as much as of human history, he supposed, and, in his *Refutation of Helvetius* of 1773, he accordingly took issue with the famous dictum of Helvetius's *On Spirit,* published earlier that year, that "l'education peut tout." The proposition that anything might be achieved through education is false, according to Diderot, because it presumes that men and women are everywhere identical and that differences of character depend entirely upon the circumstances of a person's upbringing. Because it appeals to a notion of human equality, it is tempting to accept the supposition that all individuals have the same capacities, but that is a delusion, Diderot contends, based on the false premise that we are all motivated only by our sensations, which, through instruction, can be refined into every sort of rational and moral judgment. It is impossible to pass directly from sensation to judgment, or, in effect, from animal reflexes to human design, he insists. Our species is uniquely endowed with reason that makes it possible for us, as distinct from other creatures, to formulate ideas and combine them into judgments; within our species, however, our mental capacities are unequally distributed. In allowing with Helvetius that our vices do not spring from our nature but are generally attributable to harmful social practices and teachings, we are not committed to the belief that all individuals have good minds and that genius may everywhere be trained. A good education can improve native aptitudes, but it can never induce them among individuals who lack them at birth.

These objections to the philosophy of Helvetius bear a striking resemblance to arguments put forward by Rousseau both in his novel the *New Heloise* and in *Emile,* published in 1762, the most notable of all eighteenth-century treatises on education. Although they were to become estranged and increasingly antagonistic toward one another after the late 1750s, Diderot and Rousseau had earlier been best of friends, and for more than fifteen years each had drawn great inspiration from the other. In opposing Helvetius's sensualist ideas about the formation of the human intellect and character, Rousseau had also been drawn to the conclusion that genius cannot be instilled by tuition and that education ought to cultivate the natural dispositions and qualities of children rather than impose their tutors' designs and expectations upon them. Yet in their common objections to Helvetius, the two men were not in full agreement.

Rousseau opposed materialism in general, whereas Diderot took issue only with that crude form of it which, as he understood it, reduced all thought to passive sensation. Rousseau mistrusted teachers partly because they merely pretended to speak on God's behalf, whereas Diderot came to think that God Himself had been invented by man. Rousseau subscribed to a theory of "negative education," as he put it, building from the solitude of Robinson Crusoe, an idea that meant nothing to Diderot. But in contrast with Helvetius, Rousseau and Diderot both believed that education ought fundamentally to accord with human nature instead of recasting it. They both subscribed essentially to a doctrine of self-education, through which pupils would come to intellectual and moral maturity by following their intuitions and being true to themselves rather than by precept and instruction. They both showed a deep mistrust of the superstitious idolatry kindled by the mysteries of Revelation that passed for a Christian education, proffered by priests in the light of Holy Writ. They both thought education ought to arise endogenously, out of natural curiosity, marking the development of our faculties, and never from bookish, still less religious, indoctrination.

If in these respects *Emile* foreshadows the *Refutation of Helvetius,* it is plain that Diderot had himself pursued such notions still earlier,

independently of Rousseau, particularly in his *Letter on the Blind* and *Letter on the Deaf and Dumb,* which appeared in 1749 and 1751 respectively. In each case, Diderot had attempted to establish that human powers of perception do not themselves spring from sensory experience. He had shown how, in the absence of some of their faculties, individuals could still comprehend the ideas that those faculties shape, how it is possible to form mental images without sight and to converse without sound. The late eighteenth-century teaching of sign languages to the deaf, in classes established by the Chevalier de l'Epee in Paris or Dr. Braidwood in Edinburgh, for instance, owed much to such notions, and the deep structural grammar of Chomskeian linguistics today is similarly inspired by the idea that fundamental human capacities are not determined by the contingencies of their exercise.

Diderot's philosophy of education in accordance with nature embraces at least one other feature that is equally central to Rousseau: its primitivism. In contrasting the trappings of culture and the civilized morality of European society unfavorably with the free expression of the natural proclivities of Tahitian savages, Diderot, in his *Supplement to the Voyage of Bougainville,* which he drafted around 1773–1774, closely follows some of the main themes of Rousseau's *Discourse on Inequality* of 1755. Like Rousseau, Diderot extols the innocence of vitality of an uncultivated state of nature, where there is no religious dogma that holds natural appetites in check, where private property is unknown and the horrors of war to which it gives rise are largely absent, where the self-serving hypocrisies of civilization do not pass for justice. The *Supplement to the Voyage of Bougainville* is among the most liberal and irreverent works of the whole Enlightenment, in decrying the missionary zeal of an effete culture of Christendom, when its crass teachings are imposed through colonization.

Far more than any text of Rousseau's, the *Supplement* also pursues the thesis that a natural education, springing from the spontaneity of impulse, is conducive to the self-development of women in particular. Whereas, in the West, wives are the sexual property of their husbands, who transform a bond of affection into a legal tie, in Tahiti women choose their husbands as much as they are chosen by them, claims Diderot. Polygamy, promiscuity, fornication, adultery, and incest are not criminal, wherever sexual partners freely give themselves to each other. In Europe, by contrast, religiously induced repression teaches men and women that the physical promptings of their own bodies are loathsome, and that the highest calling for both sexes entails a vow of chastity. No one in the eighteenth century believed more passionately that the liberation of women from the tyranny of men entailed the expression of their own sexual identity. Diderot was convinced that an education in accordance with nature is not just mental but physiological in form.

Yet he subscribed to primitivist ideals in a manner that was akin to Rousseau only insofar as he believed that peoples uncorrupted by Christian dogma would be more free and content than Europeans. As editor of the most substantial dictionary of the arts and sciences yet undertaken, he could scarcely agree with Rousseau that the refinement of secular culture had itself been responsible for the degradation of morals. On the contrary, as he makes plain in his articles on *art* and *encyclopedia* for the *Encyclopedie,* Diderot believed that the general march of the human spirit throughout history had been of great benefit to mankind as a whole. Scientific and artistic innovation had liberated us from the yoke of precedent and the tyranny of dead dogma, he asserts. The art of printing, the discovery of the compass, and the invention of gunpowder had each transformed the face of the earth and opened new horizons for human endeavor and ingenuity.

Although particularly well versed in the history of philosophy, whose ancient and modern achievements alike he extols in several of his contributions to the *Encyclopedie,* Diderot perhaps displays his greatest enthusiasm for the crafts and technologies of the mechanical arts— for the tanneries, mills, and foundries that are the workshops of the world and whose tools and instruments are illustrated in many of the volumes of plates the production of which he supervised. As he conceived it, the *Encyclopedie* brought the arts and sciences of civilization together. It encouraged the interpenetration of the liberal with mechanical arts, as if bridging what has today come to be termed "the two cultures." It was designed to promote a spirit of practical cooperation between specialists of different disciplines, to show how learning could be made useful to the public interest or common good. By way of its dissemination to readers— that is, to a whole class of literate consumers on a scale unprecedented in human history—it had

as its central aim the pursuit of a Platonic ideal of promoting virtue through knowledge.

In his *Observations on the Nakaz,* or commentary on a new code of law for Russia envisaged by Catherine the Great, dating from 1774, he was to press a case for a program of secular education in order to stimulate the civilization of that country through small-scale enterprises that in turn would lead to its economic development—intellectual and material progress thus proceeding hand in hand, he thought, not least by way of the emancipation of the serfs. On Catherine's request, moreover, Diderot developed his views on education in Russia into a full-length work, entitled the *Plan of a University for the Government of Russia.* There he puts forth a vigorous case for a scheme of public education as part of the formation of a general culture. "To instruct a nation is to civilize it," he remarks. In softening people's character, in enlightening them about their duties, it directs them away from barbarism.

Diderot's schemes of education could be both compatible with primitive morality and conducive to progress, because he believed that Nature is itself in continual flux, passing through periodic stages of growth, maturity, and decline. Supposing that our biological attributes make the establishment of society necessary, he also thought that the organic and dynamic forces that shape our behavior make our invention of morality possible, and thereby, our adoption of rules which, over generations, could give rise to the advancement of human culture. Being, in his fashion, a materialist and a determinist, Diderot showed none of Rousseau's fascination for the concept of a *free will.* Sometimes he suggests that even the idea of liberty is meaningless, there being nothing in human affairs that cannot be explained in terms of our physical constitution, our education, and the chain of events that make all our actions effects of certain causes. But in his belief that our nature must never be forced, that through their free rein our faculties raise us above all animals, and that freedom in all societies should be encouraged by the adoption of rules that express our fundamental tendencies, he subscribed to a philosophy of human nature among the most liberal and progressive of all Enlightenment doctrines. Provided that our schemes of education are compatible with our fundamental tendencies, he was convinced that men and women enjoy a wonderful capacity to transform themselves, to perfect their own natures

D

through enlightenment, to improve themselves through self-instruction.

Robert Wokler

See also CENSORSHIP; HAPPINESS; HELVETIUS; HUMAN NATURE; INDOCTRINATION; ROUSSEAU; SOCIAL AND POLITICAL PHILOSOPHY; TOLERATION; UTILITARIANISM

Bibliography
Crocker, Lester G. *Diderot: The Embattled Philosopher*. New York: Free Press, 1966.
France, Peter. *Diderot*. Oxford University Press, 1983.
Furbank, P.N. *Diderot: A Critical Biography*. London: Secker and Warburg, 1992.
Hope Mason, John. *The Irresistible Diderot*. London: Quartet Books, 1982.
——, and R. Wokler, eds. *Diderot's Political Writings*. Cambridge: Cambridge University Press, 1992.
Proust, Jacques. *Diderot et l' 'Encyclopedie.'* Paris: Armand Colin, 1962.
Wilson, Arthur M. *Diderot*. New York: Oxford University Press, 1972.

Discipline

"Discipline" is a subject much on the minds of philosophers and practitioners of education alike, as well as being in the consciousness of the public. The work of Michel Foucault (1926–1984) on discipline has had a great influence on educational philosophers; Lee Canter's Assertive Discipline Program has shaped the classroom practice of a generation of teachers; and the annual *Phi Delta Kappa/Gallup Poll* of attitudes toward education has consistently placed "discipline" as one of the top educational concerns of the public.

The word *discipline* is Roman in origin. The etymology is instructive: The Latin *discere* ("to learn") was related to *discipulus* ("a pupil"). In English, a "disciple" is one who lives according to the teachings of a master, and a "discipline" was originally a way of life to which one committed oneself. Thus it is that a subject or course of study is called a "discipline."

Modern usage has shifted the primary associations: Discipline today is most commonly thought of as something imposed from "outside" ourselves that we "internalize," though John Dewey (1859–1952) follows Jean-Jacques Rousseau (1712–1778) in describing discipline as a feature of our relations with the world.

The question of the nature of discipline is ancient. Plato (c. 427–c. 347 B.C.) and Aristotle (384–322 B.C.) both tried to explain the common human experience of finding that we often act in ways that bring us further from, rather than closer to, our stated goals. This was the problem of *akrasia*. Believing all human action to be in pursuit of what is perceived as The Good, Plato saw *akrasia* as a mistaken choice; at the time we act, we choose what seems good. Aristotle recognized that at times we knowingly make choices contrary to our long-term goals and interests; our wisdom and good judgment can be overwhelmed by the strength of immediate desire. Here we can begin to discern the shape of one modern question about discipline: Why are some people, but not others, able to persist over time in tasks against the temptations of more immediate pleasures?

Emile Durkheim (1858–1917) described discipline as metaphorically apart from us and an essential component of morality. In order to become moral members of a social group, children must experience discipline as something above and apart from them. Children must see teachers, the agents who first subject children to the discipline of their society, as themselves subject to the seemingly divine authority of social rules. Thus he admonishes teachers to apply rules inflexibly and without hesitation. Children will eventually become mature enough to consider the social value of rules, but they must first accept the norms of a particular social life.

Michel Foucault seems at times actually to accord ontological status to discipline. He describes our society as "disciplinary," one in which discipline is an active agent and real presence. In this view, the sort of conscious agency that Durkheim says we develop is an illusion; "disciplinary power" shapes us all. Whereas Durkheim celebrates discipline as one of the essential components of moral agency, Foucault sees it as an impersonal force that "installs" itself on our "docile bodies." The reasoned assent to the rules of social order that Durkheim posits as the core of morality is, in Foucault's view, impossible. Discipline establishes the social order, and we are shaped to it.

What Foucault and Durkheim have in common is the belief that discipline comes from outside us and shapes us internally. We become "moral" or "disciplined" as the standards of conduct that are imposed upon us, and to which we are at first required to conform, become our own. We become "normed" or "disciplined"; we discipline ourselves. They differ in that Durkheim rather celebrates the effect of discipline, whereas Foucault is more interested in whether and how we can resist its effects; thus do we assert agency.

Educational practice premised on this conception of discipline generally seeks to control students' behavior. Children come to school without discipline, and the teacher must impose it on them. As they obey the demands of their teachers they become "normed" to those expectations. This is the view that underwrites much of our educational practice. However, some dissenting practitioners see it as their role to help liberate their students, especially the less privileged, from its effects and to prepare them for resistance.

An alternate view describes discipline as a feature of effective agency. This view, articulated by Dewey, is quite close to the original: One chooses to submit to the discipline of a particular way of life, whether a religious order or some other structured way of living. It is necessary that the disciple, in submitting, do so voluntarily; it is just this that distinguishes the disciple from the slave. In pursuit of what Dewey calls an "end-in-view," we submit to the demands of the task itself. Discipline is interest directing will.

What directs our action is the interest we have in achieving our purposes. The discipline to which we must submit inheres in the goals we work to attain. And, paradoxically, it is just when we submit to the discipline that we become able to accomplish that purpose. In working with wood we must submit to the requirements of the material. The same is true of the "academic disciplines"; the more one submits to the demands of a discipline like mathematics or physics, the more one is said to master the subject. Likewise, when we choose to live a certain kind of life—good citizen, moral person, or bank robber—we must submit to its demands or we can never master it. Effective agency requires discipline.

Teachers who think of discipline in this way seek to connect classroom activities to student interests in the belief that children develop discipline by sticking to tasks that lead to desired ends. While Dewey's "progressive education" movement is often criticized as permissive, it is premised on the belief that self-direction requires disciplined action and is always part of education. For Dewey, there is no such thing as "discipline" external in the world. We act in a disciplined manner as we pursue our goals, or we do not.

In general, discipline is valued as a way to create and maintain order, and that seems right. But the sort of discipline we employ makes a difference in the nature of the order. If we impose order on a class (or a whole society) with discipline-as-control, that is a very different sort of order than would result from discipline imposed by the requirements of pursuing chosen common purposes.

Both prisons and monasteries have order that might, in some ways, appear similar, and we could attribute that order in each case to "discipline," believing both to be the same sort of institution. But if we overlook the fundamental differences between them, we miss an important part of human experience. A guard obtaining compliance from a resistant inmate is engaged in a very different activity than a master initiating a disciple into a chosen way of life. The student solving math problems because of discipline imposed by the teacher is in a very different state from the one who is solving the same problems because of the discipline imposed by the nature of the task and the fact that the answer to the problem will advance the child's own interests.

Discipline is seen as something that we develop with time, and how we believe that happens will strongly affect the way we educate. If it begins outside us and is internalized, teachers will seek to control students until they internalize discipline sufficiently to control themselves. If discipline is seen as an aspect of our relationship with the world, teachers will seek to provide children with engaging tasks leading to desired ends, fostering the capacity to act with discipline.

Whatever it is and however it comes to be, discipline is essential to our living lives in conformity with the expectations of others and the demands of the world. We can neither attain satisfaction in our private lives nor live as members of a social group without some form of discipline. Discipline alone is not sufficient—being a successful drug dealer may require great discipline—but it is necessary.

With respect to schools, a caveat regarding the common concern with the "discipline problem" is in order. Children can be expected to lack discipline. If we keep in mind that one apparent agreement about the nature of discipline is that it is something that we foster or internalize over time, then we will have to expect that schools will be places where there is a "discipline problem," just as we might truly, but not helpfully, conceive of kindergarten classrooms as places where there is a "height problem."

John F. Covaleskie

See also AIMS OF EDUCATION; ARISTOTLE; BEHAVIORISM; DEWEY; DURKHEIM; ETHICS AND MORALITY; MORAL DEVELOPMENT; PERSON, CONCEPT OF; PLATO; SOCRATES

Bibliography

Aristotle. *Nicomachean Ethics.* Translated by Terence Irwin. Indianapolis, Ind.: Hackett, 1985.

Canter, Lee, and Marlene Canter. *Assertive Discipline: A Take Charge Approach for Today's Educator.* Santa Monica, Calif.: Canter and Associates, 1976.

Dewey, John. *Democracy and Education: An Introduction to the Philosophy of Education* [1916]. New York: Free Press, 1966.

Durkheim, Emile. *On Moral Education: A Study in the Theory and Application of the Sociology of Education.* New York: Free Press, 1961/1973.

Elam, Stanley M., Lowell C. Rose, and Alec M. Gallup. "The 24th Annual Gallup/ Phi Delta Kappa Poll of the Public's Attitudes Toward the Public Schools." *Phi Delta Kappan* 74 (September 1992): 41–53.

Foucault, Michel. *Discipline and Punish: The Birth of the Prison.* Translated by Alan Sheridan. New York: Vintage Books, 1979.

Karnes, Elizabeth Leuder, Donald J. Black, and John L. Downs. *Discipline in Our Schools: An Annotated Bibliography.* Westport, Conn.: Greenwood Press, 1983.

Plato. *Protagoras.* Translated by C.C.W. Taylor. London: Oxford University Press, 1976.

Rousseau, Jean-Jacques. *Emile: Or On Education.* Translated by Allan Bloom. New York: Basic Books, 1979.

Domestic Education

Any education at home, for home life, or about home life. Political, social, and economic theorists have conceived in various ways of the educational importance of home and family. Domestic education (DE) predates democracy. But, related if not integral to some ideas of democracy and progressive education, DE has long been acknowledged distinctively practical and moral: a possible foundation for peace education, a debated purpose of African American education, a contested defining element in many theories of girls' and women's education, and a characteristic curricular feature of coeducation. Individuals, partners, and groups have deliberately formulated ideas of DE through thought experiments in speculative treatises, philosophical novels, and innovative practice. DE's relationship to liberal education and its significance for education generally have often been disputed. Despite its important place in social history, the concept's complicated logic and history have received little philosophical attention hitherto.

DE may be education simultaneously in, for, and about home life. But the term can apply to any education at home, which need not be either education for or education about home life. DE also may be either community education or schooling simultaneously like, for, and about home life. In contrast to home schooling, though, homelike community education and homelike schooling are not DE unless the learning sought is either for or about home life. Thus, DE has often been understood as education for home life regardless of where that education takes place. Such DE usually entails some education about home life when it includes other subjects. As education about home life, DE need not occur either at home or in a homelike setting, for teaching and learning about home life have occasionally been conceived to fulfill purposes other than mere preparation for home life. Indeed, philosophers of DE have upheld its possible significance as education for the general enhancement of life.

Education at Home

Among the most prominent arguments for conducting education exclusively at home is Jean-Jacques Rousseau's philosophical novel *Emile, or On Education* (1762). Rousseau (1712–1778) theorized that "the heart is linked with the great fatherland through the little fatherland of the home." "Domestic education" was the name he gave to "the education of nature," by which he meant education as distinguished from artificial learning offered by colleges and other manmade institutions; DE, in his view, meant education for life—not just for citizenship. Regarding the home as "a place of happy life" in the country "far from the filthy morals of the towns" and equating education with childrearing, Rousseau saw education's aim as other than children's preparation for specific public roles: more generally, to take care of themselves and their families when they grow up, to endure hardship, to live fully and feel life deeply. Johann Heinrich Pestalozzi (1746–1827) in *Leonard and Gertrude* (1781) also romanticized home as the ideal educational institution. But, whereas Rousseau argued that a father should be his son's tutor, Pestalozzi idealized mothers as teachers of housework, social arts, manners, morals, and piety to children of both sexes. However, recognizing the difficulty of mothers' performing so many educational responsibilities, this philosophical grandfather of the kindergarten did argue for the necessity of formal schools to regenerate society.

After using *Emile* as a manual for his first born son's education, Richard Lovell Edgeworth (1744–1817) declared Rousseau's theory a practical failure. Consequently turning to maternal insights such as Pestalozzi had acknowledged, he engaged his second wife and his more famous eldest daughter, the prolific bluestocking writer Maria Edgeworth (1767–1849), as collaborators in the home education of his twenty other children. Daughter and father Edgeworth's co-authored treatise *Essays on Practical Education* (1811) demonstrated the value deliberate practical experimentation might have as a bona fide medium for the development of educational thought. Recognizing that not all families could educate their children at home, they also suggested that knowledge about education at home might be a bona fide source from which to develop thought about schooling.

Education for Home Life

Contextual concerns related to sex, race, economy, and cultural changes have figured prominently in DE's philosophical history. Therefore, a particular point of difference among philosophers of education for home life has been the issue of its appropriate relationship to education for life in society at large. Rousseau's *Emile* advanced two radically different concepts of DE: (1) A boy's education for natural manhood included his preparation for a trade and for a citizen's responsibilities; (2) A girl's education for subservient wifehood excluded such preparation for productive public life. Unlike Emile's, her education must be only for home life. His future wife, Sophie, was to be educated at home by her mother to develop a feeling heart and Christian piety; to learn skill in lacemaking, pleasing conversation, modest flirtation, and guile; and to learn the art of making men's lives agreeable and sweet.

In *Vindication of the Rights of Woman* (1792), Mary Wollstonecraft (1759–1797) embraced Rousseau's notion that Sophie should be educated for home life, but faulted him for denying her Emile's education in rationality, without which a woman must be unprepared for intelligent motherhood. Also disputing Rousseau's subordination of wife to husband, Wollstonecraft conceived liberal education as essential to women's education for home life, which she thought should not preclude their education for citizenship. She argued that coeducational day schools should prepare women for equal, mutual, and rationally affectionate relationships with their husbands. Thus education for home life has not always been conceived as exclusively or even primarily about home life.

The philosophical novels of education by Louisa May Alcott (1832–1888), the trilogy of *Little Women* (1868), *Little Men* (1870), and *Jo's Boys* (1886), responded imaginatively to Rousseau, Pestalozzi, Wollstonecraft, and the Edgeworths. Alcott acknowledged education at home to be both a privilege of the few that undermined many children's chances of survival and a threat to women's life and liberty. But she also recognized the value of her own Marmee's teaching, which had aimed at four adolescent daughters' growing capacities and responsibility for learning to love and survive despite their pains, difficulties, and conflicts, especially Marmee's absence. So Alcott conceived a thought experiment about Plumfield, a private home that became an unusual "homelike school," later a homelike college. There, maternal teaching augmented even as it occurred apart from academic teaching and other practical teaching for both sexes: to foster girls' joyful expertise in and boys' respectful appreciation of women's traditional domestic skills. But Plumfield made possible for Alcott the liberatory vision of "a new and charming state of society" in which children without mothers at home need not be deprived of education for and about home life and in which both married and unmarried women, with men's understanding and respect, might freely exercise a transformative moral influence on the public world as teachers, doctors, artists, actors, public speakers, and voting citizens.

Also possessed of liberatory purpose, but with respect to race rather than sex, Booker T. Washington (1856–1915) responded to former slaves' lack of experience in childrearing and home life by conducting a thought experiment through actual practice in Alabama: Tuskegee Institute. Dismissing political struggles for African American democratic participation as premature, Washington implicitly invoked Rousseau's dualism between home and society: He constructed a concept of education that, supported by many whites, might teach African Americans to "found homes" of their own while leaving U.S. society's white supremacy unshaken. Citing their urgent needs for "food, clothing, shelter, education, proper habits, and a settlement of race relations," he argued that no "ordinary process of education" could help them. Instead of mere literary learning, they needed "proper training of head, hand, and heart," "ordinary training in how to live"; by building and maintaining Tuskegee itself as their own homelike school community, they could learn "to lift themselves up." As graduates, they would teach other African Americans such basic skills and help them develop self-reliant home communities. Thus Washington did depart from Rousseau's dualism between home and society to connect the improvement of African American homes with the improvement of African American communities that might serve and win respect from white supremacist society.

Jane Addams (1860–1935) created a thought experiment that responded to a similarly challenging practical context: U.S. urban life among formerly peasant European immigrants of all ages. Her Chicago settlement, Hull House, had a richly varied and voluntary curriculum that aimed to teach immigrants how to live peaceful home lives in a strange, often hostile new place despite intergenerational language and culture barriers within and among their families and, at the same time, how to create a just and peaceful community life despite frequent encounters with social and economic strife. Thus integrating education for home life with education for urban social life, Addams's concept of DE in the settlement house philosophically reconfigured the dualism between home and society that constituted Rousseau's

initial premises for DE.

Charlotte Perkins Gilman (1860–1935), who participated briefly in Hull House, imaginatively eradicated Rousseau's dualism together with her fictional thought experiment, *Herland* (1915). Devoid of men and boys and geographically remote from the larger world they controlled, Gilman's utopian Herland was "home" to its citizens, who were all "mothers" to the country's children whether they had physically borne them or not. Its domestic concerns were civic, scientific, artistic, and professional concerns, not merely private ones assigned to subservient people. All education there was domestic in two ways: Life in this women's homeland was nothing but an enlarged home life; no institutional schooling was necessary, as all experience was itself educational. Although a practical impossibility, Gilman's feminist utopia nonetheless made a philosophically serious case for reconceiving DE as education for broad social and environmental reconstruction, not just for private home life.

Such is Jane Roland Martin's thought experiment *The Schoolhome* (1992), which has responded to contemporary concerns about sex, race, ethnicity, poverty, cultural change, and violence. Citing the "domestic tranquility" clause of the United States Constitution, Martin has reconceptualized "domestic" by recovering its civic sense, but without reducing it to that. Revising the concept by Maria Montessori (1870–1952) of school as *casa dei bambini,* children's home, she has analyzed the "domestic" concept's relativity to one's point of view: Home can be one's personal shelter, school, country, or world. Her schoolhome would aim to prepare all children for home life in this enlarged, multiple sense. As a "moral equivalent of home," a partner to homes in which children do learn to love and survive, and a surrogate home for children without such homes, the schoolhome would reconfigure educational ends and means first experimentally conceived through Plumfield, Tuskegee, Hull House, and Herland.

Education about Home Life.

In *A Treatise on Domestic Education* (1841), Gilman's great-aunt Catherine Beecher (1800–1878) constructed perhaps the first systematic and comprehensive philosophy of school curriculum about home life. The *Plan for Improving Female Education* (1819) by Emma Hart Willard (1787–1870) had already conceived women's education as a science of domestic economy, combining housewifery with literature and fine arts. But Beecher differently conceived her Domestic Economy's subject matter to include a vast array of simultaneously theoretical and technical knowledge about proper marital relations, food, drink, clothing, house, household, health, hygiene, hospitality, childrearing, sick-nursing, religion, gardening, charity, and leisure. Such instruction would, she theorized, address her concerns about the industrial revolution's displacement of cottage industries, oppressiveness to women and children, and destructive effects upon family life by fostering new rational intelligence about the conduct of home life, relieving domestic drudgery, and bestowing unprecedented moral authority and professional expertise upon women as homemakers, "ministers of the home." However, Beecher's curricular treatise proceeded from a premise that Alcott, Gilman, and Martin emphatically rejected: that self-sacrificing Christian women schooled in Domestic Economy might best influence men's civic leadership from a paradoxically subordinate but equal position, without actual suffrage or opportunity for public employments other than teaching, nursing, charity work, and the like.

Although Beecher's curricular concept of Domestic Economy aimed to educate young women for home life, it prefigured later philosophical formulations of education about home life for broader audiences and purposes. For example, Washington proposed a coeducational domestic curriculum for partnership between African American men and women in the menial labors of home life. It taught young men industrial arts essential to home design and construction, including home furnishings, from the barest raw materials, while it taught young women housekeeping. Such DE included religious dispositions as well as scientific, agricultural, and economic skills; thus, learning at Tuskegee, as in Domestic Economy, entailed "mental development tied to hand and heart training." Similarly integrating practical with liberal learning in response to current situations, Addams's Hull House curriculum included much of Beecher's Domestic Economy. But, aiming also to help immigrants learn to make themselves at home in alien workplaces, it taught such subject matter integrally with more complex public concerns consequential to home life that Beecher excluded from Domestic Economy: for example, free democratic participation, economic need, child labor, syndicalism, public sanitation, interreli-

gious tolerance, informed citizenship, and second-language literacy.

Home Economics clearly shared Domestic Economy's purpose of educating young women for marital home life, but it had broader aims as well. Indebted to Beecher's treatise, Home Economics was a new concept of curriculum about home life first articulated by chemist-environmentalist Ellen Henrietta Swallow-Richards (1842–1911) and a few other men and women in a collective statement at the Lake Placid Conference (1902). The first home economists harked back to ancient notions of economics as household administration or domestic management and denounced the political definition of economics as production of wealth. Therefore, the philosophical foundations of Home Economics substantially predate both the field's inception and Beecher's treatise to include Aristotle's *Politics* and Xenophon's *Oekonomicus* as well as Francis Bacon's philosophy of science. Aiming to integrate the art and science of "right living," the Lake Placid Conference conceived Home Economics not only as women's schooling for marital home life, but also as women's higher education for professional life devoted to the scientific and artistic betterment of domestic living conditions. This curricular invention was thus conceived for two sorts of intellectual women: those like Swallow-Richards, who might bring scientific findings to homes, and those who might reflect philosophically upon the ethical, aesthetic, and social values of home life.

Normative questions about relations between home and society along with many other dualisms that also centrally concerned John Dewey (1859–1952) have constituted the substance of philosophical studies in Home Economics. He thought about education in the friendly company of Addams, Gilman, and innovative school teachers inspired by Beecher, one of whom addressed the Lake Placid Conference. Theorizing that schools should provide the sort of education that "the best and wisest parents" wanted for their children, Dewey embraced as a social ideal the family that was not "an isolated whole" like Emile's and Sophie's, but one whose range of associations was varied, free, and broad, in which "many interests are consciously communicated and shared." Under teachers' direction and in collaboration with Hull House, therefore, Dewey's Laboratory School at the University of Chicago taught children of both sexes alike a curriculum that integrated scientific

D

experimentation with historical reenactment of domestic occupations and technologies. Writing for the *Ladies Home Journal* (1911), Dewey defended the controversial practice of coeducation beyond elementary school, which Beecher rejected, by reasoning that it might prepare women to be "managers of households," an obvious reference to Home Economics in universities. Yet childhood education about home life, Dewey insisted, must not be mere preparation for such occupations or even only for home life, but education for democratic participation in a society undergoing radical transformation by industrial technology.

Bringing together subjects as diverse as philosophy, economics, sociology, chemistry, hygiene, design, psychology, and education, the first home economists shared Dewey's purpose of integrating the liberal curriculum with life itself. In practice, however, the highly specialized, ahistorical, scientific aspect of Home Economics—nutritional, food, and textile sciences, for example—has overwhelmed its philosophical aspect. Marjorie M. Brown has drawn upon her readings of the Frankfurt School to critique this divergence between stated aims and actual practice as the field's fatal flaw. Patricia J. Thompson, Brown, and others have also cited feminist theory to justify Home Economics' redefinition as a coeducational curricular strategy: to reconfigure the gendered division of domestic labor and to reconceptualize the home as a site where private and public issues intermingle.

Home economists have, however, tended to identify "home" with heterosexual family life even while neglecting to pose and take up philosophical questions about children's home education. In *The Stations of Solitude* (1990), Alice Koller has philosophically formulated ends and means of adult self-education for and about uncoupled home life by approaching her own as a thought experiment: "a journey toward the person one wants to become." Audre Lorde has theorized that mothering an African American son in a lesbian family entails teaching "love and survival," and feminist philosopher Sara Ruddick has conceptualized "maternal thinking" as a discipline learned while childrearing, whose transformation she has proposed for a new politics of peace. In *The Challenge to Care in Schools* (1992), Nel Noddings has made Ruddick's concept the foundation for her thought experiment redefining school as "a large, heterogeneous family," interracial, interethnic, and coeducational. Although she has

otherwise scarcely acknowledged previous thought about DE, except Dewey's, the "centers of care" around which she has reconceptualized school curriculum for all children would embrace aims and include subject matters that historically have had the name "domestic education": care for self, intimate and distant others, strangers, animals, plants, the earth, built surroundings, things, and ideas. If Noddings's educational ideal is "post-domestic," Martin's is "neo-domestic." In Martin's view, a morbid anxiety about and hatred of things domestic afflicts U.S. culture, a repression of domesticity which she has named "domephobia." Therefore, the schoolhome's curriculum would consist of domestic skills, virtues, and problems, both civic and personal; "learning to live" there would include practical activity, consciousness raising, and cultural studies occasioned and integrated by schoolhome-making, newspaper and theater production. These two contemporary philosophers of education have brought domestic educational thought into a new era whose future is still uncertain. Contrary to Beecher's hope, education about home life cannot alone remedy homes' most vicious problems, much less the world's. Yet, so long as such problems persist, DE will continue to demand philosophical ingenuity.

Susan Laird

See also Addams; Beecher; Dewey; Gilman; Girls and Women, Education of; Home and Family; Montessori; Pestalozzi; Rousseau; Washington; Wollstonecraft

Bibliography

Brown, Marjorie M. *Philosophical Studies of Home Economics in the United States: Our Practical-Intellectual Heritage.* Volumes 1 and 2. East Lansing: Michigan State University, 1985.

Edgeworth, R.L. and Maria. *Essays on Practical Education.* London: J.J. Johnson, 1811.

Koller, Alice. *The Stations of Solitude.* New York: William Morrow, 1990.

Laird, Susan. "The Ideal of the Educated Teacher: 'Reclaiming a Conversation' with Louisa May Alcott." *Curriculum Inquiry* 21 (1991): 271–97.

Martin, Jane Roland. *The Schoolhome: Rethinking Schools for Changing Families.* Cambridge: Harvard University Press, 1992.

Mayhew, Catherine Camp, and Anna Camp Edwards. *The Dewey School.* New York: D. Appleton-Century, 1936.

Noddings, Nel. *The Challenge to Care in Schools: An Alternative Approach to Education.* New York: Teachers College Press, 1992.

Thompson, Patricia J. *Home Economics Teacher Education: Knowledge, Technology, and Family Change.* Bloomington, Ill.: American Home Economics Association, 1984.

Washington, Booker T. *The Future of the American Negro.* New York: Haskell House, 1968.

Du Bois, William Edward Burghardt (1868–1963)

Multidisciplinary scholar-activist whose systematic inquiries into the conditions of African American life during the late nineteenth and early twentieth centuries had significant influence on race relations, sociological methodology, and the philosophy and program of African American higher education. In the opinion of Herbert Aptheker, during Du Bois's lifetime "no one in the United States was more expert in the area of the nature, theory, and purposes of education; and on the specific subject of the education of Black people in the United States" (1973: x). Du Bois (who preferred that his surname be pronounced Due Boyss, with the last syllable accented) was born on February 23, 1868, in Great Barrington, Massachusetts. He died in Accra, Ghana, West Africa on August 27, 1963, the eve of the U.S. civil rights movement's historic March on Washington.

After graduating from Fisk University in 1888, Du Bois, in 1895, became the first person of African descent to earn a doctorate at Harvard. His first academic appointment was at Wilberforce University in Ohio (1894–1896), where he taught Greek and Latin. Du Bois also held a brief appointment at the University of Pennsylvania (1896–1897), where he completed his renowned study of the quality of life among people of African descent in Philadelphia. His book *The Philadelphia Negro: A Social Study,* published in 1899, reported what is now recognized as the first social survey undertaken in the United States. Atlanta University, where Du Bois spent a total of twenty-three years (1897 to 1911, and 1934 to 1944), became an important center for the systematic study of African American life. During his initial tenure there, Du Bois oversaw the completion of what amounted to a virtual "encyclopedia on the American Negro problems." Of this work, Du Bois wrote that "it may be said without undue boasting that between 1896 and 1920 there was no study of the race problem in America made which did not depend in some degree upon the investigations made at Atlanta University" ([1940] 1995: 65).

Du Bois's writings in education are classic representations of public philosophy. He clearly perceived the context of education problems to be social and cultural life. Moreover, his intent was to consistently create wider contexts for understanding education in a cultural sense. Indeed, by his insistence that the educational problems experienced by people of African descent be brought into the discourse, Du Bois did significantly expand educational understanding in general. Du Bois experienced racism throughout his life. His resistance to it helped to shape a critically conscious awareness that social and cultural life in the United States is not constituted within a single public, but in multiple publics. This way of thinking about the social order in the United States made Du Bois's role as a public philosopher of education very different from that of John Dewey.

The social ideal that concerned Dewey was democracy. The role of education in Dewey's conception of democratic society was to develop within "individuals a personal interest in social relationships and control, and the habits of mind which secure social changes without introducing disorder" (1966: 99). Dewey's notion that a particular kind of education can bring about change "without introducing disorder" is problematic. Although, by his own words, Dewey understood that the United States is "composed of a combination of different groups with different traditional customs," he, nonetheless, ignored the dialectics of domination and resistance associated with these cultural differences. There is no mention by Dewey of how the power over institutionalized education held by the politically dominant members of the society is used to maintain the order he would preserve. Dewey did not confront the reality of oppressed peoples' challenge to societal power relations. For him, social change was something to be determined by the rational thinking of the politically dominant members of the society.

Du Bois and Dewey shared membership in the same society, but related to different primary cultural groups. Dewey's cultural orientation was European American; Du Bois's was African American. Consequently, Du Bois presented a quite different analysis of education's role in society than did Dewey. To begin with, Du Bois focused on the cultural contradictions in the United States, particularly between people of African and European ancestries, and the impact this conflict had on cultural identity. He saw the legislation of equal rights in voting and education as the "beginning of even more difficult problems of race and culture." He also reckoned with the question of what would become of the African American cultural identity in a United States where equality was supposedly the law of the land. As was his fashion, Du Bois posed a query: "What we must now ask ourselves is when we become equal American citizens what will be our aims and ideals and what will we have to do with selecting these aims and ideals. Are we to assume that we will simply adopt the ideals of Americans and become what they are or want to be and that we will have in this process no ideals of our own?" ([1960] 1973: 149).

Du Bois considered the cultural assimilation of African Americans into the politically dominant culture in the United States to be unacceptable. He saw a clear dilemma for African Americans—refuse to go to school, or go to school and run the risk of becoming alienated from the African American cultural community: The dialectics of power did not escape scrutiny in Du Bois's analysis, as they did in Dewey's. The exigencies of his culture, not the society dominated by whites, established imperatives for Du Bois. He was unwilling to accept any social arrangements that would restrict the ability of the African Americans to understand and appreciate their relationship to the African historical-cultural context.

The archetype of the scholar-activist, Du Bois wrote twenty-three books and hundreds of essays, articles, poems, and editorials on the experiences of people of African descent. During his college years at Fisk and Harvard, Du Bois's ambition was to become a professor of philosophy, thinking that thereby he would be able to pursue a systematic understanding of the social contradiction he termed the "color bar." He credited William James (1842–1910), one of his Harvard professors, with dissuading him from this pursuit with an admonition about the difficulty of earning a living as a professor of philosophy. Du Bois turned instead to the dis-

ciplines of history and social science and later to sociology which, at that time, was only beginning to emerge as a field of inquiry. Whatever the discipline, his investigations were always guided by a firm commitment to liberating people of African ancestry from racial oppression in all its forms.

Though defined in disciplinary contexts variously as a sociologist, political scientist, economist, and historian, in each of these fields Du Bois assumed the role of philosopher—if the task of philosophy can be said to be, as J.M. Giarelli and J.J. Chambliss (1988: 33) suggest, "the formulation of questions for reflective thought." Throughout his long life, the dominant question for Du Bois was what kind of education will uplift the person of African ancestry? He tenaciously reflected upon this question and developed ways of posing it to whomever would claim to be the definers or providers of such an education. It was over this question that Du Bois feuded for twenty years with Booker T. Washington (1856–1915) regarding the latter's advocacy of industrial schooling and contempt for college training. Du Bois fervently maintained that he agreed with Washington on many issues and was not opposed to industrial schooling for the masses. What he objected to was the strategy carried out by Washington with the backing of his moneyed, white, Northern supporters to suppress all attempts to establish schools of higher learning for African Americans.

Du Bois did not lack for courage or audacity in his efforts to hold African American educational and political leadership accountable. In the summer of 1906, Du Bois accepted an invitation to speak at Hampton. Standing before a partisan audience at Washington's own alma mater, Du Bois irreverently told those assembled that it was the Hampton philosophy of education from which he had come there to dissent. He then queried them about their fitness to be leaders of their people by musing, "When you as teachers, have learned a certain Hampton way of expressing yourselves, I am wondering and anxiously wondering, just what picture of the world and life your students are getting" (Du Bois [1906] 1973: 13). Du Bois believed that the future of African America was in its own hands and that the maturation of the first generation of African American people born after enslavement represented an especially critical moment in African history. He stood on the position that the only hope for his people was to ensure for that generation and those that would come after it "higher training in life and thought and power." The aims of such education were to achieve "abolition of the color line; the treatment of all men according to their individual desert and not according to their race" (Du Bois [1906] 1973: 15).

It was Du Bois's belief that the higher education of a "talented tenth" of the African American population would be the most efficient means of preparing the leadership needed to guide the development of the first African American generation born after emancipation. J.D. Anderson (1988) points out that in 1896 Henry L. Morehouse was actually the first to use the words "talented tenth" to describe such a philosophy and program of African American education. Nonetheless, it was Du Bois who came to be popularly associated with the term and who made the concept central to his plan for the higher education of African Americans. In his second autobiography, Du Bois wrote that he felt the "talented tenth" "through their knowledge of modern culture could guide the American Negro into higher civilization" (Du Bois [1968] 1991: 236).

Du Bois's emergence as a political leader in the United States was largely the result of his determination to wrest control of the African American intelligentsia, the "talented tenth," from the influences of Washington and the Northern industrialists/philanthropists who supported the Hampton-Tuskegee model of industrial schooling. The convening of the Niagara Movement by Du Bois in 1905 was a call to organize an African American challenge to the power that Washington wielded over the political and educational lives of people of African descent in the United States. The addition of "neoabolitionist" whites to the Niagara Movement gave rise to the National Association for the Advancement of Colored People in 1910.

Du Bois was an incorporator and founder of the NAACP. He served the organization for twenty-four years as its director of publicity and research and as editor of the *Crisis,* the organization's communications organ, from 1910 until 1934. The NAACP and the *Crisis* provided Du Bois with a platform from which to launch and disseminate potent analyses and critiques of the political and educational condition of African American people and the quality of their leadership. Notable among these debates was Du Bois's disagreement with Marcus Mosiah Garvey (1887–1940) over the emigration of people of African descent in diaspora to Liberia and what Du Bois considered to be unsound fiscal management of the huge, and to date unparalleled, mass-based organization that Garvey founded, the Universal Negro Improvement Association.

A man with a global vision, Du Bois recognized early on his kinship with African people the world over. Five years before the formation of the Niagara Movement he was secretary of the first Pan-African Congress, held in England in 1900, and a principal figure in each of the four subsequent Pan-African congresses held between 1919 and 1945.

During the frenzy of McCarthyism, Du Bois was arrested in 1950. The passive reaction to his arrest by prominent African Americans led Du Bois to rethink the "talented tenth" notion. As he put it, their general response "revealed a distinct cleavage not hitherto clear in American Negro opinion." The "talented tenth," as a class, had, in Du Bois's opinion, "become American in their acceptance of exploitation as defensible, and in their imitation of American 'conspicuous expenditure'" (Du Bois [1968] 1991: 370). Although Du Bois had succeeded in turning the direction of African American education away from the Hampton-Tuskegee model, he ultimately conceded that the higher training of the "talented tenth" to become race leaders had ultimately proved to be inadequate for the task of waging war against organized cultural oppression.

In 1961, Du Bois became a member of the Communist Party U.S.A. As a Pan-Africanist he was presented with the moral option of choosing between the West, which had opposed every African anticolonial movement, and the communist bloc, which had provided support for many African independence movements. That same year he left the United States to live in Ghana at the invitation of President Kwame Nkrumah. He devoted the final years of his life to compiling the *Encyclopedia Africana.* Today, the Du Bois Centre in Accra houses Du Bois's crypt, a museum, and library. The bulk of the Du Bois papers remain in the United States at the University of Massachusetts at Amherst.

Mwalimu J. Shujaa

See also COLONIALISM AND POSTCOLONIALISM; DEMOCRACY; DEWEY; JAMES; RACE AND RACISM; SLAVERY; SOCIOLOGY; WASHINGTON

Bibliography

Anderson, J.D. *The Education of Blacks in the South, 1860–1935*. Chapel Hill: University of North Carolina Press, 1988.

Aptheker, Herbert. "Introduction." In *The Education of Black People: Ten Critiques, 1906–1960 by W.E.B. Du Bois,* edited by H. Aptheker. New York: Monthly Review Press, 1973.

Dewey, John. *Democracy and Education.* New York: Free Press, 1966.

Du Bois, W.E.B. *The Autobiography of W.E.B. Du Bois: A Soliloquy on Viewing My Life from the last Decade of Its First Century* [1968] 11th ed. New York: International Publishers, 1991.

———. *Dusk of Dawn: An Essay toward an Autobiography of a Race Concept.* New Brunswick, N.J.: Transaction Publishers, 1940. 6th ed., 1995.

———. "The Hampton Idea" and "Whither Now and Why." In *The Education of Black People: Ten Critiques, 1906–1960 by W.E.B. Du Bois,* edited by H. Aptheker. New York: Monthly Review Press, 1973.

———. *W.E.B. Du Bois Speaks: Speeches and Addresses, 1920–1963* [1970]. 7th ed. Edited by P.S. Foner. New York: Pathfinder, 1991.

Giarelli, J.M., and J.J. Chambliss. "Philosophy of Education as Qualitative Inquiry." In *Qualitative Research in Education: Focus and Methods,* edited by R.R. Sherman and R.B. Webb. London: Falmer Press, 1988.

Lewis, D.L. *W.E.B. Du Bois: Biography of a Race, 1868–1919.* New York: Henry Holt and Company, 1993.

Duns Scotus, John (c. 1266–1308)

Franciscan philosopher and theologian, whose thought represents the last great synthesis of the high Middle Ages. Through his doctrines on freedom, epistemology, and anthropology, among others, he exercised significant influence on fourteenth-century philosophy and theology. The Scotists among scholastics were a prominent intellectual school well into the seventeenth century.

Born in Scotland, Duns Scotus joined the Franciscan order as a youth. He was subsequently educated at the universities of Oxford, Cambridge, and Paris. He achieved the highest academic rank as master of theology at Paris in 1307, and he subsequently lectured at Cologne, where he died in the fall of 1308. Scotus's two major works are his massive commentary on the four books of Peter Lombard's *Sentences* and his magisterial *Quodlibet.* In addition, he studied some of Aristotle's logical works and of his *De Anima* and *Metaphysics,* as well as a variety of other works, foremost among them being *A Treatise on God as First Principle.*

The English word *dunce* is derived from the pejorative use of "Duns" by humanists and reformers who, fatigued with the abstract intricacies of late-scholastic dialectics, slurred the sixteenth-century Scotists. Their irritation has some basis in the fact that little of Duns's thought is conceived from the practical or prudential point of view. Moreover, as his sobriquet "the Subtle Doctor" indicates, the quality of his writings challenges the most patient of students. But even though he writes preeminently from an abstract, theoretical perspective, his ideas have profound implications for the way one conceives reality and the human person.

Duns Scotus's thought is dominated by the task of forging a synthesis that remains true to both the reality of freedom, human and divine, and the demand that theology be scientific. The two generations prior to Scotus saw the overhaul of Christian theology under the influence of the Aristotelian philosophy, which had made its way into the principal Western universities. The attractiveness of the explanatory power of Aristotelian methodology and ontology proved irresistible. Along with the acceptance of Peripatetic philosophy within the Christian schools, however, came the challenge to obviate the necessitarianism that seemed intrinsic to the pagan philosopher's world view. The hallmark of Scotus's thought is his systematic, uncompromising recognition of both the contingency of God's every relation to the world and the integrity of human free will. It is with this defining characteristic in view that he develops the variety of his particular doctrines on the nature of the world and our ability to know it.

In explaining the human capacity to know God, Scotus insisted upon the possibility of the human intellect's receiving by abstractive cognition an intelligible species (an abstraction of the mind, which stands in a relationship to the act of understanding much as a visible sense image stands to an act of vision) which would serve, in its capacity as the primary object, as the source of all distinct knowledge of God, including the foundational mysteries of Trinity and Christ's redemptive acts. This doctrine concerning the scope of our abstractive intellect, at least as theoretical possibility, gives great dignity to the human mind. Indeed, Scotus considered human intellects, insofar as they are placed in ideal circumstances, to be the equivalent of angels'. Naturally, though, in the ordinary course of things, circumstances are not ideal, and our knowledge of God is constructed from data abstracted from sense experience, and so is uniformly indirect and imperfect.

Scotus's notion of our abstractive cognition was developed alongside a complementary conviction that the human intellect is, in principle, capable of the intuitive cognition of existing individuals. The idea here was that, although in the ordinary course of things we know things only insofar as we have abstracted their intelligibilities from the immediacy of their actual existence, our minds are capable of grasping things in their existential presence. However, this capacity, short of miraculous interventions, will never be exercised in the ordinary course of things, although in the next life it is by this intuitive knowledge that the blessed shall know the Divine Being.

On the vexing question of universals dealing with the truthful correspondence of our concepts with reality, Scotus was a realist. He taught that extramental things exist in their own right as individuals. Yet he also held that a nature or an essence is constitutive of the individual thing, and this element, when taken in its own right, is neither individual nor universal, but open either to being contracted to individual, extramental existence or to existing as universalized in the abstraction of some intellect. To illustrate: Only individual horses, like Traveler or Bucephalus, actually exist. Even so, one can truly say "Traveler is a horse" and "Bucephalus is a horse," and use the predicate "horse" with exactly the same meaning. The predicate, of course, is a universal and as such enjoys mental existence. As an entity of the mind, it shares with the extramental animal the common nature "horseness." Because of its indifference to and identity in either state of existence, Scotus's celebrated "common nature" provides the grounds for the objectivity of human knowledge.

Scotus developed a unique doctrine of individuation. The issue is: What is the principle by which an entity exists as an individual? The question is a difficult one for realists, like Scotus, who want to hold that our universal concepts are in some sense isomorphic with extramental existents. The problem is that the individuating principle invariably turns up as a factor that militates against the intelligibility that has become closely identified with the abstracted universal. But because of his doctrine on the common nature, however, Scotus can insist that what makes each thing an individual is an intelligible principle that transforms or contracts each *type* into a concrete *this*, an individual. The practical implications of this doctrine are profound, for it means that each thing, and especially each human person, has not only a uniqueness, but also an intelligibility and intrinsic value rooted in that principle. One of the consequences of the fact that our abilities to both understand and love are limited in the present order of things is that things always enjoy more intelligible and axiological significance than we can master. On Scotistic principles, then, any objective encounter with reality runs into the inexhaustible mystery of a plentitude of value: What exists as an individual is known to us only by abstractive cognition of universals drawn out of the entity's inexhaustible uniqueness.

In the moral sphere, Duns Scotus taught that innate to each human person is an inclination to choose what is intrinsically good. He called this basic tendency *affectio justitiae* (inclination for the just good). Humans, however, inevitably experience this benign desire in conflict with an equally basic desire for one's egoistic good (what he called *affectio commodi*). The action of moral life portrays the drama of free will tempering its natural love for its own well-being under the influence of a love for self-transcendent values. Scotus's moral theory is often characterized as either a right reason or natural law ethics, for he holds that in principle one can come to judge what is truly right or wrong on the basis of rational inquiry. Such true judgments amount to a recognition of how human actions with respect to the material world and to other persons conform to the first moral principle of loving God above all and for his own sake. Fundamental moral truths, then, are expressions of the divine will ordaining human action to the final end or goals of human existence. For Scotus, men and women stand before the divine order with a remarkable degree of autonomous freedom and rational insight.

From the practical point of view of the educator, Scotistic philosophy communicates a keen sense of the dignity of the human person, a worthiness rooted in both a basic freedom and a powerful rationality. Human liberty and knowledge, however, never exhaust the capacity of things and persons around us to serve as centers of what is true and good. As the poet G.M. Hopkins, who was greatly influenced by Scotus, wrote: " . . . nature is never spent;/ There lives the dearest freshness deep down things . . ."

William A. Frank

See also FREEDOM AND DETERMINISM; REASON AND RATIONALITY; SCHOLASTICISM

Bibliography

Bettoni, E. *Duns Scotus: The Basic Principle of His Philosophy.* Translated by B. Bonansea. Washington, D.C.: Catholic University of America Press, 1961.

Duns Scotus, John. *Duns Scotus on the Will and Morality.* Translated by Allan B. Wolter. Washington, D.C.: Catholic University of America Press, 1986.

———. *God and Creatures. The Quodlibetal Questions.* Translated by F. Alluntis and A.B. Wolter. Princeton: Princeton University Press, 1975.

———. *Opera Omnia.* 26 vols. Paris: Vivies, 1891–1895.

———. *Opera Omnia.* 11 vols. Vatican City: Vatican Polyglot, 1950–.

———. *Philosophical Writings.* Translated by Allan Wolter. Indianapolis, Ind.: Hackett, 1987.

———. *A Treatise on God as First Principle.* Translated by Allan B. Wolter. Chicago: Franciscan Herald, 1984.

Ryan, John K., and Bernardine M. Bonansea, eds. *John Duns Scotus, 1265–1965.* Studies in Philosophy and the History of Philosophy, vol. 3. Washington, D.C.: Catholic University of America Press, 1965.

Saint-Maurice, Beraud de. *John Duns Scotus. A Teacher for Our Times.* St. Bonaventure, N.Y.: Franciscan Institute, 1955.

Schaefer, Odulfus. *Bibliographia de vita, operibus et doctrina Iohannie Duns Scoti Doctoris Subtilis ac Mariani saeculorum XIX-XX.* Rome: Herder, 1955.

———. "Conspectus brevis bibliographiae Scotisticae recentoris." *Acta Ordinis Fratrum Minorum* 86 (1966): 531–50.

Wolster, Allan B. *The Philosophical Theology of John Duns Scotus.* Edited by Marilyn McCord Adam. Ithaca, N.Y.: Cornell University Press, 1990.

Durkheim, Emile (1858–1917)

French sociologist widely regarded as the founder of the sociology of education. Most of his contributions are lecture courses given either in Bordeaux or Paris from 1895 to his death in 1917 and published posthumously. His interest in education embraced not only its sociology but also its philosophy, history, psychology, ethics, and practice. Until recently his contribution has been regarded as conservative, as placing overriding emphasis on the need for discipline, consensus, and social harmony. This interpretation is now changing and Durkheim's radicalism is now being acknowledged in a reassessment of his overall project.

Durkheim's lectures on education cannot be understood without an appreciation of his general social theory and his estimation of the social crisis in France at the end of the nineteenth century. For Durkheim, society must become the object of a social science, sociology. There are two fundamental social forms, tribal (segmental) society, and complex (organic) society. It is the latter that develops institutions specifically devoted to education. These institutions establish in a "normal" society the essential elements of its culture in the new generations. The institutions of higher education, particularly the universities, also play a role in establishing a relatively independent basis for objective knowledge. However, Durkheim believed that, in France at the end of the nineteenth century, normal conditions did not prevail, and that educational institutions had an important role to play in the formation of a liberal democratic society. The approach Durkheim adopted was to provide a social scientific—that is, sociological—basis for democratic educational practice. The main danger, he argued, came from either an exaggerated individualism (which would end in anarchy) or an authoritarianism (which would end in tyranny). It is thus fair to see Durkheim as heir to the liberal political theory of the division of powers: For Durkheim the balance of powers in a liberal society is a balance of social institutions well beyond the countervailing purely political institutions. His treatment of educational institutions was to see them as political societies in miniature—institutions specifically prone to the tendency of authoritarianism of the school authorities, teachers, and elder children.

In a large historical perspective, Durkheim was critical of the way in which social and educational revolutions had failed to consolidate their creative ideas. The general problem he sought to address was, in his terms, the equivalent of a revolution, but one that had specific features: The old and new were closely entwined: there was no simple anachronistic superstructure that could be identified and removed by a single direct act. Rather what had to be achieved, he argued, was a complex structural reformulation of educational practice. Durkheim's lectures on moral education attempt to define the main elements of modern moral education and the problem of how to develop such a moral discipline in the child.

Discipline is, for Durkheim, the first element of morality. Durkheim admits that to the liberal individualist this starting point appears entirely misconceived, as a kind of policing, a purely negative activity. Durkheim suggests that discipline is essentially positive: Not only is it necessary to control appetites, but moral discipline, as long as it is not too severe, protects the individual against *anomie*—a concept developed by Durkheim to define a state of disillusionment that occurs when the connection between means and ends is broken. Genuine liberation is not a liberation from constraint.

The second element in moral education concerns altruism, or the attachment to social groups. If the family is the initial center of moral development, it is the school that is able to link the child to a national culture and identity. But there is a link between discipline and social attachment, because it is to the authority of social rules that morality must ultimately appeal. These elements are found in all traditional moral teaching, says Durkheim; what is new is that in the modern world there is a third element that is altogether different and that creates special problems. He calls this the problem of self-determination. It becomes completely impossible any longer to make an appeal to a dogmatic moral authority as the source of moral certitude, and the problem with science, even social science, is that it undercuts the traditional supports of religious authority. The paradox of the new situation is that a secular and rational education must accept the fundamental idea that the individual human being must be the object of a cult. The humanization of religion implies the deification of man. In its highest forms, education must develop a genuine knowledge of the nature of society and what must be done in order for it to realize itself in a state of well-being. In these conditions moral rules lose their authoritarian character, and consensus is reached by informed consent. Thus the third element of morality and the decisive one in a modern state is rational moral understanding.

The practice of education in the schools must also be adequate to the requirements of a democratic society. The legitimate content of education should not be justified by appeal to great personalities, even the authority of the teacher. The character of modern societies is that they are governed by the rule of law, and respect for impersonal democratic norms has to be developed. Order and social discipline in the school must also incorporate growing respect for the individual: Corporal punishment should be entirely prohibited. Teachers must demonstrate a respect for the society for which they speak and avoid either an authoritarian or an anarchic style of teaching, for these will either engender passivity or rebellion. The aim of moral education is to develop a modern citizen.

The general character of Durkheim's contribution to education was therefore conceived as an attempt to transform traditional religious education into a rational and secular one. The special feature of Durkheim's project was to insist that on the one hand such education could work only if certain ritual elements were retained from the religious tradition, while on the other the new style of education aimed to produce a self-critical citizen able to play a creative role in modern life.

Michael Gane

See also DEMOCRACY; DISCIPLINE; INDIVIDUALISM; SOCIOLOGY

Bibliography

Cladis, Mark. *A Communitarian Defense of Liberalism: Emile Durkheim and Contemporary Social Theory.* Stanford: Stanford University Press, 1992.

Durkheim, Emile. *Durkheim: Essays on Morals and Education.* Edited by W.S.F. Pickering. Translated by H.L. Sutcliffe. London: Routledge and Kegan Paul, 1979.

———. *Education and Sociology.* Translated by S.D. Fox. Chicago: Free Press, 1956.

———. *The Evolution of Educational Thought in France.* Translated by P. Collins. London: Routledge and Kegan Paul, 1977.

———. *Moral Education: A Study in the Theory and Application of the Sociology of Education.* Translated by E.K. Wilson and H. Schnurer. New York: Free Press, 1961.

E

Educational Policy and Administration

Educational policy and administration deal with the actual conduct and operation of educational institutions. A perennial problem for the philosopher of education is to demonstrate a connection between educational ideas and actual organizational processes. A possible strategy is to show that a particular ideology has become the basis for human action by showing that a proposed system of rules that the ideology advocates is actually followed. According to James E. McClellan (1968), policy-making is itself a rule-directed activity that generates the rules that govern conduct in an institution. The process of policy-making must ideally: (1) acknowledge conflicting interests, (2) be generated by an organization that carries on a public and reasonable debate, and (3) produce rules that can actually be enforced. McClellan points out the interrelatedness of the terms "policy," "polity," "politeness," and "police."

"Administration" is commonly characterized as the maintenance of the rules that govern an institution. Writers such as James M. Lipham contrast "administration" with "leadership"—with the latter being activities that change the rules of an institution. An older contrast—going back to Woodrow Wilson (1856–1924)—contrasts administration and politics, with "administration" being termed a rational activity while "politics" is termed irrational. This latter dichotomy seems to have been pervasive until recently. Notice that McClellan's definition of "policy" is programmatic in that it seeks to identify policy-making with rational debate, while Wilson sought to do the opposite.

A recent paper by Deal and Wiske sees policy-making and administration as heavily influenced by "one's vision of schools as organizations" or "school images." They identify three metaphors—the factory, the jungle, and the temple—as the bases of three contemporary "school images." The main section of this article will discuss the history of these school images in terms of the history of educational administration. The final section of this article will address parallels between the philosophical reflections on educational policy of Thomas F. Green and John Dewey (1859–1952), and the policy-making of James B. Conant (1893–1978) and his opponent Frederick M. Raubinger (1908–1989).

Administration and School Images

The metaphor of the school as a temple places the administrator in the role of a priest whose task is to enact rituals and ceremonies that maintain the faith. In the nineteenth century, states increased the power of school administrators with the enactment of compulsory attendance laws. Books on school architecture of this era explicitly referred to the school building as a temple. The school building changed from being a large room with one central authority figure to many rooms with many authority figures. William Torrey Harris (1835–1909)—a well-known advocate of Idealistic philosophy—rose to the position of superintendent of schools in St. Louis and subsequently served as U.S. Commissioner of Education (1889–1903). Harris wrote no books on educational administration, but his writings reveal a quasi-religious faith in American institutions. For Harris, people achieve identity only through social institutions. The individual must not seek an identity outside of institutional contexts, for only those activities carried on through social institutions have educational value. For Harris, any activity that seeks to be defended as having educational value must be pursued in an institutional context. Strangely, Harris failed to institutionalize his own ideas. But the temple metaphor was developed in educational administration texts written by William E. Chancellor (1867–1963) between 1904 and 1920.

Chancellor's views were even more authoritarian than Harris's. He applied Harris's faith in American institutions to a faith in public schooling. Chancellor was contemptuous of politicians and businessmen. He explicitly compared schooling to religion and superintendents to ministers. Chancellor advocated an increased authority for school administration and the abolition of school boards. Like his hero, Woodrow Wilson, Chancellor sought to separate administration from politics. Ironically, in 1920 Chancellor's career temporarily ended because he became involved in a smear campaign against presidential candidate Warren G. Harding. He was dismissed from his teaching position, hunted by a lynch mob, forced to leave the country, and had his book on Harding burned by Harding administration officials. After several years as a traveling salesman in Canada, Chancellor returned to the United States and resumed his teaching career (Mason; Russell).

Chancellor's textbooks were displaced by the texts of Ellwood P. Cubberley (1868–1941). While Cubberley was sympathetic to Chancellor's authoritarian views, Cubberley's ideology was based on a different metaphor: the factory. In an article published in 1915, the famed rhetorical scholar Fred Newton Scott (1860–1931) noted that the metaphor of the temple in educational rhetoric was being displaced by the new rhetoric of efficiency. Like Chancellor, Cubberley deplored the presence of women and minorities on school boards, but, unlike Chancellor, Cubberley idolized businessmen. As dean of the Stanford University College of Education, Cubberley sought to establish a profession of educational administration, promoted the use of intelligence tests as a selection device, and urged the increased presence of businessmen on school boards. He was influenced by the evolutionary view of history and positivist epistemology.

Cubberley saw the American educational system as the apex of civilization and the professional school administrator as one of history's greatest heroes. For him, the evolution of human society is not advanced by democratic influence, but by the enlightenment of the ignorant masses by legitimate educational authority. Cubberley saw children as the product of the school as factory—designed by professionals to meet the needs of society. (This last point would have been anathema to Chancellor.) But, like Chancellor and Wilson, Cubberley sought to free administrative decision-making from the conflicts of politics. Cubberley believed that the presence of businessmen on school boards would give the professional school administrator a free hand. (Chancellor feared that the new breed of administrator would turn out to be a new breed of mental defective.)

Cubberley's textbooks became standards for the field of educational administration, but in the late 1920s research in the social psychology of organizations began to influence writing on administration—initially in business and then later in education. By the early 1940s, Douglas M. McGregor (1906–1964)—a Harvard-educated psychologist—had emerged as one of the leading advocates of a social-psychological approach to administration. His six years as president of Antioch College (1948–1954) and his long association with the philosopher of education Kenneth D. Benne (1908–1992) gave McGregor considerable credibility as a source of a more humane approach to educational administration.

McGregor called his view "Theory Y" and contrasted it with "Theory X." The newer view was more commonly called "the human relations approach" while the older view was better known as "scientific management." Yet McGregor's work was not really a break with the past. Although he often echoed John Dewey's calls for democratic educational administration, McGregor, like Cubberley, saw schools as goal- and output-oriented, and he once suggested that student programs must be governed by "requisitions from America." In short, while McGregor opposed the authoritarian inclinations of both the temple model and the scientific management approach, his views can be seen as a more kind-hearted version of the factory model. During the 1960s and 1970s, McGregor was widely quoted in educational administration with such writers as Thomas J. Sergiovanni and Fred D. Carver clearly advocating a Theory Y approach.

McGregor studied psychology at Harvard during the 1930s—a time when Harvard psychologists sought to identify themselves as scientists and divorce themselves from philosophy. Like many early writers on organizational behavior, McGregor based his views of organizations on means-ends rationality and argued that, in a congenial work environment, employees will seek to integrate personal objectives with organizational goals. McGregor deplored the "carrot and stick" approach to management. As president of Antioch College, he sought to include students, faculty, and blue-collar workers in discussions of college policy, but his openness left McGregor vulnerable to the machinations of professional anticommunist informers who were willing to spread outright lies about student activities on the Antioch campus. In McGregor's view of management we see a tension between the rhetoric of the democratic institution and the image of the school as a factory.

In 1947, the educational historian Archibald W. Anderson (1905–1965) published a paper in which he warned that while educational administration's ideals might be democratic, the practice commonly violated this ideal. A 1960 paper by McClellan applauded administrators' efforts to develop scientific administrative theory but warned that the then-new behavioral-science-based administrative theory assumed a centralized model of decision-making. But the administrative theorists discussed by Anderson and McClellan may have been engaged in wishful thinking. During the mid-1950s a popular film (based on a popular novel) introduced a phrase into the national vocabulary that contained a new and disturbing metaphor for the school: *The Blackboard Jungle*.

The metaphor of the jungle—where all social roles are subject to political negotiations, the exercise of power, and the flux of symbolic meaning—seems to be the school image that informs the administrative theory of James G. March, a social scientist on the faculty of Stanford University. During the 1970s, March conducted extensive studies of college presidents and school superintendents. His resulting works can be understood as a rejection of most of the assumptions of educational administration theory in the twentieth century. Specifically, March rejects the assumptions that: (1) organizations exist to achieve goals; (2) individuals act on their beliefs; and (3) only actions based on goals or beliefs are rational. He sees schools as "organized anarchies" or "loosely coupled systems" that have ambiguous goals, unclear relations of means and ends, and whose decisions are made in the context of chance interactions of people, problems, and solutions. For March, actions on the basis of intuition and tradition are just as rational as actions toward a goal with a clear means in mind. His work even hints at a convergence with the long-forgotten views of W.T. Harris. March's advocate Karl E. Weick urged administrators to consider the leadership style of a clergyman as possibly more appropriate to schooling than that of a management scientist.

Rational or Democratic Policy-Making?

While the metaphors of temple, factory, and jungle do seem to identify three kinds of educational institutions, we lack any clear intuitive characterization of educational systems. And the question of the very existence of educational systems is still controversial in some circles. Philosophical inquiry about educational systems and the making of educational policy at the national level seem to involve at least three central questions:

1. Does nation N have a system of education?
2. Can policy for that system be made rationally?
3. Can policy for that system be made democratically?

Dewey wrote his little book *The School and Society* at a time when the high school was beginning to function as the institution that linked elementary school and college. In this book, Dewey advocated the formation of an educational system as a way of creating teacher training institutions with a clear purpose and that do not serve an ambiguous role as both a kind of secondary school and a kind of college. According to Thomas F. Green, the System began to take shape around 1910. The System is a well-organized institution defined by rules that operate with the rigor of an Aristotelian practical syllogism. The System as Green sees it is composed of primary and derivative elements. The primary elements are:

P1: Schools
P2: A medium of exchange
P3: A principle of sequence

While the derivative elements are:

D1: Size
D2: A system of control
D3: A distribution of goods

The System "behaves" according to such laws as:

L1: The Law of Zero Correlation
L2: The Law of Last Entry
L3: The Principle of the Moving Target

Green paints a picture of the System as a well-programmed computer that will continue to function in spite of the misguided efforts of reformers. This may be reassuring to the conservative who fears that the System will break down, but it is hardly reassuring to those who believe that the System has perpetuated social injustices. Green's L1 states that educational credentials become worthless once everyone attains them. L2 can be summarized as the claim that the least advantaged social groups cannot benefit from the System until the higher status groups have exhausted the System's resources. And L3 maintains that educational credentials over time can change from being sufficient conditions for social status to being necessary conditions. When Dewey wrote *The School and Society* in 1899, he did not have that in mind.

In his few discussions of social and educational policy, Dewey was concerned with making a case for a desirable approach to policy-making. Green deploys a Kantian transcendental argument to show how an educational system must operate. For Green, the question of rationality or desirability of the System simply does not come up. The rationality of the System is the way the system functions. By contrast, Dewey would regard a Kantian transcendental argument with considerable skepticism. For Dewey the educational policy-maker must ask if the educational system is successfully regulating public acts in the public interest. In the nineteenth century, a wide variety of schools existed with drastically different functions. Dewey favored the organization of a national system of education as an expression of the evolution of America into a democracy. In teacher education, the normal schools that taught teaching methods existed completely separate from university education departments that prepared educational researchers. Dewey's ideal was a unified college of education that integrated both functions and prepared teachers in the public interest.

Dewey would have rejected Green's suggestion that the logic of the educational system is unassailable by any external standards. He warned in a 1903 paper entitled "Democracy in Education" that the authority structure of any kind of educational institution must be evaluated by the standard of whether it impedes or encourages that freedom of thought that is necessary to democracy. Thirty-five years later, Dewey reiterated this point in a paper entitled "Democracy and Educational Administration," wherein he chided school administrators for their failure to develop structures that would allow teachers a role in decision-making.

The conflict between the rationalist and democratic views of educational policy-making is not just a debate for the philosophy of education classroom. During the 1950s and 1960s, New Jersey State Commissioner of Education Frederick M. Raubinger attacked the work of the Educational Testing Service—located in Princeton, New Jersey—and its guiding inspiration, former Harvard University president James B. Conant, as an undemocratic elite who had seized educational policy-making from public officials. Like Chancellor, Conant was fond of dismissing critics of public education as being misinformed. Raubinger, by contrast, was a firm believer in local control of education who devoted an entire chapter of his 1974 educational administration textbook to a discussion of democratic theory. In the early 1970s, Conant sought to establish the Education Commission of the States, which took as its mission the expansion of the two-year community colleges. Raubinger pointed out in 1972 that the ECS had also sought to increase the power of the fifty state governors over educational policy at the expense of education officials. Conant in his autobiography clearly advocated the expansion of the two-year college at the expense of the four-year college. Because of the influence of Conant and the ETS, Raubinger was forced to resign in 1966.

During the twenty-five years since Conant completed his autobiography, the two-year college has continued to be the subject of fierce debate. Green, for example, treats the two-year college as an institution separate from the System. The conceptual framework of this entry can illuminate controversies over this new kind of institution. The earliest type of two-year college—the junior college—was seen as a rational and democratic institution. It supposedly satisfied a public demand for access to higher education while rationally fitting into the educational system and enabling students to transfer to bachelor's programs. Gradually, a factory model of administration became the central metaphor, with greater emphasis on vocational education and a rational fit with the job market. However, recent demands on these institutions by ethnic minorities have placed faculty in a jungle environment wherein the role of the teacher is poorly defined. Cynical administrators see this situation as an opportunity to deprofessionalize teaching and expand vocational programs that do not terminate either in a degree or in the opportunity to transfer to a bachelor's program. But newer nondegree programs and the reduction of faculty can be seen as antagonistic to the demands of the community for more course offerings. Jungle-oriented administrators' attempts to save money may backfire and antagonize the community and threaten the survival of the institution. Perhaps a return to the more ministerial role by educators could even be defended as democratic.

Michael A. Oliker

See also DEMOCRACY; DEWEY; HARRIS; IDEALISM; KANT; POSITIVISM; PUBLIC EDUCATION; SCHOOL; SOCIAL AND POLITICAL PHILOSOPHY; SOCIAL SCIENCES, PHILOSOPHY OF

Bibliography

Anderson, Archibald W. "Violations of the Democratic Ideal in Current Conceptions of Administrative Procedure." *Educational Administration and Supervision* 33 (1947): 26–34.

Callahan, Raymond E. *Education and the Cult of Efficiency.* Chicago: University of Chicago Press, 1962.

Chancellor, William E. "Hypermoron as Educator." *School and Society* 5 (1917): 668–71.

———. *A Theory of Motives, Ideals, and Values in Education.* Boston: Houghton Mifflin, 1907.

Conant, James B. *My Several Lives.* New York: Harper and Row, 1970.

Cubberley, Ellwood P. *Public School Administration.* Boston: Houghton Mifflin, 1916.

Cutler, William W., III. "Cathedral of Culture: The Schoolhouse in American Thought and Practice since 1820." *History of Education Quarterly* 29 (1989): 1–40.

Deal, Terrence E., and Martha Stone Wiske. "How to Use Research to Win Battles and Maybe Wars." In *Managing Schools in Hard Times,* edited by Stanton Leggett. Chicago: Team 'em Inc., 1981.

Dewey, John. "Democracy and Educational Administration." In *The Later Works.* Vol. 11, edited by Jo Ann Boydston. Carbondale: Southern Illinois University Press, 1987.

———. "Democracy in Education" [1903]. In *The Middle Works.* Vol. 3, edited by Jo Ann Boydston. Carbondale: Southern Illinois University Press, 1977.

———. *The School and Society.* Edited by Jo Ann Boydston, with a preface by Joe R. Burnett. Carbondale: Southern Illinois University Press, 1980.

Eaton, William. "From Ideology to Conventional Wisdom: School Administration Texts 1915–1933." In *An Analysis of Texts on School Administration 1820–1985,* edited by Thomas E. Glass. Danville, Ill.: Interstate, 1986. ERIC Document ED 294 314.

Green, Thomas F. *Predicting the Behavior of the Educational System.* Syracuse, N.Y.: Syracuse University Press, 1980.

Lipham, James M. "Leadership and Administration." In *Behavioral Science and Educational Administration,* edited by Daniel E. Griffiths. The sixty-third yearbook of the National Society for the Study of Education, Part 2. Chicago: NSSE, 1964.

McClellan, James E. "Theory in Educational Administration." *School Review* 68 (1960): 210–17.

———. *Toward an Effective Critique of American Education.* Philadelphia: J.B. Lippincott, 1968.

McGregor, Douglas M. *The Human Side of Enterprise.* New York: McGraw-Hill, 1960.

———. *Leadership and Motivation.* Cambridge: MIT Press, 1966.

March, James G. "American Public School Administration: A Short Analysis." *School Review* 86 (1978): 217–50.

———. "Model Bias in Social Action." *Review of Educational Research* 42 (1972): 413–29.

Mason, Robert. "From Idea to Ideology: School Administration Texts 1820–1914." In *An Analysis of Texts on Edu-*

E

cational Administration 1820–1985, edited by Thomas E. Glass. Danville, Ill.: Interstate, 1986. ERIC Document ED 294 314.

Oliker, Michael A. "Analytical Philosophy and the Discourse of Institutional Democracy." In *Proceedings of the Midwest Philosophy of Education Society 1991 and 1992,* edited by David B. Owen and Ronald M. Swartz. Ames, Iowa: The Society, 1993. ERIC Document ED 364 493.

———. "Douglas McGregor's Theory Y and the Structure of Educational Institutions." Ph.D. diss., University of Illinois at Urbana-Champaign, 1976.

Raubinger, Frederick M. "Compact for Education: A Tale of Educational Politics." *Educational Forum* 36 (1972): 441–50.

———. "A National Testing Program: Viewed with Misgivings." *NEA Journal* 48 (1959): 29.

———, and Harold C. Hand. "Later Than You Think." Typewritten manuscript, 1967. Personal library of Michael A. Oliker.

———, Merle R. Sumption, and Richard M. Kamm. *Leadership in the Secondary School.* Columbus, Ohio: Merrill, 1974.

Russell, Francis. *The Shadow of Blooming Grove: Warren G. Harding in His Times.* New York: McGraw Hill, 1968.

Scott, Fred Newton. "Efficiency for Efficiency's Sake." *School Review* 23 (1915): 34–42.

Weick, Karl E. "Administering Education in Loosely Coupled Schools." *Phi Delta Kappan* 63 (1982): 673–76.

Wilson, Woodrow. "The Study of Administration." *Political Science Quarterly* 2 (1887): 197–222.

Elitism

Elitism is a fairly modern concept that came into popular usage as a result of the works of Gaetano Mosca, Vilfredo Pareto, and Robert Michels, referred to as the founding fathers of the Italian school of elitism. Within more recent times, it has come to take on negative connotations and has tended to be used in opposition to the notion of democratic institutions. Elitism seems to imply possession of superior knowledge or ability that catapults a group of people into control over those who do not possess such

knowledge or ability. In some cases, elitism is tied to the notion of expertise and specialization. There is some contention that while the practice of elitism is universal in scope, its prominence has been a fairly recent phenomenon.

The earliest bases for the practice of elitism were religion and heredity. According to Jeffrey Bell (1992), "For most of the period from 3000 B.C. to 600 B.C. . . . blood elites and religion elites, often in combination, dominated society by combining possessions, knowledge, and ideas into power over people." This form of elitism was overcome by the idea that human beings are capable of learning, as was particularly evident in the Confucian era. To a great extent, the concept of elitism has undergone various transformations; it has, nevertheless, maintained the notion of a minority group of persons exercising control over the majority population.

Contributions from Philosophy to the Concept of Elitism

The earliest writings of Plato (c. 427–347 B.C.) hint at notions of elitism, though many scholars have argued that his works do not support a position that may be characterized as fascist, dictatorial, or in some measure coercive. He nevertheless makes specific reference to the educational system's assuming a direct role as a "sorting machine," in which those whom he refers to as intellectually able are prepared to fill leadership roles. The net effect of his position is to set up a class system based upon some rather elitist notions primarily manifested in one's ability to be educated. Gerald Gutek describes the apex of Plato's hierarchy as being occupied by philosopher kings who have achieved such status primarily because of their "intellectual propensity."

Michel de Montaigne (1533–1592), unlike Erasmus (c. 1469–1536), was very concerned about the education of the aristocracy. He propagated the position that the aristocracy could be guaranteed of both its ascendancy and longevity if its youngest members were "properly" educated from birth. This education was not to be made available to the masses. Martin Luther (1483–1546) and John Calvin (1509–1564) are truly representative of the contributions that the religious Reformation movements made to the notion of elitism in education. Luther appeared to be nonelitist, but his support for the aristocracy in the peasant revolt and his insistence that Latin and Greek be the medium of instruction for the religious and political elite hint at his support of elitism in education. John Calvin's treatise on "predestination" hints at elements of elitism when he contends that God has not created all people equal with one another but has foreordained some to eternity and others to damnation. The "marks" for identifying the predestined elect resemble those others have identified with the upper echelons of society.

John Locke (1632–1704) and Jean-Jacques Rousseau (1712–1778) best represent the philosophy that was prevalent in the period of Enlightenment. Locke is best known for his major work *Two Treatises on Government*. This work may be seen as an antithesis to the notion of elitism, in that it sought to undermine the theory of the "divine right of kings" by contending that kings, like everybody else, are subject to the conditions of the social contract. Rousseau is well known through his *opus magnum* popularly known as "The Social Contract." He argued for the "natural good" in all men and ascribed notions of inequality and elitism to the construction of what he referred to as "social artificialities."

Benjamin Franklin (1706–1790) and Thomas Jefferson (1743–1826) are the most noted persons who influenced early American philosophical thought in education. Franklin sought to provide education for all people, and there is no hint in his writings of support for elitism in education. Jefferson, on the other hand, may be seen as revisiting the position of Plato, insofar as he contended that not only should some persons be specifically "sorted" out of society to receive preparation for leadership positions, but also that such persons should receive deference from the masses, who would recognize them for their superior intellectual capacities. John Dewey (1859–1952) counteracted much of the elitism in American educational philosophy and argued rather cogently for an educational system that sought to dismantle all obstacles to the creation of a society in which cooperation was of paramount importance.

The Contributions of Political Theorists to the Concept of Elitism

The concept of elitism is usually associated with a political tradition beginning with the works of Gaetano Mosca (1939), Vilfredo Pareto (1966, 1968), and Robert Michels (1962). It is important to note that these early proponents of the concept of elitism thought of themselves primarily as social scientists rather than social philosophers, primarily because "elitism" was both accepted and viewed as a "moral point of view and as a respectable intellectual orientation" (Field and Higley, 1980: 3). According to Mosca, elitism manifests itself in society through a significantly small minority, irrespective of the size of the entity that is in question; some checks and balances are maintained, however, to ensure that such groups do not obliterate competing groups through excessive powers. Pareto, who argued that elitism continues only when ruling elites are mindful of incorporating the positions of other elites, conceded that there is an ever-present group of elites in any given society. Michels's contribution to the body of literature on elitism is probably best summarized in his insistence on the inevitability of oligarchy in any society, organization, or group. Mosca, Pareto, and Michels, considered the "founding fathers of the Italian school of elitism" (Albertoni, 1987: 118), have undoubtedly influenced the concept of elitism in the Western tradition. The best known scholars who have referred to those works in their writings on elitism are Joseph A. Schumpeter (1950) and C. Wright Mills (1956).

Schumpeter's work is referred to as "a reformulation and application of the political elitism of the classical Italian exponents" (Albertoni, 1987: 122). Central to Schumpeter's thoughts, which are characterized as a "pluralist elitist equilibrium model" (McPherson: 1977), is the perpetual dialogue between competing elite groups to the exclusion of the masses. In essence, this dialectical relationship between varying privileged groups ensures the perpetuation of this notion of elitism, concentrated in only a few persons in society. C. Wright Mills is credited with contributing, more than any other person in the United States, to the construction of the body of literature on elitism in American society. In formulating the well-known term the "power elite," Mills contends that elitism is perpetuated through such a group, defined by "the similarity of its personnel, and their personal and official relations with one another, upon their social and psychological affinities" (C. Wright Mills, 1956: 278). Mills emphasized the necessity of consensus among the members of such a group if a system of elitism is to be enforced in any given society.

Elitism in the American Educational System

There are three main areas within education in which the notion of elitism is foremost: the is-

E

sue of choice, the sorting or "tracking" of students, and educational opportunity based upon issues of merit. There is a plethora of arguments both in favor of and against choice in education. At one end of the spectrum, there are significant groups of scholars, professionals, and lay persons alike who argue that the absence of choice gives public schools a monopoly on education and has the effective result of depriving poor children of the benefits of quality education. In fact, there is a significant group of researchers (Chubb and Moe: 1986, 1988; Coleman et al.: 1982), who argue rather strongly that the very nature of denying choice, primarily manifested in the dichotomy between private and public schooling, fosters an elitism primarily through the radically different curricula and associated activities offered by private institutions. They see this "elitism" as a positive factor and, in fact, are very supportive of such efforts. Boyd and Walberg (1990) summarize rather clearly why choice is needed in education, citing that denial of choice violates the tenets of democracy, breeds inequality in the society through differential educational opportunities, and fosters a lack of accountability.

Those who object to incorporating choice into the educational system buttress their position with three main contentions: that some schools might choose to offer a curriculum that does not meet the needs of the disadvantaged and "culturally different" within the society, thereby virtually predisposing those students to failure; schools might establish entrance requirements that are "elitist" in nature and thereby make it nearly impossible for all students to gain admission; or schools might establish rather demanding and sophisticated ground rules for parental involvement that have the net effect of frustrating primarily those parents who are from poorer or "culturally different" backgrounds. Interestingly, the issue of choice hinges largely for both proponents and opponents on the issue of elitism.

The issues of "sorting" and "equality of educational opportunity" are closely related. The works of Bowles and Gintis (1976), Giroux (1983), and Spring (1991) are demonstrative of the tremendous degree of social reproduction that takes place in schooling. Their primary argument is that by reproducing the social classes in society, one guarantees the perpetuation of the elitist class. Michael Apple (1979) and Raymond Williams (1961) are particularly associated with the notion of the "hidden cur-

riculum," which acts as the principal factor in executing that social reproduction.

The notion of elitism in education is rooted in both political and philosophical ideas with long histories. Even though there has been an effort to view the positive aspects of elitism, it still carries a rather pejorative connotation.

P. Rudy Mattai

See also CALVIN; EQUALITY; LOCKE; LUTHER; PLATO

Bibliography

Albertoni, Ettore A. *Mosca and the Theory of Elitism.* Translated by Paul Good Rick. Oxford: Basil Blackwell, 1987.

Apple, Michael W. *Ideology and Curriculum.* Boston: Routledge and Kegan Paul, 1979.

Bell, Jeffrey. *Populism and Elitism.* Washington, D.C.: Regnery Gateway, 1992.

Bowles, Samuel, and Herbert Gintis. *Schooling in Capitalist America.* New York: Basic Books, 1976.

Boyd, William L., and Herbert J. Walberg, eds. *Choice in Education: Potential and Problems.* Berkeley, Calif.: McCutchan, 1990.

Chubb, John E., and Terry M. Moe. "No School is an Island: Politics, Markets, and Education." *Brookings Review* 4 (1986): 21–28.

———. "Politics, Markets, and the Organization of Schools." *American Political Science Review* 82 (1988): 1065–87.

Coleman, James S., Thomas Hoffer, and Sally Kilgore. *High School Achievement: Public, Catholic, and Private Schools Compared.* New York: Basic Books, 1982.

Field, G. Lowell, and John Higley. *Elitism.* London: Routledge and Kegan Paul, 1980.

Giroux, Henry. *Theory of Resistance: A Pedagogy for the Opposition.* South Hadley, Mass.: Bergin and Garvey, 1983.

Gutek, Gerald L. *A History of Western Educational Experience.* Prospect Heights, Ill.: Waveland Press, 1972.

McPherson, C.B. *The Life and Times of Liberal Democracy.* Oxford: Oxford University Press, 1977.

Michels, Robert. *Political Parties: A Sociological Study of the Oligarchical Tendencies of Modern Democracy.* Translated by Eden and Cedar Paul. Introduction by S.M. Lipset. New York: Collier Books, 1962.

Mills, C. Wright. *The Power Elite.* New York: Oxford University Press, 1956.

Mosca, Gaetano. *The Ruling Class*. Edited by A. Livingston. Translated by H.D. Khan. New York: McGraw Hill, 1939.

Pareto, Vilfredo. *The Rise and Fall of the Elites: An Application of Theoretical Sociology*. Edited by A.L. Zetterberg. Totowa, N.J.: Bedminster Press, 1968.

———. *Sociological Writings*. Edited by S.E. Finer. Translated by D. Mirfin. New York: Praeger, 1966.

Schumpeter, Joseph A. *Capitalism, Socialism, and Democracy*. New York: Harper and Row, 1950.

Spring, Joel. *American Education: An Introduction to Social and Political Aspects*. 5th edition. New York: Longman, 1991.

Williams, Raymond. *The Long Revolution*. London: Verso, 1961.

Emerson, Ralph Waldo (1803–1882)

New England lecturer, essayist, and poet whose life work is a point of departure in the development of an American literary culture, and whose moral and aesthetic vision, however averred or averted, has exercised a lasting influence on American culture in general.

It is commonplace that readers of Emerson find the fewest of his views on a topic by reading the essay of that title—for example, "Education." Observations about education and schooling are scattered throughout his writings. Emerson consistently wrote against education as system or method, against formal schooling, and, at times, even against reading books.

This said, Emerson's writings, from his private journals to his published essays, comprise a philosophy of education in an affirmative sense: the reader is first oriented to what a philosophy of education is not, and therein becomes positioned to turn and reorient toward some new, unknown tuition, which is more the reader's than Emerson's. This turning, toward an always partial but sufficiently provisional perfection, one's necessary disposition in coming to know, for Emerson, is the prerequisite of any knowing worthy to be called education. Emerson considered the tuition or instruction of education as those thoughtful and remedial actions undertaken in which we are disposed to lead ourselves. On this singular point Emerson often is interpreted as providing the ideological foundations of "rugged individualism."

A broader reading of Emerson, however, is useful in clearing the way for turning to a self that is more liberal and encompassing than the old. The resources that inform this concentrically growing self are not foreign but are domestically and democratically available, despite the many dismal manifestations of American public life that Emerson cataloged.

Emerson gave most value to those ways Americans might make use of language in translating the world (nature), which includes ourselves (natures), into usable meanings. In Emerson's writing, this amounts to the appropriation of nature(s) in indigenous figurative or literary terms.

For Emerson, the newness of an emerging American culture offered the opportunity for its language to be practiced as emerging too, so that the very processes of change could be encompassed in language, selves, selves in relation to other selves, society, and culture. For Emerson, the paradigm of this more lively language was the trope. Tropes are linguistic gestures or figurative turns leading away from the literal toward broader meanings. The capacity, ability, and disposition to use language in this way is the primary characteristic of an Emersonian tuition. In Emerson, troping is the means of overturning passive relations to language in order to work with it as a companion form of life—in effect, to reconstitute the actual constitution of our selves as texts capable of troping, and through these processes to challenge our contexts.

An Emersonian tuition is not advanced by method or system, but is formed through immediate intuitions or holistic intimations of the ordinary world. This aspect of Emerson is shaped against the notion that the cultivation and function of human intellect is purely rational, a philosophical epistemology, necessarily of European derivation, or coherent through any imposed consistency or order. Rather, Emerson posits that our reception of the world is its inception, colored by an evanescent play of moods, and that our subsequent conceptions formed of this provide beginnings that lead to more fruitful engagements with our context and condition.

Emerson's illustrations and allusions provide a varied demonstration of his conviction that our reception of the world is mostly ordinary and that moments of ecstatic enthusiasm are rare and ephemeral. Emerson's valuation of both, as the immeasurable bottom and top steps of human experience, provides the scale needed to move beyond mere existential fact in the processes of self-tuition.

For Emerson, the ecstatic and the ordinary establish a composite wholeness, necessary in forming a dynamic, rhythmic, individuated, and contextual logic on which he recommends that an individual learn to stand and rely, although his most characteristic question of this condition is "Where do we find ourselves"? Out of this self-reliance comes the process of living forward, which is often the projected action of words as deeds, at times simple, unmitigated action, at other times the imagination conjugating with the world, but which is most often bending to the necessity of things: These things were for Emerson the composition of a life that is and is the instruction of a life becoming.

Decidedly, Emerson is best interpreted from a philosophical-literary perspective, particularly that of nineteenth-century romanticism. Samuel Taylor Coleridge (1772–1834) comes to mind. Emerson's work demonstratively fuses form and content in a nonpropositional way such that it has baffled philosophers quite consistently. His relentless perfectionist probing owes most to Plato (c. 427–347 B.C.), while his style of probing is reminiscent of that of Michel de Montaigne (1533–1592). It is from these influences that his work seems to derive its broad notion of education and the moral life, its valuation of the ordinary, and its philosophical-literary temper, although his source of the everyday was resoundingly American.

His earliest major work, the 1836 *Nature,* is Neoplatonic in character, notable for its moments of intense and expansive enthusiasm. The middle *Essays, First* (1841) and *Second* (1844) *Series,* indirectly treat and notably depart from many of the epistemological formulations of Immanuel Kant (1724–1804). These essays are the richest and most suggestive expression of Emerson's complex of thought and style and represent a more cautious appraisal of human prospects than was promised in *Nature.* Emerson's later essays, characterized by *The Conduct of Life* (1860), most fully acknowledge constraints on human action. Emerson's private journals establish an excellent counterpoint to his published work.

Emerson influenced Friedrich Nietzsche (1844–1900), perhaps more than has been commonly acknowledged, and the American pragmatists, especially William James (1842–1910) and John Dewey (1859–1952). His emphasis on language and the ordinary presages the later Ludwig Wittgenstein (1889–1951). Like Wittgenstein, Emerson's fusion of form, con-tent, the aesthetic, and the moral has had a greater impact on practice in the creative arts than on the professional pursuits of philosophy and education.

Allan F. DiBiase

See also DEWEY; HUMAN NATURE; JAMES; NIETZSCHE; PLATO; ROMANTICISM; WITTGENSTEIN

Bibliography

Bloom, Harold, ed. *Modern Critical Views: Ralph Waldo Emerson.* New York: Chelsea House, 1985.

Cavell, Stanley. *Conditions Handsome and Unhandsome: The Constitution of Emersonian Perfectionism.* Chicago: University of Chicago Press, 1990.

———. *This New Yet Unapproachable America: Lectures after Emerson after Wittgenstein.* Albuquerque: Living Branch Press, 1989.

Emerson, Ralph Waldo. *The Collected Works of Ralph Waldo Emerson.* Edited by Robert Spiller, Joseph Slater, et al. 4 vols. to date. Cambridge, Mass., and London: Belknap Press of Harvard University Press, 1971–.

———. *Journals and Miscellaneous Notebooks of Ralph Waldo Emerson.* Edited by William H. Gilman et al. 16 vols. Cambridge, Mass., and London: Belknap Press of Harvard University Press, 1960–1984.

Whicher, Stephen. *Freedom and Fate: An Inner Life of Ralph Waldo Emerson.* Philadelphia: University of Pennsylvania Press, 1953.

White, Morton. *Science and Sentiment in America: Philosophical Thought from Jonathan Edwards to John Dewey.* New York: Oxford University Press, 1972.

Emotivism

Emotivism claims that value judgments, especially ethical judgments, differ from scientific, factual, and logical statements by expressing emotions or attitudes. The theory could possibly be traced to the connection between ethical terms and the attitude of approval or disapproval outlined by David Hume (1711–1776). It was also hinted at in the 1920s by C.K. Ogden and I.A. Richards. Emotivism has been one of the most influential ethical theories of the twentieth century.

Alfred J. Ayer offered the first major statement of emotivism. He claimed that ethical concepts are unanalyzable because they are pseudoconcepts, insofar as they add nothing to a statement's factual content. Thus to say to someone "You acted wrongly in stealing that money" is the same as saying "You stole that money." By saying that it is wrong simply shows one's moral disapproval. Saying that a certain action is right or wrong is to express feelings. Such statements are also calculated to arouse feelings and to stimulate action. Thus the sentence "It is your duty to tell the truth" expresses feelings and conveys the command "Tell the truth." As ethical sentences make no statement at all, it is senseless to ask whether they are true or false—they are unverifiable. Ayer claimed that his conclusions about ethics apply to aesthetics as well.

Charles Stevenson developed the most sophisticated version of emotivism. Stevenson distinguishes two broad kinds of disagreements: beliefs and attitudes. The major purpose of ethical judgments is not to indicate facts but to change attitudes. The term attitudes is used broadly to include purposes, aspirations, wants, preferences, and desires. Disagreement in beliefs relates to explanations and descriptions, whereas disagreements in attitudes concerns favoring or disfavoring something. Our attitudes affect our beliefs, and vice versa. Both imperative and ethical sentences are used more to encourage, alter, and redirect aims and conduct than to describe them. For example, "This is good" means I approve of this; do so as well. An imperative ("Defend your country") is designed to gain what the speaker desires. If the speaker says, "Smith is fundamentally a good man," the judgment asserts that A approves of Smith and acts quasi-imperatively to induce in the hearer a similar attitude. Ethical agreement, therefore, requires more than agreement in belief; it requires agreement in attitude. Ethical argument usually ends when disagreement in attitudes terminates, even though some disagreement in belief may remain. Ethical terms such as "good," "wrong," and "ought" are habitually used to deal with disagreement in attitude because they have acquired a strong emotive meaning by repeated occurrence in emotional situations.

Among other contributors, Hans Kelsen (1881–1973) developed an emotivist position in legal theory. He holds that legal science is a descriptive science and that questions about values cannot be scientific; he proposes a "pure theory of law" based on analyzing legal concepts apart from value judgments. National codes of law rest on political and moral preferences and are emotive in nature.

Emotivism has come under sharp attack. First, attitudes are tenuously connected to emotions; thought, words, and deeds are more central manifestations of them. Second, one can claim that unrelieved suffering is bad even before one takes a particular attitude toward it. Even if we do not have any strong feelings or emotions about it, it does not change the evaluation of it. Third, ethical judgments are true if supported by better reasons than the alternatives.

Emotivism today is represented by R.M. Hare, who has modified it in two significant ways: (1) ethical statements prescribe; (2) they are universal prescriptions.

John Martin Rich

See also ETHICS AND MORALITY

Bibliography

Ayer, Alfred Jules. *Language, Truth and Logic.* New York: Dover, 1936, 1946.

Hare, R.M. *The Language of Morals.* Oxford: Clarendon Press, 1952.

Kelsen, Hans. *What Is Justice?* Berkeley: University of California Press, 1957.

Stevenson, Charles. *Ethics and Language.* New Haven: Yale University Press, 1944.

Urmson, J.O. *The Emotive Theory of Ethics.* London: Hutchinson University Library, 1968.

Empiricism

Empiricism is both a philosophical theory and a cultural attitude. Each has an important influence on the other, but not in a manner that is always direct or easy to discern. How empiricism relates to the theory and practice of education is an example of the complicated and subtle connections among the abstractions of philosophy, the imperatives of culture, and the practical tasks of education.

As a philosophical theory, empiricism, in all of its various forms, gives primacy to human sense experience as the basis for all substantive—that is, existential—knowledge claims. Even those forms of empiricism that allow for the possibility that the formulation of knowledge has its temporal beginnings with the conceptual manipulation of ideas or symbols maintain that the validation of these ideas or symbols is always founded on the experience of the knower.

Empiricism rejects a priori modes of existential knowing, such as reason, contemplation, revelation, or faith, on the grounds that they ignore or repudiate the central role in the epistemic process played by the human body and its material environment. Moreover, empiricism would accept the notion that substantive knowledge might stem from innate ideas or instincts only with stiff qualifications. In its strictest philosophical form, empiricism is not designed to promote any moral, social, or political doctrine, but rather to represent the most plausible, and therefore the least objectionable (as distinct from the "true") analysis of what it means to "know."

In the classical Western philosophical tradition, epitomized by Plato, reality—or what is true, good, and beautiful—is defined as immutable, as what is not subject to change. As an implication of this it is believed that reality must be absolute rather than relative, and objective rather than subjective. Said yet another way, what is true, good, and beautiful cannot be contingent on anything outside of itself, and especially it cannot be contingent on a knowing subject.

If knowledge is a function of what is real, and reality is neither relative nor subjective, then any form of perception or understanding that is rooted in contingency must be an illusion. Thus, when our perception or understanding is grounded in sense experience, there are only two possibilities. Either we are connected more or less objectively to the material world of space and time, the essence of which is its susceptibility to change; or else we have created a solipsistic universe for ourselves that allows for no objective test of validity whatsoever. In the first case we are limited to the practical benefits of science and common sense. In the second case there is only madness. In neither case, however, do we possess genuine knowledge, or the capability to acquire it.

Precisely because of the assumption that the conditions of knowledge require a stable ontology, classical Western philosophy is being-centered, rather than knowledge-centered. It begins with theories about what exists and proceeds to construct epistemologies that allow for the possibility that human beings might come to possess some degree of genuine, or "real," knowledge. Given the stipulation that truth is immutable, and the obvious inaccessibility of experience to this kind of reality, a credible theory of knowledge must ultimately be a priori, regardless of whatever other feature it might possess.

As defined by its literary canons, Western philosophy has always contained voices that were not in harmony with this classical view, such as those of Thucydides (c. 457–c. 401 B.C.), Sophocles (495–406 B.C.), and Socrates (470–399 B.C.). However, it was not until the end of the Middle Ages that the weight of official opinion began to shift significantly from being-centered to knowledge-centered conceptions of philosophy. By the time of the Enlightenment, this shift was more or less complete.

René Descartes (1596–1650) may have championed reason over experience as the highest mode of knowing, but he is widely regarded as the father of modern philosophy because he was the first major philosopher to give epistemology priority over the study of existence per se. This nominalistic attitude was a fundamental departure from Aristotle's view, which gives theoretical reason a higher status than practical judgment. The latter cannot discern being as such, but only the phenomena that occur within conscious life.

Despite this limitation, Descartes gave new authority to the knower and put the individual at the center of ontological decision-making. However unintentionally, his ideas led to the establishment of empiricism as the cornerstone of Western philosophy. Once individual consciousness is granted the status attributed to it by Descartes, empiricist attitudes are almost sure to follow. From the perspective of an individual, knowing person, what is most likely to be regarded as the feature that distinguishes human beings from other beasts is not reason, as Descartes, following Aristotle, maintained, but rather the more subjective and ethnocentric qualities of experience. When David Hume (1711–1776), undoubtedly empiricism's most ardent and renowned philosophical champion, remarked that reason is a slave of the passions, he was giving testimony to the power of experience and habit to influence our lives, and celebrating human feelings as criteria for defining what is real.

Deliberately or not, Cartesian rationalism paved the way for empiricists like Hume. It also served as the groundwork for the writings of classical empiricism that are associated with the development of modern Western conceptions of popular democracy. By focusing on the individual knower as the starting point for the philosophic enterprise, these two schools of thought combined to radically change the defining images of the Western mind. They undercut the authority of tradition and rejected any hierarchical social relationship that could not be reduced to a voluntary contractual arrangement. It is no wonder that the writings produced by these schools have been periodically censored and continue to be viewed with grave mistrust by those who espouse more communal or collectivist values.

It might be debated whether the acceptance of empiricism in philosophy was the cause or effect of other changes that were then occurring in Western culture. There is no question, however, that it has had a profound impact on how education is thought of and conducted. Depending on the purpose and point to be made, the inception of modern education can be dated from the period of the Enlightenment and the works of writers and reformers such as Jean-Jacques Rousseau (1712–1778), Johann Pestalozzi (1746–1827), Johann Herbart (1776–1841), and Friedrich Froebel (1782–1852), or from the beginning of the twentieth century and the works of thinkers such as Sigmund Freud (1856–1939) and, especially, John Dewey (1859–1952). What these works and individuals have in common is the belief that practical needs and the interests of the self, struggling to survive in a precarious material world, are more important than eternal verities or the preservation of high culture. It was exactly this empiricist attitude that led to the demise of Enlightenment (including Cartesian) rationalism. The latter maintains that, in order for experience to be possible, the knower must first have ideas or concepts. Empiricism maintains that this contention in any form is merely a prejudice, one that weighs heavily as a burden on actual practice. For someone engaged mainly in thinking, such a burden may seem to be minor. But to a person with the mind-set of a doer, the price will almost always appear to be too high.

Steeped in this attitude, modern education has historically and ideologically supported efforts to secularize authority and discredit architectonic theories of culture. These efforts have been largely successful. For the welfare of the individual and society taken as a whole, however, the consequences are mixed. In the spirit of democracy, modern educators have confidently predicted that the secularization of authority would result in the decentralization of power. Not only has this often times failed to happen, as political dictatorships and corporate monopolies clearly demonstrate, but even when power has been decentralized, the results have not always been salutary.

The kind of freedom that is promoted by modern education, and legitimized philosophically by empiricism, has a dark side. All too easily it can be vulgarized and corrupted, so as to rationalize the ruthless or self-indulgent use of power. The counter-argument given by modern education is that the best protection from this threat is to provide more education. But since the type of education that is being recommended promotes the same sort of freedom that has been found so often to be problematic, the argument seems somewhat circular.

Be this as it may, most astute observers agree that the promise and actual achievements of modern education far outweigh the risks. More important than its material benefits are its moral virtues of self-reliance, self-respect, and self-acceptance, which, at their best, breed a complementary treatment of others. Perhaps the same might be said for empiricism.

Philip L. Smith

See also ARISTOTLE; DESCARTES; DEWEY; EPISTEMOLOGY; PLATO; RATIONALISM

Bibliography

Church, Robert L. *Education in the United States.* New York: Free Press, 1976.

Dewey, John. *Types of Thinking.* New York: Philosophical Library, 1984.

Hamlyn, David W. "Empiricism." In *The Encyclopedia of Philosophy.* Vol. 1, edited by Paul Edwards, 499–505. New York: Macmillan and the Free Press, 1967.

Rogers, Arthur K. *A Brief Introduction to Modern Philosophy.* New York: Macmillan, 1923.

Skidelsky, Robert. *English Progressive Schools.* Baltimore, Md.: Penguin, 1969.

Epicureanism

Epicureanism refers to the philosophy of the ancient Greek teacher Epicurus (c. 341–c. 270 B.C.). In view of both its importance as an Athenian school for hundreds of years and its popularity in ancient Roman civilization, Epicureanism can be said to have had a significant influence in the ancient world. Unlike the practitioners of other philosophical schools at the time, followers of Epicurus remained dedicated to his teachings, and very few modifications occurred even with the passage of centuries.

Unfortunately, the ideas within the philosophy of Epicureanism have been badly distorted through historical assessment. Today, the word *epicurean* has nothing in common with Epicurus. Dictionary definitions of *epicurean* suggest that the word means given to luxury or sensual pleasure, or having luxurious tastes. That is far removed from the philosophy of Epicurus, who was in fact an ascetic who rejected the life of sensual gratifications. In one of the literary fragments attributed to Epicurus, he suggests that he would live on bread and water, while spitting contemptuously upon the pleasures of plush living.

In the few preserved writings of the Greek teacher, which consist mainly of short letters to friends, he takes a condemnatory attitude toward society, suggesting that Athenian culture was debased by materialism, superstition, and fear of the unknown. It was to free the mind from these perils that he founded his Garden School in Athens (c. 305 B.C.) and wrote, according to tradition, some three hundred treatises on living the good life.

Epicurus and his followers were not interested in the same investigative fields as other contemporary schools, such as the Academy, founded by Plato (c. 427–347 B.C.), or the Lyceum, established by Aristotle (384–322 B.C.). Epicureanism was not devoted to metaphysical speculation or scientific inquiry for its own sake, but rather to answering questions so as to enable people to live in peace of mind. The governing philosophy of Epicureanism was happiness through mental serenity. Preserved writings from Epicureans do cover scientific information—in fact, the school borrowed the modified atomic theory from the pre-Socratics Leucippus (fifth century B.C.) and Democritus (c. 460–c. 370 B.C.)—but Epicurus and his followers were not scientists. They disdained pure scientific inquiry and were not even concerned whether hypotheses were provable by experimentation. Knowledge of the heavens and earth was valuable only for alleviating fear of the unknown. For this reason Epicurus prefaced all his writing with the injunction that the aim of knowledge is to find freedom from fear and achieve *ataraxia,* peace of mind.

A cursory investigation of the most famous Epicurean writings—such as Epicurus' *Letter to Herodotus,* in which he lectures on the facts of sense perception, atoms, the soul, cosmology, meteorology, and celestial phenomena, or the *Letter to Pythocles,* outlining heavenly phenomena and meteorological conditions—would suggest the research of a scientist. The same may be said for the most famous of all Epicurean publications, *De Rerum Natura* (*The Nature of Things*), written by the Roman Lucretius (c. 99–c. 55 B.C.). This literary classic is a poetic exposition of Epicureanism with an emphasis on the atomistic and materialistic state of the cosmos. Lucretius was a devoted follower of Epicurus, and his Latin poem proposes scientific explanations for many physical phenomena.

Neither Epicurus nor Lucretius claimed to be a scientist; each viewed his role as an observer of life, helping to show others a natural explanation of the events that were not clearly understood by the populace. The people of ancient times worried about supernatural causations and the intervention of gods in the events of daily life. Epicureans refuted myth and superstition. They insisted that natural phenomena such as storms, earthquakes, and volcanoes do not occur because of the caprice of some god, but rather that all disquieting events can be explained by natural law. Like all ancient peoples, the Greeks believed that it was necessary to propitiate the gods through prayer, sacrifice, and ritual; Epicureanism insisted that such practices were unnecessary. Denying that vengeful and vindictive gods intrude into the lives of humans, causing suffering to some and offering succor to others, Epicureans rejected the notion of divine intervention in earthly affairs. They insisted that the gods take no interest in mankind, because as superior beings they live in another element and do not become enmeshed in the troublous world of humanity. For this belief, Epicureanism was branded as a school of impiety, if not atheism.

Epicurus established his Athenian school in a small park where resident-members provided for their own food, growing a variety of vegetables. For this reason the school was known as the Garden, and followers of Epicurus were proud of their self-sufficiency in providing for food. In the third century B.C., military campaigns around Athens caused food shortages during difficult times; Epicureans therefore believed in isolating themselves and followed an injunction from the leader of the Garden School to live in anonymity. In what became a distinguishing feature of Epicureanism, causing other schools to criticize its philosophy, the search for obscurity became an aim in life. Epicurus and his followers became subject to vilification because they insisted that in the interest of achieving serenity for a happy life, an individual should avoid most of the political, social, business, and religious activities of society. Epicurus expressed the idea that business affairs and politics imprison a person and that the only way to secure a quiet life is withdrawal from the mob. At the least, he added, one does not want to hold public office.

The Epicureans therefore cloistered themselves from public attention, prompting the Roman Seneca (c. 3 B.C.–A.D. 65) to say of Epicurus that he and his followers hid themselves away from Athenian society and were relatively unknown. The Garden School suggested a rural commune, where members lived simple lives and tried to avoid participation in public events. Their attitude was very much counter to mainstream Greek thinking. From the beginning of Greek history, as exemplified in the *Iliad* and *Odyssey*, the goal of life was for gallant and brave men to seek public acclaim through valiant deeds. Whether in the marketplace, the battlefield, or the political arena, one was encouraged to become active in a competitive society. Civic duty was sacrosanct to the ancient Athenians; male citizens were required to participate in the *Ecclesia* (legislative assembly) and could be chosen by lot for jury duty and many other positions of public trust. Plato and Aristotle, as well as Zeno (c. 336–c. 264 B.C.), founder of Stoicism, which rivaled the Garden School, believed that civic duty is not only a right but an obligation of the citizen.

When Epicureanism chose to adopt a philosophy of retreat from worldly affairs, it provoked a savage reaction from the Greek and later Roman society. The Roman Stoic Epictetus (c. 50–c. 120) proclaimed with righteous indignation that an Epicurean state would be subversive, causing destruction to the family. He added that it is the duty of one to serve the state and hold public office. Stoics like Epictetus used terms such as *duty* and *service in public life* to describe the *summum bonum* of living. Beginning during the lifetime of the founder of the Garden School and continuing during the entire time of its existence, critics would charge that the philosophy was selfish and egocentric.

The Roman writer Plutarch (c. 46–c. 120), in a treatise entitled "That Epicurus Actually Makes a Pleasant Life Impossible," suggested that the doctrine of the Garden was little less than a crime against humanity. Epictetus, Plutarch, and others were incensed by what they interpreted as a self-seeking, hedonistic attitude held by the Epicureans. It is true that Epicureanism may be described as a philosophy of hedonism; from founder through followers, the cornerstone of the ethical edifice was pleasure. However, Epicurean pleasure as an axiological goal was not physical enjoyment of the passing moment, as promoted in the Cyrenaic School of Aristippus (c. 435–c. 350 B.C.), but rather an avoidance of all active, dynamic sensations. Epicurus proposed that one should avoid physical pleasure and refrain from self-gratification. The type of pleasure proposed by the Garden School was pursuit of mental joys in quiet, static contemplation, bereft of the vain pursuit of worldly goods and recognition. Therefore, Epicurean pleasure can best be described as a negative conception wherein happiness is found in avoidance of fears and desires that produce pain. As long as pain is absent, pleasure may be attained through a simple life of equanimity of spirit.

Throughout history, criticism has been directed at Epicureanism for its advocacy of pleasure, but often opponents have mistakenly assumed it to be an egoistic hedonism, similar to the Cyrenaic pursuit of physical pleasure, rather than an avoidance of pain. Stoicism, the Christian Church, and other detractors also believed that Epicurean hedonism denied altruistic service and benefits to others. Epicurus answered this by denying that altruism always works for the common good. Many wars, and some of history's destructive ventures into supposedly improving the conditions of life, have been conducted by people who claimed to be working from altruistic motives. He further added that a philosophy that promotes individual needs is not necessarily counter to the public good. In a suggestion that speaks of the highest act of selflessness, Epicurus once wrote that one must be willing to die for a friend. Perhaps the difference between this Epicurean position and the attitude of the Stoics and others is the qualification that in the Garden School one admits that self-sacrifice is motivated primarily by self-interest. In addition, Epicureans would want to maintain the choice of how, when, and to whom one would confer benefits and offer sacrifice of life.

When Epicurus said that one must be willing to sacrifice for a friend, he was reiterating the Epicurean principle of the necessity of friendship for happiness. Of course the Garden School admitted that, although friendship is desirable for itself, it starts from personal need. Friends offer support and assistance in times when even the most self-sufficient individual cannot control all the conditions of life. The Epicurean doctrine taught that individual happiness is derived from the collective well-being of friends. Seneca quotes Epicurus as saying that pleasure is found in good company, and that dinner not shared with others is like the life of a lion or a wolf. As Epicurus advocated very simple fare, specifically a diet of barley meal, water, and an occasional piece of cheese, his shared table was spread rather thin, compared with the typical meal in ancient Greece.

Living in quiet fellowship in their garden setting, Epicurean friends at the Garden School differed from other Greeks in more than their eating habits. They rejected the general learning and ideals for the upbringing of children known as *paideia*. Whereas Plato, Aristotle, and other philosophers and schools advocated adherence to the noble traditions of the past, Epicureans denied the values of the classical culture. When a new student arrived at the Garden, that person was told to forget previous schooling, which had served as indoctrination in the traditional Greek *paideia*. This resulted in two unique features of the school of Epicurus.

First, subjects such as mathematics, music, grammar, rhetoric, and dialectic were dismissed as unimportant to the philosophy. Second, whereas other schools admitted only male citizens for study, Epicureans accepted men and women, resident aliens, slaves, and courtesans. Stating that the school accepted women and slaves, allowed atheistic thinking, preached egoistic hedonism, and denied Greek *paideia*, the enemies of the Epicureans began a campaign of defamation that lasted throughout the Hellenistic and Roman civilizations. After the third century A.D., and with the emergence of Christianity, little was heard of the Epicurean philosophy. Only in the late Renaissance, with the rediscovery of Greek and Roman writings such as Lucretius' *De Rerum Natura*, was interest rekindled. By the seventeenth century, led by the writings of Pierre Gassendi in France, Walter Charleton, and William Temple in England, interest in Epicureanism grew. In the late nineteenth century, additional archaeological and literary discoveries brought to light new information on the philosophy and enabled scholars such as Edward Zeller, William Wallace, and especially Hermann Usener to contribute a new appraisal of the school. In the twentieth century many writers, such as Cyril Bailey, Robert Drew Hicks, and Norman Wentworth Dewitt, have added to the scholarship so that Epicureanism has come to be recognized as one of the most important ancient schools of philosophy.

Richard W. Hibler

See also CYRENAICS; HAPPINESS; *Paideia;* PLEASURE; STOICISM

Bibliography

Dewitt, Norman W. *Epicurus and His Philosophy*. Minneapolis: University of Minnesota Press, 1954.

Epicurus. *Epicurus, the Extant Remains*. Translated by Cyril Bailey. Oxford: Clarendon Press, 1926.

Festugiere, A.J. *Epicurus and His Gods*. Translated by C.W. Chilton. New York: Russell and Russell, 1955.

Hibler, Richard W. *Happiness through Tranquillity: The School of Epicurus*. Lanham, Md.: University Press of America, 1984.

Hicks, R.D. *Stoic and Epicurean*. New York: Russell and Russell, 1962.

Lucretius. *The Way Things Are (De Rerum Natura)*. Translated by Rolfe Humphries. Bloomington: Indiana University Press, 1968.

Panichas, George A. *Epicurus*. New York: Twayne, 1967.

Epistemology

Epistemology is concerned with justifying not some particular truth or type of knowledge but knowledge in general. Predominant in American philosophy of education is the analytic position promoted in Israel Scheffler's *Conditions of Knowledge*. It does not explicitly consider the genesis, transmission, or evaluation of knowledge but assumes that objective knowledge is justified in immediate relation to a nonhuman reality.

Scheffler identified three theories of knowledge: rationalistic, empiricistic, and pragmatic. Rationalism, using mathematics as its model, is established by deductive chains linking necessary and general truths with self-evident truths. Because truths of logic or mathematics are not dependent on or refutable by experience, they are seen by many philosophers as being the firmest of all truths, called necessary or deductive truths.

In the empiricist tradition, science is taken as the basic warrant for knowledge. The relationship between elementary states-of-affairs in the world cannot be inferred by logic from self-evident truths; they are natural associations tentatively projected inductively as generalizations from our limited past experience. Empiricists focus on what we observe with our senses, presuming that these will accurately be described within coherent theoretical frameworks. Empirical science aims to put forward bold hypotheses and subject their deductive consequences to rigorous testing and criticism. Rationalists tend to focus on those deductive consequences, or on those theoretical concepts that tie our sensations together to make them meaningful, presuming a mind that organizes our perceptions of the world.

Empiricist and rationalist theories of knowledge depend on two traditional theories of truth: the correspondence theory, which says that our statements correspond directly to what is in the world, and the coherence theory, which says that a statement is true to the extent to which it coheres with all our other beliefs and knowledge structures.

Analytic philosophers combine these two theories of truth for their epistemology. Knowing comes about through a process of observation and reasoning, in which we build cumulatively on the knowledge of our predecessors. Like the mathematician Alfred Tarski, they believe that the truth of any sentence consists in its agreement with (or correspondence) to reality and its coherent fit within a consistent set of beliefs.

For most analytic philosophers, the paradigmatic instance of knowledge is propositional, and theories are rational systems of true statements. For them, knowledge sits in a narrower range than knowing how to do something like ride a bicycle, or knowing another person well, or appreciating music. Active propensities and attainments, such as learning and teaching to understand the relationship between multiplication and addition, for instance, do not count as knowledge.

The conditions of propositional knowledge are justified true belief. In other words, to know any proposition (say, Q), one has to believe that Q is true, have adequate evidence that Q is true, and Q has to be the case. One has to believe that Q is true, that is, it has to be consistent with one's past experiences in an empirical and a pragmatic sense. The belief has to correspond to the way things are in the world, once again fitting the empiricistic concern for scientific testing. And finally, one's beliefs have to be justifiable—that is, they have to fit coherently within a set of beliefs, both personal and public, once again constructed from experience and fitting rationally together.

The comprehensiveness of this set of necessary and sufficient conditions for knowing that Q, however, masks some of its difficulties. While a proposition has to be true for one to know it, how does one know that it is true? Scheffler says that the truth condition does not reflect what goes on in the consciousness of the person attributing knowledge. Rather it reflects an objective commitment of such attribution evidenced in the way specific attributions are critically evaluated. Yet it is objective only from within a publicly warranted and logically coherent set of beliefs that provide the reasons for knowing it to be true. There is no theory-independent way to reconstruct statements about what is "really there." What could count as objective evidence or warranted assertibility for one's theory? It would necessarily be bound up with more or less reasonable webs or systems of belief. Our belief in phlogiston or superconductivity or insanity is rendered at once more certain and fallible by supporting constructions of language and reasons.

Knowledge that is tied only to propositional knowledge is as much limited as it is warranted by language. It is a view of knowledge that assumes that, the more systematic knowledge is, the more likely it is to be true; it has consolidated in educational institutions into disciplines that appear to represent idealized forms of knowledge (Paul Hirst). To accept it as the prototype of knowledge authorizes standardized tests and a fairly dogmatic pedagogy. It could discourage students from coming to know outside the linguistic frame of reference of the teacher or subject discipline. Stephen Toulmin shows how it runs the danger of idealizing the logicality of disciplines and scientific theories, to such an extent that the logic of their structure determines their value rather than their adaptability to an evolving world.

Karl Popper has argued from a realist and evolutionary epistemology that this "institutionalized knowledge" is what we mean by objective knowledge. He describes it as a sort of independent third world, consisting of theoretical systems, problems, and problem-situations that emerge from the interaction between the physical world (the first world) and a world of states of consciousness (the second world). His third world consists not only of language and theories but also by-products of language such as birdhouses, consciousness, and virtual reality. Like Scheffler, he remains an analytic philosopher because he believes that the most objective knowledge we can have is that which is agreed upon through the evidence gained through testing the theories currently held to be logical and true. Yet his preference for falsifying theories rather than believing them to be true marks him as having pragmatist tendencies.

To less analytic pragmatists such as John Dewey (1859–1952) and William James (1842–1910), we must do more than operate logically upon basic truths that appear to us self-evident, and we must also go beyond reasonable generalization of observed phenomenal patterns in our past experience. Rather, our knowledge (or, as Dewey preferred to speak of it, our "knowing") arises from our continuing need to transform the environment by trying and undergoing our social practices as well as our logical theories.

James argues that we have to settle for "true" as being only an expedient in our way of thinking, a sort of temporary endorsement of reality. A statement is true if it works. To attain knowledge we should be wary of the misleading dualisms often imposed by language, especially those that make a hard and fast distinction between subjective and objective knowledge, between knowledge and what knowledge is about, between facts and values, between logic and reason. More recently, Richard Rorty argues that because knowledge is a matter of acquiring habits of action for coping with reality, it is something we do in the world, not outside it.

Rorty notes two ways in which reflective human beings try to understand themselves and their world. The first is by seeking objectivity through attachment to something that can be described without reference to any particular human beings—the scientific search for objective truth underlying science and logic. Such science and logic are valuable but need to be balanced by what he calls solidarity, by humans telling the story of their contributions to humanity, seeking as much intersubjective agreement as possible. Humans are not simply passive subjects of research, determined by their environment. Because we intentionally construct or discard knowledge, we are ethically responsible for it.

Pragmatists and postmodernists alike argue that because language and theories are manmade and therefore fallible, one cannot start from them in objectively justifying one's knowledge. Nor can one step outside them. Truth is to be understood as a constructed system of ordered procedures for the production, regulation, distribution, circulation, and operation of statements, and it is linked in a circular relation with systems of power that produce and sustain it. Humans do not simply receive knowledge; they make it, and there is no way of their attaining the sort of objectivity that Hilary Putnam described as "a God's eye view of things." Because humans are natural organisms, their knowledge is a result of an active and rational interaction with the biological and social environment, rooted in shared practices. We do not, as the analytic philosophers did, require explicit criteria to justify knowledge. Our reasons for knowing a statement or theory to be true come after the event, or from within our form of life, as Ludwig Wittgenstein (1889–1951) said. When we focus on them, they are often rational in form, but more often they operate tacitly or at an unconscious level.

Can a pragmatist have any notion of the advancement of knowledge? Why should we hold some knowledge as better than others? Jürgen Habermas believes that Rorty dismisses the force of rationality too glibly, that every utterance a speaker lays claims to has at least three dimensions of validity that transcend that particular utterance—a truth claim relating to the objective world of states of affairs, a rightness claim relating to the social world of norms and interpersonal relations, and a truthfulness or sincerity claim relating to the subjective world of experience to which the speaker has privileged access. These may seem similar to Scheffler's three knowledge-conditions or Popper's three worlds, but they differ in that the concept of a world is no longer projected by a single consciousness or a God's eye view, but by interacting subjects who raise these validity claims in communicative acts to try to bring our presumptions to awareness. Knowledge can advance through critical scrutiny of the limits and use of reason, using universal objective communication norms of language.

Michel Foucault shared Habermas's belief in the construction of the world through language. When we talk about our way of seeing the world, we are presuming a notion of evidence rather than direct contact with the way things are, to such an extent that discourse analysis may seem to be overtaking scientific experiment as the preferred path to knowledge. Foucault believes that knowledge owes as much to imagination as reason, because it first opens up an arena for action and communication by allowing us to let things appear as something. He believes, like Friedrich Nietzsche (1844–1900), that our notions of truth grow out of dead metaphors. We construe atoms as billiard balls, we see the heart as a pump or systems as chaotic, and follow through the consequences for our other beliefs and practices.

Knowledge grows through a combination of inference and imagination, the former like Thomas Kuhn's normal puzzle-solving science working within a fixed logical space and introducing no new candidates for belief, the latter more a matter of inquiry than habit, of rearranging old themes and disciplines, of "seeing things from a different point of view." The epistemology offered by Foucault, for instance in *Discipline and Punish,* is linked with power by creatively drawing historical parallels between the "normalization of knowledge" and the evolution of rituals of punishment and torture.

Any cultural tradition consists of a number of genres, ways of looking at the world, rather than the subject matters and methods of traditional analytic disciplines. The genres are not essentialistic but historically expedient and experimental ways of looking at the world. There is no ranking of these genres or disciplines according to degrees or kinds of truth, as Paul Hirst set out to do. This knowledge rooted in social practices is not founded on principles so much as a recontextualizing of concepts, concepts that have already been socially formed— "root metaphors." Foucault asks us to stand back from our immersion in social assumptions to see the strangeness of our society's practices from an archaeological perspective, and to look for what he calls discontinuities that mark out radical shifts in our ways of knowing or seeing things, our "root metaphors."

As these practices are shared with others, and as they have made us what we are, we have some common ground from which to act and understand. But it is a temporary foothold only, and cannot be guaranteed, verified, or rendered universal or grounded. It is a much less certain epistemology than the analytic view. We can offer through our interpretations of our institutionalized knowledge a history of how we constitute ourselves as human subjects. We cannot pretend to describe an external reality or objective truth.

Because our involvement in the world is textual in nature, our interpretation of language is a matter of seeing the speaker in relation to the world in which that speaker is located—that is, a matter of context. We can dissolve persons into webs of belief and desires, and we can also dissolve a belief into an attitude a person has toward a sentence. We can dissolve a sentence into a pattern of words, but we can go on to remark that only in the context of a sentence does a word have meaning. The pragmatist and the postmodernist specialize in promoting an epistemological Principle of Uncertainty. We can know anything only by temporarily presuming the constancy of certain truths. We are continually having to make choices, and must stop asking which is the real thing.

This seems relativist only from an analytic perspective. The pragmatist is a coherentist rather than an idealist, trying to remove the dualism between beliefs and objects, trying to place knowledge in a holistic frame of beliefs, values, and facts. There is no sensible distinction to be made between things as they are and things as we describe them. Language is a means of moving us to concerted action within a physical reality. What makes one interpretive theory better than another has yet to be worked out but it has to do with articulating common concerns and finding a language that becomes accepted as a way of talking about social situations, while leaving open the possibility of dialogue, or better, a conflict of interpretations with other shared discursive practices used to articulate different concerns. We are not recontextualizing objects so much as finding out how our webs of desires and beliefs can be rewoven so as to accommodate new beliefs, desires, and practices.

This frees the pragmatists and the postmodernists from having to answer the old epistemological question of "Are you representing accurately" or "Are you getting at the way the object is intrinsically?" but not from questions like "Can you fit in the belief that the litmus paper turned red or that your lover has deceived you with the rest of your beliefs and actions?" We have made a radical shift, the linguistic turn, from seeking knowledge as the path to truth about the world, to seeing knowledge as interpretation.

Felicity Haynes

See also ANALYTIC PHILOSOPHY; COMMON SENSE; CRITICAL THEORY; FORMALISM; HISTORICISM; MEANING; MODERNISM AND POST-MODERNISM; PHENOMENOLOGY; POSITIVISM; PRAGMATISM; RATIONALISM; REALISM; RELATIVISM; TRUTH

Bibliography

Dewey, John. *Logic: The Theory of Inquiry.* New York: Henry Holt and Company, 1938.

Foucault, Michel. *Surveiller et punir: Naissance de la prison.* Editions Gallimard, 1975. Translated by Alan Sheridan as *Discipline and Punish.* London: Allen Lane, 1977.

Habermas, Jürgen. *PostMetaphysical Thinking.* Cambridge: Massachusetts Institute of Technology, 1992.

Hirst, Paul. *Forms of Knowledge and the Curriculum: A Collection of Philosophical Papers.* London: Routledge and Kegan Paul, 1974.

Popper, Sir Karl. *Objective Knowledge.* Oxford: Oxford University Press, 1972.

Putnam, Hilary. *Reason, Truth and History.* Cambridge: Cambridge University Press, 1981.

Rorty, Richard. *Objectivity, Relativism and Truth.* Cambridge: Cambridge University Press, 1991.

Scheffler, Israel. *Conditions of Knowledge.* Glenview, Ill.: Scott Foresman and Co., 1965.

Toulmin, Stephen. *Human Understanding.* Princeton: Princeton University Press, 1972.

Equality

Educational equality emerged as a philosophic issue at least as early as Plato (c. 427–347 B.C.). In his celebrated *Republic,* Plato made the radical suggestion for his time that women be granted equal educational opportunity, and he extended this suggestion to social class as well. His reasoning was that the talents needed for ruling that were emphasized in his educational system were not confined to the class of aristocratic men, and that such talents should be developed in whoever possessed them. Plato, however, was no egalitarian. He did not believe that all persons need or deserve an equal education because he did not believe that there is any sense in which all persons are equal. Indeed, he ridiculed this notion of equality and identified it with democracy, which he roundly criticized.

The notion, *contra* Plato, that there is an important sense in which all persons are equal took root as a political ideal only relatively recently, in the sixteenth and seventeenth centuries, with the advent of liberal political theorizing exemplified by seminal philosophers such as John Locke (1632–1704). Today the commitment to political equality is thoroughly entrenched in the political thought, rhetoric, and institutions of all Western democracies. This is not to say, however, that such a general commitment now entails or ever did entail unanimity on the specific requirements of equality, including how education should exemplify and foster it. On the contrary, controversy regarding equality in general and educational equality in particular continues to be intense.

Equality of Educational Opportunity

The contemporary discussion of educational equality (especially in the United States) has adopted equality of educational opportunity as the locus. Couched within the liberal tradition, a strict form of equality is eschewed, on the grounds that it is undesirable, unattainable, or both. Instead, equality of opportunity to pursue one's life choices is all that can or should be required in the name of equality, and equality of educational opportunity is a prerequisite for enjoying equality of opportunity more generally. Within this shared framework, two general questions arise. The first concerns the degree to which intervention in social institutions and practices is required in order to equalize educational opportunity. The second concerns the relative adequacy of competing theories of social justice used as a basis for answering the first question.

Two basic interpretations of the principle of equality of educational opportunity may be identified with respect to the issue of intervention: "negative" and "positive." The negative interpretation is noninterventionist: It identifies equality of educational opportunity with the absence of formal (especially legal) barriers to access to public education that discriminate against individuals and groups on the basis of morally irrelevant criteria such as race, sex, and language. Although progressive when compared with overt and legally sanctioned discrimination, the negative interpretation may be criticized for insensitivity to the nonformal but powerful effects that factors such as race, sex and language have on opportunities even when formal barriers are absent. For example, providing children with equal access to books and instruction in a language they do not understand fails to provide equality of educational opportunity in any but the most meaningless sense. Thus, the negative interpretation can be quite hollow for those who lack the resources—cultural, linguistic, political, and economic—to take advantage of merely formal opportunities.

The positive interpretation is interventionist: It requires public education to go beyond mere formal equality and to take positive steps to eliminate differences in the circumstances of school children that result in persistent inequality, particularly differences associated with disadvantaging social factors. Positive interpretations differ in the degree of intervention required and, closely related, in what factors are morally permissible sources of inequality.

To illustrate the range of interpretations, consider race, natural endowment, and effort as three possible sources of unequal educational opportunities (Nagel: 1991). From among these, race is the factor most easily precluded as a morally permissible source of inequality. Natural endowment is more problematic because the intuition that natural talent is a morally permissible source of differential educational opportunities—in placement decisions, for instance—is relatively widespread. Finally, effort is the most problematic because if effort (which involves a large element of personal choice) is not a morally relevant source of differential opportunities, then it appears that nothing can be.

As the preceding examples suggest, the criticisms to which a positive interpretation is subject depend on the sources of differential opportunities that it embraces as morally permissible. At one end of the spectrum, the more factors that an interpretation judges to be morally permissible sources of inequality, the closer it is to the negative interpretation and the more likely it will be charged with being hollow. At the other end of the spectrum, the fewer factors that an interpretation judges to be morally permissible sources of inequality the more likely it will be charged with posing a threat to liberty and encouraging heavy-handed social engineering. Interpretations that exclude even personal choice as a morally permissible source of inequality may be charged with collapsing the distinction between equality of educational opportunity and equality of educational results (Burbules et al.: 1982).

Liberal Theories of Justice

As suggested earlier, determining what level of intervention is justified in the name of equality of educational opportunity turns on the broader question of the relative adequacy of competing theories of social justice. Within the liberal tradition, three theories of social justice predominate: libertarianism, utilitarianism, and liberal egalitarianism.

Libertarianism places a premium on individual liberty and, consistent with this, contends that states should be "minimalist" in their exercise of power (Nozick: 1974). Chief among the things that a state should not do is redistribute resources in order to achieve equality among its citizens.

Libertarianism is most congenial to the negative interpretation of equality of educational opportunity. Positive interpretations are precluded on the grounds that they entail unwanted and objectionable state interference in private educational choices. Indeed, given libertarians' hostility toward state-mandated and -regulated public education per se—particularly the redistributive tax schemes that support it and its unavoidable tendency to purvey what the state deems educationally important—even a negative interpretation might go too far.

Utilitarianism is the form of liberal theory made prominent by philosophers such as Jeremy Bentham (1748–1832) and John Stuart Mill (1806–1873); it has predominated through much of the nineteenth and twentieth centuries. Formally, it is an amazingly simple theory: The rightness of an action or policy is judged in terms of whether it satisfies the principle of maximizing the total good. More specific principles are judged by reference to this single overarching one.

In utilitarian theory the principle of equality of educational opportunity is justified on the grounds that it contributes to maximizing the total good, and utilitarianism has no difficulty embracing a positive interpretation of equality of educational opportunity. For example, so long as they maximize the good, interventionist educational programs that target talented disadvantaged children for extra resources in order to develop their talents are justified on utilitarian grounds, as are the redistributivist policies that are necessary to support them.

Liberal egalitarianism, as the name suggests, stresses the principle of equality. It may be distinguished from strict egalitarianism, however, by virtue of the fact that, like all liberal theories, it does not claim that inequality must always be eliminated. It claims instead that inequality is prima facie objectionable and therefore must be justified. It, like utilitarianism, embraces a positive interpretation of equality of educational opportunity.

John Rawls (1971) no doubt is the most celebrated liberal egalitarian. In his theory, equality of opportunity is required for individuals to have a fair chance to enjoy a reasonable share of society's goods—for example, employment, income, health care, self-respect, and education. He contends that people are not responsible for disadvantages over which they have no control that arise from natural and social contingencies—who their parents are, how talented they are, whether they are handicapped—and that justice requires social institutions, including education, to intervene actively to mitigate these disadvantaging contingencies to the degree possible.

Internal Criticisms

Libertarians object to both utilitarianism and liberal egalitarianism on the grounds that, because they embrace positive interpretations of equality of educational opportunity, they sacrifice liberty in order to advance equality. From the libertarian perspective, a positive interpretation of equality of education requires a large bureaucracy to devise policies, to evaluate them, and to distribute resources accordingly. Even if such bureaucracies were not notoriously poor at delivering on their promises, they are objectionable for being paternalistic and undemocratic.

Insofar as libertarians endorse the negative interpretation of equality of educational opportunity, they are liable to the rejoinder from both utilitarians and liberal egalitarians that the kind of opportunities provided by a negative interpretation of equality of educational opportunity are hollow. Furthermore, such an interpretation implicitly holds children responsible for decisions that others—parents, teachers, and counselors, for instance—make on their behalf. Insofar as libertarians reject equality of educational opportunity even under its negative interpretation, they are liable to the charge that children's educational fate is made even more precarious. If children's educational opportunities need not be equal in even a negative sense (or, indeed, if education need not even be publicly supported), it becomes solely a matter of private parental responsibility to pursue various avenues for educating their children. Children

are made totally dependent on their parents' power, wealth, ambition, knowledge, and sense of parental obligation.

Liberal egalitarians criticize utilitarians for failing to go far enough in the name of equality of educational opportunity because utilitarianism renders it too vulnerable to contingency. For example, if educational programs for the disadvantaged prove to be less effective means of maximizing the good than programs for the academically talented, then the utilitarian justification for such programs is lost and, along with it, so is the justification for equalizing educational opportunity. Consider the flurry of government support for social programs in general and educational programs in particular following the late 1960s riots in U.S. inner cities. Programs such as Head Start, children's educational television, and free school lunches were often justified on the utilitarian grounds that they would lead to a reduction of violence, an increased quality of life for all, identifying and developing talent that would otherwise be wasted, and so forth. Support for such programs has since drastically eroded, and the problem for utilitarian thinking is that it has been an accomplice in this erosion. The perception by many citizens as well as policy-makers today is that such programs do not maximize benefit and thus should be abandoned.

According to liberal egalitarians, the principle of equality of educational opportunity—principles of justice in general—should not be held hostage to maximizing the good. In this vein, Dworkin (1977) distinguishes "equal treatment" from "treatment as an equal." "Equal treatment" is the interpretation of equality implicit in utilitarianism, in which everyone's interests are given equal weight. The problem with this interpretation is that it cannot distinguish essential interests from nonessential interests, from mere preferences. As already observed, equality of opportunity, like any other principle within a utilitarian framework, is subordinate to maximizing the good. By contrast, liberal egalitarians are willing to accept—indeed, they insist on—forgoing maximizing the good in order to respect equality. In contrast to the "equal treatment" interpretation of equality, the "treatment as an equal" interpretation is sensitive to the relative legitimacy of different interests and is closely tied to the concept of "equal respect."

Utilitarians criticize liberal egalitarians for having no overarching first principle, and thus of "intuitionism" (Hare: 1981). Whereas utilitarians appeal to the principle of maximizing the good to set educational policy, liberal egalitarians must balance competing principles, including the principle of maximizing the good, and are criticized by utilitarians for having no principled (versus intuitive) way of doing this.

External Criticisms

The criticisms discussed so far are all internal to liberal theory, which is to say that they assume the overall viability of the liberal tradition. The principle of equality of educational opportunity is also the target of more fundamental criticisms advanced from other theoretical perspectives. Leftists have historically criticized liberal conceptions of justice for being insensitive to sources of inequality that are found in the underlying economic structures, particularly as they relate to social class. Critics from this perspective contend that underlying economic structures must be the focus of change if equality is to be realized, and that focusing on the meliorism associated with equalizing educational opportunity diverts attention from the real problem and, in the process, serves to legitimate vast inequality.

More recently, liberal conceptions of justice have come under increasing criticism for also being insensitive to the effects of race and sex, in addition to the effects of class. From this perspective, the principle of equality of educational opportunity requires women and racial minorities to accept a "fair application" of rules governing the institution of schooling that have been rigged by the historical operation of patriarchy and racism to be to the advantage of white men. Thus, as with class, ignoring the deeper problems associated with sex and race also serves to legitimate vast inequality.

Notwithstanding their radical critics, contemporary liberal theorists deny that the above kinds of difficulties are fatal either to liberal theory in general or its conception of equality in particular. Contemporary liberal theorists are confident that liberalism's commitment to equality is well founded and that liberal theory can be formulated so as to avoid the charge that it is insensitive to the influences of race, class, and sex. The basic idea is that fostering equality requires liberal institutions, schools among them, to be designed—or, more precisely, redesigned—so as to ensure that historically dominated groups are given an effective and equal voice in political decision-making.

Conclusion

The preponderance of current thinking is united in the view that something more substantive is required to achieve a defensible form of educational equality than what is provided by the negative interpretation of equality of educational opportunity. Beyond this, how much intervention a positive interpretation may legitimately require, or, indeed, whether the principle of equality of educational opportunity ought to be abandoned altogether as irremediably inegalitarian, remain hotly contested questions.

Kenneth R. Howe

See also DEMOCRACY; GENDER AND SEXISM; JUSTICE; LIBERALISM; LOCKE; MILL; RACE AND RACISM; RIGHTS; SOCIAL AND POLITICAL PHILOSOPHY

Bibliography

Bowles, S., and H. Gintis. *Schooling in Capitalist America*. New York: Basic Books, 1976.

Burbules, N., B. Lord, and A. Sherman. "Equity, Equal Opportunity and Education." *Educational Evaluation and Policy Analysis* 4 (1982): 169–87.

Coleman, J. "The Concept of Equality of Educational Opportunity." *Harvard Educational Review* 38 (1968): 7–22.

Dworkin, R. *Taking Rights Seriously*. Cambridge: Harvard University Press, 1977.

Hare, R.M. *Moral Thinking: Its Levels, Method and Point*. New York: Oxford University Press, 1981.

Nagel, T. *Equality and Partiality*. New York: Oxford University Press, 1991.

Nozick, R. *Anarchy, State and Utopia*. New York: Basic Books, 1974.

Rawls, J. *A Theory of Justice*. Cambridge, Mass.: Belknap Press, 1971.

Strike, K. *Educational Policy and the Just Society*. Chicago: University of Illinois Press, 1982.

Weis, Lois, ed. *Class, Race and Gender in American Education*. New York: State University of New York Press, 1988.

Erasmus, Desiderius (c. 1469–1536)

Erasmus's philosophy of education was based on the humanist creed that the individual is not born but made human through education. His views were shaped by his religious beliefs, his practical experience as a teacher, and an intuitive understanding of human nature. Indeed, the insight into child psychology manifested by Erasmus is remarkable in a man who had no close contact with children and did not grow up in a traditional family setting.

Of illegitimate birth and orphaned at an early age, Erasmus was obliged by intransigent guardians to enter a religious order when he was still a teenager. Later he obtained a papal dispensation that allowed him to reside outside the confines of a monastery. He remained true to his vows, however, and led a celibate life devoted to scholarship. Sent by his bishop to study theology in Paris, he conceived an instant dislike for the scholastic method taught there and departed without a degree. A doctorate was conferred on him in 1509 *per saltum* (that is, without the normal academic requirements having been fulfilled) by the University of Turin. After travels in Italy and a stint as instructor of Greek at the University of Cambridge, Erasmus was appointed councillor by Prince Charles (later Emperor Charles V) and settled down at Louvain, where he remained from 1517 to 1521. The departure of the imperial court for Spain and the hostility of the conservative theologians at Louvain led Erasmus to move to Basel. His efforts to escape the religious controversies of his time were in vain, however. His pioneer work as editor and translator of biblical and patristic texts and his suspected sympathy with the Lutheran movement involved him in numerous polemics. When Basel turned Protestant in 1529 the then-elderly Erasmus took up residence in Catholic Freiburg, but he returned to Basel shortly before his death in 1536.

During his years of residence at Paris, Erasmus earned his living by tutoring well-to-do students. As tutor in Paris and as lecturer at Cambridge, he prepared his own teaching materials. These were eventually published and enjoyed a wide circulation. In later years, Erasmus added to this crop of books. Although he was no longer actively engaged in teaching, he retained a lifelong interest in pedagogy. Among the textbooks and educational aids he produced are a handbook of style (*De copia*, 1512), a letter-writing manual (*De conscribendis epistolis*, 1522), anthologies of proverbs (*Adagiorum collectanea*, 1500), similes (*Parabolae*, 1514), and literary anecdotes (*Apophthegmata*, 1531), a guide to good manners (*De civilitate*, 1530), dialogues to teach boys Latin conversation (*Colloquia*, 1519), a manual for preachers (*Ecclesiastes*, 1535),

epitome of the *Elegantiae,* Lorenzo Valla's study of Latin usage (1531), and a Latin translation of Theodore of Gaza's Greek grammar (1516). Most of these works went through a large number of editions and were adopted as textbooks in schools and universities throughout Europe. The *Adagia* and the *Colloquia,* in particular, became best-sellers. The latter caused considerable controversy, however, because the dialogues added to later editions changed the character of the original book from a manual teaching Latin composition to a social commentary sharply critical of popular superstitions and ecclesiastical abuses.

Erasmus formulated his philosophy of education in a number of books dealing with curriculum, teaching methods, and, more generally, the goals of education. Two works concerned with curriculum, *De ratione studii* (1511) and *Ratio verae theologiae* (1518), a curriculum for students of theology, both evince a humanist's bias. In *De ratione studii,* Erasmus counsels early instruction in Greek and Latin based on extensive readings from the works of the "best"—that is, classical—authors. He recommends in particular Lucian, Homer, Terence, Plautus, Virgil, Horace, and Cicero. Additional knowledge of history and natural sciences was needed, he said, to build word power and enhance comprehension. Ideally, the texts chosen for classroom use should be entertaining as well as instructive and should contribute to forming not only the pupil's language but also his character.

In the *Ratio verae theologiae,* Erasmus's proposal for a curriculum reform of theological studies, Erasmus likewise urges a return to the "classics"—that is, the sources of Christian literature: Scripture and the Fathers. Here, too, he stresses the importance of a general education in the humanities and in the biblical languages to provide a historical approach to the texts under scrutiny and to give students a better understanding of the context. Erasmus deprecates the commentaries of medieval scholastics, both on account of their barbaric language and their speculative approach. The former offended the humanist's aesthetics; the latter, being ineffective in shaping the student's conscience, failed to satisfy his moral exigencies. Erasmus's insistence on the applicability of education to life (in this case, the spiritual life of the student) and his emphasis on ethics rather than logic or dialectics were shared by many humanist educators.

His views on the goals of education and the roles played in the educational process by pupil, parent, and teacher found their fullest expression in two works: *De pueris instituendis* (1529) and *Institutio principis Christiani* (1516). The latter is dedicated to Charles V. It deals specifically with the education of princes, whose power over the lives of their subjects and corresponding responsibility for their welfare made their intellectual and moral formation a matter of public interest. The prince is seen as the representative of God, a paternal figure who must have the good of his people at heart, be a moral inspiration to them, and render an account of his stewardship to God. Since in Erasmus's time heredity rather than ability determined who would be ruling a territory, Erasmus noted that education played a crucial role in reducing personal shortcomings and enhancing natural abilities, thus increasing the chances of the hereditary prince's developing into an efficient and responsible ruler.

Although the successful education of a prince was of great significance because his actions and attitudes affected a larger number of people than those of a private individual, Erasmus emphasized that all parents are under obligation to provide an education for their children. It was education that raised them above the level of mindless beasts and made them useful members of the Christian community. To create a suitable environment for the formation of their children's character and intellect was thus a debt owed by parents to God and society. Erasmus castigated fathers who failed to set a suitable example to their offspring and who were negligent or niggardly in providing a teacher for them. He chided parents who failed to protect their children from unsuitable sights and sounds, such as foulmouthed stable hands, drunken and philandering dinner guests, and silly domestics. And he criticized doting and overprotective mothers who treated their children like pets, depriving them of early childhood education because of a misplaced concern about the physical and intellectual rigors of formal education. In Erasmus's view, early childhood education was of signal importance. The formation of a child begins at birth, he notes, and physical or mental harm suffered at an early age will affect the adult. Unlearning bad habits and incorrect information is cumbersome. It is therefore essential to lay solid foundations for a child's education.

The standards Erasmus set for the teacher were high. He was to have impeccable morals, a gentle disposition, and a thorough education. Indeed, Erasmus demanded from the teacher an encyclopedic knowledge to enable him to give the pupil a well-rounded education. He (Erasmus disapproved of female teachers) was to be a fatherly friend to the pupil, aware of the child's abilities and propensities and carefully fostering his interests. The good teacher would tailor his lessons accordingly, choose materials and textbooks appealing to his pupils' interests, encourage their curiosity, and generally make work appear like play. Erasmus suggests rewarding small children with cookies shaped like letters or organizing educational games. He saw the competition between peers as a healthy incentive to succeed, but warned teachers not to disparage their young charges when they failed to achieve the desired goal. Admonition and criticism must be gentle, he says, and carefully balanced with praise. Erasmus deplored the psychological or physical abuse so common in his age. Hazing and corporal punishment were repugnant to him, and he emphasized the destructive nature of such practices. His palpable horror of flogging schoolmasters and his vivid description of instances in which disciplinarians destroyed the mental and physical health of their helpless charges or suppressed their natural desire to learn through harsh and unsympathetic treatment suggests that Erasmus himself was a victim of such methods.

In an interesting passage in *De pueris instituendis*, Erasmus weighs the advantages of private tutoring against ecclesiastic and public schools. Reflecting on his own experience at the school of the Brethren of the Common Life in Deventer and the hostile reception given to his efforts to further his education in the monastery where he resided, Erasmus had only disparaging words for church-sponsored schools. Their narrow aim, he said, was to recruit novices. In preparation for a clerical or monastic career, they stifled all creative impulses and encouraged unquestioning compliance with rules. He had misgivings also about public schools, primarily because of the average class size, which restricted personal attention. He recognized, however, that private instruction—the schooling favored by him—required a level of financial commitment that many parents were unable to make.

Although Erasmus appears to place most of the responsibility for a successful education on the shoulders of the teacher and the parent,

E

he did not entirely disregard the necessary contribution of the student. He reaffirmed the classical doctrine of the three prerequisites of excellence: talent, instruction, and practice. Thus the pupil must show a certain aptitude for learning. However, Erasmus was remarkably optimistic in his pronouncements about the human capacity for education. He asserted in effect that every individual has the potential for self-improvement and is capable of benefiting from education. On the whole, Erasmus's pedagogical theories are highly idealistic. He did not discuss unwillingness or lack of cooperation on the part of the pupil. Rather, he appeared to consider negative behavior or attitude the result of poor teaching methods.

Erasmus was primarily concerned with intellect and moral education, but he also took an interest in the social aspects of a child's upbringing. He believed that external appearance and behavior should complement and reflect a person's disposition and erudition. In his treatises entitled *De civilitate* he addressed these concerns, dealing with such mundane matters as personal hygiene, table manners, and appropriate gesture, speech, and dress. Unlike his other pedagogical treatises, which have largely retained their relevance, this little work is primarily of interest to historians and provides a fascinating and at times amusing glimpse of sixteenth-century mores. Some rules have survived the test of time (picking one's nose is still frowned upon); others, such as the reminder not to throw bones under the table, are specific to Erasmus's age. In spite of its somewhat narrow scope, the tract exemplifies Erasmus's philosophy of education. According to his recommendation that the teacher must be flexible and consider the needs of the student, Erasmus avoids dogmatic pronouncements and adapts his usually sophisticated and scholarly language to a youthful readership.

Most of Erasmus's pedagogical works address the education of boys. Erasmus grew up with the belief that girls are not as capable of benefiting from education as boys. Unlike many of his contemporaries, however, who held to their preconceived notions, Erasmus modified his views, persuaded by the example of learned women of his acquaintance. Impressed with their proficiency in Latin and their keen understanding of Scripture, he composed a dialogue in praise of educated women, which he added to his *Colloquia* in 1524. In this piece, entitled "The Abbot and the Learned Lady," a well-read and witty gentlewoman gets the better of a boorish abbot who wants to confine her to the "distaff and the needle." In her concluding words she pays tribute to the learned women of her time, specifically naming the female members of the More, Pirckheimer, and Blaurer families.

The educational methods Erasmus outlined are traditional in that they rely heavily on memorizing and imitation. He does make it clear, however, that this cannot be the end-all of education. In the *Ciceronianus* (1528) he discusses the concept of *imitatio* and, more particularly, the style and language appropriate to Christians. He emphasized that the main principle governing style is *aptum et decorum*—that is, the principle of appropriateness. This cannot be acquired simply through memorization or mechanical reproduction of rules. It requires that the student digest or internalize what he learns and reflect rather than slavishly reproduce the desirable qualities of the model author. Such a process requires creativeness and judgment. It is in this fashion, Erasmus says, that Christians should imitate pagan models and adapt them to the exigencies of their own time and circumstances.

The educational philosophy of Renaissance humanists is rooted in classical antiquity. Plato and Isocrates, Quintilian and Cicero are often cited in Renaissance theories of education, but Christian ethics form a continuous subtext. Erasmus may be regarded as the Christian humanist *par excellence*. In recommending models of style he did not confine himself to writers of classical antiquity; he also listed patristic authors like Jerome and Ambrose. In the same vein he paired his *Education of the Christian Prince* with a translation of Isocrates' counsel to a Cyprian prince. As he noted in his dedicatory preface, it was right that he, a Christian, should address advice to a Christian prince to counterbalance what Isocrates, a pagan, had written to a pagan ruler. In outlining the responsibilities of parents he stressed that it is not only good citizenship but also a Christian duty to educate one's offspring. In his treatise on good manners, he advised on behavior at the banquet table as well as in church. Many of the sample passages and suggested themes in his manuals have a Christian moral. It is clear that the aim of Erasmus's method of education was to produce not merely a learned person, but a learned Christian. His philosophy of education is therefore best summed up in the catch phrase *docta pietas,* denoting the conjunction of erudition with piety.

Erika Rummel

See also HUMANISM, *Studia Humanitatis*

Bibliography

Augustijn, Cornelis. *Erasmus, His Life, Works, and Influence.* Toronto: University of Toronto Press, 1991.

Erasmus, Desiderius. *The Adages of Erasmus.* Translated by Margaret Mann Phillips. Cambridge: Cambridge University Press, 1964.

———. *The Collected Works of Erasmus.* Toronto: University of Toronto Press, 1976–.

———. *The Colloquies of Erasmus.* Translated by Craig R. Thompson. Chicago and London: University of Chicago Press, 1965.

———. *Opera omnia Desiderii Erasmi Roterodami.* Amsterdam: North Holland Publishing, 1969–.

Soward, Kelley. "Erasmus and the Education of Women." *Sixteenth Century Journal* 13 (1982): 77–89.

Woodward, William. *Erasmus: Concerning the Aim and Method of Education.* Cambridge: Cambridge University Press, 1904. Reprint. New York: Columbia University Press, 1964.

Ethics and Morality

Although the classical roots of ethics, from the Greek *ethos,* and morality, from the Roman *mores,* appear not to make much of a distinction between their subject matters, there is considerable modern literature that suggests significant differences. One line of interpretation identifies the domain of morality with a study of the substantive rules, norms, and conventions of a social group. In contrast, in this view, the domain of ethics is identified with the study of the organization and criticism of conduct in reference to ideals. As John Dewey (1859–1952) and James H. Tufts (1862–1942) put it in *Ethics* (1908), morality is custom observed and ethics is conscience heard. Again, Dewey and Tufts, for example, identify morality with conduct grounded in group custom and ethics with systematic judgments about such conduct.

In more recent views, some analytic philosophers distinguish between normative ethics, thought of as the domain of substantive moral questions of right and wrong, good and bad, and metaethics, thought of as an inquiry into the meanings of ethical terms, the logical and epistemological status of ethical judgments, and the justification of ethical claims. Bernard Williams in *Ethics and the Limits of Philosophy* (1985) takes a competing view that identifies morality as a "special system" developed by modern, professional philosophers that places particular emphasis upon ideas of our obligations and duties and their justification. In contrast, Williams identifies the ethical domain as that broader range of concerns focused around questions about the worthwhile ends and activities of life.

Clearly, there are different ways to begin an inquiry into the domains of morality and ethics. Most modern approaches begin in a contrast between the questions "What is good?" and "What ought I to do?" The first is addressed by theories of value and the second by theories of obligation. Answers to the first question have been many and varied, ranging from notions of pleasure, happiness, wisdom, and freedom to values of love and growth. Answers to the second question, theories of obligation, fall roughly into two categories, teleological or consequentialist and deontological or nonconsequentialist.

Teleological views, from the Greek *telos,* meaning end or result, base a theory of obligation upon a theory of value such that one ought to do that act that brings about the maximization of some good. Thus, all teleological theories emphasize the results, products, or consequences of one's actions as the most crucial factor in determining what one ought to do. Again, following contemporary distinctions, there are two main varieties of teleological theory, egoism and utilitarianism.

Egoism holds that a person is obligated to perform an act if that act among all the other acts available is the one that will produce the maximum good for the actor. Ethical egoists emphasize the results that will accrue to the ethical agent.

Utilitarians view the ultimate source of obligation as the principle of utility, which holds that one is obligated to perform that action that will produce the greatest amount of good in the world. There are many varieties of utilitarian ethics. Act utilitarians hold that one is obligated to perform that specific action in that specific situation that will produce the greatest amount of good over evil in the world. Rule utilitarians apply the principle of utility to general rules instead of specific cases. Thus, rule utilitarians ask which general rule, if followed over time and across situations, will produce the greatest amount of good over evil.

All teleological theories rely on some notion of moral good and evil coming in "amounts" that can be weighed and balanced in a kind of moral calculus. In contrast, deontological theories of obligation, from the Greek *deon,* that which is binding, emphasize the motives, reasoning, or intentions of the actor, rather than the results, as the crucial consideration in making ethical decisions. As these views emphasize the form rather than the consequences of the choice, they are also called "formalist" ethical theories.

Again, two main varieties are typically distinguished. Act deontologists maintain that all ethical decisions are particular and situational, and that there are no general rules or principles on which one can rely. Thus, many act deontologists appeal to ideas of a moral intuition or to ideas of a form of unconditioned freedom as the basis of ethical choice.

Rule deontologists hold that there are standards of right and wrong composed of logically necessary rules or principles that can be determined through moral reasoning. Such reasoning can yield principles or general guidelines for ethical choice that are consistent and universalizable. The categorical imperative of Immanuel Kant (1724–1804), "Act only on the maxim whereby thou canst at the same time will that it should become a universal law" is the paradigmatic case of such a rule deontological principle.

These distinctions have dominated the modern study of ethics and led to certain ways of thinking about ethics and education. For example, in this view, ethical inquiry begins in dilemmas of value or obligation, focuses on the conditions, forms, and consequences of individual choice, and determines which ethical theory or coherent combination of ethical theories best resolves the dilemma and withstands critical counterexamples. To "do" ethics of education, then, consists of applying alternative theories of ethics to dilemmas arising out of educational practice and policy, conceived of as issues of choice, to determine which theory or combination of theories produces a consistent and justifiable resolution.

Of course, within this broad, mainstream conception of ethical inquiry there are many controversies. Is the source of ethical choice something "inner," internal, inherent, an individual "will" or "intuition," or is it something external to the agent, social and empirical? Is the aim of ethical inquiry the resolution of individual ethical dilemmas, the generation of general ethical principles, or the justification of certain modes of moral conduct? What counts as a "good" consequence and how can competing "goods" be compared? What counts as "universalization" of a principle, when are exceptions permitted, and is there a way of deciding among competing principles?

One strategy to sidestep the seemingly endless and interminable debate around these issues is to conceive of the proper domain of ethics as inquiry into the logic and language of ethical discourse instead of an inquiry aimed at the resolution of ethical quandaries. Since at least the beginning of the twentieth century, analytic philosophers have turned to these metaethical concerns. In some ways, this shift of focus reflects larger trends in intellectual life and philosophy in particular. While it could be reasonably argued that ethics was at the center of Hellenic, Roman, Christian, and classical philosophical thought, since René Descartes (1596–1650) and the rise of the empirical sciences, epistemology has become the core of philosophy. Thus, John Locke (1632–1704) wrote no systematic treatise on ethics, and the eighteenth- and nineteenth-century utilitarians, while concerned with ethics, thought of it largely as a system of rules for distributing natural "goods" understood as empirical. Political theory also has shifted from a concern with concrete forms of authority to abstract notions of citizenship grounded in "natural" laws and rights and finally to metaanalyses of the concept of "rights" itself. Thus, the linguistic turn toward metaethics is consistent with the modern idea of the appropriate province of philosophy. In what Bernard Williams calls this "special system" created by modern, professional philosophers, ethical inquiry consists of the application of the methods and tools of linguistic and logical analysis to the language of morality and ethics. Thus, this literature has produced analyses of the concept or idea of "good," purportedly neutral to substantive instances. Another line of inquiry has distinguished between the logical and epistemological status of the concepts of "ought," "can," "must," and "should." A good deal of literature focuses on the concept of "rights," its entailments and logical status.

An analytic or metaethical literature on ethics and education also has emerged. R.S. Peters and others have focused on an analysis of the concept of "education," and the ways in which educating is an inherently normative enterprise whose activities require justification in reference to ethical criteria. In this light, Peters and others have examined the concepts of "teaching," "indoctrination," "punishment," "discipline," "interests" and the ideal of an educated person. Thus, while the traditional view of ethical theory generates a view of the domain of ethics and education, applying the varieties of ethical theory to the dilemmas of educational practice and policy for the purpose of resolving conflict and guiding choice, the metaethical approach also generates an approach to ethics and education. In this view, inquiry into ethics and education consists in applying the tools of linguistic and logical analysis and the results of metaethical analyses to the discourse of education for the purpose of clarifying concepts, dissolving pseudoproblems, and informing intelligent speech.

These theoretical and metaethical approaches have dominated the study of twentieth-century ethics. Despite some obvious differences, they share some common characteristics. They both are concerned with moral reasoning understood as the analysis of moral experience in reference to principles and rules. In both views, ethical inquiry is dominated by the language of ought, should, rights, justice, equality, freedom, and related abstract concepts. Both view ethics as involving the individual in dilemmas of choice between alternative actions. Thus, moral choice is viewed as a cognitive affair requiring the kind of knowledge that will result in ethical decisions that are universalizable or generalizable.

Criticisms of these mainstream contemporary views are many and varied. Does ethics require an account of the good or the good life that is more than just a concept or a taken-for-granted unknowable that is distributed? Can we think of the good as something that "does" rather than "is," that shows itself in conduct and judgment, that is both naturally occurring, yet constructed and re-formed through practice? Can we think of ethics as an inquiry into the worthwhileness of certain ends and activities of life, in contrast to the narrower "special system" domain of the theoretical and linguistic foundations for certain obligations?

This possibility seems especially important for educational theorists and philosophers whose inquiries must always begin in some account of the differences, tensions, and interactions between *thesis*, what is set up, convention, and custom, and *physis*, nature, individual abilities, choice, and creativity. In much of the classical Hebrew, Greek, and Roman worlds, ethics was centrally concerned with these same ideas. What are the sources of our conventions, the excellences that define their practice, the virtues that sustain and vices that diminish them, their limitations and constraints? What are the possibilities or our nature or natures? What are the differences between nature as it is and nature fully developed, nature in isolation and nature in association, passionate natures and reasoning natures? What are the processes of passage between conventions and nature, between convention and nature as they are to convention and nature as they could be, and how can an account of these processes be constructed to give sense to a human life?

Alasdair MacIntyre in *After Virtue* (1981) makes perhaps the most straightforward case against modernist conceptions of ethics and for a view of ethics as a kind of educational theory. For MacIntyre, rather than questions about value or obligation, the fundamental ethical questions are about virtues and the ends of a good life for human beings. For MacIntyre, virtues are specific to social roles and duties, they inform and give quality to the way specific practices are performed and judged and bridge moral judgment and social structure. They are qualities of conduct, known through practical reasoning. And practical reasoning, or *phronesis*, is learned in relation to an account of the purposes of conduct in a complete human life. Thus, for MacIntyre, ethics is about how to get from untutored nature to our *telos*, from a state of unknowing, unpurposive behavior to a state where we may engage in purposeful conduct and judge the qualities of that conduct in reference to the essential purposes of living well. In this view, ethics is about what we are (our nature) and what we could become (our *telos*) and, most important, about the virtues that sustain and enable us in our search for a purpose throughout life. This search, this quest, is our education. For MacIntyre and this particular version of what is sometimes called "virtue ethics," ethics is inquiry into educational practices.

In this view, to be educated is to be able to produce an intelligible account for oneself in terms of a historical narrative. These narratives, very different from the arguments for justification of traditional and metaethical ethical philosophy, will describe differences about choices made and roads not taken, but they will also provide an objective way to settle such disagreements in terms of the intelligibility of the narrative. To say objective does not mean unproblematic. The educated person knows there is always more than one way to go in pursuing the good. Still, the educated person accepts the tragic nature of life in sometimes having to choose between two "goods," but recognizes that there are better and worse ways to make these choices where better and worse are defined in reference to virtues and excellences instead of formal conditions of reasoning. Was the choice made courageously or with cowardice, with grace or impudence, thoughtfully or carelessly? Living a good life is not found in the conquest of some absolute good, but rather in the quest undertaken virtuously. As MacIntyre writes, "It is in looking for a conception of the good . . . that we initially define the kind of life which is a quest for the good. . . . It is in the course of the quest . . . that the good of the quest is finally to be understood. A quest is always an education both as to the character of that which is sought and in self-knowledge" (204).

MacIntyre's view, sometimes called "virtue ethics" but which might also be called "ethics as *ethos*," is sharply divergent from most contemporary theoretical and metaethical approaches to ethics. It is also a view that joins the domains of ethical and educational inquiry. Although there are significant differences, John Dewey's treatment of ethics has much in common with this view of ethics and ethos.

For example, in *Moral Principles and Education* (1909), Dewey turns our attention away from anything distinctive about ethics as a subject matter, course of study, or segment of experience requiring a distinctive way of thinking. Instead, Dewey distinguished between "ideas about moral action," ethical theory, and "moral ideas," ideas that affect conduct and character. Since, for Dewey, all genuine ideas have this quality, indeed they are only ideas because they have this quality, all learning is moral learning. Thus, much like MacIntyre, Dewey is content to turn the "special system" of morality over to the philosophers, while focusing instead on questions involving the worthwhile ends of life and the tasks of creating institutions that can sustain our educational quests for the discovery of such ends. Thus, in *Moral Principles and Education,* Dewey focuses on the continuities between good educational theory, curriculum theory, classroom practice, and school organization and the representation and practice of ethical conduct. For Dewey, like MacIntyre, an account of the point of a practice is the source of ethical judgment. That is, while contemporary theoretical and metaethical views hold that ethics is something that can be "applied" to a dilemma arising in a specialized domain of practice, such as education, Dewey, MacIntyre, and other "virtue" or "ethos" theorists hold that the ethics of some form of specialized practice is constructed from an account of the point, purpose, or *telos* of the practice itself, where this purpose is discovered and rediscovered in the search for it. In these views, when confronted by an ethical dilemma, look not to theory, but to the institutions, the patterns of social relations, the opportunities for interaction, the structures of freedom and constraint, and the intelligibility of the narratives that shape these into a coherent whole.

Feminist ethics offer another significant alternative to the main varieties of contemporary metaethics and theoretical ethics. Though certainly not uniform, most formulations of feminist ethics question the emphasis given to individual choice, cognitive reasoning, and abstract principles in mainstream ethical theory. Again, while there are different emphases in different feminist ethical theories, most focus on choice in relationship, the integration of emotions, passions, and reason, and on an ethic of relation rather than rights. In these views, ethics is not about individual agents rationally deciding on alternative actions in reference to universal principles, but rather it concerns inquiry into forms of attachment and relation and the qualities of responsiveness and reciprocity that create and sustain practices of caring.

Among others writing on these issues, Nel Noddings in *Caring: A Feminine Approach to Ethics and Moral Education* (1984) has developed an elaborate theory of ethical caring as an alternative to mainstream ethical theories. For Noddings, the source of ethical caring lies not in a cognitive decision to follow a principled obligation, but rather in a memory of caring and being cared for and in a natural longing for goodness to preserve and extend the joy experienced in such natural relationships by meeting the other morally, receiving and responding to the other's needs and interests as one's own.

For Noddings, the ethics of caring addresses the question begged in mainstream ethical theory, "Why be moral?" Knowledge of some learned principle or moral calculus provides no motivation to meet the concrete other morally. For Noddings, we choose to meet the other morally because of the joy we've experienced and remembered that accompanies caring and being cared for and our longing to preserve that joy. Thus, caring is a premoral good and the source of an ethical ideal. Though there are important differences, caring acts much like a purpose or *telos* of human conduct, as in MacIntyre's and Dewey's views. For Noddings, "The first aim of educating is to preserve and enhance the caring relation" (172), thus the ethics of education in this view is derived from an analysis of the ways in which various educational activities, practices, and institutions bear on the preservation and enhancement of caring as the fundamental point or purpose of the enterprise of educating. Ethical inquiry in education is not applying ethical theory to educational dilemmas, but rather assessing the ethical qualities of educational events in light of a theory of the point of the educational enterprise.

Education is a normative enterprise. As such, the connections between ethics, morality, and educational theory are inherent. Debate about the appropriate domain, questions, and purposes of ethics and morality promises to keep inquiries into ethics and education as alive today as when the Greeks asked, "Can virtue be taught?"

James M. Giarelli

See also DEWEY; FEMINISM; KANT; MILL; PRACTICAL WISDOM; RIGHT, THEORIES OF THE; RIGHTS

Bibliography

Becker, Lawrence, and Charlotte B. Becker, eds. *A History of Western Ethics.* New York: Garland, 1992.

Dewey, John. *Moral Principles in Education.* Boston: Houghton Mifflin, 1909.

Dewey, John, and James H. Tufts. *Ethics.* New York: Henry Holt and Company, 1908.

Giarelli, James M. "Primers in Ethics: Reflections on a Changing Field." *Teachers College Record* 83 (1982): 323–39.

Hancock, Roger. *Twentieth Century Ethics.* New York: Columbia University Press, 1974.

MacIntyre, Alasdair. *After Virtue.* Notre Dame, Ind.: University of Notre Dame Press, 1981.

Noddings, Nel. *Caring: A Feminine Approach to Ethics and Moral Education.* Berkeley: University of California Press, 1984.

Peters, R.S. *Ethics and Education.* London: Allen and Unwin, 1966.

Williams, Bernard. *Ethics and the Limits of Philosophy.* Cambridge: Harvard University Press, 1985.

E

Evolution

The concept of evolution emerged in the eighteenth century. Earlier thinkers had recognized change as inherent in life, but few took seriously the idea that the present had emerged out of the past, and none saw the material world continuously changing in small, almost imperceptible ways over time. One of the earliest examples of an evolutionary outlook was the assertion of Immanuel Kant (1724–1804) that the universe is the product of slow change over eons of time. Geologists, too, about this time, recognized that the earth also has a history—it was not always as it now appears. Most important, of course, was the application of evolutionary thinking to living nature. In biology, evolutionary theory postulates that the various types of animals and plants have their origin in other preexisting types and that the distinguishable differences are due to modifications in successive generations.

The two most influential theorists of biological evolution during the nineteenth century were Jean-Baptiste Lamarck (1744–1829) and Charles Darwin (1809–1882). Each offered a different explanation of how evolution took place. Lamarck claimed that it took place through the acquisition of acquired characteristics; that is, organisms passed on to their offspring those characteristics they had acquired in solving problems they encountered in adapting to their environment. Darwin claimed that evolution takes place through the process of natural selection; that is, organisms produce progeny who differ slightly from themselves, and nature selects those who are adapted to the environment, eliminating those who are not fit.

Education and Educational Theory

Jean Jacques Rousseau (1712–1778) was probably the first educational theorist to adopt an evolutionary outlook. Rejecting the reigning, mechanistic, transmission theory of education (see, for example, John Locke [1632–1704] and John Amos Comenius [1592–1671], according to whom the teacher transmits knowledge to more or less passive pupils—much as one fills an empty bucket), Rousseau construed education as a process of growth in which the child passes through discrete stages of development. The key to successful education, he explained, is to have the child learn what is appropriate, or natural, to each stage of development. Rousseau seemed to think that the path of growth or development was preordained by God, and that the teacher's role was simply to facilitate that growth by following nature. Rousseau would have the teacher function somewhat as a gardener who prepares a suitable environment so that plants can grow. In the same way, the teacher is to prepare an educative environment wherein the child can grow, naturally and without interference.

The transmission theorists, against whom Rousseau fought, believed that we learn from experience, by which they meant that we receive knowledge through sense perceptions. Rousseau introduced a more active conception of learning from experience insofar as he insisted that children should explore their (carefully controlled) natural and social environments, discovering thereby the laws that govern those environments. But Rousseau provided no explanations, no guidelines, that would enable teachers to facilitate such educative experiences. It was John Dewey (1859–1952) who took that next step.

Encouraged and influenced by the biological theory of evolution that had appeared since the time of Rousseau, Dewey explicitly declared that education is a process of growth that takes place through the solving of problems of adaptation to the environment. The role of the teacher is to present students with problems that are meaningful, relevant, and significant, through the solution of which students will discover knowledge that will live "fruitfully and creatively in subsequent experience." The best, or most intelligent, way to solve problems, Dewey maintained, is the scientific method of experimentation, and this, then, is what students must learn to do. So, according to Dewey, to learn from experience consists of learning through experimentation: testing proposed, or hypothetical, solutions to real problems.

Although he was born in the same year that Darwin published his *Origin of Species* (1859) and although he claimed to have been influenced by Darwin (see his *The Influence of Darwin on Philosophy*), Dewey's educational theory was decidedly Lamarckian, not Darwin-

ian. For Dewey, education consisted of the transmission of the acquired knowledge of the society to upcoming generations, much as Lamarck had claimed that the species evolved through the transmission of acquired physical characteristics. And, like Lamarck, Dewey thought that we acquire knowledge, or behavior, via the purposive solving of problems of adaptation to our environment.

A more Darwinian educational theory, based on the principle of selection, emerged in the twentieth century out of the work of James Mark Baldwin, E. Claparede, Jean Piaget, Donald T. Campbell, and Karl Popper. Called "evolutionary epistemology," and sometimes (by Piaget) "genetic epistemology," this theory holds, first, that humans construct or create knowledge, just as they create progeny; and, second, that knowledge evolves through critical selection, through the elimination of that which is unfit, that which does not fit the facts.

According to evolutionary epistemologists, both objective knowledge (like the state of a field, in science, say) and subjective or personal knowledge (of a student, say) grow through the modification of preexisting knowledge. People make such modifications, whether in personal knowledge, or in the state of some field, when the existing knowledge is found to be wrong, mistaken, inadequate, or erroneous. Since criticism, or a critical approach toward knowledge, can facilitate the uncovering of errors, the role of the teacher here is primarily that of a critic.

In Darwinian education, the focus is on the growth of the student's knowledge. Darwinian educational theorists agree that knowledge grows through experience, but claim that this happens indirectly. That is, knowledge grows through the experience of uncovering mistakes in one's present knowledge. Such uncoveries lead one to modify or refine that existing knowledge. The role of the teacher is to educe the students' present knowledge, help them to uncover the heretofore unrecognized inadequacies in that knowledge, and then to encourage them to modify it in light of the uncovered inadequacies. The best exemplar of this Darwinian educational theory is the Montessori method, in which pupils continually modify their skills and knowledge through the process of trial and error elimination—learning from their mistakes.

Evolution and Educational Philosophy

The English philosopher Herbert Spencer (1820–1903), who was an advocate of evolution even before the publication of Darwin's *Origin of Species,* extended evolutionary theory to society, thereby creating what came to be called Social Darwinism. According to Spencer, society evolves naturally, through the mechanism called "the survival of the fittest"—that is, society progresses over time as its unfit members fail to adapt to their circumstances, and are eliminated. An advocate of laissez-faire before becoming an evolutionist, Spencer insisted that governmental welfare measures impede social progress by putting "a stop to that natural process of elimination by which society continually purifies itself." For this reason, he opposed government schooling. He did not oppose education, especially scientific education—privately provided—but claimed that education can play no role in social progress, which takes place only through the inexorable workings of the evolutionary process.

In opposition to the conservative Social Darwinism of Spencer, the American social philosopher Lester Ward (1841–1913) put forward a progressive Social Darwinism. Ward held that social evolution, unlike biological evolution, can be guided or manipulated by (properly trained) human intelligence. For Ward, education—especially scientific education—was the "great panacea" for all social ills, "the mainspring of progress." This belief of the progressive Social Darwinists that education and schooling should become the agency to guarantee social and political progress was a dramatic reversal of the belief common throughout the nineteenth century that education and schooling were to protect against social and political innovation.

Some progressive Social Darwinists, like Charles W. Eliot (1834–1926), president of Harvard University from 1868 to 1906, believed that only experts and specialists would be able to guide social development. Eliot's philosophy of education promoted a conception of limited democracy wherein the school system would sort out the talented and train them as experts to whom the rest of society would assign the responsibility for guiding social progress.

Other progressive Social Darwinists, like John Dewey, believed that the scientific intelligence necessary to guide social development could be taught to all, in elementary and secondary schools that were appropriately transformed into "progressive schools." Here, students would learn how to work together cooperatively on common problems, solving them through the scientific method of experimentation. Dewey's philosophy of education promoted a conception of participant democracy wherein people educated in such progressive schools would be able to work together on social problems and thereby reconstruct the society. Education, Dewey wrote, in "My Pedagogic Creed," is the fundamental method of social progress and reform.

All of the evolution-inspired philosophers of education—from Spencer to Dewey—were Lamarckian. None construed education as Darwinian. Recently, Henry Perkinson, building on the philosophy of critical rationalism of Karl Popper, has sketched a Darwinian philosophy of education.

Henry J. Perkinson

See also COGNITIVE DEVELOPMENT; CONSERVATISM; DARWIN; DEWEY; EPISTEMOLOGY; PROGRESS, IDEA OF, AND PROGRESSIVE EDUCATION; RECONSTRUCTIONISM, SOCIAL; ROUSSEAU; SOCIAL AND POLITICAL PHILOSOPHY; SPENCER; TEACHING AND LEARNING

Bibliography

Broughton, John M., and D. John Freeman-Moir, eds. *The Cognitive Development Psychology of James Mark Baldwin.* Norwood, N.J.: Ablex, 1982.

Campbell, Donald T. "Evolutionary Epistemology." In *The Philosophy of Karl Popper,* edited by Paul Arthur Schlipp. LaSalle, Ill.: Open Court, 1974.

Dewey, John. *Experience and Education.* New York: Macmillan, 1938.

———. *The Influence of Darwinism on Philosophy.* New York: Holt, 1910.

Hofstadter, Richard. *Social Darwinism in American Thought.* Philadelphia: University of Pennsylvania Press, 1944. Boston: Beacon Press, 1955.

Perkinson, Henry J. *Learning from Our Mistakes.* Westport, Conn.: Greenwood Press, 1984.

———. *Teachers without Goals/Students without Purposes.* New York: McGraw Hill, 1993.

Piaget, Jean. *Behavior and Evolution.* New York: Pantheon Books, 1978.

Popper, Karl R. *Conjecture and Refutations.* New York: Basic Books, 1963.

———. *Objective Knowledge: An Evolutionary Approach.* Oxford: Oxford University Press, 1972.

Richards, Robert J. *Darwin and the Emergence of Evolutionary Theories of Mind and Behavior.* Chicago: University of Chicago Press, 1987.

Existentialism

Existentialism, or philosophy of existence, names a philosophic movement of loosely related thinkers without a common set of doctrines. They have in common opposition to the systematic philosophy of G.W.F. Hegel and all its twentieth-century offshoots, including Marxism, positivism, American pragmatism, and what, in its latest incarnation, is called analytic philosophy. In the last half of the nineteenth century, the spirit of Hegelian optimism dominated in Western cultures: Witness, the political utopianism of Karl Marx, the progressive view of biological science advanced by Charles Darwin, the doctrine of positive social science advancing the cause of the alleviation of human suffering, the faith of American pragmatism that by cooperative inquiry societies might progress in the solution of human problems.

Voices emerged within that chorus of idealistic optimism to challenge the faith in progress, in science, and in the earthly triumph of human reason. In the period after World War I, which had seriously shaken the optimism of Western nations, these disparate voices of doubt became lumped under a label that proclaimed them representative of a new philosophy, existentialism.

Existentialism points to the two distinctive meanings of "being": existence and essence. Where most traditional philosophy has sought to account for existence by reference to the essences that "explain" it, existentialism attempts to restore a "factual" order to understanding: existence *is* prior to all efforts to explain it. Plato created as a central question of philosophy the relation between existence and essence, —that is, between sensible events and their meanings. Plato regarded essences as the "higher reality" and he regarded existents as copies of their essences. Through more than two millennia Western philosophers have sought to recast that relationship. From the perspective of many moderns, the problem of the relationship was resolved in an acceptable way by Plato's student, Aristotle, and updated within the Christian context of the late Middle Ages by Thomas Aquinas: Existent and essence are inseparable. First perceived as sensible events, the essence that explains them can be found by dint of human scientific effort. Both Aristotelianism and Thomism rest on the faith that the universe constitutes a rational system, which humans can come to know. It is this faith that Hegel shared, despite his belief that reality is constituted by the historically situated consciousness of human individuals.

Philosophers of existence generally agree with Hegel's historically situated starting point, but note that the historical individual is more than just a consciousness, but also a physical body possessed of feelings and a will, and that those aspects of the existent individual result in a life of aspiration and struggle, marked by joy, suffering, and ending in death, which constantly threatens to render that struggle meaningless. They find no reassurance in Hegel's faith that human problems can yield to rational understanding of their cosmic context. That, in itself, cannot relieve the anxiety or forlornness of an individual human life.

Kierkegaard

The initial existential response to Hegel came from his Danish contemporary Soren Kierkegaard (1813–1855), who made no pretense of being a philosopher. Kierkegaard's most basic concern was with Hegel's impact on Protestant religion. Hegel's rational optimism promised humans access to the workings of God's historically evolving plan for the world. Kierkegaard regarded God as radically other than human existence, so that the existent individual must choose his faith without certainty grounded in knowledge.

Although Kierkegaard points to the anxiety, fear, and anguish that accompany the individual's risk of action into an uncertain future, and the omnipresent possibility of death, the reader should not regard existentialism primarily as a philosophy of gloom and doom. Most existentialists share a sense that risk and danger give human existence its positive emotional quality. Exclusive reliance on reason as a way out of human difficulties proves existentially inadequate because it threatens to stultify the emotional life. We see that threat most directly and poignantly from an aesthetic perspective: Artists who use reason to "play it safe" often rob their work of emotional force. Kierkegaard sees the aesthetic as an important first stage on life's way. But the existential inadequacy of exclusive reliance on reason applies as well to the ethical or religious aspects of life (which represent Kierkegaard's "higher" stages). If people strive primarily to "follow the rules" and "earn their just rewards," they rob life of emotional value. Kierkegaard made heroes of Jesus and Socrates, whose lives he saw as passionate more than rational, Socrates by his embrace of skepticism, Jesus by his embrace of the outcast.

Nietzsche

A second existential voice, also unknown by that label in his own time, is Friedrich Nietzsche (1844–1900). Nietzsche's quarrel was not so much with Hegel as with the whole tradition of Western philosophy, generated by Plato and later merged with Christianity. Nietzsche pictures Plato (whom John Herman Randall describes as the "dramatist of the life of reason") as the progenitor of a decadent art, decadent because it is consciously moral—that is, it aims for the story that will point the moral, and the moral is generally that reason must control the passions. Nietzsche saw himself rather as dramatist of the life of instinct. He calls for a dramatic art that is not consciously moral, that thereby transvalues conventional values, and expresses the instincts, the life force, the will to power, of the human animal.

Nietzsche responded to the strong impact that evolutionary theories (first in the "spiritual," Hegelian form, then in the naturalistic, Darwinian form) had had on the liberal morality then dominant in Western Europe. Evolution had led to replacement of the traditional bedrock of liberal faith—the rational freedom of the individual—with hope for the progressive emergence of a higher form of human social life. The supreme ironist Nietzsche was both caught up in and resistant to that movement. He saw liberalism being transformed to "fit" with evolutionary goals, and he believed that the upshot could be the submergence of the individual in the service of societies becoming progressively more egalitarian and just.

The events in the Western world since Nietzsche's death tend to bear out his pessimistic vision. But Nietzsche couldn't tolerate his own pessimism—he wanted to be joyful and exuberant, all the things his culture militated against. In romantic fashion, he reinterpreted the workings of evolution in order to picture the unfettered individual, the person with sufficient foresight to transcend the limited vision provided by the culture, as the generator of human evolution to a higher form. Nietzsche saw, as the flaw of liberalism, its faith that individual reason could be the source of social progress. To him, rather, evolution to a higher form can best be promoted by assertion of the will to power. He would replace the rational virtues of liberal democracies with values that are fundamentally aesthetic.

Heidegger

As previously noted, the idea of existentialism as a distinctive philosophic movement came into play after World War I. The work of Martin Heidegger (1889–1976), author of the monumental *Being and Time* published in 1927, pulled together elements from Nietzsche and Kierkegaard, along with the phenomenological method of philosophizing developed by Edmund Husserl (1859–1938). Phenomenology provides a method for looking at a situation from the standpoint of a participant rather than from an "objective" point of view. While Husserl employed the method primarily to look at the contents of human consciousness, Heidegger incorporated the perspective of Kierkegaard and Nietzsche, in which consciousness emerges from a concrete human existence grounded in will and feeling.

Heidegger sees evidence of human will in the desire for transcendence, to go beyond the given, to achieve what is not yet. A human being lives primarily in the future but fears to confront the imminent possibility of death, which would bring an end to future projects. Heidegger sees the resulting everyday life of human beings as inauthentic, taken up with petty cares and pastimes, constituting a refusal to face the absence of any cosmic grounds for making the choices that constitute human living. Only when a human being encounters the feeling of anxiety or dread that pervades human choices can that person realize the significance that awareness of the omnipresence of the possibility of one's own death has for being human.

Because, from Heidegger's perspective, no accounting of the facts of a situation can determine a person's next action, all human acts contain an element of risk. (Some contemporary educational theorists have set up a category of students "at risk"—demanding special attention—but from an existential point of view all students are at risk, since the risk of choosing actions into an uncertain future characterizes the human situation.) Those people who seem to take the greater risks in life often say to their more timid acquaintances, "You've got to die some day." A further implicit rhetorical question typically characterizes a Heideggerian stance toward life: "Would you rather die fearful of taking a risk with your life, or choosing to act with awareness of the unavoidability of risk?"

In this regard, William Barrett points out that Heidegger provides "the final anatomy of the romantic individual." In a sense, this expresses both the appeal of Heidegger's philosophy and the source of strong counterreactions. Existential philosophy's romantic individuals sought to restore almost "medieval" virtues, in the face of a modern culture dominated by science and technology, by sheer dint of a heroic personality. Heidegger's philosophy, however, seems to lack the ironic sense of life of its precursors, Kierkegaard and Nietzsche. (Existentialism seems to have lost its appeal in the wake of the postmodern turn in Western cultural life. Postmodern movements have as one defining characteristic a kind of dismemberment of the anatomy of the romantic individual; those under the influence of postmodernity come to see selves as many-sided individuals, rather than integral and standing heroically against the trends of the culture.)

In a recent book, Hugo Ott demonstrates at some length that in the 1930s Heidegger came to believe that his philosophy was the spiritual core of National Socialism in Germany. The recognition of Heidegger's Nazi sympathies does not diminish his importance as a philosopher for the twentieth-century Western world, but, in retrospect, it does diminish the post–World War II importance of existential philosophy as an antidote to Nazism, laying stress on individual responsibility and commitment.

Sartre

In large part, the popularity of existentialism in the wake of World War II, both in Europe and the United States, came in response to the work of Jean-Paul Sartre (1905–1980), a hero of the French resistance. Sartre managed to temper the romanticism of Heidegger by a generally pessimistic account of existentialism.

In a poignant story in his autobiography, Sartre tells of how, at age seven, he imagined that he was on a train to Dijon. When the ticket collector asks for his ticket, he admits that he has none, but claims that he is on a secret mission to save France. Sartre finds that story an apt metaphor for his existentialism: All his life he has been a traveler without a ticket. In his old age, the ticket collector looks at him less sternly than when he was a child, but now he realizes that he has no excuse for taking his ride, and that when he arrives at his destination, no one will be waiting.

Thus, Sartre recognizes the dreadful burden that human freedom places on the individual—to choose without any "good reasons"

for one's choice. In Sartre's writing, existentialism plays a role in recalling the negative concept of freedom that had characterized liberalism from its seventeenth-century emergence until late in the nineteenth century. With the arrival of the twentieth century, a new version of liberalism, with a positive vision of freedom as the empowerment of individuals to participate intelligently in the life of society, began to replace the negative concept, under the influence of such outstanding thinkers as John Dewey (1859–1952).

Sartre counters that vision with a negative view of freedom, raised to ontological status. For Sartre, freedom is that aspect of human existence that denies to any power in the universe the capacity to dictate the future of an individual life, whether that power be God, individual reason, science, political authority, or ethical obligation. Human beings are free because the future events of their life are indeterminate and indeterminable.

Positive views of freedom set up a hierarchy of liberation, depending on a person's degree of empowerment within a culture. They set the conditions for the "victimization" of many members of a society, whose freedom has been curtailed by this or that disempowering condition of their lives.

Negative freedom, on the other hand, is the correlate of an important sense of human equality: recognizing the incommensurability of human lives. The contingencies that make each life indeterminable, if recognized, would severely limit the applicability of one person's attempts to prescribe for another. This provides perhaps the only direct point of reference of Sartre's philosophy to education: Teachers should keep before them awareness of the freedom of each student, not through any power bestowed on a student through the efforts of the teacher, but as an expression of each student's existential situation.

Existentialism and Philosophy of Education

As existentialism became fashionable in the United States in the wake of World War II and the Holocaust, several leading American philosophers of education took it up as a possible source of educational reform. Typically these authors explored the works of the leading Continental European existentialists for their possible relevance to education in America, while trying to avoid any suggestion that a thinker's philosophy had direct implications for the conduct of schooling. George Kneller produced one of the first such approaches. His book *Existentialism and Education* (1958) surveyed the ideas of five leading existentialists, and he used their ideas as a basis for critique of certain movements Kneller considered to be then dominant in American education, for which he used the labels logical positivism, experimentalism, and uncritical collectivism. Articles of this type appeared regularly in *Educational Theory*, a leading journal of philosophy of education, throughout the 1950s.

A number of other educational theorists focused on specific existential thinkers. Van Cleve Morris's *Existentialism in Education* (1966) concentrated mainly on the ideas of Sartre; Donald Vandenberg's *Being and Education* explicated primarily the ideas of Heidegger. David Denton based his critique of contemporary American education to a large degree on ideas drawn from Albert Camus, the French existentialist, essayist, and novelist. A volume edited by Denton in 1972 combined original essays on existential and phenomenological themes by American educational theorists. Maxine Greene appears in that group, in her own original works exploring primarily the relevance for education of works by literary existentialists.

To judge by the sharp falloff in references to existentialism since the 1970s, it seems that the era in which existentialist ideas strongly influenced American educators has passed. In a sense, existentialism represents one of the last active phases of modernity in Western cultures, and in many ways modernity's most self-critical phase. In this respect it may have given way before the emergence of a new epoch in cultural history, which, most generally, bears the label of "postmodernity." It seems as if modern thought, having reached its existential limits, has begun slowly, almost imperceptibly, to erode. To the extent that that process of erosion comes to dominate contemporary cultures, we do not live in a period of great optimism, lacking, so far, a clear basis for faith in the future. But from a historical perspective, existentialism has done much to preserve individuality against the prevailing tide of technical rationality that has characterized modernity.

Clinton Collins

See also HEIDEGGER; KIERKEGAARD; MODERNISM AND POST-MODERNISM; NIETZSCHE; SARTRE

Bibliography

Works on Existentialism

Barnes, Hazel. *Humanistic Existentialism: The Literature of Possibility*. Lincoln: University of Nebraska Press, 1959.

Barrett, William. *What Is Existentialism?* New York: Grove, 1964.

Bretall, Robert, ed. *A Kierkegaard Anthology*. Princeton: Princeton University Press, 1951.

Buber, Martin. *Between Man and Man* [1947]. Translated by Ronald Gregor Smith. Boston: Beacon, 1955.

Cline, Geoffrey, ed. *The Philosophy of Nietzsche*. New York: New American Library, 1965.

Grene, Marjorie. *Introduction to Existentialism*. Chicago: University of Chicago Press, 1959.

Heidegger, Martin. *Being and Time*. Translated by John Macquarrie and Edward Robinson. New York: Harper and Row, 1962.

Husserl, Edmund. *Ideas: General Introduction to Pure Phenomenology* [1913]. Translated by W.R. Boyce Gibson. New York: Macmillan-Collier, 1962.

MacIntyre, Alisdair. "Existentialism." In *Sartre*, edited by Mary Warnock, 1–58. Garden City, N.Y.: Doubleday, 1971.

Nietzsche, Friedrich. *Beyond Good and Evil: Prelude to a Philosophy of the Future*. Translated by Walter Kaufman. New York: Random House, 1966.

Olson, Robert. *An Introduction to Existentialism*. New York: Dover, 1962.

Ott, Hugo. *Martin Heidegger: A Political Life*. Translated by Allan Blunden. New York: Basic Books, 1993.

Randall, John Herman, Jr. *Plato: Dramatist of the Life of Reason*. New York: Columbia University Press, 1970.

Sartre, Jean-Paul. "Existentialism is a Humanism." Translated by Philip Mairet. In *Existentialism from Dostoevsky to Sartre*, edited by Walter Kaufman, 287–311. New York: World, 1965.

Wahl, Jean. *A Short History of Existentialism*. Translated by Forrest Williams and Stanley Maron. New York: Philosophical Library, 1949.

Works on Existentialism and Philosophy of Education

Denton, David, ed. *Existentialism and Phenomenology in Education*. New York: Teachers College Press, 1974.

Greene, Maxine, ed. *Existential Encounters for Teachers.* New York: Random House, 1967.

Harper, Ralph. "Significance of Existence and Recognition for Education." In *Modern Philosophies and Education,* 54th yearbook of the National Society for the Study of Education, Part I, edited by N.B. Henry, 215–58. Chicago: NSSE, 1955.

Kneller, George F. *Existentialism and Education.* New York: Philosophical Library, 1958.

Morris, Van Cleve. *Existentialism in Education.* New York: Harper and Row, 1966.

Vandenberg, Donald. *Being and Education: An Essay in Existential Phenomenology.* Englewood Cliffs, N.J.: Prentice-Hall, 1971.

Experience

In everyday language, experience refers to what we do and undergo in life. It is the source of the knowledge, skills, qualities, and habits that make us what we are. Common experiences give individuals in a family, group, or culture a sense of common identity. It is little wonder that philosophers return again and again to the study of experience. Everything that makes human beings distinctly human owes that distinction to its connection with human experience.

When philosophers study things, they often take them apart, identify their pieces, and try to figure out how they work. The process has its dangers, as any child who has disassembled an old clock knows too well. When philosophers take things apart, they may not get them back together again. They may concentrate on the parts and fail to see their connection, their unity.

Greek philosophers understood that experience was the source of knowledge and skill, but they left reason out of their conception of everyday experience. Experience, they believed, was little more than practice. With experience, bricklayers and painters mastered their trades, children learned to walk, and musicians conquered the musical scales. Practice was an essential to education, but practice, by itself, did not make perfect. Experience provided practical information about particular cases and specific events, but, in the Greek view, experience was a slow and inefficient teacher. It mired individuals in the practical events of everyday life. Quotidian experience did not allow individuals to see connections among events and the larger patterns that gave those events significance. To see these connections, the philosophers claimed, students must retreat from the world and employ reason. With reason, individuals might transcend practical knowledge and ascend to a higher plane the Greeks called conceptual knowledge. Reason allowed individuals to escape all that was perishable, unreliable, physical, and inferior and achieve true knowledge that the Greeks believed was eternal, certain, metaphysical, and superior.

Later philosophers took experience apart again and reassembled it in different ways. Auguste Comte (1798–1857) brought reason back into experience, elevated the importance of practical knowledge, and denied the possibility of metaphysical wisdom. He asserted that human history moves through three distinct and predictable stages: the theological, the metaphysical, and the positive. In the theological stage, societies explain reality in terms of gods and demons. In the metaphysical stage, societies explain reality in abstract terms such as essence and existence. In the positive stage, which Comte believed was just beginning in his lifetime, societies define reality in terms of scientific laws. We discover those laws, he said, through logic, observation, and experimentation.

Comte was the founder of a philosophical movement called *positivism.* Positivists believe that the scientific method is the only road to knowledge. They draw sharp distinctions between facts and values, reason and emotion, objects and ideas, the observer and the observed. Comte had little regard for either religion or traditional philosophy and was especially wary of metaphysics. He divided experience into the struggling subject of experience (the knower) and the fixed object of experience (the known). He defined knowledge as an accurate replication in the mind of objective reality in the world. In Comte's view, truth exists independent of human perception. The aim of inquiry is to ensure that internal perceptions precisely mirror external reality. Achieving an exact correspondence between perception and reality is difficult, Comte explained, because perceptions are easily distorted and human beings are easily fooled. What we learn through experience is not to be trusted unless the experience is disciplined by scientific method and reason. When disciplined, however, experience brings external reality before the mind's eye. Disciplined experience can move perception from the uncertain world of perishable facts and practical knowledge to the certain world of scientific laws, eternal principles, and essential qualities.

In the end, Comte's view was not so different from that of the Greeks. Like the ancients, Comte conceived a two-part world: a lower realm that is uncertain, untrustworthy, illusionary, and mutable, and a higher realm that is good, true, real, and immutable. The Greeks distrusted the lower realm of practical experience and hoped to escape to an upper realm of metaphysical truth. Comte also distrusted the realm of everyday experience, but he hoped to escape to an upper realm of scientific truth. He dislodged metaphysics from his philosophy but, in the process, substituted science for religion.

By the end of the nineteenth century, some philosophers, especially American pragmatists such as Charles Sanders Peirce (1839–1914), William James (1842–1910), and John Dewey (1859–1952), were growing suspicious of absolutist systems of thought that disparage primary experience. Philosophers devised absolutist systems, pragmatists said, to avoid the inevitable uncertainties of life. Experience, the pragmatists pointed out, begins in doubt and ends in the tentative resolution of doubt. Because earlier philosophers could not extinguish the uncertainty of everyday experience, they banished it to a lower realm of existence and declared it unimportant. In the process, the pragmatists argued, they distorted experience. Reality, James insisted, is not neatly stratified. What is needed, he said, is the tough-minded, inclusive philosophy that accepts the world's inherent uncertainty.

James and his fellow pragmatists put experience at the center of their philosophy. Unlike their predecessors, pragmatists posited no secure and settled order separate from, or superior to, everyday life. They examined nature without dissecting tools. Human beings, they insisted, are not mere observers of nature but a part of nature. Within nature, humans create their individual and collective worlds the only way they can, out of experience, through acts, intentions, reflections, feelings, imaginings, and will.

John Dewey devoted much of his long career to formulating and refining a philosophically useful description of experience. It was a formidable task, because the term had been used to mean so many different things. Dewey began with the common-sense notion that humans gain knowledge by interacting with their physical and social environments. These transactions always involve change. Sometimes an experience will change a person, sometimes the person will change the environment, and sometimes both are altered. The story of nature, Dewey said, is a story of these transitions. There are physiochemical transitions, when, for example, bile breaks down fat in the digestive system; there are psychophysical transitions, when, for example, a cat feels pain as it sits on a hot stove; and there are experiential transitions, when, for example, you take an aspirin for your headache or cry when watching a play.

Uniquely human experience (*experiential transition*) is just another form of change in nature. It was not Dewey's intent to diminish the significance of human experience by making it a part of nature; quite the opposite was true. He wanted to describe experience accurately so that we might understand the role it plays in human existence. Experience, he argued, is not something that transpires in the mind; it is, instead, a matter of doings and undergoings, of adjustments and readjustments, of transactions and transitions.

Life is a series of experiences because individuals continuously interact with nature. Some experiences are inchoate. You experience some things superficially, habitually, as when you pass someone in the hall and mindlessly ask, "How are you?" Perhaps you do not listen for an answer because your utterance was more of a statement than a question. You put very little into such encounters and you take little from them. You experienced the other person superficially, so you might call this a casual experience. You would not call it an "experience." Little registered. Little changed.

Other experiences involve you more deeply. You bring more to them and take more from them. There is exchange and transition, emotion and thought, struggle and fulfillment. You win the game, solve the problem, complete the task, or finish the book. The experience has many parts, but, upon its completion, there is more than consummation, there is a unity that makes the experience unique, that makes it an "experience." The stream of an experience has a beginning and an end, but it also has a quality that makes it something whole, that makes it a thrilling game or a special book. The quality that pervades the experience unifies its constituent parts.

For an example of a full and mature experience, think back to the first time you read your favorite novel. You probably remember the storyline and important characters, the text and the subtext. Those elements, though important, are just part of the experience. Perhaps you remember where you read the book, how you felt, and the character with whom you most closely identified. You may remember events in your own life that the book brought to mind and helped you redefine.

Reading the book took time. There were moments of intense interest and moments of coasting. Sometimes you were lost in the prose and other times you were not. You experienced feelings of happiness, sadness, worry, and satisfaction. Despite these temporal, emotional, and intellectual fluctuations, the book hangs in your memory as a single experience. Its varied components are united by a single quality that defines the entire event.

The quality of your experience united the psychological and temporary components in the book-reading event and it did more. It also united the subject (you, the reader) and the object (the book you read). Where, then, would we locate that special quality that made this particular book so important to you? In the mind of the reader? Certainly, the pragmatists would answer, but not only there. You needed the book to have the experience. Does the quality reside in the book? Certainly, the pragmatists would answer again, but not only there. An unread book is just a collection of ink and paper. The quality of the book-reading experience exists in the reading, in the transaction between the reader and the read. The unity is pervasive and unites subject and object, thought and feeling, problem and solution. Others who read the book have different experiences. They bring their own habits and histories to the novel and experience it in their own ways.

We have contrasted a casual, habitual experience (passing someone in the hall) with a vital and mature experience (reading an extraordinary novel). Dewey called the latter event an aesthetic experience. Other experiences have neither the mindlessness of the casual experience nor the intensity of the aesthetic. These more common events share the characteristics of the aesthetic experience, though in milder form.

All experience, Peirce contended, begins in doubt. When a habit or expectation is violated, we feel uncertain. At first, we may not even recognize what is amiss; we just feel that something is wrong. On such occasions, we stop our habitual activity to look to see what is troubling us.

Let us alter the hallway example we used earlier. Let us say that this time you are lost in

thought when you pass a friend. Again you mindlessly murmur, "How are you?" and walk on. After a few steps you let go of your thoughts and turn your mind back to the person you passed. Quite literally in this case, you stop and think. Something was different, but you do not know what. In a moment you *recognize* the problem. Your friend was silent. As you recall the event you realize that he was walking unevenly. You turn your head to check your perception. You spot your friend now some distance away, staggering. You wonder what might be wrong. Has he been drinking? Is he ill? Is he fooling around? Different conclusions call for different responses. You may ignore an acquaintance who has been drinking, help a person who is ill, and laugh at a person who is playing a joke. What do you do? You might just walk away; some people dislike uncertainty. If you are inquisitive, however, you would look for information that would solve your mini-mystery. Let us say, for the sake of this example, that your friend staggers, pauses, and falls to the ground. You conclude he is ill and run to assist. You check his vital signs and notice that he has stopped breathing. You consider many courses of action and choose one. You tell a passerby to call 911 and begin to administer the breath of life.

The situation we have invented was not an aesthetic experience, but it certainly was an "experience." Its many constituent parts had their own unity or quality. If we examine the chronology of events we discover some things about not only this experience but all experiences. There was a felt but undefined problem (you stop and think about passing your friend), an effort to define the problem (did he slur his speech? was he staggering?), a definition of the problem (he fell and lost consciousness), a consideration of possible actions (do I run for help, ask someone else to take over, or take charge?), an action (you administer first aid), and a reconsideration (did I act appropriately? what have I learned?). When you think about it, the process of your hallway heroics was not so different from what scientists do when they do science. Having said this, however, pragmatists would remind us again that the experience is more than a rational act. The human mind is a congress of faculties in which no one faculty or one mode of experience has the deciding vote. Neither the hallway experience nor a scientific discovery is an example of reason defeating emotion, but, rather, of reason, emotion, and imagination working harmoniously.

For the pragmatists, experience is a process and knowledge is one of its outcomes. Through experience we learn how things are related. Mere events take on meaning and become knowledge when they are connected in mind with other events. A sneeze becomes the sign of an oncoming cold. An uneven walk becomes a sign that a friend is ill. Knowledge is a product of experience, but it is also a part of experience. New experiences expand our stock of knowledge at hand, and that knowledge is available to us in future experience. (The hallway experience we just invented would have been different had I not assumed you knew something about first aid.) Knowledge in an indeterminate situation signifies possibilities, things to be tried. As past experiences evolve into present experiences, our stock of knowledge is expanded or refined.

For the pragmatists, education was more than an accumulation of facts. Knowledge was born of experience. Those who teach bring students and subject matter together in a way that makes experience possible. Some educators misunderstood the pragmatists to suggest that subject matter is unimportant. They thought the pragmatists were saying that thinking is easy and that students will learn if teachers stand aside and let experience happen. The pragmatists knew better. They understood that thinking is difficult, learning is a struggle, and not all experiences are educative. They advised that teachers put students to work on real problems, in authentic situations, and with genuine subject matter.

Students are not passive recipients of knowledge; they learn by doing. Doing, however, is always a discipline of mind, subject matter, and purpose. Random experience is undisciplined. It lacks fullness and quality. It rarely educates, if we mean by that term that it yields knowledge and enables us to have richer and fuller experiences in the future.

Rodman B. Webb

See also DEWEY; JAMES; METAPHYSICS; POSITIVISM; PRAGMATISM

Bibliography

Comte, Auguste. *The Positive Philosophy of Auguste Comte.* Translated by H. Martineau. London: G. Bell and Sons, 1896.

Dewey, John. *Art as Experience.* In *The Later Works, 1925–1953.* Vol. 10. Carbondale: Southern Illinois University Press, 1987.

———. *Democracy and Education.* In *The Middle Works, 1899–1924.* Vol. 9. Carbondale: Southern Illinois University Press, 1980.

———. *Experience and Education.* In *The Later Works, 1925–1953.* Vol. 13. Carbondale: Southern Illinois University Press, 1988.

———. *The Quest for Certainty.* In *The Later Works, 1925–1953.* Vol. 4. Carbondale: Southern Illinois University Press, 1984.

James, William. *The Meaning of Truth.* In *The Works of William James,* edited by F.H. Burkhardt, F. Bowers, and I.K. Skrupskelis. Cambridge: Harvard University Press, 1975.

———. *The Principles of Psychology.* In *The Works of William James,* edited by F.H. Burkhardt, F. Bowers, and I.K. Skrupskelis. Cambridge: Harvard University Press, 1981.

———. *Varieties of Religious Experience.* In *The Works of William James,* edited by F.H. Burkhardt, F. Bowers, and I.K. Skrupskelis. Cambridge: Harvard University Press, 1985.

———. *The Will to Believe.* In *The Works of William James,* edited by F.H. Burkhardt, F. Bowers, and I.K. Skrupskelis. Cambridge: Harvard University Press, 1979.

Peirce, C.S. *Pragmatism and Pragmaticism.* In *Collected Papers.* Vol. 5, edited by C. Hartshorne and P. Weiss. Cambridge: Harvard University Press, 1934.

———. *Science and Philosophy.* In *Collected Papers.* Vol. 7, edited by A.W. Burks. Cambridge: Harvard University Press, 1958.

E

F

Feminism

In 1913, Rebecca West gave her often-quoted answer to the question "What is feminism?" She replied: "I myself have never been able to find out precisely what feminism is: I only know that people call me a feminist whenever I express sentiments that differentiate me from a doormat." Since then much has been written about feminism, enough to permit us more precise though still controversial definitions.

For many, feminism is summed up as a movement for creating a society in which women can live a full, self-determined life. That characterization may seen innocuous, but the changes needed to achieve such lives for women remain revolutionary. The term *feminism* refers both to feminist theory and to social movements that advocate an end to the political, economic, social, and cultural subordination of women. A common misconception views feminism as a monolithic ideology for a single progressive movement. However, the term has a wide application, covering many different liberatory movements as well as disparate political views.

For some, feminism has seemed quite separate from any kind of politics in which men are involved; others have seen it as a movement for political reform, but not for radical social transformation; still others have urged that the liberation feminism seeks can be realized only through a socialist transformation. Cultural feminists believe that women will be freed only through the cultivation of specifically womanly values and an alternative women's culture. Some other theorists define feminism as a mode of analysis. In fact, toward the end of the twentieth century there are such differing political perspectives encompassed by the term *feminism* that it is common to speak of feminisms.

Women's political struggles in their own behalf have inevitably been influenced by other progressive movements within their respective societies. As a result, most accounts of feminist theory fall into what one theorist calls a "hyphenated model of feminism," which emphasizes the different political perspectives. Common listings of feminisms include: liberal feminism, Marxist feminism, radical feminism, socialist feminism, psychoanalytic feminism, cultural feminism, even existential feminism, and, more recently, multicultural feminism, global feminism, and postmodern feminism.

The history of modern feminism, in the Western world is usually linked with the struggle for women's suffrage, sometimes called "the first wave" of feminism. The resurgence of attention to women's emancipation in the 1960s, known as the Women's Liberation Movement, has been called "the second wave." Many object to this characterization however, for it eclipses the efforts of women outside these acknowledged movements and forgets the ways in which, as Dale Spender says, "There's always been a women's movement."

Prior to modern feminism, one finds three positions that the historian Joan Kelly has identified as characterizing what we now refer to as feminism: (1) a deliberate and conscious opposition to male defamation and mistreatment of women; (2) a belief that the sexes are culturally and not just biologically formed, that women are a social group shaped by male notions of their sex; and (3) a desire for a conception of humanity that recognizes women as fully human.

Commonly, however, the term *feminism* refers to emancipatory movements among women since the late eighteenth century. Modern feminism, initially characterized as the advocacy of women's rights to full citizenship, is said to have been born with the French and American democratic revolutions of the eighteenth century. What differentiated modern feminism from feminism of the past was the application of the democratic implications of the "rights of man and the citizen" to women as a group. The term "women's rights" became political currency in 1792 with the publication of Mary Wollstonecraft's *Vindication of the Rights of Woman,* her response to the failure of the central document of the French revolution, "The Declaration of the Rights of Man," to address women's inequality.

The term *feminist* originated in France, invented in the early nineteenth century by the sociologist Charles Fourier, who claimed that women's emancipation marked the degree of enlightenment and social progress of a society. It was a name for the "new woman." In England, *feminist* was used to describe British women campaigning for the vote in the 1890s.

In the United States, the serious fight for women's rights to control their persons, property, and earnings, and for their right to vote, began with the Seneca Falls Convention in 1848. At that time, Elizabeth Cady Stanton in her "Declaration of Sentiments" used the language of the American colonists' *Declaration of Independence* to criticize society's treatment of women. The argument for women's suffrage was a strong one: Without women's franchise there was no democracy.

The term *feminist* came into use in the United States around 1910, when women from a wide spectrum of new political groups, including blacks, immigrants, radicals, and college students, joined the suffrage movement. They had a broader vision for women than the acquisition of the vote, and feminism thus became associated with the introduction of a wider range of activities and with greater militancy. In the words of Charlotte Perkins-Gilman (1860–1935), the word *feminism* came to denote "the social awakening of women of all the world." But after women in the United States won the vote in 1920 the women's movement waned; the first Equal Rights Amendment (ERA), introduced by Alice Paul in 1923, failed to pass, leaving in abeyance other hoped-for reforms.

In the 1960s, feminism reappeared in many countries. As with the previous women's movement, the new feminism criticized major social institutions such as government, the economy, and education. But what distinguished this movement was feminists' challenge to the organization of so-called "personal life": marriage, family, and sexuality. "The personal is political" became a commonly espoused slogan.

In both North America and Europe, two forms of the new feminism emerged among educated middle-class women. In 1961 in the United States, President Kennedy established a national commission on the status of women, which documented women's second-class status. Although short-lived, it spawned fifty state commissions whose members soon found themselves dissatisfied with the progress on their recommendations and so joined with Betty Friedan to found NOW (National Organization for Women) under the slogan "full equality for women in a truly equal partnership with men." In 1967 they published their demands in a "Bill of Rights." Women in NOW tended to be politically moderate professional women with a strong pragmatic streak and little concern for ideology.

The second branch of the new U.S. women's movement was made up of younger women from other "radical" movements, such as civil rights and the effort to end the war in Vietnam. These women were suspicious of a feminism that dealt only with women's civil and political rights; the term "women's liberation" proclaimed their bolder emancipatory goal. They eschewed hierarchical organizations and favored small consensus-building groups.

Debates among these two branches centered on women's subordination, its relationship to capitalism and to normative heterosexuality. Early on, U.S. feminism discovered the significance of lesbianism, both in NOW and in the more informal grass roots organizations, for many lesbians were active feminists and leaders in the women's movement. It was obvious that lesbians were women who had "chosen" differently, and how they were treated was a measure of society's tolerance for any woman who differed from male notions of what women are, or who chose something other than the usual "homogenization" of the American woman into housewife and mother.

In the 1970s the concept of "gender" was developed by feminists as a means for drawing a distinction between the social situation of women and men in contrast to their biological differences. The distinction between gender and biological sex allowed feminists to recognize that the position of women as "gendered" subjects in society has varied across times and cultures. Shulamith Firestone wrote in *The Dialect of Sex* that male dominance "was so deep as to be invisible"; formulating the category of gender and separating it from sex was a significant breakthrough because it revealed male dominance in areas never before acknowledged. Recognizing the ways in which gender orders virtually everything in both private and public, symbolic and material, human life, including human thought and imagination, has continued to offer remarkable insights. Some of the most provocative analyses of male supremacy can be found in the early work of Shulamith Firestone, Ti-Grace Atkinson, and Kate Millett.

During the 1980s, dramatic shifts occurred in feminism in North America, because of the criticisms from black women who were justifiably angry at the ways in which white women overgeneralized from their own experiences when talking about women's oppression. In the early stages of the Women's Liberation Movement, women met in small "consciousness-raising groups" to discuss with one another their own experiences, perceptions, and feelings about matters hitherto presumed to be private, secret, or taboo. With consciousness-raising, feminists found a general method with which to critically reconstruct the meaning of women's collective social experience in their own terms from a shared perspective inside of that experience. However, as white feminists came to discover, this method soon confronted the "not me problem," in which whole groups of women claimed that the experiences described by white, middle-class, North American women did not match their own experiences. For example, some black women perceived feminism as a "white thing" because white feminists' critiques of the family and their idealizations of paid work were genuinely at odds with the lived experience of most black women.

Black women and other women of color, as well as lesbians, Jewish women, Native American women, and older women, challenged white feminists on their tendency to speak of women as a unified group, or a discrete category, and to analyze gender in isolation from other systems of oppression. Subsequently, "identity politics" has emerged as a means for ensuring that particular groups of women with distinct needs and diverse views are not ignored or overruled by others in positions of greater privilege. Thus, within late-twentieth-century feminism conflicts have arisen over who has the power to speak for women as a group, and disagreement has intensified about the meaning of feminism. As a result of these conflicts, feminists have come to appreciate the ways in which race, ethnicity, class, sexuality, and a host of other variables are indissolubly linked in the construction of women's experience and in the structures of domination.

Although the term *women* as a category or class is invoked politically by feminists, recognition is also given to our need to be clear about who is being labeled and for what purposes. With this recognition comes an expression and redefinition of feminist theory. Having begun to wrestle with the paradox that people may simultaneously be victims of one system of domination and agents of another, some feminists now define the concerns of feminism to encompass opposition to all forms of domination. Consider bell hooks's inclusive definition: "Feminism is a commitment to eradicating the ideology of domination that permeates Western culture on various levels—sex, race, class to name a few—and a commitment to reorganizing . . . society, so that the self-development of people can take precedence over imperialism, economic expansion and material desires."

And yet radical feminists keep insisting that feminism itself becomes at risk if it does not put women first, if it does not focus on the effects of race and class on women. Perhaps more than others, radical feminists have focused on the pervasiveness of violence in women's lives, including the fact that the violence is by men from all classes and races. Calling attention to endemic misogyny, they argue that feminism risks losing its practical effectiveness as well as its theoretical integrity if we abandon what Andrea Dworkin calls the "firm, unsentimental, continuous recognition that women are a class having a common condition."

Most advocates continue to use the term *feminism* to highlight women's specific oppression in relation to men. Along with women's concerns about all the other unequal relationships in society, there remains a strong impulse to see women's struggles against oppressive gender relationships as the core of feminism.

In addition to, and partly because of, doubts about the viability of the category called *women*, new skepticism has arisen within late-twentieth-century North American feminism concerning the role and even the possibility of theory. Feminist theory was initially thought to be an arm of the women's movement, but with the recognition of biases inherent in previous feminist theories, and with the acceptance of

F

European postmodern insights, there has arisen a cynicism about any theory aimed at producing broad generalizations and comprehensive social analyses. Postmodern feminism does not aim at authoritative accounts of women's subordination or emancipation, but rather has shifted from general foundational issues to more specific, detailed, and local analyses of the way in which gender entwines with other systems of domination. The problem of how to create feminist theory that reflects the reality of women and avoids a monolithic view of women remains unresolved. The task is both to maintain the category *women* and at the same time embrace the differences within this category.

The test for a feminist theory used to be: Does this help in the liberation of women? Now it seems to be: Does this reflect female experience? When one combines the second criterion with postmodernists' emphasis upon differences, it is easy to understand Virginia Held's concern that postmodern feminism is in danger of being caught in a "fragmentation that may dissipate the concentrated effort needed to strive for liberation." Furthermore, when postmodernists emphasize the belief that theorizing is political activity, many feminist activists become wary. They worry that the idea of theory as politics might replace other kinds of activism. Feminist activists point out that redescribing and creating new meaning in theory is not enough to stop battering, promote reproductive freedom, or end child abuse.

Feminism since the 1960s has been characterized by intense political activity. Feminists in the United States and Canada have raised public awareness about the amount of domestic violence directed at women and the prevalence of sexual abuse of girls. Feminists have developed health services for women, shelters for battered women, and rape crisis centers. They are responsible for identifying, naming, and urging criminal prosecution of sexual harassment, rape within marriage, and wife beating. They have persuaded law enforcement officers to adopt new guidelines for investigating violence against women, and they have challenged the law's punitive stance toward victims of rape and domestic violence.

Feminists have also directed considerable attention to pornography and violence against women and have worked to diminish the denigration of women in the mass media. Feminists who see abortion rights as central to women's self-determination have achieved decriminalization of abortion, and they continue efforts to keep issues associated with reproductive freedom before the public. They have lobbied to have safe, affordable, quality day care available for working mothers.

The alliances of straight and lesbian women within the women's movement and the feminist critique of compulsory heterosexuality have helped eliminate the stigma attached to women remaining single and have made it easier for lesbians and gay men to acknowledge their sexuality openly. Feminist rethinking of sexuality and gender roles has led to more open cultural definitions of maleness and femaleness in North America. Feminists have also worked to create at least some pockets of women-friendly culture; they have established women's presses, book stores, women's journals, magazines and newspapers, women's art galleries and music festivals.

Since 1960 in the United States and Canada, great numbers of women hold political office and a wide range of other jobs in fields traditionally limited to men. In order to tackle the wage gap between women and men, U.S. feminists pioneered the concept of comparable worth for jobs of equal skill and expertise. The numbers of women in professional occupations and those attending professional and graduate schools has risen dramatically.

Although what we call modern feminism may have originated in the countries of the industrialized West, no country has failed to feel its influence. Like the earlier struggle for women's suffrage, feminism has grown into a self-consciously international political movement. For example, in 1985, at the United Nations World Conference in Nairobi, Kenya, attended by many women of color from the West, and by Third World women, conference delegates unanimously passed a resolution on goals for the next twenty-five years. Among the resolutions were those calling for flexible working hours, government-funded child care centers, minimum wage standards, as well as a resolution asking Third World governments to construct wells, dams, and boreholes to "relieve the burden placed on women by the task of fetching water."

All over the world feminists have organized in factories, supported women on picket lines, helped print and distribute leaflets, publicized conditions at work and in peasant communities, established health services for women, and disseminated ideas through magazines, radio, and television. Women's centers have been set up in the Third World, countries such as India, Sri Lanka, Mexico, Peru, and the Philippines. Feminists have campaigned for the garment workers in Mexico, and in Mauritius they have challenged multinational capital in the free trade zones. In India, for instance in Bombay, Calcutta, and Bahir, there have been several joint conferences and meetings at which feminists and working-class and rural peasant women have come together to discuss rape, health, religion, and communalism. In Korea, where rapid industrialization has worsened social problems, feminists have helped to create service groups and community projects.

Even when women's protests and collective actions to seek access to social resources have not been initiated by feminism, women worldwide have found through feminism a language for redefining the scope of politics. And feminists better understand the range of particular issues and the varying forms of struggle for women. For example, in the United States comparable worth is a policy needed for economic independence for women; in African countries it may be more urgent to organize against brideprice; in India against bride-burning; and in the Philippines, South Korea, and Thailand against the international trafficking of women in sex tourism. In the nations of the Persian Gulf, women still lack the vote, and in Central America, more Latin American women work in domestic servant jobs than in any other type of employed labor. Feminism with a global perspective has also required women in industrialized countries to understand the global implications of our actions. For example, our fight to have an unsafe birth-control device banned in the United States must include a demand that it be destroyed rather than dumped on women in the Third World.

Education

Feminism in the Anglo-American world has brought significant changes to education. Although there remains much to be accomplished, in Canada, England, the United States, and Australia there have been profound, insightful critiques and some reforms of educational institutions as well as of educational policy and practice. Feminist scholars have critiqued traditional white-male dominated frameworks, contributed to the disciplines, and created new fields of study. The formation of women's caucuses in most professional academic societies, and the adoption of women's studies into the university curriculum along with an increase in numbers of women faculty and administrators have "disturbed if not dislodged" the patterns of power and privilege in higher education. There is now a voluminous literature on gender and education, along with a noteworthy start on work in philosophy of education.

In North American philosophy of education, a developed feminist perspective was first introduced at the beginning of the 1980s when Jane Roland Martin began to report on her answers to two fundamental questions: "What is the place of women in education?" and "What happens to educational thought when women are brought into it?" Since then, in her books *Changing the Educational Landscape* and *The Schoolhome*, Martin has pursued the questions of how the field of philosophy of education and the nature of schooling might be redefined to include women's experiences, women's values, activities, and social responsibilities. Along similar lines, Nel Noddings, another feminist philosopher of education, argues in *The Challenge to Care in Schools* for a restructuring of education based on an ethic of caring, born out of women's maternal practice and feminist consciousness. These and other feminist publications have changed the face of philosophy of education.

Barbara Houston

See also GENDER AND SEXISM; GIRLS AND WOMEN, EDUCATION OF; HOME AND FAMILY; MODERNISM AND POST-MODERNISM; WOLLSTONECRAFT

Bibliography
Anzaldua, Gloria, ed. *Creative and Critical Perspectives by Women of Color*. San Francisco: Aunt Lute Foundation Books, 1990.
———. *Making Face, Making Soul*. San Francisco: Aunt Lute Foundation Books, 1990.
Collins, Patricia Hill. *Black Feminist Thought: Knowledge, Consciousness and the Politics of Empowerment*. Boston: Unwin Hyman, 1990.
Ford, Maureen. "Being in the Know(n): The Implications of Situated Knowledges for Education." Ph.D. diss., Ontario Institute for Studies in Education, 1994.
Freeman, Jo. *The Politics of Women's Liberation*. New York: Longman, 1975.

Frye, Marilyn. *The Politics of Reality: Essays in Feminist Theory*. Trumansburg, N.Y.: Crossing Press, 1983.

Grant, Judith. *Fundamental Feminism*. New York and London: Routledge, 1993.

Held, Virginia. *Feminist Morality*. Chicago and London: University of Chicago Press, 1993.

hooks, bell. *Feminist Theory: From Margin to Center*. Boston: South End Press, 1984.

Jagger, Alison, and Paula Rothenberg, eds. *Feminist Frameworks: Alternative Theoretical Accounts of the Relations between Women and Men*. New York: McGraw Hill, 1978. 3rd ed., 1993.

Kramarae, Cheris, and Dale Spender, eds. *The Knowledge Explosion: Generations of Feminist Scholarship*. New York: Teachers College Press, 1992.

————, and Paula Treichler, eds. *Amazons, Bluestockings and Crones: A Feminist Dictionary*. London: Pandora Press, 1985. 2nd ed., 1992.

Mackinnon, Catherine. *Toward a Feminist Theory of the State*. Cambridge: Harvard University Press, 1989.

Martin, Jane Roland. *Reclaiming a Conversation*. New Haven and London: Yale University Press, 1985.

Mitchell, Juliet, and Ann Oakley. *What Is Feminism?* New York: Random House, 1986.

Mohanty, Chandra Talpade, Ann Russon, and Lourdes Torres, eds. *Third World Women and the Politics of Feminism*. Bloomington and Indianapolis: University of Indiana Press, 1991.

Nicholson, Linda, ed. *Feminism/Postmodernism*. New York and London: Routledge, 1990.

Noddings, Nel. *The Challenge to Care in Schools*. New York: Teachers College Press, 1992.

Rowbotham, Sheila. *Women in Movement: Feminism and Social Action*. New York: Routledge, 1992.

Stone, Lynda, ed. *The Education Feminism Reader*. New York and London: Routledge, 1994.

Formalism

Formalism is the view that theoretical information about an object, or practical guidance about how to treat it, is to be derived from attention to its form rather than its matter or content. The idea originates in ancient Greek metaphysics. Plato (c. 427–347 B.C.) argued that to understand an object is to graph the forms in which it "participates." Aristotle (384–322 B.C.) developed this theory by contrasting the form of an object to its matter. In Aristotle's account, the form of an object is its functional construction, the arrangement of the matter or parts that enable it to serve its purpose or engage in those activities that are essential to it. The members of a species all have the same form, while each individual has its own particular matter.

An area of study is therefore "formal" to the extent that it focuses on the structural and functional properties that instances of a type have in common and derives its conclusions from those alone. Logic and mathematics, for example, are considered formal because they are concerned with the way certain forms of argument and calculation work, without regard to what those arguments or calculations are about.

In other areas the appropriateness of formalistic thinking is more controversial, and in modern philosophy a debate has arisen about formalism in ethics. Most people agree that there is a formal aspect to the idea of justice. Justice demands that we "treat like cases alike" and "treat equals as equals." But philosophers disagree about the extent to which any practical guidance can be derived from such formal considerations, and about the appropriateness of appealing to them in other areas of ethical life.

The debate began with criticisms leveled by G.W.F. Hegel (1770–1831) at the philosophy of Immanuel Kant (1724–1804). Kant argued that in order to determine whether an action is right, we should attend to the form of the "maxim" or principle on which the agent proposes to act. The categorical imperative tells us to act only on maxims that can serve as universal laws. Suppose an agent proposes to perform a certain action in order to realize a certain end. We should ask whether everyone with this end could rationally act on this maxim. Some maxims would be contradictory or self-defeating if everyone acted on them, and those are ruled out by morality. Since the question is whether the action and the purpose, the "matter" of the maxim, can be combined in a principle that can function as a universal law, it is a question about the maxim's functional construction—in the Aristotelian sense, its form.

Debates about the formalism of this procedure for testing maxims arise at two levels. First, questions may be raised about whether the categorical imperative really is a formal principle. Kant claimed that maxims must have the form of a law, but his procedure seems to require that maxims have the form of a law for human beings who live together in community. This additional specification might be thought of as an appeal to content. Relatedly, questions are raised about whether a purely formal principle can have any determinate application. Hegel and his followers argued that the categorical imperative is an "empty formalism" that by itself tells us nothing about what we ought to do. The procedure fails to rule out any maxims, or fails to sort maxims correctly. In contemporary philosophy, feminists and communitarians have echoed these criticisms, arguing that in concrete ethical situations the important question is not what any human being ought to do, but what a member of a particular community or family or a particular person's friend ought to do. Attention to particular content is necessary. Kantians deny that these are objections: In assuming that there are certain ways in which friends, family members, or community members as such ought to act, the critics are implicitly relying on formal and universal considerations. The debate about the extent to which formal considerations govern ethical thinking thus remains unsettled.

Christine M. Korsgaard

See also ARISTOTLE; FEMINISM; HEGEL; JUSTICE; KANT

Bibliography

Aristotle. *Physics; Metaphysics; On the Soul.* In *The Complete Works of Aristotle: The Revised Oxford Translation,* edited by Jonathan Barnes. 2 vols. Princeton: Princeton University Press, 1984.
Gilligan, Carol. *In a Different Voice: Psychological Theory and Women's Development.* Cambridge: Harvard University Press, 1982.
Hegel, G.W.F. *Elements of the Philosophy of Right.* Translated by H.B. Nisbet. Edited by Allen W. Wood. Cambridge: Cambridge University Press, 1991.
Kant, Immanuel. *Critique of Practical Reason.* Translated by Lewis White Beck. Indianapolis, Ind.: Library of Liberal Arts, 1956.
———. *Foundations of the Metaphysics of Morals.* Translated by Lewis White Beck. Indianapolis, Ind.: Library of Liberal Arts, 1959.
Korsgaard, Christine M. "Kant's Formula of Universal Law." *Pacific Philosophical Quarterly* 66 (1985): 24–47.
Sandel, Michael. *Liberalism and the Limits of Justice.* Cambridge: Cambridge University Press, 1982.

F

Franklin, Benjamin (1706–1790)

"He seized the lightning from the skies and the scepter from the tyrants," says the epigram attributed to Baron de l'Aulne Turgot, stating Franklin's most celebrated accomplishments. His scientific studies of electrical phenomena and the technological application of those experiments, specifically his invention and promotion of the lightning rod, brought him fame both in America and in Europe. His leadership in the struggle of the British colonies in North America to throw off British rule, serving as minister to France from the united colonies, later the United States, brought him further honors. To Europeans of enlightened temper, Franklin appeared to be the perfect reflection of right reason and natural law, of political freedom and equality in the American style.

Over a long life, Franklin reached well beyond science and statesmanship to contribute as a worldly philosopher in many areas of activity. Born in Boston to the family of a small tradesman, he failed in successive efforts to acquire a degree of formal education and was put as an apprentice in the printing trade. Still in his youth, Franklin moved to Philadelphia, a livelier and more expansive city, where within a few years he managed to establish himself in his own printing business, a secure, prosperous base that enabled him to pursue various "philosophic" and community projects. He developed, for example, a fire company, the first in the city, a free public lending library, a coffee house club called the Junto that brought together young businessmen of the city for discussion of moral and philosophical issues, and other similar improvement efforts. These projects both benefited the community and secured Franklin's position as a leading citizen of Philadelphia. He was indeed a master at linking his private and often profitable initiatives with what he perceived as the public good. In time, his projects expanded to include the British colonies at large. He initiated the American Philosophical Society as the Junto on an expanded scale, he created a postal service for the American colonies, and he wrote and published a vastly popular almanac, *Poor Richard's,* which publicized his varied researches and inventions, from the smokeless fireplace to the lightning rod. His studies in electricity and his statesmanship in behalf of the newly declared United States brought him in time to international prominence.

One of Franklin's particular interests was in the formal education of the young, an interest arising no doubt in part from his own failed experience with the narrowly bounded classical curriculum of the existing institutions, but deriving as well from his understanding of the "realist" theories of John Locke (1632–1704) and the several Commonwealth educators in England. Franklin's "invention" in this arena was the English School, part of his 1749 proposals to create the Philadelphia Academy. He proposed that the new academy be composed of two branches of equal status, the Classical School and the English School. The one was to offer schooling in the grammar, rhetoric, and logic of the classical, Latin tradition, in preparation for college and the learned professions. The other was to include much of the same curriculum, but instruction was to be not in Latin but in English, thereby saving instructional time enormously and allowing a wide expansion of curriculum in preparing young persons for varied trades and professions. Franklin's oft-quoted explanation is from the *Proposals* (Labaree: 3, 404): "As to their Studies, it would be well if they could be taught every Thing that is useful, and every Thing that is ornamental: But Art is long, and their Time is short. It is therefore propos'd that they learn those Things that are likely to be most useful and most ornamental. Regard being had to the several Professions for which they are intended." The English School revisions in curriculum were fundamental: The study of Latin, no longer the frame of the curriculum, became "ornamental"; the study of poetry (in English) would be justified only in that it was useful in the grasp of grammar and structure of language; introduction of applied mathematics, scientific studies, and modern languages was justifiable in that these areas of study could contribute to such vocational work as surveying, accounting, navigation, gardening, teaching, and a range of other trades and professions.

To Franklin and to an emerging middle class of farmers and business people as well, the academy was ultimately the "public" school: It was open to all who could pay the tuition fee, without religious or residence strictures, for study in whatever curriculum might be determined by the student to be directly useful. The academy's English School, with its varied and flexible curriculum, institutionalized individual initiative and celebrated the will to achieve success in schooling and in life. In Franklin's view, schooling that could aid and advance the success of the individual was fundamental to ensuring the prosperity, the moral and social betterment of society at large. In a 1750 letter to Dr. Samuel Johnson, Franklin summarized these views: "I think with you, that nothing is of more importance for the public weal, than to form and train up youth in wisdom and virtue. Wise and good men are, in my opinion, the strength of a state; much more so than riches or arms" (Labaree: 4, 41). The advancement of learning, in Franklin's enlightened view, provided the basis of civic strength, the means of moral betterment and, thereby, the possibility of human progress.

John Hardin Best

See also JEFFERSON; LOCKE; VOCATIONAL EDUCATION

Bibliography

Best, John Hardin, ed. *Benjamin Franklin on Education.* New York: Teachers College, Columbia University, 1962.

Crane, Verner W. *Benjamin Franklin and a Rising People.* Boston: Little, Brown, 1954.

Franklin, Benjamin. *The Autobiography of Benjamin Franklin.* Edited by L.P. Masur. Boston: St. Martin's Press, 1993.

———. *The Papers of Benjamin Franklin.* Edited by L.W. Labaree et al. 30 vols. New Haven: Yale University Press, 1959.

Van Doren, Carl. *Benjamin Franklin.* New York: Viking Press, 1938.

Freedom and Determinism

Determinism is the theory that all events are wholly determined by previous causes. The universe is assumed to be rational and orderly. Hence, complete knowledge of the present would give total knowledge of the future. Since human choices are determined in advance, the individual could not have acted otherwise and free will is precluded. Indeterminism, on the other hand, accepts the existence and influence of external forces on human beings but maintains that we have the power to choose freely among alternatives and to act independently of restraints, thus retaining an area of freedom of choice.

Which theory one adheres to has substantial implications for one's position on major issues of ethics, morality, and educational practice. Determinists sometimes claim that determinism can be seen as compatible with moral responsibility because evil consequences of actions can be foreseen and this brings a deterrent effect that influences behavior. But they would deny the reality of free choice because motive and volition are completely caused by preceding forces. Adherents to theories of free will and human freedom would maintain that we have the ability to make voluntary ethical choices, such as choosing between right and wrong, good and bad, better and worse. The evidence they would educe to support their beliefs would include the subjective experience of freedom, the existence of feelings of guilt (indicating that one could have acted otherwise), and the notion of responsibility for personal action inherent in law, rewards, punishments, and incentives.

All of the major religions have wrestled with this difficult issue concerning human morality. At one end of the spectrum of belief lies fatalism, the belief that all events are ineluctably predetermined, that nothing we can do can affect their course in any way, and that it is appropriate to accept submissively all that happens. Fatalism is more common in eras or places where people feel themselves to be relatively powerless to control their destinies. It usually declines when people begin to feel able to exercise control over their environment and, consequently, to control their fate. Many religions and systems of faith include a belief in Fate (ancient Greeks), Fortune (ancient Romans), Kismet (Islam), or Karma (Hinduism and Buddhism)—that a force or power stronger than the human will determines the nature and quality of our lives and choices.

In Christianity, the doctrine of predestination has been in existence since the writings of St. Paul, but it received its most rigorous exposition at the hands of John Calvin (1509–1564). According to this doctrine, we are destined before birth for damnation or salvation. Nothing we do can alter this decision. Thus we are incapable of saving ourselves by our own efforts and must depend for redemption on God's grace. The doctrine effectively undermined the ability of the medieval Church to profit from good "works" like penances and indulgences, but it also complicated the issue of personal freedom and responsibility. If we are totally dependent on God's will and grace, how can we be held personally responsible for our own acts? Although the strict Calvinist notion of predestination has largely disappeared from Christian theology, its legacy remains in a variety of forms, especially in Puritan influences on North America.

The idea of the omnipotence of God casts doubt on our ability to act out of personal freedom. The idea of the omniscience of God implies that God knows all events before they occur, with the consequence that it is difficult to believe in the freedom to decide when all such decisions have already been foreseen by God. The doctrine of divine grace implies an active intervention by God into human affairs, thus casting doubt upon our control over what we suppose are our own choices and decisions. The seventeenth-century Jewish rationalist philosopher Benedict de Spinoza (1632–1677) maintained that human freedom is an impossible idea because God is identical with the world, which is necessary in all its parts. The sense of freedom that humans hold, he insisted, is due to their ignorance of the determining causes of their actions.

The major monotheistic religions (Judaism, Christianity, Islam), after many theological struggles, eventually came to the position that evil originates not with God but from the improper use of freedom by created beings. For St. Augustine (354–430), we were created in the image of God and given the gift of reason, which provides us with free will and the burden of accepting responsibility for our actions. Christian theologians suggest that, in the Bible (Genesis, chapter 3), the story of the Fall portrays man and woman trying out their freedom, committing a free act against the God who had given them the freedom to rebel. It was the creation by God of humans in His own image that invested them with the gift of nobility and freedom.

The major world religions (Hinduism, Buddhism, Judaism, Christianity, Islam) now make room in their belief system for human freedom, if sometimes only at the level of paradox. Usually it takes the form that God's omniscience covers the natural world but allows space for individual human freedom and free will, so that we are personally responsible for our actions.

The belief that we can make free choices and decisions that cannot be determined in advance has been challenged in the past by scientific determinism. Newtonian physics saw the universe as a vast machine operating according to deterministic laws of strict causality. According to classical mechanics, all events, including human acts and choices, are conditioned by a continuously linked chain of cause and effect. Natural law determines the behavior of every element of nature, including human nature. The future is totally determined by the present.

The French mathematician and astronomer Pierre-Simon, marquis de Laplace (1749–1827), created a classical version of deterministic theory with his "mathematical demon." This would be an infinitely intelligent computing machine, which would be able to know the precise position and velocity of every particle in the universe at a particular moment. Since the present state of affairs is the effect of the previous state and the cause of the state that follows, if one could know all the forces and positions of all components of the present, one could predict the future with certainty.

However, in 1927, the German physicist Werner Heisenberg (1901–1976) formulated the Indeterminacy Principle, which maintains that it is impossible to determine both the position and velocity of a particle simultaneously. The Indeterminacy Principle destroyed the conditions necessary for Laplace's demon to operate and effectively replaced classical mechanics with quantum mechanics. The orthodox version of quantum mechanics became known as the Copenhagen interpretation, named after the city where Niels Bohr (1885–1962), its chief protagonist, worked. According to Bohr, indeterminacy in nature is fundamental and not due to the inadequacy of scientific knowledge or measuring tools. Indeterminacy implies intrinsic randomness. Quantum mechanics showed that a particle can move in any of a number of ways. With a large number of particles one can predict statistically what proportion will move in a particular way, but one cannot predict the path for any single particle. Analogously, insurance companies use life-expectancy tables to predict accurately the death rates of various groups of people, but they lack the ability to predict when you or I will die. Modern scientists are now typically more modest than their predecessors about their ability to predict the future.

Evidence from the social sciences has also influenced our views on the issues of human freedom and determinism. Eighteenth-century confidence in human rationality and in our ability to solve our personal and social problems through reason and intellectual inquiry was shaken in the nineteenth and twentieth centuries by developments in psychology and psychiatry that demonstrated the power of our irrational side and our unconscious mind to affect our choices, decisions, and acts. In the early twentieth century, Sigmund Freud (1856–1939), the founder of psychoanalysis, examined a number of neurotic patients with physical symptoms. He adopted a position of multiple causation. He accepted the theory of scientific determinism but suggested that the causes of these conditions were multiple rather than single, including some unconscious psychological processes. Psychiatric evidence shows that, although we like to believe that we are the rational, conscious masters of our decisions and fate, we are often the virtual slaves of unrecognized and hence powerful unconscious forces.

Psychological and sociological studies in this century have shown the power of early life experiences and home and environmental conditions to form children's personalities and abilities, and hence largely to determine the choices, decisions, and paths they will follow in later life. The theory of behaviorism, developed in the early decades of this century, cast doubt on the idea of an autonomous, self-determining human being and emphasized the importance of antecedent stimulus conditions in determining a person's responses. The work of Ivan Pavlov (1849–1936) and J.B. Watson (1878–1958) on conditioning and of E.L. Thorndike (1874–1947) and B.F. Skinner (1904–1990) on stimulus-response connections helped to create a point of view that saw all behavior as the inevitable product of external stimuli. If everything we do is caused by forces outside ourselves, why should we be held personally accountable for our acts or feel guilty for our misdemeanors?

Some philosophers, however, maintain that causality for a human being is fundamentally different from that for other objects in nature, and that intentional action is quite different from behavior determined from without. William James (1842–1910), the American pragmatist philosopher, to some extent manifested this in his own behavior. In 1869–1870 he was very depressed and ill; he found relief by reading Charles-Bernard Renouvier (1815–1903), the Kantian philosopher, on free will. James decided that his first act of free will would be to believe in free will. He abandoned determinisms of all kind, scientific and theological. In fact, his subsequent professional life, achievements, and viewpoints were substantially affected by this solution to his personal problem.

One of the chief claims of existentialist philosophers has been that we are free to choose and that we *must* choose. The existential predicament is that we are condemned to choose and to bear responsibility for our choices. We cannot escape the situation by inaction, for to fail to make a decision still involves choice and responsibility. To fail to decide is, in effect, to choose the status quo. In the view of Jean-Paul Sartre (1905–1980), we have no essential nature apart from our existence—that is, apart from the existential choices and decisions we make from day to day. We make ourselves through our free choices. We become what we will. Moreover, our choices affect others, and hence for this we must carry responsibility. Sartre insisted that we must surmount obstacles to freedom and our own limitations by acts of conscious decision. It is through such acts of freedom, he maintained, that people achieve authenticity.

All human behavior is caused by certain forces: the laws of nature (such as gravity), one's personal history, environmental conditions, and so on. But not all causes compel us to act in a certain way. They may be necessary but not sufficient conditions for the result to follow. Only a sufficient cause compels an effect. Causal explanations can suffice when we refer to things that *happen* to us. But they are only necessary and insufficient explanations when we refer to deliberate human choices and decisions, where responsibility, blame, praise, reward, and punishment are considered appropriate. When we act deliberately, in an attempt to achieve a particular purpose, our behavior can be judged by moral criteria. Such behavior cannot be fully explained in naturalistic terms, which refer only to necessary conditions (such as the existence of a brain).

Attempts to explain fully the causes of human conduct are hampered by predictive ignorance and posterior ignorance. First, we have no scientific laws that enable us to predict with certainty what any individual person (as opposed to groups) will do in any situation. Because of our inability to describe a person fully in present space and time, infallible prediction is impossible. Second, our present psychological and sociological knowledge is inadequate to fully explain, even after exhaustive study, why a person acted in a particular way. Thus the ideas of human freedom and regular causation of human events can coexist.

There can be little question that human freedom, if it exists, is limited. What we choose is usually a function of who we are; and who we are is largely a result of what has happened to us. The fact that we must make a special effort to overcome the effects of heredity, environment, and our basic impulses, shows that we are not free from their influence. Moreover, we are often unfree even when we believe we are free. We may, for example, believe we are free merely because we do not want to do something that, in the event, we would be unable to do. Or we may feel free because we have a false belief in our power to achieve our desire, either because we overestimate our capacities or means, or because we are ignorant of obstacles to the achievement of our intentions.

Our limited freedom was described by Alexis de Tocqueville (1805–1859): "Around every man a fatal circle is traced, beyond which he cannot pass." But, he added: "Within the wide verge of that circle he is powerful and free" (*Democracy in America*: 317). Alcoholism is evidence of human limitation. The alcoholic is enslaved by the power of the compulsion. But Alcoholics Anonymous is evidence of the existence of human freedom. Alcoholics who were unfree have, through personal efforts and the support of others, regained a measure of freedom, even though it is a freedom maintained tenuously, against the constant danger of a reversion to a former state of compulsion.

We are least free when we are purposeless, or when our actions do not reflect our purposes, or when we fail to carry out our purpose through inattention, ignorance, or the pursuit of incompatible goals. We are most free when the ends we pursue have our wholehearted support and when these ends represent long-term goals, the products of mature reflection.

Educational philosophy and practice are affected by the views people hold of freedom and determinism. One of the common goals of education is to help people to learn more about themselves. Growth in self-knowledge helps us to exercise our freedoms. As we become more aware of the factors in our personal history that have affected our development, of the urges within us and the restrictions society would place on those urges, of the limitations laid upon us by our membership in various social, religious, racial, national, and cultural groups, and of the impact of our diverse talents and deficiencies, we become more able to use this knowledge to operate effectively within our circle of freedom. As we advance in self-knowledge, we are better able to perceive what we can and cannot do. Illusions of power lead to disillusionment and subsequent passivity. Illusions of impotence lead to an underassumption of responsibility. Self-knowledge also helps to save us from the rationalizations that permit us to slough off appropriate responsibilities. It is tempting to focus on abstract problems or distant causes, on which it is impossible for us to take action, instead of on problems that are near to us or to which we could make a difference. But this tempting path leads to complacency, inertia, and the loss of responsibility.

Education for freedom should include the opportunity to gain knowledge of the physical, social, economic, and other forces that exercise restraint and influence over us. If we have knowledge of the laws of nature we can anticipate the consequences of acting in certain ways and can thus guide events, to a degree, to desired outcomes. For example, we are all, on earth, subject to the impact of the law of gravity. But knowledge of its workings can alter its effects on us. We can, for example, design, build, and experience the freedom of flying in airplanes, which do not ignore the law of gravity but operate within and under its control. Knowledge of the deterministic power of nature can thus open up new dimensions of freedom.

Discussions of determinism and freedom have frequently tried to deal with the issues of justice and punishment. The notion of free will has often been tied to the concept of justice. If all is determined by God or some irresistible force, it would be unjust to punish or hold one responsible for harmful behavior, such as injuring another person. It is therefore held that justice demands notions of human responsibility, human power of personal action, and human freedom.

However, determinists may advocate and defend punishment on grounds of deterrence or restraint. According to deterrence theory, the wrongdoer, although not personally responsible, can be used as an example to deter others who might be tempted to commit the same crime. According to restraint theory, the individual can be forcibly restrained, by isolation or imprisonment, in order to protect others. In both cases, the individual, though not culpable, is sacrificed for the perceived good of the group.

It is not just—as opposed to lawful—to punish wrongdoers unless they have freely done wrong and could have acted otherwise. Only a believer in human freedom can punish with justice. A person of impaired mental capacity may escape punishment for what would normally be considered a criminal action and may instead be committed for treatment. Georg W.F. Hegel (1770–1831) considered punishment to be the criminal's right and privilege, because it showed that the latter was being honored as a rational and responsible being.

Issues of justice and punishment need to be considered in an atmosphere of proportionality and appropriateness. If we believe in human freedom, we cannot punish people justifiably unless we believe that they acted deliberately, were old enough and sane enough to know what they were doing, knew it to be wrong (or at least had the opportunity to find out that it was wrong), and were not forced to do it. Children, for example, are appropriately held responsible, and punishable, only in proportion to their age, experience, and maturity. Studies of child development reveal the complexity of children's changing views on responsibility, guilt, honor, punishment, lying, loyalty, and so on. These complexities should make us cautious about automatically applying adult standards on these issues to young children.

How we view individual culpability will be affected by our position on freedom of choice. For example, to what extent does a child brought up in an atmosphere of daily violence have alternatives to acting violently? We know that there is a high likelihood that abusers of others have been abused themselves, usually as children. To what extent should they be held responsible?

The argument is made more intractable when people take hard-line free will versus determinism positions. One may alternatively take the position that outside forces are partial causes of my acts—that I am substantially affected and influenced by my birth, upbringing, schooling, rearing, friendships, and the other events of my life. These may limit, enhance, harm, broaden, narrow, or color my actions. However, there can still be room for me to choose among competing values or actions. This is not to say that these choices are free-floating in a chaotic, uncaused universe. But, for all practical purposes, I have a measure, however small, of choice among alternatives. This measure is my freedom and the source of my responsibility.

Paul Nash

See also ACADEMIC FREEDOM; CHILDREN'S RIGHTS; EQUALITY; JUSTICE; RIGHTS

Bibliography

Bergson, Henri. *Time and Free Will* [1910]. Translated by F.L. Pogson. New York: Harper and Row, 1960.

Cranston, Maurice. *Freedom: A New Analysis*. London: Longmans, Green, 1953.

Farrer, Austin. *The Freedom of the Will*. London: Black, 1958.

Kilpatrick, William H. "The Supposed Conflict between Moral Freedom and Scientific Determinism." In *Freedom and Authority in Our Time,* edited by Lyman Bryson, Louis Finkelstein, R.M. MacIver, and Richard P. McKeon, 409–17. New York: Harper, 1953.

Nash, Paul. *Authority and Freedom in Education*. New York: Wiley, 1966.

Planck, Max. *Where Is Science Going?* New York: Norton, 1932.

Pollard, William G. *Chance and Providence: God's Action in a World Governed by Scientific Law*. New York: Scribner's, 1958.

Sartre, Jean-Paul. *Being and Nothingness: An Essay on Phenomenological Ontology*. Translated by Hazel E. Barnes. New York: Philosophical Library, 1956.

Skinner, B.F. *Walden Two*. New York: Macmillan, 1948.

Wild, John. *Existence and the World of Freedom*. Englewood Cliffs, N.J.: Prentice-Hall, 1963.

Freud, Sigmund (1856–1939)

The most influential, controversial figure in the history of psychiatry, his Viennese psychoanalytic school of thought has enormously affected psychological and cultural judgments since the late nineteenth century. Initially trained as a neurologist, his studies of hysteria under Joseph Breuer and hypnosis with Jean-Martin Charcot spurred him to unravel the hidden potency of sexuality and the unconscious in a rather closed Victorian society.

Breuer and Freud have been credited with developing the talking-out technique in psychoanalysis. Freud was also influenced in his theory of psychodynamics by the German physiologist Ernst Brücke, of the Helmholtz School of Medicine. Beginning his own lifelong self-analysis in the 1890s, Freud published his breakthrough book *The Interpretation of Dreams* in 1900. Dream analysis and interpretation of patients' free associations, generated as they reclined on a couch in his consulting room, formed much of the foundation for Freudian therapy. Other important works in explaining his theory of psychoanalysis include *The Psychopathology of Everyday Life* (1901), *General Introductory Lectures on Psycho-Analysis* (1917), *New Introductory Lectures on Psychoanalysis* (1933), and *An Outline of Psychoanalysis* (1940).

In 1908, Freud established the International Psycho-analytical Association. In 1909, he was formally introduced in the United States by G. Stanley Hall, renowned psychologist in child and adolescent studies, who invited him to lecture at Clark University in Worcester, Massachusetts. During the Nazi period, Freud, a Jew, left Austria in 1937 and spent the last two years of his life in London.

In his theories, Freud hypothesized a tripartite division for personality structure: id, ego, and superego. The id represents animallike, aggressive instinctual impulses, largely of an unconscious sexual nature, that form the repository for primary thought process. Id signifies what humans primordially desire to do and is most clearly demonstrable in dreams, fantasies, and the like. Id plays a predominant role in infancy and early childhood, the period Freud considered most critical in one's overall growth. Ego counterbalances the id by serving as a more self-regulating product of secondary, more conscious and rational, thought process. It brings the id under some tenuous executory control, though ego functions are refined only gradually as one matures. Most significant for moral development is the role of the superego—the inhibiting, prohibiting standards imposed, initially and primarily, by one's parents and later by teachers and other significant external authorities. If the child is to be "normal" and "adjusted," her superego should develop a healthy ego-ideal and conscience through struggles with guilt and repression. A substantial level of repression is necessary to transform id impulses into more socially acceptable behavior (sublimation). However, in Freudian theory psychic balance is always crucial, in that excessive guilt and repression might lead to neurotic, even psychotic, behavior. Freud also posited a psychosexual stage theory of development in which psychological problems need to be resolved at each stage in order to maintain personality structure.

F

On a broader level, Freud was vitally interested in balancing the often irreconcilable demands of individual versus social life. He points to an optimal realization of self-control through the medium of repression, which modulates personal autonomy and cultural constraints. The term *repression* is used to express that most general, largely unconscious, defense mechanism that enables human beings to keep out of consciousness those thoughts, wishes, and desires too dangerous to conscious mental processes. A form of repression referred to as sublimation is that defense mechanism that changes idlike excitations into more socially approved forms of behavior. In Freud's view, sublimation serves to build culture in the form of art, literature, and religion.

Borrowing from classical mythology and dramaturgy, Freud dealt further with morality and sex-role identity by use of the tragedy of Oedipus and Electra. Young boys' castration anxiety and identification with father facilitates their moral development. It is more problematic for young girls to achieve a strong sense of morality, as they do not experience such anxiety. Instead, they develop "penis envy"—a very controversial notion still under severe attack by some less orthodox analysts, both feminist and nonfeminist. In his characterization of female physiology, Freud appeared to extend a *prima facie* case of biological determination and differentiation into an extra-layered, psychological case of surplus-repression. Recently, such developmental psychologists as Carol Gilligan (*In a Different Voice: Psychological Theory and Women's Development*) have questioned Freud's seeming inability to assess women's psychological themes of caring and connectedness as endemic to the traditional individualism in his theory. Freud did admit that women inhabited a "dark continent" in his psychology.

Other critics have leveled a more basic assault on the way in which Freud conceptualized human relations, particularly family structures. They contend that his analysis tends to reduce human relations to the level and pattern of the psyche within the substructure of the nuclear family. In their view, Freud tended to collapse social action so as to picture it as a recapitulation of emotional sets within the psychic frame of the family. As such, according to this critique, he erroneously universalized certain internalized family matrices (such as the Oedipal and Electral complexes), thus disabling him from seeing the full impact of overarching, perhaps more dominant, external social structures of particular times and places (in his case, patriarchal Victorian society).

At the same time, many of Freud's speculative claims deal in intrapsychic phenomena that are seemingly immune to substantial intersubjective public assessment. Relying on notes taken from case studies of individual patients, he observed his subjects under rather uncontrolled conditions and situations. Also, his multiple variables of analysis have been difficult to investigate and corroborate in any thoroughgoing, scientific manner. Thus, replication studies on his original research design have remained rather problematic. Freud himself conjectured that future developments in biochemistry and neurology would amplify the scientific base of psychoanalysis.

Freud's growing pessimism about social change, which became even more pronounced following the massive bloodshed of World War I, forestalled his serious consideration of social reform on a wide scale. He postulated the term *thanatos* as a regressive propensity in organic systems, the aim of which is ultimately death and destruction. Whereas thanatos expresses aggressive instincts, eros signifies the opposite tendency toward life and the sustenance of positive potentials. However, in the Freudian scheme, thanatos and eros are perpetually in conflict and struggle, with the former prevailing in the end. In a related sense, Freud's use of the concepts of sadism and masochism reflected a similar form of explanation. Sadism expressed a union of erotic and aggressive impulses turned outward toward other people, while masochism expressed the merging of those instincts turned against oneself.

For Freud, corporal punishment was a troublesome activity. He claimed that excessive stimulation of the child's buttocks nurtured the erotogenic origins of cruelty. Those children who tended to display cruelty toward playmates and animals typically gained immense sexual gratification in activities associated with the erotogenic zones of the body. Thus, Freud warned against corporal punishment in such instances in particular.

In education, despite a cultural ideology that sought a tenuous balance between liberation and repression, Freud's influence has probably been more visible in the realm of libertarian practices. By uncovering the psychological roots of childhood neurosis, his analysis helped free the child and set the stage for tolerance and acceptance of more permissive educational arrangements. His views especially forged new pathways for discovery in the education of the emotions, creativity, and individuality.

Yet other critics have bemoaned the essential, theoretical egocentrism that seems to have been integral to Freud's psychodynamic system. By focusing on internal, individual, and differential measures of human beings, Freud established a certain set of preconceptions about human nature, human morality, and any possibilities for human change. For example, Lawrence Kohlberg's present-day dominant theory of moral development also attempts to fit humanity into assumed universal thought structures undergirded by such internal, individualistic frames of reference. Fittingly, Kohlberg (*The Philosophy of Moral Development: Moral Stages and the Idea of Justice*) saw himself as a successor to Freud in the broad tradition of psychology.

Innumerable psychologists, psychiatrists, and educators have been greatly influenced by Freud's thought and practice. Two of his earliest disciples, Alfred Adler (1870–1937) and Carl G. Jung (1875–1961) eventually rebelled against their mentor on the grounds that his theory of sexuality was overly deterministic and reductionistic and too dependent on competition, aggression, and biological views of human nature. Adler's Individual Psychology actually emphasized social interest and cooperation, and its proponents established child-guidance clinics throughout the world. Jung's Analytic Psychology focused on self-actualization (a term coined by Jung) through philosophy, religion, and self-analysis.

Other prominent Freudians and neo-Freudians include Wilhelm Fliess, originator of the theory of bisexuality; Sandor Ferenczi, who refined psychoanalytic therapy; Otto Fenichel, who elaborated on psychoanalytic theories of neurosis; Otto Rank, whose will therapy influenced generations of psychiatric social workers; Anna Freud (his daughter) and Melanie Klein, leading British child analysts in the 1940s and 1950s; Harry Stack Sullivan and his theory of interpersonal relations; Erich Fromm, of the Frankfurt school of cultural psychiatry; Wilhelm Reich, controversial psychiatric critic of authoritarianism and repressive politics in the 1930s and 1940s; Heinz Hartmann and Erik H. Erikson, in ego psychology; Ernst Kris, in art therapy; Helene Deutsch and Karen Horney, pioneers in feminine psychology; and

Herbert Marcuse, a critical social theorist and philosopher who extrapolated on Freud and Marx in the 1950s, 1960s, and 1970s.

Freud's contributions in education have been reflected, with certain notable modifications, in the work of such libertarian practitioners as A.S. Neill, headmaster of the Summerhill free school in England from the 1920s to the 1970s, who was actually more Reichian than Freudian; Margaret Naumburg, founder of the creative Walden School in New York City in 1914; and Carl R. Rogers, client-centered therapist and freedom-oriented educator since the mid-twentieth century.

Joseph L. DeVitis

See also FEMINISM; FREEDOM AND DETERMINISM; HALL; HUMAN NATURE; MORAL DEVELOPMENT; PSYCHOANALYSIS

Bibliography

Bonaparte, Marie, Anna Freud, and Ernst Kris, eds. *The Origins of Psychoanalysis: Sigmund Freud, Letters, Drafts and Notes to Wilhelm Fliess, 1887–1902*. New York: Doubleday, 1957.

Clark, Ronald W. *Freud: The Man and the Cause*. New York: Random House, 1989.

Fox, Seymour. *Freud and Education*. Springfield, Ill.: Charles C. Thomas, 1975.

Freud, Sigmund. *Civilization and Its Discontents*. Edited and translated by James Strachey. New York: W.W. Norton, 1961, 1962.

———. *The Future of an Illusion*. Edited and translated by James Strachey. New York: W.W. Norton, 1928, 1961.

———. *The Standard Edition of the Complete Psychological Works of Sigmund Freud*. Edited and translated by James Strachey. 24 vols. London: Hogart Press, 1953, 1960.

Fromm, Erich. *Sigmund Freud's Mission*. New York: Harper Brothers, 1959.

Jones, Ernest. *The Life and Work of Sigmund Freud*. 3 vols. New York: Basic Books, 1953, 1955, 1957.

Karier, Clarence J. *Scientists of the Mind: Intellectual Founders of Modern Psychology*. Urbana: University of Illinois Press, 1986.

Roazen, Paul. *Freud and His Followers*. New York: Alfred A. Knopf, 1975.

Froebel, Friedrich Wilhelm August (1782–1852)

German educator, whose kindergarten helped transform theories and practices of child nature and early childhood education, grounded his new educational ideas in philosophical Idealism, a regnant philosophy in nineteenth-century Germany. His *Education of Man,* published in 1826, provides his most extended discussion of his educational philosophy and its application to early childhood development and education.

Born on April 21, 1782, Friedrich was the youngest of five sons of Johann Jacob Froebel, Lutheran pastor of Oberwiessbach, located in Schwarzburg-Rudolstadt, a German principality. In his reminiscences, Froebel recalls the effects of his unhappy childhood, which he attributed to an authoritarian father and an unloving stepmother. Froebel felt that his childhood experiences generated feelings of loneliness, rejection, and social isolation. As a child, Froebel found solace in the natural surroundings, especially the plants and trees, of the Thuringian forest near his home. As he developed his kindergarten philosophy, two themes surfaced from these childhood experiences: children's need to be nurtured in a loving, caring, emotionally supportive home environment, and nature's importance in providing useful clues for guiding the processes of children's growth and development.

Because he believed that Friedrich would not succeed in the boy's school, Froebel's father enrolled him in a girl's elementary school at Oberweissbach that followed the traditional vernacular curriculum of Bible study, catechism, reading, writing, and arithmetic. In 1792, at age ten, Friedrich was transferred, with his maternal uncle's encouragement, to the town school at Stadt-Ilm, where he studied reading, writing, arithmetic, religion, Latin, and geography. His academic record, showing some academic difficulties, was mixed. Leaving school, he served an apprenticeship, from fifteen to seventeen, to a forester and a surveyor at Neuhaus. In reflecting on his schooling and training as an apprentice, Froebel felt that his teachers were ineffective in their teaching methods. His later forays into educational philosophy and methodology sought to remedy this deficiency by basing teaching and learning on the interest and self-activity that were stimulated by children's own natural development. Even at this stage in his own career as an educator, Froebel was enveloped in a mystical orientation to life and education. For him, all objects had double meanings—one that appeared to the senses and a second, more important, lying behind sensory perception, the true essence of the object. This epistemological view proved to be highly compatible with the Idealism he embraced as the philosophical framework for his early child-education practices.

At age seventeen Froebel entered the University of Jena, where his studies in mathematics, mineralogy, physics, chemistry, architecture, surveying, botany, and other subjects were varied but unfocused. Because of financial problems, he was forced to interrupt his higher education. He would return to pursue higher studies in 1810 at the University of Gottingen, where he studied Hebrew, Persian, Arabic, and Greek. Froebel believed that the study of these languages might provide clues to understanding linguistics as a universal process. From 1812 to 1816, he studied mineralogy at the University of Berlin with Professor Christian Weiss (1780—1856), an expert on quantitative mineral analysis. The crystallization process, following a pattern of structural development from simple to more complex forms, convinced Froebel that the same phenomenon operated in all existence. His higher studies, though fragmented and interrupted, led Froebel to develop the concept that the key to education is the principle of unity that encompasses all existence. His special interests in architecture and mineralogy, especially the process of crystallization, convinced him that more complex forms develop from simpler forms. In his educational philosophy, this led to several overarching principles: (1) All life, all existence, all objects are connected and interrelated; (2) The source of this relationship lies in its ultimate Cause, the Absolute, or God; (3) Within life, including human life, there is an internal divine essence that causes the person to seek to externalize this inner nature; (4) relationships should not be broken but should be built upon. The kindergarten curriculum, especially the gifts and occupations, were based on these principles. The gifts, an intricate series of finished but connected objects, were to stimulate children to bring the innate sense of unity to consciousness. The occupations, consisting of malleable media such as paper or clay, were the means by which children externalized their internal concepts.

Froebel's first educational position was at Anton Gruener's Pestalozzian Model School in Frankfurt. From 1808 to 1810, he studied with

Johann Heinrich Pestalozzi in Switzerland. Froebel selectively adopted certain features of Pestalozzianism. He accepted Pestalozzi's premise that children need an emotionally secure educational environment as a precondition for cognitive learning. While accepting the general strategy of the Pestalozzian object lesson based on name, number, and form, Froebel believed that Pestalozzi's object teaching was philosophically insufficient. Froebel's kindergarten gifts, a series of preformed objects such as balls, cubes, and cylinders, were based on object teaching but emphasized the object's symbolic meaning, a feature not emphasized in Pestalozzi's approach.

In 1816, Froebel established a school, the Universal German Educational Institute, at Griesheim in Germany; in 1817, he transferred the school to Keilhau, where it operated until 1829. In 1831, Froebel established schools at Wartensee and Willisau in Switzerland. After his return to Germany in 1837, he established his kindergarten, or child's garden, at Blankenburg. The kindergarten, an early-childhood school, was designed as a milieu in which children, through guided play, games, stories, and the gifts and occupations curriculum, would develop according to the preformed patterns of human growth.

Froebel's most complete treatment of educational philosophy appeared in *The Education of Man*, published in 1826. Using Idealism as its philosophical core, Froebel's book included a mixture of Christian pietistical mysticism, romanticism, and science. Froebel asserted that all existence originates with God, the universal spiritual source. Human beings are endowed by their Creator with a spiritual essence, the core of their being, and a body that positions them in the natural order. It is the spiritual essence, however, that governs human development. Each child at birth possesses an interior spiritual essence, a life force, that seeks externalization through self-activity. The kindergarten's gifts, occupations, play, games, and stories, were used to ensure that developmental plan followed the divinely ordained plan. Children's education was to follow the divine principle of interconnectedness; nothing should be taught in isolation. Froebel also believed that all that the child would become as an adult is present, or preformed, in the embryo. The pattern of children's growth is the unfolding of that which is latently present. Children, he believed, in their play, art forms, and activities, culturally recapitulate the major episodes in human history.

In 1851, Karl von Raumer, the Prussian Minister of Education, banned kindergartens as undermining traditional values. Although kindergartens functioned in the other German states, they did not function again in Prussia until 1860. After Froebel's death, the kindergarten was transported throughout the world. In the United States, the first kindergartens were established by German immigrants, who also established kindergarten training schools. The kindergarten was eagerly adopted by English-speaking American educators such as Elizabeth Peabody. Kindergartens also became part of settlement houses. William Torrey Harris (1855–1919), superintendent of schools in St. Louis and an adherent of Idealism, made the kindergarten a part of the public schools in that city. Over time, the kindergarten, though it has left behind Froebel's symbols, has become part of the American public school system.

Gerald L. Gutek

See also HARRIS; IDEALISM; PEABODY; PESTALOZZI; PROGRESS, IDEA OF, AND PROGRESSIVE EDUCATION

Bibliography

Beatty, Barbara. "Child Gardening: The Teaching of Young Children in American Schools." In *American Teachers: Histories of a Profession at Work,* edited by Donald Warren. New York: Macmillan, 1989.

Bowen, H. Courthope. *Froebel and Education through Self-Activity.* New York: Scribner, 1897.

Downs, Robert B. *Friedrich Froebel.* New York: Twayne, 1978.

Froebel, Friedrich. *Autobiography of Friedrich Froebel.* Translated by Emilie Michaelis and H.K. Moore. Syracuse, N.Y.: C.W. Bardeen, 1889.

———. *The Education of Man* [1826]. Translated by W.H. Hailman. New York: D. Appleton, 1896.

———. *Froebel's Letters on the Kindergarten, 1838–1852.* Translated by Emilie Michaelis and H.K. Moore. London: Sonnenschein, 1887.

———. *Gesammelte Pädagogische Schriften.* Edited by Wichard Lange. Berlin: Enslin, 1862.

———. *Mother's Songs, Games, and Stories.* Translated by J. Jarvis. Boston: Lee and Shepard, 1885.

Hanschmann, Alexander B. *The Kindergarten System, Its Origins and Development as Seen in the Life of Friedrich Froebel.* London: Swan Sonnenschein, 1897.

Hayward, Frank H. *The Educational Ideas of Pestalozzi and Froebel.* Westport, Conn.: Greenwood Press, 1979.

Headley, Neith. *Education in the Kindergarten.* New York: American Book Company, 1966.

Kilpatrick, William H. *Froebel's Kindergarten Principles Critically Examined.* New York: Macmillan, 1916.

Lawrence, Evelyn, ed. *Froebel and English Education: Perspectives on the Founder of the Kindergarten.* New York: Schocken Books, 1969.

Lilley, Irene M. *Friedrich Froebel, a Selection from His Writings.* London: Cambridge University Press, 1967.

Marenholtz-Bulow, Berthe Von. *Reminiscences of Friedrich Froebel.* Translated by Mary Mann. Boston: Lee and Shepard, 1895.

Ross, Elizabeth. *The Kindergarten Crusade: The Establishment of Preschool Education in the United States.* Athens: Ohio University Press, 1976.

Shapiro, Michael S. *Child's Garden: The Kindergarten Movement from Froebel to Dewey.* University Park: Pennsylvania State University Press, 1983.

Vandewalker, Nina C. *The Kindergarten in American Education.* New York: Arno Press and the *New York Times,* 1971.

Weber, Evelyn. *The Kindergarten: Its Encounter with Educational Thought in America.* New York: Teachers College Press, 1969.

G

Gandhi, Mohandas Karamchand (1869–1948)

Gandhi is universally renowned and revered as the great teacher of *ahimsa,* or nonviolence. He proposed and practiced the ideals of *ahimsa* to resist the violence of British colonial rule, first in South Africa and later in India. Gandhi's political movement to resist violence nonviolently has inspired many peace activists and leaders of the oppressed, including Martin Luther King, Jr., Nelson Mandela, Julius Nyerere, Abdul Ghaffar Khan, and Cesar Chavez.

This global fame notwithstanding, very few educators are aware of Gandhi's educational movement, specifically initiated for putting into practice a philosophy of education committed to the ideals of nonviolence. This movement spawned the creation of schools, colleges, and universities under the Gandhian umbrella of *Nai Talim* (new education), or Basic Education. In launching *Nai Talim,* Gandhi asserted that modern schools and universities, in conjunction with the economic and political institutions exported worldwide from Europe, violate and destroy indigenous peoples' cultures. Gandhi affirmed the latter for being more humane and less aggressive to the ecology and cultures of the "Other."

To once again celebrate colonized cultures' educational practices, which have evolved through practical experimentations over generations, Gandhi's *Nai Talim* movement was launched all over India in the 1930s. It called for resisting British educational philosophy and practice, imposed worldwide upon colonized peoples; deliberately weaning young Indians from cultures castigated by colonizers as "primitive," "backward," "traditional," or "nonprogressive/nonmodern." Cultural initiation in Gandhi's schools and universities ran counter to the culture and education of modernizers, European and other. The latter, warned Gandhi, posed a grave moral and ecological threat to the whole world. Uncontained, their "economic exploitation" threatened to "strip the world bare like locusts."

Gandhian education, like his economics and politics, sought to treat the disease of modernization. This social disease, spread globally by the culture of the machine, Gandhi forewarned, corrupts culture and ecology, individual and society. It damns the human soul with materialism, while seducing the human body to decay from lack of good work, physical and spiritual. Along with the degeneration of human nature, there is damage to the rest of creation, observed Gandhi. Gandhi's *Nai Talim* schools and universities, in conjunction with the political and economic institutions also conceived by him, were established to achieve "the good life," free from enslavement to the modern national economy and to the science and technology that aid in its growth, and free from the British political machinery sold worldwide as democracy. Opposing the three modern eco-political "isms"—colonialism, capitalism, and socialism—Gandhi's *Nai Talim* celebrated *Hind Swaraj,* or Indian Home Rule. This rule rests on the Hindu ideal of *ahimsa.* This ideal, warned Gandhi, is incompatible with "the good life" promised by modern industrial societies.

Gandhi initiated his "new education" experiments on the Tolstoy and Phoenix Farms in South Africa at the turn of the century. He started with his own children and those of a handful of dissidents from British oppression in South Africa. The ideal of communal self-sufficiency formed the focus of this new education. This meant self-reliance within the community to fulfill basic human needs, starting with food, clothing, and shelter. Only through such self-sufficiency, observed Gandhi, are social justice and peace possible, by helping humans escape the violence of being either oppressors or oppressed. Children and adults worked the whole morning, engaged in communal work: cultivation, cooking, cleaning, and all the other activities necessary for a flourishing household economy. The afternoons were devoted to other educational activities, which included learning the three modern Rs of reading, writing, and arithmetic. Gandhi concluded that education cannot occur apart from the daily participation of young and old alike in productive, socially just, humble, simple, and nonviolent work. His educational thought was rooted in the conviction that there is enough in the world for everyone's need, but not for anyone's greed. Modern education, like the economy for which it offers preparation, systematically promotes such greed.

It took almost three decades for Gandhi's educational experiments on the Tolstoy Farm to spawn into *Nai Talim,* the new movement conceived for the education of India's young, struggling to liberate themselves from the yoke of colonial oppression. In proposing *Nai Talim,* Gandhi observed that the very core of modern education being imposed by the British on India was essentially foreign, imported from Oxford and Cambridge, Edinburgh and London. This imported imposition completely disregarded the fact that India, with "her long established civilization, had once the advantage of an educational system of her own." Gandhi distinguished this indigenous education from the fundamentally Anglo-Indian, "pseudo-national type" imposed by the British. In describing the "greatest visible evil" of the latter, "in itself evidence of deeper defects," he pointed to the violence it had perpetrated in breaking up the cultural and historical "continuity of our existence."

The "continuity of existence" that Gandhian education sought to preserve was of diverse, agrarian, rural cultures; or "cultures of the soil," now suffering from the modern threat posed by the monoculture of the machine—transported worldwide by colonialism. The "progress" proposed by India's modernizers, Gandhi diagnosed as regress: moral, physical, and spiritual. Modern education, Gandhi observed, leaves young people ignorant of the cultural knowledge and skills practiced and perfected by their elders; uproots them from their ancestral places and soil; encourages them to march toward the industrial workplace, to fill slots within the industrial economy. Like the workplace for which it offers preparation, modern education Westernizes the hearts and minds of indigenous peoples' children, systematically transforming them into "the intimate enemy" of their own cultural norms, values, accomplishments, and ideals of "the good life."

Inspired not only by India's classical ancient texts, such as the *Taittiriya Upanishad,* but also by Tolstoy, Ruskin, Thoreau, Bondaref, Besant, Carlyle, and other Western thinkers, the curricula and pedagogy of *Nai Talim* emphasized the theoretical and practical knowledge of *agri,* or soil culture. Competence and scientific understanding of spinning, weaving, animal-husbandry, and other rural crafts constituted its core, for those have promoted regional self-sufficiency for centuries.

Instead of education for advancing national economic growth, Gandhian education celebrates "bread labor" to strengthen the local rural economy. Gandhi's education "of, by and for" bread labor calls for humble physical work that strengthens body and soul, reminding people of their debt to all the natural creation humans inherit at birth. Bread labor, observed Gandhi, forges solidarity, eroding the barriers of unjust privilege accorded by rank, class, or caste. Gandhian bread labor engages students and teachers daily in growing, cooking, and processing healthful, organically grown food; building humble, well-planned, and airy homes; making tools and equipment from materials available within their bioregions; tending animals, not only for food but also for domestic fuel, fertilizer, and natural medicines as well as building materials; constructing low-cost, ecological wells, and all other elements of daily living that promote communal and bioregional self-reliance.

These necessary elements of his experiential education continue to constitute the core of learning in contemporary *Nai Talim* institutions for primary, secondary, and higher education in India. Among the dozens of Gandhian schools and colleges still flourishing are Lok Bharati, Gram Dakshina Mandir, and Gandhi Vidyapeeth in Gujarat, and Laxmi Ashram in Uttar Pradesh. There students and teachers learn that the good life is necessarily simple and frugal. They take complete responsibility for the maintenance and cleanliness of their class-rooms, shops, laboratories, kitchens, wash-rooms, toilets, and fields. Theoretical inquiries are complemented with the growing and cook-ing of the food consumed and the daily spinning of *khadi,* or homespun, for the clothes worn by the members of the community. Concerns for reducing waste, deforestation, and other natu-ral damage influence daily decisions about what to use, produce, or consume. Service to the com-munity constitutes an integral part of the cur-riculum. Such service includes participation in the digging of wells and canals; constructing cottages, manurepits, cow-dung gas plants and smokefree mud *chullas* (stoves); and assisting with community rescue work during famines, floods, accidents, earthquakes, and other ca-lamities. Service in these schools even extends as far as taking part in local grassroots move-ments, some of which are currently resisting government as well as corporate projects for deforestation or the building of dams that de-stroy local culture and ecology.

Gandhi's legacy of *Nai Talim* schools and universities still survives and flourishes in little niches, despite the growing national flood of credentials produced by the modern, state-spon-sored educational system of India. The latter, implicitly if not explicitly, disregards Gandhi's educational proposals, as do all those modern-izers who criticize Gandhi for being out of touch with modern times. Rejecting *Nai Talim,* they promote "independent" India's quest to catch up economically with Britain and other "devel-oped" countries.

With growing awareness of the contempo-rary ecological crisis and modern forms of so-cial injustice, postmodern educators in India and abroad are beginning to turn their attention to Gandhian social thought in general, and his educational theory and practice in particular. Gandhi's forgotten truth, tarnished if not totally absurd in the eyes of all modernizers, today offers new hope to those who no longer inno-cently believe the promises of modernity for moral, social, and technological progress.

Madhu Suri Prakash

See also CIVIL DISOBEDIENCE; HINDUISM; KING

Bibliography
Alvares, C. "Gandhi's Truth." *Illustrated Weekly of India.* (October, 1983): 49–50.
Gandhi, M.K. *An Autobiography, or The Story of My Experiments with Truth.* Ahmedabad: Navjivan, 1927.
———. *The Collected Works of Mahatma Gandhi.* 90 vols. New Delhi: Govt. of India Pub.
———. *Hind Swaraj* [Indian Home Rule]. Ahmedabad: Navjivan Trust, 1989.
———. *Towards New Education.* Ahmedabad: Navjivan Trust, 1980.
Hick, John, and Lamont Hempel, eds. *Gandhi's Significance for Today.* New York: St. Martin's Press, 1989.
Leys, Wayne, and P. Rama Rao. *Gandhi and America's Educational Future.* Carbondale: Southern Illinois University Press, 1969.
Nandy, Ashis. *The Intimate Enemy.* New Delhi: Oxford University Press, 1983.
Prakash, Madhu Suri. "Gandhi's Postmodern Education: Ecology, Peace, and Multiculturalism Relinked." *Holistic Education Review* 6 (1993): 8–17.
Sykes, Marjorie. *The Story of Nai Talim: Fifty Years of Education at Sevagram, 1937–1987.* Sevagram, Wardha: Nai Talim Samiti, 1988.

Gender and Sexism
Gender
Although the terms *gender* and *sex* are frequently used as though they were interchangeable, in fact the concept of gender arises in distinction from the concept of sex. Whereas *sex* refers to the physi-ological or biological components that are taken to distinguish female from male, *gender* refers to the cultural expectations governing the attitudes and behavior of females and males. Four promi-nent theories offer explanations for the develop-ment of gender. Biological determinism posits physiological differences (male and female hor-mones are frequently cited) as leading directly to different behavior and attitudes. Social-learning theory suggests that the child's observations (par-ticularly of close family members) of females and males play a powerful role in shaping the child's aspirations and attitudes. Cognitive developmen-tal theory gives the credit for gender development to the child's differentiation between male and female in addition to personally identifying as one or the other. Psychoanalytic theory sees the child's awareness of genital differences as the core of gender development.

Gender may be loosely interpreted as what it means to be a woman or to be a man in society.

Because gender has to do with cultural norms, we must understand that different women and men experience gender (and sexism) differently. People's experiences of gender will be determined in large part by their race, class, ethnicity, and sexual preference. In other words, gender is not a monolithic, unitary concept, for it is defined differently, sometimes radically differently, in different societies. The expectations surrounding a woman's role in child-rearing, marriage, and waged work, for example, will be very much influenced by the woman's race, class, ethnicity, and religion, as well as other more specific considerations, such as whether she lives in a rural or urban community.

Monolithic accounts of gender have typically been achieved at the price of exclusivity. Such monolithic accounts typically created false generics disturbingly similar to the false male generics they critiqued, generalizing illicitly from a focus on white, middle-class women to all women, ignoring the realities of the lives of white, working-class women as well as both middle-class and working-class black women, Native women, and Asian women, for example.

We can have no assurance that taking cognizance of differences among women will be unproblematic, however. Just as the way in which gender was traditionally defined tended to re-create and celebrate the norm of male superiority together with a concomitant system of compulsory heterosexuality, so talk about race- and class-based differences in gender may re-create and celebrate the perspective of a white, middle-class female vision. The very identification and weighing of differences is frequently skewed by sexist, racist, classist presumptions, and the feminist literature is not devoid of racist and classist accounts that display white as standard and the "differences" of all others as deviant or abnormal; we also need to be aware that such presumptions not only name, but also create differences. Perceived differences, whether real or imaginary, shore up concepts of gender that often serve the interests of those in positions of power. Gender, as a social construct, is thus more aptly perceived as prescriptive than descriptive. Although gender is commonly thought to arise from the differences between women and men, it is more accurately understood as a social construct used to entrench hierarchical power arrangements.

Sexism

Sexism is the systemic and institutionalized devaluing of females relative to males and the glo-rification of males relative to females. It is a function of a power imbalance characteristic of almost all social contexts—like power imbalances generally, sexism frequently involves the abuse of power. In the academy, this power abuse takes the form of misogynist masculinist accounts of reality and knowledge; in the waged workforce it takes the form of unfair monetary recompense and undesirable working conditions; and in the home it takes the form of oppressive division of labor, wife assault, and marital rape. The lives of many males are also subject to such abusive circumstances as a function of power imbalances determined by race and class. There is now a voluminous literature on sexism that includes, but is by no means limited to, the following categories:

Linguistic Sexism

The exclusion of the female is one aspect of linguistic sexism. At the level of semantics, the so-called generic terms "man" and "he" exclude females; the literature is dramatically clear that when people encounter these words, if they perceive females to be included at all, they perceive them to be much less fully included than males. The second half of the 1960s and the 1970s examined a different level of exclusion—that of conversational interaction. The exclusion of females on this level is mirrored in male speakers' taking more speaking time than females and the inclination of both males and females to ignore the linguistic input of a female, while attributing great significance to the very same input when associated with a male.

Semantics and speech patterns are characterized by the trivialization of the female as well. Dictionaries frequently devote at least twice as much space to the word "man" as to "woman," describe "woman" in terms of "man," thus introducing an element of linguistic dependence, and describe women as intuitive, fearful, and oriented toward crafts, whereas men are described as rational, articulate, and political. Dictionaries characteristically provide a larger number of insulting, demeaning words for females than for males in spite of the fact that the overall number of words provided for males is significantly greater than the number provided for women.

Examples of linguistic trivialization of females within speech patterns abound—addressing women by their first names but men by honorific titles, inappropriate application of affectionate or intimate terminology to women, complimenting women on how they look and men on how they think, referring to a woman solely in terms of her relationship to someone else (usually a man)—"Mrs. Thomas Smith," or "the president's secretary"—constantly interrupting female speakers, and abruptly changing the topic of conversation away from that initiated by a female speaker.

Occupational Sexism
Sexism in the workforce has been identified with such issues as wages, status, and working conditions. Although some occupations and professions have taken steps to ensure equal pay for equal work, in most sectors of the labor force there are still large disparities between the wages of females and males who do essentially the same jobs. Language has frequently exacerbated this problem by trivializing the role of females in certain categories through the use of diminutives—for example, "steward*ess*," "avia*trix*," and "usher*ette*." There has been a concerted effort to introduce sex-neutral job designations, such as "flight attendant," "server," and "salesperson," an effort that has been far more successful than attempts to introduce inclusive language in the classroom or in textbooks.

Occupational sexism frequently takes more subtle forms than simply paying males and females differently for doing the same work, however. The work traditionally done by males is valued more highly than the work traditionally done by females—for example, engineering is more prestigious than nursing, and a carpenter is more highly ranked than a seamstress. Within the same occupation, the realm occupied by men is more highly valued than the realm occupied by women—for example, it is more prestigious to be a surgeon than a pediatrician, a secondary school teacher than an elementary school teacher. Within most occupational categories, it will be more difficult for women to move into management than it is for men to do so. Ironically, this is true of female-dominated occupations (such as elementary school teaching and nursing) as well as male-dominated occupations. One of the explanations provided for this phenomenon is the reluctance of senior workers to mentor or coach female employees for positions of added responsibility.

Working conditions may also be seen as indicative of occupational sexism. Women are much more likely than men to be sexually harassed on the job. The absence of daycare facilities at most job sites creates an added impediment for many women with young children. False stereotypes, such as that female workers miss more time than male workers, compound the problem. In reality, those who work at dull, boring, uninspiring jobs miss more time than those who work at interesting, challenging, prestigious jobs, regardless of the worker's sex.

Educational Sexism
The research on educational sexism centers around two main themes—classroom dynamics and the curriculum. Observations of classroom dynamics reveal that male students of all ages receive preferential treatment compared with their female counterparts. They receive more of the teacher's time, they receive more of both positive and negative feedback, and their comments made in class will more likely be followed up by a substantive response from the teacher, unlike the comments of female students, which will more likely be simply acknowledged and then dismissed. Whereas teachers often simply give girls the answers to problems they are working on, boys are more likely to receive instructions on how to solve the problems for themselves.

The teaching method used often reflects the learning style preferred by boys, but not by girls. For example, introductory exposure of elementary school children to the computer world focuses on competitive games involving high levels of symbolic violence. While young boys enjoy these games, young girls do not, preferring instead to work in small, cooperative groups in their problem-solving. If there are not enough computers for each of the students, it is the girls' access rather than the boys' that is likely to be limited.

Research indicates that these teacher-student dynamics are present in virtually all classrooms, including those of feminist teachers, and that most teachers are unaware of the antifemale bias in their classrooms, believing that they treat all their students equally, or even, in some cases, that they are discriminating against the boys.

There is an obvious overlap between certain aspects of linguistic sexism—in particular, that males enjoy more speaking time and are taken more seriously when they do speak than females—and the classroom dynamics just discussed. There is an equally strong relationship between linguistic sexism and observations regarding the curriculum. Many academic disciplines exclude women and their works, a problem that is exacerbated by the tendency of many textbook writers to use language ("he" and "man" being the worst offenders) that excludes females. Women are often trivialized in scholarly accounts—the historical treatment of the suffragist movement, often dismissed in one brief paragraph, is a case in point. It is instructive to notice that history and literary texts frequently replace the term *suffragist* with the trivializing diminutive, *suffragette*. In some disciplines, philosophy and psychology, for example, the portrayal of women has frequently gone beyond trivializing into demeaning.

Education is sometimes seen as part of the reform needed to eradicate sexism in society; in this case access to educational institutions, particularly of higher education and professional schools, is likely to be viewed as a central concern. More radical thinkers, however, are likely to view education as part of the problem of sexism, not part of the solution. In this view, schools are perceived as enormously powerful agents for socializing girls and boys into traditional stereotypic norms and identities.

While the discussion of educational sexism has been focused around research dealing with classroom dynamics and curriculum, these categories by no means exhaust the impact of sexism on education. Access to certain areas of the curriculum, particularly higher professional education, continues to be a source of concern. The use of mathematics in the elementary and secondary schools as an invisible sex filter has received a considerable amount of scholarly attention. The apprenticeship trade programs of community colleges are also a source of concern in terms of the access of women to these programs.

Just as in the workplace, the classroom is often a source of unwanted sexual attention and danger to females. Female students (and teachers) are frequently subjected to sexual harassment from male teachers and male students; unlit parking lots and unpatrolled buildings where libraries and computer terminals are housed often render it dangerous for women students to work late at night, resulting in unequal access to the educational facilities. In the case of younger female students, school buses, playgrounds, and other areas have been worrisome zones in terms of sexual harassment from male peers—some research suggests that this harassment begins as early as grade two. Furthermore, on the issue of access, there is some indication that elementary school girls have access to a mere 10 percent of the school yard, normally close to the school building itself and more likely to be supervised by teachers than the much vaster amount of space occupied by the boys.

The Relationship between Gender and Sexism

Sexism is intimately connected to the evaluation of the traits ascribed by society to the genders; the consistent glorification of the masculine and devaluation of the feminine, together with an almost universal power imbalance in favor of males, predisposes society toward sexism. Gender and sexism are linked through the power to reward those who conform to gender expectations, together with an evaluation of the masculine as superior.

Males' and females' conformity to "appropriate" gender expectations is a matter seldom left to chance (thus raising serious doubt that these expectations are rooted in innate, biological differences between the sexes); the school, the family, television programmers, clothing manufacturers and designers, toy producers, and organized sports, to mention only a few, all work to maintain an alignment of sex with gender.

Maryann Ayim

See also CURRICULUM AND INSTRUCTION; DOMESTIC EDUCATION; EQUALITY; FEMINISM; GIRLS AND WOMEN, EDUCATION OF; HOME AND FAMILY; HUMAN NATURE; INDOCTRINATION; LEARNING, THEORIES OF; PUBLIC EDUCATION; RACE AND RACISM; TEACHING AND LEARNING

Bibliography

Ayim, Maryann, and Diane Goossens. "Issues in Gender and Language: An Annotated Bibliography." *RFR/DRF Resources for Feminist Research/Documentation sur la Recherche Feministe* 22, nos. 1, 2 (Spring/Summer 1993): 3–35.

Cline, Sally, and Dale Spender. *Reflecting Men at Twice Their Natural Size.* London: Andre Deutch, 1987.

Frye, Marilyn. *Willful Virgin; Essays in Feminism: 1976–1992.* Freedom, Calif.: Crossing Press, 1992.

Garrett, Stephanie. *Gender.* In the *Society Now* Series. General series editor: Patrick McNeill. New York: Tavistock Publications, 1987.

hooks, bell. *Black Looks: Race and Represen-*

tation. Toronto: between the lines, 1992.

MacKinnon, Catherine A. "Legal Perspectives on Sexual Difference." In *Theoretical Perspectives on Sexual Difference*, edited by Deborah L. Rhode, pp. 213–25. New Haven: Yale University Press, 1990.

Martin, Jane R. *Changing the Educational Landscape.* New York: Routledge, 1994.

Rothenberg, Paula S., ed. *Race, Class, and Gender in the United States: An Integrated Study.* New York: St. Martin's Press, 1988. 2nd ed., 1992.

Sadker, Myra, and David Sadker. "Sexism in the Schoolroom of the '80s." *Psychology Today* (March 1985): 54–57.

Spelman, Elizabeth V. *Inessential Woman; Problems of Exclusion in Feminist Thought.* Boston: Beacon Press, 1988.

Unger, Rhoda, and Mary Crawford. *Women and Gender: A Feminist Psychology.* Philadelphia: Temple University Press, 1992.

Gilman, Charlotte Perkins (1860–1935)

American feminist thinker best known today as the author of *The Yellow Wallpaper* (1892). In addition to an extensive collection of fiction, Gilman wrote seven nonfiction books and over one hundred articles during her career as an author and lecturer from 1898 to 1935.

Gilman's work can best be understood as arising out of and contributing to the social evolutionary school of thought that dominated social reformist thinking, from the 1860s—when the evolutionary theories of Charles Darwin (1809–1882) gained widespread notice—until the turn of the century. Social evolutionists believed that they could take the principles of evolution from the biological world and apply them to the social world. They viewed society as a complex social organism that functions in the same way that biological organisms function, thus subject to the same rules and principles.

Social evolutionists of this period also believed that evolution and its laws were not random, but were purposive, or telic—that is, occurring toward some end or purpose. In the case of social evolution, they believed that the end was a better society. Liberal-minded social evolutionists such as Gilman further believed that if they could identify the scientific laws of evolution that applied on the social level and convince individuals and society to follow these laws, great and positive social progress would result. This belief forms the foundation of all Gilman's thinking.

Gilman's great contribution is that she focused her social evolutionary lens on women in particular. In her first and most significant book, *Women and Economics* (1898), she asks the question: Do the current roles and functions of women help or hinder social evolution? She concludes that the current state of affairs actually hinders social progress, because the duties and responsibilities that are related to being human, and thus belong to all of us as human beings, have been split into "masculine" and "feminine" in society. Thus, maintaining and caring for the private world of husband, home, and children and the qualities associated with these activities have come to be seen as essentially feminine, and activities in the public world of politics, business, art, science, and education and their associated qualities as essentially masculine.

According to Gilman, this splitting of human life and work into two separate parts is unnatural, because these qualities and duties are not in fact related to men or women biologically by sex, but rather by social convention. This split harms both men and women because it limits each sex's experience and understanding of the world. But its most important negative consequence is that it harms society by limiting the contribution that each sex can make to society, because both men and women are prevented from developing into full human beings who possess both "masculine" and "feminine" qualities.

Gilman recognized that fundamental changes would have to occur in society in order for both men and women to develop as full human beings. Gilman argued that as long as women remained responsible for all work in the home, dependent on men economically and divorced from the public world of work, they would never achieve equal humanness with men. She called for an end to the exclusion of women from public work and argued for woman's right to be economically independent and to perform satisfying human work outside the home. She believed that the traditional domestic tasks of childrearing and household industries should be organized and managed like all human work—that is, by being professionalized and specialized.

On the other side, she argued that men should be involved in the human aspects of the traditional feminine duties so that they could develop as full human beings. Gilman believed that the human responsibilities currently performed in private by women in their homes should be recognized as responsibilities of the society as a whole. To Gilman, bringing the tasks and qualities associated with the private world of home and family into the public world not only frees women from the isolation of their individual homes but also serves to humanize the public world by bringing an entire realm of experience back into the public world and thus opening it up to men's understanding and experience.

Gilman's emphasis on social betterment led her to focus a great deal of attention on the rearing of children, because she saw children as the means by which society not only continues to exist, but, more important, improves itself. Because all children represent the future of society, Gilman argues that all its members are responsible for the development of all its children, not just the children of one's private family. Throughout her fiction and nonfiction, Gilman developed her vision of a society in which the role and responsibilities of family and motherhood are primary social values and essential human functions rather than private feminine duties.

Gilman illustrates what this type of society would look like in her utopian novel *Herland* (1915). In *Herland*, she uses the fictional device of a society of women who were separated from men by a natural disaster, and who over time developed the power to reproduce without men. In this way, Gilman can describe an alternative world in which artificial sex stereotypes and roles do not exist. In *Herland*, motherhood is the primary social category, and the community functions as the family. All the women see themselves as mothers to all the children, because children's health and proper development is the central focus of the entire society. Because of this, educating and caring for children are highly respected and highly coveted jobs, and only the most talented in these areas are chosen for this special work.

In *Concerning Children* (1900), Gilman proposed that children should be cared for and educated from a very young age by trained specialists, in an environment suited to their size and needs, allowed the opportunity to follow their curiosity safely, and gently trained on how to make it lead to real learning. Gilman believed that the underlying purpose of all organisms is growth, and that learning is a natural function whereby children grow. Thus she believed that

children learn naturally. To Gilman, the foundation of learning lies in the intimate connection between knowledge and action. Understanding the connection between act and consequence is the basis for all our knowledge of the world and of our place in it. In order for a child to understand the connection between act and consequence, the child must first be able to act on ideas. The child's natural curiosity would lead the child to interact with the environment and so begin the natural sequence of learning. Thus, in Gilman's philosophy of education, one of the primary tasks of education is to create a properly structured and controlled environment so that children can act on their ideas safely and properly connect act and consequence, once they have acted on their ideas, in a way that is natural and unconscious.

The most vivid and comprehensive portrayal of Gilman's educational philosophy at work is also found in *Herland*. Growth is the fundamental principle in Herlandian life, and all Herlandians respect this process in their children. Since Herlandian society recognizes its primary responsibility for the education of all children from birth, the entire country has been scientifically designed as an educational environment for children. There is literally no separation between school and home or school and life in Herland. The children freely travel the land, safe because of its special design, inspired to learn from their environment by their natural curiosity. On hand are numbers of specially trained teachers, ready to answer questions and lead the child on to a deeper knowledge of the subject.

Gilman's portrayal of education in *Herland* embodies all the features of her pedagogical theory: an educational program based on the principle of growth, one that utilizes the child's own interest and learning pattern to foster learning through interaction with a carefully controlled and designed environment. This education, further, is unconscious to the children, although it is highly conscious to the group of educators who indirectly guide the children, always leaving them free to act on their own ideas and judgments. In this way the natural connection between knowledge and action is maintained, and as it is strengthened, the child's ability to manage her conduct increases. By following this method, Gilman believed, children will develop habits of thoughtful behavior and judicious reasoning, and grow into self-regulating, independent-minded adults who will contribute to society and further its growth.

Gilman's book *Women and Economics* was her most popular work during her lifetime, going through numerous reprintings and being translated into several foreign languages. However, her work did not have lasting effect, and all of her writings had gone out of print until a new edition of this book was published in 1966, edited and with an introduction by Carl Degler. Since then, more of her works have been reprinted, and numerous scholars have researched and written about her views on household economics, feminist utopian visions, ethics, sociology, anthropology, and educational philosophy.

Karen E. Maloney

See also DARWIN; EVOLUTION; FEMINISM; GENDER AND SEXISM; GIRLS AND WOMEN, EDUCATION OF; HOME AND FAMILY; PROGRESS, IDEA OF, AND PROGRESSIVE EDUCATION

Bibliography

Gilman, Charlotte Perkins. *The Charlotte Perkins Gilman Reader.* Edited and with an introduction by Ann J. Lane. New York: Pantheon, 1980.

———. *Concerning Children.* Boston: Small, Maynard, 1900, 1901.

———. *Herland.* Introduction by Ann J. Lane. New York: Pantheon Books, 1979.

———. *The Living of Charlotte Perkins Gilman* [1935]. Introduction by Ann J. Lane. Madison: University of Wisconsin Press, 1990.

———. *Women and Economics: A Study of the Economic Relation between Men and Women as a Factor in Social Evolution* [1898]. Edited and with an introduction by Carl N. Degler. New York: Harper and Row, 1966, Source Book Press, 1970.

———. *The Yellow Wallpaper.* [1899]. Old Westbury, N.Y.: Feminist Press, 1973.

Hill, Mary A. *Charlotte Perkins Gilman: The Making of a Radical Feminist, 1860–1896.* Philadelphia: Temple University Press, 1980.

Lane, Ann J. *To Herland and Beyond: The Life and Work of Charlotte Perkins Gilman.* New York: Meridian/Penguin, 1991.

Maloney, Karen E. "The Theory of Education of Charlotte Perkins Gilman: A Critical Analysis." Ed.D. diss., Harvard Graduate School of Education, 1985.

Martin, Jane Roland. *Reclaiming a Conversation: The Ideal of the Educated Woman.* New Haven: Yale University Press, 1985.

Scharnhorst, Gary. *Charlotte Perkins Gilman: A Bibliography.* Metuchen, N.J.: Scarecrow Press, 1985.

Girls and Women, Education of

The idea that girls and women should be taught and learn a deliberately designed curriculum.

In Plato's *Republic V,* Socrates argues that sex is a difference which, like baldness, should make no difference for education. Centuries later, when John Stuart Mill (1806–1873) argued for sexual equality in *The Subjection of Women* (1861), this ideal was still so revolutionary that he observed literate women to be "a contradiction and a disturbing element." Throughout the history of Western educational thought, both men and women have claimed that sex does and must make a difference for education. However, ignoring such claims, most twentieth-century philosophers of education have questioned neither sex equality's meaning nor its value, and some have speculated about the best means for its realization.

Anna van Schurman of Utrecht (1607–1678), possibly Europe's first "professional feminist," formally debated the question of whether girls and women should even be educated. But other men besides Plato took the affirmative position before van Schurman did: Examples include, Leonardo Bruni (c. 1370–1444), Desiderius Erasmus (1466–1536), Richard Mulcaster (1530–1611), and Cresacre More (1572–1649). Sydney Smith (1771–1845) may have been the first to argue that men's education would improve through women's education, and that to educate women would be to improve "the stock of national talents" as well as public morals. But many other men, including some of Europe's greatest philosophers, contradicted such arguments. Jean-Jacques Rousseau (1712–1778) did not doubt women's capacity for intellectual learning, but in *Emile* (1762) declared "a brilliant wife" to be "a plague to . . . everyone . . . always ridiculous and justly criticized." Immanuel Kant (1724–1804) claimed that "laborious learning or painful pondering, even if a woman should greatly succeed in it, destroy the merits that are proper to her sex." Saying women's "childish" nature fits them to be "nurses and teachers of our early childhood," Arthur Schopenhauer (1788–1860) believed women inferior because "the most distinguished intellects among the whole sex have never . . . given to the world any work of permanent value in any sphere." But, argued Mary Wollstonecraft (1759–1797), this assumption that women's mental inferiority is a natural defect, rather than socially constructed, could never be logically justified until women got an education equal to men's—through a national system of coeducational day schools.

Wollstonecraft's feminist proposal not only suggested a crucial distinction between sex, a natural category, and its social construction, gender; it also underscored a central question on which theorists of girls' and women's education have differed: Should girls and women be educated, as Plato's Socrates advocated in the fifth century B.C., together with and the same as boys and men, or as St. Jerome (340–420) advocated in the fifth century A.D., differently from them and in the company of only their own sex? This simplistic dualism underlies the frequent contemporary assumption that coeducation has rendered critical thought specifically about girls' and women's education obsolete and trivial.

Education Segregated by Sex (SSE)

St. Jerome's concern for Christian women's sexual purity led him to argue that girls should be educated far from boys' "wanton frolics." Until the late eighteenth century, most educational theorists never questioned that girls and women should be educated in religion and arts, if at all, apart from boys and men, and, unlike them, specifically for pious, servile home life. Francois Fenelon (1651–1715) proposed that girls' education should not differ from boys', and Hannah More (1745–1833) advocated an education for girls that would "exercise the reasoning faculties, teach the mind to get acquainted with its own nature, and to stir up its own powers"; still, both assumed female mental capacities to be lesser than those of men, and defined women's destiny as home management.

Thus often seeming to offer equality with one hand and take it away with the other, theorists of girls' and women's SSE did disagree about the appropriateness of their teaching and scientific study. In theoretical argument with Bruni and Erasmus, for example, Juan Luis Vives (1492–1540) agreed with Quintilian (c. 35–c. 95) that mothers must nourish children's minds and bodies, so he prescribed a classical education combined with domestic science. But he asserted, "I gyve no lycence to a woman to

be a techer, nor to have any authorite of the man, but to me in silence." Both his proposal for women's scientific study and his denial of women's right to become teachers have met significant opposition from other apologists for SSE.

For example, bluestocking Hester Chapone (1727–1801), who idealized women as companions and homemakers, proscribed their scientific education. On such premises, Clara Reeve (1729–1807), John Burton (1696–1771), and Erasmus Darwin (1731–1802) advanced the curricular concept of "female accomplishments": language, literature, history, music, dancing, singing, drawing, painting, and needlework, for the explicit purpose of imparting pleasure to home life, never for women's own "great eminence." Claiming that homemaking should not make women men's inferiors, Emma Hart Willard (1787–1870) and Catharine Beecher (1800–1878) also conceived a new subject of school study, "Domestic Economy." Willard included arts, supervised practice, and philosophical study in this subject. Later repudiating female accomplishments' frivolity, Beecher also brought sciences to bear upon teaching women an elaborate, highly rational understanding of homemaking as a "profession," in which she included childrearing.

Willard and Beecher were not the first to conceive female schooling as preparation for teaching as well as homemaking; so had Lydia Sigourney (1791–1865) and others. Whereas Sarah Fielding (1710–1768) had argued that men must educate their wives to be good mothers and to teach both in that capacity and as governesses, Johann Heinrich Pestalozzi (1746–1827) had idealized mothers as teachers, and Benjamin Rush (1745–1813) had advocated actually schooling women to claim "a principal share" as mothers in children's instruction, even to the extent of teaching their sons principles of liberty and government. According to Sigourney, Willard, Beecher, Louis Aime-Martin (1786–1847), and Pestalozzi's disciple Friedrich Froebel (1782–1852), women's ability to (learn to) teach children was innate, but men's was not. Such was Froebel's premise for an argument disputed by his own follower Bertha Maria von Marenholz-Bulow (1810–1893): Women need no higher education beyond his own program to educate them for kindergarten teaching, and higher education would actually suppress their natural capacities for the work.

Such ambiguous, controversial thought

persisted through the nineteenth century, albeit not without serious challenges that have eventually weakened the case for SSE. Indeed, some theorists who never challenged the practice of SSE did advocate equal education beyond childhood. Daniel Defoe (1660–1731) argued that men should establish women's academies to educate them for companionship with men. Mary Astell (1668–1731) in England and Mary Lyon (1797–1849) in the United States proposed that women should be educated apart from men in colleges of their own, but no differently than men. Many practical trials of their bold idea have lent persuasive power to arguments both for and against coeducation.

Coeducation

Anarchist Emma Goldman (1869–1940) remains one of coeducation's few apologists to counter St. Jerome's argument for SSE by embracing sexual knowledge, pleasure, and freedom for girls and women as well as boys and men. Also rejecting the sexual double standard, Bertrand Russell (1872–1970) argued that "the old morality" requires girls' education "to make them stupid and superstitious and ignorant." But, instead of questioning religious justifications for SSE, other apologists for coeducation have often advocated tempering the sexes' togetherness as learners with selective SSE. Thus they have made choice between SSE and coeducation other than a choice between a "gender-laden" education and a "gender-free" one: a false dilemma. Alternatively, the thought experiment *Herland* (1915) of Charlotte Perkins Gilman (1860–1935) imagined the possibility of men's learning a coherent set of values, attitudes, skills, and beliefs utterly alien, but still beneficial, to them from strong, smart, nonviolent women who had been educated and governed only by other strong, smart, nonviolent women. Recent theorists of coeducation have thus critically explored its potential to reeducate boys' and men's social dispositions and to reconstruct women's SSE within it—toward social change in behalf of girls and women, other oppressed peoples, and peace.

Educating women for lives in domestic service became an aim integral to earlier arguments for SSE within coeducation, even into the twentieth century. For example, John Drury (1596–1680) argued that girls should be schooled together with boys, but lodged separately and prepared explicitly to become "good and careful housewives, loving toward their husbands and their children." The coeducational Plumfield of Louisa May Alcott (1832–1888) aimed to prepare girls for domestic service not expected of boys or men, but also for full participation in professional, scientific, artistic, and civic life, whether married or single, with or without children. Like Alcott, John Dewey (1859–1952) defended coeducation as a means of "mutual influence," to strengthen girls' minds and civilize boys' manners. Debunking the notion of female mental inferiority and favoring women's rights to full citizenship, he considered coeducation an "absurd" issue for theoretical discussion because to him it was so obviously "an intellectual and moral necessity in a democracy"—to foster "free play of instinctive sympathy and understanding" between the sexes. However, he conceived coeducation as an opportunity to provide training "for the distinctive career of women as wives, mothers, and managers of households."

In the nineteenth century, Booker T. Washington (1856–1915) had similarly conceived SSE within African American coeducation in his thought experiment at Tuskegee Institute. But, in 1904, W.E.B. Du Bois (1868–1963) questioned "the meaning of progress" in the United States by citing the tragic case of a bright, young African American woman, denied the intellectual education for which she yearned: Endless family demands for her domestic service literally worked her to death at an early age. Yet Du Bois overlooked the theory of Anna Julia Cooper (1858–1964) that African American women's intellectual education was vital to the "regeneration and progress" of their race; in 1892 she argued that coeducation would integrate "the law of love" with that of reason and thereby correct many harms done by "the predominant man-influence."

Toward such an end, in *Three Guineas* (1938) Virginia Woolf (1880–1941) upheld for practical purposes, even as she articulated serious reservations about it, the thesis of Emily Davies (1830–1921): Women and men should have access to the same higher education, albeit university women should be educated apart from men in a college of their own. For Woolf observed that men's education had led them to war, and, therefore, she questioned whether their daughters should pursue the same education. But she also observed the private house had given women "unpaid-for education" in poverty, chastity, derision, and freedom from unreal loyalties, as explicit preparation for the

G

"unpaid-for profession" of domestic service. Suggesting such SSE might "make a difference" for peace, she argued for the moral necessity of rigorously acknowledging connections between the private house and the public world; mother-educated and university-educated, economically independent women might demonstrate that connection's creative possibilities "to protect culture and intellectual liberty" through obscure activities in an unofficial "Outsiders' Society."

Embracing Woolf's notion of educated women as self-denied outsiders, Adrienne Rich has called coeducation a "misleading concept"; critiqued U.S. higher education's exploitation, devaluation, and harassment of women; explored "what a woman needs to know" in order to survive within a male-dominated world; and proposed a new, nonhierarchical concept of coeducation, the "woman-centered university." Similarly deploring "predicaments of women" in U.S. coeducation, Maxine Greene has called philosophic attention to women's literature as a source of reflection about new educational possibilities and to the history of educational thought by and about women—for example, Sarah Grimke (1792–1873), Margaret Fuller (1810–1850), Harriet Martineau (1802–1876), and others. "The connection between the kind of subordination imposed on women and the kind of subordination imposed on schoolchildren must finally be exposed," argued Greene, in order to free coeducation from complicity in human exploitation.

Attending philosophically to girls and women more than perhaps anyone else in educational history, Jane Roland Martin has challenged philosophers of education to analyze the concept of coeducation. Her plea remains unanswered. But, laying groundwork for that effort, she herself has critiqued contemporary analytic philosophy's concept of teaching, ideal of the educated person, and ignorance of women's educational thought. Reconstructing a philosophical "conversation" about ideals of "the educated woman" and its implied critique of Western ideals of "the educated man," she has transformed taken-for-granted conceptions of educational thought's sources and methods. To correct the liberal curriculum's gender-blind assumptions and purposes, she has thus formulated a "gender-sensitive ideal" whose aim is to make "domestic tranquility writ large" the work of both sexes equally. Her thought experiment in coeducation, *The Schoolhome* (1992),

acknowledges the probable necessity of some SSE, for it suggests that girls' education toward gender equality entails boys' education toward that same end, in both the private house and the public world, perhaps occasionally correcting different gender bias effects by different means.

Susan Laird

See also BEECHER; DEWEY; DOMESTIC EDUCATION; DU BOIS; EQUALITY; FEMINISM; FROEBEL; GENDER AND SEXISM; GILMAN; HOME AND FAMILY; KANT; MILL; PESTALOZZI; PLATO; ROUSSEAU; RUSSELL; WASHINGTON; WOLLSTONECRAFT

Bibliography

Agonito, Rosemary. *History of Ideas on Woman: A Source Book.* New York: Perigee, 1977.

Ayim, Maryann, Kathryn Morgan, and Barbara Houston. "Symposium: Should Public Education Be Gender-Free?" *Educational Theory* 35 (1985): 345–69.

Cooper, Anna Julia. *A Voice from the South.* New York: Oxford University Press, 1988.

Du Bois, W. E. B. "Of the Meaning of Progress." In *The Souls of Black Folk,* chapter 4. New York: Signet Classics, 1969.

Greene, Maxine. "Predicaments of Women." In *Landscapes of Learning,* chapters 15, 16, 17. New York: Teachers College Press, 1978.

Kersey, Shirley Nelson. *Classics in the Education of Girls and Women.* Metuchen, N.J.: Scarecrow Press, 1981.

Laird, Susan. "Women and Gender in John Dewey's Philosophy of Education." *Educational Theory* 38 (1988): 111–29.

Martin, Jane Roland. *Changing the Educational Landscape: Philosophy, Women, and Curriculum.* New York: Routledge, 1994.

———. *Reclaiming a Conversation: The Ideal of the Educated Woman.* New Haven: Yale University Press, 1985.

Rich, Adrienne. *Of Women Born: Motherhood as Experience and Institution.* New York: Norton, 1975.

Shulman, Alix Kates, ed. *Red Emma Speaks: An Emma Goldman Reader.* New York: Schocken, 1972.

H

Hall, Granville Stanley (1846–1924)

American psychologist and important leader of the "child study movement." He endeavored to use the theory of biological evolution and scientific methods to increase knowledge of children and improve educational practices. Hall proposed a child-centered education, suggesting that teachers encourage the expression of primitive impulses.

Hall's philosophy of education was based on the evolutionary nature of human development. Hall's theories of development and education were influenced by a variety of evolutionary theorists. Early in his career, Hall was a proponent of the developmental philosophy of Georg Wilhelm Hegel (1770–1831). Hegel had proposed that concepts and institutions are the result of a developmental process, and thus could be understood by examining that progression. Hall then applied the idea of this developmental process to understanding the human mind.

As Hall's mentor, William James (1842–1910) had a more direct impact on his burgeoning theories. Hall was particularly influenced by James's pragmatic and empirical approach to the new science of psychology. Moreover, James was interested in exploring the mind in terms of Charles Darwin's theory of adaptation; thus he suggested that the mind is a functional organ that is involved in the adjustment between the individual and the environment.

The influence of evolutionary principles can be seen in Hall's reformation of the following recapitulation theory. Prior to Hall, Ernst Haeckel (1834–1919) had promulgated the law that "ontogeny recapitulates phylogeny." That is, during the course of embryological development (ontogenesis), an organism repeats the entire developmental sequence through which its species had evolved (phylogenesis). The theory regarding recapitulation by Herbert Spencer (1820–1903) also influenced Hall's theories. Spencer emphasized that human consciousness is a product of evolution, and that the mental life of humans also shows the consistent repetitions of its phylogenesis.

Hall's recapitulation theory emphasized that the human child's life echoes the phylogenesis of the species. From the moment of conception, he claimed, all children recapitulate every stage of development through which the human race has passed. This recapitulation occurs psychologically in the infant, child, and adolescent. Further, Hall drew heavily on the theory of Jean-Jacques Rousseau (1712–1778) that some of these developmental stages persist in behavior. Indeed, Hall noted that children regularly express antisocial impulses and cruelty. He posited that these were representative of earlier, less civilized stages of human development. According to Hall, recapitulation is necessary, and the expression of primitive impulses is cathartic. This "romantic" approach demanded that schools and teachers create an atmosphere that encouraged the expression of these impulses. Further, if these impulses were not allowed expression, they would likely be carried into adulthood.

Many were skeptical of Hall's theory of recapitulation. Edward Thorndike (1874–1949), for example, was a sharp critic, pointing out that there is not always a "concrete parallelism" between the individual's development and that of the race. Thorndike argued that similarity of embryos at certain stages in development is not sufficient evidence to support Hall's applications of the recapitulation theory to psychological development and education.

The publication of "The Contents of Children's Minds" in 1883 was the first of Hall's attempts to use the methodology of experimental psychology and the evolutionary approach to understand children and to improve education. In essence, he proposed that a combination of educational "romanticism," biological evolution, and scientific methods should be used in the service of increasing our knowledge of children and, ultimately, childrearing and educational practices. Hall claimed that education should be based on scientific study of child development. His groundbreaking use of observational and questionnaire studies of children was institutionalized in the form of the "child study movement." He proposed exploring the nature of the average child through the observation of a sample of individual children.

The child study movement had a distinct impact on education and educational psychology, and particularly on genetic (developmental) psychology. Hall's use of the questionnaire methodology allowed for a more thorough observation of children in school. The data collected from these questionnaires and Hall's numerous published discussions of educational problems helped illuminate the common problems of students in school. At the same time the child study movement served to invent the "normal" child.

Although Hall's work was accepted by many parents and teachers, it was not always popular with other psychologists. Research conducted as a part of the child study movement was thought by some to be less than scientific. Much of the disdain stemmed from the overuse of questionnaires by parents and teachers who were not necessarily connected with Hall. Despite these criticisms, Hall's research and publications were ultimately useful to educators and the psychologists working with them. First, this research advanced their meager understanding of child development, garnering diverse information about children's thinking. Questions included the children's ideas about themselves, their fears, their favorite foods, and their religious experiences. Second, many were exposed to the merits of the questionnaire and other methods (such as diary descriptions, group observations, and laboratory studies). Third, since members of the child study movement believed that both hereditary and early environmental influences were important, the significance of the educational system was

highlighted. Eventually, Hall lost interest in the questionnaire technique, and shortly thereafter, the movement disappeared.

Another major contribution Hall made was his work on the psychology of adolescence. Prior to Hall's work, a child was thought to become a "youth" during the passage to adulthood. Hall, however, emphasized that childhood and adolescence were disparate stages in human development. Prior to adolescence, much of the child's development was thought to be a continuation of embryological development. Like Rousseau, Hall believed that the child had to pass through successive phases, incorporating experiences and knowledge along the way. According to Hall, the child's long dependency on surrounding adults allowed for a more "luxuriant flowering" during the passage to adolescence.

Hall elucidated his theory of adolescence in his seminal work *Adolescence: Its Psychology, and Its Relations to Physiology, Anthropology, Sociology, Sex, Crime, Religion, and Education* (1904). This two-volume publication included the most comprehensive statement of his theory of recapitulation, which provided the basis for his insistence that education be based on the nature of the child. Hall supported Rousseau's theory of education, believing that, as children repeat the stages in the history of humans, they should be permitted to follow their natural inclinations. They should be allowed to act as "savages" before being expected to act as civilized individuals. Hall was concerned that the adolescent mind and spirit were being destroyed by the pedantic and dogmatic teaching of the educational system. Teachers should stimulate the adolescent's interest in the natural world through myths and metaphors that have excited human imagination in the distant past, and then begin to present the discoveries of science. In essence, teachers should take advantage of the ancestral residues in the imagination of adolescents.

Adolescence also included Hall's views on gender development and coeducation. He used the recapitulation theory to explain female development. According to Hall, women are psychologically more akin to a child than men, and are at all stages of development a perennial adolescent. Hall proposed that women possess larger lower brain centers, theoretically to govern maternal functions (such as milk production, fertility, general nurturing). Hall felt strongly that women should devote themselves to the natural function of motherhood, and that puberty is a critical period of preparation for this. Further, adolescence is a period during which women are highly susceptible to reproductive organ damage. Since the adolescent girl should be considered the "springboard" for the future evolution of the species, this is a critical period (approximately ages fourteen to twenty-five) not only for the individual, but for the progression of civilization as well. Coeducation would result in overexposure in the classroom (that is excessive mental activity in competition with men) possibly resulting in a loss of mammary function, lack of interest in motherhood, and decreased fertility. Thus Hall contended that biological differentiation necessitated educational and role separation starting in adolescence. Appropriate training for women should include education regarding motherhood, and additionally, education for more nurturing occupations (such as social work, home economics, and elementary school teaching).

The natural course of recapitulation would also be adversely affected in men if the educational environment discouraged the development of masculine temperament. Thus Hall argued that adolescent boys should be shielded from excessive feminine influence. Adolescent boys should be allowed expression of their male savage impulses; otherwise, if they are denied recapitulatory catharsis, they will become either wild or feminized adult men. Hall suggested that women teachers should be discouraged from teaching high school boys, because these adolescents need firm discipline and male models to emulate.

For a time, Hall's *Adolescence* was influential among teachers and parents. At the time, it served to convey some understanding and advice, useful for adults who were confused by adolescents. Hall believed that psychology could also produce useful findings for school administrators. In his two-volume *Educational Problems* (1911), he covered a wide range of topics including child-welfare agencies, school boards, teachers' salary, age of entrance, problems of public schools, and the absence of morals. As with his *Adolescence,* these volumes included a mixture of his personal and pedagogical philosophy.

Deborah M. Licht

See also DARWIN; EVOLUTION; HEGEL; JAMES; PRAGMATISM; PROGRESS; ROUSSEAU; SPENCER

Bibliography

Diehl, Lesley A. "The Paradox of G. Stanley Hall: Foe of Coeducation and Educator of Women." *American Psychologist* 41 (1986): 868–78.

Hall, Granville Stanley. *Adolescence: Its Psychology, and Its Relations to Physiology, Anthropology, Sociology, Sex, Crime, Religion, and Education.* 2 vols. New York: D. Appleton, 1904.

———. "The Contents of Children's Minds." *Princeton Review* 11 (1883): 249–72.

———. *Educational Problems.* 2 vols. New York: D. Appleton, 1911.

Ross, Dorothy. *G. Stanley Hall: The Psychologist as Prophet.* Chicago: University of Chicago Press, 1972.

Siegel, Alexander W., and Sheldon H. White. "The Child Study Movement: Early Growth and Development of the Symbolized Child." *Advances in Child Development and Behavior* 17 (1982): 233–85.

Thorndike, Edward L. "Granville Stanley Hall: 1846–1924." *Biographical Memoirs* 12 (1929): 132–80.

H

Happiness

Happiness has been highly overrated by moral philosophers, most of whom have taken it to be the greatest good or final end. One notable exception is Friedrich Nietzsche (1844–1900), who wrote: "Man does not strive for happiness; only the Englishman does that." John Stuart Mill (1806–1873) seemed to profess something similar in *Utilitarianism* when he claimed: "It is better to be a human being dissatisfied than a pig satisfied; better to be Socrates dissatisfied than a fool satisfied." Mill of course was an Englishman and a utilitarian, which suggests (1) that Nietzsche was wrong, or (2) that Mill didn't know what he was talking about—certainly not happiness conceived as the *summum bonum.* For if happiness were the greatest good, and if happiness were rightly identified with pleasure, as Mill claimed, then it apparently could not be better to be Socrates dissatisfied than a fool satisfied.

So there are at least two important and related philosophical problems about happiness: What is it? How great a good is it (conceived in that way)?

The reason it is difficult to answer these questions is that our confusions about the objectivity of value are reflected in our confusions about happiness. If pleasure, for example, were the sole intrinsic good, and happiness were identified with pleasure, as Mill claimed it should be, then it would follow that happiness is the sole intrinsic good.

Is pleasure the sole intrinsic good?

Consider the following, from Robert Nozick's *Anarchy, State, and Utopia*, pages 42–43:

> Suppose there were an experience machine that could give you any experience you desired. Superduper neuropsychologists could stimulate your brain so that you would think and feel you were writing a great novel, or making a friend, or reading an interesting book. All the time you would be floating in a tank, with electrodes attached to your brain . . . . If you are worried about missing out on desirable experiences, we can suppose that business enterprises have researched thoroughly the lives of many others. You can pick and choose from their large library or smorgasbord of such experiences. . . . Of course, while in the tank you won't know that you're there; you'll think it's all actually happening. Others can also plug in to have the experiences they want, so there's no need to stay unplugged to serve them. Would you plug in?

Most people, when asked this question, decline. Why? Answers vary, from "If that's happiness, you can have it" to "It wouldn't even be *your* life." "You wouldn't know you weren't doing what you thought you were doing; you might as well be a slug."

Such responses seem to imply one of two conclusions: (1) happiness is not the sole intrinsic good, or (2) happiness should not be identified with pleasure, but requires in addition true (or at least reasonable) belief about the realization of one's values, which is itself a value.

One position that goes part way toward reconciling this conflict is to claim that objective happiness (which includes true belief) includes subjective happiness, a view that Aristotle apparently held.

In an influential article, "Two Conceptions of Happiness," Richard Kraut has argued that a person is leading a happy life only if "he is attaining the important things he values, or if he comes reasonably close," if he knows this, and finds this life "genuinely rewarding." In this view, which Kraut calls "subjectivism," in order to be happy it is not enough that one believe that one is getting the important things one wants; one must actually get them (or come reasonably close). This is contrasted to "extreme subjectivism," according to which belief is sufficient, and "objectivism," according to which even true belief is insufficient: one's values must also be "correct."

Thus one might object that true belief concerning the realization of one's values is required for happiness, but it is not enough. Consider the following case. Suppose a man's only end in life is to amass the largest collection of bottlecaps in the world. He's worked very hard on this goal all his life, and finally achieves it: He is written up in the *Guinness Book of World Records* for the best bottlecap collection on earth. Is his a happy life?

This objection suggests that not only is realizing one's values important; one's values must themselves be worthy of pursuing and achieving. The final end of the bottlecap collector is too trivial, or perhaps irrational, and so achieving it cannot be productive of "true" happiness.

But by what standard do we judge "worthiness"?

In response to such an objection Kraut claims that we don't know what Aristotle thought he knew—how to live and so how to judge a life objectively good—and neither did Aristotle. If we did, and if happiness were the only (or at least one) way of living a good life, then happiness would have to meet objective conditions. But since we don't know what we would have to know to state and meet such conditions, we subjectivists-by-ignorance must do the best we can, just as the bottlecap collector is doing in pursuing his final end. And if he is successful, only prejudice prevents us from calling his life a happy one. So there are problems both with identifying happiness with subjective pleasure and with identifying happiness with objective virtue.

An unpopular though plausible position is that happiness even as objectively conceived and including a subjective component of pleasure or satisfaction is not the sole intrinsic good. Other things matter as much if not more: integrity, for example, or loyalty, or love.

The view of Plato (c. 427–347 B.C.) that all and only those who are just are *eudaimon* was motivated by this thought: One can be a just person (refusing to betray one's comrades, even on the rack) and be in continuous, excruciating pain. He concluded that one could be *eudaimon* even on the rack. In other words, given that *eudaimonia* is identified with justice, and justice is consistent with continuous, excruciating pain, it must follow that *eudaimonia* is consistent with continuous, excruciating pain. This is hard to swallow, or, as Aristotle claimed in the *Nicomachean Ethics*, it is "to maintain a thesis at all costs." One reason against it is that we would not (and could not, without irony) speak of the person abdicating the rack as sacrificing her happiness. If it is legitimate to substitute happiness for *eudaimonia* (which has in addition been translated as "human flourishing," "human well-being," and "well-grounded happiness"), a more plausible conclusion may be drawn from the justice-on-the-rack example: Justice (or integrity or loyalty or truth or love) is sometimes more important than happiness.

A possible objection to this view is that if justice, integrity, loyalty, truth, and love are great goods, then happiness must include them, since happiness is a comprehensive and self-sufficient good—that is, a good that includes all other important goods. This seems to be the view of both Aristotle and Mill, who conceived of happiness as the final end: intrinsically but not instrumentally good; sought for its own sake, the thing for which everything else is sought, and not itself sought for the sake of anything else. In this view, happiness is a good constituted by other goods.

Some find this view implausible. It may be true that if one values truth, integrity, and love very highly, then one cannot be subjectively happy without achieving these goods, but if objective happiness requires the realization of these goods, then it looks like there is less and less content to the claim that happiness is the sole intrinsic good, rather than some abstract complex we might more plausibly call the good life.

But now either happiness includes the subjective component of contentment or it does not. If it does, then happiness cannot compete with other valued goods. Though life would be a lot easier if such conflicts did not exist, this seems to be false. On the other hand, if happiness does not include contentment, then it's unclear why it should be called happiness at all, since it is consistent with continuous, excruciating pain.

Further, we speak not only of someone sacrificing her happiness for a greater good, but also of a person not deserving the happiness he has. If happiness were an objective, comprehensive good, then one could not be happy and not deserve it, since desert would be contained within it. So the claim that happiness is the sole intrinsic good seems to be (1) without sufficient content, or (2) false.

A common-sense view is that happiness is whatever you don't have right now that you want most. This view makes happiness logically impossible to achieve, and so irrational to aim at. But it has the virtue of explaining why happiness is so hard to come by, and why, when we get what we most want, we often no longer want it or immediately demote it in favor of other goods we still do not have. Desire, fulfilled, moves on. Or as George Bernard Shaw said, "There are two tragedies in life. One is not to get your heart's desire. The other is to get it."

Lynne McFall

See also: ARISTOTLE; JUSTICE; MILL; PLATO; UTILITARIANISM

Bibliography
Aristotle. *Nicomachean Ethics*. In *The Basic Works of Aristotle*, edited by Richard McKeon. New York: Random House, 1941.

Austin, Jean. "Pleasure and Happiness." *Philosophy* 43 (1928): 51–62.

Huxley, Aldous. *Brave New World*. New York: Harper and Row, 1932.

Irwin, T.H. "The Pursuit of Happiness." Unpublished manuscript. Personal Papers of Lynne McFall.

Kraut, Richard. "Two Conceptions of Happiness." *The Philosophical Review* 88 (1979): 167–97.

Mill, John Stuart. *Utilitarianism*. Edited by Samuel Gorovitz. Indianapolis, Ind.: Bobbs-Merrill, 1971.

Nozick, Robert. *Anarchy, State, and Utopia*. New York: Basic Books, 1974.

Plato. *The Republic*. In *The Collected Dialogues of Plato*, edited by Edith Hamilton and Huntington Cairns. Princeton: Princeton University Press, 1961.

Taylor, Charles. "Responsibility for Self." In *The Identities of Persons*, edited by Amelie Rorty. Berkeley and Los Angeles: University of California Press, 1976.

Telfer, Elizabeth. *Happiness*. New York: St. Martin's Press, 1980.

Thomas, D.A. Lloyd. "Happiness." *Philosophical Quarterly* 28 (1968): 97–113.

H

Watson, Gary. "Happiness and *Eudaimonia*." Unpublished manuscript. Personal Papers of Lynne McFall.

Wilson, John. "Happiness." *Analysis* 29 (1968): 13–21.

Harris, William Torrey (1835–1909)

Few Americans have combined educational theory and practice as successfully as William Torrey Harris. Along with Horace Mann and Henry Barnard, he was one of the three great architects of the American public school system. As superintendent of schools in St. Louis, Missouri, during the years of westward expansion following the Civil War, he created the prototype for both administration and pedagogy in America's rapidly developing public school system. During his tenure as U.S. commissioner of education, he used that office to extend his influence over the entire nation.

But Harris's accomplishments were not confined to educational administration and pedagogy. He was also an accomplished philosopher and during his lifetime perhaps the best-known translator and advocate of G.W.F. Hegel (1770–1831) in America. He never separated his roles as administrator, pedagogue, and philosopher, and, as a consequence, his influence extends across the entire spectrum of American educational philosophy and practice.

Harris was born in Killingly, Connecticut, on September 10, 1835. After an early education in the common schools of Killingly and Woodstock Academy, he entered Yale in 1854. Although successful in his studies, Harris's dissatisfaction with the impractical nature of Yale's curriculum led him to leave New Haven in 1857 without completing his degree. (Yale ultimately awarded Harris an honorary LL.D. in 1885 when he was U.S. commissioner of education).

While at Yale, Harris developed a deep interest in philosophy and psychology. Harris first accepted, then rejected, the then popular science of phrenology. His disillusionment with this early attempt to link brain physiology and psychology was caused by his rejection of the materialist ontology undergirding phrenology. In place of the materialism of phrenology, Harris developed a lifelong enthusiasm for Idealism. In 1856, during his last academic year at Yale, Harris met the American transcendentalist Amos Bronson Alcott. This encounter strengthened Harris's interest in Idealism and began a long friendship between the two philosophers.

In 1857, Harris left the safe haven of Yale and traveled to St. Louis, Missouri, the rapidly developing western center of American culture. After a brief period during which he supported himself by privately teaching Pitman shorthand, Harris became first a teacher (1858) and then a principal (1859) in the public schools of St. Louis. In 1867, Harris began his ascension to the highest levels of leadership in the St. Louis public schools. He received an appointment as assistant superintendent in that year; in the following year, the thirty-two-year-old New Englander was elected superintendent of one of the largest and fastest growing school systems in the country.

Harris's career as superintendent broke new ground in both administration and pedagogy. In 1873, he embraced Friedrich Froebel's kindergarten, and St. Louis became the first major school system to incorporate this innovation. In 1878, five years following the first introduction of the kindergarten into the St. Louis public schools, Harris's system included fifty kindergartens serving six thousand pupils. His success as an innovative educator brought him to national prominence.

While in St. Louis, Harris also acquired distinction as a philosopher. Early in his career there (1858), Harris had met Henry C. Brockmeyer, a young man with a strong interest in German academic philosophy, particularly the philosophy of Hegel. Brockmeyer turned Harris's philosophical interests toward Hegel, and, under Brockmeyer's inspiration, Harris taught himself German and perfected his command of the language. He then undertook the translation and exposition of Hegel's works in English. The two men became the driving force of a group of intellectuals known as the St. Louis Literary and Philosophical Society. This society became, in turn, the locus of the "St. Louis Movement," the most significant center of nineteenth-century American Hegelianism. Central to this movement was the *Journal of Speculative Philosophy,* founded by Harris and edited by him through twenty-two yearly volumes.

Although ill health forced him to leave his post as superintendent of the St. Louis schools in 1880, Harris continued his philosophical work in his new residence in Concord, Massachusetts. There he renewed his association with Alcott, dean of the newly formed Concord Summer School of Philosophy. Harris became an important member of the Concord School, lecturing on a variety of philosophical topics, particularly Hegelianism. At Concord, Harris did most of the research and writing for his most ambitious philosophical project, published in 1890 as a four-hundred-page book, *Hegel's Logic: A Book on the Genesis of the Categories of the Mind*.

By the time *Hegel's Logic* appeared, Harris had already accepted appointment, in 1889, as U.S. commissioner of education. He continued to exert strong influence on American education from this position until his retirement in 1906. Midway through his tenure as commissioner, he completed his most extensive publication on educational theory, *Psychologic Foundations of Education*. Following his retirement, he moved to Providence, Rhode Island, where he died in 1909.

In his combined role of philosopher and educator, Harris brought the philosophy of Hegel to bear on educational theory. Of primary importance in Harris's educational theory were Hegel's *Logic*, which focused on the dialectal pattern of reasoning, and his *Philosophy of History*, which interpreted history as the advance of the "World Spirit." From these works, Harris drew his Idealism, his pattern of reasoning, and his concern with "spirit."

Hegel had argued that history is the progress of the World Spirit from "matter" to "spirit." These two poles represent the distinction made by Immanuel Kant (1724–1804) between heteronomy and autonomy of the will. The heteronomous will is governed from without by instinct and material nature; the autonomous will is governed from within by rationality. Hegel considered the nature of spirit to be "freedom," the absolute correspondence of each individual's rational will with the total rationality of the society embodied in culture. Hegel personified the progressive advance toward this polarity of freedom as the World Spirit, and he identified the embodiment of this freedom in institutions, particularly the state.

Harris adapted this argument to educational theory by arguing that education is preparation for the "spiritual life"—that is, a life within the World Spirit, a life of social interaction. Thus education is the function by which the World Spirit is preserved and advanced. He wrote that "the great object . . . of education is the preparation of the individual for a life in institutions, the preparation of each individual for social combination."

For Harris, this function was the responsibility of four great institutions: the family, the vocation, the state, and the church. He envisioned the school not as an institution in this sense but as a mechanism that served the purposes of these four. The subordinate role of the school did not reduce its importance in Harris's view, however. The school had a vital role to fill in preserving and advancing each of the great institutions of society.

This understanding of the function of the school translated into a curricular emphasis on grammar, literature and art, mathematics, geography, and history. Harris thought these "tool" subjects to be important, especially in elementary education, to enable individuals to continue their education into adulthood through other educational agencies such as libraries, newspapers, and magazines.

Harris insisted upon disciplinary and cultural subjects and opposed the educational trend of the late nineteenth century toward narrowly utilitarian studies. He was an opponent of Herbert Spencer (1820–1903) in virtually every particular, including Spencer's advocacy of practical technological education. Harris was a champion of the classical languages, Latin and Greek, which he defended for their historic and cultural value and for their usefulness in the mastery of English. He saw technological education as overly narrow and limiting, and he minimized the importance of the growing movement for manual training.

Harris's Hegelianism translated into strong American nationalism. Hegel understood history as progress toward freedom, and Harris saw in America the vehicle for this progress. For Harris, America represented the continuation of the World Spirit in its advance toward freedom. This led Harris to support American expansion, including the imperialism of the Spanish-American War. Hegel had argued that only through the state can the individual be free, and Harris saw the advancing American state as the vehicle for freedom.

Harris shared Hegel's optimism concerning the progress of civilization. In the context of late-nineteenth-century America, this translated into approval of industrial capitalism and urbanization. Harris considered life within the city to be superior to rural life because of the increased opportunities for social interaction. The factory system brought with it increased wealth and opportunities for cultural advancement. He recognized the problems associated with the factory system, particularly the empha-

H

sis on limited, repetitive labor, but he considered this to be only a temporary phase in economic development.

In spite of Harris's emphasis on progress, he became known primarily as a conservative. Undoubtedly one reason for this perception is that his most significant work of educational theory, *Psychological Foundations of Education,* appeared late in his career, at a time when its Idealism was at variance with the empiricist trend of the times. Harris also became known as conservative because the developments he identified as progressive, the expansion of capitalism and the imperial American state, became associated with political conservatism.

However, Harris was an educational conservative in a more fundamental sense. He understood the school as basically an instrument for the social transmission of society's great institutions. His conservatism in this respect, reflected in his authorship of the very influential *Report of the Committee of Fifteen on Elementary Education* (1895), was formative in the development of the modern school curriculum. Yet it is possible to overstate his conservatism. Harris also understood the school to be necessary for the improvement of society, and many of his ideas in that respect were echoed in the Progressive Education Movement.

In one important respect, Harris set an example that can still inspire us. Through his speeches, his writings, and his actions, W.T. Harris demonstrated that philosophy could be effectively combined with educational practice in a consistent and powerful educational theory. Few have been his equal in that important endeavor.

Richard Olmsted

See also CONSERVATISM; FROEBEL; HEGEL; IDEALISM

Bibliography

Curti, Merle. *The Social Ideas of American Educators.* New York: Charles Scribner's Sons, 1935.

Harris, William Torrey. *Hegel's Logic: A Book on the Genesis of the Categories of the Mind. A Critical Exposition.* Chicago: S.C. Griggs and Company, 1890.

———. *Psychologic Foundations of Education. An Attempt to Show the Genesis of the Higher Faculties of the Mind.* New York: D. Appleton and Company, 1989.

———, A.S. Draper, and H.S. Tarbel. *Report of the Committee of Fifteen on Elementary Education.* Boston: New England Publishing Company, 1895.

John, Walton C., ed. *William Torrey Harris. The Commemoration of the One Hundredth Anniversary of His Birth 1835–1935.* Washington, D.C.: U.S. Department of the Interior, 1936.

Leidecker, Kurt F. *Yankee Teacher: The Life of William Torrey Harris.* New York: Philosophical Library, 1946.

McCluskey, Neil Gerard. *Public Schools and Moral Education: The Influence of Horace Mann, William Torrey Harris, and John Dewey.* New York: Columbia University Press, 1958.

Pochmann, Henry A. *New England Transcendentalism and St. Louis Hegelianism: Phases in the History of American Idealism.* Philadelphia: Charles Schurz Memorial Foundation, 1948.

Hegel, Georg Wilhelm Friedrich (1770–1831)

German philosopher who held appointments at the universities of Jena (1801–1806), Heidelberg (1816–1818), and Berlin (1818–1831). Between his appointments at Jena and Heidelberg, he was editor of a newspaper, the *Bamberger Zeitung* (1807–1808); following that, he was appointed rector of the Nürnberg Gymnasium (1808–1816). Hegel published four major works during his lifetime: *Phenomenology of Spirit* (1807); *Science of Logic* (1812–1816); *Encyclopedia of the Philosophical Sciences in Outline* (1817, 1827); and *Philosophy of Right* (1821). Following his death, an edition of his works was produced including volumes of his lectures on fine art, philosophy of history, philosophy of religion, and the history of philosophy.

Hegel's full compass of work contains, in addition to the above, a group of early writings, many of which are on religion, and writings from the Jena period that work out the principles of his system. There are also a number of works on specific political issues, which were published at points throughout his career. The philosophical movements and schools of the later nineteenth and twentieth centuries are incomprehensive unless understood as either extensions of or reactions to the system of Hegel and Hegelianism: from Karl Marx (1818–1883) to Friedrich Nietzsche (1844–1900) and Soren Kierkegaard (1813–1855), to Jean-Paul Sartre

(1905–1980) and Martin Heidegger (1889–1976), as well as William James (1842–1910) and John Dewey (1859–1952). This is also true of modern British philosophy, with its roots in Bertrand Russell (1872–1970) and G.E. Moore (1873–1958), who were reacting to what they found unacceptable in the philosophies of figures such as J.M.E. McTaggart (1866–1925), F.H. Bradley (1846–1924), and Bernard Bosanquet (1848–1923), whose Hegelianism dominated the British universities.

Hegel's conception of the developmental nature of human consciousness and forms of political and social life established the basis for the beginnings of social science and social thought in the twentieth century. This sense of the developmental character of human consciousness and human experience is at the basis of Hegel's conception of education. The term in German for education, around which Hegel's views revolve, is *Bildung,* a term not readily rendered into English. *Bildung* has as its root *bilden* (to form, to make). *Bildung* might best be understood as "human education," or forming or raising the individual up to the level of culture. *Bildung* is not identified with education in the sense of some formal program or curriculum of instruction in a school system. It refers to the actual process of an individual's combining, in one's own being, the values and ideas of human culture—a full level of spiritual and intellectual development that would describe a "cultivated" person in the best sense of the word.

Hegel's *Phenomenology of Spirit,* which provides the introduction and basis for his system, has been described as a *Bildungsroman*—that is, as being like a philosophical novel of the eighteenth century that gives the "inner history" or formulation of the hero's character, a work of self-understanding that is often also the spiritual autobiography of its author. In the *Phenomenology,* Hegel presents the stages of the experience of consciousness wherein human consciousness becomes consciousness of itself. In this sense, Hegel's *Phenomenology* is a conception and presentation of the education of consciousness.

In the *Philosophy of Right,* Hegel carries forth the view that education (*Bildung*) is the development of the particular individual away from what is purely subjective and unique to the individual and toward what is universal in human experience. This is a view grounded in Hegel's conception of subjective mind (*Geist*) presented in the section on anthropology in the third part of the *Encyclopedia,* the *Philosophy of Mind* (*Geist*) (secs. 395 [*Zusatz*] and 398 [*Zusatz*]). The individual, through the process of education, should lay aside the idiosyncrasies of a particular perspective or the perspective of the family, circle of friends, and society, and should attempt to grasp the existing general culture of humanity. Hegel says: "This reshaping of the soul, this alone is what education means. The more educated a man is, the less is there apparent in his behaviour anything peculiar only to him, anything therefore that is merely contingent" (*Encyclopedia* 395 [*Zusatz*]).

Hegel expands this view in his doctrine of civil society in the presentation of Objective Mind (*Geist*) in the *Philosophy of Right.* He denies that the state of nature is a state of innocence, because that implies treating education as purely external, and a form of corruption. He also denies that the pleasures and comforts of private life are absolute ends, for that would imply that education is merely a means to those ends. Hegel identifies education with that freedom obtained by the individual's going beyond the state of particular origins or immediate private needs and pleasures. He states: "The final purpose of education, therefore, is liberation and the struggle for a higher liberation still; education is the absolute transition from an ethical substantiality which is immediate and natural to one which is intellectual and so both infinitely subjective and lofty enough to have attained universality of form" (*Philosophy of Right* 187 [*Zusatz*]).

In practical terms, Hegel holds that the parents have a duty to elevate their children, but they do not have a right to countermand the interests of civil society in the forming of a common school system and ordering it for the public good (*Philosophy of Right* 277, par. 239). He stands against Rousseau's view in *Emile* of withdrawing children from common everyday life to educate them in solitude, because "it is by becoming a citizen of a good state that the individual first comes into his right" (ibid. 261, addition to par. 153).

In matters of curriculum, Hegel is a traditionalist. In a lecture, "On Classical Studies," delivered in 1809 while he was rector of the Gymnasium at Nürnberg, Hegel firmly advocates that the thorough study of "ancient languages [Greek and Latin] remains as before the basis of learned knowledge" (p. 324). The study of these languages is, for Hegel, based in the mastery of their grammar. "Strict grammar study is accordingly one of the most universal and noble forms of intellectual education" (p. 330). This puts Hegel generally on the side of the *studia humanitatis* of the Renaissance humanists, with the addition, to their conception of humanistic learning, of a study of the rising fields of natural science.

The one group in the history of American education that attempted to transform Hegel's conception of education as the development of self-activity in accord with the universal conditions of public life was the St. Louis Hegelian movement of the latter part of the nineteenth century. The leading figure of this movement, in respect to education, was William Torrey Harris (1835–1909). Harris taught school in St. Louis, Missouri, for eight years and served as a school administrator for fourteen years. He was U.S. commissioner of education from 1889 to 1906. Harris saw connections of Hegel's conception of education with democracy, and he criticized excessive emphasis on vocationalism in preference to promotion of the cultivation of the mind and development of citizenship. Harris saw Hegel's principle of the self-developing of *Geist* in the individual as the proper basis for the systems of American democracy, and for the education of the individual within it.

Donald Phillip Verene

See also DEMOCRACY; DEWEY; HARRIS; HEIDEGGER; INDIVIDUALISM; JAMES; KIERKEGAARD; MARX; NIETZSCHE; ROUSSEAU; RUSSELL; SARTRE; *Studia Humanitatis*; VOCATIONAL EDUCATION

Bibliography

Hegel, Georg Wilhelm Friedrich. "On Classical Studies." In *On Christianity, Early Theological Writings,* translated by T.M. Knox, 321–30. New York: Harper Torchbooks, 1961.

———. *Phenomenology of Spirit.* Translated by A.V. Miller. Oxford: Clarendon Press, 1977.

———. *Philosophy of Mind.* Translated by William Wallace and A.V. Miller. Oxford: Clarendon Press, 1971.

———. *Philosophy of Right.* Translated by T.M. Knox. Oxford: Clarendon Press, 1962.

Mackenzie, Millicent. *Hegel's Educational Theory and Practice.* London, 1909.

Smith, John H. *The Spirit and Its Letter: Traces of Rhetoric in Hegel's Philosophy of Bildung.* Ithaca, N.Y.: Cornell University Press, 1988.

Heidegger, Martin (1889–1976)

German philosopher, one of the leading figures in both existentialism and phenomenology, as well as a central inspiration for hermeneutics and much of what goes by the name "postmodernism." His career falls roughly into two halves, divided by his involvement with Nazism: an early phase (1923–1933) highlighted by his magnum opus, *Being and Time* (1927); and a late phase (1934–1976), consisting of a great many works with no single system or line of thinking.

Being and Time (*B & T*) is a treatise in what Heidegger calls "existential phenomenology." It aims to use the methods pioneered by the founder of phenomenology, Edmund Husserl (1859–1938), to describe human beings (and ultimately being in general) without accepting traditional philosophy's privileging of disengaged mental activity over engaged social practice. Heidegger argues that the intelligibility of human activity derives primarily from exercising capacities for prereflective action, guided and given their purpose by the implicit norms and sedimented understandings of the social milieu in which we live. Because he does not argue that all activity is action, or behavior, and because he claims that action is guided by norms and understandings, he should not be thought of as a behaviorist. Our behavior is not simply a set of motions characterizable independently of the self-understanding that it embodies. We are socialized into shared meanings, self-interpretations, ways of seeing the world, and ways of letting that world matter to us. These shared structures make up the horizon on which any object of our explicit attention shows up. Moreover, they constitute a shared world in which we always find ourselves already living with others. Thus, he gives the name "being-in-the-world" to our way of being.

Heidegger argues that this new account of the basic manner of existence of human beings dissolves some traditional philosophical problems and generates new problems of its own. Among the problems dissolved are these: skeptical challenges to the possibility of knowledge of anything beyond our own mental states; worries about the possibility of truth and reference; and metaphysical questions such as whether we have personal identity, and if we do, how. These problems are all premised upon flawed pictures of human existence. We are not "worldless subjects" trying to gain some grasp of a world essentially beyond our direct knowledge. We are neither substances nor substance-analogs, whose temporal continuity would have to be the endurance of some stuff through time. Rather, we are engaged agents already functioning "outside ourselves" in a world whose basic structures and meanings have been given to us by our culture. Our knowledge is a working mastery of the possibilities and things in that world. Finally, our personal identity resides in the self-interpretations we assign to ourselves through our basic resolutions.

The new problems are generally "existential" in character, and inspired by the writings of Soren Kierkegaard (1813–1855) and Friedrich Nietzsche (1844–1900). Because the foundation of all meaning and self-interpretation lies in our embeddedness in our culture, individuality becomes a problem. In order that we can be socialized into those cultural practices that dominate in our social milieu, we must be moldable creatures. This opens up the possibility of—and Heidegger claims, a tendency to—conformism. Pliability, when too thorough, creates a herd, each of whose members enjoys only leveled-off, insignificant possibilities. Also, Heidegger contends that we use conformism to flee from the onslaught of anxiety that arises when we confront our particularity (usually in facing up to death). We bury our anxiety in public "idle-talk." Conformist humans are inauthentic, in the language of *Being and Time,* because they do not take responsibility for who they are. Authentic people, in contrast, resolutely take up some self-understanding available in their culture, and live it out even in the midst of anxiety in the face of death.

Heidegger used the term *hermeneutic* to describe the theory of human existence central to *Being and Time.* Hermeneutics is the theory of interpretation. (The term applied originally to biblical interpretation but took on more general significance through the work of Wilhelm Dilthey [1833–1911] and Heidegger). Heidegger's account of human beings is hermeneutic in two ways: First, it assigns interpretation a central role in human life. All understanding and explanation departs from a shared, contextualizing background of social practice, and can in the end only clarify and extend—interpret—what is already there. Hence, he describes understanding as "circular." Circularity is not a defect of understanding, but rather its general form. There is no way to jump outside our personal, cultural, and historical context, to evaluate our beliefs and interpretations in an objective fashion.

This line of thought suggests that learning is not the incorporation of information from the outside, but rather the development of abilities and potentialities in which one is already involved. Heidegger's account focuses on the concepts of acquiring and developing abilities. We acquire abilities (or "potentialities") chiefly through socialization and imitation (*B & T*: I.4), almost never through deliberate devotion to rule-following. It is only once we are already enmeshed within the know-how and possibilities of some ability, that we are temporarily able to step back, focus on, deliberately reshape, and evaluate it. The molding discussed above causes us to absorb abilities in the first place from the people around us. We develop our abilities under the pressure of circumstances, when they fail to achieve their aim. It is typically in the clutch of such failures that we become aware of our abilities, their goals, and limitations (*B & T*: I.3). Such awareness gives rise to forms of reflection and learning that Heidegger calls "interpretation" (*B & T*: I.5), "deliberation," and "theory" (*B & T*: II.4). His account of these phenomena is general in nature; the details must be developed by others.

Second, Heidegger describes his phenomenological method as hermeneutic. Phenomenology is the philosophical tool of what we may call "plain description": describing things just as they show themselves to us. The topic of phenomenology, according to Husserl (in his middle phase, during which Heidegger was his assistant), is what Husserl called "noemata." These are nonnatural entities, independent of individuals, cultures, and history, which explain how experiences have the meanings they do—for example, why my thought about a unicorn is about a unicorn. The goal of Husserlian phenomenology is to shed all our personal, cultural, and historically conditioned presuppositions, and describe these noemata and how they work. Heidegger objected to this on two grounds. On the one hand, there is no way for human beings to describe anything independently of their personal, cultural, and historical backgrounds. On the other hand, human experience is made meaningful by structures, which Heidegger calls "meaning" (*B & T*: I.5), that belong to that background. Thus, Husserlian presuppositionless description, were it even possible, would be unable to describe meaning, since such description would abandon the very vantage point from which meaning is visible. Phenomenology must become, then, the expression in language of the structures of meaning—and ultimately, being, though Heidegger does not quite get this far—in which we find ourselves as a matter of fact already embedded. It is necessarily hermeneutic.

Through *Being and Time,* Heidegger established his place as one of the most innovative and powerful philosophers of the twentieth century. The next phase of his life, centering on 1933–1934, marks him also as one of the most controversial intellectual figures of the century. Heidegger became *Rektor* (roughly, president) of Freiburg University and joined the Nazi Party. He played a significant role in the reorganization of that university along the lines dictated by the Third Reich, and he delivered speeches exhorting students and teachers alike to follow the path of Hitler. This episode has given rise to a series of questions that now occupy the attention of many researchers: How intense was Heidegger's involvement in the politics of the Nazi Party? How deep was his commitment to some version of Nazi ideology? How well thought out were his social and political convictions during this period? How did his involvement with Nazism influence his pedagogy? And most important, Is there a substantial connection between his political engagement with Nazism and his philosophical thought?

The later phase of Heidegger's philosophical development is a complex series of reflections, dead ends, questions, and warnings. It is impossible to present his later thought in the fashion of a philosophical system. Three salient aspects of it are worth describing, however. Heidegger's view of our relationship to being and to language shifted after *Being and Time. Being and Time* aimed to exhibit the general features by virtue of which anything that is can be said to be (call this "being"), and to show how these features arise out of the deep structure of the human ability to understand things. This approach is broadly Kantian. Later, in stark contrast, Heidegger suggests that both the structure of human understanding and the general features of everything that is are "gifts" of the ultimate mystery of being. Put more cautiously, although human understanding and being are always keyed to one another, neither can explain the other, and, moreover, both are at bottom inexplicable. *Being and Time*'s account of language is somewhat disordered, but it seems to suggest that language is one way in which cultural meanings are embodied. Language is just another aspect of human behavior, albeit one that expresses other aspects of that behavior. Later, Heidegger (*On the Way to Language*), again in stark contrast, argues that language, like being, is ultimately inexplicable. It is not simply the expression of cultural meanings, but a deposit of being itself (the "house of being"). It gives meaning and place to whatever we experience, but we can get no grip on what produces it.

This dominant element of inexplicability that occupies center stage in Heidegger's later thought sometimes leads to almost a sort of mysticism. He claims that our fundamental attitude toward things must be one of "letting-be," in an echo of the German mystic Meister Eckhart (d. 1327). We should not try to master the basic constitution of things, indeed, not even try to understand it, but rather just accept being. Moreover, the traditional tasks of philosophy, such as metaphysics (explaining being) and epistemology (explaining how we can understand things, including being), are now otiose. They try to explain the inexplicable. At times, in fact, Heidegger suggests that philosophy itself is no longer a viable enterprise, and should surrender to the special sciences those respectable chores to which it still clings.

The preceding lines of thought may suggest a sort of quietism, but there is another element in the later Heideggerian brew: an extensive criticism of our current understanding of being. Heidegger came to think of being as possessing a history. The inexplicable gift of being has come to us in epochs: the Greek, the medieval, the early modern, and the contemporary. The distinctive character of the contemporary dispensation of being lies in what Heidegger calls "technology" (see *The Question Concerning Technology and Other Essays*). "Technology" here does not have its standard meaning as the engineered application of the results of science. Rather, it refers to the presentation of entities as items to be ordered into the total system of resources on standby for use. Since we too are entities, and thus are also so understood (as "human resources"), our enjoyment, for example, is not the ultimate goal of this ordering. That goal is simply further ordering. Thus, Heidegger constructs a frightening image of the tendency toward a totalizing incorporation of everything into one vast, pointless system. In the process, all locality is ground up and leveled off into a grid of resources. His answer to this dark vision is simply that we must wait to be saved by "a god." We cannot, after all, control the history of being.

William D. Blattner

See also EXISTENTIALISM; KIERKEGAARD; PHENOMENOLOGY

Bibliography

Dreyfus, Hubert L. *Being-in-the-World*. Cambridge: Massachusetts Institute of Technology Press, 1991.

Guignon, Charles B., ed. *The Cambridge Companion to Heidegger*. Cambridge: Cambridge University Press, 1993.

Heidegger, Martin. *Being and Time*. Translated by John Macquarrie and Edward Robinson. New York: Harper and Row, 1962.

———. *On the Way to Language*. Translated by Peter D. Hertz. New York: Harper and Row, 1971.

———. *The Question Concerning Technology and Other Essays*. Translated by William Lovitt. New York: Harper and Row, 1977.

Ott, Hugo. *Martin Heidegger: A Political Life*. Translated by Allan Blunden. New York: Basic Books, 1993.

Poggeler, Otto. *Martin Heidegger's Path of Thinking*. Translated by Daniel Magurshak and Sigmund Barber. Atlantic Highlands, N.J.: Humanities Press International, 1987.

Helvetius, Claude-Adrien (1715–1771)

French philosopher, whose *De l'Esprit* (1758) brought down the wrath of the religious establishment because of its anticlericalism and its argument that all mental life is reducible to sensations. His *De l'Homme, de ses Faculties intellectuelles et de son Education* (1772) was published posthumously.

It would be difficult to imagine a more strongly environmentalist position than the one taken by Helvetius. He argued that human beings are nothing more than the products of their education, which means that in their own hands is the instrument of their well-being. Perfecting the science of education is required if the instrument is to be rightly used.

Accompanying Helvetius's environmentalism was an equally strong equalitarianism. Here he differed from John Locke (1632–1704), whose belief in political equality in a state of nature recognized individual differences in "organization" or "parts"—what today would be called hereditary differences. Helvetius insisted that there are no such differences, that all human beings are equally disposed to understand-ing. To prove such an assertion, he claimed, we must turn to the idea that all operations of the mind are reducible to sensations. By sensations, Helvetius meant the observations by which the mind detects similarities and differences, agreements and disagreements of objects with one another and with the observer. The question How do judgments come about in sensation? was answered by saying that, in the activity of observing, to judge is to feel. In other words, sensations themselves are judgments; what we call mind is the effect of the faculty of sensation. All things can be explained by our sensations; no other faculty is necessary.

If human beings are to understand things and human relationships, Helvetius went on, they must have an interest in comparing sensations in order to grasp the similarities and differences between objects. Human beings must learn to follow the good passions, such as glory and the love of truth. Such passions we owe to a sentiment natural to human beings, which Helvetius called self-love. Yet, if directed to the wrong passions, self-love may lead us to evil. Thus we are born neither good nor bad, and both the virtues and vices we acquire are consequences of the way in which the sentiment of self-love becomes the instrument of our education. Good social consequences—for example, the love of one's neighbor—are the effect of one's love for oneself.

Helvetius's confidence in the good prospects of self-love had its counterpart in his belief that fundamental truths are by nature simple, that human beings are able to represent them clearly, and that all truths in their essential features are comprehensible to all minds. Thus the confidence that Helvetius had in human abilities to discover, represent, and learn fundamental truths was as firm as his confidence that the sentiment of self-love has adequate force to make human beings attend to the passions required to interest them in learning those truths.

Helvetius's portrayal of strong environmentalism and equalitarianism can scarcely be excelled. The tendency of his equalitarianism to emphasize similarities among human beings earned the criticism of Denis Diderot (1713–1784), who prized human differences. And his reduction of mind to sensations and its corollary that to judge is to feel has come to be seen as a notorious over-simplification. Even so, his fervent belief has endured: that, because vices and virtues are strangers to human nature, both must be acquired; and "education can do all."

J.J. Chambliss

See also DIDEROT; EQUALITY; HUMAN NA-TURE; LOCKE; ROUSSEAU; UTILITARIANISM

Bibliography

Compayre, Gabriel. *The History of Peda-gogy.* Translated by W. H. Payne. Boston: D.C. Heath, 1888.

Cumming, Ian. *Helvetius: His Life and Place in the History of Educational Thought.* London: Routledge and Kegan Paul, 1955.

Helvetius, Claude-Adrien. *A Treatise on Man, His Intellectual Faculties and His Education.* Translated by W. Hooper. 2 vols. London: B. Law and G. Robinson, 1777.

———. *De l'Esprit; or, Essays on the Mind, and Its Several Faculties.* Translated from the French. London: M. Jones, 1807.

Herbart, Johann Friedrich (1776–1841)

German educator, philosopher, and psychologist. The precocious young Herbart studied Greek with his mother under a tutor, was talented in mathematics and music, and began the study of logic at eleven and metaphysics at twelve. At the University of Jena, Herbart studied under Johann Fichte (1762–1814) but abandoned Fichte's Idealism to become one of the founders of modern philosophical Realism. From 1796 to 1799 Herbart was tutor to three boys, visited the school of Johann Pestalozzi (1746–1827) at Burgdorf, and wrote his first works on education. Then he completed a doctorate at Göttingen, and stayed on to teach philosophy and pedagogy until 1809, when he occupied the chair of philosophy in Königsberg earlier held by Immanuel Kant (1724–1804).

At Königsberg, Herbart distinguished himself by his extensive writings in philosophy, pedagogy, and psychology. He also established a pedagogical seminary and a practice school that was connected with it. This launched what was to become a widespread attempt in the late nineteenth century to make education a scientific study and to try out ideas of educational theorists in a practice school connected with a university. In Herbart's thinking, education was taken to be a subject of philosophic study, along with aesthetics, ethics, and metaphysics, and was capable of becoming a science in its own right.

Herbart's Realism—the idea that real things exist independently of the operations of the mind—has its psychological and educational expression in the idea that mind is formed by subject matter presented to it from external sources. This point of view is opposed to the "romantic" idea that mind develops from within, by "unfolding," a common metaphor. It is opposed also to what was commonly called faculty psychology, the idea that education proceeds by training "faculties," such as memory, attention, and thinking, which exist innately within the mind. Herbart was adamant in holding that these so-called faculties are arrangements and associations of what is presented to the mind. While mind does not possess faculties, it has the power to respond to external material in qualitatively different ways; such responses Herbart called "presentations," which become clarified as "ideas." Thus Herbart's educational theory emphasizes instruction, by which mind literally is built up, becomes constituted as the ideas produced in response to the material presented. As John Dewey (1859–1952) put it in *Democracy and Education*: "The 'furniture' of the mind *is* the mind. Mind is wholly a matter of 'contents.'"

Ideas of the mind relate to one another and to new presentations in a process that Herbart called "apperception." In Herbart's theorizing, ideas rise above or fall below the "threshold" of consciousness according to their power to fuse, combine, or repel one another. "Similar" ideas, Herbart thought, fuse into a strongly unified whole, powerful in resisting other ideas; "disparate" ideas also combine, but form a cluster or group rather than a strong unity. "Contrary" ideas oppose one another rather than combine. It is clear, then, why the order of presentation of subject matter is extremely important in instruction, so that ideas combine to form the strongest possible unities. In Herbart's most optimistic scientific aim, ideas were calculated to combine or oppose one another in mathematical relationships.

Herbart's idea that instruction builds the contents of the mind—which contents *become* the mind—has its moral dimension as well, by which the character of students is built: "Instruction must universally point out, connect, teach, philosophize," he writes. "In matters appertaining to sympathy it should be observing, continuous, elevating, active in the sphere of reality." Thus it is clear that Herbart's instruction aims not just to instruct in morality, but also to develop a person who will act according to moral judgments made. While character is dependent on knowledge, Herbart did not think of character as consisting of a mechanical collection of unified ideas, but as coming about in the development of the child's will, which Herbart considered to be the seat of character. Here, will is not a faculty to be trained, but a tendency to act in certain ways that can be built into the mind. Will attempts to control the objects of its desire, while interest—an emotion whose study Herbart strongly influenced—is dependent on its objects. This is to say that teachers, at least in part, can control students' interests by determining the subjects in which they become interested—the ideas found in school subjects that are capable of becoming part of students' apperceptive processes. Yet "instruction in the sense of mere information-giving contains no guarantee whatever that it will materially counteract faults and influence existing groups of ideas that are independent of the imparted information," Herbart writes. This means that interest, like all emotions, must be acquired; and it must be "felt," not merely "known," so that will is stimulated to move an individual to act. The development of interest and its active corollary, will, does not exist "naturally," Herbart believed, for life offers too many other opportunities that might shape character in undesirable ways. The building of character is too important to be left to casual mind-building. Character needs to be built through the employment of a careful educational method.

Herbart worked out a method of instruction that he thought conformed to the working and developing of young minds. In this plan he distinguished between "absorption," an activity of letting the subject matter have its way with the learner by simply acquiring its ideas; and "reflection," the combining of acquired ideas into unified wholes, as discussed above. Herbart characterized four steps in instruction: (1) "clearness" is the presentation of subject matter, whose ideas are to be "absorbed"; (2) "association" is the uniting of these ideas with others already acquired (this is mainly "absorption" with some "reflection"); (3) "system" is the arrangement of what has been associated into coherent unified wholes (called "passive" reflection); and (4) "method" is the practical application of the system to new subject matter (called "active" reflection). Herbart did not think of these steps as a procedure to be rigidly followed, but as elements in the process of thinking, by which we learn to move from in-

creasingly clarified and unified ideas to their place in modifying actions taken; or, put differently, as ways of characterizing the development of interests, leading to that conduct that judgment says needs to be taken. For Herbart, the method is not closed, but open, in that the practical application in step 4 brings about a need for a new step 1. In other words, new subject matter is needed to be absorbed by the ideas engaged in active reflection in step 4.

A quarter of a century after Herbart's death, two schools of "Herbartianism" were established by his followers. One, by Tuiskon Ziller (1817–1883) at Leipzig, elaborated on Herbart's ideas of "correlation"—the emphasis on the unification of studies—and "concentration"—the unifying of studies around a common central study, such as history or literature. It was Ziller, also, who worked out the "culture epochs" theory of child development—the notion that children's mental development follows the main epochs in the mental development of the human race, and that subject matter employed in each stage of child development should be taken from its parallel stage in the cultural development of the race. Ziller's work led to the formation in Germany of an "Association for the Scientific Study of Education."

Another school, headed by Karl Stoy (1815–1885) at Jena, established a pedagogical and practice school based on Herbart's at Konigsberg. Later, Wilhelm Rein, who had studied with both Ziller and Stoy, succeeded Stoy at Jena and developed a curriculum for German elementary schools. This curriculum was worked out in Jena's practice school, and Jena became the center of Herbartian theory and practice and attracted students of pedagogy from outside Germany, including the United States.

In the last decade of the nineteenth and the early years of the twentieth century, Herbartianism reached its high water mark in the United States, influencing many in normal schools and universities who tried to develop a science of education. America's own "National Herbart Society for the Scientific Study of Education" was organized in 1895 "to study and investigate and discuss important problems of education." Charles DeGarmo, who had published a Herbartian work, *The Essentials of Method* (1889), became the society's first president. Among other prominent American Herbartians were Charles and Frank McMurry, who wrote *The Method of the Recitation* (1897) and went on to write many other

H

volumes on educational method. The society began publishing yearbooks, which included non-Herbartian authors whose thinking was stimulated by Herbartian ideas. As examples, John Dewey's "Interest as Related to the Will" (1896) and "Ethical Principles Underlying Education" (1897) were Herbart Society publications. In 1902, Herbart's name was dropped as the society became the National Society for the Scientific Study of Education; eventually it became the National Society for the Study of Education, the name by which it is known today.

Herbart's works and those of the Herbartians are seldom read today. Yet they had an important place in the nineteenth-century development of the science of education. And Herbart's ideas have endured whenever thinking, moral judgment, and conduct are taken to be parts of the same growing reality.

J.J. Chambliss

See also FROEBEL; PESTALOZZI; REALISM

Bibliography

Cole, P.R. *Herbart and Froebel: An Attempt at Synthesis.* New York: Teachers College, Columbia University, 1907.

DeGarmo, Charles. *Herbart and the Herbartians.* New York: C. Scribner's, 1895.

———. *The Essentials of Method.* D.C. Heath, 1889.

Dunkel, Harold Baker. *Herbart & Education.* New York: Random House, 1969.

———. *Herbart and Herbartianism: An Educational Ghost Story.* Chicago: University of Chicago Press, 1970.

Herbart, Johann Friedrich. *Outlines of Educational Doctrine.* Translated by Alexis F. Lange. New York: Macmillan, 1911.

———. *Sammtliche werke.* Herausgegeben von G. Hartenstein. 15 vols. in 14. Leipzig: L. Voss, 1850–1909.

———. *Science of Education . . . and The Aesthetic Revelation of the World.* Translated by Henry M. and Emmie Felkin. Boston: D.C. Heath, 1893.

Mac Vannell, John Angus. *The Educational Theories of Herbart and Froebel.* New York: Teachers College, Columbia University, 1905.

McMurry, Charles A. *The Elements of General Method Based on the Principles of Herbart.* New York: Macmillan, 1903.

———, and Frank McMurry. *The Method of the Recitation.* Bloomington, Ill.: Public School Publishing Co., 1897.

Randels, George Basil. *The Doctrines of Herbart in the United States.* Philadelphia: University of Pennsylvania, 1909.

Heredity and Hereditarianism

Heredity is usually defined as the genetic transmission of characteristics from parent to offspring. This, however, is an oversimplification. The child does not inherit characteristics or traits from its parents. Children do not inherit musical ability, criminal tendencies, or I.Q. Neither do they inherit physical characteristics such as skin or hair color. The child inherits one set of alleles from each parent. Together they form the child's genotype. The child also inherits mitochondria that are outside the nucleus of the cell. Genes code for the production of proteins, which in turn interact with the environment to produce a phenotype. What we refer to as traits or characteristics are the phenotypes. Human beings in all their complexity are the result of this interaction of unique genotypes with unique environments.

The modern study of heredity began with the rediscovery in 1900 of the work of Gregor Mendel (1822–1884) by Hugo De Vries, Karl Correns, and Erich Tschermak. Mendel discovered the basic laws of segregation and independent assortment of paired alleles, which opened the way for the modern science of genetics. The American geneticist Thomas Hunt Morgan (1866–1945) carried on studies of heredity in *Drosophila* (fruit fly) and was awarded the Nobel Prize in 1933 for his discoveries relating to the laws and mechanisms of heredity. Morgan showed the existence of genes located at specific sites on chromosomes. These theoretical discoveries enabled George Shull, operating at the Carnegie Institution's genetics research facility at Cold Spring Harbor, New York, to develop the technology of plant hybridization. The practical result was a revolution in farming techniques that vastly increased the world's food production between 1920 and 1950. This "green revolution" led many to believe that the science of genetics would banish hunger. It also led some to an exaggerated belief in the power of genetics to explain human character traits and solve human social and political problems (hereditarianism).

Hereditarianism, or biological determinism, as it is also called, is the belief that individual differences in human beings can be accounted for primarily on the basis of genetics. Further, many hereditarians believe that racial or ethnic groups differ, on average, in socially important traits such as intelligence, altruism, and aggression. Hereditarians have explained race and class differences as reflecting differences in innate ability. *Webster's Third International Dictionary* defines *racism* as "the assumption that psychocultural traits and capacities are determined by biological race and that races differ decisively from one another which is usually coupled with a belief in the inherent superiority of a particular race and its right to domination over others." Thus, hereditarianism has been associated, from its origins, with racism.

Francis Galton (1822–1911) may be considered the father of modern hereditarianism. Galton, Charles Darwin's half-cousin, is best known as the founder of the eugenics movement. He coined the term *eugenics* in 1883 in his widely read book *Inquiries into Human Faculty and Its Development.* Galton took the word from the Greek *eugenes,* which means "to be well born." He defined eugenics as a "science" that "takes cognizance of all influences that tend in however remote a degree to give the more suitable races or strains of blood a better chance of prevailing speedily over the less suitable than they otherwise would have had." Galton noted that the Negro, Hindu, Arab, Mongol, and Teuton all have "their peculiar characters," that "are transmitted, generation after generation" (Galton: 26). He believed that whites are intellectually superior to blacks and he hoped "inferior" races would gradually become extinct.

Galton's British disciples, including Karl Pearson, R.A. Fisher, Charles Spearman, Cyril Burt, Raymond B. Cattell, and Hans J. Eysenck, have all been advocates of eugenics. In the United States, the eugenics movement was sponsored by leading psychologists such as Robert M. Yerkes, Carl C. Brigham, Lewis M. Terman, and Henry H. Goddard; it reached its peak of influence in the 1920s. By 1930, a majority of states had passed eugenic sterilization laws, which allowed for the forced sterilization of people thought to have bad genes. In 1924 the eugenics movement aided in the passage of the Johnson Immigration Restriction Act, which restricted the immigration of racial and ethnic groups thought to be biologically inferior to the Western European white Protestant stock that made up the majority of the country. In Europe, the eugenics movement peaked with the rise of Adolf Hitler and the Nazi Party. Eugenic ideology in Nazi-occupied Europe led to the sterilization of millions of individuals, death camps, and breeding farms.

On the opposite side of the spectrum are the behaviorists, or social determinists. The father of behaviorism is John Locke (1623–1704). Locke advanced the idea that the mind is a *tabula rasa,* or blank slate, at birth. Behaviorists postulate that there are no prenatal differences. The leading exponent of behaviorism in the United States was the American psychologist John B. Watson (1878–1958). Watson argued that the environment in which the child is brought up determines intelligence and character. He claimed that given complete control over the environment of a child he could guarantee to train him to become any type of specialist—"doctor, lawyer, artist" and even "beggar man and thief"—regardless of the talents or tendencies of his parents or race.

The debate between the hereditarians and the behaviorists is known as the "nature-nurture controversy." Between the two extremes are exponents of the "norm of reaction" concept. Jerry Hirsch, a behavioral geneticist, has been one of the leading exponents of this position. The norm of reaction is the range of possible phenotypes that may develop from any genotype. According to this concept, each unique genotype can develop into various phenotypes. In fact, theoretically, each genotype can develop into an infinite number of possible phenotypes. For example, a seed would grow differently in different soils or with changes in moisture and temperature. One of the most dramatic experimental demonstrations of this idea was presented by Charles R. Stockard (1879–1939), who created a cyclops fish by treating the water in which the embryos were developing. This is why we say that children do not inherit "traits" from their parents. Children inherit only alleles. It is the interaction of these alleles with the environment that creates phenotypes.

Let us take, for example, the case of mental deficiency and the genetic disease known as PKU (phenylketonuria). It has been known since the 1930s that a particular genotype causes an error in the metabolism of the amino acid phenylalanine, a common constituent of milk products, resulting in high levels of phenylpyruvic acid in the body. For reasons still not well understood, high levels of phenylpyruvic acid in the developing child result in mental deficiency. In this case, it seems particularly clear that a given genotype "causes" mental deficiency, but appearances can be deceiving. If the child is raised on a diet containing no phenylalanine, normal intelligence can develop. The genotype did not cause any phenotype. The phenotype was caused by an interaction of the genotype with phenylalanine.

The implications of this position are that there are genetic correlates to physical as well as behavioral traits. However, correlation should not be confused with causation. Genes do not "cause" a trait any more than environment does. It is the interaction between the two that results in phenotypic traits. The norm of reaction position rejects both the biological and the social determinist views. If one takes seriously the concept of the norm of reaction, it is apparent that social engineering can alter child development. However, the child is not a *tabula rasa,* to be easily molded into a scientist or a thief. The child has a genotype and there are genetic correlates of behavior. What might transform one child, say a PKU baby, from mental deficiency to mental normalcy, may not work for another child. While the advocates of this middle position reject both biological and social determinism, they have been primarily concerned with pointing out the problems and dangers of genetic determinism.

The debate between hereditarians and social determinists (sometimes referred to as environmentalists) has raged for over a century. The hereditarians have predominated during most of this time. Only during the period from 1945 to the mid seventies have social determinists held the dominant position. The debate is not entirely over the merits of scientific evidence. Nicholas Pastore was one of the first to investigate the significance of the outlook of scientists on the nature-nurture debate, in his classic study *The Nature-Nurture Controversy.* Pastore concluded that the social and political allegiances of the scientists were a significant determinant of their position on the issue. Those who favored the hereditarian view tended to be conservative. They viewed the social order as a natural result of variation in talent and character. They tended to explain class and race differences as likewise the result of innate group differences. The behaviorists or environmentalists, on the other hand, were more likely to be liberals or Leftists. They believed economic disadvantage and structural problems in the social order were to blame for group differences. They also believed in the power of social engineering to alter class and race discrepancies.

Thus, in the aftermath of World War II, when the United States economy was booming and faith in social engineering was at its height, the social determinist ideology held sway. During the period of the civil rights movement and the Great Society, social scientists were committed to an egalitarian ideology. They created a wealth of programs, such as Head Start, food stamps, Aid to Families with Dependent Children, and Affirmative Action, aimed at transforming and perfecting society.

With the economic problems of the seventies and the rise of the New Right, more conservative ideologies returned to dominate social science thinking. Beginning with the appearance of sociobiology in the mid seventies, there has been a distinct rise in the number of studies that emphasize genetic theories of crime, intelligence, alcoholism, and mental illness.

How far the contemporary resurgence of hereditarianism will go is uncertain. There have already been calls for a renewed eugenics. In 1969, Arthur Jensen called for "eugenic foresight" in governmental policies dealing with African Americans. William Shockey, Richard Hernnstein, and Lloyd Humphreys, among others, have warned of declining intelligence in the United States and called for eugenic policies to stem the tide of degeneracy. Most recently, J. Phillipe Rushton, a professor of psychology at the University of Western Ontario, has brought back nineteenth-century notions of craniometry, arguing that Asians, whites, and blacks differ in cranial capacity. He further states that numerous traits show Asians and whites superior to blacks. According to Rushton, Orientals and whites have evolved into races that are more intelligent, family oriented, and law-abiding than Negroes. The Negro race is, on the whole, smaller brained, slower to mature, less sexually restrained, and more aggressive than its white and Asian cousins. John Lynn, another prominent supporter of the new eugenics, wrote in 1974: "If the evolutionary process is to bring its benefits, it has to be allowed to operate effectively. This means that incompetent societies have to be allowed to go to the wall. . . . What is called for here is not genocide, the killing off of the populations of incompetent cultures. But we do need to think realistically in terms of the 'phasing out' of such peoples."

How far this trend will go is uncertain. There has emerged a vigorous opposition to the new eugenics that is aided by the memory of horrors that biological determinism in the form of Nazi ideology wrought. America is today the world's most successful experiment in multicultural democracy. Minority ethnic and racial groups wield far more political and social power than they did in the 1920s and 1930s. When Frederick Goodwin, director of the federal government's Mental Health Administration, announced a governmental plan in 1992 to identify 100,000 inner city children whose alleged biochemical and genetic defects would lead them to violence later in life, a hue and cry emerged from a coalition of African American politicians, civil rights leaders, and scientists that quickly scuttled the program. The call for such programs will continue, however. Clearly, the debate over heredity and hereditarianism will continue to rage.

Barry Mehler

See also BEHAVIORISM; HELVETIUS; INTELLIGENCE; RACE AND RACISM

Bibliography

Brigham, C.C. *A Study of American Intelligence.* Princeton: Princeton University Press, 1923.
Burt, C. "The Inheritance of Mental Ability." In *The Discovery of Talent,* edited by D. Wolfle. Cambridge: Harvard University Press, 1969.
Chase, Allen. *The Legacy of Malthus: The Social Costs of the New Scientific Racism.* New York: Alfred Knopf, 1980.
Galton, Francis. *Hereditary Genius: An Inquiry into Its Laws and Consequences.* [1869]. London: Collins, 1962.
Gould, Stephen Jay. *The Mismeasure of Man.* New York: W.W. Norton, 1981.
Hirsch, J. "Evidence for Equality: Genetic Diversity and Social Organization." In *Equality and Social Policy,* edited by W. Feinberg. New York: Elsevier, 1978.
Kamin, Leon J. *The Science and Politics of I.Q.* New York: John Wiley, 1974.
Pastore, Nicholas. *The Nature-Nurture Controversy.* New York: King's Crown Press, 1949.
Rushton, J.P. "Gene-Culture Coevolution and Genetic Similarity Theory: Implications for Ideology, Ethnic Nepotism, and Geopolitics." *Politics and the Life Sciences* 4 (February 1986).

Higher Education

Higher education has long been a contested term. What constitutes higher education? What is the value of higher education for society? Who should attend institutions of higher education? These are questions, asked by scholars, politicians, and the public. Crises in society and in education are often intertwined. "In any age it is that connection that makes a reexamination of the idea of the university so essential and yet so complicated" (Pelikan: 14). Indeed, in many countries, institutions of higher education, especially universities, have at times generated critiques of the wider society that have led to widespread reforms.

Higher education has always been selective. Its purpose has been the intellectual education of leaders; in Europe, originally, these were leaders in medicine, law, and theology. The first European university teachers gathered students round them to whom they taught Christian texts and commentaries written in Latin, Greek, and Hebrew. The prerequisite for studying these texts was proficiency in translating and writing those languages, most importantly, Latin. Until the nineteenth century, in Europe and in other parts of the world where Europeans had established political control, higher education prepared students not only in the moral teachings of Christianity, but also in rhetoric, logic, and the cultures of ancient Greece and Rome, including their philosophy, science, law, medicine, and literature. Although by the nineteenth century writers had begun to criticize the concentration on "liberal education" in terms of its lack of utility, when it was introduced the curriculum had been perceived as utilitarian.

Beset with the need for better educated citizens and practitioners in all fields, newly industrializing societies found themselves, in the nineteenth century, embroiled in disputes over the aims of higher education and its role in promoting the practical as well as the liberal arts. People's ways of thinking changed with the advent of factories. Indeed, "the dramatic revising by the new industrialist was to see everything as tools or instruments to be put to some use" (Fitzgerald: 105).

The assault of pragmatic instrumentalism was nowhere more keenly felt than in higher education, where, in 1852, the Englishman John Henry Newman (1801–1890) wrote an eloquent defense of knowledge as an end worth pursuing for itself. According to Newman, "That alone is liberal knowledge, which stands on its own pretensions, which is independent of sequel, expects no complement, refuses to be informed (as it is called) by an end, or absorbed into any art, in order duly to present itself to our contemplation" (Newman: 101). Newman wrote as though he were merely articulating a well-accepted, nonhierarchical differentiation between the liberal and the useful arts—"No-one can deny that commerce and the professions afford scope for the highest and most diversified powers of mind" (Newman: 100)—both of which he perceived to belong in some measure within the university. Yet his words implied a hierarchy of knowledge, and his defense of knowledge for its own sake claimed greater scope for that idea than it had previously been accorded. His words, therefore, became torches for those who wished to maintain the university as an oasis of intellectual excellence for its own sake in a desert of instrumentalism.

Newman was defending not only a curriculum but also a process of teaching by which the hegemony of well-to-do European, Christian males was perpetuated. In the intervening years, both scholars and policy-makers have challenged his assumptions. While Newman urged reflection on some aspects of teaching, such as the need to attend to the interaction of one branch of knowledge with another as it was introduced to students, he discounted the educational value of practical knowledge and personal experience in the same way that he discounted knowledge acquired for a practical goal. Newman's attitudes were challenged in his own day by those championing workers' education, who drew heavily upon the workers' practical knowledge and personal experience in their courses. In more recent years, feminist pedagogy has drawn on women's practical knowledge and personal experience, while feminist scholars have challenged the dichotomy previously assumed between the personal and the political.

Even as Newman wrote, the university was assuming a new role in the creation of knowledge. During the nineteenth century, new methods of textual research emerged in biblical and historical studies, as well as new techniques of empirical research, not only in the natural and earth sciences but also in areas that came to be defined as the social sciences. In the years that followed, university professors came to define their primary task as the creation, rather than the transmission, of knowledge. That change has led a scholar recently to declare that "the advancement of knowledge through research, the transmission of knowledge through teaching, the preservation of knowledge in scholarly collections, and the diffusion of knowledge through publishing are the four legs of the university table" (Pelikan: 16).

In the United States, where the demands for an educated populace to ensure the success of the republic led to an early challenge to higher education's selectivity, the Yale Report of 1828 represented a strong and for many years successful defense of the classical curriculum. The debate in the United States was shaped differently from that in England because the instrumental aims of higher education were more acceptable to both sides, and because the charge of "elitism" was problematic to anyone believing in the concept of the republic. Thus, by the end of the Civil War, the demands of a new and expanding society for more highly trained practitioners overwhelmed all opposition. With the passage of the 1862 Morrill Act, establishing land grant colleges and universities, and its extension in 1890, the federal government asserted its role in assisting the states to establish and maintain institutions of higher education dedicated not only to a liberal education but also to the occupational advancement of all students. Some scholars have claimed that the Morrill Act democratized American higher education; others, that it provided governmental assistance to industry in stratifying the workforce, a stratification reflected even today in the "pecking order" of higher education institutions and the lowly position of certain professional schools on university campuses.

From their inception, professional schools in the United States have provided a systematic curriculum for neophyte professionals in each field and helped practitioners deal with social problems. As more universities became involved with the production of knowledge through research, both pure and applied, the service they could provide industry, the government, and the military became clearer. The gradual application of theoretical research methods to social problems, as well as to scientific and technical problems, forged a new link, which has strengthened during the twentieth century, between the university and the business and professional communities. While this link has produced benefits, it has also had deleterious effects in eroding the power and the will of scholars working within the university to critique social and political activities. One example of this erosion may be seen in the development of nuclear power. "Among the hundreds of thousands of documents written by scientists and engineers in various countries over the first five years of nuclear fission work, not a single memorandum or letter has been found that attempts to analyze at length the consequences for society of developing reactors. Even the general implications of nuclear bombs were almost never discussed with care until around the time they were exploded on cities" (Weart: 273).

During the 1960s, there were riots in European as well as U.S. universities. Students, and some faculty members, challenged the links between universities and what was termed "the military-industrial-complex." In the United States, influenced by the civil rights movement and a growing feminist movement, students' accusations went deep to the heart of the university, challenging not only its curriculum but also its governance structure. The war in Vietnam raised students' anxiety to fever pitch, but it also narrowed their focus. After the killings of students at Jackson State University and Kent State University in the spring of 1970, student revolts in the United States came to an abrupt end. There were some tangible results from the disturbances, however. At many universities, students were invited to membership on faculty and administrative committees, including boards of trustees. The links between the universities and the military became more tenuous as universities spun off weapons research into free-standing research institutions. And the curriculum was enriched by African American studies, Asian American studies, Latin American studies, and women's studies.

The intellectual arguments used by those who struggled to change the universities during the 1960s were varied. Among them were arguments that expanded on those formulated at the end of the nineteenth century by Friedrich Nietzsche (1844–1900). In Nietzsche's view, intellectuals were not admirable. They were dangerous, insofar as they undermined the noble myths upon which societies depend. Nietzsche's critique of the intellectuals' search for truth suggested, also, that the unity of learning envisioned by Newman is impossible to achieve because it depends upon a specific perspective that not all people share: a belief in God and an acceptance of a Christian vision. Nietzsche's arguments could lead one to the conclusion that increased specialization in higher education and the loss of an overarching belief in the unity of knowledge have been in-

evitable. During the 1960s, those demanding change within the university perceived that in an environment of competing claims for inclusion in the curriculum, political power had become supremely important.

Marxist thought, which also influenced political actions in the 1960s, has for many decades been an important source for the critique of Newman's views. Marxism has encouraged a more humble claim for those who teach than Newman envisioned by locating the teacher and the taught within a web of power relationships existing between them and between them and others in a classbound society. Not only are students and teachers bound by power relationships, but university researchers are bound by them also, in the very construction of knowledge. The belief that knowledge could be generated by students as well as teachers was an axiom of the rebels of the 1960s. Through "teach-ins" on campuses they initiated a new informal curriculum infused with their own political focus. In doing so, they sought to overturn the traditional power relationships between faculty and students.

Contemporary writers have expanded on the idea that claims to knowledge and moral certitude are bids for power by specific elites. In the last two decades, for instance, feminist scholarship has challenged both the discounting of the personal female experience and the dichotomy between theory and practice espoused by Newman and twentieth-century exponents of liberal education. Challenges to the unity of knowledge have been made by authors in subaltern studies, African studies, African American studies, Asian studies, and Latin American studies, expounding on the racism of the Eurocentric world view, and the denial of the experiences of those who are oppressed. Thus, the challenges to the classical view of higher education have become more intense during the decades since the 1960s, as the role of higher education in the construction, as well as the transmission, of knowledge has become more clearly defined and as the nature of objectivity has been called into question.

The growing intensity of the challenges may be judged by the fact that "in the 1960s, it was possible to support the civil rights movement without this support having any significant implications for the universities. In the 1980s, issues related to race had a direct impact on campus—for intergroup relations, for the curriculum, for the professoriate and perhaps

H

more important, for the allocation of resources" (Altbach: 4). In the United States, the late 1980s saw a backlash in the form of racist incidents on several campuses, a slowing in the proportional increase of African American students attending universities, and attacks from supporters of the traditional curriculum who claimed that those who aimed to make the curriculum pluralistic were imposing "political correctness" on both faculty and students. Racist incidents led some institutions, such as Stanford University, to expand their goals in regard to race relations so that "students have positive and significant experiences with others whose racial/ethnic backgrounds are different from their own, and that they leave [the university] with the skills, the knowledge and the enthusiasm needed to contribute to the multicultural worlds that they will enter" (Cole in Altbach: 230).

Despite opposition to the liaison of business and industry with the universities, the links among them strengthened in the last decades of the twentieth century as government reduced its financial support for research and development at the same time that the universities became an important source of new technologies. "In the emerging field of biotechnology, the lack of corporate expertise led to unique new arrangements between industry and corporations at institutional levels [such as corporate funding of whole departments] that are affecting a number of the university's traditional values and norms" (Kenney: 29). For example, business firms have already challenged the freedom of faculty and students to publish their research results, and for faculty to recommend students to the full range of potential employees.

Access to Higher Education

Consensus occurred in many industrialized countries by the end of the nineteenth century on who should receive higher education. Although, across the centuries, a few brilliant women and a few men of non-European ancestry had been allowed to study at European universities, and at colleges and universities elsewhere founded by people of European descent, their access had never been guaranteed. During the nineteenth century, in most of these universities, political movements obtained admission for women to undergraduate and professional education. In some places, separate women's colleges and women's qualifications were established. In others, existing institutions expanded their admission and examination regulations to include women. Similar political actions led to the inclusion of more non-Caucasians in higher education, also. The examination system established by the University of London, which did not entail a residential collegiate experience, provided a way for men and women, Caucasian and non-Caucasian, in many countries to obtain a university degree. In the United States, the profusion of private degree-granting institutions included, before the Civil War, a sprinkling that admitted men and women of any race. After the Civil War, especially in the Northeast, more separate colleges were founded for women, while women's admission to state colleges and universities became widespread across the nation. Separate public and private colleges and universities for African Americans were also established in the last half of the nineteenth century, some concentrating on a liberal arts and others on a vocational curriculum. Until the early twentieth century, most of these institutions depended heavily upon enrollments in their precollege programs to maintain their economic viability. Despite the expansion of both public and private institutions during this period, only a small percentage of the total American population, and an even smaller percentage of people of color, attended colleges and universities.

In Europe, where a tradition of governmental assistance to students existed, costs were contained by the establishment of strict academic standards. In the United States, students' ability to pay was almost as important a criterion for college attendance as academic attainment. Few scholarships of any kind existed. The sense of community in early-twentieth-century American universities may be largely attributed to the socioeconomic homogeneity of the student body and to the acceptance of the "American dream" by the small proportion of lower-class students then attending a university.

Always in contention was the question, Should all postsecondary education be called "higher education"? The very term *higher education* assumes a hierarchy of learning: A student is expected to complete primary education before embarking on secondary education, and secondary before embarking on higher (or tertiary) education. Traditionally, entrance to higher education was not open to all who had completed secondary education, but only to an intellectual elite from that group who demonstrated their proficiency through examinations devised by the universities themselves, or, as in the United States in the twentieth century, by national testing services.

This narrow definition of who should be eligible for higher education did not mesh with people's understanding of who was eligible for elementary and secondary education, however. In the case of the latter forms of education, the age at which students normally undertake such education often determines the name people give it. Those democracies that have committed themselves to increasing the access of their citizens to higher education have become likely to choose the most inclusive way to define such matters, which is to use a definition based upon age and not attainment. In that situation, colleges and universities have to provide for the needs of some students whose age makes them appropriate for higher education but whose preparation in some areas may not be adequate for it. There is a continuing debate among educators themselves about the relative importance of developmental maturation on the learning process, and of the role of motivation in promoting intellectual development.

In many industrialized countries, especially the United States, the aims of higher education have expanded since the Second World War to include access for new populations. Although a theoretical underpinning for this change lay in the belief that there was a need for all qualified people in a democracy, of whatever race, class, or sex, to have equal access to higher education, there were also economic reasons for it. Post–World War II society needed a better-educated workforce than previously, and people believed that society would benefit from engaging able-bodied men and women in education rather than having large numbers unemployed as in the 1930s. In the United States, the many male (and many fewer female) veterans of World War II were rewarded for their service to their country not only with pensions, continuing health services, and military awards, but also with financial assistance in obtaining higher education, with its concomitant effect of preparing a person to obtain, for life, a higher-paying job than might otherwise have been possible. The expansion of higher education in the 1940s and 1950s, through federal funding to educate the veterans, was continued in the United States and even increased during the 1960s due to a growing awareness of the inequities in access because of race and sex. Some universities and colleges, especially those in the public sector, responded to the demand by underrepresented groups for greater access to higher education by developing open-admissions policies for all high school graduates who wished to obtain bachelors' degrees and had or could obtain the necessary financial support. Open admissions policies guaranteed open access to the freshman year but did not guarantee continuation beyond that point.

The new populations, who sometimes came less well prepared academically or prepared in subjects different from those previously expected of college students, challenged educators. They responded by establishing new institutions, enlarging existing ones, expanding their curricula, and providing additional services for the emotional and academic support of students. The problems of returning and older students, such as their difficulty learning study skills and initiating their own learning activities, have generated a new kind of professional, who specializes in both the practice and the scholarship relating to study skills. In the United States prior to the Second World War, some states had already set up junior colleges to provide two-year vocational courses for some postsecondary students who did not intend to go to college and would not otherwise have obtained vocational training. Those junior colleges, and others newly established after the war, were incorporated into systems of community colleges. They offered not only stand-alone, two-year technical and vocational courses, but also the first two years of undergraduate work (to be completed at a university or four-year college) to a diverse population of adult returnees and recent high school graduates. A variety of experimental programs in four-year colleges and universities were introduced, also, to meet the needs of nontraditional students.

Increasingly, institutions of higher education and society at large have become interested in the issue of retention. Much of the literature has concentrated on the economic cost to institutions and to society as a whole of high attrition from college and university programs. Less often discussed, but equally important, are the costs to the individual of crushed aspirations, and the dubious ethics of encouraging aspirations in people that society has little intention of permitting them to fulfill.

Among the changes in higher education after World War II were new job categories in the area of student services. As universities grew in size, faculty members became more deeply engaged with research and writing, and their interaction with students became limited to the classroom and formal office hours. Where, in

H

undergraduate colleges, small interest groups organized by students with faculty advisors had functioned well, in large-scale universities they became obsolete. Neither faculty nor university administrators, however, were willing to leave the area of student life outside the classroom—the cocurriculum as it is now called—entirely in the hands of the students. If not the faculty, then some other professionals were needed to facilitate the students' activities. Thus, cocurricular activities have become, increasingly, the domain where student service personnel, not faculty, facilitate students' emotional and intellectual growth.

Graduate and Professional Education and the Future of the Multiversity

The twentieth century has witnessed a steady increase in the number of people who wish to continue their education beyond the baccalaureate. Many professional societies now require their members to continually update their professional knowledge. Experience alone is not enough to keep doctors, lawyers, and teachers in touch with new information and technology. Business and industry require employees to attend on-site workshops, and pay for them to attend local universities for higher degrees. Some large firms have developed their own graduate-level programs. Unions sometimes negotiate further education as part of the benefit package for their members. Most of these programs, however, are specific, and oriented toward the improvement of work-related skills. Few include the liberal and fine arts, or concentrate on the skills of citizenship, caring, and developing human potential to its fullest. Nowhere in the university does anyone plan for an orderly sequence of adult learning throughout a person's lifespan.

Another critique leveled at some graduate and professional education is that the teaching process takes account of neither the students' stages of adult development, nor the demands of their adult life. Hence, there is often frustration on the part of students and teachers alike. These last issues are likely to be addressed in the future with the development of a new focus at research universities on faculty teaching and student learning, and with the evolution of information technology, which has the potential to revolutionize higher education. For several decades, open universities throughout the world have provided degree programs using distance education for students who otherwise would

not be able to attend. Open university courses may be delivered by satellite, may involve sophisticated computer hardware and software, or may be "low-tech," employing only the mailed books and essay responses of traditional correspondence courses. Whatever their format, most offer students the opportunity to control their own study times and they depend upon the initiative and persistence of the learner. The material for a course, or for a complete program of study, can be tailored to meet the needs of the individual. Potentially, the ability for students to control their own education has been increased manyfold by the advent of computer networks. Students may now use the Internet, for instance, to initiate research from their own homes.

Faculty as well as student interactions have changed as a result of new technologies. Scientists were among the first scholars to initiate new methods of investigation and communication using mainframe computers, but with the introduction of personal computers, fiber-optic networks, modems, and high-speed printers, the methods and products of scholarship in all fields began to change dramatically. *Higher education* has long been a contested term. With the advent of the latest information technology, institutions are being formed that no longer depend upon one location, or upon individuals meeting in person, or upon the acquisition of knowledge through memorization and recall. A new era has arrived that is changing both the content and the structure of higher education.

Joan N. Burstyn

See also LIBERAL EDUCATION; PUBLIC EDUCATION

Bibliography

Altbach, Philip G., and Kofi Lomotey, eds. *The Racial Crisis in American Higher Education.* Albany: State University of New York Press, 1991.

Anderson, James D. *The Education of Blacks in the South, 1860–1935.* Chapel Hill: University of North Carolina Press, 1988.

Chickering, Arthur. "The Modern American College: Integrating Liberal Education, Work, and Human Development." In *Preparation for Life? The Paradox of Education in the Late Twentieth Century,* edited by Joan N. Burstyn. Philadelphia: Falmer Press, 1986.

Farnham, Christie, ed. *The Impact of Feminist Research in the Academy.* Bloomington:

Indiana University Press, 1987.

Fitzgerald, Thomas. "Education for Work and about Work: A Proposal." *American Journal of Education* 101 (1993): 99–115.

Geiger, Roger L. *To Advance Knowledge: The Growth of American Research Universities, 1900–1940*. New York: Oxford University Press, 1986.

Gilligan, Carol. *In a Different Voice: Psychological Theory and Women's Development*. Cambridge: Harvard University Press, 1982.

Kenney, Martin. *Biotechnology: The University-Industrial Complex*. New Haven: Yale University Press, 1986.

Newman, John Henry. *The Idea of the University* [1852]. Edited by I.T. Ker. Oxford: Clarendon Press, 1976.

Pascarella, Ernest T., and Patrick T. Terenzini. *How College Affects Students: Findings and Insights from Twenty Years of Research*. San Francisco: Jossey-Bass, 1991.

Peek, Robin P., and Joan N. Burstyn. "In Pursuit of Improved Scholarly Communication." In *Desktop Publishing in the University,* edited by Joan N. Burstyn. Syracuse, N.Y.: School of Education, Syracuse University, 1991.

Pelikan, Jaroslav. *The Idea of the University: A Reexamination*. New Haven: Yale University Press, 1992.

Rudolph, Frederick. *The American College and University: A History* [1962]. With an introductory essay and supplemental bibliography by John R. Thelin. Athens: University of Georgia Press, 1990.

Solomon, Barbara Miller. *In the Company of Educated Women*. New Haven: Yale University Press, 1985.

Weart, Spencer R. *Scientists in Power*. Cambridge: Harvard University Press, 1979.

Hinduism

Hinduism is a religion of about 700 million people, and it is the oldest religion still practiced in the modern world. It has its origins in the Indus Valley Civilization (2500–1800 B.C.) and reaches its philosophic and religious perfection in the sacred Hindu text, the *Bhagavad Gita* (400–200 B.C.). If it is assumed that religions, like philosophies, can be seen as problem-solving disciplines, and if it is assumed that Hinduism as a religion is attempting to solve religious problems, then to understand Hinduism the following questions might be pursued: What problem is Hinduism trying to solve? What is the cause of that problem? What is the solution that it seeks? What is the way to that solution? What is it that guarantees that if the way is followed it will remove the cause of the problem and arrive at the solution?

The evolution of Hinduism from the Indus Valley Civilization to the *Bhagavad Gita* can be divided into four rather distinct phases. These phases can be examined in order to discover historically the problems, causes, solutions, ways, and guaranteeing principles or Persons for each of these four phases. The examination concludes with a general definition of Hinduism and with an illustration of this general definition by pointing to three famous practicing Hindus of the twentieth century who exemplify the three major ways or yogas of modern Hinduism.

The Indus Valley Civilization (2500–1800 B.C.)

Hinduism has its origins in an ancient civilization that flourished for over seven hundred years along the one-thousand-mile stretch of the banks and tributaries of the great Indus River in Western India (a river which, since the partition of India in 1947, now lies in Pakistan). The Indus Civilization consisted of some five large cities and over 150 smaller villages and settlements. The religion of these people, called "Harappans" and named after one of their larger northern cities, lay in the devotion to one or more nature deities associated with the worship of a particular kind of pipal or fig tree (*Ficus religiosa*). From the pictures on the more than two thousand stamp seals that have been found in the archaeological sites of the Indus since 1922, a rather sketchy but nonetheless exciting hypothetical re-creation of the religion of the Harappans is possible:

The Problem: The Harappans were a farming and herding people. From the evidence of their burial practices, it is thought that they probably believed in a life after death, and thus it can be assumed that the problem they faced was twofold: concern for the production of adequate food and progeny in this life and anxiety over the life to come.

The Cause: The cause of the concern for this life and the anxiety over the next is not known. However, it is sufficient to point out that the vagaries of nature as well as the periodic flooding and destruction caused by the Indus River may have been the same then as now. Further, the general absence of any certainty regarding the life after death may have warranted anxiety.

The Solution: The solution to the problem is also not known, for while more than 270 carved symbols of the Harappan language have been identified, all attempts at translation have thus far failed. Whatever name might have been given to the solution, it can be said that it would probably consist of guaranteed bountiful crops, abundant progeny (animal and human), and enjoyable future lives.

The Way: The way to the solution lay in the worship of the god or gods pictured on the stamp seals. These seals are for the most part one-inch-square steatite pictures in bas relief of the daily activities of the Harappans. We see their chief deity sitting cross-legged in yoga posture surrounded by animals, in particular the tiger, an animal subsequently sacred to the Hindu god Shiva. This seated deity has an erect penis indicating that he is a god associated with procreation and fecundity. We see him emerging from the trunk of the sacred fig tree, entangled in its leaves and branches, receiving offerings, sacrifices, and worship from his kneeling devotees. As far as later Hinduism is concerned, the Indus Valley Civilization is probably the place of the beginning of bhakti yoga, the way of devotion to a personal god.

The Guaranteeing Principle or Person: This is unknown, but very likely the god who is being worshiped, who is probably the forerunner of the Hindu god Shiva, guarantees that his devotees' efforts will not be in vain. In other words, the offerings to him of goats, bulls, and devotion will relieve his devotees' concerns for this life and their anxieties over the life to come.

The Vedic Period (1200–900 B.C.)

Hinduism also has its origins in the sacred works called the Vedas. These compositions were first brought into India beginning in about 1200 B.C. by a people who called themselves Aryans ("the noble ones"). These warrior tribesmen worshiped many different gods of heaven, sky, and earth, carrying out elaborate religious ceremonies prescribed initially in their oral tradition and subsequently in the Sanskrit texts of the Vedas ("books of knowledge"). These religious sacrifices describe the way of sacrificial action wherein offerings of food and the mysterious hallucinatory soma are made to these nature gods, such as Indra (war and the thunderstorm), Agni (fire), Varuna (a savior deity), and Surya (the sun). In return, the gods grant certain favors to the sacrificing brahmins (priests) and their patrons. An elaborate vocational class or caste system had been brought by the Aryans into India and the Vedas prescribed who did what within that class system. Thus the brahmins taught the Vedas and carried out the sacrifices; the kshatriyas defended the clan as soldiers and ruled the clan as kings and princes; the vaishyas produced the food and trade for the society; and the shudras, the serving class, performed the menial tasks for the other members of the clan. From the Vedas a rather complete picture of Vedism can be obtained:

The Problem: Together with the Harappans, the Aryans shared a concern for this life as well as an anxiety over the life to come. They carried out sacrifices to ensure an abundance of sons, land, victories in battle, and cattle as well as proper receptions into the heavenly world. Hence, the problem of Vedism concerns a fear that these bounties would not be available or forthcoming. The noble Aryan warriors were, if nothing else, a practical people dedicated to conquering others and subduing the conquered. With their bows and arrows, their two-horse battle chariots, and their gods, they were eminently successful in both undertakings.

The Cause: The causes of the concern and the anxiety lie in improprieties toward humans and the gods, in actions of immorality and neglect.

The Solution: The solutions are merely getting the goods of this life, sons, victories, and wealth, and of the next, heaven.

The Ways: The way to the solution lies through action, karma, moral action, and sacrificial action. The Vedas describe the sacrificer as a morally upright person who is willing to give the offering to god and to do it without attachment—that is, the offering is for god and not for the sacrificer. Contained in this ritual action is the root of what the later Hinduism of the *Bhagavad Gita* will refer to as "karma yoga," the way of selfless action.

The Guaranteeing Principle or Person: The Vedas employ the concept of Rta, a metaphysical principle that guarantees both the physical and the moral order of the universe. In addition, one of the Vedic deities, Lord Varuna, also sees to it that order is maintained throughout the universe. Both Rta and Varuna guarantee justice—that is, that all get what's coming to them and that as you sow so shall you reap; hence, the sacrificer's efforts in solving the problem of concern and anxiety will work when selfless action in the sacrifice removes the causes of both problems.

The Upanishadic Period (800–200 B.C.)

Hinduism also has its origins in a second set of texts sacred to all Hindus, the Upanishads ("to sit down close to"). These texts, about two hundred in all with about a dozen being chiefly significant, preach the message of the identity between a person's real Self (Atman) and the Holy Power of the universe (Brahman). In addition, several other new concepts have worked their way into these secret teachings, so secret that the pupil must sit down close to the brahmin who is teaching. Together with these new concepts—for example, samsara (rebirth), moksha (liberation), jnana (knowledge), and the law of karma—the Upanishads appear as a reformation of Vedism and a revolution in religious thinking:

The Problem: The problem is samsara, a concept that means both "suffering" and "rebirth." The object of the Upanishads will be to provide a solution to the problem of suffering—the concern for this life and the anxiety over rebirth into the next, where more suffering awaits reborn selves.

The Cause: There is a double cause of samsara: desire, which keeps the self bound to life after transmigrating life, and ignorance of the true nature of the real Self, which is identical to Brahman.

The Solution: The solution to the dual problem of samsara is moksha, liberation or enlightenment. Moksha liberates one from desire and it enlightens one as to one's true and divine Self; hence, by getting at the causes of suffering, it abolishes that suffering.

The Way: The way to the solution lies through the knowledge, jnana, of the Self. Jnana yoga, the way of knowledge of the Self, sees by mystical intuition that the Self and Brahman are identical.

The Guaranteeing Principle: The law of karma, a new concept similar to the Rta of the Vedas, guarantees that one's efforts for good—for example, using jnana yoga to reach moksha—will be rewarded, and that one's efforts for evil—for example, failing to reach liberation—will be properly punished with rebirth.

The *Bhagavad Gita* (400–200 B.C.): Hinduism

The task of the *Bhagavad Gita*, a seven-hundred-verse poem taken from the world's longest epic poem, the Mahabharata, will now be to synthesize the three previous religious traditions into a single but complex religion: Hinduism. The *Gita,* probably the most universally revered of all the sacred texts of Hinduism, is a dialogue between a human hero, Arjuna, and a divine hero, Lord Krishna. The setting is an ancient battlefield near modern New Delhi, where a horrendous slaughter is about to begin. From his chariot Arjuna has just seen the men on the "enemy" side that he, as a kshatriya warrior, is supposed to fight. But the war he is engaged in is a civil war, of brother against brother, cousin against cousin. And Arjuna has just recognized across the field men that he knows and loves, friends and relatives: The family that he had been called upon to serve and protect is now the very family that he is called upon to kill. The first of the eighteen chapters of the *Gita* ends as Arjuna casts aside his weapons and sits down in his chariot refusing to fight. His charioteer, a man who is Arjuna's friend and cousin, is in reality Lord Krishna, an incarnation of the second member of the Hindu trinity, the God Vishnu, the Preserver, and now Savior, of the world. It will be Krishna's task in the remaining seventeen chapters to counsel Arjuna, and with him all of mankind who find themselves beset with concern and anxiety, in the arts of coping with the suffering world. Lord Krishna's message is the message of Hinduism, a synthesis of the three previous historical traditions:

The Problem: The problem remains samsara: suffering and rebirth, a concept from the Upanishads.

The Cause: The cause is desire and ignorance, concepts from the Upanishads.

The Solution: The solutions remain moksha (that is, liberation, from the Upanishads) and the concept of the heavenly worlds from the Vedas.

The Ways: The yogas to the solutions are now seen as threefold: bhakti yoga, the way of devotion to God, a concept from the Indus Valley Civilization, or, in the *Gita*'s case, to Lord Krishna; karma yoga, the way of selfless action, from the Vedas; and jnana yoga, the way of mystical intuition, from the Upanishads.

Guaranteeing Principle or Person: Both the law of karma and Lord Krishna, the *Gita* maintains, guarantee that efforts toward liberation will never be in vain. And in the end Lord Krishna successfully persuades Arjuna to get up, do his duty, and escape the bondage that leads to present and future suffering.

The *Gita* will provide the foundation for understanding many of the other philosophic and religious traditions that make up, and emerge from, the complexities of early Hinduism. Thus the traditions of the Puranas, the Ramayana, the Mahabharata, the six philosophic systems, and even Jainism and Buddhism, are all better understood through understanding the *Bhagavad Gita* and its seminal place in the history of Hinduism.

In the twentieth century, three Hindus have exemplified the three different yogas of Hinduism: A.C. Bhaktivedanta (1896–1977), the founder of the International Society for Krishna Consciousness (ISKCON), upholds the *Gita* as the central message of Hinduism and believes that only through bhakti to Lord Krishna can liberation ever be achieved. Bhaktivedanta's followers, the Hare Krishnas, with their shaved heads, saffron robes, and sandaled feet, dancing and chanting the name of their beloved God, and with over four thousand devotees in the United States alone, represent Hindu bhakti yoga in the modern world. Mohandas K. Gandhi (1869–1948), represents the karma yoga of Hinduism in its most obvious modern setting. Gandhi's philosophy of satyagraha, while embodying the religious devotion of bhakti, stresses the active karma yoga search for justice and love in a world where injustices and hate prevail. Finally, the great swami ("master") Paramahansa Yogananda (1893–1952), like Bhaktivedanta, himself a Hindu missionary to the West, was the founder of the Self Realization Fellowship (SRF). In 1920 he introduced jnana yoga as kriya yoga to Western audiences, teaching that cosmic consciousness, or moksha, could be achieved in the shortened time of only three years of practice. Today SRF reports over forty-four centers throughout the world, with nine in California alone. Ancient Hinduism, with its three yogas to liberation, would appear to be alive and well in the twenty-first century.

Arthur L. Herman

See also BUDDHISM; GANDHI; ISLAM; KING

Bibliography

Basham, A.L. *The Wonder that Was India.* New York: Grove Press, 1959.

Fairservis, Walter A., Jr. *The Roots of Ancient India.* 2nd ed., rev. Chicago: University of Chicago Press, 1975.

Herman, A.L. *The Bhagavad Gita, A Translation and Critical Commentary.* Springfield, Ill.: Charles C. Thomas, 1973.

———. *A Brief Introduction to Hinduism.* Boulder, Colo.: Westview Press, 1991.

Knipe, David M. *Hinduism, Experiments in the Sacred.* San Francisco: Harper, 1991.

O'Flaherty, Wendy Doniger, ed. and trans. *Textual Sources for the Study of Hinduism.* Chicago: University of Chicago Press, 1990.

Historicism

The term *historicism*, or rather *historism* (*Historismus* in German), was used occasionally in Germany in the first two-thirds of the nineteenth century (Ludwig Feuerbach, Carl Prantl, J.G. Fichte) to distinguish a historical orientation that recognized individuality in its "concrete temporal-spatiality" (Prantl) such as pursued by the Historical School of Law (Savigny, Eichhorn) both from a fact-oriented empiricism and from the system-building philosophy of history in the Hegelian manner that ignores factuality. The Romantic writers Friedrich Schlegel and Novalis had used the term as early as 1797 and 1798 respectively without assigning it a clear definition. Eugen Dühring (1866), Carl Menger (1884), and Adolf Wagner (1892) in their attacks on the Historical School of National Economy (Wilhelm Roscher, Karl Knies, Gustav Schmoller) used the term in a negative sense to criticize the abandonment of theory in economics and the confusion of economic theory with economic history.

With the turn to the twentieth century, the term received a different and more precise meaning. Ernst Troeltsch saw in *historicism* (*Historismus*) the dominant attitude of the nineteenth and twentieth centuries, which consisted in the recognition that all human ideas and values are historically conditioned and subject to change. Historicism was now identified with cultural relativism. As Karl Mannheim defined it: "Historicism is neither a faddish notion, a fashion, nor even a trend, but rather the ground from which we observe socio cultural reality"—in other words, the condition of modern existence. Historicism was now identified with cultural crisis. The discussion on the relativity of historical values had been initiated by Friedrich Nietzsche in his essay on "The Uses and Disadvantages of History" (1872), in which he criticized the irrelevance of scholarly historical study as it had developed in

German academia and its paralyzing effect on human action. History, which to much of nineteenth-century bourgeois culture had constituted the key to understanding things human, for Nietzsche now revealed that on the one hand there is no way out of history, and on the other that history has no objective meaning.

Troeltsch, a theologian by training, faced this dilemma in his work on "The Absolute Truth of Christianity" (1902), in which he recognized that the historical study of Christianity had destroyed the claim of Christianity to be the one true religion and pointed to the pluralism of beliefs. For Troeltsch there were two ways out of this dilemma, neither of which was intellectually convincing: The one, which Troeltsch rejected, was to renounce a scholarly historical approach to the study of religion and of culture. This is the way Nietzsche had chosen, with his accompanying proclamation of the death of God. Protestant theologians from Albrecht Ritschl to Karl Barth and Emil Brunner, the proponents of a crisis theology, drew a different conclusion from that of Nietzsche, clinging to revealed truth but stressing the radical otherness and ahistorical character of this truth. For Troeltsch, however, not merely the belief in God was at stake, but also the confidence of cultural Protestantism in the solidity of the values of the Western world.

The way Troeltsch chose to solve what he termed "the crisis of historicism" was to arrive at a synthesis of Western values through a historical study of Western culture. Yet this belief in the special dignity of Western culture, to which Troeltsch clung even after World War I, was increasingly challenged in the wake of the European cataclysm of the First World War. Thinkers as different as Max Weber and Martin Heidegger stressed the total historicity of human existence. While for Heidegger there was an escape in the safe haven of ontic Being, which transcended logical thought, a remnant of the very metaphysical tradition Heidegger sought to repudiate, for Weber, committed to a logic of scientific inquiry, rational thought and science offered no answers to questions of values but revealed a world that was ethically irrational. But for Weber the questions that scholars and scientists asked always derived from their value perspectives. All knowledge thus for Weber, as for Mannheim, reflected a specific social and cultural context embedded in history. Our understanding of reality does not reflect this reality as it really is but answers the questions that the

scholar and scientist ask. What remained unshakable for Weber were not the conclusions of scientific inquiry, which were constantly revised by further research, but the logic of scientific inquiry, which was on the one hand the specific product of Western civilization, on the other hand possessed universal validity.

A basic element of historicist thought was the distinction between the cultural sciences (*Geisteswissenschaften, Kulturwissenschaften*) and natural science. Developing ideas that had been expressed earlier in the nineteenth century by Leopold von Ranke and Johann Gustav Droysen, Wilhem Dilthey sought to formulate a specific methodology for these sciences. The study of culture required the understanding (*Verstehen*) of meaning, which always took on a unique, individual form, and thus differed from natural phenomena, which were repetitive and devoid of meaning and required causal explanation. Building on this distinction, Friedrich Meinecke, in his work on the origins of historicism (1936), gave the term *historicism* a new meaning that sought to overcome the crisis of historicism by stressing the positive aspects of a radically historical approach.

Meinecke identified this approach with a specifically German intellectual tradition that replaced classical Western notions of natural law with a genetic outlook that stressed the role of uniqueness and "individuality" in history. Although certainly no supporter of National Socialism, Meinecke once more in 1936 proclaimed the superiority of the German cultural tradition and saw in the German tradition of historicism the "highest attained stage in the understanding of things human," the most important intellectual development in Europe since the Reformation. Going back to the Neoplatonism of the German classical period, particularly Johann Wolfgang Goethe (1749–1832), Meinecke sought to overcome the relativism of historicism, by seeing in every historical individuality, whether a state, a nation, or a culture, the expression of a transcendent but unique idea. Accepting Meinecke's conception of historicism, historians in recent decades have identified the term with the scholarly orientation that emerged at the German universities in the early nineteenth century with Barthold Georg Niebuhr and Leopold von Ranke and dominated the writing and teaching of history in Germany until well after World War II. Historicism was now seen not primarily as an intellectual outlook, a *Weltanschauung,* in Meinecke's sense, but as an institutionalized, professionalized enterprise that provided the "paradigm" for historical scholarship as it was practiced worldwide. In Germany this scholarship focused on the states, seen by Ranke as "thoughts of God." Because of its narrow, narrative political approach and its bias against any form of social analysis, this historicist tradition was increasingly criticized as an inadequate way of understanding the past. It was also identified with authoritarian and ultranationalist German traditions.

Apart from the German discussion, historicism also played a significant role in twentieth-century Italian thought with Benedetto Croce. Croce stressed, as did Jose Ortega y Gasset in Spain and R.G. Collingwood in England, that history is the sole key to understanding of things human. Like Meinecke, they held that a naturalistic world view is totally inadequate to understand human reality because of the uniqueness and individuality of the historical world. Giambattista Vico, who early in the eighteenth century had observed the difference between the historical world that human beings make and therefore can understand and the natural world, was seen as a forerunner of a historicist outlook. History—Croce, Collingwood, and Ortega y Gasset agreed—"is principally an act of thought." But unlike Meinecke, who believed that the individual is "unfathomable" and thus not susceptible to rational inquiry, Croce and Collingwood believed that thought itself has a rational structure and that "historicism is a logical principle," thus avoiding the radical subjectivism implicit in the German historicist concept of *Verstehen*. In postulating that history is "the story of liberty," Croce's historicism was closer to that of G.W.F. Hegel (1770–1831) than to that of Ranke or Meinecke.

Two other uses of the term should briefly be mentioned. Karl Popper in *The Poverty of Historicism* identified the term with the attempts by Hegel and Karl Marx (1818–1883) to formulate laws of historical development that were used by the Marxists to legitimize their authoritarian control. Popper's use of the term has been severely criticized as idiosyncratic, but, in fact, Popper distinguished between *historicism* (*Historizismus*), and *historism* (*Historismus*) in the German sense at a time when *historism* was still the current term in the English-speaking world. Only in the 1940s, under the impact of Croce's *storicismo*, did *historicism* replace *historism*. The Marxist-Leninists, the objects of Popper's criticism, used the term *historicism* (see

the *Great Soviet Encyclopedia*—*istorism* in Russian) in a sense similar to Popper's as "the possibility of understanding objective reality through revealing the lawlike process of its development." Most recently, the term "New Historicism" has occurred in American literary discussions. The meaning of the term remains vague at this early stage. The "New Historicists" adopt Michel Foucault's critique of power and domination, including its sexual forms, and share the postmodernist rejection of historical optimism as it was contained in both German historicist and Marxist thought, but urge a recognition of the "historical and cultural specificity of ideas" largely lost in postmodernist thought.

Georg G. Iggers

See also MARXISM; NIETZSCHE; RELATIVISM; VICO

Bibliography
Antoni, Carlo. *Lo Storicismo*. Torino: E.R.I., 1957, 1968.
Brook, Thomas. *The New Historicism and Other Old-Fashioned Topics*. Princeton: Princeton University Press, 1991.
Croce, Benedetto. *History as the Story of Liberty*. New York: Meridian Books, 1955.
Dilthey, Wilhelm. *Introduction to the Human Sciences*. Princeton: Princeton University Press, 1989.
Iggers, Georg. *The German Conception of History. The National Tradition of Historical Thought from Herder to the Present*. Middletown, Conn.: Wesleyan University Press, 1983, 1986.
———. "Historicism." In *Dictionary of the History of Ideas*. Vol. 2, edited by Philip P. Wiener, 456–64. New York: Scribner's, 1972.
Jaeger, Friedrich, and Jorn Rusen. *Die Entstehung des Historismus*. Munchen: C.H. Beck, 1992.
Lee, Dwight E., and Robert N. Beck. "The Meaning of 'Historicism.'" *American Historical Review* 59 (1953–1954): 568–77.
Mandelbaum, Maurice. *History, Man, & Reason: A Study in Nineteenth Century Thought*. Baltimore, Md.: Johns Hopkins Press, 1971.
Mannheim, Karl. "Historismus." In *Wissensoziologie: Auswahl aus seinem Buch,* edited by Karl Mannheim, 246–307. Berlin: Luchterhand, 1964.

Meinecke, Friedrich. *Historicism. The Rise of a New Intellectual Outlook*. New York: Herder and Herder, 1972.

Popper, Karl. *The Poverty of Historicism*. New York: Basic Books, 1960.

Veeser, H.A., ed. *The New Historicism*. New York: Routledge, 1989.

Weber, Max. *From Max Weber: Essays in Sociology*. Translated and edited by Hans Gerth and C. Wright Mills. New York: Oxford University Press, 1946.

Home and Family

Although home and family are not the natural, immutable, eternal entities that they were once considered to be, the story of their place in Western educational philosophy is surprisingly consistent. It is as notable for the affirmation by a small number of thinkers of home's educative role as for the denial of the educational functions of domesticity and the educational capacities of mothers.

Like other philosophical narratives, this one starts with Plato (c. 427–347 B.C.). Maintaining that the institutions of private home, marriage, family, and child-rearing will tear a city apart, in the *Republic* Plato envisioned a state in which these social arrangements were abolished, at least for the guardian class. He reasoned that if the rulers of a state were to possess wealth, children, and families, "one man would then drag into his own house whatever he could get hold of away from the others; another drag things into his different house to another wife and other children. This would make for private pleasures and pains at private events." Given that the guardians will consider themselves one big family, they "will think of the same thing as their own, aim at the same goal, and, as far as possible, feel pleasure and pain in unison" (464d).

In view of the *Republic*'s disregard for the household, it is scarcely surprising that Aristotle (384–322 B.C.), whose philosophy so often countered Plato's, began his *Politics* with a treatment of it. Remarkably enough, however, after making the household a basic constituent of the polis, and then discussing slavery and the art of acquisition in some detail in Book I while devoting only a single sketchy paragraph to a man's rule over wife and children, Aristotle quit the subject. Although he promised to return later to the topics of marriage and parenthood, he did not. More interesting still, when he discussed education in Books VII and VIII of the *Politics,* Aristotle was strangely silent about the educative activities of the household. He pointed out that children can all too easily learn what they should not—especially from slaves, he said. But instead of crediting the household members in whose care he placed children up to age seven with playing a positive role in furthering their charges' growth and development, he ignored these educational agents altogether.

The educative aspects of home and family disappear in the philosophy of Rousseau (1712–1778) too. In *The Social Contract,* published in 1762, this philosopher who also reacted so strongly to Plato's social policies called families the first model of political societies. In *Emile,* which was published that same year, he presented the private home as a necessary foundation of a healthy state and discussed the relationship between husband and wife, parent and child. Yet Rousseau was of two minds about the claims of home and family. Although in the last book of *Emile* he said that the love of one's nearest is the principle of the love one owes the state, the treatise begins with the orphaning of a newborn child. Our hero's parents are not dead. For the sake of education the author has simply dismissed them from Emile's life, putting him instead in the hands of an unmarried male tutor with whom he is to live in virtual isolation.

Rousseau's ambivalence toward home and family was marked. Acknowledging in *Emile* that there is "no substitute for maternal solicitude" (45), he dismissed Emile's mother from the scene. Insisting that it is "the good son, the good husband, and the good father who make the good citizen" (363), he removed domesticity from Emile's childhood. A close reading of *Emile* reveals that even as its author separated his protagonist from family affections, home's informal intimate atmosphere, and the chores that support daily living, he retained the curriculum that, by tradition, was home's responsibility. Nevertheless, in describing the tutor's work as "negative education," he effectively masked both the intentionality and the effort that characterize the educational activities of mothers.

The wonder of it all is that after effectively concealing home's positive educational contributions in the first four books of *Emile,* Rousseau felt free to advertise them in Book V. One can but surmise that, having shifted the subject to the education of girls and women, he then felt comfortable discussing home and family. Since, however, in Rousseau's script Emile marries Sophie and will live with her and their children in a home of his own, the pretense in the boy's case that home and family do not exist seems ill advised, to say the least. Educating Emile as if Plato's Just State had come to pass, Rousseau retained in his own philosophy the institutional arrangements that Plato had rejected, thus undermining his own position.

In *Leonard and Gertrude*, a pedagogical novel published in 1781, Johann Heinrich Pestalozzi (1746–1827) had no trouble remembering what the much-admired Rousseau had tried so hard to forget. When in *Leonard and Gertrude* Cotton Meyer is asked how a "true" school—one that would "develop to the fullest extent all the faculties of the child's nature" (118)—could be established, he advises the village lord and his aide to visit Gertrude's home and observe how she teaches her children. The impression Gertrude's teaching makes can scarcely be exaggerated. Before the aide opens his eyes the next morning, he murmurs: "I will be schoolmaster!" Returning to Gertrude's house, he asks her if it would be possible to follow in a regular school the method she uses at home, and he requests her help in so doing. In response to her suggestion that another woman might be of more assistance to him, he replies: "She will doubtless be useful, too, but there can be no substitute for your mother's heart, which I must have for my school" (135).

Commentators have been unable to see or else unwilling to report the domesticity at the center of Pestalozzi's educational philosophy. Their oversight is more than matched by his own ambivalence, however. In 1801 *How Gertrude Teaches Her Children* was published. Difficult as it is to believe, Gertrude's name is not mentioned in this didactic work nor is a mother in evidence until the discussion turns in the last fifteen pages to religion. Not only is her appearance so long delayed and so brief that few readers will take seriously Pestalozzi's protestations about the importance of her educational role; his portrayal of her as a creature "forced by the power of animal instinct" (182) and of himself as the author of the methods she follows all but guarantees that she will not be given credit for the accomplishments Pestalozzi says are hers.

The mother one meets in *How Gertrude Teaches Her Children* is the direct opposite of the Gertrude of *Leonard and Gertrude*. Far from being in the grip of animal instincts, this latter is a tower of strength, a repository of good sense, and a model of self-discipline. The mother in *How Gertrude Teaches Her Children* is, in contrast, a woman whose heart is detached from her hearth and whose love for her children is devoid of intelligence: a pathetic figure "confined within the miserable and limited sphere of her actual knowledge" (192). It seems that without ever announcing the switch, in *How Gertrude Teaches Her Children* Pestalozzi cast another woman in the good mother role. Having done so he then felt free to represent himself as the sole authority on teaching.

Whereas Pestalozzi recognized the educational significance of rational mother love and of domestic environments only to allow them to disappear from his philosophy, in *The School and Society*, first published in 1900, John Dewey (1859–1952) repressed domesticity from the start. Looking back at the home of preceding generations—one might almost say the home of Leonard and Gertrude—Dewey saw a household whose every member shared in its work. Directing attention to the discipline and character-building of that earlier form of life, Dewey asked if the teachings that used to be acquired there were available elsewhere. His answer was that they were not.

A lesser educational thinker, aware of the effects of the Industrial Revolution on the home, might have proposed measures for making schools more efficient sites for training the new factory workers. From the changing home and developing factory system Dewey derived a different educational message: If home is no longer a center of occupations and, as a consequence, a unique source of educational value has been lost to us, let school become such a center; let it not become a place where children are trained *for* work, but what home used to be—a place *of* work.

As large as Dewey's educational vision was, however, it did not encompass domesticity. Although the first three chapters of *The School and Society* give the impression that the home of the past was educative in the broadest possible sense, his conception of that home was highly selective. In his eyes it was a place of work, as of course it was. But it was also a site of the shared day to day living, the family relationships and, in the best of cases, the affections that constitute domesticity. Furthermore, while changes in the American home provided Dewey's point of departure, the attention he paid home was short-lived. Read the first few pages of *The School and*

Society and one wonders why "home" is not included in the title. Read on and one realizes that the gap is in the text.

In contrast to Dewey, Maria Montessori (1870–1952) built domesticity into her concept of school. Following Gertrude's advice that the aide do for the children in his school what their parents failed to do for them, she designed the Casa dei Bambini as a kind of surrogate home for children. Just as commentators have missed the significance of Pestalozzi's Gertrude, they have ignored Montessori's radically different idea of school, but in her case some responsibility for the lapse must be assigned to her translators. In a 1907 address at the opening of the second school she established in Rome, Montessori made the point that the word *casa* has come to have for Italians the significance of the English word *home*. Nevertheless, from the beginning English translators rendered Casa dei Bambini as House of Childhood or Children's House. Ignoring the domestic metaphor at the heart of her system, neither they nor the great majority of Montessori's interpreters seem to have realized that in a Casa dei Bambini family affections are supposed to govern relations between the "directress" and the children and among the children themselves.

Because of the changes in home and family in Western societies in the last decades of the twentieth century that have created a great "domestic vacuum" in so many children's lives, there is more reason than ever for philosophers of education to be interested in home's educative contributions. One promising response to the Deweyan question of what changes in school suffice now that home and family have been radically transformed, is the proposal that the modern schoolhouse be turned into a "moral equivalent" of home, or "Schoolhome." Modeled on an ideal home—one that bears little if any resemblance to the patriarchal, heterosexist home that Rousseau envisioned for Sophie and Emile—a Schoolhome would re-create home's domestic atmosphere and affection and teach the still relevant aspects of the curriculum that have historically been considered home's responsibility.

The Schoolhome is the direct opposite of what those who believe in home-schooling advocate. Whereas the one policy would make schools more homelike, the other would make homes more like schools. Much as Rousseau separated Emile from home and family so as to avoid the boy's *mis*education, home-schoolers would remove children from school because they perceive *school* to be miseducative. Whether, and in what respects, homes and families today are in fact educative rather than miseducative is a question that contemporary philosophers of education might well address. Since, however, many parents cannot for economic reasons, and will not for personal or political reasons, take their children out of school, it is well to remember that these two sides of the educational coin are fully compatible.

Jane Roland Martin

See also DEWEY; DOMESTIC EDUCATION; GIRLS AND WOMEN, EDUCATION OF; MONTESSORI; PESTALOZZI; ROUSSEAU

Bibliography

Aristotle. *The Politics*. Rev. ed. Translated by T.A. Sinclair. Harmondsworth: Penguin Books, 1981.

Dewey, John. *The School and Society*. Chicago: University of Chicago Press, 1956.

Holt, John. *Teach Your Own*. New York: Delacorte, 1981.

Martin, Jane Roland. *The Schoolhome: Rethinking Schools for Changing Families*. Cambridge: Harvard University Press, 1992.

Montessori, Maria. *The Montessori Method*. New York: Schocken, 1964.

Pestalozzi, Johann Heinrich. *How Gertrude Teaches Her Children*. London: Allen and Unwin, 1915.

———. *Leonard and Gertrude*. Boston: D.C. Heath, 1885.

Plato. *The Republic*. Translated by G.M.A. Grube. Indianapolis, Ind.: Hackett, 1974.

Rousseau, Jean-Jacques. *Emile*. Translated by Allan Bloom. New York: Basic Books, 1979.

Homer (Eighth Century B.C.)

Homer, who flourished in the eighth century B.C., was called "the educator of the Greeks" by Plato some four hundred years later. In this century, Werner Jaeger wrote that Homer "became the teacher of all humanity." There is little disagreement about his importance.

When it comes to such questions, however, as who he was, where he lived, how he came to write, and whether, indeed, he composed and wrote the *Iliad* and the *Odyssey* at all, and whether or not these two epic poems were the work of a single author or of two—here we have a great and contentious scholarly tradition. More important for us is the question of the meaning and significance of his work, an understanding of why it has led the canon of our culture's great books for almost three millenniums, almost impervious to the evolving standards of successive epochs. Here, again, there is no lack of contending interpretations.

Homer's works are the oldest surviving examples of Greek writing, earlier than inscriptions on pottery or coins, earlier than commercial inventories or tax records, and probably contemporaneous with the first recorded Olympic games in 776 B.C.. Homer signals the emergence of the Greek alphabet, the world's first system for converting a spoken language into writing. Whether the excellence and importance of his poems led them to be chosen as the first works to be recorded, or whether the alphabet was developed to record his works can be debated. But the stories he told were unquestionably significant to the Greeks.

He wrote of a time some four hundred years earlier, of the Trojan War (c. 1200 to 1190 B.C.) and its aftermath, with the return home of the great hero Odysseus. He wrote about a predominantly Mycenaean civilization in the late Bronze Age, though he lived at a time when that civilization had disappeared in the emerging Iron Age. Very likely, the story of the Trojan War began to be told during the war itself, and by many bards or story-tellers, who continued to improve upon the story while synthesizing various versions of it. Homer was probably the culmination of this oral tradition, who, by recording it in writing, ended its development. Little wonder there are contradictions and anachronisms within the story as well as rich layers of meaning.

Background to the war was the myth known as the "Judgment of Paris," a young Trojan prince. He is asked to choose the fairest of three goddesses: Hera, wife of powerful Zeus (who is the defender of the family and womanhood), Athena, who sprang from the head of Zeus (and represents wisdom), or Aphrodite, symbol of lust or passion. As a reward for Paris's choice of Aphrodite, she casts a spell over the beautiful Helen, who is willingly abducted by Paris. Unfortunately, Helen is the wife of Menelaus, who calls on his brother Agamemnon and all the other great leaders of the Greeks to help him regain her. They build an armada of a thousand ships, sail for Troy (Ilium), and

struggle for ten years before achieving victory. The *Iliad* recounts a dramatic episode that takes place in the ninth year of the war. Achilles, the greatest Greek warrior, and Agamemnon, the commander-in-chief, come into conflict. Agamemnon's arrogance and lack of respect for Achilles drive the great warrior to rage, and in retaliation he withdraws from battle until the plight of the Greeks becomes desperate and the Trojans come to the verge of victory. Achilles reenters the fray and drives the Trojans back into their walled city, culminating in a confrontation with their champion, the great Hector, whom he slays.

The *Odyssey*, not the *Iliad*, tells us about the famous Trojan horse, and the war's end. But it is primarily about Odysseus' ten-year journey home from the war, and the challenges he had to face, his encounters with Calypso, the Sirens, the Cyclops, Scylla and Charybdis, and others, until he is reunited with his son Telemachos, and his faithful wife, Penelope.

In these poems Homer has painted a magnificent world view, showing us how the gods or forces of nature operate. He depicts not only men in conflict with other men, but values (especially passion versus wisdom) as well, as the *Iliad* and *Odyssey*, taken together, symbolize the contrast. Most poignantly, and characteristic of the Western intellectual tradition, he shows Achilles struggling with himself, questioning his own—and his culture's—central values. Homer glorified the unity of the Greeks above their constituent city-state identity, and he buttresses this with their common belief in the Olympian gods (whom he may have helped create or define). He celebrates the courage and strength of his heroes, especially the wisdom and restraint of Odysseus, and their striving to achieve great things. These men believe they are better than their fathers—they want to excel, and be "among the foremost," and they wish their sons will be better than they. They anticipate our ideas of individualism, competition, and progress. And throughout these epics Homer catalogs in incredible detail, often poetically with similes, the everyday life of ploughing fields and tending orchards, weaving clothing and building houses, preparing food and feasting. Distant places are enumerated, almost endlessly, with their topographical characteristics; the genealogy of men (and gods) is traced, convincing us that these were real men and women, living in a concrete, material world, and not just in the imagination of a talented story-teller.

Homer gave the Greeks a textbook of their civilization to introduce the young to their history, religion, lore, and values (*Paideia*). He is not preachy or didactic. He educates the young through example and role models. He was used by conservatives to instill temperance and citizenship, the integrity of the family, the nobility of self-sacrifice. But in the striving to exceed past achievements, the valuing of contest and competition, the encouragement of individualism, and in the primacy of wisdom and critical thinking, Homer is liberal or progressive.

Homer's culture was vastly different from ours, and far away, and he lived in a distant time, but he understood the universality of the human condition. The Romans appropriated him as their educator also, and Virgil continued his story with the *Aeneid*. Dante hears his voice, and William Shakespeare (in *Troilus and Cressida*) takes up the theme. In our time, James Joyce shows us he is not yet dead. Plato tried to exile Homer from his ideal state because of his fanciful and untruthful understanding of God. But in our real world we have embraced Homer because of his inspired understanding of man.

Louis Goldman

See also ARETE; *PAIDEIA*; PLATO

Bibliography

Bowra, C.M. *Homer*. London: Duckworth, 1972.

Homer. *The Iliad*. Translated by Richmond Lattimore. Chicago: University of Chicago Press, 1951.

———. *The Odyssey*. Translated by Richmond Lattimore. Chicago: University of Chicago Press, 1965.

Jaeger, Werner. *Paideia: The Ideals of Greek Culture*. Vol. 1. New York: Oxford University Press, 1965.

Marrou, H.I. *A History of Education in Antiquity*. New York: Sheed and Ward, 1956.

Wace, Alan, and Frank Stubbings. *A Companion to Homer*. London: Macmillan, 1962.

Hook, Sidney (1902–1989)

For the last five decades of his life, the foremost champion of academic freedom in the United States. Hook was a philosopher of education and democracy. The main contours of his thought followed those of John Dewey (1859–1952), his teacher and friend. He was a great proponent of pragmatic intelligence: the method of inquiry that stresses experimental and cooperative investigation, the fallible character of all empirical judgments, and the correction of theory by reference to experience. Hook also emphasized cognate qualities of mind: intellectual candor and courage and the willingness to subject beliefs to the rigors of experimental verification. These are traits that he found wanting in much of the intellectual community. He wrote copiously and trenchantly on the nature and importance of an education that would truly inculcate these pragmatic habits of mind. These are habits on which the flourishing of democratic societies depends.

Like Dewey, Hook became engaged in numerous public controversies, and his most distinctive contributions to educational principles can be examined by considering three such issues, all of which come to a focus on the nature of academic freedom. Hook insisted that academic freedom consists of two essential elements: the freedom of qualified instructors to teach their subject matter without constraint from outside authorities and the freedom of students to be presented subject matter as free as possible from misinformation and indoctrination. Freedom to teach, then, implies that instructors must possess the learning and competence to present appropriate information to students; and freedom to learn implies that it is wrong for faculty to teach in a deliberately biased or otherwise distorted manner. To do so is clearly to interfere with the students' opportunities to learn. Academic freedom and academic excellence are therefore inseparable. These principles should govern all of academic life. The curriculum, for example, or the hiring and firing of teachers, should be predicated exclusively on academic grounds, rather than being subordinated to the goals of varying forms of orthodoxy.

The first such controversy concerned the fitness of persons to teach who did not subscribe to the principles of academic freedom. In America in the 1950s, there was intense dispute over whether members of the Communist Party should be permitted to teach in schools, colleges, and universities. Hook defended the view that they should not. He pointed out that the party is completely militant; all of its members are under strict orders from the Kremlin to indoctrinate students in the dogmas of Marxism-Leninism and to discredit all other points of view, regardless of their merit. That behavior is in direct violation of academic freedom, which requires that instructors conscientiously teach all sides of controversial issues. Party members, moreover, are in the service of a regime whose avowed intent is to overthrow American democracy by force and violence. Hence they would end freedom in all the ways that we know it.

Hook's adversaries had varying retorts: The Soviet regime is not really hostile; it is not really a threat to American security; and in any case any teacher in America should be considered innocent of any charge of subversion until proven guilty. For his part, Hook mounted formidable evidence that the Soviets were indeed powerful and implacably imperialistic, and he urged that proven membership in the party constituted certainty that the member has no respect for academic freedom and is in fact pledged to subvert it.

In the following decades, Hook became increasingly alarmed by exclusively domestic threats to academic freedom. The treatment of these threats is the second controversial issue to be examined. In the 1960s, student-led groups made demands that the universities be transformed into institutions for political action. They charged that American schools were no more than willing stooges for the perpetuation of the oppressive power structure. The students' aims varied from ending the war in Vietnam to the revolutionary overthrow of the U.S. government. Student behavior and college curricula would, accordingly, be designed to provide leadership for such overthrow, rather than to present a balanced view of controversial issues. Whether to placate student activists or deliberately to lead the politicalization of the academy, most colleges and universities in this period initiated policies and practices of a nature to subordinate academic standards to the political aims of certain groups. Affirmative action in admissions and hiring is one such policy. At the same time, the introduction of politically oriented courses in women's studies and black studies, for example, was widespread.

In a tide of writings, Hook defended the position that the schools—especially those of higher education—had not in recent decades been politically corrupt. They were, on the contrary, devoted to intellectual independence and harbored some of the most noteworthy critics of American politics and policies. By deliberately subordinating academic standards to political aims, the schools were not only undermining academic freedom but also running the

risk that they would be taken over by reactionary forces within the society.

The third controversy to be considered concerns the very idea of academic freedom. Especially in the 1970s and 1980s there were increasing claims that the disinterested search for truth was not only impossible but fraudulent. Indeed, so it is widely claimed, the very notion of truth is an anachronism. The human mind, so it is argued, is necessarily constituted of nothing but localized cultural prejudice, and the ideas and values of one culture cannot be communicated to another. This claim brought with it the attendant claim that the typical college curriculum consists of the prejudices of dead white European males, and it should be discarded and replaced by a multicultural curriculum in which each group is represented in its irreducibly unique form.

Hook replied that the Western tradition has been more pluralistic, more open to heresy and diversity, and more self-critical and self-corrective than any other. He also attacked the view that knowledge and value are simply functions of race, class, gender, ethnicity, or culture. He continued to show how education could be nonpolitical. He likewise continued to argue that any institution of learning would best serve all its constituents by honoring the principles of academic freedom.

James Gouinlock

See also ACADEMIC FREEDOM; DEWEY; PLURALISM; PRAGMATISM

Bibliography

Hook, Sidney. *Academic Freedom and Academic Anarchy.* New York: Cowles Book Company, 1969.

———. *Convictions.* Buffalo: Prometheus Books, 1990.

———. *Education for Modern Man: A New Perspective.* New York: Alfred A. Knopf, 1946. Rev. ed., 1963.

———. *Heresy, Yes—Conspiracy, No.* New York: John Day, 1953.

Kurtz, Paul, ed. *Sidney Hook and the Contemporary World.* New York: John Day, 1968.

Hostos y Bonilla, Eugenio Maria de (1839–1903)

Educated in Spain, Puerto Rican philosopher, propagandist, writer, sociologist, and educator; he revamped the public school systems of the

Dominican Republic and Chile in the late nineteenth century and advocated formal education of Latin American women. Named by Chile as its adopted son, Hostos had the honor of having the first trans-Andean train and a Chilean mountain explored by the Germans Stange and Kruger named after him. He has been called "Citizen of the Americas" and "the Apostle of Freedom" for his lifelong contributions to the enhancement of education and the political and social well-being of Latin America.

At the age of twenty-four, with *La peregrinacion de Bayoan* (1863), he initiated his public life as a staunch defender of oppressed nations as well as his life of exile from his native Puerto Rico, then a Spanish colony. In Spain, Argentina, Chile, Peru, Venezuela, the Dominican Republic, New York, and Puerto Rico, he wrote for and founded various newspapers with the express purpose of propagandizing the need for political and philosophical freedom.

Hostos joined and founded a variety of political associations to aid the cause of freedom in Latin America. In New York, he met Puerto Rican patriot Ramon Emeterio Betances (1827–1898) as well as other Puerto Rican, Dominican, and Cuban revolutionaries. Upon the death of Jose Marti (1853–1985), Hostos resolved to leave behind all other efforts to join in the armed revolt against the Spaniards in Cuba. This attempt was aborted as the old ship, the *Charles Miller*, which carried him from Boston, was forced to anchor in Rhode Island.

His concern for the fate of the Caribbean Islands never ceased. When, as a result of the Spanish-American War, Puerto Rico became a colony of the United States, Hostos formed part of a delegation to Washington. He was baptized by President McKinley's secretary of state "the arrogant man from the Tropics" on account of his stated views that "the people of Puerto Rico do not ask for mercy, they demand justice." Earlier in *Episodios nacionales,* the Spanish novelist-historian Benito Perez Galdos (1843–1920) had referred to him as a man "of radical ideas, talented and intrepid."

To the casting of new pedagogical forms for the public school systems of the Dominican Republic and Chile, he added the founding of colleges and higher institutions of learning. He assumed the formal role of rector (Liceo de Chillan, Province of Nuble in Chile, and Colegio Nacional in Asuncion, Nueva Esparta, Venezuela); professor of constitutional law, sociology, and political economy (Instituto Profesional de Santo Domingo—Centro Universitario, and University of Santiago, Chile); and introduced sociology as an independent discipline to the Dominican Republic and Chile before that field was treated as such in any other part of the world. His *Tratado de sociologia* (1901) is deemed the first integrating essay in the independent field of sociology to be published in Latin America, and his essay *Ensayo critico sobre Hamlet* (1873) is judged by some to be the best work published in Spanish or in any other language on the incomparable Shakespearean tragedy. Of all his works, however, *La moral social* (1888) is the best known as encompassing his philosophical thoughts. For Hostos, every person's calling revolves around the idea of *"el deber del deber"*— that is, duty or, better yet, the fulfillment of our moral obligation. There is only one responsibility, that of fulfilling all of the obligations that life brings, regardless of inconvenience of place, time, or condition. "Man cannot be a man unless he is good. . . . Beyond truth—the object of reason, there is justice—the object of conscience. . . . Beyond the wise man, there lives the just man; beyond science, there is morality."

Hostos has been compared to Emerson in that both advocated a "new man" whose life and mission would rest upon a political order based on liberty, an intellectual order based on the education of the people, and an administrative order founded upon the work and the fundamental coherence of all national organisms. Like Domingo Faustino Sarmiento (1811–1888), he dedicated his life to education, but in a much broader sense. It has been said that while Sarmiento's interest was to teach Argentina to read, Hostos's preoccupation as a genuine thinker, logician, and moralist was to teach all of Latin America to think. Ironically, in accord with the old dictum that "no one is a prophet in his own land," Hostos is better known and celebrated in Latin America than in his native Puerto Rico.

Ana Maria Diaz-Stevens

See also COLONIALISM AND POSTCOLONIALISM; JUSTICE; MARTI-PEREZ; MULTICULTURALISM; REVOLUTION

Bibliography
America y Hostos. Coleccion de ensayos acerca de Eugenio Maria de Hostos. Edicion commemorativa del Gobierno de Puerto Rico. La Habana: Cultural, S.A., 1939.

Carreras, Carlos N. *Hostos: Apostol de la libertad*. San Juan de Puerto Rico: Editorial Cordillera, 1971.

Figueroa, Loida. *Hostos: Ensayos ineditos*. Rio Piedras: Editorial Edil, 1987.

Hostos, Adolfo de. *Indice-Hemero bibliografico de Eugenio Maria de Hostos*. La Habana: Cultural, S.A., 1940.

Hostos, Bayoan de. *Hostos intimo*. Santo Domingo: Imp. Montalvo, 1929.

Hostos, Eugenio Carlos de, ed. *Biografia y bibliografia y coleccion de articulos y poesias*. Santo Domingo: Imp. Oiga, 1904.

Hostos, Eugenio Maria de. *Eugenio Maria de Hostos: Obras*. Coleccion Pensamiento de Nuestra America. La Habana: Casa Las Americas, 1976.

———. *Hostos (Hamlet y Romeo y Julieta) Ensayos*. Rio Piedras: Editorial Edil, 1972.

———. *La moral social*. New York: Las Americas, 1964.

———. *Obras completas*. 20 vols. Edicion Conmemorativa del Gobierno de Puerto Rico. La Habana: Cultural, S.A., 1939.

Pedreira, Antonio S. *Hostos, ciudadano de America*. Madrid: Espasa-Calpe, A.A., 1932.

Rodriguez Demorizi, Emilio. *Hostos en Santo Domingo*. 2 vols. Ciudad Trujillo, Santo Domingo: Imp. J.R., Viuda de Garcia Sucs., 1942.

Roig de Leuchsenring, Emilio. *Hostos y Cuba*. Edicion del Municipio de La Habana, 1939.

Human Nature

A multifaceted and elusive reality that resists precise definition. Human nature can be viewed from many perspectives—chemical, biological, anthropological, sociological, psychological, and so on. A comprehensive theory of human nature attempts to integrate insights from various disciplines into an overall view of what human beings are and what they should become. Every philosophy of education contains, either explicitly or implicitly, some theory of human nature: The goals one sets as an educator and the methods one selects to achieve them are determined largely by one's notion of what human beings are and by one's convictions about what they should become.

A theory of human nature assumes that there is some reality called "human nature" shared by all members (or at least by all normal members) of the species. This assumption has not gone unchallenged: Some theorists so emphasize human individuality that they deny that human beings have a common nature, while others so stress the differences between men and women that they deny that the two sexes share a common nature. This article, however, will proceed on the assumption that human nature, though difficult to define, does exist. The article will discuss six fundamental issues of human nature that pertain directly to the philosophy of education. It will explain the main philosophical options on each issue and, to facilitate further reading and investigation, will name one or more prominent proponents of each position.

Monism versus dualism

Philosophers disagree about whether human beings are ultimately composed of one kind of basic "stuff" (monism) or of two radically different kinds of reality (dualism). Monistic theories can be materialistic, idealistic, or neutral. According to materialistic monism (also called physicalism), human beings are completely physical entities. What we call the mind or soul or consciousness is simply an aspect or function of the body (more specifically, of the brain). Proponents of materialistic monism include Thomas Hobbes (1588–1679), psychologist B.F. Skinner (1904–1990), and many contemporary thinkers. Idealistic monism claims that human beings, along with everything else in the universe, are wholly immaterial. The body and the entire physical world are illusions. Idealistic monism is a central doctrine in Hinduism and in the philosophy of George Berkeley (1685–1753). Neutral monism contends that the mental and physical are two manifestations of some more basic reality. Bertrand Russell (1872–1970) held this view at one time.

Dualists claim that human beings are composites of two radically different and irreducible kinds of reality: something immaterial (the soul, mind, or consciousness) and something material (the body). Some dualists, such as Plato (c. 427–347 B.C.) and Rene Descartes (1596–1650), hold that the immaterial part of human nature can exist without the body; others, including Aristotle (384–322 B.C.) and Jean-Paul Sartre (1905–1980), maintain that the immaterial part perishes along with the body.

Monists and dualists take different views of the learning process. Materialistic monists, for example, see learning as basically an alteration of molecules in the brain. According to Skinner, for instance, learning occurs when events that follow our actions create changes in our brain that affect our future behavior. Dualists typically distinguish sense learning and intellectual learning, and claim that the latter is a spiritual process. For example, Plato contended that true intellectual knowledge is the recollection of things known by the soul before it was united to a body and entered this world; Saint Augustine (354–430) believed that knowledge of immutable truths is caused by God's illumination of the soul; Saint Thomas Aquinas (1225–1274) maintained that the soul "abstracts" intellectual knowledge from sense experience; Descartes held that God furnishes the soul with certain innate ideas.

The Self

Whether human beings are composed of one kind of stuff or two, it seems evident that each person undergoes constant change. Is there a "self" that persists through and underlies all these changes, or is the self an illusion? Most philosophers maintain that the self is real. Monists typically identify the self either with the stuff (material, immaterial, or neutral) of which a human being is made, or with the continuous process this stuff undergoes. Dualists usually identify the self with the nonphysical part of human nature; for example, Plato held that the self is the soul, and John Locke (1632–1704) said that it is consciousness. Both monists and dualists, however, have difficulty explaining precisely what the self is. If it is an unchanging substrate, what aspect of a human being can be said to be immune from change? If it is a process of change, what unifies the many processes that a human being undergoes?

The difficulties of identifying the self have led some philosophers to conclude that there is no self. For instance, the Buddha (Siddhartha Gautama, c. 563–c. 483 B.C.) maintained that what we call the self is simply an aggregate of various kinds of force or energy. David Hume (1711–1776) argued similarly that the so-called self is merely a bundle of continuously and rapidly changing perceptions.

Educators who hold that there is a self and see their teaching as directed primarily toward the student's self must reflect on what this "self" is and how it learns. Educators who deny the existence of a self will need to consider just who (or what) is the recipient of their teaching.

Free Will versus Determinism

The existence of human free will seems obvious from ordinary human experience; it seems clear that we sometimes freely choose to act as we do. However, when we examine the numerous internal and external factors influencing our decisions, it seems less obvious that, in any given situation, we could have chosen otherwise than we did. This has led some theorists to espouse determinism, the theory that every human action is determined by preceding causes and that we can never act otherwise than we do.

The common-sense view that we have free will has been defended by numerous thinkers, especially those wishing to preserve the notion of moral responsibility. Proponents of free will include philosophers as diverse as Aquinas, Descartes, William James (1842–1910), and Simone de Beauvoir (1908–1986). Other thinkers—especially those whose theories are strongly influenced by natural science—maintain that free will does not exist: If we knew all the influences acting on a person in a given situation, we would see that the person could not have acted otherwise.

Determinism takes various forms, according to the type of influence that is said to be principally responsible for a person's behavior. For example, psychological determinists emphasize the power of inner drives or desires; environmental determinists stress external events and forces; genetic determinists focus on inherited traits. These three kinds of determinism are represented, respectively, by psychologist Sigmund Freud (1856–1939), B.F. Skinner, and sociobiologist Edward O. Wilson. Some philosophers, such as Hume, attempt to reconcile determinism with the existence of free will.

Educators who believe in human freedom will have a basis for nurturing a sense of moral responsibility in their students; those who accept determinism will not blame students for their undesirable behavior, but see it as a sickness needing a cure.

Fulfilling Human Potential

The briefest look at human history or at diverse cultures makes clear the vast range of human potential. Individuals can fulfill only some of their many potentials. One of the tasks of a theory of human nature (assuming that we have some measure of freedom) is to determine which potentials are good and should be fulfilled, and which are bad and should be left unfulfilled. Some thinkers, such as the Chinese

H

philosopher Mencius (Meng-tsu, c. 371–c. 289 B.C.) and psychologists Carl R. Rogers (1902–1987) and Abraham H. Maslow (1908–1970), believed that human beings are fundamentally good and that they should therefore strive to fulfill their deepest innate potentials. Theorists like Immanuel Kant (1724–1804) and Freud believed that our human nature includes inclinations such as selfishness and aggression, and that we must learn to overcome or at least redirect these antisocial impulses.

The potentials that we choose to fulfill will eventually establish in us certain character traits (dispositions, habitual ways of acting). To become a good person means to develop good character traits (virtues); to become a bad person is to acquire bad character traits (vices).

Since education is a process of developing certain human potentials and fostering certain character traits (a point emphasized by John Dewey [1859–1952]), it is important for teachers to have a criterion for determining which potentials and traits are good and which are bad. Teachers also need to decide whether human nature is basically good. If it is good, teachers should foster the students' fundamental inclinations. But if it is not entirely good, they should try to inhibit or redirect the bad human impulses.

The Individual and Society

Among our potentials are the ability to seek our own individual good and the ability to seek the good of society. While these two goods are often in harmony, at times they conflict. In cases of conflict, should we pursue our private good or subordinate it to the societal good? Some philosophers, such as Aristotle and Aquinas, held that the good of society is paramount and that we should prefer it to our individual good. But Aristotle and Aquinas also deny a complete dichotomy between individual and societal well-being: Since we are by nature social creatures (we naturally live in society and join with others in achieving common goals), any time we promote the societal good we also, in an important sense, further our own good. Other thinkers, such as Hobbes and Freud, view human beings as individualistic rather than social: A society is a collection of individuals joined together in an uneasy compromise, who seek primarily their private welfare and help or cooperate with others only insofar as it yields some personal benefit. More recently, Edward O. Wilson and other sociobiologists have argued

on evolutionary grounds that human beings, like other animals, are genetically programmed to seek both their individual good and the good of those who share their genes, because both traits promote the survival of the species.

Ideally, education fosters both the good of individual students and the good of society. But since these goals can conflict, educators must decide which (if either) they believe to be primary. Furthermore, since part of education consists in helping students work cooperatively and live harmoniously with others, it is important for educators to be aware of whether they think such education builds on a fundamentally social human nature or goes against an individualistic human nature.

The Purpose of Life

Perhaps the most basic question about human nature is whether there is a purpose to human life and, if so, what it might be. Hindus and Buddhists see the goal of life as liberation from suffering and the cycle of death and rebirth. In Western thought, the purpose of life is often connected with belief in a personal God. According to Augustine and Soren Kierkegaard (1813–1855), for instance, the purpose of this earthly life is to live in such a way that we will be united with God forever in the afterlife. Those who do not believe in a personal God (for example, Aristotle) or in any God at all (for example, Freud) often hold that the purpose of life is to attain happiness. Happiness itself is defined in various ways, such as rational activity (Aristotle) or pleasure (Freud). Contemporary thinkers whose views are shaped by evolutionary biology tend to see the purpose of every organism—including the human organism—as survival and reproduction; such is the view of Wilson, for instance. Some existentialist thinkers, such as Sartre and Albert Camus (1913–1960), believe that life is "absurd" in the sense that it has no objective purpose (we are not "created" to achieve some goal), but they maintain that one can choose one's own goals and thereby give one's life a subjective meaning.

While it is of course possible to set certain educational goals without direct reference to one's view of the ultimate purpose of life, if education is understood as a preparation for life, the justification of any proximate goal will depend ultimately on one's view of the purpose of life. And it will most likely make a difference in a teacher's attitude toward teaching whether the teacher believes that life has an objective or a merely subjective purpose and, if objective, whether the purpose lies in this life or in a life hereafter.

Donald C. Abel

See also AIMS OF EDUCATION; ETHICS AND MORALITY; FREEDOM AND DETERMINISM; HAPPINESS; METAPHYSICS; PERSON, CONCEPT OF

Bibliography

Abel, Donald C., ed. *Theories of Human Nature: Classical and Contemporary Readings*. New York: McGraw Hill, 1992.

Mitchell, John J., ed. *Human Nature: Theories, Conjectures, Descriptions*. Metuchen, N.J.: Scarecrow Press, 1972.

Morris, Brian. *Western Conceptions of the Individual*. New York: Berg, 1991.

Radhakrishnan, S., and P.T. Raju, eds. *The Concept of Man: A Study in Comparative Philosophy*. London: George Allen and Unwin, 1960, 1966.

Stevenson, Leslie. *Seven Theories of Human Nature*. New York: Oxford University Press, 1974, 1987.

Trigg, Roger. *Ideas of Human Nature: An Historical Introduction*. Oxford: Basil Blackwell, 1988.

Humanism

A broadly defined current of thought affirming the inviolability or sanctity of the individual, people's inherent dignity, the power and worth of human personality, and the self-directed development of an autonomous self. Originating as a reform movement in education within the fourteenth-century Italian Renaissance revival of antique arts and letters, humanism has subsequently acquired many divergent associations and meanings, to the point where its historical inception has been largely obscured.

Western humanism was originally allied with the concept of education itself. Among the ancient Greeks, humanism was associated with *paideia*—the "culture" of mind shared in common by all educated persons. For Cicero, Varro, and other classical Roman authors, *humanitas* meant simply the state or condition of being "human." By extension, it meant the process of acquiring human characteristics through learning and instruction. To educate oneself therefore was to claim one's birthright as a human being. The individual's most important life work was often claimed to be one of self-definition, the shaping of one's self in the world.

More broadly, Graeco-Roman humanism denoted an anthropocentric point of view enshrining human interest or judgment as the ultimate arbiter of relevance and standards of value. The Greek sophist Protagoras, it has been argued, captured part of the essence of the humanist stance with his declaration "Man is the measure of all things." Without necessarily entailing any presumption of ethical relativism, a central humanistic tenet affirms the paramount importance of human beings in the large order of reality: Individuals matter for what they are intrinsically, prior to any accounting of what they have received or achieved. Human dignity, in other words, is intrinsic to the natural order.

Humanism in the Western cultural tradition borrowed its human-centeredness, its concepts of human rights and personal dignity, and the theme of individual autonomy from antiquity. As revived among Italian Renaissance writers in the 1400s and 1500s, classical or literary humanism sometimes took on an intense emotional coloration and a heightened emphasis upon individuality as well, partly in reaction to the corporate communalism of the Middle Ages. The term *humanista* (*umanista* in Italian) was reportedly coined by fifteenth-century university students to designate a teacher of the new *studia humanitatis*—literally, "studies of humanity"—following the precedent of words such as *canonista* and *legista,* the names given to professors of canon and civil law. Hence, a humanist was, simply, one who professed "humanism."

When fifteenth-century humanists embarked on their reform of learning, what they envisaged above all else was a rebirth of the Roman ideal in education, as outlined in Cicero's *De oratore*. That is, the goal was to produce articulate and cultured individuals who were prepared for active service in civic life. It meant that students were to be provided with a broad general training, coupled with intensive training in those skills appropriate for forensic debating, or for legal pleading. The "perfect orator," as Cicero described him, was the person who could be relied upon to defend any cause with integrity, to justify any rightful course of action, and to draw upon an almost limitless fund of detailed knowledge in his support of any just case. The orator was thus the pivot of the state: the individual who could be relied upon to assist in making principled judgments and then communicating decisions persuasively and cogently to the public at large.

The ideally educated person, following Cicero, was to be an individual possessed of such important qualities as verbal fluency, erudition, political and legal expertise, discretion, integrity, nobility of spirit, humility, and oratorical or rhetorical eloquence. Whereas early Renaissance humanists endorsed this Ciceronian model more or less intact, later humanist writers tended to downplay the civic function of the orator as an educational ideal. Instead, they began to emphasize arts and letters as intrinsically valuable ends in themselves, largely detached from the public and civic applications.

An example of early humanist education is the school of the teacher Guarino Guarini da Verona (1374–1460). In 1429 he established a school at Ferrara at the request of the local ruling lord, Niccolo Este. Guarino's humanist school eventually provided the model for dozens of others that sprang up across Italy, all of whose masters looked back to him as their mentor and chief source of inspiration. In common with his contemporary Vittorino da Feltre (1378–1446), founder of a famous school of his own, Guarino's aim always was not so much to train professional scholars as active people of affairs, people destined to exercise political and moral leadership within the various Italian city-states. The regimen of studies prescribed included virtually all of the elements of the classical education. It was intended to produce a nobility of character presumably unattained since the days of the great Roman statesmen of ancient times. The means to that end, Guarino was convinced, was thorough and systematic absorption of the moral philosophy, poetry, literature, and history of classical antiquity.

Renaissance humanism meant more than a rebirth of interest in the classical texts of a bygone era, however. More fundamentally, its concern was for the restoration or reclamation of capacities that the Greeks and Romans were believed to have once possessed and which, it was alleged, had been later lost to Western civilization. That spirit was symbolized by a conviction that humanity is free to exercise its will in the world, to project itself into nature and history, and, finally, to shape or form the world in order to improve it. Against the seeming fatalism of medieval thought, Renaissance humanism thus asserted the capacity and freedom of humanity to control the circumstances and conditions of its own destiny.

Gianozzo Manetti (1396–1459), Marsilio Ficino (1433–1499), and, in particular, Pico della Mirandola (1463–1494) numbered among the leading fifteenth-century humanist scholars who celebrated the capacity of human will or volition to impose itself upon the existing order of things so as to transform it in accordance with human values and aspirations. Much the same theme was amplified later on by the French humanist Charles Bouille (Carolus Bovillis, 1475–c. 1553). A more skeptical tone began to appear in the century following, as illustrated in the writings of Michel de Montaigne (1533–1592), Pierre Charron (1541–1603), and Francisco Sanchez (1552–1581). Yet even as late as the eighteenth-century Enlightenment, the more optimistic strain of humanist thought can be seen to resonate in the hopeful pronouncements of Europe's leading social critics and theorists, most notably among the French *philosophes*.

Over the centuries, the focus and thrust of humanist thought changed greatly. Humanism as a broad tradition within Western thought has since been claimed as the distinguishing hallmark of an astonishingly diverse range of philosophies and movements, many of them having nothing whatsoever to do with education as such. It likewise has assumed many forms: classical and literary, religious, Marxist, personalist, secular, pragmatic, evolutionary, psychological, phenomenological, and so on. In its educational expressions, however, humanism's association with broad, recurrent themes pertaining to human self-development, individual autonomy, and personal choice and freedom has been somewhat more consistent.

In modern times, Marxists have claimed that they alone are guardians of the only true humanism, as only under pure communism will it be possible, through the abolition of private property and the end of class exploitation, to eradicate alienation from self. This was the viewpoint advanced by Marx himself in his *Economic and Philosophical Manuscripts,* published in 1844. A comparable claim was advanced by F.C.S. Schiller in a 1903 work, *Humanism,* except that he argued that it is the philosophy of pragmatism that most fully exemplifies the spirit of humanism in the modern era. In his 1946 essay *Existentialisme est un humanism,* French philosopher Jean-Paul Sartre similarly sought to show that existentialism, which purportedly affirms that "there is no other universe than the human universe, the universe of human subjectivity," represents "authentic" humanism in its highest form.

Thomist philosopher Jacques Maritain, on the contrary, in his 1936 work *Humanism integral,* put forth the argument that "personalism," which affirms humanity's capacity for contemplating eternal truths and entering into a relationship with transcendent reality, is the most adequate expression of modern religious humanism. Secular humanists, like Julian Huxley in *Religion without Revelation* (1957), on the other hand, have identified "evolutionary humanism" with the agnostic's suspension of belief or the atheist's denial of God, coupled with a faith that human potential can achieve its full development without benefit of, or reference to, any higher, transcendent reality.

Humanism in education traditionally has referred to a broad, diffuse outlook emphasizing human freedom, dignity, autonomy, and individualism. Among those humanist educators who have valued spontaneity and freedom in learning, and who in some sense have been called educational humanists, brief mention should be made of the French archbishop Francois Fenelon (1651–1715); the great Moravian reformer Johann Amos Comenius (1592–1670); Jean-Jacques Rousseau (1742–1778), author of the well-known *Emile;* Johann Heinrich Pestalozzi (1746–1827), Rousseau's interpreter and disciple; Maria Montessori (1870–1952); and John Dewey (1859–1952), among many others. The penchant for "open education" and the "open-space classroom" in the 1970s in Great Britain and America, to cite yet another example, stood very much within the tradition of humanistic teaching and learning developed since the seventeenth century, if not even earlier.

Educational humanism in modern times has been represented as a reaction against any theory or set of practices that would reduce the idea of the person to something else (for example, to a set of biologically driven impulses or to environmentally conditioned stimulus-response reflexes). Humanism thus stands in opposition to all forms of psychological, social, or historical reductionism. Again, educational humanism has been construed as a way of emphasizing the primacy of "inner consciousness" and subjectivity, as opposed to approaches that "objectify" human beings as the subjects of scientific investigation and manipulation. It is further assumed in some quarters that humanism in education has to do with feelings, desires, and emotions—with "affect" as much as with rational "cognition." Some interpret educational humanism as providing a warrant for specific pedagogical practices and administrative arrangements, as, for example, those said to typify "informal" and individualized education: differentiated curricula, self-paced learning, values education, and teaching efforts directed to learners' emotional and ethical development. Possibly the most derivative meaning of humanistic education is instruction in the "humanities" (history, philosophy, poetry, languages, literature), broadly defined, as distinct from the teaching and learning of the natural and social sciences.

In its very loosest sense, educational "humanism" today is taken to be vaguely cognate with "humane" teaching and learning, with "benevolence" and a general attitude of caring and solicitude toward students. Common themes associated with modern educational humanism include freedom in learning, curricular diversity, individualized instruction and self-paced learning, the importance of developing intuition and feeling, so-called child-centered pedagogy and curricula, advocacy for children's rights, and discovery learning. Humanism is commonly taken to symbolize antipathy toward all forms of rigidity, classroom authoritarianism, and passive learning. Humanistic educators accordingly tend to emphasize the importance of active student involvement and participation, the affective development of students, and maximal freedom in the classroom setting so as to allow for the full exercise of spontaneous curiosity and inquiry.

Christopher J. Lucas

See also AIMS OF EDUCATION; *ARETE;* CICERO; DEWEY; EXISTENTIALISM; FROEBEL; MONTESSORI; *PAIDEIA,* PESTALOZZI, ROUSSEAU; *STUDIA HUMANITATIS*

Bibliography

Bowen, James. *A History of Western Education: Civilization of Europe: Sixth to Sixteenth Century,* vol. 2. New York: St. Martin's Press, 1975.

Broome, Jack H. *Rousseau: A Study of His Thought.* New York: Barnes and Noble, 1963.

Childe, Gordon. *Man Makes Himself.* New York: Mentor, 1951.

DeGuimps, Roger. *Pestalozzi: His Life and Work.* New York: Appleton-Century-Crofts, 1895.

H

Dewey, John. *Democracy and Education.* New York: Macmillan, 1916.

Grafton, Anthony, and Lisa Jardine. *From Humanism to the Humanities: Education and the Liberal Arts in Fifteenth and Sixteenth-Century Europe.* Cambridge: Harvard University Press, 1986.

Holt, John. *How Children Fail.* New York: Pitman, 1969.

Kohl, Herbert. *The Open Classroom.* New York: New York Review Books, 1969.

Lerner, Max. *Education and a Radical Humanism.* Columbus: Ohio State University Press, 1962.

Montessori, Maria. *The Montessori Method.* New York: Schocken, 1964.

McCallister, William J. *The Growth of Freedom in Education.* London: Constabel and Company, 1931.

Neill, A.S. *Summerhill, A Radical Approach to Child-Rearing.* New York: Hart, 1960.

Pratt, Caroline. *I Learn from Children.* New York: Cornerstone Library, 1970.

Rogers, Carl R. *Freedom to Learn.* Columbus, Ohio: Charles E. Merrill, 1969.

Silberman, Charles E. *Crisis in the Classroom, the Remaking of American Education.* New York: Random House, 1970.

Hypatia (c. 360–415)

Mystic and philosopher, born in Alexandria. Her father was Theon, a geometrician, astronomer, renowned philosopher, and teacher at the university. She grew up and was educated in Alexandria, mostly by her father. She may have studied at Athens under Plutarch's daughter, Asclepigenia, but this seems improbable. By 393 she was teaching at the university in Alexandria and must have been doing so for a while, for her reputation lured young Synesius of Cyrene, then about twenty-four, to Alexandria.

Synesius studied there between 393 and 395. The respect he developed for Hypatia as a scientist, mystic philosopher, and teacher is evident in his letters, in which he calls her "my most revered teacher" (Fitzgerald: Letter 160), "the most holy and revered philosopher" (Letter 4), and does not hesitate to submit to her accounts of his own mystical experiences, asking for her judgment and guidance (Letter 154). Writing to one of his friends, a former classmate, he recalls how they "had seen and heard the true and real teacher of the mysteries of philosophy" (Letter 136).

Hypatia was an accomplished author who wrote commentaries on *The Canons of Astronomy,* the *Arithmetics* of Diophantus, and the *Conics* of Apollonius, but her works have not been preserved. She lectured on mechanics and seems to have invented or perfected models of a hydroscope and an astrolabe. In philosophy she was a Neoplatonist, and in 400 she may have become the leader of the Neoplatonist school of Alexandria. Not satisfied with delivering lectures at the university, she would often make her way through the city discussing philosophy with any hearers.

She was a virtuous woman, unmarried, and, according to Suidas, "so extremely beautiful and attractive, that some among her hearers were madly in love with her. But she was not the kind to fall under the power of love, for she was long given to ascetical practices." Once, to a young man who was obviously more in love with her body than her teaching, she is reputed to have said (pointing to her pudenda as she spoke): "I know it is *this* you want, young fellow, and not the true beauty; modesty and fear of indecent exposure (which distracts the soul) require self-control." These are the only words that have come down to us.

Alexandria was a troubled city at that time. The population was equally divided among Christians, Jews, and pagans. Christianity was on the ascent, as it had become the "official" religion of the empire. But with recognition had come excesses. In 390 the temple of Serapis and the adjoining local library had been destroyed by Christian fanatics incited by Theophilus, Patriarch of Alexandria, to obliterate pagan rites and pagan learning. On the other hand, the Jews had lived in the city for at least seven hundred years; they were prosperous and influential. In contrast, Hypatia took no sides among the religious factions, for she considered philosophy the paramount spiritual way to the divine. Thus, her school enrolled Christians, Jews, and pagan sectaries of the Mysteries.

Orestes, the prefect of the city, had a difficult time keeping the factions in line. To make matters worse, Cyril, a young priest who had succeeded his uncle Theophilus as patriarch, was a brilliant but somewhat vengeful person, intent on power, which he wielded ruthlessly. He virtually ruled Alexandria.

On one sabbath day Orestes had convened the citizens to the theater to discuss some pressing affairs. Others (Socrates, *Hist. Eccl.*:VII.15) claim that the occasion for the meeting was a dance performance about whose merits the crowd had split along religious lines. While Orestes was speaking, Hierax, a teacher and follower of Cyril, entered the theater, only to be confronted by the Jews who claimed he had come to disrupt the meeting. Orestes had him arrested and tortured. Meanwhile his friends ran to inform Cyril, who called a meeting with Jewish leaders and threatened them. That night Jewish rioters sped through the city assaulting any Christian in sight and killing many. The next morning Cyril ordered his followers to expel the Jews from the city and seize their property.

Orestes appealed to the emperor. In the meantime hundreds of fanatical monks from Nitria descended on the city eager to support Cyril. A band of fifty happened upon Orestes, himself a Christian, and attacked him. His guards fled, but citizens came to his rescue—not, however, before a monk named Ammonius had hurled a stone at him and wounded his head.

Ammonius was caught and beaten to death by a lictor. Cyril countered by taking the monk's body in solemn procession to the great church of the Caesarium, where he declared Ammonius a martyr and changed his name to Thaumasius ("the Wonderful").

Reconciliation between prefect and patriarch seemed impossible, and Hypatia, who was adviser to the prefect, was blamed for the impasse. One day, as she was on her way to lecture at the university, she was snatched from her chariot by the monks and rushed to the church of the Caesarium. There she was stripped naked, and whether after she was killed or as a method of execution, her flesh was scraped from her bones with sharp oyster shells by the crazed monks and her quivering limbs delivered to the flames.

Hypatia's death took place during Lent, in March of the year 415. She was murdered, as Gibbon (*Decline and Fall*: chap. 47) says, "in the bloom of beauty, and in the maturity of wisdom." The monks were led in this cruel deed by the reader Peter, and, some say, incited by Cyril, although others exculpate him.

An epigram, perhaps the work of the poet Pallades (fl. 5th century), expresses the high regard in which Hypatia was held:

> The Virgin's starry sign whene'er I see,
> Adoring, on thy words I think, and thee;
> For all thy virtuous works celestial are,
> As are they learned works beyond compare,
> Divine Hypatia, who dost far and near
> Virtue's and learning's spotless star appear.

Ignacio L. Götz

See also: NEOPLATONISM

Bibliography

Bregman, Jay. *Synesius of Cyrene: Philosopher-Bishop*. Berkeley: University of California Press, 1982.

Crawford, W.S. *Synesius the Hellene*. London: Rivingtons, 1901.

Duckett, Eleanor S. *Medieval Portraits from East and West*. Ann Arbor: University of Michigan Press, 1972.

Evrard, Etienne. "A quel titre Hypatie enseigna-t-elle la philosophie?" *Revue des etudes Grecques* 90 (1977): 69–74.

Fitzgerald, Augustine. *The Letters of Synesius of Cyrene*. London: Oxford University Press, 1926.

Kingsley, Charles. *Hypatia*. New York: A.L. Burt, n.d.

Rist, J. M. "Hypatia." *Phoenix: The Journal of the Classical Association of Canada* 19, no. 3 (1965): 214–25.

Socrates Scholasticus. *Historica Ecclesiastica*. In *Patrologia Graeca*, vol. 67, edited by J.P. Migne. Paris, 1859.

Suidas. *Lexicon Graecum*. Milan: Joannes Bissolus Benedictur Mangius, 1499.

Wider, Kathleen. "Women Philosophers in the Ancient Greek World: Donning the Mantle." *Hypatia* 1, no. 1 (Spring 1986): 21–62.

I

Idealism

Personalistic Idealism

An *ideal* represents an "idealized" view of things—a *vision* of sorts, a mind's-eye picture of a utopian condition of affairs in which the realization of certain values is fulfilled and perfected. Ideals as such are instruments of the imagination. They are fundamentally value-oriented, abrogating "by hypothesis" certain limitations the real world imposes on the realization of value. Ideals serve as our index not of what is or will be, nor even of what can be, but of what should be. They represent a vision as to how things ought ("ideally") to stand in the world, even though they do not and indeed cannot do so.

The aspect of "idealization" attaches to all ideals. That has important consequences, since it means that we cannot expect to meet with the realization of ideals in actual experience. The object at issue with an ideal (perfect democracy, definitive science, full realization of our own potential, and so forth) cannot be brought to completed actualization in this world. Ideals are merely visions of things about which there is always an element of the visionary. In its very nature, the ideal provides a contrast to the real: There is always some tincture of the imaginary about our ideals. They are not objects we encounter in the world; it is only through thought, and specifically through the imagination, that we gain access to the ideal.

There are, of course, very different types of ideals—personal, moral, political, social, religious, cognitive, aesthetic. A taxonomy of ideals would be complicated indeed, seeing that there are bound to be as many different kinds of ideals as there are kinds of values. Even "purely theoretical" issues can have their ideal aspect, as is attested by the cognitive ideal of "perfected science"—a body of knowledge capable of answering our questions about nature in a way that satisfies such abstract desiderata as truth, comprehensiveness, coherence, elegance, and the other characteristic features of "the systemic ideal."

Commitment to an ideal is inappropriate if it occasions the pursuit of values to become unbalanced. Here, as elsewhere, health is a question of harmony and balance–of giving the diverse elements of a rational economy of values a chance to flourish in their proper place. An ideal functions as simply one component within a system, which makes it possible to strike a reasonable balance between the different and potentially discordant values. The cultivation of ideals is profitable only within the setting of a concern for the overall "economy" of the system of values whose interaction imposes mutual constraints. And the health of such an economy is destroyed when one element is aggrandized by expanding its scope at the cost of the very life of others. Unreasonable dedication to an ideal is a dangerous thing. Public order is a great good. But when, like Maximilien Robespierre (1758–1794), one sacrifices multitudes on its altar, things have gone too far. Like other powerful tools, ideals can be abused. Excesses are possible even—perhaps especially—in the pursuit of virtue.

As Aristotle observed, things can go awry through the neglect of due balance in the pursuit of perfectly sound and appropriate values. Family loyalty can engender nepotism, patriotism can inflate to jingoism, prudence can degenerate into avarice. And so the prospect of misbegotten ideals arises, whereby in the pursuit of some valued goals, one allows other values to be trodden under foot. The Nazi ideal of "racial purity" reflects such a misbegotten desideratum, in which perfectly good values such as communal solidarity, pride in one's heritage, and group loyalty were overdeveloped into something monstrous, usurping the space created by abandoning other less parochial and more humane values.

The stress on ideals must accordingly be tempered by this recognition of the need to harmonize and balance values off against one another. In the realm of values, too, there must be a Leibnizian *harmonia rerum* where things are adjusted in an order of mutual compossibility.

Ethical Idealism

What do ideals do for us? What useful role do they play in the system of things?

The answer runs something like this. Man is a rational agent. He can act and he must choose among alternative courses of action. This crucial element of choice means that our actions will be guided in the first instance by considerations of "necessity" relating to survival and physical well-being. But to some extent they can, and in an advanced condition of human development must, go beyond that point. And then they must be guided by necessity-transcending considerations, by man's "higher" aspirations—his yearning for a life that is not only secure and pleasant but also meaningful in having some element of excellence or nobility about it. Ideals are the guideposts toward these higher, excellence-oriented aspirations. As such, they motivate rather than constrain, urge rather than demand.

The validation of an ideal is derivative. It does not lie in the (unrealizable) state of affairs that it contemplates—in that inherently unachievable perfection it envisions. Rather, it lies in the influence that it exerts on the lives of its human exponents through the mediation of thought. The justification and power of an ideal inhere in its capacity to energize and motivate human effort toward productive results—in short, in its practical efficacy. Ideals may involve unrealism, but this nowise annihilates their impetus or value, precisely because of the practical consequences that ensue upon our adoption of them.

Ideals are visionary, unrealistic, and utopian. But by viewing the world in the light of their powerful illumination, we see it all the more vividly—and critically. We understand the true nature of the real better by considering it in the light reflected from ideals, and we use this light to find our way about more satisfactorily in the real world. The power of ideals lies in the circumstance that the efficacy of our praxis can be enlarged and enhanced by looking beyond the limits of the practicable. Ideals can render us important service when we "bring them down to earth."

The trio "liberty, equality, fraternity," which constituted political ideals for the ideologues of the French Revolution, illustrates the points of the preceding paragraph. Their devotees looked to a new order, where men, freed from the restrictive fetters of the ancient regime, would work together in cheerful cooperation for the common good. Hoping to overcome the deficiencies of the old order, they envisioned a transformation that could find no accommodation amid the harsh realities of an imperfect world.

To adopt an ideal is emphatically not to think its realization to be possible. We do (or should!) recognize from the start that ideals lie beyond the reach of practical attainability. Ideals accordingly do not constitute the concrete objectives of our practical endeavors but rather provide them with some generalized direction. Moreover, objectives are simply things we want and desire—for whatever reason. There is no suggestion that they are inherently valuable or worthy. But by their very nature, ideals are held by their exponents to be objects of worth. An ideal of mine is not just something I want; it is a condition I am committed to considering as deserving of being sought. By their very nature, ideals are seen not as mere objects of desire (*desiderata*) but as desirable objects (*desideranda*): What counts with them is not what one finds that people do want but what one judges to be worthy of wanting.

Ideals are in a way akin to such quasi-fictive reference devices as the equator or the prime meridian, which we do not actually encounter in physical embodiment on the world's stage. They are "navigation aids" as it were—thought constructions that we superimpose on the messy realities of this world to help us find our way about. The utility of an ideal lies in its capacity to guide evaluation and to direct action in productive ways. The crucial role of ideals is as a tool for intelligent planning of the conduct of life. To manage our own affairs satisfactorily—and to explain and understand how others manage theirs—often calls for exploiting the guiding power of ideals.

Nevertheless there are limits here. In theoretical matters idealization can provide a powerful and useful instrument (we can approximate reality by making calculations for ideal gasses and perfectly elastic springs). But in matters of practical action, idealization can prove counterproductive when we allow the better to become the enemy of the good. In life we have to choose between the available alternatives (the ideal house or the ideal candidate just may not be on offer). And theoretical idealization does not help us to effect the necessary interoptimizations. (Knowing what an ideal bridge hand is like does not help us to bid the one we are actually dealt.) Overcommitment to idealizations does actual damage.

Social Idealism

The social idealist position as nowadays considered has two major versions:

Ideal Social Contact Theorists (such as John Rawls): A social arrangement is seen as valid (appropriate) to the extent that a society's members would—if perfectly rational—opt for it in ideal circumstances (the members being equally "powerful," not acting under pressure or duress, equipped with all relevant information, and so forth). In this approach, validation turns on considering an arrangement's place in a social contract achieved under ideal conditions.

Ideal Social Process Theorists (such as Jürgen Habermas): A social arrangement is seen as valid (appropriate) to the extent that it is arrived at by a society's members through the processes and procedures that would govern an ideal discussion—that is, a quest for consensus among perfectly rational agents acting in ideal circumstances (all equally "powerful," not acting under pressure, equipped with the relevant information, and so forth). In this approach, validation is a matter of the ideal appropriateness of the process by which an arrangement is arrived at.

No doubt, the millenarians among us would yearn for a society organized on the principle of having people do what ideally rational agents would do in idealized conditions. But most of us recognize that this is simply pie in the sky. A pragmatic theory is clearly more realistic than its idealized rivals, seeing that it requires no recourse to perfectly rational agents and ideal circumstances. It is willing and able to function in "the real world," pivoting its operation on a factor (the minimization of serious dissatisfaction and discontent) that is readily understood and relatively simple to assess.

To begin with, one must distinguish between an ideal and an idealization. An ideal as such belongs to the practical order. It is something that can and perhaps should be a guide to our actual proceedings, providing a positive goal—or at least a positive direction—of appropriate human endeavor. It represents a state of things whose realization—even if only in part—is to be evaluated positively and that should, by its very nature, be seen as desirable. Like "liberty, equality, fraternity," an ideal represents a state of affairs whose pursuit in practice is to be regarded as eminently "a good thing." By its very nature as such, an ideal is something toward whose realization right-thinking people would deem it appropriate to strive.

An idealization, on the other hand, is something quite different. It involves the projection of a hypothesis that removes some limit or limitation of the real (a perfectly elastic body, for example, or a utopia composed only of sensible and honest people). An idealization is accordingly a thought-instrument—a hypothetical state of things that it may be profitable to think about, but toward whose actual realization in practice it may be altogether senseless to work for. And so, while idealization can prove helpful in theoretical matters, in practical matters it can often do damage.

Ideals, in sum, are constructively action-guiding, while idealizations need by no means be so. A world of eternal springtime might be nice to have if we could get it. But it makes no sense to expend effort and energy in that direction. A positively evaluated idealization does not necessarily constitute a valid ideal.

The situation differs in this regard as between theoretical and practical philosophy. A resort to idealization in theoretical philosophy—in matters of inquiry, truth, and rationality—is something of a harmless bit of theoretical ornamentation. But in matters of practical philosophy idealization can do actual harm. No doubt, ideals can be a useful motive in the direction of positive action. But generally only as a *primum mobile*—an initiator. To hold to the hard and fast, in season and out—not just at the start of the process of decision and action but all along the line—can be dangerous and self-defeating. By diverting our attention away from the attainable realities, a preoccupation with the unrealizable ideal can do real damage in this domain where a pursuit of the unrealizable best can all too easily get in the way of the realization of attainable betterments and impede the achievement of realizable positive objectives. It might be nice for me to be a good polo player, but if that lies beyond my means and talents, it would be foolish to let that desideratum get in the way of my perfectly feasible and attainable goal of being a good tennis player. It would be a splendid thing to be a great artist, but for many individuals it would be counterproductive to let that aspiration get in the way of being a good craftsman. Similarly it might be nice to have social consensus, but it would be counterproductive to let that get in the way of social amelioration—of effecting various smaller but perfectly feasible improvements in the arrangements of a pluralistically diversified society concerned for the benefit of individuals as individuals.

On this basis, it emerges that idealization in the social dimension is something problematic. Its inherent unrealism is far more dangerous in the domain of social than individual action because of its potentially negative bearing on the interests of individuals. For individuals as such, ideals serve to provide guideposts for action, but for societies there is a large potential for conflict.

All the same, with societies and nations, as with individuals, a balanced vision of the good calls for a proportionate recognition of the "domestic impetus," concerned with the well-being of people, home and hearth, stomach and pocketbook, good fellowship, rewarding work, and so forth. But it also calls for recognition of the "heroic impetus," concerned with acknowledging ideals, making creative achievements, playing a significant role on the world-historical stage, and doing those splendid things upon which posterity looks with admiration. Above all, this latter impetus involves the winning of battles not of the battlefield but of the human mind and spirit. The absence of ideals is bound to impoverish a person or a society. Toward people or nations that have the constituents of material welfare, we may well feel envy, but our admiration and respect could never be won on those grounds alone. Excellence must come into it. And in this excellence-connected domain we leave issues of utility behind and enter another sphere—that of human ideals relating to man's higher and nobler aspirations.

Metaphysical Idealism

Metaphysical idealism is the philosophical doctrine that reality is somehow mind-correlative or mind-coordinated—that the real objects composing the "external world" are not independent of cognizing minds, but exist only as in some way correlative to mental operations. The doctrine centers on the conception that reality as we understand it reflects the workings of mind. And it construes this as meaning that the inquiring mind itself makes a formative contribution not merely to our understanding of the nature of the real but even to the resulting character we attribute to it.

For a long time, a dispute raged within the idealist camp over whether "the mind" at issue in such idealistic formulas is a mind emplaced outside of or behind nature (absolute idealism), or a nature-pervasive power of rationality of some sort (cosmic idealism), or the collective, impersonal, social mind of people-in-general (social idealism), or simply the distributive collection of individual minds (personal idealism). Over the years, the less grandiose versions of the theory came increasingly to the fore, and in recent times virtually all idealists have construed "the minds" at issue in their theory as a matter of separate, individual minds equipped with socially engendered resources.

As the accompanying table shows, idealist doctrine takes many forms. Perhaps the most radical of these is the ancient Oriental spiritualistic or panpsychistic idea—renewed in Christian Science—that minds and their thoughts are all there is; that reality is simply the sum total of the visions (or dreams?) of one or more minds.

TABLE 1

Versions of Metaphysical Idealism

I. Ontological Versions

1. *Causal idealism*
   Everything there is, apart from minds themselves, arises causally from the operations of minds.

2. *Supervenience idealism*
   Everything there is, apart from minds themselves, is supervenient upon the operations of mind (that is, somehow inheres them in ways that are not necessarily causal but involve some other mode of existential dependency).

II. Epistemic Versions

1. *Fact idealism*
   To be as a fact, is to be a language-formulable fact—that is, a truth. Every fact can be semantically captured in a language-formulated truth.

2 *Cognitive idealism*

To be as a truth is to be knowable. Every truth can—potentially—be cognitively captured as an item of knowledge. Truth stands coordinate with the cognitive potential of mind.

3 *Strong substantival idealism*

To be as a thing or entity is to be actually discerned (discriminated, identified, perceived) by some knower. (This is simply a restatement of Berkeley's idealistic thesis that "to be is to be perceived.")

4 *Weak substantival idealism*

To be as a thing or entity is to be discernible (discriminable, identifiable, perceivable). Any real thing (entity, object) can—in principle—be discerned by some knower; it must—in principle—be of a nature that admits cognitive access.

5 *Explanatory idealism*

An adequate explanation of the nature of physical ("material") reality requires some recourse to mental characteristics or operations within the substantive content of the explanation.

6 *Conceptual idealism*

Reality is to be understood in terms of the category of mind: Our knowledge of the real is grasped in not merely mind-supplied but indeed even in to some extent mind-patterned terms of reference. Our knowledge of fact always reflects the circumstances of its being a human artifact. It is always formed through the use of mind-made and indeed mind-invoking conceptions and its contents inevitably bear the traces of its manmade origins. Whatever we have any knowledge of we know in terms of mind-construed terms of reference *in whose conceptual content* there is some reflection of its origin in operations characteristic of mind.

It is quite unjust to charge idealism with an antipathy to reality, with ontophobia, as Ortega y Gasset (1883–1955) called it. For it is not the existence but the nature of reality that the idealist puts in question. It is not reality but materialism that classical idealism rejects—and even here the idealists speak with divided voice. Berkeley's "immaterialism" does not so much deny the existence of material objects as their unperceivedness.

There are certainly versions of idealism short of the spiritualistic position of an ontological idealism that (as Immanuel Kant [1724–1804] put it in *Prolegomena*, sect. 13, n. 2) holds that "there are none but thinking beings." Idealism need certainly not go so far as to affirm that mind makes or constitutes matter; it is quite enough to maintain (for example) that all of the characterizing properties of physical existents resemble phenomenal sensory properties in representing dispositions to affect mind-endowed creatures in a certain sort of way, so that these properties have no standing at all without reference to minds. Weaker still is an explanatory idealism that merely holds that an adequate explanation of the real always requires some recourse to the operations of mind.

Positions of the generally idealistic type have been espoused by numerous thinkers. For example, George Berkeley (1685–1753) maintained that "to be (real) is to be perceived" (*esse est percipi*). And while that does not seem particularly plausible because of its inherent commitment to omniscience, it seems more sensible to adopt "to be is to be perceivable" (*esse est percipile esse*). For Berkeley, of course, this was a distinction without a difference: If something is perceivable at all, then God perceives it. But if we forgo philosophical reliance on God the issue looks different, and then comes to pivot on the question of what is perceivable for perceivers who are physically realizable in "the real world," so that physical existence could be seen—not so implausibly—as tantamount to observability-in-principle.

The three positions to the effect that real things just exactly are things as philosophy or as science or as "common sense" takes them to be—positions generally designated as scholastic, scientific, and naive realism, respectively—are in fact versions of epistemic idealism exactly because they see real things as inherently knowable and do not contemplate mind-transcendence for the real. Thus, for example, the thesis of naive ("common-sense") realism that "external things exist exactly as we know them" sounds realistic or idealistic according to whether one stresses the first three words of the dictum or the last four.

There is also another sort of idealism at work in philosophical discussion, an axiological idealism that maintains that values play an objective causal or constitutive role in nature and denies that value is wholly reducible to something that lies in the minds of its beholders. Its exponents join the Socrates of Plato's *Phaedo* in

I

seeing value as objective and as productively operative in the world.

Any theory of natural teleology that regards the real as explicable in terms of value could to this extent be counted as idealistic, seeing that valuing is by nature a mental process. To be sure, the good of a creature or species (their well-being or survival, for example) need not be actually mind-represented. But nevertheless, goods count as such precisely because if the creatures at issue could think about it, they would adopt them as proposed. It is this circumstance that renders any sort of teleological explanation at least conceptually idealistic in nature. Doctrines of this sort have been the stock in trade of philosophy from the days of Plato (c. 427–347 B.C.) to those of Gottfried Leibniz (1646–1716), with his insistence that the real world must be the evaluative best possible. And this line of thought has recently surfaced once more in the controversial "anthropic principle" espoused by some theoretical physicists.

Then too, it is possible to contemplate a position along the lines envisioned in the *Wissenschaftslehre* of Johann Fichte (1762–1814), which sees the ideal as providing the determining factor for the real. In such a view, the real is not characterized by the science we actually have but by the ideal science that is the *telos* of our scientific efforts. In this approach, which Wilhelm Wundt (1832–1920) characterized as "ideal-realism" (*Idealrealismus*; see his *Logik*, vol. 1, 2nd ed., 1895, 86ff.), the knowledge that achieves adequation to the real (*adaequatio ad rem*) by adequately characterizing the true facts in scientific matters is not the knowledge actually afforded by present-day science as we have it, but only that of an ideal or perfected science. In such an approach—which has seen a lively revival in recent philosophy—a tenable version of "scientific realism" requires the step to idealization, and realism becomes predicated on assuming a fundamentally idealistic point of view.

Over the years, many objections to idealism have been advanced. Samuel Johnson thought to refute Berkeley's phenomenalism by kicking a stone. He conveniently forgot that Berkeley's theory goes to great lengths to provide for stones—even to the point of invoking the aid of God in their behalf. G.E. Moore (1873–1958) pointed to the human hand as an undeniably mind-external material object. He overlooked that, gesticulate as he would, he would do no more than induce people to accept the presence of a hand on the basis of the hand-orientation of their experience. The "Harvard Experiment" of C.S. Peirce (1839–1914), of letting go of a stone held aloft, was supposed to establish scholastic realism because his audience could not control their expectation of the stone's falling to earth. But an uncontrollable expectation is still an expectation, and the realism at issue is no more than a realistic thought-posture.

Kant's famous "Refutation of Idealism" argues that our conception of ourselves as mind-endowed beings presupposes material objects because we view our mind-endowed selves as existing in an objective temporal order, and such an order requires the existence of periodic physical processes (clocks, pendula, planetary regularities) for its establishment. At most, however, this argument succeeds in showing that such physical processes have to be assumed by minds, the issue of their actual mind-independent existence remaining unaddressed. (Kantian realism is an intra-experiential "empirical" realism.)

It is sometimes said that idealism is predicated on a confusion of objects with our knowledge of them and conflates the real with our thought about it. But this charge misses the point. The only reality with which we inquirers can have any cognitive commerce is reality as we conceive it to be. Our only information about reality is via the operations of mind—our only cognitive access to reality is through the mediation of mind-devised models of it.

Perhaps the most common objection to idealism turns on the supposed mind-independence of the real. "Surely," so runs the objection, "things in nature would remain substantially unchanged if there were no minds." This is perfectly plausible in one sense, namely the causal one—which is why causal idealism has its problems. But it is certainly not true conceptually. The objection's exponent has to face the question of specifying *just exactly what* it is that would remain the same. "Surely roses would smell just as sweet in a mind-denuded world!" Well . . . yes and no. Agreed; the absence of minds would not *change* roses. But roses and rose-fragrance and sweetness—and even the size of roses—are all factors whose determination hinges on such mental operations as smelling, scanning, measuring, and the like. Mind-requiring processes are required for something in the world to be discriminated as being a rose and determined as being the bearer of certain features. Identification, classification, and property attribution are all required and by their very nature are all mental operations. To be sure, the role of mind is here hypothetical. ("*If* certain interactions with duly constituted observers took place, *then* certain outcomes would be noted.") But the fact remains that nothing could be discriminated or characterized as a rose in context where the prospect of performing suitable mental operations (measuring, smelling, and so forth) is not presupposed.

The preceding inventory of versions of idealism at once suggests the variety of corresponding rivals or contraries to idealism. On the ontological side, there is materialism, which takes two major forms: (1) a causal materialism that asserts that mind arises from the causal operations of matter, and (2) a supervenience materialism that sees mind as an epiphenomenon to the machinations of matter (albeit not a causal product thereof—presumably because it is somewhere between difficult and impossible to explain how physical processes could engender psychological results). On the epistemic side, the inventory of idealism-opposed positions includes (1) a factual realism that maintains linguistically inaccessible facts, holding that the complexity and diversity of fact outruns the limits of the reach of the mind's actual or possible linguistic (or, generally, symbolic) resources; (2) a cognitive realism that maintains that there are unknowable truths—that the domain of truth runs beyond the limits of the mind's cognitive access; (3) a substantival realism that maintains that there exist entities in the world that cannot possibly be known or identified: incognizables lying in principle beyond our cognitive reach; and (4) a conceptual realism that holds that the real can be characterized and explained by us without the use of any such specifically mind-invoking conceptions as dispositions to affect minds in particular ways. This variety of different versions of idealism/realism means that some versions of the one will be unproblematically combinable with some versions of the other. In particular, a conceptual idealism maintaining that we standardly understand the real in somehow mind-invoking terms of reference is perfectly compatible with a materialism that holds that the human mind and its operations ultimately root (be it causally or superveniently) in the machinations of physical process.

Perhaps the strongest argument favoring idealism is that any characterization of the real that we can devise is bound to be a mind-constructed one: Our only access to information about what the real is, is through the mediation of mind. What seems right about idealism is inherent in the fact that in investigating the real we are clearly constrained to use our own concepts to address our own issues; we can learn about the real only in our own terms of reference. But what seems right about realism is that the answers to the questions we put to the real are provided by reality itself—whatever the answers may be, they are substantially what they are because it is reality that determines them to be that way. Mind proposes but reality disposes. But, of course, insofar as one can learn about this reality, it has to be done in terms accessible to minds. Accordingly, while metaphysical idealism has a long and varied past and a lively present, it undoubtedly has a promising future as well.

Nicholas Rescher

See also EPISTEMOLOGY; ETHICS AND MORALITY; EXPERIENCE; METAPHYSICS; POSSIBILITY; PRACTICAL WISDOM; PRAGMATISM; RATIONALISM; REALISM; REASON AND RATIONALITY; ROMANTICISM; SOCIAL AND POLITICAL PHILOSOPHY

Bibliography
Personalistic Idealism
Brightman, Edgar S. *A Philosophy of Ideals.* New York: Henry Holt, 1928.
Royce, Josiah. *The Philosophy of Loyalty.* New York: Macmillan, 1908.
———. *The World and the Individual.* New York: Macmillan, 1990.
Stuart, Henry Cecil, ed. *Personal Idealism.* New York: Macmillan, 1902.

Ethical Idealism
Mead, George Herbert. *Mind, Self, and Society.* Chicago: University of Chicago Press, 1934.
Rescher, Nicholas. *Ethical Idealism.* Berkeley and Los Angeles: University of California Press, 1987.
———. *Moral Absolutes.* New York: Peter Lang, 1989.

Social Idealism
Dewey, John. *Philosophy and Civilization.* New York: Minton, Balch, 1931.
Habermas, Jürgen. in *Moral Consciousness and Communicative Action.* Cambridge:

MIT Press, 1990.

Rawls, John. *A Theory of Justice*. Cambridge: Harvard University Press, 1971.

Stebbing, L. S. *Ideals and Illusions*. London: Halsted, 1948.

Metaphysical Idealism
For the history of metaphysical idealism see:

Willmann, Otto. *Geschichte des Idealismus*. Braunschweig: F. Vieweg and Sohn, 1894–1897; 2nd ed., 1907.

For the German tradition see:

Hartmann, Nicolai. *Die Philosophie des deutschen Idealismus*. Berlin: W. de Gruyter, 1923, 1929.

Kronenberg, M. *Geschichte des deutschen Idealismus*. Munich, 1909, 1912.

Royce, Josiah. *Lectures on Modern Idealism*. New Haven: Yale University Press, 1919.

For British idealism see:

Ewing, A.C. *Idealism: A Critical Survey*. London: Methuen, 1934.

———. *The Idealist Tradition*. Glencoe, Ill.: Free Press, 1957.

Pucelle, J. *L'Idealisme en Angleterre de Coleridge a Bradley*. Neuchatel: La Baconniere, 1955.

Contemporary defenses of idealist doctrines are presented in:

Foster, John. *The Case for Idealism*. London: Routledge and Kegan Paul, 1982.

Rescher, N. *Conceptual Idealism*. Oxford: Blackwell, 1973.

Sprigge, Timothy. *The Vindication of Absolute Idealism*. Edinburgh: Edinburgh University Press, 1983.

Ignatius of Loyola (1491–1556)

Founder of the Society of Jesus (the Jesuits) in 1540, also founder of Jesuit educational work, organizer of missionary endeavors and church reform, Christian mystic, author of the *Spiritual Exercises* and of the *Constitution of the Society of Jesus*, the principles of both of which greatly influenced his educational philosophy and the worldwide network of Jesuit schools.

The philosophy of education of Ignatius was heavily influenced by his own personal experiences, by the Judeo-Christian religious heritage, and by the Graeco-Roman cultural heritage; it is fully comprehensible only in the light of those influences.

Born into a Spanish Basque noble family, Ignatius entered upon a court career and was seriously wounded in battle in 1521. During his enforced convalescence he underwent a religious conversion. He then gave himself to a life of prayer accompanied by profound spiritual experiences, and by the growing ability to discern and judge successfully the various influences, religious and psychological, working upon his personality and upon the choices he was called upon to make. Those experiences and his reflection upon them are the source for his religious, philosophical, and psychological insights, and for the practical advice that went into the *Spiritual Exercises*. The purpose of the *Exercises*, in turn, is to bring a person to an interior freedom that makes it possible to make fundamental decisions about one's life without being influenced by inappropriate attachment.

Desirous of serving God and helping others, Ignatius realized that he needed a formal academic education to do so, and he therefore set himself to school at Barcelona, at the universities of Alcala and Salamanca, and finally at Paris, where, at the age of forty-three, he was a master of the university. Meanwhile he had gathered around him a group of fellow students and graduates of Paris whom he directed in the *Spiritual Exercises*. They decided to offer themselves as a body to the service of the Church, and in 1540 the Church approved the group as a new religious order called the Society of Jesus. Those first members then elected Ignatius as the general superior or head of the order and charged him with the task of drawing up constitutions for its corporate existence and work.

Very quickly the Society of Jesus witnessed to its concern for serious learning by establishing houses of study for the young men who were applying for membership. Within a few years, by 1548, the society, convinced of the need for and usefulness of education for both sacred and civil society, began to establish schools for lay students. As those schools spread across Europe—and even into Asia and the New World—with astonishing rapidity, Ignatius wrote into the *Constitutions* principles and practices for what became the single largest corporate endeavor of the Jesuits. By the time Ignatius died, in 1556, there were almost forty Jesuit schools in existence.

Because it was a corporate work of the Society of Jesus, the Jesuits established the first true educational system in the world. That system linked the schools geographically through a common foundation. It also linked them in philosophy and practice through a set of common principles and procedures drawn from the *Spiritual Exercises* and from the fourth path of the *Constitutions* and codified in a common "Plan of Studies" (the *Ratio Studiorum*). It was not so much new curricula or new methods that distinguished the Jesuit schools, but rather the collaborative planning and activity of a large group of men imbued with a common philosophy of life and of education that, together, they attempted to transmit to their students.

The central purpose at which Ignatius aimed in the educational activities of the Society of Jesus was to prepare students to take a part, ideally a leading part, in the life and activities of their religious, cultural, and sociopolitical milieu, influencing it through the principles and practices of the Christian tradition. This aim was set forth very directly in a letter by Ignatius in 1551 on the founding of Jesuit schools: "From among those who are now merely students, in time some will depart to play diverse roles—one to preach and carry on the care of souls, another to government of the land and the administration of justice, and others to other occupations. Finally, since young boys become grown men, their good education in life and doctrine will be beneficial to many others, with the fruit expanding more widely every day."

Such results would come from the study of the twin traditions of classical Greece and Rome and of Christian philosophy and theology. As content for the Jesuit educational system, Ignatius chose the former, in part because it was the common coin of educated people of that time; he chose the latter because it contained a perennially valid way of expressing the truths arrived at either by reason or by faith or by both together.

As times changed, the use of Graeco-Roman learning could, of course, also change to other means of acquiring an experience of the human condition, and philosophy and theology could also change in their expressions as they developed further insights. What was to remain constant, however, was the aim of acquiring the appropriate means of communicating to others that experience and those insights.

In Part IV of the *Constitutions of the Society of Jesus,* Ignatius set down, at times inextricably mingled, both the principles and the procedures for using that content to arrive at the desired end. The most important of the perennially desired features of Jesuit education would include the following: Education, to be truly complete, must aim to know, love, and serve both humanity and God. Such an education, then, was to be both intellectual and moral. In a Jesuit school, any faculty or discipline could play a part, provided it contributed in the way proper to its own intrinsic nature, to the general purposes of that education. The several parts of a curriculum were to be so arranged and integrated that a person always proceeded from the less to the more comprehensive and unifying elements. Because theology was the unifying discipline, par excellence, it held a special place. This was not in the sense of numbers of hours or courses, because, as a matter of fact, they were usually rather few, but rather in the sense of an atmosphere or outlook that understood that a relationship to God was the most important of all the relationships that make up human life. At the same time, God was to be sought and seen in all human endeavors. While teaching handed on the heritage of the past in the context of the present, research would address questions of the future. Teachers were to be interested in the personal growth of their students, both as individuals and as part of the community of the school. Classroom methods and procedures were to be the best available, no matter where they came from. As a matter of fact, a certain number of the procedures set down by Ignatius came from his experiences at the University of Paris, which he had highly esteemed. Lastly, any such procedures were always to be adapted to the circumstances in which a school found itself, whether of time, place, culture, person. This threefold combination of Ignatius's educational philosophy, the specific directives for all Jesuit schools in the *Ratio Studiorum,* and the principle of adaptive freedom made the Jesuit schools, no matter where located, recognizably part of a worldwide system and yet attuned to local needs.

In addition to its specific provisions, one of the early editions of the *Ratio Studiorum* (1597) set forth the underlying philosophy of Jesuit education in a brief statement of its purposes. The Society of Jesus conducted schools "first, because they supply man with many advantages for practical living; secondly, because they contribute to the right government of public affairs and to the proper making of laws; third, because they give ornament, splendor and perfection to the rational nature of man; and fourth, and what is most important, because they are the bulwark of religion and guide man most surely and easily to the achievement of his last end." That sixteenth-century phrasing, when put into contemporary terms, expresses the practical, the social, the humanistic, and the religious aims for education that flowed from the principles set down by Ignatius.

By 1740 the Jesuits were conducting more than eight hundred schools, most of them in Europe but with others located in both Asia and Latin America. At the temporary suppression of the Society of Jesus in 1773, they were all lost. At the restoration of the society in 1814, the Jesuits again took up the work of education. Now, in the 1990s, in the United States the Society of Jesus sponsors twenty-eight colleges and universities and forty-six high schools. They form part of an international endeavor in more than six hundred and fifty Jesuit educational institutions at every level in sixty-five countries around the world. All told, close to two million students attend those schools.

John W. Padberg, S.J.

See also: Aims of Education; Ethics and Morality; Higher Education; Humanism; Jesus of Nazareth; Liberal Education; Moral Development; *Paideia;* Religious Education; Scholasticism; *Studia Humanitatis;* Thomas Aquinas

Bibliography

Dalmases, Candido de. *Ignatius of Loyola, Founder of the Jesuits.* Translated by Jerome Aixala. St. Louis: Institute of Jesuit Sources, 1985.

Donahue, John W. *Jesuit Education: An Essay on the Foundation of Its Idea.* New York: Fordham University Press, 1963.

Farrell, Allan P. *The Jesuit Code of Liberal Education.* Milwaukee, Wisc.: Bruce, 1938.

Ganss, George E. *St. Ignatius' Idea of a Jesuit University.* Milwaukee, Wisc.: Marquette University Press, 1956.

Ignatius of Loyola. *The Constitutions of the Society of Jesus.* Translated with an introduction and a commentary by George E. Ganss. St. Louis: Institute of Jesuit Sources, 1970.

———. *The Spiritual Exercises.* Translated with a commentary by George E. Ganss. St. Louis: Institute of Jesuit Sources, 1992.

O'Malley, John W. *The First Jesuits.* Cambridge: Harvard University Press, 1993.

Wulf, Frederick, ed. *Ignatius of Loyola: His Personality and Spiritual Heritage.* St. Louis, Mo.: Institute of Jesuit Sources, 1977.

Individualism

Something of an umbrella term, covering ideas ranging from the notion that people are and ought to be motivated to pursue their own advantage, to the idea that all people are valuable and so have fundamental rights that it is the principal demand of morality both in its self-regarding and others-oriented forms to guarantee. Any individualist conception, then, argues that the well-being of individuals is to be considered prior to the well-being of the communities of which the individuals are a part. The epistemological outcome of this moral stance is that people are to assess received opinion for themselves and accept only such opinion that they are convinced is correct on grounds that they accept. Thus, individualism can function as a personal or social ideal both morally and epistemologically. Morally, individualism appeals to the rights of persons as basic to personal or social views, while epistemologically, individualism appeals to skepticism as the rational basis of these views. Individualism as an ideal has been thought particularly American.

The European origins of the American ideal of individualism are found mainly in eighteenth-century thought. The moral thinking of Immanuel Kant (1724–1804), rooted in the Christian ideal of each individual counting as uniquely valuable, sought to have all individuals treated as ends in themselves, and not merely as means to the will of others. Thus, Kant argued for each person's individuality as central to the concern of all with whom that person interacted. Kant captured this idea in his admonition that individuals are to give themselves, as a categorical moral imperative, the law that they are always to act such that they can will their actions to be universal law. This, for Kant, was the rational response to the demands of morality. Thus, Kant's individualism was both moral and epistemic: moral because of its concern with the well-being of all individuals and epistemic because of its insistence that each in executing this moral stance autonomously obeys the rational demands of consistency and impartiality.

Adam Smith (1723–1790), the Scottish political economist, argued for a kind of economic individualism. Instead of attempting to regulate the welfare of the individuals who compose the state, the government was to realize that the wealth of the nation depends upon its maximizing the freedom of individuals' initiative to better their own lives. For Smith, the only legitimate curb on this individualism was the constraints of the free market, rewarding the efficient production of goods that are desired. Smith's individualism, then, promotes two ideas, one psychological, the other moral and economic. The first, derived from the thinking of Thomas Hobbes (1588–1679), is the idea that individuals are motivated solely by egoism. The second is that the welfare of all is best served when individuals attend to their own advantage. Thus, for Smith, individualism was natural and also morally appropriate—a view much in vogue in the highly capitalistic America of the 1980s.

Despite its apparently social character, the thinking of Jean-Jacques Rousseau (1712–1798) is helpful in understanding the political origins of individualism. Rousseau's conception of the social contract upon which society is founded is legitimated only by the freely given consent of each individual member of that society agreeing to live under it. This consensual model of society can be perpetuated only by the continual agreement of each individual in the society to each piece of legislation for that society. Individualism, then, is the political engine of Rousseau's ideal of society.

In the nineteenth century, John Stuart Mill (1806–1873) and Friedrich Nietzsche (1844–1900) contributed much to the European understanding of individualism. In his essay *On Liberty*, Mill argued for the sovereignty of individuals over their own minds and bodies. But he did not believe that this view committed him to the self-seeking ideas of Adam Smith. Rather, Mill argued for the freedom of individuals to explore moral, religious, and feminist ideas and to express those ideas in their individual lives. This personal freedom was central to the utilitarian principle of maximizing the greatest good for the greatest number. In this way, Mill believed that each individual gained dignity as a person. And, this commitment to the moral appropriateness of individualism has embedded in it Mill's commitment to an epistemological individualism, for exploration of the eccentric views individuals might take required, for Mill, a willingness to adopt a skeptical approach to the orthodoxies of the day. Conformity for conformity's sake was anathema to Mill. And it was just that herdlike behavior on the part of society in general that was loathsome to Nietzsche.

In Nietzsche's writing, the ideal of individualism is taken to an extreme. True individuals, for Nietzsche, must be prepared to turn their backs on society, making lives of their own in isolation if necessary. It is for this exercise of the individual's "will to power" that society exists. The rest of society, too cowardly to exercise their will, are contemptible and so unworthy to be counted as individuals. Thus, not all individuals are worthy of respect for Nietzsche; only the few capable of the exercise of the will to power matter—a conclusion very different from Mill's. For Nietzsche individuals are set against the society of which they are a part, whereas for Mill they are the constituents of the society, each and every one mattering for the society's well-being.

In the Europe of the twentieth century, the existentialist thinking of Jean-Paul Sartre (1905–1980) contributed greatly to conceptions of individualism. Sartre's phenomenological thinking urged individuals to be conscious of the choices they make, for these choices constitute their essential being. Sartre's individualism is an individualism of self-expression and can lead to the anguish of isolationism on the part of those pursuing it. Avoidance of this freedom to choose by individuals led Sartre to condemn them as guilty of bad faith, for this was to avoid one's responsibility to others. Individualism, in this view, is self-expression autonomously self-imposed by individuals as the morally appropriate response to life.

American thinking about individualism developed in parallel with much of this European heritage. Benjamin Franklin (1706–1790), for many the American ideal man, believed that individualism appropriately expressed the character of the best sort of man—namely, self-made. Contrary to many of his American contemporaries, Franklin, like Adam Smith, argued for the autonomy of economic man. Indeed, Franklin's *Autobiography* is the narrative of an individual immersed in his private economic purposes, albeit that later he engaged in philanthropy toward his beloved Philadelphia. In the nineteenth century, Abraham Lincoln (1809–1865) and Ralph Waldo Emerson (1803–1882) contributed greatly to American thought about the nature of individualism.

Lincoln, though himself the epitome of the self-made man, in arguing for the freedom and equality of all, identified himself with the Enlightenment tradition of Kantian moral thinking rooted in the Christian tradition of the unique worth of all individuals. Yet Lincoln's individualism was couched in a republican framework. As his Gettysburg address made clear, what gives the expression of individualism meaning is service to the society of which the individual is a member. Thus, Lincoln's individualism, unlike Franklin's, is ultimately to be understood in communitarian terms.

Emerson, on the other hand, argued for a kind of rugged individualism that pitted the individual against society. Like Mill, Emerson thought conformity the enemy of the exercise of individualism, especially the conformity exacted by the small-town American of his day. Self-reliance was Emerson's antidote to conformity, a self-reliance that generated property for the individuals who worked toward it. Thus, individuals' main responsibility was to themselves, and that responsibility was primarily economic. But Emerson, again like Mill, was concerned with intellectual and religious individualism. Trusting oneself as the sole legitimating source of what one thought and believed was the hallmark of Emerson's ideal individual. Thus Emerson's individualism, unlike Mill's, was a celebration of the isolated individual's hard work, both moral and economic, a forerunner of today's "work ethic" mentality.

In twentieth-century America, this mentality of the work ethic has found moral corroboration in the ethics of Ayn Rand (1905–1982). Rand argued that individuals best express their true nature by pursuing selfish actions. Because this is how they are, and because individuals want to express themselves as fully as they can, Rand further argued that individuals ought to take responsibility solely for their own fulfillment and enjoyment. For Rand, then, individualism is incompatible with any form of communitarianism. Individualism is opposed to altruism, so that for Rand, unlike Kant, there is no sense of mutual respect among individuals. Such thinking seems to underlie much of the late-twentieth-century capitalist economic thinking that propels today's celebration of the work ethic mentality. In the extreme competitiveness of the economic thinking of Milton Friedman (b. 1912), individualism is expressed in maximizing one's own aggrandizement regardless of cost, even at the expense of disregarding other individuals. Reversing Kantian thinking, Rand and Friedman view individuals as expendable resources in the Hobbesian market of the war of all against all. The pursuit of individualism has thus become a destructive pursuit in recent years, rather than the constructive ideal it was imagined to be in eighteenth-

century Europe. This eventuality is the result of America's ignoring the educational philosophy of John Dewey (1859–1952).

Dewey's framework for thinking about individualism was, as usual, to attempt to reconcile the apparent contraries of individualism and socialism—or communitarianism in today's terminology. Dewey wanted to abolish the idea that one was either an individualist or a socialist. Rather, Dewey believed that the notions of individualism and socialism were obverse sides of the same coin. Dewey believed that because individuals grow up in a social milieu their education must be in the context of a social intercourse about shared meanings and values. For Dewey, the idea that individualism leads to isolationism, so that education is gained by self-referential legitimation, is the very reverse of the truth. And, this epistemological stance is supported by Dewey's moral stance on individualism. Dewey argued against what he saw as the cause of the Depression of his day—namely, the predominance of an unregulated self-interest that was destructive of the community of purpose that provides moral meaning to the lives of those who constitute the community. Thus, Dewey argued against the rugged individualism of Emersonian self-reliance and for the kind of consensual model of society adumbrated in Rousseau's thought. Thus, Dewey's reconciliation of individualism and socialism is achieved when individuals in concert with each other shape the communities of which they are members to suit what they perceive to be the common good. In essence, like Rousseau and Mill, Dewey hoped that individuals would learn that what serves their particular interests is what serves the common interest, a view now popular once more as an educational ideal.

In his renunciation of asocial individualism, Dewey argued for a kind of individualistic education that relies crucially on social forms of meaning and value. Today Robert Bellah et al., in *Habits of the Heart,* published in 1985, have called for the moral education of the individual to ideals of service, stewardship, and cooperation. Such an education is very different from the prevalent view of moral education as an education in the individual's development of the capacity to implement the moral principles appropriate to the dilemma at hand. Rather, the socially responsible view of moral education for the individual depends more on the development of moral character in which such moral virtues as sharing, compassion, and caring predominate. These virtues, it has recently been argued, are preeminently feminine virtues, which, for some, explains their nonappearance among the masculine virtues thought necessary to the pursuit of competitiveness or naked self-aggrandizement. What is now needed, if the communitarian critique of individualism is to be attended to by educators, is a return to the old ideal of character education, understanding that individualism's virtues must now be compatible with the values of communitarianism. Such an education does not lead individuals to believe that the pursuit of their own well-being must be prior to the pursuit of that of the society. Rather, the pursuit of such individualized notions as rights, economic security, self-interest, or personal freedom can be encouraged only when every individual in the society benefits from their pursuit.

Victor L. Worsfold

See also COMMUNITY; DEWEY; FEMINISM; KANT; MILL; RIGHTS; ROUSSEAU

Bibliography

Bellah, Robert, et al. *Habits of the Heart.* Berkeley: University of California Press, 1985.
Dewey, John. *Democracy and Education.* New York: Free Press, 1966.
———. *Individualism Old and New.* New York: Capricorn Books, 1962.
Gilligan, Carol. "Remapping the Moral Domain." In *Reconstructing Individualism: Autonomy, Individuality and the Self in Western Thought,* edited by Thomas C. Heller, Morton Sosna, and David E. Wellbery. Stanford, Calif.: Stanford University Press, 1986.
Lukes, Steven. *Individualism.* Oxford: Basil Blackwell, 1973.
Noddings, Nel. *Caring: A Feminine Approach to Ethics and Moral Education.* Berkeley: University of California Press, 1984.
Rawls, John. *A Theory of Justice.* Cambridge: Harvard University Press, 1972.
Watt, John. *Individualism and Educational Theory.* Dordrecht: Kluwer Academic Press, 1989.

Indoctrination

The concept of indoctrination has its origin in the Middle Ages, where it was used to refer to the teaching of Christian "doctrine." Indoctrination is now largely seen by philosophers and other educators as a negative and coercive process in which students are taught what to think as distinct from how to think.

Philosophers of education generally regard indoctrination as the purposeful inculcation of beliefs, attitudes, values, ideas, and loyalties in a student by a teacher, parent, or other significant figure. As such, indoctrination implies a lack of regard for the truthfulness of what is being taught and the intellectual autonomy, or rationality, of the student.

I.A. Snook provides a useful generic definition of indoctrination as follows: "A person indoctrinates P (a proposition or set of propositions) if he teaches with the intention that the pupil or pupils believe P regardless of the evidence" (47). Snook's position is an exemplary instance of the emphasis that many philosophers of education place on the intentionality of the teacher or parent when analyzing a possible instance of indoctrination.

For educational philosopher Harvey Siegel (1988), education and indoctrination involve both the acts of "teachers"—in the general sense—in relation to the "students"—those who are being given beliefs. In this sense, indoctrination is the opposite of education. For Siegel, education develops within an individual the capacity to think critically and to use reason to distinguish right ideas and actions from wrong ones. Education provides students with the ability to judge their ideas and ideals in relation to the normative criteria of "reason," which stands neutrally apart from those ideas and ideals. According to Siegel, an act is educational when it is entered into voluntarily and is redeemed by reason—either at the outset or as the final outcome of the educational activity. Conversely, an act is one of indoctrination when it is not entered into voluntarily, and the beliefs being inculcated are not made defensible by reason. Indoctrination is often carried out through coercion.

Siegel's position on the importance of "rationality" over "ideology" is reflected in his (and others') belief that there can exist neutral, nonpolitical, and nonideological ideals and ideas. He advocates the concept of "critical thinking" as one such "neutral universal." Yet progressive and critical educational theorists have convincingly argued just the opposite. Criticalists, in fact, assert that no social domain, least of all education, is neutral or devoid of ideological relations (Giroux; McLaren 1993).

For criticalists, the student or teacher as social actor both creates and is created by the surrounding social universe. There exists no ideal, autonomous, pristine, or aboriginal world to which social constructions must necessarily correspond. There is always a referential field in which signs and symbols are situated relationally. And this particular referential field (such as language, culture, place, time) is always already implicated discursively in relations of power. There exists no pure, subjective insight outside of discourse itself. Students and teachers do not stand before the social world as much as they live in the midst of it.

From the perspective of the criticalist, all educational acts are acts of knowing and as such are bound up (in origin and in outcome) in ideology and politics. In the end, the main disagreement that exists at the heart of the debate remains: Which is primary, ideology or reasoning? From a critical perspective, the "rationality" versus "ideology" argument creates a false dichotomy between these two concepts. Ideology is coexistent with decisions, actions, reflection, experiences, and ideological self-reflection. Our ideas and ideals emerge from ideological and context-dependent social practices. Ideology and rationality are therefore coterminus and mutually constitutive.

According to the criticalists, one cannot "not have" an ideology, but one can adapt or change one's ideological imperatives based on critical reasoning. While there exist no ideas that totally escape embeddedness in ideology (that is, in language), critical reasoning can help identify (in order to prevent) the most debilitating consequences of one's ideological situatedness.

Historically in the United States, it has been groups or individuals whose teaching focuses on religious beliefs or political ideologies that have been the main target of accusations of indoctrination. Yet just as these religious and (generally) Leftist/progressive educators are accused of teaching dogma (such as a literal interpretation of the Bible, in the case of Christian fundamentalists) and ideology (such as political correctness in the case of Leftist educators), the prevailing—yet "invisible"—dominant ideology of free market capitalism is rarely mentioned and less often problematized, or even conceptualized, as an ideology. Because it is naturalized ideologically it remains, for the most part, unquestioned in school curricula.

In the 1930s, the reconstructionist wing of John Dewey's progressive education movement, under the leadership of George Counts, began to articulate a radical new interpretation of American democracy based on social justice and socialism. This movement called for sweeping social change and saw the schools and teachers as the instruments of that change. It was argued that teachers could no longer remain neutral given the deteriorating economic and social conditions of the country. This movement wanted to inculcate a new vision of society (one that witnessed a growing popularity in the 1930s) within schools.

Social reconstructionists held that there was already a prevailing articulation (a hegemony, to use Antonio Gramsci's terminology) of society inculcated or indoctrinated into children and workers. This was accomplished primarily through state-sponsored schooling and took the form of the "American dream"—today's poststructuralists might describe this as America's "guiding fiction"—which causally connected intentionality and achievement. Such a fiction held out the promise that financial success would follow hard work and dedication to the job. The project of the social reconstructionists involved presenting and arguing for a new, more just social order based on equality and justice, or "counter-indoctrination" as Horace M. Kallen (8) called it (a counter-hegemony, really). The central questions raised by the social reconstructionists included: Whose hegemony is prevailing? What are the social and economic consequences? What role do educational institutions play?

The social reconstructionists were acutely sensitive to the liberal and conservative charge of "indoctrination!" However, they claimed that they were not indoctrinators because "they encouraged discussion, stressed scientific method [reason], and were utterly opposed to any distortion or suppression of evidence" (Snook: 19).

While it was argued by social reconstructionists that a vision of the world is always being indoctrinated or inculcated by dominant groups over subordinate groups, they failed to place enough emphasis on resistance by nondominant groups. Often oppressed groups assert their own counterhegemonic view of the social order as they begin to make sense out of their lives (McLaren 1989).

Today's critical educators agree with the social reconstructionists that the current social/economic order is oppressive to most people (as members of the working class, as women, as people of color, and so on). They further argue that elites exercise hegemonic control and practice indoctrination in schools and in society at large (see Herman and Chomsky) and that oppressed groups struggle against this in varying degrees. But at this point they diverge, for contemporary criticalists emphasize individual and group agency and activity in the struggle between the oppressed and the oppressor. They argue that dominant power relations are not reproduced in the same form generation after generation (as the reconstructionists held), but rather that they are dialectically reinitiated each generation in slightly different forms, and that this "space" should give hope to social progressives and radicals.

Most mainstream philosophers and theoreticians still view indoctrination with grave concern (Peters; Siegel) yet see traditional education as it is currently practiced as generally free of undue ideological influence and removed from the consequences of indoctrination (Kallen; Snook). Some even fail to mention—or to be consistent about the fact—that they are themselves living under a particular ideological system with its own resultant doctrines.

The ideological situatedness of an argument or idea does not necessarily preclude its validity or plausibility, or foreclose discussion with people who hold competing ideologies. Rational discussion among people is possible, and indoctrination may be avoided, provided that both the overt and tacit ideological dimensions of the propositions put forward by the interlocutors are identified and freely challenged on ontological, ethical, and epistemological grounds, as the situation demands. This does not guarantee an ideologically free dialogue, but it does establish the grounds for making discussants more accountable for the political, ethical, and social consequences of their arguments and actions.

Peter McLaren
Marc Pruyn

See also CRITICAL THEORY; CRITICAL THINKING; RECONSTRUCTIONISM, SOCIAL

Bibliography

Counts, George S. *Dare the School Build a New Social Order?* New York: John Day, 1932.
Dewey, John, and Evelyn Dewey. *Schools of Tomorrow.* New York: E.P. Dutton, 1915.
Giroux, H. *Border Crossings: Cultural Workers and the Politics of Education.* New York: Routledge, 1992.
Gramsci, Antonio. *Selections from the Prison Notebooks of Antonio Gramsci.* Edited and translated by Q. Hoare and G. Smith. New York: International Publishers, 1971.
Herman, Edward S., and Noam Chomsky. *Manufacturing Consent: The Political Economy of the Mass Media.* New York: Pantheon, 1988.
Kallen, Horace M. *Education versus Indoctrination in the Schools.* Chicago: University of Chicago Press, 1934.
McLaren, P. *Life in Schools: An Introduction to Critical Pedagogy in the Foundations of Education.* New York: Longman, 1989.
———. *Schooling as a Ritual Performance: Towards a Political Economy of Educational Symbols and Gestures.* New York: Routledge, 1993.
Peters, R.S. "Education and the Educated Man." In *Proceedings of the Annual Conference, 1970.* Philosophy of Education Society of Great Britain, 5–20.
Rugg, Harold. "The American Scholar Faces a Social Crisis." *Social Frontier* (March 1935): 10–13.
Siegel, Harvey. *Educating for Reason: Rationality, Critical Thinking, and Education.* New York: Routledge, 1988.
Snook, I.A. *Indoctrination and Education.* London: Routledge and Kegan Paul, 1972.

Intelligence

The word *intelligence* refers by origin to the capacity for "bringing things together" (Latin *inter* and *legi*), finding or creating new order, and bringing that order into memory and conduct. Intelligence is traditionally described as the capacity to judge (Latin *ius*, law; *iustus*, just) and to reason (Latin *ratio*). Hence in Aristotle's biological classification of living things, man is distinguished from the other animals as *rational*.

The nature and powers of human intelligence have been a central preoccupation among the classics of Western philosophy, from Plato (c. 427–347 B.C.) and Aristotle (384–322 B.C.) to Immanuel Kant (1724–1804) and G.W.F. Hegel (1770–1831). To bring the subject closer to the concerns of education this introduction places it first, as Aristotle did, in relation to the special character of human life and history.

Many animals show intelligence; they can learn to modify the patterns of their inherited behavior, and in some measure their environments as well. Some such learning, moreover, can be transmitted, along with the nurture of the young and the association of adults. A clear contemporary account is that of Donald R. Griffin's *Animal Minds* (1992). But such behavior always reaches some plateau, higher in some animals than in others, beyond which it does not grow. Only in human history have the capacities for learning, invention, and expression led to a nonbiological *cultural* evolution, unique in our planetary history. A classic account is that of V. Gordon Childe (1892–1957), *Man Makes Himself* (1936); for the context in evolutionary theory, see the present author's "Three Evolutionary Stages" in *The Language of Nature* (1964).

The biological evolution of human intelligence has been an essential part of a major transformation of our ancestry. It first created small societies that increasingly shared a public world, made possible by the capacity for articulate communication. From Hegel: "Language is self-consciousness existing for others." Such a distinctively social world is one both of material culture—of shared tools and their products—and of the other face of culture: shared science, modes and rules of conduct, belief, and expression communally enjoyed. Because it can evolve and give form nongenetically, culture is treated by anthropologists as "second" nature, shaping and reshaping much of the human character.

First, stones and sticks found in nature became tools, then tools to make other tools and inventions; it is a long story that brings us today to an elaborate material culture, one that includes the jet engine and the surgeon's laser-knife. In this history new modes of conduct and association, of knowledge and belief have evolved, interacting with material cultures, ideas leading to further ideas. As Benedict de Spinoza (1632–1677) put it: "The matter stands on the same footing as the making of material tools." Like all evolution, that of culture has been uneven and sporadic, and many branches of it have failed the test of survival. Over hundreds of millennia, however, human history has increasingly outpaced any purely biological changes. From George Herbert Mead (1863–1931): "The scientific method is, after all, only the evolutionary process grown self-conscious." Through migration and invention, our species has increasingly transformed a wide range of terrestrial environments, and, unlike any other species, supported a population growth rate that has doubled in intervals shortening from millennia to mere decades. In this often chaotic growth, intelligence has enhanced the destructive arts as it has the constructive. Yet this "slaughter-bench of history"—as Hegel called it—has never significantly obstructed population growth.

Intelligence can be identified, quite generally, as the capacity we can bring to resolve the problematic in experience, those difficulties or novelties that interrupt our untroubled, free-flowing competencies that Friedrich Nietzsche (1844–1900) referred to as our "joyous science." John Dewey (1859–1952) made this the central focus in his lifelong engagement with the theory of inquiry, brought together in his *Logic: The Theory of Inquiry* (1938). After intelligent engagements with the problematic, enjoyed as successful, such episodes become deliberately sought after for curiosity and enjoyment, not first to fill known needs. The reactions to small copper spheres, found first among the ashes of some ancestral fires, were surely just aesthetic—their first use perhaps as jewelry. Only later would come the copper needle, the bronze hammer, and in due course the great age of metals. Leisure allowing, these sorts of learning and invention have themselves become individual and social commitments. Thus intelligence has created its own traditions: those of the arts, sciences, and of reflective morality. But these commitments have made their ways unevenly, among practical engrossments often more demanding.

In both personal and political decisions, inquiry is directed toward the nature and consequences of alternative courses of action, toward their acceptability to established interests and beliefs, and toward new interests they may in turn suggest. Thus toward inquiry and debate properly called ethical, the definition of ends. From curiosity about the natural world and the means of human existence there have evolved the sciences. Closely linked to both these major kinds of interest is always a third, that of elaborating the many means of expression and communication, from prosaic discourse to the fine arts and those of instruction.

For what may be called the "anatomy" of intelligence—the diverse functions that enter into its operation—there is a kind of synopsis in the writings of the famous French encyclopedist Jean le Rond d'Alembert (1717–1783). The operation of the mind, he says, involves the interaction of three different "manners in which our soul operates on the objects of its thoughts." These are "memory, reason, and imagination," each word taken in a wide, generic sense. In the grand scheme of the *Encyclopedia,* these aspects of thought, each predominating in turn, correspond to history, philosophy (the sciences), and the arts.

In a like-minded but far more analytical discussion, William James (1842–1910), in his *Psychology* (1890), described the work of intelligence as that of organizing experience through the interaction of two capacities, which he calls "sagacity" and "learning." Sagacity is the ability to focus attention on specific objects and situations, thus to discern in them essential features, putting them together in classes or categories that link them, in turn, to others important to our purposes. Learning, by contrast, is the ability to relate such categories of things to each other, for the recording and retrieval of experience, by relations of analogy and contrast, by causal connections, by narrative association, and others. In such ways we organize our experience in webs or networks of association that can guide further experience and, in turn, grow and be modified by it.

Considered thus, the operation of intelligence is a constructive process, one of attempting to find fresh experience and fit it into the web of previously acknowledged order and established belief, then of testing hypotheses so constructed by seeking still further experience, and on occasion some reconstruction of the web itself. Speaking thus of science, Niels Bohr (1885–1962) said, "The Task of Science is both to extend the range of our experience and to reduce it to order." The first major philosopher of modern times to recognize this active or constructive character of human intelligence was Immanuel Kant. Responding in part to Kant's arguments, a group of Americans, led initially by Charles Saunders Peirce (1839–1914), developed Kant's basic thesis in less formalistic and more diversified ways. William James was one of these, as were George Herbert Mead and John Dewey.

When once the central work of intelligence is thus recognized as a kind of workmanship, new questions may arise as to its scope and power. Here the work of the architect has often provided a paradigm. Even though a structure has been planned and built rationally, it may take different forms all initially passing the test of practicality. Such differences depend, evidently, on the mode of design that the architect brings to his work, his prior commitments as to style, thus his *preconceptions.*

So also in scientific inquiry, not alone in matters of individual or political decision, "architectonic" differences may lead along the way to divergent arguments and conclusions. Each may apparently be consistent with available evidence, each put forward as correct by its advocates. Such divergence of beliefs may be understood as transient, to be resolved in the light of evidence or argument still to be found.

But as in ethics and politics, scientific preconceptions may be held to stubbornly as reflecting different systems of belief that seem to lie beyond the power of further experience or argument—of intelligence—to reconcile. That intelligence can somehow maintain such relativism, yet never in principle overcome it, may seem a hard saying—one we need not further here explore.

From an initially value-free discussion of education as the vehicle of cultural reproduction and evolution, this discussion has shifted to one that is necessarily value-centered. Because of the varied and uneven ways in which formal education has summoned up and transmitted the works of intelligence, it appears itself as increasingly problematic. Research on such matters, as related at least to science education, is critically appraised by George L. Hills (1989). Conspicuous educational failures invite inquiry into just those teaching arts that seek to advance students' own investigative curiosity and talents. Such investigations may remind us of earlier traditions that emphasized the *Selbstatigkeit*—self-activity—essential to critical understanding. The word is that of Friederich Froebel (1782–1852), Romantic philosopher and founder of the Kindergarten movement. In *The Education of Man* (1887), he fully recognized, for childhood education, the deep and central importance of active play as "the highest phase of child development." Far more critically developed, this minority tradition is best represented by the work of John Dewey. But his influence and sometimes successful following failed—as he himself acknowledges in his late *Experience and Education* (1938)—to define and establish, in institutionally robust traditions of practice, something essential: the complex art, required of those who teach, of understanding and supporting the always varied investigative and reflective talents of their students. This art is often confused, by the fallacy Dewey called "either-or," with merely laissez faire practices. Such understanding points to a need it does not yet meet: to evolve the modes of educational practice it invites. It is teachers' own investigative talents that are at stake.

Children (adolescents, adults) will often confront their teachers with well-established preconceptions that stand in stubborn opposition to those that the subject matter seemingly requires. Students' common-sense "sagacity" and "learning" evidently must first be understood on their merits, then with help in finding ways of testing their preconceptions and perhaps restructuring them. To give such support for students' sometimes divergent presuppositions is a pedagogical task for which many traditional ways of teaching, predominantly the fact-giving and explanatory, are radically inappropriate.

As discussed so far, the term *intelligence* refers to the complex, primarily human, talents discussed above. The term is also frequently used in a comparative sense. One argument, one decision, or the person making it, may be judged more or less intelligent than another. In this comparative—and euphemistic—sense, "intelligence" has received much attention in educational research and pedagogy, beginning at least as far back as Francis Galton (1822–1911). For the study of children's intelligence, Alfred Binet (1857–1911) and Theodore Simon (1873–1961) invented tests for the estimation and comparison of children's age-dependent mental abilities. These tests, and their later extensive elaborations, aim to sample achieved knowledge and skills of kinds conventionally attributed to intelligence. They have little to say about the functional nature of intelligence or the diversity of its manifestations among different societies or different individuals in the same society, or about the ways in which educational practices can be optimally attuned to its nurture.

David Hawkins

See also CRITICAL THINKING; HEREDITY AND HEREDITARIANISM; POSSIBILITY

Bibliography

Alembert, Jean le Rond d'. *Preliminary Discourse to the Encyclopedia of Diderot.* Translated, with an introduction and notes, by Richard N. Schwab. Indianapolis, Ind.: Bobbs-Merrill, 1963.

Bohr, Niels. *The Philosophical Writings of Niels Bohr: Vol. I, Atomic Theory and the Description of Nature.* Woodbridge, Conn.: Ox Bow, 1934, 1987.

Childe, V. Gordon. *Man Makes Himself.* London: Watts, 1936.

Dewey, John. "The Existential Basis of Inquiry: Biological." In *Logic: The Theory of Inquiry,* 23–41. New York: Holt, 1938.

———. *Experience and Education.* New York: Macmillan, 1938.

Froebel, Friedrich. *The Education of Man.* Translated and annotated by W. N. Hailmann. New York: Appleton, 1887.

Griffin, Donald R. *Animal Minds.* Chicago: University of Chicago Press, 1992.

Hawkins, David. "Three Evolutionary Stages." In *The Language of Nature,* 255–75. San Francisco and London: Freeman, 1964.

Hills, George L. "Students' Untutored Beliefs about Natural Phenomena: Primitive Science or Common-Sense Education?" *Science Education* 73 (1989): 155–86.

James, William. "Reasoning." In *Psychology.* Vol. 2, chap. 22. New York: Holt, 1890.

Mead, George Herbert. "Evolution Becomes a General Idea." In *On Social Psychology.* Chicago: University of Chicago, 1956. Rev. ed. 1969.

Spinoza, Benedict de. "On the Improvement of the Understanding." In *The Chief Works of Benedict de Spinoza,* 1–41. Translated, with an introduction by R.H.M. Elwes. London: Bell, 1883. Reprint. New York: Dover, 1955.

Intuitionism

Intuitionism is the view that human beings have direct awareness or knowledge of moral values. While many have embraced such a position, its best known proponents have been British philosophers, initially responding to the challenges of egoism and materialism put forward by Thomas Hobbes (1588–1679). Most prominent of these are Ralph Cudworth (1617–1688), the Earl of Shaftsbury (1671–1713), Samuel Clarke (1675–1729), Joseph Butler (1692–1752), Francis Hutcheson (1694–1746), and Richard Price (1723–1791). In the twentieth century, H.A. Prichard (1871–1947), G.E. Moore (1873–1958), and W.D. Ross (1877–1971) are its chief proponents.

The assertion that human beings have direct knowledge of moral values raises many questions. The first concerns what human beings have this knowledge. In the Platonic tradition, one might say that only a select few have such capabilities. But the British philosophers mentioned above opted for a more democratic route; they held that normal, mature humans were capable of such knowledge.

A second question raised by the thesis concerns the content of the knowledge. What sort of moral values are normal humans capable of knowing? Moore held that we know directly what is good and evil, and that our judgments of what actions are right or wrong are derived from this knowledge. Most of the older intuitionists claim that we have direct knowledge of what is right or wrong. But among these philosophers, additional distinctions are necessary. Some (for example, Butler and Prichard) say that we have direct knowledge of the rightness or wrongness of particular acts in particular situations. Others (for example, Price and Ross) say that normal, mature humans have knowledge of what kinds of acts are generally right or wrong. Still others suggest that people have knowledge of the general standard by which the rightness or wrongness of all specific acts is determined. The first of these views is the boldest, attributing to people knowledge of what ought to be done in very particular situations; for this reason, perhaps, it has fewer proponents. The second view is more modest, saying merely that normal people know what characteristics are morally relevant—what characteristics contribute to making an act right or wrong. This view allows us to affirm general moral rules or ethical generalizations with confidence; but since in particular situations more than one rule may be applicable and those rules may conflict, we cannot be certain what particular act ought to be performed.

The third view is bold in that it supposes that people know a single, universal standard of right or wrong, but it is modest in that it acknowledges that applying the standard to particular cases may be difficult. Neither the second nor the third position implies that normal people can always be sure what they ought to do in specific situations; yet each attributes to people important moral knowledge. Some argue that the third version of intuitionism must be endorsed by anyone who believes in a single, fundamental moral principle, whether that principle is utilitarianism, Kant's categorical imperative, or something else. For either we have an infinite regress, or proof stops somewhere; and where proof stops is likely to be at the fundamental principle.

There is a third question raised by intuitionism. How do people apprehend moral truths? It is surprising that the British intuitionists, reacting to Hobbes, agreed that moral knowledge cannot simply be revelation from God—and that in spite of the fact that they were religious. They held that moral knowledge must be accounted for by showing how it can be acquired by the exercise of some human faculty. This led to the development of two schools of intuitionism. Moral sense theorists, such as Shaftsbury and Hutcheson, held that people's awareness of moral values must be conceived as a form of sense perception; grasping the difference between right and wrong is comparable to perceiving the difference between a red thing and a blue thing. Rational intuitionists, such as Clarke, Balguy, and Price, maintained that it is understanding or reason that enables people to grasp moral values; it is comparable to comprehending mathematical axioms.

Intuitionists interpreted Hobbes as saying that people are essentially selfish and that moral qualities such as benevolence and gratitude are approved only because they promote self-interests; against Hobbes, they held that moral qualities are intrinsically good. Moral sense theorists wanted to show that benevolence, gratitude, and other moral traits are natural. Shaftsbury argued that self-knowledge reveals that not all human actions originate from selfish motives. Benevolent and grateful actions please us, and kindness and gratitude become themselves objects of affection. Hutcheson argued that moral goodness procures approbation in a way that natural goodness does not. For example, people's attitudes toward kindness and generosity are different from their attitudes toward health and sagacity. Having observed natural goodness, we desire the object; but having encountered moral goodness, we approve of the agent. This is the way that normal humans are structured; they have a moral sense. Hobbeseans, of course, will say that the approval of moral traits is rooted in self-interest; people praise beneficence, for example, because they want to encourage others to treat them in this manner. But Hutcheson retorts with a series of counterexamples. In one, he asks readers to imagine themselves as beneficiaries in two different cases. In the first, the reader is the heir of a miser; in the second, treated generously by a friend. From the perspective of self-interest,

I

the cases are equal. But anyone's approval of the friend will be much greater. So the sense that determines our approbation is independent of self-interest.

Rationalists wanted to show that benevolence, gratitude, and other moral acts are demanded by reason. Awareness of moral truths is comparable to understanding that from "if A, then B" and "A," one can deduce "B." Moral knowledge is grasping the fitness of certain kinds of behavior between persons: fidelity between promisor and promisee; assistance between one who can help and one in need; and reciprocation between beneficiary and benefactor. Just as we need not posit an intellectual sense to explain our grasp of logical truths, so too we need not posit a moral sense here; reason alone is sufficient.

Moral sense theorists and rationalists were critical not only of Hobbes but also of each other. One criticism that moral sense theorists directed at rationalists concerned moral motivation. Merely apprehending something as true gives one no motive to act. Yet, moral sense theorists contended, part of what it is to affirm a moral judgment is to have some motive to act on it. Moral sense theorists also claimed that rationalists must give an implausible account of moral errors. Those who deny the obligatoriness of beneficence or gratitude are, according to rationalists, guilty of denying a conceptual truth. But to most this mistake does not seem to be conceptual. Rationalists had criticisms of their own. They accused moral sense theorists of making morality too subjective. This is because moral sense theorists made rightness depend on moral approbation, and moral approbation itself depends as much on the psychological makeup of individuals as it does on the objective qualities of acts. If perceivers were created different, morality would be different. In addition, rationalists say that the picture of human nature painted by moral sense theorists threatens the freedom necessary for morality. For moral sense theorists depict normal humans as structured in such a way that they naturally and of necessity exhibit moral approval in appropriate circumstances. But freedom of choice is an essential component of morality.

The most common objection aimed at all versions of intuitionism appeals to the wide variation of moral beliefs: different cultures have different beliefs, and within the same society people disagree. Intuitionists have been united in rebutting this objection. First, there is more agreement than is apparent; for example, nearly everyone affirms the goodness of helping another in need. Second, some disagreement is merely apparent; for the same principle applied in different circumstances will yield different particular prescriptions. Third, some moral disagreements result from disagreements about nonmoral facts. In such a situation, there is agreement about the underlying principles, but disagreement about that to which they are applied. Finally, just as some people are unable to see or to hear, so too some are morally obtuse. Even a former president, Thomas Jefferson, joined the defense of intuitionism, making most of the points just mentioned in a remarkable letter to Thomas Law (dated June 13, 1814).

If intuitionism is correct, moral education can be more than indoctrination; real understanding can be achieved. Of course, the form that such education is likely to take will vary depending on what it is that one believes normal humans can know (rightness of specific acts in particular situations or general right-making characteristics) and how they come to know it (moral sense or reason). For example, we might expect those who believe that people can know what they ought to do in particular situations to emphasize case studies, learning from stories and novels, and the like. By contrast, those who believe that people can know only general moral rules might emphasize studying various societies in order to discover the common underlying precepts.

Terrance McConnell

See also: ETHICS AND MORALITY

Bibliography

Hudson, W.D. *Ethical Intuitionism.* New York: Macmillan, 1967.

Jefferson, Thomas. *The Writings of Thomas Jefferson,* vol. 14. Washington, D.C.: Thomas Jefferson Memorial Association, 1904.

Moore, G.E. *Principia Ethica.* Cambridge: Cambridge University Press, 1903.

Prichard, H.A. *Moral Obligation.* Oxford: Oxford University Press, 1968.

Raphael, D.D., ed. *British Moralists 1650–1800.* 2 vols. Indianapolis, Ind.: Hackett, 1991.

Ross, W.D. *The Right and the Good.* Oxford: Oxford University Press, 1930.

Sinnott-Armstrong, Walter. "Intuitionism." In *Encyclopedia of Ethics,* edited by Lawrence W. Becker, 628–30. New York: Garland, 1992.

Islam

The leading issue in the philosophy of education of Islam is the relationship between religious and secular knowledge. This affects both the content of knowledge and its transmission. If Islam represents the truth, then what is the purpose of acquiring knowledge that comes from outside of the Islamic religion? It might seem that there is no need to appeal to any source of authority outside of that approved by the Muslim tradition, and that the way in which knowledge is transmitted could be on the lines of communicating religious truth to an audience. Such assumptions would be misleading, though, and, to understand why, it is useful to look briefly at some aspects of how education developed in the Islamic world. It will then be seen that the links between education, religion, and pedagogy in that world are far more complex than might superficially appear.

There are a number of sources of authority to which Muslims can appeal, and to a degree they vary in accordance with the type of Muslim at issue. For the majority in the sunni community, religious truth reposes in the Qur'an, the traditional sayings of the Prophet (*hadith*) and the consensus of the community, generally expressed in the form of law (*shari'a*). The shi'i community would replace the role of consensus with the opinion of a properly constituted individual, and might well consult a different form of law and *hadith,* but for both groups the Qur'an has enormous significance as representing the words of God transmitted to the Prophet Muhammad, the final prophet and the recipient of the very last in the series of religious revelations. Yet as with any religion, it is not always easy to reconcile the apparent demands of faith with the practical difficulties of life, and it became necessary to interpret the rules of religion in order to establish satisfactory rules of behavior in societies that came to differ greatly from those that initially received the Qur'an. The rapid expansion of the Islamic world led to the rule by Muslims over Christians, Jews, Persians, and those within a Greek-based culture of considerable sophistication, and a whole range of both religious and secular knowledge became available to Muslims in a potentially threatening form. It became necessary to persuade unbelievers of the truth of Islam, and these unbelievers often had sophisticated reasons for adhering to their original religious doctrines. A considerable body of astronomical, medical, philosophical, mathematical, and scientific knowledge was found to exist in the wider world, and it also became necessary to decide how much was to be accepted into the Islamic world. If the unbelievers possessed certain kinds of knowledge apparently superior to that existing in the world of Islam, then wherein lay the superiority of Islam? How should Muslims react to alternative sources of authority in knowledge?

A conflict thus arose between the "Islamic sciences" and the "ancient sciences," the latter being largely derived from Greek thought. The Islamic sciences were not only religious but also included Arabic grammar and jurisprudence. The justification for studying such material seemed to be implicit in the religion of Islam itself and its national origins in a particular part of the world. Yet many Muslims sought in addition to avail themselves of the benefits of wider learning, knowledge that had been produced in a social and religious context entirely different from the Islamic. The transmitters of such knowledge were not on the whole Muslims, but rather Christians who translated Greek texts into Syriac and then into Arabic. Some Muslims argued that there was enough already in the Islamic sciences to constitute an appropriate education, and anything that came from outside could be ignored as superfluous to that which is really worth knowing. Not only is such "foreign" knowledge unnecessary, but it could also prove dangerous in that it could lead to a weakening of religious faith and a growing adherence to ideas incompatible with Islam. This approach was opposed by other Muslims, who argued that there is no reason why "foreign" ideas and technologies should be feared, as they can be reconciled with Islam and bring with them many benefits. This rather stark dichotomy has many variants, and there is a continuum of approaches to ideas from outside of the Islamic context, ranging from the very hostile to the welcoming.

This sort of debate has taken place throughout the Islamic world from almost the earliest years of Islam right up to today, and we shall examine some of its contemporary implications later. The debate has certainly characterized the direction in which much Islamic education has taken place. Two vital aspects of Islamic education are jurisprudence (*fiqh*) and theology (*kalam*), and these disciplines vary in character in accordance with the attitudes of their adherents to knowledge in its widest sense. In jurisprudence, for example, there has been a protracted debate in some schools over the permissibility of the application of analogy (*qiyas*). How far may one use one example of how to act, an example that has a solid religious basis, to work out a similar but different example through arguments by analogy? The problem with using analogy, or so it has seemed to many jurisprudents, is that it opens the door to subjective opinion and a wide extension of the letter of the law, both of which may lead to dangerous consequences. It could result in legal decisions being reached that have little to do with Islam, but that merely demonstrate the ability of the lawyers themselves to establish persuasive comparisons between different examples. Those Muslims who support the application of analogy argue that with suitable precautions it is entirely acceptable to extend the narrow range of legal prescriptions by analogy to cover a far wider gamut of cases. The jurisprudent is then acknowledging the continuing relevance of Islam by extending its application, as opposed to using reason to establish entirely new legal principles.

There were many arguments between the theological schools of the Mu'tazila and the Ash'ariyya, but a crucial difference lay in the importance they accorded to the use of reason. For the Mu'tazilites, the justification for Islamic doctrine is apparent in the rationality of that doctrine, while for the Ash'arites what makes a particular course of action right is the fact that God has declared that it is right. There is a tendency to regard the Mu'tazilites as rationalist and the Ash'arites as traditionalist, but this is far too crude a model of the distinction. The latter are enthusiastic adherents of the sophisticated use of rationality, but only within the confines of religion, which they see as defining the parameters of rationality. For the Mu'tazilites rationality has a wider sense, and religion can be shown to be rational by objective and independent proof. They appeal to those frequent passages in the Qur'an in which Muslims are urged to argue with nonbelievers, and such argument only has a point if there is a level of rationality that transcends religious differences. Islam does often portray itself as a very rational religion, one that is based upon the evidence of the Qur'an, the reading of which is supposed to incline the nonbeliever to embrace Islam. The perfection of the Book is designed to show the reader how reasonable it would be to become a Muslim, and the Book itself refers to many different forms of expression to attract different kinds of individuals.

The Ash'arites also give importance to the use of reason, but this should take place within a religious framework. It is an error to think that reason can itself justify faith. In practice this theological controversy does not have important educational implications, since the argument is not so much over the use of reason but with respect to how this use is described. For example, both Mu'tazilites and Ash'arites would value scientific enquiry and consider it important, but the latter would not accept that causal links observed in nature are really there independently of the will of God. Once it is accepted that those links depend completely on divine power, it is permissible to talk about causality and natural laws, since this is only a roundabout way of talking about God's actions. It is important, though, that while we use scientific language to make sense of the world around us we are at the same time aware of what lies behind that language, and any education in science must make this manifest. It is interesting to note that the Ash'arites won the debate in the world of Islamic theology, with the result that any scientific education is supposed to embody aspects of a religious perspective if it is to be complete—a very different context for such education than is found in other cultures.

Different kinds of education are appropriate to different kinds of people. This is a frequent theme of much discussion within the history of Islamic culture. There are Muslims who are not particularly interested in theoretical speculation, or who are capable of such thought but who are mainly concerned with their everyday tasks and do not think much about theoretical issues. For this group, assumed to be the vast majority of the community, education should provide them with what they require to function properly and should go no further. If it seeks to go further it will result in raising questions that cannot be satisfactorily answered, and so will threaten the faith and social stability of the masses. The Islamic philosophers often used Aristotelian notions of different forms of reasoning to explain differences between types of thinkers. The ordinary people are most receptive to rhetorical, persuasive, and poetical language, and one of the excellences of the Qur'an is taken to be its use of such forms of language in order to bring along to its message the largest number of people. These ways of representing the truth in fact represent what are logically rather weak forms of argument, but the majority of the audience would not appreciate this; it is important that they be addressed in the ways most appropriate to their capacities and interests. Other and more sophisticated forms of argument should be used for more intellectually advanced audiences. For example, lawyers, theologians, and grammarians are skilled in dialectical thinking, which works from premises they accept because they are the leading axioms in their areas of enquiry and they are able to work from such premises to validly derived conclusions. The highest form of reasoning is reserved for the philosophers, who work from premises that have themselves been established as conclusions of demonstrative arguments and so have entirely universal application. If the wrong forms of reasoning are applied within a particular group, that may result initially in only errors of judgment, but it can have more dangerous consequences in the longer term. It may lead people to doubt their faith, or to doubt the faith of others, or even to doubt the value of education itself.

This approach to education may seem objectionably elitist, and one can clearly see the influence of Plato's *Republic* in Islamic philosophy here. But the basis of this approach is the idea that, because everyone is different, it is appropriate to educate them differently, and indeed prudent to do so. People who are not capable of understanding difficult theological distinctions may feel that their faith is threatened when they are made aware of those distinctions. They might not understand how theologians could reconcile those distinctions with their faith, and so come to doubt their faith or the faith of the theologians.

This is potentially a serious problem for the philosophers, whose adherence to Islam was often doubted by those who became aware of their philosophical views. They argued that it is possible to reconcile religion with philosophy, but also that only philosophers can really understand how this is done—and so it is dangerous to expound philosophical ideas to those unaccustomed to them. To do so results either in a weakening of faith or in a questioning of the orthodoxy of the philosophers themselves, and such undesirable consequences can be avoided by not publicizing the work of philosophy among groups who would not really understand it. The philosophers took the fate of Socrates to heart here. Socrates was taken to have been executed because he expressed himself so clearly that everyone became aware of his

views, and they did not understand how those views were compatible with religion. Aristotle, by contrast, expressed himself in difficult and technical language, so that only philosophers could understand him, and he did not fall into danger. Education should be carefully designed to fit into the intellectual scope of the individual, and care should be taken to avoid treating everyone as though they are the same or indeed could be the same. God has created people to be different, and educationalists must respect those differences in their construction of the curriculum.

The point of such differentiation in education is to protect the different categories of thinkers from interfering in each other's route to knowledge. Ordinary believers have an unsophisticated faith that helps them to maintain an ethically acceptable lifestyle, and no intervention in their behavior is required. If the philosopher were to come and start to explain what problems exist in justifying ethical standards as derivative from God, ordinary believers would become confused and possibly dissatisfied with their previously habitual behavior; this is not in any sense a move in the right direction. It is not that under the separation of different kinds of thinkers we allow some people to remain in blissful ignorance of the truth. The truth is available to everyone, but in different ways. Different kinds of believers are urged to improve their knowledge, and this improvement can take a quantitative rather than qualitative form.

For example, the ordinary believer may improve her understanding of the Qur'an by learning more verses and meditating for longer on them, while the theologian may improve his grasp of the forms of resolution of a particular legal problem. Believers can increase their understanding but not leave the level of explanation that provides them with information appropriate to their level of comprehension. Of course, a time may come when an individual may no longer be satisfied with the sorts of solutions to questions that are provided on his level of understanding, and this may be an indication that he is now ready to move up to a higher and more theoretical type of thinking. One of the characteristics of much writing in Arabic on theoretical topics is that such works often start with a description of the sort of reader who will benefit by reading the text, and this reader is frequently taken to be a person who has reached a certain degree of under-

I

standing that is no longer sufficient to answer the sorts of questions he sees before him. The aim of the text may well be to raise him to a higher level of investigation and to provide solutions to those questions. But before such thinking is possible it is necessary for a good deal of prior learning to take place, and the notion of a curriculum according to which there is a certain order to knowledge is a strong feature of education within Islamic culture.

The fact that Islam recognizes religious knowledge as the most important sort of knowledge has had a powerful influence upon the character of education in those countries where Islam is the majority religion, and especially in the Middle East. Although it is readily acknowledged that religious and secular instruction are distinct, the methods for the former are often replicated for the latter. A good deal of religious teaching involves recitation and the learning by heart of texts and practices, and this has proved common in secular schools too. In religious instruction the teacher is not someone whom it is easy to challenge, as he is the transmitter of knowledge that cannot be challenged. Any attempt at criticizing the teacher would be taken to be a criticism of Islam, and children are not encouraged to raise questions or difficulties with the teacher that are more than technical. This attitude extends often to secular teaching, where rote learning is encouraged and active participation in the educational process by the student is actively discouraged. The idea that the student might have something of value to contribute to the lesson would be regarded as eccentric. The role of the student is to listen, learn, and be able to repeat what has been acquired in the lesson when called upon to do so. The sorts of teaching strategies that are sometimes called "progressive" have little place within Islamic education. Again, the religious model of education has had an important influence on secular education in this respect. If the teacher is the custodian of the truth, then there is no point in trying to develop the imaginative or the collaborative capacities of his pupils, since that would only result in a distortion or weakening of the truth that it is his role to transmit. Those who do not yet know the truth can do only one thing, and that is to play the role of empty receptacles, waiting to be filled by the knowledge of those who know what is lacking.

What is at issue here is not so much the content of learning as the way in which it takes place. Islam places a considerable emphasis upon the importance of learning. Muslims will frequently repeat the traditional sayings "Seek knowledge even if it is in China," "Seek knowledge from cradle to the grave," and "Seeking knowledge is a duty of every Muslim man and woman." Some of these sayings have quite radical implications. The first implies that it is obligatory to go outside of one's own culture to acquire knowledge, while the last imposes the obligation on both men and women; it is a saying that has not always been observed in the Islamic world insofar as women are concerned. The crucial issue in education, though, is often not what the object of knowledge is taken to be, but how it is to be known. Knowledge is regarded as objective and real, and the subjective and personal opinions of the individual student are not viewed as of any great significance. The notion of the autonomy of the learner and the suggestion that the relationship between the teacher and the student should take the form of a dialogue would be regarded as vacuous. Now, it is certainly true that these aims of education are often not realized in institutions that perceive themselves as liberal, but they do form part of the rhetoric of education and as such they might be expected to have some practical impact upon the educational system. Education within an Islamic context does not share these aims, but has what might be regarded as the more limited objective of producing good Muslim men and women in accordance with a clear and determinate formula.

What are the criteria of Islamic education? There is naturally no easy answer to this question, since it would in the first place depend upon the sort of Muslim one was asking. A distinction between secular and religious education lies in the fact that the aim of the latter is to produce an individual with a commitment to a particular faith rather than just a knowledge of it, and this is certainly true of Islamic education. Muslims often object to a form of multicultural education that represents Islam as just one religion among many. They want to be part of an educational system that gives priority to Islam, and that sees other religions through Islamic spectacles. They want to grow up as part of a community that sees Islamic practices as natural and that reinforces the religious education that is part of the formal curriculum. An interesting question here is what implications an Islamic education has for the rest of the school curriculum. Does it imply that some subjects, or parts of subjects, should be excluded, or that some subjects should be emphasized at the expense of others? The answer that is normally given is that the formal curriculum in an Islamic school should be the same as the secular curriculum in other schools in the country, apart of course from the religious part, but that the hidden curriculum should be very different. The atmosphere of the school, the ways in which students and teachers treat each other, the sort of language that is used, and so on should all be based upon acceptable Islamic rules of behavior. Students are thus brought up within an Islamic community and so develop both an understanding of and an affinity toward such a lifestyle.

When one examines the literature of classical and medieval Islam, one finds no specific treatments of educational philosophy that are separate from broader studies in philosophy, law, and history. There are plenty of writers who give advice on the cultivation of character, and sometimes the implications for teaching and training are specifically related to schools and colleges. On the whole, though, there was not much interest in the work of the schools from a philosophical point of view, and much more in the institutions of higher education, which came to be extraordinarily well developed and successful both in training scholars and in pursuing research. The basis of elementary education is taken to be religious, and it is the duty of parents and teachers to instill in their pupils the articles of faith and the knowledge required to avoid vices and acquire virtues. Other sorts of knowledge are useful and can be attained, but they are not of the nature of a personal religious obligation. What is of overriding importance is the lifestyle that young people develop, and a Muslim lifestyle is the only real aim of education. Secular knowledge can certainly be pursued, but not at the expense of Islam, and it must always be understood that a difference exists between religious knowledge and other forms of knowledge. As we have seen, in practice the form of education has often not distinguished between these two kinds of knowledge, which has resulted in a less critical and creative attitude to instruction than one might think desirable from a liberal perspective. But it is of the very essence of Muslim education that a strong distinction be made between the religious and the secular, and it is unfortunate that there is frequently a pedagogical confusion between them.

To a certain extent, though, it is not surprising that there is such confusion, since one aspect of education in the Islamic world that should be stressed is its view of the individual as an organic aspect of reality. This leads to a criticism of what is regarded as the over-compartmentalization of knowledge. Students may see natural science, for example, as an objective and completely accurate description of reality, and they may come to view science as a far more secure form of knowledge than religion. They may blindly accept the truth of science and at the same time criticize the assertions of faith as subjective and unreliable. Western technology may appear to be a surer guarantee of knowledge than the Qur'an, and the demands of morality far more personal and variable than the laws of science. This results in a failure to appreciate the spiritual side of reality, and leads us to relate to the world as an instrument for our purposes rather than a metaphysical reality of which we are only a part. If education glorifies the technical as an end in itself, it is radically misleading from a Muslim point of view. It is indeed important to understand nature and to adapt it to our purposes, but we should at the same time take steps to appreciate the broader context within which those processes take place.

The world in which we live has a deeper religious significance than that which superficially appears, and education should reflect this if it is to give us an accurate view of the world. We require a worldview that gives us access to what lies beneath the surface if we are to grasp the nature of our world. Secular knowledge can in that case be very misleading if it sets out to comprise the whole of reality, and any attempt to educate in entirely secular terms will be unsatisfactory. Similarly, if secular and religious education are thoroughly divorced from each other, the individual will fail to appreciate the ways in which secular knowledge is anchored in religious knowledge. The Muslim knows through her faith what the answers to the main questions about the nature of reality are, and it is incumbent upon her to use those answers to put secular knowledge within an appropriate context. This brings out the leading issue in the philosophy of education for Muslims today—how to confront modernity without abandoning faith. This problem extends right back to the early years of Islam and represents the perpetual dilemma of reconciling religion and practical life through the structure of education.

Oliver Leaman

See also AVERROES; AVICENNA; RELIGIOUS EDUCATION

Bibliography

Butt, Nasim. *Science and Muslim Societies.* London: Grey Seal, 1991.

Giladi, Avner. "Islamic Educational Theories in the Middle Ages: Some Methodological Notes with Special Reference to al-Ghazali." *British Society for Middle Eastern Studies Bulletin* 14, no. 1 (1988): 3–10.

Leaman, Oliver. *An Introduction to Medieval Islamic Philosophy.* Cambridge: Cambridge University Press, 1985.

———. *Averroes and His Philosophy.* Oxford: Clarendon Press, 1988.

Makdisi, George. *The Rise of Colleges: Institutions of Learning in Islam and the West.* Edinburgh: Edinburgh University Press, 1981.

Nasr, Seyyed Hossein. "Science Education: The Islamic Perspective." *Muslim Education Quarterly* 5, no. 1 (1987): 4–14.

Rosenthal, Franz. *Knowledge Triumphant.* Leiden: E.J. Brill, 1970.

Sardar, Ziauddin, ed. *An Early Crescent: The Future of Knowledge and the Environment in Islam.* London: Mansell, 1989.

———. *How We Know: Ilm and the Revival of Knowledge.* London: Grey Seal, 1991.

Isocrates (436–338 B.C.)

Greek teacher, Sophist, political writer, and in subsequent ages often referred to as the "father of Classical Humanism." Isocrates was the most renowned teacher of the Classical Era. And as the fountainhead of rhetorical teaching he exerted a profound influence on Western European education, especially in Rome, the Renaissance, and subsequent eras in which their example exercised authority. His career and outlook were significantly shaped by the fact that his life spanned the century beginning with the disastrous Peloponnesian War, saw the Athenian resurgence as leader of the Second Naval League, its subsequent dissolution, and ended shortly after the battle of Chaeroneia, which marked the beginning of Macedonian hegemony. These events not only induced his career choice and contributed to its spectacular success, but also set the problems to which he addressed most of his political writing.

Isocrates was born to affluent parents. His father, Theodoros, owned slaves skilled at making flutes. Through them he accumulated enough wealth to have been a *choregus*—a wealthy citizen who was required to finance a chorus for one of the festivals—and to provide his son with the best education available in fifth-century Athens. According to biographical tradition, Isocrates studied with several of the most prominent Sophists during his youth. Among his reported teachers were Gorgias of Leontini, Prodikos, and Socrates. His family's fortune, however, was lost during the Peloponnesian War, and Isocrates was forced to search for a profession. His frail constitution, weak speaking voice, and an intense fear of crowds kept him from pursuing a career in politics or in the courts. From about 402 to 393 he was a logographer, a writer of court speeches. In 392 Isocrates opened his school in Athens near the Lykeion. By the time of his death in 338, he was the premier educator in Greece and an important political essayist.

These two seemingly unrelated aspects of Isocrates' career actually form intimately interrelated parts of a single whole. The political essays were meant not only to instruct and persuade the Greeks, but were also parts of Isocrates' instructional method in his school. Moreover, their subject provided the type of content that he considered appropriate and necessary for true rhetoric and education. The political problems addressed in his essays were the incentive and the leaven for his school.

The subject of all his political essays was the salvation of Greece, which during his lifetime was destroying itself through internecine wars between Greek cities and intracity social conflict. These were two distinct but related problems. The first involved intercity relations. The second concerned the internal governance of individual cities. Panhellenism was the best solution, although ineffective, that thinkers of his age could conceive for the first problem. Like Aristotle, Isocrates believed that Greek unity was essential for survival of the Greek world. The demand for unity among the Greeks was the central theme in all his political essays, from the *Panegyricus,* in the 380s, to his last oration, the *Panathenaicus,* completed as he reached the age of ninety-seven. While the vehicle for unity shifted according to circumstances, the goal of Panhellenism remained.

In the *Panegyricus,* Isocrates argued that under Athenian leadership a new naval confederation of Greek cities should be welded together with an imperialistic crusade against the Persian Empire. He saw the proposed war as a struggle between civilization and barbarians. Most significant in his argument was his justification. In the past, bonds had been forged by geography, kinship, and history. Isocrates justified his plea for Panhellenism with culture and education: "The man who shares our paideia is a Greek in a higher sense than he who only shares our blood" (*Paneg.*: 51). Unity was to be the result of culture and education. The justice of imperialistic ventures was to reside in the superior culture and education of the Greeks.

Shortly after the Second Naval League collapsed Isocrates wrote *On Peace,* in which he urged the Athenians to forsake the idea of military hegemony. In its stead, he advised Athenian moral leadership to create the goodwill necessary for Greek unity.

Later in his life, as the possibility for Athenian hegemony receded, Isocrates looked for other agencies to unify Greece. His last hope was the rising star of Philip of Macedon. In his *Philippus,* he appealed to the king of Macedon to unite the Greeks and lead them in the war against the Persians. Isocrates' justification remained the binding power of Greek culture and education and their reputed superiority over those of the barbarians—peoples defined as those who did not share Greek culture. The proposed war with Persia was a constant in Isocrates' program, and he always saw it as a means to Greek unity. Both he and Philip failed to live long enough to witness the fulfillment of this goal by Philip's son, Alexander.

The second political issue addressed by Isocrates involved the governance of individual cities. The problem, as he conceived it, was moral and educational. He took it as axiomatic that the best should rule. All cities, he asserted, had benefited when this had been the case and had suffered when it was not. The most obvious solution, but not the one Isocrates preferred, was enlightened despotism. In a monarchy the educational problem could be confined to the schools, especially the schools for the rulers. As he illustrates in his *To Nicoles, Evagoras,* and *Archidamos,* within this political arrangement the educational objective is to develop self-control in the king. He must rule for his subjects; justice, honesty, and love of humanity must be his guiding principles. Thus, the educator of a future king must develop these virtues as far as the pupil's nature will allow. He does not go so far as to claim that *arete,* or vir-

tue, can be produced by education. His claim is more modest: that the education can improve on the natural endowment of the pupil. In these writings, Isocrates places a significant limitation on monarchy. The right to rule is not based in constitutional fact or lineage, but depends on the *arete* of the ruler. The monarch's right is based solely on personal virtue.

Isocrates, however, preferred a more democratic organization for the state. His counsel to the Athenians for reform of their democracy is presented in the *Areopagiticus.* He argued that mid-fourth-century Athenian democracy was fatally flawed. The democracy that he advocated was a highly romanticized version of that of Solon and Cleisthenes, when the best were elected to lead and citizens set aside their personal greed in favor of service to the community. Contemporary Athenian democracy, he charged, "trained the citizens in such a fashion that they looked upon insolence as democracy, lawlessness as liberty, impudence in speech as equality, and license to do what they pleased as happiness" (*Areo.*: 20). Isocrates rightly understood that contemporary Athens was afflicted with a moral problem that could not be corrected with a few good laws or in the schools. Moral regeneration of the society was necessary. As he put it, "For the soul of a state is nothing else than its polity, having as much power over it as the mind does over the body" (*Aero.*: 14). It was the ethos of the society that needed reformation. He firmly believed that a morally just society would produce morally good citizens. While his diagnosis was profound, his solution was shallow. He proposed returning to the *Areopagus* the power of overseeing the morality of citizens.

The political problems of Greece, always seen by Isocrates as moral problems, were confronted both in his essays and in his school. It was, no doubt, in the latter where he experienced the greatest success and achieved the highest acclaim. His school of rhetoric educated the leaders of Greece for more than fifty years and had a major impact on Western European education and culture for twenty-four centuries.

Dobson suggests that the early stage of his school, until the mid 370s, attracted mostly Athenian students, while its greatest ascendancy was achieved during the next twenty years. Then, owing partly to Isocrates' acclaim and partly to Athenian prominence as economic and military leader of the Second Naval League, it attracted students from the entire Greek world. Measured by most standards, his school was a success. He claimed to accept payment only from non-Athenians, and he admitted only four to ten students at any one time. It has been estimated that he taught only about one hundred students during his career of more than sixty years. Nevertheless, the tuition payments and gifts that grateful former students bestowed on him made him one of the twelve hundred most affluent men in Athens. Moreover, over forty of his students became prominent in Greek life. They included teachers, historians, statesmen, generals, and kings.

Students came to his school of rhetoric in their adolescence, after they had completed elementary schooling in writing, reading, numbers, grammar, physical education, and music, which included poetry. Typically, Isocrates' course required three or four years to complete. This was much longer than his competitors' rhetorical schools, but less time than Plato's Academy. Rhetorical training and its competitor, philosophical training, were the higher education of the classical world. The competition between rhetoric and philosophy represented more than simply competing schools. It was a conflict about *paideia,* the cultural nurturing of the young. During the fourth century, rhetoric and philosophy were engaged in an intense cultural conflict for the soul of Greece.

Isocrates' major educational ideas and methods are contained in three orations: *Against the Sophists,* written in 391 as an announcement of his new school; *Antidosis,* composed some forty years later; and his autobiographical work, *Panathenaicus.* Only the first portion of *Against the Sophists* has survived. In it Isocrates attacks his rival schools. Teachers of political discourse, both for the courts and the assembly, he notes, are just too simpleminded. They teach a few rules of argument and present their students with a number of set speeches for rote memorization. Subsequently, the memorized speeches are to be used as models, much as form letters of today are used in business. Only the proper nouns and dates need to be changed. These students, Isocrates argued, are not educated. They are simply trained to apply a few school rules to a world that often refuses to conform to the artificial reality of the school. Moreover, their training does not prepare them to make appropriate ethical decisions. They believe it appropriate to defend willy-nilly any position to display their forensic skills.

His second salvo was fired at the philosophical schools. They, he argued, claim to teach virtue, but that is far more than they can deliver. First, virtue can not be taught for, according to Isocrates, it is part of a person's natural gifts. Education may improve the student's natural gifts, but not create virtue. Second, the philosophers purport to teach virtue through the dialectic, which leads the student to *episteme.* This *episteme* is unchanging, absolute truth. It automatically leads to virtue, for as Plato argued, "To know the good is to do it." Isocrates rejects the existence of any absolute truth humans can obtain. If there is no such truth, he asserts, then the philosophical school can not possibly provide Greece with the requisite education to meet the problems of the age.

Isocrates' own educational ideas and methods are explained in *Antidosis,* restated in *Panathenaicus,* and modeled in his political essays. He presents four general objectives that guide his school. First, he endeavors to introduce his students to what he calls a "Hellenic" viewpoint. By this he means an outlook that is wider than the concerns of a single person or even a single city. He is striving to expand his students both politically and intellectually. This was to be accomplished by exercising them on a broad range of subjects that included literature, politics, ethics, geography, mathematics, and most important, history. He was one of the first teachers to insist on history, because it teaches about good and bad leaders, civic successes and failures. These subjects were not studied "as a subject" in the contemporary schools. Rather, they were introduced as writing topics required them. One can easily understand the increased motivation resulting from the "immediacy" of the subject. Isocrates' demand for a "Hellenic" outlook ensured that none of these subjects would be slighted. It is from this ideal that Western education's belief in "breadth of study" was born.

Isocrates' second educational goal was to elevate the moral tone of the thought and writings of his pupils. This was to be accomplished by insisting that their writings have permanent results—that is, that they consciously strive for lasting value. The pupil must produce works that will be "respected in all companies and for all time." Only those topics that deal with truly humanistic problems and that condemn evil and praise virtue can yield permanent results. Thus, he set his students to working on political problems, social issues, and other broadly conceived humanistic subjects.

The third Isocratean goal was to avoid artificial and pedantic methods. Students must personally engage the material. No mere memorization or slavish following of models was countenanced in his school. Here Isocrates provides a vivid look at his methods. He argues that teachers should study the methods of the *paidotribes*, the physical education teacher. This study reveals a step by step instruction: breaking down each movement, allowing the student to practice it in isolation, combining of the several movements, and finally the application of the movements in a real contest. The teacher of rhetoric is called to imitate this instruction. The student is given individual instruction in each discrete aspect of writing, bringing each product to the group for criticism and finally putting them together in a complete essay. This is aided by the introduction of models of excellent writing. The student is encouraged to study the model—not to memorize it, nor to copy it, but to analyze and criticize it in order to comprehend the principles utilized to accomplish the specific task. Isocrates often placed his own writings before his students for this kind of dissection and criticism. Similarly, each student submitted his own essays for such group examination. Group discussion and criticism were not an end; rather, they led to the correction of ideas and construction and to rewriting an improved essay.

The three above goals were instrumental for the fulfillment of Isocrates' fourth and major educational objective. His paramount goal was the production of a man with good practical judgment. The culmination of his efforts was to produce educated men "who manage well the circumstances which they encounter day by day, and who possess a judgment which is accurate in meeting occasions as they arise" (*Panath.*: 3).

The relationship between these goals becomes more apparent when Isocrates' ideas about knowledge and thought are explicated. He meets the challenge of Plato straight on. Plato had contrasted *episteme*, Truth, with *doxa*, mere opinion. Isocrates refuses this characterization. For him *episteme*, absolute Truth, is unobtainable by humans. The best truth, and only truth, available is *doxa*, which he indicates is a working theory or hypothesis based on human experience and communication. Isocrates' *doxa* bears a ready resemblance to Dewey's notion of a "warranted assertion." *Doxa* is the outcome of a particular typeof human experience, which Isocrates calls *logos*. Roughly translated, *logos* means word or speech, but for Isocrates it is much more. His *logos* included speech, persuasion, communication, inquiry, understanding of good and evil, and education. It has both an inner and an outer side. Its inner side consists of an individual's private, inner conversation—that is, the process of thought. The exterior of *logos* is interpersonal communication, debate, dialogue, and discussion. It is this double process of *logos* that produces *doxa*, practical truth or working hypothesis, on which humans can base their decisions. Isocrates' development of the concept of *logos* seems especially interesting when compared with the language-based social psychology of George Herbert Mead and the empiriocriticism of Richard Avenarius and Ernst Mach. Perhaps Isocrates was, indeed, more of a philosopher than some critics would admit.

Isocrates' reputation as a teacher is unchallenged. Evaluated by his own criterion, "Judge me by the success of my students," he was supreme in his day. His educational ideals have influenced much that is valuable in Western European education. They gave form and substance to Hellenistic education, which, in turn, overwhelmed its Roman conquerors. The educational ideals that the Renaissance rediscovered were those of Isocrates transmitted through Cicero to Quintilian. In subsequent Western education, wherever one finds the spirit of the Renaissance, one will also find the inspiration of Isocrates.

Paul C. Violas

See also: *Arete;* CICERO; *Paideia;* PLATO; PRACTICAL WISDOM; QUINTILIAN; RHETORIC

Bibliography

De Romille, Jacqueline. "Isocrates and Europe." *Greece & Rome* 39 (April 1992): 2–13.

Dobson, J.F. *The Greek Orators.* Chicago: Ares, 1924.

Guthrie, W.K.C. *The Sophists.* New York: Cambridge University Press, 1971, 1978.

Hudson-Williams, H.L.L. "A Greek Humanist." *Greece & Rome* 9 (May 1940): 166–72.

Innerd, Wilfred L. "Isocrates: Pillar of Western Education." Unpublished manuscript. Personal Library of Paul C. Violas.

Isocrates. *Isocrates in Three Volumes*. Translated by George Norlin. Cambridge: Loeb Classical Library, Harvard University Press, 1932, 1982.

Jaeger, Werner. *Paideia: The Ideals of Greek Culture,* Vol. 3. New York: Oxford University Press, 1944, 1986.

Jebb, R.C. *The Attic Orators*. New York: Russell and Russell, 1875.

Johnson, R.S. "Isocrates' Methods of Teaching." *American Journal of Philology* XLXXX (January 1959): 25–36.

Marrou, H.I. *A History of Education in Antiquity*. Madison: University of Wisconsin Press, 1982.

J

James, William (1842–1910)
Summarizing William James's views on education presents peculiar difficulties and opportunities. He wrote little explicitly on the subject. Yet practically everything he did and wrote bears implicitly and importantly on education. His academic career—from assistant professor of physiology to professor of philosophy by way of psychology—itself testifies to education in the deepest sense: self-education, self-development, self-realization, continual growth as a personal, social, and cosmic being (an expression of the difficult-to-translate Greek term *paideia*).

His writings stem directly from this impulse to realize himself. His thought about life was constantly tested by his life (he can be classed as an existentialist in the broad sense). His first book, the extensive *Principles of Psychology* (1890), is at once a book in philosophy and philosophy of education. Who are we basically—minds conjoined with bodies, or must we seek a deeper ground for our integral selves? How do our capacities for conceptual thought connect with our instinctual nature? What are the various senses in which we will our acts? How is a matrix of good habits essential to an effective voluntary career? What is it to be an agent, a self? How do we learn? How are our experiences of value and reality connected?

As James struggles in his writings with those questions—cheerfully, arduously, self-critically—he draws us into his personal self-education so that we may confront the question of our own. This personal struggle is, perhaps, the deepest thing he reveals about education. The mere instructor manipulates communication so that a body of ready-made facts or skills are built into, structured into, students (*instruere*). The educa-tor leads out, or draws out, students (*educare* or *educere*) so that we all learn what matters most to us as beings who must develop and grow, all in our own way, and one way or the other. Note that the process of education is different from that of instruction (from the Latin *instruere*), in which facts and skills are built into, structured into, students with no personal reflection required or desired from either student or teacher. James was ever an educator with little interest in instruction. When he was teaching or writing, he embodied in his every move and sentence the later observation of Alfred North Whitehead (1861–1947) that education is at its best when old and young are learning together—from each other—with zest.

If this were all we were to learn about education from James it would be a great deal, and very timely. He assumes the challenge of self-development. In our age of technology, however, much that passes for writing about education is really only about instruction: It is assumed that teachers are the rightful masters of their subject and need not learn much from their pupils. Teaching manuals typically teach teachers how to manipulate and control students so that a predetermined body of facts or skills may be built into them. In this way "agents" manipulate "patients." James's writings prod us into self-reflection: as if each of us were not an agent who must confront, each in our aloneness and togetherness, the challenge of self-development; as if we already knew which facts and skills are most essential for maturation and development. What authorizes teachers to manipulate students as if they were mere objects or malleable subjects? It is as if this technological age assumes its members have nothing to learn from the struggles for maturation and well-being recorded by the world's civilizations over the millennia.

The implicit educational significance of James's work appears most vividly in his *Varieties of Religious Experience* (1902). He teaches as a learner. He goes to great pains not to assume that he or his readers already know the essence of religious experience. He even allows himself to consider that things generally assumed to be completely unacceptable might have positive contributions to make—for example, that intoxicants and "hallucinogens" might open channels for experiences that are akin to religious ones. Likewise for the "data" turned up by "psychical research." Though James could come to no settled religious beliefs himself, he was convinced that our standard methodologies for doing research and finding out the truth about some things—logic, common sense, and scientific measuring—are not adequate for exploring certain other features of reality. There is always "something more" suggested, something more to be learned, when we touch the limits of our received methodologies. Some conventional researchers may not be seriously impeded by presuming a dualistic view of life—that there is an unalterable, hierarchical split between mind/body and thought/emotion, for example. But such dualistic thinking seriously impedes other researchers, particularly those who delve into how humans experience what is valuable and holy, topics that require empathy and a nonhierarchical synthesis of experiencing, feeling, and knowing. There may be—he suggests in one place—"a mother sea of consciousness" that our conventional mentality and calculation cannot imagine.

James did, however, write a few important pieces that deal explicitly with educational issues. The most important were published in 1899 as *Talks to Teachers on Psychology and to Students on Some of Life's Ideals.* (Certain occasional pieces, all interesting, some of which are reprinted in *Memories and Studies,* 1911, cannot be treated here.) The teacher's part comprises fifteen terse chapters: explicit applications to pedagogy of his great work in psychology, talks delivered in 1892 immediately following the *Principles* (and *Psychology: Briefer Course*). Some examples: "Psychology and the Teaching Art," "The Stream of Consciousness," "The Child as a Behaving Organism," "Native Reactions and Acquired Reactions," "The Laws of Habit," "Attention," "Memory," "The Will." With amazing concision, James applies principles of psychology to teaching and learning. For example, he writes that "the secret of will is the control of mental effort" and attention. This is James's version of what philosophers of education have long maintained: that the teacher's first job is interesting students, fixing their attention, motivating them to learn. Motivation, of course, can take many forms. Students' interest may be "stung" simply by being drawn into the vortex of the teacher's own passion for learning; only, this passion must be shown in a way that "developing organisms" can appreciate and accept. Or, they are already interested in certain things, of course, and the teacher's job is just to listen respectfully to what these interests are; then the teacher may draw students out so that they extend these interests to a broader matrix than anyone could have before imagined. James also offers wise and consoling words about the power of practice and habit. When we practice the inherent principles of a subject matter or skill, we must improve. There is a place for instruction within education. Above all, teaching requires empathy. His main desire is that teachers conceive—or, best, sympathetically imagine—the mental life of students as the sort of active unity that they themselves feel it to be.

Fittingly, James closes his book with three "Talks to Students": "The Gospel of Relaxation," "On a Certain Blindness in Human Beings," and "What Makes a Life Significant." The blindness of which he speaks is lack of empathy. He writes that he wishes he could make this second talk "more impressive." But the attentive reader will be impressed. Writing autobiographically (and including choice selections from R.L. Stevenson, Walt Whitman, and W.H. Hudson), James documents that the "fuel" that energizes and drives a life—making it significant—is a person's ideals. Such unmeasurable "entities" as ideals may look insignificant to the scientifically trained observer; they may seem completely fanciful, absurd, or childish. But they "sting" people's interest and involve them ecstatically. To miss ideals is to miss the heart in people—including students, of course. James speaks of the need for poetry and music—for countering "the haunting unreality of realistic books."

Educators are willing to grope for growth and for what makes a life significant. They understand the limits of scientific knowing and instruction, and share this understanding contagiously, putting us on the path, knowing that the process of learning, of education, is ongoing, and that the process is often more exciting and worthwhile than a collection of answers. "The facts and worths of life need many cognizers to take them in. There is no point of view absolutely public and universal. Private and incommunicable perceptions always remain over, and the worst of it is that those who look for them from the outside never know *where*." And again, in "What Makes a Life Significant?" James insists that the significance of a human life is a matter of the growing union of "reality with ideal novelty" as the person lives this growth moment by moment.

Bruce W. Wilshire

See also LEARNING, THEORIES OF; *PAIDEIA;* PERSON, CONCEPT OF; TEACHING AND LEARNING

Bibliography

Edie, James M. "The Philosophical Anthropology of William James." In *William James and Phenomenology*. Bloomington: Indiana University Press, 1987.

Fontinell, Eugene. *Self, God, and Immortality: A Jamesian Investigation.* Philadelphia: Temple University Press, 1986.

James, William. *The Principles of Psychology.* New York: Henry Holt, 1890.

———. *Talks to Teachers on Psychology and to Students on Some of Life's Ideals.* New York: Henry Holt, 1899.

Perry, Ralph Barton. *In the Spirit of William James*. Bloomington: Indiana University Press, 1958.

Wilshire, Bruce W. "Edie's Hard Nosed James and the Retrieval of the Sacred." In *Phenomenology and Skepticism,* edited by Brice Wachterhauser. Publisher not yet determined.

———. "The Intimate Otherness of the Material World: James's Last Thoughts." In *The Cambridge Companion to William James.* New York: Cambridge University Press, in press.

———, ed. *William James: The Essential Writings.* Albany, N.Y.: SUNY Press, 1984.

Jefferson, Thomas (1743–1826)

American statesman and third president, whose Declaration of Independence (1776) boldly asserted as "self-evident" truths the doctrine that "all men are created equal" and are endowed by their Creator with "inalienable rights"

to life, liberty, and the pursuit of happiness. Abraham Lincoln (1809–1865) stated that "the principles of Jefferson are the definitions and axioms of a free society"; Franklin D. Roosevelt (1882–1945) termed him America's "apostle of freedom"; and John Dewey (1859–1952) lauded Jefferson as "the first modern to state in human terms the principles of democracy."

Although Jefferson's Declaration of Independence has become a universal proclamation of the rights of all humanity as well as the pivotal document in the American struggle for independence, he did not lay claim to originality of argument, principle, or sentiment. Rather, Jefferson stated that his intent had been to set forth, in the tone and spirit demanded by the occasion, a clear and forceful "expression of the American mind" in order to "place before mankind the common sense of the subject, in terms so plain and firm as to command their assent."

Jefferson cannot be considered a "philosopher" in the sense of erecting a complete or comprehensive system of thought. He was eclectic and pragmatic in his views, influenced by ideas and values drawn from classical antiquity as well as by the modern thought of the eighteenth-century Enlightenment. He thought metaphysics a waste of time and considered Plato (c. 427–347 B.C.) the "fountainhead of meaningless mysticism." However he expressed admiration for the Stoic attitude of facing with dignity the inevitable tribulations of life and, while rejecting excess, also embraced the Epicurean ideal of purposefully seeking happiness through the disciplined tranquillity of mind and body.

In terms of modern thought, Jefferson considered Francis Bacon (1561–1626), Isaac Newton (1642–1727), and John Locke (1632–1704) "the three greatest men the world has ever produced." These men appealed to Jefferson's thirst for empirical, useful knowledge. Bacon's insistence on the value of inductive logic and the superiority of fact over speculation placed him at the fountainhead of the scientific revolution. Bacon's system of classifying all knowledge according to the faculties of the mind served as the basis for Jefferson's own scheme of cataloging his personal library, which eventually formed the nucleus of the Library of Congress. Newton seemingly had brought the scientific revolution to its fulfillment with his explanations of the natural laws governing the orderly workings of the universe. Locke, through his *Essay Concerning Human Understanding* (1690) and *Two Treatises on Government* (1689, 1690), had laid bare the laws that he thought determined the functions of the mind and the natural relationships that should exist between the governors and the governed in a properly ordered state.

To these influential thinkers could be added others who contributed to the shaping of Jefferson's thought. He was profoundly influenced by ideas advanced by leaders of the Scottish Enlightenment. Jefferson came to hold in high regard the political and moral essays of David Hume (1711–1776), but not his Tory interpretation of history. He admired the writings on moral philosophy of Hume's older cousin, Lord Kames (1696–1782), as well as the moral and economic treatises of Adam Smith (1723–1790). Influential too were Thomas Reid (1710–1796), founder of the Scottish "common sense" school of philosophy, and Francis Hutcheson (1694–1746), who espoused a "moral sense" explanation of such concepts as self-evident truths, equality, and inalienable rights.

The degree to which Scottish philosophers, especially Hutcheson, may have influenced Jefferson has become a matter of dispute among some historians since the publication of Garry Wills's *Inventing America: Jefferson's Declaration of Independence.* Contrary to most traditional Jeffersonian scholarship, Wills has argued that Jefferson's sentiments in the Declaration of Independence stem more directly from Hutcheson's moral-sense philosophy than from Lockean rationalism. Morton White, in *The Philosophy of the American Revolution,* has stressed the importance of bringing an understanding of the philosophy of the Swiss jurist Jean Jacques Burlamaqui (1694–1748) to a proper interpretation of Jefferson's language and intent in the Declaration of Independence.

Whatever the precise sources of Jefferson's thought, the basic contours of his Enlightenment philosophy are clear. Jefferson posited the existence of a benevolent Creator whose laws are to be found in the observable order and design of nature. As a deist, Jefferson rejected notions of divine intervention and miracles. He held that God had created humans as rational beings capable of discerning natural law in the human and social as well as the physical realm. Moreover, Jefferson assumed the existence in every person of a moral faculty that provides an innate sense of right and wrong. This moral sense and the ability to reason, both of which he believed could be strengthened and developed, distinguish humans from other living creatures and make possible the creation and maintenance of a social contract among equals.

In Jefferson's original wording in the Declaration of Independence, he spoke of "sacred and undeniable" truths and of rights that are "inherent and inalienable." Jefferson's belief in natural rights not only formed the core of his justification of the right of citizens to oppose unjust government, but also presupposed correlative obligations on the part of all members of society. In Jefferson's formulation, it is incumbent on each member of society to respect and protect the equal rights of others. The legitimate role of government, then, is to preserve what John Dickinson (1732–1808) had earlier called "the rights essential to happiness."

Jefferson understood that the liberty to pursue happiness could not be obtained solely through declarations and revolutions, or peace treaties and political treatises. Freedom requires legal and institutional safeguards, an informed electorate, and leaders dedicated to the public good. To that end, Jefferson advocated a variety of measures designed to protect the rights and freedoms due citizens of a self-governing, republican society. Declaring "eternal hostility against every form of tyranny over the mind of man," for example, Jefferson fought against governmental intrusion into matters of religious belief and conscience by drafting the Virginia Statute for Religious Freedom. This bill, which became law in 1786, disestablished the Anglican Church in Virginia and guaranteed the right of religious liberty.

In Jefferson's republican view, political and religious freedom could not exist without the support of intellectual freedom. Jefferson asserted, "If a nation expects to be ignorant and freed, in a state of civilization, it expects what never was and never will be." He contended that self-government necessitates an enlightened citizenry and that the state has an obligation to provide for the basic education of all citizens. His Bill for the More General Diffusion of Knowledge, submitted to the Virginia legislature in 1779, called for the establishment of schools and free education at the elementary level for all male and female children of the citizenry. The bill provided further for scholarships to enable the most able and deserving boys to advance into publicly maintained secondary schools. A few of the best and brightest secondary school graduates would then be entitled to public support in order to attend the College of William and Mary, which Jefferson hoped to modernize and liberalize.

The Virginia legislature failed to adopt Jefferson's 1779 proposal and a similar bill presented in 1817. Had his meritocratic scheme been adopted, Jefferson asserted, all citizens would have had access to the basic education required for responsible self-government, and at least a limited number of those who belonged to the "natural aristocracy" of talent and virtue would have been enabled, through advanced education, to compete with the members of the wealthy "artificial aristocracy" for the positions of trust and leadership in the republic. Although Jefferson fought intermittently for a comprehensive system of education for over forty years, he lived to see only the capstone of his system put in place. The University of Virginia, considered by Jefferson along with the Declaration of Independence and the Virginia Statute of Religious Freedom as among the three most important accomplishments of his life, was chartered in 1819 and opened in 1825.

Jefferson's philosophical positions must be gleaned in large part from his public papers and voluminous personal correspondence. His only book, *Notes on the State of Virginia* (1787), covers a vast array of information and opinion on many subjects, beginning with descriptions of the geography, flora, and fauna of Virginia, and ranging into discussions of the laws, manners, and customs of the original inhabitants as well as of the more recently arrived settlers, both free and slave. Over time he modified certain of his views as changing events and experiences seemed to warrant. However, nearly half a century after giving classic form to the sanctity of human rights in the Declaration of Independence, Jefferson pointed to what he held to be the single constant in human affairs: "Nothing is unchangeable but the inherent and unalienable rights of man."

Jennings L. Wagoner, Jr.

See also: BACON; COMMON SENSE; DEMOCRACY; EMPIRICISM; EPICUREANISM; EQUALITY; ETHICS AND MORALITY; HAPPINESS; HUMAN NATURE; LOCKE; PROGRESS, IDEA OF, AND PROGRESSIVE EDUCATION; PUBLIC EDUCATION; REASON AND RATIONALITY; RIGHTS; STOICISM

Bibliography
Honeywell, Roy J. *The Educational Work of Thomas Jefferson*. Cambridge: Harvard University Press, 1931.
Jefferson, Thomas. *Notes on the State of Virginia* [1787]. Edited by William Peden. Chapel Hill: University of North Carolina, 1954.
———. *The Papers of Thomas Jefferson*. Edited by Julian P. Boyd et al. Princeton: Princeton University Press, 1950–.
———. *The Writings of Thomas Jefferson*. Edited by Andrew A. Lipscomb and Albert E. Bergh. Washington, D.C.: Thomas Jefferson Memorial Society, 1905.
———. *The Works of Thomas Jefferson*. Edited by Paul L. Ford. New York: Putnam, 1950.
Malone, Dumas. *Jefferson and His Time*. Boston: Little, Brown, 1948–1981.
Peterson, Merrill D., ed. *Thomas Jefferson: A Reference Biography*. New York: Charles Scribner's Sons, 1986.
White, Morton. *The Philosophy of the American Revolution*. New York: Oxford University Press, 1978.
Wills, Garry. *Inventing America: Jefferson's Declaration of Independence*. New York: Vintage Books, 1979.

J

Jesus of Nazareth (c. 4 B.C.–c. A.D. 29)
Since the Enlightenment, a large number of scholars have attempted to reconstruct the life and teachings of Jesus through the employment of modern historical-critical tools on the New Testament. Their results have varied widely, from the view that there never was any person called Jesus of Nazareth to the Christian confession that he was and is the Son of God. That disagreement has not been settled by looking at textual variants, sources, forms (the smallest units) and redaction (the large edited units), or by employing the newest postmodern deconstructive theories. Yet most scholars now concede that Jesus did live in Palestine during the first century A.D., that he prophesied, perhaps did wonders, and both preached and taught.

Some textual, source, form, and redaction critics have developed ways that satisfy their criteria for getting back to the historical Jesus. Traditional Christians have found no major discrepancies between the common tradition and the historic reality. Deconstructionists share with them the sense that trying to get behind the narratives constructed on the basis of the confession that Jesus was raised from the dead is impossible, but there are differences. Traditionalists see all the information about Jesus as collected and shaped within the early Christian communities, who tell the truth as best they can. Deconstructionists insist that modern communities create their own readings of the texts. Thus in search of any philosophy of education associated with Jesus, there is reason to look again at Christian scriptures to see what kind of teacher those texts say he was or what readings contemporary Christian communities give those texts.

It is not uncommon for some scholars to look at materials other than the four Gospels (Matthew, Mark, Luke, and John) of the Christian New Testament for information about Jesus. But in any description of Jesus' philosophy of education, the data from other religious communities are rarely helpful. The earliest Jewish tradition about Jesus is most concerned with refuting claims that he is the Messiah. Only the apparent text of the Jewish historian Josephus, which was actually interpolated by third-century Christians, accepts the claim. The tradition about Jesus in the Muslim Qur'an presents him as a messenger and a prophet, but it has no interest in how he taught and little in what he taught. It accepts his virgin birth but warns that he is not God incarnate. The Gnostic Christian materials, particularly those discovered at Nag Hammadi in Egypt in the 1940s, primarily view Jesus as a divine revealer and savior who brings knowledge necessary for salvation. But within that corpus the interest is more in cosmic secrets. Only the *Gospel of Thomas,* with its 114 sayings of Jesus—many found also in the four Gospels—is basically concerned with what Jesus taught. Other Gnostic materials, found prior to the Hag Hammadi discovery, are little different.

The Christian New Testament does not contain any treatise that is dedicated to Jesus' philosophy of education, but the four Gospels do offer some sense of what it was perceived to be. The Christian communities, whose members created the Gospels and over a period of centuries and in many geographical areas selected them from other such narratives, particularly Gnostic Christian ones, saw Jesus as a divine teacher who brought truth from God. That led them to an interest both in what he taught and how he taught. From that information some conclusions can be drawn about a philosophy of education that they declared he practiced.

Because Jesus is called "rabbi" (primarily in Jn.) or "teacher" (in Mt., Mk., and Lk.) nearly fifty times, it is likely that he was often viewed as a teacher. In some ways he appeared to be a rabbi to many whom he met, the great majority of whom stood within his Jewish religious tra-

dition. His own disciples used that title (Mk. 4:38, 9:38, 10:35; Mt. 26:18). People from various circles who sought his help called out to him as a teacher (Mk. 9:17; Mt. 19:16). Some were astonished by his lessons and his authority which they saw as unlike that of their previous teachers (Mk. 1:22, 11:18, Lk. 4:31–32). His major opponents—Pharisees, Sadducees, lawyers, and leaders of synagogues—addressed him as a rabbi or teacher, possibly as a way to gain access in order to refute the genuineness of such a claim (Mt. 12:38; 22:16, 24, 36).

Jesus taught both in the Jewish temple in Jerusalem (Mk. 12:35; Lk. 19:47–20:1) and in various synagogues (Mk. 1:21, 6:2; Lk. 6:6, 12:10). He viewed temple worship as something sacred, not to be defiled by a greedy concern for money (Mk. 11:15–20). At least on occasion he expounded upon Hebrew scripture within the synagogues and elsewhere by following the patterns and customs of the times. He stood to read and sat to clarify the text or the lesson (Lk. 4:16–20). There is reason to think that he used memorization as a technique of learning, as did other teachers of Jewish law. At the same time he reshaped the expectations surrounding a rabbi. He did not wait for disciples to come to him to study; he called them out (Mk. 1:16–20). He had a movable classroom. He acted out his precepts by healing in the marketplace (Mk. 6:56), the temple (Mt. 21:14), and the synagogue (Lk. 6:6–11). In the fields he used the simple matter of plucking the heads of grain and eating them to provoke questions and make his point (Mk. 2:23–28). He taught by the seaside even when crowds forced him into a boat (Mk. 4:1–2). For him, teaching could be done anywhere that the attention of the students could be focused on something significant.

According to the Gospels of the New Testament, even a revealer of divine truth like Jesus must pay close attention to the milieu in which his students live. Unlike the Gnostic Gospels, with their remarkably esoteric terminology, the New Testament gospels depict Jesus as often using statements that have a hook—that could catch the interest of a passerby. "It is easier for a camel to go through the eye of a needle than for a rich man to get into heaven" (Mk. 10:25). Despite the studied earnestness of many who read and interpret his sayings, he probably had a keen sense of humor, a helpful attitude for any teacher. Yet there is also a mysterious quality within a number of his pronouncements; indeed one of the phrases more frequently attributed to him is a variation of "Let those who have ears hear" (Mk. 4:9, 23, 7:14, 8:18; Mt. 11:15, 13:9, 43; Lk. 8:8, 14:35, Gospel of Thomas, logia 8, 21, 24, 63, 65, 96). The poetic quality of the sayings made them memorable, although it is true that Middle Eastern culture depended more heavily on memorization of a teacher's words than do most modern North American and European settings. We do not know exactly how much the tradition of Jesus' sayings was shaped by the communities who believed in him, but we must assume that he said things well enough that many wanted to remember them.

Jesus' pithy statements and parables also indicate that he used illustrations and vocabulary familiar to his audiences. Indeed much can be learned about lower- and middle-class life, particularly within rural village settings in first-century Palestine, by paying attention to the words and phrases he employed. His parables deal with sheep (Mt. 18:12–14), fig trees (Lk. 21:29–33), a sower and weeds (Mt. 13:3–8, 24–30), sons who are to work the fields for their father (Mt. 21:28–32), a landowner seeking laborers for his fields (Mt. 20:1–16), leaven (Mt. 13:33), a woman who lost her hoarded coins (Lk. 15:8–10), marriage feasts (Mt. 25:1–13; Lk. 14:7–11), debtors and borrowed money (Lk. 7:41–43; Mt. 25:14–30), children in the marketplace talking of music (Mt. 11:16–17), and so on.

He also seems to have offered allegorical or complementary interpretations of some of the parables to make their points clear (Mt. 13:18–23, 15:15–20). He apparently knew that even using such common language did not ensure that his views would be understood, but without such language no communication would take place.

To employ some common parlance in the philosophy of education, the Gospels portray Jesus as student-centered. There is no doubt that, depicted as a divine revealer, he was deeply concerned about the content of his teaching. But he showed equal concern for those whom he tried to teach. Crowds were offered parables and sayings that piqued their interest (Mk. 42: 33–34). One-on-one encounters indicate his own powerful relationships with his students. Zacchaeus, a tax collector, was singled out. Jesus went to his house, ate with him, and taught there. Zacchaeus listened and decided to give back much of what he had collected fraudulently (Lk. 19:2–10). The Samaritan woman, from the text's perspective a half-breed

with deep moral faults, was given direct attention. Jesus discussed her life and Samaritan-Jewish relationships with her as well as making his own claims (Jn. 4:7–42). At times his efforts in such instances are so intense and heroic that they often have been interpreted by traditional Christians to be part of his divine foreknowledge. The close attention he paid to these people is enough of a rarity in human exchanges that it too often suggests primarily divine prescience.

This multifaceted picture of Jesus also demands that the teacher be viewed as a moral model, one who teaches oneself as much as any subject. Jesus did not isolate the teaching function as the delivery of objectively ascertained facts to students through a process unaffected by the teacher's person. He was a passionate instructor who warned about the dangers of the superior position. Teachers must apply the principles they teach (Mt. 5:19, 23:3).

What we today might refer to as moral values were an assumed part of the teacher's web of influence in the tradition about Jesus. There are aspects of this view of Jesus that exceed certain values expressed more commonly in his culture. He advised his disciples not to go outside the confines of Israel in preaching and teaching about the kingdom of God (Mt. 10:1–7). But the Gospels include incidents that show his concern for those who were considered to be the pariahs of his culture. He did not turn away either hated soldiers or tax collectors (Lk. 3:12–14). Jesus did not avoid feared lepers (Lk. 17:11–19) or the blind and lame (Mk. 8:22–26, 10:46–52; Mt. 9:27–31). A woman ritually unclean from continuing menstrual problems was not shunned but healed (Mt. 9:20–22). Although his innermost circle were Jewish men, they were not from the upper strata socially (four were fishermen: Simon, Andrew, James, and John—Mk. 1:16–20). Indeed women of means supplied economic assistance to his ministry (Lk. 8:1–3). He also met rich rulers of the synagogue, the Pharisees or the Sadducees (Mk. 5:22–43; Mt. 19:16–26, 22:15–46). A Syro-Phoenician woman, one well outside the limits of Israel, claimed Jesus' focus. He uttered a hard saying, "We do not give our food to dogs," but she persisted for the sake of her ill daughter. He commented that her faith was deep and sufficient (Mk. 7:24–30; Mt. 15:21–28). Jesus made his way through the land contacting people of both sexes, of varied social and economic status, and of different cultural and religious backgrounds. The earliest Christian communities did not find in him either a sexist or a racist, but a teacher of liberation from such views, lessons not always learned by traditional Christians.

The content of his teaching greatly informed how he taught. He warned his followers not to lord it over one another as Gentiles did, for the Son of Man came to serve and give his life (Mk. 10:42–45). He emphasized the faith of those he healed and sometimes urged them not to talk about what he had done for them (Mk. 8:22–26, 10:46–52). At his entrance into Jerusalem, although the crowds laid palms in his path and honored him greatly, he slipped away rather than accept their accolades (Mk. 11:1–10). His humility in teaching is most impressive to the traditionalists who believe him to be God incarnate.

This portrait of Jesus does not present a full philosophy of education by any means, but it does represent an important structure within which such a view could be built.

Frederick W. Norris

See also: AUGUSTINE; ETHICS AND MORALITY; SOCRATES

Bibliography

McAuliffe, Jame Dammen. *Qur'anic Christians: An Analysis of Classical and Modern Exegesis.* Cambridge: Cambridge University Press, 1991.

Maier, J. *Jesus von Nazareth in der talmudischen Uberlieferung.* Darmstadt: Wissenschaftliche Buchgesellschaft, 1978.

Perkins, Pheme. *Jesus as Teacher.* Cambridge: Cambridge University Press, 1990.

Perrin, Norman. *Rediscovering the Teachings of Jesus.* New York: Harper and Row, 1967.

Riesner, Rainer. *Jesus als Lehrer: Eine Untersuchung zum Ursprung der Evangelien-Uberlieferung.* "Wissenschaftliche Untersuchungen zum Neuen Testament, 2. Reihe 7." Tubingen: J.C.B. Mohr [Paul Siebeck], 1984.

Robbins, Vernon K. *Jesus the Teacher: A Socio-Rhetorical Interpretation of Mark.* Philadelphia: Fortress, 1984.

Robinson, James M., ed. *The Nag Hammadi Library in English.* 3rd ed. San Francisco: Harper and Row, 1988.

Stein, Robert H. *The Method and Message of Jesus' Teachings.* Philadelphia: Westminster Press, 1978.

Trueblood, D. Elton. *The Humor of Christ.* New York: Harper and Row, 1964.

John of Salisbury (c. 1115–1180)

Born at Old Sarum in England. John went to Paris in 1136 to study at Mont-Saint-Germain. During the ensuing twelve years he studied with many of the great minds of the twelfth century—Peter Abelard, Adam de Petit Pont, Gilbert of Poitiers, Thierry of Chartres, William of Conches, and others. He became secretary to Archbishop Theobald of Canterbury, and later to Thomas Becket, who succeeded Theobald as archbishop. During the last four years of his life, John served as Bishop of Chartres.

John's best-known writings are the *Policraticus*—the first extensive work in political theory of the Latin Middle Ages—and the *Metalogicon*—now regarded as a classic in educational theory. He also wrote a satirical poem about philosophers and courtiers, *Entheticus Major,* and historical works, the *Historia Pontificalis* and lives of St. Anselm and Becket. Here we shall focus on the *Metalogicon.*

The word *Metalogicon* is a synthesis of two Greek words: *meta,* which means "about" or "on behalf of," and *logikon,* which means "logic," or "the arts relative to words and reasoning." In the prologue, John says that his aim is to defend logic. He adds that, in doing so, he will discuss morals, because writings on philosophy that do not have an influence on conduct are "futile and false." At the same time, John admits to a certain modesty regarding the truth or falsity of his claims; he learned his modesty from Cicero and the teachers of the Later Academy, who are remembered for their skepticism.

In spelling out the sense in which the *Metalogicon* is a defense of logic, John claims that all seven of the liberal arts enable us to philosophize. The trivium (grammar, logic, rhetoric) discloses "the significance of all words," while the quadrivium has "unveiled the secrets of all nature." John's account of his own education gives only a brief mention of the study of the quadrivium; for the most part, the teachers with whom he studied were masters of logic, grammar, eloquence, and theology. The main concern of the *Metalogicon* is with the arts of the trivium.

To unpack John's assertion that his aim is to defend logic, we will follow his characterization of its nature. Logic, he says, may be thought of in two senses: In its broadest sense, logic is the science of verbal expression and reasoning; in a more restricted sense, logic is the study of the rules of reasoning. Yet because in

Greek *logos*—from which "logic" stems—means both "word" and "reason," logic involves "all instruction relative to words." Such instruction deals with oral words, and thus includes the study of eloquence; it also deals with written words, and thereby includes grammar.

When John turns to discuss instruction, grammar comes first. It may be thought of as the cradle out of which all of literature and learning grow. While grammar is a human invention rather than a thing of nature, grammar "imitates" nature. John says that the things that nature fashioned—by working with the four elements, or by combining matter and form in certain ways—are named and have their properties described by the rationality of human beings. Nature has made rational human beings as well as the things in whose midst they dwell: By their powers of observation and reason, human beings are able to imitate nature by distinguishing, naming, classifying, and quantifying its handiwork.

In arguing that logic should be studied by every student of philosophy, John shows a familiarity with Aristotle's *Organon*. Demonstration, probable logic, and sophistry are included in his discussion of logic. Demonstration, he says, "rejoices in necessity." Probable logic considers propositions that are "best known" and "most probable," while sophistry has the objective of deluding its adversaries—it "wears a disguise of probability or necessity." Demonstration is employed when, possessing the principles of a science, we deduce conclusions from them. Thus demonstration "teaches the truth" and is independent of people's opinions of its propositions; demonstration's concern is "that a thing must be so." Probable logic includes both rhetoric and dialectic, for both employ arguments that have only a likelihood of being true. The dialectician, in arguing (or "disputing"), attempts to persuade an adversary; the orator attempts to persuade an audience. Each must be content with proving or disproving something on probable grounds.

John argues that a preoccupation with the study of logic for its own sake, if other studies are neglected, has little practical utility. In a passage in the *Metalogicon* that is often quoted by historians, John tells a story of returning to the Mont to revisit students of dialectic whom he had known twelve years before. He found them still occupied with the same questions but no wiser: "Just as dialectic expedites other studies," John writes, "if left alone by itself, it lies powerless and idle." The *Metalogicon* itself is testimony to John's insistence that, if logic is to contribute to the "fruits of philosophy," it "must conceive from an external source." The Greek and Latin classical authors drawn on virtually exhaust that literature known in the Latin Middle Ages in John's time. He cites Aristotle's *Organon*, Plato's *Timaeus*, and other Greek and Latin philosophical writings; in the liberal arts, Cicero, Quintilian, Martianus Capella, and Hippocrates, among others. The Church Fathers and numerous medieval authors on Christian doctrine are used extensively; and quotations from the Old and New Testaments are frequent.

John made an art of drawing upon classical Greek and Latin authors and using them along with Christian literature in his own applications of dialectic. As one example, in arguing that "faith" lies between "opinion" and "science," John cites Aristotle's *Posterior Analytics* and *Topics* and Cicero's *De Oratore*, and quotes from *Hebrews* and Hugh of St. Victor. The *Metalogicon* is unsurpassed for its time in its celebration of the idea that, in the pursuit and teaching of truth, Greek and Latin arts and literature must be studied along with Christian writings.

J.J. Chambliss

See also: ABELARD; DIALECTIC; LOGIC; PETER LOMBARD

Bibliography
Chambliss, J.J. "John of Salisbury's Defense of the Arts." In *Educational Theory as Theory of Conduct*, 63–69. Albany: State University of New York Press, 1987.
John of Salisbury. *Metalogicon*. Translated by K.S.B. Keats-Rohan. Oxford: Oxford University Press, 1990.
———. *The Metalogicon of John of Salisbury*. Translated by Daniel D. McGarry. Berkeley: University of California Press, 1955.
———. *Policraticus: Of the Frivolities of Courtiers and the Footprints of Philosophers*. Translated by Cary J. Nederman. Cambridge: Cambridge University Press, 1990.
Webb, Clement C.J. *John of Salisbury*. London: Methuen, 1932.
Wilks, Michael, ed. *The World of John of Salisbury*. Oxford: Blackwell, 1984.

Judaism

Judaism consists of the teachings and faith commitments valued and transmitted by communities around the world that see themselves as descendants of the inhabitants of Judea—the hills and deserts surrounding the city of Jerusalem—during the centuries before the common era.

Jewish Communities

Judea took its name from Judah, meaning thanks to God, the fourth son of Jacob by his wife, Leah, and the great grandson of Abraham and Sarah, traditionally considered the first adherents of this people's faith. The tribe of Judah was one of the twelve tribes believed to be descendant from Jacob. As part of the southern kingdom established after the rule of Solomon, residents of Judah escaped the conquest of the Assyrians in the eighth century B.C. only to be exiled to Babylonia by Nebuchadnezer in 586. Those who returned to Jerusalem in 444 established a new state under the protection of the Persian ruler Cyrus, which was to become known as Judea. Its inhabitants were known as Judeans. Their descendants became known as Jews.

Since Jacob was also known by the name Israel, or one who struggles with God, his descendants were often referred to in the Hebrew Bible as the children of Israel or Israelites. Israel thus became the name of the kingdom established by the northern Israelite tribes that were conquered by the Assyrians. Consequently, the Jewish people are sometimes referred to as the people of Israel and its ancestral home the land of Israel. The Jewish state established in that land in 1948 is also known as the State of Israel.

A biblical tradition also refers to Jacob as an Aramean (Genesis 29, Deuteronomy 26:5–11). This suggests to some scholars that Israelite ancestors are to be found among a group of wanderers associated with the great Aramean migration of the late Bronze Age (1500–1200 B.C.) known as "Habiru" (or "Apiru"). This term appears etymologically related to the term "Hebrew," which is used to refer to Israelite ancestors (Genesis 14:13, Exodus 1:15, 19, and so forth). Jews are thus sometimes referred to as Hebrews. Hebrew is also the language of the Bible and the most central language used by Jews to communicate with one another throughout the ages.

Sephardic Jewry

Although the northern tribes were assimilated by the Assyrians, the southern tribes maintained a separate identity both in exile and upon return to Jerusalem in 444 B.C. Exiles remained in Persian Babylonia, becoming the basis for a leading Jewish community during the first centuries of the common era and later flourishing under Islamic influence from around the ninth to the fifteenth centuries of the common era. Jewish communities under Hellenistic influence also grew in North Africa, eventually to be ruled by the Muslims.

The greatest of these communities prospered in southern Spain, to which Jews had migrated together with Muslims during the fourteenth and fifteenth centuries of the common era. Thus Jews under Islamic influence and their descendants took the name of their leading historic community, the Hebrew for Spanish, *Sepharadi*. After the Spanish Inquisition and expulsion of Jews from Spain in 1492, some Sephardic Jews made their way to southern and northern Europe, as well as to the New World. Many from North Africa and the Middle East immigrated to Israel after the establishment of the Jewish state in 1948. During this period others migrated to France, which is home today to the fourth largest concentration of Jews, after those of North America, Israel, and Russia.

Jewish communities tracing their roots to preexilic settlements in the land of Israel have also existed in Yemen, India, Ethiopia, and even China.

Ashkenazic Jewry

Hellenized Jews under Roman rule established communities in Southern Europe to which Jews gradually migrated after the destruction of the Temple in Jerusalem by the Romans in 70. From there communities were established throughout the Roman Empire, especially in Provence and along the Rhine, that later took the Hebrew name for that region, Ashkenaz. Ashkenazic Jews eventually migrated east and lived for more than a thousand years among the Slavs, Poles, Balkans, Ukrainians, Russians, and other Eastern Europeans.

During the late nineteenth and early twentieth centuries, immigrants left these regions because of poverty and persecution, bound for North and South America, South Africa, Australia, and the land of Israel.

Jewish Teachings

These diverse and disparate communities share not only a common ancestry but common teachings as well. These are recorded in texts referred to by the Hebrew word for teaching, *Torah*. Traditionally, it is believed that the Torah was revealed to Moses by God at Mt. Sinai in two forms, written and oral. The Written Torah includes the whole of the Hebrew Bible, which consists of texts accepted as canonical by third-century rabbis; they were composed between 2,000 and 200 B.C. The Oral Torah consists of rabbinic teachings composed between 200 B.C. and the present, with special attention to law codes, case law, and rabbinic lore recorded in the *Mishna* around 200 and interpreted in the *Talmud* by around 600.

Written Torah

Although the Written Torah is usually understood to consist of the whole of the Hebrew Bible, including prophetic and later writings, most important is the Pentateuch, or the five Books of Moses. Indeed, so central are these five books that they are often referred to exclusively as the Torah even though the term can also be used to refer to the entire biblical, rabbinic, and exegetical corpus. These books have been read publicly by Jews on Mondays, Thursdays, Sabbaths, and festivals, since the return to Jerusalem in 444 B.C. To this day they are copied meticulously from one scroll to the next by specially trained scribes and are kept in designated cabinets on the most sacred spot of the synagogue.

The first four of these books tell the story of the growth of the people of Israel, beginning with the creation of the world and encompassing the migration of Abraham and Sarah to the land of Canaan, the enslavement of their descendants in Egypt, and their ultimate redemption and return to their ancestral home. The books also contain divine commandments—*mitzvot*—according to which this people would govern itself in its own land. The fifth book consists of the final exhortations of their leader, Moses, in which both the lore of the people's journey and the law they were enjoined to live by is reviewed.

These five books, or some portion thereof, are depicted as having been revealed to Moses by God, who is portrayed as the creator of the universe and the author of morality. Human beings are viewed in these texts as being like God in that they have the freedom of will to control their own behavior and the intelligence to understand the difference between right and wrong. Life, especially human life, is a prime value according to these teachings. The right path, therefore, is identified with that which will affirm life, while evil is seen as the road to death.

The people of Israel are enjoined by these texts with the special task of communicating this vision of goodness to humanity. A variety of restrictions are imposed on juridical, business, dietary, and sexual practices that implement and provide daily reminders of these teachings.

The Torah also establishes occasions for studying, practicing, and celebrating its central tenets. This is accomplished first through daily worship. Second, the Sabbath is celebrated weekly, on which day the Torah is studied and creative work is forbidden in recognition of divine rest after the creation of the world.

Third, Israelites went up to the central Temple in Jerusalem during three annual pilgrimage festivals, to make animal sacrifices in commemoration of the harvest cycle and of important events in their history. *Pesah* (Passover) is a spring planting holiday on which the exodus from Egypt is reenacted. *Shavuot* (Pentecost) is the spring harvest festival, which recalls the giving of Torah by God. *Sukkot* (Tabernacles) is the fall harvest festival, which retells the story of desert wandering and arrival home to the land of Israel.

Fourth, it is assumed that people will not always adhere to the path set forth in the Torah. Therefore, ten days of penitence are set aside annually beginning with *Rosh Hashana* (New Years) and ending on *Yom Kippur* (Day of Atonement). During this period the ram's horn is sounded as a call to return to this path, and a day of fasting is observed on which forgiveness is asked from friends, family, and God for sins committed during the previous year. Finally, a sabbatical was observed every seventh year, during which the land was to lie fallow to replenish its resources, and a Jubilee was celebrated every forty-ninth year, during which land was returned to its original owners and slaves were freed to return to their families.

Central to all of these practices and celebrations is the Jubilee pronouncement, "Proclaim liberty throughout the land to all its inhabitants" (Leviticus 25:10). To be human is to be created in the image of the Creator, with intelligence to understand the ways of Torah and the freedom to follow them. We are, therefore, responsible beings with the capacity to do good as well as evil. "I have given you today a choice," wrote the deuteronomist (Deuteronomy 30:15-20), "between good and

evil, between life and death. . . . Choose life!"
The purpose of Torah is to teach this conception of liberty and to provide practical strategies for celebrating it.

Oral Torah

The second Jewish commonwealth existed in the land of Israel from the time of the return in 444 B.C. until the destruction of the Temple in Jerusalem by the Romans in 70. Toward the end of this period, two groups dominated the political landscape of the Jewish people. The Sadducees consisted of the priestly class and their supporters, who saw the sacrificial cult of the central Temple as the cornerstone of Jewish worship, much as their ancestors had during the first commonwealth before the Babylonian exile. The Pharisees grew from a class of scribes who emphasized the teaching of Pentateuch in local assembly halls or synagogues according to practices that took shape in exile, where there was no temple. They adhered to a democratic orientation that placed authority to decide matters of law in those with knowledge of it. Like the prophets before them, they took seriously the exegetical imperative (Deuteronomy 17:9) for the "priests, levites, and judges" of each generation to teach Torah, interpret the law, and pass judgment.

Around the first century of the common era, these pharisaic teachings began to be organized orally into exegetical traditions known as *midrashim*—from the Hebrew *darash,* or "interpret"—and legal aphorisms known as *mishnayot*—from the Hebrew *shinun,* or "repeat." The scholars of these oral traditions became known as *rabbanim,* or rabbis—from the Hebrew *rav,* or "master teacher." During the third century of the common era the mishayot of the school of Rabbi Akiba, a revered leader of Jewish resistance to Hadrianic persecutions, were edited into a compendium by Rabbi Judah, a student of Akiba's school and a leader recognized by both Jews and Romans. This compendium, which became known as the *Mishna,* served as the basis in both the land of Israel and Babylonia for developing tractates of case law that became known as the *Gemara*—Aramaic for "that which is learned." The *Mishna* together with the *Gemara* became known as the *Talmud*—Hebrew for "that which is studied." Various collections of *midrashim,* the Babylonian and Palestinian editions of the *Talmud,* and commentaries on them all, became the textual record of the Oral Torah.

Rabbinic Judaism and Early Christianity

With the destruction of the Jerusalem Temple by the Romans in 70, the heirs to Israelite religion were faced with a spiritual crisis of crippling proportions. The Temple was not only the center of the sacrificial cult, it was also the symbol of God's special relationship with those who atoned for their sins through that form of worship. Without the Temple, people would have no way to expiate their guilt for abandoning God's teachings. This would be not only psychologically devastating, it would also ultimately lead to the impossibility of following the Torah.

Two competing traditions evolved to respond to this crisis. One drew on the prophetic teaching (such as Isaiah 9:1–7, 11:10; Ezekiel 37:15ff; Hosea 3:5; Amos 9:5) that God would reinstate the davidic dynasty at the end of days to obliterate injustice. During the period of the Second Jewish commonwealth, these ideas evolved into the belief that God would send a *Messiah*—from *Mashiah,* or "anointed one"—to announce direct divine rulership over the world. Some held that the message of this "anointed one" would supersede previous revelations.

Although there were numerous messianic sects during this period, the followers of Jesus of Nazareth led in the Sadducean emphasis on sacrifices by suggesting not only that their leader was this messianic figure, but also that his death on the Roman cross represented the ultimate sacrifice for human sinfulness. The early Christians held that, in His grace, God had sent His son as the final sacrifice. Divine forgiveness and ultimate salvation were now to be dependent upon acceptance of this sacrifice in one's heart as atonement for one's sins.

The rabbis took an approach to this dilemma that was rooted in their pharisaic heritage. They held that, at least until the messiah would announce the restoration of the Temple, divine service by means of animal sacrifices would be replaced by "service of the heart"—that is, by self-examination through the study of Torah, both written and oral. Thus, the rabbinic worship service is composed of formulaic responses to three central biblical quotations dealing with the themes of creation, revelation, and redemption. The most sacred services climax in public recitation of selections from the Pentateuch and the Prophets. Worship, in short, became a form of study. Moreover, study of *midrash* or *Talmud* came to be concluded with recitation of a prayer in praise of God. Study, in other words, also became a form of worship.

Rather than sacrifice, the antidote for sin was now to be found in Torah study and its consequences, the improvement of character through the practice of that which is learned. Christianity and Judaism, then, are competing heirs to the sacrificial cult of biblical religion. The former sought to replace the Israelite notion of salvation through animal sacrifice with a personal acceptance of the ultimate sacrifice of Jesus. The latter sought to recover from the demise of the Temple through the study, practice, and celebration of Torah. Both traditions see the world as in need of repair. But the rabbis taught that repair is to be accomplished not by means of vicarious atonement made possible by the crucifixion of Jesus, but rather by means of the improvement of human character made possible through education.

Jewish Faith

The Torah, both written and oral, speaks not only of the obligations—*mitzvot*— it also tells the story of a continuing relationship between observers of these *mitzvot* and their God. Obligations are spelled out in terms of law, or *halakha*. The nature of God is explored through lore, or *aggada*. It follows that, although observant Jews consider themselves duty-bound to follow certain practices, faith commitments are considered to be a matter of conscience, not law. In fact, neither biblical nor rabbinic lore deals with the subject of divinity systematically. Nevertheless, they share a set of assumptions about God without which the legal sources of those traditions would make little sense. More systematic treatments of Jewish theology would have to wait until the philosophers and mystics of the medieval period.

Rationalism

The twelfth-century philosopher Moses Maimonides adumbrated one version of these assumptions, which can be summarized as follows:

> There is a Creator who alone created and creates all things. He has no body, no form. He is eternal. He alone is to be worshiped. The words of the prophets are true. Moses was the greatest prophet. The source of the Torah divine. The Torah is immutable. God knows the deeds and thoughts of men. God rewards and punishes. The Messiah will come. God . . . will resurrect the dead. (*Siddur Sim Shalom*: 327).

Maimonides represents one strand of medieval Jewish theology, which attempted to reconcile the faith of the Hebrew Bible and the rabbis with Greek pagan philosophy—especially that of Aristotle, and, to a lesser degree, that of Plato. The twelfth-century thinker Yehuda Halevi challenged this rationalist approach by claiming that efforts to synthesize the teachings of Aristotle with those of the Torah result in a vision of God more in tune with philosophy than the teachings of the patriarchs Abraham, Isaac, and Jacob.

Mysticism

Rather than attempting to translate theological beliefs into philosophical discourse, Jewish mystics extended biblical and rabbinic lore by choosing poetry, metaphor, parable, and storytelling as more apt techniques for alluding to divinity. Perhaps the most influential such attempt to capture the relationship between God and the world is found in the teachings of the sixteenth-century mystic of Safed, Isaac Luria.

The Spanish Inquisition that expelled Jews and Muslims from Spain in 1492 left a deep longing to explain how a good God could allow such evil to be perpetrated. Luria was especially concerned with this question, and he advanced a version of the biblical creation myth that envisaged the world as created out of a cosmic catastrophe. The vessels God used to transform His holy essence into material being were, according to this account, unable to contain the divine glory. They burst, and the sparks of divine essence that remained were hidden within the souls of every human being. The Torah was given, according to this view, as an antidote for this divine error. Through its observance, the divine sparks can be drawn out of humanity and the world can be made whole once again.

Modernism

In the medieval world, Jews lived as separate corporate entities, usually recognized by local fiefdoms or principalities. They exercised no individual political rights but enjoyed considerable collective autonomy. During the nineteenth century, Jews in Central and Western Europe experienced the process of enlightenment that led to the birth of modernity. They also experienced political emancipation as part of the rise of European nationalism, and became eligible as individuals to become citizens of the nation states where they resided.

In consequence, autonomous, premodern Jewish communities that were the locus for both the political and religious identity of Jews were challenged. Politically, Jews sought citizenship in the nations in which they resided. This led to the erosion of the authority of the rabbinate that had constituted the leadership of the autonomous communities of the medieval period. Religiously, Judaism faced intellectual challenges from Cartesian and empiricist philosophy and from the rise of natural science. Responses took the form of religious denominationalism and the rise of Jewish nationalism.

The first to react to these developments were the architects of Reform Judaism, who argued that in the modern period Jews must be free to pray in their local vernaculars, be citizens of their local nations, and base their religious practices on individual choice.

Orthodox Judaism responded to reform by arguing that modernism posed a threat to Jewish continuity and should be opposed. In the extreme, the orthodox have maintained rigid adherence to Jewish law without any intentional compromise with modernity. Neo or Modern Orthodoxy followed the teaching first advanced by the eighteenth-century Jewish philosopher Moses Mendelson and popularized by the nineteenth-century rabbi S.R. Hirsch. According to this view, Jews should remain committed to traditional practice in the home but accept modernity in public, at least in outward appearance.

Historical or Conservative Judaism has taken Hirsch's approach a step further by accepting the influence of modernism on tradition both in and out of the home. This approach has sought to define a traditional core of Judaism through the study of Jewish history using the tools of modern scholarship. Reconstructionist Judaism grew out of American Conservatism during the mid twentieth century. Under the influence of Mordecai Kaplan, it holds that Judaism undergoes a Deweyan sort of development with each passing generation and that each age must reconstruct Judaism out of traditional sources to suit its own felt needs.

Enlightenment came later in Eastern Europe, where emancipation came hardly at all. As a result, Jews in that region tended less toward religious reform of Judaism and more toward political reorganization of the Jewish people. The consequence was the rise of Zionism, the movement that led to the creation of a Jewish state by the United Nations in 1948 in the national homeland of the Jews, the land of Israel. Political Zionists have argued that the Jewish religion should be abandoned in the wake of modernism and that Jewish identity should be recast wholly in terms of secular citizenship in a Jewish state.

Cultural Zionists have claimed that the Jewish community in its homeland should serve as a cultural center for Jews around the world and that rabbinic religion should be replaced by the spiritual values found in the Hebrew language and literature. Religious Zionists have viewed the creation of a Jewish state as the "beginning of the flowering of redemption," a precursor to messianic times. They have tended to support theocratic legislation in the state of Israel.

Jewish Education

Each of these modern Jewish movements operates educational institutions that reflect its point of view. In Israel, where Jewish education is compulsory, there are two state educational systems, secular and religious. Youth movements, usually aligned with political parties, have also been especially important educational venues in Israel until recently. In the Diaspora, where Jewish education is completely voluntary, there are essentially three types of educational institutions.

Supplemental schools operated by synagogues and other communal agencies assume that youngsters will acquire a secular education in a state-sponsored or nondenominational independent school. Offering anywhere from two to ten hours of instruction per week, their mission is to provide initiation to the substance of Jewish life, including language, law, lore, history, and culture.

All-day schools were initially preferred primarily by the Orthodox and, outside North America, the Zionists. During the past twenty years, they have become educational venues for most Jewish denominations. These institutions offer both secular and Judaic instruction in a single institution. The amount of time spent on curricula dealing with Jewish concerns as well as the approach taken to the subject matter will depend on the perspective of the school.

Many orthodox schools, for example, have students study religious subjects in the morning and secular material in the late afternoon. In these schools, modern Hebrew is considered a secular subject, and the religious curriculum is confined to the study of traditional sources, such as Talmud for the boys and weekly Torah reading for the girls. More liberal schools, on the other hand, might study Judaica in the afternoon, or split the week with some Judaic study in the morning as well. They will also tend to be coeducational and to place greater emphasis on the Hebrew language and Jewish history. These schools may devote less time than the orthodox to Jewish studies, although not usually less than ten hours per week.

The third sort of Diaspora Jewish education is informal. North American Jewry in particular has pioneered a unique system of summer camps and youth groups that has been especially successful at transmitting Jewish commitments to young people. A most recent addition to this genre is the educational trip to Israel, which combines the features of summer camp with touring of sights of historical and sociological significance.

H.A. Alexander

See also BUBER; JESUS OF NAZARETH; PHILO OF ALEXANDRIA; RELIGIOUS EDUCATION

Bibliography

Bickerman, Elias. *From Ezra to the Macabbees: Foundations of Post Biblical Judaism.* New York: Schocken, 1975.

Chazan, Barry. *The Language of Jewish Education.* New York: Hartmore House, 1972.

Cohen, Shaye. *From the Macabbees to the Mishna.* Philadelphia: Westminster Press, 1987.

Guttman, Julius. *Philosophies of Judaism.* New York: Schocken, 1973.

Hayes, John H. *Introduction to the Bible.* Philadelphia: Westminster Press, 1976.

Hertzberg, Arthur. *The Zionist Idea.* New York: Atheneum, 1969.

Levy, Hans, Alexander Altman, and Isaak Heinemann, eds. *Three Jewish Philosophers.* New York: Meridian Books, 1961.

Moore, G.F. *Judaism in the First Century of the Christian Era.* New York: Schocken, 1971.

Neusner, Jacob. *Judaism: The Evidence of the Mishna.* Chicago: University of Chicago Press, 1981.

Radvsky, David. *Modern Jewish Religious Movements: A History of Emancipation and Adjustment.* New York: Behrman House, 1979.

Scholem, Gershom. *Major Trends in Jewish Mysticism.* New York: Schocken, 1973.

Seltzer, Robert. *Jewish People, Jewish Thought: The Jewish Experience in History.* New York: Macmillan, 1980.

Siddur Sim Shalom. Edited by Jules Harlow. New York: Rabbinical Assembly, 1985.

Twersky, Isadore. *A Maimonides Reader.* New York: Behrman House, 1972.

Urbach, E.E. *The Sages: Their Concepts and Beliefs.* Jerusalem: Magnes Press of the Hebrew University, 1975.

J

Justice

The concept of justice has been of enduring interest to philosophers and educators. Numerous understandings have been advanced. These perspectives provide frames for considering the nature of the good life and the good society and for exploring the links between education and these ideals.

Greek Roots

Plato (c. 427–347 B.C.), in the *Republic,* put forward a vision of justice that combined personal and social harmony. In the just state, individuals are educated to fulfill roles that align with their particular capacities and with social needs. Of particular importance was the education of the guardian class who governed the state. Their rational pursuit of the form of the good enabled individuals to pursue the good society and to reject the corrupting influences of private interests. Similarly, soldiers' and workers' educations aligned with their roles and personal capacities.

Aristotle (384–322 B.C.), like Plato, used the concept of justice as a tool to provide an account of the good life and the good society. However, instead of focusing on abstract ideals, as Plato did, Aristotle prized the development of practical reason. He explored the nature of both universal justice (a form of complete virtue) and particularistic justice (which pertained to context-specific matters of distributive justice and retributive justice). Just distribution and retribution were determined in accordance with merit. Just arrangements reflected a mean between receiving either more or less than is deserved. Those who were superior were to receive greater benefits in proportion to their superiority. Aristotle believed that man's reason should guide judgments of distribution and retribution and that the nature of "just" treatment was context-dependent.

The Enlightenment and Early Modern Period

Many thinkers of the eighteenth and nineteenth centuries shared Aristotle's belief that one must evaluate specific acts and their empirical consequences when considering matters of justice. Unlike Aristotle, however, many of these theorists' context-specific judgments focused on social utility. David Hume (1711–1776) believed that public utility was the motive that led individuals to design systems of justice. These conventions protected rights and thus provided a desirable kind of security. However, Hume felt that neither utility nor rationality was the source of the moral judgments tied to just and unjust acts. Hume wrote that the moral content of justice could be traced to moral sentiments, to sympathy and concern for others in the society. This orientation has informed the thinking of many moral educators who emphasize the development of moral sentiments and who question the links between abstract reasoning abilities and ethical behavior.

Rather than emphasizing an intuitive approach to moral judgment, utilitarians emphasized rationality. Though their primary emphasis was on utility, John Stuart Mill (1806–1873) and others recognized justice as a central moral concern. Their commitment to justice stems from the social utility they believed it would promote.

Immanuel Kant (1724–1804) took a different approach. He believed that justifications based on approximations of social utility inevitably reflect decision-makers' self-interest and that this corrupts moral judgments. Similarly, Kant rejected Hume's belief that sympathy or other emotions could provide adequate moral guidance. One's emotions are not the product of reason and are thus both unreliable and uncontrollable. Consequently, Kant worked to develop an ethic in which the principles of justice were determined prior to a vision of the good. Without this independence, he argued, models of justice would be determined by the very norms and values they were being asked to judge. By developing a reasoned conception of categorical duties that did not privilege a particular vision of the good, a system of laws could be created that permitted individuals to pursue their own conception of the good without constraining other individuals' right to do the same. This reasoning led Kant to formulate the test of moral principles he referred to as the categorical imperative.

Contemporary Theories of Justice

John Rawls's theory of distributive justice has reignited interest in theories of justice among contemporary philosophers. Like Kant, Rawls wants to develop a set of abstract moral principles for evaluating social institutions. However, rather than emphasizing pure reason, as Kant does, Rawls considers the principles we could expect rational individuals to accept if they did not know their social class, social status, physical abilities, or intelligence, but did know all relevant facts about society and had a strong understanding of the social and behavioral sciences. This "veil of ignorance," he argues, provides a fair setting in which to examine alternatives. His ideal is a process of "reflective equilibrium" whereby intuitions are harmonized with principles of justice. Rawls concludes that rational individuals would select a system he labels "democratic equality," which provides equal basic liberties, respect to all, and equal distribution of opportunity and income unless unequal distribution improved the position of the least advantaged.

The implications of this perspective for education are substantial. First, schools would protect basic liberties such as freedom of thought and speech. Next, they would work to secure equality of fair opportunity, demanding both that those with similar skills have access to similar careers and that life circumstances, being born into a poor family for example, would not diminish one's opportunity for development. Once these concerns were met, policies and practices would be guided by the desire to maximize the welfare of the worst off. This would not necessarily mean that relatively successful students would be neglected. If analysts believed that a special program for gifted students benefited the least well off citizens through gains in national productivity more than a subsidized dropout-prevention program, for example, the gifted program might be funded. This example also illustrates the complexity of using philosophical perspectives to inform educational decision-making. Because of the multiple and uncertain effects of policies, those who share philosophical commitments do not necessarily support the same policies, and those with differing philosophical beliefs may promote the same policies.

A variety of alternative visions of justice are also considered by philosophers. Some pursue meritocratic notions of justice, which emphasize equality of opportunity, and argue, in a modified Aristotelian manner, that distribution should be determined by ability and effort. Like those committed to Rawls's system, these analysts often support extra compensatory services for poor students. Some differences might arise over issues such as tracking. Meritocrats might want to reward those who show greater ability and effort, while proponents of democratic equality might focus more directly on the needs of the least well off.

Libertarians provide still another interpretation of justice and a different frame for educators. They believe that government programs that target support for disadvantaged individuals interfere with a free-functioning market, and they wish to limit government's role to ensuring that "careers are open to talents." In addition, this commitment to free markets might lead libertarians to support relatively unregulated school-voucher programs.

Michael Walzer criticizes modern political philosophers for attempting to identify a single abstract formula that is independent of community values and that applies to all questions of distribution. He argues that matters of distributive justice should be further classified as belonging to different spheres (money and commodities, education, kinship and love, and so on). Since our values regarding fairness and merit differ in these settings, our distributive systems should vary as well. Similarly, there might be multiple spheres within education. The principles that lead to a just system of finance might differ dramatically from those surrounding a just curriculum or a just admissions policy.

In addition to focusing on the developing of just educational policies and practices, some moral educators have revived Plato's and Aristotle's emphasis on fostering the development of just individuals. Lawrence Kohlberg puts forward a six-stage theory of moral development. His model, which draws heavily on Plato, Kant, and Rawls, provides ways to conceptualize, measure, and promote individual students' moral development. Kohlberg also combines Rawls's vision of justice with John Dewey's notion of democratic communities in an effort to develop what he calls "Just Community Schools."

Alternatives to Justice

Many educational philosophers argue that schooling that aims to promote the good life and the good society should be based on principles other than justice. For example, policymakers committed to utilitarian goals some-times argue that educators' emphasis on equality constrains the pursuit of academic excellence. Alternatively, Carol Gilligan, Nel Noddings, and other feminist educators assert that the emphasis on abstract principles of justice has obscured human caring as an ethical priority. Some who seek a return to "traditional" values write that the concern for justice has led to bureaucratic efforts to promote students' rights and that this orientation undermines educators' authority and prevents schools from providing students with sound moral guidance. Finally, many who are committed to justice and in particular to equality note the limited ability of schools to overcome the effects of other social forces. They caution against placing too much hope in the belief that schools can bring about a just and equal society.

The meanings assigned to the concept of justice and the educational implications of these understandings vary considerably. Over time, the notion has been used in different ways to frame discussions of the good life and the good society. As a result, debates regarding the meaning of justice and its implications for education mirror, in a fundamental way, the central issues with which we grapple as a culture.

Joseph Kahne

See also ARISTOTLE; CHILDREN'S RIGHTS; CIVIL DISOBEDIENCE; EQUALITY; KANT; LIBERALISM; MORAL DEVELOPMENT; PLATO; RIGHTS

Bibliography

Aristotle. *Nicomachean Ethics*. Translated by M. Ostwald. New York: Macmillan, 1962.

Gilligan, C. *In a Different Voice: Psychological Theory and Women's Development*. Cambridge: Harvard University Press, 1982.

Kant, I. *Groundwork of the Metaphysic of Morals*. Translated by H.J. Paton. New York: Harper and Row, 1964.

Plato. *The Republic*. Translated by F.M. Cornford. Harmondsworth, England: Penguin Books, 1955.

Power, F.C., A. Higgins, and L. Kohlberg. *Lawrence Kohlberg's Approach to Moral Education*. New York: Columbia University Press, 1989.

Rawls, J. *A Theory of Justice*. Cambridge: Harvard University Press, 1971.

Walzer, Michael. *Spheres of Justice*. New York: Basic Books, 1983.

K

Kant, Immanuel (1724–1804)

The main ideas of Kant's critical philosophy are prefigured in the life and work of Socrates, as he defends himself in the *Apology* against accusations of impiety and corrupting the youth. Is the unexamined life worth living? Should questioning the foundations of conventional beliefs be a crime? Should we value wealth and power more than wisdom? Is it a good idea to replace human wisdom with someone's claim to superhuman wisdom? Socrates makes it clear, through his distinctive method and by his personal example, that there are no satisfactory answers to these questions unless we take a critical approach to experience. A critical attitude is at the heart of philosophy from the beginning.

Like Socrates, Kant wanted to know what he did not know as a way to avoid fruitless intellectual endeavors—warning against entanglements with ideas of reality that take us into a realm in which experiences do not count and any notion can hold sway. Like Socrates, Kant refused to be lured into theological or metaphysical speculation while there were urgent practical decisions to be made in the world of experience. By drawing limits to what could be considered genuine human knowledge, he was able to focus on answers that could serve as a basis for action in the world in which we find ourselves. Both philosophers realized that a critical orientation is implicitly an emphasis on the practical and on human development.

These themes can be found in Kant's earliest statement of the outlines of a critical philosophy, *Dreams of a Spirit-Seer as Illustrated through the Dreams of Metaphysics* (1766). This is Kant's first effort to catch his intellectual balance in a society caught up with spirits.

Spirits filled the social world of Kant's contemporaries and shaped his educational experiences. The young were drilled in religious exercises designed to test their spiritual commitment, when they were not being drilled in Latin to test their competence as students. From firsthand experience Kant describes this as "childhood slavery." Spirits also filled university lecture halls. The official academic philosophy of the day, traceable to Gottfried Leibniz (1646–1716), posited the world of spirits as ultimate substance and viewed the physical world as a derivative, "well-founded illusion."

Spirits were at large even in society. Conversations revolved around "spirit-seers" (*Geistersehers*) like Emmanuel Swedenborg, who claimed to see events elsewhere (as they were happening) and to communicate with the departed. Could he really see the Stockholm fire as it was occurring, although he was far away? Could he really ask questions of a departed soul and have them answered? Could he really retrieve information everyone thought was lost?

Kant wonders whether there ever has been "a philosopher who did not at one time or another cut the sorriest figure" talking at length about the human spirit and denying "the veracity of all such spirit apparitions." Suppose even one of these examples were to be accepted. "What startling consequences would follow!"

The world of metaphysicians is very much like the world of spirit-seers. Metaphysicians claim to know ultimate reality and actually believe that their ideas of spirit or of matter are what the world is ultimately and finally like (apart from human interpretations that are conditioned by space and time). What are we to make of these dreams?

Kant resolves to treat the matter critically. This means drawing the boundaries more carefully between the knowable and the unknow-able and between the world that has a claim on our moral energies and the world in which we squander our efforts and resources. Initially critical of the claims of Emmanuel Swedenborg to be in contact with other-worldly spirits, Kant becomes critical of the conditions under which knowing and acting meaningfully occur.

A radical transformation is required to get beyond entanglements with other worlds and properly focus on this one. Kant calls for a "Copernican revolution in philosophy" to change the nature of the debate over the real-ity in which we are implicated. In effect, this means getting over both rationalism and skep-ticism, which are habits of mind that have kept philosophy in an ongoing, fruitless debate for two millennia. Both positions assume that hu-man concepts must conform to ultimate reality in order for genuine knowledge to exist. Ratio-nalism claims that human reason can know the nature of ultimate reality and that human con-cepts can grasp it. Skepticism denies this can happen and thus calls into question all human knowledge. Rationalism claims that theoretical knowledge of ultimate reality can give us prac-tical guidance on what we should be doing in this world. Skepticism denies it and leaves us with a cynical attitude on the status of moral values.

Kant's Copernican revolution is an-nounced in the *Critique of Pure Reason* (1781). It is a proposal to resolve the debate by aban-doning the assumption that concepts must con-form to ultimate objects (things in themselves) for genuine knowledge to exist and by asking instead how (under what conditions) it is pos-sible for objects to conform to human concepts. What does it take for any object to be real for us in the world of experience that we share? Are there concepts that are so fundamental for hu-man thinking (such as substance and causality) that we cannot be aware of and know any ob-ject without using these categories? If we come up with a list of such categories, show that they are indispensable for thinking, and specify the conditions under which they apply, we will have uncovered the structure of the reality of the human world. This will enable us to draw boundaries between the knowable and the un-knowable and release ourselves from the point-less exercise that rationalism and skepticism demand we perform. These basic concepts will be part of any experience of knowing objects. They will be the forms in which we find any

construction of human reality. The materials come from the world as it is presented to us in experience—through the senses and in our per-ceptions. Categories are meaningful in relation to the world we are in and meaningless if exer-cised in a sphere beyond human experience. We will know when we have transgressed the boundaries of meaningful discourse, Kant ar-gues at length in the "Dialectic" of his first *Critique,* because we will lapse into contradic-tions when we exceed the (phenomenal world) conditions under which knowledge claims are legitimate.

In this way, Kant redirects philosophical activity toward the world of experience. Like Nicolaus Copernicus (1493–1543), he reverses the perspective and switches the terms of the debate, making possible a more careful and systematic gathering of knowledge in the world in which human beings actually live.

After the Copernican revolution in phi-losophy, we can proceed confidently with knowledge claims based on experience, and avoid becoming ensnared in what Kant calls "the logic of illusion." A line is drawn between the metaphysics of experience (phenomena, the world that is real for us) and transcendent meta-physics (noumena, a world beyond the human capacity to know). The former is the realm in which human categories meet and shape the world as it is given to us in sensory experience (perceptions in space and time). The latter is the domain in which categories shape entities pro-duced by the imagination with reference to con-ditions outside of space and time—creating anything at will. In such a domain, debate is not meaningful. Nevertheless, the noumenal world is filled with entities and creatures that human beings say they know are there. This includes God, the cosmos, the ultimate constituents of nature, the soul, free will, divine judgment, and immortality.

Kant knows some will be disappointed if they cannot plunge headlong into the transcen-dent and know ultimate reality. For those people, Kant already had left some advice at the end of *Dreams of a Spirit Seer:*

> Human reason was not meant to try and part the highest clouds in heaven or lift from our eyes the curtains in order to re-veal to us the secrets of the other world. The curiosity-seekers who are so anxious to enquire into these, should be given the most natural reply: that it would be more

advisable if they please show some patience until they get there. Our destiny in the future world most likely depends on the way in which we manage our jobs in this world.

Does this critical approach destroy the basis for religious faith? On the contrary, Kant argues that it strengthens the position of religious faith because it denies the arrogance of a reason that would claim to know ultimate reality and derive marching orders from it. "I have found it necessary to deny knowledge in order to make room for faith," he states in his preface to the first *Critique*. Like Socrates, Kant believed that if a person does the right thing in this world, there is no reason to worry about how one will fare in the next. But whatever this faith might involve, it cannot mean violating or undermining the morality of the world we experience.

Although there were serious disagreements over the nature of the metaphysical and religious commitments that followed from Kant's approach, it was widely accepted as a watershed for modern thought. The critical philosophy became a turning point that had an influence on all future formulations of philosophical issues. It provided an alternative to the endless debate between rationalism and skepticism, and resolved the cultural crisis resulting from the conflict between modern science and religion. Moreover, because Kant emphasized the active side of the process of knowing, with human beings organizing (through categories and concepts) the world they were to know, he anticipated and grounded the participant/observer theories of twentieth-century science.

The growing consensus on the significance of Kant's theoretical work helped to create an interest in the practical implications of his approach. Is there a Copernican revolution in ethics that runs parallel to the revolution that came with his first *Critique,* and if so, what does it mean for values and practices?

In the *Critique of Practical Reason* (1788), Kant makes it clear that moral judgments are projections of what this world would be like if everyone behaved morally; they are not projections of the proper order of things in a world different from the one we know. Moral questions are about what is right to do in this world, not about what to do in preparation for the next world. It is reasonable to hope that moral actions will be rewarded, but it is not reasonable to bank on it based on some dubious claim to knowledge.

How do people act in the moral world? What are the imperatives they take seriously? What is the right thing to do if we take the moral experience of this world as a point of departure? Within moral experience, we know that there is an important difference between the way we treat human beings and the way we treat things. Knowing this difference is fundamental to knowing what it is to be human. Human beings are treated as ends in themselves, not merely as instruments for purposes they do not share.

This principle is central to the human experience of morality. It is expressed directly in one of the formulations of the "categorical imperative" in what was to become Kant's most popular work, *Foundations of the Metaphysics of Morals* (1959): "So act as to use humanity, both in your own person and in the person of every other, always at the same time as an end, never merely as a means." Other formulations say the same thing with more or less emphasis on universalizability of conduct, respect for autonomy, and recognition of the value of community.

In the *Critique of Judgment* (1790), the last of his three *Critiques* and written especially for the purpose of summing up the approach of critical philosophy, Kant talks about "moral teleology," the idea that there is "a final purpose that we must aim at in this world." This "moral teleology concerns us as beings in the world and therefore as beings bound up with others in the world." This final purpose is "the *highest good in the world* possible through freedom."

Freedom movements that swept across the world during the next two centuries were based on the belief that human beings should not be used merely as means—that people should have a chance to develop themselves and should have a say in their destinies. They should not have their lives used up for the purposes of others. In other words, they should be treated as human beings, as ends in themselves. The highest good in this world is possible only through their freedom.

Kant's critical philosophy is related both historically and theoretically to the concerns expressed in freedom movements. Intellectuals active in these movements found a theoretical foundation for practical conclusions they were ready to draw about the value of equality in relation to freedom. The critical philosophy also becomes a basis for thinking about what counts as human development once the overt forms of oppression are removed. In fact, the idea of aesthetic education in the third *Critique* sparked an ongoing discussion among poets and philosophers. What would it mean to value the development of the full humanity of all human beings?

While Kant's philosophy had this progressive effect, it also had a conservative effect as a result of his endorsement of retribution in *Metaphysical Elements of Justice* (1797). Although retribution was not mentioned in any of the formulations of the categorical imperative, the conventional world of Kant's contemporaries came to treat the idea as if it were the centerpiece of the critical philosophy.

For many of Kant's contemporaries, the moral life is about duty and retribution. It is the combination of a stern sense of duty and strict acts of retribution for those who do not obey the call of duty. Enforcing this discipline becomes the meaning of human life. For some it even is to betray the meaning of human life to fail to carry out acts of retribution. From this point of view we are obligated to devote all our resources to completing acts of retribution—no matter what the cost or consequence might be. In the background is a God who is the ultimate moral enforcer, with rewards and punishments distributed exactly in proportion to how much virtue or vice there is in each person. Human beings are supposed to lead lives in such a way that there is little left for God to do. In this way, retribution comes to take over human life.

It is important to note that when Kant sides with this conventional view of moral experience, it is in his own conventional work, *Metaphysical Elements of Justice*. Here he merely searches for the assumptions of the criminal justice system he found in his own society. He comes to the conclusion that retribution must be so important that human beings should be prepared to sacrifice everything in life in order to carry it out—upon pain of abandoning their moral nature as human beings. "If they fail to do so [carry out the punishment], they may be regarded as accomplices in this public violation of legal justice." This is exactly what Kant's contemporaries wanted to hear. They wanted retribution to be grounded in the critical philosophy and quickly made Kant the principal proponent of a "modern" theory of retribution.

Kant did not find a contradiction, or even a tension, between the values of human development and retribution. It remains for later generations to discover the difficulty of balancing commitments to education and criminal justice. If there is need for a philosophical framework that gives guidance about the nature of this moral choice, the three *Critiques* and the *Foundations* point us in the direction of the development of all human beings, with emphasis on aesthetic education. On the other hand, the *Metaphysical Elements of Justice* presents the conventional view of criminal justice and ties our humanity (and our resources) to a willingness to finish the job of retribution. Because the expansion and deepening of the human spirit became the theme of his *Opus Postumum*, and retribution disappears, there is at least one indication of the choice Kant finally made for himself. In his last notes about the world of spirits, Kant reaffirms the boundaries that separate us from the all-devouring spirits of another world and reorients us toward the development of the human spirit in this one.

Thomas Auxter

See also ETHICS AND MORALITY; JUSTICE; METAPHYSICS; RATIONALISM; SKEPTICISM; SOCRATES

Bibliography

Allison, Henry. *Kant's Transcendental Idealism.* New Haven: Yale University Press, 1983.

Ameriks, Karl. *Kant's Theory of Mind.* Oxford: Clarendon Press, 1982.

Auxter, Thomas. *Kant's Moral Teleology.* Macon: Mercer University Press, 1982.

Beck, Lewis White. *Commentary on Kant's Critique of Practical Reason.* Chicago: University of Chicago Press, 1961.

———. *Early German Philosophy: Kant and His Predecessors.* Cambridge: Harvard University Press, 1969.

Cassirer, Ernst. *Kant's Life and Thought.* Translated by James Haden. New Haven: Yale University Press, 1981.

Kant, Immanuel. *Critique of Judgment.* Translated by Werner S. Pluhar. Indianapolis, Ind.: Hackett, 1987.

———. *Critique of Practical Reason.* Translated by Lewis White Beck. Indianapolis, Ind.: Bobbs-Merrill, 1956.

———. *Critique of Pure Reason.* Translated by Norman Kemp Smith. New York: St. Martin's Press, 1963.

———. *Dreams of a Spirit-Seer.* Translated by John Manolesco. New York: Vantage, 1960.

———. *Foundations of the Metaphysics of Morals.* Translated by Lewis White Beck. Indianapolis, Ind.: Bobbs-Merrill, 1959.

———. *Kants gesammelte Schriften.* Berlin: Walter de Gruyter, 1902.

———. *Metaphysical Elements of Justice.* Translated by John Ladd. Indianapolis, Ind.: Bobbs-Merrill, 1965.

Kemp Smith, Norman. *Commentary on Kant's Critique of Pure Reason.* 2nd ed. New York: Macmillan, 1923.

Murphy, Jeffrie. *Kant: The Philosophy of Right.* London: Macmillan, 1970.

O'Neill, Onora. *Constructions of Reason.* Cambridge: Cambridge University Press, 1989.

Kierkegaard, Soren Aabye (1813–1855)

Justly regarded as the prime mover of the existential movement in philosophy, Kierkegaard was born in 1813 in Copenhagen. At the behest of his father, who was a brilliant, melancholic, and deeply pious individual, Kierkegaard took his doctorate in theology at the University of Copenhagen. In his late twenties, Kierkegaard began his short but mightily prolific career as a writer. An author who was as poetic as he was philosophical, Kierkegaard wrote a number of masterworks including *Either/Or, Fear and Trembling,* and *The Sickness unto Death.* For reasons as complex as his philosophy, he wrote many of his greatest works pseudonomously. Kierkegaard was a highly polemical individual, who, over the course of his career, attacked both the public press and the Danish State Church. He died of undetermined causes in 1855.

Kierkegaard was a strident critic of the then regnant philosophy of his day—German Idealism. According to G.W.F. Hegel, the most celebrated philosopher of this school, philosophical knowledge is higher than faith. On this and a number of other points, Kierkegaard vehemently disagreed with Hegel. In his own inimitable and often highly oblique style, Kierkegaard argued that Christendom had forgotten what it means to have faith. An ardent admirer of the Athenian gadfly, Kierkegaard often remarked that what the world needed was neither more progress nor more knowledge but rather another Socrates—that is, someone capable of delivering others of false knowledge, or, as Kierkegaard saw it, false conceptions of faith. To no small extent, Kierkegaard played the role of a Christian Socrates.

Kierkegaard's views on education were dialectical. On the one hand, he believed that acquiring knowledge about the world without a corresponding increase in self-knowledge was productive of nothing more than unwarranted snobbery. On the other hand, his writings stand as a veritable advanced course in the development of self-knowledge. In order to appreciate Kierkegaard's ambivalent attitude toward education it will be useful to consider a distinction that he draws in his philosophical magnum opus, *Concluding Unscientific Postscript.*

Writing under the pseudonym of Johannes Climacus, Kierkegaard distinguishes between an objective and subjective approach to life. Objectivity involves the suppression of self-interest. The objective individual is always trying to see things from a disinterested perspectiveless perspective. In contrast, the subjective or inward individual makes no excuses about taking an infinite personal interest in matters of infinite personal interest. Whereas the objective thinker will try to take a dispassionate approach to matters of faith, subjective individuals will accept and affirm their passions. While Kierkegaard readily acknowledged that an objective approach is appropriate to certain subject matters, such as logic, mathematics, and science, he thought that people had become too much inclined toward objectivity, too much inclined to muting the very passions that he took to be essential to self-knowledge.

To the extent that educators encourage students to believe that the acquisition of knowledge and the objective approach to life are the truth and the way, Kierkegaard was wary of education. According to Kierkegaard, the highest good is being properly related to God and, as he saw it, being properly related to God has very little to do with the acquisition of knowledge or academic degrees.

Kierkegaard the cultural observer judged his age to be passionless and spiritless or, as he often put it, devoid of inwardness. Both in philosophical theory (Hegel) and in everyday practice there was, Kierkegaard observed, a growing conviction that there is nothing within us that can not be expressed in outward form. In other words, you are exactly what you have and do, which Kierkegaard thought was to concede that there is no such thing as having a private and personal relationship with one's Creator. By crafting images such as his Knight of Faith (*Fear and Trembling*), who is a spiritual virtuoso of the highest order and yet outwardly appears like everybody's next door neighbor, Kierkegaard argued that the inner and outer are incommensurable; or, more to the point, that our individual relationship to God cannot be read off the outward manifestations of our life.

Kierkegaard theorized about and practiced a method of indirect communication. On this count he wisely insisted that effective communication and thus pedagogy require taking the subjectivity of your audience into account. In other words, one must know whom one is talking to. The individual who wants to communicate must write "merrily for the merry" and, as Kierkegaard could have continued, abstractly for the abstracted. Kierkegaard had the literary gifts to practice what he preached. Depending upon his audience he wrote in a number of different styles: as a philosopher, ethicist, aesthete, journalist, and theologian. As a footnote, it should be remarked that among Kierkegaard's contributions to philosophy must be reckoned his elegant raising of the question of the relationship between style and philosophical content.

Kierkegaard held that the truths that matter in life cannot be publicly broadcast and committed to memory. Acquiring these truths, which Kierkegaard took to be of an ethico-religious nature, requires something more than merely getting the right mental representation. The task as Kierkegaard envisioned it was not so much one of forging ideas that mirror reality but rather of becoming truly related to an idea. Kierkegaard's approach to education has left him open to the charge best expressed by Alasdair MacIntyre in his *After Virtue* that Kierkegaard despaired of the possibilities for rational suasion and practiced what can only be termed a sophisticated form of manipulation.

Gordon D. Marino

See also EXISTENTIALISM; HEGEL; SOCRATES

Bibliography

Hannay, Alastair. *Kierkegaard.* London: Routledge and Kegan Paul, 1982.

Kierkegaard, Soren. *Concluding Unscientific Postscript.* Translated by Howard and Edna Hong. Princeton: Princeton University Press, 1993.

———. *Either/Or.* Translated by Howard and Edna Hong. Princeton: Princeton University Press, 1990.

———. *Fear and Trembling.* Translated by Alastair Hannay. New York: Penguin Press, 1985.

———. *The Sickness unto Death.* Translated by Alastair Hannay. New York: Penguin Press, 1989.

MacIntyre, Alasdair. *After Virtue: A Study in Moral Theory.* Notre Dame, Ind.: University of Notre Dame Press, 1981.

Manheimer, Ronald J. *Kierkegaard as Educator.* Berkeley: University of California Press, 1977.

Marino, G. *Kierkegaard in the Present Age.* Marquette, Mich.: Marquette University Press, 1994.

King, Martin Luther, Jr. (1929–1968)

The son and grandson of college-educated Baptist Ministers, Martin Luther King, Jr., carried on an African American pragmatic tradition that emphasized the use of intellectual skills to pursue group advancement. Born in Atlanta on January 15, 1929, King was exposed to many educators and religious leaders with advanced degrees and strong commitments to racial advancement. As a student at Morehouse College in 1944, he was inspired by President Benjamin E. Mays, who insisted that black students prepare themselves for a life of service to the race. In 1947, King expressed his evolving educational views in an article entitled "The Purpose of Education," prepared for the Morehouse student newspaper. Asserting that education prepared one to "Think intensively and to think critically," he insisted that these were not sufficient: "The most dangerous criminal may be the man gifted with reason, but with no morals." King concluded that "intelligence plus character" must be goals of education, which should not only provide the "power of concentration, but [also] worthy objectives upon which to concentrate."

One of the first of his race to receive a doctoral degree in systematic theology, King saw his theological studies at Crozer Seminary and Boston University as a source of ideas that would enrich his preaching and social ministry. He considered pursuing an academic position but decided that his initial postgraduate position would be as a minister of a Southern church. In 1954, he became the pastor of Dexter Avenue Baptist Church in Montgomery, Alabama. The following year he quickly rose to national prominence as a leader of a successful bus boycott movement. For the next dozen years, King devoted himself to the expanding Southern civil rights movement, serving as president of the Southern Christian Leadership Conference.

Through his public career, King expressed his belief in the importance and moral basis of education and in the application of intellectual skills to the solution of social problems. King's personalist theology and his egalitarian dream of a "beloved community" led him to call for the revamping of educational institutions so that all members of society could benefit. Because of his belief in equality and potential in every person, King condemned segregation in schools and racial discrimination as destructive of human personality. "The unrealized capacities of many of our youth are an indictment of our society's lack of concern for justice and its proclivity for wasting human resources," he once asserted. "As with so much else in this potentially great society, injustice and waste go together and endanger stability."

Beyond simply calling for equal access to educational opportunities, King consistently reaffirmed his belief that academic training should benefit society rather than simply the individual. Although he resisted the elitism and obscurantism that were often associated with advanced educational training, he believed that every individual has the ability and obligation to serve society. "You don't have to have a college degree to serve," he remarked in a sermon delivered shortly before his assassination in Memphis on April 4, 1968. "You only need a heart full of grace."

King remained an idealist throughout his life. His commitment to social change was formulated using a vocabulary he acquired largely in academic institutions. In his final book, *Where Do We Go from Here? Chaos or Community?* (1967), he argued that "education without social action [is] a one-sided value because it has no true power potential," adding that "social action without education is a real expression of pure energy."

Clayborne Carson
Angela Brown

See also MINORITIES; RACE AND RACISM

Bibliography

Ayres, Alex, ed. *The Wisdom of Martin Luther King, Jr.* New York: Meridian Books, 1993.

Bennett, Lerone, Jr. *What Manner of Man: A Biography of Martin Luther King, Jr.* New York: Pocket Books, 1974.

Carson, Clayborne et al., eds. *The Papers of Martin Luther King, Jr., Volume 1: Called to Serve, January 1929–June 1951.* Los Angeles: University of California Press, 1992.

King, Martin Luther, Jr. *Where Do We Go from Here: Chaos or Community?* New York: Harper and Row, 1967.

Muse, Clyde. "The Educational Philosophy of Martin Luther King, Jr." Ph.D. thesis, University of Oklahoma, 1978.

K

L

Learning, Theories of

Explanations of the changes occurring in behavior and mental processes that result from being in the world. Theories of learning present accounts of these changes by describing both the resources newborn children bring with them into the world and the principles that explain how these congenital factors participate in the creation of experience. An examination of the various theories of learning reveals obvious differences in how learning is explained. The greatest of these differences among theories of learning is accounted for by the role assigned to the a priori. Since there are three conceptions of the a priori at work, theories of learning can be classified by means of three major categories. Within each category there will be differences, but those differences will not be as great as the differences among categories.

Empiricist theories of learning base explanations on the analytic conception of the a priori, the truth of which can be established solely by the rules of language. Under this conception, the a priori is true in all possible worlds, come what may in actual experience. Because empiricists want explanations of learning as it occurs in this world, theories must include statements verifiable by sensory experience. Scientific knowledge is thus built of general analytic statements and synthetic data reports.

This approach is implicit in the associationism of David Hume (1711–1776), and it was given its most developed expression by B.F. Skinner (1904–1990), who viewed the newborn child as possessing only respondent (reflexive) behavior, a genetic endowment, and the capacity to be reinforced. With proper schedules of reinforcement, genetic differences become negligible. Children actively interact with their environment and are shaped by these encounters according to the law of operant conditioning: Behavior that is reinforced becomes more frequent. Descriptions of learning, for empiricists, are never stated in terms of unverifiable references to mental processes, or causes of behavior. Hume had argued that causal claims are proscribed in the science of behavior because they appeal to nonobservable concepts.

Two types of operant behavior characterize the behavioral approach to learning. Stimulus generalization is the process by which learners adapt behavior learned in one situation to different but similar situations. The parallel process is stimulus discrimination: Learners respond to finer and finer details in the environment and thereby develop more and more effective operants (learned behaviors) for operating within that environment.

Contemporary behaviorists can be divided into two types: Operant behaviorists hold to the traditional approach of describing behavior. Cognitive behaviorists view behavior as evidence for neuro-processes that explain learning. Cognitive behaviorism depends on the existence of a viable account of causation. Recent work on the nature of statistical explanation in science presents an account of causality acceptable to empiricists. Cognitive behaviorists can view such conclusions as providing philosophic legitimation for studies of learning that include unobservable elements and make references to causes of behavior.

Jean Piaget (1889–1980) rejected the empiricists' view of science and adopted the Kantian conception of the synthetic a priori, upon which he based his stage theory of development. While analytic statements are known a priori, these are not the only form the a priori may take. Some statements are true of the world—that is, synthetic—but do not have their truth established through experience, that is, a priori. Synthetic a priori structures are true of experience but do not derive from experience. Kant (1724–1804) objected to Hume on the basis that we experience the world in terms of our already existing cognitive structures. For example, Kant claimed that we must experience the world in Euclidean terms because that is the way the mind understands space. This makes the empiricists' claims about theory-free observation unacceptable.

Kant was describing mature thinkers, but Piaget wondered about the processes involved as children's thinking develops into the capacity for mature thought—that is, formal operational reasoning. Learning is movement through four innately ordered and qualitatively distinct stages: sensory motor, intuitive or preoperational, concrete operations, and formal operations. Stage changes are explained by the process of adaptation, which is composed of two reciprocal subprocesses, assimilation and accommodation. Learning occurs because: (1) new elements in the environment are assimilated by means of one's current cognitive structures, or (2) as we experience the world, gaps and incongruities occur that produce disequilibration. Equilibration is restored by accommodation, the process of modifying cognitive structures. The innate and automatic tendency to reestablish equilibration leads individuals to move through the four qualitatively different cognitive stages identified. Since, according to Piaget, equilibration is an automatic process, thinking as reflective problem-solving under the conscious control of free agents should not be attributed to this theory. Some researchers working in the Piagetian tradition believe that the original characterization of the four stages may require modification.

The theory of Lawrence Kohlberg (1927–1987) regarding how children learn moral concepts appealed to six distinct moral stages that roughly paralleled Piaget's four cognitive stages. Stage changes are explained in terms of the Piagetian processes of assimilation, accommodation, and equilibration, though these explanatory processes are seldom made explicit in textbook accounts of Kohlberg's theory. Like Piaget, Kohlberg interviewed children and attempted to identify the various qualitatively different argument forms being used as children attempted to construct solutions to the moral problems presented by the interviewers.

Piaget's research and subsequent developments in artificial intelligence, information processing, and neuroscience have coalesced into cognitive science. It is generally agreed that the durable and revealing results of Piaget's work are major factors in the effort to codify various cognitive studies into cognitive science. For many years, some empiricistically oriented psychologists have wondered if operant behaviorism had been too radical with Ockham's Razor. Cognitive science seemed to contain elements relevant to understanding learning, but the operant-behaviorists' criterion of cognitive meaningfulness proscribed these.

The third view of the nature of the role of the a priori emerged from the search for an alternative to the analytic and synthetic conceptions of the a priori. A common assumption of these two diverse conceptions of the nature of the a priori is that the a priori must be certain beyond all doubt. Since everything cannot be doubted at once: (1) logically, at the very least, some language must be assumed in which the doubted is expressed, and (2) psychologically, one could not function if one's *loco standi* were to vanish completely. The pragmatic a priori consists of those elements in a problematic situation that are not doubted and that provide the epistemic context in terms of which the doubted is investigated. This conception of the a priori is relative, in that what is undoubted in one context may become the doubted in another. While critics fear that this conception of the a priori allows science to become a collection of personally relative beliefs, pragmatists hold that the social nature of inquiry leads to entrenched or institutionalized habits of thought, which have more recently been referred to as paradigms. Those who hold this conception of the a priori view the history of any inquiry as a repository of experience with the undoubted in that inquiry. Through historical analysis the explicit and implicit meaning that constitutes the a priori for inquiry is subordinated to intelligence.

Jerome S. Bruner holds that children are thrown into a language game in which they must learn to function, and that it is the goal of learning theory to investigate the processes by which they develop meaning. They come into the world curious and seeking competence (which is more than simply the capacity to be reinforced and less than possessing latent ideas such as quantity). The metaphor is that of being pushed onto a stage where a play is in progress. Children do not know what the play is about or what character they are to play. They focus on action and the consequences thereof, especially human interactions. Narrative reports of experience impose linear order on events and are particularly concerned with identifying the unusual or exceptional. In this way, children use the construction of narratives to discover the canonical sociocultural patterns within which they must operate. The focus of this view is on child development as a process of constructing and reconstructing meaning.

Empiricism and pragmatism come into direct opposition over the question of the epistemic value of folk psychology. In the dim past, early humans used their intelligence to survive and prosper. Learning to describe, explain, and predict environmental events, including the behavior of others, has great survival value. Experience enhanced this emerging lore of common-sense or folk psychology—that is, the rough generalizations and rules of thumb about mental states such as beliefs and desires that are entrenched in language.

B.F. Skinner, in *About Behaviorism*, attempted to reduce some of the content of folk psychology to operant behaviorism by showing how the ordinary language meanings of mentalistic concepts could be reformulated in terms of empiricistic psychology. He seemed not to object to the use of folk language as long as language users realized that such talk reflected bad linguistic habits formed before the science of behavior was fully developed. Others see folk psychology as much more harmful to the development of scientific psychology. Eliminative materialists hold that folk psychology is theoretical psychology that requires substantial revision if a major impediment to understanding how people learn and think is to be removed. They further believe that folk psychology will ultimately be replaced by neuroscience. They argue that while the average person believes in the folk-physics principle that the motion of objects results from forces acting on those objects (the impetus theory of motion), Newtonian physics shows this to be a false belief. If the conclusions of folk physics are wrong, then how can we assume the correctness of folk psychology? Why would folk psychology be the one folk theory that was correct?

Bruner, in *Acts of Meaning*, argues that while the term "folk psychology" originated as a term of derision, the idea behind it is valid. He takes cultural analysis to be an essential element of psychological research because it is through participating in culture that mental capacities are developed. Through such participation in culture meanings become shared. Psychological studies should be focused on the meaning-making and meaning-using aspects of our existence in culture because these cannot be fully explained by methodologies that approach learning by trying to remain outside of human subjectivity. Bruner holds that learning can be understood only by making the idea of the Self as an agent in culture the basis of such studies.

This debate over the epistemic significance of folk psychology has meaning for the philosophy of education. Ordinary language analysis has been used as a device for clarifying the meaning of many terms used to describe education. The term *teaching*, for example, has been the focus of numerous analyses, each of which has sought to help improve the practice of teaching by better revealing the nature of teaching activities. If, as Bruner argues, everyday conceptions are valuable resources for scientific research, then such analyses should be done and these results used for further research. If, as the eliminative materialists argue, everyday conceptions of mental phenomena are incorrect and prevent paradigm shifts toward correct accounts of how we think, then one wonders if ordinary-language analyses of *teaching* and other terms have served to misdirect thinking. Whether folk psychology is a great resource for describing and explaining human learning, or a major obstacle to the further development of cognitive science, is ultimately an issue over the proper conception of the a priori upon which to base the study of learning.

Jerome A. Popp

See also BEHAVIORISM; COGNITIVE DEVELOPMENT; EMPIRICISM; EPISTEMOLOGY; HEREDITY AND HEREDITARIANISM; HUMAN NATURE; INTELLIGENCE; KANT; POSITIVISM; TEACHING AND LEARNING

Bibliography

Bruner, Jerome S. *Acts of Meaning.* Cambridge: Harvard University Press, 1990.

Churchland, Patricia Smith. *Neurophilosophy: Toward a Unified Science of the Mind-Brain.* Cambridge: MIT Press, 1986.

Churchland, Paul M. "Eliminative Materialism and the Propositional Attitudes." *Journal of Philosophy* 78 (1981): 67–90.

Falvell, James. *The Developmental Psychology of Jean Piaget.* New York: D. Van Nostrand, 1963.

Ginsberg, Herbert, and Sylvia Opper. *Piaget's Theory of Intellectual Development.* Englewood Cliffs, N.J.: Prentice Hall, 1969.

Kavathatzopoulos, Iordanis. "Kohlberg and Piaget: Differences and Similarities." *Journal of Moral Education* 20 (1991): 47–53.

Kohlberg, Lawrence. "From Is to Ought: How to Commit the Naturalistic Fallacy and Get Away with It in the Study of Moral Development." In *Cognitive Psychology and Epistemologies,* edited by T. Mischel, 151–235. New York: Academic Press, 1971.

Laudan, Larry. *Science and Values.* Berkeley: University of California Press, 1984.

Salmon, Wesley C. *Scientific Explanation and the Causal Structure of the World.* Princeton: Princeton University Press, 1984.

Skinner, B.F. *About Behaviorism.* New York: Alfred A. Knopf, 1974.

———. *Science and Human Behavior.* New York: Macmillan, 1953.

Stich, Stephen P. *From Folk Psychology to Cognitive Science: The Case against Belief.* Cambridge: MIT Press, 1983.

Leisure

The ultimate links between education and leisure in the Western world are established at the outset of history by the fact that the Greek word for leisure (*schole*) is the root from which we derive the word *school.* Leisure was employed by intellectuals of fifth- and fourth-century Greece in learned disputation, and places in which these disputations occurred, the distant forerunners of modern universities, became known as schools. In particular Plato (c. 427–347 B.C.) and Aristotle (384–322 B.C.) use *schole* in both senses, and they can be regarded as responsible for the shift in meaning. Plato saw his Academy as a place where citizens were trained for service in the state, and though his ideal education included music and gymnastics, sometimes seen as leisure pursuits, there is a seriousness about his program less evident in that of his less puritanical successor. Aristotle states boldly that "we conduct business in order that we may have leisure" (*Nicomachean Ethics:* x.7.6), and he sees abstract contemplation, which might be regarded as leisure activity, as the highest form of virtue. There is something of this tension between two attitudes to leisure in the subsequent history of education.

Education at Rome was more practical than in Greece, but nevertheless both in Cicero (106–43 B.C.) and Quintilian (c. 35–c. 90) there is a pleasing insistence on the education of the whole man at the expense of the rather artificial training in rhetoric that occupied a large place in the Roman curriculum. Educated Roman men and women had a great deal of leisure at their disposal as a result of the institution of slavery, and they would seem on archaeological evidence to have used their leisure wisely, although some literary works paint lurid scenes of debauchery and gladiatorial spectacles. *Ludus* in Latin can mean both a school and a game. The decline of the Roman Empire coincided with the rise of Christianity. Leisure became less easy to enjoy with the threat of barbarian invasions. Christianity, with its concentration on the next world, was hostile to pleasant idleness in this world. Aristotle fell out of favor, and Neoplatonism became the dominant philosophy.

John Cassian (c. 366–435) defined the sin of sloth as an inability to work or pray, and the Middle Ages did not offer much opportunity for leisure, although plenty for work and prayer. There are few depictions of leisure in medieval art; even for the small proportion of the population who were literate, books were difficult to obtain, and reading could hardly be a leisure pursuit. Conversation could be, and both Giovanni Bocaccio (1313–1375) and Geoffrey Chaucer (c. 1340–1400) give an insight into the way in which all sections of society could pass their time in talking. The feudal aristocracy did not encourage their inferiors to amuse themselves, and there are records of games like football being banned as distractions from more useful pursuits like archery. Hunting and jousting were preserves of the rich. Leisure was probably better understood in the Islamic world, which kept alive the study of Aristotle.

The Renaissance brought about new inventions like printing and a new interest in the full potential of the human spirit. It ought to have led to a further flowering of leisure pursuits, and certainly literature, drama, the fine arts and learning all flourished. But the Renaissance almost coincided with the Reformation, and the Protestant work ethic was inimical to leisure. Under the Commonwealth in Britain (1649–1660) it was forbidden to enact plays on the stage or to dance under the maypole on the village green. In America, Puritanism and the hardship of life did not encourage leisure pursuits among the early settlers.

Prosperity and the collapse of religious fervor in the eighteenth century gave people more free time in which to enjoy themselves. Artists painted portraits of leisure scenes. The opening up of world markets for tobacco, tea, and coffee encouraged opportunities for relaxation. Houses and gardens were planned for enjoyment. While formal education languished, young aristocrats were sent on Grand Tours to improve their taste. The eighteenth century saw the beginning of such games as cricket. For the majority, living in villages with little education and a great deal of hard work, opportunities for leisure were limited.

The Industrial Revolution at the beginning of the nineteenth century coincided with the Evangelical Movement, another religious awakening. Industrial workers had less leisure than agricultural laborers, but the middle and upper classes had more varied opportunities and were anxious to escape from the cities. Walking, climbing, and bathing all became fashionable. Travel no longer became the prerogative of the rich. Above all, organized games were encouraged, especially in schools and universities, since religious leaders felt that these involved a virtuous use of leisure, encouraging unselfishness and team spirit as well as bodily health and strength.

Thomas Arnold (1795–1842), headmaster of Rugby, is usually credited with making sport an important part of the curriculum. Although Arnold was prominent in educational reform, and although his school gave its name to one variety of football, Arnold himself had little interest in sport. It was his successors who developed the cult of athleticism. This cult had inbuilt limitations. It was excessively masculine; girls could hardly participate. It was mainly British; Europe and the United States were less enslaved to sport in the curriculum. By organizing team sports and by implication downgrading music, painting, and other extracurricular activities as unmanly and individualistic, schools decreased rather than increased the amount of leisure time in which a student could develop individual tastes. Plato, who saw education as a means of developing good citizens, would have approved.

Plato too would have encouraged the participation in sport of all levels of society. But the poor were at a disadvantage in that they could not afford time off work to compete at the highest. Hence we have professionalism in sport and the paradox of people who work at leisure. In the late twentieth century we have other paradoxes. Unemployment has become a scourge almost as bad as the overwork that soured the lives of peasants and workers. Leisure has become a business in areas other than sport, although in Latin *business* (*negotium*) was defined as the negative of leisure (*otium*). Revolutions in technology have led to there being far more time for leisure and far more ways in which to enjoy leisure, and yet education for leisure appears to have gone into reverse. Most people in most countries measure educational success in terms of qualifications gained, of providing training for future careers, and of increasing individual or corporate wealth. In disrepute are Aristotelian notions of happiness, of education as an end in itself, of theoretical discussion as the highest virtue, and of working in order to enjoy leisure.

Tom Winnifrith

See also ARISTOTLE; PLATO

Bibliography

Barrett, C., and T. Winnifrith. *The Philosophy of Leisure*. London: Macmillan, 1989.
Huizinga, J. *Homo Ludens: A Study of the Play Element in Culture*. Translated by R. Hull. London: Routledge, 1949.
Pieper, J. *Leisure: The Basis of Culture*. Translated by A. Dru. London: Faber and Faber, 1952.

Liberal Education

Liberal education, or "liberal arts," refers to a long-standing and prominent form of education in the history of Western culture. Although the meaning of liberal education has been the object of much debate and disagreement during the twentieth century, an underlying historical and modern continuity can be ascertained in the connection between liberal education and a certain understanding of freedom.

Various historical periods, such as the later Middle Ages, have witnessed fierce debate over the meaning of liberal education. But there have also existed eras of consensus about the meaning of liberal education, such as between the fifth and tenth centuries when the curriculum of seven liberal arts (grammar, rhetoric, logic, arithmetic, geometry, music, astronomy) and the purpose of transmitting literacy, numeracy, and the cultural tradition prevailed. The modern discussion about liberal education has been characterized by disagreement and misunderstanding that began to appear in the mid eighteenth century, grew steadily during the nineteenth century, and became widespread by the beginning of the twentieth century. Thus, in 1908 Abraham Flexner concurred with the president of Cornell University in stating: "The college is without clear-cut notions of what a liberal education is and . . . this is not a local or special disability but a paralysis affecting every college of arts in America" (7). As a result, there currently exist a variety of descriptive definitions and normative judgments of liberal education in academic and popular discussion.

One of the most common definitions is that liberal education is undergraduate education that is not useful or vocational. This distinction applies particularly to vocations that do not require extensive educational preparation. The complexity of this apparently simple definition and its link to the origins of liberal education will be discussed below. Another common definition, which explicitly incorporates a normative judgment, lies in denoting liberal education, in effect, as good undergraduate education. This denotation reflects the depth of misunderstanding in modern debate because it tends to arise when discussants wish to establish consensus on the descriptive meaning of liberal education but have deep disagreements that are merely transposed to a debate over what kind of undergraduate education is good.

That denotation also reflects the pronounced tendency in modern discussion of liberal education to confuse or interweave descriptive definitions and normative judgments, a fact contributing to the general misunderstanding and disagreement over the topic. This interweaving is evident in regard to another prominent modern definition: that liberal education is a "classical" education. The meaning of "classics" in this regard has changed markedly over the past two centuries. What has remained constant is that the purpose of liberal education, understood in this way, is to induct students into the cultural tradition. This induction into

"the best which has been thought and said"— to use the often quoted phrase of Matthew Arnold (1822–1888)—is regarded quite favorably by some. Others initially agree with the descriptive meaning, but vehemently oppose the normative judgment of this induction into the cultural tradition. Such disagreement on normative grounds often leads the opponents to redefine liberal education, resulting in confusion over the nature and source of disagreement.

The confusing and interweaving of descriptive and normative senses appears in regard to another prominent modern definition: that liberal education is education associated with liberalism. This approach has not infrequently induced discussants to confound their definition and judgment of liberalism with that of a form of education that antedates liberalism. Intellectual historian Paul Kristeller provided insightful commentary on this point in a brief debate with Charles Frankel at Columbia University in 1975.

The interweaving of descriptive and normative senses appears as well in still another prominent modern definition: that liberal education is an education that liberates or frees. Although this denotation can be found in ancient, medieval, and early modern writings, it appeared with increasing frequency during the Enlightenment and became quite popular in the course of the nineteenth and twentieth centuries. This popularity attests to the modern approbation for liberation or freedom, while the continuity of this denotation throughout the tradition of liberal education demonstrates the ambiguity of liberation and freedom. For example, liberal education, understood by some as an education that liberates some from ignorance, is said to imply the prescription of studies, while others regard such prescription as the opposite of liberating education. In this fashion, contradiction or misunderstanding results even though discussants have agreed that liberal education means an education that liberates or frees. A debate in 1885 between James McCosh (1811–1894), president of the present Princeton University, and Charles W. Eliot (1834–1926), president of Harvard University, exemplifies the nature of such disagreement, which became commonplace in the twentieth century.

The modern popularity and historical continuity of this last definition suggest that there is a particularly strong and intimate connection between some notion of freedom, or liberation, and liberal education. The etymology of the term bears this out. Liberal education, or liberal arts, in English is the direct translation from Latin of *artes liberales*. This term was conventionally employed beginning at least as early as the first century B.C.when the first extant written reference to it appears in *On Discovery* of Marcus Tullius Cicero (106–43 B.C.). Cicero employs the term as though it were commonly used in his day, so it may be inferred that *artes liberales* was conventional by that time. The term itself appears to be derived from the Greek terms *technai eleutheriai, epistemai eleutheriai,* or close cognates that were employed by Greek writers of the fourth and third centuries B.C.

The adjectives *liberalis* in Latin and *eleutherios* in Greek mean "of the free person." When linked with *artes* in Latin, or *technai* or *epistemai* in Greek, the term literally signifies the arts or sciences of the free person, the education of the free person. In this way, liberal education can be seen by virtue of its etymological origins, historical continuity, and modern popularity to have a particularly close relationship with a notion of freedom. The original and the most historically and philosophically influential analysis of this relationship was put forward by Aristotle (384–322 B.C.) in *Politics* (1337b2–1338b3).

Aristotle begins by stating a series of conditions each of which makes a human pursuit or education "illiberal" (*aneleutherios*). The precise enumeration of these conditions is somewhat obscure, but four appear to be paramount. The first condition is when pursuits or studies deform or harm the body, mind, or soul, limiting the capacity of any of the three within its domain. This condition pertains, for example, to athletic games that brutalize or tend to injure the body, thereby preventing one from pursuing future athletic endeavor. Among Aristotle's contemporaries, boxing was often placed in this category, while some modern educators would categorize football in this way. In terms of academic studies, the condition may be found in indoctrination, which tends to prevent the mind from thinking autonomously or pursuing further intellectual investigation.

A second condition is when pursuits or education are undertaken in order to earn money. Here again Aristotle's rationale seems to be that such endeavors tend to prevent the body, mind, or soul from acting within its particular domain to its full capacity or as freely as it otherwise might. This is because earning money is the end to which the pursuits or education are the means, and earning money therefore guides and delimits the direction of the pursuit or education. Translated into modern curricular terms, this condition means that studying computer science in order to find a good job is illiberal. And playing football in college in order to become a professional is doubly illiberal: both because football tends to injure the body and because it is played ultimately not for the enjoyment or for physical development, but for gain. It is worth noting that some modern observers have interpreted this condition as revealing the "class bias" of Aristotle or liberal education. But this condition does not necessarily imply that liberal education is only for the wealthy. Aristotle's essential claim is that the purpose of making money introduces a constraint upon the pursuit or education and thereby distinguishes it from the kind he is talking about and calling "liberal."

The third condition is concentrating upon or specializing in a pursuit or a study with the goal of attaining perfection. Here, too, the rationale is that concentration or specialization introduces a purpose that tends to constrain or prevent the body, mind, or soul from acting within its particular domain as freely as it otherwise might. Hence, studying for a Ph.D. in computer science appears to be doubly illiberal: both because it is a credential sought for getting a job and because it is a specialized study. Furthermore, pursuits or education conventionally regarded as liberal may become illiberal by virtue of this third condition. Whereas one may study Shakespeare in a literature course without deforming the mind or trying to earn money, this study may become illiberal if it is part of a concentrated study of Shakespeare undertaken with the intent of mastering the subject, as in a Ph.D. course.

The fourth condition is when a human pursuit or education is undertaken for the sake of others—that is, in order to please or to obey others. Thus, studying computer science because one's parents told one to, makes this study illiberal, quite apart from trying to make money or specializing in the subject. Once again, the rationale here is that constraints or purposes that tend to prevent the body, soul, or mind, from acting to its full capacity within its particular domain, or as freely as it otherwise might, make a human pursuit or education illiberal.

This rationale, as implied throughout the discussion above, provides the common foundation for each of these four conditions of illiberality; it also explains the association between liberal education and freedom. Each of these four conditions refers to a limitation or constraint that prevents a human pursuit or education from being engaged in for its own sake—that is, from being its own end. The pursuit or education becomes a means to another end. Consequently, the serving as a means to another end is a general characteristic that makes a pursuit or education illiberal in Aristotle's view, and these four conditions are specific expressions of that characteristic. The useful—serving as a means to another end—is opposite to the liberal, and Aristotle virtually states as much. But he also notes that subjects conventionally considered useful may become liberal, and vice versa, although some pursuits and studies, such as boxing or indoctrination, appear to be intrinsically illiberal. Nevertheless, what fundamentally matters is the purpose for which the pursuit or education is undertaken. Computer science has often been studied illiberally, but it becomes a liberal study if pursued for its own sake and not for the sake of earning money, of becoming expert, or of obeying one's parents, and not at the expense of one's physical or mental health.

Now, if "illiberal" refers to the limiting, constraining, or preventing of a human pursuit or education from being its own end—that is, from being pursued for its own sake—then "liberal" refers to the absence of such limitations or constraints. In a liberal pursuit or study, one is free to pursue the endeavor wherever it leads, without being constrained or guided in a particular direction by an inducement or barrier external to that pursuit or study. Here is the reasoned explanation for the pervasive link between freedom and liberal education that is reflected in etymology, historical tradition, and modern debate. A pursuit or education is liberal if it is engaged in freely, for the sake of its intrinsic appeal, and not out of external constraint or inducement. A pursuit or education is liberal if it is engaged in by one who is free.

This reasoned association between freedom and liberal education is then elaborated by Aristotle in *Politics* (1337b23-13383b3) in regard to leisure (*schole*). Here it is important to see that Aristotle carefully distinguishes leisure from relaxation and from play or amusement. Relaxation and amusement are conventionally regarded as "free time," but in fact they have the purposes of rest and refreshment in order that one may return to work. Thus, relaxation and amusement have an end beyond themselves.

Leisure, by contrast, refers to free time that is unconditionally free, which is to say that there is no higher end or purpose that is being served during this time. What is done during unconditionally free time is not constrained or limited by serving a further end. Consequently, what one chooses to do during such time, leisure, indicates what one thinks is intrinsically worth doing and most worth doing in its own terms. Therefore, the choice of what to do during leisure time indicates one's view about what is most worth doing and about the ultimate purpose of life. This reasoning leads Aristotle to maintain that the choice of what to do with leisure, or unconditionally free time, is the most difficult choice, because it requires one to decide what life is all about and what is most worth doing. By the same token, this difficulty applies to choices about liberal education, the education for one who is free.

Here then is the long-standing and general conceptual frame for liberal education that is evidenced by etymology, historical tradition, and modern discussion. Understanding this general frame does not, however, resolve the difficult choice about the specific content of liberal education. This choice depends upon one's estimate of human nature and may be a matter of disagreement. In fact, such disagreement has occurred periodically and vehemently throughout the history of Western education, as noted at the outset. The dispute has predominantly involved two opposing viewpoints.

On the one hand, a tradition extending from Plato (c. 427–347 B.C.) and Aristotle has tended to regard intellectual activity as the highest and most satisfying kind of human endeavor, and therefore has identified contemplation, reflection, and the scholarly search for truth with liberal education. The curricular implications of this tradition have been to view academic research and graduate study as the purest form of liberal education, with undergraduate logic and mathematics providing the foundation for that advanced study. Institutionally, this tradition has favored a university form of organization, which is reflected in Plato's Academy, the medieval *universitas,* and the modern research universities that achieved dominance in the nineteenth century.

On the other hand, an opposing tradition, extending from the rhetors Isocrates (436–338 B.C.) and Cicero, has regarded virtuous citizenship and leadership of the polity as the highest human endeavor and thus has interpreted liberal arts as the education appropriate to that endeavor. In curricular terms, this interpretation has produced an emphasis upon general knowledge with far less concern for the thoroughness and acuity that characterizes the more philosophical view. The arts of language and communication are stressed by the rhetors, in contrast to the arts of logic and mathematics emphasized by philosophers. Institutionally, the latter tradition has envisioned liberal education ending at about age twenty, whether in the Roman *scholae,* the Renaissance humanist colleges, or the modern liberal arts college. At that point, it is thought, the young person should join the polity and gain experience in citizenship and leadership.

Although there have been intense confrontations between these two historical traditions of the education for the free person, the latter has predominated in the understanding of liberal education for longer periods of time. During intermittent, briefer eras, the more philosophical tradition has been predominant. One such brief era is the modern epoch, because the ascendance of the research university in the course of the nineteenth century, especially in the United States, has resulted in the philosophical interpretation of liberal education becoming normative over the past century.

Nevertheless, a great deal of debate and disagreement has accompanied this development, for the rhetorical tradition of liberal education has not easily been displaced. In addition, the closing decades of the twentieth century have seen a resurgence of academic and popular interest in rhetoric, general education, citizenship, and the polity, and these topics have begun to reassert themselves in the curriculum. Thus, the confrontation and dispute between the two long-standing interpretations of the education for the free person appear to be reinvigorated at the close of the twentieth century.

Bruce A. Kimball

See also: ARISTOTLE; ARNOLD; CICERO; FREEDOM; LEISURE; LIBERALISM; RHETORIC

Bibliography

Actes du quatrieme Congres internationale de philosophie medievale. Arts Liberaux et philosophie au Moyen Age. Montreal: Instit d'Etudes Medievales, 1969.

Aristotle. *Complete Works of Aristotle: The Revised Oxford Translation.* Edited by J. Barnes. Princeton: Princeton University Press, 1984.

Flexner, Abraham. *The American College: A Criticism.* New York: Century, 1908.

Grafton, Anthony, and Lisa Jardine. *From Humanism to the Humanities: Education and the Liberal Arts in Fifteenth- and Sixteenth-Century Europe.* Cambridge: Harvard University Press, 1986.

Kimball, Bruce A. "The Historical and Cultural Dimensions of the Recent Reports on Undergraduate Education." *American Journal of Education* 96 (1988): 293–322.

———. *Orators and Philosophers: A History of the Idea of Liberal Education.* New York: Teachers College Press, 1986.

Oakley, Francis. *Community of Learning: The American College and the Liberal Arts Tradition.* New York: Oxford University Press, 1992.

Scaglione, Aldo. *The Liberal Arts and the Jesuit College System.* Philadelphia: 1986.

Wagner, David L., ed. *The Seven Liberal Arts in the Middle Ages.* Bloomington: Indiana University Press, 1983.

Liberalism

Political philosophies are best characterized by their enduring themes. Among the durable themes of liberalism are that human beings are equal as citizens and that citizens have rights that constrain the scope of government action. These rights include freedom of religion, freedom of speech and press, and privacy. In the United States they are expressed in that quintessential liberal document, the Bill of Rights. The idea that people have equal rights is expressed in the view that all citizens are entitled to the equal protection of the law, a view expressed by John Locke (1632–1704) in his Second Treatise of Government, and captured in the Fourteenth Amendment to the U.S. Constitution. Many modern liberals include among their list of rights certain welfare rights such as a right to housing, a minimal income, adequate health care, and education.

Other characteristic, but less universally shared, liberal doctrines include the notion that government rests on the consent of the governed, the view that tyranny is prevented by the separation and dispersion of power, and a support of market economics as that type of economics most consistent with liberal values. The liberal commitment to freedom is often expressed not only in a commitment to limited government, but also in such values as self-ownership, individual autonomy, and democratic decision-making.

Since liberals have recognized that a free, self-governing society presupposes an educated citizenry, they have been supporters of mass education, although some liberals have also been concerned with the potential of a government-operated school system to stifle diversity.

Liberals have seen public schools as instruments of equality, arguing that a free public education along with a nondiscriminatory employment market promotes equal opportunity. Liberals have also seen schools as places where children can become autonomous individuals and make autonomous choices among various conceptions of a good life. Liberals often promote educational reforms that seek to realize these ideals and employ them as standards by which to judge current practice.

Certain debates are characteristic within liberalism. One concerns how to distinguish between a private sphere and the legitimate domain of democratic authority. A second concerns the relationship between liberalism and capitalism. Historically, liberals viewed a right to private property as on a par with such rights as freedom of religion or freedom of speech. However, for more than a century, liberals have grown suspect of any absolute right of private property. They have noted the potential of capitalism to generate inequalities of wealth and power that are inconsistent with freedom and equality. Liberal educators have worried that training students for the jobs provided by the class structure of a capitalist economy is inconsistent with developing the capacity for democratic citizenry. Thus many contemporary liberals are supportive of governmental regulation of economic affairs toward the achievement of liberal ends. Most hold that it is permissible for government to use its power of taxation to redistribute wealth and to guarantee a basic level of support to all its citizens. Some are agnostic as to whether liberalism is more consistent with capitalism or socialism, and some incline toward socialism.

A final liberal tension is that between autonomy and pluralism. Many liberals have seen limited government as preventing the views of any one community from being made obligatory for others and as granting parents significant independence to educate their children apart from governmental interference. This interpretation is often taken by those who support the right of parents to provide their children with a religious education, and it may be presupposed by some views of multiculturalism as well. However, those liberals who emphasize autonomy may wish to limit the right of parents to dominate the outlook of their children and may see public education as a means of overcoming the parochialism of a child's parents and community. Put differently, liberalism can be construed as supportive of a kind of moral particularism consisting in the right of individuals and communities to self-determinism. However, its emphasis on such values as equal rights and autonomy promotes a universalizing ethic that may be in tension with this moral particularism.

Below the views of Locke, Jean-Jacques Rousseau (1712–1778), John Stuart Mill (1806–1873), and John Dewey (1859–1952) are discussed. These writers have been especially important to the development of liberalism. In each of the cases, three questions are addressed: (1) What are the central concerns of the theorist? (2) What are the theory's central doctrines? (3) What kinds of criticisms have been leveled against the theory?

Locke

John Locke wrote in England in the second part of the seventeenth century. Locke's era was characterized by two significant problems. First was the competition between various Christian sects for religious and political preeminence. The second was the struggle between Parliament and the monarchy. Two of Locke's central projects are to defend religious tolerance and to locate political sovereignty in the legislature. Locke deals with the first question in *A Letter Concerning Toleration*. There he argues that religious faith is not properly coerced; he argues for a doctrine of the separation of church and state in which religious groups have no right to use the power of the magistrate to enforce religious convictions, and for a conception of limited government where matters of faith are beyond the scope of secular authorities.

Locke's *Two Treatises of Government* contain an argument for the familiar doctrine that government rests on the consent of the governed. People, claims Locke, are naturally free and equal. Civil authority is created by a social contract in which people agree to submit to the authority of the legislature in exchange for the benefits, largely civic peace and security, of civil society. Nevertheless, people continue to have rights apart from government, in that government may not arbitrarily deprive them of life, liberty, or property.

Central to Locke's view is a doctrine of self-ownership. No one is a natural slave. People own themselves. Thus no one may claim authority over another without that person's consent.

Locke has often been criticized for his individualism, particularly as this is expressed in his image of people existing in a state of nature prior to civil society. This objection may, however, be misconceived. Locke's main point in his discussion of a state of nature is to claim that there is no natural authority. This argument is targeted against the pretensions of the monarchy to rule by nature and divine right. It is neither a sociological nor historical thesis.

Locke's claim that there is a right to private property may also be questioned. Even in the modern era, some liberals have argued that redistributive taxation is a form of slavery in which some are compelled to work for the benefit of others. Others, however, have argued that freedom and equality are best pursued by a government that protects individuals against the economic power of large corporations and secures for everyone basic economic rights. Today, while few liberals are socialists, there are also few who hold to an absolute right of private property.

Rousseau

Rousseau was born in Geneva in 1712. His principal writings include *The Social Contract,* a discussion on the nature of civil society, and *Emile,* a work on education. Rousseau, more than anyone else, is the philosopher of the French Revolution. His *Emile* is still an important source of ideas for the romantic tradition in education. His political writings represent an alternative to the dominant Lockean interpretation of liberalism.

A central theme of Rousseau's work is captured in the opening line of Chapter I of *The Social Contract:* "Man was born free, and he is everywhere in chains." Rousseau's philosophy is characterized by an idealization of man in the "state of nature" and by the conviction that society is the source of inequality and of every other form of evil. Rousseau's *Emile* thus attempts to describe an education according to nature in which Emile's natural tendencies are allowed to develop apart from the corrupting influence of society.

The concern of *The Social Contract* is to inquire whether there is a form of government that preserves man's natural freedom, equality, and goodness. The problem is to discover a form of association that "will defend the person and goods of each member with the collective force of all" but in which each "obeys no one but himself, and remains as free as before."

Rousseau's solution to this problem is a republic in which each individual cedes his rights unconditionally to the community. Each person thus becomes subordinate to the general will, and, should the general will conflict with someone's individual will, the individual will can be coerced. Rousseau characterizes this as being compelled to be free. People are considered free in Rousseau's republic because they are subject to the individual will of no one individual. Each "gains the same rights as others gain over him." They are free also because they are lawgivers to themselves. The right to make law is not transferred to any sovereign, but is retained by the people.

Rousseau's republic is thus a far more robust civic community than the loose association of individuals that characterizes Locke's civil society. Rousseau's social contract constitutes more than an association. It constitutes a people. Some authors have claimed that Rousseau gives more weight to the liberties of the ancients, equal political liberties in service to the values of public life, than to the liberties of the moderns, such as freedom of thought and conscience. Rousseau's commitment to the importance of the role of citizen in his republic leads to a heightened concern for a social and educational system that cultivates the civic virtues. Thus, in Rousseau the liberal commitments to freedom and equality take a much different form than in Locke.

Rousseau's vision of an education according to nature may be naive in its assumption about the essential goodness of human nature and neglectful of the extent to which human beings are socially constituted. Also, Rousseau's vision of civil society seems authoritarian. It has little room for pluralism and little protection for the individual against the government. It legitimates coercion in the name of the general will.

Mill

John Stuart Mill's classic work, *On Liberty,* was published in 1859. Mill takes the existence of democratic sovereignty for granted. Moreover, he rejects any appeal to natural rights in favor of utilitarianism, the greatest good for the greatest number. Mill's concern is with the tyranny of the majority and the tendency to uniformity and mediocrity inherent in democratic societies. He emphasizes developing a doctrine that distinguishes the proper sphere of governmental or social authority from the private sphere. His central doctrine is his principle of liberty, which holds that the sole justification for governmental interference in the affairs of an individual is to prevent harm to others. Mill also argues for freedom of opinion, holding that truth is best sought in a marketplace of ideas characterized by open criticism and debate, and he argues for the wide scope for individuality.

Mill is also an early advocate of what are now called voucher plans. He argues that government ought to pay for education and may compel parents to provide it for their children, but, since government-operated schools promote majority views and conformity, governments should not operate schools.

Like most liberals, Mill can be criticized for promoting a form of individualism that dissolves the fabric of community. Other critics claim that his principle of liberty is too vague to successfully distinguish a public from a private sphere. Mill's utilitarianism is sometimes criticized by arguing that the greatest good for the greatest number permits individual rights to be violated to promote the average good. Finally the marketplace of ideas is sometimes criticized for being open largely to the voices of social elites with the power and resources to make themselves heard, but not to oppressed and dominated people.

Dewey

John Dewey wrote principally in the first half of the twentieth century. His era saw the rise of Marxism and socialism as political forces, two world wars, and the Great Depression. His concern was to interpret liberalism for industrialized societies.

A dominant theme of Dewey's philosophy was the centrality of science and the scientific method to democracy. He sought to promote democracy not just as a form of government, but also as a way of life in which citizens brought the problem-solving potential of the scientific method to bear on their common problems. Dewey's pedagogy thus emphasized problem solving using the scientific method. The central aim of education and society was to promote growth.

Dewey was a persistent critic of the class structure of capitalism. By locating control over production in the capitalist class, capitalism separates thinking and acting. Educationally this separation of thought and action results in a curriculum in which some are educated in subject matters divorced from the affairs of real life, and others are merely trained. Dewey was a persistent opponent of educational dualisms rooted in any separation of thought and action.

Dewey retained liberalism's emphasis on free inquiry. Free inquiry is essential to the scientific and democratic spirit. However, he was a persistent critic of those strains in classical liberalism that he felt limited the capacity of people to grow and to engage in cooperative problem solving. He thus opposed liberalism's commitment to a right of private property, holding that its ultimate consequence was to deny democratic participation to the vast majority, and he criticized the excessive individualism of classical liberals.

Dewey was sometimes criticized for an excessive faith in science and in the scientific method. He may also be criticized for weakening the classical liberal's commitment to individual rights. Leftists sometimes criticized him for a view of social reform that emphasized teaching people to think scientifically over using schools more aggressively to promote a new social order. However, Dewey's emphasis on teaching thinking by teaching problem solving via the scientific method and his objections to educational practices that reflected a division between thought and action have had a durable impact on American education.

Post–WWII Interpretation

Liberalism in the post–World War II period is best represented by John Rawls, whose 1971 work, *A Theory of Justice,* has been central in the debates about liberalism for the two decades since its publication.

Rawls's view, which he terms *justice as fairness,* is a modern statement of a social contract theory. Rawls asks what principles of justice would be selected by rational, self-interested agents under conditions of impartiality. We are to imagine ourselves in an "original position," in which we do not know such things about ourselves as our race, social class, religion, or conception of a good life. Rawls argues that behind such a "veil of ignorance" rational individuals would choose principles of justice that made the least advantaged as well off as possible, since they might find themselves to be among the least advantaged. People would thus choose religious tolerance, because they might turn out to be members of a minority religion, and they would choose equal opportunity because they might be members of a minority group.

Rawls proposes two principles of justice. The first requires the greatest liberty consistent with an equal liberty for others. The second requires equal educational opportunity and careers open to talents (nondiscriminatory hiring). It also requires that inequalities in wealth must be to the advantage of those receiving the smaller share.

An important feature of this form of liberalism is the insistence that social arrangements be impartial or neutral between competing conceptions of the good life. This neutrality is usually seen as a broadened statement of the principles underlying religious toleration.

In his more recent formulations of justice as fairness, Rawls has represented justice as fairness as an "overlapping consensus" about politics between people who have different and incommensurable views of a good life. This understanding of liberalism rejects seeing it as the political application of a comprehensive philosophy such as pragmatism or utilitarianism. It results from applying liberal principles of tolerance even to these historically liberal positions. Rawls claims that liberalism has three crucial commitments. First, it is committed to a constitutional regime in which basic equal rights are protected. Second, such rights cannot be overridden either in the service of the average welfare or to promote some preferred conception of a good life. And, third, society supports a minimum level of welfare adequate to permit everyone to participate in this system of rights and opportunities.

This form of liberalism suggests certain educational doctrines. The idea of neutrality precludes public schools from favoring one religion or one view of a worthwhile life against others. Instead, a good education might prepare students to choose their own conception of a good life and provide a wide range of options to consider. Civic education in liberal schools would emphasize developing a strong sense of justice. Schools would provide equal opportunity, and any inequalities in resources would be justified in that they are to the advantage of the least advantaged.

Justice as fairness can be criticized in ways analogous to the criticisms of earlier forms of liberalism. Communitarians claim that it is excessively individualistic and that the doctrine of neutrality erodes community. Some feminists have juxtaposed an ethic of caring and relationships to an ethic of justice, arguing that liberalism is a male outlook. Leftists often argue that the doctrine of equal rights serves to cloak forms of domination that result from unequal wealth and power. Rawls has also been criticized by those within a Rousseauian tradition for being insufficiently interested in the development of strong democratic communities.

Summary and Responses to Criticisms

Liberalism promotes a civic ethic emphasizing freedom and equality. It characteristically institutionalizes these values in legal protection of various rights against government coercion, such as rights of free speech or freedom of religion, and in such notions as equal protection of the laws and equal opportunity. Modern liberalism has also generally advocated the support of a minimum standard of living sufficient to permit the meaningful exercise of these rights.

Criticisms of liberalism can be grouped into two main types. One line of criticism accuses liberalism of making impossible more robust, usually democratic, communities. This strain of criticism is expressed in such perspectives as Marxism, fascism, advocates of "strong democracy," civic republicanism, and communitarianism. The liberal response to such criticism is to claim that demands for "thicker" communities are inherently oppressive. Such communities can only represent the triumph of the views of some over the views of others about religion or about the nature of a good human life. They can be accomplished only by coercing dissenters.

The second line of criticism claims that liberalism privileges the interests and the views of some over others. Marxists, for example, claim that liberalism is the ideology of the ruling class, that it obfuscates domination and repression, and promotes the interests of the capitalist class. Some feminists have claimed that liberalisms's emphasis on such values as fairness and justice to the exclusion of caring and relationships marks it as male in character. Multiculturalists may accuse liberalism of being Eurocentric.

The liberal's response to such claims is complex. To the charge of inequality, liberals may argue that they seek equality under the law and equality of opportunity, but not equality of condition. Others, such as Rawls, may claim that liberalism requires society to guarantee sufficient resources so as to permit participation in the system of rights and opportunities. Some, such as Dewey, find socialism to be the economic system most consistent with liberalism.

To the claim that liberal views are male or Eurocentric, liberals may respond in two ways. Some such as Rawls have recently argued that liberalism is merely a political doctrine, not a comprehensive moral system. As such, it is the political view most consistent with a diversity of values and cultures. It is a competitor neither with caring nor with non-Western cultures. Liberals also argue that behind such criticisms lies an implicit appeal to liberal doctrines of tolerance and equality. Multiculturalists, for example, often seem to appeal to liberal conceptions of tolerance or impartiality in their arguments for cultural pluralism.

It also seems that few critics of liberalism wish to reject liberalism's legal expressions. Few, for example, seek the repeal of the Bill of Rights or the Fourteenth Amendment. To the extent that this is true, liberalism would seem to have had a significant impact on the political values even of its most vocal critics.

Kenneth A. Strike

See also CAPITALISM; CIVIC EDUCATION; DEMOCRACY; DEWEY; INDIVIDUALISM; JUSTICE; LOCKE; MARXISM; MILL; ROUSSEAU; SOCIALISM

Bibliography

Ackerman, Bruce. *Social Justice in the Liberal State*. New Haven and London: Yale University Press, 1980.
Dewey, John. *Democracy and Education*. New York: Macmillan, 1916.
———. *Liberalism and Social Action*. New York: Capricorn Books, 1963.
Locke, John. "A Letter Concerning Toleration." In *Great Books of the Western World*. Vol. 25, edited by Robert Maynard Hutchins, 1–22. Chicago: University of Chicago Press, 1955.
———. *Two Treatises of Government*. New York: Cambridge University Press, 1960.
Mill, J.S. *On Liberty*. Indianapolis, Ind.: Bobbs-Merrill, 1956.
Rawls, John. *A Theory of Justice*. Cambridge: Harvard University Press, 1971.
Rousseau, Jean-Jacques. *Emile*. Paris: J. Gillequin, 1911.
———. *The Social Contract*. Baltimore, Md: Penguin Books, 1968.
Strike, Kenneth A. *Educational Policy and the Just Society*. Urbana, Ill.: University of Illinois Press, 1982.

Literacy

Literacy is a question both of reading and writing skills and of the conditions of their production; that is, coding and decoding language cannot be separated from the who, where, how, and why of these practices. Since the meaning of literacy is not univocal but shifting and situated within specific historical and sociocultural contexts, any single definition of it is laden with significant ethical, social, and political implications.

According to literacy historians, for the past two centuries Western notions about the nature and importance of literacy have been deeply influenced by classical conceptions of the "well-educated man" and by liberal social theories concerning progress and schooling. The classical view sharply distinguished between the educated aristocratic elite and the "dispossessed" unlettered majority. Embracing a mimetic conceptual framework based on the textual tradition of the Christian Bible and Greek and Roman classics, this definition offered a conception of reading and writing as instrumental to the development of spiritual, aesthetic, and intellectual qualities. By contrast, the Progressive movement espoused a more interactionist approach, in which language was regarded as inseparable from socialization. In that view, literacy was removed from its everyday context and became equated with widespread public schooling, literacy instruction concentrating on cognitive development and self-expression. At the same time, in response to increased industrialization, a pragmatic notion of reading and writing, defined as "functional literacy," became similarly emphasized. Its aim was to develop specific reading and writing skills to meet the needs of an advanced technological society. This "scientized" literacy made claims of objectivity, neutrality, and validity across cultures and social contexts.

Within academic circles, literacy has traditionally been synonymous with the "alphabetization of the mind." This view devolved around the polarization of oral (nonliterate) and script or print (literate) societies and the search for certain intrinsic properties of literacy assumed to be independent of social and historical context. In his discussion of literacy as the major phenomenon demarcating Platonic from Homeric Greek culture, Eric A. Havelock (1963) posited that the fixed quality of script facilitated the recognition of inaccuracies and contradictions, thus resulting in the disengagement of the knowing subject from the object to be known. Such a distancing is deemed to foster rational, analytical, and critical modes of thought, abstract language use, categorization, a conceptual understanding of space and time, and to effect the separation of myth from history. In producing these higher-order skills, literacy becomes requisite to building an abstract and coherent theory of reality and to developing an integrated sense of self. The severing of subject from object as a measure of higher-order cognitive processes came to be perceived as indicative generally of the differences between oral and literate societies and their alternative modes of understanding and communication.

Recently, however, the above view of literacy has been criticized for its entrenchment within a rigid normativity, in which the self-actualization of the individual is sought in terms of an unproblematic ethos of intellectual, moral, spiritual aspiration to a full democratic life. According to Harvey Graff (1987), the presumption of a direct correlation between literacy skills and individual progress, mobility, liberty, social order, and socioeconomic development constitutes a "literacy myth." He and others have argued that such a definition of literacy masks the hegemony embedded in its practices: Certain characteristics of a writing culture are thus imputed to those who are literate—that is, to those who possess skills that are standardized, abstract, and largely schooled—while those possessing other verbal and epistemological competencies, particularly oral ones, are consigned to the category of "illiterate" or "nonliterate." When thought of in this way, literacy serves to preserve the status quo and maintain a social hierarchy.

Current research on language and culture has disputed any logical connection between literacy and its effects. Literacy is no longer seen as necessarily linear, progressive, or autonomous; nor is the mere possession of literacy skills automatically linked with what they were formerly thought to have achieved. Brian Street (1984) has constructed an "ideological model" of literacy, in which reading and writing are contextualized socially and culturally. Within this framework, researchers have challenged the dichotomization of literacy and orality predicated upon the presumed greater objectivity, precision, and complexity of writing, contending instead that characteristics of literacy and orality overlap and interweave. Similarly, the commensurability of schooling, literacy, and higher-order cognitive skills has been questioned. Sylvia Scribner and Michael Cole (1981) recognized that multiple meanings and varieties of literacy stem from different social practices within cultures, and that schooling provides a particular set of competencies. Shirley Brice Heath (1983) argued that the specific beliefs and behaviors of a community are related to and reinforce particular language experiences of communities. This acknowledgment of the sociocultural context of literacy is also emphasized by Scollon and Scollon (1981), who understand the relationship among writing, culture, identity, and worldview in terms of different forms of discourse as embodying "forms of consciousness." Thus alterations in patterns of language use signal changes in the ethnocultural identity of a group or individual. Hence, literacy becomes a term whose meaning is plural and ideologically contingent.

The notion of literacy as a neutral educational value has been repudiated by other literacy theorists such as Paulo Freire (1970), who asserted that a truly emancipatory literacy must stress the transformation of existing power relations within a specific sociohistorical setting in order to effect significant political change and to enable human agency. Within Freire's paradigm, literacy practices emanate from the concrete individual experiences of the oppressed as they seek to acknowledge the "writing of the world before the word." Henry Giroux (1983) extended this explicitly political dimension of literacy to include the struggle for the epistemological terrain upon which the complex intersections among knowledge, ideology, power, and identity are contested.

To define literacy within particular sociohistorical and cultural contexts, to recognize its embeddedness within distinct ideologies, is to conceive of it as both a technology for social change and a means of social control. This dual focus characterizes contemporary feminist, poststructuralist, and postcolonial perspectives on literacy, which attempt to re-envision the concept within a dialectic of accommodation and resistance to power structures.

Deanne Bogdan
Claudia Eppert

See also: COGNITIVE DEVELOPMENT; INTELLIGENCE; LIBERAL EDUCATION; PROGRESS, IDEA OF, AND PROGRESSIVE EDUCATION

Bibliography

Freire, Paulo. *Pedagogy of the Oppressed.* New York: Continuum, 1970.

Giroux, Henry. *Theory and Resistance: A Pedagogy of the Opposition.* South Hadley, Mass.: J.F. Bergin, 1983.

Goody, Jack. *The Domestication of the Savage Mind.* London: Cambridge University Press, 1977.

Graff, Harvey. *The Legacies of Literacy: Continuities and Contradictions in Western Culture and Society.* Indianapolis: Indiana University Press, 1987.

Havelock, Eric A. *Preface to Plato.* Cambridge: Belknap Press, 1963.

Heath, Shirley Brice. *Ways with Words: Language, Life, and Work in Communities and Classrooms.* Cambridge: Cambridge University Press, 1983.

Kintgen, Eugene R., Barry M. Kroll, and Mike Rose, eds. *Perspectives on Literacy.* Carbondale: Southern Illinois University Press, 1988.

Mitchell, Candace, and Kathleen Weiler, eds. *Rewriting Literacy.* Critical Studies in Education and Culture series. Edited by Henry A. Giroux and Paulo Freire. Toronto: Ontario Institute for Studies in Education Press, 1991.

Scollon, Ron, and Suzanne B.K. Scollon. *Narrative, Literacy, and Face in Interethnic Communication.* Norwood, N.J.: Ablex Press, 1981.

Scribner, Sylvia, and Michael Cole. *The Psychology of Literacy.* Cambridge: Harvard University Press, 1981.

Street, Brian V. *Literacy in Theory and Practice.* Cambridge: Cambridge University Press, 1984.

Stuckey, J. Elspeth. *The Violence of Literacy.* Portsmouth, N.H.: Boynton-Cook/Heinemann, 1991.

Locke, John (1632–1704)

English thinker, one of the main sources of the Enlightenment and of modern Western philosophy. His influence in theory of knowledge, political theory, theology, and education was extensive during the final decades of his life and has remained so ever since.

Although he believed the right kind of education to be the great humanizing factor, Locke was not sanguine about the ease of its achievement: It all depends on the educator, the process of education, and the willingness of those to be educated to become responsible for their own education. To be responsible for one's own education in effect means that one is responsible for one's own humanity, for becoming a person rather than a creature driven by unexamined fears and hopes, needs and desires. This doctrine of responsibility rests on a commitment to thoroughgoing individual autonomy. Insistence on individual autonomy kept Locke from becoming a naive proponent of the widespread eighteenth-century belief in progress resting on the presumed efficacy of social engineering.

When he published, during the last two decades of the seventeenth century, his writings were both lauded and vilified. Some enthusiastically praised his *Essay Concerning Human Understanding* (1689) as indicating the end of obscurantism, the beginning of the triumph of the "new science," and (in its "new logic") the proper method for educating one's children; others condemned it as leading to skepticism and atheism. Before it was published, his *Two Treatises of Government* (1689) was the intellectual justification for the "Glorious Revolution" (1688–1689) among those of its leaders who were privy to its principles. Published after the revolution, it was a call to renew the revolutionary effort that Locke believed to have stopped short of its intended radical aim, which was to create the conditions to allow all British citizens the freedom to realize their humanity to its fullest extent.

Locke published *Some Thoughts Concerning Education* in 1693, the period during which he had few expectations of amelioration of humanity's lot through political means. If he meant its publication as a new tactic to undercut the misguided ambitions of the politically powerful, there were early indications that he might be successful. It became a popular work, which saw its fifth English edition within twelve years and exerted its influence in much of Europe through translation into French (1695),

Dutch (1698), German (1708), Swedish (1709), and Italian (1735).

All of Locke's major theories are informed by the doctrine of human autonomy, a doctrine given shape through what Locke identifies as a person's fundamental characteristics, those of rationality and freedom; and in all these works he diagnoses the human condition as one that by and large prevents actualization of both characteristics. Since Locke took prejudice (accepting something on the authority of anything but one's own reason) and habit to be the main obstacles to the expression of reason and freedom, prejudice and habit—though part of every human being's life—become antihuman forces that bind one to superstition and tradition. Education can help overcome prejudice and create such habits as are conducive to ever fuller actualization of reason and freedom. In this sense, proper education, for Locke, is the great humanizing power.

The education in question is that of both children and adults. Adults need to be reeducated because, subject to prejudice from childhood on, they have firmly adopted as truths beliefs they never questioned and have formed patterns of behavior they don't recognize as unreflectively habitual. The child must be educated by a new kind of parent and tutor, the unprejudiced kind who knows both the use and abuse of habit. Proper education of children is primarily the subject-matter of *Some Thoughts Concerning Education*. Precepts for adult reeducation are scattered throughout the *Essay Concerning Human Understanding* and in what Locke wrote as a chapter of one of its later editions but was posthumously published as an independent work, *Of the Conduct of the Understanding* (1706). Locke's positions on the education of both adults and children must be considered, for if there are no reeducated adults there are no proper teachers for children.

In addition to those about rationality and freedom, two important doctrines at the basis of Locke's educational theory are, first, that all knowledge begins with experience, and, second, that at birth each human mind is a blank slate. These four doctrines together constitute the grounds for Locke's conclusion that by nature all human beings are equal: At birth, all are potentially rational and free; none bring along a store of inborn knowledge; all are subject to having their blank slate inscribed by the experiences that their context provides. Locke does believe in some inequalities from birth on:

There are natural differences in temperament, strength, and intelligence. But none of these legitimize a doctrine of natural social or political inequality, or require fundamentally different forms of education; and none precludes achievement of education's goal, that of autonomy or self-government.

This egalitarianism dictates that children of the poor as well as of the rich receive sufficient education to enable them to achieve personal autonomy. To make this possible for the poor, Locke proposed the establishment of "work schools." These were meant to be places in which children learned a trade (such as weaving) and in which the sale of the product would allow local governments to feed these children well and to hire teachers. The teachers were to be responsible not only for the trades of their "scholars," but also for a context conducive to literacy and to rational adoption of ethical, political, and religious precepts and practices.

For Locke's educational theory, there is a flip side to this idea of natural equality with its egalitarian repercussions. This is its implied notion of universal vulnerability. Children do not choose their parents, or the physical and cultural circumstances into which they are born, and so they cannot determine the nature of the context that will inevitably inscribe its experiences on their blank slates. But that is not the most important consideration. For whether we are born into a situation of economic, social, or political oppression, or into the milieu of the wealthy and powerful, the initial outcome in either case tends to be a new prejudiced being. When the children of the deprived see priest or king pass by, their parents force them to kneel or in some other way convey submission; once they reach the age when they might reflect on these acts, their experiences have habituated them to take these as "naturally" required. When the children of the powerful are old enough to be aware of the deference paid by the masses, their experiences have habituated them to expect nothing else and they take this homage as their "natural" right.

Young children do not even have a choice in the matter. They don't possess the criteria to judge what beliefs or actions are rationally warranted and comport with their natural freedom. One becomes aware of such criteria only through a particular exercise of freedom—namely, that of reflection (through introspection) on the way one's mind works during actual episodes of reasoning to true conclusions. Young children are not naturally given to introspection; the constant barrage of their context imposing itself on them through their sensuous experience tends to make them outward- rather than inward-looking. The wrong kind of education enhances this process, the right kind breaks it down. But for the latter to occur, there must be the right kind of educators. Such educators initially come on the scene through adult self-reeducation.

Adults need to reeducate themselves because, Locke believes, they have most likely in childhood been "principled." To "principle" children is to present them with beliefs and doctrines not for their examination but for their unquestioning acceptance. Those in power so principle their children through prejudice supported by self-interest, while those suppressed do so through superstition aided by the fear of loss of the little they possess. The process is one that leaves reason inactive and freedom undeveloped. Hence the outcome of wrong education is not personal autonomy but the unenlightened, still only potentially human being.

Life itself, however, militates against total lack of enlightenment and complete suppression of autonomy. Thus some adults (usually those naturally more "spirited") are led to question what they have accepted on faith, especially if they expand their experience through reading and travel. History may then reveal that kings were not always believed to possess God-decreed rights, and travel may confront them with Christians who believe Christ is bodily present in the Eucharist or with "heathen" countries whose people nevertheless keep their promises. To dogmas whose opposite they had perhaps never imagined (like those concerning the divine right of kings, the symbolic presence of Christ in the Eucharist, the necessity of a certain religion for the very possibility of social order) experience itself then gives its opposites. Reason begins to stir in the question, Which of these beliefs are true? Since it is not possible at one and the same time to accept contradictory beliefs, and since the truth of neither is obvious, acceptance of both can come to be suspended. Once that happens, a part of the slate inscribed by experience has been cleaned, prejudice is being overcome because habitual acceptance is broken, and self-reeducation has begun. Required now are the principles by which to discern truth from falsehood, and to build a new position.

Here Locke is much influenced by his French predecessor Rene Descartes (1596–

1650). For these principles, both turn to mathematics because of the simplicity of its subject matter, a simplicity that virtually precludes prejudice, superstition, and continuing error. What controversy could there be about "2 + 2 = 4" that may not be settled by rational demonstration? And if there were controversy, how would the demonstration of its truth proceed? One would begin by taking the conclusion, the concept "four," and breaking it down to its foundational component parts, the concepts "unity," "addition," and "equality." Each of these parts is simple; that is, none can be further broken down, none has been generated through combination of simpler parts. One aspect of being rational is the ability to "grasp" or "see" or "understand" such simple ideas. This is the ability to have intuitive knowledge. Such intuitive knowledge Locke holds to be infallible, and the items so known he believes to be self-evident. Self-evident items are clear and distinct—characteristics that then come to function as the criteria of all knowledge (see the entry on Descartes). In areas in which we are capable of certainty, all complex or deductive knowledge rests on intuitive knowledge. In arithmetic, the entire number series and its various permutations are generated through combining the foundational concepts of "unity," "addition," and "equality."

Locke's insistence on the importance of mathematics is not for the sake of making people mathematicians, but for the sake of actualizing their rationality. Once we have made our mathematical demonstrations, we can see through "reflection" on our procedures—that is, through introspection—how reason has gone about its business in establishing these truths. We then come to understand that we always begin with experiencing complexity; that we cannot understand these complexities as we initially experience them; that we must break them down ("decompose" or "analyze" them) into their component parts until no further breakdown is possible; that if, at this stage, the items are characterized by clarity and distinctness, we must then be able to have an intuitive grasp of them; and that on this foundational intuitive knowledge we can begin to develop clear and distinct complexity. The complex knowledge so developed may or may not coincide with the complexity from which we set out to begin with. If it does so coincide, the initially experienced complex item may be accepted as truth. If it does not, then it must be rejected as false, and the newly constituted complex item must take its place.

Once people become proficient in this activity, they can transfer it to any area in which general knowledge is attainable, particularly to ethics and politics. At work here is a specific form of Locke's egalitarianism—namely, his belief in the universality and uniformity of reason: All persons are defined by their rationality, and the reason of each works like that of all the others.

The importance of all of this for the reeducation of adults is profound. All knowledge begins with experience, and whatever we initially experience is complex. We cannot immediately know the truth of complex items and, as rational creatures, we may not accept or act upon that which we do not understand. Whatever parents or teachers may have told us, whatever social conventions priests or kings may have imposed, it must all be able to withstand the test of reason. That is, all persons must be able to reduce the beliefs that inform their culture's practice to clear and distinct simple elements and, out of these, must be able to reconstitute those beliefs. If this can be done, the beliefs are authorized by reason and the practices based on them worthy of acceptance. If it cannot be done, then the beliefs are shown up to be prejudices or superstitions, and the practices irrational, habitual behavior.

To the extent that one engages in this rational activity, one establishes oneself as a person, because this activity actualizes one's rationality and freedom. It is a process of reeducation the result of which is freedom from the prejudices and habits acquired during vulnerable childhood. In effect, the process consists in cleaning the slate inscribed by experience. In this sense education establishes one's humanity, as rational and free, and so it is the great humanizing factor. It is a humanity characterized by personal autonomy, for it is each person's own reason that judges the complexities experienced, and it is each person's own reason that authorizes or condemns the beliefs and practices of one's context.

If, through observing reason's procedures in mathematics, people apply these procedures to the beliefs that underlie the commonly accepted activities of their daily lives, they publicly establish themselves as autonomous beings. If they apply them to the realm of politics, they will come to see that in political theory the concept "individual" or "person" plays the foundational role occupied by "unity" in mathematics. From it, they will then develop the concepts of "property," "justice," "rights," and so on, and will relate them to demonstrate that rulers are given their power by autonomous persons who combine to form a sovereign people to which rulers are responsible. They will come to see that the power of rulers exists in order to preserve the people's life, liberty, and property. They will be free in mind and, if not in body, will recognize their right—their duty—to throw off the yoke of the rulers who believe they have absolute power over those they rule. What Locke's properly educated persons will never pronounce legitimate is an absolute master in the temporal realm. Here Locke's educated person anticipates half of the slogan of the French Revolution, which was to occur a century after Locke wrote his educational works: *ni maitre*.

Persons so educated are proper tutors for children. The word *tutor* should here be taken to include parents in their activity of bringing up their children as well as teachers charged with the formal process of education.

There are two precepts that these tutors must constantly observe. The first is that the one principle they may, and are obliged to, instill in children's minds is Never accept anything on someone else's authority. The second is that the only other principle they may, and are obliged, to inculcate is Adopt only such beliefs and activities as your own reason has sanctioned. In effect, these two principles are to become habits. Children must be trained to adopt a habitual attitude of distrust of whatever those around them would have them believe and do, and they must be trained to think for themselves. Acquiring the first of these habits will place children in the position to conduct what we met in discussing the adult's reeducation as the process of analysis. The second will constitute the complex process of reasoning that consists of both analysis and composition. Since the process of education has as its end the production of autonomous individuals, it is clear that Locke's basic problem now is How can habituation result in autonomy? In order to understand Locke's solution, several factors need to be considered.

The first of these is the role of parents, especially during the period in which children are still very young and incapable of reasoning. Parents then have a preparatory role to play, which is to make the efficacy of these two precepts possible. Human beings tend to be creatures of habit, and habitual behavior is established at a very early age. Parents are to see to it that no such behavior gets established. They must keep the child from anticipating recurring connections between particular experiences. As examples, if the child cries for food, asks for toys, or demands attention, food or toys or attention may occasionally be given at that time; but more often not, these should be forthcoming when the parent, not the child, deems the time right. And the right times will have to be varied so that the child does not come to expect a particular form of behavior always to elicit a particular response. The conditioning involved in this process is that which aims at the child's not becoming conditioned to be a creature of habit.

Second: As children grow older, their tutors must introduce them to mathematics, "not so much as to make them mathematicians, as to make them reasonable creatures." Here the parallel with adult reeducation begins to surface. In both cases, mathematics is the simplest area in which to practice the technique that will lead one initially never to accept as true whatever complexity one finds through daily experience, but to test it for truth through analysis and composition.

Third: Once a measure of proficiency has been reached in mathematics, children are ready to deal with real-life issues such as ethics and politics. This part of education may not become a matter of submission to a tutor's lecturing, or of memorization of case histories. Instead, they must be presented with particular cases; they must reason about them with their tutors, who will ask them what are the particular "foundations" for these cases, and whether, given these foundations, these are cases of proper behavior, of justice.

How does this process involving habituation lead to the emergence of an autonomous being rather than a creature of habit? Locke's answer includes various aspects. When children begin to gain proficiency in mathematics, they must be encouraged to reflect on the ways their reason works in solving mathematical problems. Practice in mathematics has, thus, two results: It makes children aware of the workings of their reason, and that very practice itself begins to make the process of reasoning one that is adopted habitually. In this process, it is the child's reason that becomes conscious of its own mode of operation. And since human beings are essentially rational beings, the process is one of the child's becoming self-conscious. At this stage, children can determine themselves to be guided by their own reason's principles in all affairs of life. If they follow that course, they opt for autonomous action and establish themselves as persons.

There is, however, nothing automatic about the success of this process of education. Children may be presented with examples conducive to reasoning but they cannot be forced to reason about them. Whether they will or not depends on their own free action. If they decide to reason, they can be encouraged to reflect on the process of reasoning, but whether they will do so is, again, an act of self-determination. Finally, if through reflection they become conscious of the principles of reasoning, it is still up to them whether or not they will apply these principles in their lives; it is up to them whether they in fact will establish themselves as autonomous individuals. Improper education does not totally preclude the emergence of autonomous action, nor does proper education guarantee it. All proper education can do is to help children actualize their humanity, to establish themselves as persons. In this respect, the education of the child becomes like that of the adult: In both cases it is in the end a matter of self-education. For Locke, no one can be made a person by another. In the end, we are all, if successful, self-made.

Peter A. Schouls

See also CIVIL DISOBEDIENCE; DESCARTES; EMPIRICISM; EQUALITY; EXPERIENCE; HUMAN NATURE; INDIVIDUALISM; PERSON; PROGRESS; REASON; REVOLUTION

Bibliography

Axtell, James L. *The Educational Writings of John Locke.* Cambridge: Cambridge University Press, 1968.

Locke, John. *An Essay Concerning Human Understanding.* Edited and with an introduction by Peter H. Nidditch. Oxford: Clarendon Press, 1975.

———. *Of the Conduct of the Understanding.* In *The Works of John Locke.* Vol. 3. London, 1823. Reprint. Aalen, 1963.

———. *Some Thoughts Concerning Education.* Edited and with an introduction by John W. and Jean S. Yolton. Oxford: Clarendon Press, 1989.

Schouls, Peter A. *Reasoned Freedom: John Locke and Enlightenment.* Ithaca and London: Cornell University Press, 1992.

Tarcov, Nathan. *Locke's Education for Liberty.* Chicago: Chicago University Press, 1984.

Logic

Logic has been seen as furnishing the structure of reason and as identifying the canons of correct inference. It has been variously seen as incorporating the laws of thought and as reflecting the norms of argument. It has been taken as the key to true metaphysics and has been viewed as no more than a formal calculus, a set of elements and rules whose applications are to be rigorously distinguished from the formal items themselves. Logic is traditionally seen as having been invented by the Greeks, although both Chinese and Indian logicians developed rich independent traditions, and thinkers from many cultures have discussed issues that the study of logic reflects.

Seen as furnishing the structure of reason, logic has been central to education wherever reasoning was taken as essential to learning. The view that logic is crucial to the developing rational capacities predates Plato (c. 427–347 B.C.) and extends until Jean Piaget (1896–1980) at least, whose developmental stages reflect abstract mental operations rooted in fundamental categories of judgment. Logic as the basis of correct inference has had a similarly rich history, including early attempts to codify such norms, as in Aristotle (384–322 B.C.), and extending to logic-driven theories of inquiry, as in John Dewey (1859–1952).

Although many early Greek thinkers such as Zeno of Elea (born c. 490 B.C.), Socrates (470–399 B.C.), and Protagoras (c. 490–c. 421 B.C.) created careful logical arguments, the credit for creating the first systematic logic is reserved for Aristotle. Aristotle's theory of syllogism, as presented in his *Prior Analytics,* is a "term logic"; that is, the salient level of analysis is that of terms within a proposition rather than propositions taken as a whole. The terms may be designated as subject (S) and predicate (P), as in the standard representation of the four categorical propositions: A, E, I, and O, upon which the theory of syllogism is based:

A: All S is P;

E: No S is P;

I: Some S is P;

O: Some S is not P.

The terms S and P are to be thought of as naming natural kinds, kinds of things that naturally exist in the world, as in "All dogs are canines."

In 1787, Immanuel Kant maintained that Aristotle's logic had "not been able to advance a single step, and is thus to all appearances a closed and completed body of doctrine" (*Critique of Pure Reason:* 17). Kant's estimation of the durability of logic reflected the tradition from Plato onward. Logic has been generally seen to embody timeless and necessary truths.

Logic was always associated with schools of higher learning: syllogism with Aristotle's pupils in the Lyceum, and proportional logic with the Stoics, who built on the ideas of the Megarian school (c. 430–c. 360 B.C.). It was taught in the universities at Paris and Oxford as early as the thirteenth century. The teaching of logic fell to the lower faculty of arts in the trivium: grammar, logic, and rhetoric. Medieval logic reflected the commentaries on ancient logic by Arab scholars such as Abu ibn Sina, known as Avicenna (980–1037) and Ibn Rushd, called Averroes (1126–1198), as well as scholastic philosophers such as Peter Abelard (1079–1142) and William of Ockham (c. 1285–1349), who developed the technical concepts, metaphysical assumptions, and rhetorical analyses found in the ancient texts. Scholastic philosophers discussed topics such as the supposition of terms: the analysis of syllogistic terms through the distinction between meaning and reference, later to become one of the major concerns of modern logicians, particularly, Gottlob Frege (1848–1935). Another area of concern was that of implication (*consequentia*), in which modern work in modal logic associated with C.I. Lewis (1883–1964) was foreshadowed.

The *interregnum*—lasting roughly from the middle of the fifteenth century until the revival of the study of logic by Gottfried Wilhelm Leibniz (1646–1716) on the Continent and Sir William Hamilton (1788–1856) in England—saw a renewed focus on logic as a practical concern of educated persons. The complex discussions of medieval logicians were simplified and logic was codified, facilitating its role within the core university curriculum. Manuals of logic replaced scholastic disputation; one of the most famous was the *Port Royal Logic* (1662) by Antoine Arnaud and Pierre Nicole. Among the contributors to the movement to simplify scholastic accounts of logic and to incorporate rhetorical elements within the teaching of logic were Lorenzo Valla (1407–1457) and Peter Ramus (1515–1572). Ramus was a critic of Aristotle who was extremely influential in education. His attempt to replace scholastic terminology and disputation with more ordinary language and rhetorical concerns was not readily accepted by many of his contemporaries, a situation that foreshadows the current debate on the role of informal logic, logic devoid of supporting mathematical elements, within contemporary logic instruction.

Psychologism, the analysis of logical relations in psychological terms, is characteristic of the *interregnum*. Rene Descartes (1596–1650) assimilated logical necessity to psychological certainty. John Locke (1632–1704) saw judgments as mental operations rather than as logical propositions. The faculty of judgment was based upon reflection, the inner awareness of internal mental states that was the complement to sensation, the inner representation of external states. For Locke, the act of judgment reflected psychological correlates for logical categories such as identity and difference. The active operation of the mind in forming complex ideas reflects such traditional logical categories as mode, substance, and relation.

The work of Descartes and Locke set the stage for a three-hundred-year tradition in which logic was seen as an indication of the underlying structure of the intellect. This is best reflected in the work of Kant, who used the forms of logical judgment as a clue to the categories that he took to underlie all experience. It is evidenced in the work of contemporary experimental psychologists such as P.N. Johnson-Laird. Psychologism was attacked by Frege and is now considered to be a fundamental error in philosophical logic, confusing the "is" of psychological practice with the "ought" of normative inquiry. Recent studies have shown divergence between the empirical facts of actual reasoning and the norms of logic (Nisbett and Ross).

Kant not withstanding, syllogism does not offer a complete theory of logical inference. Construing the terms as naming natural kinds, as in the Aristotelian tradition, creates difficulties for arguments that refer to possibly nonexistent kinds, such as hypothetical entities. Modern logic construes the categorical propositions as statements about sets that may be empty. Based in the work of Augustus De Morgan (1806–1871) and George Boole (1815–1864), John Venn (1834–1923) offered an account of the standard categorical propositions that furnish the connection between logic, elementary set theory, and mathematics:

A: The set of things that are both S and not-P is empty.

E: The set of things that are both S and P is empty.

I: The set of things that are both S and P is not empty.

O: The set of things that are both S and not-P is not empty.

The later history of set theory and logic reflects the depth of this move; the two disciplines have been linked since then as the theoretical core supporting the understanding of reasoning of all sorts, particularly mathematical reasoning.

Logic extends beyond relations between terms or sets. The Stoics had developed the beginnings of a propositional logic: a logic that explores the relation between entire propositions, rather than between their terms, when they defined the hypothetical syllogism: If A then B, and if B then C, then if A then C.

Propositional logic was significantly advanced by philosophers including Charles Sanders Pierce (1839–1914) and Ludwig Wittgenstein (1889–1951) and by the development of truth table definitions of the connectives linking propositions. All propositional connectives can be reduced to one, for example "neither nor," which is defined in terms of a truth table for propositions "p" and "q" such that "neither p nor q is true" if and only if both p and q are false and in no other case. On the basis of this single connective we can define the standard connectives "not," "and," "or," and "if then." Propositional logic includes classic inference patterns such as:

If p and if p then q, modes ponens;

If not q, and if p then q, then not p, modes tollens;

If p or q and not p, then q, disjunctive syllogism.

The strength of propositional logic is not derived from the number of such inference patterns contained in it, although it contains all of them. Its strength is in the clarity of its basis and the depth of the understanding it affords. Propositional logic exhausts the logic capacity of all electronic computers; "nand-nor" logic gates embedded in chips permit propositional functions to be modeled in electrical circuits.

Propositional connectives reflect set-theoretical operations: "and" is identified with class produce and "or" with class union. In modern logic based on formal languages, the traditional quantifiers "all" and "some" are associated with conjunctions and disjunctions, respectively, across the domain of objects to which the constants of the formal language refer. The categorical propositions on this reading become:

A: For all x, if x is S then x is P;

E: For all x, if x is S then x is not P;

I: There is an x such that x is S and x is P;

O: There is an x such that x is S and x is not P.

Relations are defined as sets on the domain as well: unary relations (properties) are defined as sets of individuals; binary relations as sets of pairs; tertiary relations as sets of triples, and so on. If among the binary relations we include the relation of set membership and the identity relation, the result is first-order predicate logic with identity, the core of modern logic within which significant portions of mathematics may be defined and its rules of proof understood.

Predicate logic has other advantages as well. The argument John is taller than Peter, and Peter is taller than Paul, therefore John is taller than Paul, easily seen as valid in predicate logic, is neither demonstrably valid nor even expressible in syllogistic logic. One of the strengths of modern logic is the ease with which the logical structure of relations is made coherent, rendering suspect the metaphysical analyses of ordered relations such as space and time typical of Idealist philosophers such as F.H. Bradley (1846–1924).

Central to modern mathematical logic is the distinction between the syntax of the formal language and its semantics: possible interpretations of the formal language in mathematically well-defined models. The study of the relation between formal languages and their interpretations is associated with Alfred Tarski (b. 1902), reflecting studies of the foundations of mathematics by thinkers such as Frege and Giuseppe Peano (1858–1932). Logic, seen through the needs of mathematics, involves the issue of the size of the domains of mathematical entities such as the natural numbers which serve as models for formal languages. Mathematics requires infinite sets of objects, among them infinities that transcend the size of the natural numbers, as demonstrated by George Cantor (1848–1925). Exploring the size of the domains of mathematical models in which logic is complete—that is, where truth and provability coincide—has been one of the focuses of mathematical logic in the twentieth century, notably in the work of Thoralf Skolem (1887–1963) and Alonzo Church (b. 1903).

Logicians have extended modern logic in a number of nonmathematical dimensions as well. These include modal logic, the logic of possibility and necessity, a topic of concern to logicians from Aristotle onward; deontic logic, the logic of normative judgments; and epistemic logic, the logic of belief.

The philosophic tradition, for the most part, saw logic as certain. In logic, per se, the notion of certainty was associated with provability. This reflected discussions of necessity and other modalities within Aristotle, the medievals, and Leibniz, and looked forward to both demonstrable proofs within formal languages and to metaproofs in the style of mathematicians.

During the first three decades of the twentieth century, mathematicians and logicians attempted to show that mathematical proof could be reduced to logical proof, thereby offering the former the cogency that was seen as characterizing the latter. Bertrand Russell and Alfred North Whitehead's *Principia Mathematica* (1910–1913) furnished the foundation for the project to define a formal system that contained in its set of consequences all and only true mathematical statements. The foundation of the formal system was, however, problematic, as shown by a paradoxical construction discovered by Russell: the set whose members are nonmembers of itself.

The project, identified with David Hilbert (1862–1943), was seen to be deeply problematic as well. Kurt Gödel, in 1931, showed that if a formal system is powerful enough to contain number theory there are some statements expressible in it that are undecidable. Since these statements are, if true, unprovable, truth in a formal rendering of mathematics can not be reduced to provability. A corollary of Gödel's Theorem is that the consistency of a system can never be proved within the system itself.

These problems are not unrelated to perennial problems in logic such as the Paradox of the Liar: "One of themselves, even a prophet of their own, said, The Cretans are always liars, evil beasts, slow bellies. This witness is true" (King James Bible, Epistle of St. Paul 1:12–13). The problem of such self-referential paradoxes is exhibited by the following sentence: The sentence that you are now reading is false.

Mathematical logic has had little direct impact on education compared with traditional logic, which through the theory of syllogism or in more complex rhetorical and argumentational guises has always had a central place in higher education. Logic courses in universities today generally include some aspects of modern logic. This was facilitated by the development of systems of natural deduction, as in the work of Gerhard Gentzen (1909–1945). These replace axiom-based representations with logical transformations based on simple and definable steps that reflect plausible and easily mastered strategies of argumentation. Natural deduction systems became the mechanism for teaching logic to college undergraduates in courses throughout the United States and elsewhere.

In recent years, logic courses have exhibited a greater concern for arguments in natural language and a reemphasis on the fallacies of argumentation drawn from the rhetorical tradition. Such courses are called informal logic courses to distinguish them from standard logic courses, which rely on some combination of natural deduction, canonical representations of traditional logic, and elementary set theory. Logic courses frequently include elements of inductive reasoning and the logic of scientific inquiry, frequently based on the work of John Stuart Mill (1806–1873).

Courses in critical thinking, which had often reflected compendia of elementary logic, rhetoric, and the philosophy of language such as Monroe Beardsley's *Practical Logic* (1950) or Max Black's *Critical Thinking* (1946), increasingly rely on informal logic in place of formal logic. Critical thinking approaches have been modified for use in primary and secondary school settings by contemporary philosophers such as Robert Ennis, Matthew Lipman, and Richard Paul.

Mark Weinstein

See also ARISTOTLE; ARNAULD; AVERROES; AVICENNA; CRITICAL THINKING; DESCARTES; KANT; LOCKE; MILL; RHETORIC

Bibliography
Agazzi, Evancro. *Modern Logic: A Survey.* Dordrecht: Reidel, 1981.
Beardsley, Monroe. *Practical Logic.* New York: Prentice-Hall, 1950.
Black, Max. *Critical Thinking.* New York: Prentice-Hall, 1946.
Bochenski, I.M. *History of Formal Logic.* Translated and edited by Ivo Thomas. Notre Dame, Ind.: University of Notre Dame Press, 1961.
Copi, Irving M. *Introduction to Logic.* 7th ed. New York: Macmillan, 1986.
Edwards, Paul, ed. *The Encyclopedia of Philosophy*, vols. 3–4; 5–6. New York: Macmillan, 1967.
Fraassen, Bas van. *Formal Logic and Semantics.* New York: Macmillan, 1971.
Haack, Susan. *The Philosophy of Logics.* Cambridge: Cambridge University Press, 1978.
Kant, Immanuel. *Critique of Pure Reason.* Translated by Norman Kemp Smith. New York: Macmillan, 1965.
Nisbett, Richard E., and Lee Ross. *Human Inference.* Englewood Cliffs, N.J.: Prentice Hall, 1980.
Quine, W.V.O. *Methods of Logic.* 3rd. ed. New York: Holt, 1972.

Love

Some prominent thinkers believe that the history of culture has to a large extent been written by the emergence and development of a fundamental set of ideas. By that reckoning, the history of the world is to no small extent a history of ideas. In the history of ideas, no idea looms larger than the concept of love. The idea of love has been central to the explanations of a wide range of phenomena including wisdom, madness, philosophy, art, the bonds of society, the essence of humanity, and our highest obligations.

Philosophers since G.W.F. Hegel (1770–1831) have recognized that ideas do not exist outside of time. Like languages, ideas evolve. The notion that the contemporary English term "love" calls to mind is quite different from, say, the ancient Greek conception of *eros,* and yet the Greek idea of love is, as it were, embedded in our own.

Plato (c. 427–347 B.C.) was arguably the greatest theoretician of love (eros). In his dramatic dialogues the *Symposium* and the *Phaedrus, eros* is depicted as both a desire and life force. This desire takes many forms, but, whether or not the lover recognizes it, *eros* is ultimately a longing to possess the Beautiful and the Good. Depending upon our stage of development, we see Beauty and Goodness in different objects. Thus the sensualist and the philosopher are both driven by the same desire, it is just that one glimpses Goodness and Beauty in the human body and the other in philosophical truth.

In both the *Republic* and the *Laws,* Plato unfolds his views on education. In his account, the practice of dialectics should be the core of any curriculum intended to develop leaders. Dialectics is a process whereby two or more individuals critically examine their philosophical views together. But note well that, for Plato, this process of examination, which many people find quite threatening, is one best practiced when there is love between the truth-seekers. Thus, for Plato, love provides both the impetus and the context for the process of education.

Though the term *eros* had strong sexual overtones for the Greeks, it was still a word that could be and was used to refer to a desire for impersonal objects of love, such as truth. The ancients had access to another more personal and less egocentric concept of love, marked by the term *philia,* which is best translated as "friendship" or "fondness." Aristotle (384–322 B.C.) described *philia* as "wishing for anyone the things which we believe to be good, for his sake but not for our own" (*Rhetoric*: II, 4). Unlike *eros, philia* imbues the idea of love with qualities involving others.

In his *Metaphysics,* Aristotle argued that the Prime Mover, which is essentially the pure activity of thinking about thinking, moves the universe as an object of love. Aristotle is, however, careful to add that the Prime Mover can in no way love or even think about either the cosmos or its denizens, for the cosmos is an imperfect object of thought. Thus for Aristotle love is, among other things, an axial cosmological principle. Aristotle's ruminations on the Prime Mover had an immense impact upon Christian theology.

The Christian concept of love, or, as it appears in the Greek of the New Testament, *agape,* combines aspects of *eros* and *philia* with the Hebraic idea of love. *Agape* is the term used to translate Jesus' commandment to love our neighbors as ourselves, and, then again, to love our enemies. In the New Testament, *agape* is used to describe, among other things, the essential, self-sacrificing nature of God, the highest obligation of humanity, and God's greatest gifts. In literature of every age, love is often depicted as a force that will sunder us from our senses and thus from truth. But in the New Testament increased understanding of the highest matters—that is, God—is intimately bound up with an expanding capacity for love. Indeed, according to St. Augustine (354–430), one of the greatest Christian theologians, God extended his love to humanity precisely so that we would come to love and know Him.

With the Enlightenment, reflections on love became less theological and more psychological. The naturalist approach to love reaches fruition in the works of Sigmund Freud. Freud was a quintessentially modern thinker, and yet he resuscitates many aspects of the ancient Greek concept of love as *eros*. For Freud all love is the expression of sexual desire, which he termed "libido." Libido is a biologically based instinct. The accumulation of libido causes tension and anxiety and the release brings forth an experience of pleasure which, in combination with freedom from suffering, Freud identifies with happiness. Like *eros*, libido is plastic in the objects it can take and in the activities in which it can be released. The theories of Freudian revisionists notwithstanding, the concept of libido is foundational in Freudian psychology. For Freud it is libido or love that drives us out of ourselves and forms the mortar of society. It is also central to Freud's explanation of both the continuity and intensity of mental events.

The concept of sublimation is central to Freud's theory of education. Sublimation is the process whereby sexual drive or libido is released in socially acceptable, nonsexualized activities. Thus, the student who is able to engage in and so enjoy a creative writing class is sublimating sexual energies (love). For Freud, sublimation requires both the successful resolution of the Oedipal complex and the ego's use of the mechanism of repression.

It should be noted here that Freud and other naturalists are highly critical of the Christian claim that we ought to love everyone, nonpreferentially. According to Freud and other naturalists, such unrealistic edicts degrade the idea of love, for love is something precious that should be bestowed only upon people whom one values. Also, according to Freud, we have only a determinate quantity of love, and thus the only way that we could love everyone would be in a highly attenuated sense.

Gordon D. Marino

See also AUGUSTINE; FREUD; JESUS; PLATO

Bibliography
Aristotle. *Nicomachean Ethics, Metaphysics, Rhetoric.* In *Aristotle: Collected Works,* translated by J. Barnes. Oxford: Oxford University Press, 1984.
Freud, Sigmund. *Civilization and Its Discontents.* Translated by James Strachey. New York: W.W. Norton, 1961.
Nygren, Anders. *Agape and Eros.* Translated by Philip Watson. Chicago: University of Chicago Press, 1982.
Outka, Gene. *Agape: An Ethical Analysis.* New Haven: Yale University Press, 1972.
Plato. *Symposium, Phaedrus, Republic, Laws.* In *Plato: Dialogues,* 4th ed, edited by B. Jowett. Oxford: Oxford University Press, 1967.
Singer, I. *The Nature of Love.* Chicago: University of Chicago Press, 1984.

Luther, Martin (1483–1546)

Born in Eisleben of peasant ancestry, Martin Luther was the recipient of a strict upbringing under the rule of his father, a copper worker. Educated in his early years in the cathedral school at Magdeburg under the guidance of the Brethren of the Common Life, Luther subsequently studied liberal arts at Erfurt, where he was exposed to the influence of William of Ockham (c. 1290–c. 1349). Fulfilling a vow made during a thunderstorm, Luther entered the monastery in 1505.

In 1512 he was appointed to a lectureship on the Bible at Wittenberg. His conflict with the Papacy over the means of salvation began a few years later, around 1517. The conflict ultimately resulted in the Reformation, religious wars, social upheaval, and the emergence of a number of religions, collectively termed "Protestant."

The Roman Catholic Church held a dominant position in education, as well as in society at large, in Europe as the sixteenth century dawned. Consequently, the religious rupture that occurred as a result of the Reformation had major ramifications for all social institutions, including education.

In 1520 Luther penned three pamphlets that led to his excommunication by Pope Leo X. In one of them, "To the Christian Nobility of the German Nation Concerning the Reform of the Christian Estate," Luther asked the nobles for help in his struggle with the Papacy. The nobles' response ultimately led to a state church system and to an extension of the power of the princes in social matters, including education, in their territories. The letter reflected his position that civil government is empowered by divine authority to be the guardian of the intellectual, moral, and religious well-being of its citizens. Hence, the state's rulers are responsible for maintenance of law and order, and for the protection of the lives and property of their subjects. Overseeing the educational "system" in their territories became, then, one of their chief responsibilities.

This increased role of the secular authorities in the governance of schooling was due in considerable part to the removal—in Protestant lands—of the Papacy from such a role. Prior to the Reformation, the Catholic Church had held a prominent position in the control of education at all levels. The vacuum created by Luther's early successes led to his recommendation, based on ideological and pragmatic reasons, that civil government assume a leadership role in the conduct of schooling. His concern with growing social discord, especially the Anabaptist controversies, led to a second influential letter, published in 1524, and entitled "To the Councilmen of all Cities of Germany That They Establish and Maintain Christian Schools." In this letter, Luther took note of the disuse into which the former cathedral and conventual schools had fallen. Observing the failure of the people to be ready or willing to finance these schools voluntarily, and the inability of the Reformation churches to assume responsibility, Luther appealed to civil government to take the lead. It is fair to note that Luther was also concerned with the opposition to secular learning on the part of several leading reformers, such as Carlstadt and Munzer, and with the closing of the schools at Wittenberg for a year. The decision of fathers to refrain from sending their sons to school in order to have them work, thereby capitalizing on the opportunity to make money amid the rising tide of commercialism, frightened Luther. Accordingly, he begged his readers "in the name of God" not to take the "subject lightly." He called on the aldermen to provide appropriate schools for the young, for the sake of Christ and of society. The city councils were enjoined to accept this charge because parents either neglected their responsibility or were unqualified or unable to carry out the divine mandate of educating their offspring. Further, Luther averred, society needs an educated citizenry for its welfare and that of its citizens.

By 1524, Luther was contending with fellow reformers as well as with the Papacy. He strongly advocated, in opposition to some Reformers' positions, the study of Latin and the liberal arts, for spiritual and secular purposes. Libraries, in particular, received Luther's approbation. Books on the arts, law, medicine, and science, as well as theology, were to be housed therein. Learning, he maintained, was necessary for Christianity and the Scriptures, but also for civil order and the "proper regulation of households."

That Luther remained anxious about the state of education can be seen by his "Sermon on Keeping Children in School," written in 1530 while the important Diet of Augsburg was in session. Intended for preachers and pastors as a stimulus to them to carry out their God-given responsibility of admonishing their hearers on the importance of sending their children to school, the document called attention to parental negligence in this regard. Common people, Luther contended, were too often limiting their concern for their children to bodily wants, bypassing the important eternal and social aspects of having children schooled. The sermon contained a prediction of dire things to come, even to having the "pope restored to power," if children were not properly educated.

Luther's educational efforts, as one would expect from a religious reformer, included an array of writings and translations. Mention must first be made of his translations of the Bible into German, translations that were both popular and highly praised. Catechisms designed for religious instruction were penned in the late 1520s. One, known as the *Shorter Cathechis,* served as the basic textbook of religious instruction. It was a brief summary of the essential teachings of the Bible, and came into being as a result of the ignorance of both pastors and parents as to Christian teachings and training that Luther discovered in visiting churches in the late 1520s. Designed as an aid to instruction, not as a textbook for children, it followed the question and answer format.

The *Larger Catechism* elaborated on the basic teachings of its smaller relative. It, too,

was divided into five parts: (1) the Ten Commandments; (2) the Creed; (3) the Lord's Prayer; (4) the Sacrament of Baptism; and (5) the Sacrament of the Altar or Lord's Supper.

Aided considerably by his educational advisor, Philipp Melanchthon (1497–1560), Luther conceptualized and implemented a comprehensive system of schools. First, there were the "lower," or primary, schools, supported by compulsory attendance requirements, for boys and girls. These schools featured reading and grammar, and the Holy Scriptures. Planned to enable the masses to discharge their domestic, religious, and social duties, they were followed by the secondary schools, which enabled their graduates to pursue careers in either church or state. These in turn were succeeded by the universities, which contained the final preparations for learned vocations. Luther urged preservation of the arts and languages (Latin, Greek, and Hebrew), and exulted over the expulsion of much of Aristotle from the curriculum of higher education, because many of his writings were opposed to the "word of God." Dialectic, disputations, and canon law were also removed from Luther's course of study.

Teachers held an esteemed place in Luther's hierarchy of values; indeed, the dignity of the office approximated that of the preacher. Luther strongly urged that a man serve as a teacher before ordination to the ministry. Turning to pedagogy, Luther exhorted primary teachers to capitalize on the active natural inquisitiveness of children, calling on teachers to come down to the level of the children in their instruction. He followed his own advice on the subject, as is witnessed by his use of twenty woodcuts in the first edition of his *Shorter Catechism,* published in 1529. Recommending the use of "simplicity and repetition," Luther admonished teachers to see that their students were first familiar with the words of the text and then to teach their meaning, proceeding from the concrete to the abstract, from the simple to the complex. Finally, contending that it was only natural to emphasize religious instruction and make the "Scriptures prominent in schools of every grade," he called on parents not to send their children to institutions where that sentiment did not prevail.

Overall, Luther was a firm advocate of the importance of Christian education, from humanitarian, social, and domestic views as well as the eternal. Parents and civil rulers had the religious obligation to instruct first for the sake of God, then for secular pursuits. It was God's will that these human agents take their God-given mandate seriously.

There are, as would be expected, several dilemmas in Luther's educational teaching, caused to some extent by the ever-shifting events of the Reformation. For instance, the thrust of his 1530 sermon on keeping children in school reflected a shift from his early 1520s concern for the spread and understanding of the Gospel to ensuring the Reformation's survival. He was, in a sense, a humanist, yet the major mission of his primary schools was to teach doctrine through the Catechism. In this matter, one finds the divergent educational objectives of the Renaissance humanists (the pursuit of wisdom) and the Reformers (the drive to teach pure doctrine).

The social conflicts of the 1520s, in particular the Peasants' Revolt, tempered his early idealism. Parents, "bishops in their own homes" in the early years, evolved to a stage where he believed many of them could not be trusted with their new freedom. Civil government became ever more the guardian of the children's education; Luther ultimately supported the transfer of educational authority from voluntary to compulsory, from associative to institutional, as well as from private to public. Rulers were authorized, for example, to compel their subjects to memorize the Catechism; governments tightened the regulations pertaining to the support of schools when citizens failed to respond appropriately in a voluntary fashion.

There was, indeed, a paradox in Luther's educational program, one that should not be unexpected. His pedagogical thought rested on his image of man as a fallen sinner; yet he suggested permanence of and trust in human institutions. *In fine,* though, one must stand in awe in beholding his educational, as well as his other accomplishments, achieved in an era of severe social strife.

James W. Garrison
Thomas C. Hunt

See also CALVINISM; RELIGIOUS EDUCATION

Bibliography

Bainton, Roland H. *Here I Stand: A Life of Martin Luther.* New York: Mentor, 1950.

Bruce, Gustav M. *Luther as an Educator.* Westport, Conn.: Greenwood Press, 1979.

Kittelson, James M. "Luther the Educational Reformer." In *Luther and Learning,* edited by Marilyn J. Harran, 95–114. London: Associated University Presses, 1985.

Lohse, Bernhard. *Martin Luther: An Introduction to His Life and Work.* Philadelphia: Fortress Press, 1986.

Luther, Martin. *Luther's Works.* General Editors: Jaroslav Pelikan, vols. 1–30; Helmut T. Lehmann, vols. 31–55. St. Louis and Philadelphia, 1955–1976. "A Sermon on Keeping Children in School" (1530), vol. 46, 207–58. "To The Christian Nobility of the German Nation Concerning the Reform of the Christian Estate" (1520), vol. 44, 123–217. "To the Councilmen of All Cities in Germany That They Establish and Maintain Schools" (1524), vol. 45, 347–78.

Painter, F.V.N. *Luther on Education.* St. Louis: Concordia Publishing House, 1889.

Strauss, Gerald. *Luther's House of Learning.* Baltimore: Johns Hopkins University Press, 1978.

M

Macaulay, Catharine (1731–1791)

Historian, republican reformer, and educational and social theorist; an influential Whig historian of seventeenth-century England, eloquent opponent of aristocratic privilege, and pioneering advocate of coeducation. Her most important writings were *The History of England from the Accession of James I to that of the Brunswick Line* (1763–1783) and *Letters on Education* (1790), but she also published several other works on historical, political, and philosophical topics.

Catharine Sawbridge was one of four children born to John Sawbridge, a reclusive antimonarchist, and Elizabeth Wanley Sawbridge, who died in Catharine's infancy. Little is known of her upbringing, except that her father refused to provide his daughters with the tutors he granted his sons. She had access to his library, however, and developed there the love of classical history and passion for democratic political reforms that guided her in later life. She also formed a close attachment to her younger brother and political ally John Sawbridge, later a radical Whig alderman, lord mayor of London, and member of Parliament.

At twenty-nine, Catharine Sawbridge married George Macaulay, a member of the Scottish circle in London and a physician in his mid forties, who seems to have encouraged her work on her eight-volume *History of England, from the Accession of James I to That of the Brunswick Line*. The first of eight volumes appeared three years after they married, and the second three years later. Dr. Macaulay died in 1766, leaving Catharine to raise their one daughter. Between 1767 and 1771 she completed three more volumes of the *History* and began a series of radical pamphlets that in-

cluded *Loose Remarks on . . . Mr. Hobbes' Philosophical Rudiments of Government and Society* (1767) (against Hobbes's authoritarianism) and *Observations on a Pamphlet Entitled "Thoughts on the Cause of the Present Discontents"* (1770) (a critique of Edmund Burke's antireformism). Her characteristic blend of idealism and sharp sarcasm brought her much publicity, and contemporary political cartoons often posed "defenders of liberty" by volumes of Macaulay's *History*. In the 1770s, she moved for her health to Bath, where she continued her writing and met and corresponded with contemporary proponents of reform and revolution, among them the American patriots Benjamin Franklin, James Otis Warren and Mercy Otis Warren, and George and Martha Washington. After the American Revolution, she traveled to the United States in 1785 to gather material for a projected history of the Revolution and stayed with the Washingtons at Mt. Vernon.

Macaulay's opponents found a female intellectual and political reformer difficult to bear, and James Boswell recorded Samuel Johnson's dismissive remark in 1776: "She is better employed at her toilet than using her pen. It is better she should be reddening her own cheeks than blackening other people's character." In 1778 she married and retired to Berkshire with William Graham, a twenty-one-year-old surgeon's mate without rank or wealth; the union was a happy one, but her detractors claimed to find it scandalous. In the reactionary atmosphere of the post–French Revolutionary era, her writings fell into obscurity after her death in 1791. The year before, she had published *Letters on Education with Observations on Religious and Metaphysical Subjects* (1790), a three-part treatise on theology, the nature of an ideal society, and humanist education, which became her most reflective and comprehensive work.

In the first section of *Letters* Macaulay presents a model of education from infancy onward, with comments on the equality of the sexes, the proper social and physical environment for young people, and romantic love. Macaulay's work contributed substantially to an extended Enlightenment debate on education, and she took careful note of her predecessors, including John Locke (*Some Thoughts Concerning Education*, 1696), Jean-Jacques Rousseau (*Emile*, 1762), Madame de Genlis (*Adele et Theodore*, 1782), Francois Fenelon (*Traite de l'Education des Filles*, 1687), and Claude Helvetius (*De l'Homme, des ses facultes intellectuelles et de son education*). Like them, she discussed children's health, modes of reward and punishment, and ways to encourage intellectual curiosity and independence of character. She shared with Locke, Rousseau, and de Genlis the assumption that children should not be beaten, encouraged in luxury, or permitted to depend on servants, but her position mediated between Locke's training in self-discipline and Rousseau's laissez-faire "naturalism." With Locke, she emphasized the need to teach through personal example and to adapt curricula to children's temperaments, and the necessity of befriending and trusting them as rational beings. With Rousseau, she wished to limit meat-eating, teach compassion for animals, postpone religious discussion until later life, and warn pupils of the evils of the world, lest they suffer them without preparation. Locke's education was designed to produce a successful man, and Rousseau's a practical and happy one. Macaulay's was intended to nurture a virtuous and widely intelligent person.

Macaulay thought it would be desirable to have government-supported education, beginning with "public nurseries for infants of all ranks, where a perfect equality was preserved in all the regulations which affect the health and well being of the race," but she feared that existing governments would use public education to control and indoctrinate. She placed great emphasis on the need for physical health, an emphasis shared by Locke, Rousseau, and de Genlis, and one that was desperately needed in eighteenth-century Britain. Like most others who surveyed the field, she condemned virtually all of the literature written for children, and she reserved special venom for the "virtue is the

path to success" genre and plots that portray "the constant union of virtue with personal charms." She opposed the views of most contemporary educational theorists, including Helvetius and to a lesser extent Rousseau, that children should be taught to perform actions for extrinsic future rewards.

Like Fenelon, Locke, and Rousseau, Macaulay advocated a teaching method that would appeal to children's natural interests rather than impose authoritarian discipline, and one that sought to inculcate simplicity and clarity of speech. Her fervent emphasis on children's need for independence reflected an essentially political contempt for the weaknesses of aristocracy, and rationalism as well as compassion prompted her to warn against the common practice of terrorizing children: "Other means will be found to prevent [children] from running into mischief, than the trite caution of not doing this or that action, lest they should die and be put into a hole." She also wished children to appreciate the simple, everyday variations of life, and wanted them to respect a simple and nondoctrinal form of rational deism, exemplified through benevolent and ethical behavior. Above all, she advocated compassion for the real needs of humans and animals, and a latitudinarian tolerance for any traditions that exhibited simplicity, liberality, and good sense. Children who are kindly treated, she believed, are most likely to become kind in their turn.

Macaulay's greatest innovation, however, was her steadfast advocacy of women's full and equal education. Locke had held that women should engage in physical exercise but not receive a liberal education, and Rousseau denied them education of any sort. Macaulay, by contrast, outlined the first equitable system of education for both sexes. The sexes should not be separated, she believed, nor should their education be different; girls' feet should not be constrained in unnaturally tight shoes (an eighteenth-century practice), and boys as well as girls should learn manual skills such as needlework. She advocated physical exercise for both boys and girls, and noted that the diseases of adult women were often furthered by the rearing of middle-class girls to artificial delicacy and frailty. Like most women reformers, Macaulay, who believed that the ability to captivate and flatter men is ultimately degrading to women, was disgusted by affectations of weakness, and she commented with asperity on Edmund Burke's arch pronouncement in *The Origin of Our Ideas of the*

Sublime and the Beautiful (1756) that "we are more inclined to love those we despise."

Even more harmful than proscription of female physical vigor, Macaulay contended, was the virulent prejudice against women's intellectual development. She considered men physically stronger than women, but admitted no other differences of character or intellect between the sexes, for "knowledge is equally necessary to both sexes in the pursuit of happiness," and "all those vices and imperfections which have been generally regarded as inseparable from the female character, do not in any manner proceed from sexual causes, but are entirely the effects of situation and education."

The *Letters* strongly influenced Mary Wollstonecraft, who described Mrs. Macaulay in her 1792 *Vindication of the Rights of Woman* as "the woman of the greatest ability, undoubtedly, that this country has ever produced." Like Macaulay, Wollstonecraft opposed the charge that a learned education would distract women from other "duties," and criticized the practice of calling a vigorous mind "masculine." Both attacked the double standard that makes sexual behavior the sole criterion of female conduct, lacerated convention and social hypocrisy, and attacked the practice of keeping women in sexual ignorance. Both denounced women's civil disabilities, and quoted sardonically from the hostile pronouncements of chauvinist authors, a method since employed by many feminist critics.

At the end of her own polemic, *A Vindication*, Wollstonecraft expressed sorrow that Macaulay had been unable to live to read *A Vindication*, acknowledged the extensive nature of her debt to her, and observed that Macaulay "had been suffered to die without a sufficient respect being paid to her memory." But she hoped that "posterity, however, will be more just; and remember that Catharine Macaulay was an example of intellectual acquirements supposed to be incompatible with the weakness of her sex." Macaulay's contributions to British Enlightenment thought and political history have never been adequately appreciated, but recent feminist histories of education have acknowledged the striking originality of her arguments in the *Letters*.

Macaulay tended to slight more practical forms of education and disregard issues of social class, and later polemicists and reformers championed the cause of women's education and gender equality with greater rhetorical fervor, but

Macaulay's early insistence on coeducation and her categorical denial of innate sexual differences—both straightforward consequences of Enlightenment humanism— anticipated a wide range of "liberal" and "radical" positions, and her vision of a sexually egalitarian education was virtually unique in her time.

Florence Boos

See also FEMINISM; GIRLS AND WOMEN, EDUCATION OF; HELVETIUS; LOCKE; ROUSSEAU; WOLLSTONECRAFT

Bibliography

Boos, Florence. "Catharine Macaulay's *Letters on Education* (1790): An Early Feminist Polemic." *University of Michigan Papers in Women's Studies* 2.2 (1976): 64–78.

———, and William Boos. "Catharine Macaulay: Historian and Reformer." *International Journal of Women's Studies* 3.1 (1980): 49–65.

"Catharine Macaulay." *Dictionary of National Biography.* Vol. 12, 407–9.

Donnelly, Lucy Martin. "The Celebrated Mrs. Macaulay." *William and Mary Quarterly* 6 (1949): 173–207.

Macaulay, Catharine. *History of England, from the Accession of James I to That of the Brunswick Line.* Vols. 1–8 [1763–83].

———. *The History of England, from the Revolution to the Present Time, in a Series of Letters.* Vol. 1. Bath, 1778.

———. *Letters on Education with Observations on Religious and Metaphysical Subjects.* New York: Garland, 1974.

———. *Loose Remarks on Certain Positions to be Found in Mr. Hobbes' "Philosophical Rudiments of Government and Society"* [1767].

———. *Observations on the Reflections of the Right Hon. Edmund Burke on the Revolution in France, in a Letter to the Earl of Stanhope* [1790].

———. *A Treatise on the Immutability of Moral Truth.* London, 1783.

Schnorrenberg, Barbara. "Catharine Macaulay Graham: The Liberty of Luxury." *Studies on Voltaire and the Eighteenth Century* 303 (1992): 391–93.

———. "An Opportunity Missed: Catharine Macaulay on the Revolution of 1688." *Studies in Eighteenth Century Culture* 20 (1990): 231–40.

Staves, Susan. "The Liberty of a She-Subject of England: Rights Rhetoric and the Female Thucydides." *Cardozo Studies in Law and Literature* 1.2: 161–83.

Makarenko, Anton (1888–1939)

Anton Makarenko was an educator and author in the former Soviet Union in the 1920s and 1930s. He is best known for his work in dealing with a major problem facing Soviet society after the war and revolution—large numbers of orphaned, homeless, and often violent youth. One way in which the government attempted to deal with the threat posed by these juveniles was to set up youth colonies. Makarenko participated in this effort by first establishing the Gorky Colony in 1920 and later, in 1927, the Dzerzhinski Commune. What occurred at these two colonies is portrayed by Makarenko in *The Road to Life* and *Learning to Live*, popular novels that made him famous.

Makarenko's contribution may be looked at from two perspectives. First, as distinct from what happened at many other such settlements, Makarenko was able to achieve practical results and instill a sense of discipline and order into the chaotic lives of his charges. In addition, they found purpose in life through cooperative, constructive labor that included producing their own food as well as manufacturing items needed in the larger society. In his writing, Makarenko emphasizes the psychological changes that took place in the young people and how they eventually acquired an enthusiasm for work and an excitement in meeting challenges as a group.

Second, there evolved in Makarenko's thinking an idealized conception of society, education, and the family. This ideal focused on an interrelated network of "collective" bodies. Although Makarenko had not carefully studied Marxist philosophy and tended to be disdainful of "theoreticians," he was strongly critical of the "individualism" embedded in capitalist societies. In these contexts, Makarenko saw each person seeking as much freedom as possible from the control of others in order to gain private wealth and advantage. Motivated by greed and self-interest, each was in competition against the other with no sense of shared concern or mutual responsibility.

In contrast to this, Makarenko posited the idea of an organized community of "personalities" pursuing a clear and common objective—a "collective." Makarenko viewed the ideal family and school as the first collectives for the nurturing and upbringing of children. Education would center on the process of developing a spirit of collective life in preparation for participation in the interconnected collectives of socialist society. He saw his work at the Gorky Colony and the Dzerzhinski Commune as the development of experimental models that could set the stage for the eventual collectivization of society as a whole.

Makarenko had little use for the educational theory and psychology officially endorsed in the Soviet Union in the 1920s that stressed "child-centeredness" and the cultivation of the "interests" of the child. He was often in conflict with the educational authorities on this and other issues, but his views did come into official favor during the Stalinist era in the 1930s. The important thing for Makarenko was to discover the most effective techniques for absorbing a child into the collective whole. This meant that a child must not only conform to the collective will, but also develop a devotion to it and to the collective's mission. However, Makarenko did not think that this meant undermining or distorting the formation of human personality. For him, great tasks could be accomplished only through group effort, not by means of autonomous individuals freely charting their own paths in the world. Accordingly, being a participating member of a collective that was in the process of pursuing and achieving a particular goal would bring about the most substantial realization of a person's potential. Makarenko often spoke of the collective in aesthetic terms as an object of beauty, a kind of living organism in which the various components contributed to achieving its proper form. For this to occur, obedience to the collective was essential. Since the ultimate source of authority is to be found in the decisions of collective bodies, morality can have as its source only collective opinion. Challenges to this authority by appeal to independent criteria of right and wrong, personal conscience, or some higher authority would constitute deviance that had to be purged.

Makarenko criticized traditional Western ideas, such as the value placed on the autonomy of the individual and the importance of treating persons as ends rather than only as means. He also challenges us to reconsider how we should understand the relation between the individual and the group and the meaning of such concepts as "freedom," "authority," and "morality." These are among the areas where Makarenko met much opposition and where many Western (and non-Western) thinkers would find significant problems with his views and his picture of what society might become.

Bruce F. Baker

See also FREEDOM AND DETERMINISM; MARXISM; SOCIALISM

Bibliography

Bowen, James. *Soviet Education: Anton Makarenko and the Years of Experiment.* Madison: University of Wisconsin Press, 1962.

Goodman, W.L. *A.S. Makarenko, Russian Teacher.* London: Routledge and Kegan Paul, 1949.

Lilge, Frederic. *Anton Semyonovitch Makarenko: An Analysis of His Educational Ideas in the Context of Soviet Society.* Berkeley and Los Angeles: University of California Press, 1958.

Makarenko, A.S. *A Book for Parents.* Translated by Robert Daglish. Moscow: Foreign Language Publishing House, 1954.

———. *Learning to Live.* Translated by Ralph Parker. Moscow: Foreign Language Publishing House, 1953.

———. *Problems of Soviet School Education.* Edited by V. Aranksy and A. Pisunov. Translated by O. Shartse. Moscow: Progress Publishers, 1965.

———. *The Road to Life.* Translated by Ivy and Tatiana Litvinov. Moscow: Foreign Language Publishing House, 1955.

Mann, Horace (1796–1859)

American common school reformer, who believed that sending all children to state-regulated schools could both control and perfect society. Mann's faith in the power of schooling drove his work as the first secretary (superintendent) of the state board of education in Massachusetts (1837–1848), where he built the nation's first statewide common school system. As common school campaigns developed in every state and grew into one of the major social reform movements of the antebellum era, Mann's widely publicized speeches and writings shaped a nationwide ideology of educational reform.

Mann believed that the challenges posed by urbanization, immigration, and industrialization—historians call them the forces of modernization—demanded a concerted response. Something had to be done. As modernization changed the patterns of life in Mann's native Massachusetts and other Northeastern states, he could see these forces offering at once the blessings of progress and the curses of dislocation. Not just in Boston and New York City but in lesser cities and towns as well, crime and degradation seemed to be increasing along with economic development. The distance between rich and poor seemed to be widening. The traditional community controls that had worked well in small towns and rural areas appeared to be breaking down. Yes, something had to be done, Mann was convinced, and he set out to rally people to the task.

Over the course of his life, Mann championed a wide range of reforms, including temperance, prison and asylum reform, and abolition. As a graduate of Brown University, a lawyer, a state legislator and senator, and a member of the U.S. Congress, he had the background, opportunities, and connections to advance his causes in a variety of political arenas. Mann's campaign to establish common schools in Massachusetts was only one stage of his career, just as educational reform was but one movement in the mid-nineteenth-century cycle of social reform.

But Mann threw his greatest energies into educational reform, for he believed it to be the most fundamental. "Having found the present generation composed of materials almost unmalleable," he wrote, "I am about transferring my efforts to the next. Men are cast-iron; but children are wax."

Mann read educational reform into a Bible verse he first encountered as a youth reared in the Calvinist faith: "Train up a child in the way he should go: and when he is old, he will not depart from it" (Proverbs 22:6). Rejecting the fire and brimstone of Calvinism at an early age, he turned to Unitarianism as a more rational, humane faith. Calvinism left him intense and driven for life, Mann confessed, but Unitarianism allowed him to take an optimistic view of human progress.

Reinforcing Mann's religious faith was his belief in phrenology, a nineteenth-century behavioral psychology that divided the mind into thirty-seven different "faculties" (such as benevolence, aggressiveness, and self-esteem), each of which could be strengthened or weakened by the proper mental exercise. Under the influence of common schools, Mann believed, children could learn to control their "evil pas-

M

sions" and develop their "positive propensities" as they grew into adulthood. The people of an entire nation could gradually become more perfect, generation by generation.

These optimistic views were especially appealing to Americans whose backgrounds and attainments were similar to Mann's. Native-born, Protestant, economically successful Americans paid close attention to the Massachusetts school reformer, for many felt sure they were among the nation's most "nobly endowed," and many shared Mann's sense of obligation to help the less fortunate. From the standpoint of self-interest, people at Mann's level of society also had the most to gain or lose from modernization. Indeed, Mann's views offered reassurance to those with the greatest stake in maintaining the existing political and economic system, for Mann attributed poverty, crime, and other problems to ignorance rather than to anything inherently wrong with the system.

Mann spoke most persuasively to citizens who shared his belief in activist government that was willing to intervene to improve society. This view of the proper role of government was closely associated with the Whig Party, which held that the federal and state governments should involve themselves in local affairs to improve schools and other social institutions. The Democratic Party, by contrast, advocated less government rather than more, arguing that people should be free to make their local schools as good—or as bad—as they wished. Given these differences in political outlook, common school campaigns often divided Americans along traditional party lines, despite the insistence of Mann, a well-known Whig politician, that educational reform was nonpartisan.

The controversies that surrounded his efforts only made Mann more determined to refine his message and broaden its appeal to different constituencies. First in his speeches and then in his writings, Mann promised something to almost everyone. To those concerned with the political destiny of the nation, Mann presented common schooling as the only way to produce a literate electorate essential to republican government. To working people he held out common schools as the "balance wheel of the social machinery" and the "creator of wealth undreamed of." To those who already had wealth, Mann offered a stable society whose members respected one another's property rights. Business owners were promised reliable employees. People who worried that the nation might frag-

ment along economic, political, and religious lines, as was the case in Europe and Great Britain, heard that common schools would quell prejudice and promote unity. And so the rhetoric continued, until it came as no surprise that Mann unabashedly touted common schools as the "greatest discovery ever made by man."

But could the mere acquisition of academic knowledge and literacy skills transform people in all the ways Mann catalogued? Were reading, writing, arithmetic, and the other subjects really so powerful? Of course not, he replied. The ultimate power of schooling resided in moral and religious education, for the ultimate purpose of schooling was character training. Trying to persuade those who remained skeptical that schooling could do so much, Mann returned again and again to his central theme: common schooling as a means of moral uplift.

Children who went to common schools would emerge literate, to be sure, but far more important they would possess such character traits as honesty, respect for authority, and self-discipline. Such virtues would permeate the curriculum of common schools. The school day would begin with the reading of a passage from the King James Bible, "without note or comment." Moral lessons would flow from every subject. Teachers, carefully selected and professionally trained in normal schools, would exert loving discipline and serve as moral exemplars.

Morality and religion were closely linked in Mann's mind, as they were in the minds of most Americans during the first half of the nineteenth century. In the context of the times, morality without religion was no morality at all. But in an increasingly diverse nation, where Catholics, Jews, people of other non-Protestant faiths, and people of no religious faith were becoming more numerous every year, how could schools provide a common moral and religious education?

Mann believed the answer lay in removing specific religious doctrine from the schools while retaining a common, nonsectarian creed as the basis for moral education. The nonsectarian creed he had in mind, though, was not a distillation of principles from religions around the world. It was instead a broad, nondenominational rendition of the "precepts and the doctrines of the Christian religion." Who could object to such a foundation for moral education? Mann asked rhetorically.

As common schools became established in Massachusetts and other states, the question became more than rhetorical. Catholics registered the strongest protests, pointing out that Mann's nondenominational Christianity really amounted to nondenominational Protestantism. Catholic students who attended common schools had to endure textbooks filled with slurs against their faith, ridicule from Protestant teachers and students, and daily readings from a Bible translation significantly different from their own Douay version.

In state after state, Catholics withdrew into their own schools, even as legislatures withdrew financial support from Catholic and other religious schools. Mann regretted the loss of Catholic students, for many were immigrants or the children of immigrants—the very kind of children he thought needed character training the most. Still, Mann and other reformers watched with satisfaction as common schools triumphed.

Mann's major legacy is his conviction that a state institution, common schools, could usher in a better-controlled, more perfect society. Mann believed in common schooling as a panacea. He never doubted he was right. And although Mann's confidence in the power of schooling blinded him to its limitations, both his faith and his myopia have proven contagious. Successive generations of Americans have regarded public schools as the institution best equipped to solve whatever social problems seem pressing at the time, from assimilating immigrants to reducing unemployment to slowing the spread of AIDS.

As much as Mann believed in schooling, though, he also recognized other, often more direct ways to reform society. After he resigned his Massachusetts education post in 1848 to serve in the U.S. Congress, he refocused his energies on the abolition of slavery—a highly controversial cause that Mann had deliberately downplayed while he was active in school reform. As secretary of education, he had been unwilling to risk jeopardizing the common school campaign by appearing to be radical on the issue of race.

Yet on that very issue, Mann finally lost patience with the gradual process of reforming society by reforming schools. While saying goodbye to Massachusetts teachers in his *Common School Journal* (1848), he made a significant admission: Before people could be educated, they had to be free. Mann then went to Washington to fight the social evil of slavery head-on. His choice of a reform strategy more direct and more immediate than common schooling represents another side of Horace Mann's legacy.

Joseph W. Newman

See also Behaviorism; Human Nature; Moral Development; Progress, Idea of, and Progressive Education; Religious Education; Slavery

Bibliography

Church, Robert L., and Michael B. Sedlak. *Education in the United States: An Interpretive History.* New York: Free Press, 1976, chs. 3–4.

Cremin, Lawrence A. *The Republic and the School: Horace Mann on the Education of Free Men.* New York: Teachers College, Columbia University, 1957.

Curti, Merle. *The Social Ideas of American Educators.* New York: Charles Scribner's Sons, 1935, ch. 3.

Katz, Michael B. *The Irony of Early School Reform: Educational Innovation in Mid-Nineteenth-Century Massachusetts.* Cambridge, MA: Harvard University Press, 1968.

Mann, Horace. *Annual Report[s] of the Board of Education.* Boston: Wentworth and Dutton, 1838–1849.

———. *Lectures on Education.* Boston: Ide and Dutton, 1855. Mann also founded and edited the Massachusetts *Common School Journal.*

Messerli, Jonathan. *Horace Mann: A Biography.* New York: Knopf, 1972.

M

Marti-Perez, Jose (1853–1895)

Born in La Habana, Cuba. Early on he identified with the struggle for independence from Spain, became a vocal antiimperialist, and is revered as the "apostle" of Spanish American nationalism. By the age of sixteen he had served time in prison for his political activities. Banished to Spain, he was influenced by the philosophical works of Karl Krause (1781–1832) and received a doctorate from the University of Zaragoza. He served as pro-counsel for Uruguay in the United States. He worked as a journalist in Spain, France, and Venezuela, and he was a professor of literature in Guatemala before settling in New York City, where he spent most of his life.

Marti became the leader of the Cuban independence movement, organizing and recruiting Cuban exiles for an invasion. On May 18, 1895, speaking about the United States, he said, "I have lived inside the monster and know its entrails." He died the following day leading a charge against the Spanish at Dos Rios. A sculpture by Anna Vaughn Hyatt Huntington (1876–1973), possibly inspired by Esteban Valderrama's painting depicting this scene, can be found at the entrance to Central Park in New York City at Avenue of the Americas and Central Park South.

Marti wrote essays, plays, and poems in both Spanish and English. His style of writing was a precursor to the modernist movement, with a direct, simple, and concise prose that broke with the overwrought style of Hispanic literature. He interpreted the United States for Latino readers and put together the first Latino magazine for children, *La Edad de Oro (The Age of Gold)*, where his most famous poem, "Los Zapaticos de Rosa" (The Rose Colored Slippers), appeared. It is the story of a child's altruism and human kindness. His most famous essay is "Nuestra America" (Our America). In it he disparages learning that is not ethnically diverse and criticizes education that is alien. He states, "Our Greece must take priority over the Greece which is not ours. We need it more." From verses written by Marti, Joseito Fernandez later wrote the music to "Guantanamera" (Woman from Guantanamo), which became a folk music standard. In the poem, Marti writes, "I am a sincere man, from where the palm trees grow, who throws his lot in with the poor of the earth." The United States was the "Other America," a "harsh selfish civilization." He was anti-Eurocentric, yet deeply rooted in classical European and Euro-American literature, especially the writings of Ralph Waldo Emerson and Walt Whitman. He was both admirer and critic of education in the United States. Marti began his own school, "La Liga" (The League), near Cooper Union in New York City, where he taught Afro-Cuban tobacco workers while propagandizing for the independence movement of Cuba and Puerto Rico.

Marti's impact on the Cuban Revolution's educational system is pervasive, and his ideas are pursued by Cuban educational authorities nationally. Emphasis is on vocational training and the application of knowledge over rote learning. He advocated equal access for boys and girls, saying, "Education should be so common among women that the one who has it is not noticed nor does she notice it." He admired military training for youth as protection against imperialism and militarism, and he proposed that schooling include work in agriculture and adult education classes in the evenings and on weekends. Marti championed schools in the countryside and literacy training. He favored a ban on Roman Catholic teaching in the schools, and he became critical of U.S. racial attitudes and annexationist tendencies. There is a Center for Studies on Marti at the University of Havana.

Andres I. Perez y Mena

See also COLONIALISM AND POSTCOLONIALISM; DEMOCRACY; EMERSON; HOSTOS Y BONILLA; MULTICULTURALISM; REVOLUTION

Bibliography
Kirk, John M. *Jose Marti: Mentor of the Cuban Nation.* Tampa: University Presses of Florida, 1983.
Marti, Jose. *The America of Jose Marti.* Edited by Juan de Onis. New York: Noonday Press, 1954.
———. *Inside the Monster.* Edited by Philip S. Foner. New York: Monthly Review Press, 1975.
———. *Obras Completas.* Edited by Gonzalo de Quesada y Mirada. La Habana, Cuba: Tropico Edition, 1936–49.
———. *On Art and Literature.* Edited by Philip S. Foner. New York: Monthly Review Press, 1982.
———. *On Education.* Edited by Philip S. Foner. New York: Monthly Review Press, 1979.
———. *Our America.* Edited by Philip S. Foner. New York: Monthly Review Press, 1977.
Ripoll, Carlos. *Jose Marti, the United States and the Marxist Interpretation of Cuban History.* New Brunswick, N.J.: Transaction Publishers, 1984.
Santonvenia y. Echaide, Emeterio Santiago. *Lincoln in Marti: A Cuban View of Abraham Lincoln.* Chapel Hill: University of North Carolina Press, 1954.
Turton, Peter. *Jose Marti: Architect of Cuba's Freedom.* London: ZED Books, 1986.

Marx, Karl (1818–1883)

German philosopher, economist, social theorist, and radical political activist whose works influenced socialist and communist political movements throughout the world. Often writing in collaboration with Friedrich Engels (1820–1895), Marx helped create modern social theory. Despite the many criticisms and misunderstandings to which he has been subject, he remains one of a handful of intellectual personalities who—by his own work and by that of countless "Marxists" who have built on his ideas—have decisively affected politics and intellectual life over the last century.

Historical Materialism

Marx built on the heritage of German Idealist philosophy, which held that human nature is not individual and given in advance but a collective product, based in human activity and evolving over time. Marx distinguished himself philosophically when he added other critical elements to this philosophy. First, he separated the process of human self-becoming from any religious source, rejecting theology as a mystification of social pain. He also discarded Idealism's focus on mental processes, concentrating instead on collective human action.

Philosophically, Marx organized these intuitions into a comprehensive theory of human existence: historical materialism. Historical materialism claims that the "mode of production" is the central organizing force of every society and the most important determinant of historical change.

A mode of production consists first in forces of production: the tools and techniques used in interacting with nature to meet human material needs. A mode of production also includes "relations of production," the forms of human organization that shape our interaction with nature. The essential aspects of the relations of production can be identified by determining who owns or controls the forces of production, how the products are distributed, who controls the labor process, and who does the essential material labor.

The mode of production is the center of social life for a number of reasons, most importantly because it shapes class struggle and encompasses the development of the productive forces.

Marx believed that the mode of production naturally divides social life into antagonistic classes, groups determined by their position in relations of production, ownership, and control. In all but the most primitive societies, an exploited class performs the bulk of the productive labor; a ruling class controls or owns the forces of production, governs how much of the economic surplus will be distributed, or controls the process of production. Where a fundamental division of labor and social position exists, there arise essentially antagonistic interests. One's class position—structured by the mode of production—sets a multitude of conditions in one's life. Because of one's class, one has particular resources, choices, friends, expectations, and problems.

Class divisions also create class interests. Members of the ruling class have an interest in protecting and enhancing their superior power and their unearned wealth. The producing classes have an interest in lessening exploitation, increasing their power, and eventually overturning the system. Capitalists want to pay lower wages and get more labor from their employees. Workers want the opposite. Slaveowners want docile laborers and slaves want freedom. Class interests, in turn, will (sooner or later) lead to class struggle, which itself will shape history.

The mode of production also sets the limits to and provides the resources for all other human activities. The level of technological, scientific, and productive development determines how much time and energy we have for activities other than simply meeting our survival needs: for art, religion, philosophy, or science. Further, technology provides basic experiences of everyday life. The more science, for instance, the less trust in superstition. The more production is socialized and geographically interdependent, the less meaningful small political boundaries can be.

Marx also suggested that people manifest a widespread desire to continually develop the forces of production. If social relations of production interfere with that development, they will be removed. Political revolutions and social change serve to expand our technical, scientific, and productive power.

Marx believed that technological progress was lessening the labor time necessary to meet biological needs, and continually expanding our sense of a normal standard of living. Simultaneously, the cumulative effect of class conflicts eventually leads to human liberation. The exploitation built into class society tends to make those societies unstable, for exploitation gives rise to resistance. The fulfillment of material needs leads to the development of new needs. Human beings will not rest until they have reached a social form that supports unfettered, creative self-transformation.

Marx's theory definitively rejects the individualism of eighteenth-century philosophy and economic theory, which held that human nature is determined not by social relations but by individual choices, experiences, or desires. For Marx, each individual is necessarily born into some particular mode of production, and a corresponding political, social, and cultural system.

For Marx, historical materialism was a distinct, in some ways "scientific," theory of human life. His opponents' ideas, as well as the dominant conceptions of class-ruled social life, he considered "ideological." They were inadequate or mistaken because they ignored or misrepresented the historical or social nature of their object; they were put forward and accepted because they served the interests of the economic or political ruling class. These ideological theories often supported oppression or exploitation by representing them as inevitable or by masking their existence. Talk about Truth, Rights, and Goodness, he claimed, was often a mask for class interests, a rationalization of the existing distribution of power and wealth.

Alienation and Freedom

Marx believed that a fulfilling society must allow people to make maximum use of their capacity for creative activity. When that process can proceed with as little unnecessary hindrance as possible, then human freedom is being realized.

The progressive realization of human freedom requires first that we bring our relations with nature under rational control, replacing drudgery with mechanized production. With the development of technology by capitalism, Marx believed, it would soon be possible to have a life of freedom, beyond scarcity and toil. However, to utilize these emerging resources the alienation endemic to capitalism had to be overcome. "Alienation" refers to the way specifically human abilities and products come to limit or oppress the human beings who are their source. Marx observed that the people who perform the productive labor in capitalist society are contributing to the wealth and power of those who are exploiting them: as the factory owners accumulate profits, the factory laborers become increasingly impoverished. Moreover, the essentially human act of productive labor is degraded into boring, damaging, exhausting tedium. Workers under capitalism are alienated whether they realize it or not. However, Marx was confident (perhaps mistakenly so) that objective alienation would inevitably lead to subjective dissatisfaction and, eventually, to class struggle.

Capitalism

The capitalist economic and social system was the center of most of Marx's writing, as well as of his extensive radical political activity. Marx describes capitalism first and foremost as a mode of production in which the producers and expropriators found in all class societies take the form of proletariat and capitalists. As a class, the proletariat is initially composed of peasants who are forcibly driven off their land and thus economically compelled to join in capitalist production. Members of the proletariat own only their labor power and must work for wages to survive. The capitalist ruling class owns concentrations of the means of production. These concentrations originated in precapitalist wealth, or from profit on trade, colonial exploitation, or war.

Unlike all precapitalist economies, capitalism centers on the production of commodities—objects produced in order to be bought and sold rather than consumed by the people who make them. Owning neither land, natural resources, nor machines to produce with, wage laborers must buy the necessities of life. The capitalist class, in turn, uses its accumulated wealth to produce not to satisfy people's needs, but in order to generate profit.

For Marx, the key to understanding any mode of production lies in the way the ruling class exploits the laboring class. In different social settings, the surplus labor—the amount of labor beyond what is used to meet immediate material needs—is appropriated by an economically dominant class.

Unlike slavery or feudalism, under capitalism there is often a fair amount of political freedom and mobility. Capitalist exploitation is therefore a hidden form of unequal exchange. Marx's analysis here turns on two notions: the labor theory of value and "surplus value." The first notion, derived in part from John Locke (1632–1704) and Adam Smith (1723–1790), is that commodities exchange relative to the amount of labor it takes to produce them. Treating labor itself as a commodity, Marx analyzed workers' wages as a form of unequal exchange: the amount of labor needed to "produce" a worker (food, shelter, and so forth) was less than the worker produced in a given day. Wages paid for the daily reproduction of the worker, but the worker produced more than what was necessary for that reproduction. The difference between these two sums was the basis of the capitalist's profit. The worker is (politically, though not practically) free to work or not as she chooses, and gets paid for her work. *But the wage is less than the value of what the worker produces.* What looks like a fair exchange is exploitation.

With the theory of exploitation, Marx identified the key source of class struggle in capitalism. The capitalist strategy is to speed up the production line, demand greater output, and lengthen the working day relative to wages paid. Workers seek to raise the socially necessary labor time required in order to produce labor power—that is, to try to raise the socially accepted value of labor. This theoretical model matches the historical realities of the early years of capitalist development in Western Europe (as well as the newly developing capitalisms of today).

Marx observed that capitalists have another basic strategy of raising the rate of surplus value: to decrease the amount of labor time necessary to reproduce the worker through the development of ever more efficient and sophisticated forces of production. The more sophisticated the production techniques, the less time it takes for the worker to produce commodities equal in value to his wages, and the more of the working day is left for surplus value.

The social changes encouraged by the dynamic of exploitation are relevant to Marx's theory of capitalist development.

For Marx, capitalist development involves continual expansion: the reinvestment of profit into ever larger economic enterprises. Increasing investment in technology demands that production occur on a progressively greater scale. More profit must be made to compensate for the greater amount of capital invested. For these reasons, there is a natural tendency for capitalist enterprises to increase in size and to develop new technologies. With expansion of production, capitalism must seek new markets, by replacing production for use with commodity production at home and by penetrating noncapitalist societies abroad. The constant drive to develop means of production also stems from competition among capitalists. The key to competition is producing goods more cheaply. While this is partly accomplished by lowering wages, the major drive is to introduce increasingly sophisticated production techniques. For these reasons, capitalism is the only mode of production in which the drive to develop the forces of production is built into the relations of production.

This constant development of the forces of production gives capitalism its power as a form of social life and its crucial role in human history. Through its development of productive forces, capitalism offers human beings the capacity to meet their material needs with less labor and to produce new objects—and thus create new needs—on a previously unknown scale. This is why capitalism so easily brushes aside precapitalist social relations at home and abroad. Marx was of course bitterly critical of the human costs of the triumph of capitalism: the raging poverty suffered by the creators of wealth, alienation at work, the destruction of the environment, and the suffering imposed by the capitalist cycles of booms and busts. Yet by forcing the continual expansion of human productive powers, capitalism provides the resources that can be used to create a truly free and fulfilling society.

Because capitalism is geared around the private interests of an ever-smaller ruling class, it is inherently unstable. While production is national and international in scope, control of the production process and of the surplus continues to be held in private hands. From a point of view of the needs and interests of society as a whole, these conditions give rise to too much needless suffering.

More concretely, there arises a series of economic crises—a pattern of hyperexpansion leading to contraction, booms followed by busts, expanding industries followed by dramatic surges of unemployment and business failures. After every depression, capital gets more concentrated, the productive forces more developed, and both the local and the international economy more dominated by capitalist social relations. Small producers are constantly supplanted by the vastly more efficient technologically developed capitalist firms. People must earn a living by investing or laboring. And the entire system is subject to greater and greater fluctuations, since more and more of the world is part of the capitalist system. Expansion leads to crisis, and then to more expansion. This spiral of capitalist development leads inevitably, Marx claims, to concentration and monopolization, periods of high unemployment and poverty, technological development, and the attrition of small businesses and farms.

Marx's compelling analysis of the dynamic and effects of capitalism was far ahead of its time. At least for this particular period of competitive capitalism, his claims about the leading role of the mode of production were confirmed. The interests generated by the economic structure did give rise to predictable actions and social changes. The entire social fabric became subject to the logic of capitalism. Human relations in general took on the form of commodities; historical change was accelerated by rapid development of technology; education and socialization were adapted to producing workers, owners, and consumers. Competition, the drive for "success," and the freedom to buy, sell, and consume were enshrined as the highest social values. Religion, family life, the physical structure of cities, political institutions—all were reformed to meet the needs of a society dominated by commodity production.

Politics, Revolution, Socialism

Eventually, Marx believed, the severity and repetitive nature of unemployment and poverty, combined with the fact that more and more of the working class would be living socially homogeneous lives, would create a radical political climate. Differences of age, sex, nationality, region, religion, or culture would become unimportant. Class identity would determine self-understanding and values. Even if workers' absolute standard of living improved, the gap between them and the ruling class would increase. These experiences would create a growing class consciousness among workers: an awareness of shared interests and common situation. Finally, a cataclysmic economic crisis would spark the final socialist revolution, a revolution led by industrial workers.

Since it is their labor that is the source of social wealth, Marx believed, only the working class has the potential social power to overthrow capitalism. Other groups may dislike capitalism, but none are central to the social structure. As the potential inheritor of immense technological development, the working class has resources for the realization of human freedom. Once productive powers are unchained from the logic of profit, they can be directed to human fulfillment. As the enemy of the ruling class, the proletariat has an interest in eliminating all forms of oppression that politically divide workers. Racism, ethnic hatred, male chauvinism, and so on only distract attention from the "real" enemy. After capitalism is eliminated, they will disappear. For these reasons, the proletariat is the "universal" class in the sense that the redress of its wrongs will signal the liberation of all of humanity.

Marx's views on socialist revolution were influenced by his direct experience of the various European uprisings of 1848, the First "International" of workers' organizations and radical political parties, and the revolutionary Paris Commune of 1871.

After the revolution, Marx envisaged a set of social relations that would end systematic class antagonisms and harmonize personal fulfillment and social justice. The technological development of capitalism would drastically shrink the amount of time necessary to meet material needs, even needs that had grown with the increase of the productive forces. The means of production would be subject to democratic, egalitarian relations of production. They could then serve human needs rather than private profit. Also, the systematic ideological distortions of capitalist society would be eliminated. In short, social life would be characterized by freedom, equality of power, a just exchange of labor for money, and rational organization. As society fully adjusted to the revolutionary changes, it could move toward "communism." Here people no longer work for wages, even "fair" wages. Creative activity comes to be the dominant mode of self-expression, and people function under the maxim "From each according to his ability, to each according to his needs."

Postcapitalism political life was to be democratic, giving ordinary citizens some direct control over all critical social decisions, as well as representative, with representatives recallable by popular vote at any time, having a salary equal to no more than that of the average factory worker, and conducting governmental deliberations in an open and accessible way. With the eventual end of class domination, political life would simply become a matter of rational, nonconflictual administration. Unlike in class-dominated societies, there would be no need for political power to pretend to serve the interests of all of society while really managing the economy in the interests of only the ruling class.

Given the sad history of self-proclaimed "Marxists" who became totalitarian, it is important to stress that any fair reading of Marx's writings refute any claim that he did or would have supported tyranny. While Marx's theory had many errors and limitations, an attraction to dictatorships is not one of them.

Roger S. Gottlieb

See also MARXISM; SOCIALISM

Bibliography

Avineri, S. *The Social and Political Thought of Karl Marx.* Cambridge: Cambridge

University Press, 1970.

Cohen, G.A. *Karl Marx's Theory of History: A Defence.* Princeton: Princeton University Press, 1978.

Elster, Jon. *Making Sense of Marx.* Cambridge: Cambridge University Press, 1985.

Gottlieb, Roger S. *Marxism 1944–1990: Origins, Betrayal, Rebirth.* New York: Routledge, 1992.

Marx, Karl. *Capital.* Vols. 1–3. New York: International Publishers, 1967.

———. *A Contribution to the Critique of Political Economy.* New York: International Publishers, 1970.

———. *The Economic and Philosophical Manuscripts of 1844.* New York: International Publishers, 1964.

———. *Grundrisse.* New York: Vintage, 1973.

———, and Frederick Engels. *The Communist Manifesto.* Chicago: Gateway, 1954.

———, and Frederick Engels. *The German Ideology.* New York: International Publishers, 1947.

Miller, Richard. *Analyzing Marx.* Princeton: Princeton University Press, 1984.

Schmitt, Richard. *Introduction to Marx and Engels: A Critical Reconstruction.* Boulder, Colo.: Westview, 1987.

Marxism

Marxism may be defined as the set of ideas originally formulated by Karl Marx (1818–1883) to provide a critical explanation of the development and structure of capitalist society, ideas that were systematized and applied to changed circumstances by his followers.

Marxism as a term was first used by the opponents of Marx and famously rejected by him in 1882 when referring to the caricature of his ideas then offered by his followers in France: "What is certain is that, as for me, I am no Marxist." The term continues to be fiercely contested, not least by the followers of Marx, as the century since his death has witnessed a number of schisms occasioned by attempts both to systematize his ideas and to see their application to modern conditions. Each disputant has sought to claim fidelity to some particular aspect of Marx's authority, but disputes have been settled as often by force of arms as by force of argument. For their part, the opponents of Marxism have sought to demonstrate the flaws of Marx's ideas by pointing to the consequences of their application in the so-called socialist countries. The recent demise of official communism and a declining level of industrial and political struggle in the advanced industrial societies has coincided with a withdrawal of thinkers associated with Marxism—from the public sphere to the academy—with the result that many writers have concluded that Marxism is now discredited as a political movement and coherent doctrine of social change.

It should be no cause for surprise that Marx's theories have always been dependent upon others for their interpretation and application. Perhaps the most remarkable feature of the rapid development of Marxism following Marx's death in 1883 was that most of the important writings for which he is now known were then unavailable: the full text of the *German Ideology;* the *Contribution to the Critique of the Hegelian Philosophy of Law;* the *Economic and Philosophic Manuscripts of 1844;* the *Foundations of the Critique of Political Economy (Grundrisse).* All were unknown until the 1920s or 1930s and could therefore have had no influence upon the first generation of Marx's followers. Moreover, Marx's work at the time of his death was radically incomplete: Projected works on philosophy and political theory remained unwritten, and even the mass of economic studies were left in a state of almost indecipherable chaos.

At the time of Marx's death, his thought was known mainly through his *Communist Manifesto* (1848) and *Capital* (1867); Marx was known primarily as an economist, and Marxism was first approached through the medium of economics. The need to locate that economics in a larger framework of a general conception of society, and the absence—at least in Marx's published writings—of such an analysis, made the matter of interpretation quite crucial. In the absence of direct evidence of Marx's own philosophical development, these later writings tended to reinforce an economic determinism, a belief that the overthrow of capitalism and its replacement by socialism would be an inevitable consequence of its internal contradictions, in particular its tendency to economic crisis.

Though both Marx and Friedrich Engels (1820–1895) had maintained a keen interest in the class struggles of their lifetime, their organizational links with the working class had been constrained by the very real limits of working-class political organization during that period. It was only after Marx's death that political systems in the advanced world expanded to encompass mass political parties that sought the support of the majority of the population; it was only at that point that Marxism made its entry as an important factor in national politics. It was this emergence of a modern polity and the development of working class political parties in the late 1870s and 1880s that led first Engels, and later such figures as Karl Kautsky (1854–1938) and George Plekhanov (1856–1918), to attempt to provide a systematic exposition of Marxist ideas by supplementing the perceived gaps in Marx's legacy to yield a comprehensive world view to sustain a powerful and growing political movement.

Thus was born the conversion of Marx's ideas into the ideology of Marxism, an ideology, moreover, that sought application not only to circumstances that Marx foresaw but did not live to see, but also to circumstances—the application of his ideas to economically backward societies, for example—that he could not have been expected to anticipate. The development of mass working-class parties receptive to the ideas of socialism gave an opportunity for the ideas of Marx to gain widespread influence; they also tested the ambiguities and silences in Marx's thought and made his ideas uniquely in need of, but also vulnerable to, the interpretations and application of his followers.

The political parties that collectively constituted the Second International sought to integrate into a comprehensive theoretical perspective and political program the demands and aspirations of their respective labor movements, to convert the workers' movement to socialism. This task required the translation of Marxist theory into the language of the workers' movement, thus meeting the demand for an ideology, a set of beliefs, that would situate and orient that movement and its struggle in the world: That ideology came to be known as Social Democracy.

However, the opportunities afforded those parties carried particular difficulties when they tried to work out the relation between their theory and practice, in particular how they conceptualized the relationship between their day-to-day political tasks and their declared final aim, the revolutionary overthrow of capitalism. Here the ambiguities and silences in Marx's corpus became most evident, for while Marx had advocated the central importance of the proletariat in the revolutionary transfer of political power, he did not rule out the utilization of class alliances in that struggle. Similarly, while he was uncompromising in his hostility to capitalist society and in his belief that it is impossible to reform such a society, he was not indifferent to the form of political rule in such a society, nor dismissive of struggles to improve the conditions of the lives of workers within it.

These ambiguities were complemented by a tendency within Marx's work to limit the importance of the political: first, in terms of his dismissal of any separation of the "political" from the "economic," "social," or "cultural"—that is to say, because of his treatment of social theory as a totality; and second, because of his view that political emancipation—by which he meant the achievement of suffrage and civil liberties—would not in and of itself constitute nor necessarily bring about his desired end of human emancipation, which required the revolutionary transformation of the social and economic order.

The first generation of Marxists, the most important of whom were Karl Kautsky, Georgi Plekhanov, Eduard Bernstein (1850–1932), and Antonio Labriola (1843–1904), had little or no knowledge of Marx's early philosophical development and writings, or of the importance of these to his economic theories and understanding of historical development. Their attraction to Marxism was framed by the cultural and philosophical climate of the time (Darwinism, positivism) and by those writings by Marx that were available and that, crucially, were complemented by the prolific writings of Marx's lifelong collaborator and first interpreter, Frederick Engels. Indeed, it was the latter's *Anti-Duhring* (1878), *The Origin of the Family, Private Property and the State* (1884), and *Ludwig Feuerbach* (1888) that were chiefly responsible for drawing this generation to Marxism: Such works were seen to complement Marx's economic writings.

These writers drew upon the prevailing influence of natural science, and especially Darwinism, to create an evolutionist, scientistic socialism that came to be distilled into an objective, scientific study of the facts of economic life that revealed to the subjects of that study their future—in the face of which revelation they had no other choice than to adopt a moral position: to side with historical progress or vainly to resist its advance. This view of Marxism as a theory of social development concerned with identifying the laws of motion of capitalist society that would lead to its inevitable collapse was supplemented by appeal to either philosophical or ethical support drawn from elsewhere—from Kantianism or positivism, or to the later writings of Engels. In this latter case Marxism developed into an ideology characterized by its unified, all-encompassing system. That uniformity, however, disguised the inevitable difficulties in combining a revolutionary doctrine with a political movement immersed in a nonrevolutionary environment.

It was on this point that the first fundamental schism of the modern socialist movement was brought about. By challenging the prevailing economic determinism of Social Democracy, Eduard Bernstein denied both that the economic forces of capitalism would inevitably lead to its shipwreck and that the working class would be propelled to revolution. He considered Marx's predictions to be quite wrong: "Peasants do not sink; middle class does not disappear; crises do not grow ever larger; misery and serfdom do not increase." There was, in fact, said Bernstein, a contradiction between the theoretical premises and everyday practice of Social Democracy, a contradiction that should be resolved by freeing the party from the utopian and insurrectionary phraseology of the old theory and unifying the opportunities to be found in its successful practice with a more realistic understanding of socialism.

Though strongly criticized by Kautsky and Plekhanov, as well as by the radical Left of Social Democracy in the persons of Rosa Luxemburg (1870–1919) and V.I. Lenin (1870–1924), Bernstein's views were eventually to prevail, as it was his ideas that most accurately reflected the actual behavior of Social Democracy in this period (though its Marxist leaders were loath to admit it). Social Democracy's deterministic and evolutionary interpretation of Marxism allowed it to lapse into a quiescent fatalism; its interpretation of its revolutionary role consisted in its acquiring state power by way of achieving a parliamentary majority and then being prepared to use force against the anticipated "slaveowners rebellion" of the old ruling class. Its road to power was ensured by two objective laws: the breakdown of capitalism, and the evolution of economic conditions that would constitute the working class as a majority prepared and able to constitute itself, via its political representatives, as a majority class.

The illusions of Social Democracy were exposed by the outbreak of war in 1914 and of revolution in Russia in 1917, events that forced political action and eventually division upon Social Democracy. The leading parties of the Second International gave support to their national governments' prosecution of the war, thus bringing about the ignominious collapse of the International—only the Russian, U.S., Serbian, Italian, Bulgarian, and Rumanian parties remained true to the antiwar principles previously expounded by the International. Then in 1917 the Russian Revolution marked for the first time the seizure of state power by an avowedly Marxist party, the Bolshevik Party. At that point the Marxist orthodoxy of Kautsky and Plekhanov entered a terminal decline, while the radical Marxists, who hailed the workers' state in Russia as the embodiment of working-class democracy, entered into a fratricidal struggle with those social democrats who retained their allegiance to and hopes in the parliamentary system.

As chief organizer of the October 1917 Bolshevik Revolution, Lenin was to become the most important and influential interpreter of Marx, his authority being derived from his creation of a revolutionary party that had successfully seized state power in Russia and his influence extending to a number of fundamental revisions of what had hitherto been Marxist orthodoxy: He reconceptualized the relation between political party, leaders, and masses in a new way by stressing the importance of a vanguard revolutionary party; he typified the epoch as one shaped by the rivalries between the imperialist powers; he applied the Marxist theory of revolution to the economically backward conditions of Russia by seeking to unite the struggles of the proletariat and peasantry; he emphasized the pivotal importance to Marxism of the new form of state initiated in Russia—the Soviets, or workers' councils; and, finally, he emphasized the importance of the national question to Marxist political practice. The success of Lenin's politics and the isolated example of what became the Soviet state tended to disguise the continuities between Lenin's theoretical positions and those of Social Democracy. For example, when Lenin expounded his views on party organization in *What is to Be Done?* (1902), he quoted favorably and extensively from Kautsky when seeking to demonstrate the separation of actual working class consciousness from any development of a socialist consciousness, which latter had to be developed by intellectuals grouped in a party. It was the political achievement of the Bolshevik Revolution that set Lenin apart from Social

M

Democracy—and that was a tribute to his political perspicuity and to the uniqueness of circumstances in Russia rather than to his theoretical uniqueness.

The Russian Revolution was an amalgam of working-class urban socialism and peasant-agrarian populism forged into revolutionary unity by the political and intellectual leadership of the Bolshevik Party. The success of that alliance made the revolution possible and successful, but at the same time ruled out socialism and the preservation of proletarian political hegemony—which was subsequently to collapse into a substituted rule of the Communist Party. Following civil war, foreign intervention, and international isolation, and once the revolutionary upsurge in Europe had ebbed, the Russian regime degenerated into a repressive and authoritarian dictatorship. With that degeneration, orthodox communism, too, entered an intellectual demise, becoming little more than a mouthpiece for the Soviet state and supporting the worst atrocities of the Stalinist counterrevolution. That this was claimed both by apologists for Joseph Stalin (1879–1953) and by anticommunists to be the inevitable consequence of applied Marxism should be no surprise: They each had their own reasons for the distortion and caricature of Marxism that this represented.

Kautsky and the Social Democrats had raised the question of the relevance of the Russian experience to the social and political circumstances of Western Europe, but their views had been discredited by their failure to oppose the war effectively and by their willingness to trade revolutionary for governmental aspirations. A more reputable opposition to the degenerated orthodoxy that passed for Marxist ideology in communist orthodoxy was registered by Leon Trotsky (1879–1940) and his followers, who sought to identify the precise point at which the Russian revolution had collapsed into Stalinist counterrevolution, and by what came to be known as Western Marxism.

Western Marxism was marked by the two events catastrophic to the evolution of Marxism as a political movement: the emergence of Stalinism out of the Russian Revolution, and the triumph of fascism in Western Europe. Marked by these severe defeats, it sought to account for the detour that history had apparently taken, and in so doing was forced to question some of the fundamental premises of

Marxism, not least of which was the posed unity of theory and practice. Excluded from the Stalinized communist movement and secluded from the working-class movement in general, the theorists of Western Marxism became specialists located in academic life, and their interests typically shifted from politics and economics to questions of epistemology and aesthetics. The locus of this work was directed toward contemporary thought and culture rather than to questions of class struggle, capitalist economy, political rule, or revolutionary change. Such thinkers as Georg Lukacs (1885–1971), Karl Korsch (1886–1961), Antonio Gramsci (1891–1937), Walter Benjamin (1892–1940), Herbert Marcuse (1898–1979), Theodor Adorno (1903–1969), Jean-Paul Sartre (1905–1980), and Louis Althusser (1918–1990) produced a vast body of diverse work marked by an opposition to capitalist society but whose radical edge was sublimated away from class struggle to cultural theory.

Of these thinkers, Lukacs, Korsch, and Gramsci are set apart by their earlier immersion in the political struggles of the post–World War I epoch. The work they produced in that period, though prefiguring the motifs of Western Marxism, in fact bridged the two periods—albeit that later they were to recant (Lukacs), desert (Korsch), or be rendered impotent (by imprisonment, Gramsci). Lukacs, for example, produced in his *History and Class Consciousness* (1923) a key text of Western Marxism that was clearly set against the revolutionary background of the period: Its themes pulsed with the optimism of its time. Lukacs's achievement was to reestablish the importance of Marx's early writings by demonstrating their relationship to his later works, and by placing at the center of Marxism the liberatory function of the proletariat. Furthermore, his essentialism allowed him to escape—or to avoid—the preemptive judgment of any particular epoch, while his theory of reification demonstrated how this liberatory function had been thwarted by the very ability of bourgeois society to shape and distort the consciousness through which it is perceived.

Other of the Western Marxists were also to offer interesting insights into the changed culture of modern capitalism: Gramsci's theory of ideology and of the role of intellectuals, and his analysis of civil society; Althusser's structuralism; Marcuse's pessimistic account of (one-dimensional) consciousness and his theory of Eros. But it was Lukacs's thought that most closely integrated the original philosophical preoccupations of Marx with the changed culture of modern capitalism. His theory of party provided what had been missing in Lenin—a nondogmatic account applicable to the conditions of advanced democratic societies. And his theory of reification provided a point of connection between Marx's notion of commodity fetishism and his embryonic theory of alienation with the everyday lived experience of the modern working class. In this way, Lukacs reintegrated philosophy and psychology with Marx's economics.

None of this answers the question of whether this reunification demonstrates Marxism's continued relevance. Indeed, it might be judged that, in laying such stress upon the need to instantiate the unity of theory and practice in the form of the consciousness of the proletariat, such an interpretation merely advertises its complete irrelevance or redundancy, as it is the apparent separation of Marxist ideas from the working-class movement that is such a marked condition of the modern world. Class divisions may persist, class inequalities may widen, the class character of the state may become increasingly explicit: but if this has little or no effect upon the consciousness of the working class, if it is not expressed through class or political struggles, then does that not signify the very failure of Marxism as a political doctrine?

Yes, if success is the sole determinant of a political doctrine's claim to authority. But that is not necessarily the case; a doctrine may be a total failure and yet not be in error. In the case of Marxism it is necessary to establish whether it can give an account of its political failure in terms that do not contradict its truth or meaning. Lukacs's theory of reification begins to do that, just as his uniting of Marx's theory of alienation with Lenin's theory of the party point Marxism toward a more open and creative model of political praxis. It remains to be seen whether, in the light of the collapse of orthodox communism, these insights may play any further role in the "ruthless criticism of all that exists."

Stephen M. Perkins

See also CAPITALISM; DEMOCRACY; EVOLUTION; MARX; POSITIVISM; RECONSTRUCTIONISM, SOCIAL; REVOLUTION; SOCIALISM

Bibliography

Anderson, Perry. *Considerations on Western Marxism*. London: New Left Books, 1976.

Bernstein, Eduard. *Evolutionary Socialism: A Criticism and Affirmation*. New York: Schocken Books, 1961.

Callinicos, Alex. *Making History: Agency, Structure and Change in Social Theory*. Cambridge: Polity Press, 1989.

Gouldner, Alvin W. *The Two Marxisms: Contradictions and Anomalies in the Development of Theory*. London: Macmillan, 1980.

Jacoby, Russell. *Dialectic of Defeat: Contours of Western Marxism*. Cambridge: Cambridge University Press, 1981.

Kolakowski, Leszek. *Main Currents of Marxism: Its Origins, Growth and Dissolution*. Oxford: Oxford University Press, 1978.

Lukacs, Georg. *History and Class Consciousness: Studies in Marxist Dialectics*. London: Merlin Press, 1971.

McLellan, David. *Marxism after Marx: An Introduction*. London: Macmillan, 1979.

Miliband, Ralph. *Marxism and Politics*. Oxford: Oxford University Press, 1977.

Perkins, Stephen. *Marxism and the Proletariat: A Lukacsian Perspective*. London: Pluto Press, 1993.

Schorske, Carl E. *German Social Democracy, 1905–1917: The Development of the Great Schism*. Cambridge: Harvard University Press, 1983.

Meaning

Plato (c. 427–347 B.C.) in the *Theatetus* (197–198a) spoke of knowledge as something one couldn't just possess. To retrieve and use knowledge, one needs reason. Philip Phenix similarly wrote that rote memorization is relatively inefficient if the symbols learned are not significant to the learner. For him, significance depends less on reason than on meaning.

Michael Polanyi agreed, saying that all human thought comes into existence by grasping the meaning and mastering the use of language. To grasp meaning one has to interiorize external things, or pour oneself into them. Meaning arises either by integrating clues in our own body or by integrating clues outside. We cannot learn to ride a bicycle by memorizing the laws of physics that govern its balance. The laws have to be made meaningful by getting on the bike and trying the different actions that keep it upright. The language of physics is less necessary to bike riding than is an understanding of balance, which is learned physically and socially at the same time. Helen Keller in 1908 spoke of how meaningless her world was without language. She did not know that she was. She lived in a world that was a no-world. Since she had no power of thought, she could not compare one mental state with another.

Polanyi illustrates the necessity and insufficiency of language for meaning with an example of learning to detect pulmonary disease on X rays. As the student listens for a few weeks, examining pictures of different cases, a rich panorama of significant details will be gradually revealed of physiological variations and pathological changes, of scars and signs of acute disease. The X rays begin to make sense. At the very moment when he has learned the language of pulmonary radiology, the student will also have learned to see the X rays meaningfully. The immediate experience of the X-ray's meaning is coincidental but not identical with the focal awareness of it that is present in thought. Knowledge is focal awareness, what we are conscious of and can talk about. Knowing is the tacit integration of knowledge.

Polanyi argues that it is our subsidiary awareness of anything that endows it with meaning, with a meaning that bears on an object of which we are focally aware. The tacit knowing that gives us meaning consists in subsidiary things bearing on a focus by virtue of an integration performed by a person.

We could not formulate strict laws for deriving general laws from individual experiences, because each instance of a law will differ in every particular from every other instance of it. To form class concepts essential to meaning we must presume that indeterminate and global process of tacit knowing. In applying our conception of any class of things, whether pains, pronouns, or persons, how can we identify objects or feelings that seem to be different in crucial respects?

Tacit knowing cannot be reduced to its explicit articulation because it can be articulated through an indeterminate number of language systems. When the student looks at the X ray, he may focus on it with an artist's eyes and see forms of light and shade, or, as a photographer, he may be conscious of the quality of the picture. The medical information will be part of the subsidiary knowing that will inform his focusing on it in those ways.

How do we get meaning from unfamiliar sequences of words and letters such as "Bullets are earnest lullabies," or "The spot is moving from reft to light"? We involuntarily make sense of the data, proceeding on the assumption that there is a text to be recovered. We must move beyond the sense stimuli to treat the uttered noises as things people wanted to assert for various reasons. We reason that they must have meant "left to right" or that bullets are a sort of earnest lullaby though the emotional associations are so different.

To understand unusual meaning, we have to put the statement into some context, to try to understand why the speaker would have said it. What someone means by an utterance depends not only on what she believes, but also on what she intends, and what she intends will depend on what she desires. We have to adopt a holistic approach that conceives of a speaker's behavior and attitudes as a single interconnected and interdependent system. Our interpretation requires us to adopt what Daniel C. Dennett calls the intentional stance: We must treat the noise-emitter as an agent whose actions can be explained or predicted on the basis of the content of his beliefs and desires and other mental states.

Similarly, when we say we understand other minds, or understand an unfamiliar object placed before us, our meaning is dependent on our assumption that the world does fit together in meaningful ways. Our actions generally satisfy us. We recognize them in the main as the product of processes that are reliably sensitive to ends and means. They are thus rational, but not necessarily in the sense of being the product of serial reasoning. Donald Davidson calls this the principle of charity, though it could equally be Platonic reason in our capacity to make satisfying connections. Meaning could not get off the ground without it.

The requirement of context makes it virtually impossible to locate the meaning of meaning precisely. It cannot be understood by being reduced to some other notion such as that of the speaker's intentions or to reference, nor can the meaning of words be understood in isolation from whole sentences, or sentences in isolation from a language, a speaker, a community, or a world. It can be understood only in terms of its interconnections with other notions.

Davidson says that meaning forms a basic, interdependent triad with beliefs and truth. In interpreting a speaker, beliefs and utterances are identified, certainly in the first instance, in relation to the objects and events in the speaker's environment—that is, in relation to the world in which both speaker and interpreter are located. But in doing this the interpreter is also relating those utterances and beliefs with her own beliefs and utterances. The overall truth of our beliefs, and the overall agreement of those beliefs with the beliefs of others, is thus a presupposition of the very possibility of interpretation of meaning—of being able to make sense of ourselves and other speakers.

Dennett warns us that meaning requires mind and intention, but we shouldn't assume a single Boss that focuses our subsidiary awareness. The ultimate "point of view of the conscious observer" does not have to be a single self in control of organizing meaning, but it is probably a temporary set of highly structured but flexible regularities and recipes that give the physical hardware of the brain a huge interlocking set of habits or dispositions to enable it to react with or make sense of the world, like the artist or doctor viewing the X ray.

The number of selves that provide meaning is indeterminate, as is the number of possible interpretations of meaning. "We cannot suppose that we could first determine what a speaker believes, wants, hopes for, intends and fears and then go on to a definite answer to the question that his words refer to. For the evidence on which all these matters depend gives us no way of separating out the contributions of thought, action, desire and meaning one by one. Total theories are what we must construct, and many theories will do equally well" (Davidson: 240–41).

Other philosophers, particularly W.V. Quine and Michael Dummett, agree that truth and meaning are paired, but they approach the problem from a different perspective. They believe that whatever there is to meaning must be traced back somehow to experience, the given, or sensory stimulation, something intermediate between belief and the usual objects our beliefs are about. Once we take this step, however, says Davidson, we open the door to skepticism, for we must then allow that a great many of the sentences we hold to be true may in fact be false. We cannot separate out the world from the way we see it. There is no separation between seeing something and then seeing it as something, the seeing of a fact and then interpreting it. Its significance allows us to see it—we see it through its meaning. This means that there is not a separate level of meaning.

There is rather a change in the appearance of spoken or written words when their meaning is established. The meaningful use of a word that causes it to lose its physical character makes us look through the word at its meaning. In the sentence "The bag was split so the notes were sour" the individual words make sense, but together they have no meaning outside the context of a Scottish bagpipe. Some philosophers have spoken of meaning as a mirror of nature. But the mirror of meaning is not a mirror that re-presents the world. The world is not reflected in meaning. Rather on a Davidsonian account, the world is the mirror of meaning. Within the world, meaning is constituted; only within the world do things appear as meaningful.

Felicity Haynes

See also EXPERIENCE; REASON AND RATIONALITY; TRUTH

Bibliography

Davidson, Donald. *Inquiries into Truth and Interpretation.* Oxford: Clarendon Press, 1980.
Dennett, Daniel C. *Consciousness Explained.* Canada: Little, Brown, 1991.
Phenix, Philip. *Philosophy of Education.* New York: Holt, Rinehart and Winston, 1958.
Polanyi, Michael. *Knowing and Being.* Chicago: University of Chicago Press, 1969.
Quine, W.V. *The Roots of Reference.* La Salle, Ill.: Open Court, 1973.

Metaphysics

Metaphysics, the study of "being qua being," has a convoluted history. Its prominence has waxed and waned through time, and its self-understanding has changed at different epochs.

The first difficulty faced in any attempt to understand metaphysics is the problematic nature of its name. It has often been interpreted as indicating an arcane study that seeks to go "beyond" the physical. Contemporary usage has carried this to such an extreme that bookstores will classify as "metaphysical" texts dealing with the occult or with some form of spiritualism. Such associations have little to do with the branch of philosophy that carries the name.

Aristotle (384–322 B.C.) first gave systematic articulation to this study. He indicated its importance by calling it "first philosophy" (*Metaphysics*: 1026a, 24, 30). In another passage, he referred to it as "theology" (*Metaphysics*: 1026a, 19), since it incorporates reflection on the highest kind of being.

Much of what Aristotle wrote was lost in the centuries following his death. A recovery of his texts led to the preparation of a standard edition (ca. 70–50 B.C.). Andronicus of Rhodes, the editor, placed a series of texts in sequence after those known as the "physics." He named them "the texts that come after the physics" (*ta meta ta physika*). Andronicus's label quickly took on the connotation "beyond the physical."

For Aristotle, "first philosophy" dealt with that which is most fundamental: "being as being" (*Metaphysics*: 1003a, 21–22). This study was to be contrasted with those that isolate specific aspects of reality for detailed study. For example, medicine deals with bodies as afflicted with disease, meteorology with the weather, and mechanics with bodies in motion. "First philosophy" seeks rather to characterize "what is" in a general sense, prior to its compartmentalization by the specialized disciplines.

Several conflicting currents were in existence at Aristotle's time. The first great movement in the direction of metaphysics had been made by Parmenides (515–450 B.C.). Parmenides' text is a poem that opens with the central character being carried away from the deceptive world of appearances into a higher realm of "being," one that is free from the errors that mar the ordinary human world. This "Way of Truth" can be revealed only by "reason," as it turns away from the "seeming" associated with the senses. In a puzzling fragment, Parmenides seems to be saying that there is a congruence between what is and what can be thought. "Being" in the fullest sense will resemble the objects of thought. His conclusions are that whatever "is" in the truest sense must be one, unchangeable, and indivisible.

Parmenides established a paradigm that was to return in many guises. This paradigm combines two elements: (1) the primacy of thought: "Being" is understood in terms of what approximates objects of reason in clarity, simplicity, and atemporality. (2) the disparagement of ordinary experience: A sharp demarcation is established between "appearance" and "reality."

The break with the Parmenidean paradigm began with Plato (c. 427–347 B.C.). Plato used

stories, not so much to provide an alternative world to which we should escape, but rather to highlight important truths about the world within which we live. Plato, using the example of a line divided into four segments (*Republic*: 509d), suggested a multifaceted approach to the question of what is most real. Plato's line holds together percepta, objects of sense experience, and ideas, objects of reason. The world is populated not only by natural entities and artifacts: Any intelligible discussion of our world must recognize that mathematical concepts (number, geometrical figures) as well as ideals (justice, love) are also in an important sense "real."

Plato thus mitigated the sharp bifurcation between the objects of everyday experience and those of refined cognition. Nonetheless, he continued to privilege the objects of reason, what he called the "Forms," as ultimately having primacy over the objects of sense experience.

Aristotle's own contribution to metaphysics was to move even further from the Parmenidean paradigm. Aristotle's father had been a physician, a biographical fact that seemed to mark him with an appreciation for biology. Aristotle also spent twenty years in Plato's Academy. The result of these influences was a biological Platonism. For Aristotle, the fundamentally real was the individual organism. But organisms are never completely unique; their structural and behavioral patterns are modeled on a Form, the species to which they belong.

For Aristotle, "What is *ousia*?" was the central question of metaphysics (*Metaphysics*: 1028b 5–6). *Ousia* is often misleadingly translated as "substance." A better translation would be "entity" or "primary being." What is it, Aristotle is asking, that can most fully be said to be? His first response is to be generous. A great diversity of things must be admitted "to be." Many sorts of things—atoms, numbers, ideals, plants, animals, stars, and planets—belong to the realm of being.

Nonetheless, to bring order to such a complexity, Aristotle sought to identify an exemplaric sort of being. Aristotle was here following a common procedure for explaining concepts that are exceedingly complex. The category, "bird," for example, includes within it creatures so tiny as to be indistinguishable from insects, and others that are larger than humans. It includes both creatures who can and cannot fly. To understand what "bird" means, we highlight an exemplaric instance, say a robin or bluebird, that manifests as fully as possible the cluster of traits that go into defining what it is to be a bird. Such a procedure has the advantage of not giving a sharply bifurcated analysis that separates the things of experience into those which are "real" and those which are mere "appearance."

What is most fully real is not hidden behind appearances. The exemplaric being is the organism as a member of a species. Aristotle's writings seek to preserve the tension between the biological side of his temperament, which highlights concrete individuals, and the Platonic side, which emphasizes the essence or Form that explains why entities fall naturally into kinds. Without the former, we lose the immediately experienced world. Without the latter, intelligibility (the ability to make general claims) disappears. Metaphysics thus serves to keep us alive to the full richness of existence.

Questions about "being" led Aristotle to seek an explanatory principle that would provide an adequate answer to the question of why there is the sort of world we live in at all. By a series of arguments, in both the *Physics* (Book 8, chapters 5–6) and the *Metaphysics* (Book 12, chapters 6–8), Aristotle came to admit that there must be a First Mover, or Ultimate Cause. This line of reflection is usually thought to belong to metaphysics.

Aristotle formulates a rival to the Parmenidean paradigm. The Aristotelian model understands metaphysics as combining two sorts of inquiries: (1) an attempt to articulate a general doctrine that answers the question What is being? and (2) a line of inquiry that seeks an ultimate explanation for beings.

The Aristotelian model was championed during the Middle Ages by Thomas Aquinas (1225–1274). Although Aquinas follows Aristotle, he does make an important emendation to the Aristotelian tradition. For Aristotle, "being" meant primarily a "something" whose defining traits could be articulated. For Aquinas, this means that Aristotle's metaphysics is primarily a metaphysics of "essence." It is overly concerned with the defining traits (essence), while paying too little attention to the surprising fact of its coming into being (existence). All beings are contingent for Aquinas; that is to say, they could very well not have existed at all. The paradigmatic instance of being is thus transformed from a noun, "the entity," to a verb, the act of being (*esse*). Of course, all entities are entities of a sort, and thus have essential characteristics. Essence is not denied, but now it is understood correlatively with existence. Only in God do we find the purity of *esse*. God is pure activity, sheer being understood as *esse*. This explains God's ineffability. Intelligibility is linked to essence. Unlike creatures whose contingent status indicates a distinction between existence and essence, no such distinction is present in the divine.

The modern period (1600–1900) is marked by an anti-Aristotelian character displayed by a revival of pre-Aristotelian strains: an atomistic mechanism, an emphasis on thought rather than being, and a fascination with disclosing what is hidden behind appearances. Rene Descartes (1596–1650) signals an important shift. Worried that the dependence on sense knowledge or on tradition could not provide absolute certainty, Descartes sought a starting point that would serve as a directly grasped, secure foundation. This kind of absolute certainty he found in his famous phrase "I think, therefore I am." "Subjectivity," the thinking subject, now became the pivot around which philosophical reflection would revolve.

Metaphysics itself came to be associated with pure thought attempting to demonstrate that God exists and that the soul is distinct from the body. Such a discipline could be engaged in only by those whose mind "can easily withdraw itself from commerce with the senses." Disconnected from its roots in experience, modern metaphysics turned to the construction of speculative systems based on the model of geometry. Baruch Spinoza (1632–1677) exemplified this trend when he published his *Ethics Demonstrated in Geometrical Order* (1675). This mode of philosophizing was systematized by Christian Wolff (1679–1754). Wolff's textbooks followed the deductive method. He subdivided metaphysics into various disciplines, including "rational theology" (studying questions relating to the existence of God) and "ontology" (a term he coined to describe the generic description of existence).

The deductive approach, minimizing the importance of direct experience, could not long go undisputed. The most significant challenge came from within the Wolffian school itself, which spawned the most important Enlightenment philosopher, Immanuel Kant (1724–1804). Kant claimed that he had been awakened from his Wolffian "dogmatic slumbers" by reading the British empiricist David Hume (1711–1776). The prefaces to the first and second editions of his *Critique of Pure Reason* (1781, 1787) mounted a direct attack.

Metaphysics is there described as "despotic" and "dogmatic." It is a "battlefield" of "endless controversies." The aim sought by metaphysics, to transcend "the limits of possible experience," is an impossible fantasy whose attempt leads its adherents to mere "random groping," and, what is worst of all, a "groping among mere concepts." Kant's own aim was nothing short of "completely revolutionizing" the then prevailing foundations for metaphysics by examining critically and carefully the origin, extent, and limits of human knowledge.

After Kant, modern metaphysics, seeking by deductive reasoning to gain access to truths independently of experience, was no longer credible. To be sure, the temptation to provide great speculative syntheses lingered on into the nineteenth century, most famously in *The Phenomenology of Spirit* (1807) by Georg W.F. Hegel (1770–1831). But such a synthesis as Hegel's was historical and incorporated experience as a necessary component. The Kantian critique had been felt. No longer could thinkers share in the Wolffian optimism about an elaborate system based on a deductive model isolated from the impact of experience.

By the end of the nineteenth century this criticism was carried to its artistic and devastating apex by Friedrich Nietzsche (1844–1900). His *Twilight of the Idols* (1889) savaged the "reason" of philosophers for having transformed the vibrancy of life into "concept-mummies" such as "being."

The devastation of such critiques did not still the human desire for information about the world. The void left by the undermining of nonempirical metaphysics was quickly filled by a movement known as Positivism. For the positivists, the only valid source of information about the world was science. Auguste Comte (1798–1857) suggested that history had progressed through three stages, the "theological," the "metaphysical," and the "positive" or scientific. The first two were prominent in a world not yet fully mature. Their explanations depended on either the will of the gods or on nonempirical forces. Only in the final, positive stage was knowledge properly understood as empirically derived facts correlated to the general laws of nature.

Positivism unleashed a barrage of propaganda against its predecessor. Metaphysics came in for harsh criticism, for example, in *Philosophy and Logical Syntax* (1935) by Rudolf Carnap (1891–1970), and in the very popular *Language, Truth and Logic* (1936) by A.J. Ayer. By the beginning of the twentieth century, modern metaphysics had effectively been overcome.

The older metaphysics, however, based on an Aristotelian concern with being, rooted in experience rather than in deductive reason, was poised for a return. Positivism's success was counterweighed by a sense that there was a gap between the objects of science and the ordinary experience of "being." The world as described by scientists seemed more and more distant, foreign, and unlike that of ordinary experience.

Edmund Husserl (1859–1938) and William James (1842–1910) helped break the stranglehold of positivism. Husserl developed the "phenomenological method" for describing "phenomena," whatever is given to consciousness, not simply the already purified, restricted objects of science. James introduced "radical empiricism," an attitude that took the varied data of immediate, ordinary experience seriously. With these two men, the full complexity of lived experience could once again become a subject for philosophical examination.

The twentieth century, still sensitive to the critiques of modern metaphysics, has not witnessed a full-fledged flourishing of the discipline. Nonetheless, metaphysics has made impressive contributions.

Martin Heidegger (1889–1976) announced in his *Being and Time* (1926) that Being is the fundamental theme of philosophy. Western philosophy had forgotten Being in its fullest sense, concentrating instead on beings. Only the present-at-hand is focused on, and that is viewed instrumentally as potential tools or utensils. That is inadequate. "Being and the structure of Being lie beyond every entity and every possible character which an entity may possess." The surest mode of access to Being is via a phenomenology of that entity whose mode of existence is to ask questions about Being. This is the human or *Dasein*. Heidegger's project thus becomes a "universal phenomenological ontology" that takes its departure "from the hermeneutic of *Dasein*." The rich texture of this phenomenology, highlighting the nature of "being-in-the-world," "being-unto-death," the importance of possibility, of temporality, of anxiety, and the contrast between authentic and inauthentic existence, has proven to be a watershed for inspiration and commentary.

In the English-speaking world, it was Alfred North Whitehead (1861–1947) who brought metaphysics to a new culmination. His *Science and the Modern World* (1925) together with *Process and Reality* (1929) work out a comprehensive, revived metaphysics. He returns to an Aristotelian sense of understanding being, but now it is an understanding informed by evolutionary biology and by the quantum and relativity revolutions in physics. The opponent against whom Whitehead writes is a static, atemporal ontology. Whatever is, is in process. The world is made up, not of static "things" but of "events," complexes that develop in time. "We must start with the event as the ultimate unit of natural occurrence" (*Science and the Modern World*). Whitehead's metaphysics is organicist, in the sense that it recognizes events as organized complexes linked together in multiple interrelations, and temporalist, in the sense that events both endure and change as they live out their processes in time.

Metaphysics is inherently related to reflection on education. The Parmenidean paradigm and the Aristotelian orientation each carry in their wakes certain corollaries for education. Someone who supports a sharp appearance/reality bifurcation will want education to avoid association with the everyday and focus on eternal, unchanging truths. Those who prize thought over being will tend to suggest an educational scheme aimed at "minds" and mental training, minimizing the role of the body. Those, on the other hand, whose metaphysics accepts the full reality of ordinary experience will want education to be immersed in the practical and specific. They will tend to emphasize the importance of habits and character development in education.

Raymond D. Boisvert

See also ARISTOTLE; COMMON SENSE; DESCARTES; HEGEL; HEIDEGGER; IDEALISM; KANT; PLATO; POSITIVISM; SCHOLASTICISM; SCIENTISM; WHITEHEAD

Bibliography

Aune, Bruce. *Metaphysics: The Elements.* Minneapolis: University of Minnesota Press, 1985.
Bahm, Archie. *Metaphysics: An Introduction.* New York: Barnes and Noble, 1974.
Coreth, Emerich. *Metaphysics.* Translated by Joseph Donceel. New York: Herder and Herder, 1968.
DeGeorge, Richard, ed. *Classical and Contemporary Metaphysics: A Source Book.* New York: Henry Holt, 1962.
Emmett, Dorothy. *The Nature of Metaphysical Thinking.* London: Macmillan, 1945.
Hamlyn, D.W. *Metaphysics.* Cambridge: Cambridge University Press, 1984.
Heidegger, Martin. *Being and Time* [1926]. Translated by John Macquarrie and Edward Robinson. New York: Harper and Row, 1962.
Neville, Robert, ed. *New Essays in Metaphysics.* Albany: State University of New York Press, 1987.
Taylor, Richard. *Metaphysics.* Englewood Cliffs, N.J.: Prentice Hall, 1963. 3rd ed., 1983.
Whitehead, Alfred North. *Science and the Modern World.* New York: Macmillan, 1926.

Mill, John Stuart (1806–1873)

The foremost English philosopher of the nineteenth century. His thought and example have been inspiration to subsequent thinkers and reformers, including those in the field of education. Mill believed, indeed, that the solution to all human problems lay in education. He declared that civilizations should devote themselves to education as they had hitherto been devoted to religion. His ambitions for education were almost unlimited: Under appropriate conditions, human nature and institutions could be perfected, and mankind could attain a state of nobility, generosity, and happiness far surpassing its current "wretched" state. Although his confidence in the ease with which such goals might be achieved diminished in his later years, he maintained the essential faith throughout his life.

The implications of these convictions for the theory and practice of education were by no means clear, however. His foundational conceptions of human nature and learning were systematically ambiguous. Unwittingly, he oscillated between two incompatible philosophies of mind. On the one hand, Mill affirmed and elaborated the associationist psychology that had been articulated in detail by his father, James Mill (1773–1836), a follower of Claude Helvetius (1715–1771). According to this theory, the mind is a passive receptacle of sensations. These sensations become amalgamated into complex ideas in accordance with the alleged laws of the association of ideas. These laws are inherent properties of mind, and their workings are not determined by human choice. According to this theory, the educator would so far as possible determine the entire detailed sequence of experiences that occur for the student, and in this manner the complete mentality and character of the student would be formed.

In contrast most of Mill's writings presuppose that mind is composed of inherent active faculties. By exercising such faculties, the individual develops and perfects them. The formation of mind and character, accordingly, is largely an individual and self-generated process. The principal requirement for conducting it is freedom from outside interference. Mill's habitual vocabulary for discussing the growth of the individual is that of the active exercise of faculties and their release from needless subordination to external control. His other philosophy, associationism, prescribes an exacting and deliberate control of every phase of the educational environment. Mill is justly famous as one of history's greatest defenders of freedom of inquiry and expression. This freedom rests less comfortably with the associationist psychology than with the belief in the efficacy of liberated human capacities.

Mill's own education illustrates this dichotomy of educational philosophy. He had no formal schooling whatever. His father attended to his education from the age of three, when Mill began the study of Latin. In all regards, this procedure was intended to exemplify the principles and practices of associationism. This father/son education lasted continuously until Mill was fourteen, and during this time the astoundingly precocious boy mastered more fields of knowledge than are aspired to in any known Ph.D. program. As undergone by Mill himself, however, this education could not be described as associationist. His father's principal method was to set his son on specified problems and to insist that he determine their solutions by himself; and James Mill offered assistance only on those occasions when John's struggles were exhausted. In practice, then, this education was one of asserting and exercising native powers.

Mill was never aware of the equivocal nature of his philosophy of education. In any case, he was consistent regarding educational aims. The general aim is nothing less than the perfection of the race. He had a much richer conception of human nature than did his liberal predecessors. Excellence consists not only of intellectual attainment; Mill was also especially concerned with moral improvement, and he re-

peatedly urged the development of altruism and noble moral virtues as explicit educational aims. He also urged the unfolding and enriching of all dimensions of one's nature: He believed that all instincts, passions, feelings, desires, and emotions are amenable to deliberate education; there is no characteristic of human beings that cannot be molded by education. We needn't suppress destructive desires, but rather transform them into constructive capacities. The resultant nature would be whole, unified, and individualized. Mill had a loathing for conformity, lack of independence and initiative. At the same time, he deeply honored boldness of mind and the willingness to experiment.

He also insisted that the cultivation of feeling and aesthetic sensibility are especially important constituents of education. His father had regarded such experience with contempt, but Mill found that a good life must include them abundantly, and that all positive human traits are enhanced by our sensitivity to human feeling and a cultivated love of beauty.

The questions of how such aims are to be accomplished, who is responsible for seeing to them, and to which populations they are to be addressed are more vexing. Because of his having two distinct educational psychologies, it is not surprising that Mill does not offer systematic proposals for implementing these aims. He proposed a new science—ethology—that would study the laws and conditions of the formation of character; this science would serve as the basis for education. He intended to launch this science himself, but he never did so.

Regarding the assignment of responsibility, Mill is characteristically emphatic in rejecting state-controlled or state-prescribed education, for he always feared the state's intrusions in personal liberty and its tendency to demand uniformity. He did allow, nevertheless, for a tax subsidy available to each family for the cost of elementary education, and he advocated that the state require standardized achievement tests at each level of education.

At some point in history, presumably, everyone will be capable of the highest reaches of learning and character development; but in Mill's time he favored universal education only at the elementary level. He was persuaded that in any known culture the resident populations are unequally prepared to acquire and utilize education. Elites, accordingly, are needed to provide whatever education can be effectively appropriated.

James Gouinlock

See also: FREEDOM AND DETERMINISM; HELVETIUS; INDIVIDUALISM

Bibliography

Garforth, F.W. *John Stuart Mill's Theory of Education*. New York: Barnes and Noble, 1989.

Gouinlock, James. *Excellence in Public Discourse*. New York: Teachers College Press, 1986.

Mill, John Stuart. *Autobiography* [1873]. New York: Liberal Arts Press, 1957.

————. *On Liberty* [1859]. Indianapolis, Ind.: Hackett, 1978.

————. *A System of Logic, Ratiocinative and Inductive* [1872]. 8th ed. London: Longmans, Green, 1956.

Milton, John (1608–1674)

One of the world's preeminent poets, a political theorist, theologian, teacher, author of textbooks on grammar and logic, and educational reformer.

Milton encountered a humanist curriculum at London's celebrated St. Paul's School and a scholastic and Aristotelian one at Christ's College, Cambridge. In a university exercise he contemptuously described the Cambridge curriculum as a "Lernian bog of fallacies" generated by a "monkish disease" (c. 1632). Years later he lamented the fate of undergraduates, who are "fed with nothing else, but the scragged and thorny lectures of monkish and miserable sophistry" (1642).

After Cambridge, Milton spent five years in self-directed study and then fifteen months touring Europe. Returning to London, he took in several students. The curriculum resembled the humanist one of St. Paul's rather than the scholastic one of Cambridge, although it was more practical than either. Drawing upon classical writers and his own experience as a teacher, Milton advocated educational reform in *Of Education* (1644), written at the request of the Comenian reformer Samuel Hartlib (c. 1600–c. 1670).

Milton offered two versions of the goal of education. The first reflected a Baconian optimism in the potential of method to reverse the effects of the fall: "The end of learning is to repair the ruins of our first parents by regaining to know God aright." We attain knowledge of God by studying in ascending order the works of nature and humanity. The second version echoed early humanist programs: A complete education "fits a man to perform justly, skillfully, and magnanimously all the offices, both public and private, of peace and war." Milton's curriculum was noteworthy for its rigor (Greek and Latin, for example, were to be mastered in the early teens, and Italian, Hebrew, Syriac, and Chaldean to be picked up shortly thereafter), its pragmatic nature, and its emphasis on physical exercise. Milton's program was radical in the etymological sense of going to the roots. He claimed models in Pythagoras, Plato, Isocrates, and Aristotle, and he saw his schools as replacing the medieval invention of universities. While there might need to be centers for advanced study of medicine and law, his academies would be dispersed throughout the country and house boys from twelve through twenty.

While Renaissance schools began with logic and metaphysics, Milton deferred these subjects as beyond the interest and capacity of children. He condemned also the standard practice of forcing children to compose prose and verse in ancient languages before they had either the requisite linguistic proficiency or anything to say. Instead the boys began with classical writers on education and arithmetic and geometry. They turned next to classical works on agriculture, both for the simplicity of their language and the practicality of their content. Cartography, physiology, and natural history followed. Next they moved to trigonometry and thence to fortification, architecture, engineering, and navigation. Then they began botany, mineralogy, zoology, and anatomy. Though unconventional for its time, the program thus far looked to the past, with an exclusive diet of classical authors. The next element was distinctively new: Milton recommended that reading be supplemented by listening to and observing such skilled workers and professionals as fishers, artisans, sailors, architects, and engineers.

Only at this relatively advanced stage Milton advocated the study of lyric poetry and moral philosophy, again from classical sources. Pupils were to study the elements of politics and law, to prepare themselves for public leadership. As students approached the end of the course of study, Milton found them ready for tragedy and epic, logic and rhetoric, oratory, and the theory of poetry—studies that typically came very early. The older students were also to "ride out in companies" to learn by experience what they studied in books, going so far as to practice navigation at sea.

M

From the beginning, nearly four hours a day were to be devoted to exercise (conceived in military terms: the use of the sword, wrestling, marching, fortifying, besieging, encamping) and to music in its ancient function of composing the spirits to valor and equanimity. This exercise fit Milton's vision of liberal education. While he separated professional schooling from his proposed academy, he maintained an ideal of the complete gentleman, versed in classical learning, ready to take up or supervise the practical arts, and endowed with physical strength and courage.

Milton's interest in education extended beyond his tract. He wrote in 1642 of a wish to be "doctrinal to a nation." His many prose political works were designed to educate his countrymen to citizenship in a republic, a goal that turned out to be premature. Moreover, his great epic *Paradise Lost* is pedagogical in theme and structure. Half of the twelve books unfold as lessons taught by angels to the first parents mentioned in *Of Education*. If Milton the reformer advocated pragmatic education, Adam learned from Raphael that it is best to learn "that which before us lies in daily life" (8.193), and the poem ends with Michael's assurance that with regeneration Adam and Eve will have attained "the sum/ Of Wisdom" (12.575–76).

Stephen M. Fallon

See also: COMENIUS; HUMANISM; SCHOLASTICISM

Bibliography
Bundy, Murray W. "Milton's View of Education in *Paradise Lost*." *JEGP: Journal of English and Germanic Philology* 21 (1922): 127–52.
Clark, Donald Leman. *John Milton at St. Paul's School: A Study of Ancient Rhetoric in English Renaissance Education.* New York: Columbia University Press, 1946.
Fletcher, Harris Francis. *The Intellectual Development of John Milton.* Urbana: University of Illinois Press, 1956–1961.
Melczer, William. "Looking Back without Anger: Milton's *Of Education*." In *Milton and the Middle Ages*, edited by John Mulryan. Lewisburg, Pa.: Bucknell University Press, 1982.
Milton, John. *Of Education* [London, 1644]. Reprinted in most collections of Milton's prose.
Samuel, Irene. "Milton on Learning and Wisdom." *PMLA: Publications of the Modern Language Association* 64 (1949): 708–23.

Minorities

Like many other social scientific concepts, the term *minorities* has an everyday use and a number of everyday meanings. In daily discourse it tends to be interpreted exclusively in numerical terms. In that view, the term refers to a distinctive group, smaller than another distinctive group, or groups, within a definable social context. Members of the minority group are said to form a coherent and identifiable collectivity by virtue of the fact that they share at least one distinctive characteristic. By definition, this characteristic is in relatively short supply within the particular social context in question and those who possess it can be differentiated from the majority group along this line.

This distinguishing trait might be physical, biological, religious, linguistic, ideological, political, professional, or sexual in nature. Accordingly, the discriminating variable—whether it be color of hair, age, sexual orientation, allegiance to political party or soccer team—is not assigned particular salience other than providing a dividing line between the "minorities" and "majority." Within this definition, numbers determine which group (or groups) is (or are) assigned minority status. What is more, the division between "majority" and "minorities" is reckoned to be value-free and innocuous.

The term *minorities* assumes a value-laden and potentially more insidious character when social scientists adopt it as an analytical term. From that perspective, the limitations of the everyday definition, with its emphasis on statistical aggregations, are plain to see.

Consider, for instance, those groups such as blacks in South Africa, Catholics in Northern Ireland, and women in Britain. Each has been designated a "minority"; but each is numerically stronger than, respectively, Afrikaaners, Protestants, and men. However, what unites these and other groups assigned minority status is the common experience of political and economic subordination within their respective societies. Each is subjected to underprivilege, oppression, exploitation, and disadvantage. What animates this conception of "minorities," then, is a group's relative lack of political and economic power. Those who constitute social and political minorities are singled out for unequal treatment and discrimination and are denied those opportunities for social and economic development afforded other members of the society.

In contrast to "common-sense" notions about the idea, the social definition of the term *minorities* insists that the relative size of groups is nothing more than a contingent variable. Rather, what distinguishes minorities from the majority is their relative access to scarce resources. It follows from this that the criteria used to distinguish the minority group are not arbitrary. On the contrary, they derive, in particular, from the differential power relations associated with class, race, sex, religion, and nationality.

One of the most important elements of this social definition is that it recognizes that members of minorities are stigmatized in common discourse and attendant practices. Simply put, "they" are distinguished from "us." Members of minorities tend to be represented as "the other" and designated as socially and politically peripheral. Those members who are constituted as minorities often find that they are seen as outsiders in an ideological rather than geographical sense. For this reason, minorities are central in maintaining the fiction of a national identity and way of life.

In the field of race relations, where the term *minorities* constitutes a key concept, Stephen Castles and Mark Miller (1993) make the important point that ethnic minorities tend to form only in those societies that wish to retain firm boundaries between the indigenous population ("us") on the one hand, and immigrants and their descendants ("them") on the other. In contrast, ethnic communities emerge in societies that are more amenable to the conception of cultural pluralism. In the former scenario, minorities are often viewed as undesirable and divisive and the commitment of the majority is to maintain singularity and uniformity in all its social and political institutions. In the latter, there is a genuine political commitment to reshape the society in ways that integrate multicultural perspectives.

Quite clearly, social scientists tend to agree that processes of exclusion and stigmatization constitute powerful impulses in the formation of minorities. At the same time, it is wrong to see members of minorities simply as the passive victims of state and institutional forms of discrimination. It is more accurate to note that while the existence of minorities always implies some degree of exclusion and marginalization, the realization of a shared identity and consciousness also plays some part in the formation and maintenance of minorities. Although members of minority groups forge a common identity, often as a reaction to exclusion, this process of self-definition—based, perhaps, on class, race, sex, sexual orientation, religion, or language—also takes on its own momentum.

The orientation and priorities of educational systems articulate with and reflect broader patterns of social relations. For this reason, then, the social definition of the term *minorities* has important implications for education. Arguably, these center on two discrete but interdependent concerns. First, if minorities are defined primarily in terms of their differential positioning with regard to scarce resources such as education, how is access improved either without impairing the quality or without violating conceptions of equality of opportunity? Second, to what extent can the legitimate demands of, say, antiracists, feminists, gays, and other minorities be incorporated into the concerns of the educational system without its degenerating into a form of relativism where anything and everything goes? The dilemma facing educational systems in complex state societies is both real and demanding. Too much allowance for diversity can lead to fragmentation and loss of control; too little, to alienation, unrest, and loss of control.

Barry Troyna

See also ALIENATION; COMMUNITY; EQUALITY; FEMINISM; MULTICULTURALISM; RACE AND RACISM; RIGHTS

Bibliography

Cashmore, E. Ellis, and Barry Troyna. *Introduction to Race Relations.* 2nd ed. Lewes, U.K.: Falmer Press, 1990.

Castles, Stephen, and Mark J. Miller. *The Age of Migration: International Population Movements in the Modern World.* London: Macmillan, 1993.

Raphael, S. "Introduction: The 'Little Platoons.'" In *Patriotism: The Making and Unmaking of British National Identity.* Vol. 2: *Minorities and Outsiders,* edited by R. Samuel, ix–xxxix. London: Routledge, 1989

Said, Edward. *Orientalism.* London: Routledge and Kegan Paul, 1978.

Tajfel, H. "The Social Psychology of Minorities." In *"Race" in Britain: Continuity and Change,* 2nd ed., edited by C. Husband, 232–74. London: Hutchinson University Library, 1987.

Troyna, Barry. *Racism and Education: Research Perspectives.* Buckingham: Open University Press, 1993.

M

van den Berghe, P. L. "Minorities." In *Dictionary of Race and Ethnic Relations*. 3rd ed., edited by E.E. Cashmore, 191–93. London: Routledge, 1989.

Wagley, Charles, and Marvin Harris. *Minorities in the New World*. New York: Columbia University Press, 1958.

Modernism and Postmodernism

The debate between modernism and postmodernism emerged in the latter half of the twentieth century during an era when both the theoretical framework and the political hegemony of the Western European tradition began to be challenged. Modernists defend traditional ideals of freedom and reason, while postmodernists question the existence of universal truths or disinterested knowledge apart from relations of power.

Rene Descartes (1596–1650) initiated modern philosophy by searching for a secure foundation for all knowledge through the method of universal doubt. After subjecting all of his beliefs—those derived from authority, religious tradition, custom, common sense, sense perception, and even mathematics—to radical questioning, Descartes discovered one idea that resisted all attempts to doubt it: "*Cogito ergo sum*" (I think, therefore I am). The impossibility of doubting the existence of his own thinking self led Descartes to conclude that all knowledge is grounded in the clear and distinct ideas of the individual rational mind, which, if not obscured by tradition, superstition, imagination, or emotion, can accurately represent universal truths about objective reality.

Throughout the seventeenth and eighteenth centuries, rationalist and empiricist philosophers debated about the methods by which these clear and distinct ideas can be discovered and about the way in which human knowledge is related to the Truth as seen in the mind of God; but they all assumed that the individual rational mind is capable of understanding universal principles and that freedom is the ultimate reward of the quest for truth. These beliefs, combined with a philosophy of history as the progressive realization of freedom, inspired the revolutionary movements of the Enlightenment and continued to be the dominant presuppositions of Hegelian and Marxist philosophies during the nineteenth century. The unprecedented violence and barbarism of the twentieth century, however, led to skepticism about the power of speculative reason to grasp truth and about history as the story of inevitable progress.

Critics of the modern tradition have attacked it on epistemological, political, and pedagogical grounds. In *Philosophy and the Mirror of Nature* (1979) Richard Rorty attempts to deconstruct the tradition of modern epistemology by criticizing its central metaphor—the image of the mind as a kind of mirror—and its notion of truth as correspondence between thought or language and the world. Following the American pragmatists, Rorty argues that language and thought are more like tools for coping with experience than pictures of reality. He advocates the end of epistemology and the beginning of a new kind of "edifying" philosophy, or "hermeneutics," that would not seek to represent an independent reality but would simply try to keep the conversation going in the broadest possible sense. Rather than specialists in a particular field or method, philosophers would be redefined as "all-purpose intellectuals" or "culture critics." Education, from this point of view, should be seen as helping students to get in touch with their own potentialities, not with something nonhuman called Truth or Reality. This can best be accomplished, says Rorty, by initiating them into an intellectual community through conversation with teachers who define themselves in terms of books and ideas that have influenced their lives. Human solidarity replaces objectivity as the educational ideal.

Jean-Francois Lyotard's *The Postmodern Condition* (1984) presents a different view of the implications of postmodernism for education. Lyotard defines modernism as the attempt to legitimate science by appealing to "metanarratives"—that is, philosophical accounts of the progress of history in which the hero of knowledge struggles toward a great goal such as freedom, equality, or the creation of wealth. Postmodernism, defined as skepticism about all the grand narratives of legitimation, represents a radical break with the tradition that has played an important role in the development of Western educational institutions. Lyotard warns that the criterion of efficiency of performance is rapidly replacing legitimation through metanarratives, and as a consequence education has been transformed into the production of skilled experts to fill slots in the economy. He thinks that the "Age of the Professor" is coming to an end, since computers can perform all of the traditional tasks of the teacher once grand narratives disappear. While recognizing that the computerization of society may lead to totalitarian control, Lyotard holds out the hope that it could also lead to free public access to all available information, which would encourage radical freedom and innovation rather than conformity. Lyotard's vision of the educational ideal in a postmodern society, in contrast to Rorty's, emphasizes individual autonomy rather than solidarity with one's community.

There has been a great deal of controversy about the political implications of the deconstruction of modern philosophy. Some postmodernists identify the universal claims of modernism with the experience of a dominant elite (mainly white European males), connecting epistemological privilege with sexual, racial, political, and economic privilege. Jacques Derrida attacks "logocentrism," the tyranny of the Western philosophical perspective, which he argues has suppressed, excluded, or marginalized all otherness and difference in the modern tradition. His proposal of a "logic of *différance*" celebrating plurality, contingency, and diversity has encouraged some feminists and minority groups to ally themselves with the deconstructionists in their struggle for equal rights.

On the other hand, it has been argued that postmodernism's emphasis on differences and opposition to universality can easily degenerate into cynical relativism if not balanced by a search for common theoretical ground as a rational basis for action. In *The Philosophical Discourse for Modernity* (1987), Jürgen Habermas defends modernism, redefined as a still-unfinished project that keeps alive the Enlightenment hope for a more just, equal, and rational society, grounded in the ideal of free and open communication rather than in absolutes or totalizing theories.

The debate between modernism and postmodernism has resulted in bitter conflicts in education about the core curriculum and "political correctness." Postmodern advocates of diversity argue that all students should be exposed to the perspectives and contributions of many cultures other than their own, both temporally and geographically. They should also become aware of the heterogeneity of their own societies and learn not just to tolerate but also to value differences of race, ethnicity, class, sex, and sexual preference. The ideal of "multicultural literacy" challenges the modernist assumption that the perspective of historically dominant groups is superior or objectively true. It is also viewed as an important counterweight to the natural human tendency to fear differences, given that students must learn to live and work in a rapidly changing world. In addition to demanding curricular reform, some postmodernists defend campus speech codes restricting the use of racial slurs or other expressions offensive to certain groups on the grounds that this language creates a climate that interferes with equality of educational opportunity.

Critics of postmodernism are outraged at what they see to be the politicization of education. Allan Bloom's *The Closing of the American Mind* (1987) argues that women's studies, African American studies, and other attempts to diversify the mainstream curriculum have resulted in the lowering of standards and the corruption of the ideal of objective Truth. E. D. Hirsch's *Cultural Literacy* (1987) insists that students need to master basic concepts in their own tradition before being exposed to other cultures. Dinesh D'Souza's *Illiberal Education* (1991) attacks the politics of race and gender as a new form of totalitarianism in which freedom of thought and expression are stifled in the name of tolerance of diversity. Defenders of multiculturalism reply to the charge that they are making education too political by saying that educators have always had to make controversial decisions about what to include in the curriculum and what kind of speech and behavior to tolerate. Whether or not this fact is acknowledged, they maintain, education is and always will be political.

It is likely that the debate between modernism and postmodernism will continue for some time to come. Modernists defend the existence of objective standards of quality that ideally would guide choices about course requirements and ethics, but they have not succeeded in developing educational principles or programs that command universal agreement. Postmodernists argue that students should be taught not to depend upon fictional ideals of objectivity, but no comprehensive postmodern philosophy of education has yet been produced. Perhaps this is not surprising in a movement that defines itself in terms of the critique of tradition. It remains to be seen whether a constructive phase of postmodernism will emerge out of the attempt to deconstruct modern philosophy and culture.

Carol J. Nicholson

See also EMPIRICISM; EPISTEMOLOGY; FEMI-
NISM; MULTICULTURALISM; PLURALISM;
PROGRESS, IDEA OF, AND PROGRESSIVE EDU-
CATION; RATIONALISM; SKEPTICISM; TRUTH

Bibliography

Aronowitz, Stanley, and Henry A. Giroux.
*Postmodern Education: Politics, Culture,
and Social Criticism*. Minneapolis: University of Minnesota Press, 1991.

Bernstein, Richard J. *The New Constellation:
The Ethical-Political Horizons of Moder-
nity/Postmodernity*. Cambridge: MIT
Press, 1992.

Bloom, Allen. *The Closing of the American
Mind*. New York: Simon and Schuster,
1987.

D'Souza, Dinesh. *Illiberal Education: The
Politics of Race and Sex on Campus*.
New York: Macmillan, 1991.

Gless, Darryl J., and Barbara Herrnstein
Smith, eds. *The Politics of Liberal Edu-
cation*. Durham, N.C.: Duke University
Press, 1992.

Habermas, Jürgen. *The Philosophical Discourse of Modernity*. Translated by F.
Lawrence. Cambridge: MIT Press, 1987.

Hirsch, E.D. *Cultural Literacy*. Boston:
Houghton Mifflin, 1987.

Lyotard, Jean-Francois. *The Postmodern
Condition: A Report on Knowledge*.
Minneapolis: University of Minnesota
Press, 1984.

Nicholson, Linda J. *Feminism/Postmodernism*.
New York: Routledge, 1990.

Rorty, Richard. *Philosophy and the Mirror of
Nature*. Princeton: Princeton University
Press, 1979.

Montaigne, Michel de (1533–1592)

French philosopher, mayor of Bordeaux from
1581 to 1585, author of three books of *Essays*
(1580–1588) and of a *Travel Journal* (unpublished during his lifetime), reporting on his trip
to Germany, Switzerland, and Italy in 1580 and
1581. His *Essays* are a major masterpiece of
French literature and a true mine of reflections
on the most varied subjects; here we will concern ourselves with his views on education.

Montaigne declares that "the greatest and
most important difficulty in human knowledge
seems to lie in the branch of knowledge which
deals with the upbringing and education of children," and he expressed admiration for those

ancient states (such as Sparta) that made a serious effort to perform this difficult task well.
But education must be of the right kind: teaching not so much "letters" as good judgment and
understanding, and more practical skills than
useless quibbles. "I would rather make of [my
student] an able man than a learned man,"
which implies that the teacher, too, must have
"a well-made rather than a well-filled head."

Not one's memory but one's life must
profit from teaching; so whatever one is taught
must be appropriated and modified in a personal way. "The stomach has not done its work
if it has not changed the condition and form
of what has been given it to cook." Nothing
should be taken "on mere authority and trust,"
and it is all right to forget where one has learned
certain "ways of thinking" so long as one
knows "how to make them his own."

Because one is one's body as much as one's
soul, and because body and soul work together,
they must be educated together. "The soul is too
hard pressed unless it is seconded, and has too
great a task doing two jobs alone." And any
education must come primarily through example and exercise: Just as one cannot become
a dancer by simply learning about dancing, one
cannot become a just, wise, or honorable person without practicing justice, wisdom, and
honor. Montaigne had direct experience of this
maxim as a child, when his father, wanting him
to learn Latin well, had everyone around him
speak nothing but Latin for the first few years
of his life—which strategy made the boy extremely proficient in, and also attracted to, the
language. So he wants a tutor "right from the
start, according to the capacity of the mind he
has in hand, to begin putting it through its
paces, making it taste things, choose them, and
discern them by itself; sometimes clearing the
way for him, sometimes letting him clear his
own way."

The world itself must be a textbook for this
sort of teaching, and no matter is to be considered too small or unimportant to learn from it.
"A page's prank, a servant's blunder, a remark
at table, are so many new materials." The student "will sound the capacity of each man: a
cowherd, a mason, a passer-by; he must put
everything to use, and borrow from each man
according to his wares, for everything is useful
in a household; even the stupidity and weakness
of others will be an education to him."

This emphasis on the many occasions
available for learning naturally leads to the cen-

tral concept of Montaigne's philosophy of education: diversity. On the one hand, teaching must be individualized and made to fit the needs of each student. "If, as is our custom, the teachers undertake to regulate many minds . . . with the same lesson . . . , it is no wonder if . . . they find barely two or three who reap any proper fruit from their teaching." On the other hand, and even more important, teaching must overcome the students' limitations by making them appreciate different customs, rules, and tastes, and turning them into more flexible, adaptable people. For this purpose, it is especially useful to travel: "I should like the tutor to start taking [his student] abroad at a tender age." And one must not even be afraid of excess, since that is part of life, too: "Provided his appetite and will can be kept in check, let a young man boldly be made fit for all nations and companies, even for dissoluteness and excess, if need be."

Finally, education should be fun. Once more, Montaigne refers here to his own experience with his father's techniques, which included teaching him Greek "in the form of amusement and exercise. We volleyed our conjugations back and forth, like those who learn arithmetic and geometry by such games as checkers and chess." And he contrasts this strategy with the harsh discipline current in the schools of his time. "Go in at lesson time: you hear nothing but cries, both from tortured boys and from masters drunk with rage." A teaching respectful of children's likes and inclinations, and even ready to give them "healthful foods . . . sweetened," will develop into a "gay and sociable wisdom" and a philosophy than which "there is nothing more gay, more lusty, more sprightly, and I might almost say more frolicsome." Students will flower into adults at ease with themselves, armed "with graceful pride, an active and joyous bearing, and a contented and good-natured countenance."

Ermanno Bencivenga

See also AIMS OF EDUCATION; HUMAN NATURE; INDOCTRINATION; LEISURE; NIETZSCHE; PLEASURE; PRACTICAL WISDOM; ROUSSEAU

Bibliography

Montaigne, Michel de. *Complete Works.* Translated by Donald M. Frame. Stanford: Stanford University Press, 1948.

Montessori, Maria (1870–1952)

Shortly after receiving her diploma, Maria Montessori, the first woman to graduate from medical school in Italy, undertook research that led her to visit asylums where young children were locked up with the criminally insane. While reading up on the education of "deficients," she discovered the writings of Jean-Marc-Gaspard Itard (1775–1838) and Edouard Seguin (1812–1880). Profoundly affected by their ideas, she went on to study pedagogy and physical anthropology and to acquaint herself with the major works in educational theory of the past two hundred years. In quick succession thereafter Montessori gave a series of lectures on special methods of education at a teacher training institute in Rome, became director of a medical-pedagogical institute, and taught in the Pedagogic School at the University of Rome. Then, in 1907, she opened the first *Casa dei Bambini*—a school for "normal" children who were running wild in Rome's tenements while their parents were at work. Two years later the Italian-language edition of *The Montessori Method* was published and in a short while several more schools were established. These were so successful and Montessori's book was so well received that people across the world began flocking to Rome to observe her ideas in action. Montessori, in turn, made several triumphal speaking tours in the United States.

When, after 1917, her American reputation waned, Montessori continued to lecture to huge audiences and to give training courses throughout Europe. Despite the speeches on education and peace that Montessori began giving in 1926, and notwithstanding the central role that education for independence played in her system, from 1925 to 1934 her schools in Italy had Benito Mussolini's backing. When in 1935 that dictator finally closed them down, she moved to Holland to continue her work and to deliver the addresses that would later be collected in *Education and Peace*. In 1939 Montessori left her new home for India, where, during World War II, she trained over one thousand teachers while giving the lectures that formed the basis for such works as *The Absorbent Mind* and *The Discovery of the Child*. Returning to Europe after the war, she spoke, wrote, traveled to conferences, and gave training teacher courses until the very end. At the time of her death she had thrice been nominated for the Nobel Peace Prize.

When Montessori first visited the United

States in 1913, a news article referred to her educational ideas as having already taken their place in history next to those of Jean-Jacques Rousseau (1712–1778), Johann Heinrich Pestalozzi (1746–1827), and Friedrich Froebel (1782–1852). Her claims to admission to the pantheon of educational philosophers were even then being contested, however. William Heard Kilpatrick (1871–1965), a member of the faculty of Teachers College, Columbia University, and a disciple of John Dewey (1859–1952), challenged them first in a speech to the International Kindergarten Association and then, with Dewey's blessing, in a short monograph addressed to teachers and school superintendents. In that 1914 work, Kilpatrick asked where among other systems of education Montessori's belonged. Placing Montessori in "the Rousseau-Pestalozzi-Froebel group," he faulted both her logic and her knowledge of educational theory and practice before saying that, in her thinking, Montessori belonged to the mid nineteenth century. Using Dewey's ideas as the yardstick by which to assess Montessori's, and judging that hers consistently fell short of the master's, Kilpatrick assured readers that they owed Montessori "no large point of view." He then concluded: "They are ill advised who put Madam Montessori among the significant contributors to educational theory. Stimulating she is; a contributor to our theory, hardly if at all."

Reducing Montessori's educational theory to seven "characteristic elements," Kilpatrick critiqued her doctrine of education as development and her doctrine of liberty for the child; the related ideas of self-expression and auto- or self-education; the exercises in practical life she built into the child's curriculum; her theory of sense training; and her approach to teaching the 3Rs. One important element of her system that he did not see fit to mention was her ideal of sexual equality. Unwilling to allow one sex to be the servant of the other, Montessori required both sexes to learn how to do the domestic work both needed done; thus, both boys and girls in the Casa dei Bambini set tables, served soup, and cleaned house. Nor did Montessori's rejection of stereotypical sex roles stop there. The "new woman," she said in her inaugural address at the opening of the second Casa dei Bambini in Rome, "shall be, like man, an individual, a free human being, a social worker." Kilpatrick did not remark on the element of love, either, although Montessori clearly intended that there be an affectionate relationship between teacher and children and among the children themselves. She also wanted the children to feel respect and affection for nature and to come to love and value all living things. And he failed to make note of the joy that, as a byproduct of learning in the Casa dei Bambini, was a familiar feature of life therein.

In 1918 the historian of educational thought Robert R. Rusk reached an opposite conclusion from Kilpatrick's. This lecturer in education at Glasgow University also saw reflections of Rousseau in Montessori's work. And whereas Kilpatrick considered Seguin's influence to be grounds for condemning her, Rusk represented Seguin's work as fertile soil from which she had imaginatively drawn implications about the education of all children. Along with many others, Rusk criticized Montessori for overrating the importance of the special devices for sensory training she had introduced into early education. However, his final verdict on her contribution to educational theory is reflected in his decision to include a chapter on her system in a text entitled The Doctrines of the Great Educators.

Over the years, Montessori's ideas have been admired by many besides Rusk and condemned not only by Kilpatrick. Friends and foes alike, however—at least English-speaking ones—have misread a central element of her theory. Speaking at the opening of the second Casa dei Bambini in Rome, Montessori said: "We Italians have elevated our word 'casa' to the almost sacred significance of the English word 'home,' the enclosed temple of domestic affection, accessible only to dear ones." Nevertheless, from the beginning, Montessori's term for school has been rendered in English "The House of Childhood" or "The Children's House." Indeed, in 1912 the speech containing her cautionary note was published as Chapter III of the first English-language edition of The Montessori Method under the title "Inaugural Address Delivered on the Occasion of the Opening of One of the 'Children's Houses.'"

Read casa as house and one's attention is drawn to the child-size furniture in the schools Montessori established, the exercises in dressing and washing, the self-education, and perhaps the extended day. Read casa as home and one discovers a moral and social dimension that transforms one's understanding of Montessori's theory. A common criticism of her educational thought has been that it ignores interpersonal or social education. When her system is reinterpreted, however, its elements take on a different configuration: Where small individuals were seen busily manipulating materials designed especially for learning, there emerges a domestic scene with its own special form of social life and education.

If Montessori's inaugural lecture is not in itself convincing evidence that she conceptualized school as home, her use in later years of the image of a womb—a child's very first home—should be decisive. In *Education and Peace*, Montessori distinguished a negative concept of peace as merely the cessation of war from a positive one. Introducing an analogy to good health—which, she said, is not simply a matter of the absence of disease but is based on a strong, well-developed body relatively resistant to infection—she argued that positive or genuine peace requires a transformation of moral life. Peace, wrote Montessori, is not "a partial truce between separate nations, but a permanent way of life for all mankind." How is this to be achieved? Because she believed the hope of altering adults to be vain, the child must be the starting point for the transformation.

Considering the child a spiritual embryo, Montessori told European audiences that the child "must no longer be considered as the son of man, but rather as the creator and the father of man." The spiritual embryo's promise will only be fulfilled if the child is allowed to develop normally, Montessori insisted. Since its psychic life begins at birth, the problem of peace becomes, then, one of educating young children. Just as the physical embryo derives its nutriments from the womb, the spiritual embryo absorbs them from its surroundings. Put children in the wrong environment and their development will be abnormal and they will become the deviated adults we now know. Create the right environment for them and their characters will develop normally. The "second womb" is what she called the young child's proper environment. From at least age three, the *Casa dei Bambini* was to be that second womb.

What is the character of the institution she called home? One dwells in a house. One feels safe, secure, loved, at ease—that is, at home—in a home: at least, in the kind of home envisioned by Montessori. Montessori was well aware that not all homes are safe and loving. In addition, this delegate to the 1896 International Women's Congress in Berlin knew that the sexual equality she was building into her idea of school was not an attribute of the ordinary Italian home. However, she did not dream of modeling her school on just any home. Maintaining in her inaugural address that the *Casa dei Bambini* "is not simply a place where the children are kept, not just an *asylum,* but a true school for their education," she indicated that even in its homelikeness it was to be educative.

One clear implication of Montessori's concept of school as home is that the inhabitants of school constitute a family. Just as the model for school in Montessori's theory is an idealized version of home, an exemplary family serves as the model for the relationship in which those attending school stand to one another. When it does, the social nature of Montessori's system becomes apparent. Instruction in a *Casa dei Bambini* is definitely individualized. However, like the individual members of the family of Montessori's imagination, even as the children are treated as individuals and their individuality is allowed to flourish, they feel connected to one another and concerned about each other's welfare.

Although Montessori's name is usually associated with the education of young children, in *From Childhood to Adolescence* she applied her idea of school as home to the case of teenagers. In that work she proposed that adolescents live together in the country away from their private homes, and that they run a modern farm, a country store, and "The Rural Children's Hotel." Directed by a married couple who would exercise "a moral and protective influence on the youths," this home away from home would be an ongoing commercial enterprise. Conserving "the tradition of the past when personal talent was expressed in the fabrication of each object," the store would sell not only the produce of the young people but also that of poor neighbors. "Mixing business with friendship," it would also serve as a kind of social center.

Ignoring the context in which Montessori developed her ideas, most interpreters of Montessori's thought have not realized that the *Casa dei Bambini* was meant to compensate for the domestic vacuum in the lives of children whose mothers were required to work each day outside their own homes. Even those who were aware of its origins apparently did not realize that the *Casa dei Bambini* was intended as a surrogate home for children. In consequence, the uncanny relevance for future generations of Montessori's idea of school has never fully been appreciated. To borrow a phrase that William James (1842–1916) introduced in a very different context just three years after Montessori delivered her inaugural lecture, the *Casa dei Bambini* was Montessori's "moral equivalent" of home. Because fathers have left home each day to go to work ever since the Industrial Revolution, and many families are headed by single mothers, the exodus of women to the workplace greatly expands this concept of school's range of application.

One reason why Montessori's domestic imagery has been neglected is that it violates basic cultural expectations about the role of school in society. Implicitly dividing social reality into two parts—private home and public world—members of Western industrial and postindustrial societies take the function of school to be that of transforming children who have heretofore lived their lives in one part into members of the other. Assuming that the private home is a natural institution and that, accordingly, membership in it is a given rather than something one must achieve, they see no reason to prepare people to carry out the tasks and activities associated with it. Perceiving the public world as a human creation and membership in it as something at which one can succeed or fail, and therefore as problematic, they make preparation for carrying out the tasks and activities associated with the public world the main business of education.

Montessori wanted the *Casa dei Bambini* to form children for life in the public world. But she knew that a public world hospitable to peace in the positive sense would have to be very different from the one of her acquaintance, and that those living in it would have to have been formed by a very different kind of school. Envisioning school as an extension of the private home and the world as continuous with school and home, she left no room in her system for the radical dichotomies so often drawn between school and home, home and world, world and school.

Montessori may not have been the only or even the first person in the history of Western educational thought to reject a radical separation between school and home. Because, however, she is the one who built domestic imagery into her theory, even as her educational practice acknowledged the importance of the atmosphere, affections, and curriculum associated with home and domesticity, the system that Kilpatrick claimed had nothing new of

importance in it is nothing short of revolutionary.

Jane Roland Martin

See also DOMESTIC EDUCATION; FROEBEL; HOME AND FAMILY; PESTALOZZI; ROUSSEAU

Bibliography
Kilpatrick, William Heard. *The Montessori System Examined.* Boston: Houghton Mifflin, 1914.
Kramer, Rita. *Maria Montessori: A Biography.* Chicago: University of Chicago Press, 1976.
Martin, Jane Roland. "Romanticism Domesticated: Maria Montessori and the Casa dei Bambini." In *The Educational Legacy of Romanticism,* edited by John Willinsky, 159–74. Waterloo, Ontario: Wilfrid Laurier University Press, 1990.
Montessori, Maria. *The Absorbent Mind.* New York: Dell, 1984.
———. *Education and Peace.* Chicago: Regnery, 1972.
———. *From Childhood to Adolescence.* New York: Schocken, 1973.
——— *The Montessori Method.* New York: Schocken, 1964.
———. *The Schoolhome: Rethinking Schools for Changing Families.* Cambridge: Harvard University Press, 1992.
Rusk, Robert R. *The Doctrines of the Great Educators.* 3rd ed. New York: St. Martin's, 1965.

Moral Development

It needs to be stated at the outset that ethics, moral behavior, and moral development are human activities, involving people-to-people relations. A hamster who destroys its litter if there is a runt in it would certainly not be called a "bad mother," since the behavior is an automatic reaction built into the animal as a response to external anomalies.

The question that is first addressed is whether philosophers have established universality and prescriptiveness as criteria for moral decisions. Lawrence Kohlberg, a psychologist, has postulated an invariant sequence of moral development that parallels Jean Piaget's stages of cognitive development. Kohlberg's position is that philosophers have established universality and prescriptiveness as criteria for evaluating moral decisions. This philosophical position is contrasted with John Dewey's position. A brief consideration of personality, intelligence, and morality follows. It concludes with a contemporary analysis of ethics and moral development, seen as part of a theory of communication, control, and organization.

Kohlberg's Model of Moral Development

One of Kohlberg's major concerns was to join philosophy and psychology in the study of moral development. He wrote:

> I claim, persuaded by some of my philosopher friends, that an ultimately adequate *psychological* theory as to why a child does move from stage to stage is an ultimately adequate *philosophical* explanation as to why a higher stage is more adequate than a lower stage and are one and the same theory extended in different directions (Kohlberg 1971: 5).

The psychological explanation is concerned with the universal development of morality through an invariant sequence, while the philosophical explanation involves why a higher stage in the sequence is more desirable than a lower stage. This philosophical explanation depends upon an isomorphic relation that Kohlberg saw between psychology and philosophy. Higher forms of psychological functioning involve increased differentiation and organization. Philosophical systems of morality are more adequate in relation to their inclusion of universality and prescriptiveness. The claim of principled morality is that it defines the right for anyone in any situation.

To provide support for his psychological theory, Kohlberg established empirical data. Over a period of twelve years, he did both longitudinal and cross-sectional studies of moral development in different cultures: the United States, Great Britain, Canada, Taiwan, Mexico, and Turkey. At the beginning of the longitudinal studies, the subjects (all boys) ranged in age from ten to sixteen. The age range at the conclusion was twenty-two to twenty-eight. His procedure was to present the subject with an ethical dilemma and then to analyze the reasoning through which a decision was reached. It is to be noted that what was considered important was the reasoning, not the decision itself. These studies continued after Kohlberg's death in 1986.

An example of one ethical dilemma appears as follows:

In Europe, a woman was near death from a very bad disease, a special kind of cancer. There was one drug that the doctors thought might save her. It was a form of radium [for which] a druggist was charging ten times what the drug cost him to make. The sick woman's husband, Heinz, went to everyone he knew to borrow the money, but he could [get together only] about half of what it cost. He told the druggist that his wife was dying and asked him to sell it [for less] or let him pay later. But the druggist said, "No, I discovered the drug and I am going to make money from it." So Heinz got desperate and broke into the man's store to steal the drug for his wife.

Should the husband have done that? And why? (Montgomery 1972: 178).

In analyzing the decision-making processes of his subjects, Kohlberg derived six stages of moral development that he considered to be universally applicable. Although the sequence of this development is invariant (except for stages 5 and 6—a person may reach stage 6 without going through stage 5), the rate of development may vary, so that children from isolated villages developed more slowly than children from urban environments.

The six stages entail the following:

Stage 1. Action is motivated by avoidance of punishment and "conscience" is irrational fear of punishment.

Stage 2. Action is motivated by desire for reward or benefit. Possible guilt reactions are ignored and punishment is viewed in a pragmatic matter.

Stage 3. Action is motivated by anticipation of disapproval of others, actual or imagined-hypothetical (for example, guilt). (Differentiation of disapproval from punishment, fear, and pain).

Stage 4. Action is motivated by anticipation of dishonor—that is, institutionalized blame for failure of duty, and by guilt over concrete harm done to others. (Differentiates formal dishonor from informal disapproval. Differentiates guilt from bad).

Stage 5. Concern is about maintaining respect of equals and of the community (assuming their respect is based on reason rather than emotions). Concern about own self-

respect—that is, to avoid judging the self as irrational, inconsistent, nonpurposive. (Discrimination between institutionalized blame and community disrespect.)
Stage 6. Concern about self-condemnation for violating one's own principles. Differentiates between community respect and self-respect. Differentiates between self-respect for generally achieving moral principles and self-rationality respect for maintaining moral principles.) (Kohlberg 1971: 30–31).

Stages 5 and 6 were later considered to form one stage, indicating one's arrival at "Principled Morality," the highest stage of moral development. (Kohlberg 1986). This will now be referred to as stage 5/6.

A concern to be addressed is the relationship Kohlberg draws between moral theory in psychology and philosophy. There are two important questions that arise in any consideration of his work. Is Kohlberg's psychology based on structuralism? Are there limitations to structuralism as an explanation for human behavior? Kohlberg attributes the six-stage sequence to an invariant genetic structuring process of the individual as he interacts with the environment. Might these six stages be attributable to similar conditions of human existence?

Structuralism explains human behavior by describing cognitive operations through which the individual interprets his world. These operations evolve in a fixed sequence and are the same for all men (Kohlberg 1986), although some attain higher levels of operation than others. Variety in human behavior comes via the ability to apply the operations in differing situations, much as the rules of chess provide the framework for an almost infinite possibility in games. How, however, does a fixed cognitive matrix allow the formation of new concepts? How do you explain the development of operations entailing reorganization of all previous cognitive operations, not only changing a rule in chess that makes it an entirely different game, but also developing, creating, and generating rules? As an example, did Einstein use structural operations in his thinking to a significantly greater degree than "ordinary" individuals? Kohlberg's structuralism does not allow for going beyond previous experience. P.B. Rice states:

> We cannot say outright, then, that ethical principles are a priori either in the linguistic sense or in the existential sense. This

may express adequately the structure of the linguistic and normative habits that to date have withstood the buffeting of experience through a variety of conditions . . . (but) even apart from these there is always the possibility of discovering new capacities for experience and new ways of integrating conduct. (Rice 1955: 193)

Such possible limits pose some serious complications for Kohlberg's theory. Accepting for the moment the experimental design and interpretation of Kohlberg's longitudinal study that seventy-five boys did pass through a sequence of moral development, is it necessarily the case that the structure of their thinking will remain the same, even if they have reached stage 6, or is it possible that in the future they may transcend the limits of the moral structure Kohlberg has delineated? Accepting for the moment that the subjects will not make such a transition, is it possible that there is an individual, not included in the sample, who has transcended the moral system? Finally, has there been a philosophic explanation of moral decision-making that does not involve any stage suggested by Kohlberg? If there is, then it is sufficient evidence to show that Kohlberg's theory is not universal.

One alternative to explain Kohlberg's results is to attribute them to conditions of existence. By not providing an analysis of the child-rearing process or the possible effects of the culture at large in those societies he studied, Kohlberg has not discounted the possibility that his stages may be explainable through the experiences of the child. As an instance, despite parental influences, what is the likely generalization in regard to punishment that a ten-year-old child, particularly a boy, might make to the story "Little Red Riding Hood" or the song "Three Blind Mice"?

Dewey and Kohlberg Contrasted

Dewey offers a strong argument that universality and prescriptiveness have not been established as criteria for moral decisions. Dewey's moral theory provides a means of evaluating Kohlberg's experimental technique; Dewey's moral theory does not fit conveniently into any of Kohlberg's six stages.

Primary to Dewey's moral philosophy is its base in experience. Reflective thinking stems from the conditions of the environment, whether it be thinking in the physical sciences or morality. It begins with the perception of a disturbance, a signal from noise, sensed by an individual. For Kohlberg, disturbance can provide the impetus for moving from stage to stage. However, once one reaches stage 6, the principled or categorical stage, the function of doubt as a trigger to thinking appears to atrophy. "The claim of principled morality is that it defined the right for anyone in any situation." In Kohlberg's system, a person at stage 6 need no longer appeal to experience. In Dewey's system, without an appeal to experience, thinking is impossible.

In a different manner, Kohlberg's discounting of experience appears throughout all six stages. In analyzing his data, he was concerned with the process of reaching the decision, not the content of the decision. A decision is more adequate morally in accordance with the process used, not in reference to the nature of the decision or its consequences in experience. Is it possible to have two people at stage 6 reach different decisions, although each is operating via a "universal principle"?

One consequence of the above is that Kohlberg's system was being suggested as beneficial in alleviating strife among nations, since the right is not defined in terms of cultural norms (NICH: 22). Even as late as 1986, Kohlberg's concepts were being promoted to be of utility in American and Soviet "exchanges." However, his theory may block communication among nations who have derived different imperatives. For how is it possible to negotiate matters which are beyond doubt?

Dewey's explanation as to the origin of the appeal to universality and prescriptiveness and the consequences of such an appeal are as follows:

It is clear that the various situations in which a person is called to deliberate and judge have common elements, and that values found in them resemble one another. It is also obvious that general ideas are a great aid in judging particular cases. . . . Through intercommunication the experience of the entire human race is to some extent pooled and crystallized in general ideas. They are thought of as if they existed in and of themselves and as if it were simply a question of bringing action under them in order to determine what is right and good. Instead of being treated as aids and instruments in judging values as the latter actually arise, they are made superior to them. They become prescriptions, rules (Dewey 1960: 136).

Experience carries over from one situation to another, and experience is intellectually cumulative. Out of resembling experiences general ideas develop, and differentiation and organization. In this case, however, differentiation and organization are not isomorphic with universality and prescriptiveness, as they are in Kohlberg. Rather, as a generalization becomes prescriptive it diminishes the occasions for further differentiation and organization. In effect, growth comes to a halt. Dewey states:

The philosophic significance of the doctrine of evolution lies precisely in its emphasis upon continuity of simpler and more complex organic forms until we reach man. . . . The doctrine of organic development means that the living creature is a part of the world, sharing its vicissitudes and fortunes, and making itself secure in its precarious dependence only as it intellectually identifies itself with the things about it, and forecasting with future consequences of what is going on, shapes its own activities accordingly. . . . Knowledge is a mode of participation, valuable in the degree in which it is effective. It cannot be the idle view of an unconcerned spectator (White 1972: 273).

Thus, for Dewey, knowledge at all levels involves a reference back to experience; it does not for Kohlberg. In 1915, Dewey wrote a short book, *German Philosophy and Politics,* in which he uncannily pinpointed the type of thinking that led later to the Third Reich. At the base of this thinking was a moral system that did not involve an appeal to experience. Let the German writer Heinrich Heine (1797–1856) speak for himself:

It seems to me that a methodical people, such as we, must begin with the reformation, must then occupy ourselves with systems of philosophy, and only after their completion pass to the political revolution. . . . Then will appear Kantians, as little tolerant of pity in the world of ideas, who will mercilessly upturn with sword and axe the soil of our European life to extirpate the last remnants of the past. . . . The hour will come. As on the steps of an amphitheater, the nations will group themselves around Germany to witness the terrible combat (Dewey 1915: 84–85).

Or, quoting another German writer:

> To no nation except the German has it been given to enjoy in its inner self that which is given to mankind as a whole. . . . It is this quality which especially fits us for leadership in the intellectual domain and imposes upon us the obligation to maintain that position. (Dewey 1915: 35)

Is stage 5/6 thinking involved in the above?

An argument stating that philosophers have not established universality and prescriptiveness as criteria for moral decisions has been offered. Important to this argument is the negation of the contention that universality and prescriptiveness are isomorphic to differentiation and organization. At stage 5/6, increased differentiation and organization are not possible. Kohlberg may not have realized that he was a neo-Kantian, but we need to be careful to recognize his thinking as such. The fate of German thought was to wreak such crimes by man against man that thinking about the era brings serious questions about man's moral adequacy. And, though philosophy requires circumspection, in this case it is not unduly rambunctious to ask whether we have learned anything.

Contrasting Dewey with Kohlberg provides a means of evaluating Kohlberg's experimental technique. At this point, two important questions need to be asked: What constitutes moral experience? Do Kohlberg's ethical dilemmas constitute moral experiences? For Dewey, moral experiences are within the ongoing activities of the individual. They start with a desire arising from a field of activities, entailing evaluation of the desire and establishment of means to attain a particular end.

In two important respects, Kohlberg's ethical dilemmas do not constitute moral experiences. First, there are no criteria for gauging whether or not the dilemmas introduced by Kohlberg were sufficiently meaningful to create doubt within the thinking of the subjects. Did the ten year olds questioned have sufficient appreciation of such terms as *death, cancer,* or *husband and wife* to be involved in a moral dilemma derivable from their own experience and disruptive enough of that experience to entail thinking? Second, in Dewey's terms, a moral experience involves inquiry into the situation at hand for the purpose of transforming that situation. With Kohlberg's example, Heinz has already terminated the moral situation. The

subjects were asked to comment only upon his actions. They were not given the option to inquire into alternative action. Hence, ethical dilemmas do not constitute moral experience as Dewey conceived it.

In 1983, it was learned that some graduate students from Harvard University were involved in "moral development" workshops with prisoners. As time progressed and some prisoners changed their "reasoning" concerning particular "moral dilemmas," recommendations would then follow to the parole board that certain men had attained a higher level of moral development and should be considered for parole. Is this what men's moral adequacy consists of? Giving "more adequate reasons" for their decisions? It is well known that some anti-social, psychopathic personalities are excellent conartists. They are able to lead others into believing that they are now able to "make it" in the outside world. The Kohlberg experiment brings into serious question not only the moral adequacy of the prisoners and the parole board but of the moral adequacy of the thinking responsible for the development of this particular program.

It seems that a more fruitful method of studying moral behavior and development than the approach used by Kohlberg is to engage in long-term study and observation of subjects within their daily activities. Only in this way can there be guaranteed the selection of the significant by the subject, rather than by the experimenter. Only in this way can reflective inquiry be observed in an open-ended situation rather than in one that has already been resolved, as in Kohlberg's dilemma where the solution is given. Kohlberg maintains that his stages are inclusive of all philosophic thinking in ethics. However, we find it is difficult to include any of the stages in Dewey's thinking concerning how principles arise. Its appeal to experience, its emphasis on reflective inquiry and evaluation, its consideration of the means–end relationship are not considered by Kohlberg. In such an event, it is fair to ask whether Kohlberg's stages are indeed universal.

Personality, Intelligence, and Moral Behavior and Development

The recent work on the Nazi personality examines a relatively large group of nearly two hundred psychological protocols of the Rorschach records of rank-and-file Nazis, many of which have been previously unavailable (Zillmer et al. 1989, 1990, 1991, 1995). The rank-and-file

Nazis were more likely than upper-echelon participants to be the direct perpetrators of many of the atrocities.

The Rorschach test itself is a projective test of personality. The subject is asked to interpret the standard designs and ink blots. His interpretation is then analyzed as a measure of emotional and intellectual functioning and integration (Zillmer et al. 1994: chap. 3, 23–34). Personality is simply striking or dominant characteristics, those that are relatively consistent over time and across different situations (Zillmer et al. 1994: chap. 3, 34–39). To most psychologists, personality is the readiness for behavior rather than the behavior itself (Zillmer et al. 1993: chap. 3). This is also a definition of character.

Zillmer et al. (1995) "clearly suggest that a majority of the Nazis were not deranged in the clinical sense and that common personality characteristics, while undesirable to many are not pathological in and of themselves in the American population" (chap. 9, 25). A further critical area of inquiry was the evaluation of intelligence, or, I.Q. scores, of the Nazi perpetrators, using the Wechsler test for adult intelligence. I.Q.s were used to "estimate an individual's present level of cognitive functioning and are highly correlated with academic success" (Zillmer et al. chap. 3, 14). Parts of the subtexts were wisely eliminated to reduce cultural bias (Zillmer et al. 1994: chap. 3, 14). The mean I.Q. for twenty-one Nazi Nuremberg defendants was 128. Twelve were "very superior," with I.Q.s between 128 and 143. Six were "superior," with I.Q.s ranging from 120 to 127. The remaining three defendants were two "bright normals," I.Q.s 113 and 118, respectively, and one had an "average" I.Q. of 106. The mean I.Q. of college graduates is 118, and of doctoral students 125. The conclusion reached is that it should be obvious to the reader that intelligence and morality are completely unrelated (Zillmer et al. 1995: chap. 3, 21).

Consider the following: One of the defendants was asked if he had considered not obeying orders. He answered: "No, from our entire training the thought of refusing an order just didn't enter one's head, regardless of what kind of an order it was" (Zillmer et al. 1995 chap. 9, 36). Note the word *training*. Distinction needs to be made between training, assimilation or integration of previous experience, and education, growth and development, going beyond the given, development of new concept formation (Steg 1971, 1987, 1988).

To summarize, it is not intelligence per se that makes for moral behavior. Nor is personality in itself an explanation for the horrors perpetrated by the Nazis. Personality, intelligence, and morality are completely unrelated, though training and education are both critical in their development. Individuals are thus responsible for their own actions. No mental illness was present, except in the case of Hess, who could be considered paranoid. One further note: One needs to study how Hitler managed the corruption of the superego of the Germans. The real horror is that the German perpetrators did it, believing in "good faith" that they were doing the "right thing."

Human Evolution: An Adapting Moral Development

What remains is a discussion of the sense in which evolution has resulted in human beings who adapt environments to themselves, rather than merely adapt themselves to existing environments. Human evolution leads to a system of controls that is organizing its environment: an adapting control system as distinguished from the evolution in which natural selection ensures survival of the species best adapted to the environment—an *adaptive control system*. In an adapting system, moral development makes rules and their environments, rather than adapting to rules already alleged to be part of the nature of things.

When a system is of an adapting nature, it is organizing elements external to the system. A qualitative distinction needs to be made between an adaptive and an adapting nature of a control system. The adapting control pattern requires understanding of environmental reality as part of a system of controls that adapts the milieu, while an adaptive system of control, such as in a tadpole, or a frog, or process controls in industry, do not. Through evolution and continuous adaptation to the environment, as a result of mutations selected by the inexorable effect of the survival of the fittest, nature has provided human beings with a control system of an adapting nature. Animals adapt themselves to the environment with the aid of involuntary changes in their physical structure. Human evolution is presently at a point where human beings adapt the environment to their needs through voluntary acts, requiring knowledge and understanding of reality. Human civilization has gone beyond adaptive controls. The fittest survived in an adaptive system, which is nature's way, and requires no understanding of reality on the part of the evolving species. The adapting system makes changes in the immediate environment, and works toward survival even in a hostile milieu. In essence, an artificial environment is created by human beings to form a shield against the effects of the natural environment.

Evolution under an adapting control system involves voluntary acts, knowledge, and understanding of reality that result in survival even in a hostile environment. There is a shift in emphasis in the elements of the environment and their effect on the evolutionary process. Thus, in the evolutionary processes of the adaptive type, the survival of a species depends on its adaptation to the natural environment, and on the ability of the species to overcome any hostile species. But in the adapting control system of the human species, the ability to overcome any hostile species and the natural environment is subordinated to the human capacity for socializing.

If, as stated above, animal and machine control is adaptive and human control can also be adapting, what then is the nature of the control in relations between human beings? Control of relationship between human beings depends on "factual knowledge" and "understanding" as part of the adapting mechanism characteristic of human beings, and it is possible to evaluate the adequacy of a set of rules by reference to results. An adapting control eliminates disturbance through understanding, reflective thought, and is thus a creative control. Consciousness is the acquired characteristic of an adapting control. Thus training is not sufficient nor satisfactory for moral behavior. Training enables the individual to have some skills, some tools at his disposal. Training is thus a primary prerequisite (Steg 1964, 1971, 1987, 1988). But such behavior will not go beyond previous experience. Besides training, the way to moral behavior requires creating and sustaining relationships. It is important to emphasize the place of knowledge and judgment in such conduct, to emphasize the fundamental psychology of thought, what it is and what it does. The question arises whether one can educate for ethical behavior. Is virtue, is "good conduct," a result of training, thus a habit of right action, of rule-following behavior, or is it knowledge? Communication in an adapting control system relates to a relationship between human beings and comprises a special condition that implies mutual understanding, awareness, conscious-

ness, and reflective thought. This characteristic is acquired by each new generation from the previous one by means of the educational process. Thus the educational process has a prerequisite, mutual understanding.

Ethics and morals, as interpreted by a particular set of rules, in turn, mirror the understanding of reality on the part of the social group that lives and abides by these moral rules. Human history is a continuous succession of forms generated by the adapting controls of humans in relation to their natural environment, including humans as part of the environment of the individual. Primitive, feudal, capitalistic, or communist societies are all expressions of the same adapting control system. The degree of understanding that has been achieved by a particular group of people will determine its form of society, but it will not change the adapting nature of control in any and all human societies.

Thus, while the educator is working under what might be characterized by the term *is*, the object of the education is working under what might be characterized under the term *ought*, and, at times, the hostility of the younger generation toward the older, or of the new society against the old. Since mutual understanding, awareness, consciousness, and reasoning result in a continuously changing pattern, freedom of choice becomes a basic requirement of the educational process in an adapting control system.

D.R. Steg

See also: COGNITIVE DEVELOPMENT; DEWEY; ETHICS AND MORALITY; EVOLUTION; HUMAN NATURE; VALUE AND EVALUATION

Bibliography
Dewey, John. *German Philosophy and Politics*. New York: Henry Holt, 1915.
———. *Theory of the Moral Life*. New York: Holt, Rinehart and Winston, 1960.
Kohlberg, Lawrence. "How to Commit the Naturalistic Fallacy and Get Away with It in the Study of Moral Development." In *Cognitive Development and Epistemology*, edited by T. Mischel. New York: Academic Press, 1971.
———. *Moral Judgment Scoring Workshop*. Centre for Moral Development and Education. Cambridge: Harvard University, 1986.
Montgomery, M.B. *Morals, Passions and the Stubborn Man: A Dissertation in Ethical*

Theory. Unpublished Ph.D. dissertation, University of Pennsylvania, 1972.

NICH (National Institute of Child Health and Human Development). *The Acquisition and Development of Values: Perspective on Research*. Bethesda, Md.: NICH, 1968.

Rice, P.B. *On the Knowledge of Good and Evil*. New York: Random House, 1955.

Steg, D.R. "Control Theory, Human Activity, and Social Development." In *Proceedings, VIth International Congress of Cybernetics*. Namur, Belgium: 1971.

———. "Ethics, Moral Development and Experience." Unpublished paper presented at Middle Atlantic States Philosophy of Education Society, Rutgers University, New Jersey, 1987.

———. "Ethics, Moral Development and Reasoning." Urbana, Ill.: American Society for Cybernetics, 1988.

———. "Some Aspects of Teaching and Learning." In *Proceedings of the Philosophy of Education Society*. Edwardsville: Southern Illinois University Press, 1964.

———. "Systems Rules and Ethics." In *Proceedings of the Philosophy of Education Society*. Edwardsville: Southern Illinois University Press, 1966.

White, M. *Science and Sentiment in America*. New York: Oxford University Press, 1972.

Zillmer, E.A., and R.P. Archer. "The Rorschach Records of Nazi War Criminals." Unpublished paper presented at the XIIIe Congress International du Rorschach et des Methods Projectives. Paris, July, 1990.

———, R.P. Archer, and B. Castino. "The Rorschach Records of Nazi War Criminals: A Reanalysis Using Current Scoring and Interpretation Practices." *Journal of Personality Assessment* 53 (1989): 85–99.

———, M. Harrower, B. Ritzler, and R.P. Archer. "The Rorschach Records of Nazi War Criminals: Historical Perspectives and Current Research." Unpublished Symposium presented at the fifty-first annual meeting of the Society for Personality Assessment. New Orleans, Louisiana, March, 1991.

———, M. Harrower, B.A. Ritzler, and R.P. Archer. *The Quest for the Nazi Personality*. Hillsdale, N.J.: Erlbaum, 1995.

Multiculturalism

An educational reform movement that aims to equalize educational opportunities for diverse racial and ethnic groups. In the United States, multiculturalists focus on widening the perspective on North American history by a fair portrayal of the history of minority contributions to the formation of the United States so that they can figure equally with those of Euro-Americans. The relationship between the majority and minority has been infused with polar opposite perceptions of the national reality. Ethnocentric educators, along with some minority educators, have developed public school-based curriculums that focus on the contributions of Euro-Americans at the expense of minority contributions.

Multiculturalism's intention is to provide a means for the open examination of history by providing a forum for the analysis of Euro-American ethnocentric suppositions. It therefore goes beyond the crosscultural model of the examination of cultural artifacts, food sampling, dressing in native attire, or the hanging of pictures of minority leaders in classrooms. Multiculturalism aims at undermining the ideological basis of national chauvinism, which is a necessary development in which national boundaries begin to lose their importance and are replaced by multinational trading blocs such as the European Economic Community or the North American Free Trade Agreement. These regional trading blocs are leading the way into the global economy.

Multiculturalists view all societies as historically constituted from many different people. Consequently, culture is seen as dynamic, not static. Multiculturalists value cultural pluralism, linguistic diversity, and diverse cultural ideologies, and multiculturalism is gender inclusive. Most important, multiculturalism views culture as emanating from the home into the school classroom. The student is not viewed as an isolated being, and the school is not a laboratory where the student is infused (treated) with culture. The school becomes a place where learners arrive to clarify their presuppositions about themselves and others. They learn to question their ethnocentricity, and their radical stereotyping. Educators anticipate that it will lead to less interracial aggression nationally while also leaving the student capable of comfortably contributing to transnational economic development.

The idea of multiculturalism has two forces that labor against one another. The leading force is the experience of assimilating European immigrants during the nineteenth and early twentieth centuries. This then evolved into a sociological assimilationist paradigm of society that failed to include nonwhites. The counterforce is represented by minorities who saw assimilation as an idealistic paradigm held out for Europeans only. In reality most minority members were marked by either their color or their accent, and this gave rise to the assertion by W.E.B. Du Bois (1868–1963) that the problem of the twentieth century is that of the color line. The assimilationist model became intermeshed with the public school curriculum, and, as a consequence, most Euro-Americans tended toward accentuating a Eurocentric reality. Generally, a controversy was inevitable between those still holding to the Euro-American paradigm of assimilation and the experience of minorities. These minority voices lay silenced by the Anglo-American hegemony over the institutions of cultural reproduction such as schools, colleges, museums, and universities. Minorities in the past spoke mostly to one another, countering this hegemony among themselves, but as integration took hold a clash ensued as the legal basis for segregated speech ended and minority voices now became unleashed. The majority found its cultural institutions under siege as minorities' views were found unpalatable. These outspoken minorities are reminiscent of Shakespeare's Caliban, who in the *Tempest* says, "The red plague rid you for learning me your language!"

American sociology has not invested itself in a dynamic theory of wide-ranging transculturalization with a syncretic model of societal development as suggested by the Cuban anthropologist Fernando Ortiz. Anglo-American sociologists have not encountered a society of "mestizaje" (Native American–European intermarriage) or "muletage" (African-European intermarriage), as has occurred in Latin America. Syncretism has been confined to the analysis of religiosity in the United States, whereas in the Afro-Latin Caribbean it has been extended from the analysis of religious artifacts to the concept of race mixing and cultural reproduction. Most minorities such as African Americans, Native Americans, Filipinos, and Latinos (composed mostly of Puerto Ricans, Mexicans, Dominicans, Central Americans, and Cubans) have a different national culture from one another and from that held by Euro-Americans. The importance of the syncretic societal paradigm is that it offers every culture a place as a contributor to the North American na-

tional culture as it evolves into the future. Syncretism offers a convergence for diversity that ultimately embraces all cultures.

Some of the issues that multiculturalism addresses are gender-inclusive education that not only focuses on the contributions of women but also addresses the issue of sexism. At the Board of Education of the City of New York, sexual orientation has been included as part of multiculturalism. In bilingual/bicultural education, the learner's culture is intricately tied to the curriculum. The learner in this manner is not psychologically deformed by an assimilationist model, such as English as a Second Language, where the premise is that the learner's culture is ignored as if the individual dropped his cultural baggage at the border. Certainly, multiculturalism is opposed to the English Only Movement and views it as xenophobic and possibly racist.

Another aspect of multiculturalism is Afrocentric education, in which the focus is not solely on the African but embraces a conscious acknowledgment of African contributions to world history. As an example, Egypt is a continuation of Nubian civilization, and is an African civilization not separate or apart from the rest of Africa. The Middle East is a Euro-centric misnomer and should be known as Western Asia and tied to the continent where it naturally belongs. Again, Ancient Greece has some of its roots in Ancient Egypt, which predates Greek city-states. This effort by the Afro-centrist then extends itself to other people who bring to the United States a rich history of Native American peoples as well as descendants of the Inca, Mayan, and Aztec civilizations. A last example: The federated system of the United States has its origins from among the Native American Seneca nation of New York State and not from England. These issues are not to be studied at the expense of Europe but at the level of historical inquiry and redefinition so that all learners have a sense of their legitimate role in the world.

It will be difficult for many educators to encourage this multicultural perspective. Some have the tendency not to teach aspects of history that illustrate vividly how the majority's dehumanized behavior victimized and deformed the minority. Teachers will need to be compassionate about the horrors of slavery, of genocidal practices—from outright massacres of Native Americans to medical research experiments on minorities. There are a wide range of segregationist practices, the systematic defamation of minority leaders, unfair employment practices, unequal application of the law, red lining by banks, and imposition of English on tribal lands and in conquered territories. Multiculturalism requires a questioning of how one perceives a reality that is all too often uncomfortable for the complacent. Much of the criticism of multiculturalism is based on how a rewriting of the social history of the United States would contribute to creating a society without historical cohesion, which might then lead to "anomie," a sense of not knowing who one is and why each person feels that he or she is who others say they are, a condition minority members know all too well.

Andres I. Perez y Mena

See also COLONIALISM AND POSTCOLONIALISM; MARTI-PEREZ; RACE AND RACISM

Bibliography
Abalos, David T. "Multicultural and Gender Inclusive Education in the Service of Transformation." *Latino Studies Journal* 2 (1991): 3–18.
———. "Multicultural Scholarship and the Rediscovery of the Feminine as the Principle of Liberation and Transformation." *Journal of Multicultural Education of New Jersey* 1 (Spring 1993).
Fantini, Mario D., and Rene Cardenas. *Parenting in a Multicultural Society.* New York: Longman, 1980.
Lynch, James. *Education for Citizenship in a Multicultural Society.* New York: Cassell, 1992.
Schlesinger, Arthur M., Jr. *The Disuniting of America—Reflections on a Multicultural Society.* New York: W.W. Norton, 1992.
West, Cornel. *Prophetic Thought in Postmodern Times—Beyond Eurocentrism and Multiculturalism.* Monroe, Maine: Common Courage Press, 1993.
Wurzel, Jaime S., ed. *Toward Multiculturalism—A Reader in Multicultural Education.* Yarmouth, Mass.: Intercultural Press, 1988.

Mysticism

Viewed from within, mysticism represents the vital, experiential heart of the world's great spiritual traditions. Mystics teach reverent, open, and respectful ways for us to connect, or reconnect, with reality at the deepest, most profound levels. Mystical experiences, also known as "enlightenment" or "illumination," bring about the discovery of our "interbeing," our perpetual interdependence with all that is. Viewed from without, mysticism may appear to be mysterious, other-worldly, or occult, and may be perceived as puzzling, as harmlessly irrelevant, or as dangerously subversive. These reactions of puzzlement or confusion are not altogether surprising when one realizes that "ineffability" is a constitutive feature of mystical experiences.

Mystics around the world and throughout the ages all agree on the ineffable, nondiscursive, verbally inaccessible nature of their mystical experiences. Therefore, any attempt to write or talk about mysticism attempts to describe the indescribable—in some sense we are already bound to fail. And yet we also have a vast, worldwide treasury of just such attempts. Experiences termed "mystical" seem to have occurred throughout the world during all periods of recorded human history. A rich and varied mystical literature spans at least three thousand years of human history, while mystical teachers and shamans represent long-standing oral traditions with ancient lineages.

Mystical literature includes poetry, devotional texts, interpretive narratives, philosophical writings, and a wide range of instructional accounts, many transcribed from oral teachings and providing detailed procedures, techniques, and methods of practice. Within the literature, one finds striking similarities in the writings by mystics from diverse times and traditions. Compare, for example, two sets of opening lines from mystical poets: one from William Blake's eighteenth-century English poem "Auguries of Innocence," the other from a thirteenth-century southern-Chinese Zen Master named Shiqi Xinyue. First, Blake's familiar stanza:

> To see a World in a Grain of Sand
> And a Heaven in a Wild Flower
> Hold Infinity in the palm of your hand
> And Eternity in an hour

Then Shiqi Xinyue:

> In an atom of dust, a galaxy of worlds
> In a half a second, eighty thousand
>   springs (translated by J.C. Clear)

Both poems capture a recurrent central feature of mystical experiences, namely the mystic's inexplicable yet powerful and convincing shift out of such seemingly fixed and pervasive human categories as time and space, the transformation of consciousness that derails and goes beyond all the systems of mental representations we ordinarily project upon the phenomenal world.

When we look at efforts to provide discursive definitions of mystical experiences, we again find recurrent similarities. Walter T. Stace surmises that the oldest extant textual definition is found in the *Mandukya Upanishad,* dating from before 600 B.C. This text describes a mystical experience as one of "pure unitary consciousness wherein awareness of the world and of multiplicity is completely obliterated. It is ineffable peace. It is the supreme good. It is One without a second." At the end of the twentieth century, Charlene Spretnak's definition reflects a Western scientifically informed perspective. She defines a mystical experience as one that occurs when "an individual experiences direct awareness, purposively or unexpectedly, of the larger reality, which includes the perceiving being and is not something apart from him or her. In such moments the universe reveals a dimension of its nature that is inaccessible to mundane, discursive consciousness. One perceives being as a unitary ground of form, motion, time, and space, such that one experiences an enormously spacious sense of the immediate. Perceptual boundaries between the inner and the outer dissolve, and an intense awareness of the whole, as a benevolent and powerful presence, is common."

Spretnak's definition parallels Stace's list of seven features common to most forms of mysticism: (1) ineffability; (2) paradoxicality; (3) a feeling that what is apprehended is holy, sacred, or divine; (4) feelings of blessedness and joy; (5) a sense of utter reality or objectivity; (6) a sense of Oneness; and (7) that all things are expressions of this Unity.

Mystics and mystical practices exist in all the major world religions and spiritual traditions. In some religions, such as Hinduism and Buddhism, mysticism functions as the constitutive center for the whole religion. In other cases, mystics form a distinctive group of practitioners within the larger religious tradition, such as the early Daoists (Taoists) within Confucianism, the Sufis within Islam, the Kabbalah and Hasidim within Judaism, the contemplative and monastic orders within Catholicism, and the Quakers within Christian Protestantism. Most

religious founders seem to have been persons with significant mystical experiences, as presumably were many other "prophets," "saints," "shamans," and "seers."

The spiritual traditions and shamanic lineages of "first peoples," such as Native Americans and indigenous peoples of Africa, Australia, and elsewhere, tend to practice nature-oriented or creation-centered forms of mysticism. Over a period of twenty thousand years of earth-based practices of spirituality, Native Americans viewed the entire natural world as animated by a single, unifying life force. Shamans, as well as respected elders, appear to meet criteria analogous to those characteristic of mature mystics in other traditions. For example, they exhibit the achievement of that profound reconciliation of inner- and outer-directed understanding that marks the advanced stages of mystical development wherein one reaches a sense of "cosmic union" with all forms of life, as well as with the earth, the stars, the moon, and the universe. The Hopi term *navoty* conveys this idea of being in perfect harmony with the processes of the universe.

Recent research into the rituals and symbolic arts associated with ancient Goddess spirituality and with primordial mythology has also uncovered evidence for creation-centered forms of mysticism in which practitioners envisioned themselves as active participants in the creative processes of an alive and sacred earthbody.

Mysticism does not imply theism. For instance, Buddhism, a major mystical tradition, is nontheistic. Nor is mysticism confined to religion in any narrow sense. Nonreligious persons, poets, philosophers, and scientists give convincing accounts of their own mystical experiences. Such persons do, however, exhibit a strong sense of "the sacredness of life." They have a deep transformative attitude of awe or reverence toward the universe. Consider Ludwig Wittgenstein's remark: "That the world is, is the mystical."

Even religious mystics sometimes find that their mystical experiences defy or break with the orthodoxies of their religious institutions. It is certainly the case that the mystical experiences of practitioners can lead these mystics into "heresy" with respect to "official" established doctrines, sometimes so much so that they leave them behind in order to found a new religion or a new religious order, as when Jesus of Nazareth (first century A.D.) broke with Judaism, or Shakyamuni Buddha (c. 484–403 B.C.)

went beyond Hinduism, or George Fox (1624–1690) started the "Society of Friends" (Quakerism).

Indeed this pattern among mystical adepts of going beyond the established doctrines is to be expected when we consider that the achievement of mysticism is essentially one of going beyond all conditioned forms of knowledge and discursive knowledge claims, including those propounded by mystics themselves.

Thus, even though it can never be adequately described, the goal of mystical education is in one sense quite clear—namely, the student's own mystical experience. The methods or "paths" used to achieve this encompass almost every educational means known to humanity.

Since mystical experiences and insights seem simply to happen to people in ways beyond their control, one could leap to the mistaken conclusion that education has no place in mysticism. Quite the contrary is true. The mistake would be analogous to inferring that, because creative insights or new discoveries in science and art cannot be willed or controlled, there is no point in studying science or practicing the arts. Most mystical traditions are also teaching traditions.

Within Hinduism, the primary purpose behind Yoga is to teach techniques that Yogis can use to move themselves into mystical states. Within Buddhism, famous teaching lineages abound, and the Bodhisattva ideal, central to Mahayana Buddhism, is basically that of a tireless teacher striving to bring all sentient beings to "enlightenment."

Much of Christian devotional literature is filled with instructional teachings. For instance, during the sixteenth century, Saint Teresa of Avila (1515–1582) wrote her *Way of Perfection* in order to meet the needs of her sister nuns for a manual of practical mystical instruction. In this book and in her later work, the *Interior Castle,* she makes it clear that she believes that mystical experiences are within the reach of all her "sisters" and "daughters" if they follow the "Way" she has delineated for them. At the beginning of the twentieth century, Evelyn Underhill (1875–1941) wrote *Practical Mysticism* as a popular text for the achievement of mystical experience by any ordinary person who is willing to follow her instructions. Both Underhill and Teresa of Avila believed, along with mystic teachers throughout the world, that we cannot describe the ineffable nature of the universe, but we can educate people to experience it for themselves.

Ann Diller

See also Buddhism; Hinduism; Taoism

Bibliography
Cleary, J.C. *A Tune Beyond the Clouds.* Berkeley, Calif.: Asian Humanities Press, 1990.
Easwaran, Eknath. *Meditation.* Tomales, Calif.: Nilgiri Press, 1978, 1993.
James, William. *The Varieties of Religious Experience.* New York: Penguin Books, 1902, 1985.
Nhât Hanh, Thích. *The Sun My Heart: From Mindfulness to Insight Contemplation.* Berkeley, Calif.: Parallax Press, 1988.
Otto, Rudolf. *Mysticism East and West.* Translated by Bertha L. Bracey and Richenda C. Payne. New York: Meridian Books, 1932, 1960.
Schimmel, Annemarie. *Mystical Dimensions of Islam.* Chapel Hill: University of North Carolina Press, 1975.
Spretnak, Charlene. *States of Grace.* San Francisco: Harper San Francisco, 1991.
Stace, Walter T. *The Teachings of the Mystics.* New York: New American Library, 1960.
Suzuki, David, and Peter Knudson. *Wisdom of the Elders: Honoring Sacred Visions of Nature.* New York: Bantam Books, 1992.
Underhill, Evelyn. *Practical Mysticism.* New York: E.P. Dutton, 1915, 1992.
Van Over, Raymond. *Eastern Mysticism.* New York: New American Library, 1977.
Weber, Renee. *Dialogues with Scientists and Sages: The Search for Unity.* London: Routledge and Kegan Paul, 1986. Arkana edition, 1990.
Wilber, Ken, ed. with Ann Niehaus. *Quantum Questions: Mystical Writings of the World's Great Physicists.* Boulder, Colo.: Shambala Publications, 1984.

M

Nationalism

Nationalism refers to the often intense commitment felt by a people toward a nation-state or a potential nation-state. Nationalist sentiment is commonly expressed in citizens' acts and ways of thinking reflecting loyalty to one's nation. Nationalism is also present in "nationalist movements," wherein groups of people seek to establish a nation-state reflecting either the distinct culture and practices of a particular ethnic group, or the distinct moral, political, or religious beliefs of a particular group. Thus, we speak of French nationalism among French citizens, and of Pan-Indian nationalism among indigenous peoples who believe they will receive justice only once they are a sovereign nation.

Nationalism arose with the creation of nation-states in the late eighteenth century in Europe and the United States. As capitalist institutions grew on both continents, the accumulation of wealth among traders and manufacturers allowed a decisive challenge to the existing monarchies. The redistribution of power led to the construction of the nation as the fundamental political unit, replacing the feudal kingdom and city-state. Nationalism accompanied the formation of nations: It initially fueled combatants in the French and American revolutions, and it was subsequently fostered—often through schooling—by government officials in an attempt to build national identity. In the United States, for example, instruction in a specifically American form of the English language and republican morals was prescribed by early political and educational leaders.

With the nation replacing the province and city-state, Western political philosophy began to focus upon reconciling the interests of the individual and the larger nation, extending previous discussions focusing upon the individual and the city-state. Within European and U.S. debates, a range of perspectives developed concerning the means of building strong, just, and free nations. Nationalism has been conceived in strikingly different ways—as the source of freedom or as its antithesis—leading to importantly different verdicts on its role in education.

The most positive conceptions of nationalism, like the one delivered in 1808 by Johann Fichte (1762–1814) in *Addresses to the German Nation,* often portray nationalism as an expression of the distinctive and noble characteristics of a nation's people; national characteristics are here considered a unique mix of racial characteristics and a particular culture. Given this laudatory conception of nationalism, Fichte recommends educational practices intended to inculcate the child fully in the national culture. Respecting the child's will only allows the development of a weak character, for the most positive aspect of the child's nature lies in her ability to obey and thus assimilate the strengths of her nation's culture. Children are well educated to the degree that they have been molded to have a "stable, settled, and steadfast character."

A more cautious endorsement of nationalism is developed in the work of G.W.F. Hegel (1770–1831), particularly in *The Philosophy of Right,* published in 1821. Hegel shares with Fichte the fundamental assumption that it is culture that raises humans above animals. The established practices, beliefs, and institutions of a society embody in a concrete form the principles of truth, goodness, and justice for citizens of the society. The government represents the most concrete embodiment and highest statement of those principles. Nationalism, or citizen commitment to the government, thus represents an act of wisdom, and Hegel consequently recommends that children have ethical principles instilled so that they feel them instead of thinking them. However, for Hegel there is no inconsistency between instilling national culture and a reflective endorsement of the nation. Upon reaching the age of reason, Hegel expects the adult to reflect on the value of the nation. Using the principles of the culture, the adult will learn to reflect on the value of the government, and the wise person will understand the government to be the historically necessary and best expression of the culture, deserving one's commitment.

In many philosophies, trust of nationalism decreases with a deemphasis upon the importance of culture in the construction of standards of knowledge. Where Hegel believed the standards of rationality were contained within the national culture, other philosophers locate the source of rational thought in the innate reasoning and observing powers of the individual and tend to be more suspicious of nationalism. John Stuart Mill (1806–1873), for example, considered nationalism an essential element of a society—making it possible for citizens to understand each other's values and to care for one another. Yet the most fundamental message in Mill's *On Liberty* (1859) is a fear of nationalism. Mill hopes for a society of free-thinking individuals in which disagreements will be rationally adjudicated in a public forum. Free inquiry and public debate, not the accepted beliefs of one's culture, form the surest route to truth. Irrational commitment to one's nation and the homogeneity of opinion associated with nationalism both stand in the way of this vision. Mill thus hopes for schooling that will prepare individuals to reason, and he opposes government control over the school curriculum, fearing that such control amounts to "a mere contrivance for moulding people to be exactly like one another."

Influenced by both Mill and Hegel, John Dewey (1859–1952) developed a type of liberalism that maintains Mill's distrust of nationalism but nonetheless accepts nationalism as a positive phenomenon. Dewey considers nationalism an expression of commonalities people gain by participating in shared institutions, practices, and beliefs. He argues for a system of government and education corresponding to these organically developed commonalities. However, like Mill, Dewey does not trust the national culture to embody the highest standards of truth and goodness. For Dewey, citizens' cooperative employment of the scientific method, involving both the empirical testing of beliefs and public debate, are basic to democratic decision-making.

Dewey, consequently, fears an imposed sort of nationalism, wherein the government or news media employ nationalistic imagery to sway the populace. Where nationalistic symbolism is used to prevent the cooperative use of the scientific method, leading to decisions made on the basis of patriotism alone, Dewey considers nationalism a threat to democracy itself. Thus, Dewey's educational proposals focus on pedagogies calling upon students to employ the scientific method consistently in group decision-making—leading them to be thoroughly at home with scientific ways of thinking. Like Mill, Dewey favored a decentralized educational system allowing teachers to adjust their curriculum to relate to the specific students in their classrooms.

Within philosophical debates in Europe and the United States, the most critical view of nationalism has been developed by Karl Marx (1818–1883) and Friedrich Engels (1820–1895). Nationalism, in the socialist view, is an ideology imposed by the dominant class leading the working class to mistakenly identify their interests with the national good and consequently with their oppressors, the employers. Nationalism operates to keep the working class from realizing, in Marx's words, that "the proletariat has no country." The working class of one nation has shared interests with the working class of other nations; liberation comes with the overthrow of capitalism throughout the world.

Despite the rejection of nationalism in an established capitalist society, socialists have been divided in their support of a second form of nationalism: the nationalism of some socialist movements, dedicated to overthrowing the established governments of their nation and attaining national sovereignty and socialism within one country. In Marx's own works, nationalist movements are sometimes criticized for abandoning an internationalist perspective and are sometimes seen as a necessary step toward international socialism. Given the distrust of nationalism in socialist traditions, its most powerful educational recommendations, such as those developed by Brazilian philosopher Paulo Freire in *Pedagogy of the Oppressed* (1968), focus upon developing critical dialogue among workers, so they may both unmask the dominant ideology and be reeducated to trust their own decision-making abilities.

These debates on the appropriate relationship between the individual and the nation have had extremely important consequences. The works of Fichte and others expressing similar endorsements of nationalism have rightly been seen as precursors to fascism, since the individual's good is thought to be entirely unified with the good of the nation. The safeguards to abuse of governmental authority supplied by freedom of speech are allowed no place where nationalism is deemed the ultimate value. Similarly, the suspicions of nationalism and defenses of free inquiry found in the works of Mill and Dewey continue to play a critical role in defending freedom of speech in many industrialized countries. And the socialist pedagogies recommended by Freire have informed adult literacy programs, intended to aid workers' understanding of their place in society, in Brazil, Chile, Nicaragua, and the United States.

The European and American debate on the nature of nationalism, however, has suffered from too exclusive a focus upon the internal character of the nation and too little consideration of the role that nationalism plays in relations between nations. Historically, the character nationalism assumed in one country owes as much to relations between nations as to a government's relationship to its citizens; for both France and the United States, for example, nation status operated to consolidate and exert military and diplomatic power vis-à-vis enemies.

While internally focused theories of nationalism aided the construction of laws and practices within nations, the neglect of international relations offered no moral guidance in mediating relations between nations—allowing the use of nationalism to sanction wantonly aggressive acts. The military conquests of German fascism were justified by reference to nationalistic conceptions like those articulated by Fichte. Similarly, appeal to nationalism justified the colonization of African and Latin American countries by both European governments and the United States. For example, U.S. genocide of American Indians and military interventions in Latin America have been justified by reference to the exceptional character and mission of the United States. While philosophical theories cannot be expected to prevent such tragedies, they can offer moral guidance intended to correct such blatant wrongs. The traditional focus in nationalism debates on citizen-nation status neglects the rights of noncitizens.

Philosophers' difficulties in understanding nationalism as an international phenomenon have been due partly to the absence of adequate theories with which to describe the development of the world political economy and the place that individual nations play in that development. Dewey took a step toward an international view by arguing for "transnationalism" as opposed to nationalism, suggesting that nationalism is a destructive form of thinking insofar as it pits people from different nations against one another. Marxism made an even more important step in supplying an account of international economic relations where national developments are placed within a global history of capitalist development. Both of these steps were limited, however: Dewey focused on ethical principles guiding cooperation between nations, neglecting the historical developments whereby the dominance of some nations was won partly at the expense of other nations and groups. Marx takes the historical progression from feudalism to capitalism in Europe to be universal, demarcating the inevitable progression through which all countries move as capitalism extends throughout the globe. Such universalism, however, describes countries in Europe and North America much better than the progression characterizing the history of many other countries; Russia, for example, progressed from feudalism to socialism, apparently missing the "necessary" stage of capitalism.

Like Marx's work, Hans Kohn's important studies, *The Ideal of Nationalism* (1944) and *The Age of Nationalism* (1962), adopt an internationalist perspective while assuming a universalistic picture of national development. For Kohn, nationalism represents a modern idea that began in Europe and spread across the globe along with the extension of democracy and industrialization. Nationalism relies upon the will of the people—even in apparently despotic countries—and requires the efficient relations of the modern industrialized society. Like Marx's work, Kohn's conception of nationalism relies upon a universalistic belief; industrial democracies are assumed to be the most progressive form of government, toward which all nations and contemporary nationalist movements tend, and nationalism is the idea motivating this historical progression.

Kohn's celebratory conception of nationalism serves to deemphasize the historical processes in which industrial democracy in colonial nations was only part of the picture, complemented and in part made possible by often despotic colonies whose wealth was siphoned off by the dominant countries. As the nationalism of colonial powers fueled imperialist policies, many people subject to these expansionist policies were forced to pursue national organization in reaction to colonialism. Indigenous peoples and African tribes have developed nationalist movements in an international context where parity with other nations requires national sovereignty. The process of "decolonization" on the African continent, whereby formerly white-ruled nations like Zimbabwe have been transformed into African-led nations, is a process of nation-building that is motivated not simply by ideals of modernization and democracy.

Similarly, in the United States, most American Indians are committed to establishing the national sovereignty of Indian tribes in response to a history of genocide as well as economic and political control. The 1980 statement of the Indigenous People's Fourth Russell Tribunal claims that "indigenous peoples have the right to exist as distinct peoples of the world, and they have a right to possession of their territories and the right to sovereign self-determination." Here nationalism is not simply the extension of democratic principles and industry but rather a defensive response to a history of conquest. Consequently, there is a need for an understanding of international relations that captures the role nationalism plays both in supporting imperialist conquest and in motivating national resistance movements. Universalistic conceptions of national development are ill suited to capturing such asymmetrical relations.

Anthony Giddens, in *The Nation-State and Violence* (1987), has attempted to develop an understanding of nationalism that avoids the universalistic assumptions in both Marx's and Kohn's works. Giddens has attempted to develop a theory of international historical development that, like Marxism, places nationalism within the context of the world capitalist economy, but, unlike Marxism, does not adopt a strict economism. In Giddens's view, European nations and the United States developed with the development of the bourgeoisie as a class. With the backing of the capitalist class, national governments acted to secure boundaries and gain a monopoly of power—through the law, police, and military—within those territories. Nationalism, developed as part of this political, economic, and martial process, assumes forms specific to particular nations depending upon a broad range of specific historical factors, from the cultures and languages of groups within the nation to the wars between nations over trade or territory. In this view, colonialist nationalism is seen as closely related to the nationalism of decolonialization.

Giddens's work, however, takes only the first step toward refashioning conceptions of nationalism to include international relations. His goal is to describe existing power relations in the world, and such an understanding is a prerequisite to developing an ethics of international relations and an ethics by which to guide educational prescriptions regarding nationalism. But contemporary philosophical thought has yet to address the meaning that historical descriptions of colonization and decolonization have for the ethics of nationalism. Dewey's and Tufts's suggestion that "the criteria of the greater good of all must be extended beyond the nation" signals a valuable starting point, but this generous sentiment is insufficient in considering the respective responsibilities of nations to one another, especially when the relative wealth and power of some nations has been achieved through the exploitation of others.

Frank Margonis

See also CAPITALISM; DEWEY; HEGEL; INDIVIDUALISM; LIBERALISM; MARX; MILL; SOCIALISM

Bibliography

Dewey, John, and James Tufts. *Ethics* [1932]. In *John Dewey: The Later Works, 1925–1953.* Vol. 7, edited by Jo Ann Boydston. Carbondale: Southern Illinois University, 1985.

Fichte, Johann Gottlieb. *Addresses to the German Nation.* Translated by R.F. Jones and G.H. Turnbull. Chicago: Open Court Publishing, 1922.

Freire, Paulo. *Pedagogy of the Oppressed.* Translated by Myra Ramos. New York: Continuum, 1970.

Giddens, Anthony. *The Nation-State and Violence.* Berkeley: University of California Press, 1987.

Hegel, Georg W.F. *Philosophy of Right.* Translated by T.M. Knox. London: Oxford University Press, 1967.

Jaimes, Annette, ed. *The State of Native America: Genocide, Colonization, and Resistance.* Boston: South End Press, 1992.

Kohn, Hans. *The Age of Nationalism*. New York: Macmillan, 1962.

———. *The Ideal of Nationalism*. New York: Macmillan, 1944.

Marx, Karl, and Friedrich Engels. *The Communist Manifesto*. In *The Marx-Engels Reader*, edited by R. Tucker. New York: W.W. Norton, 1972.

Mazrui, Ali, and Michael Tidy. *Nationalism and New States in Africa*. Nairobi: Heinemann, 1984.

Mill, John Stuart. *Utilitarianism, On Liberty, and Considerations on Representative Government*. Edited by H.B. Acton. New York: E.P. Dutton, 1972.

Naturalism

In contemporary philosophical discourse, refers to a pair of views: (1) the opinion in ontology that whatever exists or occurs is "natural"; and (2) the corresponding monism of inquiry, the view in epistemology that all objects are susceptible to treatment within a science whose methodology is continuous with that practiced in the "natural" sciences. Naturalism is characterizable, therefore, as the doctrine that knowledge is acquirable only by way of the scientific method. Not only are beliefs generated by other methods perceived by naturalists as suspicious posturings; they are also suspected of pushing the envelope of intelligibility. Naturalism should not, however, be confused with materialism, the view in ontology that all being is material being; while consistent with materialism, naturalism makes no commitment on the subject of what may count as "natural" save that it should make itself susceptible of inquiry via the scientific method.

In eras past, the philosophical debates surrounding naturalism focused on the question whether there is more to reality than the natural world. The naturalist position squarely denied a supernatural or spiritual creation, value, control, or significance. The natural order, it maintained, constitutes the whole of reality. As the naturalist position developed and gained defenses and adherents, primarily in the late nineteenth and twentieth centuries, proponents fostered an association between science and the natural world, urging a definition of the natural as that which is susceptible to scientific investigation. To such an extent has naturalism been associated with science that many of those involved in discourse on ethics have sponsored, and continue to urge, a scientific method for ethics. The growing success of science at explaining an increasingly bewildering variety of phenomena was itself an impetus for naturalism, and an argument its adherents routinely extended in its behalf.

Naturalism today comes in two varieties. The first affirms (1) as a consequence of (2); the second affirms (2) as a consequence of (1). I will call the first epistemological naturalism, the second ontological naturalism. While the preponderance of academic philosophers today would readily assent to (1), there is genuine and heated debate, especially among contemporary investigators of cognition, concerning both the meaning and the implications of (2). A classic debate in metaphysics has in the twentieth century been (appropriately enough) resuscitated as a debate in the philosophy, and in particular the epistemology, of science.

Introduction

A recurring theme in the history of philosophy is a tension between the tendency to view the human organism as an "ordinary" part of the realm of the natural and the opposing tendency to view human practices and human reason as phenomena apart from the natural, the study of which requires special tools and organs distinct from those appropriate to the study of other objects. The former tendency has come to be associated with naturalist positions, such as classical empiricism, positivism, and pragmatism; the latter tendency has in the past gone under many heads, among them Platonism, rationalism, dualism, intuitionism, and spiritisms of all varieties.

The long and venerable tradition of naturalism traces its lineage back to classical roots. Indeed it is a commonplace to identify naturalism in terms of the procedure of inquiry practiced by Aristotle (384–322 B.C.). But whereas for Aristotle it was a "natural" matter to proceed in philosophy as he did, the teaching of philosophical naturalism in the modern era rubs against the grain of inclinations with wide scholarly appeal. The origins of contemporary sensibilities can be traced partly to the details of the intellectual history of the period intervening between the classical era and the Enlightenment, wherein the speculative currents of the Augustinian traditions of thought, in competition with more modest schools of naturalism and skepticism (the latter a forebear of Humean empiricism), intertwined with approved Church doctrines, ultimately winning the blessing of "legitimate" intellectual authorities determined to instill Christian orthodoxy. The result was a strain of scholasticism strongly resistant to naturalistic antidotes and surviving (even thriving) today in modern rationalist thought. The robustness of this scholasticism is partly due to the fact that moderations of a naturalistic sort are vulnerable to offensives of a skeptical nature, since the official naturalist line includes the position that there can be no antecedently held guarantees of the products of rational inquiry. Thus scholastic argumentation is perceived in some quarters, even among contemporary philosophers, as the only genuine alternative to the view that knowledge of the natural order is impossible. Cartesian science, along with its intellectual descendants, is developed expressly with the skeptic as the primary philosophical foil. Yet another source of contemporary counternaturalist inclinations is the institutionalized fragmentation of discourse in the contemporary research institutions of the academy. While the fragmentation reflects genuine divisions of intellectual labor, it is also perceived as strongly marking "real" distinctions among spheres of inquiry, thus suggesting distinctions among investigative methodology.

For disciples of Aristotle, the relationship of scientific inquiry to academic philosophy (with the latter understood as a discipline whose proper subject matter is the totality of truth) is the relationship of identity: There was no distinction between natural science and philosophy. For Aristotelians, past and present (and no less so for Aquinas, who believed one could establish a host of theological truths, including the existence of God, by attending to commonplace empirical matters of fact), the world is an organic whole with human intellect and functioning constituting no less legitimate a natural phenomenon than fire or flora, and no more legitimate a natural phenomenon than deity itself. For the majority of contemporary minds, on the other hand, the set consisting of nature's qualities is fragmented into the genuinely natural ("physical") traits and the transnatural (the many-layered non- or transphysical). Consequently, the structure of knowledge, mirroring as it must the structure of nature's qualities, is also fragmented, with knowledge dividing along familiar disciplinary lines—into that to do with the physical, that to do with the mathematical, that to do with the mental, that to do with the moral, and so on. This epistemic pluralism is the philosophical position with which naturalism is to be contrasted in the contemporary debates, and against which it actively presses.

This debate is especially heated among those who study human cognition. Some among them hold to the view that cognition and mental phenomena are a "special" realm of the natural. This view is articulated by proponents of the "special sciences" thesis, who reject the unity of science and instead adopt the view that each science addresses a particular domain in a hierarchical structure of subject matters constituted by levels of natural qualities; we may call this view neofunctionalism (following Wilson 1985). Others among contemporary cognitive theorists hold that cognitive phenomena are "reducible" to "physical" phenomena; these are the physicalists. It might be supposed that whichever view should win the day, naturalism will have been vindicated, since even neofunctionalists countenance only natural entities and the scientific investigation thereof. We ought not, however, be unquestioningly sanguine about such a victory; it is arguably little more than a terminological one. For, should the first party to the debate win their case, the realm of the natural will have been fragmented; reality will consist of "levels" of properties—as the proponents of the view have it—the interconnections of traits at each level independent of the interconnections of traits present at any other. And thus, in the respects that matter most to epistemology, the "levels" view is only minimally different from that in which the "natural" and the "supernatural" are different realms of being. The primary difference between today's dominant neofunctionalist view and old-style antinaturalism is only slightly more than a mere verbal difference: It is that contemporary neofunctionalists distinguish among the properties or traits of natural objects (stressing the metaphysical distinctions marked thereby), whereas the old dualisms distinguish among objects themselves.

Thus the new debate in naturalism concerns whether there are seams in the natural order among classes of natural traits. A very small, practically invisible, minority of philosophers holds to the thesis that even if cognitive phenomena are not reducible to the canonically accepted paradigms of "physical" phenomena (that associated with the characters on the embarrassingly short rolls called time and again in the philosophers' narratives of microphysics), even so the mental is no less physical for lack of inclusion in these narratives. This minority argues that classical thermodynamic phenomena are likewise irreducible to microphysics, but are no less physical for all that. This school of thought, also identifying itself as physicalism because it countenances no trait useful to science as nonphysical, adheres most strictly to the spirit of naturalism, according to which the objectionable aspect of scholastic thought is the postulation of metaphysical gulfs or chasms in the orders of being and quality.

Despite occasional revivals—classical British empiricism, Humean empiricism, American pragmatism of the first half of the twentieth century, and even contemporary Quinean holism—naturalisms favoring the unification of knowledge have tended to wage a losing battle against forces attempting to fragment the operation and the interdependence of the sciences, favoring an autonomy for the "special sciences." This also perhaps is partly due to naturalism's vulnerability to skeptical offensives. But the vulnerability alone cannot explain completely naturalism's failure to gain wide subscription, for the most recent champions of real distinctions among the sciences are professed adherents of empiricist methodology.

Defenses
Naturalism is the thesis that the only beliefs meeting stringent enough criteria for certification as knowledge are those derivable from scientific method, or a method continuous with careful application of the built-up body of public procedures of hypothesis testing and confirmation fundamental to human epistemological enterprises. Scientific methodology is a battery of procedures of inquiry consisting of the systematized and refined canons of rationality and intelligibility present in the techniques of behavior and habits of inference evolved in the commonly held practices of human beings and required for survival, even if overlaid (however remotely or recently) with myth and ritual. Most prominent among these canons are two: (1) nature is, in all its parts, even those respecting moral and mathematical practices, intelligible to the human mind; and (2) every natural event has a natural cause, or set of natural causes, that explains it fully. Characteristic of contemporary naturalism is a disposition toward the selection of a particular class of categories with which to describe natural phenomena. This is the class of categories encompassing events, relations, qualities, and stretches of

natural process—the class required for event-causal explanations of other natural events. Implicit in this choice is a rejection of alternative categories for scientific explanation of natural phenomena, such alternatives as the categories of substance and sufficient reason, employed by Aristotle no less than by Rene Descartes (1596–1650) or Gottfried Leibniz (1646–1716). This choice rules out of court as unintelligible such questions as whether there is an ultimate ground of all existences, questions not fully characterizable in terms of events, qualities, and relations. Such questions, the naturalist submits, are incurably confused.

When called upon to present argument for or justification of their faith in scientific methodology as sole determinant of justified belief, naturalists have typically given one of three defenses:

(1) Since the totality of objects and processes in the world coincides with the totality of natural objects and processes, there can be no need for another method in addition to the scientific method for inquiry, which is ideally suited to investigation of natural phenomena.

This is ontological naturalism; its defense of the epistemological component of naturalism is rooted in a denial of heterogeneity in the class of beings, a stubborn refusal to take the terms "natural" and "nature" as terms of distinction. The defense itself, however, if it is not to be construed merely as a proposal for how we should deploy terminology, is a substantive claim. As such it itself requires defense. But it is doubtful whether it can be given a defense that naturalists themselves can endorse. It is an open question today whether (1) can be defended on scientific grounds alone.

A second line of defense is:

(2) Respect for the human spirit demands naturalism. Antinaturalism insinuates an insidious denigration of the physical as the lowest stratum in the hierarchy of Being, most vile and corrupt as well as inept and deceptive. The cure for unjustifiable vilification of the natural is its exaltation, and therewith the promotion of the means for its investigation—the scientific method—which has wrought a profound transformation in the physical and biological sci-

ences. Human reason, its canons systematized in the scientific method, is responsible for these advances; due respect for human reason requires no illiberal limits be placed on what human scientific capacity can accomplish by way of accessing truth.

This position was occupied by many American pragmatists of the first half of the twentieth century, prominently by John Dewey (1859–1952) and Sidney Hook (1902–1989), who understood naturalism as the intellectual component of the social and political impulse for democracy:

> Democracy cannot obtain adequate recognition of its own meaning or coherent practical realization as long as antinaturalism operates to delay and frustrate the use of the methods by which alone understanding and consequent ability to guide social relationships are attained (Krikorian: 3).

This second defense contains less philosophical argument than polemic. A philosopher can be sympathetic to attempts to redeem the human spirit from the fires of Roman Catholic condemnations without thereby becoming philosophically committed to naturalism, whether in its epistemological or ontological versions. A rationalist or intuitionist can be a strong champion of human reason, a genuine patron of free and public inquiry, an ardent opponent of special pleadings from authority or canon, an indefatigable foe of superstition and dogmatism, and a staunch adversary of obscurantism, without becoming thereby a living contradiction.

Finally,

(3) An honest reflection on human capacities for inquiry demands rather greater modesty regarding claims to knowledge than antinaturalists usually recognize. Human access to knowledge of nonnecessary matters of fact, in contrast with matters of reason, is limited to empirical methods of inquiry since the only contact with such matters is through observations of the familiar nature. Hence scientific method is the only method suited to investigation of nonnecessary matters of fact.

Clearly, (3) is an empiricist argument. As such it is at once unnecessary and yet too weak. First, not necessary: It is possible to advocate naturalism without demanding empiricism as well. Some (notable among them W.V.O. Quine) hold that scientific method involves the use of superempirical induction principles: considerations of simplicity, fecundity, and so on. If science cannot do without these, then scientific method cannot meet empiricist standards. Even so, a scientific method with rationalist considerations might nonetheless produce theories describing an ontologically "seamless" world, without gulfs, chasms, or levels, thus satisfying naturalism's desiderata. Second, (3) is too weak: Even if adopted it does not establish naturalism. It is consistent with a thesis of autonomy for the special sciences and hence with the hierarchy of natural traits mentioned above; an autonomist is free to embrace (3) so long as said autonomist will brook no method but an empirical (presumably the scientific) method for inquiry at each level. Finally, it is problematic. It suggests there are other methods for acquiring knowledge—namely those methods appropriate to mathematical claims (claims of the *a priori*). But if these are legitimate, then how is it possible to rule out "nonscientific" methods on the grounds of modesty of means? If a principled version of (3) is accepted, then there can be no nonempirical methods of discovering mathematical truths—a proposition at which many philosophers (many among them naturalists) will balk.

Criticism

Most problematic for naturalists has been to give an adequate account of the mathematical and the moral. It is recognized that if naturalists cannot make sense, in satisfactory fashion, of mathematical and moral activities and investigations within the framework of scientific inquiry, then naturalism must be considered a failed experiment. While there are many who would gladly do away altogether with the realm of the moral, and fewer who would deny reality to mathematical objects (and truth to mathematical claims), there are many more who cannot do without either. Attempts to give noncognitivist, naturalistic accounts of the moral, according to which moral imperatives and claims have no truth values, have met with much criticism. More recent attempts to cast moral and political imperatives in contractarian terms, and to ground the latter in rational preference theory, have met with more success among those who will not relinquish moral truths.

Another problematic aspect of naturalist argumentation is that it presupposes that there is a unique method that is scientific method, despite appearances to the contrary among such diverse disciplines as chemistry, sociology, and psychology. Philosophers of science today, however, are not in agreement on the universality of one unique scientific method among the scientific subdisciplines. Neofunctionalists and other adherents of autonomy for the "special sciences" presumably do not approve of the methods they perceive to be operative in physics for, say, psychology, since they hold (though not uncontroversially) that physics is reductionistic whereas psychology should not be so. While the claim of uniqueness may in fact be true, no argument has been advanced for it. Consequently we have no clear account of how actual scientific method is uniquely suited to the task of ascertaining truth. Classical philosophy of science typically focuses on "idealized" procedures of investigation. And naturalists never discuss the distinction.

There is still an open question whether naturalism requires justification, or whether the burden lies with antinaturalists to prove their case. Some naturalists, resting their position on a principle of burden, have maintained that, since scientific method is simply the refinement of principles of reasoning that have developed in the course of human evolution, scientific method should be given a place of privilege, if only for its "naturalness." Even if this were true, however, it is not clear that adoption of scientific method rules out all antinaturalist principles, such as those of rationalism or intuitionism. An argument is required to establish that adoption of scientific method implies the abandonment of extraempirical principles, such as the rationalist principles of simplicity and fecundity.

Moreover, the very fact of coexistence of antinaturalism with naturalism in current debates casts doubt upon the claim that naturalism has been victorious in an evolutionary "war" among procedures. And even should we believe the battle has been won, we should be wary of concluding that, therefore, the victor in the evolutionary war is rationally to be preferred to its competitors. It is, after all, well known that evolution by process of natural selection does not in every case favor traits beneficial to the organism in which they evolve.

Organisms often evolve traits that contribute toward their extinction. Finally, burden-of-proof claims are rarely uncontroversial, and always difficult to establish. It is philosophically precarious to rest one's case on a burden of proof.

Other naturalists, taking more seriously the challenge for justification, have suggested that, once science's favored choice of categories (the categories of event causation) has been adopted, then naturalism follows therefrom. It must be noted, however, that neofunctionalism is consistent with this choice of categories, whereas Aristotelian categories of substance and final causation are not. Adoption of the argument, therefore, commits the naturalist to the (somewhat undesirable) consequence that Aristotle did not adhere completely to the scientific method as officially approved by contemporary naturalists, while somehow standing in an ancestral relationship to it. Finally, it would appear that the choice of categories must itself be argued for and not taken for granted. Philosophical advocacy of any method, whether scientific or otherwise, must be argued on epistemological grounds—via arguments that adoption of the favored method is more productive of truth than adoption of its competitors. This requirement cannot be waived for scientific method. We may indeed be convinced of the value of the scientific method; even so we can recognize that the interests of philosophy demand science too make a case for itself. The task of epistemology, according even to Quine, the most famous opponent of positivism but a naturalist in his own right, is to attain a logical clarification of the successful investigative procedure that is scientific method, and hence to "defend science from within, against its self-doubts" (Quine: 3).

Finally, there are suggestive hints, but never orderly argumentation, for the claim that science "after all is but systematic, extensive, and carefully controlled use of alert and unprejudiced observation and experimentation in collecting, arranging, and testing evidence" (Krikorian: 12). Contemporary sociologists and feminists have argued that, to the contrary, the actual practice of science is, and can be no more than, a battery of ethno- and phallocentric biases and procedures, functioning to advance theories that maintain existing structures of power and advance the interests of the most powerful. Against the backdrop of the many evidences of bias produced by these contemporary critics of institutional science and scientists, an undernuanced naturalist claim that the actual practice of science is "nothing but" the best in human use of reason stands as a naive position at best.

And here matters more or less stand, with the choice of naturalism being more a matter of philosophical temperament than the considered result of weighing evidence for the case. Even among those who advocate some "scientific" method, there is no clear agreement on the nature of that method. Thus the challenge for naturalists still remains: (1) to clarify the meaning and implications of the scientific method; (2) to address issues raised by skeptics as to the adequacy of this method for advancing knowledge; and (3) to defend the integrity of scientific method in light of the sociological data of bias, whether racially, politically or gender based, common among the persons of scientists.

Mariam B.C. Thalos

See also ARISTOTLE; DESCARTES; DEWEY; EPISTEMOLOGY; FEMINISM; INTUITIONISM; POSITIVISM; PRAGMATISM; RATIONALISM; SCIENCE, PHILOSOPHY OF; SKEPTICISM

Bibliography

Block, Ned, ed. *Readings in the Philosophy of Psychology.* Vol. 1. Cambridge: Harvard University Press, 1980.

Danto, Arthur. "Naturalism." In *The Encyclopedia of Philosophy.* Vol. 5, edited by Paul W. Edwards. New York: Macmillan, 1967.

Harding, Sandra, and Merril Hintikka. *Discovering Reality: Feminist Perspectives on Epistemology, Metaphysics, Methodology and the Philosophy of Science.* Dordrecht: Reidel, 1983.

Hook, Sidney. *The Quest for Being and Other Studies in Naturalism and Humanism.* Westport, Conn.: Greenwood Press, 1961.

Krikorian, Yervant, ed. *Naturalism and the Human Spirit.* New York: Columbia University Press, 1944.

Murphy, Arthur. "Review of *Naturalism and the Human Spirit.*" In *Journal of Philosophy* 42 (1945): 400–17.

Quine, W.V.O. *The Roots of Reference.* LaSalle, Ill.: Open Court Press, 1974.

Strawson, P.F. *Skepticism and Naturalism.* New York: Columbia University Press, 1985.

Tuana, Nancy, ed. *Feminism and Science.* Bloomington: Indiana University Press, 1989.

Wilson, Mark. "What Is This Thing Called 'Pain'?—The Philosophy of Science behind the Contemporary Debate." *Pacific Philosophical Quarterly* 66 (1985): 227–76.

Neoplatonism

In its primary sense, Neoplatonism refers to the doctrines found in Plotinus's cryptic and condensed lecture notes collected by Porphyry, called *The Enneads.* The theses in this work were developed by followers such as Porphyry (c. 232–305), Proclus (c. 401–485), and Iamblichus (c. 250–330). The thought of Plotinus itself, however, is a development of the philosophy of Plato, and there is accordingly a secondary use of "Neoplatonism" signifying developments of the philosophy of Plato (c. 427–347 B.C.) by later philosophers who found an affinity between Platonism and theism or mysticism. The most popular theme of Neoplatonism, the theory of emanation and return, holds that the entire universe is an emanation from an ultimate entity named "The One" and that people can ascend toward a union with The One in a state of "no otherness." Careful examination reveals that emanation and return is compatible with the doctrine of the unity of being, the essential core of the Jewish Kabbalah, Christian mysticism, and Islamic Sufism. In mystical union, there is no alienation between persons and God. Consequently, Neoplatonic themes were the essential core of the mystical dimension of medieval philosophy, and its antisubstance theory became the ontological framework of the systems of many later metaphysicians who had mystical tendencies.

For Plotinus, three analogies illustrate the specifics of his system. First, matter is analogous to a mirror, and differentiation in material constituents is like images in the mirror, deriving their reality from their source, which is the incorporeal soul. Second, The One is analogous to a nonphysical sun from which, without being affected, there are increasing lesser reflections or rays, while from each ray there is a lesser reflection—The Intelligence, The Soul, and the sensible images. Third, The One is analogous to an eternal source, an overflowing spring of water, which, although having no origin, is nevertheless the source of everything else. From it emanate rivers that flow in different directions.

Metaphysics: The Primary Hypostasis of The One, The Intelligence, and The Soul; Production of Matter as Reflection of The Soul

Metaphysics, for the ancients and medievals, investigates classification of beings or the categories. Plotinus takes categories to be purely ontological structures, while Proclus takes them as logical instruments. Following Plato, Plotinus explicitly postulates five ontological greatest genera: Being, Rest, Motion, Same, and Other. But in fact the most important divisions of reality for him contain The One and the rest of the world, as well as the separation of reality into the Intelligible and Sensible realms. For Aristotle, the categories include substance (both primary and secondary) and the nine accidents: quantity, quality, relation, place, time, posture, possession, action, and passion. Plotinus, choosing an ontological reading of Aristotle's categories, holds that Aristotle's application of the same category of substance to both realms is absurd, as there is no place in the Aristotelian categories for the Intelligible. Plotinus needs to reject not only categories but also two principles that follow from them. The first core of Aristotle's view, what he calls the first substance, or a concrete particular, is the basis of realization of all entities. Simply stated, an accident like the quality red is not an eternal form existing in itself, but is realized by the mediacy of an apple that is a red apple. Unless there is this apple, this redness does not exist. This procedure places the sensible entities as the ground of realization of the universals, turning the Neoplatonic system on its head. Another principle following from the doctrine of the categories that Plotinus needs to reject is the position that the only type of substantial change is generation and destruction; no substance can blend or be united with another substance. In contrast, for Plotinus's metaphysics of processes, entities descend from The One and also ascend toward The One. Here we have a genuine process metaphysics that allows immanence of The One in the world and a mystical union in which there is no otherness between the Soul and The One.

It should be noted that Plotinus uses the expression "one" in the following two senses: The One that is beyond being, and the one that is a unity predicated of each individual form. While the entire cosmos is emanated from The One in the first sense, the one in the second sense is prior to all individuals and prior to numbers. In the same manner that the Platonic Form of the Good is the source of other Forms, the One, as the first of three hypostases—that is, realities—emanates the other two—that is, The Intelligence and The Soul. Unlike the Platonic Form of the Good, The One of Plotinus is not a form, nor an individual existent like a conscious God or an apple. As The First, It cannot be a being. It is beyond existence; It is omnipresent in every entity as its ultimate cause, both as the efficient cause and the final cause, which for him is the cause of completion or perfection. Nothing is good for the One. It is not even good for Itself, but It is a good to others. It does not think in the sense that an entity thinks of another entity, because for The One there is no otherness. Unlike the God of monotheism, Plotinus's One does love itself but not its product because love implies need.

One's emanation of the Intelligence is sometimes referred to as The One turning to Itself, even though as a simplicity The One cannot be the object of any knowledge. The Intelligence contains an infinity since it is a multiple unity and emanates The Soul. There are different senses of the term *soul*. In one sense, there is The (World) Soul, as Cosmos is an entity in itself. In another sense, there are individual souls of celestial and earthly bodies. Each individual soul has two layers, that which recollects its upward origin and that which reflects lower in its sensible images. Matter itself is a reflection of the soul in its lowermost form. In the soul, multiplicity pervades over simplicity. But all souls communicate by nonsensory means and thus integrate into one soul. For Plotinus the world of actual existents is identical with the world of cognitive knowledge of The Intelligence (*nous*). As an imitation of the world of true being, the sensible world is beautiful and is the best possible realm of existent matter—a mirror of reality. The basic procession of order of being is by an involuntary and overflowing type of emanation that embeds the agent in the patient without affecting the agent. Production of an entity is the result of knowledge by prior contemplation of true realities. Plotinus notes the soul's desire to govern as well as its will for isolation. Even in its embodiment the soul in a sense is in the celestial realm. Souls as a consequence of their separation are morally different from one another.

For Plotinus primarily, eternity belongs to the unchangeable, and time is applicable to the contingent entities. But in a secondary sense, we have in fact within us a glimpse, although not a total experience, of time and eternity. Time is that in which movements occur. It is generated simultaneously with the universe. Thus the origin of time is due to the soul when it separated itself from the intellect and different events happened to it, but our experience of time is formed by analogy, using the experience of movement rather than rest. It follows that time is the life of the soul in a movement from one state to the other, and it is measured by movement instead of being the measure of movements. By inner reflection, we can relate to the eternal within us, contemplate toward eternity. Eternity is a unity, and like beauty and truth has a common existence with the primaries. The universe is eternal and there is no temporal beginning.

In Plotinus the primary beauty is without any form. The One is above beauty and can be mentioned only as a beauty that is beyond beauty. Beauty is due to participation in an immaterial form or principle that integrates it into a unity. Beauty is not ultimate, for the love of the Good is free from the violent passion associated with Beauty. The final goal is to assimilate one with the Good, as infinite love demands infinite object.

Ethics and Theodicy: Providence, Fate, Love, and Happiness

Events in the world cannot be attributed to mere chance and accidents. Because the Universe is produced by the Intelligence, it has an intelligent order. Moreover, every existent in the universe is a necessity and according to the world order, which is just and wise. Thus if any part seems imperfect when viewed in itself, in the larger macrocosm that part, because of the exact way that it is, contributes to the cosmos being the best of all possible composites. Providence exists only if there are other entities; otherwise it would have no field of action. Consequently existence of imperfect entities is necessary because of the existence of the Good. Evil is necessary because it is falling short of the Good. In addition to evil, inferior beings like animals still lie inside of the natural plan. Sense experiences, too, are less noble than contemplation, but the soul and its works are in harmony with each other and a unity emerges out of the opposites. Thus, even though providence does not directly produce evil it takes it into account—along with chance circumstances—in the light of the universal order. Thus neither moral nor wicked acts are caused by providence, but they are realized according to providence.

Plotinus mentions the absurdity of someone censoring a play because not all its characters are heroes. What happens to the play if the inferior characters are eliminated? It is, indeed, the author of the play who assigns roles to characters, but this assignment is partially due to the fact that the role of good or evil is applicable to particular persons. In this sense they are responsible for their acts. Plotinus notes that the higher dimension of the Soul seeks to know The One in a mystical union that is an ecstasy, a flight of the alone to the alone. This kind of knowledge has pragmatic use, as only reasonable souls can be free. The person who is able to contemplate is a knower and takes part in the process of production. There is an upward contemplation, where contemplation ascends from nature to the soul, and then its Intelligence; in this mode the contemplation becomes united to the contemplators. Moreover all actions aim at contemplation since the agent is motivated by contemplating the result of actions in his mind. Each person is primarily a soul using a body. By love too, the individual soul has a possibility of uniting with a higher realm. Each individual soul has a love which in its noble state implants the desire appropriate to the individual soul in question, as well as a longing of the Soul toward pure beauty. Since all souls are related, so the love of individual souls is not cut off from the love of the Universal soul, but is in fact included in it and leads it to The Good.

But Plotinus is not against the body as body because the origin of the body is based upon soul's contemplation of the soul; persons should attend to bodily needs and constructively discipline the body. The pain of the body does not affect the noble part of the contemplative soul. But the happy sage regards his body as a musical instrument to which he tends and cares; but he gives up the body gracefully at death in the same spirit of a musician who is ready to give up his lyre, which was useful to him while he was playing music.

The ethical doctrine here is related to Plotinus's aesthetics, as he notes that The Good has no need of beauty whereas beauty is in need of The Good. Moreover good presupposes actuality and truth, whereas with physical pleasure one is often pleased by expectation of a pleasure like eating or sex, even when such an expectation is not realized. Ultimately salvation is achieved when the higher dimension of the soul turns its attention away from worldly affairs toward the Intelligence in order to restore its divine image. This is done by attempting to train the lower soul voluntarily to accept the dictum of reason and then to withdraw one's attention from it. Salvation is within our power and requires self-discipline. Since not all parts of the soul have descended into the lower realm, the upper part is able to have the intellect, which is concatenated with action. Here freedom exists in the context of the knowledge of the necessity of action, not in the conscious willed ignorance of desires affected by passions that blind us to our original affinity with The One. Even though dialectical training in philosophy is an essential beginning of this journey, ultimately the aim is an encounter as a person "sees" the Intelligence as if it were an object of sense. In this path we should turn to The One, which is our primordial origin and source. The mode is a union through love with our transcendent source.

Parviz Morewedge

See also ISLAM; JUDAISM; METAPHYSICS; MYSTICISM; PLATO

Bibliography

Armstrong, A.H. *The Architecture of the Intelligible Universe in the Philosophy of Plotinus.* Cambridge: Cambridge University Press, 1940.

Goodman, L., ed. *Neoplatonism and Jewish Thought.* Albany: State University of New York Press, 1992.

Lloyd, A.C. *The Anatomy of Neoplatonism.* Oxford: Clarendon Press, 1990.

Morewedge, P., ed. *Neoplatonism and Islamic Thought.* Albany: State University of New York Press, 1992.

O'Meara, D.J., ed. *Neoplatonism and Christian Thought.* Albany: State University of New York Press, 1992.

Plotinus. *The Enneads.* Translated by S. MacKenna. New York: Penguin, 1991.

———. *Plotini Opera.* Edited by Paul Henry and Hans-Rudolf Schwyzer. Paris: Desclee, de Brouwer, 1951–1973.

———. *Plotinus.* Translated by A.H. Armstrong. Cambridge: Harvard University Press, 1966–1988.

Rist, J.M. *Plotinus: The Road to Reality.* Cambridge: Cambridge University Press, 1967.

Wallis, R.T. *Neoplatonism.* New York: Scribner's, 1972.

Nietzsche, Friedrich Wilhelm (1844–1900)

N

Nietzsche, a German philosopher, is best known for his vitriolic critique of traditional Christian morality. His critique of contemporary education, however, is at least as constant a theme throughout his writings.

Indeed, Nietzsche's attack on morality at times takes the form of an attack on the way in which he and his contemporaries have been educated. Morality, he contended, is relative to one's particular upbringing, not an eternally valid code of principles derivable from human nature or reason. The morality inculcated by his own culture, with its emphasis on suppression of natural instinct and its analysis of human behavior in terms of the concept of sin, was psychologically and culturally disastrous. The result was a society of timid souls, eager to ascribe sinfulness to others in an effort to minimize their own sense of guilt, and fearful of any departure from convention that might render them morally suspect in the view of others. The educational emphases of millennia had inculcated these pathetic tendencies, and Nietzsche was convinced that the only positive course available to Western culture was to attempt to reeducate moral habits, beginning with oneself.

The fundamental conviction guiding Nietzsche's analyses of education is the view that education achieves its purpose only to the extent that it has real impact on human life. In "On the Advantages and Disadvantages of History for Life," Nietzsche evaluated the contemporary rage for historical education on the basis of this standard, concluding that emphasis on history could have either positive or negative impact on lived experience. Study of history could benefit the living by producing inspiring monuments, evoking reverence, and developing critical judgment that can be used in the direction of life in the present. The contemporary insistence that history be "scientific"—and thus extremely methodical and complete—had damaged the ability of scholars and their students to gain these advantages that history offers for the conduct of living. Instead, the rage for "scientific" history was damaging to contemporary students by: (1) exaggerating the distinction between the inner person and outer acts, thereby weakening the personality of the student who took history seriously; (2) deceiving students into believing their own age more just than previous ages; (3) disrupting students' instincts and sense of self by presenting a standardized "cultivation" as the ideal; (4) making students feel that they are latecomers in history who can see their own lives only with irony; and (5) encouraging cynicism and, ultimately, extreme egoism.

"Schopenhauer as Educator," although ostensibly a paean to Arthur Schopenhauer (1788–1860), offers a similar critique of contemporary, standardized education. The primary aim of education, Nietzsche argued, should be the production of those rare individuals, or geniuses, on whom genuine culture depends. The most important aspiration of an educational system, therefore, should be to equip those showing potential for greatness with models like Schopenhauer, who can inspire them to their own creative individuality and provide them with a realistic awareness that genius is seldom appreciated in its time. Schopenhauer was also a model in demonstrating the distance between the creative work of genius and the career of the professor, ultimately a civil servant whose intellectual freedom is constrained by all who have power over the professor's job.

The elitism implicit in Nietzsche's essay on Schopenhauer characterized his discussions of education throughout his career. Nietzsche's elitism is evident especially in his characterization of scholars, whom he sees as petty individuals engaged in petty tasks. In *Twilight of the Idols* (1888), a work of his final year of productive work, Nietzche summarizes his view in the form of a parody of doctoral examinations. "'What is the task of all higher education?' To turn men into machines. 'What are the means?' Man must learn to be bored. . . . 'Who serves as the model?' The philologist: he teaches grinding" (*Twilight of the Idols*: 532).

Although many of Nietzsche's discussions of education are formulated as critiques, *The Gay Science* (1882; fifth book added 1887) and *Thus Spoke Zarathustra* (Parts I–II, 1884; Parts I–IV, 1891), works of his middle period, offer positive visions of an alternative to contemporary scholarship. "The gay science" (*die fröhliche Wissenschaft*) refers to a lighthearted approach to scholarship, in contrast to grim research into details of narrowly conceived projects whose possible relationship to lived experience is ignored. Nietzsche proposed that scholarship be seen instead as an artistic enterprise, in which scholars are aware that the truth, like a living being, cannot be captured in fixed formulas. Such scholars would see their work as akin to that of artists. Rather than attempt-

ing to uncover buried truths underlying the world of our experience, they would focus on the world as it appears to us, and their work would emanate from their aesthetic appreciation of this world.

Nietzsche recognized that his "gay science" might sound to some like an abandonment of education's "deeper" aims, particularly that of achieving a firm knowledge of reality. Nevertheless, he believed that his scholars would show more intellectual integrity than contemporary scholars showed, whose behavior belied their professed belief in an insight offered by Immanuel Kant (1724–1804) a century earlier. Kant had asserted that our minds condition all knowledge, and that human beings will never, therefore, come to know reality as it is independently. The truth for human beings is always relative truth, in reference to themselves. Nietzsche's scholars would take this claim as their premise; and if "superficial" by reigning standards, they would be "superficial—out of profundity" (*The Gay Science*: 38).

Thus Spoke Zarathustra, a fictional work in biblical style, is a chronicle of Zarathustra, a prophet who descends from his mountain hermitage to teach his wisdom to others. Zarathustra is thus a teacher, and the work reports both his teachings and his second thoughts about the status of his teaching vocation. Although complex from a literary point of view, one aspect of the work is its concern with certain issues of education, including the following: (1) How much should a teacher sacrifice precision for the sake of making subject matter comprehensible to students? (2) How important is the teacher's own conviction to the teaching effort? (3) Can one's own insights be communicated to others without utter distortion of their meaning? (4) To what extent does education necessitate a teacher's use of indirect methods of communication? In a sense, too, Zarathustra as fictional character can be seen as one who teaches his readers by demonstrating the ways in which his whole person is involved in his teaching effort and his own learning is a response to his pedagogical failures.

Beyond Good and Evil (1886), as well as Nietzsche's other works following *Thus Spoke Zarathustra*, elaborates the complaints of "Schopenhauer as Educator." Contemporary education, far from working to ensure the development of "philosophers of the future" who would take responsibility for the further direction of culture, puts obstacles in the way of philosophical development. Pressured to become a specialist, the potential philosopher is discouraged from taking a comprehensive view. Surrounded by the democratic sentiment that all should be educated equally, the would-be philosopher is discouraged from recognizing what Nietzsche takes to be real qualitative differences among individuals' talents. Inwardly disposed to maintain intellectual conscience, such an individual hesitates along the way, fearing the loss of self-respect. Worst of all, scholars, recognizing the truth that they are mere beasts of burden, are motivated by resentment toward those gifted with genuinely independent minds.

Nietzsche's late works are rather vague regarding solutions to this crisis in education. They primarily aim to expose the errors of various pseudosolutions, like commitment to "objectivity" (a posture that involves studied dissociation from the concerns of life) or skepticism (a stance of pseudosophistication that Nietzsche sees as symptomatic of nervous exhaustion). Ultimately, Nietzsche believes that the solution must lie with the rare individuals that the current educational system fails to support. Genius cannot be taught, but culture can recover only by means of the leadership of genius. Nietzsche encourages those who have the potential for genius to stand against their time and educate themselves. In any case, he considers the best education to be a form of self-education in which one treats one's life as a grand experiment. Only in this way will those with potential for greatness respond to their true calling, that of legislating new values for their era.

As for educational institutions, Nietzsche urges them to return to their basic tasks of helping students learn to see, to think, to speak, and to write. These, he claims, are the preconditions of noble culture. Ultimately, he urges, all educators should learn from those who teach dancing: "Thinking wants to be learned like dancing, *as a kind of dancing*" (*Twilight of the Idols*: 512).

Kathleen Marie Higgins

See also Elitism; Existentialism; Kant; Tragedy

Bibliography

Cooper, David. *Authenticity and Learning: Nietzsche's Educational Philosophy.* London: Routledge and Kegan Paul, 1983.
Golomb, Jacob. "Nietzsche's Early Educational Thought." *Journal of Philosophy of Education* 19 (July 1985): 99–109.
Gordon, Haim. "Nietzsche's Zarathustra as Educator." *Journal of Philosophy of Education* 14 (1980): 181–92.
Nietzsche, Friedrich. *Beyond Good and Evil.* Translated by Walter Kaufmann. New York: Random House, 1966.
———. *The Gay Science.* Translated by Walter Kaufmann. New York: Random House, 1974.
———. *Kritische Gesamtausgabe Werke.* Edited by G. Colli and M. Montinari. Berlin: Walter de Gruyter, 1975ff.
———. *Thus Spoke Zarathustra.* Translated by Walter Kaufmann. In *The Portable Nietzsche,* edited by Walter Kaufmann. New York: Viking, 1968.
———. *Twilight of the Idols.* Translated by Walter Kaufmann. In *The Portable Nietzsche,* edited by Walter Kaufmann. New York: Viking, 1968.
———. *Untimely Meditations.* Translated by R.J. Hollingdale. Cambridge: Cambridge University Press, 1983.
Rosenow, Elijahu. "Nietzsche's Concept of Education." In *Nietzsche As Affirmative Thinker: Papers Presented at the Fifth Jerusalem Philosophical Encounter, April 1983,* edited by Yirmiyahu Yovel, 119–31. The Hague: Martinus Nijhoff, 1986.

Nihilism

Nihilism in the philosophical sense is the view that there is no inherent value to be found in the world, or beyond it, and that there is no intrinsic goal or purpose to human existence. The major implication of this view for the philosophy of education is that any received values that have not already been perceived as null and void may have to be "suspended" in order to clear the ground for the responsible creation of new values.

The philosophical idea of nihilism goes back to the German thinker F.H. Jacobi (1743–1819), who in an essay from the 1780s entitled "Idealism and Nihilism" argued that Kantian philosophy leads to a view of the human subject as "everything" and the rest of the world as "nothing." In a letter to the philosopher Johann Fichte (1762–1814) in 1799, Jacobi criticized the extreme subjectivism of German Idealism and branded the whole movement as "nihilism." This tendency in German thought reached its culmination in Max Stirner's *The Ego and His Own* (1844).

Nihilism was an important force in the development of Russian culture and politics in the latter part of the nineteenth century, thanks to the influence of I.F. Turgenev's novel *Fathers and Sons* (1862) and the works of F.M. Dostoevsky. However, the most influential confrontation with the problem of nihilism has been on the part of a thinker much concerned with education: Friedrich Nietzsche (1844–1900).

With his ideas of "the death of God" Nietzsche claims to have discovered that the values that have sustained the development of Western culture hitherto (values rooted in the Greek, Roman, and Judeo-Christian traditions) have "devalued themselves" and are no longer tenable. He distinguishes between "passive" nihilism, which realizes that human existence and the world have no intrinsic worth but have been invested with value by successive moral and political systems, and "active" or "creative" nihilism, which sees such worthlessness not as grounds for despair but as providing the opportunity for the creation of new values—but this time by the individual rather than by the society. Nevertheless, these new values are not to be created *ex nihilo* or arbitrarily: Nietzsche sees us as heirs responsible to rich cultural and intellectual traditions from which elements can be selected for the fashioning of meaningful existences. A key feature of his thinking here is the idea that our lives can be made meaningful to the extent that we fashion the "givens" of our existence into works of art that are integrated into the greater work of culture as a whole.

In his early work *Schopenhauer as Educator* (1874), Nietzsche sees the educator as one who liberates the student by removing the layers of social and cultural accretions that obstruct the unfolding of the student's true individuality. The educator must then assess the relative strengths of the student's various talents, determine which is the strongest, and help provide optimal nourishment for that greatest gift—while at the same time preventing the dominant talent from inhibiting the development of the student's subsidiary abilities. Nietzsche's later writings suggest that the main knack the educator needs to develop is that of knowing, in the event that the received basis of the student's worldview has not crumbled spontaneously, at which point to inject a dose of nihilism to undermine the student's framework of beliefs. Another important task is to provide through one's way of life a model on the basis of which students can learn to fashion their own existence.

Socrates (c. 470–399 B.C.) believed that no true learning could take place until the ground of the student's soul had been cleared of unexamined opinions and prejudices. In this sense one can see nihilism—as long as it is carried through to its fruitful phase—as a creative rather than a destructive force in the educative process.

Graham Parkes

See also EXISTENTIALISM; NIETZSCHE; SOCRATES

Bibliography

Nietzsche, Friedrich. *Schopenhauer as Educator.* In *Untimely Meditations.* Translated by R. J. Hollingdale. Cambridge: Cambridge University Press, 1983.

Nishitani, Keiji. *The Self-Overcoming of Nihilism.* Translated by Graham Parkes with Setsuko Aihara. Albany, N.Y.: SUNY Press, 1990.

Rosen, Stanley. *Nihilism.* New Haven and London: Yale University Press, 1969.

Norm

A social norm is a rule, standard, or pattern for action against which conduct—either one's own or that of others—is approved of, disapproved of, or measured to determine its excellence or faults. A norm, in that sense, is not a statistical average or modal tendency of behavior in a social group. It is not even a formulation of what is usual. Rather, it is a shared standard of desirable behavior: a standard of what ought to be done, not a frequency measure of what is done. Behavior we discover to be frequent, even usual, in a social group may, nevertheless, violate the social norms of the group.

Where the norms of a society are frequently violated, one is likely to find a widespread sense of guilt, especially if the norms are important or strong ones. Persons aiming to disobey such norms will generally try to conceal their actions. That acts of bribery are undertaken in secret, for example, advertises the presence of normative boundaries and shows that the participants know where those boundaries lie. Secrecy may satisfy a desire merely to avoid discovery and public disapproval. In such cases, norms of prudence operate. But if the desire for secrecy expresses a reluctance to commit a moral breach, then at issue is a norm proscribing bribery. Its violation is likely to produce guilt, even if the act remains concealed.

The norm persists even in the presence of its violation.

Conscience is the reflexive application of norms. It is present when the self stands in judgment upon the conduct of the self. Thus, the formation of conscience can be seen as the process of norm acquisition. So also can entry into every academic discipline, craft, or social practice. These too can be viewed as occurring by the acquisition of norms. To become a historian, lawyer, teacher, physician, gardener, golfer, and so on, is not merely to acquire a body of knowledge or skill, but also to come to judge one's conduct and that of others by the norms of historians, lawyers, teachers, physicians, gardeners, golfers, and so forth. Becoming a musician, for example, is at the very least coming to judge the excellence of one's own performance by the standards of judgment used by musicians.

From the perspective of the student, therefore, the central problem of education is the acquisition of norms; from the perspective of the educator it is their public promulgation or transmission. The acquisition of norms proceeds to the formation of reflexive judgment through three stages. It may begin in mere compliance with a rule, develop into a form of habitual conformity to it, and eventually take shape as obedience. Mere compliance is evident when behavior is made to accord with the rule simply because the alternatives are more onerous and weighty or because the rule embodies a prescription so trivial as to matter hardly at all. Mere conformity is exemplified when, as is common with rules of grammar and customs of dress, behavior accords with the rule without reflection or even without any knowledge of what the rule of practice may be. Obedience to a norm in any full sense occurs only when the norm is allowed to govern, not merely because it is custom or habit but because it formulates a rule of right or good—that is, because it states what ought to be.

This last phase in the full acquisition of a norm leaves it an open possibility that the norm can be redeemed by reasons, and thus become not simply a rule of custom or practice but a rationally justified rule that ought to be obeyed. Thus, the movement from compliance to obedience through habitual conformity is a movement from the external imposition of a norm to its internal, autonomous, and rational authorization, a movement from the status of a rule that stems from some external tutor to its status as the self-legislation of an independent agent. In this progression lies the sociological expression of the Kantian insight that, insofar as we are rational creatures, the moral law presents itself to us as objective legislation, as a law of nature, even though it is self-given. Here also is an expression of the view of Emile Durkheim (1858–1917) that morality, whether in the form of the right or the good, though met as something perfectly objective, must, in a state of autonomy, come to be affirmed by the self as rationally vindicated. Whatever is my community's rule of conduct must become my own. Finally, this movement from compliance to obedience and rational endorsement incorporates critical judgment on the norms of practices. That is to say, given any social practice, craft, or profession, there will be norms to guide the rational assessment of those practices. The reflexive debate upon these norms, when systematically pursued, might be described as the philosophy of law, history, teaching, sociology, politics, and so forth.

Whether or in what measure a particular norm has been acquired by any individual cannot be established by showing that his behavior matches what the norm requires. Such evidence is always insufficient. Proof of norm acquisition must be found rather in a person's disposition toward violations of the norm. That behavior accords with what the norm requires might establish compliance to external authority or conformity resulting from habit, but not obedience to the norm. When departures from the norm are confronted with the attitude that such behavior needs correction, however, then we know that the rule has become not simply a rule of social convention, but a rule of right or rectitude. Whether the response to error is response as to a "social gaff" or response as to a serious violation of morality or craft will tell us what status is accorded to the norm as a guide to behavior. In short, if we are to empirically detect educational success in transmitting social norms, it is more important to observe response to error than frequency of compliance.

Durkheim, though usually described as a major figure in the history of sociological thought and almost never listed among major philosophers, is, nevertheless, the principal philosopher of social norms. Durkheim was concerned to establish sociology as a discrete science, the fundamental facts of which cannot be reduced either to psychology or to any of the physical sciences. To the question "What are social facts?" Durkheim's answer was "social norms." And so in *Suicide,* the social facts to be confronted are not the different frequencies of suicide in Catholic and Protestant communities, as modern empiricists have sometimes supposed, but rather the social norms that produce such frequencies. The fundamental realities of any society are its social norms. They constitute the building blocks of social systems.

Of equal importance to the idea of social norms is Durkheim's distinction between the empirical and the normative community, a distinction between the way things are and can be discovered to be in any society and the way things would be were they all that the shared norms of a society suggest they ought to be. In this sense, the norms of a society are its ideals. They provide the standards against which the actual community is to be assessed.

Thomas F. Green

See also COMMUNITY; CRITICAL THEORY; DISCIPLINE; DURKHEIM; MORAL DEVELOPMENT; SCIENCE, PHILOSOPHY OF; SOCIOLOGY

Bibliography
Durkheim, Emile. "Individualism and the Intellectuals." In *On Morality and Society,* edited by Robert Bellah, 43–57. Chicago: University of Chicago Press, 1973.
———. *Moral Education.* Translated by Everett K. Wilson and Herman Schnurer. New York: Free Press, 1973.
———. *The Rules of Sociological Method.* 8th ed. Edited by George Catlin. New York: Free Press, 1965.
———. *Suicide.* Glencoe, Il.: Free Press, 1951.
Nisbet, Robert A. *The Sociological Tradition.* New York: Basic Books, 1966.

P

Paideia

Denoted in its etymological origins in early Greek the "rearing" of a child (*pais*) by its mother or "nanny." By the fourth century B.C., *paideia* had come to mean teaching or education generally, and was understood to refer most properly to the education that began at the age of five to seven with the start of schooling outside the home. With that alteration in meaning, the term came to signify both the content and processes of teaching, training, and education, and also their results—namely learning, culture, and accomplishments.

The education in question was invariably understood to be general, rather than technical, and directed above all at forming the child or youth into an admirable or good (*agathos*) human being. Indeed it was often taken to embrace everything apart from natural endowment that contributes to a person's goodness (*arete*), formal instruction or schooling being considered only a part of this. Thus the experience of the civic and cultural life of one's city, including not only its festivals and public art, but even its architecture, was generally regarded as an aspect of *paideia*. A related view, characteristic of the Classical Period and espoused most notably by Simonides (556–468 B.C.), Protagoras (c. 490–c. 421 B.C.), Plato (c. 427–347 B.C.), and Aristotle (384–322 B.C.), was that the instruction in living provided by the laws of one's *polis*, or city-state, was itself a fundamentally important aspect of *paideia*. The term *paideia* is associated especially with the Hellenistic Age, however, for it was only then, in the generation after Aristotle and the demise of the independent city-state under Alexander the Great (356–322 B.C.), that Greek education attained a definitive form incorporating the innovations of the late Classical Period.

A further expansion of the meaning of *paideia* occurred in the Hellenistic Age, owing to the character of Hellenistic education and to its place in Hellenistic civilization. Because Hellenistic education was essentially literary in content, and because *paideia* or *paideusis* (*auxesis,* in Hellenistic Greek) had long had as one of its primary senses the content of education, it also came to signify literature and indeed the whole of the Greek cultural tradition embodied in literature. Because the unity of the Greek world of the Hellenistic Age was largely cultural, and was sustained through the spread of Greek schools and gymnasia, *paideia* also took on the meaning of "civilization," or that which separates a "civilized" people from a "barbaric" one, and the Greeks in particular from "barbarians." Finally, what civilizes was understood to make a person not only better, but also more truly or fully human. This view reflected a broad acceptance of the idea, which was already highly developed in the teachings of Aristotle, that what defines a species is the most admirable potentialities, or *aretai* (virtues), inherent in its nature, though present only in potentiality without culture or *paideia*. In the case of human beings, the defining potentialities were held to be those pertaining above all to the capacities for reason, and a "man of *paideia*" was thus understood to be a person of good judgment in all matters. Hellenistic education parted company with Aristotle and the philosophical tradition, however, in taking the study of human existence as it was represented by the great poets to provide the training that could form such judgment. Hellenistic *paideia* was thus "humanistic" in a twofold sense: It was an education in the "humanities," or "arts and letters," but also an education thought to "humanize" or nourish the best or most truly human traits of the student.

The development that culminated in Hellenistic *paideia* may be described most simply as the evolution of an education in athletics and music into one that was literary and increasingly technical in fact, though not in theory. It had its beginnings in what Aristophanes called the "old education" of Athens, an education for a leisure class of knightly warriors, dating to the latter half of the sixth century B.C. The members of this aristocracy devoted their leisure (*schole*) to athletics by day and to song by night, and the "schooling" they acquired through affiliation with a private tutor was thus devoted to athletic and musical training and to general moral instruction. The traditional virtue of "valor" had been transplanted from the field of battle to the arena of sport, and it served as the dominant aim of this training, though its more comprehensive ideal was the man both beautiful (*kalos,* meaning physically beautiful) and good (*agathos*).

With the democratization of Athens came a democratization of education through the introduction of group lessons in schools and the addition of instruction in letters or writing. This resulted in three subjects being taught by three teachers rather than by one, with the general moral component falling largely to the *pedagogue,* the slave belonging to the child's family who led the child from one teacher to another. In time, the significance of gymnastic training and music declined, and music in the larger sense of the "arts of the Muses," including above all the recitation and mastery of Homer and the other poets, grew in importance.

With the advent of schools of rhetoric and philosophy in the fourth century, a higher learning, including a highly technical course of instruction in rhetoric, developed. Hellenistic education embraced the rhetorical tradition, thereby preserving the place of Homer as "the educator of the Greeks," but in doing so it also embraced an increasingly technical study of literature and an almost exclusive preoccupation with the intellect. Nevertheless, its ideal continued to be the balanced development of the whole person.

The enduring influence of Hellenistic *paideia* was ensured by its adoption by the Romans, and by the early Christians as part of a system of Christian *paideia* that combined the classical curriculum with biblical revelation. It lived on in the Byzantine Empire in the East, in schools and universities conducted entirely in Greek, until the fall of Constantinople in 1453.

Randall R. Curren

See also Arete; ARISTOTLE; CICERO; HOMER; HUMANISM; ISOCRATES; PLATO; SOPHISTS

Bibliography
Beck, F.A.G. *Bibliography of Greek Education and Related Topics.* Sydney: F.A. Beck, 1986.
———. *Greek Education.* London: Methuen, 1964.
Downey, Glanville. "Ancient Education." *Classical Journal* 52 (1957): 337–45.
Jaeger, W. *Paideia: The Ideals of Greek Culture,* vols. I–III. New York: Oxford University Press, 1939–1944.
Marrou, H.I. *A History of Education in Antiquity.* Translated by George Lamb. London: Sheed and Ward, 1956.

Peabody, Elizabeth Palmer (1804–1894)

American transcendentalist, common school advocate, proponent of the philosophy of infant education of Friedrich Froebel (1782–1852), and founder of the nineteenth-century movement to establish kindergartens in the United States.

In 1835, Peabody published *Record of a School: Exemplifying the General Principles of Spiritual Culture,* which described her work with Bronson Alcott at the Temple School and placed her at the center of nineteenth-century debates on educational reform. Over the course of the next four decades, she wrote books and articles on curriculum, pedagogy, teacher training, and the educational responsibilities of the family and society. Writing and lecturing extensively on the need for kindergarten as the first phase of "the elevation of the moral life of society," she raised funds to support teacher training and model schools, founded and edited the *Kindergarten Messenger,* served as president of the American Froebel Union and the Boston Froebel Society, and was a member and lecturer in the Concord School of Philosophy. In Boston in 1860, Peabody opened the first English-language kindergarten in the United States. Her *Guide to the Kindergarten and Moral Culture of Infancy* (1863), written with her sister Mary Tyler Mann, was widely considered the most authoritative work on the theory and methods of the kindergarten during the 1860s and 1870s.

Elizabeth Palmer Peabody was born in Billerica, Massachusetts, on May 26, 1804. Her father, Nathaniel, a former teacher at Philips Andover Academy, was a student of dentistry at Harvard. Her mother, Elizabeth (Palmer), a former teacher at the North Andover Seminary for Young Ladies, was the headmistress of a girls' boarding school. The Peabody family had long been prominent in Massachusetts political and cultural life. Elizabeth, her brother, and two sisters thus grew up within a highly literate local society in which Ralph Waldo Emerson (1803–1882), Bronson Alcott (1799–1888), Henry David Thoreau (1817–1862), Julia Ward Howe (1819–1910), Margaret Fuller (1810–1850), William Ellery Channing (1780–1842), as well as other notable writers and thinkers of the time were not only part of the cultural milieu but also often family friends.

The Peabody children received their formal education at the small school their mother founded in Salem following her husband's completion of his Harvard studies. Elizabeth proved to be a particularly gifted student and, unusual for young women of the 1820s, was encouraged to pursue further education. She became a private student of Emerson's, with whom she studied Greek, and was tutored in history and philosophy by Channing. After assisting at her mother's school, Peabody opened her own class for young children at the age of sixteen. This was followed by teaching positions in Maine and other Massachusetts towns until she and her sister Mary were able to establish the Beacon Hill School in Boston in 1825.

From the first, Peabody's philosophy of education was shaped by the Transcendental movement and New England Unitarianism. In opposition to the Calvinist doctrines of the eighteenth century, the Transcendentalists denied that humanity was inevitably damned through original sin. Since the Transcendentalists understood the divine as the guiding principle in all nature, they reasoned that individuals had been given the potential to transcend evil. God-given human nature was perfectible and responsive to cultivation. Children, they believed, were not innately depraved but innocent and malleable—in need of careful guidance and loving nurturance rather than a Calvinist regime of restraint and repression. The social doctrines of New England Unitarianism, as interpreted in

Channing's influential sermons, were compatible with this transcendental vision of natural perfectibility and human progress. Societies as well as individuals could advance spiritually through their institutions.

Like many of her contemporaries, Peabody was convinced that education could not only provide spiritual salvation for the individual but also produce morally responsible citizens capable of realizing democratic national ideals. Peabody incorporated these tenets in the organization of her earliest classrooms. In an effort to acquaint students with models of the ethical life, she provided exposure to the best of human creation in art, literature, and history. To capture the imagination, she guided her students in dramatic play and creative writing. She also began to develop a theory of pedagogy that valued children's individual emotions. As she wrote, her teaching experience had convinced her that "nothing is permanently remembered which does not touch the heart or interest the imagination" (*Record:* 7). According to Peabody, forcing children to memorize strictures for behavior and adhere to them through fear was ineffective. Children, she believed, should be lovingly guided toward a realization of transcendent goodness that they could freely accept for themselves.

During her early career, Peabody published a series of history textbooks and guides for teachers that reflected these pedagogical convictions. This prompted Bronson Alcott to ask her to become his assistant at the experimental Temple School in 1934. While Alcott assumed the role of head teacher, Peabody served as administrator, fund-raiser, teaching assistant, and what might be described as early classroom ethnographer. She took extensive notes, describing daily activities, pedagogical practices, classroom organization, materials, student work, and Alcott's conversations. Peabody's notes became the basis for *Record of a School* (1835), which evoked considerable interest in transcendental educational methods. The impact of the Temple school, however, was eventually obscured by controversy. There were questions about the propriety of Alcott's rumored discussion of human reproduction in relation to Christ's birth. In the second edition (1836), Peabody avoided direct reference to the rumor and defended the way Alcott "conversed with (the older students), and by a series of questions, led them to conclude for themselves upon moral conduct" (*Record:* 121). However, when

Alcott's *Conversation with Children on the Gospels* (1836) was published later that year, its preface included a disclaimer stating that Miss Peabody and the author sometimes disagreed on classroom discussion topics.

Peabody returned to her own school in 1837 and became active in organizing teacher-training institutes and normal schools, lecturing, and writing. During this period, she also joined Fuller's Ladies Cultural Discussion group (1839–1844), opened a Boston bookstore to promote transcendentalist literature and make foreign-language texts (several of which she translated herself) more widely available (1840–1850), and served as editor of *The Dial* (1842–1843). In her writing she detailed plans to reform the standard grammar-school history curriculum, argued for the need to educate girls as rigorously as boys, and supported the common school campaign.

In 1859 an article on the German kindergarten appeared in the Unitarian journal *Christian Examiner,* and Peabody recognized the emphasis on guided play, creative industry, and the malleability of childhood as strikingly similar to her own philosophy of early childhood education. She immediately began to channel her considerable energies toward advocating for kindergartens as part of the larger common school movement, and she opened a kindergarten with her sister Mary in Boston in 1860. The publication of *Guide to the Kindergarten* in 1863, derived from research similar to that which had led to *Record of a School,* initiated a national kindergarten movement. Peabody became the movement's acknowledged leader.

During the late 1860s, Peabody traveled to Germany to study kindergartens first hand and to entice German kindergartners to come to the United States to train American teachers. She succeeded in placing former students of Froebel's in model kindergartens in Boston, New York City, Washington, and California. Gradually, a national network of teachers and teachers-in-training emerged. As her extensive correspondence indicates, Peabody kept individual members of this network informed of each other's progress, and she continued to recruit new student teachers and to raise funds and organize community groups to support kindergartens until well into her eighties.

As kindergartens gained greater popularity in the mid 1870s, Peabody served on the National Education Association's committee on kindergarten with Bronson, Alcott, Henry Bar-

nard (1811–1900), and William Torrey Harris (1835–1909) and, working through the Froebel Society of Boston, organized a model Centennial Kindergarten for the 1876 American Centennial Exposition in Philadelphia. Differences about the nature, goals, and practices of early childhood education emerged on both occasions. Throughout, Peabody maintained her transcendentalist principles. Cultivation and nurturance of the child's moral potential and creative faculties, she argued, were the foundations of true Froebelian method and would meet the needs of children of all classes.

Although Peabody's persistent activism was admired by many of her contemporaries, she was also subject to criticism leveled at women of her time who dared to enter public political debate. Nathaniel Hawthorne (1804–1864), husband of her sister Sophia, saw her as a humorous spinster hopelessly involved in causes; the caricature by Henry James (1843–1916) of the elderly committee woman Miss Birdseye in *The Bostonians* (1886) was widely thought to have been based on Peabody. Yet Peabody's work was greatly respected by her fellow common schoolers. Horace Mann (1796–1859), who had married her sister Mary Tyler Peabody, collaborated extensively with her. Henry Barnard published several of her articles in the *American Journal of Education* and chose Peabody as his collaborator on *Kindergarten and Child Culture* (1881).

While Peabody is best remembered as the founder of kindergarten in the United States, her contributions to larger nineteenth-century educational debates and her influence on twentieth-century theorists in early childhood education have been underestimated. Peabody's work was integral to the common school movement, and Susan Blow (1843–1916), Kate Douglas Wiggin (1856–1938), and Lucy Wheelock (1857–1946) all began their careers as her students or protégées. Following Peabody's death on January 5, 1894, Wiggin described her as "that noble and venerable woman Elizabeth Peabody, the revered and eminent champion of childhood" (154).

Susan Douglas Franzosa

See also ALCOTT; FROEBEL

Bibliography

Baylor, Ruth M. *Elizabeth Peabody: Kindergarten Pioneer*. Philadelphia: University of Pennsylvania Press, 1965.

Fleming, Alice. *Great Women Teachers.* Philadelphia: J.B. Lippincott, 1965.

Peabody, Elizabeth Palmer. *Aesthetic Papers.* Boston: Periodical Publications, 1849.

———. *Education in the Home, the Kindergarten, and the Primary School.* London: Sonnenschein, 1887.

———. *Guide to the Kindergarten and Moral Culture of Infancy* (with Mary Tyler Mann). Boston: T.O.H.P. Burnham, 1863.

———. *The Kindergarten and Intermediate Class.* New York: E. Steiger, 1877.

———. *Kindergarten Culture: 1870 Report.* Washington, D.C.: United States Bureau of Education, 1870.

———. *Lectures in the Training Schools for Kindergartners.* Boston: D.C. Heath, 1886.

———. *Record of a School: Exemplifying the General Principles of Spiritual Culture.* Boston: Russell, Shattuck, 1835.

———. *Reminiscences of Rev. William Ellery Channing, D.D.* Boston: Roberts Brothers, 1880.

Shapiro, Michael Steven. *Child's Garden: The Kindergarten Movement from Froebel to Dewey.* University Park: Pennsylvania State University Press, 1983.

Synder, Agnes. *Dauntless Women in Childhood Education, 1836–1931.* Washington, D.C.: Association for Childhood International, 1972.

Tharp, Louise Hall. *The Peabody Sisters of Salem.* Boston: Little, Brown, 1950.

Weber, Evelyn. *The Kindergarten: Its Encounter with Educational Thought in America.* New York: Teachers College Press, 1969.

Wiggin, Kate Douglas, ed. *The Kindergarten.* New York: Harper and Brothers, 1893.

Person, Concept of

One of the most interesting and controversial topics in twentieth-century philosophy is the question, What must a being be like to be a person? There are numerous perspectives on the nature of the person, and while personhood is perhaps at its deepest level a metaphysical notion, one can focus on one or more aspects of the idea. For example, we can speak of persons in the legal sense, in the socio/political (cultural) sense, in the religious sense, in the strictly metaphysical or ontological sense (where the questions of personal identity are a major issue), in the moral sense, and so on.

In each of these conceptions, a definition is wanted. Thus, for example, we might define a metaphysical person as a being possessing, say, consciousness or rationality or self-consciousness, or some combination of the three. A person in the legal sense might be defined as any being for whom there is provision in the law regarding rights or responsibilities. Under this definition, a business corporation having the right under the law to issue stock would be a legal person. A person in the socio/political sense may perhaps be defined as any member of a given culture who is taken to be a person within that culture. In this brief essay, the concept of moral personhood will be the primary focus of attention.

The general question of personhood can be asked now specifying the moral sense: What must a being be like to have moral rights and responsibilities? The thrust of the question is that a person, taken in the moral sense, will be defined as a being possessing moral rights and responsibilities. As can be seen, this definition is not culture-specific—that is, it is intended to apply to any culture in which the concepts of moral right and moral responsibility have a footing. Nor is the definition species-specific. In fact, the reverse is the case, since the crucial point here is to leave open exactly the sort of being to which the epithet "person" applies.

Further, as specified, the definition makes it clear that a person is defined with reference not simply to moral rights or moral responsibilities, but rather with reference to both. This is significant in that it forestalls establishing either a rights-based morality alone or a duty-based morality alone on the basis of the definition of persons, where in the former a sufficient condition for moral personhood could be the possession of moral rights alone.

To ask what a being must be like in order to have moral rights and responsibilities is to ask what attributes or characteristics or qualities are necessary or sufficient for the title "person" to be applied. Personhood, then, is conditioned by one or more of these attributes.

It is instructive to work through the paradigm case of the person and ask what sorts of characteristics this being possesses that make it possessive of moral rights and responsibilities. The case is, of course, that of adult human beings. A caution is due here, since there is some question whether all adult human beings are persons (or are always persons). A human will be a person just in case that he or she possesses the person-making qualities. From what is said here it follows that having a human genetic code may be neither a necessary nor sufficient condition for personhood. But, taking this as a lead, we can ask after some physical characteristics of humans.

Is having arms or legs or shoulders or kidneys or a heart or a brain required for having moral rights and responsibilities? The answer is that none of these body parts are in themselves necessary for personhood except to the extent that any or all are necessary for whatever qualities are required for the ascription of personhood. So, for example, one would not exclude any human with no arms from the class of persons solely on the basis of the absence of arms. Similarly, having or not having legs appears irrelevant to the question of moral personhood, as does the possession of eyes, ears, fingers, hair, and so on. This line of thought can be extended to character and personality traits as well, where it would be thought perverse to deny personhood to humans simply because they are not generous or wise or open-minded or reflective or sympathetic or creative or clever.

The same cannot be said of the brain, perhaps; not only is the brain necessary for human life as we know it, but the brain is thought to be necessary for many or all of the qualities defining personhood, such as self-consciousness. On the other hand, though the brain may be the operational organ for self-consciousness, it is not logically impossible that some beings other than humans have self-consciousness but no brain. What this would show is that possession of brain itself would not be a necessary condition for personhood, though presumably the being with self-consciousness but no brain would have some other operational organ for self-consciousness.

Let us now look at a number of conditions for personhood that have appeared in the literature on this topic. One of the forerunners in the meaning and use of the term person is John Locke (1632–1704). He writes, "We must consider what Person stands for; which, I think, is a thinking intelligent Being, that has reason and reflection, and can consider it self as it self, the same thinking thing in different times and places, which it does only by that consciousness, which is inseparable from thinking, and as it seems to me essential to it" (*Essay:* book II, chap. XXVII). Here we see that consciousness,

self-consciousness, and rationality are preeminent. In fact, these three proposed conditions are echoed throughout the literature on personhood.

A number of other proposed "conditions" for personhood found in recent writing on the topic include complex communication, the ability to view another being as a person, being the sort of being another could view as a person, ability for self-motivated activity, freedom of will, capacity for love, intentionality, having a conception of moral right and wrong, and being sentient.

A question arising from any list of conditions for personhood is the following: Is there any (set of) sufficient condition(s)? Some philosophers, such as Daniel C. Dennett and Roland Puccetti, caution that there probably is no set of conditions such that any one or more would be thought sufficient for personhood. There are others, however, who disagree. Immanuel Kant (1724–1804), for example, seems to have thought that rationality is a sufficient condition for personhood. Michael Toole believes that self-consciousness is sufficient for a right to life, where "person" is defined as a being with such a right. And there have even been proponents of the view that being human itself is a sufficient condition. The great majority of writers on the topic, however, seem agreed that the conditions mentioned in the previous paragraph comprise a workable set of necessary conditions for personhood for situations in which the category of moral personhood is of relevance. So, for example, in coming to grips with the question of whether children have a moral right to education, the concept and conditions of moral personhood would be of practical importance.

Another question arising in this issue is whether persons are to be decided upon or discovered. How shall the conditions listed above be viewed? Are they to be seen as more or less objective, given what is requisite for moral personhood, or are they to be construed as those conditions arising from the culture in which the writers on personhood have been educated, given the values that these writers accept? In the first view, one might say a moral person is a natural kind, whereas in the second one would say perhaps that the concept of moral personhood is relative to the culture in which the concept is employed. In the second view, then, persons in, say, Scotland would be all and only those individuals toward whom the term *person* is correctly applied as judged by the members of the Scottish community. This may, of course, change, as the community changes its ideas of what is important for personhood. Personhood in the "natural kind" view would be an absolute, something we can discover, timeless and immutable. From the perspective of deciding who are persons (or deciding on the conditions of personhood), personhood is relative, what Richard Rorty in *Philosophy and the Mirror of Nature* would call part of the "conversation" of humanity, working through, over and over, how the world shall be constituted.

With all of this said, the further question of the nature of moral rights and responsibilities is not answered. Perhaps one is likely to say that until we answer this question, we cannot anyway define "moral personhood."

Michael F. Goodman

See also CHILDREN'S RIGHTS; ETHICS AND MORALITY; HUMAN NATURE; RIGHTS

Bibliography

Callahan, Daniel. *Setting Limits.* New York: Simon and Schuster, 1987.

Dennett, Daniel C. *Brainstorms.* Cambridge: MIT Press, 1978.

———. *The Intentional Stance.* Cambridge: MIT Press, 1987.

Fletcher, Joseph. *Humanhood: Essays in Biomedical Ethics.* Buffalo, N.Y.: Prometheus, 1979.

Goodman, Michael F. *What Is a Person?* Clifton, N.J.: Humana Press, 1988.

Kant, Immanuel. *Groundwork of the Metaphysic of Morals.* Translated by H.J. Paton. New York: Harper and Row, 1964.

Kohlberg, Lawrence. *The Philosophy of Moral Development.* San Francisco: Harper and Row, 1981.

Locke, John. *An Essay Concerning Human Understanding.* Edited by P.H. Nidditch. Oxford: Oxford University Press, 1975.

Lomasky, Loren. *Persons, Rights and the Moral Community.* Oxford: Oxford University Press, 1990.

Melden, A. I. *Rights and Persons.* Berkeley: University of California Press, 1977.

Parfit, Derek. *Reasons and Persons.* Oxford: Clarendon Press, 1984.

Perry, John. *Personal Identity.* Berkeley: University of California Press, 1975.

Puccetti, Roland. *Persons: A Study of Possible Moral Agents in the Universe.* London: Macmillan, 1968.

Regan, Tom. *Matters of Life and Death.* 2nd ed. New York: Random House, 1986.

Rorty, Amelie, ed. *The Identities of Persons.* Berkeley: University of California Press, 1976.

Rorty, Richard. *Philosophy and the Mirror of Nature.* Princeton, N.J.: Princeton University Press, 1979.

Scott, G.E. *Moral Personhood.* Albany: State University of New York Press, 1990.

Searle, John. *Intentionality.* Cambridge: Cambridge University Press, 1983.

Strawson, P.F. *Individuals.* London: Methuen, 1959.

Tooley, Michael. *Abortion and Infanticide.* Oxford: Oxford University Press, 1983.

Wellman, Carl. *A Theory of Rights: Persons under Laws, Institutions, and Morals.* Totowa, N.J.: Rowman and Allanheld, 1985.

P

Pestalozzi, Johann Heinrich (1746–1827)

Swiss educator, whose educational innovations such as the object lesson and simultaneous instruction reformed elementary education. His *Leonard and Gertrude,* published in 1781, *How Gertrude Teaches Her Children,* published in 1801, and other writings reshaped educational ideas and practices. Teachers trained at his institutes at Burgdorf and Yverdon disseminated Pestalozzian ideas throughout Europe and the Americas.

Johann Heinrich Pestalozzi, born on January 12, 1746, in Zurich, Switzerland, was the son of Johann Baptiste Pestalozzi, a physician from a middle class Protestant family of Italian ancestry, and Susanna Hotz Pestalozzi. His father's death in 1751, which reduced the family's income, caused his mother to entrust the household's management to Barbara Schmidt, a dependable servant and important model in young Pestalozzi's life. Pestalozzi was influenced by his grandfather, Andreas Pestalozzi, a minister in the village of Hongg, to dedicate his life to assisting the poor. According to his own recollections, he grew up overly protected, isolated from peer contact, shy, introspective, and physically uncoordinated. From 1751 to 1754, he attended a local primary school where he studied the traditional curriculum of reading, writing, arithmetic, and religion. In 1754, he began classical studies at the Schola Abbatissana, then transferred to the more advanced Schola Carolina and the Collegium Humanitatis, where he studied Latin, Greek, Hebrew, literature, rhetoric, philosophy, and theology. In 1763, admitted to the Collegium Carolinum, he concentrated on languages and philosophy. There, he was influenced by Jean Jacques Bodmer, professor of history and literature, who advocated revitalizing Swiss life by modeling simple peasant virtues. Pestalozzi and other followers of Bodmer's organized the Helvetic Society and published *The Monitor*, a reform journal, urging a Swiss renascence. The society's activities offended Zurich's officials, who suppressed *The Monitor* and briefly jailed Pestalozzi and other members.

Completing his formal education, Pestalozzi sought a career that would fulfill his goal of ameliorating the condition of the poor. His inadequacy at public speaking caused him to abandon a career in religious ministry. In 1767 he studied farming with Johann Rudolf Tschiffeli, a physiocratic proponent of scientific agriculture, at an experimental farm near Kirchberg in Berne canton. In 1769 Pestalozzi married Anna Schulthess, daughter of an upper middle class Zurich family and sister of his friend Caspar Schulthess. In 1771 he purchased a farm, called Neuhof, near Birr in Berne canton; it was the location of his first educational experiment. In 1770, his only child, Jean Jacques, named after Rousseau, was born. Pestalozzi used Rousseau's didactic novel *Emile* to guide his son's education, but he decided that Rousseau's method needed reformulation according to a psychology of learning. His *How Father Pestalozzi Instructed His Three and a Half Year Old Son*, published in 1774, described his experiment in educating his son. He now had developed several insights that shaped his educational philosophy: (1) Rousseau's ideas on natural education, while essentially valid, needed revision to include a more psychologically based strategy for guided child development; (2) Education, through the regeneration of individuals, could bring about larger social and economic reform.

In 1774 Pestalozzi launched his first educational experiment, opening what he hoped would be a self-supporting agricultural and handicraft school at Neuhof. The school enrolled fifty children, many of whom were orphans or indigent. In addition to their farm chores and handicraft production, the children were taught reading, writing, and counting by a group method that Pestalozzi called "simultaneous instruction." Group instruction was an alternative to the conventional recitation, a form of simplified tutoring in which a teacher taught each child individually. Between 1775 and 1778, Pestalozzi's *Essays on the Education of the Children of the Poor* and *The Evening Hours of a Hermit* appeared in the journal *Ephemerides*, to publicize and raise funds for his school. By 1779, however, financial losses forced the school's closing. Despite his seeming failure, the Neuhof experience contributed the following beliefs to Pestalozzi's evolving philosophy of education: (1) It was highly unlikely that schools could be economically self-supporting; (2) Children could be effectively and efficiently instructed in groups and could learn skills and subjects concomitantly rather than in isolation.

Concentrating on writing, Pestalozzi hoped that his publications would offset the financial losses he incurred at Neuhof. His well-received didactic novel *Leonard and Gertrude*, published in 1781, marked his first systematic effort to articulate his educational philosophy. In the novel, which portrayed his conviction that education could stimulate personal and social regeneration, the heroine, Gertrude, an exemplary mother and educator, leads a successful reform of a destitute Swiss village. The next year, in 1782, he published *Christopher and Elizabeth*, a less successful sequel to *Leonard and Gertrude*, consisting of dialogues in which Christopher, the father, leads family discussions.

From 1782 through 1784, Pestalozzi, publishing his own newspaper, *Ein Schweizer Blatt*, (the *Swiss News*), editorialized for a new educational system based on natural principles. His *On Legislation and Infanticide*, in 1783, condemned the practice of killing or abandoning unwanted children. He also wrote several children's books, including *Illustrations for My ABC Book* (1787) and *Fables for My ABC Book* (1795). His *Researches into the Course of Nature in the Development of the Human Race*, in 1797, articulated a broad philosophical base for his educational ideas.

In 1799 the new Swiss government, the pro-Napoleonic Helvetian Republic, appointed Pestalozzi director of an orphanage at Stans, location of a battle between opposing French and Austrian armies. He was responsible there for eighty children, some of whom had been recently orphaned by war. His work at Stans generated an important educational insight, the necessity of creating a home-school environment in which children experienced emotional security provided by caring adults. He incorporated into his general method the principle that schools should be emotionally secure environments and that emotional security is a precondition for successful cognitive learning. In 1799 the orphanage was closed when opposing French and Austrian armies again battled in its vicinity.

In 1799 Pestalozzi was appointed assistant to Samuel Dysli, schoolmaster of Burgdorf's working-class primary school. Dysli and Pestalozzi disagreed over the use of corporal punishment, rote memorization, and the catechetical method. Assisted by the Helvetian government, Pestalozzi was provided with a castle where, from 1800 to 1804, he operated his Burgdorf Institute, which included a boarding school and a teacher-education center. In 1801, Pestalozzi's most systematic book on educational philosophy and method, *How Gertrude Teaches Her Children,* described how, at Burgdorf, he had developed sensation as a key element in his methodology. All learning, he claimed, is based on sensory experience, a process he called *Anschauung,* defined as conceptualization from sense impressions. Using *Anschauung,* Pestalozzi designed his "object lessons" in which children, guided by teachers, examined the form (shape) and number (quantity and weight) of objects, and then named them only after direct experience with them. Sensory instruction, based on object teaching, was the most widely adopted part of Pestalozzi's method. His educational philosophy, however, rested on two basic assumptions: (1) Children need an emotionally secure (affective) environment for successful (cognitive) skill and subject learning; (2) Instruction should follow the generalized epistemological process by which individuals formulate concepts through the process of sensation. Because he stressed conceptualization based on sensation, historians of education have positioned Pestalozzi in the genre of sense realism.

To diffuse his method, Pestalozzi made teacher preparation an integral element in his institutes at Burgdorf and then later at Yverdon. He trained Joseph Neef (1770–1854), who introduced Pestalozzianism to the United States in the early nineteenth century, and Friedrich Froebel (1782–1852), the kindergarten's founder. As his reputation grew and translations

of his books reached a larger audience, Pestalozzi's institutes attracted such prominent educators as America's common school leaders, Horace Mann (1796–1859) and Henry Barnard, and the scientist-geologist-philanthropist William Maclure (1763–1840). In 1804, Pestalozzi relocated his institute to Yverdon, where he continued his educational work until 1825. He died on February 17, 1827, and is buried at Neuhof, site of his first school.

Pestalozzi's enduring significance in education rests on his educational philosophy emphasizing children's holistic physical, mental, and psychological development; his emphasis on sensationalist epistemology; his reforms of elementary and teacher education; and his anticipation of more child-centered progressivism in education. Pestalozzi's philosophy emphasized the General and the Special methods. The General Method, designed to create an emotionally secure learning environment, was a necessary condition for the Special Method of sensory instruction using objects.

Pestalozzi's theory of moral education rested on his premises of how individuals develop into educated, economically self-sufficient, and emotionally healthy persons. Emotional security, he believed, originates in concrete human instincts rather than preaching abstract moral principles. Applying his concept of moral development to schooling, Pestalozzi challenged conventional nineteenth-century practices of physical and psychological coercion.

Pestalozzi criticized conventional schools' verbalism, bookishness, rote memorization, and practice of ignoring that human beings learn through sensation. Since human beings come to know about the objects in their environment through their senses, Pestalozzi reasoned that instruction should be based on sensory learning. His Special Method used Object Lessons, in which children, guided by trained teachers, observed and analyzed the objects in their immediate environment—minerals, plants, animals, and the artifacts made by human beings. Each object could be studied through a series of "Form, Number, and Name" lessons.

Pestalozzi's Object Lessons encouraged curriculum enrichment in natural sciences and geography, two previously neglected areas. Led by teachers on field trips through the surrounding countryside, children had direct opportunities to study the local topography, economy, and society.

Pestalozzi stimulated innovations in classroom management and instruction. The conventional method, the recitation, located children all in one room, with one child at a time appearing before the teacher to recite a previously assigned lesson. Pestalozzi's use of group instruction corrected what he saw as the verbal recitation's inefficient use of time and its failure to bring children together as an integrated, interactive social group.

Pestalozzi's educational philosophy was diffused throughout Europe and the Americas by those he trained as teachers and by visitors to his institutes at Burgdorf and Yverdon. Because Pestalozzi wrote in German, his method was first transported to the German states. Johann Gottlieb Fichte's *Addresses to the German Nation,* in 1808 urged Prussia's adoption of Pestalozzian education to regenerate the country after its defeat by Napoleon's armies. Incorporating selected Pestalozzian elements in its educational reform of 1809, Prussia dispatched teachers to train with Pestalozzi. England's Home and Colonial School Society, organized in 1836, promoted Pestalozzianism by establishing a model school to demonstrate the method and a training school to prepare Pestalozzian teachers.

In the United States, Pestalozzianism experienced three distinct phases: (1) William Maclure's and Joseph Neef's initial introduction; (2) Henry Barnard's efforts to publicize the method; (3) Edward A. Sheldon's development of Pestalozzian-based teacher education at the Normal School at Oswego, New York.

In the early nineteenth century, William Maclure, a philanthropist who had visited Pestalozzi at Burgdorf, was determined to use the Pestalozzian method to diffuse scientific knowledge to the American agricultural and working classes. In 1806, Maclure contracted with Joseph Neef, Pestalozzi's former assistant, to introduce the method in the United States. Neef established several Pestalozzian schools in Pennsylvania and Kentucky and wrote *A Sketch of a Plan and Method of Education* in 1808, and *The Method of Instructing Children Rationally in the Arts of Writing and Reading* in 1813, based on Pestalozzian pedagogical principles. Neef conducted a Pestalozzian school at Robert Owen's communitarian experiment at New Harmony, Indiana, from 1824 to 1826. Other Pestalozzian educators at New Harmony were Marie Duclos Fretageot and William D'Arusmont.

American Pestalozzianism's second phase involved the efforts of Henry Barnard (1811–

1900), a common school leader and the first U.S. Commissioner of Education, to popularize the method. Barnard, editor of the *Connecticut Common School Journal,* published *Pestalozzi and Pestalozzianism* in 1859. Bronson Alcott (1799–1888), William C. Woodbridge, and William Russell also incorporated Pestalozzianism into their educational activities.

The work of Edward A. Sheldon (1823–1897) and his associates at the Oswego Normal School in New York constituted Pestalozzianism's third major phase in the United States. Sheldon and his associates, Margaret Jones, a former teacher at the Home and Colonial Training School in England, and Herman Krusi, Jr., the son of one of Pestalozzi's assistants, incorporated Pestalozzi's object lessons, featuring form, number, and name lessons, into Oswego's training program. Published lesson plans from Oswego were used by teachers throughout the country. In 1865, the National Teachers' Association's endorsement of object teaching brought national attention to Oswego's version of Pestalozzianism.

Selected Pestalozzian elements could also be found among early-twentieth-century progressive educators, who opposed formalism and excessive verbalism in schools. Pestalozzi's General Method, designed to cultivate an emotionally secure learning environment, resembled American progressivism's emphasis on children's interests and needs. Francis W. Parker's nature studies, William H. Kilpatrick's project method, and Harold Rugg's "child-centered school" resembled Pestalozzi's focus on children's interests and on direct activities as the basis of learning.

For education today, Pestalozzi's major contribution was his philosophy of "natural education," which stressed the dignity of children and the importance of a child-centered curriculum. Pestalozzi's General Method, the creation of an emotionally secure learning environment, anticipated modern child psychology. Contemporary concepts such as the "child-centered school," "child permissiveness," and "hands-on-process learning" originated with Pestalozzi.

Gerald L. Gutek

See also FROEBEL; PROGRESS, IDEA OF, AND PROGRESSIVE EDUCATION; ROUSSEAU

Bibliography
Anderson, Lewis F., ed. *Pestalozzi.* New York: McGraw-Hill, 1931.

Barlow, Thomas A. *Pestalozzi and American Education*. Boulder, Colo.: Este Es Press, 1977.

Barnard, Henry, ed. *Pestalozzi and Pestalozzianism*. New York: Brownell, 1862.

Dearborn, Ned H. *The Oswego Movement in American Education*. New York: Teachers College Press, Columbia University, 1925.

De Guimps, Roger. *Pestalozzi: His Aim and Work*. Syracuse, N.Y.: Bardeen, 1889.

Downs, Robert B. *Heinrich Pestalozzi, Father of Modern Pedagogy*. Boston: Twayne, 1975.

Gutek, Gerald L. *Joseph Neef: The Americanization of Pestalozzianism*. University: University of Alabama Press, 1978.

———. *Pestalozzi and Education*. New York: Random House, 1968.

Hayward, Frank H. *The Educational Ideas of Pestalozzi and Froebel*. London: R. Holland, 1905.

Heafford, Michael R. *Pestalozzi: His Thought and Its Relevance Today*. London: Methuen, 1967.

Jedan, Dieter. *Johann Heinrich Pestalozzi and the Pestalozzian Method of Language Teaching*. Bern: Peter Lang, 1981.

Monroe, Will S. *History of the Pestalozzian Movement in the United States*. Syracuse, N.Y.: Bardeen, 1907.

Pestalozzi, Johann Heinrich. *The Education of Man—Aphorisms*. New York: Philosophical Library, 1951.

———. *How Gertrude Teaches Her Children*. Translated by L.E. Holland and F.C. Turner. Syracuse, N.Y.: C.W. Bardeen, 1894.

———. *Leonard and Gertrude*. Translated by Eva Channing. Boston: D.C. Heath, 1891.

———. *Pestalozzi's Letters on Early Education*. Addressed to J.P. Greaves and translated by Christian F. Wurm. London: Sherwood, Gilbert, and Piper, 1827.

———. *Pestalozzi's samtliche Briefe*, vols. 1–12. Edited by the Pestalozzianum and Zentral-bibliothek. Zurich: Rascher, 1946.

———. *Pestalozzi's samtliche Werke*, vols. 1–28. Edited by A. Buchenau, E. Spranger, and H. Steebacher. Berlin, 1927.

Pinloche, Auguste. *Pestalozzi and the Foundation of the Modern Elementary School*. New York: Charles A. Scribner's, 1901.

Silber, Kate. *Pestalozzi: The Man and His Work*. London: Routledge and Kegan Paul, 1960.

Walch, Mary R. *Pestalozzi and the Pestalozzian Theory of Education: A Critical Study*. Washington, D.C.: Catholic University Press, 1952.

P

Peter Lombard (c. 1100–c. 1160)

Born in Italy, educated at the School of St. Victor's, and a teacher of theology in the Cathedral School at Paris from about 1140, Peter Lombard became bishop of Paris sometime during the last decade of his life. A collection of his sermons and two biblical commentaries are extant, yet he is best remembered for his *Four Books of Sentences,* completed in 1157 or 1158.

His *Sentences* attempt a comprehensive and systematic presentation of Christian doctrine. The scope of the main problems of theology and their sequence was customary by his time; yet in the *Sentences* was a prototype of the theological-philosophical *Summas* that later scholastics would develop more acutely. Book I treats of God; Book II, creation, grace, and sin; Book III, incarnation and redemption; and Book IV, the sacraments. While the *Sentences* are largely a compilation rather than an original work, the work came to be widely adopted as a text for courses in theology. About 1222, the *Sentences* were officially incorporated into the course of theological studies at the University of Paris, where students were required to write commentaries on them in order to receive a degree in theology. Among the theologians who studied him, we may mention Alexander of Hales (c. 1186–1245), Bonaventure (1221–1274), and William of Ockham (c. 1290–c. 1350) as authors of commentaries on the *Sentences*. A sense of the pervasive character of Peter Lombard's influence may be seen in a comment by Roger Bacon (c. 1214–c. 1294), who said that one of the seven sins of the study of theology in his time was the preference for the *Four Books of Sentences* over the Bible. The influence of the *Sentences* on theological studies continued for four hundred years.

The method employed is exemplified in Book I, Chapter I, of the *Sentences*. Here the question is on man's knowledge of God and the Trinity. After stating the question, Peter Lombard quotes the Scriptures (four times), Augustine (thirty-one times), Ambrose (once), and Hugh of St. Victor (once). On God, he concludes that "the truth of God is known in many ways through things which have been made." On the Trinity, Peter concludes in a like manner that while "no sufficient knowledge of the Trinity can be had . . . we are aided . . . in the faith of invisible things by the things which have been made." Elsewhere in the *Sentences* he quotes other fathers, yet Augustine was his favorite.

Apparently Peter Lombard was influenced by the method of Abelard (1079–1142): We see in both the contrasting of authorities and arguments, with the ultimate aim of reconciling opposing texts. (It is possible that he was a student of Abelard's, but we do not have certain evidence.) The pervasive spirit of the *Sentences* lies in the strong belief that authorities and arguments can be successfully contrasted, and that opposing texts on questions can be reconciled. Later theologians such as Thomas Aquinas (1225–1274) made use of Aristotle's philosophy in working out a more nearly complete dogmatic theology. And where Peter Lombard was sometimes hesitant in stating doctrines of his own, Aquinas was more bold in stating doctrines as reconciliations of various authorities and arguments. Even so, a definite sense that questions on opposing texts and arguments can be resolved was a fundamental part of Peter Lombard's legacy to generations of theologians. Very seldom has a text been studied by so many students for such a long period of time as was the case with the *Four Books of Sentences*.

J.J. Chambliss

See also AUGUSTINE; SCHOLASTICISM; THOMAS AQUINAS

Bibliography

Brady, Ignatius. "Peter Lombard." In *The Encyclopedia of Philosophy.* Vol. 6, edited by Paul Edwards, 124–25. New York: Macmillan, 1967.
Kearney, Eileen F. "Peter Lombard." In *The Encyclopedia of Religion.* Vol. 2, edited by Mircea Eliade, 257–58. New York: Macmillan, 1987.
Peter Lombard. *The Four Books of Sentences.* Book 1, Distinction III. In Richard McKeon, *Selections from Medieval Philosophers,* 189–201. New York: Charles Scribner's Sons, 1929.
Van Dyk, John. "Thirty Years since Stegmuller: A Bibliographic Guide to the Study of Medieval Sentence Commentaries since the Publication of Stegmuller's *Reportium.*" *Franciscan Studies* 39 (1979): 255–315.

Phenomenology

Phenomenology is an approach to philosophy that examines the basic conditions of subjective experience. Best understood as a method of philosophical investigation, phenomenology seeks to articulate invariant structures of experience that govern the course of subjective awareness. As an analysis of experience, phenomenological inquiry restricts itself solely to what is presented to awareness within the field of lived experience—to the "phenomena" given for consciousness as appearances for consciousness. The central issue for phenomenology is the manner in which the phenomenal "contents" of experience are presented to subjectivity within the sphere of conscious life. Through strict attention to the manner in which phenomena are presented for consciousness, phenomenology reveals the basic structure of experience, a structure that accounts for our basic abilities to know and act upon the world.

As a method for philosophical research, phenomenology provides philosophy with a particular starting point. Phenomenological philosophy holds that lived experience is the origin of every philosophical problem; progress in philosophical thinking is therefore to be achieved by returning to this origin. Every philosophical problem emerges as a problem only for an inquiring subject, out of the person's own lived experience; phenomenology therefore calls for radical reflection upon the lived processes of subjective life. The purpose of this reflection is to understand how philosophical questions originate within experience, within the field of subjective awareness. By its turn toward the concrete nature of lived experience, phenomenology seeks to achieve insight regarding the ways in which traditional philosophical questions have been posed. For example, when we pursue the question of the foundations of certainty of our knowledge, we already suppose the course of our ordinary, prephilosophical experience of the world; the phenomenologist therefore approaches this problem by attending to the ways in which our common-sense notions of certainty and uncertainty are gained within the course of ordinary experience. Phenomenological inquiry reveals how the philosophical question of certainty is framed on the basis of a prephilosophical acquaintance with the conditions of "normal" and reliable experience; to clarify these ordinary foundations of certainty, as they are experienced within the course of mundane life, is already to resolve the philosophical issue of certainty.

As a method for philosophical research,

phenomenology resists approaching the problems of philosophy as they have been traditionally posed; rather, phenomenology attempts to reformulate these problems by attending to the conditions of lived experience out of which they have first emerged. This return to the concrete nature of lived experience is the sense of the basic "motto" of phenomenology: "To the things themselves." To clarify the origin of a problem within "the things themselves," within the course of subjective experience, is to approach the problem from a standpoint that is critically informed. Phenomenology attacks the problem explicitly as a problem for and about subjective experience; this orientation to lived experience provides the motivating insight of phenomenological philosophy.

As a philosophical movement, phenomenology arose in the early part of the twentieth century. Although the term *phenomenology* can be traced farther back in the history of philosophy—most notably, to G.W.F. Hegel's *Phenomenology of Spirit* (1807)—the movement called phenomenology is basically understood as a more recent development. The German philosopher Edmund Husserl (1859–1938) is considered the central figure and founder of the contemporary movement. Husserl's work has exercised wide influence within twentieth-century European philosophy; Husserlian concepts and methods are utilized by philosophers such as Martin Heidegger (1889–1976), Jean-Paul Sartre (1905–1980), and Maurice Merleau-Ponty (1908–1961). Husserl's phenomenology is understood as a forebear of the philosophical movements of existentialism and hermeneutics; it is also associated with the poststructuralist movement of deconstruction, although most accurately as a point of ideological departure. The phenomenological movement, however, is by no means a unified "school" of philosophy. It offers no single set of results that might be understood as a doctrine or system; rather, phenomenology is more accurately characterized as a network of associated, though divergent, schools of thought. Phenomenological philosophies share not so much a final, determinate, philosophical position as much as a similar conception of their starting point. Phenomenological thinkers have taken diverse philosophical positions; however, they rely in common upon a basic idea of method developed by Husserl. In what follows, we shall briefly sketch Husserl's conception of phenomenology, for the sake of exploring its relevance to the philosophy of education.

The basic subject matter of phenomenology is lived experience; phenomenological inquiry seeks to explore the course of experience as such, precisely as it is experienced. A working definition of experience might be: open and continuing awareness of the self and world, which present themselves as familiar and already meaningful spheres of existence. Phenomenology investigates experience explicitly as this course of awareness, attending strictly to "phenomena"—the given appearances presented for consciousness. Through phenomenological method, the course of experience is brought to relief as a current of subjective awareness. Experience is the progress of a consciousness, alive to a world already familiar in its established meanings. The chief purpose of the phenomenological method, as a specialized attitude adopted toward experience, is to bring the course of experience to the foreground as such. One might question the need for this special approach to experience—experience is already given! Indeed, but in the ordinary, practical, unreflective attitude of daily life, the course of experience is taken for granted, pursued without being explicitly noticed. Within the standpoint of daily life, which Husserl calls the "natural attitude," the course of experience maintains a particular translucency: We do not see our experience; we see through it. Our attention is directed through experience to the themes of our concerns. As long as experience proceeds smoothly, it maintains its translucency, and its surface as a stream of appearances escapes direct attention. We rarely notice experience as such, much less isolate it as a theme for prolonged investigation. We direct our attention immediately through experience, to the manifold issues of daily life. Within the natural attitude, the surface of experience is self-effacing, seen through but rarely seen, taken for granted as a window to the world.

The primary exercise of phenomenological method therefore consists in a "setting aside," "suspension," or "bracketing" of the natural attitude. If we hope to inquire explicitly into the course of experience, we must abstain from that attitude by which our experience goes for the most part unquestioned. Ordinary belief in the world, ordinary concerns for the world, and ordinary judgments regarding the actuality of the world, are set aside through the adoption of the phenomenological "epoche." The epoche, as a particular attitude adopted toward experience, allows the phenomenologist to view her experience explicitly as that stream of appearances normally seen through. Her experience follows its ordinary course, but she now attends to it strictly as a course of experience. Although it is certainly an interruption of the natural attitude of daily life, the phenomenological epoche differs from the attitude of doubt or denial adopted by Rene Descartes in the *Meditations*. Within the phenomenological epoche, the reliability of ordinary experience is not questioned, nor need its certainty be "secured." Ordinary belief in the world is suspended, but not so that it be proven valid; the commonsense validity of this belief is not in question. Rather, the phenomenologist distances herself from ordinary belief in the world, in order to clarify how its validity, as belief, is already ensured. Within the epoche, belief is revealed as a particular attitude of consciousness, sustained with regard to what is given for consciousness, and how it is given, within the course of ordinary experience.

As a suspension of one's "natural" belief in the world, the epoche purposes merely to maintain critical distance from the course of one's own experience. This distance is maintained so that, for example, belief might be examined as a particular modality of consciousness. Within the epoche, the stream of experience is brought forth as a theme of investigation in its own right, in resistance against its normally self effacing translucency and familiarity. The phenomenologist maintains her awareness of self and world, precisely so that self and world can be examined as phenomena, as meant, as intended within the course of experience; the phenomenologist, however, suspends her ordinary concern with these issues. Her attention is directed strictly to the structure of experience— to the manner in which the self and world are presented purely as phenomena: as appearances for consciousness, laden with meanings for consciousness. What is decisive is the way in which these phenomena, in the natural attitude, are experienced as already bestowed with meaning. Within the natural attitude, the self and world are given as already established in their meanings, as familiar "objects" of experience. Furthermore, within the natural attitude, the self and world are given according to an overall familiar "style" of appearance. The phenomenological epoche explicitly reveals for consciousness, for the first time, this prefamiliar structure of its own experience of these meanings. Within the epoche, the structure of experience, as the overall manner in which phenomena are meaningfully presented for consciousness, is brought to attention in its own right.

With the natural attitude suspended in this manner, experience is "reduced" to a field of immediately given phenomena. Within this reduced sphere of experience, phenomenological investigation pursues two basic paths of inquiry. The first is entitled "eidetic analysis," or analysis of structures essential to any meaningful experience of a given theme. (The term *eidetic* is derived from the Greek *eidos*, "form," "appearance.") For the sake of eidetic analysis, within the epoche, the phenomenologist employs a method of investigation that Husserl calls "free variation" or "imaginative variation." Attending to some theme of experience as it is given—say, a cup of coffee on a kitchen table—the phenomenologist employs her imagination in an attempt to vary the manner in which the phenomenon is ordinarily given. This exercise in imaginative variation is pursued until it exhausts itself, running up against the limits of what can meaningfully be varied with regard to the structures of appearance. One cannot, for example, coherently imagine a perceptual experience in which a perceived object is simultaneously viewed from more than one perspectal angle: The coffee cup is seen, and can be seen, from only one angle at a time. The method of imaginative variation clarifies the manner in which the ordinary course of perceptual experience is governed by invariant and essential structures of appearance. To name but a few of these structures:

1. Every experience necessarily features the structure of consciousness as "intentionality"; every experience involves a subjective act (or *noesis*), which is correlated with the intended theme of that act (or *noema*). Every experience, as an act of seeing, hearing, desiring, affirming, denying, and so on, is necessarily a seeing of, or a hearing of, some appearance intended for that act. Every act of consciousness involves, over and against it, yet inseparable from it, an appearance of the object seen, heard, desired, affirmed. By necessity, every phenomenon, or every appearance for consciousness, displays this bivalent structure of intentionality, the correlation of *noesis* and *noema*.

2. Every phenomenon, as a correlation of act and theme, is given to experience at any one moment from a single perspectival aspect of its whole makeup (as outlined above). For example, in any perceptual experience, the object perceived is strictly presented to perception from only one angle at a time. Strictly speaking, I never see the whole cup, from all of its angles at once; rather, I strictly see only this side of the cup, that face of it that is turned toward me. If this insight seems trivial at first glance, its significance is critical for understanding the course of experience in the natural attitude. Within the natural attitude, I always perceive "more" than what is strictly given to appearance: I perceive the whole cup—not the side of the cup. This is to say: On the basis of what is strictly given to appearance, I always intend more meaning than that which is strictly presented to me. Phenomenological reflection reveals how the course of experience relies upon an active but unreflected bestowal of meaning upon those appearances that are strictly given. There is always more seen—more meaning intended—than meets the eye. To account for this surplus of experienced meaning, a further structure of appearance is examined:

3. "Horizonality." Although the perceptual phenomenon is strictly given from merely a single perspectival angle, in the natural attitude I perceive the whole object. Even as I strictly see only that partial, single aspect of the object, I bestow upon that aspect the meaning of the whole object; I intend it as the whole object. This is to say, in phenomenological terms, that I perceive the single aspect of the object along an intended, "inner horizon" of the full meaning of the object. The inner horizon of the object, bestowed as a meaning upon the aspect of the object directly given, completes my perceptual experience of the object as a whole. Beyond this inner horizon of the perceived object, however, eidetic analysis reveals that every phenomenon is also intended along an "outer horizon." The outer horizon of the object leads experience beyond that object spatially as well as temporally. Imaginative variation re-

veals the impossibility of perceiving a theme that is not given against the background of an outer horizon, even if this background is imagined as an empty space or a time devoid of future or past events. In the natural attitude, this outer horizon is perceived as the overall field of phenomenal appearance given in the present, emerging from the past, anticipating a future; the coffee cup is now perceived as located on the table, in the kitchen, in the apartment, in the world, where it has been, and where it will remain. Our ordinary sense of objectivity—of the actuality of perceived objects—is sustained through our awareness of the object's givenness along this outer horizon of appearances. Realized in its full meaning, the outer horizon of perceptual experience received the name of "world." Phenomenological reflection reveals the meaning of the "life-world" as the all-encompassing, spatiotemporal horizon of all possible perceptual experiences. The structures of ordinary experience, correlated as an overall field of appearances, constitute the essential structure of the life-world, the world as experienced in the setting of daily life. Familiarity with the preestablished sense of the life-world is decisive for the course of experience in the natural attitude; the familiar sense of the life-world, more than any other intended meaning, accounts for and sustains the translucency of ordinary experience. Settled into the life-world, as a domain of familiar meanings, our experience finds itself "at home," such that we find ourselves at home in experience.

As these examples illustrate, eidetic analysis has sought to clarify the essential structures of appearance that regulate the course of experience. For Husserl, however, eidetic analysis is merely a preparatory task which opens up a second, philosophically crucial path of phenomenological inquiry: demonstration of the necessary subjective constitution of these "essences." Since these invariant structures of appearance compose the objective structure of the experienced world, they serve as foundations for any rational understanding of the world. Acquaintance with the invariant structure of the life-world is the basis of any rational awareness of the world as a realm of objective being. Therefore, according to Husserl, the ultimate task for phenomenology is demonstration of the absolute necessity of these structures for any possible consciousness. To demonstrate how these structures of appearance arise necessarily from the course of subjective experience would be tantamount to demonstrating the absolute universality of reason. The issue for this second, "transcendental" analysis of experience, therefore, is to account for the manner in which the eidetic structures of experience are constituted by subjectivity, necessarily and universally, within the course of experience.

This notion of transcendental constitution is most difficult, and it is easily and often misunderstood. Sufficient exposition of the meaning of transcendental phenomenological constitution is beyond the scope of this discussion. The basic issue, however, might be briefly indicated: The structures of experience are themselves given for experience, within experience; this givenness implies their availability to consciousness as complex formations of meaning—phenomena in their own right. As meanings given for consciousness, these structures of experience indicate their own origins within experience; they are in a certain sense artifacts—meanings that are originally constituted by subjectivity within the course of experience. Transcendental phenomenology seeks to demonstrate the manner in which this constitution takes place, assumed within the progress of experience, and it seeks to demonstrate the absolute necessity of this constitution of the structures of experience. At stake, for Husserl, are the deepest issues of reason, objective knowledge, and the intersubjective accessibility of a common experienced world. In its turn toward transcendental analysis, phenomenology takes up the classical problems of "first philosophy"—problems concerning the possibility of universal reason.

Our survey of Husserl's phenomenology is complete. Husserl's followers, within and beyond the phenomenological movement, have revised Husserl's methods, and have achieved diverse philosophical positions. In their work, however, a basic idea of phenomenology remains intact. Experience is to be studied in its own right, as the origin of our access to the world, and as the origin of the meaning of the world as we experience it. Phenomenological philosophy, it would seem, should have much to offer for the philosophy of education. Briefly,

we shall indicate a few points of possible contact between phenomenology and the philosophy of education, and we shall cite works that have pursued these possibilities.

First and foremost, phenomenology offers a method for descriptive analysis of basic educational processes. Learning and teaching are particular modes of experience, and phenomenological methods can be adopted for the sake of investigating their structures as such. The bulk of phenomenological research within the philosophy of education has been devoted to this sort of descriptive analysis. (See Chamberlin, 1969; Curtis and Mays, 1978; Mitchell, 1990; Morrison, 1988; Stanage, 1987; Denton, 1974; and Donald Vandenberg in Soltis, 1979.)

Furthermore, education, as a basic activity of human subjective life, occurs in a variety of settings, institutional and otherwise. In the case of institutional education, a phenomenological sociology of educational institutions can attend to the placement, roles, and functions of these institutions within the wider setting of the sociocultural life-world. Phenomenological analysis of educational institutions, as social settings for the processes of education, can contribute to our understanding of the purposes and challenges faced by these institutions.

Existential phenomenology and existentialism, as outgrowths of the original Husserlian phenomenological movement, employ Husserl's concepts and methods to various degrees. Existential phenomenologists, however, give priority to the basic issues of situated, embodied, intersubjective human existence. Existential phenomenologists generally express distrust of what they see as a tendency toward idealism in Husserl's work; they greet with suspicion the idea of transcendental phenomenology, and limit their inquiry to what amounts to eidetic analysis of the basic conditions of human existence. Philosophers of education have utilized the works of existential phenomenologists to examine the existential import of education within the basic situation of human beings in the world. From an existential-phenomenological point of view, education is understood as a chief factor in the ongoing project of human self-determination. Educational processes of teaching and learning are examined as ways in which human being-in-the-world achieves its self-understanding; education as a whole, as the process through which the individual comes to realize her situatedness within a particular cultural world, is examined as an instrument of social coexistence. (Many of the works cited below contain essays that express an existential-phenomenological orientation to the philosophy of education, as well as essays that express a more Husserlian point of view.)

A final note regarding the overall relevance of phenomenology to philosophy of education: Assuming that a philosophy of education pursues issues beyond the specific focus of "applied" educational theory, phenomenology is already a philosophy of education. Prior to its application to educational theory, phenomenology solicits our attention to the concrete processes through which we, as subjects for the world, confront and resolve the sense of the world as we experience it. If the confrontation and resolution of meaning is itself the meaning of education, then education is not merely a specific form of experience; education is the meaning of experience as a whole. If the broadest sense of education is the process through which we, as human beings, develop awareness of ourselves, the world, and other people, then the course of ordinary experience is already a course in education. Education is the core of experience. Phenomenology, as philosophical reflection of the lived processes of experience, is already reflection upon the nature of education.

Michael McDuffie

See also EPISTEMOLOGY; EXISTENTIALISM; EXPERIENCE; HEGEL; HEIDEGGER; MODERNISM AND POSTMODERNISM; SARTRE

Bibliography

Chamberlin, J. Gordon. *Toward a Phenomenology of Education.* Philadelphia: Westminster, 1969.

Curtis, Bernard, and Wolfe Mays, eds. *Phenomenology and Education: Self-Consciousness and Its Development.* London: Methuen, 1978.

Denton, David E., ed. *Existentialism and Phenomenology in Education: Collected Essays.* New York: Teachers College Press, 1974.

Gallagher, Shaun. *Hermeneutics and Education.* Albany: State University of New York Press, 1992.

Husserl, Edmund. *Cartesianische Meditationen,* [1929]. In *Husserliana,* vol. 1. Den Haag: Nijhoff, 1950. English version: *Cartesian Meditations.* Translated by Dorion Cairns. The Hague: Nijhoff, 1960.

———. *Ideen zu einer reinen Phanomenologie und phanomenologischen Philosophie.* Erstes Buch: *Allgemeine Einfuhrung in die reine Phanomenologie* [1913], neu herausgegeben von Karl Schuhmann. Den Haag: Nijhoff, 1976. English version: *Ideas Pertaining to a Pure Phenomenology and to a Phenenological Philosophy.* Vol. 1, *General Introduction to a Pure Phenomenology,* translated by F. Kersten. The Hague: Nijhoff, 1982.

———. *Die Krisis der europaischen Wissenschaften und die transzendentale Phanomenologie: Eine Einleitung in die phanomenologische Philosophie* (1934–1937), herausgegeben von Walter Biemel. Den Haag: Nijhoff, 1954. English version: *The Crisis of European Sciences and Transcendental Phenomenology: An Introduction to Phenomenological Philosophy.* Translated by David Carr. Evanston, Ill.: Northwestern University Press, 1970.

Mitchell, John G. *Re-Visioning Educational Leadership: A Phenomenological Approach.* New York: Garland, 1990.

Morrison, Harriet B. *The Seven Gifts: A New View of Teaching Inspired by the Philosophy of Maurice Merleau-Ponty.* Chicago: Educational Studies Press, 1988.

Pinar, William F., and William M. Reynolds, eds. *Understanding Curriculum as Phenomenological and Deconstructed Text.* New York: Teachers College Press, 1992.

Schutz, Alfred. "Some Leading Concepts of Phenomenology." In *Collected Papers.* Vol. 1, *The Problem of Social Reality,* edited and with an introduction by Maurice Natanson. The Hague: Nijhoff, 1962.

———. "Some Structures of the Life-World." In *Collected Papers.* Vol. 3, *Studies in Phenomenological Philosophy,* edited by I. Schutz. The Hague: Nijhoff, 1970.

Soltis, Jonas F., ed. *Philosophy of Education since Mid-Century.* New York: Teachers College Press, 1979, 1981.

Spiegelberg, Herbert. *The Phenomenological Movement: A Historical Introduction.* The Hague: Nijhoff, 1960.

Stanage, Sherman M. *Adult Education and Phenomenological Research: New Directions for Theory, Practice, and Research.* Malabar, Fla.: Krieger, 1987.

P

Philo of Alexandria (c. 25 B.C.–c. A.D. 40)
Also known as Philo Judaeus, Hellenistic philosopher schooled in Judaism and Greek philosophy, whose concept of God's nature and relationship with humanity formed the philosophic underpinning of Christianity, Judaism, and Islam until the seventeenth century. In several of his works, he discussed the nature of the ancient course of secondary education, the *enkuklios paideia,* or encyclical studies.

Philo was fond of expressing his thoughts in allegorical form, referencing people and events of the Hebrew Scriptures. Accordingly, he expressed his understanding of the role of secondary education by pointing out that when Abraham's wife, Sarah, was barren, he mated with the servant, Hagar the Egyptian, but when Sarah conceived he no longer consorted with Hagar. This, Philo, contended, was an adequate model for the role of the encyclical studies: They encompass things the child learns while as yet unready for higher studies but that are abandoned at the proper time for philosophy. The encyclical studies are the vestibule of philosophy, drawing their matter from the sensible world and unable to claim fully to get at the truth. Nonetheless, their subject matter is infinite and they cannot be fully comprehended in a lifetime of study. At one point, Philo admits that encyclical education also has value in tempering abstract justice with law and custom, and in helping individuals cope with the demands of daily life. But the weight of his emphasis is clearly on encyclical studies as instrumental, and he felt that they should be studied in youth rather than in maturity.

He agreed with Greek tradition about specific subjects to be included in the encyclical studies, but his understanding of the Jewish tradition often led him to conceptualize them uniquely. In the first place stood grammar, a matter first of learning reading and writing, then to encompass the reading of the great writers of prose and poetry. He saw this study as producing intelligence and a wealth of knowledge, as well as reverence for the best of the past. In the main, however, he thought it valuable in a negative way: Because it exposed the faults and calamities to which the gods and heroes were alike prone, it armed the student against pride and vain hopes. Positive models of virtue were to be found mostly in the Pentateuch. Music brought harmony to the soul; geometry supplied a love of equality and proportion while teaching logical thinking and creating a love of justice by emphasizing logic. Arithmetic in Philo's conception broadened out to include what we would call numerology, useful in understanding and interpreting the Hebrew Scriptures. Astronomy was admitted to the syllabus, not only in its role in studying the physics of the heavens, but also for prophesying the future in ways that we today dismiss as astrology. Rhetoric brought mastery of words and thoughts and, by emphasizing the construction of arguments, made a person truly reasonable, though it was dangerous because unwise study of it might foster sophistry. Finally, dialectic showed how to distinguish truth from falsehood by probing arguments.

While other ancients, Quintilian excepted, generally agreed on seven as the age at which formal study should begin, Philo opted for a later age. He felt that the child reaches the use of reason at seven but is still apt to be incompletely reasonable and prone to make poor moral decisions. Exposure to the encyclical studies should therefore wait until the individual child was truly ready. Philo used the term "ten years old," not intending it in a literal sense but as a perfect number significant of readiness. When this formal secondary education began, Philo contended, it would be obvious that students learn through instruction, natural intelligence, and application. The latter two are more significant, and teachers should limit themselves to displaying the extent and possibilities of knowledge rather than on drilling the student in specific facts and skills. He had a low opinion of schoolteachers in general, finding them apt to take credit for results achieved by the students' natural abilities and practice. The work of learning embraces the lesser activity of analyzing and making distinctions, which Philo likened to the rooting of a pig, and the much higher and more productive task of thinking and meditating, which he likened to the ruminating of a cow.

Much of what is distinctive about Philo's educational concepts is traceable to his moving back and forth between the more linear and abstract Greek thought tradition and the more concentric and concrete Hebrew tradition. Often the true liquor of his thought has to be carefully distilled from complex allegories. In the hands of Clement of Alexandria and Origen, his notion of the encyclical studies as gateway to philosophy became the idea of the encyclical studies and philosophy as the gateway to theology, a relationship that decisively shaped the thought system of Western Christianity.

Joseph M. McCarthy

See also CLEMENT OF ALEXANDRIA; JUDAISM; *Paideia*

Bibliography

Colson, F.H. "Philo on Education." *Journal of Theological Studies* 18 (1916–1917): 151–62.

Conley, T. *"General Education" in Philo of Alexandria.* Berkeley: University of California Press, 1975.

Goodheart, H.L., and E.R. Goodenough. "A General Bibliography of Philo." In *The Politics of Philo Judaeus,* edited by E.R. Goodenough, 125–348. New Haven: Yale University Press, 1938.

Mendelson, Alan. *Secular Education in Philo of Alexandria.* Cincinnati: Hebrew Union College Press, 1982.

Philo of Alexandria. *The Essential Philo.* Edited by Nahum M. Glatzer. New York: Schocken Books, 1971.

———. *Philo.* Translated by F.H. Colson, G.H. Whitaker, and Ralph Marcus. London: William Heinemann; Cambridge: Harvard University Press, 1929–1971.

Radice, Roberto, and David T. Runia. *Philo of Alexandria: An Annotated Bibliography, 1937–1986.* Leiden: E.J. Brill, 1988. See also their annual bibliographic updates in *Studia Philonica Annual,* 1989–.

Wagner, W.H. "Philo and *Paideia." Cithara* 10 (1971): 53–64.

Williamson, Ronald. *Jews in the Hellenistic World: Philo.* New York: Cambridge University Press, 1989.

Philosophy and Literature

Philosophers of education in the United States have paid little attention to possible relationships between philosophy and literature. Like European philosophers, they seem to have taken for granted Plato's view in the *Phaedrus* that those who cultivate "the garden of letters" are inferior to "lovers of wisdom" or those who engage in the "serious pursuit of the dialectician." Ralph Waldo Emerson (1803–1882), who today is recognized as one of our first philosophers, is generally thought of as a literary artist, indirectly related to the British Romantics and at once to Immanuel Kant (Cavell: 3–49; Poirier: 67–94). For all his concern for American scholarship, the growth of mind, the significance of reading, he was not seriously attended to by spokespersons for the common school, who felt challenged and mocked by much of what he said.

If there was a philosopher whose work was used as a lens by certain American educators, it was probably G.W.F. Hegel (1770–1831), who exerted a powerful influence on William Torrey Harris (1855–1909), the founder of the St. Louis Hegelians and later a prominent educational writer and administrator. John Dewey (1859–1952) was also strongly influenced by Hegel's view of historical consciousness and the dialectics of change; but neither he nor Harris was likely to seek resources in imaginative literature when it came to posing philosophic problems. In a rare evocation of a literary artist in a philosophic context, Dewey did once mention Walt Whitman, who often saw himself as a kind of Hegelian. Dewey wrote that democracy, "a name for a life of free and enriching communion . . . had its seer in Walt Whitman" (*Experience and Nature:* 184). For all his interest in particularities, however, and in the lived situations "in which we find ourselves" (*Art as Experience:* 263), he seldom turned to literature *qua* literature.

He did work to break with Platonism as he developed a conception of philosophy as "thinking what the known demands of us— what responsive attitude it exacts" (*Democracy and Education:* 381)—or viewed philosophic inquiry within an experiential and social matrix. Rejecting merely "spectator" approaches, he linked philosophy to educative action; it was to make a difference in human lives. This did not, perhaps, because of old intellectual habits, unseat traditional philosophies. The dominant conception was of philosophy as a "mirror of nature" (Rorty 1979), a representation of what was universally and objectively true. The social concerns of experientialism, the focus on scientific method and intelligence, the demand for critical thinking, the devotion to the making of a democratic community: These did not appeal to schoolmen interested in establishing institutions that would maintain public order and at once prepare children to play their required parts in an industrial society. Dewey's progressive ideas did have tangential effects on thinking about teaching and learning in various sections of the country, although mainly with regard to private schools. Experientialism or pragmatism, at the beginning of the twentieth century, cannot be said to have seriously challenged the idea of philosophy as reflective of a higher truth oriented to the discovery of large integrations and encompassing certainties.

Imaginative literature, especially in the early part of the twentieth century, was often considered equally referential: It too was to bring the reader in touch with something purer and more ennobling than the everyday. The emphasis was laid uncritically on the canonical tradition, or what Terry Eagleton describes as "English." Even where minimal attention was paid to literature, English texts provided the major content of the curriculum. American fiction was acknowledged as respectable only after the First World War. In any event, like their English counterparts, American curriculum makers were convinced that literature could effect a "more subtle communication of moral values" than the tired religious ideologies. "Since," writes Eagleton, "such values are nowhere more vividly dramatized than in literature, brought home to 'felt experience' with all the unquestionable reality of a blow on the head, literature becomes more than just a handmaiden of moral ideology; it *is* moral ideology for the modern age." American educators may not have been as concerned as the British with lightening the oppressiveness of working-class lives; but behind them lay the McGuffey Readers, with their use of literature chosen for its didactic powers. Shakespeare's plays, romantic poetry, Dickens's novels: All were generally taught for their elevating, improving qualities. In public schools committed to mass education, these were the qualities that were expected to sustain adjustment.

In the mid twentieth century, at about the time the dominant philosophy in American academic life (and eventually in the world of educational philosophy) was becoming analytic or focused on concept clarification, the approach to imaginative literature was moving from the so-called humanistic or explicitly ideological to what was called the "New Criticism" (Richards; Wimsatt and Brooks: 555–698). This meant a largely technical concentration on works, mainly poetry, viewed as closed universes, complete in themselves. Attention was turned to the internal unity and purely aesthetic life within the literary work; biographical, moral, and social associations were excluded by the need to concentrate on the "work itself." There are odd resemblances between the formalist specializations in philosophy and the work being done in literary criticism at the time.

Richard Rorty finds Hans Reichenbach to be one of the major influences on the "Age of Analysis." A historian of scientific philosophy,

he was an unabashed positivist (Rorty 1982: 213–14). To pay heed to Reichenbach on what was being supplanted is to understand why there was so little effort at the time to connect philosophy to literature. With Reichenbach, writes Rorty, philosophy teachers assumed that "the philosopher of the old school is usually a man trained in literature and history, who has never learned the precision methods of the mathematical sciences or experienced the happiness of demonstrating a law of nature by a verification of all its consequences" (215). At philosophy of education conferences, where attention was shifting from pragmatism and experientialism to logical and linguistic puzzles and problems, to (as Wittgenstein [1958] put it) "a battle against the bewitchment of our intelligence by means of language," empirical tests for meaning barred serious discussion of literary meanings. Dewey's view that "the realm of meanings is wider than that of true-and-false meanings" was set aside. So was the view that "poetic meanings, moral meanings, a large part of the goods of life are matters of richness and freedom of meanings, rather than of truth" (*Experience and Nature:* 411). Efforts to make use of literary works were frequently met with charges of lack of precision and rigor, charges that most often led to retreats.

The period after the Second World War was, of course, soon to be marked by an increasing interest in Continental philosophy. That meant for some a discovery of the so-called human sciences, of existentialism, phenomenology, hermeneutics, and (in time) critical theory (Gadamer; Habermas; Heidegger; Merleau-Ponty; Palmer; Ricoeur; Sartre 1956, 1949). Because of their concern for problems of human existence, consciousness, intentionality, and freedom, many of these philosophers were drawn to imaginative literature, drama, and poetry. Jean-Paul Sartre, for instance, wrote fiction and drama, embodying many of his philosophical ideas. Albert Camus became best known for his philosophical novels, such as *The Plague, The Stranger,* and *The Fall.* Graham Greene's novels and even Ernest Hemingway's were perceived as interrogating the world in an existential vein.

For Maurice Natanson, theories of literature have arisen out of phenomenology and existentialism. He wrote that "the microcosm given to us in a literary work is founded on and in turn illuminates the transcendental structure of common sense experience" (82). The task of literature from this point of view was the "reconstruction of mundane existence." Engagements with works of literature were believed to wrench people from submergence in the taken-for-granted and look through new eyes at their experience in the world. Sartre, taking the view that readers had actively to participate in literary works and to bring them alive in their own consciousness, said that there was a "moral imperative" at the heart of the aesthetic imperative in literature. "For, since the one who writes recognizes by the very fact that he takes the trouble to write, the freedom of his readers, and since the one who reads, by the mere fact of his opening the book, recognizes the freedom of the writer, the work of art, from whichever side you approach it, is an act of confidence in the freedom of men" (*Being and Nothingness*: 63). The idea was that, through an imaginary presentation of the world as it demands freedom, a novel could urge a reader on to make choices, to repair what was lacking, to become what he was not yet.

This approach to literature would appeal only to those philosophers who saw themselves "doing" philosophy with respect to open human questions, social restiveness, educational purposes. As educational and other philosophers did, in some measure, turn to issues of what Ludwig Wittgenstein (1958) called "ordinary language" and, as time went on, to different kinds of "language games," there was an acknowledgment of a wider range of symbol systems. Nelson Goodman, for instance, has written about the "*languages* of art" (1976), challenging traditional notions of representation and expression. When he writes about "art and understanding," he stresses the affinities among the diverse "languages" and says that the aesthetic experience, wherever it occurs, is dynamic rather than static. "It involves making delicate discriminations and discerning subtle relationships, identifying symbol systems and characters within these systems and what these characters denote and exemplify, interpreting works and reorganizing the world in terms of works and works in terms of the world" (241). The major differences between the arts and other modes of understanding had to do with the "difference in domination of certain specific characteristics of symbols" (264). The point was that the old dualisms were being challenged: All had to do with the comprehension of the world.

On the side of literary theory, a great many shifts were taking place, even apart from what existentialism and phenomenology had begun. There was a slow abandonment of the "New Criticism" and the formalism associated with it. Little by little, critics and teachers began focusing on the part of the reader in realizing works of literature and achieving meaning through engagements with them. The initial stage of the change was generally overlooked because the text, *Literature as Exploration,* by Louise Rosenblatt, appeared in 1938 as a John Dewey Lecture under the aegis of the Commission on Human Relations. Scarcely noticed by academic critics, it did not seriously challenge the dominating mode. It took more than two decades before what was sometimes described as a pragmatic approach, or a "reader response" approach to literature, brought the study of imaginative works into a significant relationship to the doing of philosophy (Bruner; Iser).

According to this view, readers have deliberately to release themselves into the "as/if" world created by a writer without a preconception that a meaning is hidden within it. Using their imaginative capacities, they lend their own lives to the characters involved and to the landscapes on which those characters enact their story. Often, readers are enjoined to single out the perspectives that compose the text: the perspective of the author, of the narrative voice, of the various characters. Each one can be looked through; each one is likely to disclose another dimension of the social reality the book presents. Striving for a coherence among these perspectives, readers are required to use their imagination to cross the gaps that inevitably exist between such ways of seeing, say, as that of the slaveowner in Toni Morrison's *Beloved* and that of the escaped slave, Sethe, who slits her own baby's throat rather than allow her to return to slavery, or between Creon and Antigone, or between Isabel Archer and her "collector" husband, Gilbert Osmond, in Henry James's *Portrait of a Lady.* There is, ordinarily, no way to reconcile such perspectives; there is only a sense of incompleteness, an enhanced tendency to ask difficult questions, to interrogate the world. This can happen when it is recognized that works of literature, when attentively read, become objects of experience. Reader experience is shaped in response to the engagement; new connections are made; new possibilities opened. What is referred to is not some objective reality toward which all are supposed to aspire, but human subjectivity, human experience itself.

P

This change from an orientation to universality and objectivity affected and still affects both philosophy and literature. It is partly due to winds of change like these that a philosopher like Richard Rorty has chosen to go beyond conceptual clarification and old epistemological puzzle-solving to pragmatism and hermeneutics, the points of view of Martin Heidegger, Dewey, and Wittgenstein. The interest in hermeneutics or interpretation has coincided with a rising interest in constructivism, in the making of meanings. At once, it is overlapping a rising interest in interdisciplinary study and interdisciplinary teaching. As Clifford Geertz puts it, there is a growing "ethnography of modern thought" (155). He speaks not only of intellectual vantage points but of "ways of being in the world"; and he writes of the connections between studying Yeats's imagery, an absorption in black holes, a measurement of the effect of schooling on economic achievement, and of how all this signifies taking on "a cultural frame that defines a great part of one's life." Louise Rosenblatt's later work (1978), detailing a "transactional theory of the literary work" and emphasizing the ways in which the informed reader-critic can bring to bear "ever wider and richer circles of literary, social, ethical, and philosophical contexts" (174), connects with the ethnographic view. At once, like Wolfgang Iser, stressing what can happen to experience when a reader grasps a text, when layers of personality are brought to light never recognized before, she is illuminating a participative mode of reading and cognitive-imaginative action that renders encounters with literature deeply relevant to philosophy of education.

It must be said, as well, that the rise of feminism in literary criticism and in philosophy of education has had a good deal to do with bringing literature to the attention of philosophers. Deane Bogdan, Jane Roland Martin, Lorraine Kasprisin, Betty Sichel, and others are most engaged with the identification of philosophical and educational problems in novels and short stories. Betty Sichel, for instance, consulted Virginia Woolf in an examination of caring and the range of communities under the title "Education and Thought in Virginia Woolf's *To the Lighthouse*"; as the fascination with story and narrative increases in connection with pursuits of meaning, there are likely to be increasing connections made between dimensions of educational philosophy and imaginative literature.

Meanwhile, such scholars as Martha Nussbaum make increasingly clear what is described as "the contribution made by certain works of literature to some important questions about human beings and human life" (5). As a philosopher, Nussbaum turns to Henry James, Marcel Proust, Samuel Beckett, and others for increasingly deepening insights as to ethical action and moral points of view. On the educational side, Nel Noddings and others interested in the particularities of educational and community life open doors to the extensive use of imaginative works. On the side of literary theory, the concentration on texts and textuality has led to consideration of the transformational effect of reading imaginative works; and this cannot but hold implications for educational thinkers. Robert Scholes, who begins his study of the "protocols of reading" with a quotation from Roland Barthes (1970) saying that reading is "rewriting the text within the text of our lives," makes the important point that reading is not only an academic experience. It is also, he writes, "a way of accepting the fact that our lives are of limited duration and that whatever satisfaction we may achieve in life must come through the strength of our engagement with what is around us. We do well to read our lives with the same intensity we develop from learning to read our texts. We all encounter certain experiences that seem to call for more than a superficial understanding" (Scholes: 19).

Education has to do with widening the perspectives through which people can look at their lived situations and understand them; it has to do with heightening their consciousness of their own thinking; it has to do with disclosing the possibilities of action in the world. Even as new ethnographies are explored, there is a sense of a new cartography as well. "Now the adventure of the *detour* begins," writes Giovanna Borradori, after interviewing a number of modern philosophers, "a restless wandering along the edge of an ever-mobile frontier, that never ceases to disarrange and recompose the profile of a new history" (25). Educational philosophers may begin participating in this adventure and breaching old boundaries as they reach toward new modes of understanding, new modes of being, new modes of saying. Muriel Rukeyser said it in this way—a way for ending, a way for beginning: "The river flows past the city. Water goes down to tomorrow making its children. I hear their unborn voices. I am working out the vocabulary of my silence" (135).

Maxine Greene

See also CRITICAL THEORY; DEWEY; EMERSON; EXISTENTIALISM; EXPERIENCE; PHENOMENOLOGY; PRAGMATISM; SARTRE

Bibliography

Barthes, Roland. *Writing Degree Zero* and *Elements of Semiology*. Boston: Beacon Press, 1970.

Borradori, Giovanna. *The American Philosopher*. Chicago: University of Chicago Press, 1991.

Bruner, Jerome. *Actual Minds, Possible Worlds*. Cambridge: Harvard University Press, 1986.

Cavell, Stanley. *In Quest of the Ordinary*. Chicago: University of Chicago Press, 1988.

Dewey, John. *Art as Experience*. New York: Minton, Balch, 1934.

———. *Democracy and Education*. New York: Macmillan, 1916.

———. *Experience and Nature*. New York: Dover, 1958.

Eagleton, Terry. *Literary Theory*. Minneapolis: University of Minnesota Press, 1983.

Gadamer, Hans-Georg. *Truth and Method*. Boston: Seabury Press, 1975.

Geertz, Clifford. *Local Knowledge*. New York: Basic Books, 1983.

Goodman, Nelson. *Languages of Art*. Indianapolis: Hackett, 1976.

Habermas, Jurgen. *Knowledge and Human Interests*. Boston: Beacon Press, 1971.

Heidegger, Martin. *Poetry, Language, and Thought*. New York: Harper and Row, 1973.

Iser, Wolfgang. *The Act of Reading*. Baltimore: Johns Hopkins University Press, 1980.

Merleau-Ponty, Maurice. *The Primacy of Perception*. Evanston: Northwestern University Press, 1964.

Natanson, Maurice. *Literature, Philosophy, and the Social Sciences*. The Hague: Martinus Nijhoff, 1962.

Nussbaum, Martha C. *Love's Knowledge*. New York: Oxford University Press, 1990.

Palmer, Richard E. *Hermeneutics*. Evanston: Northwestern University Press, 1969.

Poirier, Richard. *The Renewal of Literature*. New York: Random House, 1987.

Richards, I.A. *Practical Criticism*. New York: Harvest Books, 1929.

Ricoeur, Paul. *Interpretation Theory*. Fort Worth, Tex.: Texas Christian University Press, 1976.

Rorty, Richard. *Consequences of Pragmatism*. Minneapolis: University of Minnesota Press, 1982.

———. *Philosophy and the Mirror of Nature*. Princeton: Princeton University Press, 1979.

Rosenblatt, Louise M. *The Reader, the Text, the Poem*. Carbondale: Southern Illinois University Press, 1978.

Rukeyser, Muriel. *Out of Silence*. Evanston: Triquarterly Press, Northwestern University Press, 1992.

Sartre, Jean-Paul. *Being and Nothingness*. New York: Philosophical Library, 1949.

———. *Literature and Existentialism*. New York: Citadel Press, 1956.

Scholes, Robert E. *Protocols of Reading*. New Haven: Yale University Press, 1989.

Sichel, Betty A. "Education and Thought in Virginia Woolf's *To the Lighthouse*." In *Proceedings of Philosophy of Education Society*, 191–200. Urbana: University of Illinois Press, 1993.

Wimsatt, William K., and Cleanth Brooks. *Literary Criticism: A Short History*. New York: Vintage Books, 1967.

Wittgenstein, Ludwig. *Philosophical Investigations*. London: Oxford University Press, 1958.

Philosophy of Education, History of

Philosophy originated in ancient Greece under the pressure of questions about the nature of *arete* (translated as "virtue"). The Sophists (fifth-century B.C.) claimed that they could teach virtue, thereby challenging the traditional wisdom, which held that virtue is a natural possession of the few—the "nobly born," whose virtues were celebrated in the epics of Homer (c. 850 B.C.) and the odes of Pindar (518–438 B.C.). In the dialogues of Plato (c. 427–347 B.C.), Socrates (c. 470–399 B.C.) is portrayed asking the question, Can virtue be taught? Discussion made it clear that no one knew the nature of virtue. Thus another question naturally arose: What is the nature of virtue itself? Socrates goes on to ask whether virtue is one thing or many things, and how we can know what it is. These are matters of philosophy in that they are questions about the life worth living (ethics), knowing (epistemology), and the nature of reality (metaphysics). At the same time they are matters of education, in that answers to these questions can be found only in an educational process that aims to find out the nature of virtue. Thus such questions as what is worth knowing and how we can know it have both a philosophical and an educational dimension. It is clear that, in their origins, philosophy and educational theory stood on common ground. Ideas on clarifying and elaborating the meaning of philosophical questions became theories to be tested. Finding out what thinking makes us do—the practical meaning of philosophical ideas—became an activity of education. Philosophy of education, like philosophy in other contexts, is thinking that results in ideas that unsettle things, that brings about something different from that which once had been taken as settled. Beginning in curiosity about the nature of things, philosophy of education is thinking about what to do in education. Philosophy of education is not thinking that stands apart from action, but thinking that aims to make a difference in human conduct. The ancient Greeks did not use the term *philosophy of education* in their writings. Yet they first envisaged what later thinkers came to call philosophy of education.

In its origins, philosophy attempted to provide a unity in thought that is lacking in the ways reality comes to us, unorganized and fragmented. Yet unity in thought stands only as a possibility for the way things are experienced; what and how things actually are experienced can be found out only when ideas go to work, get tested in reality. So it is in philosophy of education: Any unity that thinking proposes must be tried out in specific processes of education.

The Educational Theory of Plato and Aristotle
The educational thinking of Plato may be taken in two ways. (1) As philosopher of the life of drama (or dramatist of the life of philosophy). Here Plato leaves the philosophical-educational questions unanswered in a final sense. His dialogues are dramas of the life of reason, showing us that we do not know what we think we know, claiming that an admission of our ignorance is a necessary condition for knowing, and holding forth the possibility that further dialogues will clarify the nature of virtue. The conditions for knowing portrayed in his dialogues alert us to find ways of educating ourselves and others. If we ever succeed in knowing virtue, we must gain it through a process of self-examination and clarification in dialogues with others. (2) As philosopher-educator who shapes individuals from childhood to maturity. Inquiry

into the nature of virtue continues in the *Republic,* where Socrates and his companions pursue the nature of Justice. When an impasse is reached, Adeimantus presses Socrates to continue the inquiry in order to prove that justice is good, "whether gods or men know it or not."

This leads to a long philosophic journey, in which Justice is taken to be "written small" in each individual and "written large" in the state. However, once Justice is discerned to be that virtue by which each member of the state is doing what each is naturally fitted to do, the pursuit is not over. What is necessary, Socrates argued, is knowledge of the Idea of the Good. To know the Good would be to know the source of all reality, the nature of that reality, the shape of things and the ways things take shape, including Justice and the other virtues. The pursuit of the Good is an educational matter as well as the highest ethical matter. The way in which children are educated in seeking the highest Good has its counterpart in the way in which the state is formed; education is the conjoint growth of the individual and the state. Plato does not know the Good, but he takes the activity by which we strive to know it to be the ideal by which human beings are educated to be citizens.

Aristotle (384–322 B.C.) shared Plato's idea that human beings are social animals, that they can be human only in the life of a community. Like Plato, Aristotle was a naturalist, holding that human beings are a part of nature. Our reason cannot overcome the limitations set in the nature of things, yet reason can cooperate with nature by striving to find nature's meanings. What human beings feel, know, and do are attempts to discover the nature of things, which lies potentially within us. What individuals discover is something they share with a larger nature. While they are limited to discovering what nature makes possible, their discoveries become part of social custom to be passed on, by education, to the young.

Aristotle criticized Plato's Idea of the Good as the one virtue that would unify all knowledge claims, and instead engaged in investigations into the nature of distinct subject matters. He worked out the idea of distinct sciences; each takes its shape according to the nature of its subject matter. One kind of subject matter forms the practical sciences, which study things that are changing and whose nature is found out by doing something, by taking action. In holding that the conduct by which we discover the highest good (an understanding of ethics) is doing something in a community (an undertaking of politics), Aristotle shows that striving for virtue is a social undertaking, an activity of education. Only in what we do can we find out what is good for us. Like Plato, Aristotle argued that the good must be discovered. Yet, unlike Plato, Aristotle held that the changing character of human behavior is something from which we cannot escape by bringing it under the exact control of the Idea of the Good. Thus the virtue we seek does not exhibit the exactness of geometry, a standard that Plato used in thinking of the Idea of the Good. Rather, we must learn to work with probabilities and not expect certainty in the practical activity of discovering virtue.

Epicureanism and Stoicism

The Epicureans and Stoics established schools in Athens that proved to be lasting alternatives to those of Plato and Aristotle. Epicurus (341–270 B.C.) founded the first about 306 B.C. In his school, women, men, and slaves lived a communal life dedicated to seeking happiness through *ataraxia* (peace of mind). One of Epicurus' teachings was that in order to experience peace of mind we need to live free from trouble. Certain studies help us do that. For example, we study natural science, not so much for the knowledge gained in itself, but in order to free ourselves from the myths and superstitions that religion teaches us. We gain knowledge, therefore, to provide peace of mind. We aim for peace of mind, Epicurus taught, by avoiding experiences that give us pain, such as sexual experience and physical and sensual gluttony, and by limiting greed for such things as, social stature, power, and fame. Therefore Epicureans argued against participation in the political and social affairs of society. The aim was to live in obscurity, in a congenial atmosphere of friends, devoting time to gaining peace of mind. Where each person in a community of friends respects the peace of mind of others, it is friendship, rather than laws, that holds the community together. Now this approach is different from Plato's and Aristotle's philosophies of conduct, wherein the effort to educate ourselves involves living in the sort of community that is a deliberate political undertaking. Rather than taking on the problems of the political community, Epicureans attempted to ignore those problems; in such a manner they hoped to avoid the pain that they alleged would be experienced by dealing with them.

Stoicism took its name from the painted colonnade, the *stoa poikile,* where the founders of the school taught. Zeno of Citium (342–280 B.C.) was its founder around 300 B.C. While the Stoics had less of an orthodoxy than the Epicureans, they shared certain views. Stoicism was predominantly a moral philosophy. Its ideal was reason, which turned out to be a moral ideal as well as a rational one, in that the life of reason is the highest virtue. In looking at reason as a way of life rather than merely an activity of the mind, the Stoics shared with Socrates the idea that knowledge is virtue, by arguing that reason is both the end and the means of life. Learning to live according to reason, therefore, is the highest educational ideal. "Nature" is another name for the reality in which human beings have a place, and since that reality is endowed with rationality, human beings can strive for the best that is in their nature only by learning to live according to reason. The highest desire proper to human beings is to conform to the nature of things. After human beings develop to the age of reason, the Stoics held, their actions are determined by reason alone. In this they differed from Plato and Aristotle, for whom both emotion and reason are at work in conduct. Yet the Stoics shared with Plato and Aristotle the idea that human beings are at home in nature, as well as the belief that the quest for understanding the nature of which we are a part is a striving to educate ourselves along with others.

Rhetoric in Greek and Roman Educational Theory

The classic characterization of the orator was "the good man speaking well." This was the ideal of creating orations that would stand alongside the work of the poets in embodying the pursuit of the highest virtue. Like the poets, the orators worked to portray the nobly born striving for the best that nature and custom make possible. Rhetoric grew to maturity alongside philosophy. Isocrates (436–338 B.C.), a teacher of rhetoric, made claims also in behalf of philosophy. For Isocrates, the virtuous person was one who made the most of the community's established opinions and long-standing customs in order to determine which courses of action to take. He criticized Plato's search for the Idea of the Good as a futile quest; philosophy has a less lofty but practically significant goal: to arrive at workable opinions in the absence of ultimate truth. Aristotle found a place for rhetoric in the enterprise of philoso-

P

phy; he taught rhetoric in his school, and his treatise on the subject is one of its classics. Aristotle's *Rhetoric* is closely allied with his *Ethics* and *Politics:* As an art by which we learn to persuade others, rhetoric displays the probabilistic kind of reasoning by which we understand the nature of the good that is sought in community action.

The Roman rhetorician Cicero (106–43 B.C.) followed Aristotle in holding that orators must work with probabilities rather than certainties. Oratory is more than a skill to be attained by studying the theories of rhetoricians. It is a way of action in which the orator celebrates the virtues that are learned through an education in the subject matters of philosophy and by living a life devoted to the pursuit of the highest virtues. Thus Cicero's orator is a philosopher as well, whose orations attempt to persuade others to pursue the virtues by which the philosopher-orator has lived.

Quintilian (c. 35–c. 90), like Cicero, emphasized a sense of the orator at work in the midst of probable judgments, saying that oratory attempts to talk about what is "like truth." Quintilian insisted that the orator has a difficult time in striving for the best without any assurance of victory. The necessity of virtuous conduct, rather than merely talking about virtue, is portrayed in Quintilian's idea that oratory does not merely address questions of virtue. Rather, oratory itself is a virtue: In the act of speaking lies the subject and the object of oratory. As the dialogues of Plato are both a way of seeking virtue and examples of virtue in action, so the art of oratory consists of seeking the virtue by which the orator tries to live and exemplifying that virtue in orations delivered.

The term *paideia,* difficult to translate directly into English, encompasses the unity of thought and action that we have discussed in the educational aims of philosophy and rhetoric. The Romans called it *humanitas.* On one side it means the highest educational ideal; on the other side it stands for the means for reaching the ideal. This characterization holds true so long as the two sides are distinct in thought but joined in reality. We may think of *paideia* as an ideal of ends and means joined in idea and action so as to shape mind and character. *Paideia* is "humanistic" in the sense that human beings are held to be responsible for shaping their own ideals and finding the ways to realize them. This is so, even when chance is not on our side, or when tragic events do us in. And *paideia* is

"naturalistic" in that there is no extranatural authority to guide us, no reality beyond nature to serve as our standard. Human beings must make their standards, for better or for worse, in the natural world to which they belong.

Philosophy in Early Christian Educational Thinking

In Christianity, an extranatural source of human existence and of the highest virtues put humanistic and naturalistic *paideia* in a position subordinate to the true *paideia,* which comes from God. Greek philosophy and Roman rhetoric represented the highest ideals to be found in human teachings, but the divine teachings of Christ are higher in the order of Being. The former teach us, but only in imperfect and incomplete ways, while the latter teach us in the ways of God. Clement of Alexandria (c. 150–c. 215), one of the founders of Christian philosophy, held that the humanism and naturalism of classical education cannot fully educate us; they come up short of the education that is needed, and must be superseded by the word of God. The pride of a philosopher who is seeking virtue must be replaced by the humility of a Christian. Rather than beings who can place our trust in human rationality, human beings are creatures of God who are mere children in the eyes of Christ. Taking its place alongside the highest reality, our reasoning is like the play of children.

Augustine (354–430) followed the founders of Christian philosophy and established the relationship between human and divine teachings that was to prevail in Western Christian culture in medieval institutions. Philosophers, when they have God's assistance, may make important discoveries; when they strive for the highest wisdom by use of reason, they go astray, for human weakness gets in the way. To strive for the virtues of Christian doctrine, human beings must restrain their pride and learn the way of piety, which begins with humility. Augustine took Plato's search for the Good to be an attempt to know and love God, and Plato's Ideas became thoughts in the mind of God. According to Augustine's philosophy of history, whatever has taken place prior to the coming of Christianity is a preparation for Christianity itself; if it is useful for Christian doctrine, Christians may take it as their own. The fundamental tenet in Christian doctrine taught by Augustine may be stated as follows: The only things worthy of love for their own sake are the Father, the Son, and the Holy Spirit; all other things are to be used for the sake of them. This holds, of course, for all subject matters we study: In principle, non-Christian subject matters are not suspect, so long as their relationship to the highest objects in Christian doctrine is respected. Subject matters of poetry, philosophy, and rhetoric are to be taken as means to Christian ends, never as ends in themselves.

With the collapse of Roman civilization and the disappearance of its educational institutions, by the sixth century Christians faced a situation in which the non-Christian materials came to be largely forgotten. The new educational institutions that arose seized the opportunity to realize the ideal of a "purely Christian culture," one largely devoid of the teachings of the ancient philosophers. Some Christian educators argued that religious culture was the only culture that deserves to be taught. Certain materials from classical antiquity survived in this environment, but stripped of their original humanism and naturalism they were diluted versions of the ancient subject matters put to the service of Christian doctrine. The Christian character of the new educational institutions had the consequence of shaping the fundamental attitude toward the literary materials of classical Greece and Rome in all renaissances that were to come: Thereafter, those materials would only be admitted on Christian terms.

Renaissances of the Twelfth and Thirteenth Centuries

Certain materials in classical literature gradually made their way back into the West in the eleventh century, and by the twelfth century we may speak of a renaissance. John of Salisbury's *Metalogicon* (1159) reveals a familiarity with Latin poets, grammarians, and rhetorical writings. John's work was a Christian defense of the arts of verbal expression and reasoning and, like the ancient rhetoricians and philosophers, he argued that they are to be studied for their influence on human conduct. Thus he criticized those who pursue dialectic for the sake of verbal jugglery but who never seem to know anything. Logic, to be effective, must be used in the pursuit of knowledge and in the teaching of knowledge already gained. John was familiar with Aristotle's distinction between demonstrative logic and probable logic. In showing the influence of his famous teacher, Peter Abelard (1079–1142), who had used logic to clarify questions in Christian doctrine, John argued that the arts are useful for the study of temporal things, as well as eternal truths, to which we

have access through faith. The wide range of humanistic studies addressed by John can be illustrated in an institutional setting in the School of Chartres. John described Bernard of Chartres, master there in the early twelfth century, as a grammarian and a Platonist. Thierry of Chartres, a chancellor of the school, wrote a manual of the seven liberal arts. In addition to the "literary" studies—grammar, rhetoric, and logic—he brought the "scientific" studies—arithmetic, geometry, music, and astronomy—to support biblical teachings; for one thing, he argued that Plato's final cause is to be identified with the Holy Spirit.

Alongside the humanistic studies, another method was making its way. It came to be called Scholasticism, essentially the application of reason to theological studies. Under a number of masters, including William of Champeaux (1070–1121) and Abelard, a genre of subject matter known as "Sentences" grew up. They were a collection of questions of Christian doctrine dealing with the conflicting answers given by authorities, to be resolved by logic. This enterprise of logic culminated in a work by Peter Lombard (c. 1100–c. 1160), *Four Books of Sentences,* which became the standard textbook in theology. The growth of logic as the arbiter of all intellectual activity came to overshadow the other arts in the curriculum of the universities that grew to prominence in the thirteenth century. What is more, with the influx of Aristotle's materials, it became more difficult to keep Christian theology free from "pagan" philosophy. By 1254 Aristotle's logical works, natural philosophy, and part of his treatise on ethics were prescribed for the Bachelor's and Master's degrees in the arts curriculum at the University of Paris. The mostly Aristotelian course of studies was preliminary not only to all advanced studies; in the minds of theologians such as Albert the Great (c. 1200–1280) and Thomas Aquinas (1225–1274), logic and the rest of the Aristotelian corpus were essential to the study of theological questions.

Aquinas's distinction between philosophy and dogmatic theology has endured in Christian philosophy and theology down to our own time, and his writings stand out as a classic representation of Scholasticism. The distinction goes as follows: Philosophy and the other sciences that reason works out rely on the natural light of reason; the philosopher works with principles established by reason and argues to conclusions that are the consequences of reason.

The theologian accepts principles on faith; they are taken as revealed by God to human beings. Starting with revealed principles the theologian uses reason and argues to conclusions. Some principles properly belong to philosophy alone in that they are known by reason and have not been revealed, while other principles properly belong to theology alone in that they cannot be known by reason but only by revelation. Yet some truths belong to both philosophy and theology in that they can be established by reason and have been revealed. Thus philosophy and theology sometimes express the same truths; but each science deals differently with the same truths. An important conclusion to draw from Aquinas's distinction between the two sciences is that no truth reached by reason alone may contradict a revealed truth. Aquinas's accommodation of the rational human sciences with theology meant that it was acceptable for Christians to study philosophy and the other sciences of human reason.

Renaissance Humanism, Fourteenth to Sixteenth Centuries

By the fourteenth century, there was a renewed interest in Greek and Latin literature, which had been studied very little in the medieval universities. This literature consisted of grammar, rhetoric, poetry, history, and moral philosophy. This literature was read and interpreted in their original languages. The term *humanism* in this Renaissance was derived from the *studia humanitatis,* which stands for the subject matters mentioned above. Renaissance humanism was less a philosophical system that opposed itself to Scholasticism and more an educational curriculum that emphasized the *studia humanitatis* and, for the most part, excluded logic, metaphysics, natural philosophy, mathematics, astronomy, law, and theology—the essential curriculum of the medieval universities. The humanists emphasized the technical aspects of the arts of grammar and rhetoric, along with poetry, oratory, and history—the literary expressions of these arts. Thus they renewed an ancient tradition that had lived in the poets and rhetoricians of classical Greece and Rome.

It is instructive to contrast the treatment of ancient writings in Renaissance humanism and in Scholasticism. The latter took the ancient philosophical writings to be authorities in philosophy and useful in clarifying Christian doctrine. Aristotle's logic was the method for establishing authoritative conclusions in the human sciences and in theology; both philosophy and theology contain the truth, and the proper use of logic makes that truth evident. In contrast, the *studia humanitatis* were taken by the humanists as the arts and literature of writing and speaking; the writings of the ancients were looked upon as perfect vehicles of human expression. The appeal of such a literature led to a search for manuscripts that had lain unread for centuries; the passion for scholarship yearned to regain the ancient writings in their original form, to cleanse them of accretions and to correct translations that were unworthy of them. The humanists studied classical authors as writers of incomparable classics, not as authorities in philosophy and theology. In principle, this means that the ability to speak and write clearly and logically is evidence that one comprehends a subject; the best examples of human expression serve as unified wholes, combining language and thought in a compelling and compact way, forging a union of erudition, eloquence, and integrity. Those humanists who sought the highest virtue by imitating Cicero, and who were so obsessed with Cicero as the supreme Latin stylist that they imitated his gestures and peculiarities of speech, were called "Ciceronian apes" by Desiderius Erasmus (c. 1469–1536). He argued that the way a Christian humanist should imitate Cicero is by attempting to speak as Cicero would speak if he were living as a Christian, using his oratorical abilities to address Christian concerns.

The Renaissance remained largely a Christian age, as the humanists attempted to live according to Augustine's dictum that non-Christian things should be put to Christian uses. They were able to place the non-Christian virtues embedded in the *studia humanitatis* alongside the virtues expressed in Christian literature without serious concern that one set of virtues might contradict the other. As a consequence of their scholarly and literary achievements, however, the renaissances made available a literature with ideas and critical ways of thinking that came to challenge the Christian culture in whose terms that literature had reentered Western society. The virtues of classical antiquity gradually came to speak for themselves, and in the Enlightenment of the eighteenth century, philosophers would feel free to see themselves as "pagans" in opposition to their Christian culture.

Empiricism and Rationalism in Early Modern Philosophy

Francis Bacon (1561–1626) advocated an inductive method of investigation based on the idea that a study of the particulars of experience leads to universals. He contrasted this with what he took to be Aristotelian and Scholastic method, and thus challenged it as a source of authority. According to Bacon, the logic of authority is a false method, a method of argument and disputation, not a method of inquiry and discovery. Rather than taking conclusions already reached as the basis of thinking, individuals must learn that such conclusions are suspect; nature, Bacon thought, is more subtle than reason, and we need to develop a method of knowing that gets hold of the particular subtleties of nature. Instead of following the tendency of the mind to build things out of itself, the structure of the mind must be built out of the things of nature. Bacon's appeal to firsthand experience was an effort to let facts speak for themselves and lead to an understanding of nature.

In contrast, Rene Descartes (1596–1650) worked out a rationalistic method, beginning with what the mind can grasp clearly without doubting what it sees. The mind must be free to proceed by deduction from what is known intuitively to conclusions about particular things. Descartes's method sought to avoid the limiting of reason by sensory experience. For him, the ideas that thought alone first grasps will show the way to the nature of sensory things. Descartes stood Bacon's method upside down by holding that what is most evident are not empirical matters but logical conceptions that are self-evident to individual minds. Concepts of reason are primary; to know what is in nature, we must first see the reasons for its existence in our minds.

Despite their difference, empiricism and rationalism shared a common ground in their criticism of certain claims to authority. Each espoused an individualism that was an inheritance of the Christian conception of the worth of individual souls. Yet individualism had been made subordinate to the authority of religious doctrine in the institutions of medieval society. The following requirement was shared by empiricism and rationalism: Individuals must be responsible for using a method to gain knowledge, and each person is responsible for the knowledge so gained; simply to accept claims offered by others is to ignore one's responsibility as an inquirer. Thus empirical and rational methods of knowing carry with them a moral responsibility, to apply each method in a way that is true to oneself by learning to be free from dependence on others. Reality must be discovered by and ultimately reside in individual minds, either as a result of applying a Baconian method of induction, or as clear, undoubted intuitions as logical starting points, as in Descartes's rationalistic method. Truth does not come to the mind on the authority of others, but individual minds must work to find it. Beginning in doubt about the truth of existing knowledge-claims, individuals engage in inquiry to establish the sciences by which the nature of things is known.

In emphasizing the moral responsibility of individuals to employ empirical and rational methods, the early modern philosophers made a problem out of knowing. No longer were human beings taken to be a part of nature, in a way that knowing itself is no less natural than feeling or breathing, as in the thinking of Plato and Aristotle. Instead, whether in sense-perceptions entering the mind or intuitions grasped by reason, mind finds itself detached from nature and becomes a sort of stranger to the nature it is trying to know. Rather than being at home in nature, mind stands apart from nature, looking on.

The imperative that individual minds must do their own reasoning had its social counterpart in the idea that political organizations are social contracts freely agreed to by all individuals concerned. In a state of nature, individuals would not survive by themselves; thus they enter into contracts with one another for mutual benefit. However, in doing so, they surrender part of their natural freedom as individuals. Thus the social contract is "less natural" than the original condition of freedom, and when certain individuals do not live up to the terms of the contract, other parties to the contract may assert their natural freedom by forming another. John Locke (1632–1704), in his treatise on government, held that human beings, in a state of nature, would be equals as well as free and independent from one another. This is a moral equality in that no individual is subordinate to another, none has more than another. It is not a "biological" or "psychological" equality. Taken together with his argument that our knowledge originates in sensory experience, which means that no one is born in possession of innate ideas, Locke's espousal of natural equality contributed to an "environmentalism" in educational thinking. If our minds are "blank tablets" at birth, and if we are free and equal living with one another, then our natural condition is such that what we become is an out-

P

come of our education: Our biological and psychological differences are less important than our original ignorance, freedom, and equality.

Method of Criticism in the Enlightenment

Locke's empiricism, by which perceptions enter the mind, was joined with a rationalism according to which the mind reflects, using the ideas that have gained entry. Intuitive knowledge comes when the mind perceives immediately that ideas agree or disagree, as when the mind just knows that black is not white. Demonstrative knowledge comes when agreement or disagreement comes, not immediately, but with intervening ideas, then with one another, as when we know that the three angles of a triangle are equal to two right angles. While our ideas originate in experience, once they are present in the mind, the aim of gaining intuitive and demonstrative knowledge is no less rationalistic than the method of Descartes.

Enlightenment thinkers were heirs of Locke in that they cherished the kind of understanding that comes with an increasing accumulation of empirical details together with the efforts of reason to make sense of them. Yet they went beyond Locke and worked out a critical method from which nothing was safe from criticism. Not content to criticize political institutions only, they took on the religious establishment. Enlightenment thinkers, critical of society's dominant institutions, customs, and habits, saw their proposals for enlightened public education fall stillborn in the face of authoritatian resistance to a critical method. At the same time, their criticisms helped pave the way for a more enlightened and democratic way of life. Sensitive to the self-diminishing and authoritarian hold that existing political, religious, and educational institutions had on human beings, Enlightenment criticism required nothing less than a democratic revolution for its criticisms to bring down those institutions. For instance, the preliminary outline for Denis Diderot's *Encyclopedia* (1751) proposed to subject everything that human minds could take into account to critical scrutiny. In doing so, they would inquire into all arts, sciences, and works of the imagination; theology did not stand above the other sciences but, like them, was to be subject to reason. However, it was not reason alone that they wanted to further; rather, "reason" was taken as one of the powers of the mind, to be joined with "memory" and "imagination" in the search for understanding. Not at all sanguine about the prospects for overcoming ob-

stacles in the way of improving the human condition, Enlightenment thinkers were not optimists, promising the triumph of understanding over myth and superstition. Theirs was a more modest position, holding that if progress is to come to pass, it will do so only through the agency of human intelligence. Neither fate nor providence is to be trusted to bring about the needed changes.

Their critical spirit enabled them to see equality and freedom as possibilities to be sought in actual social conditions, rather than as an imagined original condition of human beings in a state of nature. Taking this idea seriously means that human nature is a moral and social condition that human beings must strive to bring into existence, rather than a nature that existed in some past or that is destined to come to pass in some future. This sense of nature as an ideal to be actualized has a radical corollary for human knowing and education. It lies in the idea that our knowing refers to what might be, not to what has been and now is. Thus we are to be educated to be critical of our past and our present, in order to bring about improved conditions in the future. The past that lives on in the present has its customs and institutions which inhibit our freedom and perpetuate conditions of inequality. Thus the Enlightenment spirit was alive in the new United States of America in the thinking of those who exhibited the critical spirit of the Enlightenment. For them the real revolution lay ahead, to be won if the young are taught how to think, rather than what to think. And in France, Marquis de Condorcet (1743–1794), drafting a work on prospects for human progress, held that only a method of intelligence might remedy the conditions of inequality. These conditions, he argued, are due mainly to deficiencies in the "social art," not the result of "natural inequality."

The eighteenth century also spawned a sense of the limitations of reason in the midst of hopes that it could be used to improve human conduct. Expressed in different ways by Giambattista Vico (1668–1744) and Jean-Jacques Rousseau (1712–1778), this sense was not anti-rationalistic; rather, it emphasized the point that reason, while necessary, does not suffice to explain the plight of human beings. In his *New Science,* Vico argued that the first human beings were not rational beings who wrote philosophy and made social contracts; instead, they were simple-minded creatures possessed of large imaginations. Even so, they had a metaphysics—a "poetic" metaphysics, by which they made heroes. Thus the heroic tales recounted by Homer were not invented as "rational" poets would do; they were "true" stories, created by an imagination not yet capable of deliberately "making up" a story. Only later, when human beings became capable of a "rational" metaphysics, could thinkers believe that Homer was deliberately inventing an account. "Poetic" and "rational" came into being in different historical conditions, and were an important part of those conditions. Vico attempted to let each speak for itself, rather than judging one by the other.

Rousseau also acknowledged the importance of reason, but claimed that the very methods by which rational methodology does its work get in the way of understanding. His *Discourse on the Origin of Inequality* (1755) chronicled the development of the human race from a simple way of existence, in which each was treated as an equal with others, to a complex way of life in which inequality has come to be an essential feature of the fabric of society. The good features of original human nature are scarcely recognizable in the prevailing conditions of modern society. The predicament of modern human beings in pursuit of an education according to nature is dramatized in *Emile* (1762), in which the tutor takes Emile away from the existing society and creates a special society that is closer to nature. Yet, as Emile is educated from his original a-moral, a-social, and a-rational way of being in childhood to morality, sociality, and rationality, he comes to realize that he has been educated for a world that does not exist. At the end of the story, Emile realizes that he will not be at home in modern society. Rousseau asks whether the better nature sought by Enlightenment thinkers is a meaningful ideal, and thereby casts doubt on the possibility of improving the human condition by the use of intelligence.

Nineteenth-Century Responses to Enlightenment Ideas

In the early nineteenth century, there were different and sometimes conflicting responses to the Enlightenment idea that, by learning to use their intelligence, human beings might ameliorate the conditions that stand in the way of extending freedom and equality. On the one hand, an increasingly democratic spirit may be seen in movements for popular education. Horace Mann (1796–1859), for example, argued that the right to an education should be placed along-side the other basic human rights spelled out in the Declaration of Independence. At the same time, the nationalistic motive that played a large part in establishing popular education opposed the Enlightenment habit of questioning the existing political and social order. As an example, Johann Fichte (1762–1814) argued that restructuring schools in the German nation should aim to oppose individual self-seeking by teaching young people that they can find their own interests only in those of the nation.

G.W.F. Hegel (1770–1831) enlarged the scope of attention given to the limits of rationality earlier addressed by Vico and Rousseau. In Hegel's historical account, "reason" in the Enlightenment sense of understanding is *verstand*. There is another way of knowing, *vernunft*, an insight into what has taken place, which comes only at the end of an activity. As we are living, we may have some control over what we are doing, but our rationality cannot assure us of the way things will turn out. Only after a historical process reaches a turning-point can we look back and say, "Now we understand the way things turned out; this is what things have come to mean." *Verstand* is the kind of understanding by which empirical and rational methods are used to gain reliable knowledge. *Vernunft*, however, is not entirely under our control; it is akin to the work of poets, who use imagination to gain a kind of insight that is different from *verstand*. In the work of imagination, as in the working out of history, one cannot determine exactly what the outcome will be. While both kinds of reason had a place in Hegel's philosophical system, others tended to emphasize the *vernunft* form of reason. This emphasis, commonly called "romanticism," had a large place in poetry and other literature in which "feeling" was prized over "thought" and was expressed in the idea that the human spirit is more authentic when it gives voice to what it immediately sees and feels than when it works according to empirical and rational methods of knowing.

Romanticism also had an influence on a revised conception of childhood, seeing a certain wisdom in the simplicity of children that is lost to adults who try to understand everything. This interest had its origins in Rousseau's assertion that children are not just small versions of adults; rather they grow through distinct ages in which they have their own ways of thinking and being in the world that are fundamentally different from adult ways. The increased interest in the nature of childhood eventually led to studies in child and adolescent psychology; special attention to early childhood education was an outgrowth of the romantic spirit.

The empirical evidence in support of the idea of evolution in Charles Darwin's *Origin of Species* (1859) enabled thinkers to take seriously the idea that species—the forms of plant and animal existence—have come into being through time. Thus the long-standing belief that the nature of species is fixed and unchanging came under attack. To take seriously the idea that nature's forms have come into being as a historical process is to acknowledge that the nature of things requires a method of inquiry that tries to take into account the history of its own development. Thus John Dewey thought of scientific method as "the evolutionary process grown conscious of itself."

Relations between Philosophy and Science in the Nineteenth Century

Philosophical idealism, in a variety of forms, came to prominence in the nineteenth century. Idealists regard mind, or types of mental activity, as basic to understanding. The world of nature exists as an object of mental activity. We have seen the rationalistic method in modern philosophy; emphasizing rationalism in opposition to empiricism, idealism was heir to Descartes. In its argument that the empirical cannot be known except for categories by means of which the mind orders objective reality to bring about knowledge, idealism was indebted to Immanuel Kant (1724–1804). Certain forms of idealism owed much to Hegel, in emphasizing that the nature of mind itself, along with the mind's objects, have come into being as a historical process. What the mind knows, then, is its own history as revealed in the ideas, customs, and institutions that are manifestations of mind actualizing itself over time. For Hegelian idealists, mind is more like an organic process than an "entity" or "substance" whose nature has been established once and for all time. Even though there are similarities between Hegel's idea that mind has come into being historically and Darwin's idea that forms of living things have evolved, idealists tended to oppose the idea that the emergence of mind can be accounted for by natural evolution alone. A characteristic position taken by idealist philosophers was that the knowledge gained by the sciences is dependent on mental activity, and that mind has an activity to do that cannot be accounted for by scientific principles. Some idealists contrasted science

with philosophy, saying that philosophy has its own categories of understanding, its distinct subject-matter. In that sense, philosophy itself may be called a science—the "science of sciences," or the "ultimate science."

Herbert Spencer (1820–1903) reversed the idealist's order of priorities, holding that in all things science is capable of providing the knowledge that is of most worth. For Spencer, science is the highest philosophy. His aim was to work out a systematic science of all human activities; every art has its science. Spencer conceived of the evolution of living forms as a law, not restricted to biology, but to be applied generally to all phenomena. What is more, evolution is not just development, it is change for the better, it is progress. His idea that progress in life forms has its parallel in progress in society, in commerce, literature—indeed, in all phenomena subject to human understanding—expressed an optimism according to which all problems can be settled by the furthering of science. Spencer's optimism was widely shared and, together with his scientism, became part of the nineteenth-century movement to develop sciences of psychology, society, and education.

A naturalistic empiricism emerged in response to idealism and scientism. This approach to philosophy was naturalistic in its willingness to take seriously the possibility that the moral makeup of human experience, as well as its biological forms, is an outcome of natural evolution. It was empiricistic in its insistence that while "reason" is as important as "sense" in our deliberations and knowings, the test of an idea is not to be found in another idea, but in the consequences of trying out the idea empirically. The American philosopher Chauncey Wright (1830–1875) exemplified naturalistic empiricism in his criticism of Spencer's scientism. Spencer was not true to empirical science, Wright argued, because he raised the findings of particular sciences into metaphysical first principles. For Wright, evolution is not a law to be applied, but a hypothesis to be tested. Whether or not society evolves according to a "law of progress" is an idea that will have to be tested in the context of actual empirical societies, not a principle whose truth will inexorably be illustrated in existing society. Spencer acted as if scientific principles are summaries of truth when, in the practice of scientists, they are finders of truth. For Wright, ideas are hypotheses that we put to work in an attempt to make truth-claims. They are neither summaries of truth nor are they principles from which truths are deduced.

Philosophy of Education as a Distinct Study

Even though the practice of relating ideas of philosophy and education is at least as old as Plato's dialogues, that practice was not recognized as a distinct study called "philosophy of education" until the nineteenth century. And not until Paul Monroe's *Cyclopedia of Education* (1911–1913) did "philosophy of education" as a substantive entry appear in a major reference work. Philosophy of education as a distinct study had its origins along with other subject matters of education, such as educational history, psychology, administration, and sociology. In its development as a distinct study, philosophy of education has taken on a substantive and professional life of its own, forging a sometimes-uneasy existence between the profession of philosophy on one side and the variety of educational studies and practices on the other. In its modern dress, philosophy of education has taken its professional place mainly in college and university departments, schools, and colleges of education; the subject first appeared in the curriculum in the form of courses and, eventually, as graduate programs.

In its nineteenth-century origins as a distinct study, three conceptions of philosophy of education may be discerned. One followed the lead of Spencer and others who were advocates of scientism, arguing that education could become a science if it were treated inductively; here philosophy of education would become a scientific method for making inductions. The second, following the lead of idealism, took the position that reason must complete the work that science is not capable of doing; philosophy of education aims to make visible the larger reality from which the fragmentary nature of the sciences comes. The third, working in the pathway of naturalistic empiricism, took philosophy of education to be neither an inductive method of science nor an ideal of a world larger than science, but an approach to experience that suggests ideas to be tested in educational contexts. Taking philosophy to consist of ideas of what is possible, philosophy of education consists of ideas of what to try out in education. This approach was worked out most extensively in the writings of John Dewey (1859–1952).

By the 1930s and continuing into the 1940s and 1950s, one way of relating philosophy and education was prominent: the idea that philosophy is the "foundation," or basic study, from which philosophy of education is derived. In building philosophies of education, this meant that philosophical propositions of metaphysics, epistemology, and axiology have "implications" for philosophy of education. While philosophers were not clear as to whether "implications" is to be taken in a strict, logical sense or in some other sense, they did think it is important to make explicit the conceptions of reality, knowing, and valuing on which propositions in the philosophy of education are to be grounded. In this view, philosophy of education is derived from philosophy, and practice in education is derived from philosophy of education. In principle, the idea that educational practice can ultimately be grounded in philosophy stands on an alleged unity that holds among metaphysics, epistemology, and axiology in particular philosophies. Thus distinct philosophic positions—for example, idealism, realism, pragmatism—differed from one another in their basic propositions of reality, knowing, and valuing; yet each represented a rational unity from which a unified educational theory-and-practice could be derived.

Eventually the "philosophic positions" approach came under attack. Instead of looking first to the content of philosophy to define educational problems, one argument went, philosophers need to look more closely at the educational process itself and ask what is going on there; how may the educational process be examined critically, and which ideas derived from critical examinations might be tested in educational situations? Inasmuch as philosophers themselves disagree as to the content of philosophy, another argument went, is it not a mistake to suppose that philosophical positions provide the sort of unity needed for the direction of educational practice? Insofar as we cannot know in advance where a philosophical question will take us, we cannot determine in advance what a philosophical position will mean for education.

Accompanying these criticisms was the analytic movement in philosophy, an attempt to clarify the ambiguous language and faulty logic in educational discourse. Absent from the writings of analytic philosophers was a systematic view of philosophy; instead, they developed linguistic and logical methods for clarifying the language of education. The primary aim was to treat philosophy as careful, controlled thinking that attempts to clarify the ways we think and what we think about. For example, analysis of a central education concept such as "teaching" may begin with a distinction between "intentional" and "success" senses of teaching, and move on

P

to consider what counts as cases of successful teaching. By analyzing the concept of teaching, analytic philosophers pursue the larger goal of informing ways of thinking about teaching.

Existentialist and phenomenological concerns have also been addressed by philosophers of education who have sought methods for transforming individual consciousness. Existentialist philosophers take the "inner awareness" of one's own existence to be the heart of human reality. This awareness must be made by reflecting on and clarifying the nature of existence in order to seek the limitations and possibilities there. Phenomenologists share existentialism's attention to the need for developing inner awareness, but attempt to avoid the idiosyncrasies of subjectivism by developing cognitive methods that bring about publicly verifiable results. Thus existentialism emphasizes the noncognitive elements of human existence, while phenomenology tries to establish the cognitive elements in the world that is there. In both, the connection to philosophy of education lies in the ways in which we can become ourselves: for existentialism, in overcoming alienation from ourselves; for phenomenology, in learning ways of knowing things that are present to our awareness.

Marxism, critical theory, and critical thinking also have made serious contributions to the literature in philosophy of education. In addition, philosophers of education have been active in the critical examination of virtually every human and social problem besetting modern society: alienation, civil rights, colonialism, gender and sexism, human rights (of children, minorities, women), social justice, radical school reform, and others.

In the last decade of the twentieth century, philosophy of education scarcely resembles a discipline with a distinct purpose and a clearly established agenda. It is more accurately characterized as a field of study defined by the variety of its research and interpretive projects. In one sense, the entry of analytic philosophy, existentialism, and phenomenology into philosophy of education, along with the inquiries into areas of human and social concerns mentioned above, indicates a richness of subject matters under investigation. From an interest in analysis of concepts to the various concerns for human and social problems, we can see a wide and colorful array of projects addressed by philosophers of education. At the same time, the variety of projects is evidence for an individuality

of effort that exists in the absence of a community of philosophers who search for the nature of *arete*. Missing in the present world of diversity of interests is the classic sense of a quest for philosophic unity.

J.J. Chambliss

See also PHILOSOPHY OF EDUCATION, LITERATURE IN; PHILOSOPHY OF EDUCATION, PROFESSIONAL ORGANIZATIONS IN

Bibliography

Adams, John. *The Evolution of Educational Theory*. London: Macmillan, 1928.

Chambliss, J.J. *The Origins of American Philosophy of Education: Its Development as a Distinct Discipline, 1808–1913*. The Hague: Martinus Nijhoff, 1968.

Dewey, John. *Philosophy and Education in Their Historic Relations*. Transcribed from Dewey's lectures, 1910–1911, by Elsie Ripley Clapp. Edited and with an introduction by J.J. Chambliss. Boulder, Colo.: Westview Press, 1993.

Jaeger, Werner. *Paideia: The Ideals of Greek Culture*. Translated by Gilbert Highet. New York: Oxford University Press, 1943, 1944, 1945.

Kaminsky, James. *A New History of Educational Philosophy*. Westport, Conn.: Greenwood Press, 1993.

Monroe, Paul, ed. *Cyclopedia of Education* 5 vols. New York: Macmillan, 1911–1913.

Philosophy of Education, Literature in

To a large extent the literature in philosophy of education is coterminous with the literature of general philosophy. The scholar in philosophy of education, then, needs to pursue those sources available in philosophy. These include many philosophical dictionaries, encyclopedias, and journals. Summaries of what they contain are found in the *Encyclopedia of Philosophy* in articles entitled "Philosophical Bibliographies," "Philosophical Dictionaries and Encyclopedias," "Philosophical Journals," and "Philosophy, Historiography of." The same *Encyclopedia* also contains articles on "Philosophy of Education, History of," and "Philosophy of Education, Influence of Modern Psychology on."

The field of education as a focus for academic study also encompasses many journals, encyclopedias, and dictionaries. A reference librarian is the best consultant on such matters, since information is constantly being updated. There are at least five guides to educational literature as well as two general guides to information in the social sciences that include information on education. Currently, two of the best general guides are *A Bibliographic Guide to Educational Research* and *A Guide to Sources of Educational Information.*

The best single source of articles and books on current philosophy of education is the *Philosopher's Index.* All the major journals dealing with philosophy of education are indexed here by subject and by author, along with abstracts of the articles. There is a book review index included in each volume that lists books alphabetically by author's last name. Books on philosophy of education that have been reviewed in philosophy journals or journals devoted mostly to philosophy of education will be included. Philosophy of education books reviewed in journals not dealing primarily in philosophy of education, such as *Teachers College Record* or *Harvard Educational Review,* will be missed.

The next best source of articles and books on current philosophy of education is the Educational Resources Information Center (ERIC) system. This is a national information system designed and supported by the U.S. Department of Education for providing access to the results of programs, research and development efforts, and related information. Through a network of clearinghouses, each responsible for an area, ERIC brings information to research libraries. ERIC collects reports of programs, conference proceedings, bibliographies, professional papers, curriculum-related materials, reports of research and development from schools, state educational organizations, businesses, government agencies, and foreign sources. Abstracts are provided. The parts that make up ERIC are provided to libraries in bound form. Two major parts of ERIC are *Resources in Education* (RIE) for documents on microfiche and *Current Index to Journals in Education* (CIJE) for citations to periodical articles. Most research libraries have specific handouts about how to use ERIC for database searches on their computer systems. Because electronic systems change so frequently, it is not appropriate to go into any detail here, except to mention that there is a *Thesaurus of ERIC Descriptors* that leads to subject terms that can be used widely among educational sources.

Beyond the ERIC system, there are other indexes and abstracts on both general and more specifically topic-oriented dimensions of educa-tion, such as the *Education Index, Educational Administration Abstracts, Higher Education Abstracts, Psychological Abstracts, Child Development Abstracts and Bibliography, State Education Journal Index, British Education Index,* and the *Physical Education Index.*

In ERIC materials, philosophy of education articles and books are not indexed as precisely as in the *Philosopher's Index.* The ERIC system omits about half of the important journals in philosophy of education, and the same is true of the *Education Index.* ERIC and the *Education Index* also include articles under subheads such as "Education, Philosophy" and "Philosophy" that are more related to the concept of philosophy as a general term than as an academic discipline. Hence, "'Techno-Arrogance and Halfway Technologies: Salmon Hatcheries on the Pacific Coast of North America.' Focus; V3N1 p. 35–39 1993" appears in the CIJE for September 1993 under the subject index "Philosophy." The expert bibliographer in philosophy of education can expect no more than 15 percent correct designations from printing out everything on the ERIC CD from the nearly four thousand entries between the years 1982 and 1993. This electronic means of screening, however, is still clearly a great expediter when compared with individually screening the hundreds of thousands of articles listed in tables of contents and journal indexes, the alternative to using electronic screening.

Since the forming of the Philosophy of Education Society in the United States (1941), philosophy of education has been the subject of a semiannual volume of the *National Society for the Study of Education Yearbook* on a number of occasions. Philosophy is the topic of Part 1 of 1942, 1955, 1972, and 1981 of the *NSSE Yearbook* and plays a significant role in Part 2 of the 1985 and 1992 volumes. Other research-oriented materials with significant contributions from philosophy of education include all three editions of the *Handbook of Research on Teaching* (1963, 1973, 1986).

A major source of scholarly writing in philosophy of education is Section A, the Humanities and Social Sciences volumes of *Dissertation Abstracts International.* Entries in philosophy of education will be found in two places: under Education, Philosophy of, and under Philosophy, Religion, and Theology, Philosophy. The researcher's judgment will be critical under both categories: Not all the entries under Education, Philosophy of, are academic philosophy of education, and very few of the dissertations under

P

the category Philosophy are in philosophy of education. *Dissertation Abstracts International* is published monthly, and each abstract gives the title, author's name, institution, and the name of the dissertation director. This latter, along with membership lists of the American Philosophical Association and the Philosophy of Education Society, can sometimes be helpful in deciding whether or not the dissertation is clearly a contribution in academic philosophy or philosophy of education. A membership list is published annually in the *Proceedings and Addresses of the American Philosophical Association* and approximately every third year in *Philosophy of Education,* the proceedings of the annual meeting of the Philosophy of Education Society.

The following are quarterly journals, semiannual publications, and annual publications in philosophy of education. Where possible, the educational philosophy of each publication is either quoted verbatim or paraphrased from editorials. Some of the publications have no stated editorial policy. The first group of publications is in philosophy of education only. The second group is of publications primarily or importantly related to philosophy of education.

Publications in Philosophy of Education

Educational Philosophy and Theory (1969–). Philosophical debate on issues of major interest and concern in the discourse of contemporary education. Themes shared by educational institutions, systems, and schools across all countries are particularly appreciated. Space is given to responses to papers already published in this journal. Special issues will be developed as particularly discernible central themes emerge.

Journal of Aesthetic Education (1966–). Publishes articles devoted to the following areas: aesthetic interest and public policy, including problems of cultural administration and the character of cultural services; problem areas critical to arts and humanities instruction at all levels of schooling, including higher education (literature, film, music, the visual and performing arts); an understanding of the aesthetic character of humanistic disciplines and the art of teaching and learning.

Journal of Philosophy of Education (formerly *Proceedings of the Philosophy of Education Society of Great Britain*) (1966–). Articles have a close bearing on education, but may vary from an examination of some fundamental philosophical issue in its connection with education to a detailed critical engagement with

some current educational practice or policy from a philosophical point of view.

Philosophy of Education; Proceedings of the Fiftieth Annual Meeting of the Philosophy of Education Society (1958–).

Proceedings of the Far Western Philosophy of Education Society (1952–).

Proceedings of the Philosophy of Education Society of Australasia.

Proceedings of the South Atlantic Philosophy of Education Society.

Studies in Philosophy and Education (1960–1976; 1989–). The key criteria are clarity and excellence in philosophical argumentation on important educational and related topics. Lengthier manuscripts are allowed. Book reviews with author rejoinders are a regular feature.

Publications Related to Philosophy of Education

Discourse; Australian Journal of Educational Studies (1980–). Focuses on cultural, political, economic, philosophical, historical, and policy studies in education.

Educational Foundations (1987–). Seeks to help fulfill the stated mission of the American Educational Studies Association to enhance scholarship concerning educational foundations by providing a vehicle for publication of articles and essays that feature analysis of foundations, of methodology, of the applications of such methodology to key issues of the day, and of significant research that evolves from and unifies the foundations disciplines, all focusing on the interdisciplinary nature of the educational foundations fields.

Educational Studies (1970–). *Educational Studies* is a journal of reviews and criticism in the foundations of education.

Educational Theory (1951–). Publishes scholarly articles and studies in the foundations of education, and related disciplines outside the field of education, that contribute to the advancement of educational theory.

Journal of Moral Education (1971–). Provides an interdisciplinary forum for consideration of all aspects of moral education and development. It contains philosophical analyses, reports of empirical research, and evaluations of educational strategies that address a range of value issues and the process of valuing both in theory and practice at the social and individual level.

Teaching Philosophy (1975–).

Thinking: The Journal of Philosophy for Children (1979–).

Aspects of the above publications change periodically. For the most current listings, see the *Philosopher's Index*. Many other education and philosophy publications accept contributions on philosophy of education, but there is no way to predict where they may appear in the literature.

Thomas Whitson Nelson

Bibliography

Encyclopedia of Philosophy. Edited by Paul Edwards. New York: Macmillan, 1967.
Philosopher's Index. Bowling Green, Ohio: Philosophy Documentation Center, Bowling Green University, 1967–.

Philosophy of Education, Professional Organizations in

Professional organizations of educational philosophy in Australasia, Britain, and the United States are the result of moral and social philosophy's evolution into the various social sciences (Kaminsky; Bryson 1932) and an extensive social and political discourse over the industrial order and the role education should play in that order (Cremin; Barcan 1980; Silver).

By the 1890s, the twilight of the Victorian period, urban manufacturing centers in Australasia, Britain, and the United States had become slums. It was evident to the newly affluent professional and middle classes that a remedy for the damage generated by industry and urbanization was beyond their ability or the ability of private charity to provide. Nevertheless, the Victorians' enormous faith in the accumulation and analysis of factual data (Mayhew; Hunter) led them to believe that if the problematic elements of society were codified it would be possible to specify the political action and social legislation necessary to ameliorate the social damage generated by industrialism and urbanization. Charitable and intellectual societies were formed to accumulate the factual data necessary to address the seemingly intractable social dilemmas (Abrams; Haskell; Soffer). The evolution of intellectual authority into professional societies provided the template and precedent for the organization of educational psychology into its various professional organizations.

The political and social debate that played itself out between liberal (conservative) and social democratic (radical) thought and conduct was a central element of the period's intellectual history (Kloppenberg). Fundamental questions about the political and social role of education were an important element in that debate. Liberals held that good government was minimal government (Mill 1848), freedom was the absence of social and economic restraint (Spencer 1892), and morality (measured in terms of economic success) was a matter of individual virtue (Sidgwick). Thus an education would instruct individuals in the graces of a civilized society (deference, manners, thrift, saving, temperance, moderation, and so on) and the requirements of economic self-interest (Connell). In contrast, social democrats held that the key to economic progress was altruism. Freedom was not merely a matter of absence of restraint, it was a matter of the assurance of equal opportunity. For them the control of institutionalized economic oppression masquerading as liberty was the means for the realization of equality of opportunity, community, and justice (Kloppenberg). Dissolving the monopolies of learning was a central educational concern of social democrats (Dewey; Tawney 1918, 1922; Horne 1964, 1972). Public education was a predominant tactic for extending democracy into the social and economic elements of everyday life. The intellectual agendas of the professional organizations of educational philosophy on various parts of the globe developed in response to the fundamental elements of this Victorian debate. These agendas played themselves out differently in various places.

From its inception, the professional discourse of educational philosophy has played out one side or the other of the social and political debate between liberals and social democrats. In the United States, the John Dewey Society was decidedly social democratic. The American Philosophy of Education Society adopted a stance somewhere between its social democratic progenitors and their more conservative colleagues in Britain. The Philosophy of Education Society of Great Britain took the conservative side of the debate, demonstrating a Victorian faith in liberalism and liberal education. The Philosophy of Education Society in Australasia embraced both social democratic and liberal elements of the debate and found its stance within the context of Australasia's unique history.

Professional Organization of Educational Philosophy in the United States
The John Dewey Society
The John Dewey Society (JDS) was the first professional organization of educational philosophy. It was established at the Hotel Traymore, Atlantic City, New Jersey, 1935

(Harap; Johnson). Faced with the Depression and the anticipated economic collapse of Western industrial society, the JDS was formed to study and discuss the role of the public school in reconstructing American society. Its organization and establishment were sponsored by the National Education Association's Department of Superintendence. William H. Kilpatrick's "discussion group," a group of New York professors and homespun nationalists who met to discuss issues of social reform in social democratic terms, provided the society with its intellectual and organizational leadership.

The JDS had sympathies for the Progressive Education Association, but its educational covenant was more closely related to the social reform mission of the American Social Science Association (ASSA). The JDS and the ASSA were interested in child-centered literature, but they were more interested in books with a social-democratic agenda, such as Margaret Mead's *Coming of Age in Samoa* (1928), than they were in the soft, romantic, and apolitical literature of the Progressive Education Association.

The official publication of the JDS was its yearbook series, begun in 1937 with a volume edited by William H. Kilpatrick entitled *The Teacher and Society*. The yearbook series was intended to study the important problems that confronted the school in American society. But the yearbook series was too slow and cumbersome. The primary voice of the society became *The Social Frontier (SF)*, a radical journal appearing in October 1934 under the editorship of George Counts and his two associate editors, Norman Woelfel and Mordecai Grossman. The *SF* explored social reconstructionist and social-democratic ideas, but its editorial policy turned Marxist as the Depression developed. In an article entitled "Teachers and Labor" (1935), the editors acknowledged that their proposals for social and educational reform mortgaged progress to revolution.

The *SF*'s radical editorial policy alienated support for both the *SF* and the JDS. Liberals and social democrats withdrew their support from both organizations. Liberals and conservatives led by R. Bruce Raup withdrew their support for both organizations to form a professional organization that was more in tune with their politics.

The Philosophy of Education Society
In November of 1940, R. Bruce Raup circulated a letter calling for the formation of the Philoso-

phy of Education Society (PES), an academic society focused upon the concerns of philosophy and education, free from the Left political and social posture that had damaged the JDS. The following February, in Atlantic City, New Jersey, the PES was formally inaugurated. Raup, of the Teachers College, Columbia University, was elected president, and an executive committee was appointed, composed of Lawrence Thomas, Stanford University; H. Gordon Hullfish, Ohio State University; and John Brubacher, Yale University. Theodore Brameld became secretary-treasurer, and was the remaining member of the social-democratic Left. This was to be a society for educational philosophers, not educational activists (Axtelle; Benne).

By the 1950s, the PES had become the dominant professional organization of educational philosophy. The society prospered despite the relatively diffident support of the American Philosophical Association (Macmillan; Kaminsky). In the early 1950s, with the assistance of the JDS, the University of Illinois and the PES agreed to publish a journal (Anderson 1951, 1959). *Educational Theory* was launched in 1951. The University of Illinois also sponsored the publication of PES *Proceedings*, papers from its annual conference.

A few years later, in 1960, Francis Villemain produced another journal dedicated to the philosophy of education, *Studies in Philosophy and Education*. The journal followed Villemain's career until it suspended publication. *Studies in Philosophy and Education* recently returned to publication with the support of the graduate school of education at the University of California, Los Angeles.

PES has established a secure place for itself in the years since 1950. The American Philosophical Association has continued the Association for Philosophers of Education and has held sessions at their annual meetings for those interested in philosophy of education. The American Educational Research Association has formed a special-interest group for those interested in philosophy of education at their annual meetings. It plays an active part in the Council of Learned Societies in Education. Moreover, educational philosophy continues as an important part of the knowledge base required by the National Council for Accreditation of Teacher Education (Macmillan).

PES never set itself the same type of grand political goals to which the JDS subscribed. Nevertheless, PES continued John Dewey's original intellectual project; it gave education a philosophical lineage, provided educators with academic respect, and gave them an ideology (Feuer).

Great Britain

The professional organization of educational philosophy in Great Britain originated in the same Victorian discourse over the social and political order that predicated the American society (Seaman). But the absence of support for education as an academic discipline in the English university establishment delayed the professional organization of educational philosophy until the middle 1960s. Britain's professional organization was much more at ease with conservative Victorian assumptions about society and the role of education in that society.

In the period after 1900, philosophical discussions of education adopted an uncompromisingly Victorian tone. It was a version of education that was conservative and elitist. The work of the radical utilitarians persuaded Britain's philosophers of education that education was an irreducible element of any real democracy. Herbert Spencer's writings on education (1861), the state (1892), and the evils of social welfare (1873), convinced them that government sponsorship of mass education was neither commendable nor advisable. Like Bertrand Russell, the English were unconvinced that mass education could be delivered to all without reducing education to the lowest possible common denominator (Benn and Peters).

L.A. Reid took educational philosophy's first chair in 1947 at the London Institute of Education. Reid was drafted from the chair of philosophy at Armstrong College, now the University of Newcastle upon Tyne (Reid: chaps. 4, 11). Reid made a major contribution to the discipline's domestic literature and established a small department at the institute. R.S. Peters later developed Reid's department into the most intellectually significant and professionally powerful department in Britain and the Commonwealth (Simon 1983, 1991).

Richard Stanley Peters was a reader in psychology and philosophy at Birkbeck College. Lionel Elvin, director of the London Institute of Education, managed to inveigle Peters to accept the chair of educational philosophy at the institute in 1962 (Elvin). Preparatory work for the organization of the Philosophy of Education Society of Great Britain was accomplished in the 1963–1964 academic year (Philosophy of Education Society of Great Britain [PESGB]). The Aristotelian Society was the organizational template; the public and schoolies were not encouraged to seek membership. "The Steering Committee was composed of Professor R.S. Peters, Professor L.A. Reid, Mr. C.H. Bailey, Mr. R.F. Dearden, Mr. M. A.B. Degenhardt, Mr. P.H. Hirst, Miss B.H. Hosegood, Mr. T.W. Moore, Mr. K. Neuberg, Dr. L.R. Perry, Mr. H.T. Sockett and Mrs. J. White" (PESGB). The first annual general meeting was held on December 13, 1964 (PESGB). The steering committee suggested the following officers: L.A. Reid, president; R.S. Peters, chairman; Paul Hirst, secretary, and Mr. K. Neuberg, treasurer (PESGB). The first volume of the *Proceedings of the Philosophy of Education Society of Great Britain* was published in 1967. R.S. Peters was the journal's editor.

R.S. Peters and the Philosophy of Education Society of Great Britain played an instrumental part in determining who would be appointed to chairs in Britain. Paul Hirst held the chair of educational philosophy at King's College London and later the chair at Cambridge; Leslie Perry held the chair at Warwick and King's College London; Ray Elliot and Robert Dearden held chairs at the University of Birmingham; Hugh Sockett held a chair at the New University of Ulster and later at the University of East Anglia; and Richard Pring held a chair first at Exeter and then at Oxford. They were all students or colleagues of R.S. Peters at the London Institute of Education, and influential actors in the society.

Australasia

The intellectual ideology of the Philosophy of Education Society of Australasia (PESA), which draws its membership essentially from Australia and New Zealand, is heavily influenced by Australia's origins (Kaminsky). Australia's history has been called meager, shameful, and uninspired—tales of brutal convicts, doomed expeditions, and unremarkable or, at best, tragic heroes (Horne 1964; Summers; Hughes; Hazzard). Part of the nation's response to its convict history was the development of an economically and socially segregated educational system (Barcan 1980, 1988; Burnswoods and Fletcher). A significant portion of PESA's philosophical work was a reaction to Australasia's socially segregated system of education.

After the Festival of Britain in 1951, a domestic version of Australian identity began to emerge in the academic and commerical press. In the contentment and prosperity of the post–

World War II period, intellectuals articulated their own identity and history. Books such as Donald Horne's *Lucky Country* (1964), Humphrey McQueen's *A New Britannia* (1970), Russell Ward's *Australian Legend* (1958), and Ronald Conway's *Great Australian Stupor* (1972) were seminal parts of the new identity and ethos. The establishment of educational philosophy was part of the construction of a new Australasian ethos. It was part of the attempt to disentangle Australia and its institutions from their British parentage.

The intellectual works of two immigrants from Great Britain, John Anderson and C.D. Hardie, were seminal elements of the invention of Australasian educational philosophy and the establishment of its professional organizations. In 1927, John Anderson accepted an appointment as professor of philosophy at Sydney University. Anderson's radical intellectual stance brought him into conflict with the church, welfare socialism, jingoistic patriotism, censorship, and the "new education" (Passmore). His *Education and Politics* was an important philosophical contribution to Australian educational thought. Anderson was responsible for encouraging Australasia's philosophers and philosophers of education to speak with their own voice. C.D. Hardie became Australasia's first professor of educational philosophy. He was appointed to the chair of education at the University of Tasmania in 1946 shortly after his book *Truth and Fallacy in Educational Theory* was published in Britain. Although he did little to establish chairs or lectureships in educational philosophy throughout his career, he struggled to free educational discourse from the constraints of metaphysics.

Australasia's invisible college of educational philosophers had a strong domestic literature in place when its professional organization was finally established in 1970. At Armidale Teachers College, Margaret Mackie followed her own mind and the inspiration of John Anderson to write at length about education in a philosophical tone. She wrote *Education in the Inquiring Society; An Introduction to the Philosophy of Education* (1966); *Educative Teaching* (1968); *What is Right?* (1970); and *Philosophy and School Administration* (1977). Les Brown published *General Philosophy in Education* (1966); James Gribble published *Introduction to Philosophy of Education* (1969); and D.C. Phillips wrote *Theories, Values and Education* (1970) at other places in Austra-

lia. In the 1960s the New Zealander Ivan Snook published "Education and the Philosopher: A Reply to J.P. Powell," (1966); "Philosophy, Education and a Myth" (1966); and "Philosophy of Education: Today and Tomorrow" (1969).

What would become the society's journal was launched about a year before the society was established. The first number of *Educational Philosophy and Theory* appeared in May 1969. It was the work of Les Brown, then associate professor of education at the University of New South Wales.

In the same year a professional organization was foreshadowed. In 1969 Les Brown, Anna Hogg (principal lecturer at Sydney Teachers College), R. Precians (Macquarie University), and W.E. Andersen (senior lecturer at Sydney University) drafted a constitution, helped make plans for an inaugural conference, and announced a call for members. In May of 1970 at Bassar College, University of New South Wales, the Philosophy of Education Society of Australasia held its inaugural conference. The executive committee was composed of Les M. Brown, president; Anna Hogg, vice president; W.E. Andersen, secretary; and R. Precians, treasurer.

Les Brown was the president of the society and editor of the journal, but a troubled relationship between the journal and the society was a major focus of the discipline's politics. In 1973, *Educational Philosophy and Theory* was in financial difficulty; the society came to the journal's economic assistance. Influential members of the society assumed that they would play a more significant editorial role in the conduct of the journal, but that was not the case. Unable to compromise with the society, Brown repaid the journal's debt in 1976 and returned the publication to his personal control. In 1981 the society formally disassociated itself from the journal, and the publication and the society became caught up in a not so friendly rivalry between academic generations and alternative social and political philosophies.

The society and the journal remained parallel institutions until 1986, when, under the editorship of James S. Kaminsky, then senior lecturer at the University of New England, the management of the journal was passed to the society. In 1989 the editorship was transferred to Professor David Aspin, Dean of Monash University.

The society remains committed to a number of social issues generated in the sixties—Aboriginal rights, sexism, gay rights, multiculturalism, and so on. The Philosophy of Education Society of Australasia remains a merchant of nonstandard educational ideas to a conservative and centralized educational establishment.

Conclusion

In the United States, Britain, and Australasia since the middle 1960s the discourse of educational philosophy's professional organizations has become more complex. It has been conducted against the often confusing counterpoint of Marxist scholars who rejected the possibility of social reform in favor of more drastic solutions, philosophical analysts who attempted to change the terms of the debate by anchoring educational questions in the realm of epistemology or objective morality—beyond the vitriol of social reform—and romantic existentialists who attempted to transcend questions of social reform by asserting the priority of an "openness to Being." The organizations themselves have become mature members of the academic establishment. After years of declining membership in the 1970s and 1980s, the organizations seem to have acquired a new vitality. Memberships in the professional organizations of educational philosophy are stable if not improving in the 1990s, the various organizations' journals have healthy subscriptions and are financially viable, and the organizations themselves have become active players in agencies of educational accreditation and studies of education, their members playing an increasingly visible and important role in education's interaction with governmental organizations.

James S. Kaminsky

See also PHILOSOPHY OF EDUCATION, HISTORY OF; LITERATURE IN

Bibliography

Abrams, Philip. *The Origins of British Sociology: 1834–1914.* Chicago: University of Chicago Press, 1968.

Anderson, Archibald W. "Fostering Study in the Theory of Education." *Educational Theory* 9 (1959): 16–23, 49.

———. "The Task of Educational Theory." *Educational Theory* 1 (1951): 9–21.

Anderson, John. *Education and Politics.* Sydney, Australia: Angus and Robertson, 1931.

Axtelle, George E. Taped interview. Philosophy of Education Society, Archives, 1965.

Barcan, Alan. *A History of Australian Education.* Melbourne: Oxford University Press, 1980.

———. *Two Centuries of Education in New South Wales.* Kensington, N.S.W.: New South Wales University Press, 1988.

Benn, S.I., and R.S. Peters. *The Principles of Political Thought* (also published as *Social Principles and the Democratic State*). New York: Free Press, 1959, 1965.

Benne, Kenneth D. Taped interview. Philosophy of Education Society, Archives, 1966.

Brown, Les M. *General Philosophy in Education.* New York: McGraw-Hill, 1966.

Bryson, Gladys. "The Comparable Interests of the Old Moral Philosophy and the Modern Social Sciences." *Social Forces* 11 (1932): 19–27.

———. "The Emergence of the Social Sciences from Moral Philosophy." *International Journal of Ethics* 42 (1932): 304–23.

———. "Sociology Considered as Moral Philosophy." *Sociological Review* 24 (1932): 26–36.

Burnswoods, Jan, and J. Fletcher. *Sydney and the Bush.* New South Wales: New South Wales Department of Education, 1980.

Connell, W.F. *The Educational Thought and Influence of Matthew Arnold.* London: Routledge and Kegan Paul, 1950.

Conway, Ronald. *The Great Australian Stupor.* Melbourne: Sun Books, 1972.

Cremin, Lawrence A. *The Transformation of the School.* New York: Alfred A. Knopf, 1961.

Dewey, John. "School and Society." In *Dewey on Education,* edited by Martin S. Dworkin. New York: Teachers College Press, 1959.

Elvin, Lionel. Interview with the author, 1989.

Feuer, Lewis S. "John Dewey and the Back to the People Movement in American Thought." *Journal of the History of Ideas* 20 (1959): 545–68.

Gribble, James. *Introduction to Philosophy of Education.* Boston: Allyn and Bacon, 1969.

Harap, Henry. "The Beginnings of the John Dewey Society." *Educational Theory* 20 (1970): 157–63.

Hardie, C.D. *Truth and Fallacy in Educational Theory.* New York: Teachers College Press, 1942, 1962.

Haskell, Thomas L. *The Emergence of Professional Social Science.* Urbana: University of Illinois Press, 1977.

Hazzard, Shirley. *The Transit of Venus*. New York: Viking Press, 1980.

Horne, Donald. *The Australian People*. Sydney: Angus and Robertson, 1972.

———. *The Lucky Country*. Penguin, 1964, 1965.

Hughes, Robert. *The Fatal Shore*. London: William Collins and Sons, 1987.

Hunter, Robert. *Poverty*. New York: Harper and Row, 1904, 1965.

Johnson, Henry C., Jr. "Reflective Thought and Practical Action: The Origins of the John Dewey Society." *Educational Theory* 27 (1977): 65–75.

Kaminsky, James. *A New History of Educational Philosophy*. Westport, Conn.: Greenwood Press, 1993.

Kilpatrick, William, ed. *The Teacher and Society*. First yearbook of the John Dewey Society. New York: D. Appleton-Century, 1937.

Kloppenberg, James T. *Uncertain Victory*. New York: Oxford University Press, 1986.

Mackie, Margaret D. *Education in the Inquiring Society: An Introduction to the Philosophy of Education*. Hawthorne, Victoria: Australian Council for Education Research, 1966.

———. *Educative Teaching*. Sydney: Angus and Roberts, 1968.

———. *Philosophy and School Administration*. St. Lucia, Queensland: University of Queensland Press, 1977.

———. *What is Right?* Sydney: Angus and Roberts, 1970.

Macmillan, C.J.B. "PES and the APA—An Impressionistic History." *Educational Theory* 41 (1991): 275–86.

McQueen, Humphrey. *A New Britannia*. New York: Penguin Books, 1970.

Mayhew, Henry. *London Labour and the London Poor* [1851], vols. 1–4. New York: A.M. Kelley, 1967.

Mead, Margaret. *Coming of Age in Samoa*. New York: William Morrow, 1928, 1968.

Mill, John Stuart. *On Liberty* [1859]. New York: Appleton-Century Crofts, 1947.

———. *Principles of Political Economy*. [1848], vols. 1 and 2. New York: D. Appleton, 1891.

Owen, Robert. *A New View of Society*. London: R. and A. Taylor, 1818.

Passmore, John. "Anderson, John." In *The Encyclopedia of Philosophy*. Vol. 1, edited by Paul W. Edwards. New York: Macmillan, 1967.

Phillips, D.C. *Theories, Values and Education*. Melbourne, Victoria: Melbourne University Press, 1970.

Philosophy of Education Society of Great Britain. 1964. First annual general meeting, December 1964. Secretary, Paul Hirst. Archive: Philosophy of Education Society of Great Britain.

Philosophy of Education Society of Great Britain. 1964. Meeting of the Steering Committee. Secretary, Paul Hirst. Archive: Philosophy of Education Society of Great Britain.

Raup, R. Bruce. Private letter. Philosophy of Education Society, Archives, 1940.

Reid, Louis Arnaud. N.d. *Yesterday's Today; Journal into Philosophy*. Unpublished autobiography.

Russell, Bertrand. *Education and the Modern World* (also *Education and the Social Order*). New York: W.W. Norton, 1932.

Seaman, L.C.B. *Victorian England*. London: Methuen, 1973, 1985.

Sidgwick, Henry. *The Methods of Ethics*. London: Macmillan, 1874, 1907.

Silver, Harold. *Education as History*. London: Methuen, 1983.

Simon, Brian. *Education and the Social Order*. New York: AMS Press, 1991.

———. "The Study of Education as a University Subject in Britain." *Studies in Higher Education* 8 (1983): 1–13.

Snook, Ivan. "Education and the Philosopher: A Reply to J.P. Powell." *Australian Journal of Education* 10, no. 2 (1966).

———. "Philosophy, Education and a Myth." *Australian Journal of Higher Education* 2 (1966).

———. "Philosophy of Education: Today and Tomorrow." *New Zealand Journal of Educational Studies* 4, no. 1 (1969).

Soffer, Reba N. *Ethics and Society in England*. Berkeley: University of California Press, 1978.

Spencer, Herbert. *Education*. New York: D. Appleton, 1861, 1897.

———. *The Man Versus the State* [1892]. Caldwell, Idaho: Caxton Printers, 1940.

———. *The Study of Sociology*. New York: D. Appleton, 1873, 1904.

Summers, Anne. *Damned Whores and God's Police: The Colonialization of Women in Australia*. Ringwood, Victoria: Penguin Books, 1975, 1976.

Tawney, R.H.. "Keep the Workers' Children in Their Place." In *The Radical Tradition*, edited by Rita Hinden. London: George Allen and Unwin, 1918, 1964.

———. "The Problem of the Public Schools." In *The Radical Tradition*, edited by Rita Hinden. London: George Allen and Unwin, 1918, 1964.

———. *Secondary Education for All*. London: Hambledon Press, 1922, 1988.

Veblen, Thorstein. *The Theory of the Leisure Class*. New York: B.W. Huebsch, 1899, 1922.

Villemain, Francis. Taped interview with the author, 1988.

Ward, Russell. *The Australian Legend*. Melbourne: Oxford University Press, 1958.

Physical Education, Philosophy of

The philosophy of physical education is a field of applied philosophic inquiry that focuses on the educational values of human movement in five contexts—sport, dance, exercise, games, and play. While informal and sporadic contributions have been made to this field of scholarship for centuries (the likes of Homer and Plato commented on the value of motor skills), formal attempts at a systematic philosophy of physical education did not occur until much later.

Modern physical education was born at the start of the progressive education period, an era of pedagogical ferment and experimentation that lasted from approximately 1875 to the mid 1950s. When William James, Edward L. Thorndike, John Dewey, and other reformers attacked educational traditions that placed order over freedom, work over play, effort over interest, prescription over election, mind over body, and narrow intellectual content over a broader range of subjects, the way was cleared for the rise of physical education.

Its advance was swift. Even though physical activity had long been known to have therapeutic value, there was previously little appreciation of the ways in which sport, dance, exercise, games, and play might dramatically improve the entirety of human life—both instrumentally and, more important, intrinsically. Physical education philosophers were needed to analyze and articulate the possibilities of something that came to be called the "New Physical Education," a field oriented toward broad educational goals rather than narrow health-related benefits.

A raft of literature described the ambitious purposes of early-twentieth-century physical education. Thomas D. Wood and Rosalind Cassidy (1927), Jesse Feiring Williams (1927), and Charles McCloy (1940) were among the prominent spokespersons of the period. While Wood was the most original thinker of this group, it was Williams who had the greatest impact on the profession. His *Principles of Physical Education* appeared in eight editions and influenced at least two generations of physical educators. A disciple of Dewey, Williams saw physical education gymnasiums and play fields as laboratories for learning, as places where a whole host of social values could be taught. For example, Williams believed that lessons in democratic living, fair play, responsibility, and determination could be transmitted through experiences in games and play. This, as he so often said, was an education "through," not "of" the physical. Williams and other philosophers of physical education during the Progressive Era saw physical education as a full partner in the educative process.

These writers, however, did not present an entirely convincing philosophic case for the centrality of physical education in the schools. In truth, these individuals were more educationalists than philosophers. Their interests lay more in the improvement of teaching and learning than the acquisition of philosophic insight, and the stimulus for their work came more from the discoveries of science than any philosophic advances. When discussing holism, for instance, they would cite empirical evidence from biology and psychology about the organic unity of human beings but refrain from analyzing the philosophic errors of dualists such as Plato and Rene Descartes or the philosophic insights of nondualists like Dewey.

Many of the advances of the Progressive Era in education were short-lived. During the latter half of the twentieth century, those promoting physical education became unsure of themselves and frequently waffled when asked to describe its educational mission. That was due to any number of factors, among them difficulty in delivering on the broad promises made by Williams and other progressive physical educators; the durability of mind-body dualism and a re-emphasis on intellectual skills and content; fiscal constraints that put particular pressure on the nonacademic fields like art, music, home economics, and physical education; internal battles over whether the curricular focus should rest on biological objectives like physical fitness or affective, cognitive, and psychomotor outcomes; and a new philosophy of sport literature that employed a systems or schools-of-thought approach—one that was uninspired and, for many practitioners, difficult to utilize.

The schools-of-thought approach was promoted most vigorously by Davis (1961) and Zeigler (1964). They analyzed physical education on the basis of various philosophical systems—realism, idealism, pragmatism, naturalism, and so on. While these authors deduced which schools of thought were more and less friendly to the purposes of physical education and drew out the implications of each one for such day-to-day matters as curriculum development and teaching methodology, they did little to fortify physical education's tenuous place in education or to inspire its uncertain practitioners. Many felt that the schools of thought or systems were misleadingly artificial (for example, there were serious disagreements and differences within realism, idealism, and the other "isms"); that the deductions drawn from the claims of each school were selective (for example, depending on what type of idealism one considered or whom one quoted, either positive or negative deductions could be drawn about the role of physical education); and that objectively sound pedagogical conclusions were difficult to reach. (Different philosophic positions within systems, to say nothing of diverse claims between schools of thought, were often portrayed as including elements of truth. Reaching conclusions was seen by many readers as largely a subjective matter of selecting philosophical stances based on personal taste.) For these reasons, among others, this brand of educational philosophy did not endure for long.

In the early 1970s, the focus of philosophic attention shifted unmistakably from the value of physical activity in education to, simply, the value of physical activity. This was a movement from applied to basic research. It tackled such fundamental problems as the relationship between people and their bodies, the kind of intelligence needed for successful motor performance, the significance of nonsedentary skills in achieving the good life, the cultural importance of play and games, the presence (or absence) of political and social class influences in games, the possibility that sport is art or at least like art, the idea that contemporary sport performs many of the same functions as religion, and the potential of sport and dance as avenues for human expression and nonverbal communication, to cite only a few examples. Many of these research topics have been addressed by articles in the *Journal of the Philosophy of Sport*. Morgan and Meier (1988) and Vanderwerken and Wertz (1985) produced useful anthologies that contain much of the best work of this disciplinary research period.

While this basic research approach continues to hold sway, there are some indications of renewed interest in applied philosophy of physical education. In recent years, several texts that translate disciplinary research for school settings have appeared. Among these are volumes written by Arnold (1988), Kirk (1992), and Kretchmar (1994). These authors grapple with basic questions related to the education of human beings. Is intentional, skillful movement itself a form of knowing and, if so, what is the significance or value of this insight? Are games and play trivial matters that should be regarded as frills (at least in adult life), or should they be considered activities in which important individual and cultural advances take place? Should physical education emphasize fitness and health and highlight the fact that it provides important means to the good life, or should it emphasize intrinsic or end values such as the knowledge and freedom that are experienced in creative, high-level dance and sport performances? Has the physical education curriculum been largely free of ideology and political influence? If not, how does ideology show up in sport, dance, and exercise curricula?

Philosophers in physical education are still working on what it means to educate the whole person and how best to do this. Though over a century has passed since the onset of the Progressive Period in education, and in spite of the fact that systematic work in the philosophy of physical education has been in existence for decades, it is still not clear whether physical education can and should play a central role in overall human education. This will probably remain undecided until more insight and consensus are achieved on the questions of what an exemplary human being is and what the good life requires. If answers move in the direction of depicting excellent persons as reflective and verbal and the good life as sedentary, physical education will have less and less to do with mainstream education. On the other hand, if it is thought that people should be able to explore, discover, celebrate, express themselves, invent, and create nonverbally as well as verbally, out of their chairs as well as in them, then physical education's value may rise.

R. Scott Kretchmar

See also LEISURE; PLATO; PROGRESS, IDEA OF, AND PROGRESSIVE EDUCATION; WORK

Bibliography

Arnold, Peter J. *Education, Movement and the Curriculum*. London: Falmer, 1988.

Davis, Elwood Craig. *The Philosophic Process in Physical Education*. Philadelphia: Lea and Febiger, 1961.

Journal of the Philosophy of Sport. Vols. 1–20. Champaign, Ill.: Human Kinetics, 1974–1993.

Kirk, David. *Defining Physical Education: The Social Construction of a School Subject in Postwar Britain*. London: Falmer, 1992.

Kretchmar, R. Scott. *Practical Philosophy of Sport*. Champaign, Ill.: Human Kinetics, 1994.

McCloy, Charles. *Philosophical Bases for Physical Education*. New York: F.S. Crofts, 1940.

Morgan, William J., and Klaus V. Meier, eds. *Philosophic Inquiry in Sport*. Champaign, Ill.: Human Kinetics, 1988.

Vanderwerken, David L., and Spencer K. Wertz, eds. *Sport Inside Out: Readings in Literature and Philosophy*. Ft. Worth: Tex.: Texas Christian University, 1985.

Williams, Jesse F. *The Principles of Physical Education*. Philadelphia: W.B. Saunders, 1927, 1964.

Wood, Thomas D., and Rosalind Cassidy. *The New Physical Education: A Program of Naturalized Activities for Education toward Citizenship*. New York: Macmillan, 1927.

Zeigler, Earle F. *Philosophical Foundations for Physical, Health, and Recreation Education*. Englewood Cliffs, N.J.: Prentice-Hall, 1964.

Plato (c. 427–347 B.C.)

Athenian philosopher and head of the Academy, arguably the first institution of higher learning in Western culture. All his literary and philosophical production was in the form of dialogues. The exact order of their composition is not known, although there is agreement on their general chronology. The collection of letters attributed to him is spurious, except, perhaps for the seventh letter and possibly the second and the thirteenth. The Platonic Academy continued to exist until A.D. 529, when the philosophical schools were closed by Justinian.

Socrates was the overwhelming influence in Plato's life and thought. In most of Plato's dialogues Socrates is the main speaker, and Plato himself never appears as one of the interlocutors. The dialogues themselves were possibly conceived at first as Plato's interpretation of Socrates' conversations and later as an explication of what Plato considered to be the necessary metaphysical presuppositions and political consequences of Socrates' ethical convictions and educational practices. Although the difference between Socrates' thought and Plato's own philosophy becomes clearer as Plato's literary and philosophical career progresses, the demarcation between the two is nevertheless problematic and often conjectural.

In Plato's dialogues, Socrates is the paradigmatic educator. He is shown to stress above all the moral value of rational self-examination, identified by him as "the care of one's soul" (*Apology* 29e, 30ab). The aim of Socrates' examination of his interlocutors was to bring them to recognize for themselves the contradictions in their beliefs, in order eventually to "purge them" of such contradictions. Socrates attached no value to opinions uncritically accepted. Hence the dialogical and ironic nature of Socrates' educational practice, as Plato understood it: Typically, Socrates would not give answers but only ask questions, in order to draw out the consequences implied in his interlocutor's beliefs. In Plato's later dialogues, the Platonic Socrates takes on a more positive approach, although it is disputed to what extent the ironic element is kept.

Influenced as he was by the Sophists, Socrates nevertheless set himself apart from them by the firm belief, on which his whole educational attitude was predicated, that man is *not* the measure of all things, and that there is a real and not merely conventional or idiosyncratic distinction between true and false, and between good and bad. Knowledge, especially moral knowledge, should be attained by direct apprehension of the *eidos*, of configuration, of the moral quality inquired into. Socrates' method of refutation could not, however, by itself, yield positive results. At best, a set of beliefs could be presumed consistent so long as it had not been refuted; but consistency is only necessary, not sufficient, for truth.

Aware of the shortcomings of the Socratic method, Plato developed, from the *Meno* onward, his conception of the analytical or dialectical method as nondeductive and hypothetical. This is to be the main method of philosophy (and of education); it aims at finding "the reason why"—that is, the premises upon which a conclusion, presumed true, can be based, rather than deducing conclusions from premises that appear self-evidently true. Plato postulated the necessary premises of Socrates' moral convictions in what became known as his doctrine of ideas. Everything that appears to our senses, as a moral trait, or a mathematical property, or a natural being or quality, is only a "reflection," or embodiment, in a material and spatially extended medium, of nonmaterial, rational patterns or "ideas" that exist independently of their deficient—because not fully rational—materializations. Only ideas are fully real, because only they are fully rational. (Plato's ideas are not to be confused with Locke's, which are the source of the modern English "idea" as a mental representation.) Material things "participate in" or "imitate" ideas, and "fall short" of them precisely inasmuch as material things, unlike ideas, are particular, mutable, and context-dependent. But they have, nevertheless, a measure of rationality, insofar as they do participate in the ideas (*Phaedo, Republic* V).

In the *Meno,* Plato introduced the distinction between knowledge and (true or correct) opinion: Both correspond to the facts of the matter, but knowledge alone implies the capability of providing a rational explanation (*Meno* 97d–98b). In the *Phaedo* and the *Republic,* with the introduction of the doctrine of ideas, knowledge in the strictest sense is correlated with the ideas, since only ideas are fully rational, and the material world is said to be the object of opinion only. Degrees of reality and degrees of cognition are not, however, directly equated: There can be opinionlike (that is, not fully justified) apprehension of nonmaterial objects, as in the mathematical sciences (*Republic* VI 510b).

Learning is the development of rational knowledge, not the acquisition of pieces of information. These can never add up to anything more than a body of true, but not fully justified, opinions, thus lacking the essential characteristic of knowledge: the understanding of the reason why. In the strict sense, there can be learning only of ideal entities, which alone are unqualifiedly what they are and alone are susceptible of full rational justification. Sensible

objects that bear the same name as the idea, albeit derivatively, "remind" us of that idea. "Through" the sensible object, which is, say, beautiful only with qualifications (beautiful here but not there, at one time but not at another, in comparison with this but not in comparison with that, in the eyes of someone but not in the eyes of someone else, and so on; *Symposium* 211a), we grasp the nonmaterial, nonsensible idea, which is what it is to be beautiful without any qualifications. This grasping of the idea is also an insight into the logical relations between ideas.

In the *Meno* and in the *Phaedo,* learning—that is, the passage from opinion to knowledge—is described as reminiscence. In the famous "geometry lesson" (*Meno* 82b–85b), an illiterate slave-boy is brought by questioning to recognize the incommensurability of the diagonal with the side of the square. Socrates poses the boy a geometrical problem: How to double the area of a given square? The boy's initial answers are wrong, and Socrates leads him to the recognition of their wrongness. The right answer is actually proposed to the boy by Socrates himself, but, so long as the boy cannot see why the answer is right, it is, for him, a mere opinion. Knowledge will gradually develop as the boy, on being questioned by Socrates, will come to see "the reason why." Socrates' questions themselves provide him only with opinions whose validity he has to consider for himself.

Knowledge is innate, but it is in the soul only in a latent state. The soul is "in a state of having learned" (*Meno* 81c); that is, it has within itself all knowledge (in the strict sense, as what is capable of full rational justification). But Plato is careful not to specify, except in mythical terms, the supposed process by which the soul first "acquired," as it were, that knowledge. The extent to which Plato's mythical descriptions can be taken literally is a subject of great controversy (*Meno* 81c–e, *Phaedo* 72e, *Phaedrus* 246a–249d). Learning shares with reminiscence the character of a recognition. Socrates' question, typically requiring a yes or no answer, is to be answered by introspection, by the interlocutor "looking into himself" and finding the answer there. It confronts the learner with something he recognizes as familiar, as something he finds already within himself, although he has been unaware of it. If the question did not arouse in the student a sense of familiarity with the expected answer, there would be no reason—other than irrelevant psychological pressure—to answer one way rather than the other.

Learning as reminiscence is a process of gradual clarification of opinions one already has within oneself in a confused and indistinct manner. Questioning forces the respondent to turn his attention to connections and implications he had not previously considered, but which, once made to face them, he is capable of recognizing for what they are. Full knowledge is attained, if at all, only when the whole web of rational interconnections is fully comprehended; but, for the most part, learning is, in Plato's dialogues, a partial affair, in which one starts from what is imperfectly apprehended (because given by the senses or uncritically held as mere opinion) and makes one's way toward a more coherent and adequate, but still imperfect, apprehension of reality. On the other hand, Plato forcefully stresses in the *Republic, Symposium, Phaedrus,* and elsewhere, that such a process of approximation to the full truth must presuppose that there is such a thing as the full truth, that only ideas are what they are fully and unconditionally, and that these are the nonmaterial objects of true and perfect knowledge.

In the later *Theaetetus* (149ff.), Socrates is made to describe himself as a midwife: He himself cannot give birth; he can only help others, who "are pregnant in their souls," to deliver, and check to see if the newborns are sound or stillborn (that is, whether they can withstand refutation). Knowledge can come only from "inside," as a result of a conscious effort. There is no learning without personal effort, which gives knowledge an element of intimate and unshakable personal conviction. But these, although necessary, are not sufficient: knowledge is of what truly is, not of what appears to be, persuasive as it may be.

The simile of the Cave (*Republic* VII 514a–516c) is an allegorical description of "our nature in its education and lack of education." In this best known and most influential of Plato's parables, we are likened to men in an underground cave, chained so that they see only its wall and are prevented from seeing its entrance and the light behind them. Some way toward the entrance of the cave a fire is burning, and between the prisoners and the fire there is a low wall, behind which men carry above them statues and other artifacts. The shadows of these are thrown onto the wall facing the prisoners. Because they cannot turn round, the prisoners take the shadows on the wall to be the true and only reality. If someone were to release one of them from his bonds and force him to turn round and look at the objects behind him, he would at first be dazzled by the light. Pained and perplexed, he would think that the shadows he had seen before were more real than the objects that cast those shadows. If he were dragged up, against his will, out of the cave and into the light of the sun, he would need time to accustom himself to the brightness, looking first at reflections in the water, then at the stars, and finally, after much preparation, at the sun itself. Only then would he realize that all he had seen before was due to the sun, which alone is the source of all light and all being, and that all along he had been dealing with mere reflections of true reality.

Education is "an art of conversion" (518d). Knowledge is not put in the souls, just as men do not put sight into blind eyes. Rather, the mental faculties are to be turned in the right direction, away from the sensible, material, contingent, and partial, and toward the intelligible, ideal, necessary, and absolute. Although the intelligible is by nature clearer, one's habits and prejudices will make one prefer the imperfect and cognitively inferior world of one's acquaintance. Truth is self-evident, nevertheless it may be rejected as too incompatible with one's received beliefs. It must, therefore, be approached by degrees.

In this context, Plato seems to think that the process of education inevitably involves some measure of coercion, having its start in the deliberate action of "someone" (no doubt typified by Socrates). However, from other passages it may be understood that the mutability, the relativity, and the contradictions in the material world may in themselves be enough, at least for philosophical souls, to prompt "the turning of the eye of the soul." In any case, it is sufficiently clear that the senses have a positive educational and epistemological role: The objects of the senses are perceived as inherently deficient, and it is precisely this deficiency that impels us toward their ideal models.

Hence the importance of the mathematical sciences for the higher curriculum (*Republic* VII 522ff.). Arithmetic, geometry, stereometry, astronomy (that is, celestial mechanics), and music (acoustics) do have practical applications, but their chief educational function is to help turn the student away from the sensible toward the intelligible. These sciences deal with embodiments in different media of abstract relations. Their educational value lies in that, although they refer to sensible entities—dots or units, lines and areas, volumes, bodies in movement, and sounds—they nevertheless deal with them not as sensible but as the abstract relations they represent. The theorems proved by the mathematician are primarily true not of the material example (not because it is inaccurate, but because it is sensible, mutable, and particular); strictly speaking, they are true of the abstract configurations, which are the real object of mathematical proofs. Moreover, collections of units, areas, bodies, movements, or sounds, can embody the same configuration. The mathematical sciences force us to realize that the same idea can be variously embodied in different media, and that things that seem to us completely disparate may in reality be the same. Such mathematical preparation should pave the way to the understanding of how all the diverse cases of, say, justice are what they are—namely cases of justice—despite their apparent unlimited variety.

But even if the mathematical sciences were to purge themselves of all reference to sensible examples (as was in fact done in modern times), they would still not be philosophy. Mathematical sciences are deductive—that is, they start from assumptions supposed to be evident and proceed to consequences whose strength depends on the assumptions made. But these assumptions are themselves in need of justification. (Modern axiomatic mathematics, in which the first assumptions are not taken as evident but simply as agreed upon, escapes Plato's critique by giving up all claim to truth.) The philosopher does not deduce consequences from assumed principles deemed evident, but works "up" from those principles to their assumptions, not "down" to their consequences, until he comes to the principle that is in no need of further justification. That there is such a principle is required by Plato's firm anti-Sophistic conviction that there is a real difference between opinion and knowledge. The grasping of this first principle (identified by Plato as the Idea of the Good) enables the philosopher both to see each and every thing for what it is and in its proper intelligible context, and to have a synoptic understanding of the whole of reality.

A strictly intellectualistic interpretation of Plato's philosophy and educational views would be misguided, and would leave unexplained Plato's central contention that intellectual truth is a motive in its own right. Although Plato does oppose reason to passion, the opposition is not between pure contemplation and blind drive. In some contexts (*Phaedo, Symposium*), Plato

considers the soul as one and undivided; in others (*Republic* IV, *Phaedrus, Timaeus*), he distinguishes in it three parts or functions: reason, "spiritedness," and appetites. As usual, Plato stresses different points of view according to the needs of the argument. Thus, at *Republic* X (611c), he makes clear that the heterogeneity of the soul is due to its "association with the body." But in all cases Plato characterizes reason as a driving power in its own right, which can oppose the other forces in the soul. Reason is not merely instrumental, fitting means to ends, but also normative and motive, having ends of its own and striving to achieve those ends. Reason is thus not neutral in respect of ends, but it has interests of its own, and is, in the last analysis, its own justification.

In the *Symposium*, Plato takes a sunnier view of the educational process. He sees a gradation in the soul, at once cognitive and emotional, from cognitively obscure drives and appetites closely associated with the body, such as the sexual drive, hunger, and thirst, through anger and "spiritedness," to the intellectual drive toward contemplation. The *Symposium* (206–12, also *Phaedrus* 246–57) describes the ascent of the soul, all the way from sexual attraction to the forceful attraction to the beautiful in itself. Viewed from the vantage point of the contemplation of the idea of the beautiful, all the previous stages are understood as the same drive toward the idea, in different degrees of clarity. The clearer the emotion, the more forceful it is, and the intellectual love of the idea is also the strongest. Plato stresses that the eye cannot be turned round without turning round the whole body (*Republic* VI 518c): Intellectual and emotional education are inseparable.

This drive toward rational, ideal reality is also perceived as a drive toward self-fulfillment. But, for Plato, one's fulfillment is not one's empirical nature. The true nature of things being in their ideas, one's true nature too is transcendent. One's drive toward fulfillment is a drive toward a perfection that one cannot find within oneself, but must look for in the objective reality that is the object and the goal of one's rational faculty.

This love of the beautiful in all its degrees of manifestation is so powerful that it overflows in the desire for procreating the beautiful. At first it manifests itself in the desire for physical procreation; as one ascends the ladder, this desire is distilled into the desire for procreating the beautiful in the souls—that is, in the educational drive. The educator is attracted by the possibility, inherent in the educand, of realizing the objective beauty latent in the educand's soul, which has to be drawn out and developed. Politics as the art of guiding the citizens of the state toward perfection and happiness, in the measure of their several abilities, is the next rung in the ladder. The last is the contemplation of the ideal reality; this is also the apex of emotion, as true intellectual love. (This concept will be of great influence in the history of philosophy, of theology, and of education, notably on medieval Neoplatonic and Aristotelian thinkers and later on Spinoza and many others.)

The vision of the ideal reality and the irresistible desire to imitate it provide the educator with the motive as well as with justification and authority. The source of all educational authority is knowledge in the strictest sense, personified in the philosopher. This knowledge implies educational *eros,* or passion, as a drive to bring others to their possible perfection.

The philosopher returns to the cave with a changed perspective on human affairs. The moral and educational force of a doctrine of transcendent ideas is that human life is not to be evaluated in its own terms. One's empirical desires are not conducive to true happiness and success. As nobody wants to be unhappy, this doctrine has the consequence that people can be mistaken about their happiness and their (true) desires, and he who really knows can (and should) set them right. One's true desires transcend one's physical existence, and true happiness and success are to be evaluated by nonutilitarian criteria that are independent of, and higher than, one's empirical life and desires. This is the moral and educational meaning of the conversion of the soul: a change of perspective, according to which one comes to value rationality for its own sake and to assess one's own life from the point of view of the interests of reason—that is, as a life totally based on true knowledge in the strictest sense.

It is clear, however, that such intellectual and moral aims cannot be understood, let alone achieved, but by very few. Most people will not develop such a degree of rationality as may enable them to be guided by their own reason. It is the ultimate aim of the philosophical state to ensure that those capable of philosophy attain it and that those incapable lead a life that is as much as possible close to it. It is best if one can follow reason "from within"; but if one cannot, one must be made to follow it "from outside"—by force if necessary—for one's own good.

The Platonic ideal state of the *Republic* comprises three functions, to be discharged by the citizens according to their abilities and preoccupations. They are classified according to the dominant trait in their souls: Those whose main trait is the appetite will discharge the productive and economic functions of the state; those whose dominant trait is "spiritedness" will be in charge of the external and internal defense of the state; and those whose dominant passion is knowledge will, by strength of their knowledge, rule the state.

The education of the majority of the citizens, who will discharge the productive functions, does not need much reform. Selection for further education will be made on the basis of continuous assessment of ability. Class is in itself irrelevant, although Plato does think it likely that ability has a strong genetic component, even to the point of advocating eugenics (*Republic* V 459). In the *Timaeus* (86d), where he is concerned with natural science, Plato emphasizes the physiological basis of character. He expressly considers sex distinctions irrelevant, while allowing for differences in physical strength between men and women and for women's child-bearing and child-rearing roles (*Republic* V).

Rationality is to be developed gradually, at first by means that are only semirational, or, rather, imitations or embodiments of rationality in physical media. The beginnings of education are in gymnastics and "music" (that is, music and poetry) and, even earlier, in regular movements during gestation and early infancy. These are meant to develop, on the lowest level, regularity and orderliness. Plato attached great importance to the education of pleasure. A state is unified when its citizens take pleasure in the same things, and children are to be accustomed to enjoy right pleasures (*Republic* V 462b, *Laws* II 653a). This semirationality will form the substrate of good habits and right opinions on which later and higher education will act as the clarification of emotions, bringing eventually to the understanding of the reason why they are good and right.

The main vehicle for the instillation of right opinions is poetry (including mythological poetry and drama)—that is, literature in its various forms. This is the source of both Plato's emphasis on education through poetry and his violent attacks on poetry and the poets (*Republic* II–III, X). Poetry and drama put forward views on God or the gods and on human affairs, setting up models for imitation and identification. These models are flawed in at least two respects, morally and epistemologically. Myths about gods are not true in the obvious sense that they do not give us an adequate representation of divinity. Such a representation would amount, in fact, to a philosophical treatment of the divine attributes of unity, truthfulness, and goodness. The ultimate goal of human life is the imitation of God, so far as humanly possible. But an abstract conception of divinity could hardly serve as a model for imitation, insofar as such attributes are incomprehensible to the majority, and it is not immediately clear how human virtues relate to it. Myths about heroes and demigods are not true in a literal sense, but they fulfill an important educational function in providing larger-than-life characters presented (or tacitly accepted) as ideals for direct emulation. But even a cursory inspection of such myths will show that most of their heroes are not fit for the role.

Stories about men pose a different problem. These stories, in the form of epic poems and tragedies (the novel does not emerge as a literary genre until Hellenistic times), deal with men's actions and their appraisal of themselves as happy and successful or unhappy and unsuccessful in the wake of their actions. Plato thinks most such stories are false, and as such improper from an educational point of view, not because they did not happen or could not have happened (some of them did happen), but insofar as they put forth an immanent moral point-of-view: In them, one's actions are evaluated as good or bad in their own terms and according to their empirical consequences. For Plato, however, this is unacceptable: No description or evaluation of the material world in its own terms can be adequate. Moral criteria, like the criteria of reality, cannot be immanent. One should judge one's life by nonempirical, transcendent standards, and it is by them that one rightfully considers oneself happy or unhappy. The representation in words or on stage of the moral quality of an action is doubly deficient: It is necessarily a selective (hence truncated and biased) representation of the moral quality of an empirical action, which is in itself a particular (hence inadequate) materialization of the moral idea in question.

Poetry, like music and gymnastics (and like rhetoric—that is, pseudo-argumentative literature, with which Plato deals in the *Gorgias* and the *Phaedrus*), works through nonrational or semirational means. It achieves its psychological effect by aesthetic, rhetorical, emotional, or empathic means, in themselves irrelevant to the view presented. The outcome of the plot (in the case of tragedy) and, in general, the effect of the work on the soul of the hearer or spectator is not decided on the merits of the argument but by the emotional reaction it provokes. Poetry persuades by rhyme not by reason, and cannot thus lead to knowledge. All this apart from the psychological damage caused by the very act of imitation, in words and action, of unacceptable characters. Epic poetry, insofar as it has in it a narrative element, is somewhat better on this count: The narrative element secures some minimal measure of distancing between the performer (in this case the reciter) and the characters depicted.

Poetry, then, if it is to fulfill its educational purpose in the state, must be reformed (and so must music). On the above criteria, Plato found most epic and tragic poetry inadmissible, and he advocated its banishment from the ideal state. And yet, poetry (like gymnastics and music)—reformed along Platonic lines—is indispensable in early education. Moreover, Plato thought the great majority of people incapable of reaching full rationality, and for them literature in all its forms is to remain the main educational and moral influence. Plato's dialogues themselves are educational works aiming, through their literary aspects, at leading the soul from a nonphilosophical to a more philosophical state.

Although for Plato, as for Socrates, only philosophy and the philosophical life are to be truly valued, Plato did not totally dismiss popular, unphilosophical virtue—and in this he apparently differed from his master. Unphilosophical virtue is based on right opinion, and like right opinion it has pragmatic value: It allows social and political order. The ideal state, as delineated in the *Republic,* is based on true knowledge, and this knowledge is personified in the philosopher-king (not necessarily one only); the *Republic* explicitly envisages a community of philosophers who take turns in leading the state. In the later *Politicus* (or *Statesman*), Plato considers the actual possibility of such a philosopher-king. The true king, in his capacity as leader and educator, would be able to consider each particular case directly in the light of his knowledge without the mediation of laws, which are of necessity generalizations that cannot provide for every single case. He would do this out of genuine care for his subjects, as a good shepherd for his flock, not out of self-interest, like Thrasymachus' shepherd in *Republic* I 343. But the shepherd is not one of the flock; if there were such a Good Shepherd of the human flock, he would be divine, not human. Human societies must be strictly reared and governed by laws whose goodness is to be measured by the degree in which they resemble true knowledge. Once established, utmost care must be taken in changing them, lest any change be for the worse. The *Laws*, Plato's last work, is a comprehensive model of such legislation.

Citizens reared in such laws will be at least unphilosophically virtuous. But, insofar as their virtue is based on customs and opinion, it is intrinsically deficient, and forever in danger of being lost should circumstances change. Such an education has pragmatic and political value, but does not in itself lead to real virtue. Whether for the older Plato education can ever hope for more, is an open question.

Samuel Scolnicov

See also: AIMS OF EDUCATION; *Arete;* CIVIC EDUCATION; DISCIPLINE; EPISTEMOLOGY; ISOCRATES; NEOPLATONISM; *Paideia;* REASON AND RATIONALITY; SOCRATES; SOPHISTS; TEACHING AND LEARNING; TRUTH

Bibliography

Brisson, Luc. "Plato 1958–1975." *Lustrum* 20 (1977).

Brisson, Luc, and H. Ionnidi. "Plato 1980–1985." *Lustrum* 30 (1988).

Cherniss, Harold. "Plato 1950–1957." *Lustrum* 4–5 (1959–1960).

Friedlander, Paul. *Plato.* Translated by H. Meyerhoff. London: Routledge and Kegan Paul, 1958–1969.

Grube, G.M.A. *Plato's Thought.* London: Methuen, 1935; Paperback, Athlone Press, 1980.

Guthrie, W.K.C. *A History of Greek Philosophy,* vols. 4–5. Cambridge: Cambridge University Press, 1975–1978.

Jaeger, Werner. *Paideia: The Ideals of Greek Culture,* vols. 2–3. Translated by Gilbert Highet. Oxford: Oxford University Press, 1939–1945.

Marrou, H.I. *A History of Education in Antiquity,* chap. 6. Translated by G. Lamb. New York: Sheed and Ward, 1956.

Nettleship, R.L. *The Theory of Education in Plato's Republic.* Oxford: Oxford University Press, 1935.

Peters, R.S. "Was Plato Nearly Right about Education?" *Didaskalos* 5 (1975): 3–16.

Plato. *The Collected Dialogues of Plato.* Edited by E. Hamilton and H. Cairns. Princeton: Princeton University Press, 1963. (Separate dialogues are published in various translations by Penguin.)

Scolnicov, Samuel. *Plato's Metaphysics of Education.* London: Routledge, 1988.

Stenzel, Julius. *Platon der Erzieher.* Leipzig: F. Meiner, 1928.

Pleasure

Pleasure is a feeling we refer to in explaining and justifying action. To understand pleasure philosophically is to understand how feeling, explanation, and justification are systematically interlinked. Philosophical accounts of pleasure typically fail to meet this condition of adequacy. Accounts typically distort the picture of pleasure by overemphasizing either the felt aspect of pleasure or its explanatory-justificatory role. The ambiguity of the word *pleasure* contributes to this distortion. Many associate the word with the bodily sensations involved in sensory pleasure, but one may enjoy—get pleasure from—a variety of experiences and activities, such as the enjoyment of playing chess, in which the enjoyment need not involve any experience of bodily sensations at all.

We will begin by focusing on the explanatory-justificatory side of pleasure. We often refer to our desires to explain and justify our actions, and one way to accommodate pleasure's explanatory-justificatory role is to see pleasure as involving desire. Such a conception of pleasure seems clearly correct. When, for example, you eat bittersweet chocolate and enjoy the bittersweet taste, the explanation of your pleasure would seem, at least in part, to be that you are getting something you want. The obvious objection is that there are things we desire that we do not enjoy getting. When you are sitting in the dentist's chair, you are satisfying your desire to have dental work done, but you are not enjoying it. The difference between the cases of the dentist and the chocolate is that you desire dental work only as a means to an end, while you desire to taste the bittersweet taste for its own sake. This suggests that pleasure consists in satisfying a desire for something for its own sake.

This is a common suggestion. It is also an incorrect one, and seeing why reveals the true complexity of the explanatory-justificatory side of the concept of pleasure. Consider this example. Suppose you have never been deep-sea fishing and that you desire to go for its own sake. But imagine that you find the entire experience of deep-sea fishing distasteful. You get seasick; you are disgusted by the crowded, noisy deck from which you must fish; you are repelled by the necessity of barehandedly catching the small, live fish used for bait, and are even more repelled by having to impale the living bait by the gills on your hook. Your desire to fish survives the shock of these experiences, and you continue to fish even though, as you admit, you are not enjoying it. You continue to fish because you hope you *will* get pleasure. Your desire to fish is waning. It persists, but it persists despite your experiences.

You do not get pleasure from deep-sea fishing because two crucial elements are missing. The first is that your activity of deep-sea fishing does not reinforce and sustain the desire to fish. Compare the chocolate example: When you eat the chocolate, the experience of the taste makes you want that experience. Reflection on the chocolate example also reveals the second missing element. When you taste the chocolate, that experience causes you to believe that you are tasting bittersweet chocolate. So: The experience causes you to want it, and causes you to believe that you are getting what you want. In contrast, your deep-sea fishing does not make you want it, and there is a clear sense in which you certainly do not believe that you are getting what you want. You formed your desire to go deep-sea fishing because you conceived of the activity as thrilling and exciting, and you do not believe that you are experiencing deep-sea fishing so conceived. Instead, you believe that you are seasick; that the crowded, noisy deck is disgusting; that catching live bait is repellent. These are not experiences you want.

Pleasure consists in a certain harmony between causation and satisfaction. An enjoyed experience or activity causes (or causally sustains) a desire that it also satisfies. The desire is the desire that the experience or activity be of a certain sort. The experience or activity ensures the satisfaction of this desire by causing one to believe that the experience or activity is of the desired sort. (More precisely, the experience or activity ensures that it will seem to one that one's desire is satisfied; the desire is really satisfied only if it is true that, as one believes, the experience or activity is of the relevant sort.) This picture of pleasure as a harmony between causation and satisfaction illuminates the explanatory-justificatory role of pleasure, since we often explain and justify our actions by appeal to beliefs and desires.

But what about pleasure as a feeling? In explaining pleasure as a complex of desire and belief linked by causation, we seem to have left out the feeling. To leave out the feeling is not only to ignore the sensory side of pleasure, it is also to fail to adequately account for its explanatory-justificatory side. After all, the feeling is what we are aiming for when we pursue pleasure; it is the prospect of the feeling to which we appeal to explain and justify our actions. The answer to this objection is that it presupposes far too sharp a distinction between the sensory, on the one hand, and the cognitive and affective, on the other. Imagine tasting the bittersweet chocolate. When the taste makes you want the experience, the sensory and the affective are mixed together in the state of "experiencing/desiring the taste." The experience and the desire arise together in a single state of "experiencing/desiring," a state with both sensory and affective aspects. The same is true for belief: When you taste the bittersweet chocolate, the experience of the bittersweet taste and the belief that the taste is bittersweet are mixed together in the state of "experiencing/believing" that the taste is bittersweet. Indeed, the most accurate picture of pleasure represents it as a state in which experience, belief, and desire are all intermixed.

It is this mixed state that we seek when we seek pleasure. That state is "the feeling of pleasure." A life without such feeling would be an empty and unbearable one. The feeling of pleasure so conceived clearly plays a role in the explanation and justification of our actions. But it is not the only consideration that plays such a role. We also, for example, appeal to virtue, duty, self-fulfillment, and happiness to explain and justify action. Pleasure is just one explanatory-justificatory element among many.

Richard Warner

See also HAPPINESS

Bibliography
Gosling, J.C.B. *Pleasure and Desire*. Oxford: Oxford University Press, 1969.
———, and C.C.W. Taylor. *The Greeks on Pleasure*. Oxford: Oxford University Press, 1982.

MacIntyre, Alasdair. "Pleasure as a Reason for Action." In *Against the Self-Images of the Age*. New York: Schocken Books, 1971.

Ryle, Gilbert. "Pleasure." In *Proceedings of the Aristotelian Society, Supplement*. London: Harrison, 1954.

Warner, Richard. "Enjoyment." *Philosophical Review* 40 (1980): 507–26.

———. *Freedom, Enjoyment, and Happiness*. Ithaca, N.Y.: Cornell University Press, 1980.

Pluralism

The term *pluralism* (from Latin *plus, pluris*: "more") is used descriptively to indicate a diversity as a fact, normatively to signal a value commitment to articulated diversity as a means or as an end, or philosophically and theoretically to provide an account by appealing to a diversity of principles or basic realities and their interaction.

Pluralism in philosophy may argue for a plurality of ultimate principles or basic kinds of elements or substances, such as mind and matter for Rene Descartes (1596–1650). Alternatively, it may assert a plurality of things existing in their own right (whether all of the same kind or not). By contrast, monism may deny either or both of these views. An early monist was Parmenides (born c. 540 B.C.), for whom the apparent diversity of reality constituted only one thing.

Pluralism in the political sphere is concerned with promoting individual liberty and rights, and opposing monolithic state power. Many argue that for this, the individual needs to be integrated in a community, and different group interests must be recognized. They also stress the importance of relatively autonomous and cross-cutting economic, political, and other organizations, such as workers' associations, political parties, and religious groups, as well as the separation of the legislative, executive, and judicial powers of the state.

J.S. Furnivall (1957) has used the term *plural society* to refer to a particular form of pluralist social organization. This was the European colony consisting of many "racial" groups, each with "its own religion, . . . culture and language" (304). It was a radically segmented society in which individuals became isolated and atomized, the whole being held together only by the economic motive and the rule of the colonial power. It lacked a common cultural tradition and a common "social will," individuals from different groups meeting only in the marketplace to buy and sell. Furthermore, the social will and the particular cultural tradition within each of the "racial" and cultural sectors had been undermined. Economic forces were supreme, the society having been transformed "from a social organism into a business concern" (306), and tensions having arisen between sectors or groups and between individuals.

All societies are plural in a broader sense, insofar as they are articulated in various ways, into, for instance, the supraordinate and the subordinate, those with particular forms of knowledge and those without, old and young, male and female, employers and employees. Important dimensions by which societies are articulated include "race," ethnicity, and culture. "Race" is a social construction whereby phenotypical features are accorded particular social significance. Ethnicity, too, is constructed: It is a sense of peoplehood, or an attributed peoplehood. "Race" or culture may be the "basis" of this construction, and one can speak of "racial," ethnic, or cultural pluralism. "Cultural pluralism" or "multiculturalism" may describe the de facto occurrence of cultural diversity in a given society. They may also be used normatively to indicate that cultural diversity is positively valued and all cultures are equally respected.

Horace Kallen (1956) probably did most to promote the notion of cultural pluralism, linking it to pluralism in the philosophical and political sense. Culture refers to everything that the group creates or elaborates and passes on as part of its "heritage." As Kallen says, "A group's culture embraces the total economy of their life together" (44). At its core is the group's interrelated cognitive, normative, and linguistic systems, the group's "worldview," including centrally its image of itself in the world.

Philosophically, Kallen rejects both the monism of Benedict Spinoza (1632–1677), according to which there is but one infinite substance, of which all else is but modes or affects, and the monadism of Gottfried Leibniz (1646–1716), for whom there is a plurality of absolutes, each complete in itself. Instead, for Kallen there is a plurality of open, interdependent beings, human individuals, groups, and societies. Thus diversity is inescapable in social life. Every individual is unique. Each culture is living and constantly changing, and every society manifests some degree of cultural diversity. This diversity contains the seeds of conflict. But equally, the possibility for constructive cross-cultural interaction, communication, and enrichment is inbuilt. For Kallen, cultural pluralism means unity in diversity, the orchestration of diversity. The "road to peace is the road of cultural parity" (45), the road of democracy.

The unity of the diverse cultures is necessarily of the nature of a project, a becoming, a working toward, and so is always a pluralistic and changing unity. People interrelate without merging their identities, and sustain their identities by communication rather than segregation. Group "boundaries are . . . artifacts" (52), and people can widen, multiply, or even change their allegiances. By widening one's culture and one's awareness of other values, one can become "a citizen of the world" (53) without losing one's own citizenship.

Kallen perhaps overstates individual freedom and underestimates the force of history and of structural factors, in particular the unequal distribution of power in society. This does not, however, gainsay the basic reality of cultural diversity and interdependence, and the need for mutual openness and respect facilitating constructive interaction.

The objection of cultural relativism has been brought against Kallen. However, cultural pluralism does not imply a radical relativism, for all cultures involve notions of error, truth, and rightness. All cultures are equivalent systems responding to the common basic realities and imperatives of human life, albeit in differing circumstances. Cultural pluralism is relational rather than relativist, holding that individuals and groups are interdependent and best served if they respect each other's cultures, rights, and freedom.

Milton Gordon (1964) has distinguished structural pluralism from cultural pluralism, structural pluralism referring, not to the presence of several cultures, but to the existence in one society of several separate, total sets of crystallized or patterned social relationships. Gordon equates structural pluralism with the existence of several separate groups or communities each with its own network of institutions or organizations permitting "primary group relations to be confined within its borders throughout the life cycle" (39). Primary, in contrast to secondary, group relations are "personal, informal, intimate, and usually face-to-face," involving "the entire personality, not just a segmentalized part of it" (31). Gordon argues

that structural pluralism is socially dysfunctional or conflictual. Some, such as Brian M. Bullivant (1981), also argue that cultural pluralism is inherently conflictual and unstable: The greater the diversity the greater the threat to the integration and viability of the society.

However, in neither case does the threat come from segmentation or diversity as such: The integration of complex systems is a function, not of uniformity or indivisibility, but of the interdependence of the component parts, and it requires mutuality and openness (see Figueroa). Conflict arises rather from such factors as the extent to which the policies, practices, and worldview of each sector, especially the more powerful ones, are closed, distorting, or subordinating; the extent of social inequality and restricted freedom; and the lack of a genuinely democratic system in which the rights of all are respected, and all participate in decision-making about, not only private, but also public matters.

Peter Figueroa

See also DEMOCRACY; EQUALITY; MULTICULTURALISM; RACE AND RACISM; TOLERATION

Bibliography

Bullivant, Brian M. *The Pluralist Dilemma in Education: Six Case Studies.* Sydney, Australia: George Allen and Unwin, 1981.

Figueroa, Peter. *Education and the Social Construction of "Race."* London: Routledge, 1991.

Furnivall, J.S. *Colonial Policy and Practice: A Comparative Study of Burma and Netherlands India.* London: Cambridge University Press, 1948, 1957.

Gordon, Milton M. *Assimilation in American Life: The Role of Race, Religion, and National Origin.* New York: Oxford University Press, 1964.

Kallen, Horace M. *Cultural Pluralism and the American Idea: An Essay in Social Philosophy.* Philadelphia: University of Pennsylvania Press, 1956.

Positivism

Positivism began as a hopeful attempt to extend a scientific approach to social and philosophical problems. It ended as a "generalized term of abuse" (Phillips: 95). Tracing this rise and fall may help provide more specific understanding of the contributions and deficiencies of the movement and the lessons that can be drawn from them.

Comtean Positivism

The French philosopher Auguste Comte (1798–1857) is usually taken to be the founder of positivism. In the nineteenth century, Comte advocated the application of a scientific approach to social phenomena, coining the term *sociology* to refer to the new science of society modeled after Newtonian physics. Comte's view of a properly scientific or "positive" approach to knowledge (that is, one "founded on well-established facts") was as follows:

> We have no knowledge of anything but Phaenomena; and our knowledge of phaenomena is relative, not absolute. We know not the essence, nor the real mode of production, of any fact, but only its relations to other facts in the way of succession or similitude. These relations are constant; this is, always the same in the same circumstances. The constant resemblances which link phaenomena together, and the constant sequences which unite them as antecedent and consequent, are termed their laws. The laws of phaenomena are all we know respecting them. Their essential nature, and their ultimate causes, either efficient or final, are unknown and inscrutable to us (Mill: 6.).

This approach to knowledge was modeled on natural science and directed against traditional religious claims of understanding the essential or ultimate nature of things. Comte viewed a "theological" stage of understanding as the most primitive of three stages through which all fields of knowledge advance. In the theological stage, events are explained in terms of the will of spirits or gods or other beings. Animists who see a volcano as an expression of the Spirit of the Mountain, or monotheists who see it as God's will, adopt such explanations. So do those who see a person's behavior as caused by their inner desires or intentions. In the second, "metaphysical" stage, explanation is couched in terms of abstractions that are taken as real things, such as "essences, quiddities, virtues residing in things" (Mill: 16). Explaining performance on school-like tasks as caused by "intelligence," or creative behavior as caused by "creativity," are modern examples. Each simply names the pattern of behavior and then attributes its cause to the named "thing."

For Comte, both theological and metaphysical explanations are inevitably superseded by a third, "positive" stage, in which explanation is couched in terms of scientific laws stating relationships between prior and posterior conditions. Evolution through these stages was thought to take place first in those fields that are most general, simple, and independent, such as astronomy, physics, and chemistry, and, building on those, to gradually work up to the more special, complicated, and dependent fields such as physiology (biology) and social physics (sociology). (Mathematics was put at the head of the list as a sort of special case.) Later in his life Comte gathered a cult of followers dedicated to his beliefs and advocated a society based on a religious belief in positivism, with moral regulation provided by a positivistic philosophical elite (Collins and Makowsky: 26–31).

Logical Positivism

Logical positivism flourished in the early decades in between the two World Wars. It is usually associated with the Vienna Circle, a group of scientists, mathematicians, philosophers, and social scientists, including Moritz Schlick, Otto Neurath, Herbert Feigl, and Rudolf Carnap, many of whom later fled Europe. Logical positivism married modern logic (as developed by Frege and Russell) to Machian empiricism. The result was an approach that placed more emphasis on the language of formal logic than had Comte, but which retained the emphasis on developing testable scientific laws based on observable fact.

Logical positivism, like Comte's earlier positivism, was antimetaphysical. It aimed at eliminating metaphysical arguments and dogma, such as those associated with Continental idealism, as so much meaningless verbiage. As Michael Scriven put it:

> The Vienna Circle or *Weiner Kreis* was a band of cutthroats that went after the fat burghers of Continental metaphysics who had become intolerably inbred and pompously verbose. The *kris* is a Malaysian knife, and the *Weiner Kreis* employed a kind of Occam's Razor called the Verifiability Principle. It performed a tracheotomy that made it possible for philosophy to breathe again (Quoted in Phillips: 101).

The verifiability principle suggested that the meaning of a proposition is the set of experiences that are equivalent to the proposition's being true. Given this conception of meaning, any proposition that is not empirically verified by the expected set of experiences is literally meaningless. In essence, the principle says, "If you cannot show how to test the truth of a statement by seeing if it is verified by an expected set of experiences, then it is just a lot of hot air." The logical positivists also tended to assume that there are basic experiences or simple atomic facts to which appeal could be made in cases of disagreement. These two elements, the need for (potentially) observable verification for a statement to be meaningful, and the givenness of basic facts or observations, constituted the core of logical positivism. B.F. Skinner's behaviorism furnishes a good example of an educational approach heavily influenced by this approach. His arguments against "inner" mental and neural causes are virtually identical to the logical positivist's arguments against metaphysical explanations (Skinner: 27–31).

Neither of the core elements of logical positivism has fared well in subsequent debate. The verifiability principle succumbed to the limitations of induction: Because the next observation may always be the exception to the rule, no number of observations can ever verify a rule as "really" true. As Popper pointed out, logically speaking, statements may only be disproven by evidence, never proven. Even this "naive falsificationist" conclusion was softened by Lakatos, who argued that, strictly speaking, theories cannot even be disproven, since they or the dissonant facts can always be reinterpreted to remove apparent contradictions. "Sophisticated falsificationism" suggests that "theoretical programs" be evaluated in terms of their relative success in extending their theoretical and explanatory reach compared with competing programs. The verifiability criterion has, thus, been found to be much too strong to hold up for even the best-tested scientific beliefs.

Belief in atomic facts or observation statements also succumbed, like verificationism, when it was argued that such apparently firm ground as very simple and particular statements of fact depends on a wealth of other beliefs and background assumptions that are always open to challenge. Maybe the electron microscope one is looking through is not working properly? Or perhaps it behaves differently than it is

thought to? Rather than being considered as given and independent of the theory being tested, facts have come to be understood as "theory laden." The attempt to retreat to simple perceptions, rather than observation statements, such as by saying, "That's just the way I see it," was also rejected, since facts then become merely subjective, which is just what the logical positivists were trying to avoid.

Logical positivism's standards of meaning, modeled on a particular understanding of natural science, were so stringent that they were in danger of defining science itself as meaningless. If scientific theories are not logically verifiable, as it appeared they were not according to the logical positivist's conception of verification, then they are meaningless. And, if science has to appeal to raw perceptions as its evidential base, then the conclusion seems to be that science is merely subjective. The same reasoning undermined logical positivism itself, since its own assertions were apparently not verifiable. Were they, too, merely metaphysical and, thus, meaningless? While this is precisely what the earlier Ludwig Wittgenstein (1961) concluded, it was not what the logical positivists wanted to hear. Like the Shakers (who banned sex), the logical positivists eliminated themselves as a movement by trying too hard to eliminate the evils they opposed.

Vulgar Positivism

Although positivism was rejected in philosophical circles, in a broader sense Comte's dream of a religion of science came true. The influence of a broader movement of logical empiricism, or the "positivistic temper," grew in the social sciences, in education, and elsewhere in U.S. society, until at least some time in the late 1960s or 1970s. During this period the social sciences attempted to become much more rigorous and scientific, using mathematical models, computer simulations, and more complex methods of data analysis. The social sciences aped physics (as understood from a distance), and educational research aped the social sciences in adopting increasingly rigorous methodological standards. Educational and other governmental agencies adopted evaluation standards at least loosely based on positivistic assumptions about verifiability and appeal to atomic facts.

The political reaction to these trends seems to have been based on the fact that emphasis on narrow technical procedures and interpretation-free facts became ways of protecting existing authority, giving its conclusions the legitimacy of "science." Focusing on narrow technical issues and on rigorously measurable facts became a way of invalidating broader questions about aims and eliminating more subtle observations or differences in interpretive assumptions. While positivism began in opposition to established religious dogma, it ended up (in its watered-down, widely institutionalized form) as a way of eliminating questions that authorities might find uncomfortable. This is undoubtedly why positivism has become a "generalized term of abuse."

Conclusions

Although positivism has been rejected as a philosophy of science, its emphasis on logical rigor and empirical testing remains valuable. So too does its skeptical stance with respect to explanations that appeal to the intentions of inner agents (which must, presumably, require other inner agents to explain their behavior) or to dormitive explanations that simply rename a pattern of behavior and then suggest that the named thing is an inner cause of the behavior. Being hard nosed and skeptical are valuable qualities that should clearly not be rejected along with positivism. Rejection of positivism also does not imply that science (natural or social) should be rejected, only that a particularly rigid understanding of science has failed.

The larger lesson to be drawn from the rise and fall of positivism may be that it is all too easy to become what you hate. Like so many apparently successful movements, positivism began in opposition to dogma and ended as dogma itself. This lesson is interesting because it applies to antipositivists as well. Those who oppose a scientific approach to social affairs, such as by arguing that generalization is impossible with respect to social phenomena, are unwittingly adopting a verificationist view of generalization very much like that of the positivists. Thus, those who adamantly oppose everything positivism stood for may be in danger of repeating some of the most objectionable "errors" of the positivists themselves.

Eric Bredo

See also BEHAVIORISM; MEANING; SCIENCE, PHILOSOPHY OF; SCIENTISM; SOCIOLOGY

Bibliography

Collins, R., and M. Makowsky. *The Discovery of Society.* New York: Random House, 1972.

Comte, A. *The Positive Philosophy.* New York: AMS Press, 1974.

Lakatos, I., and Al Musgrave. *Criticism and the Growth of Knowledge.* Cambridge: Cambridge University Press, 1970.

Mill, J.S. *Auguste Comte and Positivism.* Ann Arbor: University of Michigan Press, 1961.

Phillips, D.C. *The Social Scientists Bestiary: A Guide to Fabled Threats to, and Defenses of, Naturalistic Social Science.* Oxford: Pergamon Press, 1992.

Popper, K.R. *The Logic of Scientific Discovery.* New York: Basic Books, 1959.

Skinner, B.F. *Science and Human Behavior.* New York: Free Press, 1953.

Wittgenstein, L. *Tractatus Logico-Philosophicus.* London: Routledge and Kegan Paul, 1961.

Possibility

Possibility is a central and distinguishing feature of utopian critiques of education. Distinct from those paralyzing forms of critique that posit educators as dupes and schools as inevitable sites of domestication, theorists of possibility look forward to the time when schools can become places of hope, support, and transformation. From the vision of education of Mary Wollstonecraft (1759–1797), which would advance the struggle for women's rights, and the call for schooling to serve the needs and aspirations of New World Africans by W.E.B. DuBois (1868–1963), to George Counts's hope that schools might indeed build a new social order, and Maxine Greene's assertion that schools are the most likely places where (and teachers the most likely people with whom) children come to experience the dialectic of freedom, possibility is that which informs the work of progressive educators and critics in universities, in schools both rural and urban, in child-care centers, in auto shops, in advanced English and remedial mathematics classes, in laboratories, in studios, and in innumerable other public spaces where people come together and consider what life together might be like.

Current interest in possibility as a transformative element in educational theorizing is perhaps most evident in a growing body of literature identified under the rubric of critical pedagogy. In the tradition of John Dewey (1859–1952) and George Counts, critical educational theorists seek to advance the project of social democracy through works in schools. As Henry Giroux puts it:

> A revitalized discourse of democracy should not be based exclusively on a language of critique, one that, for instance, limits its focus on the schools to the elimination of relations of subordination and inequality. This is an important political concern, but in both theoretical and political terms it is woefully incomplete. As part of a radical political project, the discourse of democracy also needs a language of possibility, one that combines a strategy of opposition with a strategy for construction of a new social order. (31)

An integral part of such a critique of schooling is a commitment to explore visions of education that would enhance the possibility of human freedom and expand the range of social forms that encourage and make possible the realization of a variety of differentiated human capacities. Student empowerment, therefore, becomes a central concern of any critique committed to a project of possibility. This necessarily entails concerted efforts to make student experience the focus of pedagogy. To participate in discussions, debates, and struggles over the establishment of a just and democratic social order, students, in this view, need to be provided with opportunities to explore how the sense they make of their own experiences enables or disables their ability to participate in control of their lives, to analyze social contradictions, and to discuss democracy as a means to social justice rather than an end in itself (Shannon: 157). In other words, the practice of a critical pedagogy, aimed at cultivating a commitment to possibility, is one that enables students to understand their participation in the production of knowledge, culture, and society more fully.

Yet what is implicit in this theory of hope too often remains unrealized in practice. As a reminder to those who become overly enamored of the language of possibility, Roger Simon issues this clarion call:

> The idiom of possibility stands empty. Accused of meaningless rhetoric, it can only be rescued from the dismissal of convention and cynicism by developing its substance, sketching both its form and therefore its limits. This is not a task to be completed by one person. As I attempt to clarify for my-

self the question of what might be an adequate notion of education as a moral practice, I am at the same time seeking to join with others in what must be a collective and democratic venture (13).

Finally, as Maxine Greene reminds us, any such venture requires "a consciousness of the normative as well as the possible: of what ought to be, from a moral and ethical point of view, and what is in the making, what might be in an always open world" (xi).

Donald Dippo
Esther Fine

See also CRITICAL THEORY; DEWEY; PHILOSOPHY AND LITERATURE; RECONSTRUCTIONISM, SOCIAL

Bibliography

Giroux, Henry. *Schooling and the Struggle for Public Life: Critical Pedagogy in the Modern Age.* Minneapolis: University of Minnesota Press, 1989.

Greene, Maxine. *The Dialectic of Freedom.* New York: Teachers College Press, 1988.

Shannon, Patrick. *The Struggle to Continue.* Portsmouth, N.H.: Heinemann, 1990.

Simon, Roger. *Teaching against the Grain: Texts for a Pedagogy of Possibility.* Toronto: OISE Press, 1992.

Practical Wisdom

The intellectual insight and judgment held very widely in classical thought to be a necessary condition for true *arete,* or goodness. It was called *phronesis* by the Greeks, a term deriving from *phrenes,* or "midriff," which was the part of the body believed to be the seat of thinking. Called *prudentia* in Latin, *phronesis* is most commonly translated into English as "practical wisdom" or "prudence," but also as "sound judgment." The notion that there is an intellectual element of this kind in goodness is somewhat at odds with modern intuitions, but quite understandable in light of the differences between the modern concept of moral goodness or virtue and *arete,* which is translated most frequently, though somewhat misleadingly, as "virtue." The term *arete* embraces not only good intentions or desires, but rather the totality of personal attributes required for success in pursuing the proper ends of action: a discerning and resourceful intellect having the right ends in view. Practical wisdom is part of what enables a person to do, and not merely wish or attempt, good deeds, and is thus a part of complete goodness or virtue as the Greeks understood it.

As the virtue of judging and choosing well in disparate circumstances, and in matters both private and public, practical wisdom was held by the time of Plato (c. 427–347 B.C.) to be not only one of the four "cardinal" virtues, along with justice, courage, and temperance, but also a vital ingredient in these other three. It was understood to entail not only excellence in practical reasoning, but also knowledge of the proper ends of action, and a sensitivity and timely responsiveness to the particulars of the situation at hand and to the full range of considerations relevant to it. These considerations were understood within the tradition of Socrates (c. 470–399 B.C.) to include not only those relevant to the actor's self-interest, but also those made relevant by the virtues of self-restraint. Conceived as sound judgment in statesmanship and in the conduct of one's life, practical wisdom was thought to require a grasp of particulars that only experience can provide; it also became a leading ideal of the higher education that emerged in the fifth and fourth centuries B.C. in Athens.

So described, the concept of practical wisdom presupposes that living well and happily requires living in accordance with the dictates of reason rightly employed, and also that among the dictates of reason are the requirements of justice and virtue generally. The convergence implied by these grounding assumptions, between living in accordance with right reason, living well, living happily, and living virtuously, is implicit in the Greek concept of "sound" judgment. Greek philosophy in the Socratic tradition not only accepted this convergence and defended it through theories of moral knowledge and arguments for the importance of reason to human well-being, but also aimed in its teaching to promote sound practical judgment in both politics and private life.

This conception of sound judgment was incorporated into the Christian tradition through the development of a highly detailed and deeply Aristotelian account of *prudentia* by St. Thomas Aquinas (1225–1274). In modern philosophy, however, the belief in the convergence of reason, morality, and happiness weakened, and the concept of virtue itself became narrower and lost its central place in moral thought and practice. The agenda of moral philosophy also underwent profound changes: Greek moral philosophy had been focused on the nature of the best or most desirable life for a human being, and was intended as a guide to conduct, but in the modern era moral philosophy became more narrowly preoccupied with foundational issues. The work of Immanuel Kant (1724–1804) provides a good illustration of this. Two ambitions that guided Kant's project were the development of the very Platonic idea of Jean-Jacques Rousseau (1712–1778) that one is free or autonomous only through moral law, and the overturning of the "Newtonian" account of human nature of David Hume (1711–1776), which had demoted reason from the dominant position assigned it by the Greeks. Kant thus provided himself with a suitable, if controversial, basis on which to preserve the concept of practical wisdom. Yet he concerned himself with the foundations of moral judgment in a way that almost entirely excluded any concern with the role of judgments about what one is to actually do in concrete circumstances. Thus, while it would be incorrect to say that the developments of the modern era have made the concept of practical wisdom irremediably obsolete, it is nevertheless true that the term *practical wisdom* has fallen into disuse. *Prudence,* though still used, has retained its original sense only among theologians.

The development of theoretical accounts of practical wisdom began with the Sophist Protagoras (c. 490–c. 421 B.C.), who took virtue to be a well-developed capacity of practical reasoning, and with Socrates. As the latter is presented in the early dialogues of Plato, he began with the argument that knowledge of good and evil is necessary for virtue, since without it one would not choose what is beneficial and fine. He added to this the argument that such knowledge is also sufficient for virtue, since one could not know what is beneficial and choose what is not, without having inconsistent beliefs about the relevant objects of choice. Thus, he concluded that each of the virtues is a form of knowledge, analogous to a craftsman's, of how to use well, in the pursuit of happiness, the ordinary goods, such as wealth and strength, that are available to one. He identified this knowledge as a knowledge of good and evil, and suggested that it is not only necessary but sufficient for happiness, yielding the convergence of virtue, happiness, and intelligent living on which the notion of practical wisdom rests.

Accepting the basic outlines of this position, Plato addressed himself to the problems of moral epistemology and psychology inherent in it, and in doing so developed a view in which practical and theoretical wisdom coincide in the intellectual apprehension of the transcendent "Form" of goodness. In the *Republic,* he identified wisdom with good counsel, and both of these with knowledge, on the grounds that those who counsel well are enabled to do so through knowledge. In the management of the city this can be nothing other than knowledge of the good of the *polis,* which cannot be had, he insisted, without knowledge of goodness itself.

Plato held in both the *Republic* and the *Laws* a developmental theory of rationality, according to which the ascent, which is proper to human nature, from a preoccupation with the desires of appetite, to a desire for honor, and finally to a desire for knowledge is very much subject to fortune in one's natural endowment and the quality of the nurture, training, and education one receives. Because he believed that the desires and corresponding part of the psyche one is dominated by shape one's perception of what is good, he held that those who have character types dominated by desires for things that fall short of a person's highest good (that is, by desires of the appetitive and spirited parts of the psyche, rather than the rational) will lack virtue and be unable to grasp what is best and most conducive to happiness. Those in whom reason and rational desire for what is most worthy of choice have been successfully cultivated will be able to examine their ends rationally and recognize the goodness of those ends. They will enjoy rational self-control, a freedom to effectively pursue what is most pleasant, and a superior capacity to live well grounded in a wide view of the proper place of their various desires in a good life. They will have at least a prospect of attaining practical wisdom, through experience and higher education, whereas those who have not acquired virtue will be capable of no more than a narrow, instrumental form of practical reasoning.

Aristotle (384–322 B.C.) adopted Plato's view of the prerequisites for the development of virtue and reason, and also his view that the acquisition of habits or virtue is a prerequisite for the wider view of one's ends and the comprehension of what is good, which are required for practical wisdom. He rejected Plato's theory of forms, however, and developed, on a more common-sensical metaphysical and epistemological basis, the view of human nature associated with Plato's developmental theory of rea-

son. In doing that, he provided himself with one part of an alternative to Plato's theory of moral knowledge, another important element of which was a view of moral insight and judgment in which the well-rounded grasp of the salient particulars of a situation is fundamental. In this respect, he may be seen as attempting to meet the challenge, posed by Parmenides (c. 515–c. 450 B.C.)—to show how there can be knowledge when the objects of ordinary experience appear different from different perspectives—by holding that wisdom consists in a comprehension broadened by an appreciation of as many of those perspectives as possible. It was not, as Plato held, a knowledge of a reality beyond appearance that is the same through and through, however one looks at it.

With this innovation, Aristotle elevated the role of perception, and made better sense than Plato did of the idea that practical wisdom is acquired gradually through experience and acquaintance with good models. The acquisition of practical wisdom does not depend for him, as it did for Plato, on any one discrete act of intellectual apprehension, but rather on a process of filling in the gaps in one's moral and practical insight, which takes place largely through communing with virtuous and trusted friends who can enable one to see where those gaps are. In Aristotle's view, habituated virtue becomes full virtue not only with the recognition and acceptance of the goodness of the ends that one already pursues, assuming one was fortunate in birth, nurture, and training; but through an accretion of moral insight and responsiveness, which can take place simultaneously with the refinement of one's habits once a foundation has been laid by one's early training.

This idea, that sound judgment is grounded in the synthesis of individually incomplete perspectives, also led Aristotle to arguments for the superior wisdom of collective decision-making. Because "democracy" meant something different for him than what it does for us, he did not describe these as arguments for democracy, though we have good reason to.

In the twentieth century we find something close to Aristotle's conception of practical wisdom or practical intelligence (*nous praktikos*), applied especially to the collective wisdom of a democratic community, in the concepts of "intelligence," "social intelligence," and "democracy" of John Dewey (1859–1952). Dewey described intelligence as involving a good estimation of the possibilities in a situation, an effective adaptation of means to ends, a conscious choice of ends themselves, and generally an exercise of practical judgment in the face of uncertainty, which he contrasted with a quest for certainty through reason. He rejected Aristotle's moral absolutism, but shared and developed his view that communication is an essential remedy to the deficiencies of individual intelligence.

More recently, a renewed interest in the Aristotelian concept of practical reasoning was stimulated in the late 1950s and 1960s by the work of G.E.M. Anscombe and G.H. von Wright, and it found its way into contemporary philosophy of education through the work of Thomas Green and Joseph Schwab. In "Teacher Competence as Practical Rationality," Green outlined a conception of teacher competence in instruction as a form of "wisdom," or excellence in diagnosing and improving the premises of students' practical reasoning. Schwab, in "The Practical: A Language for Curriculum," proposed reconceiving the field of curriculum as a practical discipline as opposed to a theoretical one, and he identified the method of "the practical" as deliberation aimed at choosing the best action in a concrete situation. Both works have exercised a continuing influence, and the extraordinary renaissance in Aristotelian scholarship in the years since their publication offers hope for a sustained recovery and reassessment of the idea of practical wisdom.

Randall R. Curren

See also *Arete;* ARISTOTLE; DEWEY; ETHICS AND MORALITY; PLATO; SOCRATES

Bibliography

Aristotle. *Nicomachean Ethics, Politics*. In *Complete Works of Aristotle*. Edited by J. Barnes. 2 vols. Princeton: Princeton University Press, 1984.

Bodeus, Richard. *The Political Dimensions of Aristotle's Ethics*. Translated by J.E. Garrett. Albany: State University of New York Press, 1993.

Dewey, John. *The Quest for Certainty*. In *The Later Works of John Dewey, 1925–1953,* vol. 4. Carbondale: Southern Illinois University Press, 1981–1991.

Green, Thomas F. "Teacher Competence as Practical Rationality." *Educational Theory* 26 (1976): 249–58.

Plato. *Laches, Philebus, Protagoras, Republic*. In *The Collected Dialogues of Plato*. Edited by E. Hamilton and H. Cairns. Princeton: Princeton University Press, 1963.

Schwab, Joseph J. "The Practical: A Language for Curriculum." *School Review* 78 (1969): 1–23.

Sherman, Nancy. *The Fabric of Character: Aristotle's Theory of Virtue*. Oxford: Oxford University Press, 1989.

Thomas Aquinas. *Introduction to St. Thomas Aquinas*. Edited by Anton C. Pegis. New York: Modern Library, 1948.

Pragmatism

The major classical American pragmatists are Charles Sanders Peirce (1839–1914), William James (1842–1910), John Dewey (1859–1952), George Herbert Mead (1863–1931), and C.I. Lewis (1883–1964). They evince vastly differing degrees of interest in the philosophy of education. One cannot really glean a philosophy of education through the writings of Lewis or Peirce; James and Mead have much to say on educational theory, providing the material for a solid pragmatic philosophy of education. Dewey is by far the most prolific and best recognized in this area. The collective corpus of the writings of these pragmatists, however, together provide a common pragmatic vision of the nature and role of education, and it can be said in a sense that each of the pragmatists, through his particular degree of interest in education, speaks in a general way for all. The pragmatic vision of education to be presented, then, is a general perspective that draws from and synthesizes the collective corpus of the writings of the above pragmatists.

That the pragmatists share a common vision of the nature and role of education is to be expected, for their views on education stem from a common vision of the nature of humans and their relation to the world in which they live. This common background must be briefly explored, for it provides the foundation for their common approach to philosophy of education. It provides, as well, a perspective for correcting certain pervasive misunderstandings concerning their approach.

Two dominant strains in pragmatism are its focus on activity and on scientific method. The human as "active agent" is used by pragmatism in two senses. First, it is actively used at the level of the use of knowledge to change society or the environment. This is a level frequently intended in pragmatism. Yet, this level, if erroneously taken as the sole sense of active agent, leads to the often-heard condemnation of pragmatism as overly concerned with action, as indicating an antitheoretical attitude that makes knowing only for the sake of doing. The second, and more technically important aspect of "active agent" indicates the manner in which humans know the world through the structures of the meanings they have created by their responses to their environment. Here the focus on the role of humans as active is not on what one should do with knowledge but on what knowledge is, on human activity or response as built into the very structure of meaningful awareness. However, in this appropriation, the goal-directed interactional element between humans and their environment, the first aspect of humans as active agent, is incorporated in the very heart of the internal structure of meaningful awareness. Knowledge can be actively used to change the world around us. But, even more fundamentally, knowledge, as well as the meanings that allow us to gain knowledge, are structured by possible purposive activity.

This understanding of the nature of knowledge relates directly to the pragmatic focus on science. The concern with the method of science is not just with the application of knowledge but also with the way knowledge is obtained. The focus of pragmatism on scientific method involves a recognition that theory and practical activity are interrelated. Knowledge is not contemplative or other-worldly, as opposed to a lesser realm of practice. Rather, meanings, beliefs, and knowledge incorporate an awareness of human activity and its consequences. In this way the temporal spread of human existence itself embodies the dynamics of experimental method. The stretch of experience is inherently experimental, incorporating the method of scientific inquiry in a broad sense. This experimental method has several stages.

The very first stage of scientific inquiry requires human creativity. We are not mere passive spectators gathering ready-made data, but rather we bring creative theories that enter into the very character and organization of the data grasped. Secondly, there is directed or goal-oriented activity dictated by the theory. The theory requires that certain activities be carried out, certain changes brought about in the data, to see if anticipated results occur. Finally, the test for truth is in terms of consequences. Does the theory work in guiding us through future experiences in a way anticipated by its claims? Truth is not something passively attained, either by the contemplation of absolutes or by the passive accumulation of data, but by activity shot through with the theory that guides it. And the theory itself is constituted by possible ways of acting toward the data and the anticipated consequences of such theory-laden activity. This role of purposive activity in thought and the resultant appeal to relevance and selective emphasis that must ultimately be justified by workability are key pragmatic tenets.

The relationship between pragmatism and practice and pragmatism and science indicates that reason is not sacrificed to practice, but rather rationality is "brought down to earth" and encompasses the entire human being as active agent engrossed in the world. Humans are not passive spectators of the world around them but actively interact with it in the very process of coming to understand it. In focusing on scientific method as the lived experimental activity of the scientist, pragmatism avoids the reductionism of nature that results from past philosophies that have absolutized the contents of science. Pragmatism arose in part as a reaction against the "modern world view" Cartesian understanding of the nature of science and of the scientific object. This understanding resulted from the general fact that the method of gaining knowledge that was the backbone of the emergence of modern science was confounded with the content of the first "lasting" modern scientific view—the Newtonian mechanistic universe. Such a confusion, based largely on the presuppositions of a spectator theory of knowledge, or knowledge as a passive accumulation of facts, led to a naively realistic philosophic interpretation of scientific content. This resulted in a quantitatively characterized universe and in either dualistic causal accounts of knowledge in terms of correlations between mental contents and material objects or reductionist causal accounts in terms of stimulus-response. Mind is not something set apart from nature. Nor does pragmatism, in rejecting all dualisms, hold that the human can be reduced to the contents of science, with the behavioristic model of stimulus-response in one of its several versions to which this ultimately leads.

Accordingly, mind, thinking, and selfhood are not aspects of some mental substance. Neither, however, are they reducible to the material functioning of the brain and the nervous system.

Mind, thinking, and selfhood are emergent levels of activity of organisms within nature. Meaning emerges in the interactions among conscious organisms, in the adjustments and coordinations needed for cooperative action in the social context. Mental processes are part of a process that is going on between organism and environment, and language itself is possible because of the communicative interactions on which the existence of meaning is based. In communicative interaction, individuals take the perspective of the other in the development of their conduct, and there thus develops the common content that provides community of meaning. In this way there emerges not just consciousness but self-consciousness.

To have a self is to have a particular type of ability, the ability to be aware of one's behavior as part of the social process of adjustment, to be aware of oneself as an acting agent within the context of other acting agents. Not only can selves exist only in relationship to other selves, but no absolute line can be drawn between our own selves and the selves of others, since our own selves are there for and in our experience only insofar as others exist and enter into our experience. The origins and foundation of the self, like those of mind, are social or intersubjective. In incorporating the perspective of the other, the developing self comes to take the perspective of others as the group as a whole. Yet, in responding to the perspective of the other, it is this individual as a unique center of activity that responds. In this way the individual and the community form a dynamic, developing, and inseparable relationship.

Pragmatism, in focusing on lived experimental activity, stresses that the contents of science are not a substitute for, or more real than, our lived qualitative experience, but rather they are conceptual articulations of ways in which the operations of nature can be understood, products of creative intelligence in its attempt to understand its world, and they are verified in the richness of qualitative, everyday experience. In this way, a proper understanding of the lessons of scientific method further reveals that the nature into which the human organism is placed contains the qualitative fullness revealed in lived experience, and that the grasp of nature within the world is permeated with the action-oriented meaning structures by which the human organism and its world are interactionally bound, both at the level of common-sense experience and scientific reflection. And, it is only within this context that the pragmatic focus on the human biological organism and organism-environment adaptation can be understood. The human being is within nature. Neither human activity in general nor human knowledge can be separated from the fact that this being is a natural organism dependent upon a natural environment. But the human organism and the nature within which it is located are both rich with the qualities and values of our everyday experience.

The universe is not a fixed, rational whole, but neither is it one of which the human does not have the ability to make sense. Intelligibility is a possibility of human endeavor; it is not prefixed; it is not guaranteed. The universe is not given to us as meaningful, but it is capable of becoming meaningful through intelligent inquiry. But no amount of intelligent inquiry can lead to a stagnant, fixed whole, for experience of reality includes not only the stable but also the precarious, not only continuity but novelty, not only lawfulness but chance spontaneity. The world we live in is one of process and change, not fixity and finality. There should be neither the wholesale optimism geared toward final completion, nor the wholesale pessimism of being adrift in a hostile universe. Rather, there are ongoing problematic situations that need to be resolved.

Solutions to present problems will give rise to new problems down the road. But experimental method is by its very nature self-corrective if used properly. When explanations, interpretations, solutions to problems cease to work, new ones must emerge in light of the data that defined them. Belief itself is understood in terms of activity, habits of action or tendencies to act. Peirce related the irritation of doubt with hesitancy and irresolution, and understood this as bringing about thought and the estimation of new possibilities to allow for ongoing activity that gives rise to settled belief and new habits. No resolution is absolutely final, but rather part of an ongoing process, for any resolution of belief may give rise down the road to another doubt with a new starting point for a new estimation of possibilities. Belief itself is a rule for action and there are times when the use of a rule runs into difficulties, giving rise to problematic situations.

The various features of pragmatism discussed thus far are embodied in the pragmatic understanding of democracy. Both Dewey and Mead stress that democracy is not a particular body of institutions or a particular form of government, but rather the political expression of the functioning of experimental method. Any social structure or institution can be brought into question through the use of social intelligence guided by universalizing ideals, leading to reconstructive activity that enlarges and reintegrates the situation and the selves involved, providing at once a greater degree of authentic self-expression and a greater degree of social participation.

The development of the ability both to create and to respond constructively to the creation of novel perspectives, as well as to incorporate the perspective of the other—not as something totally alien but as something sympathetically understood—is at once growth of community and growth of self. Thus Mead holds that democracy involves a particular type of self. And, in this way, democracy provides for a society that controls its own evolution. Any authentic organization involves a shared value or goal, and the overreaching goal of a human society is precisely this control of its own evolution. Thus, the ultimate "goal" is growth or development, not final completion. This in turn indicates that neither democracy nor the working ideal of universality can imply that differences should be eliminated or melted down, for these differences provide the necessary materials by which a society can continue to grow. Though society indeed represents social meanings and social norms, yet social development is possible only through the dynamic interrelation of this dimension with the unique, creative individual. The creative perspectives of individuals offer the liberating possibilities of new reconstructions. The liberating is also precarious. But the liberating, the precarious, the novel, occurs within the context of tradition, stability, continuity, community.

Like all facets of human life, values emerge as both shared and unique. Though the social context itself affects the vital drives and the energies operative within a situation, and though neither the emergence of moral norms and practices nor the emergence of brute valuings occurs apart from the social interaction of concrete organisms, yet the creative advancement of the individual in its uniqueness brings unique tendencies and potentialities into the shaping processes of social change; brings creative perspectives to the resolution of the conflicting and changing value claims; and restructures the very moral behavior or moral practices and the institutionalized ways of behaving that

helped shape its own developing potentialities. More intelligence is social intelligence, though social intelligence is not possible without individual creativity. Moral freedom lies in the ability to regulate and reconstruct conduct through the creative development of universalizing norms and ideals. This is at once growth of the self. Dewey, then, can point out that growth itself is the only moral "end," that the moral meaning of democracy lies in its contribution to the growth of every member of society, and that growth involves the rational resolution of conflict, conflict between duty and desire, between what is already accomplished and what is possible.

A true community, as by its very nature incorporating a dynamic process involving pluralism, is far from immune to hazardous pitfalls and wrenching clashes. But, ideally, these conflicts can be utilized to provide the material for further growth. Thus Dewey emphasizes that temporary conflict provides the occasion for transition to a more extensive reintegration. When, however, there is lacking the reorganizing and ordering capabilities of intelligence, the imaginative grasp of authentic possibilities, the vitality of motivation, or sensitivity to the "felt" dimensions of existence, all of which are needed for ongoing reconstructive growth, then irreconcilable factionalism results. And the development of these capabilities lies in the educational process.

What will solve present problems and provide the means for ongoing growth of the self and the community is human intelligence with its creativity, sensitivity, imagination, and moral awareness geared to the human conditions in all of its qualitative richness, and the possibilities contained therein for betterment. It is these human skills which must be developed. And this in turn requires the education of the entire person. Further, it involves the education of the society at large, for the ongoing dynamics of community development requires collective intelligence at work.

A true community, then, to maintain itself as a community, requires universal education and requires as well an understanding of the educational process that is concerned with the education of the whole person. That in turn indicates that education is not fundamentally the transmission of information but rather development of the skills of experimental inquiry. Education must provide the skills of experimental inquiry needed not just for the adequate exploration of specific subject matter but also for the possibility of the interrelated ongoing reconstruction and expansion of the self, values, and the institutions and practices of the community.

The proper method of education is, in fact, for pragmatism, the road to freedom, for we are free when our activity is guided by the outcome of intelligent reflection, when we do not let ourselves be passively pushed this way and that by external factors but can take what comes to us, reconstruct it through intelligent inquiry, and direct our activity in terms of the unique synthesis of the data brought about by our unique creativity. To the extent that we do not passively respond but intelligently participate, independently think, we are free, for we, not external factors, determine the nature of our responses. As morally responsible beings we are free, but moral responsibility does not involve the learning of rules and regulations, the following of rigid principles handed down. Rather, it involves the ability to recognize moral problems and to reconstruct the moral situation according to experimental method in order to bring about a reintegration of value experiences. Thus, in learning to think, we are learning at the same time to be free moral beings.

To be free moral beings in an authentic sense, however, we must also cultivate a deepening attunement to the "felt" dimensions of experience and to the general pulse of human existence, in which the diversity of valuings is ultimately rooted, and toward the development of an understanding of which valuings and claims of the valuable should be shaped. This requires a sensitivity to the aesthetic dimension that pervades human existence, to experiencing what Dewey calls the qualitative character of an experience as a unified whole. The enhancement of this can itself not be separated from the method of experimental inquiry, for the qualitative character of an experience as a unified, integrated whole involves a sense of its own little past and a sense of the creatively organizing and ordering movement that brings to fruition its internal integration and fulfillment. In learning to integrate an experience through goal-oriented experimental activity, one enhances its aesthetic dimension. And the enhancement of the aesthetic dimension enhances other dimensions, for the aesthetic involves the emotional, and the emotional enters into the unity of attitudes and outlooks. Here again, education should not begin with the attempt to introduce great works of art and elicit an appreciation, but with the cultivation of the impulses toward art, the impulses toward the objectification of emotional value, which are to be found within the child.

The sense of history is crucial also. But again, an adequate historical awareness involves not a passive recovery but a creative, imaginative reconstruction of a present oriented toward a future in light of the possibilities provided by the past. The creative play of imagination and intelligence can extend and reintegrate experience in productive ways only if it is not capricious but, rather, seizes upon real possibilities that a dynamic past has embedded in the changing present. Students thus must learn to live in the present through the appropriation of a living tradition that they creatively orient in light of a projected future.

Pragmatism is radically opposed to what has been a dominant strain in philosophy of education based on what is loosely called the associationist type of psychology. In this view of consciousness, knowledge is gained by the association of an idea with other ideas. Consciousness is a sort of vast container into which facts are stuffed. Thus teaching is concerned with the transmission of facts and "ready-made" ideas. The curriculum is oriented toward the laying out of these ideas; the goal of education is their accumulation.

Because of its opposition to this view, pragmatism is frequently interpreted as being opposed to content, as sacrificing content to method. The pragmatic focus on method does not ignore content, however, but rather provides a unifying thread for dealing with the vastly varied and huge amounts of content to which the child is exposed. Learning to think is not learning to memorize facts, or concepts, or the great thoughts of the past. Rather, it is learning to solve problems through the gathering, evaluation, and interpretation of evidence; through understanding relationships between the causes that instigate and the consequences which follow. It is not enough for children to learn the accumulated achievements of the past; they must learn to achieve through inquiry. Because this method calls upon individual creativity, and because students vary in their individuality, different problems will "speak" to different students.

This concern with individual creativity in the process of problem-solving has led to the misplaced charges, first, that the pragmatic approach to education is lacking in rigor, and, second, that pragmatism views knowing as only for the sake of doing, that theory has given way to crass practicality. The development of the skills of experimental inquiry requires utmost rigor. The early impulses of children must be carefully developed so that they do not turn into habits of awareness that are at the mercy of whim, random stimuli, mindless behavior, or passive acceptance. Natural inquisitiveness, imagination, and the sensitivity of the child must be developed through the educational process to provide rigor in the use of creative intelligence. The impulses of children must be molded into self-controlled, goal-oriented, problem-solving activity that encourages "thinking for oneself," providing the basis for freedom. Further, as can be seen from the pragmatic understanding of the relation of knowledge and activity, theory is not sacrificed for practice, but rather theory embodies practice, and the operation of reason cannot be isolated from the concrete human being in its entirety. A successful educational process requires that the impulses and emerging habits of the child all take on a functional unity, for the educational process involves the growth of persons as a unified whole.

Again, critics of this position have wrongly interpreted growth as mere accumulation. This leads to charges that the development of morally detrimental activity or unfounded beliefs could be considered instances of growth. It has been seen, however, that the pragmatic understanding of growth involves reintegration of problematic situations in ways that lead to widening horizons of self, of community, and of the relationship between the two. In this way, growth, and hence proper education itself, has an inherently moral and aesthetic quality.

Further, it was seen that growth of self and growth of community go hand in hand. The educational process requires that students and teachers alike understand themselves as part of an ongoing community process. Creativity, in all its varied dimensions, functions within the context of community and in turn changes and should enrich the community within which it functions. Thus, beginning teachers should not be apprentices imitating a master, unreflectively putting to use materials and regulations passed on to them. Rather, teachers should approach students creatively, experimentally, exploring the interests, atti-

tudes, creativity, and capabilities of the students, and thus entering into the enriching dynamics of community life. While any classroom and any school is itself a little functioning community, the classroom and the school are also part of a wider community. Thus, the context within which creativity emerges, and that which should in turn gain enrichment from such creativity, is ultimately the community at large. In this way, the proper educational process can be a means for guiding social change, and social change can in turn provide an enriched context for the educational process. Ultimately, the educational process cannot be limited to the school context, for the educational process in a broad sense pervades the life of an individual.

The above understanding of the role of education in the fostering of the reconstruction necessary for the ongoing development of a true community has several suggestive concrete implications for the problems facing American education. America seems to be moving from the ideal of the grand melting pot to the ideal of the grand accumulator of aggregates. Within the multiculturalism of today, many want not to assimilate but to isolate in terms of their heritage and customs. The debates and arguments over these two alternatives are wrongheaded in both directions, for both extremes are destructive of the dynamics of true community. And neither alternative is what is called for by the insights of American pragmatism. The multiculturalism of today offers the opportunity for the enrichment of all, but only if the collection of aggregates is woven into the dynamic interplay of a pluralistic community. The uniqueness of diverse cultures, as representative of the individual perspective, must be maintained not through separation from, but through a dynamic interplay with, the common perspective, bringing about a resultant enrichment of each. For this to occur, however, students from diverse cultures cannot sit in different classrooms, nor is a solution to be found by merely locating them within the same classroom or by lectures to all on the importance of tolerance. The answer to divisive selfishness and factionalism is not sacrificial external tolerance. Rather, the educational process must provide the vehicle by which the sympathetic understanding of diverse cultures through the incorporation of diverse perspectives leads to the internalized tolerance of enlarged selves.

An important vehicle for achieving this goal is the focus on the educational process as nourishing the skills of creative intelligence or experimental inquiry, attunement to the sense of values, and the expansion of the imagination. These cannot be adequately developed through different courses focusing on each, for one does not educate the whole person through an accumulation of aggregates. Rather, all have to be brought to bear on, and in turn be nourished by, diverse subject matter. Educating the entire person through the development of these skills in one sense fosters the dimension of commonalty, for regardless of the particular types of content particular cultures may prefer to focus upon, the development of the skills of experimental inquiry transcends any particular content. Yet, in another sense it fosters the expression of, and sympathetic understanding of, diverse cultures. For the diverse senses of value operative in diverse ways of marking out the significance of the problems and issues within the content to be dealt with, as well as in the evaluation of the consequences of the proposed solutions, can lead to a sympathetic understanding of diverse perspectives and sensitivities within the common endeavor of problem-solving.

This is perhaps most clearly brought to light in a discipline that is too often reduced to a series of facts—history. Diverse perspectives within the present are situated within the pasts from which they have emerged, and the common endeavor of identifying problems, issues, and possible alternative solutions within historical situations can bring forth culturally diverse, historically rooted sensitivities to these problems and issues and possible solutions. This can bring about at once the enrichment and enlargement of the selves involved in this common endeavor and a heightened attunement to the human condition and the felt value dimensions of existence.

When the educational process allows individuals to remain oblivious to the value dimension pervasive of concrete human existence, then artificial values will be substituted. When the educational process fragments the individual, then the holistic skills needed for the reconstruction and expansion of values necessary for community growth cannot occur, and the result is factionalism, intolerance, or at best external toleration. If the educational process fails to utilize the enriching potentialities of multiculturalism, then the destructive alternatives of assimilation or isolation will reign supreme.

The education of the whole person provides education for life in a true community, for it provides the tools for ongoing adjustment between the new and the old, the precarious and the stable, the novel and the continuous, creativity and conformity, self and other. Further, it nourishes the common "end" that must characterize a community, even a highly pluralistic one, for it helps bring to fruition the universalizing ideal of ongoing, self-directed growth. This results in the authentic reconstruction of free individuals within a free community. Such reconstruction involves the dynamics of experimental method embedded in the very nature of human awareness of the world. And the proper functioning of experimental method requires the proper nourishment of the whole person, for the proper functioning of experimental method is, for pragmatism, precisely the artful functioning of human experience in its entirety.

Sandra Rosenthal

See also DEMOCRACY; DEWEY; JAMES; MEANING; MULTICULTURALISM; PLURALISM; POSSIBILITY; VALUE AND EVALUATION

Bibliography
Dewey, John. *Contributions to the Educational Frontier: The Later Works,* vol. 8, edited by Jo Ann Boydston. Cardondale and Edwardsville: University of Southern Illinois Press, 1981–1989.

———. *Democracy and Education: The Middle Works,* vol. 9, edited by Jo Ann Boydston. Carbondale and Edwardsville: University of Southern Illinois Press, 1976–1983.

———. *Experience and Education: The Later Works,* vol. 13, edited by Jo Ann Boydston. Carbondale and Edwardsville: University of Southern Illinois Press, 1976–1983.

———. *Moral Principles in Education: The Middle Works,* vol. 4, edited by Jo Ann Boydston. Carbondale and Edwardsville: University of Southern Illinois Press, 1976–1983.

———. *The Public and Its Problems: The Later Works,* vol. 2, edited by Jo Ann Boydston. Carbondale and Edwardsville: University of Southern Illinois Press, 1976–1983.

P

James, William. *Psychology: A Briefer Course: The Works of William James.* Edited by Frederick Burkhardt. Cambridge: Harvard University Press, 1975–1987.

———. *Talks to Teachers on Psychology; And to Students on Some of Life's Ideals.* New York: Holt, 1900.

Mead, George Herbert. *Mind, Self, and Society.* Chicago and London: University of Chicago Press, 1963.

———. "The Relation of Play to Education." *University of Chicago Record* I (1896).

———. "The Teaching of Science in High School." *School Review* 14 (1906).

Progress, Idea of, and Progressive Education

Progress may be defined as a process in which there are a sequence of stages of development, with the later stages taken to be superior to the earlier. Thus progress means change for the better, an improvement that is a moral advance.

Disagreement about the origins of the idea of progress exists among historians. One point of view, set out by J.B. Bury in *The Idea of Progress* (1932), made the claim that the ancient Greeks and Romans were innocent of the idea. This position became almost commonplace until the publication of Ludwig Edelstein's monograph *The Idea of Progress in Classical Antiquity* (1967), in which a compelling case was made for the origins of the idea among the ancients. Edelstein found the principle underlying the idea of progress stated in a fragment of a poem of Xenophanes (c. 570–c. 480 B.C.), and he traced the fortunes of the idea into the Hellenistic period (323–30 B.C.).

In both the ancient and modern history of the idea, progress has appeared in many guises; for while all claims in behalf of progress are in agreement on the general claim that it is an improvement, there is fundamental disagreement as to the specific way in which progress comes to pass. Whether nature or the work of human beings brings about improvement leads to the question, Does "finding" that which is better mean finding what is already there in nature, or do human beings "make" what is taken to be better?

As a classic example of the sense that inquiry into the nature of things reveals what is there, we may take the conception of distinct sciences worked out by Aristotle (384–322 B.C.), for whom knowing comes about in a process of observation and reasoning, in which we build on the knowledge-claims of our predecessors. Here the objects of knowledge are found, rather than made, by human intelligence in a process in which later knowing is superior to earlier knowing. A modern example of science as knowing what is there is found in the writings of Herbert Spencer (1820–1903), who made progress synonymous with the process of natural evolution. In his view, progress is inherent in the evolving nature of things; this means that improvement in all things—including the arts, the sciences, even society itself and its institutions—is part of an evolution that human beings are capable of understanding. As in Aristotle, Spencer's view limits human intelligence to finding the ends for human existence that already exist in nature; intelligence has no place in making the ends that it tries to understand.

The idea that human beings have a voice in making, rather than merely finding, what is taken to be better, may be seen in certain writings of the eighteenth-century Enlightenment. In those writings, "nature" was conceived as an ideal to be pursued, not as a universe of already-existing objects to be known. This was taking a critical stance toward existing knowledge-claims, along with a search for the ends of human existence, which could be gained only by rebuilding the existing society. John Dewey (1859–1952) later put this critical spirit in a succinct way in saying that the object of knowing "is a made object, not a found object." Dewey's criticism went beyond objects of knowing to take into account any beliefs and institutions of society which were satisfied with understanding that which exists. Dewey's criticism, like that of the Enlightenment thinkers, was for the purpose of creating ends of human existence and making institutions in which those ends would come to life in social reality. In this view progress is a possibility—an idea of what is to be made—rather than something coming to pass that is inherent in the nature of things. Whether what is sought will come to pass is an empirical question, one that can be answered only by attempting to make conditions in reality that are true to the idea.

In historical studies of the idea of progress, much evidence is presented showing that the expansion of science has made a contribution to the idea. Yet the idea does not depend on the development of science alone. Arguments in behalf of greater happiness and an enhanced sense of community, among other meanings of progress, have been accompanied by an appeal to greater scientific achievement in certain historical situations, while in other situations the claim that scientific achievements impede improvement has been made. It is clear, then, that the general concept of progress has taken on fundamentally different specific meanings in its history.

Progressive Education

Inasmuch as education is the sort of activity that aims to bring about improvement in conduct, it is not surprising to find that the idea of progress has had a profound influence there. And as one would expect from observing the fortunes of the idea of progress itself, there have been profound differences between (1) those who have taken the aim of progressive education to be primarily that of understanding the most reliable and intellectually defensible knowledge-claims on which existing society is based; and (2) those who have taken the aim of progressive education to consist of a critical examination of existing knowledge-claims in order to seek ideas for bringing about changes in the existing society. In the first, progress is marked by the possession of a certain body of knowledge that prepares us for change; in the second, progress is made possible, not by possession of already-existing knowledge alone, but by an ability to make knowledge when it is needed in order to bring about change.

In the intellectual and social history in which the idea of progress has been related to the theory and practice of education, one does find examples of these two views of progress. The first has been supported by those who believe that the best hope for progress lies in cultivating minds to be well-informed in up-to-date-knowledge and disciplined in the intellectual methods by which that knowledge has been gained; such knowledge and methods are essential to preparing young people to make further advances in knowledge. The second view has been supported by those who believe that ideas for change are experimental, and that no particular body of knowledge already in our possession necessarily prepares us for change. Proponents of the second view argue that young people need experience in bringing about change and that educational practice should actively engage students in learning how to bring about change.

Even though there are proponents of these two differing conceptions of how progress comes to pass, for the most part the existing literature on progressive education does not relate the idea of progress to educational theory and practice in an explicit way. For example, in the most extensive history of progressive education, Lawrence Cremin's *Transformation of the School: Progressivism in American Education, 1876–1957,* published in 1961, "progressivism" refers to a pluralistic movement in American intellectual and social life rather than to conceptions of progress. In this account, progressivism consisted of manifold ways of using the schools to improve the lives of individuals. The study of child and adolescent development, evolutionary theory, and the emerging social sciences provided substance for progressive policies and practices. Attempts to make education itself an object of scientific investigation also had a place in progressive education. We may take progressivism in education to be an example of what Morton White called a "revolt against formalism" in American life. The challenge to existing political forms led to reforms such as initiative, referendum, and recall, the popular election of U.S. senators, and a Progressive party. In their own way, progressive educators were reformers who criticized existing educational institutions and developed new forms of curriculum, administration, organization, and methods of teaching. The aim was to bring about changes that would free individuals from environmental insults that are intellectually, morally, and socially repressive, and to cultivate existing abilities by putting them to work for progressive ends.

In the studies of Cremin and others, we find that the term *progressive education* refers to diverse and sometimes conflicting educational theories, policies, programs, and practices. It is important, therefore, that the term not be used as if it were a proper noun, pointing to one entity. The meaning of progressive education is not encompassed by any one philosophy or by any particular meaning of progress, and its origins are not to be associated with any one person. What the diversity of policies and practices had in common was not any specific educational theory or conception of progress, but a protest against formalisms in intellectual and social life. Some programs opposed the formalism of measuring children by adult standards and aimed to prolong childhood. As examples,

Marietta Johnson's Organic School, founded in Fairhope, Alabama, in 1907 and Caroline Pratt's Play School, founded in New York City in 1914, were inspired by the notion that children have the potential for natural growth if they are enabled to create their own standards rather than being taught to imitate those of adults. The Laboratory School at the University of Chicago (1896–1904) was an experiment that tested certain ideas in pragmatic philosophy articulated by John Dewey. Elsie Ripley Clapp's community school in Kentucky (1929–1934) tried out the idea that communities can be deliberately educative rather than merely "have schools."

The thinking of eighteenth and nineteenth-century European reformers also influenced American progressive educators, especially in the late nineteenth and early twentieth centuries. The ideas on child nature popularized by Jean-Jacques Rousseau (1712–1778), efforts by Johann Pestalozzi (1746–1827) to socialize children in a humane way, the attempts of the philosopher Johann Herbart (1776–1841) to develop a science of pedagogy, and the concern of Friedrich Froebel (1782–1852) for the inner life of the child provided ideas that were prominent in the literature of progressives. Again, the variety of ways in which the ideas and material were taken from these reformers spawned diverse educational programs and practices. And different social aims guided educational progressives as they worked on matters such as child and adolescent development and children's interests, and as they spoke out in behalf of creating situations in which children participated in planning their own educational activities. For example, pragmatists aimed to make possible a democratic way of life in which meanings found by individuals would free them to seek a social good in common with others. On the other hand, certain romantically minded individualists thought that children's natural freedom is good in itself and would be diminished by the imposition of any social aim. These differences were sometimes generalized as "society-centered" and "child-centered" conceptions of education.

While it is fair to say that explicit consideration of the idea of progress is absent from much of the literature on progressive education, it should be pointed out that the ambiguous legacy of the idea is implicit in that literature. Only the most general conception of progress, which holds that improvement of the human condition is possible, appears to be common to educational progressives. The specific ways in which it is thought that progress comes to pass are as manifold in education as in the larger history of the idea itself.

J.J. Chambliss

See also DEWEY; EVOLUTION; FROEBEL; HALL; HERBART; NATURALISM; PESTALOZZI; PRAGMATISM; ROUSSEAU

Bibliography
Bode, Boyd H. *Progressive Education at the Crossroads.* New York: Newson, 1938.
Bury, J.B. *The Idea of Progress: An Inquiry into Its Growth and Origin.* New York: Macmillan, 1932.
Counts, George S. *Dare the School Build a New Social Order?* New York: John Day, 1932.
Cremin, Lawrence A. *The Transformation of the School: Progressivism in American Education, 1876–1957.* New York: Alfred A. Knopf, 1961.
Dewey, John, and Evelyn Dewey. *Schools of Tomorrow.* New York: E.P. Dutton, 1915.
Edelstein, Ludwig. *The Idea of Progress in Classical Antiquity.* Baltimore: Johns Hopkins Press, 1967.
White, Morton. *Social Thought in America: The Revolt against Formalism.* Boston: Beacon Press, 1957.

Psychoanalysis

It has been said that Freud's impact on the history of human thought ranks with those of Copernicus and Darwin both in the scope of his influence and in the repercussions of his ideas on human narcissism. Copernicus revealed that we are not at the center of the cosmos. Darwin established that we are not special creations above and beyond the biological kingdom. And Freud demonstrated that we are not masters of our own mind. The ideas of psychoanalysis have significantly influenced psychiatry, psychology, literature, art, and the social sciences. Psychoanalysis is a comprehensive philosophy of human nature, an epistemologically unique method for exploring the human mind, and a powerful system for psychotherapeutic change that is unsurpassed in its influence on the mental health profession. As a psychological theory of the normal as well as the abnormal mind, it has been applied to all dimensions of human activity—the family, marriage, child-rearing, vocational and avocational choice, humor, group behavior, business, religion, politics, and war. In fact, a basic tenet of psychoanalysis is that no obvious distinction exists between "normal" and "abnormal." We all struggle, but never fully succeed, to become masters of our internal world.

The Unconscious

The foundation of psychoanalytic theory is the concept of the unconscious. Although surely not the first to suggest that there are mental processes outside awareness, Freud indeed was a pioneer in mapping an elaborate blueprint of this realm. In the topographic model of psychoanalytic theory, the mind often is compared with an iceberg. Consciousness is but the small tip rising above the waterline. The unforeseen, massive bulk of the iceberg—the unconscious world—lies hidden below. The principle of intrapsychic determinism states that every conscious thought, feeling, and behavior is derived from this unconscious domain. Even presumably trivial and innocuous occurrences—such as brief lapses or blocks in memory, minor errors and omissions, or slips of the tongue (the so-called Freudian slip)—hint at powerful unconscious feelings and fantasies that gave rise to them. Exploring the meaning of these seemingly inconsequential *parapraxia* reveals not only that they are intrapsychically determined, but also intrapsychically *over*determined. Every behavior, no matter how simple or mundane, arises from a complex aggregate of unconscious ideas and emotions.

Although the iceberg metaphor has merit, the unconscious is anything but a frozen, static entity. Psychoanalysis is a psychodynamic theory. It depicts the mind as an arena filled to the brim with intrapsychic collisions, struggles, mediations, and transformations. According to the topographic model, the unconscious and conscious minds are entangled in an ongoing duel. The unconscious always seeks to express itself, and it must be allowed expression in some way, shape, or form; but it cannot be allowed to articulate any problematic feeling or idea so blatantly or forcefully that it threatens the conscious mind. Through repression and a host of other defense mechanisms (which operate outside of awareness), the unconscious is held in check but also allowed to voice itself in a disguised fashion. Sometimes the resulting compromise is pathological and constitutes any of a wide variety of mental illnesses—for example, compulsive hand-washing that betrays underlying guilt, or hysterical blindness that symbolizes the refusal to see the true source of one's problems. Under ideal circumstances, the compromise is healthy, as in the rechanneling, or sublimation of unconscious thoughts and feelings into a socially constructive activity, including almost any artistic and scientific endeavor. In fact, Freud proclaimed, the defense mechanism of sublimation accounts for the rise of civilization itself.

In the structural or tripartite model, the dynamics between the conscious and unconscious are translated into a three-part drama involving the id, ego, and superego. The id consists of threatening sexual and aggressive impulses, which are always unconscious. The ego constitutes the conscious, and often naive, sense of self-identity. Like a rider on a unruly horse, specialized sectors of the ego also attempt to tame and direct the expression of the id. This regulatory function is the ego's unconscious component, as clearly evident by the fact that we seldom are aware of the perpetual struggle between the ego and the id. The ego also serves as intermediary between the id and the superego, which is the keeper of morality, conscience, and ethical standards. Some of these standards are the ideals to which we consciously strive; other superego strictures unconsciously shape our lives. As the Great Mediator, the ego attempts to satisfy the desires of the id without offending the superego.

Apart from its relationship to consciousness and the tripartite structure, the unconscious is a dynamic world unto itself, with its own unique rules and intentions. Time does not exist: What happened dozens of years ago is as fresh and alive as if it just happened. The beliefs and feelings from childhood experiences in the family form the unconscious template that determines how one thinks, feels, and behaves in the present. In the unconscious, conventional logic also does not exist, in that opposites are not mutually exclusive. They exist side by side. One can love and hate someone at the same time. Behind every fear is a wish. Unlike conscious thought, which operates according to conceptual criteria, practical requirements, and the demands of reality (secondary process), the unconscious revolves around subjective emotions, beliefs, wishes, and fantasies (primary process). The unconscious world constitutes the individual's own unique and highly subjective psychic reality.

P

Dreams and early childhood memories provide a portal into this hidden psychic world and the unconscious processes that create it. As the "royal road to the unconscious," dreams result from the relaxing of defenses during sleep. The unconscious material that begins to surface is transformed and disguised by three psychic mechanisms. Displacement allows one thing to be substituted for another: A dream about your father actually may be a dream about your mother. Through symbolization something is represented by something else that resembles it or is associated with it: Crossing a bridge may signify a period of transition in one's life, or driving a car may portray independence. Through condensation numerous unconscious ideas and emotions may be depicted by a single element in the dream: A lion may stand for one's father, courage, sexual desire, and anger, as well as represent the specific events that occurred during a visit to the zoo years ago. In the nightmare, the mechanisms for cloaking the unconscious fail, and the hidden meanings become all too clear to the dreamer, who now must wake up in order to abort the dream.

Similar to dreams, early childhood memories are psychic constructions (usually visualizations), rather than straightforward recollections of the past. Whereas the basic scenario of the memory may be a generally accurate depiction of the actual event, the details in the memory may be unconscious symbols or elements borrowed from other similar, and probably more troubling, memories. Some recalled events may never have occurred at all; they are pure fabrications that were synthesized from bits and pieces of other memories. Being products of multiple determination as well as compromise formations that simultaneously express and disguise the unconscious, both the dream and the childhood memory are gold mines in the unearthing of the individual's psychic reality.

The Schools of Psychoanalysis
The evolution of psychoanalysis over the past century has resulted in several different schools, each endorsing its own particular view of human nature. Fred Pine (1990) described them as the "four psychologies" of psychoanalysis: the psychology of drive, ego, object relations, and self-experience. While they certainly overlap, each adds something new to the theoretical understanding of personality development and psychopathology. Pine suggested that these four

psychologies may be considered different perspectives on the same phenomena, with each illuminating distinct aspects of personality dynamics.

The psychology of drive stems from the traditional view endorsed by Freud, sometimes called "Freudian psychoanalysis," and by other prominent theorists such as Karl Abraham and Otto Fenichel. From this standpoint, individuals are seen in terms of their struggle with primitive sexual and aggressive urges. Forged from early family and bodily experiences (the oral, anal, and phallic stages of psychosexual development), these urges give rise to wishes and fantasies that are experienced as unacceptable and dangerous. Psychic life is organized around the conflict between defending against and allowing some form of expressions and gratification of these urges. Emotional experience, conscious or unconscious, revolves around anxiety, guilt, shame, and inhibition. Drive psychology often emphasizes the oedipal phase of development, when the child longs for the opposite sex parent while feeling a conflicted mixture of competition, fear, and love for the parent of the same sex.

The psychology of the ego stems from the work of such theorists as Anna Freud, Rene Spitz, H. Hartmann, Ernst Kris, and R. Loewenstein. From this standpoint, the person is viewed in terms of the ego's capacity to adapt to the environment, remain attuned to the demands of reality, and effectively control emotions and unconscious impulses. Because this psychology emphasizes how the ego evolves over time, it assumes that developmental failures may lead to defects in the ego's functioning.

The psychology of object relations comes from the work of Melanie Klein, W.R.D. Fairbairn, Margaret Mahler, Otto Kernberg, Harry Guntrip, D.W. Winnicott, John Bowlby, and Edith Jacobsen. From this standpoint the individual is seen in terms of an internal drama derived from the experiences of childhood. Past perceptions of significant others—called "objects" (usually parents)—and memories of how one responded to these people are played out in one's mind and unconsciously reenacted in current relationships. All significant early relationships are repeated with other people later in life either out of an effort to repeat past pleasurable experiences or to master traumatic ones. People may reenact how they responded to the parent, how the parent responded to them, how they wished the parent would have behaved, how they think the parent wished them to behave, or various combinations of these possibilities.

The psychology of self-experience is derived from the self psychology of such theorists as Heinz Kohut, Arnold Goldberg, and Paul Ornstein. From this perspective the individual is seen in terms of an ongoing subjective experience of self. How does one define oneself in relation to others? Is the self experienced as a distinct, separate, and unique entity, or is it overly dependent on and merged with the identity of others? Is the self experienced as integrated and whole, or disorganized and fragmented? Does one view oneself as basically "good" or "bad"? These feelings and perceptions about one's self evolve out of early relationships with significant others, particularly regarding whether these others acknowledged and accepted the child's thoughts and feelings (mirroring) or acted as positive models with whom the child could identify (idealization).

To these four psychologies we may add two more categories that often are mentioned in the literature on psychoanalysis. The neoanalysts or neofreudians included such theorists as Alfred Adler, Erik Erikson, Erich Fromm, Karen Horney, Otto Rank, and Harry Stack Sullivan. They rejected the traditional focus on sexual and aggressive drives and instead emphasized the role of social relationships in personality formation. They were concerned not just with the stages in childhood development, but also with interpersonal issues and phases across the entire life span. Deviating somewhat from the traditional emphasis on unconscious motivations, these theorists also focused on deliberate choice, self-direction, and the human's unique struggle with the responsibilities and anxieties associated with free will.

The other additional category is analytical psychology, founded by Carl Jung, whom some consider one of the best kept secrets in psychoanalysis. Once a member of Freud's inner circle, Jung soon broke from traditional psychoanalysis, much to Freud's dismay and anger. Like Freud, Jung was intrigued by the idea of the unconscious. However, he believed not only in a personal unconscious (similar to Freud's concept), but also in a collective unconscious that is a universal memory and thought process common to all humans, in all cultures, throughout human history. The collective unconscious expresses itself most clearly in dreams through universal images and symbols called archetypes. Much more of a romanticist and mystic than Freud, Jung envisioned the unconscious not simply as a repository of repressed drives and painful experiences, but also as a source of wisdom, creativity, and spirituality.

Psychoanalysis Therapy

Although there are a variety of therapeutic styles derived from the various schools of psychoanalytic thought, the fundamental principles are the same. Following the Socratic maxim "Know Thyself," the path to cure is through self-insight. The clinician's role in helping patients explore the unconscious sources of their problems can be compared to that of a forest guide. The guide has never been in the particular forest that each client presents; nevertheless, the guide is an expert on how in general to explore forests. Free association and the analysis of dreams and childhood memories help open up the unconscious realm. "Cure" occurs gradually through the release, catharsis, and working through of repressed emotions, beliefs, and memories. Paradoxically, out of a fear of what might be discovered, the patient unconsciously may slow down the journey through various psychic distractions and blockages called resistance. By making interpretations of unconscious beliefs and feelings that have risen close to awareness, including the sources of resistance, clinicians help expedite the uncovering process. Interpreting transference—the patient's unconscious tendency to reenact with the clinician childhood relationships with close family members, especially parents—is a particularly powerful technique that is the hallmark of psychoanalysis. Countertransference, which is the clinician's own emotional reactions to the patient, can be used as a "barometer" for detecting the patient's often subtle behaviors that may have triggered those reactions.

Of course, there are a variety of debates about what are the most important psychotherapeutic issues and techniques, debates that usually arise between the various psychoanalytic schools. Is it more important to interpret intrapsychic conflict over unconscious urges and fantasies or to help repair deficits in the ego or in self-experience? Do the patient's problems arise mostly from problems during the oedipal phase, infantile periods earlier than the oedipal phase, or periods after the oedipal phase, such as adolescence or midlife? Is it more important for clinicians to hide their own personality in order to create a "blank screen" (analytic neutrality) onto which the patients project transference, to be "good objects" who repair the damage resulting from the patients' parents, or to help fortify the clients' sense of self by empathically mirroring their feelings and allowing themselves to be idealized? The answers to such questions are rarely reached through either/or choices; they more likely involve a complex blending of styles and techniques that parallel the complexity of the human personality.

Criticisms

Psychoanalysis has been criticized on a number of grounds. Some claim that it is overly complex. The number of articles and books written about it over the past hundred years is so vast that no one person, or even a group of people, could master it. Has the psychoanalytic literature become so voluminous and diverse that it cannot be integrated into a coherent whole? At this point, is there really any solid agreement about what exactly "psychoanalysis" is? Others claim that it plays theoretical tricks. With its concept of the unconscious, psychoanalysis can simultaneously explain any psychological phenomenon and its exact opposite. Many skeptics find it farfetched to believe that there exists an unconscious that could carry out the complex and deliberate actions that often are attributed to it. Contrary to the opinion of some psychoanalysts, prominent philosophers have stated that psychoanalysis is not a science. Based mostly on the clinical case studies of people in treatment, the psychoanalytic epistemology has been questioned. Is the process too complex to be studied scientifically? Can we trust the report of clinicians who must be biased in what they see happening in their work? Turning psychoanalysis onto itself, perhaps we also must examine the personality dynamics and unconscious motives of people who theorize about psychoanalysis in order to see how their psychic reality has shaped their theoretical ideas.

Criticisms also have been launched against the effectiveness of psychoanalytic therapy. Is it too time consuming and expensive? Does it work for enough people or is it limited to the "YAVIS"—the young, attractive, verbal, intelligent, and successful people whose problems are not that severe? How do we know what really happened in the patient's past? Recently, tremendous controversies have arisen over Freud's "seduction theory" which stated that recollections of sexual traumas are based on fantasies rather than actual events. Evidence now suggests that many sexual traumas are indeed based on real events, and that decades of psychotherapy may have been based on a mistaken premise.

As both a science and an art, psychoanalysis continues to evolve. Psychoanalytic researchers have acknowledged the deficiencies in the case study method and have begun to test psychoanalytic concepts through rigorous scientific experimentation (see Masling 1983, 1986, 1990). Clinicians search for more effective and shorter-term treatment strategies, and for methods that help a wider population of people. And the theorists continue to reach for a solid, encompassing definition of psychoanalysis while retaining its versatility as a system for understanding human nature.

John R. Suler

See also FREUD; HUMAN NATURE; PERSON, CONCEPT OF

Bibliography

Brenner, Charles. *An Elementary Textbook of Psychoanalysis*. New York: Doubleday, 1974.

Freud, Sigmund. *Introductory Lectures on Psychoanalysis* [1917]. New York: Norton, 1989.

———. *The Interpretation of Dreams.* [1900]. New York: Basic Books, 1955.

Gay, Peter. *Freud: A Life of Our Time.* New York: Norton, 1988.

Greenson, Ralph. *Technique and Practice of Psychoanalysis.* New York: International Universities Press, 1967.

Lindner, Robert. *The Fifty-Minute Hour: A Collection of True Psychoanalytic Tales* [1954]. Northvale, N.J.: Aronson, 1982.

Malcolm, Janet. *Psychoanalysis: The Impossible Profession.* New York: Random House, 1982.

Masling, Joseph. *Empirical Studies of Psychoanalytic Theories,* vols. 1–3. Hillsdale, N.J.: Analytic Press, 1983, 1986, 1990.

Pine, Fred. *Drive, Ego, Object, and Self.* New York: Basic Books, 1990.

Public Education

The term *public education* is one that is not easy to understand clearly and completely, whatever perspective one employs to discuss it. Public education, as used herein, means formal educational experiences for the purposes of the public at large, rather than for the purposes of individuals or a particular segment of the public. Additionally, the ways in which the purposes and programs of public education are formed involve a governmental body, representing the public at large. Since the public at large is an elusive concept, the goal of reaching as much of the entire public as possible is taken herein to be the closest approximation to reaching the public at large that is possible.

Because they are the institutions that have been set up explicitly to serve the educational needs of most, if not all, of the people of the United States, this article will assess the attempts of the American public schools to reach the entire public at crucial points in their history. In the United States, public schools and public education differ from "private" education or private schools according to issues of purpose, governance, and support. As already suggested, public schools exist for the purpose of serving the entire public. In addition, they are governed by a lay political body and through a political process ostensibly responsive to concerns of that larger public. Finally, public schools are supported by tax funds and other public revenue sources. Private schools exist not for the purpose of serving the public, but almost always to serve one segment of the public, say, members of a particular religious group or of a group of academically talented students or academically oriented parents. Private schools are governed by a variety of boards of trustees representing various groups of citizens, none of whom are elected or appointed by elected officials representing the larger community within which the private schools exist. Finally, private schools are supported through tuition fees, philanthropy, or voluntary fund-raising efforts. Private schools do not depend on tax dollars as their main source of revenue.

Before undertaking further analysis of the development of public schools in the United States, it is appropriate to note that circumstances and institutional forms of public education are different in other countries. The American system of public schools is explicitly nonsectarian; religious schools have no place within American public education. Even so, the constitutional framework allows for both the encouragement and the regulation of religious (and nonreligious) private schools by government. In Australia, Canada, and in several European countries, however, direct and substantial government financial support is offered to religious schools, which are deemed to be involved in public education, and the term *public school,* as it is understood in the American context, is unknown. In these countries, terms such as *state* or *government schools* denote the institutions Americans might call "public schools." Similarly, in these countries terms such as *religious* or *independent schools* describe what Americans might refer to as private or nonpublic schools. The government involvement in religious and other independent schools in these other countries consists of both more governmental support of these institutions than exists in the United States and more governmental control over them. In these countries, then, *public education,* or the education of the public, is a term that encompasses much more than the term *public schools* does in the United States.

Returning to the consideration of public schools in the United States, a historical perspective illuminates problems that have hampered the efforts of the public schools to reach the children of all of the public. The rest of this article will look at the problems and the attempts to solve them in different historical eras.

Within the United States, the public schools were started in the Northeast in the second quarter of the nineteenth century to serve an increasingly diverse society. The name given most often to these institutions was the "common school" and the adjective *common* was relevant to the purpose of serving an increasingly diverse society. The diversity was characterized by an influx of Irish immigrants to the region, the shift of substantial numbers of citizens from rural to town settings, and the increasing employment of these immigrants and migrants in newly established mills and factories.

More specifically, common schooling was characterized by a particular approach to the finance, support, and control of education. The common schools were free, universal (open to all [white] citizens), supported by taxation (almost always a locally administered property tax), and intent on moving away from that localized system of support toward a more centralized structure involving more regionalized (or state) governance and control.

While the common school was developed to appeal to a diverse constituency of students and parents, its fundamental purpose was to achieve a kind of uniformity in its students. It was essentially a "moral" institution that sought to tame the diversity that it addressed through an instructional program based on moral elements held in common by all citizens. This system was fraught with a number of tensions. First, the common morality promulgated in the common school was less universal than it appeared. Close analysis of common schooling in Massachusetts, other New England states, and the old Northwest, has found that it was the result of a Protestant Republican ideology that was adhered to more closely by the old stock middle- and upper-class white population than by the rest of the citizens (Kaestle). Almost immediately, the common school faced opposition to its common moral curriculum from a Roman Catholic population, largely Irish, that saw itself as threatened by an institution that operated under an essentially Protestant ideology (Lannie).

While Irish immigrant Catholics represented one group that had a tenuous relationship to the public schools, others such as African Americans were even more distant from the public schools in the pre–Civil War era. This estrangement from all formal education was complete in the antebellum South, where in most states it was a crime to educate a slave, and less complete in the antebellum North, where court decisions, such as in the Roberts case in Boston, dictated that African Americans, though allowed to attend school, would attend racially segregated schools. Though the court decision was negated by a state law that mandated desegregation, the attendance practices in Boston ensured that segregation would be the norm. Thus the common school was distinctly limited in its ability to reach the entire public.

Even though the common school had its limits as an institution that provided an education to all of the public, it did function somewhat successfully as the American educational agency that provided for the public in most locales through much of the nineteenth century. At the turn of the twentieth century, however, a new set of problems emerged that were to confront the public schools, the direct successors of the common schools, with new challenges in their effort to meet the educational needs of the entire public.

The new set of problems arose out of a new challenge confronting the public schools, especially the high schools, as they moved to adjust their curriculum to meet the needs of an industrializing economy. Through most of the nineteenth century, neither a mass public high

school nor a developed industrial economy had existed. In the twentieth century, however, the industrialization of the economy demanded, according to high school reformers, a mass high school to turn out both unskilled and skilled workers and new political and economic leaders.

In response to these challenges, the high school curriculum evolved differentially—that is, by developing separate courses of study for students who would perform separate functions in the new industrial world. Specifically, academic, vocational, and commercial curricula emerged to develop, respectively, the intellectual, manufacturing, and business skills deemed necessary for the maintenance of the industrial society. Initially, the three emphases were institutionalized in three separate kinds of high schools. Rather quickly, however, factors such as the authoritarian implications of this stark separation of future leaders from their constituents and opposition from working-class activists to separate vocational high schools controlled by private employers combined to create a compromise institution, the comprehensive high school. In this institution the separate curricular tracks existed side by side, with some minimal provision also emerging for across-track student contact (Krug). The comprehensive high school, like the common school, would seek universality of access but would provide different paths to adulthood for different students. Innovations such as intelligence testing and guidance services were proffered as guarantees that the sorting of students into the various curricular tracks would take place fairly—that is, on the grounds of "objective" criteria such as test scores and grades. Studies of high schools in subsequent decades, however, questioned the adequacy of the different curricular tracks to serve the public at large, since the various tracks seemed to result in a student body that was sorted on a social-class basis as much as, or more than, on the basis of objective measures (Hollingshead).

The advent of a "progressive" approach to curriculum issues served to complicate, rather than to solve, the problems of curricular differentiation. Progressives like John Dewey (1859–1952) were committed to a thorough revamping of both school and society along democratic lines. While Dewey used industrial education as one means of meaningfully linking education to the changes wrought by industrialization in society, other educational innovators with a more narrow view (one that excluded any consideration of social changes) implemented vocational studies in ways that ensured that students would learn as much about the subservient roles workers were expected to play in society as about any changes that industrialization might mean in social arrangements. At the elementary school level, child-centered and pedagogical progressives retreated into strictly educational solutions such as the child-centered school or the project method, thereby embodying a progressive education bereft of Dewey's social change orientation (Cremin).

The economic crisis of the Great Depression of the 1930s created havoc among progressive educators, as it did in the economy and in the schools. A new group within the larger camp of progressives arose called social reconstructionists. They sought schooling for direct social change as a first priority. Dewey reacted to these new socially radical educators by chiding them for their overemphasis on social change at the expense of pedagogical innovation and intellectual exploration on the part of pupils. Taking a middle ground that seemed seldom, if ever, to be inhabited by educators, Dewey criticized the extremes of child-centered and social-reconstructionist progressives for overly emphasizing one or another aspect of a thoroughgoing approach to progressive education (Bowers).

Despite the contention among various brands of progressive education in the 1930s, the institutionalization of progressive pedagogy that emerged in the post–World War II era hardly resembled anything that any earlier group of progressives had sought. The "life adjustment movement," touted by its adherents as a curriculum to serve the middle 60 percent of the high school student body (the majority group served by neither the academic curriculum nor the vocational curriculum), came to fruition in the development of a general curriculum track that in the long view seemed to do little but water down the academic curriculum. For example, intellectually substantial studies such as algebra or geometry were replaced by mathematics courses that rehashed elementary school arithmetic, concentrating on its relevance to basic life skills such as balancing a checkbook.

The major addition to the problems of the public schools since the 1950s has been in the area of school desegregation. Starting with the 1954 *Brown* decision, the schools of the South-

ern states were found to have been illegally segregating their African-American students. Soon, the charge of segregation also was successfully levied in the courts in Northern states. The gradual desegregation implemented in response to *Brown* and subsequent court decisions reached a zenith in the early 1970s before school desegregation foundered on the rocks of busing and other school transportation and pupil assignment schemes that were vigorously opposed by white parents. Politicians who pandered to the fears of these parents for their children did nothing to help the situation.

The addition, in the past two decades, of substantial numbers of "new" immigrant groups, many of whom do not speak English, resulted in controversy over whether or not the best way to serve these populations is by a bilingual approach that emphasizes learning in their native language as well as in English, or through an approach that emphasizes the learning of English as the key to school, and life, success. In addition, the existence of large numbers of pupils of one or more of these immigrant groups in public school systems has resulted in pupil assignment problems that raise the same issues of segregation and equity that pertain to the education of African Americans.

The very recent popularity of "voluntary" desegregation plans, such as majority to minority transfer arrangements, has brought things full circle to a situation in which the pupil-assignment policies in many school districts countenance substantial degrees of racial segregation. Similarly, the development of magnet schools that specialize in one or another area of study, such as computers, or business education, or traditional curricula, occurred in response to a demand for curricular choice that has not acknowledged the unsolved problems resulting from the earlier differentiation of school curricula.

Given this brief historical overview, the conclusion is that the public schools have, at best, a mixed record in achieving the objective of public education, the education of all the public. On the positive side, the public schools have reached a substantial portion of the eligible students. Recent studies of high school dropouts put their number at less than 20 percent of the relevant age group, an achievement that puts the United States substantially ahead of most, if not all, other industrial nations (Levine and Havighurst).

From the point of view of the quality of

the curriculum that is being delivered in the differentiated public school, however, it is difficult to argue that the public at large is being well served. The watered-down character of the "general" track has recently been exposed in historical studies of urban education (Mirel). The problem of the occupational relevance of any vocational program in an era when the typical adult can be expected to change jobs several times in a working life is one that has moved vocational studies in the direction of more generally relevant work skills that often look suspiciously like traditional academic studies. Further, the complaints that students in those traditional academic studies do not do as well as their counterparts in the other industrial nations have cast severe doubt on the ability of American schools to perform this traditional task.

The ability of the American public schools to provide a complete public education has been, then, partial at best since their inception in the nineteenth century. Most recently, that partial success has been looked upon as a negative rather than a positive accomplishment. The educational choice movement, fueled by a private enterprise attitude opposed to public provision in education or any other realm, is seeking one or another way of allowing parents to receive public support to attend nonpublic schools. Thus, the very existence of the public schools as the American vehicle for public education is under direct attack. Adoption of a comprehensive choice plan, one that would provide tax dollars for parents to send their children to private schools, would certainly minimize the importance of public schools and drastically alter the ways in which American society understands the meaning and the challenge of public education.

Wayne J. Urban

See also CIVIC EDUCATION; COMMUNITY; DEMOCRACY; DEWEY; MANN; PROGRESS, IDEA OF, AND PROGRESSIVE EDUCATION; RECONSTRUCTIONISM, SOCIAL

Bibliography

Bowers, C.A. *The Progressive Educator and the Depression: The Radical Years.* New York: Random House, 1969.

Cremin, Lawrence A. *The Transformation of the School.* New York: Vintage Books, 1961.

Hollingshead, A.B. *Elmtown's Youth: The Impact of Social Classes on Adolescents.* New York: John Wiley, 1949.

Kaestle, Carl F. *Pillars of the Republic: Common Schools and American Society, 1780–1860.* New York: Hill and Wang, 1983.

Krug, Edward A. *The Shaping of the American High School, 1890–1920.* Madison: University of Wisconsin Press, 1964.

Lannie, Vincent P. *Public Money and Parochial Education: Bishop Hughes, Governor Seward, and the New York School Controversy.* Cleveland, Ohio: Case Western Reserve University Press, 1968.

Levine, Daniel U., and Robert J. Havighurst. *Society and Education.* 8th ed. Boston: Allyn and Bacon, 1992.

Mirel, Jeffrey. *The Rise and Fall of an Urban School System: Detroit, 1907–1981.* Ann Arbor: University of Michigan Press, 1993.

Quintilian (c. 35–c. 90)

Pleader in Roman courts and first public professor of Latin rhetoric in Rome, whose *Institutio oratoria,* written in retirement, is singular among ancient works of educational theory in its consideration of practical pedagogy.

Much of Quintilian's book is a treatise on the art of oratory that would have been familiar enough to any of his readers acquainted with earlier examples of the genre, such as *De oratore* of Cicero (106–43 B.C.) . Where it departed from expectations was first in his detailed consideration of educational issues surrounding the early training and preliminary studies of boys who were to study oratory, second in his espousal of a broad and liberal notion of the orator and his formation. Quintilian was by no means interested in simply training young men in the techniques of rhetoric. He claimed to be educating "the perfect orator, who can only be a good man," and therefore a person who had to possess "not merely an excellent power of speech, but all the moral virtues as well" (*Institutio oratoria:* I,i,9). He did this despite the fact that public deliberative oratory was no longer politically feasible under the Empire, panegyric orations and courtroom pleadings constituting the greatest part of the orator's function. Nevertheless, eloquence retained its prestige, and Quintilian embraced an ideal and syllabus of liberal culture traceable to Isocrates (436–338 B.C.) and hoped thus to produce an effective public man.

He did not believe that education could create virtue, but that the practice of virtue could be acquired through early home training. He therefore concerned himself at the onset with the qualifications of the nurse, since it was her voice that the child would first hear and imitate, she who would first model behavior for the child and first instruct the child in morals. Fathers and mothers bore responsibility for guiding the educational process, and he hoped that they would have the proper intellectual and moral culture. But Quintilian realized that persons other than the parents would have day-to-day contact with the child, so he urged parents to select not only a nurse carefully, but also the boy's companions, from whom he might learn things that would undermine his moral education. His concern for the nurse's role in moral formation is paralleled by his concern for her role in forming correct speech habits in her charges: She must be well enough educated to speak correctly. Moreover, she ought to be watched over by a *pedagogus,* or tutor-companion of the child, learned enough to be able to correct her pronunciation as necessary. Obviously, Quintilian envisioned his advice as pertaining to wealthy families, as children of ordinary families would have neither nurses nor *pedagogi* and would get their schooling from elementary schoolmasters (*ludi magistri*).

Primary education conducted at home before age seven taught the pupil some of the basics of literacy. Quintilian resisted the long tradition that postponed formal literary instruction until age seven, feeling that the memory is especially retentive in the early years and may usefully be put to work on basics. As much as possible, these early studies were to be conducted as enjoyable activities, even to learning the alphabet by use of toylike letters carved from ivory and to tracing letters carved into boards.

The next stage of the boy's education involved grammar schools. The *grammaticus,* or grammar master, was responsible for teaching his charges to read correctly, for explaining grammar through the study of specific poets, for commenting on various authors, and for clarifying mythological allusions. Naturally, Quintilian had high standards for these teachers of the young child, who would introduce the child to writing and to memory exercises: They must be morally unassailable models of decorum. At this age, he argued, the school was the best place for the student to continue learning, and he rejected arguments that schools corrupt morals and are inferior to individual tutorial instruction. At school the boy learned not only what was taught him but also what was taught to others, had others to emulate and compete with, and daily faced an audience.

While he believed that some students lack sufficient native ability to profit from instruction—intelligence, a strong voice, a hardy constitution, and pleasant countenance being essential prerequisites for an orator—Quintilian generally considered learning a powerful tool not simply for honing natural capacities but even for remedying some of nature's shortcomings. At the heart of his method was adapting instruction to the student's ability and interests, taking full account of individual differences and the child's readiness to move on to new material, since the student could not absorb material for which he was not prepared, nor at a rate beyond his powers. The keys to inculcating learning were drill, repetition, and stimulation by the teacher, with competition and emulation providing powerful motivation as long as students were not forced into unequal matches. Mental games were not only useful for this purpose but recreational as well, and Quintilian knew that recreation is essential to managing the pace of learning. He opposed corporal punishment on the grounds that it is degrading, counterproductive, and unnecessary. The good teacher, realizing that students are eager and able to learn, uses encouragement and rewards, praising what things he can in a student's performance, tolerating some, and changing others while being careful to give reasons for the changes. Above all, the master must interest his pupils lest he destroy their enthusiasm for learning. The teacher who could do all of these things was of crucial significance to the child's early development.

For Quintilian, the training of the orator pivoted on the study of grammar and rhetoric, but these were by no means narrowly construed, for he thought the student should complete the course of study "which the Greeks call *enkuklios paideia*" (*Institutio oratoria*: I,x,1). The language of study and of instruction at the outset was to be Greek, which he accorded a place superior to that of Latin in the acquisition of learning and general culture. The study of Latin should begin not long after, and be continued in parallel with the study of Greek. In the grammar school, the prime focus was on instruction in speaking correctly and interpreting the poets, most notably Homer and Vergil, but these were not to be mere technical exercises, and so writing and reading aloud were also taught, along with philosophy, music, and geometry. Reading was clearly a preprofessional study, emphasizing breathing, timing, and emotional color, and music was valued not only for its theoretical content and its contribution to vocalization and chironomy but also because its teaching had long emphasized the poet's broad knowledge and memorization of literature. Geometry, which to Quintilian included all mathematics, furnished intellectual discipline, familiarity with the rigorous construction of proofs, and deliverance from a superstitious approach to reality, along with facility in using numbers and symbols. Plane geometry was especially useful to the orator in instances where property boundaries were being litigated. In fact, reference was made to numbers in many court cases, so Quintilian held that the orator must not only understand mathematics but also master the technique of signing with his fingers any number he mentioned.

Some philosophy was also encouraged, since it afforded tools for the study of language and literature, because some of the poets who were in the syllabus discussed philosophical ideas and themes, and because paying attention to the teachings of wise men is crucial to forming the habit of moral conduct and reflection that will help the orator speak sincerely and credibly. Finally, he recommended attendance at a school of physical culture to foster the bearing and grace of movement desirable in an orator. All of these were to be studied simultaneously rather than sequentially, so learning may be various and not tiresome. Against those who held that subjects should be taught simply to avoid confusion, distraction, and fatigue, Quintilian replied that no age was less prone to fatigue than childhood, but he feared that the application of the mind continuously to a single subject would overwhelm the child with boredom.

These things having been mastered, the pupil, now about fourteen years old, could pass on to higher studies in rhetoric proper, the study and practice of eloquence. Quintilian attempted to clarify the practical boundaries of grammar and rhetoric lest the masters of each encroach on the others' territory to the detriment of the student's education. He could not stamp out the practice of *rhetores* (rhetoricians) leaving more and more of their preliminary work to the *grammatici,* nor prevent the *grammatici* from augmenting their status and income by teaching prose composition in addition to the poetry that was their proper province, but he recommended that the *grammatici* cover only a few preliminary exercises so that boys would not be kept in grammar school any longer than necessary nor subjected to inferior teaching by those not sufficiently knowledgeable in rhetoric. Thus the *grammatici* were to teach the child no more than to paraphrase simple fables or render passages of poetry into prose. For the *rhetores* was reserved training the child in historical narration, themes praising or condemning or comparing famous persons, and essays on more abstract themes culminating in compositions on laws and evidence.

Just as a gymnast assesses which pupils are best suited for which events, so the rhetor must take account of individual differences. At the heart of any student's abilities was his capacity for memorization, since the orators must be able to commit lengthy orations to memory and must have a well-stocked memory to call upon for quotations, allusion, and telling examples. Facility of imitation was also important. The ability not only to improve upon natural mnemonic ability but also to extend it to include form and style as well as content was crucial to the formation of an orator. Rhetors must both be able to diagnose these individual abilities and be of unimpeachable moral character, intolerant of vice in their students, even-tempered, unaffected, deft in directing studies, careful in praising and correcting, concerned to maintain classroom decorum, and able to set an example of rhetorical excellence by daily declamation. Recognizing that most parents would choose an inferior but acceptable master as one being less expensive and more inclined to teach young boys, Quintilian unfailingly recommended that parents choose the most eminent teacher available, citing the expense of rectifying the defects inculcated by an inferior teacher and maintaining that the goals of teaching should always be set high enough to stretch the capacities of students. The significance of the teacher diminishes as the student matures and is able to take increasing responsibility for his own learning activities. It is important that the teacher recognize this and design teaching strategies so as to liberate his students gradually and not keep them artificially dependent by treating mature students like children.

The third through the twelfth books of *Institutio oratoria* discuss rhetoric in exhausting detail, referring intermittently to methods of teaching. To rhetoric belonged not only what we would today recognize as rhetoric, but also the study of history, literature, logic, and professional ethics. The weight of his treatment falls on the division of oratory into panegyric, deliberative and judicial, the nature of proof, the various types of argument, appealing to the emotions, the use of humor, and figures of speech. The exercises by which an orator builds the quality of his delivery are explored in detail. At the very end, most notably in books ten and twelve, Quintilian maintains that someone who has already mastered the formalities of rhetoric ought to undertake to acquire true mastery of his art. There is some confusion here. At the outset of his tenth book he simply recommends wide reading and then passes on to critical comment on various authors, but at the beginning of the twelfth book he discusses the study of philosophy, jurisprudence, and history as necessary armament for the orator. The recommendation of the tenth book is more true to Quintilian's own ideas, the later book a belated concession to ideas expressed by Cicero, whom he greatly admired.

In addition to being arguably the most thorough textbook of rhetoric ever composed, Quintilian's *Institutio oratoria* is the work of a person whose long experience of teaching and shrewdness of insight enabled him to present ideas of enduring value to the educational enterprise. It is certainly the best educational treatise to emerge from the long Roman experience, appearing too late to reshape Roman educational practice in any major way but affording future ages a persuasive theory of the ideal public person as well as practical guidance in the conduct of elementary and secondary education. Quintilian's views were enormously influential in the Renaissance, which regarded him as the greatest authority available on educational philosophy, and his impact on Western education remained strong through the eighteenth century, most especially in the curriculum and methods of the Latin grammar schools, where his recommendation of parallel study of one's vernacular and a classical language was carried out zealously. On the debit side, his emphasis on the energy of young children and their ability to absorb instruction fostered the practice of grammar schools' forcing boys to absorb heavy doses of Latin before they were ready, and his praise of the mnemonic ability of children was used to justify excessive use of rote memorization. Yet most of his influence on educational theory and practice has been benign. His support for early childhood education, moral training, diagnosis of individual differences, and use of positive reinforcement, as well as his condemnation of corporal punishment, have guided educational practice in useful directions. And his emphasis on the orator as a person whose moral worth lies at the core of his claim to credibility has always been a model for the ideal product of liberal education.

Joseph M. McCarthy

See also CICERO; ISOCRATES; RHETORIC

Bibliography

Bonner, Stanley F. *Education in Ancient Rome from the Elder Cato to the Younger Pliny*. Berkeley: University of California Press, 1977.

Gwynn, Aubrey. *Roman Education from Cicero to Quintilian*. Oxford: Clarendon Press, 1926.

Kennedy, George A. *Quintilian*. New York: Twayne, 1969.

Marrou, Henri-Irenee. *A History of Education in Antiquity*. New York: Sheed and Ward, 1956.

Power, Edward J. *Evolution of Educational Doctrine: Major Educational Theorists of the Western World*. New York: Appleton-Century-Crofts, 1969.

Quintilian. *The Institutio Oratoria of Quintilian*. Translated by H.E. Butler. New York: G.P. Putnam's Sons, 1921; London: William Heinemann, 1921.

———. *Quintilian on Education*. Selected and translated by William M. Smail. Oxford: Clarendon Press, 1938; New York: Teachers College Press, 1966.

———. *Quintilian on the Teaching of Speaking and Writing: Translations from Books One, Two and Ten of the Institutio Oratoria*. Edited by James J. Murphy. Carbondale: Southern Illinois University Press, 1987.

Rusk, Robert R. *Doctrines of the Great Educators*. London: Macmillan, 1918. 4th ed., 1969.

Wilkins, A.S. *Roman Education*. Cambridge: Cambridge University Press, 1905.

R

Race and Racism

There is general agreement among contemporary scholars that "race" is a social construction (some would say an ideological construction) rather than a valid scientific concept. A "race" is thus a constructed category within a category system typically using real or imagined phenotypical characteristics as the differentiating criteria for defining categories of people. The categories are assumed to be naturally given, mutually exclusive, and, usually, hierarchically organized. Phenotypical characteristics are observable characteristics, such as skin color, determined by genes and environment. The closely related notion of "ethnic group" refers to a group that defines itself or is defined by others in terms of real or supposed cultural characteristics.

To say that "race" is a social construction is not to say that it is a matter only of the definition of situations, nor that it is merely ideological. There are, of course, phenotypical differences between individuals and groups. But such differences are in themselves of no particular social, cultural, mental, or psychological significance. In a racist system, however, they are given such significance and linked to group interests and identity, and to the allocation of resources. As a result, real social differences may either be maintained or created, and are racialized. Thus, "race" is a social reality. It is not the expression or result of biological factors, but of social factors.

The notion of "race" has a long history, and it has been used both as a folk and a technical concept. It is not surprising, therefore, that it has taken on a variety of meanings. The word first appeared in English about the beginning of the sixteenth century (Banton). Its Italian, Spanish, and Portuguese forms go back to the fourteenth century. There were moreover earlier words signifying similar or related concepts, such as nation (Latin *natio;* see also Greek *ethnos*). Indeed, there is evidence of classifications of people based on physical differences even among the ancient Egyptians.

As a folk concept, race tends to be undefined and treated as though self-evident, but it usually seems to make an assumption that humanity is divided into several biologically and inherently or naturally distinct groups. As a technical concept it has been used in scholarly works, and also in legislation. In particular, it has been used as a scientific and analytical concept by natural scientists, such as biologists, and by anthropologists, psychologists, sociologists, and other social and political scientists. As a purely taxonomic concept employed by biologists it is of limited usefulness and of no relevance to social and political issues.

Michael Banton (1987) has identified some five main analytical meanings of the word *race* from the sixteenth century to the present time. These are race as lineage, type, subspecies, status, and class. Several theories of "race relations" have been developed around these and other concepts. Such race relations have often been seen as sharing similarities with, overlapping with, or belonging to a wider category of ethnic relations. Some of the race relations theories, especially the earlier ones, have quite expressly assumed—while others, especially more recent ones, have often at least tacitly implied—that there really are biologically distinct races, and that the relations between them are naturally determined. But most theories since about the 1930s have sought explanations other than biological ones, and many have accepted the idea that "races" are social constructions rather than natural phenomena.

"Race" as lineage denoted "race" as a genealogical group—that is, a group with a common line of descent, irrespective of whether that line of descent might include a wide range in physical appearance because of out-marriage. Race as type held that people from time immemorial were actually divided into different "racial types"—that is, types identified by appearance. Evolution posed a problem for such an account. These two approaches sought to explain both physical and cultural differences.

Race as subspecies adopted both the notion of different types and that of common descent within each type, to provide a classification at a point in time. This understood a race as a set of individuals of similar appearance who represent a class created by shared descent. The development of that view into "race" as population—that is "a system of interacting individuals," and so with a shared "gene pool" (but not necessarily originally of common descent nor of one "racial" type)—took better account of historical developments, including interaction between groups (Banton: 70). However, while both race as subspecies and as population addressed the issue of physical differentiation, cultural differentiation was more problematic.

Race as ecologically interrelated groups moved away from understanding racial relations as biological relations. Developed by Robert E. Park between 1913 and 1939, this view applied to racial relations an understanding of the interactive processes that influence all forms of life. It stressed relative group positions and the relations between the groups. Park formulated his view specifically in terms of a race-relations cycle, according to which the structure of ethnic differentiation depends on the precontact characteristics of the groups coming together and on the patterns of contact (see Pettigrew). However, racial differences were still assumed as natural differences, and differences in power and wealth were not explained.

The notion of "racial prejudice" has also been used as an alternative to biological determinism in explaining racial relations. A prejudice is an attitude or a generalized evaluative judgment made prior to properly examining the facts and made in relation to a stereotyped image of reality. A stereotype is an overgeneralization, a rigid or generally held image, idea, or belief associated with a category, and which

is not amenable to new information or to nuance. A prejudice is thus a judgment or attitude that is indifferent toward contrary evidence. One view is that prejudice is a consequence of the development of in-groups, which inevitably tend toward ethnocentrism—that is, taking one's own group as the center of things and seeing its culture or ways as the best. Another view is that prejudices are built into a culture and are learned. Yet another is that prejudices serve important psychological functions, helping people to cope with inner conflicts and tensions.

The later development of race as status holds that unequal social status provides the explanation of the position of racial minorities, physical difference serving as a sign of group membership. This unequal social status is itself understood as "the outcome of an interaction between their own preferences and skills, and the ways they are regarded by others" (Banton: 168). However, this seems somewhat circular, and tends to take "racial minorities" and "race thinking" as given.

John Dollard saw race prejudice as irrational, while the theory of subjective expected utilities and the closely related "rational choice" theory see racial relations as rational. According to these last two theories, the basic criterion of all behavior is the extent to which it maximizes the agent's net advantage, in the agent's eyes. Banton's "rational choice" theory seeks to improve on the notion of race as status, and dismisses racism as an explanation of racial relations. These are simply one form of social relations, and social relations are determined by decisions about the allocation of scarce resources to competing ends. This theory holds that physical and cultural differences are utilized in forming racial and ethnic groups, in developing group identities, and in the competition between such groups. Unfortunately, it takes market relations as the model of all social relations, and, closely related to this, understands rationality in a narrow, instrumental, and egotistical sense.

Race as class seeks to provide a historical and political account of status and power differences in terms of the development, imperatives, and tensions of capitalism within Europe and worldwide. However, this approach takes different forms. Some continue, at least implicitly, to assume that race is an unproblematic, naturally given phenomenon. Some subordinate, or even reduce, race to class. Some see racial and class structures as separate if overlapping systems of stratification. Some treat racism as merely ideational or ideological, or as being merely an epiphenomenon, instead of grasping it in its complexity.

Contrary to Banton, whom he critiques, Robert Miles (1993), writing within a Marxist tradition, embraces the idea of racism but rejects that of race as a folk, rather than an analytical, idea. For him, racism and racialization (the viewing and treating of groups or social phenomena in racial terms) are ideological forces locating certain populations in specific economic or class positions and structuring the reproduction of the capitalist mode of production in a particular ideological manner. However, the reality of social "race" cannot be dispensed with simply by stressing the idea that people are mistaken in their everyday lives by calling upon the idea of race—any more than the phenomenon of racism can be denied simply by eschewing the word.

Racism

The key to "race" is racism, or "race thinking" as Jacques Barzun (1965) terms it, racism being, essentially, that form of thinking that divides people into "races"—although it is also a form of social organization and practice informed by such thinking. There is, however, much disagreement about the nature, scope, and origins of racism.

Unlike *race* the word *racism* is a twentieth-century invention dating from about the 1930s. The word *racialism*, which has often been used to refer to the practice consonant with racism understood as a dogma or ideology, dates from about the first decade of the twentieth century. However, racist or similar ideas are ancient, such as Aristotle's view that those who are inferior are naturally slaves. Modern racist theories started, it seems, in eighteenth-century Europe in the development of European nationalism and colonialism (Banton; Miles). They proliferated in nineteenth-century Europe.

Racism involves social structuring along lines constructed on explicitly or implicitly deterministic assumptions about race—that is, about supposed biological, "inherent," or "natural" characteristics thought to be signaled by phenotype or, broadly speaking, physical appearance. Racism may, but does not necessarily, imply overt hostility or violence. It can function as a rationalization for injustice, exploitation, and privilege. Racism takes different forms

in different places and epochs, including anti-Semitism; anti-black racism; anti-"foreigner" or anti-"immigrant" racism (as in various countries of Europe today); anti-Gypsy feeling; apartheid; and nationalistic animosity and conflict between groups or nation-states. Racism can, furthermore, be seen as belonging to a broader family of more or less similar deterministic, rationalizing thinking, including ethnicism, nationalism, sexism, and classism.

Some five closely interrelated aspects of racism can be distinguished: the cultural, the structural, the individual, the interpersonal, and the institutional (Figueroa).

Racism at the level of culture may be thought of as consisting primarily of a frame-of-reference that defines and interprets reality and especially the self and the other, the in-group and, correlatively, the out-group, and thus social identities and boundaries, in deterministic ways in terms of race, or, more specifically, of assumed phenotypical, physical, or genetic characteristics or biological inheritance. Such a frame-of-reference consists of largely taken-for-granted cognitive and symbolic systems, beliefs, assumptions, values, and attitudes. It tends to be ideological in the sense that it represents a largely unwitting distortion of reality that serves the interests of the in-group. Cultural racism may include explicitly racist theories.

Racism at the structural level refers to the way society is articulated by race so that there is differential distribution of resources, rewards, status, and power along racial boundaries. Structural racism intersects in complex ways with other structural realities like social class, ethnicity and gender—but cannot be reduced to any of these.

At the individual level, racism may manifest itself as attitudes, stereotypes, prejudice, or hostility. This may be due to individual psychological factors, but it may also be an expression of a group culture.

The interpersonal dimension of racism refers to forms of interpersonal behavior—including avoidance of contact—that are more or less tacitly informed by racist or ethnicist frames-of-reference. This can include such things as discriminatory behavior, harassment, racist name-calling, incitement to racial hatred, group slandering, racist innuendo, racist graffiti, racist jokes, and refusing to socialize with others on racial grounds. A racist joke or remark made entirely among in-group members about some racially defined out-group is a form of racist interpersonal relations. Indeed, it is largely through such in-group relations and discourse that racist definitions of the "us" and the "them" are accomplished and sustained.

The assumption has often been made that discrimination results from prejudiced attitudes. However, prejudice can exist without any immediate discrimination, and discrimination can take place where there is no immediate prejudice. Discrimination may be direct or indirect. Direct discrimination (in the context of race relations) is inequitable differential treatment, often because irrelevant criteria are taken into account, or because relevant ones are ignored. Indirect discrimination, which is an important form of covert discrimination, consists of applying the same requirement to everyone, although some groups cannot meet this requirement as well as others or not at all, and the requirement cannot be adequately justified on independent grounds. One view is that discrimination may arise from situational pressures. Thus even though a person may not be prejudiced, that person may be under social pressures to conform and to discriminate. Another view is that discrimination arises because of the gains it brings to the group. Yet another view is that once discrimination arises it may become self-perpetuating.

Racism at the institutional level refers to the way the society, or institutions within the society (such as the school), separately or interactively work at least de facto to disadvantage certain groups or to advantage others by operating within the terms of a racist frame-of-reference, or by simply failing to take account of the relevant specific differences, needs or rights of those defined as belonging to a different race.

Institutional racism may be formal and explicit, as in the case of racist laws, or publicly stated racist norms. There are, however, also more subtle or unintentional forms of institutional racism that might operate even where there is no immediate or overt prejudice or racism. Indirect racist discrimination is one form of such institutional racism. Another fundamental aspect of institutional racism is the way in which discrimination in one institution or sphere, such as the school, causes a handicap and therefore leads to systematic disadvantage in another sphere or social institution, such as the labor market. This may result in the establishment of a vicious circle of disadvantage and may reinforce negative stereotypes and the racist frame-of-reference.

Antiracism refers to the combating and deconstruction of racism under all of these aspects, and to the promotion instead of positive alternatives. It seeks to promote equality and quality especially for the subordinated or exploited "races" or ethnic minorities. It is concerned with promoting such positive goals as justice, equity, peace, solidarity, openness, mutual respect, wider and more questioning knowledge, and a greater appreciation of the rich diversity of the world. It also points to the need to address the social conditions that lead to alienation and conflict, both among minorities and among disadvantaged groups within the majority.

Peter Figueroa

See also COLONIALISM AND POSTCOLONIALISM; EQUALITY; HEREDITY AND HEREDITARIANISM

Bibliography

Allport, Gordon W. *The Nature of Prejudice*. Cambridge, Mass.: Addison-Wesley, 1954.

Banton, Michael. *Racial Theories*. Cambridge: Cambridge University Press, 1987.

Barzun, Jacques. *Race: A Study in Superstition* [1937]. New York: Harper and Row, 1965.

Dollard, John. *Caste and Class in a Southern Town*. 3rd ed. Garden City, N.Y.: Doubleday, 1957.

Figueroa, Peter. *Education and the Social Construction of "Race."* London: Routledge, 1991.

Hiernaux, Jean, ed. "Biological Aspects of Race." *International Social Science Journal* 17 (1965): 71–161.

Miles, Robert. *Racism after "Race Relations."* London: Routledge, 1993.

Montagu, Ashley. *The Idea of Race*. Lincoln: University of Nebraska Press, 1965.

Pettigrew, Thomas F., ed. *The Sociology of Race Relations: Reflection and Reform*. New York: Free Press, 1980.

Rationalism

The term *rationalism* has been used in many ways, only the most important of which will be discussed here. Etymologically, it derives from the Latin word *ratio,* which means "reason," and in its most general sense "rationalism" signifies an attitude of confidence in reasoned argumentation as a means of attaining truth. In this broad sense, however, the great majority of thinkers count as rationalists, since most are committed to the standards of rationality (clarity, logic, evidence, and so forth) as guides to knowledge. Indeed, when the term is so construed, the only thinkers it excludes are skeptics, who deny that any significant degree of knowledge is possible, and irrationalists, who claim that the sources of knowledge lie elsewhere than in reason (for example, in feeling, emotion, or faith rather than in logic or evidence).

The term, however, has also been used more narrowly as a pejorative label signifying a tendency to overestimate the possibilities of reason or to underestimate factors like feeling and faith. This pejorative view of rationalism has commonly been applied to the thinkers of the French Enlightenment, such as Francois Voltaire (1694–1778), Jean Le Rond D'Alembert (1717–1783), and Marie Jean Condorcet (1743–1794), who had sanguine views of the power of science and education to promote happiness and secure the foundations of a free society. It is said, for example, that they had naive opinions about the power of benevolence and rationality in human affairs and that they failed to appreciate either the destructive side of our nature or the importance of faith and tradition. But, as Williams (1961) points out, their naivete has been greatly exaggerated. Although they did extol reason over authority, faith, and superstition, their opposition was primarily to traditional Christianity, and many of them (such as Diderot) gave a central place to feeling or sentiment. From the seventeenth through the early twentieth century, the term *rationalism* was also used pejoratively to refer simply to any antireligious attitude backed by argument. But this sense of the term eventually gave way, first to "materialism" and subsequently to "secular humanism," which is now a favorite expression of disparagement among many Christian fundamentalists.

In its most important sense, however, rationalism is the doctrine that reason is the sole source of knowledge. In this conception, all knowledge is a priori (that is, independent of experience) and is usually thought to rest ultimately on a set of relatively simple, self-evident truths. Also commonly associated with rationalism is a commitment to innatism (a belief in inborn knowledge) and necessitarianism (the idea that things could not have been otherwise). Interpreted in this way, rationalism is standardly contrasted with empiricism (from

the Greek *empeiria,* meaning "experience"), according to which all knowledge of the world comes from sensory experience. Empiricists, it is said, also typically reject innatism and necessitarianism.

Most discussions of rationalism treat it in tandem with empiricism, emphasizing the period of the seventeenth and eighteenth centuries, when the debate between them is thought to have reached an especially sharp focus. We shall do so as well, though it is worth noting that rationalism in fact dates from antiquity and that strands of it survive in the work of some contemporary thinkers. In ancient Greece, for example, the Eleatic philosophers Parmenides and Zeno (fifth century B.C.) condemned the deliverances of the senses as contradictory and deduced the true nature of reality—which they described as a changeless and undifferentiated unity—from arguments based on pure reason. Their views helped shape the system of Plato (c. 427–347 B.C.), which was also of a rationalist cast. Plato believed that only a grasp of necessary and eternal truths (nonempirical Ideas or Forms) constituted knowledge and that the senses, which he otherwise impugned, merely help us remember the innate knowledge stored within us. Many philosophers interpret G. W. F. Hegel (1770–1831) as a rationalist too, for he famously held that the universe is an expression of Absolute Spirit, or *Geist,* from whose bosom the world-historical drama unfolds by a rational necessity and whose a priori comprehension is the highest knowledge. Finally, in our own day, Noam Chomsky has argued that the sensory data available to a child is far too meager to explain its rapidly acquired ability to learn a language. In his opinion, language acquisition requires an innate knowledge of a universal grammar, the deep structure of which is common to all languages. Based on this important strand of ideas, Chomsky refers to his theory as a "rationalist conception of the nature of language."

Turning to the seventeenth and eighteenth centuries, one must note that, until quite recently, a particular interpretation of the period has held such sway among scholars as to be dubbed "the standard theory" (Loeb: chap. 1). But because this theory is currently under fire and no consensus about it has yet been reached, it is best here simply to describe it and call attention to some of its virtues and defects.

According to long-standing lore, the history of modern philosophy, which runs from

Rene Descartes (1596–1650) to Immanuel Kant (1724–1804), is best seen as the dialectical development of a conflict between rationalists and empiricists that ends in a Kantian synthesis between the two points of view. The period begins with the advent of modern science, whose turn away from qualitative Aristotelian modes of explanation to purely quantitative ones yielded advances so impressive as to require a wholesale reassessment of the nature of knowledge. The first attempt, as the story goes, came with the three great rationalists, Descartes, Benedict Spinoza (1632–1677), and Gottfried Leibniz (1646–1716), who shared certain assumptions that they applied with increasing rigor to a common body of problems. Operating with the mathematical model they took to underlie modern science, these philosophers assumed that one could organize all knowledge into a system whose axioms are necessary truths—innate ideas, knowable with certainty a priori. Careful deductions from these axioms, moreover, would yield a comprehensive body of information, all of which shares the certainty of its starting points. From this perspective, experience has no epistemic role to play: On the one hand, all knowledge can be obtained a priori, and, on the other hand, experience cannot provide the certainty and systematic unity that knowledge demands. Descartes, Spinoza, and Leibniz are supposed to have pressed this point of view in different ways until the problems internal to it generated an intense reaction against it.

The reaction, of course, was empiricism, which went rather too far in the opposite direction. It maintained that all knowledge about the world is a posteriori, or derived from experience. Furthermore, according to empiricism, all truths about the world are contingent (that is, such that they could have been otherwise). The only necessary a priori propositions are ones expressing relations among our own ideas, rather than insights into the nature of things. (For example, we can know a priori that all bachelors must be unmarried men. But since this is merely based on our treating the ideas of "bachelor" and "unmarried man" as synonyms, it tells only how our ideas are related to one another, not how the world is.) This position, expounded with increasing purity by John Locke (1632–1704), George Berkeley (1685–1753), and David Hume (1711–1776), ultimately foundered in skepticism, which is its logical conclusion. Experience is essentially contingent. As such, it can never explain the

necessary truths about the world that many are convinced we know (for example, that the past is a guide to what the future will be like). Likewise, in the empiricist view, one's experience at any given moment consists only of the sensory data and images one is experiencing at the time. But these, according to the standard theory, can provide no basis for an inference beyond the data of the moment. In the final analysis, then, although each camp has resources the other lacks, neither provides a satisfactory explanation of knowledge.

The period culminates in Kant's effort to accommodate the claims of reason and experience while avoiding the excesses of traditional rationalism and empiricism. In Kant's account, the source of our necessary knowledge about the world is the structure of the mind, whose innate categories and forms of intuition impose a priori constraints on the objects of any possible experience. The mind structures the data that is given to it by things in themselves, thereby dictating the form that any experience must have. Thus, Kant thinks that no event can be experienced unless it has a cause, appears in a spatio-temporal framework, and is subject to numerous other such conditions. Moreover, because the structure that the mind imposes on its data is prior to experience, and not a product of it, it is possible for us to have an a priori grasp of necessary truths about phenomena (for example, that they are all caused). In one respect, then, the rationalists were right, for we *do* have a priori knowledge about the structure of experience, and the necessity involved in this knowledge cannot arise from experience itself. In other respects, they were wrong. While the mind can structure the phenomena that appear to it, it is powerless to grasp the character of noumena, or things as they are in themselves. It is therefore an illusion to suppose that there is any necessary, a priori knowledge of ultimate reality. Thus, the empiricists were right in denying a priori knowledge of ultimate reality, as they were in asserting that the only objects to be known are ones that are in principle empirically observable. In this way, Kant finds a place for both empirical and a priori elements in knowledge without falling prey to the skepticism of the empiricists or the overblown claims about reason of the rationalists.

The attractions of this account are considerable: It is a clear, relatively simple plot that progresses logically and dramatically to a triumphant denouement. Moreover, a decent case can be made for portraying Descartes, Spinoza, and Leibniz as rationalists. Descartes, for example, sounds a distinctly rationalist note when he declares in the second chapter of his famous *Discourse on the Method* that the reasonings of the geometers, which proceed by logical steps from clear and obvious truths to the most arcane revelations, led him to believe that everything knowable can be reached in the same way. In an unfinished dialogue, Descartes says again that "all the items of knowledge that lie within the reach of the human mind are linked together with a marvelous bond, and can be derived from each other by means of necessary inferences." His method for securing the foundations of this system of necessary inferences also invites a rationalist interpretation. For he proposes to treat as if false anything subject to the slightest doubt and to rest content only with ideas so "clear and distinct" as to be indubitable. But the senses, he says, are inherently unreliable, and, if true knowledge is to be achieved, the mind must be led away from the senses toward divinely implanted, innate ideas accessible only to pure reason. Even a physical object like a piece of wax is comprehended, not by the senses, but by the intellect, which alone can penetrate the purely geometrical character of its essence. Descartes also represents the basic principles of physics as necessary truths. Indeed, in *The World* he deduces them a priori from the immutability of God, thus contributing further to his depiction as a rationalist.

To many, Spinoza is an even more rigorous example of a rationalist. Although Descartes claimed that all knowledge can be deduced in the manner of geometry, Spinoza actually made a systematic effort to do it. His remarkable *Ethics*, which is expounded *more geometrico*, contains axioms and definitions that support demonstrations ranging over a host of topics from the nature of God and the laws of physics to ethics, self-knowledge, and human emotion. Furthermore, according to numerous historians, Spinoza treated his axioms and deductive inferences as self-evident, whereas he denigrated the senses. In this view, he classified all sensory information as "cognition by vague experience," which is not a form of knowledge at all. Finally, he is a strict necessitarian, who declared that we think things could have been otherwise "only because of a defect of our knowledge." (Indeed, if rationalism entails necessitarianism, then, in this respect, Spinoza was the most rigorous rationalist of all: Leibniz struggled to find

room for freedom and contingency and, though Descartes's views on the topic are obscure, his references to our "infinite freedom of the will" also appear to conflict with necessitarianism.) All of this has contributed greatly to Spinoza's reputation as a paradigm rationalist.

Leibniz also seems to fit the mold. A cornerstone of his philosophy is the Principle of Sufficient Reason, which states that there is a reason—that is, an a priori proof—for everything that is the case. In every true proposition, he tells us, the concept of the predicate is contained in that of the subject. Consequently, every truth that is not already a self-evident identity (that is, of the form "A is A" or "AB is B") can be reduced to one by the analysis of concepts. The complete concept of Julius Caesar, for example, contains the concept of his crossing the Rubicon, and this idea, as well as everything else in his concept, can be proved a priori by reducing the idea to an identity. Leibniz also deduced from his theory of truth many facts that one would not expect to be knowable a priori (for example, that no two individuals differ only numerically, that there are no gaps among species, and that every particle of the universe contains an infinity of organic beings). When we add that he vigorously defended innate ideas against Locke's attack and argued that the senses can never justify necessary truths, the picture of Leibniz as a rationalist may seem quite secure.

The truth, however, is not so simple or straightforward. Despite the aprioristic character of some of Descartes's pronouncements, his scientific essays in fact rely heavily on experimental data. To be sure, he did prove the basic laws of motion a priori. But he also said that "the further we advance into concrete details, the more necessary observations become." Thus, it has plausibly been argued that Descartes thought only the most fundamental principles of physics are knowable a priori, whereas the confirmation of most scientific hypotheses depends on experience (Curley: 412). Descartes also gave demonstrations of the existence of God, some of which contain essential a posteriori elements. (One of the proofs, for example, begins from the a posteriori premise that I exist and argues on the basis of other principles that only God could have been the cause of my existence.) Even Descartes's famous proof of his own existence, "I am thinking, therefore I exist" (*cogito, ergo sum*) rests in part on his a posteriori awareness that he is thinking. All of which is in conflict with his portrayal as a pure rationalist.

The model also fails to fit much in Spinoza. For example, although he sometimes creates the impression that his axioms are all self-evident, when questioned about this, he replied that it makes no difference so long as they are all true. Furthermore, certain of his axioms (for example, "We feel that a certain body is affected in many ways") seem undeniably a posteriori. Accordingly, numerous commentators now believe that Spinoza regarded some of his axioms as highly plausible *empirical* propositions. On closer examination, moreover, his denigration of "cognition by vague experience" turns out to be not so much a rejection of the senses per se as a stricture against their uncritical use (Curley: 413). Likewise, although in an early work Spinoza appears to make a favorable reference to innate ideas, he never develops the suggestion or relies on it in any way. In view of arguments like these, it is now common to treat the *Ethics* as a holistic system that is meant to be judged by its overall coherence, both internally and with experience.

The account of Leibniz is one-sided too. In his early years he did interpret the Principle of Sufficient Reason to mean that every truth either is, or is reducible to, an identity. But that changed dramatically. After about 1686 he held that while necessary truths can be reduced to identities (and thus be known by us a priori), contingent ones cannot be reduced to identities "by any analysis." Although he continued to maintain that every truth involves an a priori connection between predicate and subject concepts, he argued that the connection in contingent truths is infinitely complex and therefore indemonstrable. God alone can grasp it a priori—and he does so in a single stroke of thought. We lesser intellects must have recourse to experience. Accordingly, Leibniz invokes a sharp distinction between truths of reason, which are necessary and a priori, and truths of fact, which are contingent and known through experience. Moreover, aside from some very general propositions, he views the verification of most of natural science pretty much as an empiricist would. Even innate ideas require sensory stimuli to bring them to our attention, just as a shape ensconced within a veined block of marble requires the sculptor's hammer to reveal it. So, in fact, experience plays a large role in Leibniz's epistemology.

Notwithstanding these problems, propos-

als are available for defending the standard theory. Some would argue, for example, that Descartes, Spinoza, and Leibniz really were rationalists, but, like most other philosophers, simply were not consistent in their views. Likewise, one might try to accommodate the anomalous data by broadening the definition of rationalism to include a subsidiary place for experience. Thus, a "moderate rationalist" could be defined as one who thinks that sensory experience is never *by itself* sufficient for knowledge and that the knowledge it brings is inferior to that of pure reason (for example, by being less certain or by failing to ground any necessary truths). Finally, it has been suggested (Cottingham: 9) that we treat rationalism as a "cluster concept," such that a belief in only part of the cluster of ideas associated with the concept will qualify one as a rationalist, provided one places sufficient stress upon it.

But many find these suggestions inadequate to save the standard theory. Moreover, the theory has problems we have not explored here (such as whether there really was the dialectical development it postulates). The jury is still out, however, and the verdict remains to be seen. In the meantime, the virtues of the standard theory, plus the lack of an equally comprehensive alternative, will probably continue to make it the predominant choice for the classroom, where simplicity is at a premium and where, in any case, there is insufficient time for details that would damage its plot.

David Blumenfeld

See also DESCARTES; EMPIRICISM; EPISTEMOLOGY; KANT; LOCKE; REASON AND RATIONALITY

Bibliography

Chomsky, Noam. *Language and Mind*. New York: Harcourt Brace Jovanovich, 1968.

Cottingham, John. *Rationalism*. London: Granada, 1984.

Curley, Edwin. "Rationalism." In *A Companion to Epistemology*, edited by Jonathan Dancy and Ernest Sosa, 414–15. Oxford: Blackwell, 1992.

Descartes, Rene. *The Philosophical Writings of Descartes*. Translated by John Cottingham, Robert Soothoff, et al. Cambridge: Cambridge University Press, 1984, 1985, 1991.

Leibniz, G.W. *G. W. Leibniz: Philosophical Essays*. Translated by Roger Ariew and Daniel Garber. Indianapolis, Ind., and

Cambridge, Mass.: Hackett, 1989.

Loeb, Louis. *From Descartes to Kant: Continental Metaphysics and the Development of Modern Philosophy*. Ithaca, N.Y., and London: Cornell University Press, 1981.

Spinoza, Benedict. *The Collected Works of Spinoza*. Translated by Edwin Curley. Princeton: Princeton University Press, 1985.

Williams, Bernard. "Rationalism." In *The Encyclopedia of Philosophy*. Vol. 7, edited by Paul Edwards, 69–75. New York and Chicago: Macmillan and the Free Press, 1961.

Realism

Theories of realism appear throughout the history of Western philosophy. There are many significantly different forms of realism, although they all possess as a family resemblance an insistence on the independence of certain entities from the mind or human activity. In what follows, summary descriptions of these theories precede detailed discussions of the two historically most important ones.

The oldest theory is the realism of universals. It is the thesis that, in addition to particular objects—each of which exists in a single place at any particular time—there exist universals, general entities that can occur in different places at the same time, or whose reality is nonspatial altogether. According to one influential account, these universals are the properties or features of objects, properties that may be shared by numerous particulars existing in different parts of space at the same time. For example, the property of being a dog occurs in all the dogs that currently exist, have existed, and will exist—hence this property is a universal. A realism of universals thus denies the thesis, referred to as nominalism, that only particulars exist. It also rejects a doctrine called conceptualism. While conceptualists agree that the universe contains more than particular objects, they claim that the only general things to be found in it are ideas or thoughts. Conceptualists repudiate the notion of mind-independent general entities, whereas realists insist that universals are external to the mind and mind-independent.

A second form of realism consists of the claim that there is a mind-independent, external material world. This thesis is probably implicit in the common-sense view of the world (sometimes referred to as naive realism), but it has been denied by a number of influential philosophers called idealists. The defense of realism with regard to the external world consists primarily of rebuttals to the arguments of the idealists. Idealists point out that the only way of knowing anything whatsoever is through ideas, thoughts, or experiences; furthermore, they claim, these mental entities are the only things of which one is ever aware. It follows, in their view, that no one really has any idea of an external, material world: The only world one can understand is the world of one's ideas or experiences. Some idealists maintain that the very idea of a material world is filled with contradictions, which they think shows that there can be no such thing. Frequently realists defend the proposition that the external, material world exists by demonstrating how it is possible to know the reality of such a world. Or they point to ways in which its reality must be assumed if sense is to be made of ideas and experiences themselves.

The third form of realism is a variant of the second: scientific realism, a very important contemporary view. The scientific realist wishes to defend the reality of entities that are referred to in accepted scientific theories, including those that cannot be observed. Subatomic particles are a case in point. One cannot directly experience them with the senses, and can only detect them indirectly through their observable effects. But the only way it is possible to know that these effects are the products of unobservable subatomic particles is via a theory that explains the effects by reference to the particles. There are philosophers of science who deny the reality of such unobservable entities. They claim that subatomic particles and the like are only theoretical constructs that amount to useful ways of summarizing and relating the complex observational data—thus they are in effect fictions that have no reality outside a theory. On the contrary, the realist responds, these unobservables have a real, theory-independent existence.

Some scientific realists who cast their philosophical eyes on the moral sphere believe that moral properties and moral facts, which are in their view unobservable, have a reality much like that of scientific unobservables (see Sayre-McCord). One cannot, they claim, directly experience the rightness, or cruelty, of an action, but a moral theory that posits moral qualities and facts of this sort is able to provide explanations of aspects of moral experience that otherwise could not be explained. A theory that includes reference to real moral properties constitutes the best explanation of the moral phenomena, which in turn justifies reference to these properties and their causal efficacy.

There are moral realists who do not approach the question of moral properties and facts from the perspective of scientific realism. Their quite different approach is often called intuitionism (see Sayre-McCord). The intuitionistic realists claim that human beings do directly observe such features as rightness and wrongness, kindness and cruelty, and the like. These features are not physical properties detected by the senses, nor are they inferred from what is observed about physical facts. Rather, it is possible to have a direct, perceptionlike grasp of these moral entities. A major component of any theory of moral realism of this variety will be an explanation of the nature of this peculiar form of moral observation. The realist will make every effort to show that, correctly understood, appeal to intuition need not invoke any mysterious faculty of mind. Moral realists who appeal to such intuitions argue that moral facts are as much an indisputable, mind-independent part of the world as facts about physical and scientifically certifiable entities. They claim that only scientism, the myth that reality is exhausted by the properties defined and referred to by science, prevents the acknowledgment of the moral facts everyone "observes" every day.

Finally, there is a group of contemporary philosophers who may be called semantic realists. Although their semantic theories differ considerably, all of them see the meanings of words or sentences as determined by mind-independent objects or facts in the world, and all reject a verificationist theory of meaning that equates meaning with a method or conditions of verification. Some (such as Hilary Putnam) argue that the meaning of a term like *water* is to be explicated in terms of the real or essential nature of what it designates as that nature is increasingly understood by science. Others (such as Saul Kripke) argue that the referent of a proper name (what it refers to) is the object or event in the world that was an initial term in a causal chain leading to the use of the name by a speaker or writer at a subsequent time. Still others (such as Donald Davidson) claim that the meaning of a sentence is to be given, not by the conditions in experience that would justify the claim that it is true (conditions that would verify it), but by the conditions in reality that actually prevail if the sentence is true. Observations justifying the assertion of a sentence (verification conditions) might occur even though the sentence is false, or the sentence might be true even though it cannot be verified. Hence truth conditions for a sentence—conditions in reality—transcend verification conditions. Truth-conditional semantics, which explains meaning in terms of truth conditions, is therefore a realist theory of meaning.

These, then, are some of the theories—ancient, modern, and contemporary—that are classified as realist. While they differ considerably, all of them involve the assertion of the reality of a certain kind of mind-independent entity which other philosophers consider highly dubious. Given this general perspective on realism, it is easy to see that other specific forms of realism could easily be developed. In point of fact, in the history of philosophy there have been philosophers who have asserted the reality of numbers as real, non–spatio/temporal objects, while others have thought that only numerals—concrete mathematical signs invented by human beings—are required to explain mathematics. And there are thinkers who postulate the reality of possible worlds, universes that might, but need not, exist. Others believe that such notions are the stuff of fairy tales. The question of realism is always the issue of whether there is more to reality, Horatio, than you have dreamed of, or thought about, in your philosophy.

With these summary statements in mind, it will be instructive to go into more detailed discussions of two of the most influential forms of realism, the realism of universals and realism concerning the external, material world.

Plato (c. 427–347 B.C.) was the father of the realist doctrine of universals, although the inspiration for the doctrine came from his teacher Socrates (c. 470–399 B.C.). Socrates was interested in understanding the nature of the five virtues that figured in the popular Greek morality of his time. What is courage? he asked. What are justice and temperance, piety and wisdom? He demanded that the answers to these questions have a certain form; they had to be definitions identifying the property or properties common to all instances of a virtue. The answers could not take the form of examples, for Socrates wanted to know what made each of the examples a case of the virtue in question.

Thus the correct answer was a definition that revealed the common properties constituting the essence of the virtue, which essence made a particular example an instance of it.

Plato took the next step and identified this essence with what he called an *eidos*, a form. Then, for reasons presently to be discussed, he characterized this form as eternal, unchanging, nonspatial, and existing in an ideal world apart from the world of particular, spatio-temporal, changing objects. He maintained that particular objects have the qualities they do by participating in the forms that constitute these qualities in their perfect states. He sometimes characterizes the particulars as being images of the forms. Forms transcend particulars; particulars participate in or reflect forms.

Why did Plato separate forms from particulars? The first of several reasons has to do with knowledge. Knowledge cannot be accounted for, Plato believed, if there are only particulars. Take the knowledge of geometry and the example of what is known about the properties of triangles. A triangle is a three-sided figure whose sides are straight lines. Has anyone ever encountered an absolutely straight line in experience (triangles drawn in the sand or on blackboards, or even printed in books)? The answer is clearly no. The sides, even of a printed figure of a triangle, have breadth, but not absolutely uniform breadth—so they are wavy, not straight lines. But the geometer's knowledge of the properties of triangles depends on triangles having absolutely straight bases and sides. How does one come to have such knowledge? Plato was of the opinion that geometry required the reality of ideal objects, in this case an ideal triangle, which, not existing as particulars in the imperfect world, did not have the imperfections of everything in this world. The ideal objects are forms—in this case the form of triangularity—and these forms are the objects of knowledge.

Another reason Plato had for his doctrine of transcendent forms relates to his metaphysical beliefs. He was convinced that there is something inherently unstable and unreal about all changing things. They do not have any lasting identity; they are never one and the same thing for any period of time. Reality, or real things, must have an unchanging identity, and this characteristic is found only in the forms. Thus they alone are fully real, whereas the ever-mutating particulars are like shadows of the forms, insubstantial and unreal. The forms play an important role, then, in Plato's doctrine that there are degrees or levels of reality; they occupy the highest level in this hierarchy (the only thing higher, the Form of the Good, is described by Plato as "beyond being").

Given the arguments Plato offered for the reality of forms, it is clear that he did not think it is through perception that one grasps them. Perception always has spatio-temporal particulars as its objects. Moreover, knowledge, for example in geometry, is of universal and necessary truths, truths say, about all triangles and what properties they must have. Perception at best encompasses some triangles and what properties they have as a matter of fact, not as a matter of necessity. Thus knowledge of geometry and other disciplines must be derived from something other than perception. Plato referred to it as reason. It is through reason that one knows the forms.

There are grave problems with Plato's theory of the forms, many of which he himself pointed out. The most famous difficulty or objection is what is called the Third-Man Argument. Plato postulates a form to explain the fact that various particular objects resemble one another. Because they resemble one another, there must be a feature they have in common, and this common feature is the form they all participate in. But his form, although different from the particulars by virtue of having a transcendent reality, still must resemble the particulars that participate in it, for otherwise it would not explain the properties of these particulars. Images or reflections, after all, must resemble what they are images or reflections of, and the relation of resemblance is symmetrical. But now, if the original resemblance of particulars required the postulation of a form in order to explain the resemblance, the resemblance between the particulars and the form must also be explained—by postulating another form! If the particulars are men, and the initial form the form of Man, the form explaining the resemblance between men and the form Man must be another form: the third-man form. But now one needs to explain the required resemblance between the third-man form, on the one hand, and the particulars and the form of Man, on the other—and so one must postulate still another form, the fourth-man form. The regress that is thus generated continues infinitely. Given this reasoning, one must postulate, not a single form of man to explain the resemblance of individual men, but rather an infinite number of man-forms. The absurdity of this implication shows that the doctrine of forms is itself absurd. Plato himself was never fully convinced that his doctrine, for this and other reasons, was not in the end unacceptable.

Because of such arguments, together with the intrinsic strangeness of the notion of transcendent forms, Aristotle (384–322 B.C.) rejected his teacher Plato's account. Nevertheless, he retained the notion that there are forms or universals. It is often said that Aristotle brought the Platonic forms down to earth. He characterized them as features of particular objects (individual substances, he called these objects) that give them the natures they have. These features, however, occur in the many different individual substances of the same kind; hence they are universals. An individual substance is a combination of matter and form, the matter being what it is composed of and the form being the structure or characteristics of that matter. Particular substances of the same genus share the property or form that defines the genus; particular substances of the same species share the properties or forms defining the species. And objects that are the same in still other respects also share the forms that explain this identity or resemblance: Everyone reading this encyclopedia, for instance, shares the form "reader of the *Philosophy of Education Encyclopedia.*" Aristotelian forms are immanent in, rather than transcendent of, particulars.

In the eyes of most philosophers, Aristotle's theory of universals is far more plausible than Plato's. Nevertheless, many thinkers continue to have problems with the notion of something real that is essentially general, that can be embodied in two or more particulars at the same or different times. Many would agree with the seventeenth-century British philosopher John Locke (1632–1704) that "all things that exist are particulars." Thus many thinkers reject Aristotle's account of universals as well as that of Plato. Generally speaking, these thinkers fall into either the class of conceptualists or the class of nominalists.

Nominalists deny that there is anything in the world that is general in nature except words, and the latter are general only in the sense that they apply to different things. People use the word *triangle* to refer to or describe many different particular objects or shapes. They do not do so, however, because there is any one thing that the various triangles have in common. There is nothing that justifies the application

of the name to many different objects—that people do so is simply a matter of convention.

Prima facie, such a nominalist position appears highly implausible. *Why,* it will be asked, does one apply the word *triangle* to the things one does? If there is no universal embodied in the particular things called triangles, what reason does one have to apply the term to just these things and not others? Some nominalists respond that people apply general terms to things because of the resemblances these things have to one another (see H.H. Price). All particular triangles resemble one another, and for this reason people call all of them triangles. Realists reject this response. Objects, they point out, always resemble one another in certain respects. Triangles resemble one another with respect to their triangularity, but this is just another way of referring to the universal they share. Furthermore, realists argue, resemblance itself is a universal, a common feature instantiated in all those instances in which particular objects resemble one another in certain respects.

In the minds of many, nominalism fails to explain why and how people can employ general terms; it risks making the employment of these terms arbitrary. Another response to realism that acknowledges the need to explain the use of general terms is that of conceptualism. Conceptualists deny that there are objective universals but grant that there are general ideas in the mind. They argue that the use of general terms is explained by these general ideas. Once one has formed in one's mind a general idea of, say, triangularity, then any particular object encountered in experience that matches this idea is appropriately called a triangle.

What are general ideas, and how does one come to have them? John Locke proposed that they are images formed on the basis of experience. The general image, say of a dog, is one which (a) contains the features held in common by the ideas of particular dogs, but (b) omits the differences among these ideas of particular dogs. Such an idea is generated by abstracting the common features from the total experiences one has of dogs and then combining the abstracted features into the idea of dogness. For this reason, general ideas are often referred to as abstract ideas.

Locke's theory was immediately repudiated by his fellow empiricist, George Berkeley (1685–1753). Berkeley maintained that there are no general ideas of the sort described by Locke. There is no image of what the particular ideas of individual dogs have in common and which also omits all of the characteristics that vary from dog to dog or breed to breed. All ideas, he maintained, are of particular things. Generality for Berkeley is a matter of using a particular idea as a representative for all the things that resemble the dog pictures in the particular idea. David Hume (1711–1776) agreed with Berkeley's theory, and scholars often claim that Locke too developed, and indeed originated, such a theory. Whether one finds it satisfactory or not depends upon one's view of whether the notion of resemblances among particulars incorporated in it brings universals back into the picture. It is also necessary to know more about the alleged process of using one idea to stand for many things. Hume developed this notion in the terms of his doctrine of association of ideas, but many philosophers reject Hume's doctrine as nothing more than illegitimate psychologizing.

Realists have strong arguments against both nominalists and conceptualists. The essence of their position is that one cannot ignore the fact that the experience of nature is of kinds of things, similarities, and identities across particulars. Realists believe that any attempt to explain away this generality inevitably reintroduces it in another guise. Although an ancient doctrine, it has remained popular throughout the ages, attracting many adherents in the Middle Ages—who usually followed either Plato or Aristotle in their philosophical thinking—and claiming the allegiance, although not always in Platonic or Aristotelian terms, of many contemporary philosophers, for instance the Australian materialist David Armstrong.

The doctrine of realism with respect to the external world, merely assumed in most ancient and medieval philosophy, is primarily a modern development. The arguments of the idealists who oppose this form of realism must be considered first. Initially, the idealist critique developed within the classical period of British empiricism. John Locke, the father of British empiricism and himself a realist, had accepted the then-standard scientific view of the world and added an empiricist conception of knowledge to it (as Rene Descartes [1596–1650] earlier had added a rationalist epistemology to it). Accordingly, Locke maintained that there is a material world consisting of objects having all and only the properties appealed to in quantitative scientific explanations: properties such as extension and motion. The human being interacts with this external world through sense perception, a process wherein physical objects and their features produce sensations in the human mind that in turn represent the outside world (hence the term *representational realism*). Locke calls these sensations ideas (the later empiricist David Hume improved on this account by distinguishing the immediate effects of experience, sensations, from the ideas that are copies of them and that remain in the mind after the actual experiences). Both Locke and Hume, and the other major empiricist, George Berkeley, believed that the mind is immediately aware only of sensations or ideas. According to Locke, some of these mental entities, the ideas of primary qualities (ideas of spatial extension and motion), actually reveal the properties of the objects that cause them; other sensations and ideas, those of secondary qualities (color and taste and smell), although produced by the external object, do not actually reflect the properties of these objects. Hence for Locke experience provides two kinds of information about the world: Ideas of primary qualities represent some of the real properties of things in the world, and ideas of secondary qualities at least indicate that there is an object in the world that caused them.

Locke's view quickly came under attack by Berkeley. He argued that there is no way to distinguish ideas of primary and secondary qualities—and to validate the former as informative about the features of the external world—because, by Locke's own lights, it is impossible to directly observe the objects themselves and ascertain that they have the primary qualities (and only those qualities). Moreover, Berkeley maintained, the mind has no genuine idea of matter at all, the substance that is supposed to underlie and possess the primary qualities. All that anyone really has an awareness and hence knowledge of are the person's own ideas. He concluded that *esse est percipi,* to be is to be perceived (or, he added, to perceive). Insofar as the things that are perceived are ideas, and the perceiver is the mind, the only things that exist are minds and their ideas. The real world for Berkeley becomes the world of ideas, specifically those ideas that sustain lawlike regularities among themselves. This is idealism, the variety called subjective idealism because the ideas are modifications of individual minds.

Later idealists appeal to an argument reminiscent of Berkeley's—the argument from the egocentric predicament. No matter how one defines the nature of knowledge, the knowing subject experiences or in some way or other is aware of the objects of knowledge. Thus the human knower can never make contact with anything that does not have a relationship to the mind. It follows for the idealists that all objects of knowledge are mind-related and hence cannot be described as existing independently of the mind.

In addition to subjective idealism, there is an objective or absolute form of idealism—which appeals to one universal mind—developed and defended primarily by Hegel (1770–1831). Hegel began his *Phenomenology of Mind* by arguing that the objects of knowledge clearly and always reveal the presence of mind in them. Most of the knowledge of nature consists of a grasp of universal truths, but, Hegel argued, universality or generality is a mark of reason and hence of mind. Even at the level of sense perception, what one grasps is not a mind-independent particular, but rather a universal or collection of universals. The table one perceives is simply a unique collection of universals of color, shape, size, and so on. Even pointing to a so-called particular object and calling it simply "this" is to grasp it as a universal, for "this" (or "here/now") is a term one applies to an indefinite number of things—hence its generality. The objects of knowledge, even at the level of sense-perception, turn out, then, to be mind-dependent.

Hegel's argument is a historically important example of a general kind of argument often invoked against realists by idealists. The latter will maintain that what human beings claim to know is shaped by human interests and needs, or problem-situations, or concepts and categories, or optional methodologies, or social power structures, or other elements contributed by the mind. (Pragmatists such as William James [1842–1910] and John Dewey [1859–1952]) sometimes flirt with idealism by emphasizing the role of interests, problem-situations, and concepts in the acquisition of knowledge). Idealists argue that it becomes impossible to disentangle the obvious mental elements from what is allegedly contributed by the external, physical objects. Hence they conclude that the known world and all things in it are constructs of the mind, having no reality independent of the mind that comprehends and, at least to some extent, creates it.

Realists have devised a number of responses to these idealist arguments. First, there is the causal argument, which amounts to making explicit a line of reasoning Locke simply assumed to be valid. How, a proponent of the causal argument asks, is one to account for the sensations one has? And how is one to account for the regularity with which they occur? Human beings are passive in perception: Sensations just appear in the mind without any mental effort or voluntary, creative activity on the part of the subject, and for this reason it seems wrong to attribute their existence to the mind itself. The best explanation of their existence is that they are the causal product of the mind interacting with the external world, and hence that they are effects whose causes are ultimately things in the world. The subjective idealist Berkeley was forced to admit that human minds could not account for the existence of sensations; he explained it by appeal to the causal activity of God, an explanation that has the look of desperation.

The appeal to external objects as causes of sensations has another benefit: It explains the regularity of these sensations. Sensations of the same desk may occur to a person every time she goes into her study; sensations of dark clouds are often followed by sensations of rain, and so on. Postulating the existence of a material desk in the study, one that changes very slowly if at all, and attributing to it the causal ability to produce a set of sensations in the mind provides an explanation of why a person has the same sensations when periodically approaching the desk. By postulating the existence of rain clouds and rain, and the causal relation between them, it is possible to explain why the sensations of the one are normally followed by sensations of the other. Thus the realist's belief in the external material world accounts for aspects of experience it would be difficult to explain otherwise.

The problem with the causal argument is that it cannot be directly confirmed. From the standpoint of common sense, one normally attributes causality in cases in which both the cause and the effect are (thought to be) observed: One observes the fire, and one observes the results of putting paper into it; one observes water and then its effects when put on the fire. But does anyone ever observe the material object that is supposed to be the cause of one's sensations? By the empiricists' own admission, the answer is no. Thus their postulation of a world of material objects interacting with the observer is a hypothesis for which there is no observational evidence. If one is committed, as many empiricists are, to the belief that acceptable propositions are restricted to those that can be empirically confirmed, the realist explanation of the existence and regularity of sensations is suspect.

Contemporary scientific realists are not disturbed by this counterargument. It works, they claim, only if one assumes mistakenly that only those propositions that are confirmed through direct observation of their subject matter are philosophically acceptable. In their opinion, philosophers should heed the example of science. Science proceeds by developing theories, but these theories are seldom, if ever, susceptible of direct, observational confirmation. A particular theory is accepted if it offers an explanation of what is observed that assists the scientific community in predicting and controlling future observations. Frequently, the theory that works best to accomplish these ends is one that includes reference to unobservable entities. If what one infers to exist—unobservable material objects—constitutes the best explanation of what one does observe—sensations and the regularities among them—then one has every right to accept the reality of these unobservables.

Another argument used by realists to rebut the idealist's challenge has been to question the conception of sensations that led to the empiricists' predicament. At the turn of the century, the British philosopher G.E. Moore (1873–1958) argued that the empiricist/idealist view failed to distinguish between the sensation as an act of awareness and the sensation as the object of awareness. Sensing red, say, is something the mind does, and this act, to be sure, is mental in nature. But, Moore maintained, the color red, *what* one is aware of, is not mental in nature. It is something that various minds can be aware of and hence something that transcends the individual mind, whereas the act of awareness is what goes on in an individual mind.

Still other philosophers (Gilbert Ryle, J.L. Austin, David Armstrong) challenged the idealist position by rejecting the claim that one does not directly observe physical objects. There is all the difference in the world, they maintained, between observing a sensation, say a sensation of pain in one's hand, and observing a physical object like a book. The sensation has bodily location, the perception of a physical object does not (the pain is in one's hand, the book has no location within the body—it is on the table!).

One variation of this argument is the claim that idealists (and their empiricist ancestors) have misunderstood the concepts of sensation and perception. When these conceptual blunders are corrected, the realist's claim that one directly perceives physical objects will be seen as a conceptual truth that cannot be rejected without violating the very meanings of the linguistic terms used to describe perception. If the theory of direct perception is to be viable, however, realists must explain such things as the perspectival nature of perception and perceptual illusions, which tend to suggest that what is perceived directly is *not* an external object. Different people see objects differently (some see a coin as circular, others as elliptical), and sometimes what one thinks one sees does not exist at all (an oasis in the desert). Realists in recent years have developed a number of ways of explaining how such facts are consistent with the claim that it is possible to perceive physical objects directly.

With regard to the argument from the egocentric predicament (which claims that one can never know anything that does not have a relation to the mind), realists have responded by arguing that all it proves is that "everything experienced is experienced." While this proposition is true, it is in effect totally uninformative. It does not entail that everything that is real is experienced; nor does it entail that things that are experienced do not exist independently of being experienced. It may be the case, as G.E. Moore pointed out, that "being experienced" is an external relation that some objects and events have to the mind. An external relation, as opposed to an internal one, is a relation that is not essential to a thing, one it is possible to conceive of the thing's not having. To the extent that one can conceive of objects existing when not perceived or thought of, these mental relations are not essential, internal relations. Realists believe that it is possible to conceive of a world in which there are no human beings and hence possible to think of objects existing independently of mind (one realist suggested one should think of the world as it existed prior to the sixth day of creation.)

How do realists respond to the Hegelian claim that what one knows is always permeated with rational or mental elements? Most would respond by claiming that, even if it is true that such things as human interests or theoretical constructs are involved in the development of theories about reality, there are ways of deciding among conflicting theories by appeal to something independent of these human factors. It is what happens in the world, as revealed, say, through a scientific experiment that determines the acceptability of a theory. Moreover, there are certain facts of nature that one simply cannot deny, regardless of the interests or constructs that shape one's theories. That water has a certain chemical structure, that physical objects are affected by gravity, that human beings are mortal—these and many other facts are realities to which, far from being mind-dependent, the human mind must conform.

Robert L. Arrington

See also EMPIRICISM; EPISTEMOLOGY; IDEALISM; METAPHYSICS; PRAGMATISM; RATIONALISM; REASON AND RATIONALITY

Bibliography

Armstrong, David. *Universals and Scientific Realism*. Vol. 1, *Nominalism and Realism*. Cambridge: Cambridge University Press, 1978.

Austin, J.L. *Sense and Sensibilia*. Oxford: Clarendon Press, 1962.

Copleston, Frederick, S.J. *A History of Western Philosophy*. London: Burns and Oates, 1961. Vol. 1, part 3 (Plato); Vol. 1, part 4 (Aristotle); Vol. 2, chap. 14 (problem of universals in medieval philosophy); Vol. 5, chap. 1 (Hobbes); Vol. 5, chap. 5 (Locke); Vol. 5, chap. 12 (Berkeley); Vol. 5, chap. 14 (Hume).

Davidson, Donald. "Truth and Meaning." *Synthese* 17 (1967).

Hill, T.E. *Contemporary Theories of Knowledge*. New York: Ronald Press, 1961.

Kripke, Saul. *Naming and Necessity*. Oxford: Blackwell, 1980.

Loux, Michael J., ed. *Universals and Particulars*. New York: Anchor Books, Doubleday and Co., 1970.

Moore, G.E. *Philosophical Studies*. London and New York: Routledge and Kegan Paul, 1922.

Perry, R.B. "The Ego-Centric Predicament." *Journal of Philosophy* 7 (1920): 5–14.

Price, H.H. *Thinking and Experience*. London: Hutchinson, 1962.

Putnam, Hilary. *Philosophical Papers*, vols. 1 and 2. Cambridge: Cambridge University Press, 1975.

Sayre-McCord, G., ed. *Essays in Moral Realism*. Ithaca, N.Y.: Cornell University Press, 1988.

Smart, J.J.C. *Philosophy and Scientific Realism*. London: Routledge, 1963; New York: Humanities Press, 1963.

Reason and Rationality

In the Western philosophical tradition, reason and rationality have long been regarded as important intellectual ideals. In the philosophy of education, they have been similarly esteemed as central educational aims or ideals. Historically, philosophers of education whose positions otherwise diverge considerably, for example Socrates, Plato, Aristotle, John Locke, Jean-Jacques Rousseau, Immanuel Kant, Bertrand Russell, John Dewey, R.S. Peters, and Israel Scheffler, all advocate (with various qualifications) the fostering of rationality as a fundamental educational aim. No other proposed aim of education—knowledge, happiness, community, civic-mindedness, creativity, the fulfillment of potential—has enjoyed the virtually unanimous endorsement of historically important philosophers of education that reason and rationality have.

In contemporary discussions, the fostering of rationality continues to be defended by many as an important educational aim or ideal. Unlike some historical predecessors, contemporary advocates of the ideal do not understand reason as a special psychological "faculty"; in defending rationality, they do not align themselves with the historical movement known as Continental Rationalism, according to which knowledge is based on the perception or intuition afforded by such a faculty. Rather, what is advocated is that education have as a fundamental aim the fostering in students of (1) the ability to reason well—that is, to (construct and) evaluate the various reasons that have been or can be offered in support or criticism of candidate beliefs, judgments, and actions; and (2) the disposition or inclination to be guided by reasons so evaluated—to believe, judge, and act in accordance with the results of such reasoned evaluations. Students (and people generally) are rational (or reasonable) to the extent that they believe, judge, and act on the basis of (competently evaluated) reasons. Consequently, reason and rationality constitute one ideal rather than two: To regard rationality as a fundamental educational aim or ideal is to hold that the fostering in students of the ability to reason well and the disposition to be guided by reasons is of central educational importance.

The two aspects of the ideal just mentioned deserve further comment. The first—the ability to reason well—presupposes an account of the constitution of good reasons that the proponent of the ideal is obliged to provide. How do we determine that a proposed reason for some belief, judgment, or action is a good or forceful one? What are the guidelines, or principles, in accordance with which the goodness of candidate reasons are to be ascertained? What is the nature of such principles? How are they themselves justified? These questions are epistemological in nature; they call for a general account of the relationship between a putative reason and the belief, judgment, or action for which it is a reason. Such an epistemological account will have to grapple with deep questions concerning the nature of epistemic justification, the relationship between justification and truth (and so the nature of truth), the relativity (or absoluteness) of principles of reason evaluation, and so forth. In this sense, the educational ideals of reason and rationality depend, for their own justification, on an adequately articulated and defended underlying epistemology (Siegel 1988, 1989).

The second aspect of the ideal mentioned above—the disposition or inclination to be guided by the results of the reasoned evaluation of reasons—has broader philosophical implications. Here the ideal recommends not simply the fostering of skills or abilities of reason assessment, but the fostering of a wide range of attitudes, habits of mind, and character traits thought to be characteristic of the rational or reasonable person (Scheffler 1973; Siegel 1988). This extends the ideal beyond the bounds of the cognitive, for, so understood, the ideal is one of a certain sort of person. In advocating the fostering of particular dispositions, attitudes, and character traits, as well as particular skills and abilities, the proponent of this educational aim denies the legitimacy, or at least the educational relevance, of any sharp distinction between the cognitive and the affective, or the rational and the emotional. The ideal calls for the fostering of certain skills and abilities as well as for the fostering of a certain sort of character. It is thus a general ideal of a certain sort of person, which sort of person it is the task of education to help to create. This aspect of the educational idea of rationality aligns it with the complementary ideal of autonomy, since a rational person will also be an autonomous one,

capable of independently judging the justifiedness of candidate beliefs and the legitimacy of candidate values.

In contemporary discussions, these ideals are often discussed in terms of "critical thinking." Advocates of efforts to foster critical thinking in the schools sometimes conceive this aim narrowly, in terms of imparting skills that will enable students to function adequately in their jobs, and, in so doing, to be economically productive. More often, however, proponents of the educational aim of critical thinking have in mind the broader view of critical thinking as more or less equivalent to the ideal of rationality. In any case, it is only when understood in this broad way that the educational aim of critical thinking can be adequately analyzed and defended (Siegel 1988).

Perhaps the leading exponent of the ideal of rationality (and its near-equivalent, critical thinking) in contemporary philosophical discussion of education is Israel Scheffler. Scheffler urges that "critical thought is of the first importance in the conception and organization of educational activities" (1973: 1); "rationality . . . is a matter of *reasons,* and to take it as a fundamental educational idea is to make as pervasive as possible the free and critical quest for reasons, in all realms of study" (1973: 62); "the fundamental trait to be encouraged is that of reasonableness. . . . In training our students to reason we train them to be critical" (1973: 142–43). In these and many other passages in his writings, Scheffler forcefully and articulately defends the central educational importance of the ideals of rationality and critical thinking. He also regards these ideals as central to the understanding of teaching, and is the originator of what has come to be called "the rationality theory of teaching," according to which

> to teach . . . is at some points at least to submit oneself to the understanding and independent judgment of the pupil. . . . Teaching . . . requires us to reveal our reasons to the student and, by so doing, to submit them to his evaluation and criticism. . . . To teach is thus . . . to acknowledge the "reason" of the pupil, i.e. his demand for and judgment of reasons. (Scheffler 1960: 57–59; see also Scheffler 1973: 2–3)

In his defense of the educational ideal of rationality in the broad context of his work in epistemology, philosophy of science, and philosophy of language, and his application of it to teaching and to other dimensions of education, Scheffler articulates the most significant theoretical discussion of these matters among contemporary philosophers of education, and indeed among contemporary philosophers generally (Neiman and Siegel).

In the long tradition of discussion of these issues, most authors have equated "rationality" and "reasonableness"; the ideal was generally understood in terms of the fostering of both rationality and reasonableness, which were understood as equivalent or near-equivalent expressions. Recently, however, some writers have attempted to distinguish between them, and to favor one reading of the ideal rather than the other. Of particular note is Nicholas C. Burbules's effort (1991) to discredit the ideal, when understood in terms of rationality, for relying on an overly formalistic conception of rationality; and to defend the ideal, when understood in terms of reasonableness, in terms primarily of character. Burbules defends the ideal in terms of the fostering of what he calls "virtues"; the virtues he defends under the heading of reasonableness do not involve skill in reason assessment as discussed above, but rather virtues of character such as sympathy, humility, and tolerance of and willingness to enter into the worldview of others. Siegel (1991) argues that while Burbules is on solid ground in emphasizing the character dimension of the ideal, his rejection of the epistemological, reason-evaluation dimension of it is problematic. He argues further that, when purged of its formalistic connotations, which Burbules rightly criticizes, the ideal, encompassing both rationality and reasonableness in Burbules's sense, survives.

Deeper challenges to the ideal have recently been articulated by feminist critics, who argue that, as standardly conceived, the ideal harbors deep masculinist biases, and by postmodernist critics, who argue that the idea is prototypically modernist and retains all the flaws associated with modernism. Full consideration of these challenges is beyond the scope of this discussion. It should be noted, however, that the proponent of the ideal must, to be consistent, regard such challenges as centrally important, and must regard the obligation to take such challenges seriously as integral to rationality itself. In that regard, deep criticisms of the ideal, and reasoned consideration of both its praiseworthy characteristics and its indefensible ones, are exactly what the ideal itself recommends. Whether the ideal survives these important criticisms (or others) is at present an open question. It nevertheless remains central that the convictions (shared alike by defenders and critics of the ideal) that criticisms of the ideal are at least potentially significant, and that the defenders of the ideal have an intellectual obligation to consider all criticisms seriously and to acknowledge them and change their views accordingly when the criticisms are rightly judged to be of merit, are themselves underwritten by the ideal. Therefore, there is a limit beyond which any proposed criticism of rationality cannot go without undermining itself. To that degree, the ideal of rationality, at least in some formulation, cannot be coherently rejected (Siegel 1992).

Harvey Siegel

See also AIMS OF EDUCATION; CRITICAL THINKING; EPISTEMOLOGY; FEMINISM; FORMALISM; LIBERAL EDUCATION; MODERNISM AND POSTMODERNISM; PERSON, CONCEPT OF; RATIONALISM; RELATIVISM; TEACHING AND LEARNING; TRUTH

Bibliography

Burbules, Nicholas C. "The Virtues of Reasonableness." In *Philosophy of Education 1991*. Proceedings of the forty-seventh annual meeting of the Philosophy of Education Society, edited by Margret Buchmann and Robert E. Floden, 215–24. Normal, Ill.: Philosophy of Education Society, 1991.

Neiman, Alven, and Harvey Siegel. "Objectivity and Rationality in Epistemology and Education: Scheffler's Middle Road." *Synthese* 94 (1993): 55–83.

Scheffler, Israel. *The Language of Education.* Springfield, Ill.: Charles C. Thomas, 1960.

———. *Reason and Teaching.* London: Routledge and Kegan Paul, 1973.

Siegel, Harvey. *Educating Reason: Rationality, Critical Thinking, and Education.* New York and London: Routledge, 1988.

———. "Epistemology, Critical Thinking, and Critical Thinking Pedagogy." *Argumentation* 3 (1989): 127–40.

———. "The Rationality of Reasonableness." In *Philosophy of Education 1991*. Proceedings of the forty-seventh annual meeting of the Philosophy of Education Society, edited by Margret Buchmann and

Robert E. Floden, 225–33. Normal, Ill.: Philosophy of Education Society, 1991.

———. "Rescher on the Justification of Rationality." *Informal Logic* 14 (1992): 23–31.

Talaska, Richard A., ed. *Critical Reasoning in Contemporary Culture.* Albany: State University of New York Press, 1992.

Reconstructionism, Social

A social and philosophical theory stressing the need for continuous, critical examination of cultural and educational institutions and their reconstruction into forms that would allow the maximum possible self-realization of the great masses of the people.

The initial expression of social reconstructionist educational theory arose in response to the economic and political crises of the 1920s and 1930s. In a society marked by gross inequalities of wealth, where great numbers of ordinary people suffered poverty and destitution in the midst of natural and material abundance, and in a world where authoritarian regimes and political fanaticism were increasing ominously, a small but influential group of educational theorists struggled to develop a comprehensive philosophy of fundamental educational and social improvement.

Though differing in emphasis, the varieties of social reconstructionism share common elements. Though certainly not the only source, a particularly good forum for the expression of these views, especially in the early years, was *The Social Frontier: A Journal of Educational Criticism and Reconstruction,* published between 1934 and 1943. Another seminal text in the early phase of social reconstructionism is *Dare the Schools Build a New Social Order?* (1932) by George Counts (1889–1974). Other educational scholars such as Harold Rugg (1886–1960), and especially Theodore Brameld (1904–1987), were active in the early period and later developed social reconstructionism into a systematic philosophy and theory of education.

It may be said fairly that all varieties of social reconstructionism operate in the broad tradition of the philosophical pragmatism and progressive educational theory of John Dewey (1859–1952). When Dewey wrote in *Democracy and Education* (1916) of education as the "constant reorganizing and reconstructing of experience," a view that he held identified the end and process of education as well as its social and individual functions, he provided a point of critical departure for progressive educational theorists. For some educational theorists, however, the conditions of social and economic crisis were signals of serious omissions within mainstream progressive educational theory that demanded urgent revision.

In Theodore Brameld's view, the Achilles' heel of progressive educational theory and practice was the neglect of ends, and, with that, specific, programmatic plans of action. In a direct criticism of Dewey, Brameld argued that progressive education had focused too much on how we think rather than on what we should think. In Brameld's view, developed in different ways by other writers, the philosopher must be as much a visionary as an analyzer, educating the community to think of and plan for worlds that could be potential futures. Thus, while rooted in a critical analysis of what is, the social reconstructionists insisted upon the efficacy of utopian thought and the obligation of educators to assist the public in envisioning and building a new society and a new culture. Although developed in various forms, the central roles given to looking to the future, goal-seeking, and utopianism are characteristics of social reconstructionism.

How do these visions of alternative futures arise? Are some futures better than others? How will the public, a classroom of students, or any group decide on what futures are worthy of their organization and effort? First, the future must be seen as something other than a subject of idle speculation. For Brameld and other social reconstructionists, the future, just as much as the present, is a part of ontology; it is a generic trait of existence. Humans are by nature drawn to goal-seeking; goal-seeking is central to learning, and all goal-seeking, and thus all learning theory, is future-oriented. Further, goal-seeking behavior is significantly nonrational. Our goals and wants are known largely unmediated by reason, by what Brameld called "prehension" in contrast to the rational process of apprehension. It is precisely the kind of social power and energy that are attached to objects of prehension, their immediacy and felt attachment, that are required to bring utopias into existence.

Harold Rugg, another noted social reconstructionist, expressed this view over a long career focused on the cultural uses of imagination. In Rugg's view, in part echoing the criticism of Randolph Bourne (1886–1918), Deweyan pragmatism and progressivism put too much stress on science, inquiry, and experimentation to the neglect of the arts and imagination. This focus on the instruments of knowledge, the means, made progressivism compatible with an emerging industrial, corporate society. This view devalues the exercise of the social imagination, the visioning and re-visioning of alternative futures. It is these visions, the products of imagination, prehended and unbounded by the demands of ratiocination, that supply the ends and the motivation required for social groups to work collectively for cultural renewal and reconstruction. While a descriptive and analytical diagnosis of present social life is part of the task, even more important are the tasks of imagining cultural forms that would serve better the shared, communal, public goals by developing effective means of educating and organizing the public to achieve them through social reconstruction.

The relevance of educational considerations becomes apparent. First, educators have the responsibility to prepare learners with the skills and knowledge necessary for a critical analysis of contemporary culture. Beyond this and more important, educators must take the lead in developing methods and occasions for the development of group consensus of goals and futures and the methods of dialogue and shared decision-making through which organizations can be formed to make these goals manifest through social reconstruction. Groups of people joined by common experience tend to develop shared norms. However, in hierarchical, divided, class societies where individual competition rules, the possibilities for social consensus are limited. Thus, the educational challenge is to find ways to facilitate voluntary social consensus on norms, goals, and desired futures. Dissatisfied with the progressive belief that the workings of intelligence would naturally find their way to the good, and also rejecting the option of indoctrinating students with particular utopian beliefs, the social reconstructionists sought some form of what Brameld called "defensible partiality" for educating about and toward preferred futures.

Again, although expressed in different ways, these preferred futures were defined in reference to democratic ideals. Brameld challenged educators to work for a world in which "the common man" rules not merely in theory but in fact and where the material and cultural resources existing in the modern world could be directed by public control for the fulfillment of the natural values of humanity. Harold Rugg and others wrote of educating for democracy as a form of aesthetic community, rather than a mechanism for registering public opinion. George Counts, also critical of child-centered progressivism and the anemic, individualistic idea of democracy offered in mainstream varieties of progressive education, argued that the schools must take responsibility to lead in a collective struggle to democratize the economic, as well as cultural, spheres of social life.

Later curricular theorists, such as William O. Stanley and B.O. Smith, though stressing that social reconstructionism implied a modification, rather than repudiation, of social and cultural institutions, emphasized that belief in the democratic ideal demands a continuous re-examination of social ideals, beliefs, and institutions. At the core of all varieties of social reconstructionism is a belief in using democratic methods to extend the democratic ideal to schools, culture, the economy, and politics.

There have been many critics. For some, the focus on the educator's responsibility to develop group consensus on preferred futures opened the path to methods of indoctrination. Brameld's effort to distinguish indoctrination, which he rejected, from propaganda, defined as a "short cut" route through prehension to learning in the service of the good, which he believed was justified in times of crisis, did little to allay these concerns. Closely connected to these problems is the criticism that the social reconstructionists, for all their talk of the democratic ideal, placed an undue reliance on experts to formulate the problems for the public and lead them to consensus on preferred futures. The appeal to prehended goals, unmediated by reason or the claims of evidence, opens the possibility of authoritarian manipulation. The social reconstructionist's attention to adult education and, later, techniques for intercultural communication and group dynamics were responses to these concerns. Others found an incongruity between the origins of social reconstructionist thought in a reality-based analysis of a culture in crisis and the rhetorical solution of utopian futures. Drawing on the distinction made by Lewis Mumford (1895–1990) between "utopias of escape" and "utopias of reconstruction," Brameld argued that utopian thought is at the core of human nature and education for democracy.

For these criticisms and other reasons, social reconstructionism has had little influence in philosophy of education in the second half of the twentieth century. However, the growing power of conservative cultural and political movements in the 1980s sparked a renewed interest in the social reconstructionist legacy as part of a critical educational movement. The contemporary critical educational theorist Henry Giroux appeals to the social reconstructionist tradition as part of an effort to develop a new democratic public philosophy of education. Just as Brameld wrote in response to the "New Reaction" of the 1950s, Giroux writes of the obligation of progressive educators in the 1980s and 1990s to respond to the "New Right" with a substantive, goal-oriented vision of democratic public education. Giroux's use of the language of utopianism, a "provisional morality" that can justify education into preferred futures, as well as his thorough-going commitment to the democratization of school, culture, politics, and the economy are echoes of the social reconstructionist tradition.

James M. Giarelli

See also DEMOCRACY; DEWEY; INDOCTRINATION; PRAGMATISM

Bibliography

Bourne, Randolph S. "Twilight of Idols." *Seven Arts Magazine* 2 (1917): 688–702.

Brameld, Theodore. *Ends and Means in Education: A Mid-Century Appraisal.* New York: Harper and Row, 1950.

———. *Patterns of Educational Philosophy.* Yonkers on Hudson: World Book, 1950.

Counts, George S. *Dare the Schools Build a New Social Order?* New York: John Day, 1932.

Giroux, Henry A. *Schooling and the Struggle for Public Life.* Minneapolis: University of Minnesota Press, 1988.

McClellan, James E. "Theodore Brameld and the Architecture of Confusion." Chap. 3 in *Toward an Effective Critique of American Education.* Philadelphia: J.B. Lippincott, 1968.

Stanley, William B. *Curriculum for Utopia: Social Reconstructionism and Critical Pedagogy in the Postmodern Era.* Albany: State University of New York Press, 1992.

Relativism

Since a persistent complaint about relativism has been that no coherent statement of the thesis can be given, any characterization of it is controversial and runs the risk of begging the question either for or against the thesis. For example, if relativism is the view that "anything goes"—that is, that all beliefs are equally true or well justified, it has little to recommend it. Nevertheless, because the intuitions that relativism expresses have attracted many thinkers, and the thesis is currently experiencing a revival, there is good reason to attempt to describe the claim and explain its appeal. The challenge is to provide an account that is neither obviously false nor too weak to be interesting.

According to the theory of relativity, mass and velocity, once thought to be invariant or absolute, are in fact relative to inertial frameworks. Similarly, relativists hold that basic epistemic or metaphysical features, commonly held to be absolute or invariant, are relative to the cognitive resources of individuals or social groups. Perception, concepts, reasons, standards of rationality, truth, reality, and moral principles have all been held to be relative in this sense. Hence relativism is a family of views rather than a single thesis.

This account focuses primarily on the version of relativism that has generated the most contemporary discussion, namely the view that truth or reality is relative to conceptual schemes (also referred to as frameworks, paradigms, forms of life, world views, and perspectives). This form of relativism holds that truth or reality is not absolute, objective, and universal, but rather varies with the conceptual scheme being employed. According to the relativist, there is no scheme-independent way of deciding between competing frameworks, no possibility of determining truth in a way that transcends all schemes. In its strongest form, the thesis implies that a statement may be true relative to one framework and false relative to another. For example, it could be true that there are witches relative to the world view of one social group and false relative to the world view of another group. These two groups, then, are said by the relativist to live in different worlds.

Relativism should be distinguished from a variety of other claims: (1) It involves more than the simple observation that people hold different and conflicting beliefs about the nature of the world, what is morally right or wrong, and so forth. It is even stronger than the claim that such conflicting views may each be rationally held or well justified. These observations are compatible with there being at most one correct view in each case. Although relativism may be inspired by the observation of diversity of beliefs, it goes beyond this empirical fact to assert that more than one of these views may be true, even when they are incompatible. For example, it may be true both that there are witches and that there are not witches, depending on which scheme is being employed. (2) Also, relativism is a stronger thesis than the uncontroversial point that the truth of some assertions depends on the context and occasion of their utterance. Everyone agrees that the truth of "It is raining now," for example, is relative to time and place. These examples, involving indexical constructions such as "now," "here," "yesterday," and so on, have no bearing on the truth of relativism. (3) Relativism must be distinguished from nihilism or skepticism—that is, from the view that there is no truth or the claim that we cannot know what the truth is. According to the relativist, we can know the truth, but there are many "truths" rather than one truth for all.

Any plausible form of relativism must maintain a distinction between what people believe to be true and what is true; that is, it must be compatible with the possibility of error. Otherwise, "P is true for X" will simply be a roundabout way of saying that "X believes P." One advantage of the relativism that relies on the possibility of different conceptual schemes is that it meets this requirement. Presumably a conceptual scheme will contain methods of inquiry and criteria for truth within its domain. Thus someone who holds a particular belief might in fact be mistaken relative to the requirements of that person's own conceptual framework. Someone might be mistaken, for example, in holding that a particular person is a witch, although witches form part of the society's conceptual scheme, because the methods of evidence for determining witchcraft have not been properly employed.

Relativism generates a variety of puzzles that have been held to establish its incoherence. For example, when relativists assert the thesis of relativism they make the claim that it is true. If this means that the statement "all truth is relative" is (absolutely) true, relativists contradict themselves. On the other hand, if it means that relativism is true relative to the conceptual scheme of the relativist, the relativist must concede that, on its own account, relativism may be false relative to many other conceptual schemes (that of the absolutist, for example). The most common response of the relativist to this argument is simply to agree that relativism is true relative to a conceptual scheme. While this move may appear to preclude the possibility of rational debate between defenders and critics of relativism, relativists tend to hold that relativism is a logical consequence of beliefs shared by many conceptual schemes, perhaps even that of the absolutist. The relativist argues that absolutism itself cannot be adequately defended on its own terms and that relativism is the rational alternative.

Some philosophers have denied the coherence of the idea of radically different conceptual schemes, on which the contemporary version of relativism depends. If the content of one conceptual scheme can be explained using the resources of another, in what sense are they different conceptual schemes? On the other hand, if one "scheme" is totally inaccessible from the perspective of another, how could one who employed the second scheme have grounds for believing that the first is a conceptual scheme at all? Equally puzzling is the claim that a statement could be true in one scheme and false in another. It is commonly held that a necessary condition for one statement's being a proper translation of another (that is, for the two to be equivalent in meaning) is that they have the same truth conditions. Hence, if the truth conditions of the two statements vary, this would be sufficient evidence that they are not the same statement. How, then, can the same statement be true in one framework and false in another? These objections point to the difficulty of identifying and individuating conceptual schemes and of explaining the way in which the schemes in question are conflicting or incompatible.

Relativists offer a variety of responses to these problems. Some argue that, while we may not have evidence that there are genuinely alternative and mutually incomprehensible conceptual schemes, that fact does not prove that none do or could exist. We might be able to imagine ways in which such divergences could come about, and thus give content to the idea, even if in the nature of the case we cannot offer examples. Others argue that the ability to explain and understand one scheme using the resources of another does not mean that they are not genuine alternatives of the sort required by relativism. The inability to translate from one scheme to the other is too strong a requirement, it is said. The schemes are "alternative" if they countenance incompatible truth claims. Finally, some relativists require neither the failure of translation nor conflict in truth claims for establishing alternative conceptual schemes. In a situation such as this, the schemes may be pragmatically conflicting in the sense that they cannot be compatibly employed. Although users of one scheme may be able to understand other schemes, those other schemes are not (and could not now be) the basis for how they see the world or act in it. Users of the two frameworks think about the world differently even if they can understand each other's perspective. A shift from one framework to another in this sense, if it could be accomplished, would require resocialization, not merely the acquisition of a new set of concepts. This view endorses conceptual relativism but not necessarily relativism of truth.

Relativism continues to appeal to many despite the puzzles it generates. Why? Contemporary relativism appears to be motivated by both philosophical and political considerations. Philosophically, it stems from the position, familiar at least since Immanuel Kant (1724–1804), that "the world" is partially constituted by the representing mind. The relativist rejects the metaphysical realist's picture of "the world" as having a structure independent of conceptualization and perspective. This claim, however, can be accepted by nonrelativists. If in addition one holds that conceptual frameworks can vary historically and culturally, and that there are no independent criteria for choosing among competing frameworks, then relativism emerges. Politically, the appeal of relativism is its commitment to pluralism. There is felt to be something totalitarian about insisting on one truth for all. Relativists protest the tendency to turn the ways of organizing experience of one particular social order into a universal requirement, especially when such a move has the effect of suppressing effective criticism of that social order.

Alternatively, critics of relativism appear to see something positively pernicious about "the specter of relativism." It is important to note that absolutism can also support a moral and political stance. If our minds are unconstrained by reality, such that incompatible views can be equally rationally justified, then radical disagreement seems resolvable only by force. Absolutists sometimes see themselves as affirming our common humanity in the interests of political equality and rational resolution of disputes.

Hence the contemporary discussion of relativism concerns not only fundamental issues in metaphysics and epistemology but also involves competing political stances.

Emily Robertson

See also EPISTEMOLOGY; ETHICS AND MORALITY; FEMINISM; HISTORICISM; IDEALISM; MODERNISM AND POSTMODERNISM; REASON AND RATIONALITY; SCIENCE, PHILOSOPHY OF; SOCIAL SCIENCES, PHILOSOPHY OF; TRUTH

Bibliography

Gellner, Ernest. *Relativism and the Social Sciences*. Cambridge: Cambridge University Press, 1985.

Hollis, Martin, and Steven Lukes, eds. *Rationality and Relativism*. Cambridge: MIT Press, 1982.

Krausz, Michael, and Jack W. Meiland, eds. *Relativism: Cognitive and Moral*. Notre Dame: University of Notre Dame Press, 1982.

McMullin, Ernan, ed. *Construction and Constraint*. Notre Dame: University of Notre Dame Press, 1988.

Margolis, Joseph. *The Truth about Relativism*. Oxford: Blackwell, 1991.

Putnam, Hilary. *Realism with a Human Face*. Cambridge: Harvard University Press, 1990.

Siegel, Harvey. *Relativism Refuted*. Dordrecht: D. Reidel, 1987.

Religious Education

Traditionally, the concept of religious education has been used to refer to the faith-nurturing activities of a community of faith, especially those designed to initiate or induct children and young people into its central corpus of knowledge and beliefs, its traditions and practices, its perspective on moral issues, how it sees its relationship to other religious traditions, and how it responds to civil and legal obligations that are a consequence of its being part of a wider, secular society.

The essential characteristics and purpose of this conception of religious education are rooted in its being seen as both an expression of faith and an initiation into faith. For example, the rationale for engaging in such an activity will be based upon religious or theological concepts which themselves are derived from core beliefs that a community holds to be revealed truth about human nature and its relationship to divine nature. The purpose of religious education will thus be to actualize that relationship in the life of the individual adherent and in the life of the community of faith. It is inevitable, therefore, that this form of religious education will be specific to a particular religion; it will aim to induct or nurture initiates into Christian faith, Islamic faith, Hindu faith, Jewish faith, and so on. Indeed, it is the duty and prerogative of each faith community to establish its own pattern of religious education, and, although similarities will exist, each will have its own distinctive procedures of religious upbringing and, for those seeking admission to the faith from outside, procedures of religious initiation.

It is in the combination of involuntariness and voluntariness on the part of the person to be nurtured or religiously educated and the close relationship between the activities of the home and those of the faith community that the distinctiveness of each form of "faith-based" religious education may be discerned as a perfect linking of the "theory" and "practice" of a particular religion. Children of Christians, Muslims, Hindus, Jews, Sikhs, and so forth, are brought involuntarily within the ambit of faith by the circumstances of their birth. Their religion is thus an essential part of the fabric of their lives. They learn about their faith, and to have faith, in and through their domestic routines; whatever instruction they receive—from parents and from members of the faith community—becomes part, either consciously or unconsciously, of their emerging identity. In this sense they are being fashioned or shaped into faith as a natural part of their development as human beings; thus their religious education is furthered through practice. The "theory" of their faith may not be immediately understood or even appreciated, but, given the opportunity of a continuing relationship with their families and faith communities, a coalescence between theory and practice takes place. In the same manner, adults who voluntarily seek to be initiated into a faith are nurtured in it by their willing involvement in its corporate life and experience, as well as through direct instruction. In this form of religious education there is constant interaction on the part of the person being nurtured between living the faith and learning about the faith. The outcome of such a process—which is lifelong—is that questions of personal identity and personal worth (Who

am I? Where do I belong? What is my purpose?) are both raised and answered within a perspective of religious faith because the process itself is ultimately directed toward the creation of an all-embracing religious consciousness. A religious interpretation of human experience is thus established as an essentially subjective and interior experience of a lived reality that remains the norm for the interpretation of all experience.

This latter point is fundamental to understanding the long-standing relationship between religions and education. A faith-based view of religious education cannot be restricted to initiation into religious knowledge because that fails to recognize that, for most religious believers, religious knowledge encompasses, informs, and completes all knowledge. A truly religious education is, therefore, an education in which all fields of knowledge—the so-called secular subjects or disciplines—are contextualized within a single, coherent pattern of religious meaning. In other words, a first-order reason for religions being involved with education is epistemological. An equally significant reason concerns the aims or ends of education. If all knowledge is, in a sense, contingent upon revealed religious truth, the ultimate end of education must be, to use a Christian word, redemptive—that is, directed toward the restoration and redemption of human beings and human society in the light of that truth. Thus it should be religious beliefs about the nature and destiny of humanity that fulfill a normative and prescriptive function in thinking about education in general and its aims in particular. In contemporary societies, many other factors are, of course, instrumental in encouraging faith communities to establish their own schools—for example, the experience of racism, the concern to preserve cultural identity as many young people from all faiths and cultures become assimilated into, and enculturated by, a dominant secularism and materialism, the absence of religious education in the state school curriculum, and so on. While these may be persuasive reasons in their own right, it is as expressions of the more fundamental, epistemological and soteriological assumptions that religious adherents hold about their own faith that makes them substantive and persistent.

The history of education, however, bears witness to the many problems that arise when religion and education are brought into any form of relationship, and, in the modern era, the conception of religious education as a religious activity having a place within a state or public system of education has largely disappeared. Consequently, where religious education has not been excluded from the state school curriculum it has undergone a significant change in its conception. Its transformation from a religious activity to an educational activity raises, however, many administrative, philosophical, and theological problems, some of which may now be examined.

If, as indicated, one of the main points of difference between religions and education is to be seen in conflicting epistemological assumptions about the nature of knowledge, under what circumstances is it possible to recontextualize the study of a religion within an educational process based on value assumptions that may not be compatible with those of the religion itself? From the point of view of educators, this is necessary because, at least within the Western tradition of liberal education, the concept of education itself is a normative, discriminatory, or critical one that identifies criteria to which processes such as educating, training, instructing, and teaching should conform. Thus, despite the persistence of their title (which, like "Religious Education" itself, suffers from an ambiguous adjective), religious educators are secular educators concerned with the study of religion. They are secular educators insofar as the educational principles that govern their activities as educators are, in the first instance, those governing the activities of educators per se, irrespective of their subject disciplines. Such principles relate to the manner in which all subject disciplines, including religion, are to be investigated—in a manner that assists the development of cognitive perspective or rationality, promotes understanding of the structure and procedures of the disciplines, recognizes the integrity, autonomy, and voluntariness of the student, and so on. Thus, the legitimation of any educational process so conceived lies in these principles having a higher claim on how educators fulfill their task than any beliefs of a personal nature that they may hold about the subject matter they are required to teach, or any expectations that might be held by a faith community that their value assumptions should replace them. In short, a secular educational process cannot accommodate religious goals.

From the point of view of religious adherents, to study religious faith within any other context than that of its own self-understanding is to distort, reduce, or domesticate it. The view of religion implied by religious educators using such descriptions as a "field of study," a "discipline," a "form of knowledge," a "social phenomenon," a "belief system," an "ideology," or a "stance for living" is incongruent with a religious community's understanding of its own faith as the vehicle for revealed, eternal Truth. Adherents hold that their religion cannot be known or judged by its capacity to fulfill truth tests or contribute to educational goals based on criteria other than Truth itself—that is, that which is enshrined in the faith tradition and by which all truths are judged. Neither should a religion be studied for some instrumental educational purpose, but only for the purpose of gaining greater insight into Truth and strengthening one's commitment to it. To study a religion to gain "religious understanding" can only be meaningful if it refers to the level of consciousness of one's awareness and knowledge of God and of one's dependence upon Him. Furthermore, if the faith-orientation of religious education as a religious activity is removed, with what is it replaced? Is it legitimate for what is regarded by adherents as sacred religious content to be used for a purpose for which it was not intended? What is to be the purpose of the study if the intrinsic value of a religion (that is, to foster faith) is replaced by an instrumental one? And who owns the religious traditions? There is a strongly held view among adherents that the religious traditions belong to the faith communities who have exclusive rights over them and the power to decide upon how they are to be used and by whom. Similarly, in the eyes of faith communities, parents have exclusive rights over their children in matters of religious faith and have the right to object to any form of religious education that is not provided strictly in accordance with the teaching of their own faith.

In removing religious education from the context of nurture and placing it in the context of education, one set of constraints (what constitutes successful religious nature) has been replaced by another set (what constitutes successful religious education). Religious educators have needed, therefore, to accommodate religious education within a construct of educational, not religious, thought, although some have been sensitive to finding ways of bringing about a complementary rather than conflicting relationship between the two. The tendency has been to seek such accommodations by using paradigms either from the rationalistic tradition or from the humanistic tradition of education. From the former, the paradigms of "objectivity" and the notion that "reality is objectively extant and that value-free methods of studying it can be found" have been influential, especially in the use of the principles and techniques of phenomenology to investigate religion. The use of a phenomenological approach has the advantage of enabling the study to be "objective" (that is, students are required to distance themselves from their own presuppositions and beliefs through applying the technique of "bracketing") while being directed toward establishing an understanding of the subjective consciousness of the adherent and the tradition's own self-understanding. In contrast, from the humanistic tradition, the paradigms of "subjectivity" and "the need to treat wholes rather than parts and to give attention to the history of the situations studied and the subjective reports of participants" have led some religious educators to abandon the search for value-free methods of study. Consistent with the social construction theories of knowledge, they have stressed the dialectical relationship between knower and what is known, between learner and what is learned, and emphasized the necessity for students to make qualitative judgments about and evaluations of religious beliefs and practices in order to enable the study to contribute to an elucidation and clarification of their own values and beliefs.

Fundamental to the task of establishing religious education as an educational activity with a legitimate place in the state school curriculum is the need to identify the distinctive contribution that it makes to students' learning. Some have argued that this is to be found in the distinctiveness of its subject matter (that is, religion is a distinctive form of knowledge or of thought and awareness), others in its cultural and social importance (its contribution to intercultural understanding in a pluralist society), others in its moral dimensions (its illustration of the link between beliefs and actions), and others in its literary and historical value (its contribution to an understanding of great literature and national identity). More persuasive, however, is the view that the study of religion provides insight into the causal relationship between what human beings believe and what human beings become. Human beings are shaped in accordance with the beliefs they

hold about themselves and others, or, as the *Bhagavad Gita* expresses it: "Man is made by his belief. As he believes, so he is."

While it is axiomatic that religious education must represent the beliefs and values of faith communities accurately and in so doing treat religious traditions with utmost integrity, religious education's prime responsibility and function is not to produce either religious adherents or phenomenologists of religion, but to help pupils to come to terms with questions about their own identities, their own values and lives, their own priorities and commitments, and their own frames of reference for viewing life and giving it meaning. The value of the study of religion from an educational point of view is to be located in the insights it provides into humanity's most characteristic activity—namely, a search for meaning and an engagement in meaning-making through the holding of beliefs, religious or otherwise. These insights are transferable to the lives of students, where they can be used to stimulate and assist them in their own search for meaning and identity; to promote critical consciousness, self-knowledge, and self-awareness; to develop skills necessary for the interpretation of personal, social, moral, religious, and spiritual issues and experiences; to extend capacities for personal decision-making. More particularly they are able to be used to sensitize students to the significance of their own beliefs and commitments in determining the shape of their lives.

A fundamental educational concern, connected in the Western liberal education tradition with the goal of personal autonomy, is to help students acquire the knowledge, skills, and attitudes that enable them to participate consciously and critically in the processes by which they and their lives are shaped. Religious education shares this concern and makes a distinctive contribution to it by highlighting the shaping properties of beliefs and commitments and exploring the nature of demands of ultimate questions arising from the human condition and the faith-responses they prompt. This aim is not necessarily inconsistent with the aims of religion, both being committed to humanization and the realization of personhood, although each religion will define rather differently how this is to be understood and the means and the end of the process. However, given that a satisfactory convergence between the aims of religion and those of education is unlikely, the task of contemporary religious educators is to develop a pedagogy that accommodates a faith community's demands that the study of religion be contextualized within that faith's self-understanding, while allowing the outcomes of that study to be recontextualized within the student's self-understanding.

Michael H. Grimmitt

See also AIMS OF EDUCATION; EPISTEMOLOGY; ETHICS AND MORALITY; LIBERAL EDUCATION; PERSON, CONCEPT OF; PHENOMENOLOGY; PUBLIC EDUCATION; TRUTH

Bibliography

Bushnell, Horace. *Christian Nurture* [1861]. New Haven: Yale University Press, 1979.

Fowler, James W. *Stages of Faith*. New York: Harper and Row, 1981.

Fowler, James W., Karl Ernst Nipkow, and Friedrich Schweitzer. *Stages of Faith and Religious Development*. London: SCM Press, 1992.

Francis, Leslie, and Adrian Thatcher. *Christian Perspectives for Education*. Leominster, Herefordshire, U.K.: Fowler Wright Books, 1990.

Grimmitt, Michael H. *Religious Education and Human Development*. Greak Wakering, Essex, U.K.: McCrimmons, 1987.

Moran, Gabriel. *Religious Education as a Second Language*. Birmingham, Ala.: Religious Education Press, 1989.

Revolution

The expression *revolution* at once suggests both social change and social conflict. But in scholarly literature on the subject, various students of revolution have provided somewhat differing definitions of the phenomenon. Revolution has sometimes been used to refer to any significant change in either patterns of social life (for example, "sexual revolution"), economic activities (such as the shift from state-controlled to "free-market" economies), cultural values (the spread of "materialism"), or government (replacement of dictatorships or monarchies with democracies). Thomas Greene (1990) observed that, despite controversy concerning the range of processes and events that should be labeled revolutions, most scholars would agree that the term should be applied to a change in government involving replacement of personnel, political structures, and supporting belief systems.

Huntington (1968) had earlier defined revo-lution as "a rapid, fundamental and violent domestic change in the dominant values and myths of a society," including "its political institutions, social structure, leadership, and government activity and policies." Skocpol (1979) distinguished among rebellions, political revolutions, and social revolutions. In Skocpol's view, rebellions are revolts which, even if successful, result only in changes in government policies and personnel but do not result in change in major institutions, such as the form of the political system or the economic system. Political revolution results in structural change in only one institution, the form of the society's political system. Social revolutions, according to Skocpol, are conflicts accompanied by "class-based revolts from below" that result in changes both in the political structure and other social structures such as social class and economic systems.

Analyses of the various usages and applications of the term indicate that most students of the phenomenon share the view that it must be reserved for major structural (institutional) change in society. A simple replacement in personnel staffing institutions does not in itself constitute revolution, even if the personnel changeover was caused by violence, as in a military coup. Similarly, a rebellion against an existing government involving mass participation does not necessarily constitute a revolution unless it results in great structural change rather than just a change in institutional personnel. For example, historians and anthropologists have noted that the traditional Chinese peasantry was among the most rebellious but least revolutionary of the world's agrarian work forces. This observation reflected the fact that China's Confucianist culture contained the notion that the people had the right to rise up against unjust leaders and replace them. The traditional Chinese peasant rebellion, however, even when successful in ousting an emperor, virtually never advocated the replacement of the Confucianist system of government or economic or social structures with new institutions. And so the pre-nineteenth-century Chinese peasant rebellions were not revolutions.

Some scholars have identified revolution with violent radical social change, while others have argued that revolutions should be defined only in terms of great structural change that may or may not be accompanied or brought about by violent means. Events in Eastern Europe and the former Soviet Union during the late 1980s and the 1990s appear to have borne out the validity of the second point of view. These societies experienced enormous, dramatic, and rapid changes in political, social, and economic institutions with little or no violence. Revolution, then, can be brought about by a wide range of means that do not necessarily include violence.

What Factors Promote Revolution?

Analyses of revolutionary movements by various social scientists have led to the identification of five factors that appear to play crucial roles in the growth of revolutions and in determining whether or not they are successful (DeFronzo). The occurrence of revolution appears to be associated with the simultaneous development of mass frustration (a majority of a society's population become intensely discontented with the status quo); profound divisions among the society's elites (people with wealth, education, power, status, or other culturally defined prerequisites for leadership roles) that concurrently contribute to undermining the prerevolution government and to providing critically needed leadership personnel necessary to organize the discontented mass into a coordinated revolutionary force with the potential for victory; one or more unifying motivations for revolution that bind members of different social groups and even different economic classes together in a prorevolution coalition; a severe political crisis that cripples governmental administrative and coercive capabilities so that the state cannot effectively counter a revolutionary movement; and a world context permissive of revolution in a particular society because other nations are in favor of the revolution, are unconcerned about it, or are unable to intervene to prevent it from succeeding.

Theories of Revolution

Several theories of revolution have been formulated to explain the development of revolutionary movements and the conditions necessary for revolutionary success. Among the more influential are the Marxist, modernization, and structural theories. The Marxist theory assumes that a primary driving force through history has been the continuous desire to increase the human capacity to derive from the natural environment the satisfaction of critical human needs, including the basic requirements of food and shelter. As a result, tools (technology) and the way people are organized (the economic system) to use technology to secure survival and need satisfaction from the environment change over time. Technology and economic organization influence cultural values, social class structure, and social institutions such as the governmental, legal, and educational systems.

According to the Marxist theory, the social class that dominates the economic system also controls the government and is in fact a "ruling class." Revolution occurs when technological and economic changes have progressed to the point that a new economic class emerges whose role in the transformed economy has in reality become more crucial than the economic role of the class that controls the government and its mechanisms of coercion, the army and police. The ruling class uses violence to preserve its control of society and tends to resist further economic changes toward greater efficiency when such changes are perceived as threatening its interests. Conflict between the ruling class and the emergent class ultimately results in the victory of the new class and a revolution that transforms major social institutions to suit the interests of the new ruling class.

Marx anticipated that during the capitalist era the exploited industrial working class (proletariat) would rise up and depose the ruling class, the business and factory owners, and establish a socialist economic system with collective ownership of wealth and industry (Marx and Engels 1972). Marx hypothesized that a post-industrialization socialist economic system would prove far more productive than what he perceived to be the economic chaos and waste often characteristic of capitalist competition. A socialist economic system would generate enormous technological progress and wealth, the benefits of which would be far more equally distributed than under capitalism because, in the socialist era, the ruling class would be the working class, the large majority of a society's population. Poverty and the social ills caused by scarcity and blocked opportunity would be eliminated as, eventually, would be the need for the type of repressive governmental systems that had characterized all societies since the dawn of civilization. This utopian society Marx called "communism," the final stage of social development characterized by material abundance, expanding opportunities, and cooperative social relations. Various versions of Marxist theory of revolution, including that of Mao Tse-tung (1893–1976), in which, in the context of largely preindustrial China, he identified not the industrial working class but the rural peasantry as the key revolutionary force, have had enormous impacts on many revolutionary movements.

Modernization theory (Huntington) also associates the development of revolutionary movements with technological and economic change. But according to this perspective, modernization tends to generate discontent when it has effects such as undermining cherished religious and other cultural values, threatens the economic interests of powerful or large population sectors, results in unequal distribution of new wealth or opportunities, or raises but fails to satisfy the expectations of major social groups for increased economic opportunity or political participation. The probability of revolution is high when the existing government is unwilling or unable to meet the demands of large numbers of people mobilized to rebellion by their dissatisfaction with aspects of modernization.

The structural theory (Skocpol) views revolution as likely to occur in economically and militarily weak societies when such societies are unable to resist the aggressive and exploitative policies of more powerful nations. The inability of a society's government to defend the nation's interests spreads disillusionment in the population not only with the society's ruling elite and form of government but also often with the ideology (set of justifying beliefs and values) that support the prerevolution social and political order. A primary motivation for revolution in such a society, according to structural theory, is to create stronger political and military systems better capable of promoting the welfare and protecting the resources of the society in its international competition with other nations. None of these three theories, however, appear capable of explaining or predicting the simultaneous occurrence of all five of the conditions that appear necessary for a revolution to succeed.

Thomas Jefferson (1743–1826) is credited with asserting that a little revolution now and then is a good thing. Interestingly, another revolutionary from another time and place, Mao, expressed a similar point of view. Both Jefferson and Mao anticipated that, inevitably, despite the victories of their own revolutions, harmful social and political conditions would tend to recur that would require periodic popular mobilizations to bring about beneficial changes. It is possible, though, that in the twenty-first century, structural social change (revolutionary change) will occur more through the relatively nonviolent, democratic means characteristic of the 1989–90s revolutions in Eastern Europe and South Africa than through the violent conflict that characterized the American, French, Russian, or Chinese revolutions of previous eras.

James DeFronzo

See also JEFFERSON; MARX; MARXISM; SOCIALISM

Bibliography

DeFronzo, James. *Revolutions and Revolutionary Movements*. Boulder, Colo.: Westview, 1991.

Goldstone, J., T.R. Gurr, and F. Moshiri, eds. *Revolutions of the Late Twentieth Century*. Boulder, Colo.: Westview, 1991.

Greene, Thomas H. *Comparative Revolutionary Movements*. Englewood Cliffs, N.J.: Prentice Hall, 1990.

Huntington, S. *Political Order in Changing Societies*. New Haven: Yale University Press, 1968.

Marx, K., and F. Engels. "The Communist Manifesto." In *The Marx-Engels Reader,* edited by R.T. Tucker. New York: Norton, 1972.

———. *Selected Works*. New York: International Publishers, 1968.

Selbin, E. *Modern Latin American Revolutions*. Boulder, Colo.: Westview, 1993.

Skocpol, T. *States and Social Revolution*. Cambridge: Cambridge University Press, 1979.

Rhetoric

The study of the history, theory, application, and evaluation of systems of expression. The primary concern of rhetoricians has been to understand the relationship between thought and expression and, from that understanding, offer methods to enhance oral and written expression. Although many contemporary rhetoricians employ current principles of empirical research, much of that work is grounded in a history of the discipline, since rhetoric is best understood when it is examined within its social and cultural context.

Classical Rhetoric: Ancient Greece

Although societies always have been inventing, developing, and refining systems of expression as an essential feature of what makes them communities, the emergence of rhetoric as a formal discipline in the West began in Greece in the early decades of the fifth century B.C. As is also true with other cultures, ancient Greece initially developed and transmitted poetry, literature, and virtually every form of communication through oral compositional techniques. For centuries Greek "literature" was transmitted through the mentor-apprentice relationship of *aoidoi* (bards) and rhapsodes, who developed aides to memory and techniques for both composition and performance, of which the *Iliad* and *Odyssey* are our best examples. The invention of the alphabet, and the literacy that it subsequently helped to foster, facilitated the evolution of Greek culture from exclusively oral to both oral and written expression. The development of writing also influenced and hastened the development of genres. No longer requiring elaborate and detailed memory training to ensure the perpetuation of discourse, the stability of text offered by writing greatly aided the shift from poetry to prose, since the rhythm and cadence necessary as memory aids in oral composition were no longer necessary in the permanent forms of inscribed prose. Thus, prior to the early decades of the fifth century B.C., rhetorical principles facilitated the needs and preferences of specific types of discourse that would later be classified into such disciplines of symbolic expression as poetry, logic, history, and drama.

The emergence of rhetoric as a discipline in its own right, however, came to fruition when rhetoric served not only the arts of expression but also the expediency of forensic and civic issues. Out of the pragmatic need to resolve legal and political disputes in Syracuse, the Sicilians Corax (fl. 467 B.C.) and Tisias (fl. 467 B.C.) offered training in public argument and were credited with founding the discipline of rhetoric. The close relationship between education and rhetoric is apparent in its origin as well as its application in such social functions as law and politics. Prominent Sophists emerging from the tradition of Corax and Tisias—such as Gorgias of Leontini (c. 483–376 B.C.) and Lysias (c. 459–c. 380 B.C.)—established schools of rhetoric and training in speech-composition or logography. The reservations of Plato (c. 427–347 B.C.) about the value of Sophistic rhetoric is apparent in several dialogues. His ardent opposition to the popularity of Sophistic rhetoric through the words of Socrates (470–399 B.C.), his primary voice in the dialogues, is also an indirect statement of Plato's recognition of the impact of rhetoric on education, and ultimately, society. The popularity of schools of rhetoric was so widespread that philosophers such as Plato and Aristotle (384–322 B.C.) be-

lieved that the promulgation of rhetoric undermined the moral and ethical development of youth and thus posed a direct threat to the welfare of the city. Many of Plato's dialogues—the *Gorgias* and the *Phaedrus* are two of the most popular examples—are direct challenges to Sophistic education and the place of rhetoric in the curriculum. Similarly, Aristotle's *Rhetoric,* which offers the most comprehensive system of rhetoric to survive this period, is also a response to the ever-growing popularity of Sophistic rhetoric.

Although the views of Plato and Aristotle are now fully accepted as part of the rhetorical tradition, the popularity of Sophistic rhetoric as a dominant feature of Greek education continued and spread throughout Hellas. As Greeks colonized throughout the world they established not only cities but schools as well. The impact of the Hellenistic age applies also to the study of rhetoric, for knowledge of rhetoric as a feature of their notion of educational excellence (*paideia*) was pervasive. Schools of rhetoric often taught principles of expression through exercises in *declamatio*. Education exercises for youth were covered in exercises called *progymnasmata*. In these elementary exercises, young students sought to sharpen their wits by arguing and by interpreting and analyzing fables, historical themes, and other topics that lent themselves to reasoned interpretation and debate. Advanced students continued in declamation and were assigned themes ranging from legal argument (*controversia*) to more broadly based political and social topics (*suasoria*). Schools of rhetoric, popular throughout Greece, were oriented toward developing oral and written expression, but with an emphasis on stylized argument wherein audiences judged a rhetor's merits not only on the cogency of argument but also on the eloquence of presentation. Principles and systems of Greek rhetoric survived well into the Roman Empire, even enjoying a renaissance of their own called the Second Sophistic.

Classical Rhetoric: Ancient Rome
One of the clearest consequences of the spread of Greek rhetoric is seen in the colonization of Southern Italy. The establishment of Greek cities in the West brought with it the transportation of Hellenic culture and the arts, one of which was the art of expression. The exposure of Rome to Greek rhetoric not only reveals the extent of its transmission but also its impact on shaping Roman rhetoric. As was the case with

Greek rhetoric, much that we know of early Roman rhetoric was subsumed under declamation. Although less technical than its Greek counterpart, Roman rhetoric nonetheless enjoyed the same popular reception, as is revealed by the introductory comments on Roman declamation exercises by the Elder Seneca (c. 55 B.C.–c. A.D. 40). Yet, also as in Greece, the study of rhetoric in Rome had its influential critics. The patrician class of Rome, fearing that rhetoric would emerge as a source of power that would challenge the aristocracy, as it had in Athens, actually sought to outlaw schools of declamation and the study of rhetoric itself. These early efforts to outlaw rhetoric in Rome are well chronicled by Suetonius (b. c. A.D. 69) in his *De Rhetoribus*.

The career of Marcus Tullius Cicero (106–43 B.C.) is evidence of the fact that rhetoric not only survived such edicts but even became a common part of the Roman education. Lacking the conventional sources of power in Roman society—wealth, military authority, or patrician heritage—Cicero was able to employ his skill in rhetoric both to become Rome's premier advocate and eventually to hold the office of consul. Education in rhetoric, as Cicero made apparent to his colleagues, was a source of power and a weapon for advancement. In the republican society of Cicero's Rome, rhetoric became a part of higher education principally because of its social and political utility. Rhetoric was, however, also recognized for its inherent educational merit. Cicero's *De Oratore*, composed after a distinguished legal and political career, is an eloquent statement of the evolution of rhetorical education and its value to a community. Of equal importance, Cicero's many rhetorical treatises served as a foundation for the study of rhetoric in the education of Romans, to the extent that rhetoric became synonymous with higher education itself.

The transformation of Rome from a republic to an empire under Augustus (63 B.C.–A.D. 14) did more than alter Rome's political character; it changed the scope of rhetoric in education. No longer the source of political power that it had been in the republic, mastery of rhetoric was nonetheless an index of refinement and a sign of higher education. Viewing rhetoric as an important component in the education of youth, Quintilian (c. 30–c. 100) solidified the educational practices of rhetoric into the curriculum with his treatise *Institutio oratoria*. Rhetoric also benefited from the sustained patronage of emperors, who consistently endowed favorite cities with imperial chairs and sponsored prominent Sophists throughout the empire. By the close of the Empire, rhetoric was an integral feature of education and, as indicated above, a chief feature of the Second Sophistic.

Medieval Rhetoric

Just as the Roman Empire was transformed with the growth of Christianity, so too was the study of rhetoric transformed when taught under the aegis of Christian emperors. Many prominent Church leaders, both in the East and West, were suspicious of rhetoric, principally because it was so closely associated with pagan themes, was oriented toward material success, and offered no easy relationship with a religion that viewed theological doctrine as dogma. *De Doctrina Christiana* by St. Augustine of Hippo (354–430), written over a period of years between the fourth and fifth centuries A.D., provided Church leaders with a rationale for accepting rhetoric into Christian education by stripping its systems of pagan topics and themes and replacing them with an orientation that facilitated Church doctrine. With this theological perspective, the teaching of rhetoric took a new direction. Rhetoric became, for a Christian world, not a topic that promoted probability and idiosyncratic preferences but rather a system for discovering, interpreting, and preaching Christian doctrine. The three medieval arts of rhetoric reflect this shift of orientation. *Ars praedicandi* (the art of preaching) used principles of rhetoric to provide instruction on religious preaching. *Ars dictaminis* (the art of letter writing) used principles of rhetoric to facilitate the teaching of epistolary composition and was often used as the primary medium for both sacred and secular communications. *Ars poetriae* (the art of versification) applied stylistic principles of grammar and rhetoric to facilitate expression. The arts of rhetoric were treated as part of the medieval curriculum, and, as evidenced as early as the fifth century A.D. with *The Marriage of Mercury and Philology* by Martianus Capella (fl. 410–429), rhetoric became a part of the trivium.

In many respects, the growth of Christianity in the West is also a study of the growth of Christian education and the growth of rhetoric. Monastic centers throughout the Roman Empire became the repository of volumes of rhetoric. Many of these religious centers had book collections so extensive that they became intellectual centers in their own right. The spread of rhetorical education was also promoted by Holy Roman emperors. The extension of the Roman Empire by Charlemagne (742–814) is reflected in the establishment of cathedrals and attendant cathedral schools. Many of these cathedral schools also became intellectual centers, some evolving into our first modern universities. This educational growth is best understood as a sustained (if sometimes haphazard) effort to preserve and reclaim works of classical rhetoric that would otherwise have been lost, and to stabilize education with rhetoric as a central feature. The effort to make such gains is all the more remarkable when we understand that this work was transmitted by handwriting, with limited resources, and often under arduous conditions.

The survival of rhetoric in the Greek East has a much greater fluidity than the West. Far less skeptical and superstitious than their counterparts in the West, Orthodox Church leaders were much more tolerant of the study of rhetoric in the Byzantine Empire. The major concern was that pagan rhetoric be taught by Christian professors. Pagan rhetoricians who found even these restrictions unacceptable, however, were welcomed to the Arab world, which eagerly solicited Greek scholars to growing educational centers such as Baghdad. In many respects, the Abbasid period of Arab history was responsible for preserving and transmitting much of Greek literature and rhetoric. The schools of rhetoric in Arabia and the Greek East produced great commentaries on Aristotle, for example, and translated numerous copies of classical works into Arabic. Thus the reintroduction of Greek rhetoric in the West that would take place in the waning years of the Middle Ages was not only a consequence of Western crusades and Venetian mercantile expeditions but also of the spread of Arab culture into the West from Africa and through Spain. The reawakening and rediscovery of Greek in the West was the result of a confluence of these factors that resulted in the revival of classical rhetoric in the Renaissance.

Renaissance Rhetoric

The study of rhetoric in the Renaissance is one of the most complex tasks challenging historians of rhetoric. The rise of cities throughout Europe, the rediscovery of Greek culture, the efforts to "purify" Latin back to its classical form and away from medieval expression, the rise of the vernacular, and the persistent tension between the Church and secular forces all had an impact on the study of rhetoric. Of prime importance here, however, is that the emergence of the Renaissance was also a sign of the rise of the universities; in that light the study of rhetoric is best understood. Continuing to maintain its place in the trivium, rhetoric was studied again as a classical subject not only by means of the rediscovery of Greek and the "purification" of Latin but also through the rediscovery of classical texts. Many of the previously lost works of Cicero and the *Institutio oratoria* of Quintilian, for example, were found, and these, coupled with the discovery by Francesco Petrarch (1304–1374) of the lost letters of Cicero, introduced new substance into the study of rhetoric.

Attention to rhetoric was directed toward stylistic expression and the study of rhetoric and poetics were closely aligned, to the extent that rhetoric as a process of discovery came to mean the discovery of lines of elegant expression. Out of this concern for and glorification of the human condition came both an appreciation for the value of rhetoric—a system that Renaissance thinkers considered to be a method for uniting wisdom with eloquence—and its placement in the newly evolving disciplines called the "Humanities." It is particularly important to note, however, that the concern for humanistic inquiry was often grounded within and judged by the standards of Christian doctrine—that is, scholasticism. The rise of Jesuit education is an index of the growth and pervasiveness of scholasticism, as well as its continued role in religious education.

The Emergence of Modern Rhetoric

The rise of the scientific method would challenge not only the tenets of scholasticism but also the principles of classical rhetoric that were subsumed under it. Sixteenth-century educational reformers such as Peter Ramus (1515–1572) advocated curricular changes that separated the study of logic and reasoning from rhetoric, relegating to rhetoric's province the study of style and expression. Curricular changes were only one sign of a reorientation of rhetoric in education, for efforts were being directed to inquiries that would explain human communications by means other than deference to classical texts. Such educational reforms were particularly evident in England, where advances in British logic and rhetoric challenged many of the principles of classical rhetoric. Thinkers such as Francis Bacon (1561–1626) began to apply principles of faculty psychology as a way of explaining processes of human communication and, in doing so, reoriented rhetoric away from its classical tenets to an understanding of the relationship between mental operations and expression. *The Philosophy of Rhetoric* by George Campbell (1719–1796), *Lectures on Rhetoric and Belles Lettres* by Hugh Blair (1718–1800), and *Elements of Rhetoric* by Richard Whately (1787–1863) are three examples of British rhetorics that apply nascent principles of psychology to explain rhetorical operations. Blair's work, immensely popular in the classroom, became a standard for its concern with the study and refinement of taste and artful expression both in England and in the United States.

Curricular changes, the popularity of Blair's rhetoric, and the growing interest in the oral performance and interpretation of literature through the elocutionary movement all directed the study of rhetoric to issues of style as the primary topic of concern. Manuals of rhetoric in American schools of the nineteenth century reflect the study of rhetoric as stylistic expression and became the dominant topic of classes of composition, which used tenets of rhetoric as a way of teaching oral and written expression.

Twentieth-Century Education in Rhetoric
Rhetoric in the early decades of the twentieth century was subsumed under the study of the newly formed department of "English." As English moved to emphasize written expression exclusively, and the study of literature particularly, the study of rhetoric became relegated to introductory composition classes. In 1914, however, a small group of professors, disturbed over the lack of attention to speech, left "English" and formed a national organization dedicated to the study of oral communication. These speech professors saw in rhetoric systems of effective expression, to the extent that rhetoric became the theorctical orientation of their emerging field. Concurrently, philosophers and emerging psychologists began to turn their attention to the study of discourse as a way of understanding ethics, argument, and the role of the community. Embracing the emergence of psychology and the social sciences, the field of speech communication began to integrate the principles of classical rhetoric with social sciences as a way of testing and refining principles

of oral expression. The field of English, emphasizing literature as the area of intellectual concern, still found itself obligated to teach writing. Professors of composition within English departments, seeing a close affinity between rhetoric in speech and the need to develop a theoretical base for writing instruction, began to reclaim the study of rhetoric as appropriate also for the study of written expression. In doing so, English professors of rhetoric taught the history of rhetoric; they also began, as had their counterparts in speech communication, to study rhetoric with a social-scientific emphasis, particularly in the areas of cognitive psychology and empirical methodology.

The study of rhetoric in the later decades of the twentieth century is a study both of the rediscovery of the history of rhetoric in the most traditional sense of the humanities and of rhetoric in current practice, using the principles of social-science research. The effort of English departments to expand their interest from canonical literature to include cultural studies and critical theory has also provided the opportunity to integrate rhetoric back into English studies. The intent of current educational programs to maintain this synthesis consciously in the study of rhetoric is recognition of the mutual benefits that result from the cooperative efforts of different orientations. Such attention to rhetoric in the latter half of the twentieth century has resulted in the emergence of professional organizations, journals, and newly created divisions within existing organizations, such as the Modern Language Association. The growth of rhetoric is evidence of its integration back into education, where concerns over literacy and expression in general are likely to remain important topics.

Richard Leo Enos

See also ARISTOTLE; AUGUSTINE; CICERO; PAIDEIA; PLATO; QUINTILIAN; SOPHISTS; STUDIA HUMANITATIS

Bibliography
A Short History of Writing Instruction: From Ancient Greece to Twentieth-Century America. Edited by James J. Murphy. Davis, Calif.: Hermagoras Press, 1990.

Berlin, James A. *Rhetoric and Reality: Writing Instruction in American Colleges, 1900–1985.* Carbondale and Edwardsville: Southern Illinois University Press, 1987.

———. *Writing Instruction in Nineteenth-Century American Colleges*. Carbondale and Edwardsville: Southern Illinois University Press, 1984.

Conley, Thomas M. *Rhetoric in the European Tradition*. New York and London: Longman, 1990.

Enos, Richard Leo. *Greek Rhetoric before Aristotle*. Prospect Heights, Ill.: Waveland Press, 1993.

Golden, James L., Goodwin F. Ferquist, and William E. Coleman. *The Rhetoric of Western Thought*. 3rd ed. Dubuque, Iowa: Kendall/Hunt, 1983.

Kennedy, George A. *Classical Rhetoric and Its Christian and Secular Tradition from Ancient to Modern Times*. Chapel Hill: The University of North Carolina Press, 1980.

Murphy, James J. *Rhetoric in the Middle Ages*. Berkeley, Los Angeles, London: University of California Press, 1974.

The Present State of Scholarship in Historical and Contemporary Rhetoric. 2nd ed. Edited by Winifred Bryan Horner. Columbia: University of Missouri Press, 1990.

The Rhetorical Tradition: Readings from Classical Times to the Present. Edited by Patricia Bizzell and Bruce Herzberg. Boston: Bedford Books of St. Martin's Press, 1990.

Speech Communication in the 20th Century. Edited by Thomas W. Benson. Carbondale and Edwardsville: Southern Illinois University Press, 1985.

Vickers, Brian. *In Defence of Rhetoric*. Oxford: Clarendon Press, 1988.

Right, Theories of the

A theory of the right purports to give an account of the right—that is, of what is right or wrong, the nature of judgments of right and wrong, and the relations between the right and other parts of our normative worlds. There is little agreement, however, between defenders of the various competing theories of the right. It is not even clear that it is possible to provide a general characterization of the domain of the right that is neutral regarding the different theories. The determination of the right is one of the central controversies in contemporary moral philosophy.

A distinction between the right and the good is the appropriate starting point for a general characterization of the concept of the right.

We might commend some act as being right or as being good. The context will usually determine whether the commendation in question is moral or nonmoral (though there is some controversy as to how we should distinguish between these two). We might applaud an answer to a question and commend it as good or right, without intending any moral judgment or approbation thereby. Similarly, there may be good or right ways of playing the piano, tuning a car, or good and right places and times to be. For the most part, theorists of the right are concerned to give an account of the moral right. We evaluate actions, motives, dispositions, institutions, and the like as good and right, and a theory of the right should explain these judgments and assist us in making them. We shall restrict our attention, then, to accounts of the moral right.

When we commend an act as right, we often say that it is *the* right act, whereas there usually is no claim to uniqueness implicit in judgments of good ("*a* good act"). But appearances may mislead, as many accounts of the right allow for the possibility of there being several different right acts in certain circumstances. However, right and good differ in that goodness allows of degrees and right does not. We can say of an act that it is better than another, but not that it is "more right." "Good" is a comparative term—better or worse—whereas "right" serves to classify acts (motives, and so on) into all-or-nothing categories—right or wrong.

This contrast between the right and the good points to another. If something is the right thing to do, then it is usually thought that we ought to do it or that we have a duty or obligation to do it. Certainly, it would be wrong not to do something that is right. By contrast, if something is good, it need not be the case that we have a duty to do it or even that it would be wrong not to do it. As we shall see below, the relationship between the good and the obligatory is a matter of considerable controversy in contemporary moral theory.

To act rightly, to do the right act, is, on virtually all accounts, always permissible. By contrast, it may not always be permissible to do something good—as, for example, when something else is required or when doing good would require acting unjustly. Further, acting rightly, it is usually thought, is expected of everyone; it is the least that is asked of moral agents. There need be no praise or special commendation for right action in this sense. Praise is held in reserve for supererogatory acts, those "over and above the call of duty." So to act is to do more than the minimum; merely to do the right act is often to do the minimum.

The concept of *the* right should not be confused with that of *a* right. We talk about the rights that people have—for example, the right to life, to liberty, to vote, to property, to privacy. (Other beings or entities—such as groups, corporations, nations, states, and animals—may also have rights.) The analysis of the concept of a right is a matter of some controversy, as is the attribution of rights. On no serious account, however, is the concept of the right confused with that of *a* right. On some account, it is even possible that it may sometimes be right to violate the rights of some people—for example, to kill someone in order to save thousands of others. Further, it has recently been claimed that the possession of (certain) rights may permit someone to do something wrong—for example, a right to liberty or to property may permit someone to refrain from telling the truth or giving to charity, where so refraining is wrong. Such "a right to do wrong" would not, of course, imply that sometimes it is right to do wrong. Although it is controversial to suggest that rights can protect wrongful action, it is not incoherent to claim this, and this shows another way in which the right is distinct from that to which we have a right.

Lastly, the domain of the right overlaps, and may even be coextensive, with that of justice in the broad sense of this notion. Justice, in this sense, concerns all those things owed to others, such as respect for their rights, fair dealing, honesty, veracity. Justice is also thought to be the minimum that we demand of people, that which they have a duty to do, and that which it is wrong not to do. Again, the relationship between the just and the good is a matter of acute controversy.

There are numerous competing theories of the right and considerable controversy among their partisans. In contemporary moral theory, a contrast is often drawn between deontological and teleological (or consequentialist) theories. Sometimes the distinction between the two sorts of theories is made in terms of consequences: Teleological accounts characterize the goodness or rightness of acts (motives, and so forth) entirely in terms of beneficial consequences, whereas deontological theories also take into account the intrinsic character or worth of the act. John Rawls, in *A Theory of Justice* (1971),

characterizes the distinction between these competing sorts of theories in terms of the manner each understands the relation of the good and the right. For him, a deontological theory "does not specify the good independently of the right, or does not interpret the right as maximizing the good" (30). The controversy between deontologists and consequentialists is one of the reasons that the very characterization of the right is no small matter. The tendency of many consequentialists to think of the right as equivalent to the best or to that which maximizes the good alters the conception of the right that many moral philosophers claim to find in ordinary discourse. If consequentialists are right, then the separation between the right and the good may be less sharp than most contemporary moral theorists believe.

Leaving aside the quarrel between partisans of deontology and consequentialism, a dispute largely about the structure of morality, we might mention the main competing theories of the right in contemporary philosophy. There is first a set of theories developing from the classical and early modern natural law tradition. Thomistic natural law theory, founded by St. Thomas Aquinas (1225–1274) and now the official moral philosophy of the Catholic Church, provides an account of the right, one that is well developed and applied by Thomist moralists to moral questions arising in wide areas (such as medicine, business, war, education). A related theory, particularly influential in the United States today, is what might be called natural rights theory. Partisans of this theory trace their ancestry less to the medieval natural law tradition than to John Locke (1632–1704). The language of natural rights comes very naturally to Americans, invoked as it was by Thomas Jefferson, Thomas Paine, Abraham Lincoln, and others. Robert Nozick's controversial defense of libertarianism in *Anarchy, State, and Utopia* (1974) is partly responsible for the attention given to natural rights theories in contemporary moral philosophy.

We may think of natural law and natural rights theories as determining the right by an appeal to principles which, it is claimed, are to be found in nature, accessible to human reason (for instance, Jefferson's "self-evident" truths). Thomas's theory starts with the fundamental principle or natural law that every agent seeks good and shuns evil. Eighteenth-century natural rights theorists claim for all persons basic rights to life and liberty (and, in some accounts, property). The right is then determined by reference to these natural laws or rights. In this view, it is wrong, for instance, to take another's life or possessions when that is a violation of a particular natural law or natural right, even if great good would come of it.

This distinction we draw between natural law and natural rights theories is not meant to be precise. Often, it is not clear how to characterize some theorists, such as Locke or Jefferson. For some moral issues, however, the difference between the two may be important, as what we have called natural rights theories tend to be more individualistic than their natural law counterparts; the former often give individuals the power to determine what to do with their lives or possessions in contexts where natural law theories leave no room for choice. Many modern natural rights theorists would leave to the individual the choice, such as of self-development, suicide, and the like; Thomists, by contrast, would forbid suicide and view self-development as a virtue.

Kantianism, related in several ways to the natural law and natural rights traditions, is especially influential in contemporary moral philosophy. Based on the moral and political writings of Immanuel Kant (1724–1804), Kantianism is paradigmatic of a so-called deontological moral theory. In *The Groundwork of the Metaphysics of Morals* (1758), Kant sought "to seek out and establish the supreme principle of morality." One of the formulations of this principle enjoins us to treat other persons always as ends and never as means. Arriving at the proper interpretation of this principle is not simple, but most agree that it forbids treating others as mere instruments of one's ends, that it requires one to accord to others a certain status or respect. The principle imposes strict constraints on our behavior that may never be violated, whatever the consequences. In this view, the right constrains the pursuit of the good.

The influence of Kant's writings in the Anglo-American world is, in part, a reaction to the influence of utilitarianism, the moral theory founded by Jeremy Bentham (1748–1832) and developed by John Stuart Mill (1806–1873). This school also asserts that there is a single, supreme principle of morality. But the principle they endorse is teleological or consequentialist: Act so as to maximize the aggregate utility of all (where utility is understood in terms of pleasure, happiness, well-being, or preference-satisfaction). Some versions of utilitarianism characterize right action as that which brings about the greatest total utility in the circumstances. Such a theory interprets the right as the best, essentially collapsing the right into the good.

Rawls's famous work on justice, and especially its emphasis on the priority of the right over the good, is also a reaction to utilitarianism. There are as well many Kantian themes and arguments in his work. But *A Theory of Justice* (1971) is responsible for the revival of contractarianism, or social contract theory, in contemporary ethics. This tradition, in its classical or contemporary forms, is too diverse to permit of a simple characterization. The main idea is that the terms of morality (or, at least, of justice) are whatever principles and dispositions would be the object of an ideal agreement by rational agents ("a social contract"). Most contractarian moralists (such as David Gauthier, T.M. Scanlon, Gregory Kavka) follow Rawls in giving priority to the right over the good. But at least one, John Harsanyi, believes that ideally rational agents would agree on a form of utilitarianism.

The main contemporary theories of the right, then, are those that are identified with the natural law and natural rights traditions, various versions of Kantianism, moral contractarianism, and utilitarianism and other forms of consequentialism. The latter may be thought of as limit cases of accounts of the right, insofar as they essentially collapse the right into the good. There are other accounts, of course, and some of these do not fit all that neatly into these categories. And some contemporary moralists eschew theory altogether and claim that no systematic account can do justice to the nature and structure of our moral judgments and practices.

The central criticism of theories of the right that accord priority to the right over the good is that it may not always be reasonable to do so. The literature is filled with examples, hypothetical and real, of situations where one can do good only by acting wrongly. Stealing from the rich in order to benefit the poor may bring great benefits to many. And, in some circumstances, killing an innocent person may prevent the loss of thousands of lives and thus be tempting. However, all these acts seem to use people as mere means. If the right constrains us from using some in order to benefit others, then these acts seem proscribed. Punishing some in order to deter others is, according to some, the best or only justification of punishment. And setting up a schooling system to educate the gifted along with the less talented may be best, even if it restrains the development of the gifted. But these practices also seem to use some as mere means to the ends of others. Many critics of deontological theories think that the wholesale condemnation of valuable practices shows these theories to be irrational or unacceptable.

Recently, other critics have also attacked these theories of the right, although from a different angle. The recent popularity of virtue ethics has focused attention on the other moral values, such as benevolence, courage, and moderation. Partisans of this general approach question the almost exclusive interest paid by modern and especially contemporary moral theorists to justice and the right. They would have us study the classical notion of a virtue (*arete*) found in the writings of Plato (c. 427–347 B.C.) and Aristotle (384–322 B.C.).

Similarly, many contemporary feminist philosophers have focused attention on characteristically male preoccupations with rights and the various categories of the right to the exclusion of other parts of morality. Some, influenced by the research of Carol Gilligan, have conjectured that men and women characteristically approach moral problems differently.

Christopher W. Morris

See also INTUITIONISM; JUSTICE; KANT; RIGHTS; UTILITARIANISM

Bibliography

Brandt, Richard B. *A Theory of the Good and the Right*. Oxford: Clarendon Press, 1979.

Donagan, Alan. *The Theory of Morality*. Chicago: University of Chicago Press, 1977.

Finnis, John. *Natural Law and Natural Rights*. Oxford: Clarendon Press, 1980.

Frey, R.G., ed. *Utility and Rights*. 2nd ed. Oxford: Blackwell, 1994.

Kant, Immanuel. *Groundwork of the Metaphysics of Morals* [1758]. Translated by H.J. Paton. New York: Harper and Row, 1964.

Nozick, Robert. *Anarchy, State, and Utopia*. New York: Basic Books, 1974.

Rawls, John. *A Theory of Justice*. Cambridge: Harvard University Press, 1971.

Ross, W.D. *The Right and the Good*. Oxford: Clarendon Press, 1930.

Scheffler, Samuel, ed. *Consequentialism and Its Critics*. Oxford: Oxford University Press, 1988.

Rights

R

Rights may be identified by their functions, limits, and importance. Several approaches may further an understanding of rights. These include noting the good rights do, and the evils they guard against; tracing the origins and development of rights; evaluating attempts to define rights, citing conditions for having rights, distinguishing categories of rights; considering criticisms of rights; citing responses; and marking out unresolved rights issues. A consideration of these approaches follows.

The Good Rights Do and the Evils Against Which They Guard

Rights provide positive benefits and guard against evils. In their positive role, rights contribute to "a single status society" (Feinberg 1973: 67). Rights help bring about freedom, dignity, decency, democracy, individual fulfillment, and fair and equitable distribution of resources.

Rights enable people to stand up with dignity and, if necessary, to demand what is their due, such as their pay check, without having to grovel, plead, or beg, or without having to express gratitude when they are given their due; and to express indignation when what is their due is not forthcoming. Making claims for one's rights is an important part of having rights.

Rights also protect individuals against evils, such as racism, sexism, anti-Semitism, child abuse, spouse abuse, terrorism, violence, hunger, poverty, inadequate health care, and lack of education. Rights provide a shield against evil to helpless underserved and undervalued children and adults. In the exercise of both their positive and negative functions, one aim for using rights is to provide standards of conduct to which reasonable people may appeal when they attempt to resolve value conflicts. Rights accordingly function as justifying reasons for acting, possessing, or claiming. Rights set standards and provide moral standing to individuals. Rights thereby guide the formation of other social and political norms.

Rights are generally absent in three settings. One is unchecked violence. Situations in which cruelty, torture, or abuse are rampant dampen the prospects of rights' permeating the moral landscape. Rights do not flourish in moral anarchy, where anything goes; nor, secondly, in a relationship where deception prevails. A third setting in which rights are generally absent is in a desert or such situation where individuals barely ever interact in mutually beneficial ways with one another. Rights have no use in a desert island society, such as the one Daniel Defoe depicts in *Robinson Crusoe* before Friday arrived. Rights are made by, for, and against people. One has no rights against nonhuman events or agents, such as earthquakes, bears, sharks, tigers, or viruses. Thoughtless violence resists rights discourse, as the Holocaust attests. Rights function where there is no excessive brutality, sparseness, or deception. For these are not the friends of rights.

The Origin and Development of Rights

Rights have several sources. In the Villey-Golding hypothesis (Golding 1978: 44–50), rights (as distinct from right), originated with William of Ockham (c. 1285–1347), who associated rights with individual powers (Golding 1978). In an alternative view, the concept of rights predates the later Middle Ages. In Sophocles's play *Antigone,* the heroine claims the right to bury her brother. In Plato's *Crito,* Socrates presents arguments against having a right to escape from prison. However one settles this issue, rights seem to have become more prominent since Ockham.

A traditional source of rights is the concept of positive law, which dates to Thrasymachus, Socrates' opponent in the *Republic* of Plato (c. 427–347 B.C.). A theme of positive law is that justice is whatever those in power decide, providing that they can enforce the law and punish noncompliance. In this view, rights are enforceable claims.

A second tradition identifies rights with natural law or a higher law, an appeal to reason, or "higher" religious values. This law claims to provide a rational standard for evaluating other laws and for canceling or annulling laws that are inconsistent with higher norms.

Natural law exposes and confronts evils among some existing legal rules and rights. An example of a gross evil is the Tuskegee syphilis experiment involving nearly four hundred black men with syphilis who, between 1932 and 1972, went untreated although antibiotics were available. Their rights to life were violated. Similarly, slavery, the Holocaust, rape, and abuse are serious rights violations. People's rights depend not only on their having enforceable claims, but on claims of another kind. People who are unjustly deprived of their rights make claims in a metaphorical sense, in which they cry out for relief from suffering.

Natural law, however, rests on dubious theological or metaphysical assumptions. Justice William O. Douglas, for example, defended released time for sectarian religious instruction on the grounds that "we are a religious people, whose institutions presuppose a Supreme Being" (Douglas 1954), a contestable statement.

A further source of rights is the social contract, a promise, tacit or explicit, to live by agreements rather than the arbitrary use of force. An example is Socrates' refusal to escape from an Athenian jail for the reason that he agreed to live by Athenian law.

Attempts to Define Rights

On the basis of these traditions, efforts are made to define rights, to specify their conditions, and to categorize them. Rights are defined either as powers, valid claims, claims, liberties, immunities, entitlements or trumps (Dworkin). Some definitions are incompatible with others, such as rights as trumps and rights as permissions. Trumps are decisive. Permissions are revokable. Moreover, counterexamples easily arise to any one of these definitions. Permissions, like privileges, are easily overruled, unlike entitlements that one stout-heartedly claims. Nevertheless, some definitions illuminate the concept of rights.

Conditions of Rights

Another approach is to characterize the conditions that enable rights to function. The first of six conditions of any right is freedom. As freedom is linked to free will in individuals, rights are attributable primarily to individuals rather than to groups.

One objection to the right to be free is expressed through the dilemma of a child's right to go to school, which the child is at the same time required to attend. How can the right to be free be a right if it implies a requirement on the part of the right-holder? One response is that, as with a right to get married, one has to fulfill certain requirements prior to exercising one's right to get married, such as having a blood test. Similarly, a child has a right to go to school for an education, but the child is required to fulfill preconditions for exercising that right, such as attending school and paying attention.

A second condition of any right is that it implies correlative obligations on other relevant persons. The right to vote, for example, implies that a state has the obligation to provide adequate police at polling booths. A third condition of any rights is that they accord with rationally defensible principles of justice. To St.

Augustine (354–430), "there is no right where there is no justice" (Augustine: 882). A fourth requirement for having rights is the presence of adequate, relevant resources. One cannot be obligated to do more than what is humanly and individually possible. An example of the violation of the resource requirement is to say that patients in need of scarce organ transplants have a right to them. A fifth condition of any right is that it be enforceable. Sixth, rights imply appropriate compensation to those who suffer from rights infringements in certain situations that are morally unavoidable.

Categories of Rights

Rights are also categorized into two or more kinds. One writer distinguishes option rights and welfare rights (Golding 1968: 521). Another divides rights into security rights, liberty rights, and subsistence rights. A third writer distinguishes will-based rights from interest-based rights (MacCormick: 305–17). Rights distinctions also raise questions about the powers and limits of rights. If Mary lacks money with which to buy textbooks for her high school chemistry course, does her right to education imply that another student, Henry, who sits near her, has an obligation to share the text?

Three Models Help Orient Rights

One way to help draw boundaries around the concept of rights is to consider activities in the social life of a community where the language of rights is at work. The first of three models is an ownership model. A paradigm is evident in one's ownership of one's body. Ownership implies nearly exclusive freedom and control over what is owned. If one has any rights at all, one has rights "in and to one's body" (Thomson 1971: 47–53), a recognition that to have rights is to own something. This model, however, identifies rights with "individual possessiveness" (McPherson), the sometimes overdrawn extension of ownership to other things. Inadequate regard is paid to rights to social security, health care, and education.

An alternative use of rights occurs in a person's memberships in associations and organizations, including clubs and the use of city and state roads, which may be identified as the club membership model. As long as members pay their dues, and maintain their decorum, respect the premises or roadways, and abide by the rules, they are pretty much free to do as they wish. This model also has drawbacks. Individu-als in clubs, societies, and institutions seem not to be obligated to care for one another. Responsibilities to others are minimal.

A third use of rights, designed to remedy defects of previous models, is a partnership model. In this view, people live with—and have trust and confidence in—one another. They live with the Three Musketeers' adage, "All for one and one for all." Rights, as they have developed through various traditions, are not exclusively ownerships or memberships in clubs and societies. Rights are also partnerships based on agreements that demonstrate people's caring for one another's common interests. These interests include "living well," as the ancient Greek philosopher's adage held. And living well implies a life of freedom, decency, dignity, mutuality, reciprocity, respect, and self-respect. To have rights is to own something, to be a member of social institutions, and to form and sustain partnerships that enable people to live well with others. A difficulty, even with the third model, is that there may be bad partnerships as well as good ones.

Rights Criticized

Rights are sometimes extended, inflated, and abused. These excesses and abuses of rights have led to criticisms. One critic recoils at the inflationary use of rights (Sumner: 9). Another writer regards rights as contributing to the "tyranny of rules" (Toulmin: 31–39). A third writer contends that rights are "witchcraft" (MacIntyre: 66–67). A fourth writer regards "rights talk" as contributing to "the impoverishment of political discourse" and claims that rights without responsibilities lead to Lone Ranger morality, a form of barren and brazen individualism (Glendon). To yet other critics, invoking rights in some medical malpractice suits generates adversarial relations between patients and physicians, which signals a breakdown of trust and confidence between patients and doctors. An older critique cites rights as expressions of greed, aimed at the exclusion of the poor. Powerful states and individuals use rights to oppress the disadvantaged.

A Response to Critiques of Rights

One response to various criticisms is to consider metaphors that are used to characterize rights. A metaphor is an analogy using a word picture designed to clarify something that is unclear or unknown. One metaphor of rights is that they are inalienable. The inalienable character of rights means that a person cannot be deprived of rights "without a grave affront to justice" (Cranston: 67). Rights metaphors also include comparisons of rights to stop and go traffic lights; to doors, which a right-holder may open or close; to keys or padlocks, which a right-holder may lock or unlock at pleasure; to weapons which a person may use to achieve protection against being injured or killed; to permissions, passes, passports, or to roadways enabling a person to move or to travel unhindered. One may also compare rights to political trumps (Dworkin) or to American-style credit cards, which give a person the power to make purchases.

One type of rights metaphor merits special attention: moral and political manifestos, declarations, proclamations, and the Bill of Rights. A notable example is the Declaration of Independence, with its trilogy of rights. This declaration sets forth the political concept that government depends upon the consent of citizens. The sole justification for governments to exist is to implement people's rights to "life, liberty, and the pursuit of happiness." Rights so conceived avoid pitfalls that accompany the abuse of rights. Rights enshrined in political manifestos contribute toward achieving worthwhile goals. Perhaps in the future, as blacks, women, and children achieve recognition of their rights, some kinds of animals will also have their rights recognized. The process of recognizing rights may begin with some wise manifestos and continue toward their implementation.

General and Special Rights
A second related response to criticisms of rights is to distinguish general and special rights, or rights as end-state rights and instrumental rights, and to test for their mutual consistency. One may regard legal, political, medical and educational rights as instrumental or as special rights, and regard rights to "life, liberty and the pursuit of happiness" as general, end-state rights. For some aspects of rights language, a useful purpose is served in making a tentative distinction between these kinds of rights. General and inclusive rights, like the trilogy of rights in the Declaration of Independence, imply more particular, instrumental rights like the right to vote, the right to a free press, the right not to be tortured, and rights to the pursuit of social and economic security, health care, and education. For rights to provide mutual costraints against excesses, one

may adapt Immanuel Kant's notion of the relationship between concepts and percepts. General manifesto rights (concepts) without reference to special rights (percepts) are empty; and specific rights without general rights are blind and purposeless.

Unresolved Rights Issues
Several unresolved rights issues include the question of group rights versus individual rights. Some rights defendants in parts of Africa claim that the rights of families, groups, and societies rather than individuals are uppermost. For example, the right of a tribe to require female circumcision overrides an individual's right to decide otherwise. Some Western thinkers from John Locke to Nozick maintain that rights belong exclusively to individuals (Nozick).

A second issue concerns the relationship of rights to virtues and responsibilities. One response to rights critiques supplements rights with virtues, such as generosity, patience, understanding, compassion, courage, and wisdom together with an appropriate sense of responsibility. A third related issue is that of rights versus communitarian virtues. In this view, rights are antithetical to the cultivation of virtues in communities. To communitarians, trustworthiness and good character are morally preferable to the institution of rights and rules. A fourth issue is whether or not there are intellectual rights, rights other than moral, legal, and political rights. Those who defend intellectual rights refer to rights to think, to know, to inquire, to infer, to believe, to examine, and to doubt. Feinberg includes intellectual rights under the rubric of "appropriateness rights," such as "the right to believe in the absence of evidence." These rights fall outside a legal model (Feinberg 1992: 228).

A final issue is whether having a right implies being right. Can one be wrong or unwise in the exercise of one's right? One writer discusses this issue in relation to children's rights (Houston: 143–55). Some critics argue that one can have and exercise rights, and be wrong. According to Searle, a teacher's right to academic freedom does not imply that the teacher has a right to use the classroom "to endorse any belief" (Searle: 62–63). Some rights defenders argue that to have rights implies that one is not wrong in exercising one's rights (Thomson 1990: 1). Those who defend the connection between having a right and being right contend that a function of rights consists in the justification of action. Rights provide justifiable reasons for making claims.

A role of rights is to help one to decide in some telling cases the difference between right and wrong. To say "You have no right to pollute the environment" or "You have no right to abuse people" (such as by engaging in racist, sexist, anti-Semitic, or abusive behavior) or "You have no right to suppress ideas" implies that polluting the environment, abusing people, or suppressing ideas is wrong. Rights and wrongs are to morality, politics, and education what true and false statements are to science, epistemology, and "systems of thought" (Rawls: 3–4). This view of rights, while defensible for some types of cases, remains contestable for others.

Bertram Bandman

See also CHILDREN'S RIGHTS; COMMUNITY; FREEDOM AND DETERMINISM; INDIVIDUALISM; JUSTICE

Bibliography

Augustine. *Concerning the City of God.* Translated by H. Bettenson. London: Penguin Books, 1972.

Cranston, M. *Are There Human Rights?* 2nd ed. New York: Taplinger, 1972.

Douglas, W.O. "The New York Released Time Case." In *Approaches to the Philosophy of Religion: A Book of Readings,* edited by D.J. Bronstein and H.M. Schulweis. New York: Prentice Hall, 1954.

Dworkin, R. *Taking Rights Seriously.* New York: Basic Books, 1973.

Feinberg, J. *Freedom and Fulfillment.* Princeton: Princeton University Press, 1992.

———. *Social Philosophy.* Englewood Cliffs, N.J.: Prentice Hall, 1973.

Glendon, M.A. *Rights Talk: The Impoverishment of Political Discourse.* New York: Basic Books, 1991.

Golding, M.P. "The Concept of Rights: A Historical Sketch." In *Bioethics and Human Rights: A Reader for Health Professionals,* edited by E. Bandman and B. Bandman. Boston: Little, Brown, 1978.

———. "Towards a Theory of Human Rights." *Monist* 40 (1968): 521–49.

Hart, H.L.A. "Are There Any Natural Rights." In *Human Rights,* edited by A.I. Melden. Belmont, Calif.: Wadsworth, 1971.

Holmes, O.W. *The Common Law.* Boston: Little, Brown, 1963.

Houston, B. "Are Children's Rights Wrong Rights?" In *Proceedings of the Philosophy of Education Society,* edited by B.A. Alexander. Urbana, Ill.: Philosophy of Education Society, 1993.

McCloskey, H. "Rights." *The Philosophical Quarterly* 15, no. 59 (1965): 115–27.

MacCormick, N. "Children's Rights: A Test Case for Theories of Rights." *Archiv Fur Rechts Und Sozialphilosophie* 62 (1976).

MacIntyre, A. *After Virtue.* 2nd ed. Notre Dame, Ind.: University of Notre Dame Press, 1984.

McPherson, C.B. *The Political Theory of Possessive Individualism: Hobbes to Locke.* Oxford: Oxford University Press, 1962.

Nozick, R. *Anarchy, State and Utopia.* New York: Basic Books, 1974.

Rawls, J. *A Theory of Justice.* Cambridge: Harvard University Press, 1971.

Searle, J. "The Storm over the University: A Further Exchange." *New York Review of Books* 38, no. 9 (1991).

Sumner, W. *The Moral Foundations of Rights.* Oxford: Clarendon Press, 1981.

Thomson, J. "In Defense of Abortion." *Philosophy and Public Affairs* 1 (1971): 47–66.

———. *The Realm of Rights.* Cambridge: Harvard University Press, 1990.

Toulmin, S. "The Tyranny of Rules." *Hastings Center Report* 11 (1980): 31–39.

Romanticism

The word *Romantic* has been used in so many ways that it would be foolhardy to assign any one meaning to it. Even so, since the late eighteenth century, Romantics have been recognized as those who celebrate and actively pursue the senses in which imagination has a primary place in human experience, over and against an emphasis on reason. The most commonly recognized flourishing of Romanticism is the phase of English poetry that began with William Blake's *Songs of Tomorrow* in 1789, includes Samuel Taylor Coleridge and William Wordsworth, and ended with the death of John Keats in 1821 and Percy Bysshe Shelley in 1822. Their writings will provide the heart of our characterization of Romanticism, while their predecessor Giambattista Vico (1668–1744) and the German poet Friedrich

Hölderlin (1770–1843) will also have a place in our account.

Imagination as Maker of Reality

While the Romantics differed from one another, they shared a sense that the imagination works with an insight into the nature of things that cannot be overcome by or subordinated to the logic of rationality. Keats gives voice to the limits of rationality in saying, "I have never been able to perceive how any thing can be known for truth by consequitive reasoning." Yet Keats was certain of "the holiness of the Heart's affections and the Truth of Imagination—what the imagination seizes as Beauty must be Truth—whether it existed before or not." What the Romantics thought of as the "common world," or the "familiar world"—what Reason knows as truth, and tries to make familiar to us—is the world that Imagination must go beyond, by making a kind of beauty that enriches the familiar. It is not that Romantic poets interpret the familiar; rather, through seen, heard, or felt things, they make beauty as a quality of existence. Listening to a nightingale, Keats hears an individual, living bird, yet beyond it he hears a kind of ideal, a nightingale timeless in the beauty of its song: "Thou wast not born for death, immortal bird!" Shelley sketches a portrait of what poetry does: "It purges from our inward sight the film of familiarity, which obscures from us the wonder of our being. It compels us to feel that which we perceive, and to imagine that which we know." Thus we must go beyond the perceived object and feel it (to really perceive it *is* to feel it); and we must go beyond what we know by "consequitive reasoning" and imagine it (to really know it *is* to imagine it).

In going beyond perception and the knowing of reason, we reveal beauty and truth by creating them; we do not "find" beauty and truth as if they already exist, but must make them with our imagination. There is a kind of mystery in the working of imagination, in that we can not know what we are making until we have made it. The subject matter of poetry startles the poet. Keats writes: "Poetry should be great and unobtrusive, a thing which enters into one's soul, and does not startle it or amaze it with itself, but with its subject matter." Thus the Romantics did not lack a subject matter, as their critics charged. Their subject matter was a world which they made, not a world which they found. And in making their world, they created possibilities, beauties which

ought to exist, even if they do not appear in the common, familiar world that is there. As George Santayana once wrote, Shelley's subject matter can be characterized in four words: "What ought to be." The world that is made by the imagination—what ought to be—takes on an existence of its own, which has the potential of freeing us from a dependency on the familiar. If the Romantics had known G.W.F. Hegel's epigram "What is familiar is not known because it is familiar," they might have added, "And what is known is not familiar simply because it is known."

The Romantic tendency to be mindful of the ways in which Reason sets up obstacles to our natural yearnings is seen vividly in Blake, who detects, in grownups, even in infants, "In every voice, in every ban, / The mind-forged manacles I hear—." Wordsworth's lines make of Blake's "manacles" a "prison-house": "Heaven lies about us in our infancy! / Shades of the prison-house begin to close / Upon the growing Boy." The beauty and innocence of childhood as expressions of nature—of the ways we ought to be—are endangered by the closing in of the prison-house, as Wordsworth continues: "The Youth . . . / Still is Nature's Priest, / And by the vision splendid / Is on his way attended./ At length the Man perceives it die away. / And fade into the light of common day." And Coleridge compared the simplicity of a poet to that of a child: "The poet is one who carries the simplicity of childhood into the powers of manhood; who, with a soul unsubdued by habit, unshackled by custom, contemplates all things with the freshness and the wonder of a child."

However, Nature by itself does not suffice for the making of beauty. Hölderlin tells us that the poet must "attend to" an "inarticulate" Nature: "But wildflowers growing / On soil as wild / We mortals on to the lap of the gods / Have all been sown, / But scantily nourished, and dead / That soil would appear, did not someone / Attend to it, raising up life, / And mine is that field." Hölderlin's poet, "raising up life," making Nature his field, is in kinship with Keats's poet who makes subject matter, and with Shelley's poet who imagines that which he knows.

The Romantic idea that, by the work of Imagination, poets make their reality rather than interpret a given reality, was anticipated in Vico's *New Science*. There he claims that, in their development, human beings were poets before they were philosophers; as sublime poets, early human beings had large imaginations but small abilities to reason as philosophers do.

Those early human beings wondered about things and gave them substance after their own ideas, "Just as children do, whom we see take inanimate things in their hands and play with them and talk to them as though they were living persons." While lacking rationality, Vico holds, such human beings had a "metaphysics," a poetic metaphysics, by which they gave expression to a kind of wisdom, a poetic wisdom. They created things according to their own ideas and, by creating them, came to believe in them. Poetic metaphysics was unable to understand things as rational metaphysics understands them; in their own way, they made things before they knew what they were making. The world of poetic wisdom was unhampered by the world of "rational wisdom" in which the Romantic poets made their poetry. Dwelling in a world that rationality attempted to render common, it was not possible for the Romantic poets to be "sublime" as Vico's early poets were. Yet the Romantics did sense the necessity of enabling Imagination to create things not common to the world of "consequitive reasoning." And like Vico's poets, Romantic poets made subject matter without knowing what they were making; after it is made the subject matter startles the poet.

Romanticism and the Education of Children

Not confined to poetry, the spirit of Romanticism influenced many dimensions of culture. As we have seen, the innocence, beauty, and promise of childhood appealed to Blake, Coleridge, and Wordsworth. It is not surprising, then, that the Romantic vision of childhood entered into educational theory and made a place in childhood education. This is not to say that anything approximating a Romantic "school" of educational theory came into existence. It is to say, instead, that Romanticism influenced educational thinking. A variety of approaches to the education of children emerged, especially in the late nineteenth and early twentieth centuries, which prized the imagination of children more than a rational understanding of them, and tried to create schools in which children's natural curiosity and activity were allowed to have free play.

It has become part of the conventional wisdom that Romantics in education are heirs to Jean-Jacques Rousseau (1712–1778). It is true that Rousseau's assertion in *Emile*— "Childhood has its ways of seeing, thinking, and feeling which are proper to it. Nothing is

less sensible than to want to subordinate ours [the ways of adults] for theirs"—was shared by Romantics in education. And the study of child development, which flourished in the late nineteenth and twentieth centuries, may be seen as an attempt to understand childhood's way of seeing, thinking, and feeling. Yet Romantics in education must take issue with the way in which Rousseau manipulates the environment in which Emile's education takes place, saying: "Doubtless he ought to do only what he wants; but he ought to want only what you want him to do." And Romantics in education would also take issue with those child developmentalists whose understanding of child nature leads them to prescribe what children need. When Rousseau and developmentalists act as if they know what is good for children in specific stages of development, they deny children the opportunity to enable their natural powers to go to work amid the materials of their environment and find out what is good for themselves. As Keats's poet did not know his subject matter until he made it, so children will not know what they do until they do it. From the Romantic point of view, to impose into the education of children what adults think is good for them is a presumption against the nature of childhood and a failure to trust imagination to make its way in a precarious world.

In the space remaining, the ideas of certain educators whose work and writings capture a sense of Romanticism will be featured. The title of Caroline Pratt's book, *I Learn from Children*, is suggestive of the Romantic sense of childhood that was alive in her Play School (opened in 1914 in New York City). Pratt saw children as natural artists who clarify their ideas by the ways they act on them. The student, Pratt writes, "is dominated by a desire to clarify this idea for *himself*. It is incidental to his purpose to clarify it for others." This suggests that others ought not be in the business of clarifying the ideas of children. Harold Rugg and Ann Shumaker, in *The Child-Centered School*, touted the faith that the creative impulse lies within the child, and they pointed to the educational meaning of this faith: "Every child is born with the power to create . . . [and] the task of the school is to surround the child with an environment which will draw out this creative power." A faith in the child's creative power of expression was echoed by Margaret Naumburg, whose Children's School (also opened in 1914 in New York City) was established on the "apparently unlimited desire and interest of children to know and to do and to be." A.S. Neill, discussing his Summerhill School (opened in 1921 in England) in *Hearts Not Heads in the School,* states well the Romantic sense in contrasting "We" (the proponents of freedom in education) with "They" (the proponents of systematic state schools): "We say: Here is a child; let's watch him and see what he is and what he wants to do. They say: Here is a child who can't know what's good for him. Let's fit him into our great schooling machine."

Although he criticized what he took to be extreme forms of "child-centered" education, John Dewey gives voice to one of the enduring themes of Romanticism when criticizing the early-twentieth-century passion for measuring children's "intelligence," achievements—indeed, whatever qualities of their lives could be reduced to quantitative terms. "Even if it be true that everything which exists could be measured," Dewey writes, "that which does *not* exist cannot be measured. . . . The teacher is deeply concerned with what does not exist. . . . What already exists by way of native endowment and past achievement is subordinate to what it may become. Possibilities are more important than what already exists, and knowledge of the latter counts only in its bearing upon possibilities." The emphasis upon possibilities rather than present existents and, what is more, the idea that the fate of possibilities is not only unknown but must be determined by human action, partakes of the Romantic sense that what is genuine subject matter to each of us is a world that we make, not a world that we find.

J.J. Chambliss

See also EXPERIENCE; POSSIBILITY; PROGRESS, IDEA OF, AND PROGRESSIVE EDUCATION; ROUSSEAU

Bibliography

Barth, J. Robert, S.J., and John L. Mahoney, eds. *Coleridge, Keats, and the Imagination: Romanticism and Adam's Dream.* Columbia: University of Missouri Press, 1990.
Bowra, C.M. *The Romantic Imagination.* New York: Oxford University Press, 1961.
Chambliss, J.J. *Imagination and Reason in Plato, Aristotle, Vico, Rousseau, and Keats.* The Hague: Martinus Nijhoff, 1974.
Dabundo, Laura, ed. *Encyclopedia of Romanticism: Culture in Britain, 1780s–1830s.* New York: Garland, 1992.
Dewey, John. *The Child and the Curriculum.* Chicago: University of Chicago Press, 1902.
———. "Progressive Education and the Science of Education." *Progressive Education* 40 (1928): 197–204.
Hartman, Gertrude, and Ann Shumaker, eds. *Creative Expression: The Development of Children in Art, Music, Literature, and Dramatics.* New York: John Day, 1932.
Neill, A.S. *Hearts Not Heads in the School.* London: Herbert Jenkins, 1944.
Pratt, Caroline. *I Learn from Children.* New York: Simon and Schuster, 1948.
Rugg, Harold, and Ann Shumaker. *The Child-Centered School.* New York: World Book, 1928.
Vico, Giambattista. *The New Science.* Translated by Thomas Goddard Bergin and Max Harold Fisch. Ithaca, N.Y.: Cornell University Press, 1968.

Rosenkranz, Johann Karl Friedrich (1824–1879)

German Hegelian philosopher, whose one book on the philosophy of education, *Pädagogik als System: Ein Grundiss* (1848), introduced to readers in translation by Anna C. Brackett in William Torrey Harris' *Journal of Speculative Philosophy,* had such an influence that the American philosopher of education William Heard Kilpatrick concluded that "it seems rather probable that the translation [of Hegel] . . . [by] Rosenkranz . . . gave the term philosophy of education its first strong hold in America" (61). For nearly forty years, Rosenkranz's interpretation and application of Hegel to education were widely assigned and studied in several American colleges and universities: DePauw, Illinois State Normal, University of Illinois, Indiana University, University of Michigan, University of Nebraska, the New Jersey State Normal School, Ohio State University, and others.

In 1824, Rosenkranz began his study of philosophy with F. E. D. Schleiermacher at the University of Berlin, but he did not long remain a Schleiermacherian. After continuing his studies at Heidelberg and Halle and being introduced to Hegelian philosophy by Leopold von Henning, he became a Hegelian. In 1833 he was called to Königsberg to succeed J.F. Herbart to the chair of philosophy and pedagogy, the chair that Immanuel Kant had held for thirty-four years prior to Herbart's twenty-four-year tenure. Rosenkranz remained in Köningsberg until his death in 1879.

In Germany, Rosenkranz was viewed as a right-wing Hegelian, in the company of Karl Göschel and J.E. Erdman, as opposed to the left-wing Hegelians such as David Friederich Strauss and Ludwig Feuerbach. For the Americans, Rosenkranz was neither a left-wing Hegelian (such as Karl Marx and Friedrich Nietzsche) nor a right-wing Hegelian (such as, F.H. Bradley, Bernard Bosanquet, Josiah Royce, W.T. Harris, and W.E. Hocking), "but formed a part of the 'center'" (Buchner: 205). He "accommodated Hegel's Absolute to the traditional theism of Christians . . . refused the option of turning Hegel head over heels and positing matter as the only reality . . . [and] interpreted Hegel as the theorist of liberty and not of political absolutism" (Krolikowski: 18). In a letter printed in the *Journal of Speculative Philosophy*, Rosenkranz indicated that "Hegel not only does not deny God, freedom, and immortality, but he teaches them as the highest consequences of his speculation." He saw himself as being "perhaps the German philosopher who has contended most against atheism and materialism" (1872: 177).

Rather than emphasize humanity's subjection to either God or the state in the guise of the unfolding Absolute World Spirit, Rosenkranz emphasized nature's subjection to humanity. For Rosenkranz, humans have mind, and mind is essentially free and knows what is rational. Mind uses "nature as a subordinate instrument." While both nature and mind are rational, mind is clearly superior to nature, for "in nature there exists instinct but not will" (1871: 243). Only humanity can be free, for freedom, he maintained, can be achieved only through willing and thinking.

Rosenkranz maintained that the inductive method of the empiricists was confused and inferior to the deductive method. Those who believed that nature could be studied empirically and inductively were mistaken. He argued, for example, that the atom, a favorite concept of the empiricists, was not a subject of experience but a hypothesis. Natural science that claimed to be empirical and inductive was in actuality metaphysical and deductive. Once the empiricists had deduced the atom, they also had to postulate other concepts such as the void so that still another concept of motion could be postulated (1874: 10–11). Rosenkranz argued that science conducted according to the rules of the inductive method had become "an entirely methodless, inorganic reflection, narration—an entirely capricious combination—in which the reader must be glad if the authors show that they have not wholly forgotten the principles of formal logic, and, at least, attend to a fixed order" (1874: 10–11).

The St. Louis Hegelians apparently believed that the empiricists' gains in the field of education had gone far enough. When Anna C. Brackett presented her first installment of her translation of *Pädagogik* in 1872, she explained that "it is very certain that too much of our teaching is simply empirical, and as Germany has, more than any other country, endeavored to found it upon universal truths, it is to that country that we must at present look for a remedy for this empiricism" (290). The presence of universal truths allowed the deduction of other necessary truths until one had a full-blown system free from an empirical contamination. When Harris edited Brackett's translation for Appleton's International Education Series in 1886 under the title *The Philosophy of Education*, he called special attention to one of those truths, the principle of *Selbst-Entfremdung*, which, he claimed, lay at the foundation of Rosenkranz's work. It was a principle that held that the development of self, of personality, is an educative process that entails more than the development of the nervous system and the formation of good habits.

The writings of Rosenkranz were important and useful for Harris and others because they provided a philosophy of education that served as an answer or an alternative to then emerging empirical sciences of human and social behavior. His was a philosophy that placed the individual above society but, at the same time, did not deny the importance of society. As Richard Edwards wrote, "Where our common writers give us empirical directions, with some show of a skin-deep reason, Dr. Rosenkranz strikes at the very root of the matter, and in a single sentence . . . makes the whole subject luminous, by stating some law, not only of universal application, but of high practical utility" (16). Henry Barnard included a selection of *Pädagogik* in his *American Journal of Education* and reported that "although Rosenkranz has published less on the prolific subject of Pedagogy than his professional contemporaries, his views are regarded as singularly comprehensive and profound—at once philosophical and practical" (5).

Erwin V. Johanningmeier

See also: HARRIS; HEGEL

Bibliography

Barnard, Henry. "Rosenkranz and His Pedagogy." *American Journal of Education* 28 (1878).

Brackett, Anna C. "Preface to Pedagogics as a System." *Journal of Speculative Philosophy* 6 (1872): 290.

Buchner, Edward F. "Rosenkranz." In *Cyclopedia of Education*. Vol. 5, edited by Paul Monroe. New York: Macmillan, 1913.

Edwards, Richard. "Karl Rosenkranz's Pedagogics as a System." *Illinois School Master* 7 (1874): 16.

Harris, William Torrey. Editor's preface to Karl Rosenkranz's *Philosophy of Education*. New York: D. Appleton, 1886.

Hoffding, Harald. *A History of Modern Philosophy*. Vol. 2, translated from the German by B.E. Meyer. New York: Macmillan, 1950.

Kilpatrick, William Heard. "Tendencies in Educational Philosophy." In *Twenty-Five Years of American Education*, edited by I.L. Kandel. New York: Macmillan, 1924.

Krolikowski, Walter P. "Arnold Tompkins: Midwest Philosopher & Education." Ph.D. diss., University of Illinois, 1965.

Rosenkranz, Karl. "Correspondence [Rosenkranz to the St. Louis Philosophical Society]." *Journal of Speculative Philosophy* 5 (1872): 177.

———. "Correspondence [Rosenkranz to the St. Louis Philosophical Society]." *Journal of Speculative Philosophy* 6 (1872): 175–81.

———. "Hegel's History of Philosophy." Translated by G. Stanley Hall. *Journal of Speculative Philosophy* 7 (1874): 10–11.

———. Introduction to Hegel's *Encyclopedia of Philosophic Sciences* (written for the edition of the encyclopedia published in J.H. von Kirchmann's *Philosophische Bibliothek*, c. 1870). Translated by Thomas Davidson. In *Journal of Speculative Philosophy* 5 (1871): 243–50.

For a complete bibliography of Rosenkranz's works as well as a bibliography of commentaries compiled by Benjamin Rand, see *Dictionary of Philosophy, Psychology, and Cognate Subjects*. Edited by James Mark Baldwin. New York: Macmillan, 1905.

Rousseau, Jean-Jacques (1712–1778)

Swiss philosopher, political theorist, novelist, essayist, and musician. His *Emile* and *The Social Contract*, both published in 1762, forced his flight from France to avoid arrest for treason and impiety. Yet they became two of the most influential works in the history of education and political theory. He is often considered a founder of the nineteenth-century Romantic movement.

Rousseau's diverse contributions have been subject from the beginning to uncommonly heated debate. Critics have called him antiintellectual, proto-Marxist, proto-fascist, the father of the French Revolution's "Terror," sexist, even literally crazy. Defenders have cited him for being the first true defender of childhood as something more than an incomplete adulthood, for his belief in the goodness of human nature, for his critique of human freedom, for the bravery of his support for democratic government while living in an absolute monarchy, and for exquisite sensitivity to the natural environment. The debate continues unabated today.

Life

Rousseau's life was in many ways an unhappy one. Though born in Geneva, his ancestors were French. His mother died giving him birth. After an altercation, his watchmaker father had to flee Geneva, leaving his ten-year-old son with relatives. Locked out of the city one night at fifteen, Rousseau began the wanderings in Europe that would last off and on throughout his life. In Italy he converted to Catholicism and then, returning to Switzerland, back to Protestantism. He intermittently lived with an older woman, Madame de Warens, who became his mistress. Later, he attempted tutoring children but, according to his own account, failed. He also wrote several operas, one quite successful, tried and failed to get a position at the French king's court, and received patronage from several noble families. He set up a household with a serving woman, Therese Le Vasseur. With her he had, according to his account, five children, all of whom he sent to an orphans' home, though whether such childbearing and giving up of children actually occurred has been subject to extended debate.

Rousseau finally obtained some literary fame in 1749, winning a prize offered by the academy at Dijon. Thereafter he gained widespread fame for his essays and for several major works, including a novel called *Julie,* a political treatise called *The Social Contract,* and *Emile.* The last two works forced him to flee France for his life, and he spent almost a decade in exile, first in Switzerland, then in England (invited there by the English philosopher David Hume). Subject to ill health throughout his whole life, during this period he began suffering from hallucinations, paranoia, and at times even madness, possibly the result of uremic poisoning. Despite these difficulties and the chaotic social relationships they produced, he continued to work on his *Confessions* and other autobiographical essays. During the last years of his life he was allowed to return to France, where he continued to write, while drifting in and out of madness, until his death.

Educational Philosophy

Rousseau wrote a number of works containing educational ideas from the 1740s onward. An early manuscript treatise (the "Favre") has come down to us; and there are passages of educational interest in *Julie,* in *The Government of Poland,* and elsewhere. However, *Emile* is Rousseau's most comprehensive treatment of his philosophy, and the centrality of education to that philosophy is underscored by the subtitle of the work, *Or On Education.* He explicitly stated that it was his "best work." In form it is unusual, a mixture of narrative passages and analytic arguments. Commentators have disagreed whether to treat it as a romance, a *bildungsroman* of Emile's childhood and early adult years, or as a patchwork treatise on one or another of various philosophical topics such as psychology, theology, or politics. These viewpoints, however, fail to recognize the uniqueness both of Emile and of Rousseau's method. Though Emile may at first strike the reader as a particular literary character, he in fact is intended to represent nothing less than the general philosophic character of humanity. Moreover, the way in which Rousseau presents him, as a thought-experiment that takes a child at birth and raises him in unique circumstances until married, might best be viewed as an archaeology of human nature. Finally, Rousseau's use of language differs from the more customary deductive method of philosophy. He repeatedly warns his reader that he does not use language as other writers do; rather, he defines his terms contextually, their meaning deriving from the ideas directly related to the one being expressed and not from some independent, authoritative dictionary. This rhetorical character of his style has often led unwary readers astray.

Emile is one of the most genuinely original works in the history of education, yet it reflects a solid grounding in previous educational philosophy. Although Rousseau received no formal education, he read widely on his own. He was especially influenced by the Greeks and Romans, and *Emile* reveals a unique modern use of ideas that were given their first full development in the works of Plato, Aristotle, and the Sophists. From Plato Rousseau derived a universal, holistic principle that sets the framework within which to treat all human problems, including education. From Aristotle he took a circumstantial, functional interpretation of those problems and invented his widely influential conception of the stages of human development. From the Sophists he drew an operational method that governs both the rhetorical form his argument takes and the substantive means by which Emile gains his knowledge. How he can weave together such apparently self-contradictory strands—narration and analysis, particular and general, ancient and modern, holism, functionalism, and operationalism—is best seen by looking at the structure and development of the argument of *Emile.*

The first few pages of Book I provide an overview of the issues Rousseau will treat and they outline how the work will proceed. He begins with his central problem, given in the form of a famous paradox: "Everything is good as it leaves the hands of the Author of things; everything degenerates in the hands of man." (His *Social Contract* begins with an even more famous paradox—"Man is born free, and everywhere he is in chains"—and proceeds with the same method.) As he later makes clear, Rousseau views this "good" as the formal principle of his whole thought. Like Plato, he sees the universe as an ordered whole, a harmony that precedes and gives both definition and meaning to all its parts, including humanity. His initial paradox, consequently, raises the problem of the source of disorder in human affairs. His answer, a response that influenced Immanuel Kant and the Enlightenment, is that although the "Author of things" created humans individually, it was they who collectively created society, a force distinct from human nature with the power to "stifle" that nature. To solve the problems raised by such "social institutions," Rousseau turns to an examination of education, which gives us "everything we do not have at our birth and which we need when we are grown." He then lays out four central features he will explore throughout his work.

He states, first, that education has three sources: nature, the internal development of our physical and mental constitution, over which we have no control; things, our external physical environment, over which we have limited control; and humans, our external social environment, over which we potentially have the most control. Second, the character of these sources determines the end of education: An individual, to be in harmony with himself, to find happiness, must follow the guidance of the first source, because it is fixed, and align the other two, insofar as possible, with it. The aim of education, therefore, is the self-development of the individual unrestrained by artificial limitations, especially those created by social institutions. Rousseau recognizes that one of his most important tasks is to demonstrate how people raised primarily for themselves can live harmoniously with others in a social setting. Third, such an aim means that the form education takes must be "individual and domestic" rather than "public and common." The best example of the latter, he says, is Plato's *Republic,* which, although he calls it "the most beautiful educational treatise ever written," errs because it seeks to "denature man," to replace natural habits and purposes by social ones, to make a citizen. *Emile,* by contrast, is intended to show how a natural education would work. Last, the content of education is the "common calling" of all humans—that is, finding one's own proper place within the natural and the (reconstructed) social orders. Consequently, the proper educational study is "the human condition" in general. Emile is not to be fitted to any particular circumstance, whether natural or social; rather, his natural flexibility will be cultivated to make him fit in anywhere. He represents a modern transformation of the Greek "golden mean," an individual who, by avoiding both excess and deficiency, most fully develops all inner potentials and thereby has, in Rousseau's phrase, the richest "sentiment of our existence."

The rest of Book I concerns the child before it achieves self-consciousness. The guiding image here is the child as a plant, and the book naturally divides into two parts: the first on how one should "cultivate" such a child and the second on the child so cultivated. The first covers mothers' natural treatment of their babies—Rousseau favors nursing, attacks swaddling and the use of nurses as mother-substitutes, and argues against letting babies dominate their parents through their cries—and fathers' duties. Rousseau then offers himself as Emile's sole "parent," his tutor. The second part of Book I describes Emile's first year and a half. He is a child of average physical and mental gifts who is raised in a rural setting with simple food, clothing, and environment, and taught to be comfortable in a wide variety of settings. He expresses himself in the natural language of cries, laughter, and other noises that convey his true needs for healthy growth but, Rousseau insists, must never lead to his dominance of those around him. This age concludes with Emile learning to walk and talk, two features that lead him to become conscious of himself.

If Book I is the age of growth, Book II is the age of sensation. Emile is now viewed not as a growing plant but as an active animal, and Rousseau traces his development up to the age of twelve to thirteen. The book has four sections. In the first, Rousseau develops his "fundamental maxim": "The truly free man wants only what he can do and does what he pleases." At this stage of development, happiness, the goal of the child, consists in the greatest ratio of natural pleasures to pains, and to seek or flee these sensations becomes Emile's central motive. Freedom as the power to act on one's pleasures and pains is the means to that goal. Power, however, is not the sole criterion of freedom. The maxim's balancing of power and desire in the creation of freedom indicates the ubiquitous principle of order, the harmonious universal whole with which the work began. Nature, therefore, which has not been disordered by human society, becomes Emile's teacher. The necessity of natural laws not only teaches him his "proper place" in the "chain of being" (a hierarchical conception of God's creation dating back to medieval theology) but also forms the model of reformed social laws that Emile will later learn to obey as his duty.

This maxim provides the two main sections of the book, an examination of desires and powers, passions and actions, with each treated in both its conventional and natural manifestations. Rousseau begins by analyzing children's natural needs, those privations of the means of survival that lead to natural desires. He makes a famous distinction here between *amour de soi,* that self-love which is "good and useful" for the individual's self-preservation, and *amour-propre,* that selfishness which arises when one compares oneself with others and which, unregulated by reason, generates "emulation, jealousy, envy, vanity, avidity, and vile fear—all the most dangerous passions" (ones, Rousseau complains, that have become adults' chief motivators in educating children.) Since children lack the mature reasoning power to deal with such passions, Rousseau argues against John Locke's exhortation to "reason with children." Rather, the tutor will place the child solely under the laws of necessity and let Emile's actions in the physical world and the consequent reactions that flow from those actions shape his mind. Several justly famous passages demonstrate this approach—for instance, children's solely physical understanding of the character of property rights as evidenced in the confrontation with Robert the gardener, their lack of moral understanding in the discussion of La Fontaine's fable "The Fox and the Crow," and their misunderstanding of the point of the famous tale of Alexander and his physician.

The book's third section turns to Emile's natural powers, focusing on physical exercise and the development of the five senses. Regarding the latter he presents a psychology of learning that, at first glance, appears to be a passive, sensationalist one similar to Locke's. Yet as he develops his conception of "common sense," a sixth sense growing out of the five physiological senses, he reveals an activist, even constructivist, view of psychology that gives great latitude of mental invention to Emile in judging his relations with his physical environment. The pragmatic judgments of the consequences of physical activity that Emile learns in the natural circumstances of Book II become the basis for all his later judgments, even the moral and social ones of Books IV and V. Here the activity of judging involves comparing the varieties of sensory experience so that one can "learn, so to speak, to sense." An extensive use of games and play, including visual art, is depicted to show how Emile grows in judgment.

The last section sums up this age by presenting a sketch of the "mature child." The "final examination" of the child of this age is presented in the story of the son of one of Lord Hyde's friends who, when asked by his father, knows exactly the position of a kite solely from its shadow on the ground. Such a child is completely at home in his natural surroundings.

The age of sensation passes into the age of reason in Book III, lasting from roughly ages twelve to fifteen. Once more the perspective shifts as the child's natural powers exceed his desires, and Rousseau views Emile no longer as a sensitive animal but as a rational one. The principle of action now is curiosity, not pleasure and pain, which leads to choosing among those alternatives in the physical world that will lead, either immediately or more distantly, to well-being, not just to the self-preservation of the previous book. The transition from sensory to rational knowledge is summed up in the discussion of refraction at the end of this book. The multiple perspectives Emile takes on a stick that appears to be broken when standing in water provide the sensory comparisons he needs in order to form not only the simple ideas of sensation that were the subject of Book II but also the complex ideas, the propositional conclusions, characterized as mature reasonings that are the subject of this book. Given this conception of science, Emile's intelligence will be prepared for the problems of adulthood presented hereafter.

Book III is divided mostly into a discussion of "natural arts" (roughly, the natural sciences) and "industrial arts" (the application of natural sciences in social circumstances). The intellectual power that Emile gains through his scientific curriculum—studies that progress through astronomy, geography, magnetism, physics, statics, and chemistry—is the ability to invent solutions to practical, physical problems. Where earlier one's own natural strength was power, here one's mental ingenuity is power, *savoir-faire.* The tutor teaches Emile the sciences through an inductive, experimental method. Anticipating much of John Dewey's conception of problem-solving, Rousseau has Emile encounter difficulties in his daily life and invent solutions for them that secure his comfort. For instance, when the tutor artfully "loses the way" in a forest one day shortly before lunch, he lets Emile "discover" the way home to a meal from the direction the shadows fall. Critical to his method, however, is the absence of formal presentation of scientific subject matter. In typical fashion, he declares, "I hate books. They only teach one to talk about what one does not know." Thus, he does not teach Emile to read but sets up situations, such as the latter's receiving a letter, that will motivate him to want to learn to read. Emile's first book comes at this age, *Robinson Crusoe,* which provides the model of someone who is "above all prejudices and order[s] one's judgments about the true relations of things," a natural model for Emile as he prepares to enter society.

The second half of the book, a discussion of the "industrial arts," provides the bridge to the human, nonphysical world. Concerned heretofore with his relations to natural things, Emile now considers economics, the utility of other things made by humans, a consideration that forms a physical basis for social, nonphysical, and therefore nonnecessary relationships. Here, as in the case of the confrontation with Robert the gardener, social relations must be translated into the conceptual perspective of the student. He finds that manual labor is the most "natural" activity, given a social setting, and decides to become a carpenter in order to earn a living and keep his freedom. By the end of Book III, Emile has the power to enter any physical situation and adjust it to fit his proper pleasures and utility insofar as the situation is amenable to individual intervention, as well as the power to recognize that if a situation is beyond his capacity for influence, he must, as a result, accept the consequences unflinchingly. With such a naturally ordered upbringing, Emile is now prepared to enter the disorder of society.

Books IV and V, which compose well more than half of *Emile,* mark a distinct break from the first three books. Up to age fifteen, the growing child has been kept in the country, but the onset of puberty, which has been delayed by carefully screening out all unnatural stimulation, requires that he be introduced to humans and their social institutions. Up to now, passion has been natural in that its cause was internal, its purpose being self-preservation; the onset of sexuality, however, gives rise to the potential for many passions that are unnatural, ones caused externally by comparison of self with others. This distinction between *amour de soi* and *amour-propre,* introduced in Book II, raises the central problem of *Emile.* The next ten years will trace how Emile uses the natural habits and knowledge acquired earlier as the basis for an orderly moral and social life. Where formerly he was educated in relation to things, he must now be educated not just about but, more important, within society. He has moved beyond being just a growing rational animal: He has become a "moral being," and necessity no longer rules. A new plan of education is needed.

In keeping with the whole book's general movement from broader to narrower perspectives on issues encountered, Book IV explores these new relations by looking at humanity first in general and then in particular. Only after he is armed with criteria derived from such an overview of his common humanity can Emile go on to discover, in Book V, the proper individual to love. Consequently, Book IV examines three issues: Emile's relation to humanity as a whole, humanity's place in the universe, and Emile's general relation to other individuals. In the first section, the first passion Emile feels connecting him with other humans as humans is friendship, not sex, because the most common human experience is suffering. Friendship grows out of both our pity for others who suffer and our gratitude to others for recognizing our suffering. These natural passions, however, can easily lead to the unnatural ones of prejudice and pride, which stimulate *amour-propre* by leading one to be overly critical of others and to believe oneself superior. At this point the curriculum introduces history, a form of "practical philosophy," and fable, which serves to "instruct him without offending him," as the appropriate antidotes for these two diseases of the soul. From this point onward, the various subject matters Emile "studies" are always viewed from such a "moral" perspective.

The middle section of this book is devoted to the tutor's telling Emile the story of the Savoyard vicar, a Catholic priest he once met who broke the vow of celibacy yet was able eventually to find inner peace and moral harmony. Often criticized as an irrelevant intrusion, the vicar's "Profession of Faith" is, in fact, essential, for it contains the principle of the entire work. He seeks to resolve this issue: If (as has been presented in Books I through III) the principle of the physical world is the law of necessity, what is the proper principle of the human world, of thought and passion? After reviewing the endless debates of philosophers, the vicar says he decided to use his own reflections, his "inner light," to find the answer. Recasting Rene Descartes's famous principle as *sentio, ergo sum,* he discovered that in his sentience, in his ability to distinguish among physical relationships, he not only exists but is an active being. After making sure of the rules and instrument to be used for his observations—that is, his mental faculties—the vicar turns to the external world and from it deduces God's existence. Two "articles of faith" set forth God's key characteristics: He is an ultimate will, the prime mover, and a universal intelligence, an agent ordering the cosmos according to law. This regularity, "the preservation of the whole in its established order," provides the principle of not only the nature or order of things but also the structure or rationality of the argument of *Emile*.

Turning to humanity, the Vicar states his third "article of faith": Humans are like God in that they are free to choose actions undetermined by physical necessity, which is how evil arises. Yet the vicar discovers a second meaning of freedom beyond that of choice: Humans are most truly free insofar as their activities are regulated by the natural law of universal order directed at the preservation of the whole. Herein lies the crucial problem of humanity: The issue of freedom is how to make the use of choice into right use, not abuse. This is what Emile's education is all about. First, the tutor must establish in his pupil necessary habits based on natural laws; then, building upon these, the two must together establish social habits and moral actions based on regularity, on reason, and not on passion, on the vicious principles of *amour-propre*. The vicar's story concludes with a description of the failings of institutionalized religions, including Christianity, and an affirmation of natural religion.

Now that Emile can grasp this rational principle of universal order set forth by the vicar and can join it to the sure interpretive agency of his natural conscience unspoiled by social conventions, he is ready for direct experience of human individuals and their passions. They leave for Paris to seek the ideal woman for Emile to marry. This Sophie—in Greek, "wisdom"—becomes for Emile a "model" capable of "repressing his senses by his imagination." In Paris, his curriculum focuses on "taste," the aesthetic question of what deeds and words are pleasing to humans; and he studies manners, languages, and literature, especially the books of the ancients (they were closer to nature). The book concludes with a long meditation by the tutor on what he would do "if I were rich," the essence of which is that he would live no differently than if he were poor because the real pleasures of life are those closest to nature, which do not require the artificial stimulants of wealth.

The last perspective needed for Emile is that of love. Where Rousseau treated humanity as a whole in Book IV to establish the principles of morality, now he turns to the major division in that whole and treats each sex as a new whole, exploring how male and female differ and what their proper relations should be in general, the particular relationship of Emile and Sophie, and, finally, the political consequences of the creation of their family.

The argument of the first major section, "Sophie, or the Woman," follows that of *Emile* as a whole: From physical to moral concerns, from general to specific and common to proper. Rousseau's principle is simple: "In everything not connected with sex, woman is man. . . . In everything connected with sex, woman and man are in every respect related and in every respect different." The physical differentiation of the sexes, moreover, has moral consequences, and the resulting incomparability renders the debate over sexual equality literally meaningless because no common standard of measure exists. The relation between the sexes is not one in which the male, because physically stronger, should dominate the female in a master/slave fashion; rather, each is both active and passive in relation to the other, depending upon circumstance. The mutual dependence that grows out of each seeking to please the other produces a distinctive union, a "moral person" which is an organic whole greater than the sum of its parts. The union of man and woman is not just that of the man's strength added to the woman's observation but that of strength made stronger through observation and observation made more keen through strength. Each is more within the interaction of the whole than either is when acting alone. Through woman, man becomes most fully man; through man, woman most fully woman; and both together reflexively become most completely human. In the rest of the section, Rousseau gives an extended description of Sophie's education, which is intended to exemplify his position that physiological differences of sex have moral consequences and both of these need recognition in education. One should note, finally, that Rousseau's argument here in favor of sexual difference and against sexual equality—he attacked Plato's *Republic* for advocating it—has been the source of great debate over Rousseau's work, especially recently, and has even led some commentators to reject his entire contribution to education.

In the book's second section, Emile at

twenty-one meets a sixteen-year-old Sophie (whom the tutor has artfully put in his way). They court for a year and become engaged. The tutor now seeks to take Emile away for two years. With the onset of sexual passion, Emile must learn to balance it with virtue, with moral strength, if he is to remain free, a master rather than slave of his passions. His happiness depends upon his choosing to extend "the law of necessity to moral things." If he can so choose, he will attain the highest human freedom, autonomy. Very reluctantly and only out of friendship for his tutor, Emile agrees to leave Sophie.

In the third section, "On Travel," Emile's search for his proper place in life reaches the last phase. Where he began with his physical relations to things in Books I through III, then explored his moral relations to humans as humans in Book IV, now he turns to his civil relations, those with humans as civil beings, as citizens. This movement has successively refined the common ground of his relationships until he is now approaching his proper place in society. The summary of Rousseau's *Social Contract* that follows reflects this same approach: First comes the issue of government in general, then that of the different kinds of governments, and finally that of particular governments, which leads Emile back to his homeland. In addition, the discussion reveals that the social contract, like the marriage contract, produces a new "moral and collective body," one that acts with a "common and general will." Incidentally, this conception of a general will and the democratic state that grows out of it have had an extraordinary influence in the history of political theory and practice, from the French Revolution onward.

After two years of inquiry, Emile—Rousseau's average, natural individual—concludes that his proper place is a common place—namely, the whole world. He has been educated to live anywhere; no particular spot on earth and no particular position in society is peculiarly his. Even his property is not really his; he can live with or without it, indifferently. His proper pleasures are independent of circumstance, are those common to humanity. Even though he has been raised "uniquely for himself," he is most truly himself when he is most natural—that is, when he has the most in common with other equally natural selves. Then he has the most virtue, the greatest goodness, and the highest possible human happiness: he re-flects the orderly union of self and other. He is, in short, free.

Emile returns home. The book concludes with his marriage to Sophie, an example of union of self and other that demonstrates that Emile has at last mastered himself, has become autonomous. In the birth of their first child, Rousseau is obviously expressing his hope for the future freedom of others.

Problems

Even the most sympathetic reader of *Emile* will note some major issues the text raises. For one, it provides virtually no account of abstract reasoning or of the formal disciplines of knowledge (though the reader might be able to gather something of an outline for them). As noted, his treatment of women, based on the explicit rejection of their equality with men, raises central questions about the value of his work. Frequently commented on, too, is the absence of a family setting, which makes it unclear exactly what consequences the work has for real-world education. That leads to an even larger question—namely, that the individual tutor-disciple relationship cannot be replicated in the world at large; consequently, one of the most troubling practical questions Rousseau's work raises is the institutionalization of his recommendations, even if one were substantively in agreement with them.

Influence

Despite these problems, Rousseau's work has had extraordinary educational influence. Beginning late in the eighteenth and continuing into the nineteenth century, educational reformers began to view children in a new light. Johann Pestalozzi built his elementary schools in Switzerland on principles laid down by Rousseau, and in Germany Friedrich Froebel started the concept of a "children's garden," or kindergarten, for education. Nevertheless, Rousseau's posthumous appropriation by leaders of the French Revolution, which led to vast social upheavals, greatly damaged his reputation in the subsequent century. In the twentieth century, however, his influence has expanded greatly. In France, the educational movement called *l'ecole active* drew heavily on his ideas. His fellow Genevan, Jean Piaget, spent an entire career experimenting with Rousseau's conception of stages of cognitive development. In Russia, Nikolaevich Tolstoy founded a school explicitly indebted to Rousseau's principles.

In England, Homer Lane and A.S. Neill each founded schools based upon the assumption that by nature children are good and that skillfully practiced "negative education" is the best.

In the United States, Rousseau's influence has been even more extensive, though often mediated through movements based on the work of Europeans like Pestalozzi, Froebel, Piaget, and Neill. In the period between 1900 and 1945, Rousseauan ideas were especially popular, notably in the "child-centered" wing of the Progressive movement. John Dewey acknowledged Rousseau's contributions in getting educators to treat children as children, not just incomplete adults. More recently, the work of John Holt reflects a Rousseauan respect for children as children. Finally, suggestive of the difficulty in assessing Rousseau's complex influence are the testimonials to his importance given by educational psychologists who normally appear to be irreconcilably opposed. The behaviorist B.F. Skinner declared that Rousseau was the first to recognize the importance of environment in the formation of individual behavior; the developmentalist Piaget based his work on the idea of stages of growth; and the humanistic psychologist Carl Rogers developed an educational philosophy based on empathy, caring, and trust, features central in Emile's tutor.

Clearly Rousseau still requires our continued attention, however much or little he wins our agreement.

David B. Owen

See also DEWEY; FROEBEL; LOCKE; MORAL DEVELOPMENT; PESTALOZZI; PROGRESS, IDEA OF, AND PROGRESSIVE EDUCATION; WOLLSTONECRAFT

Bibliography
Annales de la Societe Jean-Jacques Rousseau. Geneve: 1906–.
Brumbaugh, Robert S., and Nathaniel M. Lawrence. "Rousseau: *Emile*, a Romance of Education." In *Philosophers on Education: Six Essays on the Foundations of Western Thought*, chap. 4. Boston: Houghton Mifflin, 1963.
Cassirer, Ernst. *The Question of Jean-Jacques Rousseau.* Translated by Peter Gay. New York: Columbia University Press, 1954.
Claparede, Edouard. "J.-J. Rousseau: Sa philosophie de l'education." *Revue de metaphysique et de morale* 20 (mai 1912): 391–416.
Cranston, Maurice. *Jean-Jacques: The Early Life and Work of Jean-Jacques Rousseau, 1712–1754;* and *The Noble Savage: Jean-Jacques Rousseau: 1754–1762.* Chicago: University of Chicago Press, 1991.
Jimack, Peter D. "Le genese et la redaction de l'*Emile* de J.-J. Rousseau: Etude sur l'histoire de l'ouvrage jusqu'a sa parution." In *Studies on Voltaire and the Eighteenth Century,* edited by Theodore Besterman. Geneve: Institut et Musee Rousseau, 1960.
Kevorkian, B. *L'Emile de Rousseau et l'Emile des ecoles normales.* Neuchatel, Suisse: Delachaux et Niestle, 1948.
Martin, Jane Roland. *Reclaiming a Conversation: The Ideal of the Educated Woman.* New Haven: Yale University Press, 1985.
Rousseau, Jean-Jacques. *Emile, or On Education.* Translated by Allan Bloom. New York: Basic Books, 1979.
———. *Oeuvres completes.* Edition publiee sous la direction de Bernard Gagnebin et Marcel Raymond. Tome 4: *Emile. Education. Morale. Botanique.* Textes etablis et annotes par John S. Spink et al. Bibliotheque de la Pleiade, no. 208. Paris: Gallimard, 1969.
Shklar, Judith. *Men and Citizens: A Study of Rousseau's Social Theory.* 2nd ed. Cambridge: Cambridge University Press, 1985.
Starobinski, Jean. *Jean-Jacques Rousseau: Transparency and Obstruction.* Translated by Arthur Goldhammer. Chicago: University of Chicago Press, 1988.

R

Russell, Bertrand (1872–1970)
Bertrand Russell, who helped define the nature of philosophy and mathematics during the twentieth century, was also a major contributor to the philosophy of education. Russell wrote two books on teaching and learning as well as many essays on education. In the 1920s, he and his wife founded a school that applied his principles of educational theory.

Russell was a rationalist who called his philosophic perspective "logical atomism." By this he meant that ideas should be analyzed until they could be dissected no further. At this point the logical atom of analysis has been reached. The combination of Russell's commitment to rationalism and his logical atomism contributed to Russell's skepticism. Skepticism applied to teaching and learning may be viewed as one of Russell's most important contributions to the philosophy of education.

Russell had lost both of his parents by the age of four and went to live with his grandparents (his grandfather was Lord John Russell, a prime minister of Great Britain). Russell was educated by tutors at home, and he did not attend a public or private school. Just before his seventeenth birthday, he was sent to an Army crammer school to prepare for examinations that would enable him to attend Cambridge University. These early experiences influenced Russell's perspective on education.

Russell's first marriage was childless. His second marriage to Dora Black in 1921 led to the birth of two children, John and Katherine. Russell's interest in the education of his own children led to the publication of his first book—*On Education: Especially in Early Childhood* (called *Education and the Good Life* in its American edition), published in 1926.

In *On Education* Russell makes a distinction between education, which pertains to character, and instruction, which pertains to knowledge. He begins his work by identifying some postulates of educational theory and then describes what he believes to be the aims of education.

Russell agrees that the ideal system of education should be democratic, but he fears that democracy unchecked in education can lead to negative consequences. He opposes democratic procedures that would lead to a "dead level of uniformity," since "some children are more clever than others"; those should be prepared for higher education.

Throughout his life, Russell feared what he called "the herd instinct." Democracy must place checks on unlimited majority rule to be effective; this is particularly true of democracy in education. Russell opposed pragmatism as a philosophy, in part, because he believed that it turned the search for truth into a referendum that could be affected by the herd instinct. This perspective made him skeptical of progressive education even though his approach to education may clearly be labeled as "child centered." *On Education* reflects Russell's commitment to feminism, which he demonstrated in many ways in his lifetime. He argues that men and women should be educated in the same way for the same purposes.

The aim of education should be to form character, which consists, Russell argues, of four components: vitality, courage, sensitiveness, and intelligence. The development of each of these leads to the formation of character. Vitality creates a context for living that makes other kinds of achievement possible. Courage consists in both the ab-

sence of fear and the ability to control it. It is possible, Russell believes, to "educate ordinary men and women so that they shall be able to live without fear." Sensitiveness requires that persons learn to respond to events with appropriate emotions. Intelligence consists of the ability to acquire knowledge and not just the storing of it in one's mind. Intelligence can be generated by encouraging rather than discouraging curiosity, and it should result in open-mindedness. Russell felt that schools often teach to hinder rather than to encourage the formation of character.

Russell's call for sex education in the schools in *On Education* was controversial in its day. Russell discusses the existence of unwanted pregnancies, lack of information about birth control, and lack of understanding of sexual hygiene as one of the consequences of poor information about sex.

Because their two children had reached school age in 1927, the Russells created a private school called Beacon Hill. Russell avoided sending his children to state schools or private ones because he believed that these institutions indoctrinated students into militarism, nationalism, and religion. Russell also wanted to avoid the use of private tutors because he did not want his children to experience the kind of lonely education he had been given as a child.

Beacon Hill school reflected Russell's own belief in hard work and concentration as well as his more liberal precepts about child development. Russell sought to create a balance between too much structure and unbridled freedom. He felt that children need discipline but he also wished to provide them with emotional freedom. "Too much control over emotions," he wrote in *New Hopes for a Changing World,* "is deadening and causes loss of vitality." Russell felt that society often tries to curb emotions believed to be undesirable. Russell's approach to education at Beacon Hill combined his commitment to scholarship, rationalism, and skepticism with an approach that was child-centered, used experiential methods, and contained a strong commitment to aesthetics.

In 1932 Russell published his second major educational work—*Education and the Social Order*. This volume reflected his experiences at Beacon Hill and may be said to have been influenced by the wisdom of practice. *On Education* had relied heavily on behaviorism as a means of instructing young children. It demonstrated only a minimal acceptance of psychoanalytic theory. Russell's experience at Beacon Hill, his growing acquaintanceship with the methods of Maria

Montessori (1870–1952), and his continued study of Freudian psychology moved him away from behaviorism.

A central problem posed by Russell in this work is whether education should train good individuals or good citizens. He saw these as competing objectives. Russell concluded that individual development can occur in education and be combined with a necessary minimum of social coherence. But this can occur only under specified conditions. These include the elimination of large-scale wars, the elimination of superstition, and the avoidance of too great a commitment to uniformity. Russell was generally pessimistic about whether these prerequisites can be achieved. He believed, however, that human beings can be rational and that reason applied to education can result in a better world, in which individuality and citizenship can be reconciled.

In *Education and the Social Order,* Russell continues to express fear of unbridled democracy in education. Aristocracies erred, he argues, in believing that intellectual superiority is an inherited trait. Democracies are mistaken when they regard "all claims to superiority as just grounds for the resentment of the herd."

Russell argues that teachers need an understanding of psychology and considerable training in the art of teaching. Throughout his writings on education he argues for the necessity of teacher education. He also states that teachers must be allowed to relax the curriculum where necessary in order to pursue topics of interest to students. Russell offers some specific suggestions for curriculum. He argues that world history should replace national history. This is part of his ongoing commitment to globalism. History should emphasize events of cultural importance rather than wars. Literature should be taught through intensive rather than extensive reading. Students should study material that they find enjoyable and should not be forced to read books chosen only by the teacher. Curriculum, Russell argues, should be designed by teachers and not by administrators, because the latter will tend to put more into the curriculum than can be taught. On the other hand, teachers who construct courses of study must be careful not to include only those topics that can be taught by rote memorization simply because they are easier to teach. Russell would eliminate those subjects that serve no useful purpose. He cites the teaching of historical detail, the study of Latin grammar, and advanced mathematics (for general audiences) as examples of topics that are not important.

In *Sceptical Essays* Russell argues for a commitment to the idea "that it is undesirable to believe a proposition where there is no ground whatsoever for believing it to be true." The acceptance of this idea would revolutionize the social order, including education. In this volume Russell continues to be skeptical about both private and public education. Both the state and the church wish to instill beliefs that would be dispelled if they were exposed to free inquiry. The church indoctrinates children with religious dogma and the state seeks to indoctrinate children into nationalism, patriotism, and militarism.

In an earlier volume (*The Prospects of Industrial Civilization*) Russell had argued that the "governors of the world believe . . . that virtue can only be taught by teaching falsehood. . . . I disbelieve this, absolutely and entirely." In contrast to this, Russell argues that education be used to inculcate freedom of opinion because of the doubtfulness of all beliefs. Only when this can be accomplished can schools become the kinds of institutions that will be effective in creating effective and rational citizens. Education must develop in students the habit of "forming . . . opinions on the evidence, and holding them with the degree of conviction which the evidence warrants."

Bertrand Russell provides in his writings, and by the model he created at Beacon Hill School, a perspective on education that is child-centered in focus, experiential in methodology, and that offers support to an ongoing commitment to rationalism and skepticism in education.

Michael J. Rockler

See also CIVIC EDUCATION; DEMOCRACY; FEMINISM; MONTESSORI; RATIONALISM; SKEPTICISM

Bibliography

Clark, Ronald W. *The Life of Bertrand Russell.* London: Jonathan Cape, 1975.

Russell, Bertrand. *Education and the Good Life.* New York: Boni and Liveright, 1926. Published in London as *On Education: Especially in Early Childhood.*

———. *Education and the Social Order.* London: George Allen and Unwin, 1966. Published in New York as *Education and the Modern World.*

———. *New Hopes for a Changing World.* New York: Simon and Schuster, 1951.

————. *Skeptical Essays*. London: Unwin Books, 1928.

————, with Dora Russell. *The Prospects of Industrial Civilization*. London: George Allen and Unwin, 1923.

Ryan, Alan. *Bertrand Russell: A Political Life*. New York: Hill and Wang, 1988.

Sappho (Late 7th–Early 6th Century B.C.)
Greek poet from the island of Lesbos. Little reliable information about her life survives: She was from a prominent family, had brothers and probably a daughter, and may have spent time in exile. Her work was edited by Alexandrian critics in the Hellenistic period and came to nine book-rolls, including one book of wedding poetry. Two poems survive through quotation, and papyri from Egypt have yielded long fragments of eight other poems. Short quotations and papyrus scraps offer brief glimpses of many more.

Greek communities in the archaic age (c. 650–480 B.C.) were small and independent. Aristocracies held power in many places, although social upheaval was common. Writing was known and used, but performance of poetry was a central feature of social and ritual life. Choral performance, song, and dance by groups of young men or young women formed an important part of education. Songs included myth and history, with models for approved behavior; dance taught men and women grace and the right public demeanor. Apart from public performance men sang solo at small drinking parties (symposia), and there were women's gatherings at which the participants sang.

Sappho's wedding poetry was sung choral poetry. She probably trained the unmarried women who performed it. Some fragments suggest that she composed songs for other ritual occasions as well. But it is her personal poetry for which she is famous, mainly love poetry concerning or addressed to other women. Its intensity and exaltation of beauty have given it influence disproportionate to the number of surviving lines. Poem 31, the best known, describes the effect on "Sappho" (the speaker of the poem) of a glimpse of another woman. The anguished response coexists with poetic control and produces a sense of intimacy and distance at once. Poem 1 is a prayer to Aphrodite to come as she has before and promise "Sappho" release from unrequited love. In poem 16 Sappho proposes the relativistic view that what one loves is loveliest. Helen, the conventional supreme beauty, is adduced but gives way in the poem to the woman whom Sappho longs to see. Poems 2 and 96 evoke erotic landscapes. Poem 94 reminds a woman who is leaving "Sappho's" company to remember the beautiful things they shared. In these poems men are absent or dismissed.

Sappho must have performed these poems to an audience. The great question is who made up the audience. One reconstruction holds that Sappho had a circle of young, unmarried women around her who went through a period of initiation in her company. The initiatory period was characterized by homosexuality as a preparation for marriage and also by education in poetry and singing. Sappho loved one or another among these young women, and the others formed couples among themselves. This initiatory "school" (for which there is no evidence) is compared to Spartan male initiatory practices connected with military training and portrayed as an aristocratic relic of age-class initiation. But the (scanty) evidence of the fragments suggests that Sappho sang to a circle of friends. Her relationship to the women she loved is unknown. In the sex-segregated society of Lesbos a women's culture seems to have flourished, including song, poetry-making, training of younger women for choral performance, and eroticism. Alcaeus, a contemporary poet, mentions women gathered at a sanctuary ritually judging one another for their beauty.

Sappho's poetry, remarkably, was transported from its setting in a women's group to mainstream culture. Other women must have popularized it by constant resinging. The powerful impression of Sappho's personality that emerges from the text means that the poems could be sung to evoke her presence by women who were no longer in her company.

Eva M. Stehle

See also: HOMER; *Paideia*

Bibliography

Burnett, Anne Pippin. *Three Archaic Poets: Archilochus, Alcaeus, Sappho.* Cambridge: Harvard University Press, 1983.

Campbell, David A., ed. *Greek Lyric I: Sappho, Alcaeus.* Loeb Classical Library. Cambridge: Harvard University Press, 1982.

Snyder, Jane. *The Woman and the Lyre: Women Writers in Classical Greece and Rome.* Carbondale: Southern Illinois University Press, 1989.

Sartre, Jean-Paul (1905–1980)

Born in Paris, Jean-Paul Sartre served in the French army during World War II. Although committed to understanding the human condition, Sartre was also an activist, frequently lending his name and support for the benefit of the marginal members of society. An accomplished writer, author of novels, plays, occasional works, and masterful intellectual biographies, Sartre was offered, but refused, the Nobel Prize for literature. This essay, however, will focus on his philosophy, beginning with a brief general description and concluding with a chronological sketch of his moral views.

Sartre's philosophy is associated with existentialism. The origin of the term is obscure, but Sartre accepted the label in a popular address to students published as *Existentialism is a Humanism* (1947). Although loose in language and dated in context, this work remains an excellent introduction to his thought.

The term *existentialism* is meant to signify a renewed emphasis on the existing thing—specifically, human existence. This emphasis follows upon the distinction between essence, the necessary structure of a thing, and existence, the contingent act of a thing's presence in the world. Sartre, however, does not deny that things have structures; his point is that all essences arise from the presence and activity of human existence.

These notions are developed with care in *Being and Nothingness* (1956). The term *nothingness* in the title of the work refers to human consciousness. Sartre traces our grammatical ability to form negative judgments and negative sentences to the inner quality of negation that characterizes human consciousness. Evidence of this quality of negation is shown by our capacity to live in self-deception. In a more general sense, Sartre would have us see that, while it is true to say that a chair is a chair, it is not true to say that a self is a self. What we call our "self" is an ideal that we continually pursue but never reach. Furthermore, our "I" or "self" is something that we construct over a period of time.

Sartre also refers to consciousness as intentional. The term *intentionality,* as well as the term *phenomenology,* which Sartre uses to describe his early philosophy, are both indebted to Edmund Husserl (1859–1938). For Husserl, consciousness goes out to its object in the sense that it goes out to a structure or an essence; for Sartre, however, consciousness spontaneously goes out to the concrete, existing thing.

Sartre's emphasis on spontaneity and freedom are frequently misunderstood. One has to keep in mind that we are thoroughly situational beings. We do not choose our parents, but we do adopt an attitude to them as well as to our body and the other relatively fixed aspects of our environment.

In *Being and Nothingness,* Sartre uses the term *for-itself* rather than the term *human being,* and the term *in-itself* rather than the term *thing.* He does this in order to stress that the human reality is not merely one thing among other things in the world. Thus consciousness is a "for-itself" because it makes the in-itself (matter) exist for the sake of consciousness. Sartre's intention is to avoid both idealism, the view that the world is a projection of the human mind, and naive realism, the view that the world would exist independently of whether humans ever existed. Sartre's position is that the world exists independently of our conceptions about it, but not independently of the "advent" of human consciousness within matter.

As *Being and Nothingness* develops, the for-itself and the in-itself gradually become more concretely related to each other. By the end of the book, it becomes clear that Sartre's aim is to describe the world as the totality of matter's relations to the human conscious body. Thus, for Sartre, the origin of the structures, meanings, and values that we find in the world arise neither from God nor Nature, but from the presence and activities of human beings.

The second part of this essay will be a brief chronological study of Sartre's major philosophical writings from the perspective of the gradual development of his moral thought.

In *Existentialism is a Humanism,* Sartre considers the case of a young man who is trying to decide if he should join the French resistance in World War II, or, as the only child, stay home and take care of his elderly mother. Sartre says that the choice involves two different moralities—namely, whether an individual should take private or common needs as a goal in life. For Sartre, no advice or deductive analysis of the situation can conclusively resolve the issue. Whatever the young man decides, his particular choice is also the choice of an entire moral system, and he bears the responsibility not merely for the act, but for the moral system itself.

Being and Nothingness does not explicitly deal with ethics, but, indirectly, moral concerns arise, particularly in relation to Sartre's notion of bad faith and the so-called fundamental project. Let us first consider bad faith. Sartre agrees with Freud that our early childhood experiences are frequently crucial, for these experiences fix, to a great extent, the context in which our freedom matures. For Sartre, however, bad faith takes the place of Freud's unconscious. That is, we frequently make choices that we then attempt to hide from, and the attempt to sustain these "self-deceptions" leads to abnormal behavior.

We adopt self-deceptions and other patterns of bad faith in order to guarantee for ourselves a strange success in life. Suppose that I want to be a writer, and that I dream of writing a "great novel." In good faith, I recognize that all that I can do is write my best novel, and that its success, as well as its recognition of being "great," is beyond my control. In bad faith, however, I do not want to take the risk of making a great effort that may not succeed. I do not write, but I continue dreaming and talking about writing. I may drink or do other things to distract myself from my own lack of effort. My bad faith is that I believe both that I could

write the "Great American Novel" and that my "not writing it" is merely a temporary condition. I can pass my whole life in this way, and I can thus live with an image of myself that the world can never disprove.

Stressing again the notion that our individual ethical choices involve an entire way of life, Sartre, toward the end of *Being and Nothingness,* refers to human freedom as a fundamental project. Sartre calls human freedom a fundamental project because he views freedom as holistic and as having the character of a gestalt. Further, this gestalt is a "project," because it gives our individual acts a certain direction: It is the general way we relate to people and to the world.

Once we adopt a fundamental project we are responsible for it, because we sustain it in existence through our daily choices and because we can change it. But as we grow older and surround ourself with the effects of our past choices, it becomes difficult to change. Sartre refers to these changes as "conversions," and he maintains that we are always capable of them, although at great cost to ourselves. "When I deliberate," Sartre says, "the chips are down" (*Being and Nothingness:* 454). The chips are down, because usually our deliberations do not challenge our fundamental project—for example, our choice of profession or style of life.

In the early novel *Nausea* (French, 1938; English, 1949; 1965), Sartre had already given a literary description of our ability to change our fundamental project. Antoine Roquentin experiences a general feeling of uneasiness, "the nausea," that he only gradually identifies as his ability to change the direction of his life.

Although we can change what we might call the direction of our acts, we cannot change our general situation. Freedom is thoroughly situational: We do not choose to be born; we do not choose our language, our country, or whether we are born poor or rich. What we can choose is our attitude toward our situation. Consider the case of a mother who frequently takes a child to the opera. The mother's "taking-the-child-to-the-opera" is a situation about which the child is not free. In the concrete, however, the child either gradually conforms to or resists the mother's influence, and thus grows either to love or to hate the opera.

Sartre's notions of freedom and morality evolved during his life. One of the reasons for this evolution was his growing awareness of the special kind of limitations that circumstance placed upon the freedom of oppressed people and minority groups. In *Anti-Semite and Jew* (1948) Sartre became aware of the degree to which the anti-Semite fixes the condition in which Jews must choose their Jewishness. When society has a global view of a group as "tainted" or as "inferior," it is impossible for that group to totally escape or surpass that view of itself.

This point is developed in detail in the extensive and important work *Saint Genet: Actor and Martyr* (1963). The young orphan, Genet, innocently takes something not belonging to him, and the adults in his community call him a thief. Genet can confess his "crime," but then he must live his life as a confessed thief. He can attempt to deny that his "taking" was intended as an act of thievery; but then he defies the adult community that, as an orphan, he badly needs. Genet's choice is to accept his place in society as an evil: He sees that society needs evil, and he chooses to love the evil that society pretends to hate. He turns this choice into poetry, and he thus is able to belong to the very society that he criticizes.

Both in *Anti-Semite* and in *Genet*, Sartre attempts to reveal what he calls a "Manichaean" element in our social structures. This fourth century Christian sect held that evil and good are equal positive forces. The moral task for the Manichaean is thus simple: To fight evil is to do good. For Sartre, however, this is the general form of bad faith. By concentrating on the elimination of evil, we distract ourselves from the burden of actually changing the world for the better. It is, for example, easier to imprison criminals than to find the means for properly educating people.

In the difficult, complex, and unfinished *Critique of Dialectical Reason* (1976), Sartre attempts to sketch how our collective efforts produce and sustain the basic social structures that characterize our history, at least our Western history. It is, of course, impossible to stand outside of our history in order to judge it. For Sartre, however, the Soviet invasion of Hungary in 1956 signaled the end of the viability of Russian socialism, and gave a perspective from which to judge our history.

The failure of Russian socialism also allows us to see the defects of the democracies that opposed this socialism. Sartre criticizes Western democracies because their advocacy of a pluralist society masks a strong, monistic movement that keeps a segment of society always poor and the majority of people perpetu-ally afraid of becoming poor. Our institutions thus sustain a mass self-deception that keeps poverty in existence while allowing efforts to eliminate it. Manichaeism is thus latent in our institutions, and through it we keep bounds on our freedom.

Although there are no a priori criteria for judging whether something is right or wrong, morality, for Sartre, is not arbitrary. Through countless human efforts we have forged notions of human dignity and freedom, and the way of good faith is to continue, as best as we can, in this direction. By our individual and collective actions, or by our consistent lack of effort, we forge not only the truth of our own individual lives, but also the truth of what it means to be human. Sartre writes: "Tomorrow, after my death some men may decide to establish Fascism, and the others may be so cowardly or so slack as to let them do so. If so Fascism will then be the truth of man, and so much the worse for us" (*Existentialism is a Humanism*: 358).

Joseph S. Catalano

See also EXISTENTIALISM; PHENOMENOLOGY; PHILOSOPHY AND LITERATURE

Bibliography

Catalano, Joseph S. *Commentary on Jean-Paul Sartre's "Being and Nothingness."* Chicago: University of Chicago Press, 1980.

———. *Commentary on Jean-Paul Sartre's Being and Nothingness.* Vol. 1, *Theory of Practical Ensembles.* Chicago: University of Chicago Press, 1986.

Caws, Peter. *Sartre.* London: Routledge and Kegan Paul, 1979.

Danto, Arthur C. *Jean-Paul Sartre.* New York: Viking Press, 1975.

Rybalka, Michel. Bibliography contained in the *Philosophy of Jean-Paul Sartre*, edited by Paul A. Schilpp. La Salle, Ill.: Open Court, 1981.

Sartre, Jean-Paul. *Anti-Semite and Jew.* Translated by George J. Becker. New York: Schocken Books, 1948.

———. *Being and Nothingness.* Translated by Hazel Barnes. New York: Philosophical Library, 1956.

———. *Critique of Dialectical Reason.* Vol. I. *Theory of Practical Ensembles.* Translated by Alan Sheridan-Smith. London: New Left Books, 1976; Verso, 1982.

———. *Existentialism is a Humanism.* In

Existentialism from Dostoevsky to Sartre, edited by Walter Kaufmann. New York: New American Library, 1975.
——. *Nausea.* Translated by Robert Balkick. Penguin Books, 1965.
——. *Saint Genet: Actor and Martyr.* Translated by Bernard Frechtman. New York: George Braziller, 1963.

Scholasticism

A particular intellectual methodology that gained importance in the late medieval period but continues to the present, the philosophical and theological movements that utilized this method, and the system of thought developed by those movements. At times, scholasticism has incorrectly been viewed as synonymous with medieval philosophy and theology and as necessarily rooted in Aristotle. In fact, the movement is considerably more complex than such facile definitions suggest. The relationship between philosophy and theology differed considerably in the writings of various scholastics, and many of the system's early philosophers, most notably Anselm (1033–1109), were influenced by Platonism and Neoplatonic thought, received through Augustine (354–430).

As a method, scholasticism originated in the rational investigation of problems in philosophy, theology, medicine, law, and the liberal arts. The method seems to have developed among canon lawyers in the twelfth and thirteenth centuries as they sought to reconcile seemingly conflicting positions in attempting to codify the Church's massive collection of conciliar documents and papal decrees. Utilizing a specific manner of examining a problem from opposing points of view, it sought to arrive at solutions that reconciled fact and reason with accepted authority, including Christian faith. Underlying this was the belief that the educational process (*ordo doctrinae*) ought to follow the natural process of discovery (*ordo inventionis*).

The two primary components of scholastic method were *lectio* and *disputatio*. *Lectio* consisted in the public lecture, in which the master commented upon a particular authoritative text or commentary. In theology, the Bible was the official text, while Cicero (106–43 B.C.) was the authority in rhetoric, and Aristotle (384–322 B.C.), generally, in philosophy. The goal was not simply to explicate the text, but to grapple meaningfully with the problems it raised. This involved an awareness of all the arguments that could be set forth for and against the particular question or position (*sic et non*). Students would listen, and take notes.

Lectio, which typically took place in the morning, provided the material upon which the second component, the *disputatio,* would be developed in the afternoon. A question based on the morning's commentary would be posed by the master. Objections raised by students (*videtur quod non*) would be answered by a more advanced student, frequently called a bachelor. After the intellectual give and take, the master would re-frame the argument, present his own solution (the *determinatio*), and deal with the major objections raised. The goal of this dialectical approach was to ensure that all aspects of a particular question were thoroughly aired. The method itself was significantly affected by Aristotle's *Posterior Analytics*, as philosophers after its translation in the middle of the twelfth century were able to explicate his understanding of scientific method.

As a historical movement, scholasticism is generally divided into medieval, modern, and contemporary periods, with appropriate subcategories. In addition, the ninth through early eleventh centuries are sometimes seen as a prescholastic period in which societal and intellectual developments helped to lay the foundation for scholasticism. These included the development of episcopal and monastic schools under Charlemagne (742–814) and Alcuin (c. 732–804), as well as the revival of the *trivium* and *quadrivium* as curricular movements. While these developments did not lead to any significant evolution of dialectical method, they established a basis of learning that would aid scholasticism's development after the dissolution of the empire, with its attendant political and social disorder.

It was in the context of the great medieval universities that scholasticism came to full flower. The key event was the advent of the new Dominican and Franciscan orders in institutions that had heretofore been dominated by secular clergy and members of the older religious orders. Of these, the University of Paris was most important. Here, the mendicant orders initially were received coldly. Their refusal to join the dispersals of the university in 1229–1231 and 1253 provoked great hostility as other faculty came to view them as usurpers seeking to wrest the university from those who had traditionally controlled it.

The final resolution to the conflict in 1261 left the friars in control of the faculty of theology, with a faculty of arts to which only seculars could belong. Functionally, this spurred a period of great intellectual creativity in the higher faculty, as the mendicants sought to develop integrated understandings of both religious and secular dimensions of the universe. Indeed, it is impossible to understand the philosophical developments of scholasticism during this period without realizing its integral relationship to theology and the extent to which philosophical inquiry was motivated by a desire to reconcile reason and revelation, as well as to demonstrate the degree to which religious truth was accessible solely by human reason.

The problem of greatest concern to scholastic philosophers was that of universals, which concerns the relationship between thought and objects. Can human thought, expressed in general concepts, accurately describe the external world of particular objects? For the early medievals in scholasticism's formative period, during the eleventh and twelfth centuries, the approach was an ontological one, expressed in the question "What, if anything, in extramental reality corresponds to the universal concepts in the mind?" (Copleston: vol. 2, 139).

One answer, which might be labeled that of extreme realism, was to insist that mental concepts exist independently of the particular sense objects that exhibit such qualities. The sense objects are real insofar as they share in these independently existing ideas. The greatest proponent of this approach was Anselm of Canterbury, known for his arguments for the existence of God. In the *Monologium,* he develops proofs for God's existence based in the degrees of perfection found in creatures. In his famous "ontological argument," contained in the *Proslogium,* he moves from the idea of God to God as a reality, an example of the power that he gives to ideas as representative of existent reality.

Even more radical was William of Champeaux (1070–1121), who maintained that the same essential nature is completely present simultaneously in all the individual members of the species, who differ from each other only accidentally. While William later modified his views as a result of Abelard's critique, positions like his were common in early medieval scholasticism.

Proceeding from a more nuanced perspective was the Franciscan thinker Bonaventure.

Born Giovanni Fidanza in Tuscany c. 1217, he joined the Franciscans around 1240 and studied under Alexander of Hales, from whom he imbibed the Augustinian tradition that would run through his own writings. A professor at Paris, he was elected minister general of his order in 1257. Able to convince the pope to rescind his nomination as Archbishop of York in 1265, he was later appointed Bishop of Albano and Cardinal in 1273. He was present at the Council of Lyons, but died at its conclusion in 1274.

It is impossible to separate Bonaventure's theological and philosophical thought. For him, philosophy held interest only insofar as it supported theological inquiry, and not for its own sake. His philosophical speculation is most fully developed in areas like natural theology that can be related explicitly to Christian revelation. Here, we see the Augustinian dimensions of Bonaventure most clearly. In raising the question of the existence of God, he does not set out proofs. Rather, he insists that knowledge of God's existence is impressed on all rational minds. Since the soul is, by its nature, the image of God, it has knowledge of God naturally inserted in it. Only in the light of such knowledge of Absolute Being can humans analyze any created being. Similarly, ethical decisions are made on the basis of the highest God, whose divine law transcends our minds but is nonetheless stamped upon them.

While Bonaventure's Augustinian world view is leavened, especially in his later works, by a familiarity with Aristotle, he remains nonetheless an extreme realist in outlook. The intense subjectivity of his approach stands in contrast to the more objective stance of a contemporary like Thomas Aquinas.

A second approach to the problem of universals was moderate realism. Its proponents insisted that, while particular things seem most real to observers, universals are most real in themselves. Such universals are what give particular things their common natures. The knowledge of universals comes from consideration of the external world. For the moderate realists, the dictum that nothing is found in the intellect without first appearing in sense knowledge is key. Two of the most noted proponents of this position were Albert the Great and Thomas Aquinas.

Albert the Great (1206–1280), a German Dominican, was a man of broad intellectual interests that included natural science. While his philosophy was a mixture of Aristotelian and Neoplatonic elements, he was one of the first to recognize the importance of Aristotle and Arab commentators such as Avicenna (980–1037) and Averroes (1126–1198). For example, he adopted the Aristotelian proof for the existence of God as the prime mover. Important in his own right, he also achieved eminence as the teacher of Thomas Aquinas, and his insistence on the importance of Aristotle bore fruit in his most illustrious student.

The greatest of the scholastic philosophers, Thomas Aquinas (1225–1274), entered the Dominican order in Italy in spite of family opposition so great that his brothers had him kidnaped and kept a prisoner at the family castle in the hope of dissuading him. Thomas was probably at Paris from 1245 to 1248, during which time Albert the Great had been sent there to found a Dominican house of studies. It was during this time that he came under Albert's influence. While Albert arguably had the greater curiosity of the two, Thomas had greater systematizing and speculative power. The synergy between these two towering intellects was to be very fruitful.

In 1252, Thomas, who had been sent to Cologne, returned to Paris, studying and lecturing there until 1259. After an interlude of teaching theology at the *studium generale* (house of studies) attached to the papal court from then until 1268, he returned to Paris and taught there until 1272. In that year he went to Naples to found a *studium generale* and remained there until the pope summoned him to the Council of Lyons in 1274. On his way there, he died at the monastery of Fossanuova.

As Etienne Gilson has argued in *The Christian Philosophy of St. Thomas Aquinas,* the philosophy of Thomas is explicable only within the context of his theology, in which it is rooted. For Thomas, philosophy provides neither ultimate nor sufficient knowledge. Hence, he begins with a consideration of the supreme Existence, God, who is existence itself. This is in contrast to the idea, found in both Plato and Aristotle, of God as primarily Thought or Idea. His philosophy is realist and concrete. Rather than presupposing a notion from which reality is to be deduced, he starts from the world as it exists, asking questions about the nature and shape of its existence. He creates a philosophy by reflection upon sense experience, insisting that the object of the human intellect is the essence of any material thing.

For Thomas, all physical bodies are composed of a passive principle called prime matter and an active one called substantial form. The first actualization of potentiality is the unique substantial form of the body. In all created substances, there is a real distinction between activities, powers, or faculties, and their essential natures.

The unique substantial form of human persons is the rational soul, which possesses three spiritual powers. These are the thinking intellect, which allows for reflection, the agent intellect by which sense experience is grasped and organized, and the will, which freely determines itself.

Ethically, human beings have the natural right to organize with others to pursue personal happiness within the broader context of the common good. The individual, however, is not autonomous in such pursuits. Rather, the individual is to be guided by conscience, natural and positive law, and the private and public virtues. Because Thomas sees human authority and the state as natural, he necessarily views them as having divine justification and authority. Thomas's ethics thus have a distinctly social dimension.

In his philosophy of God, Thomas insists that the human mind can know a great deal as a result of rational examination of visible things in the universe. God can be seen as the first efficient cause by which all creation comes into being, as well as the final ultimate cause toward which all creation is oriented. God has no nature other than the fullness of pure being (*esse*), without any sort of potentiality or limitation. This is in contrast to human persons, who always experience a tension between their inner nature and the actuality of their existence (*esse*) borrowed from God.

Thomas's comprehensive writings mark the high point of scholasticism. His ability to address a wealth of philosophical and theological issues in creative and innovative ways demonstrates the power of scholastic method at its best. In both the breadth and depth of his writings, Thomas Aquinas displays prodigious intellect.

The Franciscan philosopher John Duns Scotus (c. 1266–1308) stands as a bridge between this culmination of medieval scholasticism and its final period. While his philosophy is intimately related to his theological positions, it nonetheless is somewhat less explicitly Christian than that of his immediate predecessors.

His epistemology is based on the belief that the primary object of the intellect is not the divine essence, as those rooted in Augustinian thought held, nor, as most Aristotelians insisted, in the essence of material things, but rather is pure being, perceived prior to any manifestation it might have in reality.

For Scotus, prime matter is not pure potentiality, as is the case for Thomas, but an actuality that can receive further perfection. This is because he sees matter as a positive reality, and hence, as something. Every being has a common nature that is made individual and particular by a principle of individuation that he calls *haecceitas* ("thisness"). Here again, he differs from both Augustinian and Aristotelian perspectives.

Ethically, Scotus asserts the absolute freedom of God's will and the preeminence of human freedom. A logical corollary of this position is Scotus's insistence on the primacy of the will over the intellect.

Scotus as positive philosopher harkens back to the high scholasticism of Thomas and Bonaventure. In his more critical aspects and in his voluntarism, however, his work prepares the way for the more radical thinkers of the fourteenth century.

The final scholastic solution to the problem of universals came with the development of conceptualism by the English Franciscan William of Ockham (c. 1285–1347) in the last period of medieval scholasticism. Ockham insists, in contrast to the realists, that there are no universal ideas either in the divine mind or in things. Whatever exists, by its nature, is singular and individual. While a concept can stand as a sign for reality, it can refer to one thing or many. As a sign, it is a mental reality, and is individual and unique. It is universal only insofar as it can stand for many. Thus, its universality is purely functional and has no reference to a common nature or essence. It follows that Ockham's epistemology is based on knowledge of a universe of unique singulars that bear only a de facto relationship to each other.

Like Scotus, Ockham's ethic is voluntaristic, going so far as to say that God could command someone to hate Him. Good and evil are determined by the will of God rather than by any intrinsic natural intelligibility.

In many respects, Ockham is a precursor of modernity. He anticipates the rise of modern science in his abolition of any meaningful connection between the world's absolutely singular entities. He also prepares the way for the religious revolutionaries of the early modern period (Martin Luther [1483–1546], for example, considered himself an Ockhamist). His critical spirit encouraged a severe limitation in philosophical thinking of the extent to which Christian belief could be deduced by human reason, and, by extension, in the final separation of philosophy and theology as disciplines. Thus, he anticipated subsequent religious critics who would insist on divine revelation as the only font of religious truth.

Ockham was arguably the last major medieval scholastic philosopher. The most important philosopher of the fifteenth century, Nicholas of Cusa (1401–1464), stands as a bridge between the Middle Ages and the Renaissance world. The most important element of his philosophy was the notion of unity as the harmonious synthesis of opposites.

With the coming of the Renaissance, scholasticism's reputation suffered a marked decline, largely as a result of the second-rate quality of thought exhibited by the method's proponents. Many rejected the discoveries of the new natural sciences and espoused a view of scholasticism that was ossified and static. Only a few showed any evidence of original thought. Among these were Cardinal Cajetan (Tommaso de Vio) (c. 1468–1534) in Italy and the Jesuit Francisco Suarez (1548–1617) in Spain. The former's exposition of Thomas's doctrine of analogy remains an authoritative treatment, while Suarez's extensive writings included commentaries on Aristotle and Thomas, as well as original works on legal and political philosophy.

Scholasticism remained a peripheral philosophical methodology, relegated largely to Catholic seminaries and universities for nearly three hundred years. The replacement of original thought by a plethora of commentaries and manuals made its marginalization from mainstream intellectual currents inevitable.

With the revival of medieval studies in the middle of the nineteenth century, scholasticism was rediscovered by scholars in Spain, France, Germany, and Austria, largely through the writings of Thomas Aquinas. Finally, in 1879, Pope Leo XIII, whose philosopher brother had been influenced heavily by one of the early Italian neoscholastics, issued his encyclical letter *Aeterni Patris,* in which he called for the restoration of Christian philosophy, with special attention to the work of Thomas. To further this end, he established the Roman Academy of St. Thomas and the Institut Superieur de Philosophie at Louvain, which became major centers for the study of scholastic philosophy and theology. He also created a commission to edit an edition of Thomas's work, sparking a wave of textual analysis that eventually also resulted in critical editions of the works of Bonaventure, Alexander of Hales, Scotus, and Albert the Great.

In the twentieth century, the neoscholastic approach has been utilized by a variety of scholars on both sides of the Atlantic. Perhaps the most famous of these are Etienne Gilson (1884–1978), whose landmark historical treatments have established a base for much of contemporary neoscholastic thought, and Jacques Maritain (1882–1973), who has sought to apply this philosophical tradition to contemporary questions.

More recently, both philosophers and theologians have attempted to utilize scholastic reasoning within the context of modern and contemporary philosophy. The movement known as transcendental Thomism, for example, seeks to reconcile the method and content developed by Aquinas with a post-Hegelian world. Scholars such as Emmerich Coreth, Joseph Marechal (1878–1944), Pierre Scheuer (1872–1957), and Karl Rahner (1904–1984) have utilized this approach.

Thus, scholasticism, in contemporary times, again has become a dynamic mode of conducting philosophical and theological inquiry. Its venerable history marks it as one of the most influential intellectual methodologies in the history of the Western world: Its ongoing development is testimony to the strength of both its content and mode of analysis.

F. Michael Perko, S.J.

See also ANSELM OF CANTERBURY; BONAVENTURE; DUNS SCOTUS; THOMAS AQUINAS; WILLIAM OF OCKHAM

Bibliography

Adams, Marilyn McCord. *William Ockham.* Notre Dame, Ind.: University of Notre Dame Press, 1987.
Copleston, Frederick. *A History of Philosophy,* vols. 2 and 3. Garden City, N.J.: Image Books, 1963.
Gilson, Etienne. *The Christian Philosophy of St. Thomas Aquinas.* New York: Random House, 1956.
———. *History of Christian Philosophy in the Middle Ages.* New York: Random House, 1955.
———. *The Philosophy of St. Bonaventure.* New York: Sheed and Ward, 1938.
Maritain, Jacques. *St. Thomas Aquinas.* Cleveland, Ohio: World, 1958.
Pieper, Josef. *Scholasticism.* New York: Pantheon Books, 1960.
Rahner, Karl. *Spirit in the World.* New York: Herder and Herder, 1968.
Saint-Maurice, Bieraud de. *John Duns Scotus.* St. Bonaventure, N.Y.: Franciscan Institute, 1955.
Weisheipl, James A. *Thomas d'Aquino and Albert His Teacher.* Toronto: Pontifical Institute of Medieval Studies, 1980.

School

A place where people, especially children and youth, are expected to be taught, to study, to learn, to develop character, and become productive citizens of their society. For virtually all people in developed or developing nations, *school* is a familiar word that typically calls to mind a specific place or places and the experiences associated with those places. But any attempt to define *school,* especially if the etymological trail that leads back to the discovery that the modern word *school* has its origins in the Greek word for "leisure" is avoided, quickly becomes frustrating, complicated, and not very useful: The purposes, methods, and even the curriculum of schools in modern industrialized nations are very different from those of the sixteenth and seventeenth centuries; then the school was not, as it is now, an "instrument of the state" but largely an "instrument of religion" (Cubberly: 13). What is now known as school is not a universal and immutable institution but is, historically speaking, a relatively new institution. Like the family, it has suffered and enjoyed many transformations, assumed a variety of forms, and adopted a variety of styles. The peculiar form now familiar in the developed and developing nations has its origins in the mid nineteenth century. It is an invention designed to serve the needs and interests of a newly emerging nation-state committed to an industrial economy.

Most commonly, *school* is used either as a noun to indicate a place where instructional, indoctrinational, training, or educational processes are organized and administered, or as a verb to indicate what someone, usually a teacher, does for, to, or in behalf of, students. One can school others, be schooled by another, or even school oneself. One can be schooled successfully or unsuccessfully in one subject or another, or well schooled in a subject. To say that one is schooled or well schooled in one subject or another usually means that one knows that subject or is proficient at some art or skill. It is also to say that one has received training, instruction, or education, but it does not necessarily mean that one has attended school. One can be very well schooled without ever having attended a school.

Rarely is *school* used by itself. *School* becomes a meaningful word as it is modified by an adjective, becomes part of a prepositional phrase, or is linked to another noun. There are public and private schools, good and bad schools, sectarian and nonsectarian schools, traditional and progressive schools. Some adjectives indicate the age of those who attend the schools: nursery, elementary, middle, junior, high, or adult. Other adjectives indicate either the subjects taught and studied or the skills taught and practiced: grammar, Latin, vocational, business, trade, dance, music, art, or whatever. In books mainly written for those who plan to work in schools, *school* is rarely, if ever, clearly defined but is often linked to other words. Examination of these kinds of texts reveals that the school exists in a social order and that school and society are related to each other. In a variety of ways, the society influences the school and the school is expected to serve the society. Such texts show that the school can be conceived of as an organization, sometimes as a "loosely coupled organization," as a bureaucracy, as a social institution, or as an educational institution. To consider it as a social institution is typically to conceive of it as a preparatory or an intermediate institution that takes the child from the family and prepares it for adult responsibilities, citizenship, and work.

All societies, whatever their stage of development, establish systematic ways to teach their children to maintain their society and its traditions, to equip them for survival, and, at times, even to pursue their own interests. In societies untouched by economic diversification and specialization, primary education usually occurs as children observe and assist adults in life's basic processes. As ways for tending to basic life processes become diverse and complex, social institutions are created to protect and to maintain

valued and necessary social functions. Socialization and division of labor appear. Individuals are either allowed to choose occupations or assigned specific responsibilities, and education becomes a formal process—it becomes schooling. Some are assigned the role of teacher and others the role of student. The place where they fulfill the expectations of those roles is typically called "school." Thus, a school is usually a designated place, usually but not necessarily away from the home, where children and youth—those who have not yet attained their legal majority—are sent, at times voluntarily and at other times not, to learn with others of approximately the same age what their elders and society's authorities believe they should learn. Those who learn how to behave as they are expected to behave and learn what they are expected to learn are said to have developed good character. Those who are sent to school are called students or pupils, and students are expected not only to learn how to read, write, and count but also to value and honor that which the society deems to be in its interest. Children who learn, either alone or with siblings, from a teacher in the home, do not attend school. They are tutored, and the teacher is called a tutor.

The first schools on the North American continent had their origins in the Protestant Revolt. Once Martin Luther's revolutionary notion of the priesthood of all believers was accepted, there was no question about the necessity of schooling. Clearly, each individual had to know how to read, for each individual was to be able to read Scripture in order to learn how to find salvation. In the sixteenth and seventeenth centuries, the clear distinction between the secular and the sacred, between church and state, that now obtains in the United States of America did not then exist. To the extent that there was such a distinction, the state was frequently the servant of the church.

In seventeenth century New England, it was a full decade after the beginning of the Great Puritan Migration and two decades after the Pilgrims arrived, before the authorities issued any directives about education. That now famous Massachusetts Law of 1642 is evidence that what would now be called home schooling was ineffective. The 1642 law may have been the first law in the English-speaking world to require that all children be taught to read, but it required neither the establishment of schools nor that children attend school. It required the officials of the various towns to determine whether parents and masters were ensuring that their charges were being brought up "in learning and labor and other employments profitable to the Commonwealth," and also to determine whether all children were being taught "to read and understand the principles of religion and the capital laws of the country" (quoted in Cubberly: 17). A subsequent law enacted in 1647, known as the "Old Deluder Satan" Act, specified that towns of fifty or more households appoint one of themselves to teach all children to read and write if the children were available for instruction, and that the wages of the teacher be paid by the parents, the master of the children, or by the inhabitants of the town. It further specified that once a town had grown to one hundred or more households, a grammar school be established to prepare youth for the university. These laws required compulsory education and required the establishment of schools, but they did not require that children and youth attend school.

Compulsory school attendance appeared on the European continent before it did in the American colonies. In the seventeenth century, several German states, notably Saxe-Gotha, Wurttemberg, and Saxony, adopted compulsory school attendance laws, while in France, the States-General asked the Catholic Church to open schools in all towns and villages and to require compulsory attendance (Butts: 208). Compulsory schooling, as understood in the latter half of the nineteenth century and during the twentieth century, did not appear in the United States until the mid nineteenth century, when Massachusetts enacted the first compulsory school law in 1852. The last state, actually then a territory, to enact a compulsory school attendance law was Alaska, in 1929. Compulsory school laws typically apply to children between the ages of five or six and sixteen.

The form and substance of schools and schooling have always been related to their time, place, and society. As one travels from country to country, visits schools, observes students, and discusses educational topics with teachers, the many similarities and differences among schools are easily seen. Everywhere students study many of the same subjects: language, history, mathematics, science. Teachers always want better facilities and materials for their students. Students complain that their studies are too difficult, not sufficiently interesting, or that their assignments are too many.

Parents and public officials always seem to want the students and the teachers to do more. Each nation's schools has its unique characteristics, which reflect the unique traditions and cultures of its people. For two reasons, schools are always shaped and directed by the major social and political environments in which they exist: First, citizens expect schools to conform to the ever-changing perception of what is in the national interest. Second, parents and guardians want schools to satisfy the current, real-life interests and needs of children as well as to prepare them for success later in life.

The editors of *The Social Foundations of Education* related that "in its very essence, the school is an institution established by society for the purpose of preparing the young to participate in that society." They further observed that like other social institutions, "the family, the church, or the government, the school is a social institution whose fundamental character is determined by the society it serves" (Stanley et al.: 2). Thus the aims and objectives of schooling, the curricula, the teaching methods, and the learning strategies that are used and employed, and the ways in which schools are organized, administered, and supported, all vary from time to time and from place to place.

While there is near universal agreement that the school is meant to be an educational institution, and that it is "an extensive and elaborate human institution," there is also universal agreement that "schooling is not the same as education." It "is a technology designed to domesticate the 'natural processes' of education and bring them within reach of human regulation and control. Insofar as this domestication has been successful, schooling has also become a formalized instrument for achieving the political goals of the modern 'state'" (Hamilton: 279–85). Social, intellectual, professional, and political developments in the twentieth century have had a profound influence on the manner and substance of schooling. It has been maintained that the colonization of public education by psychology contributed greatly to the process whereby education was reduced to schooling, schooling was reduced to instruction, and learning was reduced to specific skills and performances as defined, assessed, and measured by psychologists (Johanningmeier: 162). It has also been argued that schools have traditionally engaged in education, child care, and training, and that "schools should drop their educational function in order to do a better job of child care and training" (Bereiter: 391).

Whether it is publicly or privately supported, whether secular or religious, whether a for-profit or a not-for-profit institution, the school is but one of the many educational institutions that compose, to use a term and conception used by Lawrence A. Cremin (1988), the educational configuration: churches, families, the workplace, the peer group, workers' and farmers' organizations, museums, libraries, social clubs, professional associations, laborers' organizations, the various forms of the media, and a variety of other organizations, formal and informal. Many organizations—for example, churches, civic organizations, museums, libraries, professional associations, and laborers' organizations—have many of the same features as schools. They have deliberately organized and planned activities designed either to teach specific skills or to convey specific information to further the interests of the organization and the interests of their membership. Many have a curriculum, courses of study, classes, teachers, specific and specified methods of instruction, schemes for evaluating the progress of those they are trying to educate as well as their own efforts, and they award diplomas, badges, medals, certificates, or credits. Their deliberately planned educational enterprises may be designed for children, for adults, or for both, but the school is the only institution that children and youth are required to attend, if not by circumstance or convention, by law.

As important as what students are expected to learn and value in school are the reasons for the founding of schools and the purposes of schooling. Among scholars there is considerable agreement that schools are founded and designed more to satisfy the interests of society than to satisfy the interests of children and youth. Advocates of state-sponsored schooling have argued that schools are needed to ensure the desired measure of law and order, and that it is incumbent upon the civil authorities to assume responsibility for the founding and maintenance of schools. Martin Luther, for example, in his *Letters to the Mayors and Aldermen of All the Cities of Germany in Behalf of Christian Schools* (1524), emphasized the civil as well as the spiritual importance of schooling. He argued that "even if there were no soul, and men did not need schools and the languages for the sake of Christianity and the Scriptures, still, for the establishment of the best schools everywhere, both for boys and girls, this consideration is of itself sufficient, namely, that society, for the maintenance of civil order and the proper regulation of the household, needs accomplished and well-trained men and women." Luther also instructed the mayors and aldermen that many parents were too negligent, too ignorant, or too poor to be responsible for the necessary education of their children. The princes and lords, he complained, were capable, but too busy "with the weighty duties of cellar, kitchen and bedchamber" to tend to the education of the young. Consequently, education was the responsibility of the civil authorities.

Samuel Harrison Smith shared with Samuel Knox the prize for submitting the best essay on the subject of a system of education for the new American republic, in a contest sponsored by the American Philosophical Society for Promoting Useful Knowledge in 1795. He was among those who believed that the state had the right to insist that all children be educated by the public. He argued that the effects of compulsory education were so obviously beneficial that the state could expect "'a general acquiescence' from the people should it exercise this duty." It was, he maintained, "the duty of a nation to superintend and even to coerce the education of children."

Ellwood P. Cubberley (1919) was a historian of education whose texts were widely used by teachers and school administrators for at least a quarter of a century. He wanted teachers "to see the educational service in its proper setting as a great national institution evolved by democracy to help it solve its many perplexing problems." He viewed the school, historically and contemporaneously, as an institution designed to benefit not the child as much as the state. Early in the twentieth century, he cited with approval George H. Martin, an early historian of education in Massachusetts, who wrote: "It is important to note here that the idea underlying all this legislation was neither paternalistic nor socialistic. The child is to be educated, not to advance his personal interests, but because the State will suffer if he is not educated. The State does not provide schools to relieve the parent, nor because it can educate better than the parent can, but because it can thereby better enforce the obligation which it imposes" (quoted in Cubberley: 19).

At the same time Cubberly was writing, Ella Arvilla Merritt, a member of the

Children's Bureau staff, effectively rejected the notion that "the cure of our children was entirely an affair of the home." For her, "It was a great step forward when, after much opposition, the idea that it is the duty of the State to furnish schools for its children and to see that they attend those schools, gradually found expression in our public school system and our compulsory education laws" (quoted in Cremin: 297–98). The school was, however, neither solely responsible for, nor completely capable of, supervising and caring for children. It was but an instrument of the state. Only the state had the requisite power. According to Cremin, "her most fundamental point" was that "little by little we have been forced to recognize that neither the home nor the school, unaided can properly guard the welfare of the child. We need the strength of the State to protect him from carelessness and selfishness, for the child is weak, and his natural protectors, individually are weak also" (297). She claimed that "government was better equipped than any other agency" to assume responsibility for determining what constituted good care. The school was the instrument and the servant of the state.

Robert Paulsen, drawing on the work of the anthropologist Ralph Linton, concluded, "A survey of educational history supports an anthropological thesis that the realistic adaptation of dominant-status adults to new conditions has been more responsible for the development of universal education than the 'needs' of children as children."

The commitment to the proposition that the state has the right to educate created the conditions that eventually allowed instruction, as conceptualized by modern psychology, to dominate how schooling was conceived, organized, and evaluated. The public school, eventually framed within what Ernest R. House (1983) described as the "technological perspective," became the arena in which education and instruction vied for preeminence, and instruction won.

Erwin V. Johanningmeier

See also CURRICULUM AND INSTRUCTION; LUTHER; NATIONALISM; PUBLIC EDUCATION; RELIGIOUS EDUCATION

Bibliography

Bereiter, Carl. "Schools without Education." *Harvard Educational Review* 42: (1972) 390–413.

Butts, R. Freeman. *A Cultural History of Western Education*. New York: McGraw-Hill, 1947, 1955.

Cremin, Lawrence A. *American Education: The Metropolitan Experience, 1876–1980*. New York: Harper and Row, 1988.

Cubberley, Ellwood P. *Public Education in the United States: A Study and Interpretation of American Educational History*. Boston: Houghton Mifflin, 1919.

"Education and Instruction." In *Cyclopedia of Education*. Vol. 2, edited by Paul Monroe. New York: Macmillan, 1911.

Hamilton, David. *Towards a Theory of Schooling*. London: Falmer Press, 1989.

House, Ernest R. *Philosophy of Evaluation*. San Francisco: Jossey-Bass, 1983.

Johanningmeier, Erwin V. *The Foundations of Contemporary American Education*. Scottsdale, Ariz.: Gorsuch Scarisbrick, 1987.

Luther, Martin. "Letter to the Mayors and Alderman of All the Cities of Germany in Behalf of Christian Schools." In *Three Thousand Years of Educational Wisdom,* edited by Robert Ulich. Cambridge: Harvard University Press, 1963.

Paulsen, Robert. "Cultural Anthropology and Education." In *Readings in Socio-Cultural Foundations of Education,* edited by John H. Chilcott, Norman C. Greenberg, and Herbert B. Wilson. Belmont, Calif.: Wadsworth, 1968.

"School." In *Cyclopedia of Education*. Vol. 5, edited by Paul Monroe. New York: Macmillan, 1913.

Smith, Samuel Harrison. "Remarks on Education: Illustrating the Close Connection between Virtue and Wisdom." In *Essays on Education in the Early Republic,* edited by Frederick Rudolph. Cambridge: Harvard University Press, 1965.

Stanley, William O., Othanel B. Smith, Kenneth D. Benne, and Archibald W. Anderson. *Social Foundations of Education*. New York: Holt, Rinehart and Winston, 1956.

S

Science, Philosophy of

The philosophy of science did not emerge as a branch of philosophy distinct from epistemology until the nineteenth century. William Whewell argued in his the *Philosophy of the Inductive Sciences* in 1840 that knowledge derives not only from experience; the knower also actively contributes concepts to "the colligation of facts." In contrast, J.S. Mill in his 1872 *System of Logic* insisted that all knowledge is sensory in origin and that science is the result of organizing particular facts using exclusively inductive methods. Whewell remained obscure for decades, while Mill influenced the emerging philosophy of science.

At the turn of the century, the Austrian philosopher and physicist Ernst Mach dominated the scientific world. Mach, following David Hume (1711–1776), argued that we can know absolutely nothing beyond the analysis of our own sensations. Theories for Mach were merely instruments for inferring future sensations from past and present sensations. Mach was an antirealist for whom causality was just a habit of thought.

Between 1910 and 1923, A.N. Whitehead and Bertrand Russell published *Principia Mathematica*, the greatest advance in logic since Aristotle. This work was conceptually foundationalist. It assumed that arithmetic is reducible to logic. The strategy was to begin with logical constructs like sets and set membership and then logically construct entities with the formal properties of the integers. Russell used the new logic to develop a foundationalist version of traditional empiricist epistemology. Russell began with what he called "sense data" and proceeded to analyze everyday objects like trees as sets and sets of sets of sense data.

Mach and Russell influenced the logical positivists of the Vienna Circle in the 1920s and 1930s. The circle included Moritz Schlick, Rudolf Carnap, Herbert Feigl, Otto Neurath, and Kurt Gödel. Logical positivists sought to provide indubitable foundations for scientific knowledge by combining Mach's analysis of sensations with Russell's logic. It was assumed that there were hard positive facts and that logic provided a priori certainty with regard to all valid relations between concepts. The central task of logical positivism was to combine the supposed certainty of facts with that of concepts to yield an indubitable foundation normative for all "rational" scientific inquiry regardless of how, descriptively, science was actually practiced. Logical positivists never doubted that science needed distinctively philosophical foundations beyond what the scientists themselves could provide. Logical empiricists were committed to a host of sharp dualisms such as the theory/fact, fact/value, and subject/object dichotomies.

The central doctrine of logical positivism was the verifiability criterion of meaning. It was assumed that logical tautologies were necessarily true while nontautological propositions, to be meaningful, must be verifiable. The verifiability criterion of meaning was used to refute theology and metaphysics because, it was claimed, their characteristic propositions were meaningless because empirically unverifiable.

Logical positivism evolved into logical empiricism for at least two reasons. First, the verifiability criterion of meaning was not empirically verifiable. Second, scientific laws formulated as unrestricted universal propositions cannot be conclusively verified by a finite set of observations. Two canonical problems for the logical empiricists were confirmation and explanation. Both problems involved connecting the logical propositions and abstract terms of theory to an empirical foundation.

In his *Logical Structure of the World* (1967), Rudolf Carnap tried to carry out Russell's original program in detail. In this study theoretical propositions and terms that were not immediately related to experience were reduced by a system of definitions to terms that did. This project floundered for reasons already stated. In "Testability and Meaning" (1936), Carnap, realizing that verification as the definitive and final establishment of truth was an impossibly demanding criterion, concluded that "we shall speak of the problem of *confirmation* rather than of the problem of verification."

Hans Reichenbach in his 1938 *Experience and Prediction* argued for a context of discovery versus context of justification distinction, and limited the philosophy of science to developing normative foundations for the latter. Psychological and sociological questions were assigned to the context of discovery.

During the war years, Carl G. Hempel developed a syntactical and purely formal logic of confirmation. The problems of confirmation are part of the more general problem of induction traceable to Hume. Generally we would like to say that all universal lawlike statements are confirmed by their positive instances. Suppose the law states "All ravens are black." As a universal logical statement this may be written (x) (Rx then Bx)—that is, for all x if x is a raven, then x is black. Anything that satisfies the antecedent condition of being a raven (Rx) and being black (Bx) is a confirming instance. This formal model of confirmation encountered a series of "paradoxes of confirmation." Formulating and attempting to solve these paradoxes was a major area of study for decades. Hempel himself noted one paradox. The statement "All nonblack things are nonravens" is logically equivalent to "All ravens are black." Written formally, (x)(Rx then Bx)=(x)(-Bx then -Rx). By logical equivalence, the Washington Monument is a confirming positive instance of the universal law "All ravens are black." In order to preserve the logical formulation, Hempel formulated the equivalence condition that said that whatever confirms one of two equivalent sentences also confirms the other. Hempel insisted there was no paradox, only a "psychological illusion." Hempel's response is typical of the logical empiricist strategy of ignoring psychological or sociological considerations.

One influential alternative to Hempel's model of confirmation was the principle of "falsificationism" introduced by Karl Popper in his 1959 *Logic of Scientific Discovery*. Popper sought a principle of demarcation between science and pseudoscience. He did not feel that it was necessary to provide a theory of meaning. Popper argued that if there was nothing that could refute a given statement, then it had no scientific content. The logical pattern of confirmation written formally is:

T then E

E

―――――

T

where T = some theory and E = some empirical evidence. This is a logically invalid formulation known as "the fallacy of affirming the consequent." The following pattern of logical inference, known as *modus tollens*, is logically valid:

T then E

not E

―――――

not T

This is the pattern of falsification. Popper rejected the problem of induction and verification altogether. He argued that only the falsity of a theory can be inferred from empirical evidence and that all inference is deductive, therefore the most rational procedure was that of conjecture and refutation.

Hempel also developed a "deductive-nomological" model of explanation. Hempel's basic idea was that when some description of empirical phenomena (the explanandum) can be deduced from universal laws (explanans) and specific initial contextual conditions, it had been explained.

Logical empiricism dominated the philosophy of science until Thomas Kuhn's *Structure of Scientific Revolutions* (1962). Kuhn asserted that the history of science is not merely descriptive, but interpretive and often normative. Kuhn denied the context of discovery versus context of justification distinction, claiming that the actual history of science discloses that there is no "logic" of justification at all. There is only the psychological, sociological, and historical process of competition between different research "paradigms." Kuhn naturalized philosophy of science. For naturalists there is nothing outside natural existence that can be appealed to in understanding the world. Naturalism rejects any notion of transcendent a priori logic. Rationality understood as a natural occurrence is grounded in our biological makeup, or perhaps it is a social construction. Naturalized logic involves means-ends reasoning, is goal directed, and purposeful. Naturalism rejects any sharp distinction between theory, values, and facts. Naturalized philosophy of science suggests that there is no distinctively rational philosophical foundation for the practice of science beyond what the practitioners themselves eventually evolve. Many of Kuhn's theses remain highly controversial, but few would argue that as a result of his work philosophy of science has entered a postempiricist era.

During the 1970s there were two prominent critics of Kuhn's work. Imre Lakatos and Larry Laudan attempted to develop an account of science that accepted historical, psychological, and sociological perspectives while preserving standards for rational progress beyond natural growth. Following Popper, Lakatos conceded that falsification could always be avoided by invoking suitable "auxiliary hypotheses." Lakatos proposed that we view "research programmes" as a succession of theories with a "hard core" of laws that could not be abandoned without abandoning the program. Around the hard core was a "protective belt" of "auxiliary hypotheses." If the development of auxiliary hypotheses led to theoretically or empirically "progressive problem shifts," then the "research programme" was itself rationally progressive, otherwise it was degenerative. A theoretically progressive problem shift is one that leads to new predictions of fact. An empirically progressive problem shift meant that occasionally new facts were actually discovered.

Laudan abandoned the notion of a priori and formal logic, opting for a complete instrumentalism. Laudan focused on "research traditions" and argued that rational appraisal consisted in "the problem-solving effectiveness" of the series of component theories making up the tradition. Laudan distinguished empirical from conceptual problems, perceiving conceptual problems as more important. Acknowledging the role of conceptual problems made metaphysics and even theology of possible importance to the discovery and justification of scientific claims, a major break with the positivist tradition. Like Lakatos, Laudan followed Popper in seeking a criterion of demarcation, one in which the psychology and sociology of knowledge needed to be invoked only if scientific beliefs could not be "explained in terms of their internal rational merits."

The 1970s and early 1980s saw the emergence of alternative accounts of science that were less narrowly philosophical. In the 1930s, Robert K. Merton had written a classic sociological work on science, technology, and society in the seventeenth century that opened up the possibility of historically studying the culture of science. Merton left the analysis of "methodology" and the "substantive findings" of science to the logical empiricist. Merton did, however, concentrate on the cultural norms that the scientists themselves used to evaluate their own work. Merton's work was easy for the logical empiricist to marginalize. It was not until the "strong program" of the Science Studies Unit at the University of Edinburgh in the 1970s that the sociology of science achieved prominence. This program was naturalistic and concerned with the content of science. The program argued for the social construction of all knowledge. Since the appearance of Bruno Latour's and Stephen Woolgar's *Laboratory Life: The Social Construction of Scientific Facts* in 1979, case studies of actual laboratory life, its practices, beliefs, and values has played a significant role in inquiry into scientific inquiry.

Some like Ronald B. Giere (1988) approve the development of semantic and social constructivist theories of science, but bemoan the continuation of antirealist stances in the philosophy of science. Giere prefers uniting semantic and social constructivist theories of science to the work in recent decades in cognitive psychology to develop a "naturalistic realism." Finally we note that feminist philosophers of science like Sandra Harding and Evelyn Fox Keller have used the sociology and psychology of science to argue that the construction of science is gender biased.

So what has all of this to do with educational philosophy and the field of education? The answer is, very little. Educational practitioners, including educational researchers, much like practicing scientists in other fields, have generally found logical empiricism to be of little value to them. There has been more interest in postempiricist philosophy of science, as a review of articles in *Educational Researcher* will show. There is very important work to be done in applying the philosophy of science within the field of education. Unfortunately, very few in the field of education have the technical training to use it effectively. A question that philosophers of education must ask themselves is the following: If the efforts of philosophers of science to provide normative foundations for the practice of science were ignored by actual practitioners of science, then how should philosophers of education conceive their task in the field of education?

James W. Garrison

See also EMPIRICISM; EPISTEMOLOGY; NATURALISM; POSITIVISM; RATIONALISM; SOCIAL SCIENCE, PHILOSOPHY OF

Bibliography

Carnap, Rudolf. *Logical Structure of the World*. Berkeley: University of California Press, 1967.

Giere, Ronald B. *Explaining Science: A Cognitive Approach*. Chicago: University of Chicago Press, 1988.

Kuhn, Thomas S. *The Structure of Scientific Revolutions*. Chicago: University of Chicago Press, 1962.

Latour, Bruno, and Stephen Woolgar. *Laboratory Life*. Beverly Hills, Calif.: Sage, 1979.

Laudan, Larry. *Progress and Its Problems.* Berkeley: University of California Press, 1977.

Mill, J.S. *A System of Logic.* London: Longman, 1872.

Popper, Karl. *Logic of Scientific Discovery.* London: Hutchinson, 1959.

Reichenbach, Hans. *Experience and Prediction.* Chicago: University of Chicago Press, 1938.

Whewell, William. *History of the Inductive Sciences.* 3rd ed. London: Cass, 1967.

Scientism

A nineteenth-century term to designate the creed or faith of a scientist, now used only pejoratively to indicate an inappropriate extension of or admiration for science. "Science" (as in "Science tells us that evolution never ceases") means both (a) a vast congeries of conceptual systems—theories, data, techniques, methods, rules, and so forth, and (b) a social system— teachers, researchers, students, technicians, publicists—devoted to the advancement of (a). Scientism, in turn, is the belief that all significant questions may be formulated and answered somewhere in (a), and that the forms of organization found in (b) represent the highest point in the supreme human art of politics.

Behaviorism is one manifestation of scientism, evident, for example, when learning is defined as change in behavior. In all European languages, the concept of "learning" is equivalent to "coming to know." Ontologically speaking, that is what learning is. But knowing is a dispositional state or condition, thus not directly observable. To know that learning has occurred requires observation of behavior. When the logical empiricists say that science is concerned only with observables, it follows, for them, addicted as they are to scientism, that learning = change in behavior.

That bit of scientism in educational thought is relatively benign, for teachers, parents, all those concerned with education are well advised to pay close attention to children's behavior. When a school system, however, defines its main goal as increasing scores on statewide achievement tests by 10 percent, scientism has seriously distorted an educational program. The goals of a school system should be defined by what we want children and youth to have made their own at successive points in their school career: what skills we shall try to help them acquire; what ideas and information we insist that they come to know; what values we want them to embody; what experiences we want them to undergo, with outcomes, in the more important cases, up to them, not us, to determine. Progress toward few of those goals is measurable by standard achievement tests; the more important of them are not measurable at all. But school officials infected with scientism cannot admit that they are seeking goals not statable as measurable objectives. Hence, they put all their energies into effecting a 10 percent gain in test scores; thus they are guilty of reductionism, another, more vicious and widespread, form of scientism.

Pointing to instances of confusion and bad judgment in educational theory and practice is, unfortunately, all too easy, as is charging "scientism" when such are discovered. Showing exactly what is wrong in some particular case of scientism is quite another matter. When logical empiricism was deposed as the reigning philosophy of science (leaving residues in psychology and the social sciences, of course), its opponents used the full apparatus of scientific logic to present their arguments. Something very like scientific demonstration is required to show the mistake in defining learning as change in behavior. When school superintendents state educational goals as measurable objectives, that piece of wickedness would seem derived, actually, less from infatuation with science than from their subservience to capitalists, whose goals and lives reduce to numbers on quarterly balance sheets. And when arguments are presented for correcting educational errors, confusions, and crimes labeled "scientism," the audience addressed is always presumed to operate under the rules of objectivity, rationality, impartiality, and open-mindedness we have come to expect (if, alas, not always to find) in the community of science.

"Scientism" is a natural response to the arid mechanization of teaching, the absence of attention to spiritual values, and the obsession with numbers found all too often in today's schools. That response, however, may be name-calling rather than diagnosis. In the Progressive Era it was said, "There's nothing wrong with democracy that more democracy cannot cure." In the same spirit one might claim that the only cure for scientism in educational theory and practice is more assiduous practice of real science—more critical theory, more relevant arguments, a better organized community of scholars working more directly and cooperatively with the public they serve.

James E. McClellan, Jr.

See also ANALYTIC PHILOSOPHY; BEHAVIORISM; EMPIRICISM; POSITIVISM; SCIENCE, PHILOSOPHY OF

Bibliography

Gould, Stephen J. *The Mismeasure of Man.* New York: W.W. Norton, 1981.

McClellan, J. "The Concept of Learning: Once More with (Logical) Expression." *Synthese* 51 (1982): 87–116.

Richards, Stewart. *Philosophy and Sociology of Science.* 2nd ed. Oxford: Basil Blackwell, 1987.

Sorell, Tom. *Scientism: Philosophy and the Infatuation with Science.* London: Routledge, 1991.

Skepticism

The broadest general meaning of *skepticism* is that it is a critical attitude questioning various knowledge claims and the evidence for them, offered in different domains such as religion, science, philosophy, art, or politics. The great variety of human opinions, the conflicts among the many opinions, and the changes over time in what has been accepted as true, has made people skeptical about many views. The term *skeptic* originally comes from the ancient Greek term for "inquirer." More particularly, "skepticism" is a philosophical outlook that develops from examining the reasons and the evidence for various views that people hold. This outlook has been systemized into a series of questions about the reliability of our conclusions derived from sense information or from different kinds of reasoning.

The skeptics challenge the positive view of others by pointing to possible ways in which these views might be false or dubious. We sometimes experience our senses deceiving us, leading us to believe that we see or hear or feel something which, in fact, we do not. Our senses may be defective (which anyone who wears eyeglasses or uses a hearing aid realizes). Our senses may be defective without our being aware of it. Hence the views we derive from our sense experiences are open to some question unless we can be absolutely sure that no deception is occurring, and that there is no defect in our sense organs. How can we gain such assurances? If we use other sense information, gained perhaps from instruments, or from other observers, that data too is open to question as to its veracity. Similarly, our views based on our reasoning can be challenged. How can we be sure that in any given case we are reasoning correctly? We all are aware that we sometimes make mistakes in adding and subtracting. Also, we may be under the influence of drugs or alcohol, or we may be too drowsy "to think straight." Any means we might use to check up on our reasoning can again be questioned. If we employ a calculator, can we be sure it is functioning correctly? If we employ a computer, it may have a glitch or a defective program. And our mind, insofar as it is like a computer, may be misprogrammed. So, the skeptic asks, is there anything of which we can be absolutely sure, any view that cannot possibly be false?

From ancient times, some philosophers have put forth various kinds of skeptical doubts about the accepted views of their society and time. Socrates (c. 470–399 B.C.), as portrayed by Plato (c. 427–347 B.C.), was a constant gadfly and questioner. He said at one point that all he knew was that he knew nothing. Following from this assertion, a school of skeptics developed in Plato's Academy around 300 B.C., presenting a series of arguments that supposedly would lead people to this kind of Socratic skepticism (called "Academic Skepticism" after Plato's Academy, where it developed). The Academic Skeptics denied that we could have any certain, unquestionable knowledge about the real nature of the world. All that we obtain are probabilities. Much of our knowledge of this kind of skepticism comes from the description of it by Cicero (106–43 B.C.) in his *De Academica.*

A more radical skepticism developed in ancient Alexandria in the first century B.C.; it questioned whether one could even be sure that nothing could be known, or that one view was more probable than another. This kind of skepticism, called Pyrrhonism after a legendary ancient doubter, Pyrrho of Elis (c. 360–275 B.C.), was elaborated into a massive series of ways of doubting (tropes) that could be raised against knowledge claims in general, and against any particular kind of knowledge—scientific, theological, mathematical, or moral. The Pyrrhonian skeptic said that when one realizes all of the reasons for doubting, one would suspend judgment, and in so doing would achieve peace of mind (*ataraxia*). In that state, one could accept appearances without judging whether things are really as they appear, and could live according to one's natural inclinations and the mores of one's society without having to judge if one's actions were correct. The detailed statement of Pyrrhonian skepticism has survived in the writings of Sextus Empiricus (c. 200–300).

Skepticism as a systematic form of doubting seems to have disappeared during the Middle Ages, but it was revived during the Renaissance and the Reformation. Sextus' writings were translated into Latin and published in 1562 and 1569, and Cicero's *De Academica* was also rediscovered. The battery of reasons for doubting were quickly employed in the theological controversies of the time, and also supplied many reasons for doubting the then prevalent Scholastic philosophy and science. Writers like Michel de Montaigne (1533–1592) popularized skepticism as a way of questioning all dogmas, and presenting faith as the only way to find certainty.

Modern philosophy and modern science began with doubting. Galileo (1564–1642), Francis Bacon (1561–1626) and Rene Descartes (1596–1650) all used skeptical materials to challenge the accepted views. Descartes presented his "method of doubt" as the prelude to finding truth. By using skeptical questioning to its limits, one would finally find a truth so certain that none of the doubts of the skeptics could assail it—for Descartes, "I think, therefore I am." Descartes then built a new philosophy to justify modern science, which he claimed to be indubitable. Subsequent philosophers offered ways of doubting Descartes's claims. In the eighteenth century, David Hume (1711–1776) presented a far-reaching skeptical attack on both the rational philosophies from Descartes onward and the empirical theories of John Locke (1632–1704) and George Berkeley (1685–1753). Immanuel Kant (1724–1804) claimed after Hume that he had found a new answer to skepticism, an answer that was immediately subject to attacks by new skeptics. Philosophy over the next two centuries can be seen as a continuing struggle with skepticism. In spite of the enormous advances of science, skeptics have raised basic skeptical problems against claims to absolute, certain knowledge. Skeptical arguments applied to the claims of Judeo-Christian theologians have caused many to doubt various formulations of these religious traditions. The ongoing questioning of skeptics has, however, had the positive effect of prod-

ding people to try to find better and better evidence for their views and beliefs.

Richard H. Popkin

See also DESCARTES; EPISTEMOLOGY; MONTAIGNE; SOCRATES

Bibliography

Annas, Julia, and Jonathan Barnes. *The Modes of Scepticism.* Cambridge: Cambridge University Press, 1986.

Burnyeat, Myles, ed. *The Skeptical Tradition.* Berkeley: University of California Press, 1983.

Hume, David. *Enquiry Concerning Human Understanding.* Edited by L.A. Selby-Bigge. Oxford: Oxford University Press, 1975.

———. *A Treatise of Human Nature.* Edited by L.A. Selby-Bigge. Oxford: Oxford University Press, 1978.

Laursen, John C. *The Politics of Skepticism in the Ancients, Montaigne, Hume and Kant.* Leiden: Brill, 1992.

Popkin, Richard H. *The History of Scepticism from Erasmus to Spinoza.* Berkeley: University of California Press, 1979.

———. "Skepticism." In *Encyclopedia of Philosophy.* Vol. 7, edited by Paul Edwards, 449–61. New York: Macmillan, 1967.

Schmitt, Charles B. *Cicero Scepticus.* The Hague: Nijhoff, 1972.

Sextus Empiricus. *Outlines of Pyrrhonism* and *Adversus Mathematicos.* Translated by J.D. Bury. Loeb Library. Cambridge: Harvard University Press, 1933–1949.

———. *Selections from the Major Writings on Scepticism, Man, and God.* Indianapolis, Ind.: Hackett, 1985.

Slavery

Slavery in its generally accepted sense is a social institution upon which some human beings are owned by others as personal property. Moses Finley (1968, 1980), following Roman law, defined slavery in terms of the dominance/subordinance relationship between master and slave. This usage emphasizes the powerlessness of the slave and the slave's submission to the absolute control of the owner/master. Under the ownership of another person, the slave may be treated as any other form of movable property. The slave may be bought, sold, given away as a gift, willed or lent to others, used to pay debts, or otherwise manipulated for personal use. For most scholars, the identification of the slave as legally recognized property is considered the major difference between slavery and other forms of servitude or forced labor. Because slavery has usually been involuntary, some form of coercion must be used to maintain the subservience and obedience of the slave.

For Orlando Patterson, another major scholar, the property identity of the slave is perhaps less important than the dishonor that accrues to slave status. Noting that slaves were usually aliens with no birth rights in the dominant society, he argued, as did Finley and others, that the slave's position was tantamount to social death. Slaves had no social identity apart from their relationship with their masters, were culturally isolated from their native lands, and were set apart by law or custom from free people. Slaves lived and functioned only at the will of their masters, who usually had the power of life and death over them. Each slave was thus a dishonored being, stripped of human social identity and nobility. But, argued Patterson, both slaves and masters were engaged in a parasitic relationship. The slave received life, livelihood, and an identity from the master. In turn, the owning of the slave conferred honor, prestige, and status on the master, within the framework of the dominant society.

Some scholars ignore or bypass the personal identity and power issue and focus on the economic aspects of slavery. These scholars concur with a distinction made by Finley between fully slave-based societies and those with some slaves. Slave-based societies are those in which the entire economy (or a dominant part of it) depends on the productive activities of usually large numbers of slaves. Marxist scholars identify such societies as having a "slave mode of production," a particular method of organization of labor. To these scholars, slavery represents a stage in the evolution of economic systems and the societies based on them, a stage that theoretically preceded feudalism and free labor.

Slaves have existed in many other societies, but their labor did not constitute significant components of the total economy. These were largely domestic slaves involved in little or no productive activity, although they might supplement the work of other, more productive workers. They are best known from studies in some periods of Greco-Roman history, in the Muslim world, and in parts of Africa and Asia.

Since the 1960s, a great deal of information about the varying practices of forced servitude in many parts of the world has been collected. A wide range of customs, practices, beliefs, laws, and attitudes about slaves and slavery developed in different regions. Features of slavery varied considerably from one society to another and at different times. They also varied internally, particularly between urban and rural settings. This complexity has made it difficult to define or characterize the institution in a way that would be applicable to all situations. As a result, scholars continue to debate among themselves about what specific sociocultural features, found in different societies, distinguish slavery from other forms of servitude, such as debt bondage, indentured servitude, serfdom, clientage, or other types of unfree labor.

Origins and History

It is fairly clear now that the origins of slavery rest in the earliest histories of warfare and conquest. People conquered or captured became spoils of war, like other material objects, horses, livestock, precious metals, cultivable land, storerooms of food, and other goods. As an alternative to killing their victims, some conquerors opted to put them to work as domestic servants, agricultural workers, craft workers, and, in time, producers of manufactured goods. Forced servitude following conquest was institutionalized and became the major source of slaves in the Old World.

Records show that some variant of slavery has been found in virtually all of the civilizations of Antiquity, particularly in the conquest-based empires of Egypt, Mesopotamia, Greece, Rome, the Indus Valley of India, the ancient empires of China and Korea, and the Muslim empire. Many other peoples, like the Slavs (from whom the term originated), have been primary victims of conquest and enslavement. There were also similar patterns of forced servitude among some native societies of the New World, North and South America. But we do not know as much about these indigenous systems as we know about Greek and Roman slavery, Muslim slavery, and more modern forms of slavery developed in the New World.

Once early slavery had been institutionalized, it was found useful for many different functions. Slaves served as household servants and as agricultural and other laborers, doing tasks commanded by owners/masters in both urban and rural areas. In Roman times, skilled slaves functioned as physicians, pharmacists, shield- and sword-makers, accountants, tax assessors, wine-makers, and in many other occupations. Some slaves were owned by the state and worked as secretaries, record-keepers, accountants, and in other civil bureaucratic posts. Other slaves worked as artisans and craftsmen, frequently along with their owners. Slaves were also used in the military by many ancient and medieval societies. In some societies, trained slaves, like the Mamluks of Egypt and the Turkish Janissaries, served as political leaders. Female slaves were used as domestic servants but also served as concubines and entertainers. Along with female slaves, eunuchs and other male slaves often functioned primarily as displays of conspicuous consumption, as markers of the wealth and status of their owners.

As the functional uses of slaves were recognized, and indeed they became a perceived necessity, demand for them increased and a trade developed that could supply slaves even without the disruptions of warfare. In some areas, slave trading and even the breeding of slaves became important sources of this form of property. In time, other variations on the institution developed. Many societies, for example, had debt slaves, people who sold themselves, or a child, into slavery (usually temporarily) to pay off debts. Poverty in fifteenth- to early-eighteenth-century Russia forced thousands to sell themselves voluntarily into a form of "perpetual, hereditary slavery" (Hellie) which certainly changed the nature of the institution, as such slaves were no longer aliens. And its "voluntary" nature raises into question its definition as slavery. Slavery became important to some societies as a means of punishing criminals and other malefactors. Such individuals would be sold away from their natal societies, and possibly permanently ostracized. Finally, political enemies of threatened leaders were sometimes captured and shipped off into the commercial slave trade.

Certain specific features help scholars to compare and analyze the ways by which slave systems varied. The most important and distinct of these was the right to, and availability of, manumission—that is, to obtain freedom. Other features include the right to legal marriage, the right to own or possess property, the right to an education or training, the right to a wage (Roman *peculiam*), the right to practice the religion of the host society, the right to sue an owner for cruelty and to change owners, the right to bear firearms, and the right of female slaves to some form of protection when they bear children by their masters. In all of these features, North American slavery differed from Old World slavery and its Latin American extensions. It also differed in that it was exclusively racial slavery; it was a system that came to identify and reserve slavery solely for people of African ancestry. Among Old World slaves, one could find members of all races.

Issues and Debates
In North America, the works of Frank Tannenbaum (1946) and Stanley Elkins (1959), comparing North American and Latin American slavery, initiated scholarly debates about the degrees of harshness and severity of different slave systems in the Western Hemisphere. Later historians, like David Brion Davis, looked at the role and functions of slavery in the context of American social and political ideologies (1966). At the same time, scholars began debating the economic feasibility of slavery, and how and why it declined in the New World (Foner and Genovese). Critical to these studies has been the question of the relationship of slavery to the industrial revolution and the growth of capitalism.

Many American scholars have examined the relationship between slavery and the development of the idea of "race." Liberal ideologies and notions of human progress and their relationship to slavery have commanded the attention of some scholars whose interests are more philosophical. More recently, scholars have been looking at abolitionism and its impact on popular ideologies about freedom and slavery. Other contemporary historians have turned to studies of the cultures created by slavery, and the influence of enslaved people and the tropical cultures they brought from Africa to New World societies.

Comparative studies from around the world are increasing and helping scholars to sharpen their focus on the institutions of slavery, forced labor, and other forms of servitude in human history.

Audrey Smedley

See also COLONIALISM AND POSTCOLONIALISM; MINORITIES; RACE AND RACISM

Bibliography
Davis, David Brion. *The Problem of Slavery in Western Culture.* Middlesex: Penguin, 1966.

———. *Slavery and Human Progress.* New York: Oxford University Press, 1984.

Drescher, Seymour. *Capitalism and Antislavery.* New York: Oxford University Press, 1986.

Elkins, Stanley M. *Slavery.* New York: Grosset and Dunlap, 1959.

Finley, Moses I. *Ancient Slavery and Modern Ideology.* New York: Viking Press, 1980.

———. "Slavery." In *Encyclopedia of the Social Sciences.* New York: Macmillan and Free Press, 1968.

Foner, L., and E. Genovese, eds. *Slavery in the New World.* Englewood Cliffs, N.J.: Prentice-Hall, 1969.

Hellie, Richard. *Slavery in Russia, 1450–1725.* Chicago: University of Chicago Press, 1982.

Oakes, James. *Slavery and Freedom: An Interpretation of the Old South.* New York: Alfred A. Knopf, 1990.

Patterson, Orlando. *Slavery and Social Death.* Cambridge: Harvard University Press, 1982.

Phillips, William D., Jr. *Slavery from Roman Times to the Early Transatlantic Trade.* Minneapolis: University of Minnesota Press, 1985.

Tannenbaum, Frank. *Slave and Citizen: The Negro in the Americas.* New York: Alfred A. Knopf, 1946.

Watson, James L., ed. *Asian and African Systems of Slavery.* Berkeley: University of California Press, 1980.

Westermann, W.L. *The Slave Systems of Greek and Roman Antiquity.* Philadelphia: American Philosophical Society, 1955.

Social and Political Philosophy

Many of the great works of social and political philosophy, including Plato's *Republic,* Aristotle's *Politics,* and John Dewey's *Democracy and Education,* put education at the center of their investigations. The questions of what to teach, how to teach, and the need for developing "educated" citizens to live and work in society, go to the heart of the assumptions that characterize the major perspectives in social and political philosophy: liberalism, conservatism, communitarianism, Marxism, fascism, anarchism, feminism, postmodernism.

Beyond this, in most advanced societies, education, institutionalized in schools, is one of the foremost social benefits regulated and provided by the state; and it is typically seen as the central arena for opportunities that determine later success in life. As a result, a concern for principles of justice and equality, and for certain rights, fundamentally places questions of education within the context of broader social and political values. Equally, then, through debates about education we can often read the underlying differences between contending political views.

Educational thought in this sense is a holographic topic: It contains within it the essential elements of broader social and political outlooks. And a philosophy of education, therefore, is always at least nascently a social and political philosophy itself. A corollary of these observations is that by examining some of the changing ways in which certain educational topics have been discussed, we can learn something important about competing social and political philosophies. Five topics will suffice to introduce some of the major facets of these debates.

Authority

Many philosophers of education, as well as others in education, have pondered the question of authority. It seems that any educational relation that involves a teacher and student raises questions of authority: What entitles a teacher to require students to read certain books, reply to certain questions, and so on? How can students identify authorities on whom to rely for credible information or perspectives? What are the potential abuses of authority, to which teachers and students should be vigilant? The common answers to such questions usually require both a theory of rationality and of consent: A credible authority is one whose expertise, impartiality, and dependability can be established through the application of rational standards; a legitimate authority is one to whom others voluntarily cede their respect and obedience. Such an analysis of authority in the educational domain parallels an analysis of political authority in the larger social domain.

This analysis has been challenged, not simply because authority can be, and is, abused through deceptiveness, self-interest, or capriciousness (that is, through patently illegitimate exercises of authority), but because the very criteria of legitimacy (rationality and consent) are thought to be distorted. The rational qualities and capacities according to which authorities are judged (valid knowledge within a field, careful reasoning and explaining, impartiality and fairness to competing points of view, and so on) are, from this standpoint, simply the artifacts of a particular system of knowledge that, because it is dominant, represents itself as the obviously reasonable and correct one—but which in fact excludes other cultural or epistemic outlooks that do not meet its particular standards. The standard of consent, similarly, is thought to be compromised because, while an individual student-teacher relationship might appear to be a consensual one pursued out of reciprocal concern and respect, in fact such relations (especially in institutionalized settings) are primarily shaped by bureaucratic and other constraints that legitimize the exercise of power and privilege in both parties' minds.

At stake in this debate is whether one wants to establish educational relationships in which authority can be credibly and fairly sustained, or whether one regards exercises of authority—however well intended—as inevitably compromised and counterproductive. Can there be educational relationships without authority?

Equality and Equal Opportunity

If education is a social good, and if access to education is a necessary precondition for access to a range of other social opportunities, as well as for personal satisfaction and happiness, then questions of who can be educated, and how, become fundamental issues of social justice. In the philosophy of education, and in the field of educational policy generally, this debate has usually been played out in terms of commitments to principles of equality or of equal opportunity.

Commitments to equality would usually lead to positions stressing that people deserve, to the greatest degree possible, educational experiences that provide them the same resources, the same qualities of enjoyment and purposefulness, the same kinds and degrees of success and satisfaction, as those that others receive. Strong outcome-oriented views of equality would insist that people should be able to learn the same subjects, develop the same or comparable degrees of expertise, and encounter the same avenues for later life chances, however they might choose between these different avenues.

Commitments to equal opportunity, on the other hand, tend to value equality, but only in terms of providing access to the conditions in which educational success is possible; they tend

to grant much greater significance to the differential exercise of effort as a determinant of whether educational opportunities are actually undertaken and pursued successfully. From a social policy standpoint, equal opportunity views range from what are often called formalist views of equal educational opportunity, in which the responsibility of society is only to provide access to certain resources in a nondiscriminatory way, to actualist views of equal educational opportunity, in which the obligations of society also extend to the provision of compensatory programs of various types, so that educational opportunities not only exist, but also are realistically available to all. Both formalist and actualist proponents (to varying degrees) might hope that equality of educational attainments result from equality of educational opportunities; but they differ strongly in their willingness to hold equality of outcomes as a criterion of whether opportunities are equal.

In these debates, furthermore, there have been large differences in what "equality" in education has been taken to be. One view, stressing equality as sameness, would emphasize a strict equivalence among what and how students are taught, the degrees of achievement they attain, and so on. Another view, stressing equality as comparability, might desire a high degree of cultural or regional variation in what and how students are taught, but seeks comparable levels of achievement, satisfaction, and access to other benefits of life. Yet another view, stressing the initial variation among students' levels of ability, might simply pursue equal progress from those different initial starting points. Another view, abandoning the goal of strict equality or even equalization of outcomes, might simply aspire to the common minimal attainment of some basic level of learning, however much some students may go beyond that, and however unequal the overall distribution of educational outcomes remains.

At stake in this debate are fundamental values about the relative importance one gives to equality as a social principle, weighed against other kinds of social values (self-determination, allowance for diversity, excellence even at the cost of greater inequalities, and so on), and the precise meaning of the term *equality* being applied. In the sense that education is an inherently uncertain, open-ended endeavor, in which personal effort and interest are determining variables, can equality ever be ensured as a result?

Freedom

Perhaps no concept in social and political philosophy is more centrally involved in questions of education than that of freedom or liberty. At its heart, becoming educated means becoming enabled to undertake future activities in life: participating in certain kinds of relationships with others, taking pleasure in certain kinds of experience, conceiving projects and being able to complete them successfully, and so on. The very phrase "liberal education" implies a kind of learning that frees up one's understanding and outlook on the world. And even when one understands education in terms of a more conservative socialization model, it is still justified in terms of the quality of living it makes possible in later life.

The hoary distinction between "freedom from" and "freedom to" helps in understanding this sense of education. Education as a path of freedom from certain constraints means, first of all, an education that makes people aware of those constraints, and that informs them of alternative ways of thinking and living available to us. Education as a path of freedom to act, to choose, or to create, means an education that provides people with knowledge and abilities as well as the sense of purpose and efficacy that are necessary to prompt them to act, choose, or create for their own ends and for the well-being of others.

In contemporary terms, freedom is often conceived of in terms of the construction of an identity or identities that define our selves, our aims, and our relations with others. People are free to the extent that the identity that defines them is one that allows them the latitude to appreciate and explore other identities (even if they do not in fact choose to do so). In the social context, and especially in educational settings, identities are constantly being defined and redefined for people, and the process of shaping or reshaping one's identity is never a purely voluntaristic endeavor; but education is a liberating experience to the extent that it provides opportunities for the exploration of alternative identities and provisional experimentation with them.

At stake in this discussion is the extent to which education serves, and should serve, to provide an orientation to and grounding in a particular form of life, and the extent to which it should allow, even encourage, challenges to that form of life. The presumed interest of people in having a degree of latitude and au-tonomy to choose or alter the conditions of their lives assumes a broad social and political value placed on freedom that is not shared by all such philosophies: What appears as freedom to some is relativism or anarchy to others. Can education satisfy both demands at the same time?

Democracy

In any democracy, the capacity of citizens to consider and decide intelligently the issues put before them is crucial to whether such a system can endure. This capacity, in turn, is typically seen as an educational problem, and, more specifically, often a problem of schooling for citizenship. For some authors, such as Dewey, this meant that schools should be laboratories of democracy: microcosms of the sort of decision-making and civic interaction that a society would want its young, as they grow, to learn to participate in. For others, this means that schools should be concerned with the inculcation of a particular set of beliefs, values, and patriotic virtues. For yet others, education for democracy cannot take place in schools; political education must take place in the context of political life, and schools, given their other aims, are not able to provide the conditions of an authentic political culture—or, it is thought that students of a certain age are not yet able to participate in or learn from such experiences in any full sense.

For social and political philosophies of a critical bent, schools are antidemocratic places: Designed, planned, and managed with the general purpose of preserving social inequalities, on the whole, and inculcating values of conformity and rule-following, schools are (in this view) the last place one would look for a model of democracy. For other critics within this same tradition, however, schools hold at least the potential for a liberating, democratic education because they do espouse the values of democracy, and this creates the opportunity for democratically minded teachers to create niches of alternative, progressive educational possibilities.

If education promotes democratic values and participation in a political order, it appears to do so in different ways, and to different degrees, for different groups. For a democracy that is also a strongly pluralistic society, the centripetal forces drawing citizens into a common political arena are counterbalanced by centrifugal forces pulling them apart, into interest groups, contending parties, expressions of regional suspicion and chauvinism, and—with a strong resurgence lately—into religiously based group identities that are to varying degrees millennial: groups less interested in political negotiation and compromise in this worldly arena than they are in the assertion of interests that will not be compromised, because they are motivated by a vision of a future (worldly or otherwise) in which everyone will be like them.

At stake in this debate is whether a "democratic" education can be made compatible with a strong pluralistic society. Dewey finessed the question by including a conversational model of interaction and cooperation within his conception of democracy. More recently, however, we have become more aware of the intractable divisions and incommensurable systems of belief and value that threaten the vision of tolerant pluralism that democratic theorists have embraced. Can education for democracy avoid the twin pitfalls of either imposing a specific set of civic virtues and beliefs, even for groups to whom they might be repugnant, or of witnessing the balkanization of schools and communities into self-contained islands of mutual suspicion and misunderstanding?

Rights

Within theories of education drawing from liberal traditions in social and political philosophy especially, the question of rights typically plays a key role. For an author such as John Rawls, rights derive from a theory of justice; for other philosophers, rights derive from a social contract; for others, certain rights are natural, inherent to human nature. In all of these models, rights are properties of individuals, recognized and enforced by a community. Education, in these views, has to do both with acquiring the capacity to appreciate and exercise certain rights of one's own as well as appreciating and respecting the rights of others. Moreover, the existence of rights is thought to constrain the means and ends of education itself (for example, in restrictions against corporal punishment).

Authors from a more communitarian perspective reject the model of individual rights, or situate them within a web of social relations and interests that can supersede them. Liberal rights theory, from this perspective, tends to fractionate groups into self-interested, self-protective individuals at the expense of the bonds of filiality and identification with a larger whole,

which are the actual cement of social cohesion and cooperation.

The multiplicity of rights, and the bearers of rights, that are continually invented by modern liberal culture gives some support to the communitarian concern. For many, it has become virtually impossible to discuss political conflicts or interests outside the discourse of rights and conflicting rights. By ascribing rights to oysters, to trees, and to fertilized ova, modern political culture has created irreconcilable political debates because they are framed in terms of conflicts among rights, each of which is viewed as inviolate. When this political theory is overlaid with the actual political dynamics of interest-group politics, rights talk becomes a second-order medium in which first-order political interests are exalted and promoted.

Is there, for example, a right to an education? From whence does it derive? Who possesses this right? What obligations does this right put on others? Is education a right because it enables and supports the exercise of other rights and obligations toward others? Or is education a value for other reasons than its being a right?

At stake in this debate are the grounds on which society defines its commitments to provide for the education of people, and the grounds on which people see it as in their interest to pursue educational opportunities. Whether these grounds are seen as the protection and promotion of individual rights, or whether these are seen as protecting and promoting a more encompassing set of social relations and identifications, will determine, among other things, the kinds of education that might be available. Can a rights-driven view of education still preserve the communitarian impulse that binds persons to one another? Conversely, can a communitarian view of education protect the diverse interests of people in the face of a powerful collective interest?

Summary

In the case of each of these educational concerns, different social and political philosophies (and of course there are many perspectives not discussed here in detail) provide different conceptions and substantive arguments to inform the educational problem. What does a social and political philosophy contribute to a philosophy of education?

First, a social and political philosophy provides a view of the person and of the person's relationships to others: whether there are enduring qualities of human nature that are true of people in general; whether identity is a wholly or partially fungible, self-created construction; whether people possess rights, and if so of what provenance; whether humans are unique from a normative standpoint; whether people are properly viewed as, fundamentally, separate and self-interested, or as relational creatures bound inextricably to specific others, from whom they derive their sense of personal identity and significance.

Second, a social and political philosophy provides a view of freedom and possibility: what the horizons are of human choice and creativity; whether greater freedoms are always to the good; whether freedoms for some can be made compatible with comparable freedoms for others, or whether these are always destined to conflict; where constraints on freedom come from, when they are legitimate or illegitimate, and if illegitimate how they can be challenged.

Third, a social and political philosophy provides a view of social institutions and norms: where these come from; what makes them legitimate; what their appropriate weight is, judged against standards of freedom and personal self-determination; how they can be changed, and, if so, in what directions; whether some institutions, such as the family, have a unique, ineluctable benefit to human existence and social organization.

Fourth, a social and political philosophy provides a view of social aims in a broader sense: what kinds of social organization are most desirable; which are likely to be most stable and enduring; which are likely to ensure the greatest protection for the pursuit of personal well-being; which are least likely to foment violence and irreconcilable conflict; which have the greatest tolerance possible for diversity, while also securing sufficient consent and commonality to promote coherence in a society.

Fifth, a social and political philosophy provides a view of the state, laws, and the political process: what forms of government and association are possible, and which of these are the most desirable; where the normative weight of law comes from; what prerogatives the state holds toward the exercise of force, and what are the legitimate expressions of this prerogative; where political power comes from, and how it is best exercised; the legitimate forms into which people may organize themselves as political entities within the state.

All of these concerns go to the heart of how and toward what ends education should proceed. The authority of a teacher, both as a means of guiding learning and (for many students) as an early exemplar of the authority of a state or political leader, must be bound by a concern for the appropriate exercise of power and privilege, with the student's learning in mind. The content of learning, the curriculum, is an embodiment of what a society, or a subcommunity within it, defines as worthwhile knowledge and as the necessary basis for participation in its social order; yet at the same time, what is learned must prepare students for new, unanticipated circumstances and, in most cases, must prepare them to encounter and coexist with others who value and believe things quite different. The aims of learning grow out of a vision of human possibilities, as individuals and in relation to others, strengthening the capacity of people to define and effectively pursue goals of their own, while also strengthening the ties between people through bonds of commonality, concern, and mutual appreciation.

Nicholas C. Burbules

See also COMMUNITY; DEMOCRACY; EQUALITY; FREEDOM AND DETERMINISM; JUSTICE; PLURALISM; POSSIBILITY; RIGHTS

Bibliography

Aristotle. *The Politics*. In *The Basic Works of Aristotle*, edited by Richard McKeon, 1127–1316. New York: Random House, 1941.

Aronowitz, Stanley, and Henry A. Giroux. *Education under Siege: The Conservative, Liberal, and Radical Debate over Schooling*. South Hadley, Mass.: Bergin and Garvey, 1985.

Burbules, Nicholas C., Brian Lord, and Ann Sherman. "Equality, Equal Opportunity, and Education." *Educational Evaluation and Policy Analysis* 4 (1982): 169–87.

Dewey, John. *Democracy and Education*. New York: Macmillan, 1916.

Glendon, Mary Ann. *Rights Talk: The Impoverishment of Political Discourse*. New York: Free Press, 1991.

Gutmann, Amy. *Democratic Education*. Princeton: Princeton University Press, 1987.

Martin, Jane Roland. *Reclaiming a Conversation: The Ideal of the Educated Woman*. New Haven: Yale University Press, 1985.

Nyberg, David, and Paul Farber, eds. "Authority in Education." *Teachers College Record* 88 (Fall 1986).

Plato. *The Republic*. In *Collected Dialogues of Plato,* edited by Edith Hamilton and Huntington Cairns, 575–844. Princeton: Princeton University Press, 1961.

Rawls, John. *A Theory of Justice.* Cambridge, Mass.: Harvard University Press, 1971.

Sandel, Michael. *Liberalism and the Limits of Justice.* New York: Cambridge University Press, 1982.

Strike, Kenneth A. *Liberty and Learning.* Oxford: Martin Robertson, 1982.

Walzer, Michael. *Spheres of Justice: A Defense of Pluralism and Equality.* New York: Basic Books, 1983.

Social Sciences, Philosophy of

The philosophy of the social sciences is usually understood as the philosophical study of the theories, methods, and aims of the social sciences. Exactly what constitutes a social science is unclear, although economics, political science, psychology, sociology, and anthropology are usually included. Oftentimes history, geography, linguistics, and demography are included, and sometimes law and education. Among English-speaking philosophers, the philosophy of the social sciences has usually been seen as a subfield of the philosophy of science instead of aesthetics or ethics. This view assumes that there is something about the social that is distinctly amenable to scientific theories, methods, and aims as opposed to, say, those of humanistic sciences (such as poetry, narrative, and drama). As a result, debates among philosophers about the philosophical study of the social sciences have usually followed those in the philosophy of science in general. More precisely, the core debates have taken the form of epistemological boundary wars over the question of whether social science practice and discourse can be subsumed within the discourses of the philosophy of science. Books, anthologies, and journal articles in this vein commonly deal with questions like the following: Are sciences of the social possible? If so, are the theories, methods, and aims of the social sciences the same as those of the natural sciences? Do the social sciences aim at causal explanation and prediction or must they settle for interpretive understanding?

Twentieth-century debates have been prefigured by at least two nineteenth-century strands of thought: (a) The German Romantics, including Schleiermacher, with their insistence on a sharp distinction between the *Geisteswissenschaften,* the study of Ideas and Spirit that aimed at *Verstehen,* or interpretive understanding, and *Naturwissenschaften,* which aimed at causal and nomological (law-like) explanation and prediction; (b) Marx (and Engels) who, instead of examining the history of Hegelian Geist, aimed "to unmask human self-alienation" by dialectical methods that examined the real relations in the material environment and not merely people's ideas about themselves. The concern was with overcoming the illusions of consciousness involved in "almost all ideology" (Easton and Guddat: 408). Unmasking and ideological critique gave Marx and Engels a decidedly activist aim expressed in the famous statement that "the philosophers have only interpreted the world in various ways; the point is, to change it" (Easton and Guddat: 402).

Max Weber conceived interpretive understanding, or *Verstehen,* as supplementing rather than replacing empirical observational methods. As Weber put it, "A sufficient condition for explanation . . . [is to provide] an interpretation which does not contradict our nomological knowledge." Weber believed that *Verstehen,* or empathetic understanding of an agent's reasons for acting, could provide causal explanations, but that those explanations could never be complete.

A variety of perspectives can be linked to these beginnings. The ontological hermeneutics of Hans-Georg Gadamer draws from the tradition of *"verstehende soziologie"* and philosophy reaching back through Weber to Schleiermacher. The central idea of ontological hermeneutics is that personal identity is ontologically constituted by our prejudices (that is, prejudgements). Initially these prejudices are derived unreflectively from the social customs of our nation, community, and family. Our prejudices provide the necessary forestructure for interpreting the acts of others. Understanding for Gadamer is not through empathetic identification with the other but rather is something constructed intersubjectively between them by "fusing horizons" of our constituting prejudices. Ontological hermeneutics is, unlike earlier versions of hermeneutics, productive of new meanings rather than merely reproductive. Gadamer accepts a sharp separation between the

Geisteswissenschaften and *Naturwissenschaften*.

The neopragmatist Richard Rorty exemplifies a different legacy of hermeneutics. Rorty argues that the aim of all inquiry is not to produce representations that accurately mirror external social reality. The different theoretical and methodological vocabularies of the natural and social sciences do not necessarily represent two distinct ontological realms. Methodologically, for Rorty "'Explanation' is merely the sort of understanding one looks for when one wants to predict and control" (196). All inquiries, scientific and otherwise, aim at helping us cope with the practical world by developing better interpretive vocabularies for hermeneutic understanding. Humanistic studies might serve us just as well as a source of social insight. There is no "*the* scientific method," nor any sharp difference between theory and practice. As Rorty puts it, "If we get rid of traditional notions of 'objectivity' and 'scientific method' we shall be able to see the social sciences as continuous with literature—as interpreting other people to us, and thus enlarging and deepening our sense of community" (203).

Marxist poststructuralism and feminist thinkers have raised issues of power and domination to the forefront in various ways. The critical theory of the Frankfurt School, which emerged in the 1930s, as a rich blend of various influences including the left-Hegelianism of the early Lukacs, the early Marx, and phenomenology, reinvigorated philosophical awareness of the importance of practice. The outstanding contemporary exponent of critical theory, Jürgen Habermas, distinguishes three dialectically related levels of "cognitive interests": the empirical-analytic sciences resting on the "technical" cognitive interests of explanation and prediction; the "practical" cognitive interests of interpretive understanding in terms of internal "reasons;" and the "critical" or emancipatory cognitive interests concerned with the kind of ideological critiques that expose knowledge constructions that are oppressive.

The language of critical theory was an important resource in reintroducing politics into social sciences, but it was feminist thinkers, among others, who actually did the deed. More and more, the politics of research practice shape the role of philosophical analysis in the social sciences. Social scientists, through their practical engagements with, and the growing participation in their ranks of, groups usually excluded from Western philosophical discourse (women, children, working-class people, non-Western peoples, and so on) have been forced into ongoing reappraisals of the philosophical underpinnings of their knowledge-making practices. Instead of asking themselves if what they are doing is really "science," many social scientists have begun to reconstruct the discursive practices, category systems, and philosophical concepts with which they have constituted their social worlds and accomplished their research. Encounters with sorcerers engender reconsiderations of epistemology. Basic concepts such as "self," "emotion," "space," "time," "causality," "decisions, "objectivity," "method," and conversation and argument are unpacked, dissolved, or reconstructed. Attention is directed to domains of practice slighted in English-speaking philosophical discourse, such as gender, the body, popular culture, or the senses other than vision. Foundational dichotomies—modern-primitive, expert-lay, society-nature, human-animal, science-nonscience—are made problematic.

The works of philosophers are resources for social scientists in these endeavors—or, more precisely, the philosophical work is appropriated and reinvented to serve new purposes defined by the practical engagements of the social scientists. What this implies is that the philosophy of the social sciences must be understood in historically and socially specific terms. As Said suggests, "All intellectual and cultural work occurs somewhere, at some time, on some very precisely mapped-out and permissible terrain, which is ultimately contained by the State" (169).

A useful example of this point is the case of positivism. Beginning in the 1920s, logical positivists such as Moritz Schlick and other members of the Vienna Circle and G.E. Moore at Cambridge, building on A.N. Whitehead's and Bertrand Russell's powerful new logic, sought methods to "duly combine" the certainty of predicate logic with the certainty of nonlogical "sense data" to achieve the aim of deductively certain nomological explanations. For the logical empiricists, all statements had to be empirically verifiable in order to be meaningful. Rejecting metaphysics and the associated idea of real causal structures behind sense data, the logical empiricists assumed a sharp set of dualisms including the theory/fact and value/fact distinctions. By the late 1960s, the program of logical empiricism had been largely dismantled within philosophy (the term itself lingering on only as a kind of insult). A brief list of sources for the devastating counterarguments to various logical empiricist positions would include (a) dismissal of the verifiability theory of meaning; (b) dismissal of the idea that scientific theories are purely formal systems wherein the nonlogical terms can be separated into "theoretical" and "observational"; (c) the loosening of the strictures of the deductive nomological covering law model of explanation. Other antipositivist arguments owed much to the later Wittgenstein. Most notable among the philosophers of social science directly influenced by Wittgenstein was Peter Winch.

In spite of being killed and buried by philosophers, positivism, in zombie (or perhaps vampiric) fashion, remains an active force in the social sciences. Notions of verifiability and a rigid fact/value distinction have become politically and bureaucratically institutionalized in systems of "expert" control and decision-making, and a rigid separation of "theory" and "observation" is reified in conventions of describing and reporting research. What such situations suggest is that philosophy of social science practiced as strictly philosophical discourse is not sufficient for the philosophical study of the social sciences. The philosophical study of institutional arrangements and modes of practice are also required.

James W. Garrison
Jan Nespor

See also CRITICAL THEORY; DIALECTIC; EPISTEMOLOGY; PHENOMENOLOGY; POSITIVISM; SCIENCE, PHILOSOPHY OF

Bibliography

Davidson, Donald. "Actions, Reasons, and Causes." In *Essays on Actions and Events*. New York: Oxford University Press, 1980.

Easton, L.D., and K.H. Guddat, eds. *Writings of the Young Marx on Philosophy and Society*. Garden City, N.Y.: Doubleday, 1967.

Gadamer, Hans-Georg. *Truth and Method*. 2nd rev. ed. New York: Crossroad, 1991.

Rorty, Richard. "Method, Social Science, and Social Hope." In *Consequences of Pragmatism*. Minneapolis: University of Minnesota Press, 1982.

Said, E. *The World, the Text, and the Critic*. Cambridge: Harvard University Press, 1983.

Weber, Max. *The Methodology of the Social Sciences*. Translated and edited by Edward A. Shils and Henry A. Finch. Glencoe, Ill.: Free Press, 1949.

Socialism

During the last two centuries, socialism as a political philosophy and an economic system has been defined and redefined by social theorists and political groups throughout the world. The earliest use of the term, as found by the English social and cultural historian Raymond Williams, is in William Hazlitt's *On Persons One Would Wish to Have Seen* (1826), in which the author recalls a conversation that took place two decades earlier and refers to "those profound and redoubted socialists, Thomas Aquinas and Duns Scotus." A more contemporary use of the term can be found in the English Owenite *Cooperative Magazine* of November 1827; the French use of *socialism* as a political concept appeared in 1833. Since then, the word *socialist* has been associated, confused, and contrasted with many other political terms, including *communist, anarchist, syndicalist, collectivist, social democrat, populist, radical,* and *leftist.*

While proponents since the early nineteenth century have embraced an emphasis on the root word, *social,* and on a view of human nature as socially produced and changing, they have constructed differing interpretations of the root word, and consequently of the meaning of *socialism* itself and the strategies that seem most appropriate for its advocacy. This has sometimes led to acrimonious disputes and outright splits by those claiming to be adherents. At times the debates have obscured the much more significant differences between socialism and other political and economic orientations.

Socialists generally emphasize an opposition to capitalist, market-driven relations of production and overly individualistic, competitive theories of social relations, viewing them in tandem as preventing the full realization of civil liberties, social justice, and basic equality of wealth, power, and income, in particular for skilled and unskilled laborers. Socialists instead advocate social (nonprivate, public) ownership and management of the means of production, exchange, and distribution, and promote an alternative vision of communal (cooperative, collective) harmony. The capitalist organization of society and the hegemony of capital over the state may have been necessary in the evolution of the modern industrialized society, representing significant progress from prior centuries of scarce resources and feudalism. By the nineteenth century, however, the potential existed for there to be enough material goods for everyone, especially if shared in more equitable ways. Socialism thus represents the next, inevitable stage of societal development, the resolution of the contradictions inherent in capitalism. (For those who adhere to a traditional historical materialist view, communism is considered to be the "final stage" of socialism.)

More specifically, the capitalist system needs to be supplanted because its basic characteristics (such as private ownership of property and the profit motive, wage labor and the social class system, and the dominance of production in every area of social life) foster irrational social purposes, the systematic waste of public resources, and deleterious effects on global, community, and personal relations. The capitalist drive to increase aggregate production for the sake of profit rather than need and its separation of conception and execution (mental and manual labor) at the workplace creates alienated and inhumane living conditions, especially for those who are poor or from the working class. As compared with capitalism, socialism is considered both materially and morally progressive since it would provide for the more equal distribution of social goods, allow workers and clients to have greater control of their social, economic, and political lives, and alleviate human exploitation and suffering throughout the world. Its appeal was succinctly and directly stated by Eugene V. Debs, the most prominent American socialist of the early 1900s, when he wrote: "I am for socialism because I am for humanity." When the United States entered into World War I, Debs expressed the more radical side of the socialist vision: "I am not a capitalist soldier; I am a proletarian revolutionist. I am opposed to every war but one; I am for that war with heart and soul, and that is the world wide war of the social revolution. In that way, I am prepared to fight in any way the ruling class may make necessary, even to the barricades."

The point of origin of the socialist perspective, then, is the critique of and challenge to capitalist political economy. However, the exact meaning of socialism continues to be a matter of some dispute and in some radical circles has undergone significant revisions, especially during the last several decades. In the past, for example, socialist theory has been marked by a kind of economic reductionism, in which all social and cultural phenomena (the superstructure) are understood and determined by their origins in the economy (the materialist base). More recently, while maintaining the priority of a materialist perspective, a number of radical theorists have highlighted the mediated and dialectical nature of the base-superstructure relationship and the relative autonomy and contradictions that occur between and within the economic, political, and cultural spheres.

Moreover, there has been an updating of a central insight of Karl Marx, that the working class, first and foremost, is in fact compelled by the conditions of its existence to struggle for socialism. For one thing, in the capitalist modernity significant divisions are created within the working class itself. These class factions have enormous implications for the class struggle that Marx, Friedrich Engels, and other early socialists failed to anticipate. In addition, many individuals do not identify themselves solely or even primarily in terms of their social class. This has meant an incorporation of other social categories (such as race, sex, ethnicity, religion, and sexuality) when determining the allegiances of individuals and groups and, more practically, when agitating for institutional restructuring. Thus, the emphasis on working class struggles, movements, and organizations and the focus on industrial workers as the emancipatory force in radical social change have been broadened to include other oppressed and marginalized groups. For instance, although not without some resistance in radical circles, the feminist critique of male domination and its insistence that the personal is political has increasingly been fused with the socialist perspective. The concerns of other social movements, such as those involving people of color, gays and lesbians, agricultural workers, and environmental, antinuclear, peace, and consumer activists, have also been linked with the old class and labor politics that marked the socialist movement since its earliest days. Among an increasing number of socialists, then, the oppressive structures of patriarchy and racism have been placed alongside (and linked to) that of capitalism.

It is the case as well that the work of the Frankfurt School, Raymond Williams, Terry Eagleton, Michael Apple, Henry Giroux, and others have moved the socialist perspective away from a sole focus on political economy.

The importance and power of culture has been included in more recent socialist theory and in particular the ways in which it (art, literature, mass media, technology, schooling, and so on) has been implicated in the reproduction (and contestation) of twentieth-century capitalism. In addition, although a strong centralized (democratically controlled) organization is still viewed as essential for matters of planned growth, finances, external trade, foreign policy, the management of existing state forces, and the protection of civil rights and liberties, more recently (in part as a result of the experiences of East European nations that embraced a form of socialism) there is concern about the ways that a centralized state bureaucracy can function to stifle freedom and justice. Thus, socialist theorists and activists have focused more on the processes of participatory democracy, the development of caring communities, and the enhancement of self-realization. Nevertheless, while all of the revisions mentioned above are significant in coming to grips with the character of post-industrial socialism, arguing for socialism still means centering in particular on the need for radical social critique, the end of the exploitative social class system, the role of the working class as an instrument of transformation, and the fundamental, systematic restructuring of economic and political institutions.

In order to usher in the new social(ist) order, radical activists have always been strong advocates of educational work to take place alongside other forms of more directly political agitation and organization (such as union organizing, demonstrations and strikes, running for political office, and writing and distributing books, pamphlets, and newspapers). While it was presumed that workers would learn much of what they needed to know about capitalism from their experiences at the workplace, more formally organized educational activities were needed as well to advance workers' understanding of and challenge to the complexities of dominant social and economic relations. Of course, the specific character of education from a socialist perspective depends on various contexts, including the student population (adults or children), the form of education (such as study groups of workers, labor college classes, party local lectures and discussions, weekend schools for children, or public school teaching), the local community, the historical moment, and so forth. Still, some general characteristics can be highlighted.

The early socialists focused primarily on the need for an extension of educational opportunities in general and for the adequate provision of schools for the working class in particular (in terms of physical facilities, class size, free texts and other supplies, penny lunches, trade schools, and so on). Universal, free education was considered to be a significant democratic achievement. It was hoped that such public education would enhance an understanding of the political economy and, as a result, further the socialist cause. However, Marx sensed from the start that, as he wrote in his "Critique of the Gotha Program" (1875), there would be grave problems in "appointing the state as the educator of the people," that what would result would surely be quite "remote from socialism." The proper education of working-class adults and children in a capitalist society needed to emanate from the working class itself, perhaps with the assistance of what Antonio Gramsci, the Italian theorist and political activist, later referred to as "organic intellectuals." It also needed to be closely linked to the conditions of work and the lived experiences of workers, so as not to become an alienated and unproductive educational experience occurring in a scholastic ivory tower.

When public schooling for children and adolescents became more commonplace at the turn of the century in industrialized societies, socialists offered stinging critiques of the class-biased nature of the education that was provided and suggested reforms of contemporary practice. They also sponsored their own educational activities, which provide concrete indications of their educational philosophy and practices. Unlike most other radical theories of pedagogy, undergirding education from a socialist perspective has been a clearly articulated theory of social formation and the explicit goal of advancing the conditions, principles, and values associated with socialism. Such an end product differentiates socialist educators from those who have been influenced more by the pragmatic, experimentalist approach of John Dewey in the early 1900s, or the more extreme child-centeredness of William Kilpatrick in the 1920s and the radical ("free school") reformers of the 1960s. Although socialist educators clearly have much in common with the social reconstructionist perspective of George Counts and Harold Rugg in the 1930s, generally speaking they do differ in the extent to which they refer explicitly to "socialism" as a primary (ultimate) goal of their instruction.

S

This is not to say that there has been unanimity on pedagogical issues among those educators who have identified themselves as socialists. Like the debates centering on the meaning of socialism itself, there have been differing views regarding what education from a socialist perspective should look like, or, to put it another and significant way, what kind of education would be most appropriate to advance the socialist cause. In particular, socialist educators of adults and children have disagreed on the degree to which socialism should be an explicit, direct goal of teaching. Some have suggested that, because of all the countervailing capitalist influences in people's daily lives (such as public schools, mass media, and religious organizations), educators should be rather overt about the nature and value of socialist tenets. In its extreme form, this has led to a dogmatic and didactic form of teaching in which "the ABCs of Socialism" is adopted as the curriculum. Brazilian educator Paulo Freire's critique of traditional practice as "banking education" would be just as relevant in this case. Other radical educators have expressed the faith that progressive teaching (such as emphasizing critical thinking, problem solving, and decision making) would in fact ultimately result in an enlightened embrace of socialist interpretations. This approach has been criticized by some socialists as based on a watered-down reformism that minimizes the hegemonic influences in individuals' daily lives, gives primacy to instructional strategies at the expense of content, and fails to instill an advocacy for fundamental changes in the social structure. In the actual practice of socialist educators, a path somewhere between these two viewpoints is typically followed, or the attempt is made to blend them together, as the complex tensions of politics and education, theory and practice, ends and means, content and process, knowledge and skills, are worked out.

Whatever the specific instructional approach and curriculum adopted, however, education from a socialist perspective is guided by a commitment not just to personal understanding and change but also to the radical transformation of the social structure. Such social transformation is not viewed as divorced from the personal but rather as intimately linked to an enhancement of our networks of human relationships. This more social goal can be considered one of the hallmarks of a socialist education. Whether taught as dogma or as background for more active student learning, it is deemed necessary, as one prominent socialist educator put it in 1911, to address "*what* is not just and true and beautiful in things as they are, *why* there is no justice, truth or beauty in people's lives, and *how* to bring justice, truth and beauty into the world." Children and adults need to be freed "from the many prejudices" and introduced to "a new social ethic founded upon the conception of society in which profit and wage slavery are to be removed."

The central theme of education from a socialist perspective, then, is that the social structure must be transformed to eliminate capitalism. Other more specific socialist curricular themes can be mentioned as well. Although these themes are clearly outdated, it may be instructive to list the themes that predominated in the American Socialist Sunday schools for children that existed in the period between 1900 and 1920. (These themes were never articulated and listed together in the following way, but they are suggested by a reading of relevant documents.) They are (a) the place of the individual in the social world and in particular the interdependence and indebtedness of the individual to countless others, especially workers; (b) the dignity of labor and an allegiance to the interests of the working class; (c) cooperative and collectivist social and economic relations; (d) an internationalist perspective, in particular the sense of viewing oneself as inextricably linked to the interests of workers in other nations; (e) antimilitarism to prevent the "wickedness and wastefulness" of war; (f) a revisionist interpretation of history and the social sciences, so that, for example, the laboring class is perceived as an instrument for social progress; (g) collective and cooperative relations as "natural" to human existence but as having been distorted and suppressed by the capitalist system; (h) social equality and justice for all, in particular workers but also for other oppressed groups; (i) an awareness of serious social problems (such as poverty, housing, unemployment, unhealthful and unsafe work conditions, and the despoliation of nature) and a commitment to agitate for their alleviation; (j) an emphasis on community that views the everyday conditions of individuals' lives (including issues of health, the environment, and so on) as of vital concern to all; (k) the depiction of the Cooperative Commonwealth (socialism) as fostering the ideal conditions of human life; (l) the crucial role of education and self-education in the overall program to understand and transform social and economic relations; and (m) a generally critical approach toward everyday life, dominated as it was (and is) by capitalist institutions.

While socialism at the millennium may be in a crisis, it is not in fact vanquished as an idea and as a practice. For those who oppose the conditions and experiences of capitalism, it may in fact be the only viable alternative, the only long-term vision of radical democracy and equality, of genuine social sharing and self-management. What proponents perhaps need to consider, however, is a transformed kind of socialism, one that is more inclusive of other oppressed groups besides workers, one that is more responsive to the dangers of a centralized state bureaucracy, one that deals more broadly with the effects of political economy in people's lives, and one that embraces feeling and imagination as much as it does fact and organization. Different socialism for different contexts may also be needed. What is clear in particular is that socialist theory needs to be constantly updated and revised, as the world that its earliest adherents observed and experienced grows more and more distant.

Kenneth Teitelbaum

See also CAPITALISM; FEMINISM; MARX; RACE AND RACISM; RECONSTRUCTIONISM, SOCIAL; REVOLUTION

Bibliography

Buhle, Mari, Paul Buhle, and Dan Georgakas, eds. *Encyclopedia of the American Left.* New York: Garland, 1990.

Harrington, Michael. *Socialism.* New York: Bantam, 1972.

Kaye, Harvey J. *The Education of Desire: Marxists and the Writing of History.* New York: Routledge, 1992.

Levine, Andrew. *Arguing for Socialism: Theoretical Considerations.* Boston: Routledge and Kegan Paul, 1984.

Norton, Theodore Mills, and Bertell Ollman, eds. *Studies in Socialist Pedagogy.* New York: Monthly Review Press, 1978.

Teitelbaum, Kenneth. *Schooling for "Good Rebels": Socialist Education for Children in the United States, 1900–1920.* Philadelphia: Temple University Press, 1993.

Williams, Raymond. *Keywords: A Vocabulary of Culture and Society.* New York: Oxford University Press, 1983.

———. *Resources of Hope.* London: Verso, 1989.

S

Sociology

Sociology was originally conceived of by Auguste Comte as the science of society. It would find the laws governing society analogous to those of physics. So conceived, sociology would include all of the social sciences, taking its place at the top of the hierarchy running from physics to chemistry to biology to sociology. Of course, it did not work out that way: Sociology had to accept a more modest role as it was incorporated into the university. In fact, some have described it as what was left after the established disciplines had taken what they wanted. The question arises as to what, if anything, unites sociology or differentiates it from other social sciences. One answer—similar to Comte's—is that it deals with a unique object, "society," which is the cause of the diverse phenomena being studied. The various social sciences are then complementary parts of this larger sociological enterprise, even though they do not recognize it. Another answer is that sociology deals with certain general forms of social relationship, such as superordination and subordination, whose workings can be seen in a variety of specific endeavors. By that account, sociology adopts a particular viewpoint that is different from that of the other social sciences. A third approach, adopted here, is that sociology is united by the recurring themes evident in its history. Some of these themes will be suggested in the following discussion of the development of sociological theory.

Modern sociology began to emerge in early-nineteenth-century Europe as an outgrowth of the rise of science and urban-industrial society. No doubt as a result of these origins, the central problems of the field have continued to involve (a) the relations between modern economic organization and social relationships considered more broadly; (b) the nature and causes of progress, social evolution, or long-run change; (c) the relationship between science and religion, or between scientific and moral concern, especially as this relates to sociology itself. Work in the early or founding period was largely programmatic, philosophical, and hortatory in character. It tended to suggest that some ultimate unity or balance of economic and social concerns was possible, that social evolution was ultimately tending toward such a utopian state, and that a science of society was both scientific and moral because it could help bring about such conditions.

Comte

The work of August Comte (1798–1857) can be viewed as a response to moral disorder in France, which pitted the rising middle class, which opposed the old feudal order, against the old nobility who opposed the new, emerging order. Comte's more "positive" approach suggested that both order and progress were possible, if only scientific understanding were applied to social affairs. Order could be addressed by understanding the way society worked as an organic whole, rather than as a set of disconnected pieces. Comte argued that the division of labor arising in industrial society had a number of advantages, such as better utilization of a diversity of talents and the uniting of people through dependence on one another's efforts. However, it also led to social fragmentation: "while each individual is in close dependence on the mass, he is drawn away from it by the expansion of his special activity, constantly recalling him to his private interest, which he but dimly perceives to be related to the public" (Comte).

Comte proposed the study of "social statics,"—that is, "the investigation of the laws of action and reaction of the different parts of the social system" as a way of addressing such problems (219). Social governance based on such laws would make it possible to foster a more "spontaneous harmony between the whole and the parts of the social system" (222).

Progress was to be addressed by the study of "social dynamics." Here Comte "discovered" the "law of three stages," which suggested that societies inevitably progress from dominance by religious to metaphysical to scientific ideas, these ideas being the chief cause of change. Progress occurred first in fields like astronomy and physics, and only later in more special, complex, and dependent fields like sociology. Sociology was, then, a capstone science, representing the culmination of man's understanding of the world by coming to understand himself. It is itself a momentous step in social evolution. The implication of the study of these static and dynamic laws was, roughly, that, while there are short-run requirements for order, progress is inevitable in the long run. Furthermore, sociology could contribute to both. As Gouldner noted, "What was needed was a

view that was both romantic and scientific" (98). As a new, objective science, sociology would be an instance of such progress. At the same time, belief in the demonstrable fruits of such a science would help regain order by building moral consensus. Comte advocated moral rule by a scientific elite (the future sociologists), whose secular "religion of humanity" would replace traditional religion.

Marx

Karl Marx (1818–1883) was concerned with the overthrow of capitalism in his native Germany, rather than with a Comtean idea of its more balanced development. As a result, he developed a more revolutionary interpretation of social functioning and social evolution, and of social inquiry itself. For Marx, social relationships in modern (that is, capitalistic) society are inherently conflictual. To see society as a whole one needs to understand the historical character of its division of labor, which is largely determined by the technology (and resources, and so forth) of the time. Once a division of labor develops, it creates a set of antagonistic classes, such as capitalists and workers, based on ownership versus nonownership of the means of production. Other characteristics of a society, such as the character of the state or its legal and moral order, derive from the conflict between these opposing classes, mostly serving the interests of the dominant class. Alienation is inherent to such a system, since workers must sell part of their lives to serve the interests of owners, turning themselves and the fruits of their labor into alien objects. Thus Comte's desired part/whole harmony was impossible under capitalism.

Marx also viewed social progress as inherently revolutionary rather than evolutionary. It occurs as a result of the narrowly self-interested actions of capitalists, who, acting so as to better compete with one another, create the conditions of their own eventual overthrow by uniting workers in common oppression. As a result, each capitalist contributes both to the necessary functioning and to the final destruction of capitalism. Contra Comte, Marx saw the ultimate cause of these changes as the result of changes in material conditions, such as new technologies and ways of working, rather than ideas: "The mode of production of material life determines the general character of the social, political and spiritual processes of life. It is not the consciousness of men that determines their being, but, on the contrary, their social being determines their consciousness" (Marx: 51).

Despite these differences in view, Marx shared Comte's long-run optimism, believing that a harmonious socialist society would emerge from capitalism's demise, in which men would be their own employers and the alienation of man from man—and from himself—would be eliminated. Where Comte sought an objective science of society (adopted as a kind of religious mission), Marx emphasized the inevitability of class interest in shaping knowledge. However, he saw the interests of the working class as less vested in the current system, hence ideas consistent with their interests could be more universal. In this way Marx retained belief in scientific objectivity with belief that the goal of philosophy—or sociology—was not simply to describe society, but to change it.

Spencer

In England, Herbert Spencer (1820–1903) responded to industrial society in a way no less radical but in an opposite (that is, libertarian) direction. Rather than seeking the overthrow of capitalism in favor of socialism like Marx, or its centrally directed balancing like Comte, Spencer sought to free it from governmental restraint. Spencer viewed modern societies as composed, like biological organisms, out of the successive joining of different simpler units into more complex wholes. Thus diverse families are unified into clans, which are unified into cities and those into states. At each level different units exchange with one another, and, given their respective capabilities and advantages, gradually come to perform different interrelated functions in a common division of labor. Such an interrelated complex may then enter into exchanges with comparable systems, creating possibilities for further differentiation and integration.

While Spencer acknowledged that higher-order systems have properties of their own, his individualistic view placed primary emphasis on lower-level systems, since "the properties of the units determine the properties of the aggregate" (52). Viewing higher-order systems as naturally evolving out of a long history of interaction rather than from any central planning, Spencer tended to emphasize the wisdom of nature as opposed to Comte's emphasis on human reason. He also emphasized that these interdependencies make intentional social change likely to create unforeseen consequences. Spencer be-

lieved that suffering is natural and inevitable and that collective action to alleviate it, such as public philanthropy, only prolongs the agony. He argued against public education for similar reasons.

Social evolution, for Spencer, occurs in accord with a universal "law of progress" that states that evolution progresses "from a state of relatively indefinite, incoherent, homogeneity to a state of relatively definite, coherent, heterogeneity." But although evolution moves toward increasing complexity, some societies may remain stuck at a simple level, while complex societies may evolve along different lines. Spencer thought that individuals and societies evolve at different rates, but someday, if things are left alone long enough, the two will be in equilibrium.

In its classical period, running roughly from 1890 to the 1930s, the messianic view of sociological science tended to be toned down as sociology became "no longer the avocation of stigmatized social reformers but the vocation of prestigious academicians" (Gouldner: 135). During that period, the first sociology departments were started, and scholars originally trained in other fields gained university positions as "sociologists." Much of the growth occurred in the United States, coinciding with a broad movement for progressive social reform and rapid growth of universities, but much of the most influential thinking was still European. During this period the dominant sociological ideas became less utopian. Sociologists came to terms with the notion that no perfect balance between economic and social concerns was likely to be possible. Emphasis on evolutionary progress toward an ideal society was also deemphasized in favor of bilateral comparison of the cultural character or social functioning of traditional versus modern or European versus non-European societies. Finally, the role of sociology as an empirical science, separate from moral philosophy, was emphasized, and exemplary empirical studies conducted.

Durkheim

Like Comte, Durkheim (1858–1917) was concerned with the integration of French society during a time of moral uncertainty when some embraced modern utilitarianism and others sought a return to traditional religion. Durkheim argued, as had Comte, that it was possible to have both modernity and moral order—in moderation. For Durkheim a society was a kind of superordinate organism with its own personality. To understand social phenomena one needed to understand the functioning of this organism, using social facts to account for social facts, rather than reducing it to individual psychology or biology. Borrowing from Spencer, Durkheim contrasted traditional societies with simple divisions of labor to modern societies with complex divisions of labor. He argued that despite appearances, modern forms of social organization are not inherently divisive. They are as normal as complex biological organisms, and have their own form of social solidarity. Thus modern society is not necessarily morally confused, it simply has its own type of solidarity, which needs to be reinforced.

The problems of modern society are not inherent in a complex division of labor, but are caused by more specific "pathological" conditions. These can be studied empirically, such as by studying changing suicide rates. Implicit in Durkheim's analysis was the notion that modern society would never be perfectly balanced. Some local diversity in values, along with a certain suicide rate, is normal, because it is necessary for overall social functioning. Nevertheless, a coherent moral order was needed to regulate individual aspirations, bind people together, and foster individual autonomy. Durkheim's remedies for the lack of social integration in French society involved strengthened forms of communal life linking the family and state, such as occupational associations like guilds, and morally revitalized schools. In both instances, Durkheim was concerned with how to invest social institutions with the full conviction of traditional religion, but on a secular basis. He thought this could be done by recognizing that society, the only empirical superordinate being, is the secular analog of God. Seeing this helps give social obligations the same strength they have in traditional religion, but without dogma or metaphysics.

Durkheim shared Comte's belief that it is possible to have an objective science of morality that also contributes to moral order, but he argued for an empirical science independent of philosophy. Durkheim attempted to integrate descriptive and normative concerns by studying social "pathologies" empirically, but he was unable to define the difference between pathological and normal levels very clearly. Research on social organization, suicide, deviance, religion, and education is all greatly indebted to Durkheim's work, which has also strongly influenced structural-functionalism in sociology and anthropology.

Weber

Max Weber (1864–1920) was centrally concerned with the historical rise of capitalism and the rationalization of Western civilization, like his fellow countryman Karl Marx. However, Weber's reaction to the tensions between economic and social life was much more ambivalent, emphasizing the advantages and disadvantages of modern organization as well as the interplay of material and ideal causes. One might say that Weber saw all the conflict and alienation that Marx saw, but was much less optimistic about ever eliminating them. Weber was concerned with the ways in which rational and nonrational action are related to one another. He defined sociology as the science of social action, where social action occurs when individuals take each other's expected responses into account when acting. Such action may arise out of habit or emotional impulse—or it may be the result of rational planning. If it is rationally thought out, then it may involve acting to bring about a given end, or to exemplify a certain value. In this way Weber developed a typology of social action that he used to classify various types of relationships and to describe particular regimes.

Weber's analysis of social stratification was based on a similar analysis of the interplay of economic class and social status. He viewed status groups—defined by patterns of consumption rather than production—as of potentially equal importance to classes, arguing that while changing economic conditions provide opportunities for new status distinctions, existing status distinctions may also be used to regulate economic opportunities. Thus, the basis for a group's or class's dominance over others may depend on multiple factors, economic and cultural, rather than being reducible to economic factors alone. Weber also emphasized the interplay of ideal and material factors in long-run social change, in contrast to Marx's emphasis on material factors. He argued that the Protestant ethic provided some of the necessary motivation and legitimation for the rise of capitalism, rather than being a merely dependent factor: "Not ideas, but material and ideal interests directly govern men's conduct. Yet very frequently the 'world images' that have been created by 'ideas' have, like switchmen, determined the tracks along which action has been pushed by the dynamic of interests" (Gerth and Mills: 280).

Weber also refused to adopt either a positivistic or an interpretive approach to research, instead viewing sociology as "that science which aims at the interpretive understanding of social behavior in order to gain an explanation of its causes, its course, and its effects" (Weber 1964: 29).

Mead

A more optimistic mood prevailed in the work of G.H. Mead (1863–1931) and his close colleague, John Dewey (1859–1952). Where Weber was resigned to a split between modern organization and traditional ideals, and Durkheim sought to reduce it by infusing modern organization with moral purpose, Mead and Dewey sought to reform modern society by making it more democratic—so it could keep reforming itself. For Mead and Dewey, belief in Darwinian evolution did not imply the need for passive adaptation to the natural environment (contra Spencer). Rather, what is evolutionarily distinctive about human beings is their intelligence, their ability to alter their environment intentionally.

The key insight from G.W.F. Hegel was not that Reason is acting in history—which even Marx believed in his own way—but that mind develops through dialogical social relations, which can be conceived of in entirely naturalistic ways. Mead helped unite these natural and cultural views of mind by developing a connected account of how children's minds (and selves) develop through social interaction, beginning with simple signs and a "conversation of gestures" like that occurring among animals, and later moving to the reflexive use of significant symbols used in human conscious thought. In the latter, one is able to "take the role of the other" so that "the vocal gesture . . . has the same effect on the individual making it that it has on the individual to whom it is addressed or who explicitly responds to it, and thus involves a reference to the self of the individual making it" (Mead: 158).

One implication of this active and socially constructed view of mind was that intelligent social reform is possible because people can reflect on and change their environments, including their own social environments. Secondly, since mind and self are socially constructed, such reform needs to take account of the indirect educative and moral effects of changed institutions and not merely the effects on immediate goal attainment. Thus, intelligence can be used in social reform with an eye to creating the conditions promoting further intelligence needed for further reform.

Mead's focus was on how institutions might need to be altered, not on how good they are because they have done well in the past. Mead also did not view society as an organic whole or thing, but as a set of diverse and partially conflicting institutions with differing tendencies of action. In fact, this incoherence is what makes selective choice possible. The implication is that rather than bemoaning the split between present realities and traditional ideals, the practical thing is to find ideals latent in present conditions and act to realize them. Mead also rejected belief in evolutionary progress toward some ideal society. Postulating such an ideal would be to close off continuing social problem-solving. Mead would also have rejected a categorical division between descriptive and normative sociology. As Dewey put it, in a statement with which Mead would surely have concurred, "Social theory is . . . comparable not to physics but to engineering, where the 'laws' are statements of the relations of means to consequences which are desired and striven for. . . . The phenomena are still in process and knowledge of them is part of the same process" (Dewey: 235).

During its modern phase—roughly between the late 1930s and some time in the 1970s—sociology became a more autonomous science. It became internationalized, established a broad base in university curricula and in governmental and foundation budgets, and was staffed by practitioners trained in sociology itself. The dominant orientation during this period was Parsonian structural-functionalism, which became virtually identified with modern sociology. This provided an overarching conceptual tent for a variety of specific empirical investigations, leading to some division between "grand theory" on the one hand and empiricist data-grinding on the other.

During this period the reformist impulses in sociology were softened even more, at least in Parsonian and empiricist aspects. Tensions between economy and society were dealt with in the early Parsons by acting in accord with dominant social values, or, in the later Parsons, through improved socialization and control. Social evolution, or "modernization," tacitly took U.S. society as the model toward which other societies could aspire, so that social progress in effect ended in contemporary American society. Pretensions toward pure science also developed in sociology, with great increases in theoretical formalization and statistical refinement. Toward the end of the modern phase, a variety of theoretical orientations came to prominence in reaction to structural-functionalism. These are briefly discussed as "anti-Parsonian" theories since they functioned so much in reaction to Parson's work.

Parsons

Like many of the theorists considered here, Talcott Parsons (1902–1979) was concerned with the relation between utilitarianism and idealism (or instrumental rationality and moral values). However, he was chiefly concerned with this relationship in the work of other sociologists. His work can be viewed as an attempt to integrate Weberian and Durkheimian sociology, and, thereby, the traditions of sociology drawing on German Romanticism and French Functionalism. In his first major work (1937), which had a Weberian emphasis on social action, Parsons argued that the great European theorists were all seeking a view of social action that interrelated utilitarianism and idealism without reducing it to one or the other. Parsons believed that he had discovered this synthesis in their work. It basically involves understanding that elements of different levels of system—biological, psychological, social, and cultural—enter in social action. Rather than reduction to any one of these levels, one needs to see how aspects of each enter into social action. Thus the biological level provides the means for action, the psychological level selects the immediate ends, the social level determines the norms in terms of which action is oriented, and the cultural level provides the values informing the norms. This analysis helped address the very American problem of reconciling individual freedom and social order by relating individual choice, or "voluntarism," to social roles and values (as well as to the choosing organism). Properly understood, one chooses freely as an individual, but does so in the context of a social role while guided by social values. This view allowed the main threats of the post-Depression era, communism and fascism, to be criticized as reductionist, since they attempted to reduce social action to material determinacy or made it a disembodied "emanation" of culture. It also allowed some criticism of capitalism, at least in its crudest forms, by suggesting that social action is not purely a matter of individual, rational choice of means to ends, but also involves social norms and values. By adopting this view, Parsons could, in effect, call for return to a capitalism informed by the Protestant ethic, with its value on duty as a way of contributing to both economy and society.

In his later, more Durkheimian work, Parsons (1951) shifted the center of attention from individual acts to the social system. He considered that a social system must meet the needs of the other levels of system, of which it is composed or of which it is an instance. It must be able to facilitate basic adaptation (biological needs), goal attainment (personality needs), integration (social needs), and latency (cultural needs). Every social system has to fulfill these four general functional requirements. Since these needs are relatively independent of one another, social systems are likely to differentiate along these lines, creating separate institutions for each, which may then further subdivide in similar fashion. Parson's structural functionalism thus involved understanding the structure of an institution in terms of the function it performs for a whole social system, and the structure of roles in terms of the functions they perform for an institution. As long as each level of social organization does its duty and gets its job done with at least minimal adequacy, the whole system will be in "equilibrium."

Anti-Parsonian Theory

Structural functionalism's ultimately static nature—that of a closed, self-equilibrating system rather than an open, self-reconstructing one—was consistent with the finely detailed studies of individual mobility that dominated American sociology into the 1970s. However, the political unrest of the 1960s had produced reactions to this quiescent grant theory and technical social accounting, which split sociological theory into fragments along the following lines (Ritzer 1983: 441): One set of opponents developed on the materialist left. Neo-Marxist theories, which emphasized social conflict and differences in means, opposed the Parsonian emphasis on consensus and common ends. They were sometimes joined by neo-Weberian conflict theorists who emphasized the ways in which privileged strata use cultural barriers to maintain their advantages.

Another group of opponents developed

on the cultural left. Symbolic interactionists (Blumer) and ethnomethodologists (Garfinkel)—both ultimately tied back to German Idealism—emphasized the variety of conflicting interpretations and meanings that enter into social action and the socially constructed character of social "facts." In doing so they criticized the functionalist presupposition that situations are consensually defined, and the positivist presupposition that facts are given. A third reaction came from the materialistic right. Behavioristic exchange theory attempted to explain morals as emergent from rewarding and punishing exchanges (Homans), thus suggesting, in effect, that norms that do not develop out of free-market exchange are somehow artificial. As Gouldner noted, "Here Romanticism received its coup de grace from a Spencerian Positivism allied with Skinnerian Behaviorism" (139–40). Sociological theory thus came apart along lines dividing materialists and idealists, structuralists and interactionists. The heirs of Marx and Weber, Mead, and Spencer, had declared their seemingly irreconcilable differences from the heirs of Comte and Durkheim. Or, putting a good face on it, one could say that sociology had become a "multi-paradigm science" (Ritzer 1974).

Sociological theory from some time in the 1970s might be considered to have entered a postmodern phase in which dealing with these fragments and doubts has been one of the main issues. During this period, the problem of action and the problem of order seem to have reemerged in new forms. The problem of action was reflected in new questioning of science and instrumental-rationality, which many saw as contributing to social problems rather than being the keys to their solution. The problem of order arose as larger-scale social organizations, from multinational empires on down, came into question in a time of resurgent particularism. Both of these tendencies, even if only temporary, contrasted with much earlier history in which science and larger social units tended to be triumphant.

Doubts about science and instrumental-rationality were expressed in sometimes bitter methodological wars pitting natural-scientifically inclined "positivists" against more cultural, historical, or literary "interpretivists." The critique of "abstracted empiricism" that Mills had suggested in the 1950s became the battle cry of the second generation of "critical theorists" in the 1970s who suggested that not

only had "positivistic" sociology lost its critical edge, it had also become part of the dominant, socially reproductive ideology. In effect, sociological science was contributing to contemporary social problems rather than solving them.

Questions of global unity and order versus local diversity and freedom were reflected in debates between "macro" theorists who sought to use broader social-structural arrangements to explain local and evanescent patterns of social interaction, and "micro" theorists who sought to use local interaction to explain the continual re-creation of persisting structures. This led to discussions about how to interrelate "macro" and "micro," "structure" and "agency," or "system" and "life-world," as they were variously termed and conceived. For some at least, the grand theoretical metanarratives, like Parsons's structural-functionalism, were understood as ideological instruments of domination.

The irony in this is that a science developed to combat ideological dogma and the social problems attendant on narrowly instrumental action in modern society may have itself caught this disease—an insight that has given rise to reflexive sociology (Bourdieu & Wacquant; Gouldner). Viewed in that way, methodological and orientational fragmentation in sociology may simply be part and parcel of the more general uncertainty about how to proceed in the postmodern world. If so, the next great theoretical success may come not from an abstract solution to these methodological or theoretical dilemmas, but from a broader and deeper reflection on the problems of contemporary life. This was the pragmatists' simple suggestion, which it may be worthwhile to revisit (Joas).

Eric Bredo

See also DURKHEIM; EVOLUTION; MARX; MARXISM; MODERNISM AND POSTMODERNISM; PROGRESS, IDEA OF, AND PROGRESSIVE EDUCATION; SOCIAL SCIENCES, PHILOSOPHY OF

Bibliography
Alexander, J.C. *Twenty Lectures: Sociological Theory since World War II*. New York: Columbia University Press, 1987.
———, B. Giesen, R. Munch, and N.J. Smelser, eds. *The Micro-Macro Link*. Berkeley: University of California Press, 1987.
Blumer, H. *Symbolic Interactionism: Perspective and Method*. Englewood Cliffs, N.J.: Prentice-Hall, 1969.
Bourdieu, P., and L. Wacquant. *An Invitation*

to *Reflexive Sociology*. Chicago: University of Chicago Press, 1992.

Carneiro, R.L., ed. *The Evolution of Society: Selections from Herbert Spencer's Principles of Sociology*. Chicago: University of Chicago Press, 1967.

Comte, A. *Positive Philosophy*. London: Ball, 1896.

Dewey, J. "Syllabus: Social Institutions and the Study of Morals." In *John Dewey: The Middle Works, 1899–1924*, edited by J.A. Boydston. Carbondale: Southern Illinois University Press, 1983.

Durkheim, E. *The Division of Labour in Society*. Translated by W.D. Halls. London: Macmillan, 1984.

———. *The Elementary Forms of the Religious Life*. New York: Free Press, 1965.

———. *Moral Education: A Study in the Theory and Application of Sociology*. New York: Free Press, 1973.

———. *The Rules of Sociological Method and Selected Texts on Sociology and Its Method*. Translated by W.D. Halls. New York: The Free Press, 1982.

———. *Suicide: A Study in Sociology*. New York: Free Press, 1951.

Garfinkel, H. *Studies in Ethnomethodology*. New York: Prentice Hall, 1967.

Gerth, H., and C.W. Mills. *From Max Weber: Essays in Sociology*. New York: Oxford University Press, 1946.

Gouldner, A.W. *The Coming Crisis in Western Sociology*. New York: Avon Books, 1970.

Homans, G.C. *Social Behavior: Its Elementary Forms*. New York: Harcourt, Brace and World, 1961.

Joas, H. *Pragmatism and Social Theory*. Chicago: University of Chicago Press, 1993.

Marx, K. *Karl Marx: Selected Writings in Sociology and Social Philosophy*. London: McGraw-Hill, 1964.

Mead, G.H. *Mind, Self, and Society: From the Standpoint of a Social Behaviorist*. Chicago: University of Chicago Press, 1934.

Parsons, Talcott. *The Social System*. New York: Free Press, 1951.

———. *The Structure of Social Action: A Study in Social Theory with Special Reference to a Group of Recent European Writers*. New York: McGraw-Hill, 1937.

Ritzer, G. *Sociological Theory*. New York: Alfred A. Knopf, 1983.

———. *Sociology: A Multiple Paradigm Science*. Boston: Allyn and Bacon, 1974.

Spencer, H. *The Study of Sociology*. New York: Appleton, 1891.

Weber, M. *Basic Concepts in Sociology*. New York: Citadel Press, 1964.

———. *The Protestant Ethic and the Spirit of Capitalism*. New York: Scribner's, 1905.

Socrates (470 or 469–399 B.C.)

Though he did not write anything and our only chronicle of Socrates' life originates from his contemporaries, Socrates symbolizes teaching excellence and the ideal teacher. Socrates' declaration that "the unexamined life is not worth living" is the heart of his life's calling; but it pertains to only one aspect of life, the moral domain.

Socrates was born during the golden classical age and heard Pericles' incomparable eulogy to Athenian democracy, the funeral oration for those who had died during the first years of the Peloponnesian War. Socrates' life spanned Athenian military victories and then her defeats, the glories of participatory democracy and then rule by a ruthless oligarchy, social hegemony and then radical social transformation. He lived through an explosion of scientific and intellectual knowledge and witnessed the creation of architectural splendor and unrivaled theater.

Socrates conducted dialogues not only to improve the souls and lives of his interlocutors, but, as important, to test himself and to improve his own soul. Wherever he was in Athens, in the streets, the Agora, the gymnasium, or other public places, Socrates spoke with anyone who tolerated his questioning. Instead of holding private dialogues, the two discussants, Socrates and his interlocutor, were surrounded by young men who enjoyed listening to how Socrates questioned and then verbally defeated all contenders. Socrates asked politicians about the meaning of justice, generals about the meaning of courage, lovers about love, poets about poetry. Although they all claimed to be experts or to know the matter under discussion, powerful, successful, and respected men were unable to answer Socrates' questions. It is no wonder that after many years prominent people became indignant and put Socrates on trial for heresy and corrupting youth. In the *Apology*, Socrates justifies his life and likens his mission to that of a gadfly, forcing Athens and its citizens to question their lives, their souls, and motivating them to live virtuously.

Interpretation of Socrates' beliefs and his

contribution to educational thought is hampered not by a paucity of evidence, but by the abundance of writings in which Socrates has the leading role: comedy by Aristophanes, dialogues by Xenophon, Isocrates, Aeschines of Sphettus, evidence from Aristotle, and the early dialogues of Plato. Of all the diverse accounts of Socrates' "teaching," only the Socrates of Plato's early dialogues was intellectually challenging and morally uplifting enough to remain an educational ideal for more than two thousand years. But when accepting Plato's account of Socrates, it is necessary to recognize that the historical Socrates is the protagonist of only the early dialogues, not of Plato's middle or late periods, when Plato (who often still uses the name "Socrates") propounds a number of theories that are wholly alien to the thought, educational ideas, and life of the historical Socrates. It is only the historical Socrates of the early dialogues that is of concern here. These early dialogues include *Apology, Charmides, Crito, Euthyphro, Gorgias, Hippias Minor, Ion, Laches, Protagoras,* and the first book of the *Republic.* In addition, a few sections of other dialogues complete a portrayal of the historic Socrates, such as the first part of the *Meno,* Alcibiades' speech in the *Symposium.*

Through the brilliance of Plato's early dialogues, Socrates' life and teaching are reborn for each new generation. These dialogues do not allow readers to distance themselves from Socrates, but engage readers in the dialectical sparring, thought, and action. In the *Protagoras,* the reader visits the home of the wealthy, powerful Callias, and with celebrities of society, listens to the dialogue between Socrates and the wise man Protagoras about whether virtue can be taught. In another dialogue, the *Meno,* the reader is present when the indulged Meno asks Socrates whether virtue is teachable, the result of practice, given by nature, or occurs in some other way. In the *Laches,* Socrates challenges first one and then another famous Athenian general, Laches and Nicias, to state the meaning of courage. These dialogues do not result in the necessary definitions of virtue terms, but end *aporia,* with no agreement between the protagonists.

Though Socrates never propounds a doctrine or theory, his contributions to education are important. First, the method that was Socrates' trademark for conducting dialectical exchanges with interlocutors and defeating them in verbal contest has taken its place among teaching methods as the Socratic method. The Socratic method, in contrast with the techniques of the Sophists, the paid, itinerant teachers of Classical Greece, is not merely a tool with which to defeat others in verbal battle, but also a means of motivating interlocutors to examine their sincerely held beliefs and moral doctrines. This dialectic is therapeutic in that it rids the soul of misconceived and incoherent beliefs and forces interlocutors to recognize the consequences of a life based on these beliefs.

Second, rather than considering education to be the acquiring of information and skills, Socrates makes virtue the central aim of education. The virtuous life cannot be based on habit, the unthinking acceptance of societal values, or the didactic lectures of teachers. The practice of virtue requires the continual examination of sincerely held beliefs and an ongoing search for the meaning of virtue, a meaning that is general and abstract and would encompass all particular instances of virtue. Teachers lecturing and students passively acquiring information cannot affect and change the human soul. To emphasize his rejection of teacher-centered education, Socrates emphatically declares that he is not a teacher.

Unlike other Athenian teachers, in particular Sophists, Socrates was unwilling to accept official students or receive payment from interlocutors. Rather, Socrates claimed that his questioning of everyone who would submit to cross-examination was a mission ordained by the gods. That mission, though it had qualities of a priestly calling, was not the propagation of a doctrine, but a stimulating of people to search themselves, to recognize their incoherent beliefs, the consequences of their beliefs, and their lack of self-knowledge. Though he unequivocally accepted certain moral beliefs to guide his own life and dialectical interchanges, Socrates never taught or transmitted a dogma.

Noble and powerful Athenians respected and adored Socrates. Though at one time he had sufficient wealth to purchase his own armor and weapons with which to fight at the battle of Potidaea, later, no matter the weather or occasion, Socrates wore a thin cloth garment and walked without sandals. Neither his body nor facial features possessed the beauty, harmony, and balance idealized by classical sculptors. What a strange sight he presented, a person totally devoid of external pretensions and physical beauty, surrounded by people who cultivated the very characteristics he lacked. The beautiful and dissolute Alcibiades explained Socrates' attraction by likening Socrates' external appearance to *seleni* and the internal beauty and harmony of Socrates' soul to golden and beautiful gods that exist within the interior of these molded figures.

In Plato's early dialogues, Socrates' personality and character are richly portrayed: Socrates gregariously and steadfastly pursues people and shuns the beauty of nature. He displays nobility and self-control, humor and irony, earthiness and asceticism, self-awareness and curiosity, wisdom and ignorance. Henry James once said that a certain novel's protagonist "assured you that he was not economizing his consciousness. He was not living in a corner of it to spare the furniture of the rest. He was squarely encamped in the centre and he was keeping open house." Similarly, Socrates was always fully alive and never economized his consciousness. Even after drinking all night at Agathon's celebration of victory, Socrates was still fully conscious. While all his other companions slept to recover from their *symposium,* Socrates arose and went off to the gymnasium to continue to discuss virtue and the moral life.

Socrates argues that material comfort, success, respect, and professional competence are nothing unless based on a rational search to improve one's soul, character, virtue, and morality. Without testing sincerely held moral beliefs, everything else in life has little value.

Socrates was an expert par excellence of a method of arguing known as the *elenchus,* by which the many inconsistent, unfounded, and false beliefs of an interlocutor are exposed. A famous Sophist, the respected teacher Gorgias, once claimed that he did not teach students what is right and wrong, but only rhetoric, the ability to persuade and influence the public and gain political power. But after being questioned by Socrates, Gorgias finally admits that he teaches right and wrong if a student does not already possess such knowledge. Since Gorgias holds two inconsistent opinions, that he does not teach right and wrong and that he does teach right and wrong, Socrates compels him to decide which belief he sincerely accepts.

At first, this technique appeared to be great fun, in that bystanders laughed to see powerful people, politicians, poets, and craftsmen, unable to respond successfully to Socrates' questions. When interlocutors fumbled for answers, contradicted themselves, then became angry and even cursed Socrates, bystanders were

entertained and pleased. Those who became Socrates' interlocutors, however, saw these dialectical wrestling matches from a different perspective and often felt that they were Socrates' victims. For no one was able to withstand Socrates' dialectical skills; Socrates was always the victor.

Sophists of the fifth and fourth centuries were adept at reasoning and were easy victors in verbal battles with anyone but Socrates. For example, though the brothers Euthydemus and Dionysodorus were masters of eristic arguments, Socrates criticized them and likened their performances to that of jugglers and practical jokers. To these brothers, it was of little importance whether their "lessons" affected their students' character in a positive way or contributed to a student's moral beliefs and judgments. These Sophists only aimed at winning an argument no matter what methods they used. Similarly, Antiphon and the anonymous writer of the *Dissoi Logoi* revealed that one could argue equally well on either side of an argument. The concern here was not with which position was right or true or just, but with winning the argument. Even when Socrates seems to use these methods, there are subtle differences from the eristic arguments of Sophists. In particular, the aim of the Socratic dialectic is not winning or political power, but the curing of diseased souls. However, for Socrates, a reasoned, questioning approach to life and the possession of coherent moral beliefs was not sufficient.

Consistency between word and deed was a hallmark of Socrates' life and teaching. When Socrates stated that the unexamined life is not worth living, he did not refer only to the state of one's soul or to examined moral beliefs, but to acting on those virtues and beliefs, no matter the situation or hardship. When the legal authorities of the oppressive oligarchy ordered Socrates to commit a heinous crime, Socrates merely ignored their treacherous command, without concern for the personal consequences of his decision. While not accepting any external limitations on his right to speak and question, Socrates acknowledged the right of the state to prosecute and convict him for such action.

Though Socrates recognized people's complacency and lack of moral knowledge and moral commitment, he did not merely lecture or scold. Rather, he motivated others to investigate and question themselves. Those who normally preach and lecture to society should not, according to Socrates, assume that their own moral beliefs and behavior are beyond reproach. Socrates included himself with those who had to continue to investigate their lives. For Socrates continually claimed that he was ignorant and needed to search for moral knowledge.

Socrates maintained that scientific speculations are useless since they do not reveal how to perfect the human soul or how a person should live. At first, when he heard Anaxagoras' theory that mind is the ultimate principle of the universe, Socrates was enthusiastic and thought Anaxagoras provided the key to understanding human life. But when he continued to study these speculations, Socrates realized that they could not explain how to improve the human soul. Though science may explore the nature of the universe or perfect crafts such as medicine, it cannot tell human beings what moral beliefs should govern their lives and what is the best life.

What type of knowledge did Socrates seek? Only knowledge that would allow human beings to achieve the good, virtuous, and just life. From ancient times until the present day, one of three qualities, it has been assumed, ensures happiness and the good life: first, honor and success; second, pleasure; and third, knowledge. Of the three, Socrates argues that only knowledge guarantees happiness. His paradox, virtue is knowledge, continues to puzzle interpreters. Socrates' arguments and life seem convincing demonstrations that virtue is knowledge, but it is not clear what such knowledge is. When, at his trial, Socrates said that ignorance is most blameworthy and should be feared more than death, and that his only knowledge was recognition of his ignorance, the paradox is even more puzzling. Socrates argued that whereas most people really do not have knowledge, they presume to know. Unlike those who practice this self-deception, Socrates fully recognized and admitted his lack of knowledge. His statement of ignorance remains a paradox, since he also claims to be the wisest man in Athens. However, this wisdom was not based on some doctrine or knowledge of absolute truth, but his awareness of what he did not know, his self-knowledge, and mastery of a method, which continually could reveal the limitations and fallacies of unwarranted, sincerely held beliefs.

While awaiting death, Socrates talks with his old friend Crito, and resolutely states that it is better to suffer wrong than to do wrong.

When fearful of suffering and punishment or of losing possessions and friends, most people follow orders even if it means deserting their moral beliefs. Socrates did not fear anything except failing to lead the virtuous life or to search for the good and just life. Even during his trial, during the final days before his death, and on the very day he took the poison, Socrates reiterated his contentment and that he did not fear death. For how could someone fear what was unknown? This was not merely a form of detachment that allowed him to accept his impending death. During this period, he continued to live his life in exactly the same manner as he always had, discussing the same themes, such as a person's responsibility to persevere in the search for the virtuous life no matter the time or place.

Socrates died with nobility and grandeur, but Socrates' death actually marked a new beginning. Even though twentieth-century thinkers tacitly scorn Plato's theory of Forms, most would not deny the existence of one Form, the Form of the ideal teacher. The primary representative of that Form is Socrates, his life and teaching.

Betty A. Sichel

See also Arete; DIALECTIC; PLATO; SOPHISTS

Bibliography

Hamilton, Edith, and Huntington Cairns. *The Collected Dialogues of Plato.* Princeton: Princeton University Press, 1961.

Teloh, Henry. *Socratic Education in Plato's Early Dialogues.* Notre Dame, Ind.: University of Notre Dame Press, 1986.

Vlastos, Gregory, ed. *The Philosophy of Socrates.* Garden City, N.Y.: Anchor Books, 1971.

———. *Socrates, Ironist and Moral Philosophy.* Ithaca, N.Y.: Cornell University Press, 1991.

Sophists

In the fifth century B.C. the term *sophist* came to be used to refer to a class of professional educators at Athens who offered instruction for fees to young men, and who in addition gave public displays of eloquence and published writings expounding their doctrines and methods of teaching. The term *sophist* was related to two Greek words, *sophos,* or "wise man" and *sophia,* meaning "wisdom," "skill," or "understanding"; its basic meaning was "someone who makes others wise." But the wisdom so purveyed was of a particular sort and was intended to have a special function in Athenian society. The majority of the Sophists were not Athenians but Greeks attracted to Athens, as the cultural center of Greece, in order to achieve personal fame and wealth from the teaching they offered.

In Periclean Athens, success in politics depended to a very large extent on the ability of an individual to speak persuasively before the Assembly and in the law courts. What the Sophists provided was in essence a training for a successful political career. This in turn was seen as involving two requirements: first, technical skill in the presentation and use of words and arguments, for which the appropriate name was rhetoric; and second, knowledge and understanding of the content or subject matter of the debate in question, this last involving an ability to handle moral and political arguments and, on occasion, both factual and philosophical considerations that might be relevant to the questions at issue.

It follows that the importance of the Sophists may be discussed under two separate headings—their function in the social and political history of Athens within the framework of the history of education, and their significance within the history of Greek philosophical thought, and so within the history of philosophy as a whole down to and including modern times. From the middle of the fifth century B.C. onward some form of elementary school education for boys who were the sons of Athenian citizens living in Athens was practically universal, although the evidence is not clear as to whether in fact it was legally compulsory. After the conclusion of the period of elementary education, perhaps on average about the age of fourteen years, formal schooling came to an end. For older students, the Sophists in the fifth and early fourth centuries B.C. provided a selective education for a fee. That in turn was largely replaced by schools of philosophy and rhetoric from the middle of the fourth century onward, though still only for a small proportion of the total male population. The Sophists, then, may be seen as having fulfilled in some ways the social function of present-day colleges and universities.

In the history of philosophy, the Sophists come between the Presocratics and Plato (c. 427–347 B.C.). The latter, to whom we are indebted for a great deal of our information about the Sophists, treated them with virtually unqualified hostility, maintaining that they taught merely the art of fallacious discourse together with the commendation of immoral practical doctrines. Throughout his writings, Plato contrasts Socrates with the Sophists, although we can now see that Socrates was himself very much a member of the same intellectual movement as the Sophists. Indeed it would almost be true to say that, for Plato, Socrates and Socrates alone was the ideal Sophist! However it is above all Plato's hostility to the non-Socratic Sophists that has dominated the historical picture almost down to the present day and has given us the current meaning of the term *sophist* as "a dishonest and fallacious reasoner." But more recently there has been at least the beginnings of a change. A closer examination of the evidence about the various doctrines propounded by the Sophists suggests that they proceeded from genuine intellectual principles that were in fact meant as serious attempts to grapple with real philosophical problems.

Part of the difficulty in arriving at a sound view of the nature of the Sophistic movement is the inadequacy of the sources surviving from Antiquity. The Sophists themselves produced numerous writings, but the majority of these probably did not survive after the deaths of Plato and Aristotle (384–322 B.C.). All we have are two or three anonymous writings in summary form, parts of a papyrus version of a treatise by Antiphon, and two important versions of a technical philosophic treatise by Gorgias. For the rest we depend on brief fragments in quotation preserved by later writers, often not taken directly from what the Sophists themselves had written, extensive but probably distorted accounts of doctrines in Plato's dialogues, and extremely brief doxographic accounts repeated again and again in later writers. To the modern reader, the philosophic interest of many of the brief statements referring to individual Sophists will often seem obvious beyond the possibility of challenge. In a number of cases these are of considerable interest in relation to present-day discussions. But this in turn introduces the danger of distortion by finding in the teaching of individual Sophists doctrines that are almost certainly no more than modern developments.

The first and the best known of all the Sophists was Protagoras of Abdera in Thrace, who spent most of his time teaching in Athens and who died in his seventies soon after 421 B.C.

His most famous doctrine was that man is the measure of all things, of things that are as to how they are and of things that are not as to how they are not. By man, we are told, he meant men as individuals, and the principle thus enunciated became almost a slogan for the doctrines of relativism that were shared in one form or another by the majority of the fifth-century Sophists. But the precise interpretation of Protagoras' doctrine as a whole remains controversial. It seems to have applied both to sense-perceptions and to moral judgments. In one view it meant that there is no truth apart from what seems true to any one individual at any one time—in other words, complete subjectivism of knowledge. But in another view, all perceptions are true, even when they differ radically from individual to individual, because they are necessarily perceptions of something that is the case in the objective world. This world is then composed of contradictory and conflicting facts and properties, each perceived at least on occasion by different percipients. Sometimes what is perceived depends to a very large extent on the state or condition of the percipient.

Associated with the man-measure doctrine was also the contention that concerning every situation there are two opposed arguments to be put forward; this he made the basis of a specific method of arguing that he taught to students—namely, how to argue both sides of a question. Associated with this method was his proclamation of the need to convert the weaker of two arguments into the stronger or better. That in turn seems to imply that it is the way in which an argument is presented that is important, rather than its actual objective validity. Another doctrine of immense importance was his contention that as a result of teaching and practice all men, or at least all men in a Greek-style city-state, share in certain qualities or rather understandings of what is just in human relations, in such a way as to fit them to offer opinions on political questions and so to participate in the processes of democracy. Such qualities are not possessed by all men by nature but are acquired as a result of learning from their experience of social processes.

The doctrines of the other Sophists active at Athens in the fifth century B.C. were hardly less important than those of Protagoras, but they may be outlined more briefly. Gorgias of Leontini in Sicily traveled extensively throughout the Greek world and was particularly famous for his teaching and his practice of rhetoric. He propounded elaborate stylistic doctrines concerned, above all, with the use of verbal antitheses, and he insisted that, if he is to be successful, the orator must always take account of the time and situations with which he is dealing. He also developed a doctrine of "justified deception," for which precise details are lacking in the tradition that has come down to us. It provided a theory for the writing of fiction as in a Greek tragedy, and it implied that not all deception is justified. He was also the author of a famous treatise "On Nature" in which he argued that nothing is: Even if it is, it cannot be known, and even if it can be known, it still cannot be communicated to another person. This was clearly an important approach to the meaning of the verb "to be" in its philosophic sense, and seems to have involved at least a rudimentary distinction between "meaning" and "reference" of the type developed in the last century by Gottlob Frege. In other words, its purpose was probably to make a contribution to linguistic theory, rather than simply to deny the presence of any reality, the so-called nihilistic interpretation that has long been traditional among scholars.

Prodicus of Ceos was famous for his rationalizing account of the origins of religious beliefs, explaining belief in gods as the result of the personification of natural forces in the world around us. This was a revolutionary doctrine in Athens of the fifth century B.C. and Protagoras also had said that he was unable to be certain about the existence and nature of the gods, for which doctrine he was prosecuted before the courts. It was of course for similar alleged religious unorthodoxy that Socrates was condemned to death in 399 B.C. In addition, Prodicus was famous for his insistence on the need to draw sharp distinctions between words of different meanings, apparently basing this on a doctrine that each word should be related to some one thing only and to no other. Hippias of Elis claimed for himself a mastery over the whole sphere of human knowledge, and his writings clearly covered a very wide range, including the earlier history of philosophy and mathematics as well as technical discussions of the arts and crafts useful in everyday living. He also made much use of the important distinction between convention and nature (*nomos* and *physis*), maintaining that by nature all men (or perhaps all men with intellectual interests) are akin, whereas convention acts like a tyrant and constrains men into groups contrary to nature. The opposition between convention and nature has been regarded by many as typical of the Sophistic movement as a whole.

Antiphon of Athens became famous as a Sophist after the recovery, between 1915 and 1922, of a series of papyrus fragments of his work "On Truth." These expound the doctrine that what is required by law is contrary to the demands of nature, and that where it is safe to do so we should follow the dictates of nature rather than the laws and regulations of the city. These last are fetters on nature—the advantages that nature prescribes make for the freedom of the individual. The rejection of restraints in favor of individual freedom has had an abiding appeal down the ages, not least indeed at the present day. But a second treatise by Antiphon was entitled "On Concord" (*Peri Homonoias*). Here he seems to have argued in favor both of internal harmony within the individual's own soul, and also of harmony among citizens within society. Both of these would seem to require at least some restraint upon individual impulses.

The priority of nature over manmade laws and conventions was supported by at least two other Sophists, Callicles, known only from the discussion in Plato's *Gorgias,* and Thrasymachus, known likewise only from the first book of Plato's *Republic.* Callicles argues that, for the most part, nature and *nomos* are opposed to each other. Conventional laws are made by the majority who are weak. By nature it is right that the stronger should possess more than the weaker, and the abler more than the less able. This view was to be used by Friedrich Nietzsche (1844–1900) in the last century as a model for his own vision of the man who is above other men. Thrasymachus in Plato's *Republic* puts forward the view that true justice is the interest of the stronger. Conventional justice consists in seeking the interest of others than oneself. This he condemns as folly, the only sensible course of action being always to pursue one's own interest. The whole of the *Republic* that follows the discussion in the first book may be seen as Plato's attempt to reject this view of human obligation.

Among other Sophists of the fifth century B.C. at Athens should be counted Critias, a cousin of Plato, Antisthenes, often regarded as the founder or at least the ancestor of the later school of Cynic philosophers, Euthydemus and Dionysodorus, and no doubt a considerable number of others whose names have not survived. In addition, mention should be made of at least two anonymous treatises that survive and that unquestionably are derived from the Sophistic period. The work known as the *Dissoi Logoi* opens with the following words: "Twofold arguments are spoken in Greece by those who philosophize, concerning the good and the bad." The modern title is taken from the two opening words. Its basic pattern consists in setting up antilogies, or opposing arguments, about apparently opposite philosophic terms, and the whole would seem to be an application of Protagoras' doctrine of two opposing Logoi. Next is the treatise known as the *Anonymus Iamblichi* preserved in the *Protrepticus* of Iamblichus, written in the third century A.D. It defends the cause of *nomos,* or conventional law and morality, against those who would overthrow it in favor of nature.

In conclusion it is perhaps worth mentioning that the name the "Second Sophistic Movement" has come to be applied to teachers and practitioners of rhetoric under the Roman Empire, especially from the second century A.D. onward. These writers liked to claim affiliation with the Sophists at Athens in the fifth century B.C. This was probably justifiable in that they provided a valued part of higher education, although without the element of philosophical excitement that was a marked feature of the teaching of their claimed predecessors.

George B. Kerferd

See also NIETZSCHE; PLATO; RHETORIC; SOCRATES

Bibliography

De Romilly, J. *The Great Sophists in Periclean Athens.* Translated by Janet Lloyd. Oxford: Oxford University Press, 1992.

Diels, H., and W. Kranz. *Die Fragmente der Vorsokratiker,* vol. 3. 6th ed. Section C. *Aelters Sophistik.* Berlin: Weidman, 1952.

Dumont, J.P. *Les sophistes, fragments et temoignages.* Paris: Presses universitaires de France, 1969.

Guthrie, W.K.C. *A History of Greek Philosophy.* Vol. 3, *The Fifth-Century Enlightenment.* Cambridge: Cambridge University Press, 1969.

Kerferd, G.N. *The Sophistic Movement.* Cambridge: Cambridge University Press, 1981.

Sprague, H.K. *The Older Sophists. A Com-*

plete Translation. Columbia: University of South Carolina Press, 1972.

Untersteiner, M. *Sofisti testiminianze e frammenti.* Fasc. 1–4. Florence: La Nuovo Italia, 1949–1967.

———. *The Sophists.* Translated by Kathleen Freeman. Oxford: Basil Blackwell, 1954.

Spencer, Herbert (1820–1903)

Herbert Spencer was one of the most prominent intellectual figures of the nineteenth century. Educated in the homes of his father and uncle, his views on education followed from his unique educational experiences outside of any formal system, and from his ethical philosophy, first stated in *Social Statics* and enumerated in many essays reasserted near the end of his career in *The Principles of Ethics.* This philosophy was utilitarian, arguing that happiness to the greatest number is the goal of life; and in Spencer's eye, this position demands that individuals should be free from external constraint, especially by the state, in the pursuit of happiness, although the pursuit of happiness by one individual should not transgress on the rights of other individuals to do the same. This argument, which was "liberal" in the nineteenth century and "libertarian" in late-twentieth-century America, emphasized the rights and duties of individuals; and so, for Spencer, the acquisition of skills, knowledge, and moral discipline was of central concern. For if individuals are not properly socialized, they will not be capable of using and enjoying their freedom in ways that do not transgress upon the rights of others. Spencer was thus drawn into advocating a type of education that could realize his libertarian view of the "good society."

In *Social Statics,* Spencer argued that while education is essential to impart necessary "moral feelings," "sympathetic sentiments," and "exercise of faculties" for "self control," such education should be left to the "natural instincts" of parents rather than the judgments of state bureaucrats whose vested interests would dominate the kind of education implemented. Moreover, national education would evidence the biases of the upper class, who have power, and who as a consequence would take people's money to pay for other children's socialization.

These views were repeated in many essays, such as those collected in *Man vs. the State,* wherein Spencer averred that government is to "administer justice" and to protect persons and property rather than to impose education. For Spencer, "A man can no more call upon the community to educate his children, than he can demand that it should feed and clothe them" (227). The state would standardize education and, hence, reduce the variation so necessary for the survival of the species; and this standardization and conservatism would increase as education became yet another vested interest, like state-sponsored religion. In *The Principles of Ethics,* this viewpoint is toned down but still present. By that time, however, Spencer's views were clearly at variance with those of his fellow utilitarians, such as John Stuart Mill (1806–1873), who broke with Spencer and recognized the need for a national system of education. Spencer's moral philosophy was thus going against the tide of increased governmental regulation in all spheres of life. Yet, although Spencer's pleas against state-run education were ignored in the latter half of the nineteenth century, his views on how education should occur, whether in families or schools, continued to stimulate debate.

Spencer's best-known statement on education is the compilation of essays issued under the title *Education,* although the term *education* appears to denote the broader process of "socialization" by both families and schools. It is these early essays that established Spencer as a major commentator on educational policy. The first essay, "What Knowledge Is of Most Worth?" is the most famous. Here Spencer argues that the purpose of education is "to prepare us for complete living" (16), leading him to classify the most fundamental kinds of activity for such complete living: (a) activities directed toward self-preservation; (b) activities involved in direct self-preservation (such as securing an income with which to feed oneself); (c) activities for rearing and disciplining offspring; (d) activities directed toward political relations (such as political rights and duties, sense of citizenship); and (e) activities devoted to leisure, arts, tastes, gratification, and feelings. These activities are rank-ordered and nested in each other because (b) depends upon (a), (c) upon (a) and (b), (d) upon (a), (b), and (c), and (e) upon all of the rest. In Spencer's view, education should prepare individuals for these five activities, and with these criteria in mind, Spencer launched an attack on the educational systems (in both schools and families) of his time. In particular, schools "leave almost entirely out . . . that which most nearly concerns the business of life" (1860) for schools teach little about self-preservation, getting and keeping a job, raising and caring for children, becoming a good citizen, and cultural pursuits that bear "directly on the duties of life" (65). For his time, these were radical assertions, since the schools taught history, classics, language, and humanities in general. In contrast, Spencer emphasized that training in Science (with a capital S)—its methods, procedures, and substance—should constitute the core of the educational curriculum. For it is science that provides the data, methods, and principles for reasoned acts of self-preservation, effective child-rearing, proper exercise of citizenship, and heightened enjoyment of the arts. Science is thus the "knowledge of most worth." Others such as Thomas Huxley (1825–1895) and John Stuart Mill made similar arguments, but it was Spencer's advocacy that drew the most attention.

The second essay in Spencer's *Education*, "Intellectual Education," emphasizes that students should first learn to organize facts, then to develop generalizations, and, eventually, to see these generalizations as instances of more general and abstract principles. If knowledge is learned in this sequence, then it becomes pleasurable; whereas, if abstract principles are taught before the mind is ready, or if only disconnected facts are memorized, education becomes painful and, hence, ineffective. Again, this point of emphasis represented an attack on the educational systems of Spencer's time, which demanded rote memorization of facts and absorption of abstract principles unconnected to the facts of the real world. And for Spencer, this pattern of instruction violated his basic law of evolution, whereby the cognitive capacities of children grow from simple to complex and, therefore, require that education do the same. When viewed in this way, certain basic guidelines should guide intellectual education: (a) teach the simple and then combine ideas into ever more complex wholes; (b) start with the concrete and then move to the more abstract; (c) teach the genesis of knowledge as it evolved during the course of human history, which implies that one should (1) teach the empirical and then move to the rational and (2) encourage self-discovery and investigation over rigid instruction; and (d) make learning pleasurable and exciting. If a curriculum follows these guidelines, it will be successful in encouraging lifelong learning in the mode of science, and, as a result, education will prepare people for real life in a changing world.

The third essay, "Moral Education," emphasizes that learning should correspond to the natural laws of life, where organisms learn the consequences—good and bad or adaptive and maladaptive—of their actions. Family and school should, therefore, let children discover for themselves and avoid "artificial" reactions when too many proscriptions, prescriptions, sanctions, instructions, and guidelines are imposed. Only by adjusting conduct to the physical, biological, social, and ethical dimensions of the "natural" universe can children acquire the "mental discipline" necessary for a morality that corresponds to reality. Thus, Spencer felt that just as children should learn the harmful effects of fire by experience, they should learn the "natural" reactions of others to misbehavior (that is, sanctions consistently and proportionately expressed without excessive or zealous moralizing by parents and teachers). Only in that way can children acquire a "rational" conception of right and wrong coupled with a sense of proportional justice wherein punishment fits the crime. For Spencer, these guidelines do not follow from a conception that children are "morally good," but rather from his evolutionary principle that morality is learned successively and moves from simple to complex forms as experiences are built up (instead of "imposed" by the full-blown and abstract morality of adults). Only by letting children acquire morality in the course of their normal activities, Spencer argued, will they develop the self-discipline necessary for truly moral conduct, which lets each individual seek pleasures without transgressing on the right of others to do the same.

The final essay, "Physical Education," was unique in Spencer's time because it emphasized that a healthy body is essential to moral and intellectual development. For humans are an "animal," and a "good animal" is one that is physically fit. Moreover, natural exercise, using muscles and joints in normal activities, is preferable to gymnastic forms of exercise in which joints and muscles are artificially and unnaturally used and developed. Of special note is Spencer's recognition that social conventions inside and outside of schools have prevented women from engaging in natural exercise, forcing them to forgo what is basic to them as animals and, occasionally, requiring them to submit to unnatural forms of "gymnastic" exercise.

Moreover, Spencer argued that social conventions of his time violated children's need for large quantities and varieties of food, for adequate clothing, and for other physical needs.

Spencer was not the only advocate of these ideas, but he was the most persuasive. His positions were debated and discussed, and, while they were radical for his time, they were compatible with the pragmatism of John Dewey (1859–1952) and with educational thought as it was evolving in America. It is for that reason that Spencer's *Education* was his first work published in America. Although the ideas in that work are rarely cited today, they have become almost wholly incorporated into the operation of American schools.

Spencer's essays on education were published before his grand Synthetic Philosophy, which "deduced" the principles of ethics, biology, psychology, and sociology from a simple set of "first principles." They were written in his years as a commentator and journalist, but they show signs of what was to come: the emphasis on science and the concern with humans obeying "natural laws," as he formulated them. This implied for Spencer that education should not come from external authority, from the mandates of tradition, or from dogmatism. Rather, education should be enabling, allowing individuals the knowledge and self-discipline, as exemplified by the scientific method, to construct and maintain a moral community without excessive governmental regulation.

Even though Spencer invoked his principles of evolution in his analysis of education, his moral preachings on education are quite separate from his more purely scientific treatises—*First Principles, The Principles of Psychology, The Principles of Biology,* and *The Principles of Sociology*. Aside from references to the evolutionary trend from simplicity to complexity and the corresponding need to integrate ever more complex systems, the strident moral overtones of his works on education are not evident in his more scientific works. It is as if Spencer wore two hats—the shrill utilitarian and the more cautious scientist. Indeed, he hardly discusses education in his scientific treatises. In *The Principles of Sociology,* where there is a brief analysis of teachers as a part of "professional institutions," the analysis is historical and evolutionary. Spencer emphasizes that the first teachers were religious practitioners, but, with growing societal complexity, secular teachers differentiated and eventually were elaborated into a separate institutional system. There is, however, always a tension between secular and religious education in the course of societal development, but, as teachers form a profession and as the state seeks to exercise control, education is "segregated" and "consolidated" as a separate system. The fact that Spencer devotes so little attention to education in these works, especially compared with the hundreds of pages on religion, kinship, government, and work, indicates his conviction that the "natural course" of evolution would not involve a large educational establishment.

He was obviously wrong in that conclusion, and, in fact, his sociological analysis of institutions suggested why he was wrong (Turner). As populations grow, they become ever more differentiated, creating problems of regulation and control that lead to the growth of government. And, if inequalities exist within a society or external threats to a society exist, government becomes ever more centralized and begins to regulate internal system processes. In terms of his moral philosophy, Spencer did not like the evolutionary trend, but, as a scientist, he understood it. Thus, Spencer's science goes against his libertarianism, particularly the view that the state should not assume control of education. Yet, Spencer's views on the proper type of education correctly predicted the trends in instruction during the twentieth century. Indeed, as the twenty-first century approaches, Spencer's ideas still seem relevant: instruction that views science—methods, principles, and substance—as the core of the curriculum; instruction that encourages self-discovery; instruction that prepares students for real life and inevitable social change; and instruction that moves from concrete cases to general principles.

Jonathan H. Turner

See also EVOLUTION; INDIVIDUALISM; LIBERALISM; PROGRESS, IDEA OF, AND PROGRESSIVE EDUCATION; UTILITARIANISM

Bibliography

Perrin, Robert G. *Herbert Spencer: A Primary and Secondary Bibliography*. New York and London: Garland, 1993.
    See especially chapter 14, citing works on education.
Spencer, Herbert. *Education: Intellectual, Moral, and Physical*. New York: D. Appleton, 1860.

———. *First Principles* [1862]. New York: D. Appleton, 1880.

———. *The Man vs. the State* [1884]. Indianapolis, Ind.: Liberty Classics, 1982.

———. *The Principles of Biology* [1864–1867]. New York: D. Appleton, 1897.

——— *The Principles of Ethics* [1879–1896]. Indianapolis, Ind.: Liberty Classics, 1978.

———. *The Principles of Psychology* [1851]. New York: D. Appleton, 1898.

———. *The Principles of Sociology* [1874–1896]. New York: D. Appleton, 1898.

———. *Social Statics, or The Conditions Essential to Human Happiness* [1850]. New York: D. Appleton, 1888.

Turner, Jonathan H. *Herbert Spencer: A Renewed Appreciation*. Newbury Park, Calif.: Sage, 1985.

Stoicism

Primarily an ethical philosophy, supported by a physical and logical theory. Stoicism was a reaction to political instability during Hellenistic times (around 300 B.C.) and flourished in both Greece and Rome until the turn of the third century A.D. Zeno of Citium (336–264 B.C.), who had studied previously with the Cynics, a group that disdained worldly goods and standards, founded the school. Because they met in a painted colonnade, the Stoa Portico, they became known as Stoics. Zeno was followed by Cleanthes (331–232 B.C.), a yeoman, if not creative, worker who was content simply to carry on the founder's teachings. Thereafter, Chrysippus (280–206 B.C.) became head of the school, organizing and systematizing the teachings to such effect that he became known as the "second founder" of the school. This period came to be known as the "Old," or Greek, Stoa.

A second period, called the "Middle Stoa," saw Stoicism carried from Greece to Rome by, among others, Panaetius (c. 180–109 B.C.) and Posidonius (c. 135–51 B.C.). Again the ethical teachings were attractive because of rapidly changing political and social circumstances. Panaetius, considered to be the founder of Stoicism in Rome, sought to provide a moral code more in tune with the practical Roman mind. He proposed studies—history, philosophy, geography, chronology, philology, and law—that contributed directly to the attainment of virtue and truth. Panaetius was a skilled grammarian and poet; under his influence the crabbed and sparse literary style of Stoicism was reworked along the lines of the Roman infatuation with literature and rhetoric.

Panaetius' student, Posidonius, has been called the last great student in science and literature from the Greek world. He traveled widely for scientific purposes and was a confidant of influential politicians. Like Panaetius, he attempted to make Stoicism palatable to the Roman mind by emphasizing its practical, moral bearing and by clothing it in fine style. He was more a compiler of teachings, or an eclectic, often "raiding" other philosophical schools to create a great pantheistic system.

In what is called a "New," or Roman, period, Stoicism was advanced by Lucius Annaeus Seneca (c. 4 B.C.–65), Musonius Rufus (A.D. 20–90) and his student Epictetus the slave (A.D. 55–135), and Marcus Aurelius Antoninus (A.D. 121–180), the king. Marcus Tullius Cicero (106–43 B.C.), who had much to say about Stoicism, was not himself a Stoic, at least not by profession, but his career shows the Roman disposition and a Stoic inclination. As well as a "consolation for adversity," Stoicism appealed to Rome because of its cosmopolitan world view, which had an important effect on the development of Roman law.

Though the Stoics were prolific writers, only fragments remain of the early works. Much of what is known about early (Old) Stoicism comes from Diogenes Laertius, *Lives of Eminent Philosophers, Book VII*. Written in the third century A.D. on the basis of earlier writings from the third to the first centuries B.C., it is gossipy and uncritical. Cicero also comments on Stoicism, especially the teachings of Panaetius and Posidonius, in *Academica, De Finibus, De Natura Deorum,* and *De Officiis,* among other works.

The Roman Stoics remain the only substantial body of primary material about Stoic teaching. Seneca's writings, especially the *Epistles, Natural Questions,* and *Moral Essays,* are a great addition to the Stoic literature. Epictetus wrote nothing himself, but his *Discourses*—lectures, replies to students, and conversations—and the *Enchiridion* (or *Manual*), a brief summary of his teachings, were recorded by a friend and student, Arrian (Flavius Arranius). The *Meditations* of the emperor Marcus Aurelius were not meant for publication, being rather "thoughts to himself," to strengthen his courage, but by some fortunate chance they have survived.

With the death of Marcus Aurelius, nearly five hundred years of active Stoicism came to a close. But the philosophy continued to influence Western thought. The invention of the printing press in the fifteenth century led to a revival of learning and a new appreciation for literature and the ethical philosophies of Greece and Rome. What interested scholars at that time was "humanism," the idea that man is a natural being who needs only to exercise his native capacities to make his own greatness. Once again, Stoicism became an antidote for those who were frustrated by the strictures of the Church, medieval society, and scholastic scholarship.

A revival of Stoicism, a "neo-Stoicism" or Renaissance Stoicism, resulted from a rediscovery of the literary and philosophical works of Cicero and Seneca. The Flemish scholar Justius Lipsius (1547–1606) published *De Constantia Libri Due* (*Two Books of Constancie*) in 1584, a general introduction to Stoicism that emphasized the reciprocal relationship between ethics and natural philosophy. He followed that with two other books about Stoicism.

In France, Guillaume DuVair published *La Philosophie Morales des Stoiques* (c. 1585), in which he explained Stoicism mainly from the teachings of Epictetus. Stoicism was introduced into England through the studies of Joseph Hall, called "The English Seneca" because of his style and his explanation of Stoicism. Attempting to bring Stoic teachings into line with Christian morality, an impulse of many scholars at the time, Hall published *Heaven upon Earth* (1606), *Characters of Vertues and Vices* (1608), and *Meditations and Vows* (1605). Renaissance Stoicism greatly influenced seventeenth-century English literature.

The early Stoics were known as the "School of Reasoners." This referred not just to logic. They insisted that the traditional categories of logic, physics, and ethics constituted a unified, rational system. Physics was the study of reason as the law of nature; logic the study of reason as a method for discovery of the law; and ethics the study of reason as a guide for human character, action, and ends. Each of these concerns has implications for education.

Of primary interest in Stoic logic is the theory of knowledge. Like the Greeks in general, the Stoics did not have a separate category for this study apart from a wider inquiry into language, speech, and the formal principles of reasoning. Logic usually was divided into rhetoric and dialectic, and, except for some Roman teachers, the Stoics were more interested in dialectic, though some studies usually thought to be part of rhetoric, such as voice, speech, syntax, poetry, and euphony, were topics in the study of language (dialectic), for they contributed to the definition of truth. Dialectic was the study of definitions and criteria for the use of language and the discovery of truth. The criteria were divided further into the study of "presentations," the immediate datum of consciousness or experience, and the form of arguments. Knowledge was believed to be an "unerring apprehension" that could not be shaken by argument, while truth was an "apprehending presentation" from a real object firmly implanted in the mind.

The Stoics believed that all knowledge originates with the senses. In this sense they were empiricists. Further, the mind is a tabula rasa. But they were not naive empiricists. Reason has a role in determining knowledge. Though generally the senses do not deceive, error can result from hasty judging of evidence that the senses present. Consequently, rational judgment must be perfected. Notwithstanding their basic empiricism, the Stoics believed that, through "inborn ideas," the mind is predisposed to accept, reject, or withhold judgment about what the senses furnish. In practice, the Stoics added to their criteria of truth the proviso that "no objection must arise." The wise person will not agree to the truth of a perception, or act on it, no matter how vivid or persuasive it may be, until it has been examined from all sides and survives all criticism.

The Stoics also developed formal logic to go beyond that of Aristotle. They treated existence in four categories, rather than the ten that Aristotle had enumerated, and insisted that, for adequacy of description, everything had to be classified in each of the four categories. Yet they also believed that no two things are exactly alike, a "principle of individuality" that has ethical as well as logical implications. They developed a logic of propositions rather than classes and a theory of inference rather than of logically true forms. Chrysippus especially developed the hypothetical and disjunctive syllogisms, declaring them to be the only regular forms of reasoning, of which the categorical syllogism is but an abbreviation. Scholars now believe that the logic of Antiquity reached its peak in the Stoic school.

In physical theory, the Stoics followed the lead of Heraclitus, who believed that the world is a single, unitary, living thing. They distinguished between the universe and the world, the former being composed of two principles, reason and matter, or active and passive principles, and the latter coming into existence by the combination of these principles through the elements of fire, air, water, and earth. The universal exists in principle, while particular expressions of that principle, such as the world and everything in the world, are finite and material. The world is material in all its aspects and is shaped by reason.

The Stoic world view is an active materialism and a theory of change. Everything in the world waxes and wanes and is regenerated through infinite cycles of time. Only reason—the shaping principle—remains constant. Reason thus is the "natural law" under which both change and continuity are subsidiary rules. Further, the natural law is beneficial and providential; the universe contains no objective evil. Only in practice are the advantages of some things disadvantages for others. Evil has to do with ethics, not physics. It results from a failure to realize and accept one's nature or fate. Error, evil, chaos, and despair signal a misuse, or disuse, of reason. Nor does fate contradict the idea of freedom. Determinism is a physical doctrine, just an extreme form of the belief in cause and effect. Freedom relates to the will and the choices one makes through the use of will. An understanding of physics—that is, knowing what one can change and what one must accept—leads to a reasonable use of will.

Ethics is the capstone of the Stoic system. Yet there is a thoroughgoing unity in Stoic philosophy. One could begin anywhere and need to presuppose the rest of the system. The Stoics divided ethics into a concern for individual conduct and politics. The good person identifies with nature (reason) and uses reason in the conduct of life. The good is synonymous with knowledge. They divided virtue into theoretical (ideal and universal) and practical considerations, and further classified goods as primary, secondary, or "indifferent." Wisdom, courage, justice, and temperance were primary goods, justified by reason as worthy in themselves; whereas generosity, perseverance, good advice, and the like are secondary, or instrumental, virtues. Vice (or evil) generally is the opposite of these goods. The Stoics found that ideal ethics had to be adapted to practice, so between virtue and vice they recognized a large class of "indifferent things," neither good nor

evil in themselves, but to be "preferred" or "rejected" to the extent that they contribute to virtue.

Virtue can be learned. While its principle, reason, exists within every person, it must be developed through active effort in the world. Intent and effort are the primary aims of morality and the criteria by which intelligence is appraised. Results do not justify action but provide a clue to whether intelligence has been utilized. Because hasty judgment, not objective conditions, is the source of error in the world, the passions must be controlled if one is to achieve virtue. Thus, the highest state of ethical progress for the Stoics is one in which *apatheia* (apathy), or "resignation" or detachment, has been cultivated. This idea has been widely misunderstood since Stoic times. The Stoics did not deny emotional states or their utility. The doctrine of apathy has psychological force as a way of holding emotions in check by reason. Life is more difficult when persons resist what is natural and normal and act instead impulsively or on external considerations. The Stoics cultivated apathy, not as an escape, but as a way of staying in tune with the world, with what is essential in life.

Another misconception is that the Stoics neglected political and social ethics. Their emphasis seems to have been on individual virtue and independence. Yet unlike the Cynics and Epicureans, they taught that one should take part in state affairs and not avoid social life; by doing so one will be in a position to promote virtue and restrain vice. (Of course, if virtue is compromised, one should withdraw.) Generally they were indifferent to forms of government, identifying with aristocracy in the Old Stoa and equality in the Roman period. Many Stoics were influential political advisers. Some even joined resistance movements for social reform. The root principle for all details of Stoic political and social theory is the *cosmopolis,* the expression of universal reason. Those who live according to reason have everything in common and are equal. This belief had a direct effect on the shaping of Roman law; the expression of *humanitas,* or universal brotherhood; the development of international law in the late Middle Ages; and the democratic ideal of equality. Some scholars believe that Stoic political theory is the most dear to all freedom-loving persons.

The Stoic philosophy or theory of education has to be imagined from these ingredients.

They hardly considered education in the technical and professional sense common today. Their teaching was equivalent with philosophizing in general. Zeno wrote a book on education, but it is lost. Epictetus was known as one of the greatest teachers in Antiquity. His *Discourses* without doubt are the best source for an understanding of Stoic educational theory and practice (Seneca's writings also are suggestive). In the first place, the Stoics thought that virtue could be taught; in fact, the wise have an obligation to teach others. Though they were reluctant to nominate anyone as being fully wise (rational) or virtuous, they did have models of persons who had "made progress" or improvement, which also implies education.

For the Stoics, there is no other end for education than the development of reason; all else is secondary. This aim is moral—virtue is acting according to reason, which makes all education moral education. A great achievement of Stoic teaching is in the setting of moral alternatives, in the form of paradoxes that characterized the Stoics (and Cynics) from the early days. The Stoics invented the method of particular or specific cases as a means of understanding the application of the rule of nature. They also developed the diatribe, a form of critical discourse, as a way of publicly proclaiming their doctrines.

Certain predispositions are necessary for education. Students must be willing to doubt what, or that, they already know and learn something other, and they must be "mentally alert" and watchful. Self-criticism is particularly important in Stoic philosophy and education. Good teachers reflect on their inadequacies and modify their approaches. Anything in the world has potential for teaching, even imaginative materials such as poetry, which has its value not only in conveying moral lessons but also because its pleasure stimulates reason. The Stoics put great emphasis on clarity and correctness of expression and on simplicity, both in style and understanding. Repetition, which works suggestively, exercises, and practice also were emphasized. The real influence of education is intimate between the student and teacher (personal guidance), though in the last analysis it is the student who has to do the work and aspire to virtue.

The lasting influence of Stoicism is in its commitment to virtue, its use of reason and the idea of *humanitas,* its cosmopolitan view of world brotherhood, and the idea of natural law. Stoicism helped to shape Roman law, Christian ethics, international law, and democratic equality. It lives on.

Robert R. Sherman

See also DEMOCRACY; EPICUREANISM; EQUALITY; HUMANISM

Bibliography
Arnold, E. Vernon. *Roman Stoicism.* Cambridge: Cambridge University Press, 1911, 1958.
Christensen, Johnny. *An Essay on the Unity of Stoic Philosophy.* Copenhagen: Munksgaard, 1962.
Edelstein, Ludwig. *The Meaning of Stoicism.* Cambridge: Harvard University Press, 1966.
Gould, Josiah B. *The Philosophy of Chrysippus.* Albany: State University of New York Press, 1970.
Hicks, R.D. *Stoic and Epicurean.* New York: Scribner's, 1910, 1962.
Hijmans, B.L., Jr. *AEKHEIE: Notes on Epictetus' Educational System.* Assen, Netherlands: Van Gorcum, 1959.
Long, A.A. *Hellenistic Philosophy: Stoics, Epicureans and Sceptics.* 2nd ed. Berkeley: University of California Press, 1986.
Mates, Benson. *Stoic Logic.* Berkeley: University of California Press, 1961.
Pire, George. *Stoicisme et Pedagogie.* Paris: Librairie Philosophique J. Vrin, 1958.
Ressor, Margaret E. *The Political Theory of the Old and Middle Stoa.* New York: Augustin, 1951.
Rist, John M., ed. *The Stoics.* Berkeley: University of California Press, 1978.
Sambursky, S. *Physics of the Stoics.* New York: Macmillan, 1959.
Saunders, Jason L. *Justus Lipsius: The Philosophy of Renaissance Stoicism.* New York: Liberal Arts Press, 1955.
Sherman, Robert R. *Democracy, Stoicism, and Education.* Gainesville: University of Florida Press, 1973.
Tanner, R.G. "The Case for Neo-Stoicism Today." *Prudentia* 14 (1982): 39–51.
Watson, Gerard. *The Stoic Theory of Knowledge.* Belfast: Queen's University, 1966.

S

Studia Humanitatis

Renaissance learning, literally "studies of humanity," denoting a course of instruction or self-study based on the classical literature of Greco-Roman Antiquity. Early humanist scholars credited Francesco Petracco, or Petrarch (1304–1374), secretary to Cardinal Giovanni Colonna, as the individual chiefly responsible for the Italianate revival of antique arts and letters in the late fourteenth century. Leonardo Bruni (1370–1444), for example, later claimed it was Petrarch who had "restored the *studia humanitatis,* which were already extinct, and who opened for us the way whereby we could acquire learning." Similarly, Rudolph Agricola (1443–1485) wrote of Petrarch in his biography that to him "all the erudition of our century is owed."

Coluccio Salutati (1331–1406), an early follower of Petrarch, appears to have been the first to take special note of a reference to "the humanities and letters" (*studia humanitatis ac litterarum*) as it appeared in an oration by the Roman writer Cicero (106–43 B.C.). In his *Pro Archia,* Cicero had combined the common word *studium* with *humanitas* to create the phrase *studia humanitatis,* designating the arts or subjects by which one is "shaped toward humanity" during boyhood. Thus, the "humanities" in their original Ciceronian meaning were generic and nonspecific. The term referred only generally to those subjects one first encounters in youth whose study conduces to the fullest development of one's "humanness," or "humanity." In *De oratore* ("On Oratory"), Cicero cited study of the poets, geometricians, musicians, and dialecticians as examples of the elements composing an appropriate regimen of studies. To poetry, music, geometry, and dialectic, Cicero later added philosophy and "letters," or general learning, as components of his recommended curriculum. For him, the terms *artes* and *studia humanitatis* by no means denoted the specific and specialized literary curriculum later outlined in detail by leading literary humanists of the fifteenth and sixteenth centuries.

Salutati first used the phrase *studia humanitatis* in his own writings in 1369 and often thereafter. However, it was more systematically defined as an explicit curriculum in the writings of Petrus Paulus Vergerius (1349–1420) and Leonardo Bruni (1370–1444). Vergerius' didactic treatise entitled *De ingenuis moribus* ("The Education of the Gentleman"),

addressed to the Paduan prince Ubertinus, was arguably among the first treatments of the humanist approach to education. Based on a second-century essay ("Education of Children") erroneously attributed to Plutarch, Vergerius' tract spoke of the *studia humanitatis* as reconstructed liberal arts: "We call those studies liberal which are worthy of a free man; those studies by which we attain and practice virtue and wisdom; that education which calls forth, trains and develops those highest gifts of body and mind which ennoble men, and which are rightly judged to rank next in dignity to virtue only."

For Vergerius, the study of ancient history, moral philosophy, and eloquence (rhetoric) were to form the basis of an ideal liberal education, supplemented and extended by music, drawing, gymnastics, and "letters" (grammar, composition, logic, and poetry). In Vergerius' scheme, a wise teacher would feel free to experiment with different study arrangements and sequences, depending upon each individual student's interests and abilities.

In the early 1420s, Bruni, a leading humanist scholar and statesman who became chancellor of the Republic of Florence, composed two brief epistles in which he described the educational program just beginning to be known as the *studia humanitatis.* The first, a letter to Niccolo Strozzi, scion of a powerful and wealthy Florentine, urged the young man to devote himself to skill in "letters" (*litterarum peritia*) and to a knowledge of the new humanities, which encourage moral development and self-cultivation. Together, according to Bruni, the two were to be thought of as those "studies of humanity" that perfect and adorn a human being (*homo*).

Bruni's second letter, *De studiis et litteris* ("On Study and Literature"), was written to a woman of noble birth, Battista di Montefeltro, wife of the lord of Pesaro. Bruni urged Battista to absorb herself in studies that pertain to the living of the good life (*bene vivendum*). He added that she should scrupulously avoid medieval scholastic learning and concentrate exclusively upon the works of the great Latin writers of classical Antiquity. Bruni's specific recommendations afford an extensive description of the humanities as they were developing in the early Italian Renaissance. Included in his list of worthy studies were the writings of the classical historians (Livy, Sallust, Tacitus), orators (Cicero), moral philosophers, and the poets, especially Homer and Virgil. The *studia humanitatis* as Bruni characterized them thus constituted a program of classical studies emphasizing primarily literary disciples. Basically, it represented a course of study built up around history, oratory, poetry, and moral philosophy at the expense of logic, mathematics, natural philosophy, and metaphysics.

Over time, an ordered curricular structure was devised and institutionalized in classical secondary schools, or *gymnasia* (in Italian, *studio pubblico*), and in various academies. The *studia humanitatis* were the fixed point of reference, for example, for the "Pleasant House," or *Casa Giocosa,* a pioneer humanist school founded by Vittorino da Feltre (1378–1446). Opened in 1423 at the court of Gianfrancesco Gonzaga and his wife, Paola di Malatesta, of Mantua, the school enjoyed almost immediate success. Ultimately, its reputation rivaled that of many of the *studia,* or prototypical universities of fifteenth-century Italy. Included within the curriculum were the writings of Ovid, Livy, Cicero, Sallust, Homer, Plato, and Demosthenes; as well as the study of logic, rhetoric, mathematics, music, geometry, algebra, and nature studies, or natural philosophy.

Guarino Guarini of Verona (1374–1460) likewise was a successful humanist teacher whose school in Ferrara attracted students from throughout Italy and beyond. Suggestive of the growing tendency among humanist writers toward formalization, however, was a treatise written around 1460 by his son, Battista Guarino. "On the Order and Method of Teaching and Reading Classical Authors" (*De ordine docendi et studendi*) added little to the precepts of Vergerio and Bruni except to supply more detailed recommendations on the minutiae of classroom management, grading procedures, and lesson preparation.

The curriculum of the *studia humanitatis* for a time afforded explicit career opportunities for public service. It had been anticipated that those who had acquired practical wisdom, or *prudentia,* by absorbing themselves in studying the virtuous examples of Roman statesmen, would become loyal servants of kings and princes. Inspired by the noblest of motives, they would help provide the commonwealth with the wise leadership it so urgently required. Sir Thomas Elyot's *Boke named the Governour,* published in 1531, for example, held out the promise that those schooled in Greek and Roman

moral philosophy and history would come to possess a certain strength of character and integrity of judgment needed in government and public life.

Unfortunately, the growing tendency of sixteenth-century humanist authors was to place exaggerated faith in the content or substance of Renaissance learning rather than to concentrate upon the essential spirit or intent behind it. Paradoxically perhaps, the trend also was toward attention paid to the external forms of learning, not to its presumed capacity to instill judgment or moral virtue. The latter inclination, for instance, is apparent in *Il Libro del Coretegiano* ("Book of the Courtier"), written between 1513 and 1519 by Baldesar Castiglione (1478–1529), the Mantuan ambassador to Rome who was later appointed by Pope Clement VII as Nuncio to Spain. Whereas for Bruni the *studia humanitatis* were considered an integral part of one's training for civic life, for Castiglioni the humanities (*che chiamano d'umanite*) were more of an ancillary "adornment," readily acquired through vernacular translations, for those preparing to participate in the life of city-state politics.

Toward the end of the Quattrocento, emphasis upon the *studia humanitatis* had symbolized a cultural revolution, a protest against medieval formalism and intellectual aridity in all of its varied manifestations. But already in the Cinquecento and the century following, the notion of the humanities as a liberating force for human consciousness had degenerated into a somewhat devitalized and lifeless set of rigid curricular prescriptions, well illustrated in the writings of such later humanists as Jacopo Sadoleto (1477–1547) and Juan Luis Vives (1492–1540). Lost in the process of its systematization and incorporation within formal school curricula was the notion of classical learning as uniquely adapted to nourishing the *ingenium,* or "natural talent," of the individual as an autonomous and self-reflective center of conscious subjectivity. Instead, the humanities came to be regarded now more as discrete bodies of subject matter, studied less for purposes of self-development and enhancement and more for purposes of "well-roundedness" and an outward show of erudition.

By the eighteenth century, the modern sense of "the humanities" had entered English through *les humanites,* the French translation of the Latin *studia humanitatis.* By the nineteenth century, the phrase "humanities," now divested of the original intellectual and moral frame of reference within which it had had its inception, simply designated the study of philosophy, history, poetry, and languages and literature, both ancient and modern.

Christopher J. Lucas

See also *Arete*; CICERO; HUMANISM; LIBERAL EDUCATION; *PAIDEIA*

Bibliography

Bullock, Alan. *The Humanist Tradition in the West.* New York: W.W. Norton, 1985.

Kohl, Benjamin G. "The Changing Concept of the *Studia Humanitatis* in the Early Renaissance." *Renaissance Studies* 6, no. 2 (1992): 185–209.

Kristeller, Paul Oskar. *Renaissance Thought: The Classic, Scholastic, and Humanist Strains.* New York: Harper Torchbooks, 1961.

Proctor, Robert E. *Education's Great Amnesia: Reconsidering the Humanities, from Petrarch to Freud.* Bloomington: Indiana University Press, 1988.

T

Taoism

A subtle and complex facet of traditional Chinese culture. Its precise dimensions have often been debated, by Eastern and Western interpreters alike. Such debate is understandable, for Taoists have historically eschewed self-definition: The contours of their tradition have almost always been fluid and unbounded. Often the only feasible method of determining a "Taoist" viewpoint is by comparison with other traditions (especially Confucianism), from which Taoists sometimes distinguished themselves.

To most in China as well as the West, the term *Taoist* has usually (though inaccurately) been understood as referring most properly to ideas and values expressed in two Chinese texts of the classical period (that is, of the fourth to third centuries B.C.)—the *Tao te ching* (otherwise known as *Lao-tzu*) and the *Chuang-tzu*. Each was traditionally regarded as an exposition of the thought of a single great mind, though modern research has demonstrated that each is actually the product of a prolonged period of accretion, that is, that each text contains ideas from numerous minds, generations or even centuries apart.

In addition, however, the field of Taoism actually includes much more. Most important, Taoism includes a coherent religious tradition that began to evolve in late Antiquity. That tradition has never enjoyed the same celebrity or respect among intellectuals (Chinese or Western) that the "Lao-Chuang" Taoism of classical times has enjoyed. In fact, to the present, many teachers and writers continue to dismiss later Taoism as a degeneration: Many continue to call it "popular Taoism," insisting that it consists of nothing more than the superstitions of the ignorant masses. Such is certainly not the case, as extensive research of the 1970s through the 1990s has clearly demonstrated. The Taoist religion actually reflects the ideals of thoughtful men and women who were often highly educated, well to do, and deeply respected by China's cultural and political leaders. The ideals of such later Taoists reveal some of the deeper values that characterize Taoism as a whole, and its significance for issues of education, society, and culture.

At first glance, Taoist concepts and values might seem irrelevant to the philosophy of education. Certainly no Taoist writer of any period advocated any form of public education. In fact, Taoism can be sharply contrasted in that regard with Confucianism: Confucians of all periods deeply valued education as an indispensable prerequisite for social/political order and meaningful human life. Taoists disagreed, because they disputed the Confucians' notions of (1) a healthy society, (2) responsible government, and (3) desirable change. The positions of each tradition rested in turn upon contrasting assumptions regarding human nature and the nature of the world. The Confucians were essentially humanistic: They assumed that human society was the primary locus of all meaning and value. Taoists, on the other hand, always conceived the ultimate locus of meaning and value to lie not in the activities of human beings, but rather in a deeper reality, a universal natural reality that they called *the Tao*. Though "the Tao" eludes definition, the *Tao te ching* generally describes it as the creative and harmonizing impulse behind all natural phenomena: It provides all things with an environment conducive to their natural development, and is constantly at work in the world in subtle and imperceptible ways, guiding all things to a natural and healthy fulfillment. The intuitive certainty of such a reliable universal reality led certain people in ancient China to reject emphatically the Confucians' assumption that human beings are qualitatively distinct from and superior to all other living things. Such people generally remained anonymous, but for convenience we may employ the term *classical Taoist* for those who contributed to the *Tao te ching* and the *Chuang-tzu*. Those people believed that it is precisely such human peculiarities as rationality and the ability to effect change in the external world that has alienated us from the natural order and created all of the world's problems. The world, they asserted, had been in perfect harmony until humans began trying to "improve" things. So the true goal of human life, both individually and collectively, is to "unlearn" such typical but "unnatural" behavior and to return to the patterns implicit within the benign natural order.

From this perspective, the classical Taoist attitude toward education becomes clear. Just as the contributors to the *Lao-tzu* and *Chuang-tzu* were skeptical of the institutions of government, so also were they deeply cynical concerning the idea that humanity could ever devise a program or system that could create a healthy, peaceful society. From the classical Taoist perspective, acting upon such ideas could only increase disorder in the world, for the true source of all order and harmony is the natural reality of the Tao, and willful human activity of any kind—however well-intentioned—can only interfere with it. Thus, the *Tao te ching* and *Chuang-tzu* often ridicule the very notion of "learning." It is upon that fundamental premise that Taoists are generally at odds with the Confucians, as well as with most of Western thought: They reject not only the value of formal education, but also the assumptions that underlie the insistence of Confucians and Westerners that such education is even desirable. Taoist thought clearly implies that children have no need whatsoever to be molded or uplifted: Young humans, like all living things, are naturally guided to a natural fulfillment, in harmony with the rest of the world. But unlike other living things, humans have gone astray: Something about our uniquely discriminating consciousness engenders a nonholistic perception of the world. Humans (especially campaigning humanists like the Confucians) fail to appreciate the reality of the Tao, so (like virtually all Westerners of every stripe) they harbor mistaken

fears that we must act to create a good world.

The classical Taoists had such faith in the natural harmony of the world that they regarded "education" as not only unnecessary but as actually viciously destructive to individual, society, and the natural order alike. Westerners are likely to be shocked by such arguments, because the dominant Western concept of life shares the Confucians' premise that the world inherently tends toward chaos and requires the redemptive activity of human society. Whereas Westerners and Confucians thus assume a moral responsibility to educate, Taoists assume a moral responsibility not to do so.

While the classical Taoists would have had no use for any policy of organized schooling, their writings are nonetheless replete with models for education in other senses. The very composition and transmission of the materials that we find in the *Tao te ching* and *Chuang-tzu* indicate that the classical Taoists did value the verbal communication of important insights. When the contributors to those texts disparage "learning," what they are rejecting is any deliberate effort to induce an artificial transformation that would turn us yet further away from our inherent harmony with each other and the world around us. But in another sense, the classical Taoists clearly did agree on the need for some form of instruction, for they insist that most people embrace deeply misguided ideas about life. The Taoist classics (and later Chinese literature as well) are full of stories of wise people who help disabuse others of such deluded ideas. In so doing, these wise individuals help others "follow the Tao" by guiding them in a healthful direction. Thus, there is an abiding Taoist ideal of assisting others in a profound personal transformation, generally described as the attainment of true wisdom. Within that context, there is a suggestion of a positive role for a teacher, in the sense of one who has attained such wisdom and assists others in their process of reattaining harmony with the Tao.

It is within the later Taoist tradition (the so-called "Taoist religion") that we see these ideals articulated and put into effect. The earliest Taoist religious movement (second to fourth centuries) seldom seem to stress such goals. Their concerns were generally (1) integrating the sociopolitical order with the deeper forces of the world, and (2) enhancing the physical and moral well-being of individual men and women. Their ideal was the condition known as *T'ai-p'ing*, "Grand Tranquility":

It was a state in which all the concentric spheres of the organic Chinese universe, which contained nature as well as society, were perfectly attuned, communicated with each other in a balanced rhythm of timeliness, and brought maximum fulfillment to each living being. (Seidel)

Indeed, many medieval Taoists conceived their purpose to be neither individual accomplishment nor social amelioration, but actually a universal actuation of T'ai-p'ing, to effect a physical, social, political, and spiritual perfection that encompassed all people. Some even worked to extend such benefits to other living things, or even to the shades of the deceased.

Increasingly, however, the concern of Taoists came to be focused upon the spiritual perfection of individuals. Leaders provided moral guidance, and instruction in various forms of meditation. Occasional individuals saw themselves as the guardians of heavenly secrets, to be vouchsafed only to those who could demonstrate their worth in terms of ritual mastery or the knowledge of secret data concerning otherworldly forces. Such esoterism remained a characteristic of the Taoist priesthood to the twentieth century. Religious education in that context was exclusivistic, and sometimes seems to have ignored broader social concerns. Another strain of Taoism, however, worked to integrate all levels of society by incorporating local religious activities into a common liturgical framework, alongside elements of the ritual tradition of the imperial court. It was that persistent ideal of the universal integration of society that led to later Taoism's being misnamed "popular Taoism."

In general, Taoism in premodern China stressed ideals of personal spiritual cultivation. Those ideals contributed both to the acceptance of Buddhism in China and to the rebirth of Confucianism in the eleventh to twelfth centuries. Most accounts of Taoism (in Asia and the West alike) continue to perpetuate the simplistic and mistaken assertion that those ideals were the core of the sublime philosophy of *Lao-tzu* and *Chuang-tzu* but were thereafter lost, to be replaced by a foolish pursuit of physical immortality. In actuality, it is dubious whether anyone in traditional China was really intent upon achieving mere physical longevity, as opposed to a spiritual immortality. Indeed, such misconceptions project upon Chinese culture the quite alien concept of a body/spirit duality. In actuality, Taoists of all periods aspired to a state of spiritual perfection, which they describe as transcending the apparent boundaries of life and death. Occasionally, aspirants may have succumbed to romantic illusions that their efforts would magically transform them into sublime beings who were immune to death. Such beings (called *hsien*) populate much of Chinese literature. But Taoist writings of all periods insist that the goal of life is not some magical transformation, but rather the attainment of spiritual perfection through moral purification and the careful realignment of personal consciousness. Contrary to the charges of both traditional Confucians and modern Western (or Westernized) intellectuals, Taoists actually sought not to evade or escape reality, but rather to contribute to a spiritual transformation of reality, beginning with oneself.

A key issue for modern minds is whether or not anyone and everyone can follow such a path and achieve the highest goals. Most Asian systems of thought (including Taoism, Confucianism, and Buddhism) answered such questions in a way that modern minds often struggle to understand. Modern liberal beliefs insist that "everyone is equal" and therefore that "the path to success" should be "open to everyone." Most Asian traditions begin from quite different premises, which, they would argue, are much more realistic. It hardly needs noting that no Asian society has ever advanced any notion of universal equality; indeed, before contact with the modern West, few Asian thinkers of any stripe would have even entertained such notions. In China, both Confucians and Taoists began with the observation that, in real life, people are quite different, and some simply do not succeed at undertakings at which others succeed. The Chinese examination system, which recruited government officials, was certainly elitist in that it was designed to separate the sheep from the goats, certifying only those of the greatest talent and ability. And yet in another sense, the system was actually antielitist, in that anyone could enter the system, regardless of parentage, wealth, or social background. (Of course, no one ever gave any thought to the modern notion that it could or should have been open to women.)

The spiritual life for Confucianism and Taoism was understood in similar terms: Moral and spiritual perfectibility is assumed of everyone, and the undertaking of the process of self-perfection is theoretically open to anyone, but in real life most people will never attempt such things, and few will actually persevere to achieve the goal. Both Confucians and Taoists assumed that some people have a moral or spiritual talent that others lack, and that our true concern should be to identify those who possess such talent and to facilitate their development. More particularly, Taoism assumed that such people would be self-selecting: Certain individuals will distinguish themselves by their alacrity in understanding and pursuing moral and spiritual goals. And, unlike Confucianism, the Taoist religion included women in this pursuit. Stories abound of men and women of exceptional perception and dedication who succeed where others fail.

Sometimes such people pass tests of their character and determination without even realizing that they are being tested; sometimes they prove their worth not only by forgoing worldly fulfillments, but, more important, by shedding all self-centeredness and misconceptions about the spiritual life. Some texts stress that since each person is intrinsically different, mentors must mold both the content and the form of each individual's guidance to that person's unique needs. Hence, no coherent curriculum or teaching style was possible. In fact, in contrast to Zen Buddhism (which Taoism deeply influenced), Taoism never formalized the master/student relationship, or even insisted upon its necessity. Aspirants of sufficient talent might need little more than an occasional gentle nudge, and sometimes *hsien* provide such assistance without anyone even knowing it.

Taoism presented the goal of life as a highly subtle refinement of the spirit that often presupposed moral refinement but did not necessarily require any formal system of training. Taoist "education" was thus highly personalized and highly spiritualized. Historically, however, prominent Taoists were often highly educated in more traditional senses as well, not only as scholars, writers, poets, bibliographers, and historians, but also as botanists, pharmacists, chemists, and astronomers. The Taoist life was thus understood not as an alternative to all other human pursuits, but as a path toward the holistic unification of one's personal reality with all that is truly real and valuable, encompassing both society and the natural world.

Russell Kirkland

See also BUDDHISM; CONFUCIANISM; HUMAN NATURE; NATURALISM; ROUSSEAU

Bibliography
Cahill, Suzanne. "Practice Makes Perfect: Paths to Transcendence for Women in Medieval China." *Taoist Resources* 2, no. 2 (1990): 23–42.
Chuang-tzu. *Chuang-tzu: The Seven Inner Chapters and Other Writings from the Book of Chuang-tzu.* Translated by A.C. Graham. London: Allen and Unwin, 1981.
Kirkland, Russell. "The Making of an Immortal: The Exaltation of Ho Chih-chang." *Numen* 38 (1991): 201–14.
———. "Person and Culture in the Taoist Tradition." *Journal of Chinese Religion* 20 (1992): 77–90.
Kohn, Livia. *Early Chinese Mysticism: Philosophy and Soteriology in the Taoist Tradition.* Princeton: Princeton University Press, 1992.
———. *The Taoist Experience: An Anthology.* Albany: State University of New York Press, 1993.
Munro, Donald, ed. *Individualism and Holism: Studies in Confucian and Taoist Values.* Ann Arbor: University of Michigan Center for Chinese Studies, 1985.
Schipper, Kristofer. *The Taoist Body.* Berkeley: University of California Press, 1993.
Seidel, Anna. "T'ai-p'ing." In *The Encyclopedia of Religion,* vol. 14, 251. New York: Macmillan, 1987.
Sivin, Nathan. "On the Word 'Taoist' as a Source of Perplexity." *History of Religions* 17 (1978): 303–31.
Tao te ching. *Chinese Classics: Tao te ching.* Translated by D.C. Lau. Hong Kong: Chinese University of Hong Kong Press, 1982.

Teaching and Leaning
As with all matters, teaching and learning get their philosophical significance from some aspect of the human condition; in this case, it is that we are born ignorant and helpless and must acquire everything that makes life possible and enjoyable. The empirical question is "How does this happen?" The standard answer is "Each of us learns it all." But human learning does not simply happen, for the most part; much of it takes place in a teaching-and-learning context, where one person intentionally teaches another. These simple facts set the stage for philosophical confusion and investigation.

That humans learn may be their most important individual characteristic. That they teach may be their most important social characteristic. A being that cannot learn is at best a tragically deprived creature, at worst, nonhuman. Human life where teaching does not or cannot take place is almost unimaginable. Considered as a relationship, teaching and learning, as James E. McClellan said, "is one of the great modal forms of social interaction without which human life would be impossible" (94).

But how are teaching and learning related? It is difficult even to decide how to parse that question. Clearly, there is some relationship, for it is always relevant to ask, "Who taught you that?" about any learned behavior, belief, or ability, even though the question might be rejected with an answer like, "No one, I just picked it up in the course of daily living." And if one claimed to be teaching someone, a learning claim is sure to be lurking around somewhere, perhaps as a prediction, perhaps as a justification, perhaps as evidence for the teaching claim.

Philosophers have tried various ways of viewing teaching and learning in the attempt to get the relationship between them clear. Teaching, in one view, implies learning, while in another it causes learning. It has been viewed as a task (noun) for which "learn" is the achievement (verb), or it might be that learning should be seen as the intention (or goal) of the activities of teaching.

None of these attempts is fully successful at capturing the richness of the teaching-learning relationship. In every case, exceptions can be found that show why the proposed relationship cannot suffice. Teaching cannot imply learning, for example, because if the claim is taken seriously it would mean that one could not truthfully assert that teaching was going on without assessing whether learning also was going on. Yet we recognize teaching even when we are not sure whether learning is resulting; a description or report that someone is teaching does not, therefore, require a test of the students' learning, and teaching cannot, therefore, (strictly) imply learning.

Even the most sensible-sounding of these claims—that learning is (or must be) the intention of teaching—is open to challenge. Imagine a teacher who is helping his students understand a poem they have memorized; imagine further that he does not add any information to their repertoires of knowledge; no learning (in a strict sense) is intended, merely (!) an understanding of what the students have already learned or know.

It would be a mistake to say that it's not teaching going on in such a case, yet in any strict sense, learning seems far from the teacher's intention.

Such attempts seem to assume that the meaning of the concepts of teaching and learning can be spelled out in fairly simple ways. But that is a temptation to be avoided, since each of the concepts in the pair spreads out over a wide range of conditions.

Consider that first question: "How does the individual acquire everything that makes life possible and enjoyable?" The answer, remember, was, "Each of us learns it all." What is learning contrasted with here? Only innate behavior (or ideas, or thoughts, or whatever the object is), but not with any other mode of acquisition. Considered this broadly, learning is any way at all in which human beings acquire such things. Children learn to recognize their mothers, to walk, to talk, to eat with a fork, to control their anger, that Columbus discovered America, that there are monsters under their beds, everything.

If we now think of learning as a single process, we are faced with explaining the differences between learning how to play tennis and learning that pain hurts. In some sense, everything mentioned here is "learned"—but if it is the same sense, that sense does not make fine distinctions possible. Note also that any talk of "the process of learning" seems as misplaced as talk of "the process of teaching."

Teaching is equally befuddling if squeezed into such a Procrustean bed; it too must change with its object. Teaching a child how to make a bed involves very different matters from teaching it that George Washington was the first president of the United States. Any attempt to show that the same interpersonal or psychological processes are involved in the two examples must fly in the face of apparent contradictions.

As an aside, C.J.B. Macmillan and J.W. Garrison (1988) analyzed the concept of teaching for its logical structure and claimed that the concept of learning could be similarly treated. No claim was made that the same psychological processes take place in examples like those given above; but it was claimed that there is a single logical structure or process, and that that is captured by the logic of questions. Whether this conception of teaching and learning will solve most of the empirical and conceptual questions is still an open question.

Perhaps what is most important in the discussion of teaching and learning is to avoid assuming too much about the relationship between them, or about the "nature" of either of them. These are accommodating concepts that enable us to communicate in most policy-setting and practical contexts with great ease. Problems arise when we try to develop all-encompassing, high-flown theories of either learning (where psychologists are particularly tempted to pontificate) or teaching (where philosophers and curriculum specialists hold sway), for the temptation in such theory development is to unify rather than to distinguish. So the distinctions get lost and along with them, the richness—not to say fecundity—of the concepts of teaching and learning and (more important) of the human relationships those concepts try to capture.

More problematic, perhaps, are bureaucratic attempts to define either learning or teaching by giving a set of necessary or sufficient conditions that are stated as observable behaviors of the learner or teacher. Such attempts often seem to be necessitated by institutional requirements that call for clear criteria for accountability. But to put it bluntly, neither of these is a behavioral concept, and bureaucratic rules that require such a definition are doomed to misrepresent the very things they are designed to promote.

Teaching and learning are central to any discussion of education; the last-noted problems are what result when philosophical reflection is ignored altogether or is turned to other purposes.

C.J.B. Macmillan

See also CURRICULUM AND INSTRUCTION; DIALECTIC; EXPERIENCE; LEARNING, THEORIES OF; MEANING; SCHOOL; SOCRATES

Bibliography
Ericson, D.P., and F.S. Ellett, Jr. "Teacher Accountability and the Causal Theory of Teaching." *Educational Theory* 37 (1987): 277–93.
Garrison, J.W., and C.J.B. Macmillan. "A Philosophical Critique of Process-Product Research on Teaching." *Educational Theory* 34 (1984): 255–74.
Green, T. F. *The Activities of Teaching.* New York: McGraw-Hill, 1971.
Komisar, B.P. "Teaching: Act and Enterprise." In *Concepts of Teaching: Philosophical Essays,* edited by C.J.B. Macmillan and T.W. Nelson. Chicago: Rand McNally, 1968.
McClellan, J.E. *Philosophy of Education.* Englewood Cliffs, N.J.: Prentice Hall, 1976.
Macmillan, C.J.B., and J.W. Garrison. *A Logical Theory of Teaching: Erotetics and Intentionality.* Dordrecht: Kluwer, 1988.
Pendlebury, S. "Teaching: Response and Responsibility." *Educational Theory* 36 (1986): 349–54.
Plato. *Meno.* Translated by W.K.C. Guthrie. In *Plato: Protagoras and Meno.* Baltimore: Penguin, 1956.

Technology

Philosophical thinking about technology in education, such as it exists, may be placed into three categories: substantive, instrumentalist, and pluralist. These correspond to the answer implicit in each to the question of technological determinism—that is, whether technologies, from bows and arrows to writing to computers, determine human action and thought or whether the reverse is true. For substantivists, technology is at the helm of human affairs, it has inherent properties either good or ill, and consequently works to liberate or to enslave humanity. For the instrumentalist, however, tools and techniques are mere objects that await the animation of a human purpose to give them moral life; collectively or individually, someone somewhere is always responsible for technology's benefits or harm. In contrast to both, the pluralist approach avoids strong ontological commitments, focusing instead on technology's complexities; one must avoid hasty generalizations and study technological phenomena in their particular settings.

In education, the first two categories may be subdivided according to whether they lean "pro" or "anti." Protechnology substantivists argue that educators' methods and aims should follow the trail blazed by technological innovation. Some instructional design theorists even champion a paradigmatic shift in schools such that teacher preparation can largely be abandoned in favor of the technologically mediated delivery of instruction. Further, instructional programming should not be confined to imitating teachers, even the best of them. In opposition to this, antitechnology substantivists hold that on balance technology represents a malicious force. It embodies a powerful "mindset" that diminishes our basic humanity by, for example, delegitimating certain modes of expression (such as emotions and orality), making possible oppressive institutional arrangements (such as surveillance), and sanctioning the manipulation and domination of nature. For these reasons a radical pedagogy must strive to oppose and overcome it; inherent drawbacks far outweigh technology's ostensible benefits.

One of the most outspoken proponents of protechnology instrumentalism views computers and other assorted classroom tools as "objects to think with" (Papert). Technologies are more or less salutary depending upon how they are employed. If only individual instructors and designers could be trained properly and the classroom culture made amenable, both simple and advanced technologies hold great and hopeful promise. Less sanguine are the antitechnology instrumentalists, a varied group advancing a "critical theory of technology" (Feenberg). To determine the value of an educational tool, one must always look at its wider social context. In the main, it is argued, technology at present covertly serves the interests of identifiable elites, through, for example, exclusionary credentialing barriers (such as "computer literacy"), or the de-skilling of teachers and other workers. Because of its propensity to conceal domination, until its politics can be unmasked, any given technology should be regarded as "guilty until proven innocent" (Winner).

Pursuant to their prescriptive recommendations, pluralists typically draw more heavily upon survey research concerning how teachers and others have actually used educational technologies. One emerging model is a teacher-technology "partnership," wherein each party can and should determine the instructional situation. In short, technology serves as both a pedagogical "lever" and also as a "fulcrum" around which our educational practices must pivot (Kerr). At another level, some pluralists have suggested a standard of "open-endedness" as the criterion for judging the extent to which a particular technology is truly educative (Underwood and Underwood). Despite its appeal as a compromise position, however, pluralism has as yet not provided a sound basis for its scattered normative commitments. And until it does, pluralist prescriptions must be regarded as provisional and contingent.

David Blacker

See also COMPUTERS; FREEDOM AND DETERMINISM

Bibliography

Apple, Michael. "The New Technology: Is it Part of the Solution or Part of the Problem in Education?" *Computers in the Schools* 8, nos. 1, 2, 3 (1991).

Borgmann, Albert. *Technology and the Character of Contemporary Life: A Philosophical Inquiry.* Chicago: University of Chicago Press, 1984.

Bowers, C.A. *The Cultural Dimensions of Educational Computing: Understanding the Non-Neutrality of Technology.* New York: Teachers College Press, 1988.

Ellul, Jacques. *The Technological Society.* Translated by John Wilkerson. New York: Random House Vintage, 1964.

Feenberg, Andrew. *A Critical Theory of Technology.* New York: Oxford University Press, 1991.

Ferkiss, Victor C. *Technological Man: The Myth and the Reality.* New York: Braziller, 1969.

Fuller, R. Buckminster. *Operating Manual for Spaceship Earth.* Carbondale: Southern Illinois University Press, 1969.

Heinich, Robert. "The Proper Study of Instructional Technology." *Educational Communication and Technology Journal* 32, no. 2 (1984).

Kerr, Stephen T. "Lever and Fulcrum: Educational Technology in Teacher's Thought and Practice." *Teachers College Record* 93, no. 1 (1991): 114–36.

Noble, Douglas. "Computer Literacy and Ideology." *Teachers College Record* 85, no. 4 (1984): 602–14.

Papert, Seymour. *Mindstorms: Children, Computers and Powerful Ideas.* New York: Basic Books, 1980.

Sheingold, Karen, et al. "'I'm the Thinkist, You're the Typist': The Interaction of Technology with the Social Life of Classrooms." *Journal of Social Issues* 40, no. 3 (1984): 49–61.

Shriver, Donald W., Jr. "Man and His Machines: Four Angles of Vision." *Technology and Culture* 13 (1972).

Underwood, Jeanne D.M., and Geoffrey Underwood. *Computers and Learning: Helping Children Acquire Thinking Skills.* London: Basil Blackwell, 1990.

Winner, Langdon. *The Whale and the Reactor: A Search for Limits in an Age of High Technology.* Chicago: University of Chicago Press, 1984.

T

Thomas Aquinas (1225–1274)

A scholastic philosopher and theologian, a Greek scholar who knew no Greek, an epistemologist before the discipline was invented by Descartes, university bred, university centered, a teacher who is still worth learning from. In describing the scholarly life, Bernard of Chartres describes Thomas's life well: Humble in mind, searching seriously, and a life without pressure. Quiet research spent in poverty, living in lands not one's homeland. "They are accustomed to open to many the gates to obscure truths" (John of Salisbury [c. 1125–1180], *Policraticus*: vii, 13).

Thomas Aquinas was born at Rocasecca, near the Benedictine monastery of Monte Cassino in the Kingdom of Sicily (now Italy), probably in 1225. He died on March 7, 1274, at Fossanuova, near Maenza, in the Kingdom of Sicily. The middle of the thirteenth century was an exciting time. With the defeat of the Holy Roman Empire in 1214, Europe had ceased to be theocratic. The Muslim world was enjoying a series of military successes; Muslims were leaders in science and philosophy, and their writings as well as those of the ancient Greeks became available in Europe. Merchants and missionaries were beginning to explore the wider world. The efforts toward Christian religious revival centered on the cities rather than the countryside, and in the universities the diocesan clergy clashed with the new religious orders. In these years Thomas was seldom far distant from a school, a monastery, or a priory. He was an oblate at Monte Cassino (1231–1239), studied grammar, and, as his manuscripts reveal, failed to master calligraphy. During the following five years he studied grammar, logic, and physics at the University of Naples. In April 1244 he joined the Dominican order. After a brief family intervention, he studied at the Dominican house of studies in Paris, Saint-Jacques (1245–1248), and at the *studium generale* in Cologne (1248–1252). As a bachelor, he lectured on the *Sentences* of Peter Lombard in Paris (1252–1256). As a master, he taught at the university there (1256–1259), though he had to be protected by the soldiers of Louis IX at his installation. Between 1259 and 1268 he taught at Naples and then in the Papal States (now Italy), successively at Orvieto, Rome, and Viterbo. He returned to Paris in 1269, remaining there until his departure for Naples in 1272. On December 6, 1273, he experienced something that caused him to say,

"All that I have written seems to me like so much straw compared with what I have seen and what has been revealed to me." Sixteen of his theses were condemned by Etienne Tempier, bishop of Paris, in 1277. He was declared a saint in 1323 and a Doctor of the Church in 1567.

Aquinas received an excellent and traditional education from his Benedictine and Dominican teachers, one of whom was Albert the Great (c. 1200–1280). He studied the seven liberal arts, consisting of the trivium (the art of the word): grammar, rhetoric, and dialectic (logic), and the quadrivium (arts of the real): arithmetic, geometry, astronomy, and music. While at Naples, he studied the natural philosophy of Aristotle and probably his metaphysics at a time before they were taught in Paris. Thomas then studied scripture and theology in Paris and Cologne. In his more than twenty years of teaching, he employed all the pedagogical methods current in the higher education of his day. In the *lectio* (reading) a text was usually but not always read aloud (there were no printed texts) to students and explained, sometimes quite simply, at other times quite elaborately. Under this heading Thomas taught *expositiones* (which included commentaries on Job, Boethius, Dionysius, the *Liber de Causis*, and the letters of St. Paul), *postillae* (commentaries on the Psalms, Isaiah, Jeremiah, and the Lamentations of Jeremiah), a *glossa continua* (glosses on the four Gospels), *lecturae* (commentaries on Matthew and John), *commendationes* (inaugural lectures), and *sententiae* (commentaries on eleven works of Aristotle). The *quaestio* (question) called into question a received opinion, and, in resolving the doubts raised, the teacher moved toward a deeper understanding of the matter. In the *disputatio* (academic disputation) current questions were publicly discussed, and the master then gave an authoritative formulation both to the dispute and to its resolution. In the *summa* (theological synthesis) the entire range of opinion, old and new, was set forth in a series of *quaestiones* in a methodical and coherent fashion. Beginning in 1260, the Flemish Dominican William of Moerbeke (c. 1215–1286) made available to Thomas both a series of translations of Aristotle and others from the original Greek, as well as revisions of earlier Latin translations. As Robert I. Burns has pointed out, some of Thomas's works were written as missionary manuals to be used in scholarly discussions in the Muslim world.

In early 1256 Thomas gave his inaugural lecture as a master at the University of Paris. It placed his educational thought in full theological perspective. He used Psalm 104:13 as scaffolding: "From thy lofty abode thou waterest the mountains; the earth is satisfied with the fruit of thy work." God waters the mountains, and the mountains in turn fertilize the plains. So God teaches the wise who in turn teach their students. In a few pages Thomas introduced the theme of Dionysian continuity with the teacher as intermediary. Since truth comes from God, it is sublime; as mountains are the first to capture the light and protect the inhabitants from invasion, so teachers are worthy of respect for their ability to illuminate the students and protect them from error; since the mountains cannot hold all the waters poured on them, neither can teachers be all-knowing nor should they expect their students to receive all they give; since students are the recipients, they ought to be humble; since students are to be fruitful, they must go beyond their teachers.

Between 1256 and 1259, Thomas collected a set of twenty-nine *quaestiones disputatae* on truth, *De veritate*. The eleventh question was devoted to the teacher, and it constitutes his fullest treatment on the subject, though to offset its Augustinian focus it should be supplemented by *Summa Theologiae* 1, 117. While the questions asked seem and really are theological (Can God, the angels, humans be teachers? Is teaching contemplative or active?), the treatment is quite Aristotelian and philosophical. Teaching is an action as it proceeds from a teacher; learning is that same action as it occurs in the learner. All four causes are brought into play. The principal efficient cause is the learner; the instrumental efficient cause is the teacher or, more proximately, the teacher's verbal discourse. The formal cause is the rational discourse in the learner as induced by the teacher. The material cause is the learner or, more precisely, the learner's intellect. The final cause is the knowledge, which is the term of the rational discourse in the learner. Like so many concepts employed by Thomas, teaching is analogous. It refers to the generation of knowledge by way of illumination, the light of reason created by God and possibly strengthened by angelic intervention. It refers to the generation of knowledge induced in the learner by way of speech in which the object to be known is presented. It refers to the verbal discourse by means of which knowledge is generated. It refers to the knowledge that is generated as act or as habit. And it refers to discipline (itself an analogous term), the reception of knowledge from another.

Crucial to this analysis are several distinctions. Being taught by another is dependent on self-discovery; what is taught depends on what the learner already knows. Self-discovery is like natural breathing; being taught by another, like artificial respiration. One is natural; the other artful, involving the use of signs. Because physical objects can potentially be understood in a great many ways, words that focus on one meaning are more easily understood than the opaque object. Because signs are more readily intelligible than things, they are more easily grasped. Because not everything known is an object of perception (in which case the teacher, by pointing something out, functions accidentally) but depends on a series of steps, the teacher may be needed to order, focus, simplify, and exemplify the material. Even here, the signs presented must not only be signs of an intelligibility but be connected to sensible images; for, though the intellect does not employ a bodily organ, it has need of the imagination and the senses. An injured organ, such as an eye, prevents intellectual understanding of, for example, an object as colored (*Summa Theologiae*: 1, 84, 7).

The learner is active, not passive. Patients under a physician's care still have to heal themselves. Living things have an active potency, a capability of actualizing themselves (Aristotle's *De Anima*: 431a); they are not passive nor essentially dependent on an outside agent. But in teaching, learners are dependent on the teacher, who functions as a true yet secondary cause of coming to know. Furthermore, understood correctly, learning by discovery is an immanent act, while teaching is a transient act. Just as in an immanent act, the action goes on in the learner, but in the learner as moved by the teacher. The Aristotelian maxim "Action (in a transient act) is in the patient"—and not in the agent—highlights the centrality of the learner in the teaching process. The student is active in yet another sense. While the teacher may call attention to some feature of a demonstration, students must themselves see the appropriateness of the premises and see that the conclusion flows from the premises. Otherwise, what the student has is opinion or belief, not knowledge. Not that belief is a bad thing. Docility, for example, an integral part of the virtue of prudence, involves a readiness to be taught how to act, especially through the experience of others rather than simply by their demonstrations (*Summa Theologiae*: 2–2, 49, 3). Likewise, the certitude students have in the conclusions they reach arises from their own understanding. As Thomas says, the teacher is the cause of the knowledge gathered but is not the cause of the certitude with which what is known is held. On the other hand, what is simply received from the teacher can be held with an analogous certitude, but a certitude based on trust rather than on the light of the evidence. Teaching is active, though it does have a contemplative side: Insofar as teachers prepare their material, this activity is immanent, and it is also immanent because, by the act of teaching, teachers are not impoverished as they would be if they physically handed something over to another. Similarly, discovery learning is immanent; learning through being taught is transient. Teaching is analogous to creation: Creation is formally an immanent act of God, virtually a transient act.

Thomas's fullest discussion of the order of learning is found in his never-completed *Commentary on the De Trinitate of Boethius* (1255–1259). In questions five and six, there are speculative and practical sciences. This simple division turns out to be quite complicated, for it cuts four ways. On the basis of end in view, philosophy is theoretical because its end is knowing; the arts are practical because their end is action. On the basis of the human end, which is happiness, physics and rational philosophy are theoretical; moral philosophy is practical (here Thomas is using the Stoics' tripartite division). On the basis of special ends, agriculture is practical but dialectic is theoretical, though both are arts. On the basis of proximity to practice, clinical medicine is practical; classroom instruction, theoretical. The seven liberal arts do not adequately divide theoretical philosophy. The trivium and the quadrivium are all, indeed, ways of coming to know. Logic is part of the trivium; mathematics encompasses all parts of the quadrivium. But among the seven liberal arts there is no place for the mechanical arts, such as medicine and agriculture, nor for moral science or metaphysics.

For Thomas the speculative sciences are three: physics or natural philosophy, mathematics, and metaphysics. Logic plays a special role as a necessary instrument (*logica utens*) for all three. The three adequately divide the speculative realm: Physics is concerned with sensible things that depend on matter for their being and for being understood; mathematics is concerned with sensible things that depend on matter for their being but not for being understood; metaphysics is concerned with the immaterial, though the immaterial may be enmeshed in matter. The three sciences correspond to three different operations of the mind: Physics abstracts universals from particulars; mathematics abstracts form from sensible matter; and metaphysics separates through acts of judgment. Metaphysics ultimately furnishes principles that ground the other two, and physics uses mathematics. Thus, by nature, the order is metaphysics, mathematics, and physics. But the order of learning does not correspond to that order. Logic precedes, because of its universal instrumental character. Mathematics follows; for it does not require extensive experience. Then come the natural sciences, which do demand such experience. Metaphysics goes beyond the senses and imagination and yet needs their input and therefore comes last of the three. Each has its own methods. Mathematics uses a method closest to the way humans learn most easily; it is concerned with uniformities and exactness. Natural science has to be concerned with particularities and requires multiple steps in its analysis, moving from effects to causes, particulars to universals, multiples to simples. Metaphysics is synthetic and attempts to gain insights that see the connection of causes to their effects, universals to particulars, simples to the multiples they generate. George Klubertanz introduces a nuance: Certain questions in metaphysics presuppose a knowledge of the philosophy of nature, which knowledge, however, does not constitute a necessary base for metaphysics.

Some additional comments may be helpful. Thomas would take a stand for the plurality of forms of knowledge, much as P.H. Hirst does in his *Logic of Education*. Sciences are differentiated not only by their subject matter but also by the method used to come to know them. Richard McKeon, through his twentieth-century sensibilities, contrasts the ways of knowing as perceived by Thomas and Bonaventure (1217–1274). In his commentary on Aristotle's *Ethics,* Thomas inserts the moral sciences between physics and metaphysics. They cannot come before the natural sciences because they too require experience. They are to be studied later than physics because they require, in addition to experience, a soul free from passion. They should come before metaphysics because practical wisdom relates to the human world and is ordered to that higher wisdom that concerns itself with the ultimate cause of all things. Thomas's general position here may be profitably compared to that of Moses Maimonides (1135–1204) in chapters 31–34 of the first part of *The Guide for the Perplexed.* Both are heavily indebted to Aristotle. Thomas's position may be profitably contrasted with those of Cicero, Augustine, and Bacon. Cicero (106–43 B.C.) places mathematics, astronomy, and music first, for grammar and congruity of speech rely on having something to say. Dialectic, with its reasoned order, follows grammar and is followed by rhetoric, which adds the note of persuasion—all of which culminate in eloquence or wisdom. The list of studies proposed by Augustine (354–430) is a grab bag without any order: history, natural history, biology, botany, zoology, mineralogy, astronomy, medicine, agriculture, navigation, dialectics, rhetoric, arithmetic, and music. Francis Bacon (1561–1626), in book two of *The Advancement of Learning,* continues to use the traditional terminology but to his own Alice-like purposes: history, poesy, and philosophy constitute the order of knowledge. Mathematics becomes a part of physics. Physics and metaphysics divide up the four causes. The speculative is ordered to the practical, and all knowledge culminates in knowledge of the human. But all three writers are aware of the difference between the logical and the psychological order.

While Thomas spells out in some detail the order of learning for logic and the three theoretical sciences, what order is to be followed with regard to the mechanical arts is not spelled out. According to the practice of the day, medicine, law, and theology follow the seven liberal arts, but Thomas furnishes no theoretical rationale for this move.

One notable omission from Thomas's course of studies is history. It would seem that for Thomas the philosopher, like Aristotle, history is the realm of chance. Reason can discover a vertical causal ordering in things (an ordering that can then be taught); it cannot discover a horizontal ordering in time, for in time there are accidentally ordered causes, and a *regressus in infinitum* is indeed possible. As the title of his article, "Of History as a Calculus Whose Term Is Science," indicates, Bernard Muller-Thym argues for a more nuanced position.

Finally, Thomas finds a moral dimension to learning. The student's particular virtue is studiousness, and one of the contrary vices, in-

quisitiveness (*Summa Theologiae:* 2–2, 166–67). Devotion to learning is a potential part of temperance—that is, it is allied and complementary to temperance, more specifically, to modesty. Studiousness has links to Aristotle's dictum that "All men by nature desire to know" and to Albert the Great's zest for scientific discovery. But knowing has an affective side as well; for knowing is directed by appetite to this or that, and that appetite is appropriate only when knowing is not stretched beyond due measure. Thomas does not linger on the contrary vice that disposes the body to be unwilling to make the effort to know. Moses Maimonides, in *The Guide to the Perplexed,* book 1, chapter 34, presents a fuller treatment of the sluggard. Thomas spends much more space on the opposite contrary of inquisitiveness, the hankering to know, even to pry, for reasons having little to do with love of learning. "Knowledge puffs up" is the appropriate Pauline dictum. And the discussion of this vice at one and the same time harkens back to Augustine's discussion of concupiscence of the eyes (*Confessions:* 10, 34), bows to the hostility of Thomas's contemporaries to "profane science," and resonates with today's problems of selling secrets in the industrial world and young peoples' desire to experience the margins of the human.

Walter P. Krolikowski

See also ARISTOTLE; LOGIC; METAPHYSICS; PETER LOMBARD; SCHOLASTICISM

Bibliography

Burns, Robert I. "Christian-Islamic Confrontation in the West: The Thirteenth-Century Dream of Conversion." *American Historical Review* 76 (1971): 1386–1434.

Chenu, Marie-Dominique. *Toward Understanding Saint Thomas.* Chicago: Regnery, 1964.

Hirst, P.H. *The Logic of Education.* New York: Humanities Press, 1970.

Klubertanz, George. "St. Thomas on Learning Metaphysics." *Gregorianum* 35 (1954): 3–17.

McKeon, Richard. "Philosophy and Theology, History and Science in the Thought of Bonaventura and Thomas Aquinas." *Journal of Religion* 58, Supplement (1978): S24–51.

Muller-Thym, Bernard J. "Of History As a Calculus Whose Term Is Science." *Modern Schoolman* 19 (1942): 41–47, 73–76.

Thomas Aquinas. *The Division and Methods of the Sciences: Questions V and VI of His Commentary on the De Trinitate of Boethius.* Translated and edited by Armand Maurer. Toronto: Institute of Mediaeval Studies, 1986.

———. *Opera Omnia.* Rome: Ed. Leonine, 1882–.

———. *The Teacher* (Truth, *Question Eleven*). Chicago: Regnery, 1954.

Van Ackeren, Gerald Francis. *Sacra Doctrina: The Subject of the First Question of the Summa Theologica of St. Thomas Aquinas.* Rome: Catholic Book Agency, 1952.

Weisheipl, James A. *Friar Thomas D'Aquino: His Life, Thought, and Work.* Washington: Catholic University of America Press, 1983.

Toleration

Toleration is prickly, repellent, and commonly ignored. To tolerate something or someone requires having a negative attitude toward it (or him or her), being disposed to act upon that attitude, and yet refraining from doing so. Hence, those who tolerate resist their inclinations. But those who are tolerated will usually seek more than grudging restraint; they will often desire full acceptance. Toleration is thus distasteful and against the grain both for those who tolerate and for those who are tolerated.

Toleration is not inevitably laudable; even the most tolerant person or society must set limits to toleration, and cannot, for example, condone murder or abuse of persons. It is morally valuable only in certain contexts and within certain limits; one who tolerates anything and everything is morally bankrupt, because extreme permissiveness crosses the boundary from principled toleration to amoral lassitude.

Toleration occurs in the personal, social, political, and legal domains. It is frequently ordinary, unthinking practice, as when a parent tolerates messy and boisterous children or a society tolerates an abominable highway system or corrupt, self-serving politicians. Moreover, all societies in fact practice or require toleration of one sort or another, whether of the oppressed for the oppressor or of some despised class for the dominant group. Toleration is only occasionally a political doctrine and positive value. As such, it is most closely associated with the ideology of Western European liberal democracy. That ideology was formed in part by Western European history.

In the fifteenth and sixteenth centuries, Western Europe was the arena of ferocious debates over religious toleration, partly as a result of the Protestant rebellion against Catholicism. The conceptual focus of these debates was conscience, or the freedom of belief. The religious debate was settled in favor of toleration, perhaps mainly as the result of the mutual exhaustion of the participants. In the age of John Locke and John Milton, discussion of toleration shifted to the arena of politics, and freedom of speech became the central issue. With the nineteenth century and the work of John Stuart Mill, however, the arena of discussion changed to that of personal life, and the focus of the debate shifted to freedom to devise individual ways of life. Hence, the debate shifted over the centuries from conscience to speech to action, but, whatever the arena, freedom was the center of discussion, and toleration was largely its unsung accompaniment.

Toleration's reclusive nature is apparent in its historical development, for even major figures of Western liberal philosophy, such as John Locke (1632–1704) and John Stuart Mill (1806–1873), rarely mention toleration explicitly, and none analyze it in detail.

An explanation is found in the values liberals do wholeheartedly cherish, those of respect for the freedom and integrity of the individual. The focus on the individual and individual freedom is a distinguishing characteristic of Western liberal philosophy. This concern is expressed in the effort to safeguard individual lives from the intrusions of government (Locke's particular concern) and the intrusions of other persons (Mill's major theme). But genuine personal freedom requires that government, society, and other individuals refrain from intruding into an individual's affairs even when the individual is engaging in conduct that others find distasteful or immoral. If esteem for individual freedom and integrity allowed only beliefs, speech, and actions that others find admirable, that avowed veneration would be a mere hollow shell. Genuine freedom demands latitude to do that which others find immoral, distasteful, or mistaken, and thus requires toleration as its necessary condition. Toleration is overlooked because the arguments and passion of liberal thinkers are focused on the defense of freedom, and toleration is the negative image of freedom.

Toleration is also an essential component of the liberal requirement of respect for others.

That is because it allows principled disagreement, as an intermediate position between full acceptance and outright rejection. Genuine respect for others does not extend only to the beliefs and acts of others that we find correct, but must include enduring the erroneous or distasteful acts of others. Moreover, toleration also allows self-respect in these situations, because it provides an avenue for inaction combined with disagreement; hence, to tolerate the beliefs or values of others is not to accept or endorse those values, but to endure them for the sake of some further value.

At this point, the importance of toleration in moral life becomes apparent; toleration is valuable by allowing a third alternative between a stark "yes" or "no," or a stark "good" or "bad," for it provides the option of neither acceptance nor rejection but passive endurance. It is useful as an antidote to the tendency to create sharp manichean bifurcations into good and bad, right and wrong, yes and no. It allows the judgment that certain beliefs, speech, or conduct are morally wrong, but should be endured nonetheless.

Therefore, the principled toleration of Western liberalism is not lazy and uncaring; rather, it is founded on concern for freedom and respect. But principled toleration must be bounded; otherwise it does slide off into unprincipled lassitude. However, liberal thinkers and societies have encountered difficulty in their efforts to define this boundary. Locke's answer was that toleration, whether of persons or of governments, must end when natural law is violated. Mill's answer is more prosaic and more influential; he finds the limit of toleration at the point of harm to others. Thus, speech that directly causes harm to others is past the limit of toleration, as is religion that demands human sacrifice. While most Anglo-American liberals agree with Mill on this matter, there is substantial disagreement on what constitutes genuine harm and what is mere offense or irritation which, though distasteful, must be endured as a condition of freedom and respect.

Toleration is valuable because it necessarily accompanies the values of freedom and respect and because it allows a third path between full acceptance and firm rejection. It is overlooked because it is distasteful, highly complex, and plays a supporting role to more alluring values.

Gerard Elfstrom

See also LIBERAL EDUCATION; LIBERALISM; LOCKE; MILL

Bibliography

Devlin, Patrick. *The Enforcement of Morals*. London: Oxford University Press, 1965.

Fotion, Nick, and Gerard Elfstrom. *Toleration*. Tuscaloosa and London: University of Alabama Press, 1992.

Lecler, Joseph. *Toleration and the Reformation*. Translated by T.L. Westow. New York: Association Press, 1960.

Locke, John. *A Letter Concerning Toleration*. Edited by Mario Montuori. The Hague: Martinus Nijhoff, 1963.

Mendus, Susan, and David Edwards, eds. *On Toleration*. Oxford: Clarendon Press, 1987.

Mill, John Stuart. *On Liberty*. Edited by Aubrey Castell. New York: Appleton-Century-Crofts, 1947.

Milton, John. *Areopagitica, and Of Education*. Edited by Kathleen Marguerite Lea. Oxford: Clarendon Press, 1993.

Richards, David A.J. *Toleration and the Constitution*. New York: Oxford University Press, 1986.

Tinder, Glenn. *Tolerance: Toward a New Civility*. Amherst: University of Massachusetts Press, 1976.

Wolff, Robert Paul, Barrington Moore, Jr., and Herbert Marcuse. *A Critique of Pure Tolerance*. Boston: Beacon Press, 1969.

Tragedy

According to Aristotle (384–322 B.C.), tragedy originated in the dithyramb, a choral song dedicated to the god Dionysus. Aristotle was aware of a long period in the evolution of tragedy, during which it developed from an early stage of primitive plot structure and comic diction to the fully mature dramatic form we find in the works of Aeschylus, Sophocles, and Euripides in the 5th century B.C.

In the *Poetics*, Aristotle set forth a theory of tragedy that continues to be influential to the present day. He stated that tragedy is a representation of good (*spoudaioi*) human beings who are involved in a fall from happiness to misery caused, at least in part, by a "tragic flaw" (*hamartia*) on their part. Such action, he states, will achieve the *catharsis* of the emotions of pity and fear. The interpretation of the key terms, *hamartia* and *catharsis,* has been subject to much interpretative debate up to the present day. It is important to note that the focus of Aristotle's famous definition of tragedy is on the "essence" (*tes ousias*) of tragedy, and that many works we designate as tragedies do not meet all of its requirements.

In Greek literature, the term *hamartia* can mean everything from a literal missing of the mark in hurling a weapon to serious moral transgression. It is now the widely held view of experts that for Aristotle's ideal tragedy the term must mean "intellectual error," although for many other works, which do not meet all of the strict requirements of Aristotle's definition, the term can refer to a wide range of moral flaws as well.

For more than four hundred years after the rediscovery of Aristotle's *Poetics* in the Renaissance, two views dominated the interpretation of *catharsis*: "purgation" and "purification." In the second half of the twentieth century, something of a shift has taken place and the interpretation of *catharsis* as some form of "intellectual clarification" has begun to find favor. The interpretative issue is important because it relates to the ultimate effect that tragedy has on an audience: either restoration to mental health by the therapeutic purging, as in a somatic illness, of the pity and fear within us; or the purifying of the amounts of pity and fear within us so that we experience exactly the proper mean between excess and deficiency of these emotions; or our achievement of cognitive insight and clarification concerning the nature of pity and fear in human experience.

Sophocles' *Oedipus Rex* is the most important example we have of Aristotelian tragedy. In this play Oedipus is characterized by intelligence and moral courage as he abandons Corinth to avoid the oracular warning that he will commit parricide and incest; he finds his way to the kingship of Thebes by solving the riddle of the Sphinx. In Thebes he is held in high regard by the people he rules, who beg him to remove the plague that afflicts them. He shows complete integrity in unraveling the source of that plague, even though what he learns has a disastrous effect on his own happiness. Some in the past have tried to find a moral error in Oedipus and to link him to the type of tragedy discussed in the following paragraph, but the consensus of scholars today is that he is morally innocent, guilty only of not understanding the mysterious ways and power of the god Apollo.

Greek culture recognized another view of tragedy that characterizes a large number of works, both ancient and modern, that we designate as tragic. This view, found in Herodotus and Aeschylus, traces the effect of human arrogance (*hybris*), as it explodes into an act of mad violence (*ate*), and then is punished by divine or human vengeance (*nemesis*). Aeschylus' *Oresteia* is a clear example of that concept of tragedy. In the first play of the trilogy, Clytaemestra savagely kills her husband, Agamemnon, in order to become ruler of Argos. In the second play, her son Orestes returns to Argos to avenge his father's murder by killing his mother. In the final play of the trilogy Aeschylus provides a symbolic justification for Orestes' actions by having a court, at which Athena presides, exonerate him from the guilt of matricide. Another important example of this pattern of tragedy can be found in Shakespeare's *Macbeth,* in which the arrogant pursuit of royal power by Macbeth and Lady Macbeth leads to the brutal murder of kind Duncan and then to the deserved deaths of the murderous couple.

The most widespread application of the term *tragedy* has been to works that depict the failure of human beings to cope effectively with the conditions of their existence, so that they act with destructive or self-destructive violence. Among Greek tragedians, Euripides is especially the poet of such circumstances, and his *Medea* provides a clear representation of that pattern of tragedy. Medea's betrayal by her husband, Jason, awakens in her an overwhelming need to take vengeance for the insult she has suffered. When she discovers that she can exact sufficient vengeance only by killing their children, whom he needs and she loves, she is caught in a deeply troubling dilemma. She finally decides that her hatred takes priority over her love, and she murders the children so she can triumph over the man who has hurt her. Shakespeare created a number of tragic figures whose flawed capacity to deal with emotional and psychological reality ended in the tragic destruction of themselves and their innocent victims. Lear's failed attempt to accurately judge the affection of his daughters, Hamlet's incapacity to counter Claudius's villainy effectively, and Othello's psychological vulnerability to Iago's machinations, which for him overshadow Desdemona's innocence, all represent this very common dimension of tragedy.

Modern tragedy focuses its attention on this theme of psychological, emotional, and intellectual failure to such a degree that its protagonists more often appear as antiheroes than heroes. In an essay entitled "Tragedy and the Common Man," the twentieth-century playwright Arthur Miller declares that tragedy involves the struggle to find personal dignity, and that the ordinary human being of our own day is as much involved in that struggle as any king or noble of a previous age. Miller's *Death of a Salesman* can be viewed as an archetypal statement of this tragedy of ordinary human existence. His protagonist, Willy Loman, is a failed husband, father, and salesman who struggles to find some dignity in his life, which he achieves, if he does achieve it, only by his suicide.

In its long history, tragedy has continually attracted audiences who understand that it represents, in all of its various modes, a central truth about the nature of human existence.

Leon Golden

See also COMEDY; EXISTENTIALISM; FREUD

Bibliography

Aylen, Leo. *Greek Tragedy and the Modern World.* London: Methuen, 1964.

Beye, Charles Rowan. *Ancient Greek Literature and Society.* Ithaca and London: Cornell University Press, 1987.

Bradley, A.C. *Shakespearean Tragedy.* London: Macmillan, 1937.

Golden, Leon. *Aristotle on Tragic and Comic Mimesis.* Atlanta, Ga.: Scholars Press, 1992.

Henn, T.A. *The Harvest of Tragedy.* New York: Barnes and Noble, 1966.

Kaufmann, Walter A. *Tragedy and Philosophy.* New York: Doubleday, 1968.

Lesky, Albin. *Greek Tragedy.* New York: Barnes and Noble, 1965.

Miller, Arthur. "Tragedy and the Common Man." *New York Times,* February 27, 1949.

Olson, Elder. *Tragedy and the Theory of Drama.* Detroit, Mich.: Wayne State University Press, 1961.

Palmer, Richard H. *Tragedy and Tragic Theory.* Westport, Conn. and London: Greenwood Press, 1992.

Raphael, D.D. *The Paradox of Tragedy.* Bloomington: Indiana University Press, 1960.

Sewall, Richard B. *The Vision of Tragedy.* New Haven: Yale University Press, 1980.

Steiner, George. *The Death of Tragedy.* New York: Alfred A. Knopf, 1961.

Truth

Truth, by Aristotle's famous characterization, is a statement of what is that it is, or a statement of what is not that it is not. Truth, in short, is a statement representing what is actually the case, and hence the opposite of a misrepresentation of what is actually so.

Philosophers commonly draw three general distinctions regarding truth: a distinction between analytic and synthetic truth, a distinction between necessary and contingent truth, and a distinction between a priori and a posteriori truth. Analytic truth is truth just in virtue of the meanings of a judgment's constituent terms; synthetic truth is truth in virtue of something other than just meaning—for example, in virtue of an observable situation in the world. Necessary truths, in the words of Gottfried Leibniz (1646–1716), are true in "all possible worlds"; they cannot be false. Contingent truths are true only in some possible worlds; they can be false. A priori truths are truths knowable or justifiable independently of sensory experience; a posteriori truths are truths that can be known or justified only on the basis of sensory experience. The truths of logic are standard examples of truths that are analytic, necessary, and a priori; the truths of the natural sciences are standard examples of truths that are synthetic, contingent, and a posteriori. Saul Kripke and others have argued however, that some contingent truths can be known a priori.

Philosophers have focused on three topics regarding truth: (a) what truth consists in, perhaps by definition, (b) what kinds of things are the bearers of truth, and (c) what sorts of standards characterize justified belief and knowledge that something is true. Topic (c) is central to epistemology, the theory of knowledge and justified belief; it involves philosophical debates over such positions as epistemic foundationalism, epistemic coherentism, epistemic fallibilism, and epistemic skepticism. Topic (b) is central to the philosophy of language and metaphysics; it involves debates over whether truthbearers are ordinary sentences, uttered or inscribed statements, or timeless proportions. Topic (a) is the focus of this entry; it receives treatment from three prominent philosophical views about the nature of truth: a correspondence theory, coherentism, and pragmatism.

Correspondence Theories

Ever since Aristotle (384–322 B.C.), various philosophers (for example, G.E. Moore [1873–1958], Bertrand Russell [1872–1970], the early Ludwig Wittgenstein [1889–1951], and J.L. Austin), have held that truth consists in a correspondence relation between sentence-like truth-bearers, on the one hand, and some features of the actual world, on the other. True statements, according to a correspondence theory, represent how the world is in virtue of their "corresponding" to certain aspects of how the world actually is—that is, to an actually existing situation. Correspondence theorists have had difficulty giving a precise account of the kind of correspondence definitive of truth, and have not reached consensus in favor of a single such account.

Correspondence cannot be literal "picturing" or "mirroring," because many truths are not literal pictures of what they signify. Consider, for example, the true sentence, "This book would fall to the floor if it were dropped from a desktop." Consider also the true mathematical sentence, "2+2=4." It is doubtful that these truths literally picture what they are true of, or what makes them true; and it is unclear how exactly, or in what precise sense, they "correspond" to what they are true of. Correspondence theorists must, in any case, identify the kind of correlation or agreement definitive of truths of the aforementioned sorts.

Complications about correspondence have prompted J.L. Mackie and others to endorse a "simple" thesis about truth: To say that a statement is true is to say that whatever in the making of the statement is stated to obtain does obtain. Mackie rejects the influential "redundancy" view of F.P. Ramsey that the predicate "is true" is eliminable because it adds nothing to the statements to which it is applied. Mackie's simple thesis leads him to deny that the statement that S is true is nothing but a reaffirmation of the statement S. Truth, according to the simple thesis, is a distinctive relation (identified by the simple thesis) between a statement and an actual situation, and a statement that does not ascribe truth, namely S, does not automatically ascribe the truth-relation in question. Mackie's approach is a minimal correspondence theory, however, in that it characterizes truth as relational between a statement and an actual situation.

Some philosophers regard Alfred Tarski's "semantic approach" to truth as a correspondence theory, although Tarski noted that he was after, not a definition of truth, but an adequacy condition that must be met by any acceptable definition of truth. Tarski's influential adequacy condition is this: X is true if and only if P (where P stands for a declarative sentence, and X stands for the name of that sentence). For example, given Tarski's condition, the sentence "All librarians are studious" is true if and only if all librarians are studious. Since what follows "if and only if" in Tarski's condition connotes an actual situation to which the relevant true sentence is appropriately related, various philosophers have regarded Tarski's condition as indicating a correspondence requirement on truth. That, however, is a matter of controversy among philosophers. Two notable differences between Tarski and Mackie are that whereas Tarski restricts truth-bearers to sentences, Mackie does not, and that whereas Tarski is doubtful of achieving a uniform definition for ordinary, nonformal uses of "truth," Mackie is not.

Coherence Theories

Coherence approaches to truth seek to avoid reliance on talk of statement-world relations in a characterization of truth. They share the general assumption that a set of propositions' being suitably interconnected or systematic (that is, "coherent") is definitive of truth. That view was held by Benedict Spinoza (1632–1677), G.W.F. Hegel (1770–1831), and Brand Blanshard, among others. Blanshard explicitly identified coherence as not only a test of truth but also what is "constitutive" of truth. Logical implication is the strongest kind of coherence; it is the kind of coherence to which Blanshard appeals in characterizing truth. Coherentists typically regard the system of mathematical truths as offering a paradigm of a coherent system yielding truth.

Coherence theories face difficult problems about exactly when coherence yields truth. In particular, a coherence theory must avoid divorcing truth from how the world actually is. Some coherent sets of propositions fail to capture truth; that is illustrated by situations in which contrary coherent sets of propositions coexist. It seems that a coherent set of propositions will yield truth (at least as ordinarily conceived) only if it is "correlated" in some way with actual situations in the world. Coherence by itself evidently can be divorced from, or irrelevant to, what is factual. Coherentists must offer, then, an account of how their approach to truth accommodates the consideration that truth is "factual." Some coherentists recommend a kind of idealism that denies the existence of extramental facts, but such idealism is unpopular among contemporary philosophers.

Pragmatism

The American pragmatism of C.S. Peirce (1839–1914), William James (1842–1910), and John Dewey (1859–1952) is famous for attempting to characterize truth in terms of "usefulness" or "pragmatic value" of a special sort. James, in *The Meaning of Truth*, explicitly characterized pragmatists' talk of truth as talk of the "workableness" of ideas. He held that workableness definitive of truth is a matter of the "assimilation" and "verification" of ideas. In a similar vein, Peirce and Dewey identified truth with "the opinion which is fated to be ultimately agreed to by all who investigate." The common theme of the pragmatist approaches of Peirce, James, and Dewey is that truth is constituted by a certain kind of validation or verification of ideas, and that such validation or verification determines the "pragmatic" value of an idea.

Many philosophers have faulted pragmatism for confusing matters of justification (or warrant) and matters of truth. Pragmatists must explain why false propositions cannot have impeccable pragmatic value involving their being "ultimately agreed to by all who investigate." We need, in particular, an account of the alleged necessary connection between what is pragmatically valuable, in virtue of verification, and what is factual. Our ordinary use of "true" allows for validated beliefs that are, unknown to us, not true. The history of science offers an abundance of cases illustrating this point in favor of fallibilism about validation. Pragmatists have not offered a unified argument favoring a necessary connection between what has pragmatic value and what is factual.

Conceptual versus Substantive Relativism

Even if philosophers can agree on some general, rather vague notion of truth, some philosophers evidently use different specific concepts of truths: for example, correspondence, coherentist, and pragmatist concepts. This supports a kind of conceptual relativism about specific notions of truth in circulation. This relativism opposes uncritical talk of "the" notion of truth, because there evidently is no such singular thing. Conceptual relativism does not, however, entail substantive relativism, implying that whatever a person or a group believes is automatically true; it allows for nonrelativist notions of truth. Variability in notions of truth does not make mere (shared) belief a sufficient condition of actual truth. Conceptual relativism about truth does not require an "anything goes" attitude toward truth.

Paul K. Moser

See also EPISTEMOLOGY; REALISM; SKEPTICISM

Bibliography

Blanshard, Brand. *The Nature of Thought*. London: Allen and Unwin, 1939.

Devitt, Michael. *Realism and Truth*. Oxford: Basil Blackwell, 1984, 1991.

James, William. *The Meaning of Truth*. Cambridge: Harvard University Press, 1909, 1975.

Kirkham, R.L. *Theories of Truth*. Cambridge: MIT Press, 1992.

Kripke, Saul. *Naming and Necessity*. Cambridge: Harvard University Press, 1980.

Mackie, J.L. *Truth, Probability, and Paradox*. Oxford: Clarendon Press, 1973.

Moser, Paul. *Philosophy after Objectivity*. New York: Oxford University Press, 1993.

Ramsey, F.P. "Facts and Propositions." In *Truth*, edited by George Pitcher, 16–17. Englewood Cliffs, N.J.: Prentice Hall, 1964.

Tarski, Alfred. "The Semantic Conception of Truth." *Philosophy and Phenomenological Research* 4 (1944): 341–76.

Walker, Ralph. *The Coherence Theory of Truth*. London: Routledge, 1989.

T

U

Utilitarianism

The moral theory that holds that conduct must be judged solely by its consequences, or the more specific version claiming that actions should promote human welfare as much as possible. The generic theory is now called "consequentialism." Consequentialists whose conception of the good consequences to be promoted includes abstract values such as truth or beauty, are said to embrace "ideal utilitarianism." Those who endorse the species known as utilitarianism maintain that the basic value we should serve is the good of individual people.

Utilitarians have diverse ideas about the good of human beings. "Hedonistic" utilitarians, following Jeremy Bentham (1748–1832), believe that our good consists of pleasure and the absence of pain. Departing from Bentham, John Stuart Mill (1806–1873) held that "higher" pleasures, of intellectual satisfaction and moral sensibility, are more valuable than "lower" (such as physical) pleasures, and he offered a "eudaimonistic" conception of human flourishing based on the development of our distinctively human capacities.

In many contexts utilitarianism calls for radical reform or revolutionary change. It is egalitarian, in holding that the interests of servants and masters, paupers and princes, are to be weighed equally; no one's interests may be discounted. Although generic consequentialism is neither distinctively modern nor peculiarly Western, utilitarianism's impartiality testifies to its roots in the Enlightenment. Bentham and Mill, the first great utilitarian theorists, championed many reforms, from constitutional law to women's rights.

Utilitarianism is impartial as well in maintaining that one may not favor one's own wel-fare (or the welfare of those one loves): One's interests should be counted the same as any other's. Utilitarianism must be distinguished, therefore, from "ethical egoism," which holds that one should consider others' interests only insofar as that would be useful for one to do, as well as from altruistic conceptions of morality that call on us always to sacrifice our interests in order to serve others.

For the same basic reasons, utilitarians reject parochial and nationalistic approaches to deciding public policy and favor a universalistic approach. At the level of basic principle, utilitarians deny that either domestic or external policies may properly give priority to the interests of the community whose policy it is. Utilitarians are prepared to say, however, that individuals may favor family and friends and officials may favor their constituents, if in practice that constitutes an efficient division of moral labor.

Although utilitarians maintain that people should be treated as equals, they do not make it a matter of principle that people should be treated equally. Utilitarians have no fixed views concerning the social distribution of benefits and burdens. They are committed to favoring any arrangements that generate total benefits (less the burdens incurred) that are greater than could be achieved by any alternative social arrangement that is available.

This aspect of utilitarianism derives from its reference to "the general welfare." The relevant effects of conduct on all individuals affected must be summed. (This assumes that "interpersonal comparisons of utility" are possible or, in other words, that benefits and losses to one person are commensurable with benefits and losses to any other.)

In appraising social arrangements, therefore, utilitarians must determine whether the burdens that might be imposed on some, such as higher taxes, would bring greater benefits to others, such as needed services. The general welfare can be promoted by measures that reduce gaps between rich and poor. A dollar is typically worth more to the needy than to the affluent, so transfers of wealth can be useful.

But utilitarians are also committed to approving measures that would burden the less advantaged for the sake of benefits for those who are already well off, if that would maximize welfare. Thus, it is conceivable that utilitarianism would condone a system like serfdom or slavery. It is of course most unlikely that such social arrangements would in fact promote welfare more effectively than any available alternative. Utilitarians have argued accordingly. Critics may agree about those facts, but they contend that utilitarians reject such arrangements for the wrong reasons—not that serfdom and slavery oppressively exploit some in order to enrich others, but simply that the abstract sum of benefits would not be as great as it might otherwise be. Some theorists summarize such points by saying that utilitarians do not take rights seriously. There are ways in which no one should be treated, even if doing so would maximize the sum of benefits.

Utilitarians are thought to have trouble accommodating rights and obligations generally. We normally assume that past events, such as promises freely made, services rendered, and injuries done to others, establish obligations to or rights against other persons that affect how we should behave—that we must respect others' rights and discharge our obligations unless they conflict with morally more pressing entitlements or responsibilities. Utilitarians view past events differently. They believe that right conduct is determined solely by the difference for the future that the conduct makes—its "marginal utility." Utilitarians hold that past events are morally relevant only insofar as they alter the consequences of current options.

Utilitarians accordingly believe that, if there are any genuine moral rights and obligations, they are not "natural" but derivative, based on the utility of our respecting the social rules they represent. Critics do not deny that living up to one's moral responsibilities generally promotes welfare. Critics believe, however, that rights and duties, justice and responsibility are not always grounded on utility and can clash with its dictates. They may claim, for example, that the values at stake, such as dignity and autonomy, are not reducible to welfare. Furthermore, when one has incurred an obligation, one needs a special justification for breaking it, and the fact that it would be minimally less useful to perform it does not constitute a special justification.

Most contemporary theorists assume that the criterion of utility applies directly to the acts of individuals on particular occasions. The resulting theory, called "act-utilitarianism," requires that we always perform "optimific" acts. In recent years some theorists have revised utilitarianism by applying the criterion directly to social rules and only indirectly to conduct. These "rule-utilitarians" believe that right acts conform to useful social rules. One attraction of rule-utilitarianism is the idea that it can provide a utilitarian basis, in useful rules, for rights and obligations.

Utilitarians typically believe that their theory shows how moral issues can be settled by empirical investigation: All we need is reliable information about the mechanisms for promoting welfare. Uncertainties of application arise, however, because we have limited knowledge of the consequences of conduct, which can vary with circumstances and unfold indefinitely through the future. This creates a gap between the actual and predictable consequences of actions. If utilitarianism evaluates conduct on the basis of actual consequences, it might make moral demands on us of which we will forever be ignorant. Because we might justifiably be held morally accountable only for the reasonably predictable consequences of our own conduct, some utilitarians believe that the principle of utility should be formulated in terms of probable rather than actual consequences.

Critics charge that even probabilistic utilitarianism is too demanding, in various ways. First, although it does not require us always to maximize welfare, it does require us always to be doing whatever is most likely to maximize welfare. Because so many people have so many pressing unmet needs, critics say that utilitarianism would leave one no time to rest. Second, it leaves no room for "supererogation"—acts above and beyond the call of duty. Third, it implies that one is just as responsible for harm that one does not bring about but might have prevented as for harm one deliberately causes. Nonutilitarian theories avoid these objections by conceiving of morality as laying down more limited requirements for morally decent behavior.

Bentham offered no systematic defense of his utilitarianism. He believed it so clearly right that he regarded detractors as biased or confused. Mill defended his version of the theory, but he persuaded few. He assumed a consequentialistic framework—that right conduct must promote the good—and tried only to show that human happiness is the basic good. But he did not succeed in explaining why one should regard the good of others as equal to one's own. The widely respected utilitarian theorist Henry Sidgwick (1838–1900) regarded basic values, including the principle of utility, as grounded on "intuitions"; but Sidgwick failed to clarify that notion or to render its use legitimate.

Until recently, nonutilitarian theorists offered no more promising suggestions about how to appraise moral principles. That has now changed. John Rawls has developed a theory of justification along with the theory of justice for which he is well known. The former can be separated from the latter and suggests strategies that utilitarians as well as other theorists might use to defend their principles. One strategy, involving the method of "reflective equilibrium," incorporates the more persuasive arguments used by Sidgwick, Mill, and many others, that the principle of utility can account for many of our considered, reflective moral judgments.

David Lyons

See also EQUALITY; HAPPINESS; JUSTICE; MILL; RIGHTS

Bibliography

Bentham, Jeremy. *An Introduction to the Principles of Morals and Legislation.* London: T. Payne and Son, 1789. *Collected Works* ed., 1970.

Mill, John Stuart. *Utilitarianism.* London: Parker, Son, and Bourn, 1863. *Collected Works* ed., 1969.

Moore, George Edward. *Ethics.* Oxford: Oxford University Press, 1912.

Sidgwick, Henry. *The Methods of Ethics.* London: Macmillan, 1874, 1907.

Smart, J.J.C., and Bernard Williams. *Utilitarianism: For and Against.* Cambridge: Cambridge University Press, 1973.

V

Values and Evaluation

In analyzing how values are created, or how new concepts are formed, the following questions become relevant in such an analysis: What is thinking if it is new concept formation? Is it purpose that structures thought? If so, how? What is the meaning of a "qualitative, pervasive unity" in experience (John Dewey, quoted in Chambliss: 169–170), which acts as a regulative influence on thinking? And, if thinking is indeed the connecting of events as Dewey maintains (Ratner: 618), then how can one go beyond such a (purely) descriptive statement to an analysis of thinking? Another way of stating this, is that, in effect, one has to try to do for thinking what thinking can do for "values."

"Thinking" machines, computers, can in principle, and do, often perform as well as, or better than, man. The thinking techniques include those peculiar to science (both experimental and theoretical) theology, mathematics, art, and what some people call "everyday" thinking. We do not know of a thinking technique that is in principle not amenable to computer formulation (Steg: 1962, 1966, 1970, 1971, 1993, 1994).

As a matter of fact, because of the speed available in computers there are computer techniques that do not find a counterpart in human thinking. But, once one steps outside of the imperative confinement, into the choice-zone, the area where adapting behavior becomes a possibility, human capability is readily distinguished from animal or machine abilities. The symbol of choice in human thinking is value concept (Steg: 1966, 1970, 1971; Steg et al.: 1993, 1994). Animals do not determine value, they automatically follow an instinct. Computing machines have built-in, "fixed" values that

the machine cannot choose except as it is programmed to do so in a predetermined fixed fashion. The ability of man to create value, new concepts, as he grows, develops, and learns is the crucial ability that distinguishes man from machine and animal.

Let us proceed to consider some implications of the "qualitative pervasive unity" in experience that Dewey considered as all-pervasive and as exerting a regulative influence on thinking and how evaluation relates to a consideration of values.

Teleology and the Quest for Values

According to Dewey, the problem of value arose as a separate problem only when teleological considerations were eliminated from one natural science after another (Dewey 1944: 449). Four questions that Dewey posited some fifty years ago (Lepley: 5) are as fundamental today as they seemed then:

1. What connection is there, if any, between an attitude that will be called prizing or holding dear, and desiring, liking, interest, enjoying, etc?

2. a) Irrespective of which of the above-named attitudes is taken to be primary, is it by itself a sufficient condition for the existence of values?

   b) Or, while it is a necessary condition, is a further condition, of the nature of valuation or appraisal, required?

3. Whatever the answer to the second question, is there anything in the nature of appraisal, evaluation, as judgment and/or proposition, that marks them off, with respect to their logical or their scientific sta-

tus, from other propositions or judgements? Or are such distinctive properties as they might possess wholly an affair of their subject matter as we might speak of astronomical and geological propositions without implying that there is any difference between them qua propositions?

4. Is the scientific method of inquiry, in its broad sense, applicable in determination of judgements and/or propositions in the way of valuations or appraisals? Or is there something inherent in the nature of values as subject matter that precludes the application of such method?

In attempting to answer the question posed in the introduction, let us first examine the common point of departure for thinking, for "Art," from which two different kinds of handling can then take place, a theological or a scientific handling.

Furthermore, the four questions themselves form the point of departure for both a theological and a scientific handling of their own. Thus, the answers to the questions raised in the introduction are illustrated by answering the questions raised by Dewey.

A Common Point of Departure: "Art"

"Art" is to "select what is significant and reject by that very same impulse what is irrelevant and thereby compressing and intensifying the significant" (Dewey 1934: 208). "Art" is the coordination of perception in a manner that is "descriptive," but not "complete" and "total" as it may be in a photograph or a record. This in no way denies that photographers make choices when taking photographs, nor that they also enhance features when they "take" or "make" photographs. This also in no way denies that today we can hear symphonies in ways the composer never dreamed possible.

The use of the presentation of a phenomenon in this descriptive phase is influenced by the analytical phase that follows. A phenomenon can be described in many different ways, but it is only when the description has been influenced by the analysis that may follow, that we have made use of the art of description. In effect, this is probably the most important gift with which man is endowed.

The "Art" Image, Theology, and Science

Objects of perception can lead to a certain (re)action within an individual. That (re)action is translated into an artist's impression, a descriptive picture. Of course, it is strictly an individual (re)action, but the more descriptive or artistic a (re)action is, in the sense that it enhances the most characteristic features and neglects or eliminates all unimportant features, the more it does this, the more "value" it presents for both a theological or a scientific integration of a subject. For Dewey, the question as to how we find the significant (be it similarities, dissimilarities, or any other possibility), this problem is the whole problem of induction.

It is only when the descriptive, or artistic, phase is sufficiently advanced that a scientific analysis or a theological handling can follow. The value of the artistic presentation, the description, forms the very basis for what may follow, be it a theological interpretation or a scientific analysis.

The "theological" handling of a phenomenon places the emphasis on the enhanced feature of the descriptive presentation. Here the chosen, the significant, becomes the supernatural, the essence, the thing to admire, to worship, to prize, to hold dear. It abhors analysis. A "theological" handling takes it for granted that the value that is represented in the "descriptive" presentation, is above and beyond analysis. Thus, "theological" as used herein means "nonvalidated."

The scientific handling of a phenomenon is to look at the problematic critically, look critically at the enhanced significant, to think, to reason, to analyze. The scientific analysis of a phenomenon is being continually fitted into the changing state of scientific knowledge as achieved by experimentation.

The descriptive presentation of a phenomenon with its emphasis on the "significant" is at the root of both the theological handling and the scientific analysis. It is a piece of art and can take its appropriate place in an art gallery or a museum. The descriptive or artistic presentation forms the basis for the scientific analysis or the theological handling.

Without an artistic appreciation of a phenomenon, "theology" is reduced to superstition, the worship of the golden calf, and "science" is reduced to statistics, as in a Kinsey report. Value results from the enhancement of the significant. Value is something that lives and changes continuously.

A theological interpretation precludes consideration of any but theological values (see above). A scientific analysis creates the necessity for determining value in the sense that it will undertake to critically view all the enhanced features, as well as the values presented. It is then that the nature of a valuation or appraisal is required. But the valuation and appraisal is related to the totality and not to its components. The components of a presentation have no value by themselves. They have value as part of a totality. Thus, what is to be valued is the image in its entirety, an image resulting from selection, from choice, from the creation of a new concept.

In considering the four questions that Dewey posited, the qualitative approach, the description or "Art" image, and its theological or scientific handling can now be applied to the four questions themselves.

The Theological Approach

In the descriptive or artistic presentation, the words *nourishing, caring for, fostering, making much of, being loyal or faithful to, clinging to,* can be taken as equivalents for the word *prizing,* which stands for a behavioral transaction. The reason that these can be chosen as equivalents is that they all refer to human relations such as between parents and children, teachers and pupils, or government and people.

In a theological consideration, relations between parents and children, with "God the Father of all," places the supreme value on just this artistic presentation. Here the role of parenthood is enhanced to the extreme of its value. This value cannot be questioned or be subjected to analysis. It is an inherent value. The primary position is thus held by prizing or holding dear. The secondary position is held by liking or desiring.

The Scientific Approach

The descriptive or artistic presentation is the same as in the theological approach. There can be no possible substitution for it. Anything else is meaningless without it (Lepley: 6). The scientific analysis can now follow.

There is a physical phenomenon that is common to the mammalian species, born helpless, and requiring that particular capacity for prizing, and so on. The mammalian species that would not at birth possess the capacity of being on the receiving end of "caring for" (and other qualities), or would not have the capacity of growing into the giving end of "caring for" (and other qualities), when it deals with its offspring, would be incapable of survival and

thus would never become the subject of Question 1.

If we try to follow this line of reasoning to its conclusion, the capacity of being cared for has to have definite limits, implying the necessity for another capacity: "to stand on one's own feet." This applies both to the receiver and the giver. The one who is being cared for while receiving, whether or not he enjoys it, has to possess an "anticare" receiving capacity in order to survive. Similarly, the giver has to possess the "anticare" giving capacity without "ramming" it down the receiver's throat. Since the "behavioral transaction" is a function of the relative position of the giver and the receiver, the transaction has to fade gradually in direct proportion to the disappearance of the receiver's helplessness. Thus, the "value" changes every minute, just as a stock market quotation changes every minute that the quotation is made.

In human beings the tendency to conform is powerful. Obedience to authority makes it possible for many people to relieve themselves of moral responsibility, thus making it more likely that they behave with considerable cruelty. As a group, the Nazi perpetrators did things that as individuals they would not do (Zillmer et al.: chap. 1, 18). Yet, it is important to note that this is true for much of human activity, in both positive and negative ways. The desire that plays a role in activating activities may actually not be desirable at all. The desirable ties in the future, hence the need for appraisal. We can state that for a certain group of people there is a predisposition to behave with considerable cruelty. It is very scary to realize that those who "followed the leader" were not sadists.

When moral development is not internally guided, then the individual looks to the outside for values. Herman Rorschach characterized that kind of personality as an "extratensive" personality. He considered that this process of computing our behavior and even some feelings to such outside demands, this kind of conformity to external demands, is one of the major categories of personality dynamics. A quite different kind of behavior can be described as the individual's efforts to change his environment to meet his own internally defined needs or wishes. Rorschach called that process "introspection" and saw this effort to impose one's own perceptions and meanings on the world outside as a second parallel category of personality dynamics (1942).

Continuing with the Analysis

What attitudes are connected with a behavioral transaction? The value of a physical object or a service (a stove or a ride in a bus) is determined by the law of supply and demand. However, the value of a behavioral transaction has nothing to do with supply and demand. It exists only as part of interpersonal relations between individuals. Here the key is (a) perceptive ability, (b) coordination of perceptions, and (c) dependence of the individual until (a) and (b) have achieved a certain degree of independence.

The latter is never reached in humans, as members of a society. Social interrelation of the "open" kind uses this "dependence" only willingly and enjoys it, while a dictatorship "unburdens" the individual to a degree that makes for another type of enjoyment. The same applies to parent-child or teacher-pupil relationships.

Thus, neither holding dear, prizing, desiring, nor liking is primary or secondary. All of these ingredients are part of a mammalian mechanism. Let us note that a screw is as important in a mechanism as the heart of the mechanism itself.

Questions 1 and 2, reiterated below, are thus answered.

1. What connection is there, if any, between an attitude that will be called prizing or holding dear, and desiring, liking, interest, enjoying, and so on?
2. a) Irrespective of which of the above-named attitudes is taken to be primary, it is by itself a sufficient condition for the existence of values.
   b) Or, while it is a necessary condition, is a further condition, of the nature of valuation or appraisal, required?

Both parts of Question 2 have already been considered in the general consideration so that we can further amplify part (b) with a definite yes, if a scientific analysis is taken into account and if we take into consideration all the building blocks of the mammalian species.

However, obviously, a theological handling does not require an appraisal.

Consideration of Questions 3 and 4

3. Whatever the answer to the second question, is there anything in the nature of the appraisal, evaluation, as judgment or proposition, that marks them off, with respect to their logical or their scientific status, from other propositions without implying that there is any difference between them qua propositions?
4. Is the scientific method of inquiry, in its broad sense, applicable in determination of judgment or propositions in the way of valuations or appraisals? Or is there something inherent in the nature of values as subject matter that precludes the application of such method?

Both a theological handling and a scientific analysis would lead to a similar answer for question 3. For both, it is a phase reached after the problem has been given significant attention.

Digression into a Consideration of "Facts"

The "facts" of the story have little value. Consider the facts of the case in Shakespeare's *Hamlet*. If it is considered as a detective story, then it has little value. But Shakespeare has value because he laid bare all the torture and feelings of a man. It is a deep search into a man and a surrounding atmosphere.

The four questions presented above can also almost be viewed as a detective puzzle. One can ask, for instance, whether there is a relation between such and such, or are they independent? Is one primary or the other primary? Can you do this or that to it? The way the questions were phrased does not preclude either a scientific or a theological consideration.

As for question 4, both a theological handling and a scientific analysis use rationality as a tool. There is nothing irrational about the supernatural. There are certain rules that apply to the theological game as well. The inherent is the unknown. If it were known, it would not be inherent. And it is inherent until the supernatural becomes natural.

The "supernatural" is something we don't know the limitations of. A man that needs the supernatural is a man who does not prize what he lives with. For him, the supernatural is much more important. He needs it more. He does not possess the control of his perceptions, and, it can be said that cause and effect are sometimes hard to separate in this case. Thus, a "sick" fanatic who doesn't feel needles or fire—is he a victim of the supernatural, or is he "supernatural" because of his "sickness"?

Discussion

Let us go back to those building blocks that permit us to determine the limitations of prizing and caring for. The mammalian young is helpless and therefore must be able to accept help, or it would not be able to survive.

Enjoying is the physical dress of receiving or giving care. If you do not enjoy it, you cannot give or receive care. Desire is the physical dress for reproduction (giving care), contrary to the assumption that it is the other way round. For instance, desire must precede sexual activity for the mechanism to work well.

Since we have at best only partial knowledge, based on partial data, we can only guess that the condition that enables us to do this is built into the mechanisms of the species. We can certainly call the building block that does this a supernatural thing. We cannot explain it, and we do not know the limits of it. But there is nothing wrong in using the concept in such a building block. There is nothing wrong in being a believer in the supernatural. However, later on, with more data, and better instrumentation, we can state it in nonsupernatural terms, in natural terms. It can thus be substantiated that prizing, holding dear, caring are all part and parcel of it.

There is no conflict between the supernatural and the natural. The question at stake is how perceptions are coordinated. It is certainly true that fetishes, gods, and so on are all part of the supernatural. There is no argument about that. But there are no dichotomies between the natural and the supernatural. It is a question of semantics. Both the believer in the natural and the believer in the supernatural use the building blocks of Question 1. The believer in the supernatural feeds and cares for his child too, while the believer in the natural does not go out on a limb when he concludes without perfect proof. He is guessing, dreaming, imagining, and this is a part of today's supernatural block. Thus invectives that are hurled by both are simply in poor taste and are generated by a lack of sincerity.

In ancient times, all the facts existed as they do today, but their interpretation was "guesswork" and not science. The supernatural status of things unknown scientifically was thus created. A story used to be considered a supernatural phenomenon because physical science was almost nonexistent. But without physical science, a guess that a "cloud" is connected to a "possible storm" is as much of an achievement, or maybe more, as the physical science about the phenomenon of clouds and storms. An inherent valuation is as legitimate an evaluation as a logical one, if it is properly used.

If it is stated that to care or to prize is instinctive then one does not give a value other than a supernatural value to it. What is being said is, "I do not know how it works," otherwise, it would have been tagged with a name. The name could be either descriptive or nondescriptive depending on how it is used.

It can be said that seeing is a miracle. What difference is there in calling it a miracle if we do not know about it, or optics if we do know about it. But to value one's seeing ability, it must have a supernatural quality, hence calling it "the miracle of seeing," "the instinct of prizing." On the other hand, the mechanism of optics and describing the mechanism of prizing can both be described as an ingredient of the mammalian species.

We do not yet know the mechanism of creativity or imagination, so let us not give up the supernatural calling. But once the mechanism is known, let us leave off the supernatural. The supernaturalist must not be allowed to get away with what is known. Maybe the question to ask is: What is life without prizing, desiring, enjoying? What is of significance, of course, is the existence of human beings.

Law and education can be compared. In the jungle, no law protects an individual and he has to fight for himself. We have laws. This does not mean that we have done away with lawless acts, but we no longer have to worry so much about them. We no longer need to be constantly on edge about it. The same holds true in education. We worry a great deal about the three Rs.

However, some warnings must be voiced. We can teach with computers only what we are absolutely certain of and nothing else. This becomes extremely important since we have previously concluded that voluntary distortion, that the choice of the significant, the Art aspect, is a pervasive and regulative influence, and that control is impossible if error is eliminated. With computers, we can use feedback to reduce skill-drudgery in education and to free teachers and students for reflective thought, for experience in choices and creativity. But if feedback is used to control behavior, forestall revolt, and eliminate deviation, we may very soon reach George Orwell's and Aldous Huxley's worlds.

There is little difference between a man who is totally blind and a man who can see only red. Actually the requirements for education should encompass the whole spectrum, from ultraviolet to infrared. If a blind man learns about his environment by bumping into things and getting hurt until he finally knows the place as if he could see, as far as he is concerned he has full knowledge of the environment and is completely educated. But, while an educated man, or a seeing man, out of his environment will be able to see and remain educated in the new environment, without any need for additional education-bumping-into-things and getting hurt, a blind man has to reeducate himself as soon as the environment changes.

Summary

Inquiry into the how of the creation of values, and the implications of maintaining that a qualitative pervasive unity in experience acts as a regulative influence on thinking, has been presented. Questions are analyzed that seem to be essential to a consideration of values and evaluation, and a framework is established that allows for a theological and a scientific handling. The responses formulated indicate that one can go beyond the purely descriptive or the art of description, toward an analysis of thinking and the creation of values, of new concept formation with its foundation in empiricism.

Whatever consequences may follow for education or other areas of human inquiry and development would count as by-products of the theoretical inquiry.

See also COGNITIVE DEVELOPMENT; EMPIRICISM; ETHICS AND MORALITY; EXPERIENCE

D.R. Steg

Bibliography

Chambliss, J.J. "The Analysis of Experience: John Dewey and Elsie Ripley Clapp on Desire and Thinking, 1911." *Studies in Philosophy and Education* 11 (1991): 161–86.

Dewey, John. *Art As Experience*. New York: Minton Balch, 1934.

———. *How We Think*. Rev. ed. Boston: D. C. Heath, 1933.

———. "Some Questions about Value." *Journal of Philosophy* 41 (1944): 449–55.

Lepley, R. *Value, a Cooperative Inquiry*. New York: Columbia University Press, 1949.

Ratner, Joseph, ed. *Intelligence in the Modern World*. New York: Modern Library, 1939.

Rorschach, Herman. *Psychodiagnostics*. Translated by P. Lemkau. New York: Harpers, 1942.

Steg, D.R. "The Limitations of Learning Machines and Some Aspects of Learning. *Focus on Learning* 1 (1971): 43–51.

———. "A Philosophical and Cybernetic Model of Thinking." Ph.D. dissertation. University of Pennsylvania, Philadelphia, 1962.

———. "A Philosophical and Cybernetic Model of Thinking." Proceedings, 6th International Congress on Cybernetics: International Association of Cybernetics. Namur, Belgium: Palais des Expositions, Place Andre Ryckmans, 1970, 846–54.

———. "System Rules and Ethics." Proceedings Philosophy of Education Society. Edwardsville: Southern Illinois University, 1966.

Steg, D.R., I. Lazar, and C. Boyce. *Computer Assisted Education: A Communication Approach*. Philadelphia: University of Pennsylvania, 1993.

———. "A Cybernetic Approach to Early Education." *Journal of Educational Computing Research* 10 (1994): 1–27.

Zillmer, E.A., M. Harrower, B.A. Ritzler, and R.P. Archer. *The Quest for the Nazi Personality*. Hillsdale, N.J.: L. Erlbaum Associates, 1995.

Vico, Giambattista (1668–1744)

Italian philosopher who was professor of Latin eloquence at the University of Naples from 1699 to 1741. He was appointed Royal historiographer in 1735. Vico's major work, the *New Science,* published in earlier (1725) and later (1730) versions, is commonly regarded as founding the philosophy of history. It is also the first modern conception of a philosophy of mythology and of the philosophy of culture.

Vico's philosophy develops generally through three phases, from his early pedagogical orations, 1699–1709; to his work on universal law in the 1720s; to his foundation of the two versions of the *New Science*. Vico's conception of education is derived from the tradition of Italian Renaissance humanism, with its emphasis on self-knowledge as the goal of human education. As part of his duties during the first years of his career at the university, Vico delivered an oration to inaugurate each academic year. In the first oration (1699) Vico states that self-knowledge in the sense of *gnothi seauton,* "Know thyself," as inscribed on the Temple of Apollo at Delphi, is the goal of human education. He conceives the goal as the student's studying each part of the curriculum of the various fields of knowledge as a cycle. The human being knows what it is to be human by mastering all of the various kinds of know-ing distinctive to man. Thus in Vico's view self-knowledge is achieved, not by introspection, but by the individual's becoming a whole university. Vico says that Socrates (c. 470–399 B.C.) was himself a whole university.

In Vico's subsequent five orations, he explores themes concerning the value of education to the individual and to society, as well as to the church. In his famous seventh oration, published in 1709 as a little book, *On the Study Methods of Our Time,* Vico advances the first full statement of his original philosophical position. In opposition to the Cartesian and Port-Royal concepts of education as based in developing the logical power of thought in the young, Vico advocates training young minds first and foremost in the arts of memory, imagination, and topics (*topoi*).

Vico claims that to teach logic, metaphysics, and analytic geometry to the young mind damages it. These are subjects to be introduced into a curriculum once the mind has matured. Education is to be arranged in accord with the natural development of self, in which children are to be schooled in metaphor, poetry, and memory, things in which they naturally excel. Only if the mind is so developed in the powers that underlie poetic and rhetoric can the mature individual create the necessary starting points for arguments. If educated only in the techniques of evaluating abstractions and testing the validity of arguments, the mind will have no grasp of how to create beginning points for arguments through the power of metaphor and *ingenium.* Vico advocates the early study of Euclidean geometry because of its training in the use of figures and images, but he delays the study of analytic geometry because of its reliance on abstractions.

In his translation of Vico's *Study Methods,* Elio Gianturco quotes in his introduction the great Vico scholar, Fausto Nicolini, who says that this work of Vico's is "the most important pedagogic essay between Locke's *Thoughts on Education* (1693) and *Emile* (1762) of Rousseau." Vico carries further his conception of humane education in his oration "On the Heroic Mind" (1732), in which he challenges the students to master the complete cycle of studies that constitutes a university education. Although the number of studies is expanded from the list of grammar, rhetoric, history, Greek, moral philosophy, and poetry of the *studia humanitatis* of the humanists, it is an endorsement of this ideal. Vico appears to take his title from his concept in the *New Science* of the heroic age, in which he projects an "ideal eternal history" of three ages, through which any nation progresses in its rise, maturity, and fall in history. These are an age of gods (in which all the forces of nature and social institutions are formed in terms of gods); an age of heroes (in which the virtues of human conduct and social life are personified and conceived through their attachment to the figures of certain heroes); and an age of humans (a purely secular age, in which language becomes abstract and propositional—an age of Cartesian-style thinking—that is Vico's age and our own). The age of heroes is a zenith point in Vico's conception of the history of any nation. In the figure of the hero, the power of imagination is joined with virtue. Although we live in an age of humans, which is dominated, in Vico's view, by a "barbarism of reflection," and thus we cannot ourselves actually become heroic figures acting in society, we can nonetheless aspire to develop ourselves as thinkers in a heroic manner, joining our powers of knowledge and learning with virtue.

Vico's conception of education is ultimately an attempt to strike a balance between the art of civil wisdom, cultivated by the ancients, and the new sciences invented and developed by the moderns. In his last oration dealing with education, "The Academies and the Relation of Philosophy and Eloquence" (1737), Vico says: "I hold the opinion that if eloquence does not regain the luster of the Latins and Greeks in our time, when our sciences have made progress equal to and perhaps even greater than theirs, it will be because the sciences are taught completely stripped of every badge of eloquence."

In a world that Vico sees as progressively dominated by the methodology of scientific conceptions of knowledge held by the moderns, he wishes to preserve the views of Cicero, Quintilian, and Horace of the Latin and Greek world as it is brought forward in the humanist tradition. Thus Vico wishes to train students in that ideal of joining *sapientia, eloquentia,* and *prudentia*—knowledge, eloquence, and prudence. The aim of education is not simply to import knowledge of technical or scientific subjects but also to teach the student to think well, speak well, and act well. These are keys to self-knowledge and to "wisdom." As Vico says in the *Study Methods,* "the whole is the flower of wisdom." Perhaps more than any other, this line sums up Vico's conception of the aim of education—to develop in the student a vision of the whole of human knowledge.

Donald Phillip Verene

See also CICERO; CURRICULUM AND INSTRUCTION; DESCARTES; LOCKE; LOGIC; METAPHYSICS; QUINTILIAN; RHETORIC; ROUSSEAU; *Studia Humanitatis*

Bibliography

Berlin, Isaiah. *Vico and Herder: Two Studies in the History of Ideas.* New York: Viking, 1976.

Mooney, Michael. *Vico in the Tradition of Rhetoric.* Princeton: Princeton University Press, 1984.

New Vico Studies 1 (1983)– . Vol. 3 forward includes annual update of the bibliography by Tagliacozzo et al.

Pompa, Leon. *Vico: A Study of the "New Science."* Cambridge: Cambridge University Press, 1975.

Tagliacozzo, Giorgio, Donald Phillip Verene, and Vanessa Rumble. *A Bibliography of Vico in English 1884–1984.* Bowling Green, Ohio: Philosophy Documentation Center, 1986.

Verene, Donald Phillip. *The New Art of Autobiography. An Essay on the "Life of Giambattista Vico Written by Himself."* Oxford: Clarendon Press, 1991.

———. *Vico's Science of Imagination.* Ithaca, N.Y.: Cornell University Press, 1981.

Vico, Giambattista. *The Autobiography of Giambattista Vico.* Translated by Max Harold Fisch and Thomas Goddard Bergin. Ithaca, N.Y.: Cornell University Press, 1944, 1963, 1975.

———. *The New Science of Giambattista Vico.* Translated from the 3rd edition (1744) by Thomas Goddard Bergin and Max Harold Fisch. Ithaca, N.Y.: Cornell University Press, 1948. 2nd revised ed., with an introduction by Max Harold Fisch, 1968. Reprinted with corrections, 1976. Reprinted unabridged, including "Practice of the New Science," Ithaca, N.Y.: Cornell University Press Paperbacks, 1984.

———. *On Humanistic Education (Six Inaugural Orations, 1699–1707).* Translated from the Visconti (1982) edition by Giorgio A. Pinton and Arthur W.

Shippee, with an introduction by Donald Phillip Verene. Ithaca, N.Y.: Cornell University Press, 1993.

———. *On the Most Ancient Wisdom of the Italians, Unearthed from the Origins of the Latin Language.* Including the Disputations with the *Giornale de' Letterati d'Italia.* Translated by L. M. Palmer. Ithaca, N.Y.: Cornell University Press, 1988.

———. *On the Study Methods of Our Time.* Translated by Elio Gianturco. Indianapolis, Ind.: Bobbs-Merrill, Library of the Liberal Arts, 1965. Reprinted, with a preface by Donald Phillip Verene, including "The Academies and the Relation between Philosophy and Eloquence," translated by D. P. Verene. Ithaca, N.Y.: Cornell University Press, 1990.

Vocational Education

Vocational education usually refers to the practical skill training offered at the secondary-education level that leads to paid employment. More generally, it is what one learns in order to do one's work or vocation.

A number of issues derive from two uses of the term: (1) vocation from the Latin *vocatio* (a call or summons) may refer to one's work as a calling, as in, for example, "a divine call to God's service," or (2) vocation may refer to the occupation or job one holds to make a living.

At the dawn of history the chief vocation consisted of the activities performed to meet survival needs: the needs for food, clothing, protection, shelter, and so on. Children learned skills by working informally with parents or other adults. Human culture evolved to new levels of complexity as new tools and skills—including the tool of language—emerged. Over time the long-standing hunting and gathering gave way to the pasturing of domesticated animals, which in turn gave way to the settled more complex life of agriculture and commerce.

In the fourth and third millennia B.C., metal implements replaced stone tools. Great improvements took place in the skills of manufacturing and agriculture along the main river valleys of Mesopotamia and Egypt. Specialization began in crafts like metal-working, tool and weapon production, garment making, and construction. The apprenticeship system arose as the young were apprenticed to specialists to learn their skills. (Apprentice comes from the

Latin *apprendere,* to learn.) The apprenticeship system in which the young learn the practical skills of a craft under the guidance of adults continued to be the major system for producing skilled workers until the advent of factory industrialism in the nineteenth century, when many workers were reduced to de-skilled machine tenders.

A major issue emerged in the fifth and fourth centuries B.C. when Greek culture, through the influence of Plato and Aristotle, developed a dualist concept of humans and education that sharply demarcated "liberal education" from "practical or vocational training" (a dualism that dominated thinking about education in the West into the twentieth century).

When Athenian democracy was under stress in the fourth century B.C., Plato and Aristotle articulated an aristocratic ideal for saving the Greek city-states. Plato postulated the idea in *The Republic* that there are three classes of humans: Those whose nature is dominated by their physical being are destined to be workers or traders; those marked by courage or hardihood are to be warriors; only those whose nature is dominated by the rational/intellectual power of the soul are qualified to be rulers. They could create the just society in which all perform the roles appropriate to their natures.

The first two classes could receive practical training geared to improving skills as workers or warriors. A special program of liberal studies was developed for the future leaders; it consisted of systematically organized, abstract subject matter designed to sharpen and strengthen the intellect. Over time these studies became the formally organized system of the seven liberal arts: the trivium (grammar, rhetoric, and logic), which disciplined the verbal powers of the mind; and the quadrivium (arithmetic, geometry, music, and astronomy), which trained through the disciplinary language of mathematics.

In Roman, medieval, and Renaissance times, a class-divided European educational system emerged. Plato's attitude became accepted—that only the abstract liberal arts that trained the intellect deserved to be called education. Studies that improved skills of the body (man's lower nature) deserved only the lesser label of training. The system for the leisure upper class, conducted in the "dead" language of Latin, came to consist of secondary schools teaching the seven liberal arts as prerequisites for university study of the professions, such as theology, law, and medicine. Training for craftsmen was taught in the vernacular through apprenticeship. While artisans or craftsmen created objects of great beauty, complexity, and strength throughout Europe, they continued to be viewed as lower in the social order.

With the growth of commerce and urban life in the fourteenth and fifteenth centuries, the artisans and merchants created guilds to guard their secrets, to guarantee the quality of production, and to control admission to their ranks. They created three levels of training: Young apprentices, aged ten to eleven, were placed under the educational and moral supervision of master craftsmen for three to ten years; journeymen, at the next stage, could travel for advanced training with different masters under wages set by the guild. After demonstrating mastery of the craft to the guild masters, journeymen were admitted as full-fledged masters who could open their own shops.

With the growth of a merchant capitalist economy in the sixteenth and seventeenth centuries, the guilds were weakened when entrepreneurs developed the "domestic system." Guilds were bypassed as work was hired out to workers in their homes who were paid at piece rates as low as the merchant could manage.

In the New World, the United States won its war of independence in 1783. Apart from the dark stain of slavery, the new American economy was organized around small, independently owned farms, and commerce and craft enterprises. Training for working people was gained informally from parents, or through a European-type apprenticeship system. After independence, farmers, mechanics, and artisans, motivated by the desire for dignity and learning worthy of free citizens, created Lyceums and Mechanics Institutes with studies that spoke to the broader cultural interests of their members.

These were scarcely under way when the republic was torn by the trauma of the Civil War. In its aftermath came the onrush of factory industrialism powered by new science and technology. It transformed American society and dealt deadly blows to the tradition of craft apprenticeship.

Millions of impoverished European immigrants crowded into cities to find work in the new factories. A major challenge at the opening of the twentieth century was how to coordinate the labor of uneducated immigrants with the power of factory technology. A young engineer, Frederick W. Taylor, provided the needed

V

conceptual invention—Taylorism, a rationally organized assembly-line mode of production that broke the work process into easily learned, repetitive, mindless tasks. Thinking and control of the enterprise were the exclusive prerogatives of the managers and technicians at the top. Factory managers expected little from the new de-skilled machine tenders except enough of the three Rs to be able to read manuals and to follow the directions of supervisors.

But new orders of complexity arose with corporate factory industrialism. With the expansion of the railroads and steam and electric-powered machinery, new kinds and levels of skill were urgently needed. The learning required to build locomotives and power-driven machines could not be picked up informally by following mentors. Schools of engineering multiplied after the Civil War to train new cadres of technical experts. Other professional colleges were created for managers and business experts, and eventually colleges of education to teach the new army of urban teachers. Commercial schools were added at the secondary level to train women as well as men as bookkeepers, secretaries, and stenographers who could process the flow of paper and numbers in "the white-collar factories."

By 1900 American manufacturers, venturing into the markets of the world, found themselves confronted with a major competitor with marked advantages in quality and cost of product. They were confronted with the awesome power of corporate German efficiency. Investigations by the American manufacturers convinced them that the source of German superiority derived from a powerful system of carefully graded vocational training programs (twenty-one different schools for the building trades alone) neatly meshed to the hierarchical skill needs of corporate industry and commerce.

In the opening years of the twentieth century, the National Association of Manufacturers set in motion a campaign to establish a comparable system of vocational training in the United States. It was to be separate from the general education system, directed, as in Germany, by "practical men" of industry rather than "impractical educators." The purpose was to produce highly skilled, disciplined workers equipped to maximize efficiency of industrial production.

This proposal triggered a contentious debate among educators. On the one side were "social efficiency philosophers," like David

Snedden and Charles Prosser, who supported the cause of the manufacturers. On the other side were progressive social democrats led by the American philosopher John Dewey.

The debate was fueled by two competing social philosophies: social Darwinism and social democracy. The social efficiency vocationalists like Snedden and Prosser supported social Darwinist ideology. It held that society consists of isolated individuals of varying capacities and abilities. When left to pursue personal advantage in rugged competition, people will be sorted into their natural levels of competence. The newest engine of progress was the hierarchically organized corporate factory system. For maximum efficiency, those fitted to be the "foot soldiers of the assembly line" would work dutifully under the discipline and supervision of "the captains of industry." The top-down, expertly controlled system of Taylorist efficiency would enable the United States to be a winner in the competitive global market.

Snedden and Prosser argued for German-type vocationalism, which centered on detailed practical training designed and administered by industrial leaders to teach a work ethic that emphasized full acceptance of the authority of management.

This called forth an opposition, led by John Dewey, who saw in the proposal a not so subtle effort to instill a class-divided European system into American society—a system with university education for "the captains of industry" and a narrow, practical job-training for docile "foot soldiers" on the line. In such a system the demands of factory efficiency ruled out values of democracy in the workplace as irrelevant and inappropriate. Democracy for dutiful workers was to be limited to periodic voting in civic elections.

Dewey argued for a social democracy that would equip all free Americans, the working class as well as the executive class, with critical thinking skills with which to cope with turbulent change—and with the capacity to make judgments about economic and social policies. A democratic society, he said, should be based on the proposition that "the dominant vocation of all human beings at all times is intellectual and moral growth" (Dewey: 362). The moral purpose of all institutions, including industrial arrangements, is to contribute to the all-round growth of every member of society. He argued for bringing values of democracy into the workplace with policies that would "tap the brains of people at work" and would replace rigid hierarchical structures with broad worker participation. While Dewey never plotted a detailed blueprint for a social/industrial democracy, he leaned toward experiments with democratic syndicalism centered on the idea of worker ownership of individual industries.

While Dewey opposed narrow vocational training, he made the case for including occupational studies as a key part of general education for all Americans. The case for this novel idea was his conviction that human life at the opening of the twentieth century was being transformed by the power of science and technology. Getting students involved in the study of the impact of science on human work would give them vivid insight into its power. It could also give them experience with the active, problem-solving mode of learning employed by science.

Dewey opposed the pressure of the social efficiency vocationalists for premature skill training for salable skills because it could lead educators to miss the opportunity to reveal the intellectual meaning of technology-driven industry, which held both promise and threat. A narrow vocationalism without a critical liberalizing dimension could create a passive, subordinate working class ill equipped to change an unsatisfactory industrialism into something more civilized.

To illustrate his argument, Dewey created a distinctive curriculum for his Laboratory School at the University of Chicago. He made the study of the historical evolution of human occupations the integrating core. Study focused on how basic human needs, such as food, clothing, protection, communication, and transportation, had been profoundly affected by major stages in the evolution of civilization—beginning with prehistoric hunting and gathering, and culminating in the rise and expansion of science and technology.

Academic study of mathematics, literature, and science was integrated with the historical studies. Emphasis was placed on the opportunities the study of occupations provided for collaborative, problem-solving, "doing" kinds of learning. This was in contrast to the passive "lesson saying" that prevailed in urban schools. Students were to learn the habits and skills of reflective thinking in the ways they lived and learned in the school community.

Dewey's image of effective learning as an active, reflective, problem-solving process based on the model of scientific inquiry intrigued many theorists and some educators. It did not carry the day, however, in the debate over vocational education.

The social efficiency vocationalists effectively triumphed when Congress passed the Smith-Hughes Act (1917). It provided federal funding for a separate system of vocational studies in agriculture, industrial and trade education, and home economics. The trade-training emphasis was underscored by a provision stating that the controlling purpose of such education should be "to fit for useful employment." While vocational studies could be included in comprehensive high schools, they, in fact, became separate "tracks" of lower status than the "college-prep" track.

By the closing decade of the century, however, new circumstances emerged that underscored the necessity for a working integration of liberal and vocational studies.

By the 1990s, standardized factory production was being supplanted by a new postindustrialism marked by the electronics/computer revolution, a fiercely competitive global market, and serious ecological damage. For survival, the United States needed a world-class economy and workers with a world-class education.

In industry, top-down Taylorist management lacked the flexibility of response to cope with turbulent change. Critical thinking and creative response capabilities needed to be dispersed throughout the workforce. America's chief competitors, Japan and Germany, replaced de-skilled assembly-line workers with participative work teams staffed by a front-line workforce educated with both the technical and academic skills of midlevel technicians and managers.

Important American educational policy makers began calling for similar moves in the United States. They held that the traditional high school with its tracking system was dysfunctional for the kind of high-tech work that was emerging. A new "Tech Prep" was proposed that would integrate academic and technical studies in programs that combined the last two years of high school with the first year of junior college for non–college bound students. Tracking would be eliminated, as all students would take academic courses of college-prep quality, but there would be a distinctive "applied learning" emphasis for those headed for work. Practical experience in various apprenticeship programs or community service would be integrated with academic studies. Students who finished Tech Prep studies would receive a postsecondary achievement certificate. This would become the base line for career-long learning toward additional higher Technical Achievement Certificates, or study in college or universities.

The aspiration was to create a high-skill/high-wage economy in which a highly educated, highly motivated front-line workforce would work collaboratively in a new, more equal partnership with advanced-level technical and managerial personnel.

There was a growing awareness emerging with such proposals that factory-era industrialism had created serious ecological damage. To move away from destructive habits required a new *vocatio* (calling) for all workers and citizens—a *vocatio* with values and skills designed not only to improve the quality of products but also the quality of life itself on the planet.

Arthur G. Wirth

See also CURRICULUM AND INSTRUCTION; DEMOCRACY; DEWEY; HIGHER EDUCATION; LEISURE; MARXISM; SOCIALISM; WORK

Bibliography

Barlow, Melvin L. *History of Industrial Education in the United States.* Peoria, Ill.: Charles A. Bennett, 1967.

Bowra, C.M. *The Greek Experience.* New York: World, 1957.

Butts, R. Freeman. *A Cultural History of Education: Reassessing Our Educational Traditions.* New York: McGraw-Hill, 1947.

Dewey, John. *Democracy and Education.* New York: Macmillan, 1916.

Donohue, John W. *Work and Education: The Role of Technical Culture and Some Distinctive Theories of Humanism.* Chicago: Loyola University Press, 1959.

Fisher, Berenice. *Industrial Education: American Ideals and Institutions.* Madison: University of Wisconsin Press, 1967.

Jaeger, Werner. *Paideia: The Ideals of Greek Culture.* New York: Oxford University Press, 1944.

Wirth, Arthur G. *Education in the Technological Society: The Vocational-Liberal Studies Controversy in the Early Twentieth Century.* Washington, D.C.: University Press of America, 1980.

Washington, Booker Taliaferro
(1856–1915)

Through the life and career of Booker T. Washington one is able to observe closely and understand better the critical transition period in America from the close of the Civil War to World War I, especially as far as the condition of the African-Americans is concerned. The prism of his experiences, his work and his writings, exposes subtleties of life in America in that period that otherwise may be obscure.

Washington was born in 1856 to a slave mother and a white father on the Burrough's Plantation near Hale's Ford, Virginia. After the Emancipation, in 1865, his mother moved his family to Malden, West Virginia. During Washington's youth he had very little opportunity for schooling, only one hour a day for the winter months, private study on his own, and occasional tutoring at night. The circumstances of his upbringing are fully described in his autobiography, *Up from Slavery*, published in 1901.

As a young man he worked in the coal mines, and one day while at work he overheard a conversation about a school in Virginia that had been established for freed blacks. He heard also that students there could work and earn their full expenses. This conversation became the impetus for Washington to decide to leave Malden and the coal mines and to seek a new life with education and better opportunities.

In order to earn his travel expenses for the five-hundred-mile trip from Malden, West Virginia, to Hampton Institute on the Chesapeake Bay in Virginia, he continued to work a few more months in the coal mines. Meanwhile, he learned of a job in the home of a Mrs. Ruffner, the wife of a Union Army general and owner of

a salt furnace and a coal mine. It appears that the discipline and rigor required by Mrs. Ruffner were the foundation for much of Washington's progress that followed. She taught him the virtues of thoroughness and consistency, of cleanliness and trustworthiness. For a year and a half, this informal education under Mrs. Ruffner prepared Washington for Hampton Institute.

The bleak poverty of Washington's early years can be seen in his travel experiences from West Virginia to Hampton. He left home with $1.50, traveling some of the distance by train and stagecoach but walking a large portion of the way. The determination that he showed in overcoming seemingly insurmountable obstacles in reaching Hampton—extreme hunger, sleeplessness, exposure to adverse weather, and walking alone through mountain forests—would be observed later in his career as he continued to face challenges.

When he reached Richmond, Virginia, with no money, he had to sleep on the ground beneath a plant-board sidewalk. With his funds exhausted he found temporary employment unloading pig iron from a ship in Richmond's port, and he was able to survive until he reached Hampton with fifty cents.

Union Army General Samuel C. Armstrong had founded Hampton Normal and Industrial Institute, with the support of the Bureau of Freedmen, Refugees and Abandoned Lands, at the mouth of the James River on a body of water called Hampton Roads, facing the Chesapeake Bay. This location, incidentally, was only fifteen miles from Jamestown, where the first black slaves were landed in 1619. The Freedmen's Bureau was an agency of the United States Government, established in 1865 for the purpose of aiding the emancipated slaves in acquiring education, health care, and other incentives toward succeeding in their new status as free persons and full citizens. The broader mission was to protect freed blacks from abuses and poverty.

General Armstrong was a New Englander with sympathy and concern for Indians and blacks, and Hampton Institute promoted his idea of the kind of education that would benefit both groups most. He believed that their progress would be best ensured by skill training in agriculture and the manual arts, not only to become useful employees with marketable skills, but to become successful entrepreneurs as well. Accompanying this training in agriculture, homemaking, and the manual arts, Hampton emphasized personal discipline, religious training, health care, and citizenship responsibility. The basic philosophy was that the blacks should find a place in the scheme of things and where opportunities could be found, rather than prepare for other roles and professions that were not yet open to them. It was a practical and pragmatic approach, compatible with the prevailing view of blacks as a servant class with an obligation to earn respect and approval. Such education was offered at Hampton rather than a program in the liberal arts.

When Washington arrived at Hampton he was tested by one of the teachers to judge his fitness for admission. The test was to clean a nearby classroom. The test was also an introduction to the educational program in operation at Hampton. He had traveled for several weeks without adequate food, clothing, or lodging, and he felt that his appearance would cause his rejection. He seized the opportunity to clean the room, to win approval and to gain admission. He cleaned the floors and woodwork so thoroughly that the teacher could not find a speck of dust even with a white handkerchief.

Washington graduated in 1875 and returned to his coal mining community to teach. Soon afterward, he attended a teacher-training course at Wayland Academy, a Baptist institution in the District of Columbia that later became a part of Virginia Union University. Following his training at Wayland in 1879, he returned to Hampton as a teacher. Within two years, in 1881, a request came from blacks and concerned whites to send a teacher to rural Tuskegee, Alabama, to establish a school similar to the one in Hampton.

General Armstrong had enough faith and confidence in Washington's ability, and in his comprehension of the Hampton philosophy, to send him in response to the Tuskegee request. The result was that Washington was able to earn the trust of the people, to enlist the support of black and white leaders, and to solicit funds from churches and philanthropists; his success was so remarkable that his fame spread rapidly throughout the country and abroad.

Washington became a loyal advocate of the Hampton approach to schooling for blacks and a faithful disciple of General Armstrong. He was proud of Tuskegee's progress in training young blacks in cooking, blacksmithing, carpentry, painting, plastering, farming, sewing, fancy iron working, wheelwrighting, upholstering, animal husbandry, soil science, shoe repairing, tailoring, and allied trades.

He won the attention of the great philanthropists, the Huntingdons, the Mellons, the Carnegies, and the Rockefellers, and became a spokesperson for blacks in all aspects of their progress in America. His influence was felt throughout the black communities in America. Blacks discovered that politicians, public officials, foundations, and philanthropists sought Washington's approval on almost every issue regarding support for black endeavors. He and his associates at Tuskegee became known as the "Tuskegee machine," and some held them in awe, while others held them in suspicion and contempt.

Black organizations and conventions sought him as a leading platform speaker and as a counselor. He was a frequent speaker in white congregations in the North and was invited to places such as Harvard University to describe and defend his ideas about education for blacks and his strategy for black progress. Washington was consistent in his promotion of education in agriculture and the manual arts as most appropriate for blacks at that time. He was also consistent in rejecting education in the liberal arts, fine arts, and political and social strategies for black advancement. He was willing to defer political activity and social acceptance until an economic base had been established.

Early in Washington's career he became the center of a stormy controversy among blacks and the supporters of black education. His detractors were many, but the most prominent among them was W.E.B. Du Bois, a black alumnus of Fisk University with a liberal arts degree and a Ph.D. in history from Harvard. He had been born in 1868 in Great Barrington, Massachusetts, and was reared and educated in a town with less than a 1 percent black population.

Du Bois taught at black liberal arts schools, Atlanta University, and Wilberforce University, and was one of the founders of the National Association for the Advancement of Colored People, an interracial organization whose purpose was to secure equality and justice for blacks.

Washington and Du Bois were friends and collaborators during their early years, but as Washington became more vocal in his advocacy of training blacks to meet the market for jobs in the manual arts, and in deemphasizing education in the liberal arts, he and Du Bois became vigorous opponents. In his book entitled *Souls of Black Folk,* published in 1902, Du Bois was vehement in his protest against Washington's philosophy of accommodation and gradualism. In Washington's autobiography, *Up from Slavery,* he spelled out the rationale for his approach, defending the idea of securing an economic base as a priority and deferring agitation for social and political equality. He identified the black problem as one of poverty and ignorance, primarily, rendering blacks ill-prepared for a quest for equality at that time.

The political climate of the day gave fuel to the fire of controversy among blacks. Washington's enemies saw him as an opportunist who enjoyed the power that white politicians and philanthropists had conferred upon him. Washington was able to confer with presidents, dine at the White House with President McKinley, and visit royalty in Europe. In 1896, Harvard conferred upon him an honorary Master of Arts degree. Nevertheless, his opponents saw him as one who was willing to compromise with the evils of racism and black oppression for the sake of prominence and power.

When Washington began at Tuskegee, the Reconstruction was in its demise. Whites were regaining power in the South. The 1876 Hayes election had removed the Union Army from their occupation, and blacks were rapidly losing the gains they had made in the late 1860s. Moreover, the 1896 Plessy-Ferguson Supreme Court decision gave the states the right to pass laws requiring racial segregation in public travel and accommodations, in education, hospitals, and wherever it was deemed desirable. Lynching began to spread, and life for blacks became characterized by fear and humiliation. Washing-

ton's opponents believed that his philosophy gave aid and comfort to these developments, while he became famous and powerful. His followers and his opponents constituted two major factions among blacks, and the division became bitter and lasting.

There were many black educators, however, who joined Washington and fostered manual training in colleges and secondary schools, especially in the private and church-related schools that were dependent upon white philanthropists. For very practical reasons, the schools added courses in the trades, agriculture, and homemaking to both secondary and collegiate training. The poverty in black communities and the limited job opportunities compelled the schools to prepare blacks to earn a livelihood where they found openings. In addition, it was commonly understood that funds would be made available more readily to those schools that taught the manual arts and agriculture.

This apparent conflict made the question of Washington's philosophy and its justification paradoxical. On the one hand, in the wake of the slave experience blacks did need to earn a living. They did need to learn to do economical and productive farming, to build and repair their own houses and farm equipment, and to earn money in the service occupations and as skilled domestic servants. These jobs were open to them. Yet, on the other hand, in promoting this program Washington rejected the notion of preparing a black leadership class, educated in literature, philosophy, sociology, economics, and political science, on the grounds that other needs were more pressing than a crusade for social and political equality. Often Washington made comments emphasizing the importance of voting, the evil of lynching, or the injustice of racial inequality, but such were parenthetical to his principal theme of deferment of strategies toward equality.

In 1895 the leaders of business and industry in the South sponsored an exhibition in Atlanta, the Cotton States' Exposition. The purpose was to promote business for the region, and for the first time such an exposition provided space for blacks to present their products and to make their claim for recognition. Moreover, in an unprecedented move, Booker T. Washington was invited to deliver one of the opening addresses. The audience was racially mixed, including Mr. Washington's supporters and a large number of white merchants and politicians.

Washington's speech in 1895 was a clear and unambiguous statement of his overall position, of which fragments appear in all of his writings. He began by criticizing blacks who had been elected to the Congress and the state legislature, signifying that such activities were misplaced and that they should have been starting farms instead. He asked the whites to trust blacks not to engage in organized labor and to be patient. He reminded them that in matters social, the races could remain as separate as the fingers, but in things "essential to mutual progress," "one as the hand." He said that the agitation of "questions of social equality" was the "extremist folly." There was a strong plea for white support of black education and prosperity, but it was cloaked in language that guaranteed to the white listeners that the status quo politically and socially, with blacks treated as inferiors, would be unchallenged. The speech was widely acclaimed throughout the nation, and the next year Harvard awarded Washington an honorary degree.

Washington was as much of a political and social activist as he was an educator. His extraordinary success in building Tuskegee Institute in rural Alabama under extremely adverse social and political conditions earned for him unquestioned and stellar recognition as an educational pioneer. The example that he set inspired countless other blacks to attempt similar endeavors, and, while many achieved limited success, others produced some of the strongest and most productive of the historically black institutions. In 1889 when the Morrill Act (Land Grant) was revised and Southern states were required to establish Land Grant institutions for blacks, the Tuskegee model was the major influence on these schools. Washington's influence was felt throughout black education.

Following the Emancipation Proclamation, America faced a unique and unprecedented challenge: to find a way of inducting four million former slaves into independent and productive economic survival, and to prepare them for their responsibility as citizens. Washington's idea of establishing (with the necessary training) an economic base that was both practical and efficient was highly acceptable, applauded, and implemented with success. The corollary position that Washington embraced, to assure whites of the willingness of blacks to defer the struggle for political and social equality, was an incalculable price for white approval, especially with the rejection of liberal arts education for blacks.

As an educator with a relevant, effective, and successful approach to a unique and temporized situation, Washington enjoyed immense success. As a leader of thought in a critical period in America's history, Washington compromised with racism and gave aid and comfort to those who believed in the inferiority of blacks.

Samuel D. Proctor

See also Du Bois; Equality; Minorities; Race and Racism

Bibliography

Denton, Virginia L. *Booker T. Washington and the Adult Education Movement.* Gainesville: University of Florida Press, 1993.

Du Bois, W.E.B. *Souls of Black Folk.* New York: Avon Library, 1965.

Harlan, Lewis R. *The Making of a Black Leader, 1856–1901,* vol. 1; and *The Wizard of Tuskegee, 1901–1915,* vol. 2. New York: Oxford University Press, 1972, 1983.

Meier, August. *Negro Thought in America, 1880–1915: Racial Ideology in the Age of Booker T. Washington.* Ann Arbor: University of Michigan Press, 1963.

Spencer, Samuel R. *Booker T. Washington and the Negro's Place in American Life.* Boston: Little, Brown, 1955.

Washington, Booker T. *Up from Slavery.* New York: Avon Library, 1965.

Webster, Noah (1758–1843)

American educator whose textbooks provided the first uniquely American perspective on education, and whose dictionary became America's standard. Webster graduated from Yale in 1778 and formulated a plan for textbooks that would make America independent of British products. He published the *Speller* in 1783, the *Grammar* in 1784, and the *Reader* in 1785.

Webster's *Speller,* known later as the *Blue-Back Speller,* was a tremendous success. His goal was to establish a spelling standard for the entire country. He hoped that unified spelling would contribute to a unified people politically. The *Speller* changed syllabic divisions. British spellers began each syllable with a consonant. For example, they divided the word *cluster* as *clu ster.* Webster felt that a more natural division was *clus ter.* He also altered the division of words ending with *-sion* and *-tion.* The usual practice had been to divide such a word into three syllables: *na ti on.* Webster argued for two syllables only. Although these alterations sparked controversy, the *Speller* was successful beyond the author's hopes. It continued in print well into the twentieth century. During its long life, in its various forms, the *Speller* sold approximately seventy million copies.

The *Grammar* was not successful. Webster's attempt to divorce English grammar from Latin lost out in a crowded field of more traditional approaches. The *Reader,* while not approaching the success of the *Speller,* was widely used, and Webster continued to produce readers throughout his life, seeing them as tools for inculcating moral principles and patriotism.

In 1790, Webster tried an experiment in orthography. Enamored of Benjamin Franklin's design to alter American spelling, Webster published a collection of essays with a new way of spelling, tied more closely to pronunciation. As he stated in his introduction to *A Collection of Essays and Fugitiv Writings,* "The man who admits that the change of housbonde, mynde, ygone, moneth into husband, mind, gone, month, iz an improvement, must acknowledge also the riting of helth, breth, rong, tung, munth, to be an improvement." The public did not accept that drastic change, but eventually Webster succeeded in making some changes permanent: the elimination of k from words such as *musick* (music) and *publick* (public), and the change from s to c to z in words such as *practise* (practice) and *organise* (organize).

By 1807, his educational plan was to perfect the *Speller,* promote his *Elements of Useful Knowledge* and his *Philosophical and Practical Grammar;* and compile dictionaries. At this point, Webster turned to lexicography almost full time. He published his dictionary in 1828, a one-man effort that took twenty years.

In 1808, Webster converted to orthodox Christianity. This conversion gave him a new purpose for his work, as he began to see everything through a biblical perspective. It particularly affected his approach to the dictionary. The main purpose of the dictionary, in Webster's view, was to serve as a force for educating Americans in the principles of the Christian faith, principles that could remake government, schools, and other pertinent social institutions into Webster's Christian ideal. His definitions included biblical passages as examples of word usage. He also incorporated short commentaries. For instance, in the defini-

tion of education, Webster concludes: "To give children a good education in manners, arts and science, is important; to give them a religious education is indispensable; and an immense responsibility rests on parents and guardians who neglect these duties."

The influence of the *Speller* and the dictionary gives Webster claim to the title of Father of Early American Education.

K. Alan Snyder

See also AIMS OF EDUCATION; CIVIC EDUCATION; ETHICS AND MORALITY; FRANKLIN; RELIGIOUS EDUCATION

Bibliography

Babbidge, Homer D., Jr., ed. *Noah Webster: On Being American.* New York: Frederick A. Praeger, 1967.

Monaghan, E. Jennifer. *A Common Heritage: Noah Webster's Blue-Back Speller.* Hamden, Conn.: Archon Books, 1983.

Moss, Richard J. *Noah Webster.* Boston: Twayne, 1984.

Rollins, Richard M. *The Long Journey of Noah Webster.* Philadelphia: University of Pennsylvania Press, 1980.

Snyder, K. Alan. *Defining Noah Webster: Mind and Morals in the Early Republic.* Lanham, Md.: University Press of America, 1990.

Staudenraus, P.J. "Mr. Webster's Dictionary: A Personal Document of the Age of Benevolence." *Mid-America* 45, no. 3 (1963): 193–201.

Warfel, Harry R. *Noah Webster: Schoolmaster to America.* New York: Macmillan, 1936. Reprint. New York: Octagon, 1966.

Webster, Noah. *An American Dictionary of the English Language.* New York: Sherman Converse, 1928. Reprint. Anaheim, Calif.: Foundation for American Christian Education, 1967.

———. *A Collection of Essays and Fugitiv Writings.* Boston: Thomas and Andrews, 1790. Reprint. Delmar, New York: Scholars' Facsimiles and Reprints, 1977.

———. *Elements of Useful Knowledge.* Hartford: Hudson and Goodwin, 1806.

———. *A Grammatical Institute of the English Language, Part I* (Speller). Hartford: Hudson and Goodwin, 1783.

———. *History of the United States.* New Haven: Durrie and Peck, 1832.

Whitehead, Alfred North (1861–1947)

Whitehead did not write a coherent work in the philosophy of education. His major philosophical work, *Process and Reality*, does not treat education—or relevant subtopics such as teaching, learning, curriculum, or social governance. His influence in American education stems from essays on education published between 1912 and 1928 and collected in *The Aims of Education and Other Essays*. The influence of his comprehensive speculative philosophy of the organism waned during the hegemony of analytic philosophy (1950 to 1980), but recently his ideas have been rehabilitated in philosophy (Lucas; Rapp and Wiehl) and in education (Evans; Brumbaugh; Egan; Hendley). The Association of Process Philosophy, through conferences and publications, is organizing an effort to construct a process philosophy of education using Whitehead, John Dewey (1859–1952), and Henri Bergson (1859–1941) as major sources.

Whitehead's Theory

A principle in philosophy determines the functioning of a text, and in Whitehead that principle is creativity. Creativity is the key principle of novelty; novel events occur not determined by antecedents. A major factor in human mentality is the "conceptual entertainment of unrealized possibilities" (*Modes of Thought*). Whitehead uses the words "eternal objects" to stand for unrealized possibilities, and when these through becoming take form, he names them "actual entities" of actual occasions. Reality for Whitehead is process. Nature is alive with waves of energy (and emotion-feelings). Subjectivity and objectivity are always connected ("two ends of the same worm"). There is no "vacuous actuality"; there is no material substance unrelated to aliveness. Growing together ("concrescence") and perishing and regrowing are constant features of process activity.

Whitehead's method is dialectical, influenced by G.W.F. Hegel's dialectic of progress. This pattern of thesis—antithesis—synthesis was renamed by Whitehead to make the idea of progressive change in history more "happily suggestive" for intellectual progress in education. Whitehead named the dialectic in education as stages of romance (wonder, awe), precision (utility, definite action), generalization (satisfaction, resolution). He thought them cyclic and rhythmic, full of zest and adventure of connecting idea, fact, feeling, understanding, action. Education is "the acquisition of the art of the utilization of knowledge" (*Aims of Education*: 16).

What is knowledge to be used for? Whitehead, like Dewey, rejected the spectator theory of knowledge—"The merely well-informed man is the most useless bore on God's earth." The only use of knowledge of the past is to be a key to understanding the present. And the awesome present is full of creativity, novelty, and unrealized possibilities. The educator, understanding the lively rhythms of educating, will use well-achieved knowledge to celebrate the wonder, the awe, the excitement of what is not yet, the sense that change and growth lead us on to a life of the future. The future leads us. Once an organic, lush growth is felt, then the next move of the educator is to push for precision, a certain definiteness of stubborn fact and clear concept. From growth comes a development of rigor, of trimming and shaping and concrete seeing of what is in the facts and concepts. The next huge change in educative experience is the move toward generalization and satisfaction. The idea of a general ordering of highly various processes is to provide a ground for extensive connection of specific orders.

The curriculum for educating should be the best big ideas that serve to explain and to help us understand a multitude of specific facts and ideas. Educating recognizes the power of big ideas to go beyond complexity to simplify and explain. Whitehead called for scholars who comprehend the world to exhibit the habit of greatness. Big ideas through conceptual prehension have an appetition, an urge toward realization.

Whitehead's philosophical perspective is disciplinary, meaning that all knowers constitute their own personal perspectives, but each knower does so in a way that can be valid for all knowers. Knowledge is shared in the ways we use it.

Romance, precision, and generalization-satisfaction are fluid qualities of events (not mere stages). The life of the mind is rich and multiple, full of connections, contrasts, and joinings (nexus) and moving beyond what is now known. This movement is true of the humanities and the sciences and the arts in pretty much the same way. Separate disciplines are not that separate because learning is seamless, connecting and growing together. A prime value of educating is that it sustains a sense of importance within social relationships. A social harmony is based on creativity and novelty. This continuous process through which elements in the world are synthesized into new unities provides social order.

Each actual entity is a concrescence of novel togetherness, and this becoming is a creative advance. The idea of a general ordering is the primordial nature of God. God is a conceptual prehension and is not actual until the principle of concretion, as the energy for self-creation, results in values that are the actual processes of events. Within this cosmological scheme, human learning is a creative advance as unrelated possibilities form (shape) themselves into the actual entities of facts and ideas.

Whitehead's ideas are seen today as compatible with quantum physics and the biology of DNA, where wavelike energy is life itself. Perhaps what we indifferently think of as human learning is coincident with creativity. Wherever educating happens, creativity happens: Whatever we might mean by creativity is a necessary part of what we mean by educating.

"The seamless coat of learning" connects an intimate sense of the power of ideas, the beauty of ideas with a particular body of knowledge, with peculiar reference in the living person using ideas in life's activities.

How we learn and learn how to learn, how we make knowledge and construct knowledge about knowledge-making can become central to a Whiteheadian philosophy of education, a philosophy surprisingly relevant today.

Two Contemporary Significances of Whiteheadian Views—Economics: Knowledge, Work, and Wealth

In *Post-Capitalist Society*, Peter Drucker asserts that we live today in a knowledge society. Since the "information revolution" (1950–1990), work and the creation of wealth have stemmed from knowledge. Wealth is created by allocating knowledge to productive tasks. The productivity of knowledge requires increasing the yield from what is known. Advantage (to a person, a company, a corporation, a country) comes from the ability to assess, to analyze, and generally to exploit universally available knowledge. An explicit methodology for the assessment of knowledge is needed in the workplace and in educating. An example of such a connec-

tion is found in D. Bob Gowin's *Educating*. Whitehead's concept of education as the art of the utilization of knowledge takes a dramatic turn of relevance in the knowledge society and education.

Quantum Physics, Biology, Health, and Medicine

Contemporary explanations of DNA connect to quantum physics. A quantum is the indivisible unit in which waves may be emitted or absorbed. The quantum theorist David Bohm, a neo-Whiteheadian, claims that the primitive notion of movement—vibrations of subatomic particles, oscillations of electromagnetic fields, encoding of DNA energies—is the primary actuality. Movement, or process, has orders or patterns or structures ("actual entities") that are a product of process. Bohm names these the "implicate" or "enfolded" order of nature, from which the explicate order—space, time, matter, bodies—are derived as a limiting case. The human body is nothing but variants of DNA built by DNA, and the genomes are bits of information encoded. All the material of the body appears designed with intelligence as a built-in feature. This intelligence is DNA, almost as much sheer knowledge as it is matter. Everything in wavelike process is converted at the level of the neuropeptide interactions of information-sharing, events of lightning speed of an estimated fifty trillion cells. Energy vibrations to nerve impulses to brain formation is just a code, a set of signals vibrating to give an order to process reality. The brain is much more a process than a material thing. Life is a field of unlimited possibilities within which subjective participation configures such named parts as space, time, body, location—all resultants from process as eternal objects become actual entities. Understanding this process view of life can have remarkable practical applications transforming our views of health and medicine. Philosophically, DNA brings to mind the windowless monads of Gottfried Leibniz (1646–1716).

The four archic variables of any philosophy are perspective, principle, reality, and method. Whitehead's philosophy, though evolving in an emergent and creative form, shows a comprehensive structure of disciplinary perspective, creative principle, process reality, and dialectical method. Whitehead's philosophy of education is not similarly comprehensive, and his creative ideas on education focus on aims and curriculum, casual observations about teaching, almost nothing directly about learning, and a conventional, critical treatment of schools and society. Nevertheless, Whitehead's philosophical ideas are a rich historical resource for novel insights in education, economics, physics, and biology.

D. Bob Gowin

See also AIMS OF EDUCATION; DIALECTIC; EPISTEMOLOGY

Bibliography

Bohm, David. "Time, the Implicate Order, and Pre-Space." In *Physics and the Ultimate Significance of Time,* edited by David Ray Griffin. Albany: State University of New York Press, 1986.

Brumbaugh, Robert S. *Whitehead Process Philosophy and Education.* Albany: State University of New York Press, 1982.

Chopra, Deepak. *Ageless Body, Timeless Mind.* New York: Harmony, 1993.

———. *Quantum Healing.* New York: Bantam, 1989.

Drucker, Peter. *Post-Capitalist Society.* New York: Harper-Collins, 1993.

Egan, Kieran. *Romantic Understanding.* New York: Routledge, 1990.

Evans, Malcolm. In *Association of Process Philosophy of Education.* Belle Mead, N.J.: 1988.

Gowin, D. Bob. *Educating.* Ithaca, N.Y.: Cornell University Press, 1981.

Hendley, Brian. *Dewey, Russell, Whitehead : Philosophers As Educators.* Carbondale: Southern Illinois University Press, 1986.

Lucas, George R., Jr. *The Rehabilitation of Whitehead.* Albany: State University of New York Press, 1989.

Rapp, Friedrich, and Reiner Wiehl, eds. *Whitehead's Metaphysics of Creativity.* Albany: State University of New York Press, 1990.

Schilpp, P.A. *The Philosophy of Alfred North Whitehead.* New York: Tudor, 1951.

Watson, Walter. *The Architectonics of Meaning.* Albany: State University of New York Press, 1985.

Whitehead, Alfred North. *The Aims of Education and Other Essays.* New York: Macmillan, 1929.

———. *Modes of Thought.* New York: Macmillan, 1938.

———. *Process and Reality.* New York: Harper, 1960.

Willard, Emma Hart (1787–1870)

American educational reformer, whose *Address to the Public: Particularly to the Members of the Legislature of New York, Proposing a Plan for Improving Female Education* (1819) set the terms of the debate on women's education for the next fifty years and whose popular textbooks and teacher-training activities helped to shape the common school movement.

Willard's philosophy of education combined Enlightenment faith in human reason, science, and progress with the central tenets of Evangelical Protestantism. Following the ideas of John Locke (1632–1704) and his disciples, she defined rationality as the logical ordering of sensory experiences and believed that human beings should concentrate their intellectual energies on solving practical problems to improve the lot of humanity. She had great faith in the power of institutions, particularly homes and schools, to transform the American republic into a prosperous, industrial world power that would lead the rest of the nations to universal peace. However, she was fearful of national wealth, believing that it tempted individuals to indulge their selfish desires at the expense of the common good. She was certain that the only sure protection against moral corruption was the inculcation of Christian piety in the young.

The Christianity that Willard espoused was a blend of Puritanism and Episcopalian latitudinarianism. Her father, a self-taught New England farmer and Revolutionary War veteran, had rebelled against the narrow-mindedness of the Congregationalists and joined the Universalist church. Emma Willard did not share her father's universalist beliefs, nor was she attracted to the Unitarian movement sweeping over the upper classes of Massachusetts. Instead, she became a deeply pious Episcopalian. Her theological beliefs were influenced by the Anglican bishop William Paley (1743–1805) and the Puritan John Bunyan (1628–1688). She revered such Puritan values as personal holiness, hard work, integrity, and perseverance, and believed that they would reap not only eternal rewards but personal happiness and worldly success. The other main features of her theology were a belief in human beings' essential freedom and moral agency; the need for cooperation among Protestant sects; and every citizen's responsibility to make American Protestant democracy a model for the rest of the world. These beliefs were much in keeping with the New Puritanism espoused by Timothy

Dwight (1752–1817) and Lyman Beecher (1775–1863). However, Willard did not share Beecher's belligerent suspicion of the influence of Roman Catholics on American society.

Many nineteenth-century educators shared Willard's optimistic faith in the power of educational institutions to transform American society. More than most, however, she viewed the disparities between male and female schooling as both unjust and imprudent. She was confident that God had called her to lead a reform movement in women's education, the main features of which she presented in her first publication, *Planning for Improving Women's Education* (1819). Asserting that the founders of the American republic had established the most humane and just political system in human history, she argued that the nation would ensure its longevity only if it invested in its female citizens. Like other republican ideologues, she argued that mothers form the character of citizens and only those mothers who are properly educated can form the type of citizens needed by the republic. She then catalogued the deficiencies of privately funded women's institutions and argued that such schools could not maintain high standards unless they had public support. In addition, she sketched a plan for a female seminary that set a higher standard. The state should endow this latter school, she concluded, as a first step toward larger reforms in women's education.

Much of Willard's argument was not new. Since the 1780s and 1790s, conservative reformers such as Benjamin Rush (1745–1813) and Noah Webster (1758–1843) and more radical reformers such as Judith Sargent Murray (1751–1820) had argued for improvements in women's education. However, Willard was the first to argue that women's schools needed state support and supervision; she was also the first to provide a detailed description of an advanced public female seminary. She argued that public investment in female education would pay other important dividends as well, for the women who attended the seminaries she envisioned would be well prepared to teach in the common schools, an important function that they could perform more competently and cheaply than men.

The female seminary that Willard envisioned was not precisely like those provided for men, nor did she believe in coeducational colleges. Rather, she believed that the schooling of the sexes should prepare them for their different roles in society. She accepted the prevailing be-lief that God and nature had structured human society so that men have authority over women. It was reasonable for women to submit to the men, she reasoned, since her sex depended on men for protection and sustenance. She believed that despite woman's dependent position, however, she is more than a mere satellite. Instead, Willard saw the sexes as morally autonomous partners moving "in the orbit of our duty, around the Holy Centre of perfection."

Willard defined woman's "orbit of duty" largely in domestic terms. She was confident that woman's primary responsibility was to establish a home that was orderly, pious, and virtuous, and that a mother's most important duty was to rear her children to be Godly citizens. This view, which is often called "domestic" or "separate spheres" ideology, was pervasive in the antebellum era. Conservative proponents of the ideology argued that advanced schooling would unfit women for their domestic duties, while reformers such as Willard held that women needed advanced schooling to be competent homemakers. What distinguished Willard from other domestic ideologues was her broad definition of "women's sphere," which seemed to include whatever men would allow women to do. In her most daring proposal, she suggested that male legislators invite women to establish a female council to serve in the national government, with power to set policies and oversee a national budget.

Despite Willard's belief in male privilege, she viewed the natures of the sexes as essentially alike. A topic of considerable debate in America and Europe was whether women were capable of sustained rational thinking. Willard had complete faith in the rationality of women. Following Lockean principles and her own teaching experience, she developed pedagogical methods designed to develop women's rationality. This process involved teaching how the mind operates, challenging students to master subject matter requiring the use of various levels of abstraction, and communicating their understanding of the subject matter first to an individual and then to a large audience. Facility with language was central to the entire process.

Willard did not limit her reform efforts to women's education. She, along with Henry Barnard (1811–1900) and other common-school reformers, believed that public schooling was woefully inadequate and that every state should establish a system of state-supported common schools staffed by well-trained, professional, female teachers. Willard was confident that the common schools in each community could maintain high standards if student teachers received apprenticeship training and, after they were employed, had further training at teacher institutes. She urged male school boards to invite the women of each district to establish voluntary female societies designed to provide both supervision and support of the local common schools.

Willard's ideas were perhaps more broadly diffused through her schoolbooks. Apart from the Bible, the most widely read books in the nineteenth century were schoolbooks, and Willard was one of a handful of New England writers who dominated the market with her frequently reprinted geographies and histories as well as less popular astronomy and moral philosophy texts. She dissuaded teachers from the common practice of requiring students to memorize and repeat lists of words. Instead, her lessons used the students' sensory experiences, particularly those of sight, and moved them to larger, more abstract concepts. She made real advances in the use of maps to clarify historical events and eras. All of her texts conveyed her conviction that the goal of instruction is the full development of the students' rational and moral nature and her faith that each student could play a vital role in creating a great nation.

Willard's belief that nonsectarian Protestantism should be the cornerstone of American public schools was attacked by Roman Catholic Bishop John Hughes (1797–1864). Her faith in the efficacy of moral education to protect individuals from corruption was undermined by the research of Hugh Hartshorne and Mark A. May, who found little relationship between moral instruction and student conduct. The separate spheres ideology that she espoused was attacked by her former student Elizabeth Cady Stanton (1815–1902), who refused to accept a male-privileged hierarchy and demanded that women be accorded all the political, economic, and social rights granted to men. And her view that women should receive advanced schooling that prepared them for domesticity is now viewed as a relic of the past. Even so, Willard's female seminary in Troy, New York, provided a model for hundreds of female seminaries, and her academic requirements set a national standard. The leaders of the early women's colleges continued to use her domestic rhetoric and many of her administrative practices. Her teaching methods, particularly in geography, are widely practiced.

Lucy F. Townsend

See also GENDER AND SEXISM; GIRLS AND WOMEN, EDUCATION OF; HOME AND FAMILY

Bibliography

Baym, Nina. "Women and the Republic: Emma Willard's Rhetoric of History." *American Quarterly* 43 (1991): 1–23.

Beadie, Nancy. "Emma Willard's Idea Put to the Test: The Consequences of State Support of Female Education in New York." *History of Education Quarterly* 33 (1993): 543–62.

Lutz, Alma. *Emma Willard, Daughter of Democracy.* Boston: Houghton Mifflin, 1929.

Nelson, Murray A. "Emma Willard: Pioneer of Social Science Education." *Theory and Research in Social Education* 15 (1987): 245–56.

Scott, Anne Firor. "The Ever Widening Circle: The Diffusion from the Troy Female Seminary: 1822–1872." *History of Education Quarterly* 19 (1979): 3–25.

———. "What, Then, Is the American: This New Woman?" *Journal of American History* 65 (1978): 700–711.

Willard, Emma Hart. *An Address to the Public; Particularly to the Members of the Legislature of New York, Proposing a Plan for Improving Female Education.* Middlebury, Conn.: J.W. Copeland, 1819.

———. *Geography for Beginners; or the Instructor's Assistant, in Giving First Lessons from Maps, In the Style of Familiar Conversation.* Hartford, Conn.: Oliver D. Cooke, 1826.

———. *History of the United States or Republic of America, Exhibited in Connexion with Its Chronology and Progressive Geography, by a Series of Maps.* New York: White, Gallaher and White, 1830.

———. *Letters Addressed as a Circular to the Members of the Willard Association, for the Mutual Improvement of Female Teachers.* Troy, N.Y.: Elias Gates, 1838.

———. *Letters to Dupont de l'Eure on the Political Position of Women.* Albany, N.Y.: Joel Munsell, 1848.

———. *Morals for the Young; or Good Principles Instilling Wisdom.* New York: A.S. Barnes, 1857.

Wood, Diane Claire. "The Cultural and Intellectual Origins of Emma Willard's Educational Philosophy." M.A. thesis, San Jose State University, 1991.

William of Ockham (c. 1285–1347)

William of Ockham is called metaphorically, with a great insight into his role, *Venerabilis inceptor* (Venerable beginner). He stands at the entrance to the modern world, one foot planted in the past, the other hurrying toward the future. Born in Surrey, England, he became a Franciscan and, after studying theology at Oxford, was ordained a priest. He taught but never became a master. He was summoned to Avignon as a possible heretic. He fled to Italy on May 26, 1328, and was excommunicated. He joined Louis of Bavaria in Pisa and then went with the emperor to Munich, where he died. His books are, in the main, commentaries on Aristotle and the sacred writings of the Christians. But, all along the line, cracks appear in his theory of God, knowledge, ethics, and politics, with the result that a new way (*via moderna*) of seeing the human person as knower, doer, and citizen arises. The learned world coming after him continues to reveal its debt to his trail blazing.

Ockham is a theologian of the absolute liberty, power, and rationality of God. God is not an architect of the world. Though he created the world and conserves and rules it, the world is contingent. It must produce order itself. Rationality therefore allows many such orders. Humans are creators, like God, and as such are free to bring about any world they choose. Rationality does not bind. As creators, they can determine their relation to the world, other human beings, and God. And so begins a line of thought that in our day is very attractive to existentialists.

Ockham distinguishes four kinds of knowledge: knowledge that comes from testimony (we know who our mother is); from nonmethodical and changeable sense evidence; from intuitions that are necessary but nonmethodical and not about existences, like the Pythagorean theorem; and from inquiry that is necessary and true, using the method of syllogistic demonstration. It is easy to see a relation between Ockham and "How We Make Our Ideas Clear," by Charles Sanders Peirce (1839–1914), while not denying the distance is real.

Ockham is convinced that we are able to know truly and certainly only the singular things directly perceptible by the senses (*notitia intuitiva*). That did not surprise him; God also knows things singly. The mind is, moreover, active (*notitia abstractiva*) and is constructive, since it is not determined by in-tuitive knowledge; accordingly, pluralism is rational. A cause can have multiple effects, just as an effect can come from a multitude of causes. And John Locke (1632–1704) is not very distant.

Locke is a nominalist; Ockham is more correctly called a terminist or conceptualist. One of the glories of Ockham is his careful distinction between concept, proposition, and reasoning, which marks the shift from things to language. His theory of supposition carefully distinguishes "apple" ("personal supposition") as directly standing for the thing, from "apple" ("simple supposition") as a concept, which we know and can assert in a proposition, as well as from "apple" ("material supposition") having five letters and being a word in English. Surface grammar is simply not a reliable guide for determining what a proposition means. From these beginnings, much of the linguistic and conceptual analyses of Ludwig Wittgenstein (1889–1951) arises. Ockham's insistence that we know only in propositions leads to Gottlob Frege (1848–1925). His work in logic, including some evidence for material implication, points to Augustus De Morgan (1806–1871) and Bertrand Russell (1872–1970).

Ockham introduces the principle of economy as a methodological principle, or, as it is usually called, Ockham's razor: It is unjustifiable to explain with more expense what can be explained with less. More than a plea for simplicity or an aesthetic criterion, it is the principle of rationality, because the whole point of inquiry is simply to "save the appearances," the world of the single. Now knowledge is expressed in propositions, which are true and necessary. How in a contingent world can this be done? Ockham, with almost all of his successors, takes the affirmative universal, or "A" proposition, as nonexistential or hypothetical. "An apple is a fruit" becomes "If it is an apple, then it is a fruit."

All of Ockham's work on knowledge doesn't amount to a knowledge of the scientific method, although the elements are there. He rejects telic causes and emphasizes matter over form as the principle of unity in the world, though it would seem that a stumbling block would be his conception of a thing as a complex of substance and qualities. But his discussion of the intensity of qualities opens the way to quantity. When Ockham's ontology is united by John Dumbleton to the mathematics of Thomas

Bradwardine (c. 1290–1349), everything necessary for the scientific method is in place.

In his ethics, Ockham emphasizes the autonomy of the human person. It is an autonomy that is given by God, who is the exemplar of autonomy. It too involves a denial of telic cause. Humans do not have a built-in destiny, which shapes what they become (Become what you are!). As free to create their world, they are free to create themselves. Although this is not Kantian autonomy, there are resemblances, and certainly Ockham and Immanuel Kant (1724–1804) share the same concern.

Freedom is always the key word. Thus, Ockham makes Ambrose's dictum his own: The Christian religion does not deprive one of his rights. The Jewish religion was better than others because it freed men from the stranglehold of human respect. Ockham would only welcome separation of church and state.

It is easy to ignore a side of Ockham that has not yet been discovered by our contemporaries: his being a Franciscan. Literally he put his life at risk for a Franciscan ideal; namely, the distinction between *dominium* (ownership) and *usus simplex facti* (the simple use of the things of the world). The story of Cain and Abel he finds crucial for understanding what is wrong with our world. Environmentalists may find his reasons for refusing to try to own the world and for wishing to simply be allowed to use it in moderation a way of making their own case stronger.

Walter P. Krolikowski

See also METAPHYSICS; SCHOLASTICISM; THOMAS AQUINAS

Bibliography

Adams, Marilyn McCord. *William Ockham.* Notre Dame: University of Notre Dame Press, 1987.

Aicher, Oti, Gabriele Greindl, and Wilhelm Vossenkukl. *Guglielmo de Occam. Il rischio de pensare modernamente.* Milan: Fabbri Editori, 1987.

Boehner, Philotheus, O.F.M. *Ockham. Philosophical Writings. A Selection.* London: Nelson, 1967.

Hudson, Anne, and Michael Wilks. *From Ockham to Wyclif.* Oxford: Basil Blackwell, 1987.

William of Ockham. *Opera Theologica et Philosophica.* General editor, Gedeon Gai, O.F.M. New York: Franciscan Institute, St. Bonaventure University, 1967ff.

Wittgenstein, Ludwig (1889–1951)

One of the very most original and influential philosophers of the twentieth century. Central to his work was the nature of language and its role in the process of philosophizing: He played a leading role in the "linguistic turn" of modern philosophy, away from ideas and toward language, toward sentences. But his iconoclasm and the ongoing controversy surrounding the interpretation of his writings make it hard to classify him as a "philosopher of language" (or as a "linguistic philosopher"), for he differs deeply from most others so designated.

Wittgenstein developed an interest in philosophy through a background in Continental social, existential, and representational thought (particularly that of A. Schopenhauer [1788–1860], O. Weininger, F. Mauthner, G. Lichtenberg, and H. Hertz) and the foregrounding around the start of the twentieth century of certain problems of logic by Gottlob Frege, and by Bertrand Russell (Wittgenstein's friend and teacher, to study with whom he moved to England). A fusion of the most rigorous description of logic with a philosophically informed "mysticism" spawned the brilliant, gnomic, and influential *Tractatus Logico-Philosophicus* (1922). This book offered an elaboration of its prefatory dictum, "What can be said at all can be said clearly; and whereof one cannot speak thereof one must be silent," stressing that the form or structure of language itself could not be said, but only shown. Wittgenstein thus attempted to demarcate the "boundary" where the use of language shaded from clear saying (of empirical—for example, scientific—assertions) into incoherent nonsense. All attempts to speak of ethics, religion—or philosophy—must, according to the *Tractatus*, end up outside that "boundary," in nonsense.

Wittgenstein was then silent on the subject of philosophy for some years, before returning to it publicly at the close of the 1920s with a renewed interest and some strikingly new formulations of his views. His philosophical development proceeded not by means of elaboration of a basic "program," but rather as a severely enacted shift of philosophical methodology. The single most significant shift in Wittgenstein's thought was from the "early" philosophy of the *Tractatus* to the "later" philosophy that Wittgenstein developed through the 1930s and 1940s, mostly in England (where he taught, at Cambridge), and that culminated in his second classic work, *Philosophical Investigations*

(1953). This shift appeared so dramatic as to have brought some to declare Wittgenstein unique among major philosophers in having propounded two distinct philosophies. Here is an illustration of the difference in "drama" between the "early" and the "later" work, on the central issue of the structure of language:

It is clear that in the description of the most general form of sentence only what is essential to it may be described—otherwise, it would not be the general form.

That there is a general sentential form is proved by the fact that there cannot be a sentence whose form could not have been foreseen (i.e., constructed). The general form of the sentence is: Such and such is the case. (*Tractatus Logico-Philosophicus*: 4.5)

But how many kinds of sentences are there? Say assertion, question, and command? There are countless different kinds of use of what we call "symbols," "words," "sentences." And this multiplicity is not something fixed, given once for all; but new types of language, new language-games . . . come into existence, and others become obsolete and get forgotten. . . .

Here the term "language-game" is meant to bring into prominence that the speaking of language is part of an activity. . . .

Review the multiplicity of language-games in the following examples, and in others:

Giving orders, and obeying them—

Describing the appearance of an object . . . —

Speculating about an event—

Presenting the results of an experiment in tables and diagrams—

Making up a story; and reading it—

Play-acting— (*Philosophical Investigations*: 23)

We see that, in contrast to the crystalline simplicity of the *Tractatus*'s depiction of an ideal—crystalline, simple—language, Wittgenstein's later thought was expressed as a motley of considerations about the motley that lan-guage actually is. In contrast to the early focus on the essential form of logic and language, the later philosophy chiefly works by pointing out differences within and between real or imagined "language-games," by stressing how easy it is for us to fail to notice the particular contexts without which our linguistic practices cease to be of any use. The *Tractatus* gave the appearance of being a magisterial theory of logical form. *Philosophical Investigations* was fashioned rather after a dialogue with interlocutors or students.

Wittgenstein's thought has been much discussed and applied, and much misunderstood. The shift from one to another of Wittgenstein's two (or more) apparently distinct philosophies has commonly been characterized roughly as a shift from "realism" to its supposed opposite, "antirealism." But it is rapidly becoming almost a commonplace that the differences between the two philosophies have been quite deeply overestimated. The view taking shape is that, excepting differences in style, the illusion that the later philosophy is discontinuous with the earlier is founded upon Wittgenstein's own misinterpretation of his earlier work, which occurred because of his own extraordinary—perhaps excessive—standards of quality and clarity. In *Philosophical Investigations* he seemed fixated on the "grave mistakes" he had made previously. That left him unable to appreciate that he had been trying in earlier work to show precisely that the temptation to say (for example) "All of language is like this" was one that had to be entertained, examined, and finally overcome in the course of internal (or of actual) dialogue. Only in his last writings, when death from cancer impended, did he allow himself once more to note that this was a deep concern that reached back to his original insights on the logic of our language: "Am I not getting closer and closer to saying that in the end logic cannot be described? You must look at the practice of language, then you will see it" (*On Certainty*: 501). Here is the very same distinction between saying and showing with which Wittgenstein began. In the remainder of this article, then, we shall mainly treat of the insights manifest in his corpus as a whole.

As we have seen, Wittgenstein held that clarity of thought and expression was hard to obtain because we fail to notice that we are always doing things with language, that uses of language have to be contextualized within living practice if they are to be understood, and that there is all the difference in the world between the use of sentences that appear extremely similar (such as between "That sentence flows," "Time ebbs, time flows," and "The River Styx flows, does it not?"). He summed this up: "Philosophy is a battle against the bewitchment of our intelligence by means of language" (*Philosophical Investigations*: 109). As it stands, this proposition is perhaps ambiguous: Does it mean that it is language itself that (in the kinds of ways just mentioned) befuddles our intelligence? or does it mean that we can combat philosophical confusions through particular clarificatory uses of language? Arguably, both. Wittgenstein thought that it was indeed only through investigation of what it made sense to say when, and of the sources of the compulsion to misunderstand, that philosophers could begin to put an end to conceptual confusions and pacify perturbed reflective minds. He also thought that it was precisely conceptual (that is, linguistic) confusions—such as that that might be engendered by the failure to distinguish different uses of "flow"—which led to philosophical perturbation in the first place. In this way, language is both the cure and the disease.

Finding methods of "cure"—such as the construction of simplified "ideal languages" or "language-games" as objects of comparison to our actual linguistic intercourse—was far more important for Wittgenstein than arriving at dogmatic philosophical theses. Indeed, the very quest for and defense of theses was for Wittgenstein a symptom of philosophical confusion, because he held that only in scientific and other empirical disciplines could meaningful assertions (about "how things are") be made. This methodological precept, together with his lack of interest in giving arguments, has contributed to his being hard to absorb within any professional thought-community, including the discipline of philosophy.

Thus his philosophical "position" is evanescent: He can be adequately described neither as someone compelled by skeptical arguments, nor as someone endeavoring to oppose skepticism through argument and emphasis on various features of "the Real world"; rather, he held, "Scepticism is not irrefutable, but palpably senseless, if it would doubt where a question cannot be asked" (*Tractatus*: 6.51). It is tendentious to term Wittgenstein either a skeptic (or an antirealist) or a realist. We may get a better insight into this absence of a rubric under which to place Wittgenstein if we focus on the area of his thought at the center of philosophic attention: rule-following.

Wittgenstein thought it a misconception to found the compellingness of a rule either in the human mind (as though one could just decide for oneself what any given rule meant; or alternatively as though it would facilitate a philosophical explanation to say that the rules of mathematics are encoded in one's brain) or in some Platonic realm (as though the "real" rules of football—or even of mathematics—were encoded in God's brain, or had any other sort of metaphysical existence). He wrestled with the question of what it could actually be in virtue of which some way of "projecting" a rule into new cases was right and all or most others wrong. For instance, how could it be that if one were counting in 2s, and reached a number never before specifically mentioned as occurring in that series, perhaps "10,000," it was definitely correct to go on "10,002," "10,004 . . . ," rather than "10,004," "10,008 . . ."? To be sure, if we were teaching someone to count, and they proceeded in the latter, deviant, manner, we should say to them, "Look what you've done!" But what if the conversation then continued as follows:

> "You were meant to add two: look how you began the series!"—He answers: "Yes, isn't it right? I thought that was how I was meant to do it."—Or suppose he pointed to the series and said: "But I went on in the same way."—It would be no use now to . . . repeat the old examples and explanations. . . . Such a case would present similarities with one in which a person naturally reacted to the gesture of pointing with the hand by looking in the direction of the line from finger-tip to wrist, not from wrist to finger-tip. (*Philosophical Investigations*: 185)

It has been argued that Wittgenstein thought that only the agreement in reactions or conventions within a collectivity of people (a "community") could overcome this problem: that it is the way we are inclined "to go on" that alone determines what is a correct continuation of the rule. An extreme version of this view, which has recently gained notoriety because of the sponsorship of a leading philosopher of logic (Saul Kripke), commits Wittgenstein to "rule-skepticism"—that is, to the view that any way of following a rule really is as good as any other, and none can be criticized or justified, except at best in purely practical terms within the confines of some particular community. The realist reaction to "rule-skepticism" has been in large part to insist that rules are determinate, and intrinsically determine exactly how they are to be followed. What Wittgenstein actually says is that "there is a way of grasping a rule which is not an interpretation, but which is exhibited in what we call 'obeying the rule' and 'going against it' in actual cases" (*Philosophical Investigations*: 201). We see here a repugnance toward overintellectualization and a suggestion that it is in actual usage and action that one can see what following a given rule amounts to. When we are in the course of following some rule, it comes naturally to us. Wittgenstein repeatedly emphasized the prophylactic value of reminding oneself how a rule was learned: "What has the expression of a rule—say a signpost—got to do with my actions? What sort of connexion is there here?—Well, perhaps this one: I have been trained to react to this sign in a particular way, and now I do so react to it" (*Philosophical Investigations:* 198).

The foregoing brief account of Wittgenstein's "rule-following considerations" reveals how tricky it is to interpret his work, and so illustrates his philosophical methodology. For the compulsion that one feels when under the power of a rule (such as "Add two" or "Perform this kind of action") is illuminatingly related to the compulsion we feel to use certain kinds of expressions, or to formulate certain kinds of positions (theories), when doing philosophy. In fact, the latter is arguably simply a special case of the former. For example, where our grammar suggests that there must be some kind of definite phenomenon involved in "pointing to the shape of x," but there is no bodily or objective fact available to correspond to it, we tend to think (so Wittgenstein claims) that nevertheless there is some special kind of phenomenon occurring; say, a spiritual or mental one. What are we doing in such a case except trying to conform to a norm (an "implicit rule") of representation, without which we feel quite lost or perturbed? The difference, if there is one, between most cases of rule-following and many cases of its philosophical offshoot is perhaps as follows: In most cases of rule-following, we would not want to say there was any pref-

erable or actual alternative to following the rule, unless we were willing to engage in a quite different activity. Wittgenstein is not attempting to persuade us "to do arithmetic differently," or "to think a-morally," but only to understand how easily we may misunderstand arithmetic or moral thinking, and the source of the compulsion they put us under. He is reminding us of the temptation, to which we are continually subject, to misunderstand, and then to overcompensate through theory-building. Thus he specifically cautions against logicians who have claimed to offer a way of uncovering the "true foundations" of mathematics, and why mathematics therefore had to be as it was (or even, why it had to be different from how it was); and against influential thinkers who (gripped by an analogy with scientific contexts) held that the truth of some particular religion or morality was demonstrable; and so forth.

Wittgenstein's polemics were addressed then most directly to the reflective thinker, whether or not regarded as "a philosopher." His celebrated "anti-private-language argument," which followed upon the considerations concerning rule-following, urged that we are mistaken if we suppose—as he took philosophers, psychologists, and many others to do—that only individuals can describe or name their own "private" or "personal" sensations, and that therefore no one can know what others are experiencing. His alternative picture, intended not as a piece of speculative psychology or learning theory but as a means of curing one of the illusion that one has a special access to a private mental world, was that "words are connected with the primitive, the natural, expressions of the sensation and used in their place. A child has hurt himself and he cries; and then adults talk to him and teach him exclamations and, later, sentences. They teach the child new pain-behavior. So you are saying the word 'pain' really means crying?—On the contrary: the verbal expression of pain replaces crying and does not describe it" (*Philosophical Investigations:* 244).

At one point Wittgenstein is quite explicit that his discussions of training and teaching are no nascent psychology of learning: "Am I doing child psychology?—I am making a connexion between the concept of teaching and the concept of meaning" (*Zettel:* 412). What is understood when teaching (other than of particular empirical facts) is successful is the meaning of a word, or of a sentence. This simple, undramatic point is arguably as near as Wittgenstein ever came to endorsing a "theory of meaning" (or indeed a "theory of learning" or a "philosophy of education"). All a "theory of meaning" (that is, an account of what "makes possible" the meaningful use of language) can be for Wittgenstein is a description of the interrelation of the concepts of "meaning," "understanding," "explanation," and so forth. And the manner of teaching—for instance, the deep differences between the teaching of the words *"two," "God,"* and *"meaning"*—is illustrative of deep differences between the meanings, the uses, of (those) words.

These conceptual/descriptive points need bear no relation to following one specific educational practice or theory rather than another. If one were looking for a contribution to the field (of philosophy of education) made by Wittgenstein, one would do better, rather than looking at his undoubtedly evocative philosophical examples involving teaching-contexts, to look at the only book, apart from the *Tractatus,* that he published in his lifetime: the *Worterbuch fur Volksschulen.* This innovative "dictionary" was Wittgenstein's main written contribution to the Austrian School Reform Movement, in which he was a somewhat eccentric participant in the years between the *Tractatus*'s publication and his "return" to philosophy.

The only suitable closing comment on Wittgenstein's philosophy proper, however, is to emphasize that it is extraordinarily hard to do justice to its method in any summary account such as this; or indeed, in any account whatsoever. In keeping with the wish that his writing "not . . . spare other people the trouble of thinking" is the following remark:

> The right method of philosophy would be this. . . . [W]hen someone else wished to say something metaphysical, to demonstrate to him that he had given no meaning to certain signs in his sentences. . . . My propositions are elucidatory in this way: he who understands me finally recognises them as senseless, when he has climbed out through them, on them, over them (*Tractatus*: 6.53–6.54).

Wittgenstein's later belief that he had found a method (or methods) less paradoxical than this self-consuming method of his early years must be squared with his simultaneous insistence (*Philosophical Investigations*: 133) that "the real discovery is the one that makes me capable of stopping doing philosophy . . . the one that gives philosophy peace, so that it is no longer tormented by questions which bring itself in question." For there is no indication in Wittgenstein's oeuvre as to whether he thought this "real discovery" to be other than chimerical.

Rupert J. Read

See also ANALYTIC PHILOSOPHY; LOGIC; POSITIVISM; RUSSELL

Bibliography

Diamond, Cora. *The Realistic Spirit.* Cambridge: MIT Press, 1991.

Hacker, P.M.S. *Insight and Illusion.* Rev. ed. Oxford: Oxford University Press, 1986.

Kripke, Saul. *Wittgenstein on Rules and Private Language.* Cambridge: Harvard University Press, 1982.

Monk, Ray. *Wittgenstein: The Duty of Genius.* London: Jonathan Cape, 1990.

Phillips, D.Z., and Peter Winch, eds. *Wittgenstein: Attention to Particulars.* New York: St. Martin's Press, 1989.

Rorty, Richard. *Consequences of Pragmatism.* Minneapolis: University of Minnesota Press, 1982.

Shanker, V.A. and S.G., eds. *Ludwig Wittgenstein: Critical Assessments, V: A Wittgenstein Bibliography.* London: Croom Helm, 1986.

Wittgenstein, Ludwig. *On Certainty.* Edited by G.E.M. Anscombe and G.H. von Wright. Translated by D. Paul and G.E.M. Anscombe. New York: Blackwell, Harper and Row, 1969.

———. *Philosophical Investigations.* Edited and translated by G.E.M. Anscombe, with R. Rhees. New York: Macmillan, 1953. 3rd (rev.) ed. 1958.

———. *Tractatus Logico-Philosophicus.* Introduction by Bertrand Russell. Translated by C.K. Ogden. London: Routledge, 1922. Subsequently translated by D. Pears and B. McGuiness. London: Routledge, 1961. (The quotations above from this work are my own translations).

———. *Worterbuch fur Volksschulen.* Edited and translated by W. and E. Leinfelner, with A. Hubner. Vienna: Holder-Pichler-Termpsky, 1977.

———. *Zettel.* Edited by G.E.M. Anscombe and G.H. von Wright. Translated by G.E.M. Anscombe. Oxford: Blackwell, 1967.

Wollstonecraft, Mary (1759–1797)

English writer and political radical often identified as the first major feminist theorist, whose *Vindication of the Rights of Woman* (1792) argued that women and men have the same capacity for developing reason and therefore should be accorded the same rights and educated similarly.

In her brief life, Mary Wollstonecraft wrote a large corpus of works, including perhaps the most influential feminist treatise in history, *A Vindication of the Rights of Woman* (1792). Like most women of her time, she had little formal education. She was determined to become independent, and worked as a governess and taught and ran a school before she began to support herself by her pen.

During a crucial stage of her intellectual development she lived in Stoke Newington, a major center for Dissenting radicals such as Richard Price (1723–1791) and Joseph Priestley (1733–1804), both of whom served as her mentors. The intellectual circle surrounding her publisher, Joseph Johnson (1738–1809), added other important Dissenting radical philosophers, artists, and writers to her acquaintanceship, including Tom Paine (1737–1809), painter Henry Fuseli (1741–1825), artist and poet William Blake (who illustrated two of her books), and the anarchist philosopher William Godwin (1756–1836).

An admirer of the French Revolution, she lived in Paris during the Terror, which took the lives of many of her French friends among the Girondins. There she wrote a book on the French Revolution and bore a child by her lover. After returning to England she renewed her friendship with Godwin, whom she married. She died as a result of complications of the childbirth of their daughter, who grew up to become the writer Mary Shelley. Following Wollstonecraft's death and the publication of her "memoirs" by William Godwin, she was vilified as a symbol of the promiscuous Jacobin radical by the conservative society she left behind, but eventually also became a heroine for the successive waves of feminist movements around the world that followed in the nineteenth and twentieth centuries.

Education was a theme of Wollstonecraft's entire adult life. Much of her writing focused on education, including *Thoughts on the Education of Daughters* (1787); *Original Stories from Real Life* (1788), a work for children; a collection entitled *The Female Reader* (1789); her translations *The Elements of Morality* (1790) and *Young Grandison* (1790); her *Rights of Woman,* and her two fictions, *Mary, a Fiction* (1788) and *The Wrongs of Woman* (not published during her lifetime).

The Meaning and Purpose of Education

Most of Wollstonecraft's views on education, at least for men, are consistent with those of the Dissenting radicals, who were influential in the development of ideas on education and were most concerned with molding children into people of good moral character and habits. She identified John Locke (1632–1704) as her starting point and was greatly influenced by Jean-Jacques Rousseau (1712–1778), although she harshly criticized *Emile* (1762) for its treatment of women. Her emphasis on the association of ideas is traceable through Priestley to Claude-Adrien Helvetius (1715–1771) and David Hartley (1705–1757). She acknowledged the specific influence of Catharine Macaulay on her thinking as well.

Wollstonecraft shared the basic philosophic premises of the Enlightenment, including the ideas that the mind and heart are shaped by the environment and experience, and that the power to reason is implanted within people to allow them to perfect themselves individually and collectively. For Wollstonecraft, like other Enlightenment thinkers, "reason" is not mere logic, but the power to discern truth (including moral truth) through observation and thought. Human beings have not just the power to develop reason, but also the obligation to do so as a means to progress. An appropriate system of education is necessary to that purpose and education's goal should be the development of habits of mind that result in the independent ability to reason toward virtue. Training for more specific tasks or skills is secondary.

For Wollstonecraft, the chief obstacle to these goals is the system of "unnatural distinctions"—especially those of inherited class, title, race, and gender—that create patterns of inequality and hierarchy among people. She despised any form of obedience to authority based on fear of authority or even the law, because it would inhibit development of the independence and strength of mind needed for reason and virtue. The oppressed are kept from reason and virtue by their situation. She also could not imagine how members of the aristocracy or others, such as men who could demand subservience from women, could develop into rational moral beings. Oppressors cannot develop their capacity for reason because power and the experience of depending on the slavishness and dependence of subordinates corrupts their minds. Thus, far from believing that the education of women and other subordinates needed to become more like the education of the dominant groups, she thought the whole system needed changing. An error that plagues interpretations of Wollstonecraft is that her use of education is often interpreted in the narrow, twentieth-century sense—referring merely to schooling. For Wollstonecraft, in common with usage of her day, education encompasses social experience broadly in all social institutions—the family, religion, government, and the military, for example. Only by taking account of this definition can we understand her proposals either for education broadly construed, or for schooling itself.

Child Development and Education

Wollstonecraft applied her vehement rejection of submission to authority to her views on child development. Learning must be based on pleasure rather than pain, through example and conversation, leaving formal lessons and even books aside as much as possible among the very young. She rejected teaching through rote learning or memorization as cruel and counterproductive, and disliked punishment, rebukes, or other scare tactics including threats, because they instill in children a slavish fear that inhibits the development of virtue. Children must learn to love virtue and develop instinctive compassion for other beings rather than just doing what they are told is right.

Young people must take an active part in learning. Wollstonecraft did not believe people learn by example, but by firsthand experience that strengthens and exercises the mind. The analogy is important. Wollstonecraft used "strength" to refer to both mind and body, and emphasized both mental and physical exercise in girls' and boys' education.

Wollstonecraft believed that parents and other educators must understand the process of child development. She thought adults tended to treat children as more mature than they were, although she also disliked the tendency to speak down to children. She also believed children should develop in an orderly way, following a path of increasing complexity of understanding. Although she lauded Rousseau's systematic notion of education, she thought he overbur-

dened the early stages of education and marked the phases of children's education arbitrarily rather than on the basis of understanding "natural" developmental stages.

She noted favorably that authors had recently begun to write books specifically oriented toward children. She was hesitant to expose children to two types of works: romances and religious works. She worried that the former might create premature sensuality, although she wanted children to learn about their bodies including their reproductive systems. She did not think young children could understand the Bible. Above all, books should be appropriately geared toward a child's stage of development.

Education and Equality

Equality was central to Wollstonecraft's educational philosophy in two respects. First, she discussed equality with regard to both the natural capacity and need of human beings to become educated. Second, she discussed equality as a characteristic of the social context in which reason and virtue are learned. Let us explore both in turn.

Wollstonecraft's most sustained theoretical treatment of education and her program of proposals does not appear in a separate treatise on education, but in the *Vindication of the Rights of Woman,* a work on the baneful consequences of unnatural distinctions between women and men. Wollstonecraft believed that unnatural social distinctions create the differences in character and abilities that often appear so natural. Despite the common belief that men, the aristocracy or middle classes, or whites were more naturally capable than women, the lower classes, and blacks, respectively, Wollstonecraft saw no evidence to suggest either that God had given any one group of people less native capacity for intellectual and moral development than others or that any one group was less in need of the development of their human capacities. As she argued for women, unless one could prove that women had less native capacity for reason than men, women and men must have the same need and right to education. If their capacities differ, education couldn't make women's condition worse than it already was.

Wollstonecraft was discontent with the poor quality of education in general, but especially for girls. She emphasized the need for women to learn to become good wives and mothers (and for men to be good husbands and fathers), but argued that these "accomplishments" had been overemphasized to the detriment of the development of reason and virtue. Unless women were educated equally with men, society as a whole could not be improved. Wollstonecraft also discussed class inequality in education, although to a lesser extent; she believed that the same arguments had been used to exclude women and the poor from education. She thought that all classes of people needed education, and believed it more necessary to an enlightened society for all people to learn to use their reason than for a few to be brilliant.

The second role of equality in Wollstonecraft's educational ideas concerns the conditions and process of education and moral development. Wollstonecraft argued that true reason and virtue could not exist within hierarchical or unequal social relationships. Friendship, which could exist only among equals, was the ideal social relationship, and all other relationships—intimate, familial, social, or political—take the form of friendship at their best. This belief runs into its severest test with respect to relationships between adults and children, especially in the context of education and development, and parents and teachers must be careful in how they command children's respect.

Adults and children are not, however, equal, because adults have more highly developed reason, and therefore must be accorded respect. As Wollstonecraft was painfully aware, governesses, tutors, and (except in the country day schools) teachers were likely to be of lower status and poorer than their charges. Children could not learn independence, reason, or virtue if they understood their teachers to be servants or social inferiors.

Because virtue is developed in the context of social relationships, virtuous relationships could not develop between women and men if they were kept segregated from each other until after they had developed their habits of mind. She therefore argued, against Rousseau and indeed the weight of most expert opinion, that they should be educated together.

Public and Private Education

One of Wollstonecraft's central questions about formal education was whether it should take place in schools at all, and if so, what sort. Although she enjoyed her country day school experience, most educators who wrote about "public" schools were usually referring to boarding schools and colleges that boys (only)

entered after earlier private tutoring. These she regarded as corrupt and corrupting institutions, based on and perpetuating inequality and hierarchy. She also argued that public virtue must be built on private virtue, and thus children should be schooled by the domestic intimacy of their homes.

Nevertheless, by the time she wrote the *Rights of Woman* Wollstonecraft had concluded that private education—that is, tutors in the home—was not an ideal solution, especially in the existing state of society. Most parents were simply not educated enough (in the broad sense) or virtuous enough to attend to their children's education. Moreover, she thought children should be brought up and educated with their true equals—other children.

She therefore urged the establishment of a national system of day schools. She was adamantly in favor of a government-sponsored system because she did not want teachers dependent on the economic authority of a specific group of parents paying for the school. She did not trust schools run on market principles, and worried about the impact of the search for the cheapest school among those willing or able to pay at all.

According to her plan, the lower school would cover ages five through nine and would be "absolutely free and open to all classes." Select committees in each parish would hire teachers and hear complaints when they were signed by six parents. In the lower school children would be dressed alike, study the same subjects, and experience the same discipline regardless of sex or wealth.

Before Wollstonecraft listed any formal subjects of study, she emphasized that the "school-room ought to be surrounded by a large piece of ground, in which the children might be usefully exercised, for at this age they should not be confined to any sedentary employment for more than an hour at a time." Among their subjects would be botany, mechanics, and astronomy, because they could be easily rendered into forms of play appropriate to young children. They would also study reading, writing, arithmetic, natural history, and natural philosophy but, as she pointed out, gymnastic play should take precedence at that age. She added that the young children might also study some religion, history, and politics in conversational, Socratic form.

The upper schools, for children above the age of nine, would be more differentiated by sex and wealth. The first division, by implication, was to be based on wealth; that is, those "intended for domestic employments, or mechanical trades" would "receive instruction, in some measure appropriate to the destination of each individual." The ambiguity of whether this destiny was sealed by past performance or past wealth is at least partly cleared up in her description of the other upper school, where those of "superior abilities, or fortune, might now be taught . . . the dead and living languages, the elements of science, and continue the study of history and politics, on a more extensive scale, which would not exclude polite literature." In this description Wollstonecraft pushed formal education past the point received by most children, and certainly by those who followed the trades she mentioned, but the structure she proposed would do little to enhance mobility or achieve any degree of redistribution.

In the upper (trade) school, girls and boys would continue to be educated together in the morning, then in the afternoon "the girls should attend a school, where plain-work, mantua-making, millinery, etc. would be their employment"; in other words, their training would conform to already existing gender divisions of labor. The situation in the upper (academic) school would be different: Girls and boys would continue to be educated together. Because she thought that children of wealthy families tended to have years of idleness and superficiality between the conclusion of their studies and the time they married, she argued they ought to remain in school until they were of marriageable age, and those who would pursue professions would begin to be trained in them.

Wollstonecraft recognized that changes in formal education alone would not bring the changes to society she desired, but neither would the changes occur without dramatic restructuring of formal education. She believed that change in the educational system would be a "natural consequence" of the French Revolution because, like systems of government, systems of education would flow from the state of national enlightenment. But even these "natural consequences" must be the result of concerted human thought and action. As the French Revolution wore on, she seemed to become less convinced that even her reasoned appeal to its leaders would have an effect.

Virginia Sapiro

See also EQUALITY; FEMINISM; GIRLS AND WOMEN, EDUCATION OF; HELVETIUS; LOCKE; PROGRESS, IDEA OF, AND PROGRESSIVE EDUCATION; PUBLIC EDUCATION; ROUSSEAU.

Bibliography

Janes, Regina M. "On the Reception of Mary Wollstonecraft's *A Vindication of the Rights of Woman.*" *Journal of the History of Ideas* 39 (1978): 293–302.

Myers, Mitzi. "Impeccable Governesses, Rational Dames, and Moral Mothers: Mary Wollstonecraft and the Female Tradition in Georgian Children's Books." *Children's Literature* 14 (1986): 31–59.

———. "Pedagogy as Self-Expression in Mary Wollstonecraft: Exorcising the Past, Finding a Voice." In *The Private Self: Theory and Practice of Women's Autobiographical Writings,* edited by Sheri Benstock, 192–210. Chapel Hill: North Carolina University Press, 1988.

Poovey, Mary. *The Proper Lady and the Woman Writer: Ideology as Style in the Works of Mary Wollstonecraft, Mary Shelley, and Jane Austen.* Chicago: University of Chicago Press, 1984.

Sapiro, Virginia. *A Vindication of Political Virtue: The Political Theory of Mary Wollstonecraft.* Chicago: University of Chicago Press, 1992.

Todd, Janet. *The Political Writings of Mary Wollstonecraft.* Toronto: University of Toronto Press, 1993.

———, and Marilyn Butler, eds. *The Works of Mary Wollstonecraft.* New York: New York University Press, 1989.

Tomalin, Claire. *The Life and Death of Mary Wollstonecraft.* New York: Harcourt Brace Jovanovich, 1974.

Work

The term *work* in its most common contemporary usage is synonymous with a job or paid work, but work more broadly defined is human effort to bring about an end. Learning the knowledge and skills for work has been a central aim of education in all human societies, but the links between a society's philosophy of work and its philosophy of education have become especially controversial and politically charged since the Industrial Revolution. How people view work and its importance has a profound impact on how they think about and conduct education, and vice versa.

Humans have always labored to make a living. However, recent studies suggest that while earlier people labored, they did not conceive of, do, or value work in the ways most people do today. For example, Paleolithic and Neolithic people did not separate work from leisure. Work was not a part of a monetary system such as the modern system of paid labor; it usually was done in a very social setting, and it was not viewed as a curse. For most of human existence, then, work formed part of a seamless web along with sleep, play, ritual, eating, and so on; and education, too, was an ongoing, integrated, and undifferentiated process.

Contrary to popular belief, in fact, during most of human existence people have spent little time doing what we would call work. Anthropologist Marshall Sahlins, in his book *Stone Age Economics* (1972), makes a strong case that in earlier societies, because living groups were small and did not stress their natural environments, and because people had few material wants, typical hunters and gatherers spent from two to four hours per day working.

The contrast with modern life could not be greater. On the one hand are people with simple tools and limited technical knowledge who spent most of their time socializing, ritualizing, and playing. Even when they did toil, it usually was a highly sociable and leisurely activity. In contrast, people of the modern age spend most of their time preparing for work (including education) and working. Ironically, we moderns have less and less time for leisure, even though we have much greater scientific knowledge and technological prowess.

The word *leisure* comes from the ancient Greek word *schole*, which is also the root of our word *scholarship*. Leisure was not viewed by the Greeks, as it often is today, as a passive activity, a mere reprieve from toil, but instead it signified the highest of human activities, which we today often call the liberal arts. The Greeks did not belittle work, however. Hesiod (eighth century B.C.), the common man's epic poet, says in *Works and Days* that the work of the common person is vital and can be fulfilling if done properly.

Plato (c. 427–347 B.C.) agreed with Hesiod's positive and practical view of work and education, but he also created hierarchies distinguishing between kinds of work, and between work and other activities. In *The Republic,* Plato says that everyone's work is valuable, but some roles are more crucial than others. Plato leaves us with the twin legacy of placing work at the center of daily human activity and of giving higher social value to some types of work than others—and the key to determining who does what is education.

In his famous allegory of the cave from *The Republic,* Plato argues that all people should be educated to help them discover, develop, and refine their potentials. For Plato, education can serve, simultaneously, to help people to develop and thrive (liberal education) and to prepare them for their role in society (vocational education). We have struggled with the tensions between these two goals of education ever since.

In Western societies during the Middle Ages, education echoed Plato's dual emphasis: Education was for the individual (in this case the focus was on salvation rather than on Plato's enlightenment) and for social roles such as work. The Rules of Saint Benedict (sixth century A.D.), for example, attempted to reconcile the tensions built into these dual educational purposes by teaching a work discipline which, if done properly, would bring a monk closer to God. Just as Plato had attempted to reconcile work with individual good through his organic metaphor (what is good for the individual is good for the society), Catholic doctrine and educational practice provided a similar umbrella, glorification of God, to unite work and individual happiness: Through work, like most any other activity, one can find and glorify God.

Max Weber contends that the Protestant work ethic was crucial for the rise of modern market economies and the Industrial Revolution. In his famous and controversial *Protestant Ethic and the Spirit of Capitalism* (1905), Weber says that if people had not been educated to believe that individual salvation could be signified, if not won, through work, modern economies would not have developed. Whether or not Weber's complex historical thesis is correct, there is little doubt that the Protestant education for frugality, self-denial, and hard work was crucial for the radical transformation to modern life.

While the early-modern thinkers Weber points to were not particularly aware of, or did not care, how their ideas might serve economic life, educational theorists in the nineteenth and twentieth centuries were quite self-conscious in their desires that education serve social and economic ends. The great architects of the American educational system, such as Horace Mann,

Woodrow Wilson, and William McGuffey, believed that schools must properly condition children to be capable workers. While they preached the "basics," their writings reveal their astute awareness of the importance of structuring schools to be like the workplace, so that in early industrial America the great numbers of uneducated and diverse immigrants would be ready to work side by side in the factory.

John Dewey, the most influential philosopher of education in the twentieth century, tried to convince his fellow Americans to turn the balance back toward liberal education and away from too strong an emphasis on preparation for work. Yet Dewey believed that the kind of equal liberal education for the masses he espoused would be possible only in a more socialist America, and that reestablishing, in a modern secular setting, a Platonic or medieval balance between liberal and vocational education for each child would require a dramatic shift in values away from materialism.

Conflicts between Dewey and his contemporaries over the aims of education reflect a long history of tension and conflict in the West over the nature of the good life. Today these tensions and conflicts continue and are readily seen in struggles to define just what work and education are for, and how they relate to each other. We cannot decide what we believe education should look like without determining what work is, and how important it is for individuals and for our society.

Robert Sessions

See also AIMS OF EDUCATION; ALIENATION; CAPITALISM; DEWEY; DISCIPLINE; DOMESTIC EDUCATION; FRANKLIN; HAPPINESS; LEISURE; LIBERAL EDUCATION; MARX; MARXISM; SLAVERY; TECHNOLOGY; VOCATIONAL EDUCATION

Bibliography

Barrow, R. *Plato, Utilitarianism, and Education.* London: Routledge and Kegan Paul, 1975.

Bowles, Samuel, and Herbert Gintis. *Schooling in Capitalist America: Educational Reform and the Contradictions of Economic Life.* New York: Harper, 1976.

Dewey, John. *Democracy and Education.* New York: Free Press, 1966.

Freire, Paulo. *Pedagogy of the Oppressed.* New York: Continuum, 1993.

Katz, Michael B. *Class, Bureaucracy, and Schools: The Illusion of Educational Change in America.* New York: Praeger, 1971.

Sessions, Robert, and Jack Wortman. *Working in America: A Humanities Reader.* Notre Dame: Notre Dame University Press, 1992.

Tyack, David B. *Turning Points in American Educational History.* Lexington, Mass.: Xerox College, 1967.

Wilson, John. *Philosophy and Practical Education.* London: Routledge and Kegan Paul, 1977.

Index

Index lists names and subjects found in the texts of the articles of the encyclopedia. **Boldface** indicates encyclopedia entry.

506; race and racism, 523; realism, 532; reason and rationality, 536; rhetoric, 550; right, 557; Rousseau, 567; scholasticism, 581; Sophists, 620; Stoicism, 627; Thomas Aquinas, 642; tragedy, 645–646; truth, 648; vocational education, 663; William of Ockham, 677

arithmetic: Descartes, 146; Philo of Alexandria, 456; philosophy of education, history of, 465

Arjuna: Hinduism, 271

Arkansas Trial of 1981: Darwin, 135

Armstrong, David: realism, 535

Armstrong, Samuel C.: Washington, Booker T., 667–668

Arnauld, Antoine, **35–36;** Descartes, 143; logic, 367

Arnold, Matthew, **36–37;** Darwin, 136; liberal education, 352

Arnold, Thomas: Arnold, 36; leisure, 351

Arrian: Stoicism, 626

ars dictaminis: rhetoric, 551

ars poetriae: rhetoric, 551

ars praedicandi: rhetoric, 551

art: physical education, 481; values and evaluation, 656–657

"as/if" world: philosophy and literature, 459

asceticism: Buddhism, 58–59

Asclepigenia: Hypatia, 288

Ash'arites: Islam, 312

Ashkenazic Jewry: Judaism, 330

Asian studies: higher education, 265

askesis: Cynics, 132

Aspin, David: philosophy of education, professional organizations in, 478

assimilation: learning, theories of, 348

assimilationist paradigm: multiculturalism, 416

association: Herbart, 259

Association for the Scientific Study of Education: Herbart, 259

Association of Process Philosophy: Whitehead, 672

Association of Supervision and Curriculum Development: curriculum and instruction, 125

associationism: Mill, 397–398

Astell, Mary: girls and women, 243

astronomy: philosophy of education, history of, 465

asylum reform: Mann, 379

ataraxia: Epicureanism, 186; philosophy of education, history of, 463

ate: tragedy, 646

atheism, **37–38;** Diderot, 155

atheists, negative: atheism, 38

atheists, positive: atheism, 37–38

Athena: Homer, 278

athletics: *paideia,* 440

Atkinson, Ti-Grace: feminism, 217

Atlanta University: Du Bois, 165

Atman: Hinduism, 271

atom: Rosenkranz, 565

atomism, logical: Russell, 573

attitudes: emotivism, 182–183

Augustine, Saint, **38–43;** Calvin, 65; Cicero, 77; Comenius, 94; Descartes, 143–144; freedom and determinism, 223; human nature, 283; love, 371; Peter Lombard, 449–450; philosophy of education, history of, 464; rhetoric, 551; scholasticism, 581; Thomas Aquinas, 643

Augustus: rhetoric, 551

Austin, J. L.: analytic philosophy, 20; truth, 648

Austrian School Reform Movement: Wittgenstein, 682

autarkeia: Cynics, 131

authoritarianism: Durkheim, 171

authority: conscience, 110; Makarenko, 378–379; social and political philosophy, 598–599

autonomy: reason and rationality, 537

Averroes, **43–44;** Avicenna, 44; logic, 362; scholasticism, 585

Avicenna, **44–46;** Averroes, 44; logic, 367; scholasticism, 583

axiological idealism: idealism, 295–296

Ayer, A.J.: analytic philosophy, 19; emotivism, 183; metaphysics, 396

Babbage, Charles: computers, 103

Bacon, Francis, **47–50;** Jefferson, 323; philosophy of education, history of, 466–467; rhetoric, 553; skepticism, 595; Thomas Aquinas, 643

Bacon, Roger: Peter Lombard, 449

bad faith: Sartre, 579

Bailey, C.H.: philosophy of education, professional organizations in, 477

Bailey, Cyril: Epicureanism, 188

Baldwin, James Mark: evolution, 204

Banton, Michael: race and racism, 521–523

Barber, C.L.: comedy, 92

bards: rhetoric, 550

Barnard, Henry: Harris, 250; Peabody, 442; Pestalozzi, 447; Rosenkranz, 565–566; Willard, 675–676

Barnett, Samuel A.: Addams, 7

Barrett, William: existentialism, 207–208

Barrow, Robin: analytic philosophy, 22

Barth, Karl: historicism, 273

Barthes, Roland: philosophy and literature, 460

Barzun, Jacques: race and racism, 523

Bateson, Gregory: conservatism, 114

Baumgarten, Alexander: aesthetics, 9

Beacon Hill School: Russell, 574–575

Beardsley, Monroe: logic, 370

beautiful, love of the: Plato, 484–487

beauty: love, 371; neoplatonism, 432; romanticism, 562

Beauvoir, Simone de: human nature, 283

Becket, Thomas: John of Salisbury, 328

Bedford College: Davies, 137

Beecher, Catherine Esther, **50–52;** domestic education, 163; girls and women, 242

Beecher, Lyman: Beecher, 50; Willard, 675

behavior: Behaviorism, 52–54

behavioral transaction: values and evaluation, 657

Behaviorism, **52–54**; cognitive development, 86; freedom and determinism, 224; heredity and hereditarianism, 261; scientism, 593; sociology, 615

being: Buddhism, 59; existentialism, 206

being-in-the-world: Heidegger, 254; phenomenology, 453

belief: Abelard, 3; emotivism, 183; meaning, 392; pleasure, 490; pragmatism, 501

Bell, Jeffrey: elitism, 178

Bellah, Robert: individualism, 302

Benedict, Ruth: anthropology, 28

Benedict, Saint: work, 687

beneficence: intuitionism, 309

benevolence: intuitionism, 309

Benhabib, Seyla: critical theory, 118

Benjamin, Walter: Marxism, 390

Bentham, Jeremy: equality, 193; right, 556; utilitarianism, 651–653

Bergmann, Gustav: analytic philosophy, 19

Bergson, Henri: comedy, 92; Whitehead, 672

Berkeley, George: human nature, 282; idealism, 295; rationalism, 526; realism, 532–533; skepticism, 595

Bernard of Chartres: philosophy of education, history of, 465

Bernard of Clairvaux: Abelard, 4; Augustine, 42

Bernstein, Edward: Marxism, 388

Berry, Wendell: conservatism, 114

Besant, Anne: atheism, 38

Betances, Ramon Emeterio: Hostos, 281

Bhagavad Gita: Hinduism, 269, 270, 271–272

bhakti yoga: Hinduism, 270, 272

Bhaktivedanta, A.C.: Hinduism, 272

A Bibliographic Guide to Educational Research: philosophy of education, literature in, 473

Bildung: Hegel, 253

Bill of Rights: liberalism, 355

Binet, Alfred: intelligence, 308

Bion: Cynics, 131

Black, Dora: Russell, 574

Black, Max: logic, 370

Blackstone, William: analytic philosophy, 22

Blair, Hugh: rhetoric, 553

Blair, J.A.: critical thinking, 121

Blake, William: mysticism, 417–418; romanticism, 561; Wollstonecraft, 683

Blandy, Doug: aesthetics, 10

Blanshard, Brand: truth, 648

Bloom, Allan: modernism and post-modernism, 403

Blow, Susan: Peabody, 442

Boas, Franz: anthropology, 28

Bobbitt, Franklin: curriculum and instruction, 124

Boccaccio, Giovanni: leisure, 350

Bode, Boyd H.: curriculum and instruction, 125

bodhisattva: Buddhism, 61

Bodmer, Jean Jacques: Pestalozzi, 446

body, the: neoplatonism, 432–433

body, education of: Montaigne, 404

body-minded: Dewey, 149–150

Boehme, J.: Comenius, 94

Boethius: Thomas Aquinas, 640

Bohm, David: Whitehead, 673

Bohr, Niels: freedom and determinism, 224; intelligence, 307

Bolshevik Party: Marxism, 389

Bonaventure, **55–57**; Peter Lombard, 449; scholasticism, 582

Boole, George: logic, 368

Borradori, Giovanna: philosophy and literature, 460

Bosanquet, Bernard: Hegel; 253; Rosenkranz, 565

Boston University: King, 344

Boswell, James: Macaulay, 375

botany: Milton, 399

Bouille, Charles: Humanism, 286

Bourne, Randolph: reconstructionism, social, 539–540

Bowlby, John: psychoanalysis, 510

Bowles, Samuel: critical theory, 118

boys, education of: Erasmus, 198

bracketing: phenomenology, 457

Brackett, Anna C.: Rosenkranz, 564

Bradlaugh, Charles: atheism, 38

Bradley, F.H.: Hegel, 253; logic, 369; Rosenkranz, 565

Bradwardine, Thomas: William of Ockham, 677–678

Brahman: Hinduism, 271

Brameld, Theodore: philosophy of education, professional organizations in, 476; reconstructionism, social, 539

Brathwaite, Edward: colonialism and post-colonialism, 90

Brauner, Charles: analytic philosophy, 22

bread labor: Gandhi, 234

Brethren of the Common Life: Erasmus, 197; Luther, 372

Breuer, Joseph: Freud, 227

Brigham, Carl C.: heredity and hereditarianism, 261

British Education Index: philosophy of education, literature in, 473

Broad, C.D.: analytic philosophy, 21; common sense, 98

Brockmeyer, Henry C.: Harris, 250

Broudy, Harry: analytic philosophy, 21

Brown, Les: philosophy of education, professional organizations in, 478

Brown, Marjorie M.: domestic education, 164

Brown v. Board of Education: democracy, 142

Brubacher, John: philosophy of education, professional organizations in, 476

Brücke, Ernst: Freud, 227

Bruner, Jerome: learning, theories of, 348–349

Bruni, Leonardo: girls and women, 241; *studia humanitatis,* 630– 631

Brunner, Emil: historicism, 273

Buber, Martin, **57–58**

Buddhism, **58–61**; atheism, 38; freedom and determinism, 223; Hinduism, 272; mysticism, 418; Taoism, 635

Bullivant, Brian M.: pluralism, 492

Bunyan, John: Willard, 674

Burbules, Nicholas: reason and rationality, 538

Burgdorf Institute: Pestalozzi, 447

Burke, Edmund: Arnold, 36; conservatism, 112–113; Macaulay, 375

Burlamaqui, Jean Jacques: Jefferson, 324

Burnett, Joe R.: analytic philosophy, 21

Burt, Cyril: Darwin, 36; heredity and hereditarianism, 261

Burton, John: girls and women, 242

Bury, J.B.: progress, 506

Butler, Joseph: conscience, 110; intuitionism, 308–309

Butts, R. Freeman: civic education, 81

Cajetan, Cardinal: scholasticism, 584

Callias: Socrates, 617

Callicles: Sophists, 622

Calvin, John, **63–65**; Calvinism, 65; Descartes, 144; elitism, 178–179; freedom and determinism, 223

Calvinism, **65–67**; Beecher, 50, 51; Mann, 379

Campbell, Donald T.: evolution, 204

Campbell, George: rhetoric, 553

Camus, Albert: existentialism, 209; human nature, 284; philosophy and literature, 458

Canter, Lee: discipline, 198

Cantor, George: logic, 369

capitalism, **67–72**; colonialism and post-colonialism, 89; critical theory, 115–116; Harris, 251; liberalism, 359; Marx, 384–386; Marxism, 388–391; nationalism, 422; socialism, 605–606; sociology, 610–611

caring: justice, 337

Carlile, Richard: atheism, 38

Carnap, Rudolph: analytic philosophy, 19; metaphysics, 396; positivism, 493; science, philosophy of, 590

Carnegie, Andrew: Dewey, 148–149

Cartesian understanding: pragmatism, 500

cartography: Milton, 399

Carver, Fred D.: educational policy and administration, 174

casa dei bambini: domestic education, 162; Montessori, 407–408

Cassian, John: leisure, 350

Cassidy, Rosalind: physical education, 481

Cassiodorus: Augustine, 42

Castiglione, Baldasar: *studia humanitatis,* 631

Castles, Stephen: minorities, 401

castration anxiety: Freud, 228

Caswell, Hollis: curriculum and instruction, 125

catechism, larger: Luther, 373

catechism, shorter: Luther, 373

categorical imperative: justice, 336; Kant, 341

categorical propositions: logic, 368

catharsis: tragedy, 645–646

Cathedral School (Paris): Peter Lombard, 449

cathedral schools: rhetoric, 552

Catherine the Great: Diderot, 157

Catholicism: mysticism, 418

Cattell, James: Darwin, 136

Cattell, Raymond B.: hereditary and hereditarianism, 261

causal idealism: idealism, 294

causality: Kant, 340; realism, 534–535

cave, simile of: Plato, 485

celibacy: Buddhism, 60

censorship, **72–74**

Cercidas: Cynics, 131

Chancellor, William E.: educational policy and administration, 174

Channing, William Ellery: Peabody, 441

chaos: Taoism, 634

Chapone, Hester: girls and women, 242

character: Herbart, 258–259

Charcot, Jean-Martin: Freud, 227

charity: meaning, 392

Charlemagne: rhetoric, 552: scholasticism, 581

Charleton, Walter: Epicureanism, 188

Charters, W.W.: curriculum and instruction, 124

chastity: Buddhism, 60

Chaucer, Geoffrey: leisure, 350

Chavez, Cesar: Gandhi, 233

child and curriculum: Dewey, 148

child-centeredness: Makarenko, 378; progress, 508

Child Development Abstracts and Bibliography: philosophy of education, literature in, 473

child psychology: Wittgenstein, 681–682

Child Study Movement: Hall, 245–246

Childe, V. Gordon: intelligence, 306

children, education of: Locke, 363–364

Children's Bureau: school, 588–589

children's rights, **74–75**; rights, 558

Chisholm, Roderick M.: analytic philosophy, 20

choice: elitism, 180; ethics and morality, 201–202

Chomsky, Noam: rationalism, 525

choral poetry: Sappho, 577

choregus: Isocrates, 316

Christian culture: philosophy of education, history of, 465

Christianity: Buddhism, 60; freedom and determinism, 223

Chrysippus: Cicero, 76; Stoicism, 626

church: Harris, 251

Church, Alonzo: logic, 369

Cicero, Marcus Tullius, **75–79**; Aristotle, 31; Augustine, 39; humanism, 285–286; Isocrates, 319; John of Salisbury, 329; leisure, 350; philosophy of education, history of, 464; rhetoric, 551; scholasti-

conversion: Beecher, 51

Conway, Ronald: philosophy of education, professional organizations in, 478

Cooper, Anna Julia: girls and women, 243

Copernicus, Nicolaus: psychoanalysis, 508

Coreth, Emmerich: scholasticism, 585

Cornell Critical Thinking Tests: critical thinking, 121–122

corporal punishment: Freud, 228

correspondence theory of truth: epistemology, 189; truth, 648

cosmological argument: atheism, 38

cosmopolis: Stoicism, 628

Cotton States Exposition: Washington, Booker T., 669–670

countertransference: psychoanalysis, 511

Counts, George: indoctrination, 304; possibility, 495–496; reconstructionism, social, 539; socialism, 607

courage: *arete,* 29–30; practical wisdom, 497

covenant: Calvinism, 66

Cowley, Abraham: Bacon, 48

Crassus, Lucius: Cicero, 75

Crates: Cynics, 131

creationism: Darwin, 135

creative thinking: critical thinking, 121

creativity: cybernetics, 127–128; pragmatism, 502; Whitehead, 672–673

Cremin, Lawrence: curriculum and instruction, 124; progress, 507

Creon: philosophy and literature, 459

Critias: Sophists, 622

critical pedagogy: critical theory, 118; possibility, 496

critical philosophy: Kant, 340–341

critical theory, **115–119;** dialectic, 155; philosophy and literature, 458; philosophy of education, history of, 472; social sciences, philosophy of, 604

critical thinking, **119–123;** indoctrination, 303–304; logic, 370; philosophy of education, history of, 472; reason and rationality, 537; socialism, 608

Crito: Socrates, 619

Crittendon, Brian: analytic philosophy, 22

Croce, Benedetto: historicism, 274

Cross Commission: Arnold, 37

Crozer Seminary: King, 344

cruelty: rights, 557

crystallization: Froebel, 230

Cuban revolution: Marti-Perez, 382

Cubberley, Ellwood P.: educational policy and administration, 174; school, 588

Cudworth, Ralph: intuitionism, 308

cultural anthropology: anthropology, 27

cultural mandate: Calvinism, 67

cultural pluralism: multiculturalism, 445; pluralism, 491–492

cultural relativism: pluralism, 492

Current Index to Journals in Education: philosophy of education, literature in, 473

curriculum and instruction, **123–126**

Cusanus, N.: Comenius, 94

custom: ethics and morality, 199

cybernetics, **126–131**

Cyclopedia of Education, Paul Monroe's: philosophy of education, history of, 471

Cynics, **131–132;** Cyrenaics, 133; Stoicism, 628

Cyrenaics, **132–133;** Epicureanism, 187

Cyril, Patriarch of Alexandria: Hypatia, 288

D'Alembert, Jean La Rond: Condorcet, 106; intelligence, 306–307; rationalism, 525

dance: physical education, 481

Dante: Averroes, 43; Bonaventure, 55

Darwin, Charles, **135–137;** conscience, 111; Dewey, 148; evolution, 203, 204–205; existentialism, 206; Gilman, 239; Hall, 245; heredity and hereditarianism, 261; philosophy of education, history of, 470; psychoanalysis, 508

Darwin, Erasmus: girls and women, 242

Darwinism: Marxism, 388

Davidson, Donald: meaning, 392–393

Davies, (Sarah) Emily, **137–139;** girls and women, 243

Davis, David Brian: slavery, 597

Davydov, V.V.: cognitive development, 88

Day, Michael D.: aesthetics, 10

Dearden, Robert F.: analytic philosophy, 22; philosophy of education, professional organizations in, 477

Debs, Eugene V.: socialism, 606

declamatio: rhetoric, 550

Declaration of Independence: Jefferson, 323; rights, 560

deconstructionists: Jesus, 325–326

deductive method: metaphysics, 395–396; Rosenkranz, 565

defense mechanisms: psychoanalysis, 509

defensible partiality: reconstructionism, social, 540

Defoe, Daniel: girls and women, 243

DeGarmo, Charles: Herbart, 259

Degenhardt, M.A.B.: philosophy of education, professional organizations in, 477

deGenlis, Madame: Macaulay, 376

Degler, Carl: Gilman, 241

deism: Jefferson, 324

deliberation: Heidegger, 255

Demetrius: Cynics, 131–132

democracy, **139–143;** Addams, 7–8; empiricism, 184–185; liberalism, 358; nationalism, 422; naturalism, 428; pragmatism, 501–502; Russell, 574; social and political philosophy, 600–601

democracy, discourse of: possibility, 496

democracy, participatory: socialism, 607

Democratic Party: Mann, 380

Democritus: Epicureanism, 186

Demonax: Cynics, 131–132

demonstration: John of Salisbury, 329

DeMorgan, Augustus: logic, 368; William of Ockham, 677

Demosthenes: *studia humanitatis,* 631

Dennett, Daniel C.: meaning, 393; person, 444

deon: ethics and morality, 200

deontic logic; logic, 369

deontologists: ethics and morality, 300; right, 555

depravity, total: Calvin, 65

Derrida, Jacques: modernism and post-modernism, 403

Descartes, Rene, **143–146;** Arnauld, 35; cognitive development, 85; Comenius, 97; empiricism, 184; ethics and morality, 200; human nature, 282; Locke, 364; logic, 368; metaphysics, 395; modernism and post-modernism, 402; naturalism, 427; phenomenology, 452; philosophy of education, history of, 466; physical education, 481; pluralism, 491; rationalism, 526; realism, 533; Rousseau, 570; skepticism, 595

descriptive presentation: values and evaluation, 656

descriptive senses: liberal education, 352

desegregation: public education, 515

desire: Buddhism, 59; pleasure, 489–490

determinism: human nature, 283; technology, 638

determinism, biological: gender and sexism, 235; heredity and hereditarianism, 260–261

determinism, economic: Marxism, 389

determinism, intrapsychic: psychoanalysis, 509

Deutsch, Helene: Freud, 229

developmental psychology: Hall, 246

DeVries, Hugo: heredity and hereditarianism, 260

Dewey, John, **146–153;** Addams, 8; aesthetics, 11; aims of education, 12; critical thinking, 119; curriculum and instruction, 123, 124; cybernetics, 126, 128; Darwin, 137; democracy, 141; dialectic, 154; discipline, 159; domestic education, 163–164; Du Bois, 165–166; educational theory and administration, 173; elitism, 179; Emerson, 182; empiricism, 185; epistemology, 190; ethics and morality, 199; evolution, 204; experience, 211; girls and women, 243; Hegel, 253; Herbart, 258, 260; home and family, 276–277; Hook, 279; human nature, 284; Humanism, 287; individualism, 302; indoctrination, 304; intelligence, 307; Jefferson, 323; justice, 337; liberalism, 358; logic, 367; Montessori, 406; moral development, 410–412; nationalism, 422; naturalism, 428; philosophy and literature, 457; philosophy of education, history of, 471; philosophy of education, professional organizations in, 475–476; physical education, 481; possibility, 495; practical wisdom, 498–499;

pragmatism, 499, 502–503; progress, 506, 508; public education, 514–515; realism, 534; reason and rationality, 536; reconstructionism, social, 539; romanticism, 564; Rousseau, 573; social and political philosophy, 598; socialism, 607; sociology, 613; Spencer, 625; truth, 649; values and evaluation, 655–657; vocational education, 664–665; Whitehead, 672; work, 688

Dewitt, Norman Wentworth: Epicureanism, 188

Dharma: Buddhism, 60

D'Holbach, Baron: atheism, 38

dialectic, **153–155;** Calvin, 64; John of Salisbury, 329; love, 371; Stoicism, 627; Whitehead, 672

dialectic of freedom: possibility, 495

dialectical method: Abelard, 3; Plato, 483–485

dialectical thinking: conservatism, 113

Dickinson, John: Jefferson, 324

Didaskalos: Clement of Alexandria, 85

Diderot, Denis, **155–158;** Condorcet, 106; democracy, 140; Helvetius, 257; philosophy of education, history of, 468

Diet of Augsburg: Luther, 373

Dilthey, Wilhelm: historicism, 273

Dio Chrysostom: Cynics, 131–132

Diodotus: Cicero, 76

Diogenes: Cynics, 131

Diogenes Laertius: Stoicism, 626

Dionysius: Thomas Aquinas, 640

Dionysodorus: Socrates, 618; Sophists, 622

disadvantage: minorities, 400

discipline, **158–160;** Durkheim, 171

Discourse: Australian Journal of Educational Studies: philosophy of education, literature in, 474

discrimination: minorities, 401; race and racism, 524

displacement: psychoanalysis, 510

dispositions: critical thinking, 120

disputatio: scholasticism, 581

Dissertation Abstracts International: philosophy of education, literature in, 473

Dissoi Logoi: Socrates, 618; Sophists, 622

distinctness: Descartes, 145

distributive justice: justice, 337

diversity: Montaigne, 404–405

diversity, linguistic: multiculturalism, 415

DNA: Whitehead, 673

doing: Buddhism, 59

domephobia: domestic education, 164

Domestic Economy: Beecher, 51

domestic education, **160–164**

domestic violence: feminism, 218

dominium: William of Ockham, 678

Domitian: Cynics, 131

Donaldson, Margaret: cognitive development, 87

Dostoevsky, F.M.: nihilism, 436

Douay version (Holy Bible): Mann, 381
doubt: Descartes, 145; pragmatism, 501
Douglas, A.E.: Cicero, 76
Douglas, William O.: rights, 558
doxa: Isocrates, 319
dream analysis: Freud, 227
Droysen, Johann Gustav: historicism, 273
Drucker, Peter: Whitehead, 673
Drury, John: girls and women, 243
D'Souza, Dinesh: modernism and post-modernism, 403
dualism: curriculum and instruction, 123; epistemology, 191; human nature, 282–283
Du Bois, W.E.B., **165–168;** democracy, 141; girls and women, 243; multiculturalism, 416; possibility, 495; Washington, Booker T., 668–669
Dühring, Eugen: historicism, 272
Dumbleton, John: William of Ockham, 677
Dummett, Michael: meaning, 393
Duns Scotus, John, **168–170;** Bonaventure, 55; scholasticism, 583–584; socialism, 605
Durkheim, Emile, **170–171;** discipline, 158; norm, 437–438; sociology, 611–612
duty: Kant, 342: pleasure, 490; right, 555; utilitarianism, 652
DuVair, Guillaume: Stoicism, 627
Dwight, Timothy: Willard, 674–675
Dworkin, Andrea: feminism, 217
Dworkin, Ronald: censorship, 72; equality, 194
Dzerzhinski Commune: Makarenko, 378

Eagleton, Terry: philosophy and literature, 458; socialism, 606
Ebert, Roger: censorship, 73
Ecclesiastes: Erasmus, 196
Eckhart, Meister: Clement of Alexandria, 85; Heidegger, 256
Eco, Umberto: Cynics, 132
ecstatic, the: Emerson, 181
Edel, Abraham: analytic philosophy, 22, 23
Edelstein, Ludwig: progress, 506
Edgeworth, Maria: domestic education, 161
Edgeworth, Richard Lovell: domestic education, 161
educare: James, 321
Education Index: philosophy of education, literature in, 473
education of consciousness: Hegel, 253
Educational Administration Abstracts: philosophy of education, literature in, 473
Educational Foundations: philosophy of education, literature in, 474
educational opportunity: equality, 192–193
Educational Philosophy and Theory: philosophy of education, literature in, 474; philosophy of education, professional organizations in, 478
educational policy and administration, **173–178**
Educational Resources Information Center (ERIC):

philosophy of education, literature in, 473
Educational Studies: philosophy of education; literature in, 474
Educational Testing Service: educational policy and administration, 176
educational theory: philosophy of education, history of, 462
Educational Theory: existentialism, 209; philosophy of education, literature in, 474; philosophy of education, professional organizations in, 476
Edwards, Jonathan: Beecher, 51
Edwards, Richard: Rosenkranz, 565
effort: equality, 193
Egbert: Augustine, 42
ego: Freud, 227; psychoanalysis, 509
egocentrism: cognitive development, 88
egoism: ethics and morality, 199; utilitarianism, 651
eidetic analysis: phenomenology, 452
eidos: phenomenology, 452; Plato, 483; realism, 531
Elder Seneca: rhetoric, 551
Eleatics, the: dialectic, 153
election: Calvin, 65
Electra: Freud, 228
Elegantiae: Erasmus, 196
elenchus: Socrates, 618
eleutheria: Cyrenaics, 133
Eliot, Charles W.: evolution, 205; liberal education, 352
Eliot, T.S.: conservatism, 113
elitism, **178–181;** Nietzsche, 434
Elkins, Stanley: slavery, 597
Elliot, Ray: philosophy of education, professional organizations in, 477
eloquence: John of Salisbury, 328; Vico, 661
Elvin, Lionel: philosophy of education, professional organizations in, 477
Elyot, Thomas: *studia humanitatis,* 631
emanation: Bonaventure, 56
Emerson, Ralph Waldo, **181–182;** Alcott, 13; Hostos, 231; individualism, 301; Marti-Perez, 382; Peabody, 441; philosophy and literature, 457
Emile: Rousseau, 567–572
emotion: Dewey, 150
emotivism, **182–183**
empathy: James, 322
empiricism, **183–185;** epistemology, 189; philosophy of education, history of, 467; rationalism, 525–528; Stoicism, 627
Encyclopedia Africana: Du Bois, 167
Encyclopedia of Philosophy: philosophy of education, literature in, 472
Encyclopedie, of Denis Diderot: Diderot, 155
end in view: curriculum and instruction, 123
end-state rights: rights, 560
ends in themselves: Kant, 341

Engels, Friedrich: Marx, 382; Marxism, 387; nationalism, 422; social sciences, philosophy of, 603; socialism, 606
engineering: Milton, 399
English School: Franklin, 222
enkuklios paideia: Philo of Alexandria, 456; Quintilian, 518
Enlightenment, the: empiricism, 185; philosophy of education, history of, 468; progress, 506; Rousseau, 567–568
"enlightenment": Hinduism, 271; mysticism, 417
Ennis, Robert H.: analytic philosophy, 21; critical thinking, 119, 120
entitlements: rights, 558
environment: behaviorism, 52–53
environmentalism: Helvetius, 257; heredity and hereditarianism, 261, 262; philosophy of education, history of, 467–468
Epee, Chevalier de l': Diderot, 156
Epictetus: Cynics, 131; Stoicism, 626
Epicureanism, **185–188;** Jefferson, 323; philosophy of education, history of, 463
Epicurus: atheism, 38; Epicureanism, 185–186; philosophy of education, history of, 463
episteme: Isocrates, 318
epistemic justification: reason and rationality, 537
epistemic logic: logic, 369
epistemological naturalism: naturalism, 425
epistemology, **188–192;** cognitive development, 85; empiricism, 184; modernism and postmodernism, 402; philosophy of education, history of, 471; science, philosophy of, 590
epistemology, genetic: cognitive development, 87
epoche: phenomenology, 451–452
equal humanness: Gilman, 239
equalitarianism: Helvetius, 257
equality, **192–195;** King, 345; liberalism, 356–357; Locke, 363; philosophy of education, history of, 467–468; social and political philosophy, 599; socialism, 605–606; Stoicism, 628; Taoism, 635; Wollstonecraft, 684–685
equality, gender: Macaulay, 376
equality of opportunity: aims of education, 13; social and political philosophy, 599
equilibration: learning, theories of, 348
equilibrium: cognitive development, 87
Erasmus, Desiderius, **195–199;** Calvin, 65; elitism, 178; girls and women, 241; philosophy of education, history of, 466
Erdman, J.E.,: Rosenkranz, 565
Erikson, Erik H.: Freud, 229; psychoanalysis, 511
eros: Freud, 228; love, 370–371; Plato, 487
error, possibility of: relativism, 542
esse: Scholasticism, 583
essence: existentialism, 206; metaphysics, 395
eternal objects: Whitehead, 672
eternity: neoplatonism, 431–432
ethical caring: ethics and morality, 202–203

ethical dilemma: moral development, 409–410
ethical idealism: idealism, 292–293
ethical judgments: emotivism, 182–183
ethics and morality, **199–203;** Mann, 379–380; philosophy of education, history of, 462–463; Stoicism, 628
ethnic relations: race and racism, 523–524
ethnicism: race and racism, 523
ethnicity: feminism, 217; pluralism, 491; socialism, 606
ethnocentrism: multiculturalism, 415; race and racism, 522
ethnology: anthropology, 28
ethnomethodologists: sociology, 615
ethology: Mill, 398
Euclid: Alfarabi, 15; Avicenna, 45
eudaimonia: Cynics, 131; happiness, 248–249
eugenics: hereditary and hereditarianism, 261, 262–263
Euler's theorem: cognitive development, 89
Euripides: tragedy, 645–646
Eurocentrism: colonialism and post-colonialism, 89; multiculturalism, 415–416
Eusebius of Caesaria: Clement of Alexandria, 84
Euthydemus: Socrates, 618; Sophists, 622
evangelicism: Calvin, 64
evil: Sartre, 580; Stoicism, 628
evolution, **203–205;** existentialism, 207; intelligence, 306–307; moral development, 413–414; philosophy of education, history of, 470; progress, 506; Spencer, 625
evolutionary epistemology: evolution, 204
evolutionary principles: Hall, 245
excellence: *arete,* 29
exclusion: minorities, 401
exemplarity: Bonaventure, 56
existence: existentialism, 206; metaphysics, 394–395
existential phenomenology: Heidegger, 254; phenomenology, 454–455
existentialism, **206–210;** phenomenology, 451; philosophy and literature, 458–459; philosophy of education, history of, 472; Sartre, 578–580
experience, **210–213;** curriculum and instruction, 124; Locke, 365; pleasure, 490
experientialism: philosophy and literature, 457
experimental inquiry: pragmatism, 502–503
experimental method: Dewey, 150–151; pragmatism, 501–502
explanatory idealism: idealism, 295
exploitation: Marx, 383–385
extensional definition: behaviorism, 53
Eysenck, Hans J.: heredity and hereditarianism, 261

fact idealism: idealism, 294
factory metaphor: educational policy and administration, 173, 174
faculties of mind: Herbart, 258
Fairbairn, W.R.D.: psychoanalysis, 510

Galileo: skepticism, 595
Galton, Francis: Darwin, 136; heredity and
        hereditarianism, 261; intelligence, 308
games: aesthetics, 10; physical education, 481
Gandhi, Mohandas Karamchand, **233–235;** civil
        disobedience, 82–83; Hinduism, 272
Garrison, James W.: analytic philosophy, 23; teach-
        ing and learning, 637
Garvey, Marcus Mosiah: Du Bois, 167
Gassendi, Pierre: Epicureanism, 188
Gassett, Jose Ortega y: historicism, 274; human
        nature, 283; idealism, 295
Gauthier, David: right, 556
"gay science": Nietzsche, 434
Geertz, Clifford: anthropology, 28; philosophy and
        literature, 460
Geisteswissenschaften: historicism, 273; social sci-
        ences, philosophy of, 603
Gelman, R.: cognitive development, 87
Gemara: Judaism, 332
gender and sexism, **235–239;** critical theory, 118;
        critical thinking, 122; feminism, 216–
        217; minorities, 401; philosophy of edu-
        cation, history of, 472
gender development: Hall, 246–247
general ideas: realism, 532
general method: Pestalozzi, 447
general will: liberalism, 357
generalizability: critical thinking, 121
genes: heredity and hereditarianism, 262
genius: Nietzsche, 435
genocide: colonialism and post-colonialism, 90;
        nationalism, 424
genotype: heredity and hereditarianism, 261–262
gentleman: Cicero, 78; Confucianism, 109
Gentzen, Gerhard: logic, 370
geometry: Descartes, 145–146; Philo of Alexan-
        dria, 456; philosophy of education, his-
        tory of, 465; Quintilian, 518
Gewirth, Alan: analytic philosophy, 20
Gianturco, Elio: Vico, 661
Giddens, Anthony: nationalism, 424
Giere, Ronald N.: science, philosophy of, 592
gifts: Froebel, 231
gifts of being: Heidegger, 256
Gilbert of Poitiers: John of Salisbury, 328
Gilbert, William: Bacon, 48
Gilligan, Carol: Freud, 228; justice, 337; right, 557
Gilman, Charlotte Perkins, **239–241;** Beecher, 50;
        domestic education, 162; feminism, 210;
        girls and women, 243
Gilson, Etienne: scholasticism, 583, 585
Gintis, Herbert: critical theory, 118
girls and women, education of, **241–244;** Erasmus,
        198
Giroux, Henry: critical theory, 118; literacy, 361;
        possibility, 496; reconstructionism, so-
        cial, 541; socialism, 606
Girton College: Davies, 137–138
gnosis: Clement of Alexandria, 84

Gnostic: Clement of Alexandria, 84
Gnostic gospels: Jesus, 326
goal-seeking: reconstructionism, social, 539
God: Froebel, 231; Kant, 340–341, 342; metaphys-
        ics, 395; Peter Lombard, 449; William of
        Ockham, 677
Goddard, Henry H.: heredity and hereditarianism,
        261
Godel, Kurt: logic, 369–370; science, philosophy
        of, 590
gods, age of: Vico, 661
Godwin, William: Wollstonecraft, 683
Goethe, Johann W.: historicism, 273
Goldberg, Arnold: psychoanalysis, 511
Golden Rule: conservatism, 114
Goldman, Emma: girls and women, 243
good: ethics and morality, 199–200; neoplatonism,
        431–432, 433; right, 554
Good, idea of: Plato, 486
good, of individuals: aims of education, 12–13
good, of society: aims of education, 12–13
good faith: Sartre, 579
Goodman, Nelson: philosophy and literature, 459
goodness: *arete,* 29; liberalism, 357; love, 371;
        practical wisdom, 498
Goodwin, Frederick: heredity and hereditarianism,
        263
Gordon, Haim: Buber, 57–58
Gordon, Milton: pluralism, 492
Gorgias of Leontini: Isocrates, 361; rhetoric, 550;
        Socrates, 618; Sophists, 621
Gorky colony: Makarenko, 378
Göschel, Karl: Rosenkranz, 565
Graff, Harvey: literacy, 361
Graham, William: Macaulay, 375
grammar: Hegel, 253–254; John of Salisbury, 328–
        329; Philo of Alexandria, 456; philoso-
        phy of education, history of, 465;
        Quintilian, 518–519
grammar, Greek: Calvin, 64
grammar, Latin: Calvin, 64
grammar, universal: rationalism, 525
grammaticus: Quintilian, 517–518
Gramsci, Antonio: indoctrination, 304; Marxism,
        390; socialism, 607
Grand Tranquility: Taoism, 634–635
graphical user interfaces: computers, 103
Green, Thomas F.: analytic philosophy, 22; educa-
        tional policy and administration, 175–
        176; practical wisdom, 499
Greene, Graham: philosophy and literature, 458
Greene, Maxine: critical theory, 118; girls and
        women, 244; possibility, 496
Greene, Thomas H.: revolution, 547
Greer, W. Dwaine: aesthetics, 10
Gribble, James: philosophy of education, profes-
        sional organizations in, 478
Griffin, Donald L.: intelligence, 306
Grimke, Sarah: girls and women, 244
growth: Dewey, 147; Gilman, 240; pragmatism,

502; Rousseau, 568; Whitehead, 672

Guarini, Guarino: Humanism, 286; *studia humanitatis,* 631

Guide to Sources of Educational Information, A: philosophy of education, literature in, 473

"guiding fiction": indoctrination, 304

guilds: vocational education, 663

guilt: Nietzsche, 433

Guizot, Francois: Arnold, 37

Guntrip, Harry: psychoanalysis, 510

gymnastics: Plato, 487

Habermas, Jürgen: critical theory, 117–118; epistemology, 190; idealism, 293; modernism and post-modernism, 403; social sciences, philosophy of, 604

habit: Locke, 365

hadith: Islam, 311

haecceitas: scholasticism, 584

Haeckel, Ernst: Hall, 245

Hagar the Egyptian: Philo of Alexandria, 439

halakha: Judaism, 333

Halevi, Yehuda: Judaism, 333

Hall, G. Stanley, **245–247;** Freud, 227; romanticism, 246

Hall, Joseph: stoicism, 627

hamartia: tragedy, 645

Hamilton, Alexander: conservatism, 113

Hamilton, Alice: Addams, 9

Hamilton, William: logic, 367

Hampton Normal and Industrial Institute: Washington, Booker T., 667

Handbook of Research on Teaching: philosophy of education, literature in, 473

happiness, **247–250;** Beecher, 51; Cicero, 77; ethics and morality, 199; Jefferson, 323; pleasure, 490; practical wisdom, 497; Socrates, 619; Spencer, 623; utilitarianism, 653

Hardie, Charles D.: analytic philosophy, 21; philosophy of education, professional organizations in, 478

Harding, Sandra: science, philosophy of, 592

Hare, Richard M.: analytic philosophy, 20; emotivism, 183

Hare Krishnas: Hinduism, 272

Harper, William Rainey: Dewey, 148

Harrapans: Hinduism, 269–270

Harris, William Torrey, **250–252;** educational policy and administration, 173–174; Froebel, 231; Hegel, 254; Peabody, 442; philosophy and literature, 457; Rosenkranz, 564

Harsanyi, John: right, 556

Hartley, David: Wollstonecraft, 683

Hartlib, Samuel: Milton, 349

Hartmann, Heinz: Freud, 229; psychoanalysis, 510

Hartshorne, Hugh: Willard, 676

Harvard Educational Review: philosophy of educa-

tion, literature in, 473

Harvey, William: Bacon, 48

Hasidim: mysticism, 418

Havelock, Eric A.: literacy, 361

Hawthorne, Nathaniel: Peabody, 442

Hazlitt, William: socialism, 605

Heath, Shirley Brice: literacy, 361

Hebrew: Judaism, 331–332

Hebrew scripture: Jesus, 326

hedone: Cyrenaics, 132

hedonism: Cyrenaics, 133; Epicureanism, 187

hedonistic utilitarians: utilitarianism, 651

Hegel, G.W.F., **252–254;** alienation, 17; community, 101; Dewey, 148; existentialism, 206; formalism, 220; freedom and determinism, 226; Hall, 245; Harris, 250–251; historicism, 274; intelligence, 305; Kierkegaard, 343; love, 370; metaphysics, 396; nationalism, 421; philosophy and literature, 457; philosophy of education, history of, 469; rationalism, 525; realism, 534; romanticism, 562; Rosenkranz, 564–565; sociology, 613; truth, 648; Whitehead, 672

Hegelianism: Harris, 250; Hegel, 252–253

Hegelians, St. Louis: Rosenkranz, 565

hegemony: indoctrination, 304

Hegesias: Cyrenaics, 132

Heidegger, Martin, **254–257;** existentialism, 207–208; Hegel, 253; historicism, 273; metaphysics, 396; phenomenology, 451; philosophy and literature, 460

Heine, Heinrich: Cynics, 132; moral development, 411

Heisenberg, Werner: freedom and determinism, 224

Helen: Homer, 278; Sappho, 577

Heloise: Abelard, 3

Helvetius, Claude Adrien, **257–258;** Diderot, 155–156; Macaulay, 376; Mill, 397–398; Wollstonecraft, 683

Hemingway, Ernest: philosophy and literature, 458

Hemming, Leopold von: Rosenkranz, 564

Hempel, Carl: analytic philosophy, 19; science, philosophy of, 590–591

Henry, Jules: anthropology, 28

Hera: Homer, 278

Heraclitus: Stoicism, 627–628

Herbart, Johann Friedrich, **258–260;** empiricism, 185; progress, 508; Rosenkranz, 564–565

Herbertianism: Herbart, 259–260

herd instinct: Russell, 574

Herder, Johann: anthropology, 27; Comenius, 97

heredity and hereditarianism, **260–263**

hermeneutics: Heidegger, 255–256; philosophy and literature, 458

heroes, age of: Vico, 661

Hertz, H.: Wittgenstein, 678

Hesiod: *arete,* 30; work, 687

Heslep, Robert D.: analytic philosophy, 23
heterogeneity: community, 102
heterosexuality: feminism, 216
Hicks, Robert Drew: Epicureanism, 188
Hierax: Hypatia, 289
higher education, **263–269;** Durkheim, 170
Higher Education Abstracts: philosophy of education, literature in, 473
Hilbert, David: logic, 369
Hills, George L.: intelligence, 307
Hinayana: Buddhism, 60
Hinduism, **269–272;** Buddhism, 59; freedom and determinism, 223; mysticism, 418
Hipparchia: Cynics, 131
Hippias of Elis: Sophists, 621
Hippocrates: John of Salisbury, 329
Hirsch, E.D.: civic education, 81; modernism and post-modernism, 403
Hirsch, S.R.: Judaism, 334
Hirst, Paul H.: analytic philosophy, 22; epistemology, 189; philosophy of education, professional organizations in, 477; Thomas Aquinas, 642
historical relativism: anthropology, 28
historicism, **272–275**
historismus: historicism, 272
history, sense of: pragmatism, 505
history, study of: Nietzsche, 433–434; Quintilian, 519
Hitler, Adolf: heredity and hereditarianism, 261; moral development, 413
Hobbes, Thomas: children's rights, 74–75; Descartes, 143; human nature, 282; intuitionism, 308–310
Hocking, W.E.: Rosenkranz, 565
Hogg, Anna: philosophy of education, professional organizations in, 478
Hölderlin, Friedrich: romanticism, 561–562
Holocaust, the: rights, 558
Holt, John: Rousseau, 573
Home and Colonial School Society: Pestalozzi, 448
home and family, **275–277;** Montessori, 406–408
Home Economics: Beecher, 51; domestic education, 164
home life: domestic education, 161–162
Homer, **277–279;** *arete,* 29–30; comedy, 92; philosophy of education, history of, 471; physical education, 481; Quintilian, 518; *studia humanitatis,* 630
homogeneity: community, 102
homosexuality: Sappho, 577
honor: *arete,* 29; Montaigne, 404
Hook, Sidney, **279–280;** naturalism, 428
hooks, bell: feminism, 217
Hopkins, G.M.: Duns Scotus, 170
Horace: Vico, 661
horizonality: phenomenology, 453
Horkheimer, Max: critical theory, 116–117
Horne, Donald: philosophy of education, professional organizations in, 478

Horney, Karen: Freud, 229; psychoanalysis, 511
Hosegood, B.H.: philosophy of education, professional organizations in, 477
Hostos y Bonilla, **280–282**
House, Ernest R.: school, 589
Howe, Julia Ward: Peabody, 441
Hudson, W.H.: James, 322
Hugh of St. Victor: Peter Lombard, 449
Hughes, John: Willard, 676
Hughes, Langston: democracy, 140
Hullfish, H. Gordon: philosophy of education, professional organizations in, 476
Hull-House: Addams, 6–9
human nature, **282–285;** Cicero, 76–77
Humanism, **285–288;** philosophy of education, history of, 466
humanitas: philosophy of education, history of, 466; Stoicism, 628
humanity: Confucianism, 108
humans, age of: Vico, 661
Humboldt, Alexander von: Arnold, 37
Humboldt, Wilhelm von: anthropology, 27–28
Hume, David: common sense, 100; emotivism, 182; empiricism, 184; human nature, 283; Jefferson, 324; justice, 336; learning, theories of, 347; metaphysics, 395–396; practical wisdom, 497; rationalism, 526; realism, 533; Rousseau, 567; science, philosophy of, 590; skepticism, 595
Hunt, H.A.K.: Cicero, 76
Huntington, S.: revolution, 547–549
Husserl, Edmund: existentialism, 207; Heidegger, 396; metaphysics, 254; phenomenology, 451
Hutcheson, Frances: intuitionism, 308–309; Jefferson, 324
Huxley, Julian: Humanism, 287
Huxley, Thomas: Darwin, 135–136; Spencer, 624
hybris: tragedy, 646
Hypatia, **288–289**

Iamblichus: neoplatonism, 430; Sophists, 622
id: Freud, 227; psychoanalysis, 509
ideal languages: Wittgenstein, 680
ideal utilitarians: utilitarianism, 651
idealism, **291–298;** Marx, 383; philosophy of education, history of, 470; physical education, 482; realism, 533–534
idealization: idealism, 293; psychoanalysis, 511
ideas: Herbart, 258–259
ideas, doctrine of: Plato, 484
identity politics: feminism, 217
identity, shaping of: social and political philosophy, 600
ideology: indoctrination, 304
idols: Bacon, 47–49
Ignatius of Loyola, **298–300**
ignorance: Buddhism, 59
I-It: Buber, 57–58
Iliad: Homer, 277–278; rhetoric, 550

"illumination": mysticism, 417
illumination, doctrine of: Bonaventure, 56
imagination: Descartes, 146; idealism, 291; reconstructionism, social, 540; romanticism, 562–563; Vico, 661
imaginative variation: phenomenology, 452
imitatio: Erasmus, 198
immortality: Confucianism, 109; Taoism, 635
immunities: rights, 558
imperialism: colonialism and post-colonialism, 89–90; Marti-Perez, 382
impetus: idealism, 294
indeterminacy: freedom and determinism, 224
individual good: human nature, 284
individualism, **300–303;** Durkheim, 170; liberalism, 357; Marx, 383–384; nationalism, 422; rights, 560
individuality: human nature, 284; Russell, 575
individuals: Duns Scotus, 169; philosophy of education, history of, 462
individuals, socialization of: Spencer, 623
indoctrination, **303–305;** aims of education, 12; liberal education, 353; reconstructionism, social, 540
Indra: Hinduism, 270
inductive method: Bacon, 47; Rosenkranz, 565
industrial arts: Rousseau, 569
industrial education: public education, 514
Industrial Revolution: work, 686
ineffability: mysticism, 417
informal logic: critical thinking, 121; logic, 368
in-itself: Sartre, 578
innate behavior: teaching and learning, 637
innatism: rationalism, 525
inner and outer: Kierkegaard, 343–344
inquiry, theory of: Dewey, 150–151
Institute of Social Research: critical theory, 115–116
instruction: Herbart, 258–259; Taoism, 634
instruction, computer-assisted: computers, 103
instruere: James, 321
instrumentalism: Cyrenaics, 133; technology, 639
integral calculus: Condorcet, 106
integrity: happiness, 249
intellectual rights: rights, 560
intellectual virtues: Aristotle, 31–32
intelligence, **305–308;** neoplatonism, 430; practical wisdom, 498–499
intelligence testing: Darwin, 136; Dewey, 149
intelligibility: pragmatism, 501
intelligible species: Duns Scotus, 168–169
intention: teaching and learning, 637
intentional definition: behaviorism, 53
intentionality: indoctrination, 303; Sartre, 578
"interbeing": mysticism, 417
interest: Herbart, 259
International Psychoanalytical Association: Freud, 227
international relations: nationalism, 422
Internet: higher education, 268

interpretation, theory of: Heidegger, 255
intrapsychic determinism: psychoanalysis, 509
introspection: values and evaluation, 657
intuitionism, **308–310;** common sense, 100
Iser, Wolfgang: philosophy and literature, 460
Isidore of Seville: Augustine, 42
Islam, **311–316;** freedom and determinism, 223; mysticism, 418
Isocrates, **316–320;** Erasmus, 198; liberal education, 354–355; Milton, 399; philosophy of education, history of, 463; Quintilian, 517; Socrates, 617
Israel: Judaism, 330–334
Itard, Jean-Marc-Gaspard: Montessori, 405
I-Thou: Buber, 57–58

Jacob: Judaism, 330
Jacob, F.H.: nihilism, 435
Jacobson, Edith: psychoanalysis, 510
Jaeger, Werner: Homer, 277
Jainism: atheism, 38; Hinduism, 272
James, Henry: Peabody, 442; philosophy and literature, 459; Socrates, 618
James, William, **321–323;** Beecher, 51; Dewey, 147; Du Bois, 166; Emerson, 182; epistemology, 190; experience, 211; freedom and determinism, 224–225; Hall, 245; Hegel, 253; human nature, 283; intelligence, 307; metaphysics, 396; Montessori, 408; physical education, 481; pragmatism, 499; realism, 535; truth, 649
Janissaries: slavery, 597
Jansenism: Arnauld, 35
Jaspers, Karl: Anselm, 25
Jefferson, Thomas, **323–325;** civic education, 80; democracy, 140; elitism, 179; intuitionism, 310; revolution, 549; right, 555
Jensen, Arthur: heredity and hereditarianism, 262
Jerome: Erasmus, 198; girls and women, 242
Jesus of Nazareth, **325–328;** Clement of Alexandria, 84; Cynics, 131; existentialism, 206–207; Judaism, 332–333; love, 371; mysticism, 418
Jnana yoga: Hinduism, 271
Job: Thomas Aquinas, 640
John: Jesus, 326
John Dewey Society: philosophy of education, professional organizations in, 475–476
John of Salisbury, **328–329;** philosophy of education, history of, 465; Thomas Aquinas, 640
Johnson, Joseph: Wollstonecraft, 683
Johnson-Laird, P.N.: logic, 368
Johnson, Marietta: progress, 507–508
Johnson, R.H.: critical thinking, 121
Johnson, Samuel: Franklin, 222; Macaulay, 375
Jonson, Ben: comedy, 93
Josephus: Jesus, 326
Journal of Aesthetic Education: philosophy of education, literature in, 474

Journal of Moral Education: philosophy of education, literature in, 474
Journal of Philosophy of Education: philosophy of education, literature in, 474
Journal of Speculative Philosophy: Harris, 250; Rosenkranz, 564
journeymen: vocational education, 663
Joyce, James: Homer, 279
Judah: Judaism, 330
Judaism, **330–335;** freedom and determinism, 223; mysticism, 418
judgment: critical thinking, 120; Helvetius, 257; Montaigne, 404; norm, 437; practical wisdom, 497
Jung, Carl G.: Freud, 229; psychoanalysis, 511
jungle metaphor: educational policy and administration, 173, 175
junior colleges: higher education, 267
Junto: Franklin, 222
jurisprudence: Alfarabi, 13–14; Averroes, 43; Avicenna, 45; Quintilian, 519
justice, **335–337;** analytic philosophy, 20; *arete,* 30; children's rights, 74–75; equality, 193–194; formalism, 220; freedom and determinism, 226; Hostos, 281; Kant, 342; liberalism, 358–359; Montaigne, 404; practical wisdom, 497; right, 556; socialism, 605
Justius Lipsius: Stoicism, 627

Kabbalah: mysticism, 418; neoplatonism, 430
Kalam: Islam, 311
Kallen, Horace M.: indoctrination, 304; pluralism, 491
kalos: paideia, 440
Kames, Lord: Jefferson, 324
Kaminsky, James S.: philosophy of education, professional organizations in, 478
Kant, Immanuel, **339–343;** anthropology, 28; conscience, 111; Emerson, 182; ethics and morality, 200; evolution, 203; formalism, 220–221; girls and women, 241; Herbart, 258; human nature, 284; idealism, 295; individualism, 300; intelligence, 305; justice, 337; learning, theories of, 347–348; logic, 367–368; metaphysics, 295–296; Nietzsche, 434; person, 444; philosophy and literature, 457; philosophy of education, history of, 470; practical wisdom, 497; rationalism, 525–526; reason and rationality, 536; relativism, 543; right, 556; rights, 560; Rosenkranz, 565; Rousseau, 567; skepticism, 595; William of Ockham, 678
Kantianism: Marxism, 389; right, 556
karma: Buddhism, 59; freedom and determinism, 223; Hinduism, 271
karma yoga: Hinduism, 270, 271–272
Kasprisin, Lorraine: philosophy and literature, 460
Kautsky, Karl: Marxism, 388

Kavka, Gregory: right, 556
Keats, John: romanticism, 561–562
Keller, Evelyn Fox: science, philosophy of, 592
Kelly, Florence: Addams, 9
Kelly, Joan: feminism, 215
Kelsen, Hans: emotivism, 183
Kernberg, Otto: psychoanalysis, 510
Khan, Abdul Ghaffar: Gandhi, 233
Kierkegaard, Soren, **343–344;** existentialism, 206–207; Hegel, 252; Heidegger, 255; human nature, 284
Kilpatrick, William Heard: Montessori, 406; Pestalozzi, 448; philosophy of education, professional organizations in, 476; Rosenkranz, 564; socialism, 607
kindergarten: Froebel, 230–231; Harris, 250
kinesis: Cyrenaics, 132
King James Bible: Mann, 380
King, Martin Luther, Jr., **344–345;** civil disobedience, 83; Gandhi, 233
King Solomon: Bacon, 49
Kismet: freedom and determinism, 223
Klein, Melanie: Freud, 229; psychoanalysis, 510
Kneller, George: existentialism, 209
Knies, Karl: historicism, 272
knowing and doing: pragmatism, 499–500
knowledge: aims of education, 12–13; Augustine, 40; curriculum and instruction, 123–124; Descartes, 144–145; epistemology, 188–191; Locke, 363–365; meaning, 392; philosophy of education, history of, 461, 462–463; Plato, 483–486; pragmatism, 500; Socrates, 619; Vico, 661–662
knowledge and conduct: Dewey, 152
Knox, Samuel: school, 588
Kohlberg, Lawrence: Freud, 229; justice, 337; learning, theories of, 348; moral development, 408–412
Kohn, Hans: nationalism, 423
Kohut, Heinz: psychoanalysis, 511
Keller, Alice: domestic education, 164
Komisar, B. Paul: analytic philosophy, 21
Korsch, Karl: Marxism, 390
kosmopolitai: Cynics, 131
Krause, Karl: Comenius, 97; Marti-Perez, 381
Kraut, Richard: happiness, 248
Kripke, Saul: truth, 647; Wittgenstein, 680
Kris, Ernst: comedy, 92; Freud, 229; psychoanalysis, 510
Kristeller, Paul: liberal education, 352
Kriya yoga: Hinduism, 272
Krusi, Herman, Jr.: Pestalozzi, 448
Ku Klux Klan: democracy, 142
Kuhn, Thomas: cognitive development, 88–89; curriculum and instruction, 124; epistemology, 191; science, philosophy of, 591
Kulturwissenschaften: historicism, 273
kunikos: Cynics, 131

labor theory of value: Marx, 383–385

Lull, Ramon: computers, 103
Luria, Isaac: Judaism, 333
Luther, Martin, **372–374;** Calvin, 63; elitism, 178; scholasticism, 584; school, 586
Luxemburg, Rosa: Marxism, 389
Lyceum, Aristotle's: Aristotle, 31
Lyceums: vocational education, 663
Lynn, John: heredity and hereditarianism, 262
Lyon, Mary: girls and women, 243
Lyotard, Jean-Francois: modernism and post-modernism, 402–403
Macaulay, Catherine, **375–378;** Wollstonecraft, 683
Macaulay, George: Macaulay, 375
Macchiavelli, Niccolo: comedy, 92
Mach, Ernst: science, philosophy of, 590
MacIntyre, Alasdaire: community, 102; ethics and morality, 201–202; Kierkegaard, 344
Mackie, J.L.: truth, 648
Mackie, Margaret: philosophy of education, professional organizations in, 478
Maclure, William: Pestalozzi, 447
Macmillan, C.J.B.: analytic philosophy, 22; teaching and learning, 637
Mahabarata: Hinduism, 271
Mahler, Margaret: psychoanalysis, 510
Maimonides, Moses: Judaism, 333; Thomas Aquinas, 643
majority: minorities, 400
Makarenko, Anton, **378–379**
Malebranche, Nicholas: Arnauld, 35
Mamluks: slavery, 597
Mandela, Nelson: Gandhi, 233
Manetti, Gianozzo: humanism, 286
Manichean religion: Augustine, 39
Manicheanism: Sartre, 580
Mann, Horace, **379–381;** Beecher, 50–51; civic education, 80; democracy, 140; Harris, 250; Peabody, 442; Pestalozzi, 447; philosophy of education, history of, 469; work, 687–688
Mann, Mary Tyler: Peabody, 440–441
Mannheim, Karl: historicism, 272
manumission: slavery, 597
Mao Tse-tung: revolution, 548–549
March, James G.: educational policy and administration, 175
Marcus Aurelius: Stoicism, 627
Marcuse, Herbert: critical theory, 115, 117; Freud, 229; Marxism, 390–391
Marechal, Joseph: scholasticism, 585
Marenholz-Bulow, Bertha Mara von: girls and women, 242
marginalization: minorities, 401
Maritain, Jacques: humanism, 287; scholasticism, 585
Mark: Jesus, 326
Marti-Perez, Jose, **381–382;** Hostos, 281
Martianus Capella: John of Salisbury, 329; rhetoric, 551
Martin, Jane Roland: analytic philosophy, 22; civic

education, 82; domestic education, 164; feminism, 219; girls and women, 244; philosophy and literature, 460
Martineau, Harriet: girls and women, 244
Marx, Karl, **382–387;** alienation, 17; capitalism, 69; dialectic, 154–155; existentialism, 206; Hegel, 252; historicism, 274; humanism, 286; Marxism, 387; nationalism, 422; revolution, 548; Rosenkranz, 565; social sciences, philosophy of, 603; socialism, 606; sociology, 610–611
Marxism, **387–391;** critical theory, 116; existentialism, 206; higher education, 265; Hook, 279–280; liberalism, 359–360; nationalism, 422, 423; philosophy of education, history of, 472
Maslow, Abraham: human nature, 284
masters guild: vocational education, 663
materialism: Diderot, 157; Harris, 250; idealism, 297
materialism, historical: Marx, 383–384
mathematics: Avicenna, 45; Bacon, 48; Locke, 364–365; Plato, 484, 485–486
matter: formalism, 220
Matthew: Jesus, 326
Mauthner, F.: Wittgenstein, 678
maxims: formalism, 220–221
May, Mark A.: Willard, 676
Mayahana: Buddhism, 60–61
Mays, Benjamin E.: King, 344
McCarthyism: Du Bois, 167
McClellan, James E.: analytic philosophy, 21; educational policy and administration, 173, 175; teaching and learning, 637
McCloy, Charles: physical education, 481
McCosh, James: liberal education, 352
McGregor, Douglas M.: educational policy and administration, 174–175
McGuffey, William Holmes: democracy, 141; work, 688
McGuffey Readers: philosophy and literature, 458
McMurry, Charles: Herbart, 259–260
McMurry, Frank: Herbart, 259–260
McPeck, John: critical thinking, 120
McQueen, Humphrey: philosophy of education, professional organizations in, 478
McTaggert, J.M.E.: Hegel, 253
Mead, George Herbert: intelligence, 307; pragmatism, 499, 501–502; sociology, 613
Mead, Margaret: anthropology, 28
meaning, **391–393;** analytic philosophy, 18; pragmatism, 500; Wittgenstein, 681–682
mechanical arts: Diderot, 157
mechanics: Descartes, 146
Mechanics Institute: vocational education, 663
medicine: Averroes, 43; Avicenna, 45; Descartes, 146; higher education, 263
Meinecke, Friedrich: historicism, 273–274
Melanchthon, Philip: Luther, 373
memorization: Quintilian, 520

memory: Descartes, 146–147; Vico, 661

Menander: comedy, 92

Mencius: human nature, 284

Mendel, Gregor: heredity and hereditarianism, 260

Mendelson, Moses: Judaism, 334

Menger, Carl: historicism, 272

Meng-tsu: human nature, 284

Menippus: Cynics, 131

Meno: Socrates, 617

meritocracy: justice, 337

Merleau-Ponty, Maurice: phenomenology, 451

Merritt, Ella Arvilla: school, 588–589

Merton, Robert K.: science, philosophy of, 592

Messiah: Judaism, 332

metaethics: ethics and morality, 200

metanarratives: modernism and post-modernism, 402

metaphors: rights, 559–560

metaphysical idealism: idealism, 294–295

metaphysics, **393–397;** Avicenna, 45; Descartes, 146; experience, 210; neoplatonism, 431–432; philosophy of education, history of, 468–469; relativism, 543

metaphysics, pansophical: Comenius, 96

metaphysics, poetic: philosophy of education, history of, 468–469; romanticism, 563

metaphysics, transcendental: Kant, 340–341

metaphysics of experience: Kant, 340

meteorology: Descartes, 145

method: curriculum and instruction, 124; Herbart, 259

method of investigation, Aristotle's: Aristotle, 31–32

method of reason: Descartes, 145

Michels, Robert: elitism, 179

Mickunas, Algis: Buber, 58

Middle Way: Buddhism, 59

midrashim: Judaism, 332

Migration, Great Puritan: school, 586

Miles, Robert: race and racism, 523

militarism: Marti-Perez, 382

military-industrial complex: higher learning, 265

Mill, James: Mill, 397

Mill, John Stuart, **397–399;** censorship, 72; children's rights, 74; Cicero, 78; Davies, 138; equality, 193; girls and women, 241; happiness, 247; individualism, 301; justice, 336; liberalism, 357–358; logic, 370; nationalism, 422; right, 556; science, philosophy of, 590; Spencer, 623; toleration, 644; utilitarianism, 651

Miller, Arthur: tragedy, 647

Miller, Mark: minorities, 401

Mills, C. Wright: elitism, 179

Milon of Rhodes: Cicero, 76

Milton, John, **399–400;** toleration, 644

mind: Dewey, 149–150; pragmatism, 500–501; Rosenkranz, 565

mineralogy: Froebel, 230; Milton, 399

minorities, **400–402;** multiculturalism, 416

Mirandola, Pico della: humanism, 286

mirror of meaning: meaning, 393

mirror of nature: meaning, 393

Mishna: Judaism, 332

mishnayot: Judaism, 332

misogyny: feminism, 217

mitzvot: Judaism, 331

modal logic: logic, 369

mode of production: Marx, 383

Modern Language Association: rhetoric, 553

modernism: Judaism, 333–334

modernism and post-modernism, **402–404;** dialectic, 153; reason and rationality, 538

modernity: existentialism, 209; sociology, 611–612

modus tollens: science, philosophy of, 591

Mohr, Richard D.: censorship, 73

moksha: Hinduism, 271

Moliere: comedy, 92

monasteries: discipline, 159

monism: human nature, 282–283

Monroe, Paul: philosophy of education, history of, 471

Montaigne, Michel de, **404–405;** elitism, 178; Emerson, 182; skepticism, 595

Montesquieu, Alexis de: democracy; 140; Diderot, 155

Montessori, Maria, **405–408;** domestic education, 162; home and family 277; Humanism, 287; Russell, 574–575

Moore, G.E.: analytic philosophy, 19; common sense, 99; idealism, 296; intuitionism, 308–309; realism, 535; social sciences, philosophy of, 604; truth, 648

Moore, T.W.: philosophy of education, professional organizations in, 477

moral conduct: Buddhism, 59–60

moral development, **408–415**

moral education: Durkheim, 171

moral goodness: intuitionism, 309–310

moral improvement: Mill, 397–398

moral judgments: Kant, 341

moral knowledge: intuitionism, 309

moral obligation: Hostos, 281

moral order: sociology, 611–612

moral relations: Roussesau, 570–572

moral responsibilities: person, 443

moral right: right, 554–557

moral rights: person, 443

moral sciences: Condorcet, 106–107

moral sense: common sense, 99–100; Jefferson, 324

moral teleology: Kant, 341

morality, Christian: Nietzsche, 433

morals: Descartes, 144

More, Cresacre: girls and women, 241

More, Thomas: Confucianism, 109; Cynics, 131

Morehouse College: King, 344

Morehouse, Henry L.: Du Bois, 167

Morgan, Thomas Hunt: heredity and hereditarianism, 260

Morrill Act: higher education, 264; Washington, Booker T., 670

Morris, Van Cleve: existentialism, 209
Morrison, Toni: philosophy and literature, 459
Mosca, Gaetano: elitism, 178
Moses: Bacon, 47
mothering: Beecher, 51
Muir, John: conservatism, 114
Mulcaster, Richard: girls and women, 241
multiculturalism, **415–417;** liberalism, 360; pluralism, 491; pragmatism, 504–505
Mumford, Lewis: reconstructionism, social, 540
Murdock, George Peter: anthropology, 28–29
Murphy, Daniel: Buber, 57
Murray, Judith Sargent: Willard, 675
music: *paideia*, 440; Philo of Alexandria, 456; philosophy of education, history of, 465; Plato, 485; Quintilian, 518
Musonius Rufus: Stoicism, 626
Mussolini, Benito: Montessori, 405
Mu'tazilites: Islam, 312
mysticism, **417–419;** Froebel, 230, 231; Judaism, 333; neoplatonism, 430

Nag Hammadi: Jesus, 326
Nai Talim: Gandhi, 233–235
naive realism: realism, 529
Natanson, Maurice: philosophy and literature, 458–459
National Association for the Advancement of Colored People: Du Bois, 167; Washington, Booker, T., 669
National Association of Manufacturers: vocational education, 664
national chauvinism: multiculturalism, 415
National Education Association: curriculum and instruction, 125
National Geographic: colonialism and post-colonialism, 91
National Herbart Society for the Scientific Study of Education; Herbart, 259
National Organization for Women: feminism, 216
National Society for the Scientific Study of Education: Herbart, 260
National Society for the Study of Education: Herbart, 260; philosophy of education, literature in, 473
nationalism, **421–425;** colonialism and post-colonialism, 91; Marti-Perez, 381; race and racism, 523
nation-state: nationalism, 421–424
Native Americans: mysticism, 418
natural arts: Rousseau, 569
natural development: Rousseau, 568–570; Taoism, 634
natural education: Diderot, 156–157
natural endowment: equality, 193
natural goodness: intuitionism, 309
natural history: Milton, 399
natural law: Jefferson, 324; right, 556; rights, 560; Stoicism, 628
natural passions: Rousseau, 570

natural rights: Jefferson, 324; right, 556
natural science: Averroes, 43; Avicenna, 45; historicism, 273
natural selection: evolution, 203
naturalism, **425–430;** Dewey, 148; philosophy of education, history of, 470; science, philosophy of, 591
nature: Condillac, 105; Darwin, 135; Descartes, 144; Emerson, 182; ethics and morality, 200; Froebel, 230; John of Salisbury, 329; Rosenkranz, 565; Rousseau, 568
Naturwissenschaften: social sciences, philosophy of, 603
Naumburg, Margaret: Freud, 229; romanticism, 563–564
navigation: Milton, 399
navoty: mysticism, 418
Nazi party: heredity and hereditarianism, 261
Nazism: critical theory, 116; Heidegger, 256; moral development, 412–413
necessitarianism: rationalism, 525
Neef, Joseph: Pestalozzi, 447
negative education: Diderot, 156
Neill, A.S.: Freud, 229; romanticism, 564; Rousseau, 573
nemesis: tragedy, 646
neocolonialism: colonialism and post-colonialism, 90
neofunctionalism: naturalism, 426
neoplatonism, **430–433;** Comenius, 94; Hypatia, 288; leisure, 350
Nero; Cynics, 131
Neuberg, K.: philosophy of education, professional organizations in, 477
Neuhof: Pestalozzi, 446
Neurath, Otto: positivism, 493; science, philosophy of, 590
neutral universal: indoctrination, 303
"New Comedy": comedy, 92
New Criticism: philosophy and literature, 458
New Testament: John of Salisbury, 329
New Testament, Greek; Calvin, 64
Newcastle Commission: Arnold, 37
Newman, John Henry: Cicero, 78; higher education, 263–264
Newmann, Frederick: civic education, 81, 82
Newsome, George L., Jr.: analytic philosophy, 21; censorship, 73
Newton, Isaac: Jefferson, 323
Ngugi, wa Thiong'o: colonialism and post-colonialism, 90, 91
Niagara Movement: Du Bois, 167
Nicholas of Cusa: scholasticism, 584
Nicias: Socrates, 617
Nicole, Pierre: logic, 367
Nicolini, Fausto: Vico, 661
Niebuhr, Barthold G.: historicism, 273
Nietzsche, Friedrich, **433–435;** conscience, 111; Cynics, 131; Emerson, 182; epistemology, 191; existentialism, 207, 208; hap-

piness, 247; Hegel, 252; Heidegger, 255; higher education, 265; historicism, 272; individualism, 301; intelligence, 306; metaphysics, 396; nihilism, 436; Rosenkranz, 565; socialism, 606; Sophists, 622

nihilism, **435–436**; relativism, 542

nihilism, moral: atheism, 38

Nirvana: Buddhism, 59

Nkrumah, Kwane: Du Bois, 167

noble truths: Buddhism, 59

Noddings, Nel: domestic education, 164; ethics and morality, 202–203; feminism, 219; justice, 337; philosophy and literature, 460

noema: Heidegger, 255; phenomenology, 452

noesis: phenomenology, 452

nominalism: realism, 532

nomos: Sophists, 622

nonbeliever: atheism, 37–38

non-Euclidean geometries: cognitive development, 89

norm, **436–438**

normative senses: liberal education, 352

Norris, Stephen: analytic philosophy, 23

notitia abstractiva: William of Ockham, 677

notitia intuitiva: William of Ockham, 677

noumena: Kant, 340; rationalism, 526

nous: neoplatonism, 431

Novalis: historicism, 272

novelty: Whitehead, 673

Nozick, Robert: happiness, 248; right, 555; rights, 560

nuclear power: higher education, 264–265

numerology: Philo of Alexandria, 456

nurture: Darwin, 136

Nussbaum, Martha: philosophy and literature, 460

Nyerere, Julius: Gandhi, 233

obedience: norm, 437

object lessons: Pestalozzi, 447

object teaching: Froebel, 231

objectification: alienation, 17

objective happiness: happiness, 248

objectivity: Kierkegaard, 343; religious education, 545–546

obligation; ethics and morality, 200; right, 554; rights, 558–559; utilitarianism, 652

obscenity: censorship, 72

occupations: Froebel, 230; vocational education, 665

Ockham's razor: William of Ockham, 677

O'Connor, D.J.: analytic philosophy, 21

Octavian: Cicero, 76

Odysseus: Homer, 278

Odyssey: Homer, 277–278; rhetoric, 550

Oedipus: Freud, 228

Oenomaus: Cynics, 132

Offe, Claus: critical theory, 117

Ogden, C.K., emotivism, 182

"Old Comedy": comedy, 92

Old Testament: John of Salisbury, 329

Olson, David R.: cognitive development, 86

Omnes omnia omnino: Comenius, 96

One, the: neoplatonism, 430–431

Oneness: mysticism, 418

Onesicratus: Cynics, 131

ontogenesis: Hall, 245

ontogeny: Darwin, 136; Hall, 245

ontological naturalism: naturalism, 425

ontophobia: idealism, 295

open admissions policy: higher education, 267

open university: higher education, 268

operant behaviorists: learning, theories of, 347–349

operant conditioning: learning, theories of, 347

operationalism: cognitive development, 88

opinion: John of Salisbury, 329; Plato, 488

opinion, freedom of: Russell, 575

optics: Descartes, 145

oral societies: literacy, 361

oratory: Milton, 399

order: Durkheim, 171

ordinary language analysis: learning, theories of, 349

ordinary, the: Emerson, 182

ordo doctrinae: scholasticism, 581

ordo inventionis: scholasticism, 581

Orestes, prefect of Alexandria: Hypatia, 288

organicist metaphysics: metaphysics, 397

Origen: Clement of Alexandria, 84; Philo of Alexandria, 456

original sin: Calvin, 65

Ornstein, Paul: psychoanalysis, 511

orthography: Webster, 671

Ortiz, Fernando: multiculturalism, 416

otherworldliness: capitalism, 70

Ott, Hugo: existentialism, 208

ousia: metaphysics, 394–395

Ovid: *studia humanitatis*, 631

Owen, Robert: Alcott, 14; Pestalozzi, 448

Oxford English Dictionary: common sense, 99; curriculum and instruction, 124

paidagogia: Clement of Alexandria, 84

paideia, **439–440**; Augustine, 41; Clement of Alexandria, 84; Epicureanism, 188; Homer, 279; humanism, 285; Isocrates, 318; James, 321; philosophy of education, history of, 464; rhetoric, 550

paideusis: *paideia*, 439

Paine, Thomas: right, 555; Wollstonecraft, 683

Paley, William: Willard, 674

Pali canon: Buddhism, 60

Pallades: Hypatia, 289

Palmer, Elizabeth: Peabody, 441

Panaetius: Stoicism, 626

Pan-African Congress: Du Bois, 167

Panhellenism: Isocrates, 316

pansophy: Comenius, 94

Proceedings: philosophy of education, literature in, 474; philosophy of education, professional organizations in, 475

Philosophy of Education Society of Great Britain: philosophy of education, professional organizations in, 475

Phoenix Farm: Gandhi, 233

phrenology: Harris, 250; Mann, 379

phronesis: ethics and morality, 201; practical wisdom, 496

phylogenesis: Hall, 245

phylogeny: Darwin, 136; Hall, 245

physical anthropology: anthropology, 27

physical education, **481–483;** Spencer, 624–625

Physical Education Index: philosophy of education, literature in, 473

physical relations: Rousseau, 569–570

physical sciences: Condorcet, 106

physicalists: naturalism, 426

physics: Descartes, 144; metaphysics, 394; Stoicism, 627

physiology: Milton, 399

physis: ethics and morality, 201; Sophists, 621

Piaget, Jean: cognitive development, 86–87; evolution, 204; learning, theories of, 347–348; logic, 367; Rousseau, 573

piety: *arete,* 30

Pindar: philosophy of education, history of, 461

Pine, Fred: psychoanalysis, 510

Plato, **483–489;** aesthetics, 10; aims of education, 12; Alfarabi, 15; *arete,* 30; Aristotle, 32–33; Averroes, 43; Avicenna, 45–46; Bacon, 47; capitalism, 70; censorship, 72; civic education, 79; Confucianism, 109; conscience, 111; Cynics, 131; Descartes, 144; dialectic, 153–154; discipline, 158; elitism, 178; Emerson, 182; empiricism, 184; Epicureanism, 186; equality, 192; existentialism, 206; formalism, 220; happiness, 248, 249; home and family, 275; Homer, 277; human nature, 282; idealism, 295–296; intelligence, 305; Islam, 313; Jefferson, 323; John of Salisbury, 329; Judaism, 333; justice, 335; leisure, 350; liberal education, 354; logic, 367; love, 371; meaning, 391; metaphysics, 394; Milton, 399; neoplatonism, 430; pai*deia,* 439; philosophy and literature, 457; philosophy of education, history of, 461–463; physical education, 481; practical wisdom, 497; rationalism, 525; realism, 530–532; reason and rationality, 536; rhetoric, 550; right, 557; rights, 558; Rousseau, 567–568; skepticism, 594; social and political philosophy, 598; Socrates, 617; Sophists, 620; *studia humanitatis,* 631; vocational education, 663; work, 687

Platonism: Alcott, 14; Augustine, 39; scholasticism, 581

Plautus: comedy, 92

play: aesthetics, 10; physical education, 481

pleasure, **489–491;** happiness, 248

Plekhanov, Georg: Marxism, 388

Plessy-Ferguson decision: Washington, Booker T., 669

Plotinus: Augustine, 39; neoplatonism, 430–433

pluralism: **491–492;** Hook, 280; liberalism, 356; relativism, 543; technology, 639

pluralism, epistemic: naturalism, 426

Plutarch: Epicureanism, 187; *studia humanitatis,* 630

poetry: Averroes, 43; Bacon, 48; James, 322; Milton, 399; Plato, 487–488

Polanyi, Michael: meaning, 391–392

political correctness: modernism and post-modernism, 403

political science: Alfarabi, 15–16

politics: Avicenna, 45–46

Politike: Aristotle, 33

Popkowitz, Thomas: critical theory, 118

Popper, Karl: analytic philosophy, 19; epistemology, 189–190; evolution, 204; historicism, 274; science, philosophy of, 591–592

pornography: feminism, 218

Porphyry: Avicenna, 45; neoplatonism, 430

Posidonius: Cicero, 76; Stoicism, 626

positivism, **492–495;** critical theory, 116; existentialism, 209; experience, 210; Marxism, 388; metaphysics, 396; sociology, 615

possibility, **495–496;** romanticism, 564; social and political philosophy, 602; Whitehead, 672

post-capitalism: Marx, 386

postillae: Thomas Aquinas, 640

poststructuralists: indoctrination, 304

potential, human: human nature, 283–284

poverty: Buddhism, 60

power: conscience, 110; Rousseau, 568–569

practical arts: higher education, 263

practical philosophy: idealism, 293–294

practical reason: justice, 335

practical sciences: Aristotle, 31–32, 32–34; Thomas Aquinas, 642

practical wisdom, **496–499;** Aristotle, 32–34; Condorcet, 105–107

practice: experience, 210

pragmatic, the: critical thinking, 120

pragmatism, **499–506;** Dewey, 150; existentialism, 206; experience, 213; naturalism, 427–428; philosophy and literature, 458; philosophy of education, history of, 471; physical education, 482; reconstructionism, social, 539; Russell, 574; Spencer, 625; truth, 649

Prajna: Buddhism, 60

Prantl, Carl: historicism, 272

Pratt, Caroline: progress, 508; romanticism, 563

Pratte, Richard: civic education, 81

Precians, R.: philosophy of education, professional organizations in, 478
precision: Whitehead, 672
predestination: Calvin, 65
predicate logic: logic, 369
prehension: reconstructionism, social, 539; Whitehead, 672
prejudice: Locke, 364; race and racism, 522
presentations: Herbart, 258
presocratics: Sophists, 620
Price, Kingsley: analytic philosophy, 21
Price, Richard: intuitionism, 308; Wollstonecraft, 683
Prichard, H.A.: intuitionism, 308–309
Priestley, Joseph: Wollstonecraft, 683
primary process: psychoanalysis, 509
Prime Mover: love, 371
primitivism: Diderot, 156–157
Prince of Parma: Condillac, 104
principled morality: moral development, 409–410
Pring, Richard: philosophy of education, professional organizations in, 477
prison reform: Mann, 379
prisons: discipline, 159
private education: public education, 513; Wollstonecraft, 685
private property: liberalism, 356
probabilistic utilitarianism: utilitarianism, 652
probability: Cicero, 76
probability, mathematical: Condorcet, 106
probable logic: John of Salisbury, 329
Proceedings and Addresses of the American Philosophical Association: philosophy of education, literature in, 474
Proceedings of the Far Western Philosophy of Education Society: philosophy of education, literature in, 474
Proceedings of the South Atlantic Philosophy of Education Society: philosophy of education, literature in, 474
Proclus: neoplatonism, 430–431
Prodikos: Isocrates, 316; Sophists, 621
productive sciences: Aristotle, 31–32
Progress, **506–508**; conservatism, 113; Dewey, 52; Franklin, 222; Harris, 251; modernism and post-modernism, 402; philosophy of education, history of, 470; physical education, 481–482; public education, 514–515; Russell, 574; sociology, 601
Progressive Education Association: philosophy of education, professional organizations in, 476
progressive era: Addams, 6
progressive, child-centered: public education, 515
progressive, social reconstructionist: public education, 515
progressivism: reconstructionism, social, 539, 540
progymnasmata: rhetoric, 550
proletariat: Marx, 384–385
propaganda: reconstructionism, social, 540

prophecy: Avicenna, 45
propositional logic: logic, 368–369
Prosser, Charles: vocational education, 664
Protagoras: *arete,* 30; humanism, 285; logic, 367; *paideia,* 439; practical wisdom; 497; Socrates, 617; Sophists, 620–621
Protestant ideology: public education, 514
Protestant Revolt: school, 586
Protestantism: Mann, 380–381; mysticism, 418
prudence: practical wisdom, 497; Vico, 661
prudentia: practical wisdom, 496
psychoanalysis, **508–512**
Psychological Abstracts: philosophy of education, literature in, 473
psychologism: logic, 368
psychology, philosophy of: behaviorism, 52
psychology of drive: psychoanalysis, 510
psychology of science: science, philosophy of, 592
psychology of object relations: psychoanalysis, 510
psychology of self-experience: psychoanalysis, 510–511
psychology of the ego: psychoanalysis, 510
psychosexual development: psychoanalysis, 510
Ptolemy: Alfarabi, 15; Avicenna, 45
public education, **512–516**; religious education, 546; Wollstonecraft, 685
public reason: Condorcet, 106
Pucetti, Roland: person, 444
punishment: freedom and determinism, 223
pure land Buddhism: Buddhism, 61
Puritanism: leisure, 351; Willard, 674–675
purpose: cybernetics, 130
purpose of life: human nature, 284–285
Putnam, Hilary: epistemology, 190
Pyrrho of Elis: skepticism, 594
Pyrrhonism: skepticism, 594–595
Pythagoras: Milton, 399

qiyas: Islam, 312
quadrivium: John of Salisbury, 328; scholasticism, 581; Thomas Aquinas, 640; vocational education, 663
quaestio: Thomas Aquinas, 640
Quakers: mysticism, 418
qualitative experience: pragmatism, 501; values and evaluation, 655, 660
quantum mechanics: freedom and determinism, 224
quantum physics: cognitive development, 86; Whitehead, 673
questionnaire studies: Hall, 246
Quine, W.V.O.: analytic philosophy, 19; meaning, 393; naturalism, 428
Quintilian, **516–520**; girls and women, 242; Isocrates, 319; John of Salisbury, 329; leisure, 350; Philo of Alexandria, 456; philosophy of education, history of, 464; rhetoric, 551; Vico, 661
Qur'an: Islam, 311–315; Jesus, 326

Rabanus Maurus: Augustine, 42

race and racism: **521–524;** colonialism and post-colonialism, 91; equality, 192; feminism, 217; heredity and hereditarianism, 262; higher education, 265–266; Marx, 386; minorities, 401; modernism and postmodernism, 403; pluralism, 491; Washington, Booker T., 669

race relations: race and racism, 522

race thinking: race and racism, 523

racial discrimination: King, 345

racial harmony: aims of education, 13

radical empiricism: metaphysics, 396

Rahner, Karl: scholasticism, 585

Ramsay, F.P.: truth, 648

Rand, Ayn: individualism, 302

Randall, John Herman, Jr.: existentialism, 207

Rank, Otto: Freud, 229; psychoanalysis, 511

Ranke, Leopold von: historicism, 273

rape: feminism, 218

Ratio studiorum: Ignatius, 299

rational choice theory: race and racism, 522

rationalism, **524–529;** epistemology, 188–189; intuitionism, 309–310; Judaism, 333; Kant, 340; philosophy of education, history of, 467; Russell, 573

Rationalism, Continental: reason and rationality, 536

rationality: critical thinking, 120; person, 444

Raubinger, Frederick N.: educational policy and administration, 173, 176

Raumer, Karl von: Froebel, 231

Raup, R. Bruce: philosophy of education, professional organizations in, 476

Rawley, William: Bacon, 48

Rawls, John: analytic philosophy, 20; children's rights, 74; equality, 194; idealism, 293; justice, 336–337; liberalism, 358–359; right, 555, 556; social and political philosophy, 601; utilitarianism, 653

Rawson, Elizabeth: Cicero, 75

Raywid, Mary Anne: censorship, 73

Read, Herbert: aesthetics, 11

realism, **529–536;** Herbart, 258; idealism, 296–297; physical education, 482; Wittgenstein, 679

realism, representational: realism, 533

reality: metaphysics, 394

reason: Abelard, 3; Anselm, 25–26; Averroes, 44; empiricism, 184; experience, 210; meaning, 391; Plato, 484; Wollstonecraft, 683

reason and rationality, **536–539;** critical thinking, 120

reasoning: indoctrination, 303

rebellions: revolution, 547

recapitulation theory: Hall, 245

reconstruction: democracy, 141; Washington, Booker T., 669

reconstructionism, social: **539–541;** indoctrination, 304–305

redemption, human: Calvin, 64–65

reduction: Bonaventure, 56

Reeve, Clara: girls and women, 242

reflection: Condillac, 104: Herbart, 259

reflective equilibrium: justice, 336

reflective thinking: cybernetics, 127

reflexive sociology: sociology, 615

reflexology: cognitive development, 86

Reformation, Protestant: Calvin, 63–64

reformation, social: Calvin, 65

Reich, Wilhelm: Freud, 229

Reichenbach, Hans: analytic philosophy, 19; philosophy and literature, 458; science, philosophy of, 590

Reid, L.A.: philosophy of education, professional organizations in, 477

Reid, Thomas: common sense, 99; Jefferson, 324

Rein, Wilhelm: Herbart, 259

reinforcement: cybernetics, 129–130

relations of production: Marx, 383

relativism, **541–543;** minorities, 401; truth, 649

relativity, theory of: relativism, 541

religion: Mann, 379–381; minorities, 400–401

religious education, **543–547;** Durkheim, 171

Renaissance humanists: Luther, 374

Renaissances: philosophy of education, history of, 465–466

Renouvier, Charles Bernard: freedom and determinism, 224

repression: Freud, 228; psychoanalysis, 509

research: higher education, 264–265

Resources in Education: philosophy of education, literature in, 473

retribution: Kant, 342

revelation: Abelard, 3; Averroes, 44; empiricism, 184

revelation, general: Calvinism, 66

revelation, special: Calvinism, 66

revolution, **547–549;** Marx, 386

revolution, social: socialism, 606

rhapsodes: rhetoric, 550

rhetor: Augustine, 39; Cicero, 75

rhetores: Quintilian, 519

rhetoric, **549–554;** Calvin, 64; Cicero, 76, 77–78; Condorcet, 106; John of Salisbury, 328–329; liberal education, 354–355; Milton, 399; Philo of Alexandria, 456; philosophy of education, history of, 463–464, 466; Plato, 488; Quintilian, 519–520; Socrates, 618; Sophists, 622; Stoicism, 627; Vico, 661

rhetoric, Isocrates' school of: Isocrates, 316

Rich, Adrienne: girls and women, 244

Richards, I.A.: analytic philosophy, 21; emotivism, 182

right, theories of the, **554–557**

right behavior: Buddhism, 59

right concentration: Buddhism, 59

right knowledge: Buddhism, 59

right mindfulness: Buddhism, 59

right reason: practical wisdom, 497–498

School of St. Victor's: Peter Lombard, 449

schoolhome: domestic education, 164; home and family, 277

schooling: aims of education, 12

Schopenhauer, Arthur: girls and women, 241–242; Nietzsche, 434; Wittgenstein, 678

Schumpeter, Joseph A.: elitism, 179

Schurmann, Anna van: girls and women, 241

Schwab, Joseph: practical reason, 499

science, education in: Spencer, 624

science, philosophy of, **590–593**; scientism, 593

scientific analysis: values and evaluation, 656–657

scientific inquiry: historicism, 273

scientific method: intelligence, 306; liberalism, 358; nationalism, 422; pragmatism, 499–500; Spencer, 625

scientific realism: realism, 529–530

scientism, **593–594**; philosophy of education, history of, 471

Scopes Trial of 1925: Darwin, 135

Scott, Fred Newton: educational policy and administration, 174

Scribner, Sylvia: literacy, 361

script societies: literacy, 361

Scriven, Michael: analytic philosophy, 22; positivism, 493

Scudder, John R., Jr.: Buber, 57

Second International: Marxism, 388

secondary education: higher education, 266

secondary process: psychoanalysis, 509

secular educators: religious education, 545

secularization: empiricism, 185

Segal, Erich: comedy, 92

segregation: King, 345

Seguin, Edouard: Montessori, 405

Selbst-Entfremdung: Rosenkranz, 565

self: pragmatism, 500–501; Sartre, 578

self-activity: intelligence, 307

self-alienation: social sciences, philosophy of, 603

self-consciousness: alienation, 18; person, 444

self control: Spencer, 623

self-deception: Sartre, 578

self-development: James, 321

self-discipline: Spencer, 625

self-discovery: Thomas Aquinas, 641

self-education: Descartes, 145

self-evident truths: epistemology, 188–189

self-expression: Dewey, 147–148

self-fulfillment: pleasure, 490

self-instruction: Diderot, 157–158

self-interest: individualism, 302; intuitionism, 309–310; justice, 336

self-knowledge: Kierkegaard, 343; Vico, 660–661

self-love: Helvetius, 257

self-objectification: alienation, 17

self-preservation: Spencer, 624

self-reliance: Emerson, 182; individualism, 302

self-respect: toleration, 645

self-sacrifice: Beecher, 51

self-understanding: religious education, 545

Selznick, Philip: community, 101

semantic realism: realism, 530

Seneca: Cynics, 131; Epicureanism, 187; Stoicism, 627

Seneca Falls Convention: feminism, 216

sensation: Condillac, 104; Descartes, 145–146; Helvetius, 257; Pestalozzi, 447; realism, 533; Rousseau, 568

sense data: science, philosophy of, 590

sense evidence: William of Ockham, 677

sense realism: Pestalozzi, 447

sense theorists, moral: intuitionism, 309

sensory, the: pleasure, 490

Sentences: Peter Lombard, 449–450

sententiae: Thomas Aquinas, 640

sepharadi: Judaism, 330

Sergiovanni, Thomas J.: educational policy and administration, 174

sex education: Russell, 574

sexism: race and racism, 523; rights, 557

sexism, educational: gender and sexism, 237–238

sexism, linguistic: gender and sexism, 236–237

sexism, occupational: gender and sexism, 237

Sextus Empiricus: skepticism, 595

sexual abuse: feminism, 218

sexual equality: Montessori, 406

sexual orientation: minorities, 400

sexuality: feminism, 216; socialism, 606

Shaftsbury, Earl of: intuitionism, 308, 309

Shakespeare, William: comedy, 93; Homer, 279; tragedy, 646

shari'a: Islam, 311

Shaver, James: civic education, 82

Shavuot: Judaism, 331

Sheldon, Edward A.: Pestalozzi, 448

Shelley, Mary: Wollstonecraft, 683

Shelley, Percy Bysshe: romanticism, 561–562

shi'i community: Islam, 311

Shiva: Hinduism, 270

Shull, George: heredity and hereditarianism, 260

Shumaker, Ann: romanticism, 563

Sichel, Betty: philosophy and literature, 460

Sidgwick, Henry: common sense, 100; utilitarianism, 653

Siegel, Harvey: analytic philosophy, 24; critical thinking, 120; indoctrination, 303; reason and rationality, 538

signs: Anselm, 26; Augustine, 40

Sigourney, Lydia: girls and women, 242

Simon, Roger: possibility, 496

Simon, Theodore: intelligence, 308

Simonides: *paideia*, 439

simultaneous instruction: Pestalozzi, 446

sinfulness: Nietzsche, 433

Sirach: Clement of Alexandria, 85

skepticism, **594–595**; Cyrenaics, 132–133; Kant, 340; modernism and post-modernism, 402; Russell, 573, 575; Wittgenstein, 680

skepticism, Academic: skepticism, 594

standard of behavior: norm, 436
Stanford-Binet Intelligence Test: Darwin, 136–137
Stanley, W.O.: reconstructionism, social, 540
Stans: Pestalozzi, 446–447
Stanton, Elizabeth Cady: feminism, 216; Willard, 676
Starr, Ellen Gates: Addams, 7
state: Calvinism, 66; Harris, 251; school, 586
State Education Journal Index: philosophy of education, literature in, 473
status: race and racism, 521
Stevenson, Charles L.: analytic philosophy, 20; emotivism, 183
Stevenson, R.L.: James, 322
stimulus discrimination: learning, theories of, 347
stimulus generalization: learning, theories of, 347
Stirner, Max: nihilism, 435
Stockard, Charles R.: heredity and hereditarianism, 261
Stoicism, **626–629;** Cynics, 131; Cyrenaics, 132; Epicureanism, 187; Jefferson, 323; philosophy of education, history of, 463
storicismo: historicism, 274
Stowe, Harriet Beecher: Beecher, 50
Stoy, Karl: Herbart, 259
Strauss, David Friedrich: Rosenkranz, 565
Strawson, Peter F.: analytic philosophy, 20
Street, Brian: literacy, 361
Strike, Kenneth R.: analytic philosophy, 23; censorship, 72
strong substantival idealism: idealism, 295
structural functionalism: sociology, 614–615
structural pluralism: pluralism, 492
structuralism: moral development, 410
student services: higher education, 267–268
studia humanitatis, **630–632;** Hegel, 254; humanism, 285; philosophy of education, history of, 466; Vico, 661
Studies in Philosophy and Education: philosophy of education, literature in, 474; philosophy of education, professional organizations in, 476
style: Cicero, 77; Kierkegaard, 344
Suarez, Francisco: scholasticism, 584
suasoria: rhetoric, 550
subject *(inventio):* Cicero, 77
subject matter: Dewey, 147–148
subjective experience: phenomenology, 450
subjective happiness: happiness, 248
subjective idealism: realism, 533
subjective mind: Hegel, 253
subjectivity: Kierkegaard, 343; metaphysics, 395
sublimation: love, 371; psychoanalysis, 509
subordination: minorities, 400
subspecies: race and racism, 521
substance: Kant, 340; metaphysics, 394
substantivists: technology, 638
Suetonius: rhetoric, 551
suffering: Buddhism, 59
suffrage, women's: feminism, 215–216

Sufis: mysticism, 418; neoplatonism, 430
suicide rates: sociology, 612
Sukkot: Judaism, 331
Sullivan, Harry Stack: Freud, 229; psychoanalysis, 511
summum bonum: happiness, 247
Sunday schools, American Socialist: socialism, 608–609
superego: Freud, 227; psychoanalysis, 509
supererogatory acts: right, 554–555
supernatural, the: values and evaluation, 658
superstition: Bacon, 47
supervenience idealism: idealism, 294
supposition, theory of: William of Ockham, 677
surplus values: Marx, 384–385
"survival of the fittest": evolution, 205
Swallow-Richards, Ellen Henrietta: domestic education, 163
Swartz, Ronald: censorship, 73
Swedenborg, Immanuel: Kant, 339
syllogism: logic, 367–368
syllogistic demonstration: William of Ockham, 677
symbolic interactionism: sociology, 614–615
symbolization: psychoanalysis, 510
symposia: Sappho, 577; Socrates, 618
syncretism: multiculturalism, 416
synderesis: conscience, 110
syneidesis: conscience, 110
Synesis of Cyrene: Hypatia, 288
syntelia: Clement of Alexandria, 84
synthetic truth: truth, 647
system: Condillac, 104; Herbart, 259
system-makers: Condillac, 104

Tacitus: *studia humanitatis,* 630
talented tenth: Du Bois, 167
Talmud: Judaism, 331
Tannenbaum, Frank: slavery, 597
Taoism, **632–636;** Confucianism, 108
Tarski, Alfred: epistemology, 189; logic, 369; truth, 648
Taunton Commission: Arnold, 37
Tawney, R.H.: Calvinism, 65
Taylor, Frederick W.: vocational education, 663–664
Taylor, Harriet: Davies, 18
Teachers College Record: philosophy of education, literature in, 473
teachers unions: Dewey, 148
teaching and learning, **636–638;** curriculum and instruction, 125
Teaching Philosophy: philosophy of education, literature in, 474
technology, **638–639;** Heidegger, 256
Telemachus: Homer, 278
teleological argument: atheism, 38
telos: ethics and morality, 201–202
temperance: Mann, 379; practical wisdom, 497
temple metaphor: educational policy and administration, 173–174

Temple School: Alcott, 14; Peabody, 441
Temple, William: Epicureanism, 188
Terence: comedy, 92
Terman, Lewis: Darwin, 136–137; heredity and hereditarianism, 261
terrorism: rights, 557
testimony: William of Ockham, 677
thanatos: Freud, 228
theism: mysticism, 418; neoplatonism, 430
Theobald, Archbishop of Canterbury: John of Salisbury, 328
Theodore of Gaza: Erasmus, 196
Theodorus Atheos: Cyrenaics, 132
theological handling: values and evaluation, 656–657
theology: Averroes, 43; higher education, 263; John of Salisbury, 328; Philo of Alexandria, 456; philosophy of education, history of, 465–466
Theon: Hypatia, 288
Theophilus, Patriarch of Alexandria: Hypatia, 288
theoretical philosophy: idealism, 293–294
theoretical sciences: Aristotle, 32
theory and practice: pragmatism, 500
"Theory X": educational policy and administration, 174–175
"Theory Y": educational policy and administration, 174–175
Therarada: Buddhism, 60
thesis: ethics and morality, 201
"they": minorities, 401
Thierry of Chartres: John of Salisbury, 328; philosophy of education, history of, 465
things: Bacon, 48
things in themselves: Kant, 340
thinking: Condillac, 105
Thinking: The Journal of Philosophy for Children: philosophy of education, literature in, 474
third-man argument: realism, 531–532
Thirty Years War: Comenius, 93
Thomas Aquinas, **640–644;** Augustine, 42; Averroes, 43; Bonaventure, 55; conscience, 100; existentialism, 206; human nature, 283; metaphysics, 395; Peter Lombard, 450; philosophy of education, history of, 465–466; practical wisdom, 497; right, 555–556; scholasticism, 583; socialism, 605
Thomas, Lawrence: philosophy of education, professional organizations in, 476
Thomism: analytic philosophy, 24
Thompson, Patricia J.: domestic education, 164
Thoreau, Henry David: Alcott, 13; civil disobedience, 82; conservatism, 114; Cynics, 132; Peabody, 441
Thorndike, E.L.: Darwin, 136; Dewey, 149; freedom and determinism, 224; physical education, 491
Thrasymachus: Sophists, 622

Thucydides: empiricism, 184
time: neoplatonism, 431–432
Tisias: rhetoric, 550
Tocqueville, Alexis de: Beecher, 51; democracy, 141; freedom and determinism, 225
toleration, **644–645**
Tolstoy, Nikolaevich: Rousseau, 572
Tolstoy Farm: Gandhi, 233
Tommaso de Vio: scholasticism, 584
Toole, Michael: person, 444
Topics: Vico, 661
Torah: Judaism, 331–333
Torrey-Purta, Judith: civic education, 81
torture: rights, 560
Toulmin, Stephen: epistemology, 189
Toynbee Hall: Addams, 7
traditionalists: Jesus, 325–326
tragedy, **645–647**
training: aims of education, 12; school, 585
transactions: experience, 211
transcendental analysis: phenomenology, 454
transcendentalism: Alcott, 13; Peabody, 441
transference: psychoanalysis, 511
transmission theory of education: evolution, 203–204
tribal society: Durkheim, 170
Trinity, the: Peter Lombard, 449–450
trivium: John of Salisbury, 328; scholasticism, 581; Thomas Aquinas, 640; vocational education, 663
Troeltsch, Ernst: historicism, 272
Trojan War: Homer, 278
tropes: Emerson, 181
Trotsky, Leon: Marxism, 390
trumps: rights, 558
truth, **647–649;** Anselm, 26; Augustine, 40; epistemology, 188–189, 191; experience, 210–211; meaning, 392–393; modernism and post-modernism, 402; reason and rationality, 537; romanticism, 563
truth, revealed: religious education, 545
Tufts, James H.: ethics and morality, 199
tuition: Emerson, 181
Turgenev, I.F.: nihilism, 436
Turgot, Baron de l'Aulne: Franklin, 221
Turner, Nat: democracy, 141
Tuskegee Institute: Washington, Booker T., 668–670
Tylor, E.B.: anthropology, 28
type: race and racism, 521, 523
tyranny: Marx, 386

uncertainty, principle of: epistemology, 191
unconscious, the: psychoanalysis, 509–510
Underhill, Evelyn: mysticism, 419
underprivilege: minorities, 400
understanding: aims of education, 12; Montaigne, 404
Unitarianism: Mann, 379; Peabody, 441
Unitas Fratrum: Comenius, 94